AMERICAN SHORT STORY

Second Edition

VOLUME I
A–L

EDITED BY ABBY H. P. WERLOCK
ASSISTANT EDITOR: JAMES P. WERLOCK

Facts On File
An imprint of Infobase Publishing

Dedicated to my father, Thomas Kennedy Potter,
and my mother, Abby Holmes Potter.

In memory of Henry Imada of Colorado,
Teddy Miller of Minnesota,
Paul Smith of Connecticut

Storytellers all, whose stories will never end.

The Facts On File Companion to the American Short Story, Second Edition

Copyright © 2010, 2000 Abby H. P. Werlock

All rights reserved. No part of this book may be reproduced or utilized in any form or by any means, electronic or mechanical, including photocopying, recording, or by any information storage or retrieval systems, without permission in writing from the publisher. For information contact:

Facts On File, Inc.
An imprint of Infobase Publishing
132 West 31st Street
New York NY 10001

Library of Congress Cataloging-in-Publication Data
The Facts on File companion to the American short story / edited by Abby H. P. Werlock ; assistant editor, James P. Werlock.—2nd ed.
    p. cm.
    Includes bibliographical references and index.
    ISBN 978-0-8160-6895-1 (acid-free paper) 1. Short stories, American—Encyclopedias. I. Werlock, Abby H. P. II. Werlock, James P. III. Facts on File, Inc. IV. Title: Companion to the American short story.
    PS374.S5F33 2009
    813'.0103—dc22   2009004725

Facts On File books are available at special discounts when purchased in bulk quantities for businesses, associations, institutions, or sales promotions. Please call our Special Sales Department in New York at (212) 967-8800 or (800) 322-8755.

You can find Facts On File on the World Wide Web at http://www.factsonfile.com

Text design adapted by James Scotto-Lavino
Composition by Hermitage Publishing Services
Cover printed by Art Print, Taylor, Pa.
Book printed and bound by Maple-Vail Book Manufacturing Group, York, Pa.
Date printed: December, 2009
Printed in the United States of America

10 9 8 7 6 5 4 3 2 1

This book is printed on acid-free paper and contains 30 percent postconsumer recycled content.

CONTENTS

VOLUME I

VOLUME II

ACKNOWLEDGMENTS

The Facts On File Companion to the American Short Story owes its genesis to several farseeing people, chief among them James Warren, former acquisitions editor at Facts On File; Professor Alice Hall Petry, English Department chair at Southern Illinois University; Dr. Mickey Pearlman, scholar, author, and editor; and Anne Dubuisson, former agent at the Ellen Levine Literary Agency. At St. Olaf College, President Melvin R. George and Dean Jon M. Moline offered encouragement and approved a yearlong sabbatical, and Dean Kathie Fishbeck authorized a special leave as this book took shape.

A number of librarians shared with me their impressive resources and research skills: Robert Bruce, Betsy Busa, Professor Bryn Geffert, and Professor Mary Sue Lovett of the St. Olaf College Library answered a plethora of bibliographical inquiries; Jennifer Edwin of the Carleton College Library provided timely assistance with information on prizewinning stories; Professor Laurie Howell Hime of the Miami Dade Community College Library consistently contributed on- and offline research skills; and Larry L. Nesbitt, Director, Mansfield State University Library, and Nancy Robinson of the Bradford County Library, Pennsylvania, provided invaluable help with interlibrary loan acquisitions. Moreover, I owe an immense debt to the many scholars and critics whose published work on the American short story provided a significant foundation for my own research and writing. Their names appear in the bibliographies throughout the book.

The book has been greatly enhanced by the generous contributions of established scholars in diverse areas of American literature: Professors Alfred Bendixen, California State University at Los Angeles; Jacqueline Vaught Brogan, University of Notre Dame; Stephanie P. Browner, Berea College; J. Randolph Cox, St. Olaf College; Richard Deming, Columbus State Community College; Robert DeMott, Ohio University; Monika Elbert, Montclair State University; Christine Doyle Francis, Central Connecticut State University; Warren French, University of Swansea; Mimi Gladstein, University of Texas at El Paso; Harriet P. Gold, LaSalle College and Durham College; Sandra Chrystal Hayes, Georgia Institute of Technology; Carol Hovanac, Ramapo College; Frances Kerr, Durham Technical Community College; Michael J. Kiskis, Elmira College; Denise D. Knight, State University of New York at Cortland; Paula Kot, Niagara University; Keith Lawrence, Brigham Young University; Caroline F. Levander, Trinity University; Saemi Ludwig, University of Berne; Suzanne Evertsen Lundquist, Brigham Young University; Robert M. Luscher, University of Nebraska at Kearny; Robert K. Martin, Université de Montréal; Michael J. Meyer, DePaul University; Fred Moramarco, San Diego State University; Gwen M. Neary, Santa Rosa Junior College and Sonoma State University; Luz Elena Ramirez, State University of New York, College at Oneonta; Jeanne Campbell Reesman, University of Texas at San Antonio; Ralph E. Rodriguez, Pennsylvania State University; Jennifer L.

Schulz, University of Washington; Wilfred D. Samuels, University of Utah; Carole M. Schaffer-Koros, Kean College of New Jersey; Ben Stoltzfus, University of California at Riverside; Darlene Harbour Unrue and John C. Unrue, University of Nevada at Las Vegas; Linda Wagner-Martin, University of North Carolina at Chapel Hill; Sylvia Watanabe, Oberlin College; Philip M. Weinstein, Swarthmore College; and Dr. Sarah Bird Wright, independent scholar and author.

For linking me with their talented graduate students who study the short story, I wish to thank Professors Suzette Henke, University of Louisville; Keneth Kinnamon, University of Texas at Austin; James Nagel, University of Georgia; Elaine Safer, University of Delaware; Alfred Bendixen; Robert DeMott; Mimi Gladstein; and Linda Wagner-Martin. I especially wish to acknowledge the expert contributions of these graduate students whose knowledge contributed so notably to the scope and accuracy of this book. Their names appear both in the list of contributors and after each of the entries they wrote. For technical help with the inevitable computer crises, I thank Paul Marino and Van Miller of Northfield, Minnesota, and Van Miller II, of Minneapolis, Minnesota.

I am most grateful to Diana Finch, my agent at the Ellen Levine Literary Agency, for monitoring this undertaking and making a number of helpful suggestions; Laurie Likoff, Editorial Director, Facts On File, for her long-term support of the entire project; and Michael G. Laraque, Chief Copy Editor, whose veteran editing skills helped make this a better book. Most of all, I thank Anne Savarese, my former editor at Facts On File. She understood this book from the beginning, and without her intellect, insights, dedication, and sheer stamina, *The Facts On File Companion to the American Short Story* would have been impossible to complete.

In writing and compiling the entries for this book, I was fortunate to have quiet writing retreats at the homes of Verna and John Cobb, in Tuxedo Park, New York; Jean and Marshall Case, in Troy, Pennsylvania; and Tom and Abby Potter, in Tallahassee, Florida. I wish to thank them along with the many lovers of short stories who discussed their favorites,

particularly Marsha Case; Amy Gibson; Teddy, Van, Vannie, Andy, and Debby Miller; Dewey Potter; Meg and Matt Potter; Tony Wellman; and Jennifer and John Winton.

ACKNOWLEDGMENTS FOR THE SECOND EDITION

I would like to acknowledge the people without whose support there would be no second edition of this book. First and most significantly, I would like to express my gratitude to the expert contributors—a good many of them veterans of the first edition—who not only wrote excellent entries but often made valuable suggestions for additional authors and titles. Spending extra time to write on a plethora of topics were the talented and dedicated professors David Brottman, Southern Indiana University; Sanford E. Marovitz, Kent State University; Imelda Martín-Junquera, Universidad de León; Michael Meyer, De Paul University; Patti Sehulster, Westchester Community College; Carolyn Whitsun, Metropolitan State University; and Bennett Yu-Hsiang Fu, National Taiwan University. Very special thanks go to my agent, Diana Finch, of the Diana Finch Literary Agency, and my editor, Jeff Soloway, Executive Editor at Facts On File. Unquestionably, their patience, their ideas, and their support made this book possible. I would also like to thank Beth Williams of the Mansfield University Library for all her help with acquiring scores of books through interlibrary loan, and Sue Wolfe, of the Allen F. Pierce Free Library, for help with book matters great and small. Matt Strange, my guru at Autograph Systems, saved my hard drive and my data more times than I can remember. My friends in Troy and on Armenia Mountain, Pennsylvania—Mallory Babcock, Carole DeLauro, Vivian Hall, and Carol Van Zile—gave me unconditional support when I most needed it, as did friends Lindy and Don Neese in Markham, Virginia. My husband, Jim, gave me hours and more hours of his valuable time. And my mother, Abby Holmes Potter, who died while this book was in progress, never wavered in her interest in all things literary.

PREFACE TO THE SECOND EDITION

Nine years after the publication of the first edition of *The Facts On File Companion to the American Short Story,* short fiction continues to be widely read and to gain in both popularity and serious academic interest. This edition maintains the focus and main concerns of the first and has virtually doubled the size. A significant new feature of this edition is the inclusion of entries on major Canadian writers (such as Alice Munro, Margaret Atwood, Mavis Gallant, Mordecai Richler, Carol Shields, and Morley Callaghan) and their stories. Other major additions include an increased number of entries on stories by classic American writers; a significant expansion of entries on contemporary writers and stories; and updates, where relevant, on all writers, living or dead. Bibliographies have also been updated, as have the major prize lists, and new information has been added to a number of topical entries, including those on African-American, Asian-American, Hispanic-American, and Native American short fiction.

Scholars, as always, disagree over the current state of American short fiction. Many have made interesting and provocative claims in recent years. Some critics believe that, although it made a "lasting mark" in the latter half of the 20th century, postmodernism in the short story is coming to an end (Kaylor 266). Others disagree. Some feminist scholars have pointed to the ability of the short story form to express women's concerns and ethnic issues: Ellen Burlington Harrington, for instance, sees the "compressed and elastic form of the story" as particularly suitable for

women writers across the lines of "gender, race, class, ethnicity and sexuality" (12). Other scholars, such as Rocio G. Davis, J. Gerald Kennedy, Gerald Lynch, and James Nagel, have not only written on the importance of the short story and the short story cycle but also on its appeal to those of various ethnic backgrounds, both in the United States and in Canada. In his study of the short story cycles of Louise Erdrich, Jamaica Kincaid, Susan Minot, Sandra Cisneros, Tim O'Brien, Julia Alvarez, Amy Tan, and Robert Olen Butler, the scholar James Nagel notes the cross-ethnic, gender, and racial appeal of the short story: "Literature is no small social force, in the sense that it provides a window into the soul of a nation, revealing both its anguish and its bliss, its promise and its ongoing internal struggle" (258).

The American fascination with the short story and the short story cycle continues unabated. The appearance of film adaptations of short stories is indicative of the power of the genre; witness, for instance, the subsequent feature-length film adaptation of Annie Proulx's *Brokeback Mountain.* Similarly, the many important recent books on the genre testify to its vitality. Examples include *The Contemporary American Short-Story Cycle: The Ethnic Resonance of Genre* (2001), *The Postmodern Short Story: Forms and Issues* (2003), *The Art of Brevity: Excursions in Short Fiction Theory and Analysis* (2004), a reprint of Frank O'Connor's *The Lonely Voice* (2004), *Adaptations: From Short Story to Big Screen: 35 Great Stories That Have Inspired Great Films* (2005), *The Art of the*

Short Story (2005), *Short Story Writers and Short Stories* (2005), *The Cambridge Introduction to the American Short Story* (2006), *Behind the Short Story: From First to Final Draft* (2007), *The Cambridge Introduction of the Short Story in English* (2007), and *Scribbling Women and the Short Story Form* (2008).

In addition to books, journals and magazines continue to feature short stories, but it is the Internet that has truly transformed the genre by expanding the opportunity to publish and read short stories. Although the century is young and no real consensus has been reached vis-à-vis the long-range quality of online magazines, they are clearly attracting many writers and readers, and their subject matter ranges from adventure to sexuality to science fiction to horror to fantasy. The new century seems to offer an energizing climate for all forms of short fiction, perhaps because, in the words of scholar Martin Scofield, "Its ratio of insight to length is greater than that of the novel" (238).

This second edition of *The Facts On File Companion to the American Short Story* includes more than 200 new entries, many on new or younger writers (such as Junot Díaz, Dan Chaon, and Charles D'Ambrosio) and their stories (Julia Alvarez's "Ironing Their Clothes," Edward P. Jones's "Bad Neighbors," Joy Williams's "Health," Dave Eggers' "Up the Mountain, Coming Down Slowly," Lorrie Moore's "People Like That Are the Only People Here," Helena Viramontes's "The Moths," to name just a sampling). We have also added entries on many frequently anthologized stories by such classic writers as Nathaniel Hawthorne ("The Minister's Black Veil"), Bret Harte ("The Outcasts of Poker Flat"), and Robert Penn Warren ("Blackberry Winter"), as well as entries on such "rediscovered" writers as John Milton Oskison and Anzia Yzierska, again, to name only two.

Clearly, in all its many forms, the short story continues to speak to contemporary readers, perhaps because, in Ellen Harrington's words, the process of reading them "comes to symbolize the larger grasping after comprehension of the nature of reality itself" (7).

BIBLIOGRAPHY

Banks, Russell. "Introduction." In *The Lonely Voice,* edited by Frank O'Connor, 5–12. Hoboken, N.J.: Melville House Publishing, 2004.

Bloom, Harold. *Short Story Writers and Short Stories.* New York: Chelsea House, 2005.

Davis, Rocío. *Transcultural Reinventions: Asian American and Asian Canadian Short-Story Cycles.* Toronto: Tsar, 2001.

Harde, Roxanne, ed. *Narratives of Community: Women's Short Story Sequences.* Newcastle, England: Cambridge Scholars Publishing, 2007.

Harrington, Ellen Burton. *Scribbling Women and the Short Story Form.* New York: Peter Lang, 2008.

Harrison, Stephanie. *Adaptations: From Short Story to Big Screen: 35 Great Stories That Have Inspired Great Films.* New York: Three Rivers Press, 2005.

Hunter, Adrian, ed. *The Cambridge Introduction of the Short Story in English.* New York: Cambridge University Press, 2007.

Iftekharrudin, Farhat, et al., eds. *The Postmodern Short Story: Forms and Issues.* Westport, Conn.: Praeger, 2003.

Kaylor, Noel Howard. "Postmodern Narrative around the World." In *The Postmodern Short Story: Forms and Issues,* edited by Farhat Iftekharrudin, et. al., 246–266. Westport, Conn.: Praeger, 2003.

Lynch, Gerald. *The One and the Many: English-Canadian Short Story Cycles.* Toronto: University of Toronto Press, 2001.

Lynch, Gerald, and Angela Arnold Robbeson, eds. *Dominant Impressions: Essays on the Canadian Short Story.* Ottawa: University of Ottawa Press, 1999.

Martin, Wendy. *The Art of the Short Story.* Boston: Houghton Mifflin, 2005.

McSweeney, Kerry. *The Realist Short Story of the Powerful Glimpse: Chekhov to Carver.* Columbia: University of South Carolina Press, 2007.

Nagel, James. *The Contemporary American Short-Story Cycle: The Ethnic Resonance of Genre.* Baton Rouge: Louisiana State University Press, 2001.

Nischik, Reingard M., ed. *The Canadian Short Story: Interpretations.* Rochester, N.Y.: Camden House, 2007.

Scofield, Martin, ed. *The Cambridge Introduction to the American Short Story.* New York: Cambridge University Press, 2006.

Van Cleave, Ryan G., and Todd James Pierce, eds. *Behind the Short Story: From First to Final Draft.* New York: Pearson, 2007.

Winter, Per, et al., eds. *The Art of Brevity: Excursions in Short Fiction Theory and Analysis.* Columbia: University of South Carolina Press, 2004.

INTRODUCTION

"The Americans have handled the short story so wonderfully," said the Irish writer Frank O'Connor, that it constitutes "a national art form." Although by now it may seem an "old" form (since the first American short story was, arguably, published as early as 1789), it is still thriving: Witness its sales, its apparent vogue among high school students, its increased use in college courses across the curriculum, the proliferation of public short story readings at bookstores, the explosion of book clubs, and the acclaimed National Public Radio series of short story readings *Selected Shorts*. As the writer Shirley Ann Grau remarked in an interview, people are still reading the short story "like mad."

In response to readers' requests for more short fiction suggestions, an updated and revised edition of a reading group guide by Mickey Pearlman, *What to Read* (1999), includes a new chapter on short story collections. In fact, from Charles Brockden Brown and Washington Irving, through Mark Twain, Ernest Hemingway, Gertrude Stein, and William Faulkner, to Joyce Carol Oates, Raymond Carver, Sandra Cisneros, Louise Erdrich, John Edgar Wideman, and Amy Tan, short fiction—although it suffered a critical decline in the mid-20th century—has never really lost its popularity with the reading public.

To the contrary, short fiction has continued to appear in major magazines from the *New Yorker* and *Redbook* to *Esquire, Playboy,* and *Penthouse;* good story collections and anthologies are readily accessible through inexpensive paperback reprints; and, per-

haps most important of all, short stories are *short*. In an era when even many novels seem noticeably shorter than they once were, the most obvious reason for the popularity of short stories may well lie in the response I have heard hundreds of times from readers of all types: "I like to keep them on my night table so I can read one or two before I fall asleep." Younger readers—particularly those who identify themselves as "Generation Xers"—say they feel drawn to the short story not only because it is not lengthy, but also because it seems less artificially wrapped up than the novel, and thus more like "real life." Remarking on the microcosmic relationship of the story to modern life, the critic William Peden finds that the short story now appears as a "literary mirror" that reflects our postwar life, in which change, obsolescence, and destruction have become the realities:

> Unlike the traditional novelists, the short story writer usually does not bring his powers to bear on the grand questions of where are we going, why are we here. Rather, he focuses his attention, swiftly and clearly, on one facet of man's experience; he illuminates briefly one dark corner or depicts one aspect of life.

Stories have existed in one form or another, of course, for as long as people have told them and listened to them. We can picture storytellers and their audiences as they probably existed thousands of years ago, huddling together near a fire, listening to someone's story both as a form of entertainment and as a means to ward off fear of the unknown lying outside the stone walls of their enclosure or the perimeter of the firelight. The oral telling of stories conjures up in modern readers a dual image of both community interaction and private individual response.

Most scholars agree that the first written stories can be traced to numerous sources—religious stories of the Greeks, the incomparable stories of Scheherazade, the instructive narratives of the European medieval times. Throughout the Renaissance, brief tales were popular, reaching a state of art in Italy and Spain with Giovanni Boccaccio's *Decameron* and Miguel de Cervantes's *Exemplary Novels*. Many critics believe, however, that the onset of the novel in the 18th century dampened the vogue of the story. Not until the 19th century did several factors unite to give rise to a new form of tale: the appearance of the periodical, or annual—apparently originating in Germany—as well as the new forms of romanticism whose moods and effects found expressive outlets in stories and poetry.

The history of the short story in the United States is a compelling story in itself. When the Englishman Sydney Smith in 1820 asked his withering question, "In the four quarters of the globe, who reads an American book?" American writers accepted the challenge. Although critics have argued over when, and according to which criteria, the first story actually appeared (two major contenders are the pseudonymous Ruricolla's "The Story of the Captain's Wife and an Aged Woman" in 1789 and the anonymous "The Child of Snow" in 1792), Washington Irving's *The Sketch Book,* published in 1819, is generally credited as the first American book of short stories. Rather neatly predating Smith's question by a year, *The Sketch Book* includes such classic stories as "Rip Van Winkle" and "The Legend of Sleepy Hollow," both surprisingly modern in their use of self-conscious narrators and ambiguous endings.

The definitions of the short story have modified since then and provide a source for much scholarly research today, but for more than a century, students have learned its basic tenets: Most important, it is "short" when compared with the novel. Written in prose that may or may not be lyrical, it has a narrator, a plot, at least one developing character who grapples with problems, one or more themes, and a denouement. In the 20th century, writers rebelled against some of these traditional elements, particularly those of plots and tidy conclusions.

The story has also evolved into a peculiarly American form. Although certainly writers of every nationality write excellent short fiction—indeed, the modern story would be unthinkable without the Russian Anton Chekhov and the French Guy de Maupassant, to name just two influential European practitioners—no country has embraced the form as enthusiastically and as prolifically as the United States. Early U.S. writers consciously included American settings and evoked distinctively American regions and speech patterns, as some contemporary writers continue to do. The short story has remained a peculiarly American artistic vehicle, however, not only for examining the myriad voices and philosophies of this large, diverse country, but also for viewing society's preoccupations with issues of race, gender, and class; national consciousness; and the spiritual and physical position of the individual in the sometimes overwhelming welter of American life. From Irving to the present, then, the American short story provides "an index of national consciousness" (Weaver xv).

After Irving three writers of unquestionable talent further refined the short story: Edgar Allan Poe, Nathaniel Hawthorne, and Herman Melville. Poe, a literary critic as well as a practitioner of the short story, sought to define the form. With the exception of poetry, which he believed to be the pinnacle of literary expression, he judged "the Tale" as the form that afforded "the best prose opportunity for display of the highest talent," finding it superior to the novel, the essay, and, in some respects, even poetry. Poe, a superb craftsman himself, laid down guidelines for the taut, compressed, carefully considered, and thoroughly unified story. His exacting standards concerned his friend Hawthorne, who believed his own tales somewhat pale and retiring in contrast. Yet Hawthorne, too, took a painstaking approach to his art, leaving written records of his short story approach. Both writers, according to Burton Raffel, were "important exemplars, inventive, imaginative, and above all sharply aware that the untethered, uncontrolled, unmastered pen simply could not accomplish" a first-rate short story (16). Melville, despite his admiration for both Poe and Hawthorne, voiced his frustration with a thinness of characterization, particularly in Hawthorne's stories. In Melville's tales we see a movement away from romanticism toward realism, especially in the characters of Benito Cerino and Billy Budd.

The shift toward realism, with its accompanying genre, the local color story, characterized much short fiction in the second half of the 19th century. Whereas romanticism concerns itself with an idealized conception of the way things should be, realism focuses on things as they seem to be. William Dean Howells, known as "the dean of American literature" and the closest thing to a czar that American literature has ever had (Raffel 20), in the mid-1880s sounded the call for verisimilitude, or realism, in all American writing, and many writers answered this call. In the end, however, these are but labels of convenience, and, if readers look closely, they will find elements of both realism and romanticism after 1850 in such talented and differing authors as Melville, Mark Twain, and Sarah Orne Jewett. In fact, the mingling of romanticism and realism never really stopped: two so-called local colorists, Harriet Beecher Stowe and Hamlin Garland, despite their different concerns (Stowe with women and domestic life, Garland with men and war), write passages that appear almost identical in terms of both verisimilitude and idealism (Raffel 22–23).

Naturalism, another development of the literary realistic movement, called for a scientific objectivity when depicting "natural" human beings, yet its practitioners—Frank Norris and Stephen Crane, for instance—have also been called romantic and impressionistic. As Henry James pointed out, the *idea* of the writer is paramount, not the debate over a realistic or a romantic formula; the only distinction James addressed was the difference between "good" and "bad" art. James believed strongly that the value of fiction lies in its greater or lesser ability to render a direct and intense "impression of life" (Raffel 24), and nearly every critic notes that he emphasizes the word *impres-*

sion, thereby pointing to the individual quality of the writer's vision.

A number of 19th-century short story writers continued to write into the 20th century. Along with others, Kate Chopin, Jewett, Edith Wharton, Jack London—and James, who died during World War I—wrote into the new era. In many ways, the authors who did live into the new century and through World War I—not only Jewett, Wharton, and James, but also Twain, Theodore Dreiser, and Willa Cather—all implicitly or explicitly criticized the hypocrisy and conformity they saw across the United States and came to see themselves as aliens and outsiders at odds with the changing times. In any case, World War I, with its fragmentation of traditions and values, and the consequent rise of modernism, provides a sharp dividing line between the 19th and 20th centuries of American short fiction. Exactly 100 years after Irving published *The Sketch Book,* Sherwood Anderson is credited with enacting the modernist creed, "Make it new," with the publication of his short story collection *Winesburg, Ohio,* in 1919.

"Never such innocence again," writes Paul Fussell of World War I in *The Great War and Modern Memory.* The effects of the war are evident even in those writers who did not write about it—Anderson or Dorothy Parker, for instance—and even in those who did not consider themselves modernists. Anderson's ground-breaking book of stories discarded realistic representations of behavior and things, replacing them with a more allusive, mystical, and poetic form more psychologically suggestive than anything previously written in American fiction. The modernist sense of fragmentation, of postwar loss and fragile instability, is evident in the short fiction that followed his lead, whether in work by the expatriate Americans in Europe or by those who stayed at home. In Paris, for instance, Ernest Hemingway and Gertrude Stein sought radically new ways of expressing the upheaval, alienation, and disjunction they felt in the aftermath of the war, Hemingway in his terse, sharply pruned stories and Stein in her cinematic exploration of the further possibilities inherent in language and imagery. William Faulkner, in a style antithetical to Hemingway's, was every bit as experimental if not more so, stretching language as far as he could take it. Critics have observed that all the best short fiction writers of this period knew the terms from painting, from *impressionism* to *cubism*; perhaps Katherine Anne Porter's conscious use of images and symbols in her short story techniques best suggests the modernist writer's kinship with art.

Not all 20th-century writers were modernists, and many other popular practitioners of short fiction flourished—in part, in an echo of the previous century, because of American magazines. The so-called little magazines, such as the *Dial* and *Broom,* published the new and the experimental, and once again there was a call in post–World War I America for short stories to fill the widely circulated and successful magazines typified by the *Ladies' Home Journal* and *Saturday Evening Post. American Mercury* published numerous writers today considered classic—F. Scott Fitzgerald and Faulkner, for instance—and the *New Yorker,* debuting later, in 1925, also had a significant influence on the short story in following decades. O. Henry's stories continued to have enormous popular appeal, as did Ring Lardner's. Writers from the New South, from Eudora Welty and Jean Toomer to Porter and Flannery O'Connor, also were making their voices heard. The 1920s was called the Jazz Age, popularized, of course, by Fitzgerald, but it was also the heyday of the Harlem Renaissance, and it afforded significant outlets for regional writers. The 1920s left a legacy of experimentalism and diversity that future generations would, and still do, view with awe.

Historians and literary critics alike have noted the phenomenon of speaking of our eras in terms of decades; as do literary labels, such coding oversimplifies the issues. Yet the advent of the stock market crash and the Great Depression ushered in a very different sort of literature in the 1930s. It is a fact that the years 1930 to 1945, through the end of World War II, saw the greatest outpouring of short fiction in American literary history. Although the financial hardships of the Great Depression resulted in the dramatic reduction of book publication (from 1929 to 1933, published books dropped from more than 200 million a year to a little more than 100 million), an enormous increase in magazines and the introduction

of the Pocket Books paperback series stepped into the void (Watson 106). A public tired of the realities of the depression and with unpaid free time on their hands craved entertainment and thus created a huge market for short fiction. One of the most significant innovations, called proletarian, or reform, literature, was not really new but had roots in the late 19th century. Its 1930s practitioners included James T. Farrell, Ruth Suckow, Langston Hughes, and Meridel LeSueur. In fact, most of the fiction written in the 1930s hearkened back to the era of Hawthorne and the tradition of American romanticism. Writers took on the old subjects—verities, Faulkner would say—of "young Americans, initiations, death and dying, fantasies" (Watson 105). Arguably, the literary characters descended from earlier ones such as Twain's Huck Finn appear in short stories rather than novels: Hemingway's Nick Adams, Porter's Miranda Rhea, Anderson's George Willard, Faulkner's Isaac McCaslin (Watson 110). R. W. B. Lewis identified both generations as variations on the American Adam, or the innocent in the New World. Versions of this Adamic protagonist occur in the short fiction of William Saroyan, Richard Wright, Farrell, Welty, and Kay Boyle. The hard times of the depression may also have propelled certain authors back to the land itself, and to regionalism, as in the work of the midwesterners Suckow, Farrell, and Sinclair Lewis; the southerners Hughes, Toomer, Ellen Glasgow, and Erskine Caldwell; the Pennsylvanians John O'Hara and John Updike; and the Californian John Steinbeck.

The significance of the Beat writers at midcentury, although they wrote little short fiction, lies in their desire to question the status quo. Their rebellious attitude appears in somewhat altered form in the concerns of some major contemporary writers, who, distrustful of the American dream, become more and more attracted to the world of illusion as opposed to the "real" world of fact, and committed to a study of the act of writing itself. Such self-consciousness, or self-reflexivity, as it has come to be called, is evident especially in the work of writers from Robert Coover and Donald Barthelme to Leslie Marmon Silko and Bernard Malamud. Their fiction, particularly that of the former two, became less about objective reality and more about its own creative processes; the artistic process became the subject of their stories.

Notwithstanding the Beats and their similarly irreverent late 20th-century counterparts, general critical opinion seems to agree with the short story theorist Charles E. May, who suggests that two different strands developed in the short story of the latter half of the century: the stark new realistic style made famous by Hemingway and the mythic romance style made equally famous by Faulkner. The two styles combined notably in the short fiction of Porter, Welty, Steinbeck, Wright, Carson McCullers, Truman Capote, Isaac Bashevis Singer, Malamud, and others writing past midcentury. The main characteristics of this modern blending include a pronounced use of the grotesque, the employment of the traditional structures and motifs of the folktale, a tangible aesthetic concern, a fascination with dreams, a firm commitment to the power of language, the use of surrealistic imagery, and a carefully developed style and unified poetic form (May, *The Short Story* 19).

Because this combination continued into the second half of the 20th century, writers of the period between 1960 and 1990 fall roughly into two groups. On the one hand, the ultimate extreme of the mythic, romantic style is the fantastic stories—or antistories—of John Barth, Coover, Stanley Elkin, Richard Elman, and Barthelme, the postmodern writer who, more than any other, has specialized in the short story. On the other hand, the extreme of realism can be seen in the so-called minimalism of Raymond Carver, Ann Beattie, and Cynthia Ozick. The very fact that the mythic, romantic style is sometimes called magical realism, while the minimalist style is sometimes called hyperrealism, indicates that the twin streams of romance and realism are inextricably blended in the works of contemporary short story writers, including those of Hispanic-American, Native American, Asian-American, and African-American cultures—Sandra Cisneros, Leslie Marmon Silko, Maxine Hong Kingston, and Toni Cade Bambara, for example. The mid- and late 20th-century writers of urban or suburban fiction, too, sometimes blend magic and reality, as in the works of Singer, Malamud, Ozick, and John Cheever. The rise in the urban writers—Saul Bellow, for instance, writing of Chicago; Philip Roth, of New York and New Jersey; Ralph Ellison and James Baldwin, of New York, especially Harlem; Ann Petry, of New York and Connecticut—occurred simultaneously with the rise in New South writing and its more rural concerns. Robert Penn Warren, writing of Tennessee and Kentucky, and Welty, writing of Mississippi, inspired such younger writers as Peter Taylor of Tennessee, McCullers and O'Connor of Georgia, and Capote of Louisiana and Mississippi.

One of the most pronounced characteristics of post–World War II fiction has been a questioning of the traditional forms, even those of the experimental modernists. After the war, many of the "old" modernists continued to publish stories (Faulkner, Porter, and Wright, for example, lived into the 1960s). The lesson of these established writers seemed to be to write from one's own experience, and certainly many contemporary writers adhere to this principle, achieving thereby a new regionalism and a new ethnicity in short fiction. Alternatively, numerous American writers use the short story form to examine the postmodern condition, particularly by pushing that form to the edge of, or beyond, its limits. Thus such writers as Barthelme or William Gass abandon the neat sequential forms of narration in favor of fragmentation and distortion. Barth's story "Lost in the Funhouse" gives us probably the best-known postmodernist metaphor for the American condition: We cannot find our way in the distorted and illusory world that mockingly reflects our images. Characters might not—and certainly need not—develop or seem "real." Stories like these may teach us lessons about our own precarious positions in the world and about the possible inadequacy of the language we depend on for self-definition and self-realization (Weaver xv).

When examining contemporary short fiction, we need to know that for a time in the mid-20th century, the very survival of the short story sparked serious debate: Was it time to ring its death knell, or was it destined to become the most significant vehicle for expressing the dissatisfied and fragmented existence in the postwar world? Numerous critics have noted that popular interest in the short story declined after World War II, for several reasons. The clearest and most persuasive is the disappearance or reorganization of the popular magazines—the *Saturday Evening Post,* for instance—that had introduced such writers as Faulkner, Hemingway, and Welty to middle America. There no longer seemed a ready market for short fiction, although certainly the *New Yorker* provided an audience for what came to be known as the "New Yorker story," practiced by Jean Stafford, O'Hara, Cheever, Updike, and others. The late 20th century in the United States, fast paced and arguably obsessed with size and sales, tended to value the novel over the short story: If it has fewer words, it must be less important, or so the theory goes. Nonetheless, several factors during recent decades have assured the continued relevance of and audience for the short story: the rise in the publication of anthologies and their required use in the high school, college, and university classroom; the increase in the number of creative writing courses that produce short stories; and the collection of prizewinning stories in annual publications such as *Best American Short Stories.*

Perhaps one of the clearest signs of the revival of interest in short stories occurs in the vigorous and scholarly examination of the form as an enormously important genre in its own right. Such academic scrutiny began in the 1960s with the publication of Charles E. May's *Short Story Theories* (1967) and continues today with such influential short fiction studies as Susan Lohafer's *Coming to Terms with the Short Story* (1983) and Lohafer's and Jo Ellyn Clarey's *Short Story Theory at a Crossroads* (1989), as well as with May's *The New Short Story Theories* (1994). Such valuable studies not only prove that scholars take short stories seriously, but also ask theoretical questions about the special nature of the short form of fiction. The most general current debate, beginning in the 1980s, addresses the question of whether agreement on the definition and theory of such a varied form will ever occur. Students of short fiction disagree over such seemingly basic issues as length. No one has yet coined universally or even nationally satisfactory definitions that would allow clear distinctions among the short story (which can be less than a printed page in length), the short story proper, the long short story, the novella, and the short story cycle (volumes of interconnected stories). In fact, a number of critics deliberately find such definitions too restrictive. In the last few decades, these indistinct boundaries have extended still further to include novels composed of chapters that were initially published as short stories in magazines.

The debate over the appeal of the story versus the novel will continue as well. Short stories tend to nudge us slightly off balance. We feel somewhat mystified about the nature of Roderick Usher's illness in Poe's "The Fall of the House of Usher," about why Bartleby "prefers not to" in Melville's "Bartleby the Scrivener," or why Goodman Brown abandons Faith to walk into the dark New England forest in Hawthorne's "Young Goodman Brown." Why do ordinary people stone a woman to death in Shirley Jackson's "The Lottery"? Why do the hills resemble white elephants in Hemingway's "Hills Like White Elephants"? Why would Laura eat from the Judas tree in Porter's "Flowering Judas" or Manley Pointer steal a wooden leg in O'Connor's "Good Country People"? Is the grandson of Phoenix Jackson really dead in Welty's "A Worn Path"? The short story tells a different story from the one a novel tells. By focusing on a single experience or sequence of thoughts, the entire story often becomes a metaphor for a familiar if unexamined part of our own lives. As such, in Gordon Weaver's view, the story not only presents a vision of life, but also points the way to a "moral revelation" and hence a springboard to action and change (xv). In her 1977 novel *Ceremony,* Silko tells stories of the Laguna Pueblo tribe and explains the centrality of stories in the lives of all people. They can literally restore us to life, helping us to sharpen our awareness and our understanding of the seemingly mundane as well as the inexplicable and the spiritual. Rather than serving just as entertainment, they become essential to our moral and spiritual health: "You don't have anything if you don't have the stories."

This book has been several years in the planning and implementation. Focusing on American short story authors from the early 19th century to the early 21st century, *The Facts On File Companion to the American Short Story* has made special efforts to include all authors of merit, including previously ignored writers of both genders from all major cultural backgrounds. With few exceptions, these authors were born in the United States or Canada or made or make their home there. Bringing together useful information on the "universe" of the short story, the *Companion* contains author entries that include dates, biographies, lists of stories and their critical reception, and selected bibliographies. The *Companion* also contains individual entries on literary terms, themes, historical events, locales, influential magazines and critics, and major short story prize awards. We found that certain short story characters are repeatedly cited by critics and teachers as notable representatives of American experience, and we therefore provide entries on these significant protagonists. Moreover, the book includes entries on the long short story, or novella—whose connection to and difference from the short story continue to be debated—and on such short story subgenres as regionalism, science fiction, and detective fiction.

Choosing writers and stories for this book was an arduous process. We tried to achieve a representative balance between 19th-, 20th-, and 21st-century writers and between so-called classic and contemporary writers. Naturally, we regret that we could not include even more writers and even more stories. In the event, we established some guidelines to facilitate the decision-making process: In the case of the older, more traditional writers, we chose stories that appear frequently in the many anthologies available. In some cases in this book, significant writers, although closely identified with an era, do not appear simply because they primarily write novels rather than short fiction. In regard to contemporary writers, we tried to choose those who have published more than two collections, whose stories appear in popular anthologies, or who

have won literary prizes and awards, as well as those who have gained a following among younger readers and scholars. In many of the story entries, we suggest alternative ways of reading that may not occur to a first-time reader. We have also included overviews of particular categories of short fiction to provide background and bibliography for further study: The book contains entries on Asian-American, African-American, Hispanic-American, and Native American literature. The book also contains entries on critical theory, with explanations of such frequently used terms as *modernism* and *postmodernism*. Appendixes include winners of selected short story prizes, suggested readings by theme, and topic, and a selected bibliography of critical histories and theoretical approaches to the short story.

BIBLIOGRAPHY

Lohafer, Susan. *Coming to Terms with the Short Story*. Baton Rouge: Louisiana State University Press, 1983.

Lohafer, Susan, and Jo Ellyn Clarey, eds. *Short Story Theory at a Crossroads*. Baton Rouge: Louisiana State University Press, 1989.

May, Charles E., ed. *The New Short Story Theories*. Athens: Ohio University Press, 1994.

———. *The Short Story: The Reality of Artifice*. New York: Twayne, 1995.

Raffel, Burton. "Introduction." In *The Signet Classic Book of American Short Stories,* edited by Burton Raffel, 7–30. New York: New American Library, 1985.

Stevick, Philip. "Introduction." In *The American Short Story, 1900–1945: A Critical History,* edited by Philip Stevick, 1–31. Boston: Twayne, 1984.

Watson, James G. "The American Short Story: 1930–1945." In *The American Short Story, 1900–1945: A Critical History,* edited by Philip Stevick, 103–146. Boston: Twayne, 1984.

Weaver, Gordon. "Introduction." In *The American Short Story, 1945–1980: A Critical History,* edited by Gordon Weaver, xi–xix. Boston: Twayne, 1983.

A

"A & P" John Updike (1961)   First published in the *New Yorker* and subsequently collected in *Pigeon Feathers* (1962), "A & P" presents a brisk retrospective first-person narration (see POINT OF VIEW) by Sammy, a brash cashier who recounts his unsuccessful attempt to impress Queenie, one of three teenage girls who go shopping in the small seaside town grocery store where he works. Dressed only in bathing suits, Queenie and her friends immediately draw the attention of Sammy, his friend Stoksie, and the sheeplike shoppers for whom Sammy freely expresses his disdain. When Lengel, the unyielding manager, embarrasses the girls as Sammy rings up their purchase, Sammy quits, standing up for his principles and hoping to impress the girls. They have left the scene, however, and in the parking lot, he has an EPIPHANY: It reveals to him not only his present predicament but also the difficult life he will have hereafter.

With its fast-moving plot and seamless narrative, "A & P" is somewhat uncharacteristic of JOHN UPDIKE's short fiction, which more often takes a lyrical form and employs a looser construction held together by a highly metaphoric style. Nonetheless, it is his most frequently anthologized story, perhaps because of its accessibility and relevance to students, its THEME of initiation, and its pronounced concluding epiphany. Much of the story's appeal derives from the narrative voice: Sammy's lively verbal performance displays a surprising elasticity of TONE, ranging from colloquial adolescent male slang to similes that may reveal an embryonic writer. While Sammy reveals sexist attitudes, his narration seeks approval for his individualistic gesture and casts him as an unexpected hero, standing up for principles of decency toward others that Lengel fails to recognize when he chastises the girls for indecency. Initially Sammy joins Stoksie in leering at the girls; though his interest in Queenie's exposed flesh never wanes, he experiences a turning point when he observes the butcher sizing up the girls. Sammy also admires Queenie for her confident carriage—which, in quitting, perhaps he attempts to emulate—as well as her social status. Queenie embodies a socioeconomic realm to which Sammy, the son of working-class parents, desires access.

Sammy's quitting may be motivated by a combination of lust, admiration of Queenie's social status, and sentimental romanticism, but his gesture does not lack principle and quickly assumes more serious overtones. The link Sammy feels with Queenie vanishes as he crosses the supermarket's threshold for the last time and encounters not his dream girl but a premonition of the realities of married life: a young mother yelling at her children. While he has established a distance between himself and Lengel's narrow world, Sammy realizes the truth of the manager's warning that he will feel the impact of this incident for the rest of his life. Indeed, Sammy refuses to stoop to self-pity and seems to savor the experience, even as he realizes it will have numerous unforeseen repercussions that will make life more difficult in the future.

BIBLIOGRAPHY

Dessner, Lawrence Jay. "Irony and Innocence in John Updike's 'A & P.'" *Studies in Short Fiction* 25 (1988): 315–317.

Detweiler, Robert. *John Updike*. Rev. ed. Boston: G. K. Hall, 1984.

Greiner, Donald. *The Other John Updike: Poems, Short Stories, Prose, Play*. Athens: Ohio University Press, 1981.

Luscher, Robert M. *John Updike: A Study of the Short Fiction*. New York: Twayne, 1993.

McFarland, Ronald E. "Updike and the Critics: Reflections on 'A & P.'" *Studies in Short Fiction* 20 (1983): 95–100.

Petry, Alice. "The Dress Code in Updike's 'A & P.'" *Notes on Contemporary Literature* 16.1 (1986): 8–10.

Porter, M. Gilbert. "John Updike's 'A & P': The Establishment and an Emersonian Cashier." *English Journal* 61 (1972): 1,155–1,158.

Shaw, Patrick. "Checking Out Faith and Lust: Hawthorne's 'Young Goodman Brown' and Updike's 'A & P.'" *Studies in Short Fiction* 23 (1986): 321–323.

Wells, Walter. "John Updike's 'A & P': A Return Visit to Araby." *Studies in Short Fiction* 30 (1993): 127–133.

Robert Luscher
University of Nebraska at Kearney

ABNER SNOPES   Among the first in his rapacious clan to settle in YOKNAPATAWPHA COUNTY and the father of the infamous Flem Snopes, Abner Snopes is best known as a barn burner and a mule thief who appears in a number of WILLIAM FAULKNER's novels and who is the main character in the short story "BARN BURNING." In "Barn Burning," Abner is a hardened and embittered man who, resentful of his lot in life as a sharecropper, burns the barns of the planters from whom he leases land. In the novel *The UNVANQUISHED*, Abner, after deserting from the Confederate army, steals mules from both the Union and Confederate forces, changes the brands, and resells them to both armies.

See also SNOPES FAMILY.

BIBLIOGRAPHY

Beck, Warren. *Man in Motion*. Madison: University of Wisconsin Press, 1961.

H. Collin Messer
University of North Carolina

ABSTRACT EXPRESSIONISM   Twentieth-century artistic movement and literary style originating in Germany, abstract expressionism was particularly influenced by the Swedish dramatist August Strindberg (1849–1912). Although mainly associated with theater, abstract expressionism also appears in literature, painting, and music. The hallmark of abstract expressionism is its radical revolt against REALISM. Instead of representing the world objectively, the author or artist attempts to express inner experience by representing the world as it appears to him or her personally, or to an emotionally distraught or abnormal character. Frequently this troubled mental condition represents the anxiety of the modern individual in an industrial and technological society moving away from order toward confusion or disaster.

See also ABSURD; SURREALISM.

ABSURD   Dramatic and prose fiction works that portray the human condition as essentially and ineradicably ludicrous or farcical are termed *absurd*. The style has its roots in the fiction of James Joyce and Franz Kafka. The major practitioners, however, emerged after WORLD WAR II in rebellion against the essential beliefs and values of traditional culture and its literature. The absurdists' fictional modern men and women—like their real-life counterparts—see their existence as meaningless and absurd. Notable practitioners in the theatrical world were Jean Genet, Eugene Ionesco, and Samuel Beckett, European writers loosely grouped under the rubric Theater of the Absurd, and Harold Pinter, the British playwright famous for the menace lurking beneath the surface of his deceptively ordinary domestic settings. EDWARD ALBEE is the best known American practitioner. Typically this mode is grotesquely comic as well as irrational.

See also BLACK HUMOR; SURREALISM.

ADAMS, ALICE BOYD (1926–1999)   Prolific novelist and award-winning author of six story collections, Alice Adams over six decades portrayed the landscape of American women in locales from the South to the West Coast to Europe. Her protagonists are frequently artistic or professional women who wrestle with marriage, divorce, and myriad other relationships, including close friendships with other women, as they seek to define themselves and to live lives of substance. Adams's stories—which appeared in such magazines as the NEW YORKER, Atlantic, Mademoiselle, Vogue, Redbook, McCall's, and Paris Review—are collected in Beautiful Girl (1979), To See You Again (1982), Molly's Dog (1983), Return Trips (1985), After You've Gone (1989), and The Last Lovely City (1999). She won the O. HENRY MEMORIAL AWARD 25 times between 1971 and 1996 and the Best American Short Stories Award three times (1976, 1992, and 1996). In 1982 she was awarded the O. Henry Special Award for Continuing Achievement.

She was born on August 14, 1926, to Nicholson Barney Adams, a college professor, and Agatha Erskine Boyd Adams, in Fredericksburg, Virginia. She grew up in a farmhouse near Chapel Hill, North Carolina, where her father taught Spanish. Despite her early admission to Radcliffe College, Adams followed the usual pattern of the day and, soon after earning her bachelor of arts degree in 1946, married Mark Linenthal, Jr., a professor who eventually taught English at San Francisco State University. The marriage ended in divorce in 1958; Adams published her first story the following year, and her first novel at the age of 40. She remained in San Francisco for the rest of her life, and the city became one of her major settings, along with North Carolina and Virginia.

Adams is known for a spare, elegant, seemingly effortless prose style that often depicts her characters with an empathetic irony. Her frank portrayal of female sexuality and relationships is balanced by her penchant for realistic, often witty dialogue, and, although her characters are sometimes lonely, they persevere and continue with a sense of possibility and optimism. Half the stories in Beautiful Girl, her first collection, were published as O. Henry Prize winners. To See You Again, comprising 19 stories, presents a number of women who maintain their dignity as they struggle to understand themselves, and Return Trips centers on a journey motif as women remember or renew old acquaintances in old familiar places. The 14 brief romances of After You've Gone move from the California setting of the earlier work across the country to Maryland, and The Last Lovely City returns to San Francisco to consider the alternatives to failed marriages and relationships.

Alice Adams died in her sleep in San Francisco, California, on May 27, 1999. The much-praised Collected Stories of Alice Adams appeared posthumously, in 2002.

BIBLIOGRAPHY

Adams, Alice. After the War. New York: Knopf, 2000.
———. After You've Gone. New York: Knopf, 1989.
———. Almost Perfect. New York: Knopf, 1993.
———. Beautiful Girl. New York: Knopf, 1979.
———. Careless Love. New York: New American Library, 1966. Republished as The Fall of Daisy Duke. London: Constable, 1967.
———. Caroline's Daughters. New York: Knopf, 1991.
———. Families and Survivors. New York: Knopf, 1975.
———. The Last Lovely City. New York: Knopf, 1999.
———. Listening to Billie. New York: Knopf, 1978.
———. Medicine Men. New York: Knopf, 1997.
———. Molly's Dog. Concord, N.H.: Evert, 1983.
———. "PW Interviews: Alice Adams," by Patricia Holt. Publishers Weekly 213 (January 16, 1978): 8–9.
———. Return Trips. New York: Knopf, 1985.
———. Rich Rewards. New York: Knopf, 1980.
———. Second Chances. New York: Knopf, 1988.
———. Southern Exposure. New York: Knopf, 1995.
———. The Stories of Alice Adams. New York: Knopf, 2002.
———. Superior Women. New York: Knopf, 1984.
———. To See You Again. New York: Knopf, 1982.
Boucher, Sandy. "Alice Adams—a San Francisco Novelist Who Is into Her Third Book." San Francisco 20 (October 1978): 130–133.
Chell, Cara. "Succeeding in Their Times: Alice Adams on Women and Work." Soundings: An Interdisciplinary Journal 68 (Spring 1985): 62–71.
Faber, Nancy. "Out of the Pages" People, 3 April 1978: pp. 48–49.
Feinneman, Neil. "An Interview with Alice Adams." Story Quarterly, no. 11 (1980): 27–37.
Warga, Wayne. "A Sophisticated Author Gets By with Help from Her Friends." Los Angeles Times Book Review, 16 November 1980, p. 3.

ADULTERY AND OTHER CHOICES

ANDRE DUBUS (1977) ANDRE DUBUS's second collection of short stories (his first, Separate Flights, was published in 1975), Adultery and Other Choices focuses on themes of betrayal and acceptance; many of Dubus's characters are outsiders who desperately want in. The collection is divided into three sections: Part 1 involves stories of childhood and adolescence; part 2 concerns stories of military life; part 3 contains the long story "Adultery," the second installment in a three-part narrative that was later reprinted in *We Don't Live Here Anymore* (1984).

The opening three stories, "An Afternoon with the Old Man," "Contrition," and "The Bully"—as well as "Cadence," which appears later in the collection—concern the young Paul Clement (an ALTER EGO for the author) and his painful trek from childhood into manhood. Both "An Afternoon with the Old Man" and "Contrition" explore Paul's painful, deficient relationship with his father. Considered weak and inadequate by the "old man," Paul prefers to distance himself: "With his father he had lived a lie for as long as he could remember: he believed his father wanted him to be popular and athletic at school, so Paul never told him about his days" (18). Paul's attempts to negotiate the codes of adolescence reveal his fear, cowardice, and cruelty. "The Bully" is framed by two disturbing scenes: As the story opens, Paul methodically kills a stray cat; as it concludes, he darkly envisions the recent drowning death of the boy who has bullied him. Like "The Bully," which involves Paul's cruel rejection of his friend Eddie, "Cadence" is a story of betrayal: This time the victim is Hugh Munson, a fellow marine recruit whom Paul abandons after a forced training run. Despite such betrayals, Paul is often kind and sensitive, and we never fail to sense that he, too, is an outsider. Like Paul, Louise of "The Fat Girl" is a misfit; the story explores Louise's struggle for acceptance, contrasting her college friend Carrie's compassion with her husband, Richard's, cruel rejection.

The stories of military life in part 2, such as "The Shooting," further the themes of betrayal and acceptance, but some are also tales of survival. In "Andromache," Ellen Forrest must piece together her life after the death of her husband. In "Corporal of Artillery," the 22-year-old Fitzgerald reenlists in the Marine Corps, out of his sense of duty to his wife, who is recovering from a nervous breakdown, and their three young children.

In "Adultery," the final story, Jack, Terry, Hank, and Edith are all unfaithful, but it is Edith's affair with the lapsed priest Joe Ritchie—a relationship founded on compassion and love—that complicates our reading of the meaning of "adultery." "All adultery is a symptom," thinks Edith, and we sense that she is right: The infidelities of *Adultery and Other Choices* merely hint at the larger, deeper erosions and betrayals that characterize many human relationships (158).

BIBLIOGRAPHY
Dubus, Andre. *Adultery and Other Choices.* Boston: D. R. Godine, 1977.
Kennedy, Thomas E. *Andre Dubus: A Study of the Short Fiction.* Boston: Twayne, 1988.

Michael Hogan
University of North Carolina

AESOP'S FABLES According to tradition, Aesop was a Greek slave who lived around 600 B.C. The FABLES are succinct tales, such as "The Tortoise and the Hare," in which talking animals illustrate human vices, follies, and virtues (see PERSONIFICATION).

AESTHETICISM The Aesthetic Movement developed in France and during the late 19th century became a European phenomenon among those adhering to the doctrine of "art for art's sake"—that is, the purpose of a work of art is simply to exist and to be beautiful. The roots of the Aesthetic Movement lie in the German theory, proposed by the philosopher Immanuel Kant in 1790, that aesthetic contemplation is "disinterested," indifferent to both the reality and the utility of the beautiful object; it was also influenced by the view of EDGAR ALLAN POE (in "The Poetic Principle," 1850) that the supreme work is simply itself, "a poem written solely for the poem's sake." In other words, a work of art or literature need serve no moral, practical, or instructive purpose; it should, instead, appeal to viewers or readers solely on the basis of its beauty.

AESTHETICS The general term for a sense of the beautiful. Although the term may be applied to art, music, or any work that appeals to the emotions rather than the intellect, an aesthete, one especially sensitive to beauty, responds strongly to lyrically and artistically appealing works of literature. Many of KATHERINE ANN PORTER's works, for example, have a strong aesthetic appeal.

AFFECTIVE FALLACY

An essay published in 1946 by W. K. Wimsatt, Jr., and Monroe C. Beardsley, two of the architects of NEW CRITICISM, defined affective fallacy as the error of evaluating a poem by its effects—especially its emotional effects—upon the reader. As a result of this fallacy, the literary work as "an object of specifically critical judgement, tends to disappear," so that criticism "ends in impressionism and relativism." This attempt to separate the appreciation and evaluation of fiction from its emotional and other effects on the reader has been severely criticized, on the grounds that a work of literature that leaves the reader unresponsive and impassive is not experienced as literature at all.

AFRICAN-AMERICAN SHORT FICTION

Despite the debt the African-American short story owes to the "national art form," as FRANK O'CONNOR called the American short story, it, like the other genres of the African-American literary tradition, must be traced back to the site that in 1789 the freed slave Olaudah Equiano called his "nation of dancers, musicians and poets," in describing his traditional West African community of Essaka. Equiano recalled not only the integral role storytelling played in the daily life of the community but also its inextricable relationship to music and dance:

> Every great event, such as a triumphant return from battle, or other cause of public rejoicing, is celebrated in public dances, which are accompanied with songs and music suited to the occasion. . . . Each represents some interesting scene of real life. . . . And as the subject is generally founded on some recent event, it is therefore ever new. (14–15)

One may logically conclude, therefore, that the African-American short story begins with the oral lore African slaves too with them from West Africa to the "New World" as early as the 15th century.

When, as American slaves, Africans gained access to literacy and language and began creating written texts, the results resounded with fictive elements—themes, characterization, and tropes—that drew, as John Henrik Clarke noted, "on the oral literature used in Africa to teach and preserve their group history" (xv), or the oral traditions Equiano so eloquently described. An excellent example is the paradigmatic African folk hero: the TRICKSTER. Although commonly found in the Anansesem (spider tales) of West Africa, the trickster was not, as Lawrence Levine points out, represented solely in animal tales, for "tricksters could, and did, assume divine and human forms as well" (103), as evident in such heroes as the Dahomey's Legba and the Yoruba's Esu and Orunmila. Often in these tales, one finds a confrontation in which the weak uses wit to overpower or evade the strong. The direct relationship between the African-American literary tradition and African culture is offered by Henry Louis Gates, Jr., who argues that the Signifying Monkey figure found in African-American profane discourse is Esu's "functional equivalent." Moreover, Gates maintains that "unlike his Pan-African Esu Cousins," the Signifying Monkey "exists not primarily as a character in a narrative but rather as a vehicle of narration itself. Like Esu, however, the Signifying Monkey stands as the figure of an oral writing within black vernacular language rituals" (*The Signifying Monkey* 52).

In African-American literature this hero, theme, narrative mode, and linguistic ritual readily appear in the first written texts, from Equiano's *Interesting Narrative of Olaudah Equiano, or Gustavus Vassa, the African* (1789) and FREDERICK DOUGLASS's now-classic 19th-century *Narrative of the Life of Frederick Douglass* (1845) to RALPH ELLISON's American masterpiece *Invisible Man* (1952) and TONI MORRISON's award-winning novel *Song of Solomon* (1977), in which the trickster role, aptly played by the heroine, Pilate, reaches magnificent heights.

These characteristics of the trickster are first found, however, in stories about the wily acts of Brer Rabbit, Brer Fox, and High John de Conquer/Fortuneteller, who as characters are poised at all times to deceive their masters. As Darwin T. Turner notes, "These were folk tales which no individual proclaimed to be his unique creation. Certainly, individuals invented them, but later narrators felt free to modify them; for these stories about heroes—animal and human—whose character traits were well known to the listeners were the product of the race" (2). In sum, they served a communal function much in the way that stories, songs, and dance did in Equiano's "charming fruitful vale" (2).

Not surprisingly, the same desire for freedom that fueled the first English written text by North American slaves (primarily through poetry and song), injected the black voice into the antislavery movement, and created the new autobiographical genre of the slave narrative also formed the impetus of the first narrative stories (in novel form) written by African Americans: *Clotel; or, the President's Daughter* (1853), by William Wells Brown, and *The Heroic Slave* (1853), by Douglass. Other works would follow during the same decade, which some scholars now identify as the first African-American literary renaissance, including Frank Webb's *The Garies and Their Friends* (1857), Martin R. Delany's *Blake; Or the Huts of America* (1859), and Harriet Wilson's *Our Nig; Or, Sketches from the Life of a Free Black* (1859), the first novel written by an African-American woman.

Debates about who published the first African-American short story or prose narrative abound. Contending that many first appeared in early magazines and newspapers, including the *African Methodists Episcopalian Review, Colored Home Journal,* and *Anglo-African Journal,* William R. Robinson traces the publication of the first short narrative stories to the well-known 19th-century poet George Moses Horton, who wrote religious stories for a Sunday school publication. Lemuel Haynes, author of *Mysterious Development; or Russell Colvin (Supposed to be Murdered), in Full Life and Stephen and Jesse Born, His convicted Murderers, Rescued from Ignominious Death by Wonderful Discoveries* (1820), is also given this honor, as is William Wells Brown. In 1859, FRANCES ELLEN WATKINS HARPER, abolitionist orator and author of *Iola Leroy; or Shadows of the Uplifted* (1892), published "The Two Offers," the first short story by an African-American woman.

There is no debate that CHARLES W. CHESNUTT was the first professional African-American short story writer, although PAUL L. DUNBAR published the first collection of stories, *Folks From Dixie* (1898). A successful attorney who saw literature as a way of confronting racism and segregation, Chesnutt published "The Goophered Grapevine," his first short story, in the prestigious ATLANTIC MONTHLY in 1877. Steeped in folk material, his first collection of stories, *The Conjure Woman* (1899), was published by Houghton Mifflin Company, with the assistance and blessings of its editors, including Francis J. Garrison, the son of the abolitionist WILLIAM LLOYD GARRISON. It was favorably reviewed by WILLIAM DEAN HOWELLS. Ironically, because Chesnutt used a white narrator, readers were not initially aware of the author's African-American identity.

In "The Goophered Grapevine," a story framed by the ostensibly superior white narrator, Chesnutt's black narrator of the inner story, Uncle Julius McAdoo, a shrewd former field hand slave who enriches his recollection of slavery with CONJURE STORIES and voodoo tales and folk practices and beliefs, is patterned after the trickster hero. While playing the expected "darkie" role, well-masked Uncle Julius illuminates the darker side of the "peculiar institution," disrupting the romantic historical and literary conventions in which antebellum life had been enshrined by the plantation traditions of the southern local colorists Thomas Nelson Page (author of *Marse Chan and Other Stories*) and Thomas Dixon (author of *Leopard's Spots*). Chesnutt also published his second collection of stories, *The Wife of His Youth,* in 1899. By the turn of the century, Chesnutt had gained visibility and recognition for his work, although he was not considered a master of the short story during his lifetime.

By 1904, Dunbar, whose reputation for his folk poetry written in dialect had made him the most notable black poet in the United States at the turn of the century, published three more collections of stories, *The Strength of Gideon and Other Stories* (1900), *In Old Plantation Days* (1903), and *The Heart of Happy Hollow* (1904). Unlike Chesnutt, however, Dunbar embraced prevailing stereotypical images of blacks, despite what some critics also see as an element of protest in his work. His romantic portrayal of slavery (about which he learned from his parents and free blacks), with loyal slaves and benevolent masters in particular, resonates with Page's view of slavery as the "good ole days." A reviewer of *In Old Plantation Days* ranked his treatment of plantation life above that of Page: "Dr. Thomas Nelson Page himself does not make 'ole Marse' and 'ole Miss' more admirable nor exalt higher in the slave the qualities of faithfulness and good humor" (quoted in Laryea 119). Despite the fact that Dunbar is often considered more a follower than a trailblazer like Chesnutt, together they successfully initiated the African-American short story before the HARLEM RENAISSANCE of the 1920s marked the true maturation of the African-American literary tradition.

Alain Locke and LANGSTON HUGHES's declarations in their respective essays "The New Negro" and "The Negro Artists and the Racial Mountain" register the spectrum and dynamic energy of the African-American-inspired communal transformation and celebration, often called the Harlem Renaissance, that were witnessed by post–WORLD WAR I America. After proclaiming that "the Old Negro had become more myth than a man," Locke politely requested that "the Negro of today be seen through other than the dusty spectacles of past controversy" (3, 5). In contrast, Hughes pugnaciously pronounced: "We younger artists who create now intend to express our individual dark-skinned selves without fear of shame. . . . We build our temples for tomorrow, strong as we know how, and we stand on top of the mountain, free within ourselves" (1,271).

Hughes and his contemporaries, JEAN TOOMER, ZORA NEALE HURSTON, Claude McKay, Rudolph Fisher, Eric Walrond, DOROTHY WEST, and others, found a ready venue for their work in such black-owned journals and newspaper as *Crisis, Opportunity,* and *Negro World,* which sponsored annual contests to showcase talented new writers. In Harlem, the spiritual center of the "renaissance," the writers empowered their own voices by founding *Fire!,* a magazine edited by Wallace Thurman, Hurston, and Hughes, but they also sought mainstream publishers such as Boni and Liveright, the publisher of Toomer's CANE (1923). Toomer's complex landscape of southern black life transcends the debasing legacy of the plantation tradi-

tion, as seen through the penetrating eyes and heard in the haunting blues voices of the characters that people his lyrical stories, including "Karintha," "Fern," and "Blood Burning Moon."

Hurston gained attention when her story "Spunk" won *Opportunity*'s second-place prize for fiction in 1925. She added a new horizon to this landscape by looking at the black imagined self in such now-classic stories as "SWEAT" and "The GILDED SIX BITS," in which the black community (such as fictional Eatontown) surfaces as a major character, if not the very nucleus of its people's lives. In these stories, Hurston successfully demonstrates that in contrast to the way whites view "darkies," as expressed by the shopkeeper in "Gilded Six Bits"—"Laughin' all the time. Nothin' worries 'em" (98)—black life is ebullient and complex. Although Hughes uses his stories to celebrate and "sing" all aspects of African-American life, including the prevalence of the extended black family structure, as found in "Thank You, M'am," one critic notes that his first published collection, *The Ways of White Folks* (1934), "excoriates the guile and mendacity, self-deception and equivocation, insincerity and sanctimoniousness, sham, humbug, and sheer fakery of white America in all its dealings with the black minority" (Bone 253). In his best-known stories, those about the folk hero/urban philosopher Jesse B. Simple (see SIMPLE STORIES), Hughes strips bare the facade of Harlem's brownstones to show the interior lives of its residents, giving these "darker" brothers and sisters voice and wisdom. The works of two other writers of the renaissance, *Ginger Town* (1932) and *Banana Bottom* (1933) by McKay and *Tropic Death* (1926) by Walrond, feature stories set in their homelands, a Caribbean island and a Latin American nation, respectively. In the end, one may argue that stories by Harlem Renaissance writers, as typified through these authors, reveal a quest to unravel and provide "a definition of the role of black people in the world" (Litz i).

It would take the stories of the pen-wielding "native son" and paradigmatic "black boy," the Mississippi-born novelist RICHARD WRIGHT, however, to win the attention of mainstream critics. With a Marxist emphasis on class rather than race in the experience of the southern black sharecroppers (the proletariat) in such stories as "Bright and Morning Star" and "Down by the Riverside" from his first collection of short stories, *Uncle Tom's Children* (1938), Wright confirmed the "universality" and legitimacy of the African-American experience as the serious fictional subject of American REALISM and NATURALISM. This collection won him a $500 prize in a *Story* magazine contest. In "BIG BOY LEAVES HOME" and the stories in *Eight Men* (1960), particularly "The MAN WHO WAS ALMOST A MAN," the author of *Native Son* (1940), who concerned himself as much with art as with message, provided insights into the oppression experienced by those whose lives in the margin were overtly or covertly governed by the JIM CROW laws. Clearly recognized for his craftsmanship, Wright, according to Clarke, "was given the recognition that Chesnutt and Dunbar deserved but did not receive. . . . With the emergence of Richard Wright the double standard for black writers no longer existed" (xviii).

The most visible immediate beneficiary of Wright's impact was Frank Yerby. Although better known as the author of historical novels, such as *The Foxes of Harrow* (1946), which do not treat the African-American experience, Yerby won the 1944 O. HENRY MEMORIAL AWARD for his short story "Health Card," in which discrimination is the central theme. Equally significant were the other writers of the Wrightian school of literary naturalism, ANN PETRY, author of *The Street* (1946), and Chester Himes, author of *If He Hollers Let Him Go* (1945). Himes's first short story, "Crazy in the Stir," was published in *Esquire* magazine in 1934. Petry's nationally acclaimed "LIKE A WINDING SHEET" was first published in *The Crisis* (1945) and later included in Martha Foley's *Best American Short Stories of 1946;* it gained Petry a Houghton Mifflin Literary Fellowship. Her collection of stories *Miss Muriel and Other Stories* was published in 1971.

African-American writers who gained recognition for their fiction during the last half of the 20th century, from Ralph W. Ellison, JAMES BALDWIN, and Paule Marshall to ERNEST J. GAINES, ALICE WALKER, Toni Morrison, and JOHN EDGAR WIDEMAN, have all employed the short story form. In fact, to A. Walton Litz's general contention that "no important American writer of fiction has neglected the short story form,

and in the case of many writers . . . the short story represented their greatest achievement" (Clarke xviii), one can readily include African-American writers. Three anthologies of African-American short stories published in the 1990s, clearly confirm the significance of the contribution of black Americans to the genre: *Black American Short Stories: One Hundred Years of the Best,* edited by John Henrik Clarke (Hill and Wang, 1963 and 1993); *Calling the Wind: Twentieth Century African-American Short Stories,* edited by Clarence Major (Harper-Perennial, 1993); and *Children of the Night: The Best Short Stories by Black Writers, 1967 to the Present,* edited by Gloria Naylor (Little, Brown and Company, 1995). These anthologies include works by such well-known writers as Maya Angelou, TONI CADE BAMBARA, CYRUS COLTER, Samuel Delaney, Alexis DeVeaux, Rita Dove, Henry Dumas, Rosa Guy, Gayl Jones, LeRoi Jones (Amiri Baraka), Charles Johnson, William Melvin Kelley, Randall Kenan, JAMAICA KINCAID, John O. Killens, Terry McMillan, James Alan McPherson, Clarence Major, Albert Murray, Gloria Naylor, Ntozake Shange, John A. Williams, and Sherley Anne Williams. In addition, to list but a few, are the names of Don Belton, Larry Duplechan, Tina McElroy, Richard Perry, and Ann Allen Shockley.

As a genre, the short story remains a favorite among well-established writers, as is illustrated by the novelist Wideman, among whose collections are *Damballah* (1981), *Fever: Twelve Stories* (1989), *The Stories of John Edgar Wideman* (1992), and *All Stories Are True* (1993). Perhaps no other writer than Wideman so represents the distance African-American writers have traveled from Chesnutt and Dunbar to gain recognition and respectability for their stories. Not surprisingly, Wideman, who served as guest editor of *The Best American Short Stories 1996,* published by Houghton Mifflin, called attention to the best African-American short story writer of this generation, William Henry Lewis (*In the Arms of Our Elders,* 1994), by including his award-winning and widely anthologized story "Shades" in the collection.

Lewis's second collection of stories, *I Got Somebody in Staunton* (HarperCollins, 2007), which was a finalist for the 2005 PEN/FAULKNER AWARD for fiction, won the Black Caucus of the American Library

Association Literary Award, confirming his place as a major contemporary writer of short fiction. Lewis shares the vanguard with Haitian-born Edwidge Danticat, whose collection of stories, *Krik? Krak!* (Vintage, 1996) focuses, as do her novels, on her Haitian cultural heritage. Equally important is ZZ Packer, who gained national attention and rave reviews with her first collection of stories, *Drinking Coffee Elsewhere* (Riverhead Trade, 2004), which was also a PEN/Faulkner finalist and was named a *New York Times* Notable Book. Packer also edited *New Stories from the South* (2008).

Gay and lesbian African-American writers of short fiction have also carved a place for themselves. For example, Thomas Glave, winner of the Lambda Award for his nonfiction, was the second black writer to win an O. Henry Award, previously won only by James Baldwin. Glave's first collection of stories, *Whose Song and Other Stories* (City Lights, 2000), was placed at the top of the list of Best American Gay Fiction at the beginning of the 21st century. His second collection of stories, *The Torturer's Wife* (2008), was also published by City Lights Publishers. In his *Our Caribbean: A Gathering of Lesbian and Gay Writings from the Antilles* (Duke University Press, 2008) Glave introduces the works of other Caribbean short fiction writers.

BIBLIOGRAPHY

Baker, Houston A., Jr. *Singers of Daybreak: Studies in Black American Literature*. Washington, D.C.: Howard University Press, 1983.

Bell, Bernard. *The Afro-American Novel and Its Tradition*. Amherst: University of Massachusetts Press, 1987.

Bone, Robert. *Down Home: A History of Afro-American Short Fiction from Its Beginnings to the End of the Harlem Renaissance*. New York: G. P. Putnam's Sons, 1975.

Bruck, Peter, and Wolfgang Karrer, eds. *The Afro-American Novel Since 1960*. Amsterdam: B. R. Grüner, 1982.

Byerman, Keith, ed. *John Edgar Wideman: A Study of the Short Fiction*. New York: Twayne Publishers, 1998.

Clarke, John. "Introduction." In *Black American Short Stories: One Hundred Years of the Best,* edited by John Clarke, xv–xxi. New York: Hill & Wang, 1993.

Equiano, Olaudah. *The Interesting Narrative of the Life of Olaudah Equiano, Written by Himself In Classic Slave Narratives*. Edited by Henry Louis Gates, Jr. New York: Mentor, 1987.

Gates, Henry Louis, Jr. *The Signifying Monkey: A Theory of Afro-American Literary Criticism*. New York: Oxford University Press, 1988.

Gates, Henry Louis, Jr., et al., eds. *The Norton Anthology of African American Literature*. New York: W. W. Norton, 1997.

Hill, Patricia Liggins, and Bernard Bell, et al., eds. *Call and Response: The Riverside Anthology of the African American Literary Tradition*. Boston: Houghton Mifflin, 1998.

Hughes, Langston. "The Negro Artist and the Racial Mountain." In *The Norton Anthology of African American Literature,* edited by Henry L. Gates, Jr., 1,267–1,271. New York: W. W. Norton, 1997.

Hurston, Zora Neale. "The Guilded Six-Bits." In *The Complete Stories*. New York: HarperCollins, 1995, 98.

Laryea, Doris Lucas. "Paul Laurence Dunbar." In *Dictionary of Literary Biography,* edited by Trudier Harris and Thadious Davis. Vol. 50, 106–122. Detroit, Mich.: Gale Research, 1986.

Lee, Robert A., ed. *Black Fiction: New Studies in the Afro-American Novel since 1945*. London: Vision Press, 1980.

Levine, Lawrene W. *Black Culture and Black Consciousness*. New York: Oxford University Press, 1977.

Litz, Walton A. "Preface." In *Major American Short Stories,* edited by A. Walton Litz. New York: Oxford University Press, 1980.

Locke, Alain. "The New Negro." In *The New Negro,* edited by Alain Locke, 3–16. New York: Johnson Reprint Corporation, 1968.

Major, Clarence, ed. *Calling the Wind: Twentieth Century African-American Short Stories*. New York: HarperPerennial, 1993.

McMillan, Terry, ed. *Breaking Ice: An Anthology of Contemporary African American Fiction*. With a preface by John Edgar Wideman. New York: Penguin Books, 1990.

Naylor, Gloria, ed. *Children of the Night: The Best Short Stories by Black Writers, 1967 to the Present*. New York: Little, Brown, 1995.

Robinson, William R., ed. *Early Black American Prose*. Dubuque, Iowa: William C. Brown, 1991.

Turner, Darwin T. "Introduction." In *Black American Literature: Fiction,* edited by Darwin T. Turner. Columbus, Ohio: Charles E. Merrill, 1969.

Young, Al, ed. *African American Literature: A Brief Introduction and Anthology*. Berkeley: University of California Press, 1996.

Wilfred D. Samuels
University of Utah

AGRARIANS, THE

AGRARIANS, THE   A group of southern writers, including John Crowe Ransom, Allan Tate, Donald Davidson, Robert Penn Warren, Merrill Moore, Laura Riding, and Cleanth Brooks, also called the Fugitives, from the title of a magazine of poetry and criticism championing agrarian REGIONALISM that they published from 1922 to 1925. In 1930 they issued a collective manifesto, "I'll Take My Stand: The South and the Agrarian Tradition by Twelve Southerners," which espoused an agrarian economy over an industrial one. This group was also important for developing the NEW CRITICISM, in which they considered a literary work as an autonomous composition, removed from social, philosophical, or ethical considerations. This group is often given credit for energizing a literary renaissance in the South.

AIKEN, CONRAD (CONRAD POTTER AIKEN) (1889–1973)

AIKEN, CONRAD (CONRAD POTTER AIKEN) (1889–1973)   Born in Savannah, Georgia, on August 5, 1889, and educated at Harvard University, Aiken was a writer who also worked as editor, journalist, and consultant in poetry to the Library of Congress in Washington, D.C. Author of seven novels, three story collections, numerous collections of poetry, and one of literary criticism, he won numerous literary prizes—including the Pulitzer (1930) and the National Book Award (1954). Surprisingly, however, his stories have been dropped from most anthologies.

His first collection of short fiction, *Bring! Bring! and Other Stories* (1925), contains at the very least two mesmerizing stories of adolescent awakening: "Strange Moonlight" depicts the effects of a young girl's death on the preadolescent HERO, and "The Last Visit" relates a boy's final visit to his grandmother. According to Edward Butscher, looming in the background of these stories, as well as of the classic "Silent Snow, Secret Snow," are Aiken's own traumatic memories of his father's suicide after murdering Aiken's mother.

Although Aiken's second collection, *Costumes by Eros,* enjoyed less critical success, his third collection, *Among the Lost People,* contains at least three finely wrought and memorable stories: "Mr. Arcularis," "Impulse," and "Silent Snow, Secret Snow," the most famous and, until recently, the most frequently anthologized. "Mr. Arcularis" evokes the "raging inse-curity of a traumatized child now grown into a friendless old man," who lies dying on an operating table (Butscher, "Conrad Aiken" 19). The main character in "Impulse" seems a younger version of Mr. Arcularis. "Impulse" addresses the prototypical American dilemma of immature men compelling mature women to assume the features of a monstrous mother. "Silent Snow, Secret Snow," a horror story in the manner of EDGAR ALLAN POE, builds almost unbearable suspense in the reader as the young boy, Paul Hasleman, hears the soft and sibilant whispers of the falling snow creeping ever nearer until it will engulf his consciousness and probably his soul. Although critics, referring to Aiken's father's insanity as well as Aiken's fascination with psychology, commonly interpret the snow as a METAPHOR for the onset of mental disease (psychosis or schizophrenia), readers might also see the snow as the more traditional metaphor of death. The spellbinding quality, the inexorable use of the IMAGERY of coldness, and the realistic look inside Paul's mind guarantee the unforgettable effects of "Silent Snow, Secret Snow" on all readers.

BIBLIOGRAPHY

Aiken, Conrad. *Among the Lost People.* New York: Scribner, 1934.

———. *Bring! Bring! and Other Stories.* New York: Boni & Liveright, 1925.

———. *The Collected Short Stories.* Cleveland: World, 1960.

———. *Costumes by Eros.* New York: Scribner, 1928.

———. *The Short Stories of Conrad Aiken.* New York: Duell, Sloan and Pearce, 1950.

Butscher, Edward. *Aiken: Poet of White Horse Vale.* Athens: University of Georgia Press, 1988.

———. "Conrad Aiken." In *Reference Guide to Short Fiction,* edited by Noelle Watson, 18–19. Detroit: Gale Press, 1994.

Denney, Reuel. *Aiken.* Minneapolis: University of Minnesota Press, 1964.

Hoffman, Frederick John. *Aiken.* New York: Twayne, 1962.

Lorenz, Clarissa M. *Lorelei Two: My Life with Aiken.* Athens: University of Georgia Press, 1983.

Marten, Harry. *The Art of Knowing: The Poetry and Prose of Aiken.* Columbia: University of Missouri Press, 1988.

Martin, Jay. *Aiken: A Life of His Art.* Princeton, N.J.: Princeton University Press, 1962.

Spivey, Ted Ray, and Arthur Waterman, eds. *Aiken: A Priest of Consciousness.* New York: AMS Press, 1989.

Stevick, Philip. *The American Short Story, 1900–1945: A Critical History.* Boston: Twayne, 1984.

"AIRWAVES" BOBBIE ANN MASON (1989) "Airwaves" examines the way the alienation of meaningless labor breaks bonds between individuals in working-class society. The story focuses on Jane Motherall, a young woman who finds herself swarmed with messages from her culture that give her dreams of happiness she cannot fulfill in small-town Kentucky.

These messages emanate from the radio, television, and corporate culture that surrounds Jane, and she is at a point in her life when she begins to detect them. Jane has been laid off from her factory job as a presser, one who irons the manufactured clothes before they are folded and packaged. Jane used to be a folder and moved up to being a presser before she was laid off. Folding and pressing become key metaphors in this story of personal responses to the depressed economy and the unreliable low-skill jobs that are grinding Jane's town into the ground.

If one does not find reward in work, then perhaps one can find it in love, but in Jane's life Coy, the man she loves, is laid off too and leaves her because he cannot support her. Jane, before being laid off herself, wants to support him until he finds a job, but such an arrangement does not fit Coy's idea of being a man. Still, tragically, his solution is to move back in with his mother, where he cannot be a man either. When he finds work again, as a floor walker at Wal-Mart, he calls Jane back to rekindle their relationship—Jane says she cannot because now she is out of work, but Coy wants to support her, to make it possible for her to return to school part-time. But Jane knows that his job does not pay enough and that she would have to relinquish her unemployment benefits if she went back to school. She says, "You wouldn't let me support you." . . . "Why should I let you support me?" Jane wants a relationship of mutual support, but Coy wants to feel successful and maintain some power over her.

Coy has a sensitive stomach and is easily undone by the loud rock music on the radio and the tragic images of poverty he sees on TV; he is not the some-times-aggressive type that, from watching *Oprah,* Jane learns women really want. Jane uses the loud radio to try to stave off her own depression and that of everyone in her life. She sees Coy as a floor walker not just on the job but in real life as well, and he will take the least prestigious job in a corporation just to feel part of something. Jane starts losing her desire for what she is told would be a better job: waitressing at a corporate chain of restaurants where she could wear pants and get free meals. Throughout the story she grows harder and more intolerant of the lot of women in particular and working-class life in general.

If romance cannot produce happiness, perhaps one can enjoy the comforts of family. But in Jane's case, it is she who must hold her family together. Mrs. Motherall, Jane's mother, dies when Jane is 15. Jane takes care of her alcoholic father, Vernon, who is living on disability. "Living on disability" is true of her father in more ways than one. It is Jane's sense of duty to him that keeps him in contact with any human being and nourishes him on something other than junk food in front of his television. Vernon's repertoire of fatherly advice is gained mainly from TV and AM talk radio clichés: "The trouble is, too many women are working and the men can't get jobs." . . . "Women should stay at home." If this maxim were true, then Jane would be a full-time servant to her father. Vernon, even more powerless than Coy, needs to feel like a man in the same way Coy does; he manipulatively tells the unemployed Jane: "You can move back home with me," . . . "Parents always used to take care of their kids till they married." Jane knows that she, not Vernon, would be doing the caretaking if she moved back home, but she refuses by saying, "It would never work," . . . "We don't like the same TV shows anymore." And, indeed, not watching the same shows would be a central contention for two people who use the television to numb their depression.

If not romance or family for fulfillment, what about religion? Jane's brother, a raconteur bad boy just out of jail, has turned to preaching as an occupation. Jane learns that he has started to speak in tongues and wonders whether he receives airwaves directly from God. More out of curiosity than spiritual impulse or sisterly love, she goes to church to hear him preach.

She finds that he uses religion as much for retelling his adventurous misdeeds as for his journeying to find Jesus. When presented with a child to heal, he speaks in tongues, and "he probably really believes he is tuned into heaven." But Jane sees through him, realizing that in his preaching he tries to disguise clichés like "Let the Sun Shine In," from *Hair,* or "abracadabra" from childhood television shows. In the end, he tells Jane to take Coy to church and he will get them back together. Like Coy and Vernon do, he wants to be the powerful man who runs Jane's life, but she sees that her brother, too, is just too susceptible to empty cultural messages to provide any real support.

Mason elegantly details in the story the way corporate culture—with its faux-inclusive work jargon, its mind-dulling and resentment-fueling shows on radio and TV, its efficiency in using speaker boxes and intercoms to remove people from each other as they bank or order food, and its constant bombardment of people so that they do not think their own thoughts or really listen to anything—has rendered working-class life a kind of war zone, where people seek the right message to sustain themselves as their lives become shattered by poverty and lack of human connection. Her character Jane understands these problems, but her solution is not particularly liberating: She decides that she wants to be a sender of airwaves instead of a receiver, a "presser," as in *oppressor,* but in service to another institution rather than for her own empowerment. Jane decides to join the military.

At the recruiter's office, Jane is drawn to all the shiny pamphlets that promise exciting, important jobs. She takes one of each but finds the one that most appeals to her and tells the man, "Here's what I want," . . . "Communications and Electronics Operations." She is assured about her choice that "you join that and you'll get somewhere," by the man in a uniform she notes is beautiful with bright ribbons. Jane is finding a way to acquire the kind of empowerment so important to all the men in her life but without having to obtain it by proxy from them.

All the lingo in the brochure will give her a new tongue to speak; being in the military will give her a corporate job with more stability and a more respectable uniform than Wal-Mart or a big restaurant chain can provide. Her images of what her life will be are clichés from television shows: "She pictures herself . . . in a control booth, sending signals for war, like an engineer in charge of a sports special on TV. . . . She imagines herself in a war, crouching in the jungle, sweating, on the lookout for something to happen. The sounds of warfare would be like the sounds of rock and roll, hard-driving and satisfying." Her plan for herself is tragic, because it is a media-induced dream, not at all reflective of true military service. Instead of aspiring to any meaningful service, she accepts a position part of what she thinks will be excitement—something that seems different from the boredom and pain she sees as her future at home.

As is characteristic with a Mason story, the ending is left at a moment of potential, not resolution. We are not shown that Jane lives happily ever after or that she makes a tragic mistake. We are shown that she has made a decision that many working-class people make: that to leave the place is to leave the class. Jane thinks she is making a clean start, but as she is heading out to do her laundry and announce her decision to leave, she is drawn back into her dingy apartment by a forgotten dirty T-shirt, and one has to ask, Is she really going to escape, or will some sense of duty or obligation prevent her from reaching escape velocity?

BIBLIOGRAPHY
Mason, Bobbie Ann. "Airwaves." In *Love Life.* New York: Harper & Row, 1989.

Carolyn Whitson
Metrostate University

ALBEE, EDWARD (EDWARD FRANKLIN ALBEE) (1928–)

Adopted grandson of Edward Franklin Albee, owner of the Keith-Albee vaudeville theaters, Albee in his youth lived the traveling life of his wealthy Westchester County adoptive parents. Although primarily known as a playwright, Albee helped popularize the Theater of the Absurd in numerous plays that adapted NOVELLAS and stories such as The BALLAD OF THE SAD CAFE by CARSON MCCULLERS and "Bartleby the Scrivener," by HERMAN MELVILLE, as well as fiction by James Purdy, Giles Cooper, and VLADIMIR NABOKOV. From 1953, when Thornton Wilder encouraged him to try playwriting, Albee immersed himself in presentations of Theater of the Absurd plays by Europeans writing in this mode. With the production of the Broadway play *Who's Afraid of Virginia Woolf?* in 1962, Albee was hailed as a major new voice in the theater and excoriated as a writer of vulgar plays, but his vision dramatized American stories from both the 19th and 20th centuries.

"ALCOHOLIC CASE, AN" F. SCOTT FITZGERALD (1937)

Published in the February 1937 edition of *ESQUIRE,* F. Scott Fitzgerald's "An Alcoholic Case" seems perfectly suited to interpretations based on biographical comparisons to Fitzgerald's own struggles with alcohol abuse. Fitzgerald's novels and stories often mirror his personal life, and he did little in his lifetime to discourage such attention; his reckless behavior guaranteed notoriety and provided ample fodder for his fiction. As Vernon L. Parrington once observed of Fitzgerald's self-absorption and need for attention, he was "a bad boy who loves to smash things to show how naughty he is; a bright boy who loves to say smart things and show how clever he is." Indeed, since its inclusion in Malcolm Cowley's 1951 collection of Fitzgerald's stories, "An Alcoholic Case" has largely attracted biographical examinations. In a remarkably comprehensive look at the critical treatment of the story, Arthur Waldhorn illustrates how analyses of this "neglected story" have typically examined how it details the experience of alcoholism and have studied the relationship between the disease and Fitzgerald's writing. Waldhorn pursues this line of thought further by discussing the tribulations Fitzgerald faced in 1936—the institutionalization of his wife, Zelda; his mother's death; a diving injury; a mountain of debts; and his own suicide attempts—and in this way he paints the context in which this story arose. Waldhorn demonstrates that the focus has primarily been on the unnamed alcoholic cartoonist's similarity to the author, but he also devotes considerable space in his analysis to the purpose and function of the nurse in the story. He argues that "her myopic view of reality" (251) and her inability to "see her patient clearly and clinically" (251) act as stumbling blocks to both Fitzgerald's and the cartoonist's recognition and

acknowledgment of their alcoholism. Moreover, he claims that "her dodgings screen her from reality . . . [and] as her credibility as a nurse diminishes, so too does her reliability as a central consciousness" (252). Because of her failings, the story "falls short of didactic cogency and aesthetic resolution" (252). For Waldhorn, the nurse's primary function is to ensure the health and recovery of the cartoonist and, by extension, the author. But perhaps this places too much burden on the nurse and the story itself to tie up neatly the complex struggles involved with alcoholism, to provide in essence a happy ending. After all, Fitzgerald calls clear attention to the fact that she is emotionally and professionally ill equipped to deal with this case. How then can she be expected to heal her patient and sew up the narrative loose ends? Instead, the story makes more sense if we group the cartoonist and the nurse with other Fitzgerald characters who delude themselves with quixotic dreams and end up with shattered illusions, whose fantasies "crack up" against a wall of internal and external limitations. This is a bleak, almost naturalistic story not meant to uplift the characters or the reader.

Early in the story, after a struggle with the nurse over a bottle of gin, the cartoonist has the equivalent of a temper tantrum and tosses the bottle into the bathroom of his hotel room. This incident sets the theme and tone of the rest of the story, and a variation of it is repeated at the end when he puts out a cigarette "against a copper plate [from a war injury] on his left rib" (442). The cartoonist plays the disobedient child who acts out for attention and who needs a mother figure who will suffer through his outbursts yet feel sorry for him and take care of him. The nurse regrets the assignment and complains about her predicament later to her superior, Mrs. Hixton, yet she stays with him, playing the suffering maternal figure. Instead of cleaning up the broken glass initially, she withdraws into the fantasy world of *Gone with the Wind,* where she could "read . . . about things so lovely that had happened long ago" (436). Also, the world of *Gone with the Wind* is a sentimentalized and nostalgic creation where the sexes follow distinct, traditional gender roles; where women are swept off their feet by self-assured "knights in shining armor." The world in which the nurse lives inverts that, as she is expected to be the strong, capable one, and it is no coincidence that the broken gin bottle bears the name of Sir Galahad, the Arthurian knight who succeeded in the quest for the Holy Grail. The only Galahad to be found now is on a gin label; the only Holy Grail is a shattered gin bottle. As with the broken mirror of Tennyson's Lady of Shallot (another Arthurian reference), the glass of the bottle no longer reflects an ideal world, and the fragments act as "*less* than a window through which they [the cartoonist and the nurse] had seen each other for a moment" (438; italics mine); the shards do not give either insight into the other's life. Her life is far from the romantic one painted in Margaret Mitchell's novel; the fractured glass of the gin bottle and the broken glass windows of the bus she takes to work mirror a less than ideal life where she has only "a quarter and a penny in her purse" (438), where her fellow nurses gossip about her, and where her supervisor can find no one to replace the nurse in her duties. It is a broken existence. In fact, while cleaning up the glass and cutting her finger, she thinks to herself, "This isn't what I ought to be doing. And this isn't what *he* ought to be doing" (437; italics in original). She may be inspired by "the movie she had just seen about Pasteur and the book they had all read about Florence Nightingale when they were student nurses" (440), but they are idealized fantasies that will probably not materialize. Instead, her future is more likely to resemble the life of her embittered and weary superior, Mrs. Hixton, who "had been a nurse and gone through the worst of it, had been a proud, idealistic, overworked probationer" (439). Like those of the cartoonist, who intends at the end of the story to meet with the president's secretary yet cannot put on his studs and tie himself because of his inebriated state, the nurse's dreams invariably fall short. Both are hopeless cases, and thus her observation "It's not anything you can beat—no matter how hard you try. . . . It's so discouraging—it's all for nothing" (442) is not a "final, misguided insight" (252), as Waldhorn claims, but a profound and adequate summary of the limitations both she and the cartoonist face. In many ways, her statement is not significantly different in its expression of futility from Nick Carraway's metaphor about Gatsby's green light, "the orgiastic future that year by year recedes before us. . . . We beat on, boats *against* the current" (182; italics mine), never making any progress toward that imagined future.

BIBLIOGRAPHY
Fitzgerald, F. Scott. "An Alcoholic Case." In *The Stories of F. Scott Fitzgerald,* edited by Malcolm Cowley. 1951. Reprint, New York: Collier Books, 1986, 436–442.
———. *The Great Gatsby.* New York: Scribner, 1925.
Parrington, Vernon Louis. *The Beginnings of Critical Realism in America, 1860–1920. Main Currents in American Thought.* Vol. III, 1930. Reprint, Norman and London: University of Oklahoma Press, 1987.
Waldhorn, Arthur. "The Cartoonist, the Nurse, and the Writer: 'An Alcoholic Case.'" In *New Essays on F. Scott Fitzgerald's Neglected Stories,* edited by Jackson R. Bryer, 244–252. Columbia and London: University of Missouri Press, 1996.

Monty Kozbial Ernst

ALCOTT, LOUISA MAY (1832–1888)

Although Louisa May Alcott was dubbed "The Children's Friend" by her first biographer, Ednah Dow Chaney, and her reputation rested on the particular strength of *Little Women* for nearly the next 100 years, the literary detective work of her modern biographer Madeleine Stern has resulted in an awareness of the breadth of Alcott's work. In addition to eight children's novels and an original collection of FAIRY TALES, Alcott wrote three adult books and numerous short stories, many of which were published in "respectable" 19th-century periodicals such as the *Youth's Companion, Merry's Museum* (which Alcott also edited for a time), the *Commonwealth,* the *Independent,* the *Woman's Journal,* and the ATLANTIC MONTHLY. Alcott also published a number of other stories either anonymously or pseudonymously in the more torrid pages of Frank Leslie's *Illustrated Newspaper* and the *Flag of Our Union.* Whether in children's fiction, adult fiction, or sensational fiction, two elements characterize Alcott's work: a professional writer's awareness of the conventions of the GENRES in which she wrote and a commitment to societal reform. Caught up in the fervor for reform in 19th-century America, Alcott was interested in education, abolition, women's rights, and temperance, among other issues; she used to sign her letters "Yours for reform of all kinds." She included radical themes within her work, often stretching the boundaries of the genres themselves.

Born in Germantown, Pennsylvania, Alcott spent most of her life in and around Concord and Boston, Massachusetts, drawn to that area by her father's opportunity to head a school in which he could put his reformist educational theories into practice. After his Temple School closed in 1840, Amos Bronson Alcott involved his wife and four daughters in a short-lived experiment in communal living at a farm called Fruitlands in 1843–44, which Louisa satirized nearly 30 years later in her short story "TRANSCENDENTAL WILD OATS" (1873). Her father's transcendentalist (see TRANSCENDENTALISM) inclinations drew to the family such friends as Ralph Waldo Emerson and Henry David Thoreau, but little income. When Alcott's mother, the more practical Abba May Alcott, founded an employment agency in Boston in order to provide for her family, Louisa and her sisters also sought whatever work was available to 19th-century women—household servant, teacher, governess, seamstress—but Louisa was also writing. Her brief experience as a CIVIL WAR nurse resulted in the novel *Hospital Sketches* (1863), which first gained her substantial public attention and encouraged her to publish *Moods* the following year.

Alcott, however, had also submitted a sensational short story, "Pauline's Passion and Punishment," to a contest sponsored by Frank Leslie's *Illustrated Newspaper,* and its publication in 1862, along with a $100 prize, encouraged a career in the papers that published short stories, a career that lasted through the 1860s and earned substantial income for the family, even though she never attached her name to these stories. The best of them are well-crafted tales of intrigue with complex female characters, such as "A Nurse's Story" (published in Frank Leslie's *Chimney Corner* in 1865–66) and "BEHIND A MASK" (published in the *Flag of Our Union* in several installments in 1866), whose republication beginning in 1975 launched the modern reconsideration of Alcott, especially her feminism. (See FEMINIST.) With the publication of *Little Women* in 1868, Alcott found herself suddenly wealthy and

famous; "A March Christmas," an excerpt from the novel, has been reprinted so frequently that it has taken on a permanent life of its own as a Christmas story. She devoted herself increasingly to the demands of children's fiction the rest of her life, although she also was able to finish the long-abandoned manuscript of her adult novel, *Work,* which was published in 1873. Alcott died in 1888 of long-term effects of mercury poisoning, a result of the medication for the typhus she contracted during her stint as a Civil War nurse.

In all the genres in which she wrote, Alcott translated her life and reading experiences (particularly the work of Ralph Waldo Emerson, NATHANIEL HAWTHORNE, Henry David Thoreau, Johann Wolfgang von Goethe, and Charlotte Brontë) into fiction that argued for the practical application of the ideals she valued. One attitude that cuts across all genres is her feminism. Alcott herself never married, and whether she is promoting individual career choices for her women in *Little Women* or in *Jo's Boys* (1886), depicting the struggles of women limited by society in *Moods* and *Work,* or raging against those limitations in darker works such as "Behind a Mask" (subtitled "A Woman's Power"), her commitment to choice is as clear as her understanding of how to present that THEME to each particular audience. Fascinating female characters, perceptive depictions of mother-daughter relationships, multithreaded PLOT structures, and realistic detail and dialogue in her work still bring 19th-century New England to life for modern readers.

BIBLIOGRAPHY

Alcott, Louisa May. *The Journals of Louisa May Alcott.* Athens: University of Georgia Press, 1989.

———. *Louisa May Alcott Unmasked: Collected Thrillers.* Boston: Northeastern University Press, 1995.

———. *The Selected Letters of Louisa May Alcott.* Boston: Little, Brown, 1987.

Bedell, Madelon. *The Alcotts: Biography of a Family.* New York: C. N. Potter, 1980.

Cheney, Ednah Dow. *Louisa May Alcott: Her Life, Letters, and Journals.* Boston: Roberts Brothers, 1889.

Elbert, Sarah. *A Hunger for Home: Louisa May Alcott and Little Women.* Philadelphia: Temple University Press, 1984.

Keyser, Elizabeth. *Whispers in the Dark: The Fiction of Louisa May Alcott.* Knoxville: University of Tennessee Press, 1993.

MacDonald, Ruth. *Louisa May Alcott.* Boston: Twayne, 1983.

Showalter, Elaine. "Introduction to Alternative Alcott." In *Louisa May Alcott, Alternative Alcott.* New Brunswick, N.J.: Rutgers University Press, 1988, xlviii.

———. *Sisters Choice.* New York: Oxford University Press, 1991.

Stern, Madeleine. *Critical Essay on Louisa May Alcott.* Boston: G. K. Hall, 1984.

———. *Louisa May Alcott.* Norman: University of Oklahoma Press, 1950.

Christine Doyle Francis
Central Connecticut State University

ALECK MAURY

Maury is a memorable character in CAROLINE GORDON's short stories tracing the life of an American sportsman, with detail comparable to that in the hunting and fishing tales of ERNEST HEMINGWAY and WILLIAM FAULKNER. The episodic novel *Aleck Maury, Sportsman* contains most of this material, as do the stories "Old Red," "The Presence," "One More Day," "To Thy Chamber Window, Sweet," and "The Last Day in the Field." Maury, a classics teacher known as "Professor," is a southern gentleman farmer, and his devotion to the outdoors constitutes a genuine philosophy, not a hobby. Constantly escaping his home and family, Aleck is compared to "Old Red," the fox; like the fox, Aleck is hunted, but through his wiliness he evades those who would end his freedom. In ill health and old age, Aleck's ritualistic farewell to the hunt, depicted in "The Last Day in the Field," is comparable to similar scenes in Faulkner's "THE BEAR" in *GO DOWN, MOSES.*

ALEXIE, SHERMAN (1966–)

A Spokane/Coeur d'Alene Indian from Seattle, Washington, Sherman Alexie has earned high praise for his poetry and fiction, particularly for his short stories. Alexie's acclaimed *The Lone Ranger and Tonto Fistfight in Heaven,* first published in 1993, is a collection of 22 starkly lyrical and disturbing stories set in and around the Spokane Indian Reservation. His second SHORT STORY CYCLE, *Reservation Blues,* was published in 1996 and, following the same structure, features several characters from *The Lone Ranger and Tonto Fistfight in Heaven.* In 2000 Alexie published *The Toughest Indian in the World,* and in 2005 he won the O. HENRY MEMORIAL AWARD for the short story "What You Pawn I Will Redeem," part of the 2003 collection entitled *Ten Little Indians.*

In *The Lone Ranger and Tonto Fistfight in Heaven,* Alexie relates these linked stories through a powerful and direct first-person narrator (see POINT OF VIEW) who offers insights into the past as well as the present, alleviating suffering with occasional injections of wry humor, a traditional NATIVE AMERICAN antidote to pain. Thomas-Builds-the-Fire, the storyteller who has trouble finding an audience, can recall and describe, in magical realist (see MAGIC REALISM) and mythic fashion (see MYTH), events in which he participated in the distant past. Aunt Nezzy sews a traditional long beaded dress that turns out to be too heavy to wear, but she believes that the woman who can bear the weight of it will be the salvation of everyone. Jimmy Many Horses III is dying of cancer. The nine-year-old Victor snuggles next to his alcoholic parents, believing that the liquor fumes will help him sleep. Alexie transformed *The Lone Ranger and Tonto Fistfight in Heaven* into a screenplay for the film *Smoke Signals.*

Reservation Blues is again a blend of the direct and the magical, with its starting point in a long-dead blues singer, Robert Johnson, who, with his magic guitar, appears to Thomas Builds-the-Fire on the Spokane Reservation in eastern Washington. As a result, Thomas and his friends form Coyote Springs, an all-Indian Catholic rock band. The group tours the country, from Seattle to New York, in search of adventure and of their own identities.

The Toughest Indian in the World comprises nine stories that continue Alexie's focus on interracial and sexual conflicts between Native Americans and whites. Ultimately, however, they may also be viewed as love stories—between man and man in the title story, between a Navajo woman and a white cowboy in "Dear John Wayne," between a Spokane and his dying father in "One Good Man." Alexie's lyrical skill with language is frequently cited by readers and viewers alike, as particularly exemplified in this passage from "The Sin Eaters":

On that morning, the sun rose and bloomed like blood in a glass syringe. The entire Spokane Indian Reservation and all of its people and places were clean and scrubbed. The Spokane River rose up from its bed like a man who had been healed and joyously wept all the way down to its confluence with the Columbia River. There was water everywhere: a thousand streams interrupted by makeshift waterfalls; small ponds hidden beneath a mask of thick fronds and anonymous blossoms; blankets of dew draped over the shoulders of isolated knolls. An entire civilization of insects lived in the mud puddle formed by one truck tire and a recent rain storm. The blades of grass, the narrow pine needles, and the stalks of roadside wheat were as sharp and bright as surgical tools.

Ten Little Indians, Alexie's most recent collection, contains 11 sometimes exuberant, sometimes painful stories, nearly always laced with Alexie's sense of humor as the Spokane Indian characters confront the challenges of life off the reservation, most often in Seattle. The most frequently reviewed story is "The Life and Times of Estelle Walks Above," featuring a heroic feminist Spokane woman.

Alexie's 1998 novel *Indian Killer,* set in Seattle, is a contemporary examination of race relations. It features the Indian Killer, who murders white people, and the ironically named John Smith, a troubled half-white, half–Native American who seeks his true self. In 2007 Alexie published a young-adult novel called *The Absolutely True Diary of a Part-time Indian* and *Flight,* a novel that reasserts through an orphaned Native American boy, nicknamed *Zits,* the need for understanding one's history and identity as Zits time-travels through such historical moments as the Battle of Little Bighorn.

See also "Because My Father Always Said He Was the Only Indian Who Saw Jimi Hendrix Play."

BIBLIOGRAPHY

Alexie, Sherman. *The Absolutely True Diary of a Part-time Indian.* New York: Little, Brown, 2007.

———. *The Business of Fancydancing: Stories and Poems.* Brooklyn, N.Y.: Hanging Loose Press, 1992.

———. *First Indian on the Moon.* Brooklyn, N.Y.: Hanging Loose Press, 1993.

———. *Flight: A Novel.* New York: Black Cat, 2007.

———. *Indian Killer.* New York: Warner Books, 1998.

———. *The Lone Ranger and Tonto Fistfight in Heaven.* New York: Atlantic Monthly Press, 1993.

———. *The Man Who Loves Salmon.* Boise, Idaho: Limberlost Press, 1998.

———. *Old Shirts & New Skins.* Illustrated by Elizabeth Woody. Los Angeles: American Indian Studies Center, 1993.

———. *One Stick Song.* Brooklyn, N.Y.: Hanging Loose Press, 2000.

———. *Reservation Blues.* New York: Warner Books, 1996.

———. *The Summer of Black Widows.* Brooklyn, N.Y.: Hanging Loose Press, 1996.

———. *Ten Little Indians: Stories.* New York: Grove Press, 2003.

———. *The Toughest Indian in the World.* New York: Atlantic Monthly Press, 2000.

———. *Water Flowing Home: Poems by Sherman Alexie.* Boise, Idaho: Limberlost Press, 1995.

Sherman Alexie Web site. Available online. URL: http://www.shermanalexie.com. Accessed December 2, 2008.

ALGER, HORATIO (1834–1899)   A very popular author of boys' stories who wrote more than 100 books. His HEROES are newsboys, bootblacks, and similar characters who struggle against poverty and adversity, achieving success through hard work, self-reliance, and virtuous behavior. The Horatio Alger hero typically appears in such works as The Ragged Dick Series (1869), The Luck and Pluck Series (1869), and The Tattered Tom Series (1871). The theme of these stories expresses an American ideal; as a result, the true-life account of anyone who rises from "rags to riches" through personal virtue and industry may be referred to as a "true Horatio Alger story."

ALGONQUIN ROUND TABLE   In the 1920s, a number of brilliant writers and others associated with the arts and literature began having lunch together regularly at the Algonquin Hotel in New York City. Among the earliest members of this group were DOROTHY PARKER, Robert Benchley, and Robert Sherwood. Membership was by invitation only and grew to include such luminaries as Alexander Woollcott,

the columnists Heywood Brown and Franklin Adams, the playwrights George Kaufman and Marc Connelly, the songwriter Irving Berlin, the editor and founder of the *New Yorker* Harold Ross, and the writers EDNA FERBER and F. SCOTT FITZGERALD. They became famous for clever repartée distinguished by the barb and blistering insults delivered coolly to friend and foe alike.

ALGREN, NELSON (1909–1981) Born Nelson Algren Abraham, Algren wrote brutally realistic novels and stories about life in the Chicago slums. His first book, written in the depths of the GREAT DEPRESSION, was *Somebody in Boots* (1935), a proletarian or social protest novel. (See PROLETARIAN LITERATURE.) This was followed by *Never Come Morning* (1942), *The Man with the Golden Arm* (1949), and *A Walk on the Wild Side* (1956). Algren won the National Book Award for *The Man with the Golden Arm,* and *A Walk on the Wild Side* won high critical acclaim as perhaps the most influential comic novel to come out of the 1950s and as a precursor of the wild-sidedness of Ken Kesey's *One Flew Over the Cuckoo's Nest* and Joseph Heller's *Catch-22.* These novels, as well as his collection of stories, *The Neon Wilderness* (1947), depict the human casualties of a bleak urban landscape. Algren is often grouped with RICHARD WRIGHT and James T. Farrell, who wrote about similar themes in a Chicago setting.

Despite a reputation built largely on novels, however, Algren wrote more than 50 short stories that appeared in such disparate publications as the *Kenyon Review* and *Noble Savage,* the *Atlantic, SATURDAY EVENING POST, ESQUIRE, Playboy,* and *Dude.* Algren carefully chose his collection of 18 stories in *The Neon Wilderness* to include most of his best tales. He collected no others out of the dozens he wrote over the next nearly 40 years, although he included a few previously published stories, along with essays and poems, in *The Last Carousel.* Although no longer anthologized frequently, his two best stories are almost surely "A Bottle of Milk for Mother" and "How the Devil Came Down Division Street." Drug addiction, alcohol abuse, prostitution, gambling, prizefighting, and jail are the subjects of Algren's stories, both short and long. The characters are generally losers who frequent bars, brothels, and fleabag tenements or hotels. They live in a depressing, violent, naturalistic (see NATURALISM) world, but the depression is softened by Algren's sense of the gently comic and the ironic that pervades both the novels and the stories (see COMEDY; IRONY).

BIBLIOGRAPHY
Algren, Nelson. *The Last Carousel.* New York: Putnam, 1973.
———. *The Man with the Golden Arm.* Garden City, N.Y.: Doubleday, 1949.
———. *The Neon Wilderness.* Garden City, N.Y.: Doubleday, 1947.
———. *Never Come Morning.* New York: Harper & Brothers, 1942.
———. *Somebody in Boots.* New York: Vanguard Press, 1935.
———. *A Walk on the Wild Side.* New York: Farrar, Straus & Cudahy, 1956.
Cox, Martha Heasley, and Wayne Chatterton. *Algren.* Boston: Twayne, 1975.
Drew, Bettina. *Algren: A Life on the Wild Side.* New York: Putnam, 1989.
Giles, James Richard. *Confronting the Horror: The Novels of Nelson Algren.* Kent, Ohio: Kent State University Press, 1989.

ALHAMBRA, THE (1832) See IRVING, WASHINGTON.

ALIBI IKE Appearing in RING LARDNER's story "Alibi Ike," this character is a reincarnation of the hero of the FRONTIER HUMORIST tradition, carrying a bat and glove instead of a musket and powder. It does not matter to his fans that Alibi Ike, one of Lardner's best known creations, is semi-illiterate. The fact that he is a baseball player is enough to cover him with glory. He displays the virtues of speed, agility, strength, and endurance, along with the ethics of fair play and team play. He is crude and naive, with an excuse a minute, but he was a great favorite in the 1920s and became an American MYTH.

ALIDA SLADE Slade is the ruddy complexioned, dark-browed friend of Grace Ansley in EDITH WHARTON's "ROMAN FEVER." Wharton probably confused the two friends' portraits deliberately—all first-time readers have trouble distinguishing the two, despite Wharton's description of Grace as smaller and paler than Alida. The author emphasizes the similarity of their situations as women while showing their lack of knowledge of each other. Readers generally tend to have less sympathy for Alida than for Grace, but careful reading reveals the pathetic emptiness of Alida's life as young woman, wife, and widow. Both she and Grace are mothers, and both have daughters, but Alida receives the ultimate surprise at the end of the story when she learns that Grace had a secret and that Alida's daughter, Jenny, has a stepsister.

ALLEGORY   A narrative in which agents and action, and sometimes setting as well, are contrived to signify a second, related order. There are two main types: historical and political allegory, in which the characters and action represent, or "allegorize," historical personages and events; and the allegory of ideas, in which the characters represent abstract concepts and the plot serves to communicate a doctrine or thesis. See, for example, HERMAN MELVILLE's BILLY BUDD, SAILOR, in which Billy appears as a Christ figure, or JOYCE CAROL OATES's "WHERE ARE YOU GOING, WHERE HAVE YOU BEEN?" in which the teenage CONNIE represents Eve before the Fall on one hand and a decadent consumer society on the other.

ALLEN, PAULA GUNN (1939–2008)   Paula Gunn Allen grew up in Cubero, New Mexico, a small town between the Laguna and Acoma Pueblo reservations. Of German, Laguna, Pueblo, Lebanese, Scottish, and Sioux descent, she pointed out that people of the Laguna Pueblo have long intermarried with others and often referred to herself as a "multicultural event." A creative writer, scholar, and teacher, she was a pivotal force in the Native American Renaissance of the early 1970s and earned numerous accolades, including an American Book Award from the Before Columbus Foundation. Her work appears in more than 60 anthologies, ranging from mainstream publications to specialized collections that feature writings by literary theorists, women of color, and lesbians.

Allen's fiction, poetry, and scholarship reveal a range of cross-cultural sensibilities, bridging differences between such disparate perspectives as American Indian and European, reservation and urban, spiritual and academic, and traditional and mixed-blood. At the same time, in all her stories she remains firmly grounded in her mother's Laguna Pueblo culture. In nearly every tale Allen demonstrates the central position of identity and culture, and thus she interweaves personal, family, and historical accounts with mythic stories from the Pueblo oral tradition. One such storytelling figure animates all of her writing: Grandmother Spider from Cherokee and Laguna creation tales, who spins stories to ensure the survival of the people and whose intricate web sustains the relationships among the land, the communities that inhabit it, and the creative forces of the universe.

Even Allen's autobiographical novel, *The Woman Who Owned the Shadows* (1983), is actually a book about the importance of stories. Her PROTAGONIST, who feels at home neither in the Southwest nor in San Francisco, recovers from a nervous breakdown, the death of her infant son, divorce, and near-suicide by learning to understand her place in the old stories. With the aid of Grandmother Spider, she realizes that her life and the lives of her mother and grandmother parallel characters and incidents in ancient tribal narratives.

Allen is perhaps most recognized for *The Sacred Hoop: Recovering the Feminine in American Indian Traditions* (1986), a landmark collection of essays that asserts the resilience of Native women's spiritual traditions. Fusing personal, historical, and literary-critical perspectives, Allen explained the central concerns in her work, including the influence of story and ceremony on contemporary American Indian literature, the crucial role of Native American women in sustaining cultural traditions, the challenges faced by a mixed-blood writer, and the place of FEMINIST and lesbian perspectives in Native American studies.

In 1989 Allen edited *Spider Woman's Granddaughters*, the first collection of traditional and contemporary stories by Native American women. This volume distills materials from the written forms in which they had been previously published, such as "as-told-to" ethnologies or novels, and reorganizes them into sequences that reflect tribal oral traditions. Thus Delia Oshogay's rendition of the traditional Anishinabeg story "Oshkikwe's Baby" is connected to the retelling of Anishinabeg traditions in LOUISE ERDRICH's short story "American Horse"; an Okanogan COYOTE STORY is retold in "The Story of Green-Blanket Feet," excerpted from Humishima's novel *Cogewea, The Half-Blood;* and two versions of a Cochita Pueblo traditional Yellow Woman (the earth mother or corn mother figure) story appear beside modern retellings by Allen and her Laguna Pueblo cousin LESLIE SILKO.

Allen further helped to usher Native American literature into the mainstream by editing two subsequent anthologies, *Grandmothers of the Light: A Medicine Woman's Source Book* (1991) and *Voice of the Turtle: American Indian Literature 1900–1970* (1994). In these collections, she identifies connections among multiple oral and written traditions.

As Allen's often-anthologized poem "Grandmother" suggests, reclaiming lost tribal practices, or "mending the tear with string," requires not only linking one's craft to traditional Pueblo arts, such as weaving and storytelling, but also creating new patterns and new stories. Occasionally Allen assumes the role of a TRICKSTER, using humor to disrupt academic or moral pieties. Her story "A Hot Time" (*Grandmothers of the Light*) features Grandmother Spider in a wry commentary on the "supposed infirmities of old age." In *Raven's Road*, which she described as a "medicine-dyke novel" (Coltelli 33), the face of an old woman emerges in a test explosion of the atom bomb, suggesting a potent link between Yellow Woman and the uranium mined from Laguna lands. After a long battle with lung cancer, Paula Gunn Allen died on May 29, 2008, at her home in Fort Bragg, California. Her last full-length publication was *Pocahontas: Medicine Woman, Spy, Entrepreneur, Diplomat,* published in 2003, in which Allen argues that Pocahontas was not a voiceless woman subservient to Captain John Smith but a wise and exuberant visionary. *Life Is a Fatal Disease: Selected Poems 1962–1995,* a book of her last poems, was published posthumously in 2008 by West End Press.

BIBLIOGRAPHY

Allen, Paula Gunn. *Grandmothers of the Light: A Medicine Woman's Source Book.* Boston: Beacon Press, 1992.

———. *The Sacred Hoop: Recovering the Feminine in American Indian Traditions.* Boston: Beacon Press, 1986.

———. *Spider Woman's Granddaughters: Traditional Tales and Contemporary Writing by Native American Women.* Boston: Beacon Press, 1989.

———. *Voice of the Turtle: American Indian Literature 1900–1970.* New York: Ballantine Books, 1994.

———. *The Woman Who Owned the Shadows.* San Francisco: Spinsters Ink, 1983.

Bataille, Gretchen M., and Kathleen Mullen Sands. *American Indian Women: Telling Their Lives.* Lincoln: University of Nebraska Press, 1984.

Bruchac, Joseph. *Survival This Way: Interviews with American Indian Poets.* Tucson: Sun Tracks University of Arizona Press, 1987.

Coltelli, Laura. *Winged Words: American Indian Writers Speak.* Lincoln: University of Nebraska Press, 1990.

Eysturoy, Annie O. *This Is about Vision: Interviews with Southwestern Writers.* Albuquerque: University of New Mexico Press, 1990.

Jahner, Elaine. "A Laddered, Rain-Bearing Rug: Paula Gunn Allen's Poetry." In *Women and Western American Literature,* edited by Helen Winter and Susan Rosowski. Troy, N.Y.: Whitson, 1982.

Lincoln, Kenneth. *Native American Renaissance.* Berkeley: University of California Press, 1983.

Perry, Donna. *Backtalk: Women Writers Speak Out: Interviews.* New Brunswick, N.J.: Rutgers University Press, 1993.

Ruoff, A. LaVonne Brown. *American Indian Literatures: An Introduction, Bibliographic Review, and Selected Bibliography.* New York: Modern Language Association of America, 1990.

Ruppert, Jim. "Paula Gunn Allen." In *Dictionary of Native American Literature,* edited by Andrew Wiget. New York: Garland, 1994.

Smith, Lucinda Irwin. *Women Who Write.* Vol. 2. New York: J. Messner, 1994.

TallMountain, Mary. "You Can Go Home Again." In *I Tell You Now: Autobiographical Essays by Native American Writers,* edited by Brian Swann and Arnold Krupat. Lincoln: University of Nebraska Press, 1987.

Lauren Stuart Miller
University of California at Berkeley

ALLISON, DOROTHY (1949–)

Long before her seemingly sudden rise to best-seller fame with the novel *Bastard Out of Carolina,* Dorothy Allison earned a devoted gay and lesbian following with the publication of her poetry in *The Women Who Hate Me*

(1983) and her first collection of short stories, *Trash* (1988). *Trash* garnered two Lambda Literary Awards, for Best Small Press Book and Best Lesbian Book. The stories in *Trash* offer up the pain and passion of poor "white-trash" women trying to assimilate in the world of lesbian middle-class, college-educated life. In a recent interview, Allison recalls living in a Tallahassee, Florida, lesbian-FEMINIST collective in 1973, and the debt she owes those women who stopped her from burning her stories. Much material from the stories collected in *Trash* provided the basis for her first novel. *Bastard,* which was a finalist for the 1992 National Book Award, is a largely autobiographical story focusing on the extended Boatwright family through the eyes of Bone, the bastard daughter of the waitress Anney Boatwright. Bone's life is a harrowing tale of incest, abuse, and survival.

After the success of *Bastard,* Allison published the nonfiction works *Skin: Talking about Sex, Class and Literature* and *Two or Three Things I Know for Sure,* the latter a memoir in which Allison weaves together stories about her mother, aunts, sisters, and cousins. If *Trash* reflects the conflicted confusion from which emerged her desire to live, *Skin* provides a valuable demonstration of Allison's growth between *Trash* and *Two or Three Things.* In *Skin,* she analyzes, measures, and draws conclusions not only about her subject matter but also about her own philosophy. By the time she wrote *Two or Three Things,* then, Allison understood the central significance of stories to both her worldview and her art; indeed, the opening line is "Let me tell you a story" (1). Her second novel, *Cavedweller,* appeared in 1998.

In all of her work, Allison presents the lives of poor white Americans, particularly women, without romanticizing or flattening them. She draws heavily from her own painful childhood in the South and offers a prose style that is sharp-edged and riveting. Allison's work adds another dimension to southern literature and its attendant themes of tormented sexuality, victimized women and children, and men and women who cannot realize their dreams because of their class.

The first in her family to graduate from high school, Allison earned a bachelor's degree from Florida Pres-byterian College and a master's degree from New York's New School of Social Research. In the 1960s, she became a feminist activist and spent the next 20 years editing and writing for lesbian and feminist presses. She has taught at Florida State University, Rutgers, Wesleyan, and the San Francisco Art Institute. She now resides in California with her partner and their son.

See also "DON'T TELL ME YOU DON'T KNOW."

BIBLIOGRAPHY

Allison, Dorothy. *Bastard Out of Carolina.* New York: Dutton, 1992.
———. "The Salon.com Interview: Dorothy Allison." By Laura Miller. Salon.com (March 31, 1998). Available online. URL: http://www.salon.com/books/int/1998/03/cov_si_31intb.html. Accessed May 6, 2009.
———. *Skin: Talking about Sex, Class and Literature.* Ithaca, N.Y.: Firebrand Books, 1994.
———. *Trash.* Ithaca, N.Y.: Firebrand Books, 1988.
———. *Two or Three Things I Know for Sure.* New York: Dutton, 1995.
———. *The Women Who Hate Me.* Brooklyn, N.Y.: Long Haul Press, 1983.
Dorothy Allison Web site. Available online. URL: http://www.dorothyallison.net. Accessed May 6, 2009.
Sherwin, Elisabeth. "Patron Saint of Battered Women Writes, Forgives." Printed Matter (February 8, 1998). Available online. URL: http://virtual-markets.net/~gizmo/1998/dorothy.html.
Stover, Mary Ann. "Dorothy Allison Weaves Tales from the Heart." Printed Matter (February 8, 1998).
Wilkinson, Kathleen. "Dorothy Allison: The Value of Redemption." Curve Magazine (September 7, 2001). Available online. URL: http://www.curvemag.com. Accessed December 2, 2008.

Susan Thurston Hamerski
St. Olaf College

ALL STORIES ARE TRUE JOHN EDGAR WIDEMAN (1992) Originally a section of new stories written especially for the larger collection *All Stories Are True: The Stories of John Edgar Wideman* (1992), *All Stories Are True* was published separately in 1992. The title is from a statement by the Nigerian writer Chinua Achebe: "All stories are true, the Igbo say." Wideman uses this saying as a controlling METAPHOR for these stories of family, friends, and community members dealing with the pain and anguish of racism in contemporary America. The stories in the collection comment on and support one another through the power of memory and connection just as members of a family or a community sustain their own. Thus these stories do not reflect a single narrative voice but, in typical postmodern fashion (see POSTMODERNISM) many voices. As in a jazz piece, "Everybody Loves Bubba Riff" captures the orchestra of these multiple voices in a single, unpunctuated sentence as a community mourns the death of a young man. The title story, "All Stories Are True," continues stories of Wideman's mother and the fictional counterpart of his brother, Robby (here called Tommy), begun in his first short story collection, *Damballah* (1980). Other stories include "Casa Grande" and "Signs," a story about a young teacher receiving racist letters.

Tracie Guzzio
Ohio University

ALLUSION   An implied or indirect reference to a person, place, or event in history or previous literature. A terse allusion may be laden with relevant associations that amplify the emotions or ideas in a work of literature and connect them with the emotions or ideas of a previous work or historical event. In JOYCE CAROL OATES's "WHERE ARE YOU GOING, WHERE HAVE YOU BEEN?" for example, the reference to ARNOLD FRIEND's ill-fitting boots suggests an allusion to the cloven-hoofed devil and intensifies Arnold's position as the PERSONIFICATION of evil that the young CONNIE faces in her valueless world.

ALTER EGO   Literally, a second self or an inseparable friend. In literature, critics sometimes view a fictional character as the author's alter ego: In ANDRE DUBUS's short story "Cadence," for example, the young Paul Clement appears to be an alter ego for Dubus, or in F. Scott Fitzgerald's "BABYLON REVISITED," CHARLIE WALES appears to be an alter ego for Fitzgerald. The term may also apply to two fictional characters to mean a double or DOPPELGANGER. For instance, In HENRY JAMES's "The JOLLY CORNER," the kindly Spencer is determined to meet his alter ego—the calculating businessman he might have become had he stayed in New York—in the house on the jolly corner.

AMBIGUITY   Commonly, *ambiguity* characterizes a statement that, intentionally or unintentionally, contains two or more incompatible or contradictory meanings. In literature, the term also refers to a word or idea that implies more than one meaning and usually leaves the reader feeling uncertain. Writers may use deliberate ambiguity to great effect, as when two or more diverse connotations have equal relevance. (See CONNOTATION AND DENOTATION.) See, for example, HERMAN MELVILLE's use of ambiguity in "BENITO CERENO."

"AMBUSH" TIM O'BRIEN (1990)   *The Things They Carried,* referring not only to the physical objects but to "all the emotional baggage" (21) soldiers carried, is a collection of 22 related stories based on TIM O'BRIEN's experiences during his tour of duty in Vietnam in 1969–70. This book is "a work of fiction" (subtitle), and "except for a few details regarding the author's own life, all the incidents, names, and characters are imaginary" (copyright page). In 1990 O'Brien was "forty-three years old, and the war occurred half a lifetime ago, and yet the remembering makes it now." Moreover, "sometimes remembering will lead to a story, which makes it forever," and "That's what stories are for. Stories are for joining the past to the future. . . . Stories are for eternity, when memory is erased, when there is nothing to remember except the story" (38).

That O'Brien invents rather than merely reports is "not a game," but rather "a form" (179). For example, O'Brien tells the reader that "twenty years" before, when he "walked through Quang Ngai Province as a foot soldier," he "watched a man die on a trail near the village of My Khe." O'Brien "did not kill him," but he "was present," and "my presence was guilt enough." He "remember[s] his face, which was not a pretty face, because his jaw was in his throat," and he "remember[s] feeling the burden of responsibility and grief" (179). However, "even that story is made up," because O'Brien wants the reader "to feel what [he] felt" by creating a "story-truth," which is "truer sometimes than happening-truth" (179). Here is the "happening-truth" version of the story: "I was once a soldier. There were many bodies, real bodies with real faces, but I was young then and I was afraid to look. And now, twenty years later, I'm left with faceless responsibility and faceless grief" (180). Here is the "story-truth" version: "He was a slim, dead, almost dainty young man of about twenty. He lay in the center of a red clay trail near the village of My Khe. His jaw was in his throat. His one eye was shut, the other eye was a star-shaped hole. I killed him" (180). "Story-truth" is specific, graphic, and personal; it can "make things present" (180).

In "Ambush" (131–134), O'Brien tells the full story to his (fictional) nine-year-old daughter, Kathleen, who asks whether he "had ever killed anyone." Since he "keep[s] writing these war stories," she "guess[es]" that he "must've killed somebody." "It was a difficult moment" for the father, but he "did what seemed was right, which was to say, 'Of course not.'" He hopes that "someday . . . she'll ask again," but here he wants "to pretend that she's a grown-up" and "to tell her exactly what happened, or what he "remember[s] happening." First he gives only a brief summary: "He was a short, slender young man of about twenty. I was afraid of him—afraid of something—and as he passed me on the trail I threw a grenade that exploded at his feet and killed him" (131). Then he goes back to the beginning and relates in detail: "Shortly after midnight" the whole platoon "moved into the ambush site outside My Khe" and "spread out in the dense brush along the trail," and "for five hours nothing happened at all." They "were working in two-man teams—one man on guard while the other slept, switching off every two hours," and he "remember[s] it was still dark when Kiowa shook [him] awake for the final watch." The night was "foggy and hot." He lined up three grenades in front of himself, and "the pins had already been straightened for quick throwing." He knelt there for perhaps half an hour and waited. As the "dawn began to break," he remembers "looking up and seeing the young man come out of the fog." The enemy soldier "carried his weapon in one hand, muzzle down." O'Brien "had already pulled the pin on the grenade" and "had come up to a crouch." His reactions were "entirely automatic." He "did not hate the young man," he "did not

see him as the enemy," and he "did not ponder issues of morality or politics or military duty" (132). "There were no thoughts of killing. The grenade was to make him go away"; indeed, when the soldier "was about to die," he "wanted to warn him." "The grenade made a popping noise," and "the young man seemed to jerk up as if pulled by invisible wires." He "fell on his back" and "lay at the center of the trail, his right leg bent beneath him, his one eye shut, his other eye a huge star-shaped hole." O'Brien is devastated by the realization that "it was not a matter of live or die," that "there was no real peril," that "almost certainly the young man would have passed by." Later, as he remembers, "Kiowa tried to tell [him] that the man would've died anyway," that "it was a good kill," that he "was a soldier and this was a war," that he "should shape up and stop staring" and "ask [him]self what the dead man would've done if things were reversed" (133–134).

In "The Man I Killed" (124–130), the corpse is described in graphic detail as seen through the eyes of O'Brien, who is unable to reply to Kiowa when he tells him repeatedly to "stop staring" or later when Kiowa tries in vain to get him to "talk" about what happened. The "truth-story" here, however, lies not only in conveying how the narrator felt while staring silently at the corpse but also in restoring to life and inventing a biography of the young man O'Brien has killed: "He had been born, maybe, in 1946 in the village of My Khe near the central coastline of Quang Ngai Province, where his parents farmed, and where his family had lived for several centuries, . . ." (125). Dreaming people alive in stories ("The Lives of the Dead" [225–246]), whether it is the young man he has killed or Kiowa, who later dies "In the Field" (162–178), not only preserves their memory, but also compensates for the cowardice Tim O'Brien has felt ever since he went to Vietnam because he feared what his family and community might think if he had followed his own conscience and fled to Canada in 1968 ("On the Rainy River" [39–61]).

BIBLIOGRAPHY

Fussell, Paul. "Obscenity without Victory." In *The Norton Book of Modern War*, edited by Paul Fussell, 649–656. New York: Norton, 1991.

Herzog, Tobey C. *Tim O'Brien*. New York: Twayne, 1997.

Hynes, Samuel. "What Happened in Nam." In *The Soldiers' Tale. Bearing Witness to Modern War,* 177–222. New York: Penguin Press, 1997.

O'Brien, Tim. "From *If I Die in a Combat Zone.*" In *The Norton Book of Modern War,* edited by Paul Fussell, 741–756. New York: Norton, 1991.

———. *Going After Cacciato.* 1978. Reprint, New York: Broadway Books, 1999.

———. *If I Die in a Combat Zone Box Me Up and Ship Me Home.* 1973. Reprint, New York: Broadway Books, 1999.

———. *In the Lake of the Woods.* 1994. Reprint, New York/London: Penguin Books, 1995.

———. *Northern Lights.* 1975. Reprint, New York: Broadway Books, 1999.

———. *The Things They Carried. A Work of Fiction.* 1990. Reprint, New York: Broadway Books, 1998.

———. "Writing Vietnam." President's Lecture. Brown University (Providence, R.I.), April 21, 1999. Formerly available online.

Frederick Betz
Southern Illinois University at Carbondale

AMERICAN ADAM

A term coined by R. W. B. Lewis in his book *The American Adam* (1955) to describe a literary theme and phenomenon in American literature, a theme he traces from the second quarter of the 19th century into the 20th: the American as an innocent abroad, a naïf subject to the cynical manipulations of worldly, conniving Europeans. The prototypes may encounter the evil closer to home, however, and may generally be viewed as innocents with unfulfilled potential, poised on the edge of a new life; they include such characters as NATHANIEL HAWTHORNE's protagonist in "YOUNG GOODMAN BROWN," HERMAN MELVILLE's in *BILLY BUDD, SAILOR,* MARK TWAIN's in *Huckleberry Finn* (1884), and HENRY JAMES's Christopher Newman in *The American* (1877). James's tragic, innocent young woman in *DAISY MILLER: A STUDY* also exemplifies the theme. In the 20th century, Adamic protagonists who leave an EDEN-like setting to grapple with evil include SHERWOOD ANDERSON's GEORGE WILLARD, ERNEST HEMINGWAY's NICK ADAMS, KATHERINE ANNE PORTER's MIRANDA RHEA, and WILLIAM FAULKNER's ISAAC (IKE) McCASLIN. In contemporary literature, the Adamic figure appears frequently in stories featuring loners, outcasts, and misfits.

BIBLIOGRAPHY
Lewis, R. W. B. *The American Adam: Innocence, Tragedy, and Tradition in the Nineteenth Century.* Chicago: University of Chicago Press, 1955.

AMERICAN DREAM

A term originally used to define the aspiration peculiar to Americans in both life and fiction: to rise above one's situation at birth, to live self-sufficiently without financial worries, and to own land. Perhaps the best-known fictional articulation of the American dream occurs in John Steinbeck's *Of Mice and Men* (1937), in which the PROTAGONIST, George, repeatedly reminds his friend Lennie that one day they will stop working for another man, buy their own house, raise their own livestock, and "live off the fat of the land." Many writers, especially contemporary ones—TONI MORRISON, to cite just one example—demonstrate that the American dream has been accessible only to a privileged few. Others—JOYCE CAROL OATES, for example—suggest that even if attained, the dream is essentially hollow at its core. JOHN BARTH has been credited with an updated metaphor for contemporary Americans and the dream in the title of his short story "LOST IN THE FUNHOUSE."

AMERICAN REVOLUTION (1775–1783)

Relations between Great Britain and its thirteen colonies in North America had been deteriorating since the mid-1760s, when the British government passed a series of laws to increase its control over the colonies. Among these was the Proclamation of 1763 to halt the expansion of American colonies beyond the Appalachian Mountains; the Revenue Act of 1764 (the Sugar Act), which taxed molasses; the Quartering and Stamp Acts (1765), which made colonists pay part of the cost of stationing British troops in America and pay for tax stamps placed on newspapers, diplomas, and various legal documents; and the Townshend Acts of 1767, which placed duties on imported glass, lead, paper, and tea. Although the British Parliament canceled all Townshend duties except the one on tea in 1770, the basic issue of "taxation without representation" remained unresolved with many colonists who lived far from Britain and had become increasingly self-reliant. The passage in Britain of the Tea Act of 1773, which allowed the East India Company to sell its tea for less than smuggled Netherlands tea in the colonies, resulted in the Boston Tea Party later that year when patriots led by Samuel Adams disguised themselves as Indians, boarded British ships, and dumped their cargoes of tea into Boston Harbor. This revolt led to the Intolerable Acts of 1774, which closed Boston Harbor, restricted the Massachusetts legislature, and gave virtual dictatorial powers to the governor appointed by the king.

In response, the First Continental Congress met in Philadelphia in September 1774 and voted to cut off colonial trade with Britain unless the Intolerable Acts were repealed. They were not. In April 1775 fighting erupted between American patriots and British troops at Lexington and Concord, Massachusetts. The Second Continental Congress began meeting in Philadelphia in May 1775, established the Continental Army in June, and named George Washington the army's commander. In July 1775 the Congress approved the Olive Branch Petition, which declared that the colonies were loyal to the king and urged him to remedy their complaints. King George III ignored the petition and in August 1775 declared the colonies to be in rebellion; Parliament closed all American ports to overseas trade. Those actions convinced many delegates that a peaceful settlement of differences with Britain was impossible. Therefore, support for American independence continued to build. On July 4, 1776, the Congress adopted the Declaration of Independence and the United States of America was born.

Militarily, although the patriots won several victories in New England and the southern colonies during the early months of the war, the British greatly outnumbered and outgunned the Continental Army. Daring leadership on the American side provided the edge. The defeat of General John Burgoyne's forces and the surrender of 6,000 British troops to General Horatio Gates at Saratoga, New York, in October 1777 was a turning point because it convinced the French that they could safely enter the war on the American side. This crucial development gave legitimacy to the revolution as well as foreign assistance in the form of

money, troops, naval forces, and volunteers. The last major battle of the Revolutionary War was fought at Yorktown, Virginia, where combined French and American forces defeated those under the British general William Cornwallis. Almost a fourth of the British military force ship *America* (8,000 men) surrendered at Yorktown. Although this did not end the fighting, it raised to power early in 1782 a new group of ministers, who began peace talks with the Americans, and a peace treaty was signed on September 3, 1783. This Treaty of Paris recognized the independence of the United States and established the nation's borders. U.S. territory extended west to the Mississippi River, north to Canada, and south approximately to Florida. The last British soldiers left New York City in November 1783.

ANALOGY   The comparison of two people or things, at least one of them familiar to the listener or reader, to demonstrate or emphasize similarity. Thus in BILLY BUDD, SAILOR and "BARTLEBY THE SCRIVENER," HERMAN MELVILLE uses the ship as an analogy for the world in general, or Bartleby as analogous to all people who resist conformity. Critics usually discuss analogies in more specific terms, SIMILE and METAPHOR.

ANAYA, RUDOLFO A. (1937–)   Professor emeritus at the University of New Mexico, Rudolfo Alfonso Anaya, the Chicano writer born in Pastura, New Mexico, in 1937, has achieved the highest honors in literature. In fact, his first novel, *Bless Me, Última* (1972), which received the Premio Quinto Sol in 1972, has been extensively praised and considered the first Latino novel to enter the American mainstream. His aim to promote other Spanish-speaking writers in the United States is also well known. In this context, he edits a literary journal called the *Blue Mesa Review,* coedits several books and journals, and has compiled several anthologies featuring Chicano writers. Anaya has therefore been widely praised for his concern about the future of Chicano letters.

Acclaimed as the founder of modern Chicano literature, Anaya has fictionalized his childhood in *Bless Me, Última; Heart of Aztlán* (1976); and *Tortuga*

(1979), all published during the Chicano literary renaissance that began after Cesar Chavez and the United Farm Workers went on strike in 1965. These three interconnected novels form what is known as "the Southwest trilogy," which, over time, helped alleviate Anaya's painful memories of a childhood characterized by a weak physical condition and sense of alienation in a hostile English-speaking environment. On their road to maturity, his young protagonists encounter and overcome the obstacles of different urban and rural New Mexico environments. These coming-of-age novels contain autobiographical material from his youth and his working-class, Spanish-speaking, and Catholic family. While *Bless Me, Última* celebrates nature and the freedom of the vast extension of the *llano* (country), *Heart of Aztlán* recreates the dramatic move from the llano to the urban barrio (neighborhood) of Barelas in Albuquerque that Anaya himself experienced as an adolescent in 1952.

After the success of his first novel, Anaya, a high school teacher then, was offered a position as associate professor at the University of New Mexico, which he joined in 1974. Anaya's literary production belongs to almost all literary genres. He compiled most of his stories and excerpts from his first novels in *The Anaya Reader* (1995). His first screenplay was for a production by the Bilingual Educational Service: *Bilingualism: Promise for Tomorrow* in 1976. He also wrote *The Farolitos of Christmas,* which became a motion picture in 1987, and *Matachines* for television, first released on Bravo, October 19, 1989. *The Season of La Llorona,* performed first by El Teatro de la Compañía de Alburquerque in 1987, constitutes Anaya's first foray into playwriting. Later plays include *Billy the Kid* (1997), produced again as *Guillermo, El Niño* in 1998, and *Angie* (1998).

Anaya never abandons the rough landscape of the Southwest in his literary works and returns to it physically and spiritually in every novel. The literary world repeats itself together with the landscape, creating a sense of community among the characters who populate his novels: children and adults alike who jump from one to another with an easiness that helps the reader maintain interest in the story. These novels have placed Anaya among the 100 more popular young-adult authors.

During the 1980s and following the trend of rewriting the myths of the ancient Aztecs, Anaya wrote *The Legend of La Llorona* (1984), in which he presents his own vision of La Malinche from an indigenous point of view. He identifies her with the legendary figure of La Llorona, the wailing woman who appears at night to seize mischievous children because she regrets having drowned her own. He also published his own reading of the *Lord of the Dawn: The Legend of Quetzalcoatl* (1987), in which he resurrects the story of Quetzalcoatl, the plumed serpent, a Toltec deity responsible for saving his people from destruction. In *A Chicano in China* (1986), Anaya experiments with nonfiction, narrating his travels to China.

In the last decade of the 20th century a change of direction occurred in Anaya's prose writing. *Alburquerque* (1992), the novel that revives the ancient spelling of the city, an Albuquerque that lost an *r* when Anglo settlers arrived in the area, inaugurates the route toward detective fiction. As the title indicates, it is set in Albuquerque and portrays the urban conflicts, both political and environmental, of the city. It received the PEN-West Fiction Award in 1993. This same year Anaya retired from academic activity to devote his time entirely to writing and to developing a new style in detective fiction.

Anaya places the detective Sonny Baca, his hero in his next three novels and already a minor character in *Alburquerque,* in the middle of a toxic waste disposal zone. Sonny confronts political corruption and environmental degradation as he successfully solves mysterious murders associated with secret cults or rites. Thus, the trilogy formed by the detective novels *Zia Summer* (1995), *Rio Grande Fall* (1996), and *Shaman Winter* (1999) deals with both the degradation of the New Mexico landscape and a murder mystery that Baca must solve to restore the lost harmony of the area.

Magical atmospheres, environmental mysteries, and mythical encounters in New Mexico summarize the prose of Anaya, who returned to the novels of spiritual growth with *Jalamanta* (1996), the story of a New Age leader who undergoes a pilgrimage teaching ancient beliefs. *Elegy on the Death of Cesar Chavez* (2000) commemorates and celebrates the life of the revered Chicano hero who disappeared in 1993 but has never been forgotten by his fellow Chicano activists.

Anaya is better known as a novelist than a short-story writer. During the 1980s and 1990s, he published the several short stories in magazines and textbooks, most of them later collected in *The Anaya Reader* (1995). "The Silence of the Llano" takes Anaya back to the hardships of his beloved land and confirms his link with tradition as a storyteller. His narrative voice reflects the inheritance he received from the borderland. As in his novels, Anaya's short fiction focuses on the myths and traditions of his people: "The Gift" proves especially illuminating on the celebration of the Day of the Dead. *The Man Who Could Fly and Other Stories* (2006), a collection that includes some of his old short stories and introduces new ones, constitutes Anaya's latest achievement in this literary genre.

BIBLIOGRAPHY

Drew, Bernard A. *100 More Popular Young Adult Authors: Biographical Sketches and Bibliographies.* Westport, Conn.: Libraries Unlimited, 2002.

Fernández Olmos, Margarite. *Rudolfo A. Anaya: A Critical Companion.* Westport, Conn.: Greenwood Press, 1999.

West-Durán, Alan, María Herrera-Sobek, and Cesar A. Salgado, eds., *Latino and Latina Writers.* Vol. 1. New York: C. Scribner's Sons, 2004.

Imelda Martín-Junquera
Universidad de León

ANDERSON, SHERWOOD (1876–1941)

A pioneer to aspiring modernist writers in the 1920s, Sherwood Anderson suffered a decline in his critical reputation before he died and has now reclaimed a secure place as a significant influence in 20th-century American literature. In 1919 Anderson published WINESBURG, OHIO, the groundbreaking short story collection about his "GROTESQUE" characters in a small midwestern town. In 1921, along with T. S. Eliot, Anderson won the first literary award offered by the prestigious literary magazine the *Dial*. Influenced by James Joyce and GERTRUDE STEIN, who he believed had revolutionized language, Anderson in turn influenced the younger writers ERNEST HEMINGWAY and WILLIAM FAULKNER. Although Faulkner and Hemingway eventually turned against him, they continued to acknowledge their debt; Faulkner, who viewed MARK TWAIN as the grandfather of American literature, called Anderson the father of Faulkner's entire generation of writers.

In addition to seven novels, the best of which are generally agreed to be *Poor White,* published in 1920, and *Dark Laughter,* published in 1925, Anderson wrote three collections of short stories after *Winesburg—The Triumph of the Egg* (1921), *Horses and Men* (1923), *Death in the Woods and Other Stories* (1933)—and more were collected in the posthumous *The Sherwood Anderson Reader* (1947) and, recently, in *Certain Things Last* (1992). Anderson made his greatest contributions to the GENRE of the short story. Among the earliest American writers to respond to Freudian psychology (see FREUD), he rejected the traditional, carefully plotted, chronologically told story in favor of emphasizing a forgotten or subconsciously submerged moment that has deeply affected a character's life. He also introduced the SHORT STORY CYCLE, a collection of interrelated stories that do not merely stand on their individual artistic merits but extend artistic unity to the entire volume.

As illustrated in "The Egg," "HANDS," and "I WANT TO KNOW WHY," his characters, regardless of age, are not happy; most, having endured frustrated, lonely, and wasted lives, sound a bleak note that some critics speculate echoes Anderson's view of the post–WORLD WAR I situation in the United States. Anderson, a successful businessman for a while, disparagingly called himself "BABBITT," suffered hospitalization for a nervous collapse, gave up his job, and became a full-time writer. In 1913 he became part of the CHICAGO RENAISSANCE, an AVANT-GARDE group of writers that included the poets Carl Sandburg, Vachel Lindsay, and Edgar Lee Masters; the novelists Floyd Dell and THEODORE DREISER; and the LITTLE MAGAZINE editors Harriet Monroe and Margaret C. Anderson. The results of his efforts helped change the American short story. In his best fiction, Anderson managed to turn the speech of his boyhood in Clyde, Ohio (in part the model for

Winesburg), into hauntingly sensory and lyrical prose that still manages to capture readers more than 80 years after Anderson wrote the words.

See also "DEATH IN THE WOODS"; "THE STRENGTH OF GOD."

BIBLIOGRAPHY

Anderson, David D. *Sherwood Anderson: An Introduction and Interpretation.* New York: Holt, Rinehart & Winston, 1967.

———, ed. *Anderson: Dimensions of His Literary Art.* East Lansing: Michigan State University Press, 1976.

———, ed. *Critical Essays on Sherwood Anderson.* Boston: G. K. Hall, 1981.

Anderson, Sherwood. *Alice, and the Lost Novel.* London: Elkin Mathews & Marrot, 1929.

———. *Anderson Reader.* Edited by Paul Rosenfeld. Boston: Houghton Mifflin, 1947.

———. *Certain Things Last: The Selected Short Stories of Sherwood Anderson.* Edited by Charles E. Modlin. New York: Four Walls Eight Windows, 1992.

———. *Death in the Woods and Other Stories.* New York: Liveright, Inc., 1933.

———. *Horses and Men.* New York: B. W. Huebsch, 1923.

———. *The Portable Sherwood Anderson.* Edited by Horace Gregory. New York: Viking, 1949; revised edition, 1972.

———. *Short Stories.* Edited by Maxwell Geismar. New York: Hill & Wang, 1962.

———. *The Triumph of the Egg: A Book of Impressions from American Life in Tales and Poems.* New York: B. W. Huebsch, 1921.

———. *Winesburg, Ohio: A Group of Tales of Ohio Small Town Life.* 1919. Edited by Malcolm Cowley. New York: Viking, 1967.

Burbank, Rex. *Sherwood Anderson.* New York: Twayne, 1964.

Campbell, Hilbert H., and Charles E. Modlin. *Sherwood Anderson: Centennial Studies.* Troy, N.Y.: Whitson Publishing Company, 1976.

Crowly, John W. *New Essays on Winesburg, Ohio.* New York: Cambridge University Press, 1990.

Howe, Irving. *Sherwood Anderson.* Stanford, Calif.: Stanford University Press, 1951.

Rideout, Walter B. *Sherwood Anderson: A Collection of Critical Essays.* Englewood Cliffs, N.J.: Prentice-Hall, 1974.

Schevill, James. *Sherwood Anderson: His Life and Work.* Denver, Colo.: University of Denver Press, 1951.

Sutton, William A. *The Road to Winesburg: A Mosaic of the Imaginative Life of Sherwood Anderson.* Metuchen, N.J.: Scarecrow Press, 1972.

Taylor, Welford Dunaway. *Sherwood Anderson.* New York: Frederick Ungar Publishing Company, 1977.

Townsend, Kim. *Sherwood Anderson.* Boston: Houghton Mifflin, 1987.

Weber, Brom. *Sherwood Anderson.* Minneapolis: University of Minnesota Press, 1964.

White, Ray Lewis, ed. *The Achievement of Sherwood Anderson: Essays in Criticism.* Chapel Hill: University of North Carolina Press, 1966.

William, Kenny J. *A Storyteller and a City: Anderson's Chicago.* DeKalb: Northern Illinois University Press, 1988.

"ANGEL AT THE GRAVE, THE" EDITH WHARTON (1901)

"The Angel at the Grave," originally published in *Scribner's Magazine* (February 29, 1901) and in EDITH WHARTON's short story collection *Crucial Instances* (1901), combines her interest in evolutionary theory and transcendental philosophy (see TRANSCENDENTALISM) with her awareness of the tensions inherent in a woman who chooses an intellectual life over a domestic one. The story illustrates both the sacrifices and the joys that Paulina Anson experiences. The orphaned Paulina, granddaughter of the deceased Dr. Orestes Anson, returns to Anson's home, now a sacred site, where her grandmother and aunts continue to pay homage to the memory of a man who was a well-respected colleague of the transcendentalists. For a while the women cordially open the home to visitors who want to know Anson's domestic habits, but after a few years the public ceases to visit.

In the meantime, Paulina, the sole heir able to understand Dr. Anson's work, declines a marriage proposal in order to devote her life to cataloging his work and to writing his biography. Years later, when she finally presents her book to a publisher, she is devastated to learn that the public has lost interest in her grandfather's theories and that her life's work has been rejected. After this crushing disappointment, she discards her intellectual work, dons a black dress, and pursues domestic interests.

In an unexpected conclusion, a young scholar, George Corby, knocks at the family's door and asks for Paulina's assistance in tracing Dr. Anson's research on *Amphioxus*. In a gesture reminiscent of a character in EDGAR ALLAN POE's "The PURLOINED LETTER" or SIGMUND FREUD's study of Dora, Paulina "draw[s] a key from her old-fashioned reticule and unlock[s] a drawer" that holds Anson's documentation regarding this missing evolutionary link (*CI* 58). Anson's scientific journal, which Paulina has preserved, promises to reinstate the doctor in the scientific and philosophical registers, advance evolutionary studies, and revitalize Paulina through her intellectual collaboration with Corby. The story provides compelling evidence of Wharton's interest in evolutionary theory, her collaboration with Walter Berry, and her awareness of the cultural constructions of women's roles.

BIBLIOGRAPHY
Lewis, R. W. B. *Edith Wharton*. New York: Harper & Row, 1975.
Wharton, Edith. *Crucial Instances*. New York: Scribner, 1901.
Widdicomb, Toby. "Wharton's 'The Angel at the Grave' and the Glories of Transcendentalism: Deciduous or Evergreen?" *American Transcendental Quarterly* 6, no. 1 (March 1992): 47–57.

Sandra Chrystal Hayes
Georgia Institute of Technology

"ANGEL LEVINE" BERNARD MALAMUD (1955)

"Manischevitz, a tailor, in his fifty-first year suffered many reverses and indignities. Previously a man of comfortable means, he overnight lost all he had" (43). So begins Bernard Malamud's "Angel Levine," the fourth story in *The Magic Barrel* (1958), his first collection of short fiction. The story was originally published three years earlier in *Commentary* (September 1955). As does "The First Seven Years," also in *The Magic Barrel*, "Angel Levine" has roots in the Hebrew Scriptures. As "The First Seven Years" recalls Jacob's 14 years of labor to gain Rachel as his bride, so "angel Levine" initially echoes the tribulations of Job, bewildered over the extent of his suffering and grief despite his loyalty to God; "it was in sheer quantity of woe incomprehensible" (44). However, where Job is cajoled by a series of tempters who try to overcome his faith in God, Manischevitz is confronted in his living room by one Alexander Levine, a black man wearing shabby clothes topped by a derby, who claims to be a Jewish angel sent by God. If Manischevitz will request his help, Levine can assist him, but because he is still in a state of angelic internship, Levine says that he cannot restore the health of the tailor's dying wife without being acknowledged as an angel. When Levine tests him as a Jew with probing questions, Levine responds well, but the answers do not assuage his doubt, and the professed angel leaves, vaguely advising the woebegone Manischevitz that if needed he may be found in Harlem.

As he continues to suffer and his wife declines further toward death, Manischevitz relents and finds Levine in a Harlem honky-tonk. Dissuaded anew by such an ungodly atmosphere for an angel, however, he leaves, refusing to acknowledge the possibility that Levine is what he claims to be. Soon afterward, when his wife seems to be breathing her last, Manischevitz returns to Harlem and finds Levine under even more abhorrent circumstances, but seeing no alternative, he addresses the black man as an angel of God. With this remark, the two return to Manischevitz's dingy apartment building. Levine climbs the stairs directly to the roof, locking the door behind him before Manischevitz reaches it. Hearing what sounds like a rush of wings, the tailor peeks through a small broken window and sees a dark figure aloft on large black wings. When Manischevitz returns to his apartment, his wife is out of bed, dust mop in hand. "A wonderful thing," he tells her; "believe me, there are Jews everywhere" (57).

"A wonderful [wonder-full] thing," indeed, is this story, which creates its effect in a multitude of ways. It is fanciful and fantastic; it depicts profound suffering and sordid conditions yet qualifies them with poignant humor, leaving readers with relief and the pleasant sensation of having tasted the bittersweet. It is also socially rewarding through its humanistic representation of interracial harmony, especially when one considers it as having been published only a year after the Supreme Court ruled that segregated public schools are unconstitutional (*Brown v. the Board of Education of Topeka*) and a few months before Rosa Parks refused to relinquish her bus seat to a white passenger in Selma, Alabama (December 1, 1955). But Malamud's seemingly hopeful vision of black-Jewish relations in "Angel Levine" was no harbinger of imminent changes. As Cynthia Ozick has pointed out, the "redemptiveness of 'Angel Levine'" and "the murderous conclusion of *The Tenants*" (1971), a novel also by Malamud, are thematically at odds although separated by only 13 years (Field and Field 83). Yet a careful reading of "Angel Levine" shows that Malamud was not as sanguine as Ozick suggests about an early resolution to interracial conflict in the United States when he depicts Manischevitz in Harlem as the object of both anti-Semitic and antiwhite derision and scorn. In 1963 Malamud focuses more specifically on such hostility in another story, "Black Is My Favorite Color," which implies little hope of assimilation or even harmonious racial relations in the near-future. *The Tenants,* then, does not mark a change but a reinforcement of his earlier views.

Yet it would be a great exaggeration to assess "Angel Levine" chiefly in terms of black and white, which would be the result of confusing a part of the thematic design for the whole. Essentially, it is a moral tale, a story of renewed faith that overrides Manischevitz's despondency and reconfirms his trust in God as he sees his wife's health miraculously restored. He knows that such events occur only through miracles, yet they happen. As Levine's black wings lift him heavenward, a dark feather seems to flutter down before Manischevitz's eyes, but it turns white and proves to be only a snowflake. Here is an imaginative touch that recalls a scene in NATHANIEL HAWTHORNE's famous tale "YOUNG GOODMAN BROWN," where a pink ribbon, apparently belonging to Brown's wife, Faith, floats down beside him as he walks to a witches' meeting in the forest, but Malamud reverses the implication. Instead of his losing faith as Brown does, for Manischevitz faith is restored; nevertheless, the fanciful auctorial device in both stories operates similarly by drawing on the supernatural to support a moral position, for Brown a rejection of faith and for Manischevitz a strengthening of it.

Malamud, a realistic author in his own way, said: "With me it's story, story, story; . . . story is the basic element of fiction" (Solotaroff 147). For him, because humor and fantasy are as much a part of life as suffering and despair, he would not deprive them of a role in his fiction. The appearance of a black Jewish angel in the constricted life of a poor, ailing tailor and his wife is bittersweet humor, indeed, but it is necessary

for the underlying truth as well as the effectiveness of the story. Finally, if Manischevitz believes, why should not we? He and his wife receive the divine blessing, so maybe we shall too. Keep the faith, Malamud implies; keep the faith!

BIBLIOGRAPHY

Astro, Richard, and Jackson J. Benson, eds. *The Fiction of Bernard Malamud.* Corvallis: Oregon State University Press, 1977.

Field, Leslie A., and Joyce W. Field, eds. *Bernard Malamud: A Collection of Critical Essays.* Englewood Cliffs, N.J.: Prentice-Hall, 1975.

Giroux, Robert, ed. "Introduction," In Bernard Malamud *The People and Uncollected Stories.* New York: Farrar, Straus & Giroux, 1989, vii–xvi.

Malamud, Bernard. "Angel Levine." In *The Magic Barrel.* New York: Farrar, Straus & Cudahy, 1958, 43–56.

Solotaroff, Robert. *Bernard Malamud: A Study of the Short Fiction.* Boston: Twayne, 1989.

Sanford E. Marovitz
Kent State University

"ANNUNCIATION" MERIDEL LESUEUR (1935)

Written during the 1920s and anthologized often, "Annunciation" is based on MERIDEL LESUEUR's own first pregnancy. The story begins during a bleak fall; everything around the pregnant female narrator is yellow, dead, and shriveled. The pregnant woman is poor and unnamed. On one hand, perhaps, her namelessness suggests her insignificance in her bleak world, yet, on the other, it implies the universally female experience of pregnancy; she is Everywoman. (See EVERYMAN/EVERYWOMAN.) Her husband, Karl, is jobless and distant, yet she knows that the pregnancy is important and writes down her thoughts on scraps of paper she keeps in her pockets. She writes to record and explain the experience not only to herself but to others.

Just outside their small room in a boardinghouse stands a pear tree, and its importance to the woman increases daily. Through the tree's limbs, its promise of fruit, its curving leaves, she gathers strength. The tree itself speaks to her—the annunciation, an echo of the angel Gabriel's annunciation to Mary in the Bible—and she realizes she and the tree are on the same course in the "curve of creation." Through the pear tree the woman finds comfort and joy about the life growing within her.

As with so much of LeSueur's fiction, the structure of the story is circular, its rhythm repetitive. It is curved into itself, like the leaves on the pear tree or the curve of the pregnant woman's body. The woman does not venture far from her porch, her small room, yet she feels and understands her connection with life forces from the inner experience of gestation, of contemplating and listening to the pear tree. She watches the lives of the neighbors around her, and all she sees are life and "blossoming." Even the houses become "like an orchard blooming soundlessly."

At the end of the story, another woman—also nameless—offers sympathy upon news of the pregnancy. The husband, Karl, has not returned home. The pregnant woman goes without supper. But she is changed. Instead of writing on small scraps of paper, she writes on a piece of wrapping paper. Symbolically, her poverty-ridden world is enlarged; she has unwrapped the gift of the future.

Susan Thurston Hamerski
St. Olaf College

ANTAGONIST   The fictional character in direct opposition to the PROTAGONIST. In KATHERINE ANNE PORTER's "NOON WINE," for example, the protagonist, Mr. Thompson, kills Mr. Hatch, his antagonist. In WILLIAM FAULKNER's "The Bear," the protagonist is Isaac McCaslin; the antagonist Isaac finally conquers is the bear itself.

ANTICLIMAX   Sometimes used as an equivalent for BATHOS. In a second usage, however, the term denotes a writer's intentional drop from the serious and elevated to the trivial and lowly, in order to achieve a comic or satiric effect. (See COMEDY.)

ANTIHERO   The PROTAGONIST of a literary work who, instead of displaying the traditional attributes of a hero, such as dignity, courage, strength, vision, or ability, instead is graceless, petty, ineffectual, passive, and even stupid or dishonest. Contemporary usage applies the term to either male or female characters.

ANTITHESIS   A term used most frequently in poetry in reference to a parallel statement that demonstrates the polar differences between two people or things. The term also can be used in prose fiction, however, to describe two extremely different characters, values, and the like. Thus in NATHANIEL HAWTHORNE's "RAPPACCINI'S DAUGHTER," the coldly scientific Dr. Rappaccini may be described as the antithesis of his innocent and beautiful daughter, Beatrice.

"ANXIETY" GRACE PALEY (1985)   "Anxiety," published in Grace Paley's third collection, *Later the Same Day* (1985), is the story of a conversation between an older woman looking out her city apartment window and two young fathers who have picked up their kids from school. In this story, told from the point of view of the woman narrator, Paley demonstrates her well-known "ear" for dialogue and her use of the urban landscape for stories that work on two levels: on the local level of the community and on the global level of complex political and social issues. Here, Paley emphasizes the consequences for children for whom their "fathers in this society generally develop minimal attachment to their young children" (Arcana 56). So it is within the community, on sidewalks, in delis, and in parks, that Paley raises questions about how men's actions affect—or will affect—the children of the next generation.

In "Anxiety," the narrator leans out her window and watches two fathers meet their children after school. Both fathers, one of a daughter, one of a son, lift their children to their shoulders. The father of the girl, the "frailer father," Paley writes, "is uncomfortable" with his child's moving around (319). When she makes a pig sound, he becomes angry and "seizes the child, raises her high above his head, and sets her hard on her feet" (320). At this moment, the narrator intervenes and takes her authority from the fact of her age. She tells the men she recognizes they are "about a generation ahead of your father in your attitude and behavior toward your child" (320). This statement, on the one hand, appears to be a remark about their sophistication as fathers, but, on the other hand, it is a wry comment, simply stating the obvious: They are literally a generation apart from their own fathers.

Even though they are picking up their children, unlike their fathers before them, Paley identifies the men's limitations, as "the present generation of young fathers demonstrates how much further men—even those deliberately struggling toward consciousness—have yet to go in their efforts to develop the capacity for maternal nurturing" (Arcana 57).

Nevertheless, the narrator has the men's attention, in particular that of the father of the girl. She questions him about his anger toward his daughter, but first she contextualizes her questions with her political views of the world: "Son, I must tell you madmen intend to destroy this beautifully made planet. That the murder of our children by these men has got to become a terror and a sorrow to you, and starting now, it had better interfere with any daily pleasure" (320). The father says he understands her political point, and she proceeds to challenge him about the treatment of his daughter, suggesting his behavior parallels patriarchal oppression of underprivileged people and the Earth. From her perspective, though, he has not yet connected his own actions to the broader sociopolitical context of militarism and environmental destruction, so she asks him, "Why did you nearly slam this little doomed person to the ground in your uncontrollable anger" (321).

With her questions, the narrator enables the father of the girl to make a connection: He tells her his daughter's "oink" sound reminded him of an encounter with the police he had when he was younger and he felt "angry at Rosie because she was dealing with me as though I was a figure of authority, and it's not my thing, never has been, never will be" (321). The narrator invites the fathers to begin their greeting of their children again, with a clean slate; however, the girl's father immediately says to his daughter, "I don't have all day" (321), and the narrator feels compelled to "lean way out to cry once more, Be careful! Stop! But they've gone too far" because he has not understood her (322).

Instead, the narrator draws herself back into her apartment and closes the window, but she wishes to see the fathers and their children safe at home, after they pass "through the airy scary dreams of scien-

tists and the bulky dreams of automakers" (322). As a mother herself, she cannot bear to think about the dangers that threaten these men and especially their children. As do many of Paley's earlier stories, "Anxiety" demonstrates the author's "growing consciousness that women and men occupy different worlds" (Taylor 12). Here, the narrator returns to her domestic space, her apartment, after she realizes the men have heard her as best as they can. She understands that because they are men, not women with an "instinct" for nurturing life, they have not exactly heeded her warning and are not as afraid of the human-made dangers that do indeed exist in the world.

BIBLIOGRAPHY

Arcana, Judith. *Grace Paley's Life Stories: A Literary Biography*. Urbana: University of Illinois Press, 1993.

Paley, Grace. "Anxiety." In *The Collected Stories*. New York: Farrar, Straus & Giroux, 1994, pp. 319–324.

Taylor, Jacqueline. *Grace Paley: Illuminating the Dark Lives*. Austin: University of Texas Press, 1990.

Heather Ostman
Empire State College, State University of New York

APHORISM   A concise statement of a principle or the terse formulation of a truth or sentiment. The term was first used by the Greek physician Hippocrates, and the beginning sentence of his *Aphorisms* is a good example: "Life is short, art is long, opportunity fleeting, experience dangerous, reasoning difficult." Maxims, proverbs, and adages are all aphorisms.

APOLLONIAN AND DIONYSIAC   In *The Birth of Tragedy* (1872), Friedrich Nietzsche suggested that Greek tragedy resulted from the tension between the traits associated with two gods, Apollo, god of the Sun, and Dionysus, god of wine. Whereas Apollo represents the classical emphasis on reason, structure, order, and restraint, Dionysus represents the opposite qualities of instinct, irrationality, emotion, chaos, and disorder. Hence the Apollonian is often associated with classicism, the Dionysian with romanticism. The clash of these two opposite tendencies can produce CATASTROPHE and TRAGEDY.

"APRIL SHOWERS" EDITH WHARTON (1900)

In her short story "April Showers," EDITH WHARTON tells the story of Theodora (writing under the pseudonym of *Gladys Glyn*), an aspiring young writer who has just completed her first novel, *April Showers*. Through the fictional Kathleen Kyd, Wharton wastes no time in using "April Showers" to criticize both the publishing business and America's critique of sentimental writers. Wharton also uses the text, however, to stress the importance of relationships. Throughout, Wharton stresses the inherent loneliness in Theodora's task: She must write and do so alone. In fact, in many instances, Theodora is seemingly misunderstood by her own family members, including both her mother and her father. Yet Theodora's parents understand more than she gives them credit for. What appears to be a simple short story about one writer's failure to be published functions as a much larger comment on the communality of life itself, of the interactive nature of families and their function in society.

Early in the narrative, Wharton informs her readers of Theodora's solitary life. Wharton writes, "Downstairs the library clock struck two. Its muffled thump sounded like an admonitory knock against her bedroom floor" (189). In other words, a young girl is up until two in the morning, alone, working on her manuscript, even when she has promised her mother to be up early to care for her two younger siblings. But try as she may, Theodora cannot wake early enough to keep her promise to her mother. Wharton writes: "She sprang out of bed in dismay. She had been so determined not to disappoint her mother about Johnny's buttons!" (191). Even so, Theodora imagines that her expected literary success will offset her isolation and ill attention to family matters: "Her contrition was softened by the thought that literary success would enable her to make up for all the little negligences of which she was guilty" (191).

But Theodora is bent on playing the part of the misunderstood—and, of course, alienated and isolated—artist. After her late rise, Theodora hastily prepares her mother's breakfast and decides that she must bear being misunderstood only until her manuscript is accepted. Wharton writes: "It was impossible to own to having forgotten Johnny's buttons without revealing the cause of her forgetfulness. For a few weeks longer she must bear to be misunderstood; then . . . ah, then if her novel were accepted, how gladly would she forget and forgive!" (192). Even when Theodora is awake early enough to take care of the family, she cannot, because of the anxiety surrounding the unsure acceptance of her novel: "The week was a long nightmare. Theodora could neither eat nor sleep. She was up early enough, but instead of looking after the children and seeing that breakfast was ready, she wandered down the road to meet the postman, and came back wan and empty-handed, oblivious of her morning duties" (193).

But perhaps Theodora's most isolated event occurs when she journeys to Boston—alone—to discover why her novel was not published. Wharton writes: "She never knew how she got back to the station. She struggled through the crowd on the platform, and a gold-banded arm pushed her into the train just starting for Norton. It would be dark when she reached home; but that didn't matter. . . . Nothing mattered now" (194). Oblivious to her own actions—and of course to the actions and reactions of her family—Theodora chooses to suffer the trip alone. And she does not think of her family again until the train approaches Norton. Wharton writes: "Then for the first time she thought of home. She had fled away in the morning without a word, and her heart sank at the thought of her mother's fears" (194).

Even so, what Theodora fails to realize is that her isolation has been self-imposed; her father has tried, earlier in his life, to publish a novel himself. Thus, her fears of abandonment and criticism for what she thinks her parents feel is an ill-fated occupation are not justified. After learning of her father's attempt to write, Theodora feels relieved: "The doctor paused, and Theodora clung to him in a mute passion of commiseration. It was as if a drowning creature caught a live hand through the murderous fury of the waves" (196). Because of her reluctance to share her agonizing situation with her family, Theodora faces the news of her unpublished novel alone. Nonetheless, Wharton reminds us how important family is when we learn that Dr. Pace goes to meet Theodora at the train station because he remembers the pain caused by his novel's rejection. He tells her, "It took me a year . . . a whole year's hard work; and when I'd finished it the public wouldn't have it, either; not at any price and that's why I came down to meet you, because I remembered my walk home" (196).

Although "April Showers" clearly comments on what it means—or what it does not have to mean—to be a writer, Wharton uses the story to stress the importance of familial relationships. In her self-imposed isolation, Theodora bears most of the worry and all of the guilt associated with writing her novel and, consequently, ignores her family's needs. Wharton uses the ending of the story to show her readers that this action was unnecessary, however, and that Theodora is ignorant of her father's own writing ambitions. Perhaps the lesson Theodora learns is one for us all: Embrace those who can and will assist you.

BIBLIOGRAPHY
Wharton, Edith. "April Showers." In *The Collected Short Stories of Edith Wharton,* edited by R. W. B. Lewis, 189–196. 2 vols. New York: Scribner, 1968.

Chris L. Massey
Wright State University

ARCHETYPE   A literary term derived from the work of Sir James Frazer and C. J. Jung. Frazer traced elemental or "archetypal" recurring myths common to many cultures, no matter how diverse. Jung used the term *archetype* to refer to repeated kinds of experiences occurring to both ancient ancestors and modern humans alike. Thus, unconsciously, all humans share memories of recurring figures or experiences. In literature, these may include the femme fatale or Lilith figure, the evil male, the descent to the underworld, the search for the father and mother, or the rebirth of the hero. Critics generally view the death-and-rebirth theme as the most basic of all archetypal themes. The term may also be used for the first in a pattern: For instance, MARK TWAIN's Huckleberry Finn is viewed as the archetype for such subsequent fictional American males as ERNEST HEMINGWAY's NICK ADAMS or females such as KATHERINE ANNE PORTER's MIRANDA RHEA.

"ARMISTICE" BERNARD MALAMUD (1989) Bernard Malamud was 26 when he wrote "Armistice" in mid-1940. The story had remained unpublished for nearly 50 years until released posthumously in 1989 as the first of his 16 theretofore uncollected stories in a volume with the others and his unfinished novel, *The People.* When he wrote it, the United States had not yet struck out against the German onslaught in Europe that would soon expand into World War II, but Malamud was already profoundly disturbed over the plight of the Jews there as the Nazis gained control over one country after another. Until his mother died in 1929, Malamud lived in Brooklyn with his parents, who had immigrated from Ukraine early in the century; afterward he remained with his father until he rented an apartment of his own at 25 to begin his career as a writer. Like Malamud's father, Morris Lieberman in "Armistice" is a grocer with a small city store who fears not only for himself and his son, Leonard, but for Jews everywhere.

Anti-Semitism is behind the relentless distress that pervades it. "Armistice" opens with Lieberman's memory of a horrific act of violence he had witnessed as a youth during a pogrom against the Jews in his native Russia, an act that initiates the fright and stress that underlie the rest of the story. He had seen "a burly Russian peasant seize a wagon wheel that was lying against the side of a blacksmith's shop, swing it around, and hurl it at a fleeing Jewish sexton. The wheel caught the Jew in the back, crushing his spine. In speechless terror, he lay on the ground before his burning house, waiting to die" (103). This graphic description shocks readers and remains with them to the end of the story, continually reinforced by radio broadcasts of the Nazi advance in Europe and underscored by the gloating approval of their success by Gus Wagner, a German-American sausage salesman peddling his wares to the grocer.

Morris is literally addicted to the radio broadcasts; he cannot break away from the war news that informs him of what he fears to hear but for which he compulsively listens hour by hour, day by day. His son, Leonard, pleads with him to stop, as do the other salesmen with whom he trades, all of whom insist that the war in Europe has no relation to the United States, but they cannot convince him. As France gives way, Morris feels lost, and Gus's periodic stops with baskets of sausages include his increased crowing over the inevitable French surrender. When it occurs, Marshall Pétain signs an armistice for "peace with honor" according to Hitler's demands and becomes the notorious leader of Vichy France. With this news, Morris is devastated (105). Malamud must have been drafting his story immediately after these events were occurring in June 1940, while holding a civil service position in Washington, D.C. (Giroux vii–ix).

To complicate further Morris's conflict with Gus, the salesman attempts to cheat him by making small errors in his bill for meat purchased, but Leonard's checking the figures exposes his chicanery. An argument that ensues over Morris's reason for expecting a French victory—whether to support democracy or protect the Jews—reveals Gus as an anti-Semite. When Morris calls the salesman a Nazi, Gus, already angry over being caught cheating on his bill, admits his admiration for the victorious German army and curses at Leonard, leading the grocer to hug and kiss his frail son protectively. Knowing he has pushed too hard and fearing to lose future sales, Gus places several sausages on the table and leaves, saying he can wait for payment. The story does not end there, however. Whereas it begins with Morris's shocking memory, it concludes with a description of Gus driving from the store in his truck, musing disgustedly over the Jews' holding and consoling each other. "Why feel sorry for them?" he asks himself. Sitting straight with the steering wheel firmly in hand, Gus imagines himself driving a "massive tank" with the terrified Parisians on the sidewalks watching him pass. "He drove tensely, his eyes unsmiling. He knew that if he relaxed the picture would fade" (109).

The armistice to which the title of the story ostensibly refers is the one Pétain signed to end the fighting, allegedly restore "peace with honor," and give the Nazis control over France, but on a lesser scale it also represents an unspoken truce between Morris and Gus, who despise but need each other. Morris and Leonard, always defensive, can live with it because they know where they stand in a hostile world. Gus Wagner, in contrast, whose surname recalls the renowned German nationalist composer and anti-Semite Richard Wagner, cannot come to terms with his stifled humaneness. He has suppressed his sympathy in favor of an arrogant, domineering facade governed by his imagination, itself fueled by the news of glorious German conquest that he shares in name only. Unnatural restraint prevents him from sympathizing, from sharing the kind of affection that enables the grocer and his son to fear, suffer, and love openly. Gus knows this but will not face it; instead he allows the news of Nazi victory to feed his ego and dominate his relations not only with two frightened and relatively helpless Jews but with his own inner self. For him alone there can be no armistice until he surrenders to compassion and faces the truth about himself, but whether he can or will do it is left an open question.

BIBLIOGRAPHY

Astro, Richard, and Jackson J. Benson, eds. *The Fiction of Malamud.* Corvallis: Oregon State University Press, 1977.

Field, Leslie A., and Joyce W. Field, eds. *Bernard Malamud: A Collection of Critical Essays.* Englewood Cliffs, N.J.: Prentice Hall, 1975.

Giroux, Robert, ed. "Introduction." In Bernard Malamud, *The People and Uncollected Stories.* New York: Farrar, Straus & Giroux, 1989, vii–xvi.

Malamud, Bernard. "Armistice." In *The People and Uncollected Stories,* edited by Robert Giroux, 103–109. New York: Farrar, Straus & Giroux, 1989.

Solotaroff, Robert. *Bernard Malamud: A Study of the Short Fiction.* Boston: Twayne, 1989.

Sanford E. Marovitz
Kent State University

ARNOLD FRIEND Mephistophelan ANTI-HERO (in JOYCE CAROL OATES's "WHERE ARE YOU GOING, WHERE HAVE YOU BEEN?"), Friend singles out the adolescent CONNIE and hypnotizes her by pretending to be a young high school boy. His connections with the devil are implicit not only in his vulgar mannerisms and expressions but also in his ability to change shapes and, probably, in the reason his feet do not fit his boots: His feet are probably cloven hooves, like those of the devil. A stunningly frightening figure, the PERSONIFICATION of evil, Arnold Friend abducts Connie, and one doubts that she will return alive.

"ARTIFICIAL FAMILY, THE" ANNE TYLER (1975)

By the time ANNE TYLER published "The Artificial Family," her 20th story, in the summer of 1975, she was already an established writer who had published her fifth novel. Soon after Toby Scott and Mary Glover meet at a party in that story, he takes her and her five-year-old daughter, Samantha, on a visit to the Baltimore Zoo, a novel experience for the girl and one in which Toby seems to feel more at ease than either of his guests. "When she and her mother stood side by side, barefoot, wearing their long [gingham] dresses, they might have been about to climb onto a covered wagon," as Tyler herself had longed to do at about Samantha's age" (Tyler, "SJW" 13). "They presented a solid front" (Tyler, "ArtFam" 615).

It is evident almost from the time of their meeting that Toby's relationship with Mary is an uneasy one because their personalities contrast sharply enough that latent conflict is always in the air. Whereas Toby, a graduate student living along in a sizable apartment, is outgoing, affectionate, and generous to a fault, Mary is restrictive, highly ordered, and controlling. Both are devoted to Samantha, but they reveal it in altogether different ways; where Toby eagerly gives Samantha what time he can spare from his lab work and studies, Mary insists that she leave him alone and stay out of his specified study room, one that she had set up for him. But Toby treasures Samantha and heatedly tells Mary, "I don't want to be alone" (617).

Although the couple are comfortable enough together that they marry a few months after they meet, their relationship lacks the warmth and intimacy normal between newlyweds. "They were happy but guarded, still, working too hard at getting along"; in the evening Toby reads to Samantha and plays with her, but "Mary he treat[s] like glass" (617). When his parents arrive to visit for a few days around Christmas, they are quietly hostile to Mary because she was previously married, and she has given them an "artificial" grandchild, not their son's real daughter. Toby is no more comfortable than Mary around them, and both are relieved when they depart.

Mary by trade is a potter, an artist and craftsperson whom one would not expect to be overly restrictive in attitude and behavior; on the other hand, a potter has complete control over the mass of clay on her wheel, and she can shape it as she will. In a sense she is molding Samantha as if the girl were a wad of clay spinning within her controlling hands. Toby, in contrast, is a scientist who works in a laboratory all day; scientific activities are necessarily exacting in measurement and performance, yet he is far more open, imaginative, and generous with his affection and time than Mary. The marriage is soon under increasing strain because she criticizes the love and devotion he showers on Samantha, and when he reacts against Mary's criticism by denying that his attention to the child is excessive, she hides behind a fixed smile, as if she were wearing a subtle mask; she "looked carved" (619).

Before long it becomes apparent that the marriage is doomed. Instead of making Mary and Toby closer, Samantha begins taking liberties in her talk and behavior, which her mother resents, so they drift further apart. He is "spoiling" Samantha, Mary charges, when he gives her small gifts such as any caring father might give a child, and Toby is incredulous (618). He would like to have another baby, he tells her, more than one, "an armload of little girls" (619), and she replies ambiguously, "Do you?" Yet Mary also makes a sound point when she reminds him that while he treats Samantha with gifts and love, he leaves the disciplining and cleaning up to her. Of course, the girl tends to side with Toby, and Mary gradually loses the control over her that heretofore had gone unquestioned. Consequently, one day while Toby is at work in the lab, she walks out with Samantha and the few belongings with which they arrived; when he returns to find them gone, he is devastated because his greatest fear has come to pass. "She left him for good" (620) as she had left her former husband, with or without a divorce. The "solid front" that she and Samantha present when the story opens remains secure when it ends, too solid for Toby to breach it.

From reading the fiction of Eudora Welty, Tyler learned "the importance of character over plot" (Voelker 9), and indeed in "The Artificial Family" plot is minimal. A young man meets a young woman with a child; they wed, they argue a little, and the recent bride leaves with her child for good. The power of this story inheres in its effect, which in turn is attributable to its characterization. The third-person narrative point of view is limited to Toby. From the outset the readers perceive his immediate attraction to Mary and his anxiety lest he lose the phone number she gives him before leaving the party where they meet and he compulsively asks her to dinner. We know how he feels, what he thinks and fears, because the narrator describes his internal responses. In contrast, the narrative depicts the other characters objectively, so we can perceive them both as the narrator portrays them and as Toby sees and hears them, but we cannot look into their minds and hearts as we can examine Toby's. In consequence we feel with Toby as well as judge him, but we are essentially disengaged from the others. No matter how strong a case might be made for Mary and Toby's parents, then, Tyler has privileged Toby himself by enabling us to react viscerally to his predicament alone, and the effect is stunning. At the end readers are left lamenting with Toby over his irreparable loss. Desertion by family members in Tyler's other fiction, such as "Teenage Wasteland" (1983), causes lasting despondency in those who have been deserted, and Toby's loss in "The Artificial Family" illustrates her use of this emotion-laden conclusion in one of her most engaging stories with telling effect.

BIBLIOGRAPHY

Petry, Alice Hall, ed. "Introduction." In *Critical Essays on Anne Tyler*. New York: G. K. Hall, 1992, 1–18.

Tyler, Anne. "The Artificial Family." *Southern Review* 11, no. 3 (Summer 1975): 615–621.

———. "Still Just Writing" ["SJW"]. In *The Writer on Her Work*, edited by Janet Sternburg, 3–11. New York: W. W. Norton, 1980.

Voelker, Joseph C. *Art and the Accidental in Anne Tyler*. Columbia: University of South Carolina Press, 1989.

Sanford E. Marovitz
Kent State University

"ARTIFICIAL NIGGER, THE" FLANNERY O'CONNOR (1955)

"The Artificial Nigger" focuses on several themes that recur in FLANNERY O'CONNOR's fiction. It features tension between generations (an adult, Mr. Head, who is determined to prove his intellectual ability over a child); it discusses racial prejudice and overblown human egos; and, finally, its ending offers redemption and personal understanding about life to its PROTAGONISTS.

"The Artificial Nigger" begins with Mr. Head's decision to teach his grandson, Nelson, a lesson about the wicked city. The precocious child, almost his grandfather's mirror image, doubts that Mr. Head actually knows much at all about the place on which he claims to be an expert. By defiant retorts and aggressive actions, Nelson suggests the fallibility of his grandfather and defies his adult authority. In return, the old man angrily asserts his higher intelligence (a character trait symbolized by his unusual name) by stressing the child's lack of experience—a fact heightened by Nelson's inability to recognize a Negro, whom Mr. Head considers not only lower class but part of the darkness and evil ways of Atlanta. Mr. Head also attempts to elicit Nelson's approval and respect through his ability to prevent them from getting lost during the visit.

During their train ride, Mr. Head deliberately takes out his hostility toward Nelson by demeaning the boy's abilities and by suggesting his total unpreparedness for the corruption that awaits them at their journey's end. When they confront a large black/mulatto man on the train, Mr. Head is quick to exploit the boy's naïveté, his innocence regarding racial identity and the prejudice that accompanies it. Thus the boy is made to feel inferior, like the Negro, a parallel O'Connor develops in detail later in the story.

Other incidents on the train, however, indicate that it is Mr. Head as well as Nelson whose knowledge is limited. His constant talking and loud assertions are embarrassing as well as indicative of his bravado rather than his command of experiences. His prideful actions establish him as a know-it-all whose claims of expertise are questionable at best. Nonetheless, Nelson seems convinced that he would be lost without the old man's help and guidance.

When the two finally arrive in Atlanta, Mr. Head nervously begins to act as tour guide, pointing out the enticements the place offers and the intricacies of his knowledge of the city. He authoritatively points out weight machines that predict human destiny ("Beware of dark women") as well as a sewer system with dark tunnels that he hopes will bewilder and scare Nelson properly. O'Connor uses characteristic religious symbolism in depicting Nelson's association of the city sewers with "the place where I came from," thus acknowledging that the source of his humanness is in the muck and refuse rather than in the pristine country. Such acknowledgment of one's original sin is reminiscent of such NATHANIEL HAWTHORNE stories as "My Kinsman, Major Molineaux," in which a similar innocent is initiated into the ways of the world.

Unfortunately, Mr. Head refuses to acknowledge his own association with this hell-like environment, labeling it instead a "nigger-heaven" where only those of inferior social status belong. Having lost his way and wandered into a totally black area of Atlanta, he begins to see his own shortcomings and hesitates to lower himself further by asking directions from a race of people whom he despises.

Even this small act of self-humiliation proves beyond him as he forces Nelson to fulfill this task, in the process encountering the dark woman of his fortune. Again Nelson is made to feel less than adequate, and he dismisses rather than follows the accurate advice. The two proceed to wander aimlessly, following streetcar tracks in hopes of finding the train that will take them home.

O'Connor is not finished, however, for although Nelson has grown considerably and experienced a rite of passage, Mr. Head has not undergone a similar transformation. After Mr. Head cruelly leaves Nelson asleep on a curb in a white neighborhood, in an attempt to teach the self-confident little boy a lesson, the child awakens suddenly and runs in terror, seeking the security of his grandfather's presence. The practical joke having backfired, Mr. Head races after him but seconds later further alienates the child by denying he knows him.

This treachery or denial, of course, is not unpunished, for Nelson reciprocates the isolation and cold-

ness and leaves Mr. Head feeling forlorn and guilty at his rejection of his own flesh and blood. As the sun begins to set, he is suddenly illuminated with a truth similar to the one Nelson has already acknowledged: "He is lost and cannot find his way." (See EPIPHANY.) Finally depicting Mr. Head's redemption from his prideful nature, the story closes with the "artificial nigger" of the title—a plaster statue that appears in a front yard. By emphasizing the statue's combination of a wry smile and an expression of misery, O'Connor suggests its appeal to both Nelson and Mr. Head: It allows them vicariously to see their own lowness and to understand that only through mercy and forgiveness can humankind cope with suffering.

Although the story begins in darkness and ends with a sunset, the author again affirms her belief that positives can overcome negatives. Surprisingly, in this story the penalty for attaining self-knowledge is not a character's death, as it normally is in O'Connor's fiction, but rather the symbolic death of an "old Adam," the foolish one who asserts personal superiority over others, whether black or white, young or old.

Michael J. Meyer
DePaul University

ASIAN-AMERICAN LITERATURE

In its broadest sense, Asian-American literature includes the literary production (from the late 1880s to the present) by American authors identified with those ethnic groups formerly designated as "Oriental." This shifting and rapidly expanding category currently includes writers of Chinese, Korean, Japanese, Filipino, Indian, Pakistani, Vietnamese, and Cambodian heritage.

Unlike African-American literature, which arises from a more unified historical and cultural context dating back to the slave narratives of the colonial era, Asian-American literature appears, at this emergent stage in its development, to be characterized as much, or more, by the diversity of the groups it represents and the tensions among them as by what pan-Asian critics view as a commonality of circumstance and experience. Nor are scholars agreed on the delineation of their discipline: The criteria for defining "common" experience, the role of cultural and generational difference, and the inclusion or exclusion of writing by immigrants are only a few of the issues dividing the field.

Prior to the 1960s there was writing by American authors of Asian descent, but nothing that could be called a tradition of Asian-American writing. For its first 80 years, from the appearance in 1887 of Yan Phou Lee's autobiographical account *When I Was a Boy in China,* the field that we now regard as Asian-American literature was characterized by relatively scant production and publication, the lack of a broad audience, and the isolation of writers within their ethnic communities. Novelists such as H. T. Tsiang and John Okada, writing during the years preceding and following WORLD WAR II, had difficulty reaching a reading public. Tsiang's six books were self-published by the author, then peddled at leftist political meetings around New York City, while the first run of Okada's *No-No Boy* sat undistributed in a Seattle warehouse for 20 years.

Writers of short fiction fared somewhat better, especially in Chinese and Japanese communities, which published first-language newspapers that provided a forum for their work. A few, such as Edith Maude Eaton, the Canadian journalist of Eurasian descent who is acknowledged as the first Asian-American writer of short fiction, managed to reach a larger audience. Eaton, who wrote under the pen name of SUI SIN FAR, was publishing in such mainstream journals as *New England Magazine, Good Housekeeping,* and the *Boston Globe* between the late 1880s and the early 1900s. She is best known as the author of *Mrs. Spring Fragrance* (1912), her only book-length work, and "Leaves from the Mental Portfolio of a Eurasian," which appeared in the *Independent* in 1909. Her fiction is derived from personal experience and deals primarily with issues of culture contact. A couple of generations after Eaton, during the post–World War II era, HISAYE YAMAMOTO, a Japanese-American journalist and short story writer, also succeeded in achieving national recognition, despite the widespread anti-Japanese sentiment of the time. In the 1950s her work was regularly selected by Martha Foley, then editor of the Best American Short Stories series, for inclusion in its annual lists of Distinguished Fiction. In 1955 "Yoneko's Earthquake" became the first story by an Asian-American author to be included in the anthology.

The notion of a pan-Asian-American literary tradition emerged out of the ethnic studies movement of the late 1960s, when community organizers and writer-activists, such as Frank Chin, saw the political advantage of forming a national coalition of Asian communities under a common rubric and a common cause. This was, and continues to be, a challenging task, given the history of preemigration hostility among many of these groups. However, early on, Chin and his associates realized the unifying power of a common literary tradition, and having no such tradition to refer to—aside from the mainstream Eurocentric canon—set about constructing one. To this end they founded the Combined Asian Resources Project, dedicated to discovering and reissuing little-known works of Asian-American literature, including Okada's *No-No Boy.* Then, in 1974, Frank Chin, Lawson Inada, Shawn Wong, and Jeffrey Paul Chan published the groundbreaking anthology *Aiiieeeee!,* in which they attempted to prescribe a politically based aesthetic, countering what they viewed as the Asian stereotypes perpetuated by mainstream-approved publications, such as *Fifth Chinese Daughter* by Jade Snow Wong. Many of the questions of exclusion and inclusion that have occupied Asian-American literary studies were raised by the editors of *Aiiieeeee!*

In its beginnings, the political emphasis of Asian-American literature and literary studies thus tended to combine the requirements of political activism, on the one hand, and literary activity and analysis, on the other. Much of the early criticism within the field of Asian-American literary studies utilized social science methodology and a narrow adherence to sociological accuracy and didactic intent. This was, as is increasingly apparent, merely a stage of development in a yet emerging field. The old status continues to be challenged as new work by Asian-American writers is published at an unprecedented rate by mainstream presses, and a new generation of critics, such as Gayle Sato, Lisa Lowe, Rocio Davis, Dorinne Kondo, and Lydia Lin, who have a rigorous grounding in literary analysis and postcolonial and cultural studies, has moved to the fore. Consistently with general trends, many more Asian-American novels than short story collections are currently being published, as a result of the popularity of the long form, but exciting and accomplished work in short fiction has been produced by such writers as BHARATI MUKHERJEE, GISH JEN, Chang Rae Lee, Jessica Hagedorn, DAVID WONG LOUIE, JHUMPA LAHIRI, Kimiko Hahn, Karen Tei Yamashita, LOIS ANN YAMANAKA, Ruth Ozeki, Linh Dinh, Don Lee, Rattawut Lapcharoensap, and Mary Yukari Waters.

BIBLIOGRAPHY

Brada-Williams, Noelle, and Karen Chow, eds. *Crossing Oceans: Reconfiguring American Literary Studies in the Pacific Rim.* Hong Kong: Hong Kong University Press, 2004.

Chan, Jeffrey Paul, Frank Chin, Lawson Inada, and Shawn Wong, eds. *Aiiieeeee! An Anthology of Asian-American Writers.* Washington, D.C.: Howard University Press, 1974.

Davis, Rocio. *Literary Gestures: The Aesthetic in Asian American Writing.* Philadelphia: Temple University Press, 2005.

———. *Transcultural Reinventions: Asian American and Asian Canadian Short-Story Cycles.* Toronto: Tsar, 2001.

Fong, Timothy P., and Larry H. Shinagawa, eds. *Asian Americans: Experiences and Perspectives.* Upper Saddle River, N.J.: Prentice Hall, 2000.

Hagedorn, Jessica, ed. *Charlie Chan Is Dead.* New York: Penguin, 1993.

Kim, Elaine H. *Asian American Literature: An Introduction to the Writings and Their Social Context.* Philadelphia: Temple University Press, 1982.

———. *InvASIAN: Asian Sisters Represent: A Collection of Writings for Asian and Pacific American Teenaged Girls.* San Francisco: San Francisco Study Center/Asian Women United of California, 2003.

Kim, Elaine H., and Laura Hyun Yi Kang. *Echoes upon Echoes: New Korean American Writing.* New York: Asian American Writers Workshop/Temple University Press, 2003.

Kim Elaine H., and Lilia V. Villanueva. *Making More Waves: New Writing by Asian American Women.* Boston: Beacon Press, 1997.

Lawrence, Keith, and Floyd Cheung. *Recovered Legacies: Authority and Identity in Early Asian American Literature.* Philadelphia: Temple University Press, 2005.

Lee, Rachel, and Sau-ling C. Wong, eds. *AsianAmerica.Net: Ethnicity, Nationalism, and Cyberspace.* New York: Routledge, 2003.

Lowe, Lisa. *Immigrant Acts: On Asian American Cultural Politics.* Durham, N.C.: Duke University Press, 1996.

Motooka, Wendy. "Sentimentalism, Authenticity, and Hawai'i Literature." Paper presented at Pacific Writers Institute, July 6, 1977.

———. "Nothing Solid: Racial Identity and Identification in *Fifth Chinese Daughter* and 'Wilshire Bus.'" 1997. Forthcoming in *Racing and (E)rasing Language.* Edited by Safiya Henderson Holmes and Ellen Goldner.

Sui Sin Far. *Mrs. Spring Fragrance and Other Writings.* Urbana: University of Illinois Press, 1995.

Watanabe, Sylvia, and Carol Bruchac, eds. *Home to Stay.* Greenfield Center, N.Y.: Greenfield Review Press, 1989.

Won, Joseph. "The Joy Luck Club, the Woman Warrior, and the Problematics of the Exotic." Paper presented at the Association of Asian American Studies Conference, June 2, 1993.

Wong, Sau-ling Cynthia. *Reading Asian American Literature.* Princeton, N.J.: Princeton University Press, 1993.

Wong, Sau-ling Cynthia, and Stephen H. Sumida, eds. *A Resource Guide to Asian American Literature.* New York: Modern Language Association of America, 2001.

Sylvia Watanabe
Oberlin College

ASIMOV, ISAAC (1920–1992)

Isaac Asimov, a Russian-born American scientist, rationalist, and humanist, is recognized as one of science fiction's "Big Three" writers, with Robert A. Heinlein and Arthur C. Clarke. Intellectually an ardent science fiction reader in the 1930s, Asimov became bored with the usual robot themes, with machines not behaving as machines, and at age 19 determined to write a story about a robot that did the job it was designed to do. In the story, titled "Robbie," Asimov introduced the term *positronic brain,* and three stories later, in "Runaround," he created the "Three Fundamental Rules of Robotics," introducing the term *robotics* into common usage.

Writing and editing prolifically from 1939 to 1992, Asimov produced a literary legacy that includes approximately 500 volumes, consisting of science fiction, mystery, memoir, literary criticism, a college biochemistry textbook and other nonfiction texts, extensive personal correspondence, and approximately 500 boxes of personal papers, archived at Boston University. Asimov considered the "Three Laws of Robotics" his strongest influence on literature and science (*Gold* 198) and regarded the short story "Nightfall" (1941), a classic in the genre, his formal debut as a writer of science fiction. In the 1940s Asimov's rational and humanistic influence, particularly the robot stories and Foundation series, significantly contributed to the genre's radical diversion from preoccupation with machines toward a more humanistic approach to world conditions, introducing what Asimov termed social science fiction. "The Last Question" (1956), Asimov's favorite story and one that he believed rivaled "Nightfall" in popularity, explores humanity's ability to cope with and reverse entropy.

Asimov's widely ranging subject matter, including guides, essays, histories, and humor, inspired the MYTH that his work bridges all categories of the Dewey Decimal System. His numerous awards produce a similar awed response, including named awards recognizing Asimov's contributions to world and literary culture, the Asimov asteroid, *Asimov's Science Fiction* magazine, and screen credit for production and expertise in Gene Rodenberry's *Star Trek: The Motion Picture*. *The Oxford English Dictionary* credits Asimov with introducing the terms *positronic brain, psychohistory,* and *robotics*. Between 1957 and 1967, he was awarded numerous foundation and association awards and from 1963 to 1996 received multiple Hugo and Nebula Awards, including a special Hugo Award (1963) for "adding science to science fiction," *Best All-Time Novel Series* Hugo Award (1966), *Best Novel* Hugo and Nebula Awards (1973), *Best Novelette* Hugo and Nebula Awards (1977), *Best Novel* Hugo Award (1983), special lifetime Nebula Grandmaster Award (1987), *Best Novelette* Hugo Award (1992), *Best Nonfiction* Hugo Award (1995), and 1946 Retro-Hugo for *Best Novel of 1945* (1996). In addition to an earned doctorate in biochemistry from Columbia University (1948), Asimov was awarded 14 honorary doctorates from a number of universities and posthumously inducted into the Science Fiction and Fantasy Hall of Fame (1997).

Asimov's themes interweave science and the humanities. His histories, Greek (1965) and Roman (1967); guides to the Bible, Old Testament (1967) and New Testament (1969); collections of humor in the 1970s; and autobiographies (1979, 1980, 2002) suggest the breadth of his intellectual engagement, earning the titles "one-man encyclopedist" and "greatest explainer of the age" (Schaer). While Asimov purposefully resisted the popular perception of robots as machines with exceptional human abilities gone wild and emphasized their limiting, principle-based defaults, his stories, from a robotic perspective, rationally explore such philosophical issues and social conditions as paternalism, oppression, feminism, and population control. Science fiction, particularly before 1980, primarily emphasized interaction with technology, with less attention to character development.

Asimov's work has been described as plain and transparent, employing the minimalist characterization typical of the era. Literary criticism of his work is complicated by the directness of his writing style and generous use of exposition that requires little literary interpretation (Cowart and Wymer). A single review of Asimov's narrative structures as scientific concepts (Palumbo) and the evident and continuing influence of his style on the genre are perhaps the most accessible literary criticism of Asimov's legacy.

Science fiction and fantasy are complex, overlapping genres and are primarily defined by their modes of imaginative expression. Ironically, Asimov's direct writing has earned for him the rank of Grand Master in a genre that is becoming increasingly complex in the definition of what is and is not science fiction. A mythical rule of thumb seems to be, A story that claims to be science fiction and involves nails and rivets may be science fiction, but a story involving trees, magic, and water probably is not science fiction but fantasy (Card 4–5). Orson Scott Card, an award-winning science fiction writer, also notes that while readers of science fiction are "the community most willing to sample something new," it is still "traditional work that wins Hugo and Nebula awards within the field," but Card observes that current science fiction does not "resemble" the genre of 20 or even five years ago.

The only completely accurate definition of the genre is "Science fiction is what I point at when I say science fiction" (Damon Knight qtd. in Card 12).

In an evolving field of literature, with few boundaries firmly established, *speculative fiction* is the umbrella term connecting stories occurring in a setting outside familiar realities. The range includes narratives set in the future, but most stories classified as science fiction in the 1040s and 1950s and later, having plots and technologies that are no longer futuristic, retain the genre classification because of other characteristics. These distinctions may include stories contradicting known facts of history or laws of nature, stories presenting alternate worlds, stories set on Earth before history or in contradiction to archaeological record, and stories with alien characters, or involving lost kingdoms (18). Asimov's work invites readers to investigate unfamiliar places and potential realities by asking "What if?" This question challenges readers to overcome a love-hate relationship with incongruity, and readers respond, readers for whom the desire for security and familiarity is less compelling than a willingness to explore the unbelievable and incomprehensible (19).

See also "GOLD"; "MACHINE THAT WON THE WAR, THE."

BIBLIOGRAPHY

Asimov, Isaac. *The Alternate Asimovs*. New York: Doubleday, 1986.
———. *Asimov's Mysteries*. New York: Doubleday, 1968.
———. *Azazel*. New York: Doubleday, 1988.
———. *The Best of Isaac Asimov*. London: Sphere, 1973.
———. *The Bicentennial Man and Other Stories*. New York: Doubleday, 1976.
———. *Buy Jupiter and Other Stories*. New York: Doubleday, 1975.
———. *The Complete Robot*. New York: Doubleday, 1982.
———. *The Early Asimov: Eleven Years of Trying*. New York: Doubleday, 1972.
———. *Earth Is Room Enough: Science Fiction Tales of Our Own Planet*. New York: Doubleday, 1957.
———. *Gold*. New York: HarperPrism, 1995.
———. *Gold: The Final Science Fiction Collection*. New York: HarperCollins, 1995.
———. *I, Robot*. Gnome Press. 1950. Reprint, New York: Doubleday, 1961.
———. *Magic*. New York: HarperPrism, 1996.
———. *The Martian Way and Other Stories*. New York: Doubleday, 1955.
———. *Nightfall and Other Stories*. New York: Doubleday, 1969.
———. *Nine Tomorrows: Tales of the Near Future*. New York: Doubleday, 1959.
———. *The Rest of the Robots*. New York: Doubleday, 1964.
———. *Robot Dreams*. New York: Byron Preiss, 1986.
———. *Robot Visions*. New York: Byron Preiss, 1990.
———. *Tales of the Black Widowers*. New York: Doubleday, 1974.
———. *The Winds of Change and Other Stories*. New York: Doubleday, 1983.
Card, Orson Scott. *How to Write Science Fiction and Fantasy*. Cincinnati: Writer's Digest, 1990.
Palumbo, Donald. *Chaos Theory, Asimov's Foundations and Robots, and Herbert's Dune: The Fractal Aesthetic of Epic Science Fiction*. Westport, Conn.: Greenwood, 2002.
Schaer, Sidney C. "Science Writer, Robotics' Creator Isaac Asimov Dies." *The Tech* (April 7, 1992). Available online. URL: http://www-tech.mit.edu/v112/N18asimov.18w.html. Accessed June 11, 2006.

Stella Thompson
Prairie View A&M University

ATLANTIC MONTHLY, THE   First published in Boston in 1857, the *Atlantic* has maintained its reputation as an attractive and informative political and literary magazine. The first editor was James Russell Lowell, and early contributors of essays, short stories, and poetry included such literary luminaries as Ralph Waldo Emerson, Oliver Wendell Holmes, Harriet Beecher Stowe, John Greenleaf Whittier, and Henry Wadsworth Longfellow. The tradition of publishing high-quality fiction has been a consistent characteristic of the magazine throughout its history, and its editors have proven adept at discovering and publishing significant work by unknown new authors as well as established ones. Twentieth- and 21st-century writers published in the *Atlantic* have included EDITH WHARTON, MARK TWAIN, SARAH ORNE JEWETT, Dylan Thomas, PHILIP ROTH, JOYCE CAROL OATES, Robert Graves, Albert Camus, ISAAC BASHEVIS SINGER, Paul Theroux, and ANN BEATTIE.

ATOM BOMB   See COLD WAR.

"AT THE 'CADIAN BALL" KATE CHOPIN (1892)

"At the 'Cadian Ball" is a compelling story in its own right, but it is most important as an illumination of the situation that KATE CHOPIN presents in her better-known story "The STORM." Appearing in both stories is Calixta, a beautiful, sensuous young woman whose attraction to the wealthy planter Alcee Laballiere deeply disturbs Bobinot, the man she eventually marries. While the action of "At the 'Cadian Ball" predates that of "The Storm," the stories can be presented effectively in either sequence. "At the 'Cadian Ball" functions well as an introduction to the characters of the later story or as a means of looking back and discovering some explanation for the seemingly casual adultery of Calixta and Alcee. Either way, the stories are best read together, with a focus on how the choices Alcee and Calixta make in "At the 'Cadian Ball" lead to the incident that occurs in "The Storm."

"At the 'Cadian Ball" not only reveals many important details about the individual characters but also gives us a clear look at the social class structure of the characters' milieu, 19th-century Louisiana. Clearly, Alcee and Calixta are from two different worlds. Alcee is a young planter from a wealthy upper-class Creole family; Calixta is from the working-class "prairie people," the ordinary Cajuns (Acadians) of Louisiana. Calixta is shown to be set somewhat apart from her own people because of her openly sexual magnetism and flirtatious behavior, which gossip attributes rather condescendingly to her "Spanish blood." Although supposedly viewed "leniently" by her 'Cadian neighbors, Calixta is actually close to being considered not a "nice" girl. When she and Alcee Laballiere meet at the ball, held in the city of Assumption, it is not for the first time. Evidently they already have some sort of "past," for Bobinot decides to attend the ball out of nervous jealousy when he hears that Alcee may be there. Through Bobinot's thoughts, we discover that the main fuel for gossip about Calixta is an assumed scandalous liaison between her and Alcee the previous year in Assumption.

Chopin presents Alcee Laballiere as a misfit in his own society, just as she lets us see that Calixta does not entirely fit in with hers. Alcee is shown to be very different from the effete upper-class men, "with their ways and their manners," who visit his plantation in order to see his beautiful cousin, Clarisse. Alcee is hardworking, toiling long days at strenuous physical labor, impatient with social niceties, rash even in his business decisions. He is something of a gambler, choosing to risk a large amount of money and enormous personal effort on his 900 acres of rice, which a violent storm destroys in moments. Paradoxically, this destructive storm creates the emotions that drive Alcee to seek shelter with Calixta: Their passionate sexual encounter (either a distraction or, possibly, a comfort for Alcee) ultimately persuades the previously cool and distant Clarisse to declare her love for him. Alcee leaves the warmth and sensuality of Calixta to follow the "aggravating[ly]" unattainable, beautiful, but physically cold Clarisse.

ATWOOD, MARGARET (MARGARET ELEANOR ATWOOD) (1939–)

It is difficult to find appropriate words to define Margaret Atwood's significance in Canadian culture and literature. Atwood is a prolific writer who not only blazes a trail for contemporary Canadian writers but also helps Canadian literature make its mark on world literature. A versatile writer whose literary career encompasses all literary genres and experimental forms (essay, fiction, poetry, drama, criticism, children's books, political cartoons), Atwood fuses important Canadian cultural phenomena and national traditions into such a wide range of genres, creating new literary territories and reverberating sparking controversies.

Atwood's work inherits three distinct literary traditions: Anglo-American feminism, gothic romanticism, and Canadian nationalism. As a woman writer, Atwood, in most of her novels and short fictions, situates the female body in relation to women's conditions of entrapment, sexual politics, and social myths of femininity. Her first novel, *The Edible Woman* (1969), for example, exposes the feminine situation already charted by Betty Friedan in *The Feminine Mystique* (1963). The story centers on a college graduate, Marian MacAlpin, who resists marriage as she struggles to find her place between two men: her fiancé, Peter, and her mentor, Duncan. The "edible woman" in the title is a doll-shaped cake baked and consumed in the novel's conclusion. As the story questions the place of a woman in a consumer society, *The Edible Woman* also answers the question of such struggle in the novel's symbolic cake-woman climax: Peter refuses the cake Marian makes, but Duncan helps her eat it up. The cake baking, as Coral Ann Howells suggests, is "a gesture of complicity in the domestic myth and also a critique of it" (24). By refusing the marriage, Marian wins her independence from the feminine mystique. As does *The Edible Woman, Lady Oracle* (1976), Atwood's third novel, continues to question the place of a woman, particularly that of a woman artist in the patriarchal society. Atwood allows the female artist Joan Foster (a.k.a. Louisa K. Delacourt) to voice her dilemma as a woman writer in the male-dominated literary tradition. Joan returns from a suicide attempt to continue a turbulent life authoring gothic novels and engaging in romantic affairs. The novel itself is a series of stories within the framework of Joan's story told to a newspaper reporter. Different from Marian MacAlpin, who stops eating to reject society's standards of femininity, Joan Foster eats excessively to resist her mother's attempts to mold her into a svelte debutante. The "excess" and "disorder," as Karen Stein argues, characterize the gothic romance in the way that the gothic romance "features high drama, exaggeration, repetition of events, and doubling and fragmentation of characters" (59). The sexual politics also punctuates Atwood's second short story collection, *Bluebeard's Egg* (1983). The women in the collection (13 stories, 12 narrated by women) tell stories related to the Bluebeard tale of the demonic amorous villain. Some of the women (Alma, Becka, Sally) are portrayed as the conventional victims, but others (Loulou, Emma, Yvonne), like Joan Foster in *Lady Oracle,* are powerful women who represent subversive power against the Bluebeardian patriarchal domination. These women find their power through storytelling, in other words, through the artistic power of changing the male-centered perspective of constructing "his-story." Apart from these feminist concerns, the gothic sensibility and conventions pervade most of Atwood's work.

At the core of Atwoodian gothic romance and poetry lie two axes: the exterior northern gothic landscape (Stein 9) and the interior gothic fear—women's fear of men or fear of the darkness. The Canadian landscape, in Atwood's eyes, represents danger, darkness, and power (Stein 10). In her earlier poems, Atwood explores the cold, gothic Canadian landscape—an important metaphor for many other Canadian writers—in her emphasis on maps, place, and spatial details as a reiteration of Canadian identity, the identity reminiscent of Northrop Frye's provocative query "Where is here?" Topics of fear, disjuncture, dislocation, and gothic terror permeate Atwood's early poetry (especially in *Double Persephone, The Circle Game, The Animals in That Country, The Journals of Susanna Moodie*). In Atwood's first short story collection, *Dancing Girls* (1977), the 14 stories explore the gothic landscape that situates these stories: ancient sacrificial cisterns, timber wolves, the grave of a poet, and so forth. The shadow of the terror and disaster of the gothic (e.g., in "The War in the Bathroom," "A Travel Piece," and "Dancing Girl") hover over all the stories: Women fantasize about rape; heroines experience the ends of romantic relationships; a woman is placed in a mental asylum. Most of the women expect and experience danger or disaster, a state of fear not only of the exterior bleak landscape but also of the internalized suppression by men and society. Another gothic element is the presence of the aliens, foreigners, displaced derelicts, who keep their feelings private, hidden from others. In "The Man from Mars" and in "Dancing Girls," for example, foreign students cause consternation for women who see them as the Other. More gothic motifs are elaborated in her longer novels such as *Alias Grace, Lady Oracle,* and *Cat's Eye.* In *Cat's Eye* (1988), for instance, the cat's eye functions as "the nexus for all those contradictions of fear and longing, love and resistance [of] the heroine Elaine" (Howell 117). *Cat's Eye* tells and retells, through the heroine's narrative and through her paintings, the fictionalized autobiography of a successful 50-year-old artist, Elaine Risley. Rooted in gothic conventions and narrated with postmodern techniques, *Cat's Eye* situates the heroine in complex "space-time" coordinates: Elaine tells her own private history—together with fragments of Cordelia's story, her brother Stephen's story, and other people's stories—which shifts between times and spaces, between texts and paintings, and between definitions of Canadian identity in the postwar period. Pushing the feminist centrality further, Atwood blends the "I" of the woman artist with the cat's "eye" marble, the pivotal image of the novel, "which represents a number of times during the course of Elaine's turbulent journey toward maturity" (Cooke 111). The generic amalgam, the intertextual travel, often characterizes Atwood's writing.

What places Atwood in the Canadian literary tradition is her constant concern with Canadian identity. In the classical manifesto in *Survival: A Thematic Guide to Canadian Literature* (1972), Atwood begins by asking what the central preoccupations in both English and French Canadian literatures have been, and her answer is twofold: "survival and victims." The manifesto and the two themes have been further pursued by other contemporary Canadian writers.

In the collection of 10 stories in *Wilderness Tips* (1991), Canadian fantasies of the northern landscape underline three of the stories: "The Age of Lead," "DEATH BY LANDSCAPE," and "Wilderness Tips." The stories discuss Canadian popular myths about "the malevolent North" and focus on the themes of victims and survival in Canadian literature. "Wilderness Tips," for example, alludes to actual and invented stories of the North as it questions the meanings and wilderness or Canadian identity (Howells 32–37). All of the characters have different assumptions about wilderness, and throughout the story these assumptions about the Canadian wilderness are destabilized and reevaluated.

As an influential and versatile literary magnate, Atwood continues to inform, entertain, and intrigue her readers and keeps contributing stories, ideas, and criticisms to Canadian literature and society. Not only does Atwood tell stories, but she also engages in conversations with her readers, with her peer citizens, and with the world. In her novel *The Robber Bride,* Atwood writes: "She will only be history if Tony chooses to shape her into history. At the moment she is formless, a broken mosaic; the fragments of her are in Tony's hands, because she is dead, and all the dead are in the hands of the living" (461). Who is "she"? She is the woman, the historian, the storyteller, the victim, the survivor, the fragment, the Canadian, the revolutionist, the writer, the one with whom every reader can identify.

See also "HAPPY ENDINGS."

BIBLIOGRAPHY

Atwood, Margaret. *Alias Grace.* Toronto: McClelland and Stewart, 1996.

———. *The Blind Assassin.* Toronto: Toronto: McClelland and Stewart, 2000.

———. *Bluebeard's Egg.* Toronto: McClelland and Stewart, 1983.

———. *Bluebeard's Egg and Other Stories.* New York: Fawcett Crest, 1987.

———. *Bodily Harm.* Toronto: McClelland and Stewart, 1981.

———. *Cat's Eye.* Toronto: McClelland and Stewart, 1988.

———. *Dancing Girls and Other Stories.* Toronto: McClelland and Stewart, 1977.

———. *The Edible Woman.* Toronto: McClelland and Stewart, 1969.

———. *Good Bones.* Toronto: Coach House Press, 1992.

———. *The Handmaid's Tale.* Toronto: McClelland and Stewart, 1985.

———. *Lady Oracle.* Toronto: McClelland and Stewart, 1976.

———. *Life before Man.* Toronto: McClelland and Stewart, 1979.

———. *Murder in the Dark: Short Fictions and Prose Poems.* Toronto: Coach House Press, 1983.

———. *Oryx and Crake.* Toronto: McClelland and Stewart, 2003.

———. *The Penelopiad.* Edinburgh: Canongate, 2005.

———. *The Robber Bride.* Toronto: McClelland and Stewart, 1993.

———. *Surfacing.* Toronto: McClelland and Stewart, 1972.

———. *Wilderness Tips.* Toronto: McClelland and Stewart, 1991.

Brown, Russell. "Atwood's Sacred Wells." *Essays on Canadian Writing* 17 (Spring 1980): 5–43.

Carrington de Papp, Ildiko. *Margaret Atwood and Her Works.* Toronto: EWC, 1985.

Cooke, Nathalie. *Margaret Atwood: A Critical Companion.* Westport, Conn.: Greenwood Press, 2004.

Howells, Coral Ann. *Margaret Atwood.* New York: St. Martin's Press, 1996.

Jonas, George. "Canada Discovers Its 'Thing.'" *Macleans,* 25 December–1 January 1995, p. 63.

Lyons, Bonnie. "'Neither Victims Nor Executioners' in Margaret Atwood's Fiction." *World Literature Writing in English* 17, no. 1 (April 1978): 181–187.

Mandel, Eli. "Atwood Gothic." *Malahat Review* 41 (January 1977): 165–174.

Nischit, Reingard. "Margaret Atwood in Statements by Fellow Writers." In *Margaret Atwood: Works and Impact.* Rochester, N.Y.: Camden House, 2000, 305–310.

Patnaik, Eira. "The Succulent Gender: Eat Her Softly." In *Literary Gastronomy,* edited by David Bevan, 59–76. Amsterdam: Rodopi, 1988.

Rosenberg, Jerome. *Margaret Atwood.* Boston: Twayne, 1984.

Stein, Karen F. *Margaret Atwood Revisited.* New York: Twayne, 1999.

Wilson, Sharon R. *Margaret Atwood's Fairy-Tale Sexual Politics.* Jackson: University of Mississippi Press, 1993.

Woodcock, George. "Transformation Mask for Margaret Atwood." *Malahat Review* 41 (1977): 52–56.

Bennett Fu
National Taiwan University, Taiwan

"AUTRES TEMPS . . ." EDITH WHARTON

(1911) This story is a superb example of the tightly controlled and finely crafted narrative at which EDITH WHARTON excelled in both long and short fictional forms. Clearly defined characters are placed in situations that offer dramatic social conflicts. While Wharton's resolution of these conflicts may offer surprises, it never leaves any loose ends.

Mrs. Lidcote, the protagonist of "Autres Temps. . . ," returns from Europe to New York after her daughter, Leila's, divorce and remarriage. Mrs. Lidcote, herself divorced long ago when such an action made her an outcast in wealthy "old New York" society, learns from her old friend Franklin Ide that Leila is happy, because times have changed in her social set and divorce is no longer a scandal. Mrs. Lidcote cannot believe that such change is possible, but after she visits Leila and her wealthy new husband in his magnificent family home in the Berkshires, she understands that Franklin is right.

Times have not changed for Mrs. Lidcote, however; her contemporaries, who remember her past, cut her socially. Even Leila seems afraid to include her mother with her other company at an important dinner party, and Mrs. Lidcote spends the first Berkshire weekend sequestered in her room until Leila's other guests leave. Back in a New York hotel, preparing to return to her apartment in Italy, Mrs. Lidcote is approached again by Franklin, who tells her that she is wrong to live as a recluse and that she should have joined the company at Leila's dinner party. Franklin says, "It looked as though you were afraid of them or as though you hadn't forgiven them. Either way, you put them in the wrong instead of waiting to let them put you in the right."

Deciding to test Franklin, Mrs. Lidcote asks him to go with her to meet her old acquaintance Margaret Wynn, whom she has seen earlier in the New York hotel. Franklin hangs back and then lies to her, saying that she will not find her old friend at the hotel, that her daughter's "young man was suggesting that they should all go out to a music-hall or something of the sort." Just as Leila had blushed when Mrs. Lidcote asked whether her guests would "think it odd" if she joined the dinner party, so Franklin blushes when he explains why they should not look for Mrs. Wynn. Mrs. Lidcote understands what Wharton calls "the grim edges of reality" of her situation, and the story ends.

Mrs. Lidcote's strength of character is tested and found equal to the social ordeal she is forced to endure; of all the sympathetic characters in the story, she alone does not blush when forced to confront her situation. Margaret Wynn's daughter, Charlotte, blushes when her mother will not let her speak to Mrs. Lidcote at the hotel. The climax occurs in Wharton's description of Leila's blush at the end of the fifth section of the story: As Mrs. Lidcote watches her daughter's face, "the colour stole over her bare neck, swept up to her throat, and burst into flame in her cheeks. Thence it sent its devastating crimson up to her very temples, to the lobes of her ears, to the edges of her eye-lids, beating all over her in fiery waves, as if fanned by some imperceptible wind."

This closely observed blush exemplifies Wharton's technique of revealing her characters' inner psychological states through their outward manifestations. We know at once, as does Mrs. Lidcote, exactly what her daughter is thinking, although she is too embarrassed and not quite cruel enough to state those thoughts aloud. Times have changed for Leila, but Mrs. Lidcote lived in other times—"autres temps"—and society continues to condemn her according to the codes of that earlier era. The title of the story refers to the French idiom *autres temps, autres moeurs* (other times, other morés).

"AUTUMN HOLIDAY, AN" SARAH ORNE JEWETT (1880)

First published in *HARPER'S* magazine in October 1880, this early story by SARAH ORNE JEWETT initially seems a pleasing if somewhat rambling account of the first-person narrator's walk through the Maine countryside. After evoking a detailed, realistic (see REALISM) picture of the narrator's pleasure in the flora and fauna she observes on this glorious sun-filled October day, Jewett describes her friendly, gossipy encounter with Miss Polly Marsh and her widowed sister, Mrs. Snow, who is spending the day at Polly's house. Aunt Polly entertains the narrator and Mrs. Snow by recalling the antics of Captain Daniel Gunn, an apparently senile but harmless old man whom she met 50 years ago when visiting her cousin Statiry, Gunn's housekeeper. The story ends as the narrator departs with her father, the doctor, who has been seeing his patients and will take her home in his wagon.

On closer inspection, however, the story's tone—and undertone—implicitly raise issues of death, gender, and women's friendships. In her walk through the fields, the narrator conveys the combined loneliness and comfort she derives from the season and the outdoor sights: A solitary and nameless child's grave prompts a memory of a child's ruined boat she once saw, "a shipwreck of his small hopes" (639), yet, paradoxically, she enjoys her contemplations in the warm sun. When the narrator approaches Aunt Polly's house, her thoughts have been on aging and autumn, but as she sees the two cheerful old bodies" (640) at their twin spinning wheels, they convey a sense of good spirits, wisdom, and purpose. Aunt Polly then begins her storytelling, focusing on Daniel Gunn, who, in his old age, believed he was his dead sister, Patience. When he insisted on wearing her clothing, imitating the way she knitted, and attending church services and the Female Missionary Society meetings, "folks used to call him Mrs. Daniel Gunn" (643).

Underlying the kindly humor and compassion with which Aunt Polly relates the story and the community's good-natured tolerance of Daniel's behavior, however, is a more somber question. Aunt Polly wonders whether Daniel Gunn's friends and relatives would have been so tolerant had he been "a flighty old woman" (646) instead of a valued and respected man suffering the mental vagaries of old age. Only when the doctor arrives to fetch his daughter does Mrs. Snow confide to the narrator the information that Aunt Polly has omitted from her story: During her visit, Daniel Gunn's nephew Jacob had proposed to Polly, but she turned him down. The story invites unanswered questions: Why does Aunt Polly tell the story of the community's broad-minded view of this cross-dressing man? Why does she omit references to Jacob's offer of marriage? Why does the narrator value the company of the two aging sisters? And how do we account for the bleakly abrupt ending? We know only that the narrator describes Polly, "a famous nurse," as "one of the most useful women in the world" (641); that after the narrator's short "holiday," the ride home with her father took "much longer" than her walk through the country; and that when she reached home, the fine autumn day had declined into one of darkness and cold.

BIBLIOGRAPHY

Jewett, Sarah, Orne. "An Autumn Holiday." In *Major Writers of Short Fiction: Stories and Commentaries,* edited by Ann Charters, 637–647. Boston: Bedford–St. Martin's, 1993.

AVANT-GARDE

A French phrase meaning "advanced guard" or "vanguard," usually applied to art or literature that is new, original, or experimental in ideas and techniques. Such art is sometimes bizarre and often attacks established conventions. In the early 20th century, for instance, GERTRUDE STEIN's linguistic experiments were considered avant-garde, as were JOHN BARTH's later experiments focusing on fiction as a subject of fiction.

"AVERAGE WAVES IN UNPROTECTED WATERS" ANNE TYLER (1977)

The plot of ANNE TYLER's "Average Waves in Unprotected Waters" could hardly be simpler. After Bet Blevins institutionalizes her mentally incapacitated son, Arnold, because she no longer has the strength to care for him, she waits at the railroad station for the next train to take her home. Nothing exciting occurs, action is minimal, and because the predictable climax does not resolve Bet's major problem, Tyler's engaging story, one of her most highly regarded, remains open-ended. It is based not on external events but on internal conflict, on the ambivalence of a mother who has decided that she can no longer be responsible for her child yet cannot in good conscience leave him permanently hospitalized in a state institution. For nine years Bet has cared for and controlled Arnold, whose increasing strength has become too much for her; although a "staunch" woman ("Average Waves In Unprotected Waters" 33), she feels "too slight and frail, [too] wispy" (32), to continue managing him.

Bet does not know why Arnold was born with the profound mental disorder that led her husband, Avery, to abandon them soon after being informed of it by the doctor. Perhaps the cause was genetic, she muses, either Avery's fault or her own; she even wonders whether it may not be attributable to her leaving home and marrying young against her parents' wishes. "All she'd wanted was to get away from home" (33). Perhaps she should have known better, she thinks. She recalls that when she was a child herself, her father had listened every morning for the marine weather forecast and heeded it before setting out from the Maryland coast aboard his fishing boat with a group of tourists; first, he had to know "the wind, the tides, the small-craft warnings, the height of average waves in unprotected waters" (33). Bet was young then, and fear of facing the world without protection did not deter her from an early and unfortunate marriage, but it has been embedded in her mind ever since, and she discovered too late, away from home and parental care, that the "average waves" were nearly high enough to overwhelm her; apparently Avery (a name similar to the word *average*) was the first of those destructive waves. Thinking back on her childhood, she remembers only how blissful it was, and she cannot fathom as an adult why she had longed to leave home so young.

Whatever the reason, Arnold requires more care than she can provide. She dresses him neatly one morning and takes him by bus, train, and taxi to the state hospital. There she leaves him with a "flat-fronted nurse" beside one cot in a line of them that stretches along "an enormous hallway" (35). Arnold, preoccupied with the squeaky sound made by his shoe soles as he pivots on the linoleum floor, is oblivious to his mother's imminently passing out of his life forever. She touches his hair for the last time, leaves his special baby blanket with the nurse, and, without kissing him good-bye, walks with her toward the front doors. As the desexualized nurse unlocks them, Bet hears "a single terrible scream, but the nurse only patted her shoulder and pushed her gently on through" (35).

She has kept her taxi waiting to carry her back to the train station for her return trip home. Although her timing has been precise to avoid having to wait, she becomes distraught on learning when she arrives that her train will be 20 minutes late. "What am I going to do?" she twice asks the ticket agent, as if her 20-minute wait were a calamity (36). It seems that without Arnold at her side to care for, she is bewildered and lost. As her responsibility for him no longer exists, she is free for the first time in the nine years she has watched over him moment by moment. Her abrupt destabilization, with neither responsibility nor plan to occupy her, ends rapidly when several men enter the waiting room with a speaker's lectern and patriotic decorations. The mayor has arrived to speak for 20 minutes to celebrate the expansion of the station, and Bet is thoroughly relieved. "They had come just for her sake, you might think. They were putting on a private play. From now on, all the world was going to be like that—just something on a stage for her to sit back and watch" (36).

Her sudden discombobulation over being completely free is probably not surprising to Bet, who has deliberately attempted to avoid it by planning her schedule so tightly. The plan, then, serves as her protection from the unknown that inevitably accompanies complete freedom, and, in this respect, she is saved from foundering by the unanticipated entrance of the mayor and his men. Suddenly finding herself the object of the mayor's attention, she extrapolates and assumes a nonparticipatory role as the audience for a continuing play presented just for her "to sit back and watch."

According to Elizabeth Evans, this conclusion implies that Bet's "real self was tied to Arnold, who is hers no longer" (27), a viewpoint that her wrought appearance on reentering the railroad station would seem to confirm because she is "swollen-eyed and wet-cheeked" (Tyler 36) from weeping that evidently begins as soon as she leaves the hospital. But her sobbing does not continue for long. As soon as she understands that the mayor is speaking to her in a "private play," she "wipe[s] her eyes and smiles" (36). On with the show. Tyler does not foreshadow what is in store for Bet after her "private play" ends, and she returns to unprotected waters. As far as we know, however, for the indefinite future, Arnold is out of sight and out of mind. For Bet now, "all the world's a stage," and until she awakens from this illusion of theatrical security, her anxiety is over.

In Tyler's fiction, eccentricity and more serious mental aberrations, especially agoraphobia, are problems faced by numerous characters (Evans 26), but Arnold's disorder is particularly acute. The descriptions of his behavior—the way he chews gum; moans, rocks, and shakes his head; covers his mouth while eating a piece of cookie; drags his feet while walking; and so forth—are graphic and convincing. Arnold is a prominent figure, of course, because his presence alone is actuating, but the story is Bet's, not his. The narrative point of view is third-person, and hers is the central consciousness; readers visualize Arnold's erratic behavior, but they enter her mind, see what she sees, and have access to her memory. Where Arnold exists irrationally only in the present, Bet draws from the past and looks uncertainly toward the future. Whether she or the state hospital cares for him, Arnold is in protected waters, and Bet is the principal who must learn somehow to cope alone with average waves high enough to engulf her if she falters. No longer protected by the burden of responsibility

she has borne for nine years, she is vulnerable in her newfound freedom.

This story leads readers to ask how responsibility helps one manage personal freedom. The answer is contrary to one implied by several of Tyler's novels. For example, Anne Ricketson Zahlan points out that in *The Accidental Tourist* (1985) and other novels, Tyler represents "the conflicting claims of stability and freedom" in America. "Possessed by desire and anxiety, determined to live free, Tyler's wanderers resist society's repressive attempts to box them in and lock them up" (84). Bet tried this, and it did not work for long. As Alice Hall Petry perceives, characters in Tyler's novels generally "have come to rely on a strategy that exerts a genuine . . . control over their lives and the world" (16), a resolution also evident in "Average Waves." In this story caring for Arnold has been Bet's strategy, but now that she is no longer responsible for him, whether she can find a new plan for her life beyond watching what she assumes is a continuing play performed by the world for her alone remains subject to question.

BIBLIOGRAPHY
Evans, Elizabeth. *Anne Tyler.* New York: Twayne, 1983.
Petry, Alice Hall. *Understanding Anne Tyler.* Columbia: University of South Carolina Press, 1990.
Tyler, Anne. "Average Waves in Unprotected Waters." *New Yorker,* 28 February 1977, pp. 32–36.
Zahlan, Anne Ricketson. "Traveling toward the Self: The Psychic Drama of Anne Tyler's *The Accidental Tourist.*" In *The Fiction of Anne Tyler,* edited by C. Ralph Stephens, 84–96. Jackson: University of Mississippi Press, 1990.

Sanford E. Marovitz
Kent State University

AWAKENING, THE KATE CHOPIN (1899)

The Awakening, often regarded as a short novel, deals with Edna Pontellier's process of reaching maturity as a woman in both her personal and her professional life. Chopin's open discussion on women's sexuality shocked her contemporaries; even though she hides her portrayal of a frustrated woman behind an apparently simple plotline, Chopin's critics accused her of sympathizing with the fate of her protagonist instead of condemning Edna's immoral behavior.

The plot of *The Awakening* tells the story of a summer vacation during which a married woman, Edna Pontellier, falls in love with Robert Lebrun and experiences her first awakening to love, passion, and desire. This young gentleman, upon realizing that he also loves her deeply, travels to Mexico to escape from their uncontrolled passion, thus preserving her reputation. When the summer ends, Edna realizes that an unknown desire for freedom and self-fulfillment has awakened inside her. From this moment onward, she rejects her former life. She also begins to pursue her dream of self-support through becoming a painter and selling her own paintings.

During the constant absences of her husband, Edna barely keeps a social agenda; instead, she takes long walks alone and ignores the cards left at her door by the visitors she used to receive every Tuesday. She only pays visits to Mademoiselle Reisz and spends time with new acquaintances, like Alcée Arobin, a young man interested in flirting with lonely married women. Exploring the new world opened to her after her vacation in Grand Isle, Edna ignores the gossip around her libertine style of life.

Edna rebels against what being Mrs. Pontellier entails, against the duties of marriage and motherhood, against the role of submissive wife and perfect southern bourgeois. Defying her father's strict education, Edna, a Presbyterian Kentucky native, marries Léonce, a Creole, a Catholic, thereby becoming a foreigner to the culture and society of New Orleans.

Between the two models of femininity introduced by Chopin in the narrative, Edna fights against the first one, the image of the "Angel of the House" that Adèle (Madame Ratignole) represents and everyone is trying to impose on her: the notion that womanhood is completed through motherhood. Adèle poses for one of Edna's sketches, an act that symbolizes Edna's internal struggle between her admiration for Madame Ratignole and her desire to fly away from conventions. A woman devoted to her husband and children, Adèle's model acquires such an importance that even the narrative spans the nine months of her pregnancy. The last moment of epiphany for Edna coincides with her assisting her friend at childbirth:

She cannot sacrifice her own self for the sake of her children.

On the contrary, Edna willingly embraces the identity of the "New Woman," the second model of womanhood, opposed to Mme Ratignole and represented by the pianist Mademoiselle Reisz. The character of Mademoiselle Reisz, a successful unmarried artist, is ostracized by the rest of the Creole society because she does not follow the conventions of a southern woman. It is meaningful that Mademoiselle Reisz lives in an attic by herself and is often referred to as "a demented woman." Edna's atelier is also located on the top of her house, and her husband sometimes ponders whether she is growing mentally unbalanced. As the first woman to confront the traditional Creole society of New Orleans and obtain independence in the story, Mademoiselle Reisz must live alienated, separated from the "normal" people. Her difference becomes bothersome for the rest of the bourgeoisie, and were it not for her artistic talent, she would be excluded from most of the social events.

Through her refusal to go to her sister's wedding, Edna voices her awakening to the tight constraints of married life and her objections to the institution of marriage. Edna feels sick in the Gothic church of Our Lady of Lourdes, another institution that asphyxiates her as much as marriage. Besides, the Virgin Mary, submissive wife and devoted mother of Jesus, stands for the set of values that Edna has started to confront.

Obsessed with learning to swim, symbolic of her desire for independence as well as of her loss of innocence, Edna spends the whole summer in or near the water, except for the time the rest of the people take a swim. Paradoxically, she finds her freedom in the water when Robert leaves for Mexico. She finds her true self and feels reborn in the immensity of the sea, which opens a new world of possibilities for her fulfillment.

In the *Künstlerroman,* or narrative about the coming of age of an artist, Chopin gives her heroine economic independence through her art; in fact, she rents a place for herself, which she hopes to pay for by selling her sketches. Léonce, her husband, however, destroys that dream of autonomy she envisioned by disguising her moving to the apartment next door as a temporary solution to family house renovations. Mr. Pontellier through his actions constantly reminds her that she is one of his valuable possessions. Edna only learns that this has always been the case when Robert suggests the possibility of Léonce's giving her up to him, as if her life were part of a trading agreement.

Disappointed about Robert, who also wants to chain her through the bonds of marriage, Edna finds a new life immersed in water; losing earthly life, she gains freedom from a society that does not allow her self-fulfillment, where all decisions are made for her except for the last one: taking her life. The embrace of the water returns her to the beginning, to the warmth and security of the maternal womb, to a new life.

BIBLIOGRAPHY

Barker, Deborah. "Kate Chopin's *Awakening of Female Artistry.*" In *Aesthetics and Gender in American-Literature: Portraits of the Woman Artist.* Lewisburg, Pa.: Bucknell University Press; London: Associated University Presses, 2000.

Birnbaum, Michele. "'Alien Hands' in Kate Chopin's 'The Awakening.'" In *Race, Work, and Desire in American Literature, 1860–1930.* Cambridge and New York: Cambridge University Press, 2003.

Chopin, Kate. *"The Awakening" and Selected Stories.* Edited and with an introduction by Sandra M. Gilbert. New York: Penguin Books, 2003.

Imelda Martín-Junquera
Universidad de León

B

BABBITT George Follansbee Babbitt is the protagonist in Sinclair Lewis's novel *Babbitt* (1922). A conceited, arrogant, complacent businessman, he tries for a time to escape his comfortable and successful but dull and middle-class existence, but learns that he fears for his reputation and thus returns to the status quo. The name has become synonymous with the stereotype of the American businessman, whose raison d'être is to make money and avoid making waves by following conventions.

"BABYLON REVISITED" F. SCOTT FITZGERALD (1931) F. SCOTT FITZGERALD's most anthologized story, "Babylon Revisited," develops its THEME of guilt, alienation, and reparation through the PROTAGONIST CHARLIE WALES, an American expatriate who has returned to Paris from his new home in Prague in the hope that he can regain custody of his young daughter, Honoria, who has been in the care of relatives. Charlie apparently has reformed after a long period of dissipation, which the narrative suggests may have contributed to his wife's death. He is now a successful businessman, and his wife's sister, Marion Peters, has agreed to return Honoria to his care. During the reclamation visit, however, two of Charlie's alcoholic friends from the past arrive and make a scene, causing Marion to change her mind about his suitability as a guardian. The story closes as Charlie disconsolately ponders the six more months of waiting to which Marion has consigned him. There are strong symbolic suggestions that his past indulgences will permanently prevent reunion with his daughter.

Originally published in 1931 in the *SATURDAY EVENING POST*, the story was revised for Fitzgerald's fourth story collection, *Taps at Reveille*, in 1935. Fitzgerald shortened the second version and made a number of stylistic changes, but otherwise the two versions are essentially the same. The revised version did not eliminate a few inconsistencies in logic and chronology: It is unclear how long Charlie has been away from Paris or how long his period of dissipation lasted, because he mentions differing lengths of time.

Among the story's psychological complexities is the question of Charlie's conflict. Some readers see him as a man tormented by his past mistakes, attempting to atone for them in the present but still haunted by their lingering repercussions. Other readers suggest that Charlie's problem is not the conflict between his past actions and present desires but an internal division in himself. These close readers of the story find evidence that Charlie has a subconscious desire to sabotage the reformed, upstanding image he has created: successful businessman, devoted father, humble relative. The degree to which his self-destructive tendency is a healthy resistance to social coercion rather than an imp-of-the-perverse impulse is one of the story's ambiguities.

In part, "Babylon Revisited" is a fictionalized version of Fitzgerald's own confrontation with past indulgences. In 1924 he arrived with his wife, Zelda, in

Paris, where they made the acquaintance of other expatriate Americans. During a two-year stay in France, Fitzgerald's relationships with the rich and famous provided opportunities for socializing that challenged his discipline and focus. His excessive drinking led to obnoxious public displays, quarrels with friends, and marital problems. As the 1920s drew to a close, his alcoholism had become a serious health problem and Zelda had her first mental breakdown. Fitzgerald placed their daughter, Scottie, in boarding school.

While "Babylon Revisited" reflects Fitzgerald's own difficulties, many readers also see in Charlie Wales the symbolic representation of Europe's transition from the Roaring Twenties to the more somber 1930s. Americans went to Paris after World War I in search of escape or novelty, but the stock market crash in 1929 (see GREAT DEPRESSION) brought the gay times to an end. Charlie's alcoholic friends Duncan and Lorraine represent the hangers-on who refuse to admit that the world has changed.

Charlie Wales's personal suffering is at least partially created in and conditioned by a society in which appearance rather than character is the dominant value. Marion Peters judges her brother-in-law only by his friends' improper behavior. She does not understand Charlie's longing for his daughter; nor does she acknowledge the guilt he carries for his past. The strength of character that has enabled him to reconstruct his life is invisible to her. Her middle-class propriety is as shallow as Duncan and Lorraine's bohemian pleasure seeking. As a study of the historical moment or of modern society, the story emphasizes the unsatisfactory choices Charlie faces. He can enter the rigid confines of the smug middle class; embrace the rootless, self-indulgent existence of Lorraine and Duncan; or choose loneliness. Modern life as alienation is a common Fitzgerald theme.

In its ghostly evocation of the way one's past can occupy the present, "Babylon Revisited" also suggests a universal human problem: For some actions committed, there may be no complete atonement. One must live forever with the results of irreparable damage. In the last scene, when Charlie asks the bartender what he owes him, the reader perceives the IRONY:

Long after the present transaction, Charlie will still be paying for all the drinks of his past.

BIBLIOGRAPHY

Baker, Carlos. "When the Story Ends: 'Babylon Revisited.'" In *The Short Stories of F. Scott Fitzgerald: New Approaches in Criticism,* edited by Jackson R. Bryer. Madison: University of Wisconsin Press, 1982.

Gross, Seymour L. "Fitzgerald's 'Babylon Revisited.'" *College English* 25 (1963).

Hostetler, Norman H. "From Mayday to Babylon: Disaster, Violence, and Identity in Fitzgerald's Portrait of the 1920s." In *Dancing Fools and Weary Blues: The Great Escape of the Twenties,* edited by Lawrence R. Broer and John D. Walther. Bowling Green, Ohio: Bowling Green State University Popular Press, 1990.

Male, Roy R. "'Babylon Revisited': A Story of the Exile's Return." *Studies in Short Fiction* 2 (1965).

Toor, David. "Guilt and Retribution in 'Babylon Revisited.'" *Fitzgerald/Hemingway Annual* (1973).

Frances Kerr
Durham Technical Community College

"BABYSITTER, THE" ROBERT COOVER (1969)

One of the most gripping stories of recent times, "The Babysitter" reveals the sometimes violent and obscene fantasies of various CHARACTERS as they recall—or seem to recall—the events of a babysitter's evening with the children of an average suburban couple. Was the babysitter raped? Was she seductive? Did anything at all happen to her? In addition to creating suspense, ROBERT COOVER's technique—resembling WILLIAM FAULKNER's in its multiple perspectives of the same event—is brilliantly conceived, laying bare the raw chauvinism of the various male narrators and leaving the reader to determine what actually happened.

"BAD NEIGHBORS" EDWARD P. JONES (2006)

At first, race seems to be a peripheral issue in the story "Bad Neighbors." The setting is a middle- and upper-middle-class neighborhood outside Washington, D.C., where black families in the 1970s and 1980s have made their own a "good" suburb that has been vacated by white flight. Within this well-to-do community, there seem to be no contention with white culture anymore. The problem that surfaces is one of class—

the Benningtons move in, and with their broken furniture, raggedy clothes, irregular hours, and indeterminate number of children are clearly (as one neighbor expresses later) trash.

The story gestures toward being a familiar one: Sarah Palmer, a beautiful and smart high school girl, befriends the shy and younger Neil Bennington, half out of compassion, half out of curiosity about such an other. They share a love of books and trade them, and Sarah thinks Neil has a crush on her because, basically, he is nice to her, and she thinks that with her beauty and its general effect on boys, it would be unlikely that he would not have one. Sarah feels comfortable around gentle Neil, and perhaps it is the security she feels in her higher status that makes her feel safe. She is breathless about another neighborhood boy, Terence Stagg, son of the richest family and attending Howard University to become the first black doctor from the neighborhood.

The point of view seems to be a combination of the neighborhood's perspective and Sarah's. The neighborhood narration is certain that the Benningtons are the kind of black family that will drag down their aspirations to be seen as successful on any terms white culture establishes. Where the neighbors have Cadillacs, manicured yards, and ostentatious religious piety, the Benningtons represent the white stereotype of black people—dirty, without ambitions, nonpatriarchal, and perhaps criminal. The neighbors equate poverty with ignorance and laziness, for they believe in themselves as living proof of the Horatio Alger stories. If there is any crime in the neighborhood, the neighbors speculate about the Bennington children. In particular, Derek, the oldest, in his early 20s, intimidates them because he is aloof and strong and seems unguided by any conventions. Derek and the other Benningtons raise a specter of a possible common past that the social-climbing neighbors would like to forget.

Sharon is a pawn of the Palmers' plans to raise the family status even further. Her parents are grooming her to be a future wife to Terence Stagg. The Staggs are the richest and have the highest prestige occupation in the neighborhood. Sharon's friendship with Neil is worrisome to them. Terence, while self-centered and deeply certain of his own sense of privilege, will be the family's ticket to status, which would involve a son-in-law who could be a success even in the white world. For the Palmers and Staggs, being at the top in the black community still contains an awareness that their success is still a segregated success.

Sharon meets bad boy Derek only once, when going into the Bennington house to give a book to Neil—although she has more than a little curiosity about how people like the Benningtons live. Derek is ironic and mocks his bookish brother; he declares Neil's reading to be an addiction—one that distances him from the rest of the family. What lies beneath his contempt is the idea that reading will addict Neil to wanting mobility more than family, and that Neil has separated himself from the family and into the white world of the white authors he reads. Sharon has no idea how to take Derek's commentary. When Sharon leaves, Derek allows himself one personal comment to her: "You shouldn't be afraid of wearin blue. . . . Forget the red. You wear too much red." With that, Neil arrives and Derek urges him to be more attentive to his "girlfriend," though Neil insists she is not.

The action of the story ratchets up with a fight between Derek and Terence, which has been promised since the first sentence of the book. Derek is forced to park his car on the opposite side of the street because a neighbor's guest has taken the spot in front of his house. Terence rushes out of the house to defend what he insists is his father's reserved space for his Cadillac. Derek ignores him, but his sister, Amanda, berates him for his arrogance. Derek tries to stop it, reminding Terence they are neighbors and this is a free country. But Terence calls them trash, spits on the car, and insults the Benningtons' mother. Derek downs him with one punch and walks over to his house to await the police. Sharon rushes to her injured boyfriend.

To rid themselves of the Benningtons, the neighbors decide to have them evicted. It is revealed that the Bennington house is the last house on the street owned by a white man, who inherited it from his parents. His name, Riccocelli, suggests that the neighborhood was Italian-American before it became a black neighborhood. The neighbors band together to buy the house from Riccocelli when he at first says he cannot evict tenants who pay their bills. The Benningtons are forced out with two month's notice in the winter. When Derek learns from his landlord that the neighbors have bought the house expressly to evict his family, he shouts from his steps: "We got sweet innocent babies in this house, man! What can y'all be thinkin?" What they are thinking, it seems, is that class trumps race. The neighborhood is not a black community for them; it is a place to tell themselves that their money makes them something more important than their idea of what blackness is: respectable according to wealthy white definitions.

This would seem to be an appropriate ending for the story, but Jones takes us one chapter into the future: Sharon's life has been unaffected by her brush with the Benningtons; she is a student nurse, she is married to Dr. Terence Stagg, she lives in a fancy apartment in Georgetown, and her BMW is in the shop. She has fulfilled the dream her parents wanted for themselves, although she is coming to realize that Terence is too self-absorbed to be a loving husband. She has floated through her life to this point. Walking to the bus at night after a volunteer shift, she is accosted by college boys, two white and one black, who intend to gang-rape her. Out of nowhere, Derek pulls up in a car to save her, at first peacefully, and then with a knife. He tells Sharon: "I wanted to keep this clean, but white trash wouldn't let me." He grievously injures one white boy and knocks out the black one. The other white boy flees. Derek is severely stabbed in the stomach but gets into the car to whisk Sharon from the site and to her apartment. Because white boys are involved, there will be ugly trouble, and Derek does not want to taint her with his trouble.

It appears Derek has been watching over her, from afar, never asserting himself. Sharon wants to take him inside to dress his wound and have him treated, but he refuses. He confesses to her that it was not Neil who had the crush on her, but he, and that red or any color would be hers. "You make the world," he says.

In the end, Sharon is left in her apartment with a snoring Terence and a shiny bathroom in which to clean herself of the night's trauma. Red, indeed, has become her color, because Derek's blood has soaked through her clothes to her skin. Derek has loved her as she walks above a trashy world, but now he has given her a realization of what she has been missing in her successful world—selfless loyalty. Is the red that stains her passion, violence, or a call to revolt from her clean, bland surroundings?

BIBLIOGRAPHY

Jones, Edward P. "Bad Neighbors." In *All Aunt Hagar's Children*. New York: HarperCollins Press/Armistad, 2006.

Carolyn Whitson
Metrostate University

BALDWIN, JAMES (1924–1987)   James Baldwin was born in Harlem on August 2, 1924, the illegitimate son of Emma Berdis Jones. In 1927 his mother married David Baldwin, a clergyman, and subsequently had eight additional children, for whom the young Jimmy helped provide care. Greatly affected by his stepfather's growing bitterness, mocking cruelty, and rejection in an environment of racism, homophobia, and theological anguish, Baldwin, a black homosexual, suffered a crisis of identity that shaped his life and work.

His talent was recognized early by teachers and artist friends, among them Orilla Miller and the HARLEM RENAISSANCE poet Countee Cullen, who introduced him to the theater, music, film, and a wider world of books. Cullen also suggested he apply to the prestigious De Witt Clinton High School in the Bronx, to which Baldwin was accepted in the fall of 1938. Struggling with his repressed homosexuality during his high school days, he sought refuge in the church and became a boy preacher for a short time but left disillusioned. After graduation, unsuccessful jobs, and the death of his stepfather, he moved to Greenwich Village. There he met RICHARD WRIGHT, who used his influence to get Baldwin a Eugene F. Saxton Memorial Trust Fellowship in 1945. Baldwin left the United States for Paris in 1948 and remained abroad, living in France, Switzerland, and Turkey for most of the remainder of his life.

In 1947 and 1948, prior to leaving for Paris, Baldwin wrote book reviews for the *Nation* and *New Leader* and gained considerable recognition for his essay "The Harlem Ghetto" in *Commentary* (February 1948). His career was launched by his early essays, which helped him develop his own aesthetic and gain the attention of a larger audience. In particular, "Everybody's Protest Novel" (1949) and "Many Thousands Gone" (1951), which attacks Harriet Beecher Stowe's *Uncle Tom's Cabin* and Wright's *Native Son*, revealed Baldwin's lifelong concern about defined roles and racial categories and permanently alienated Richard Wright.

Assisted by numerous fellowships and grants, including a Guggenheim Fellowship (1954), a National Institute of Arts and Letters grant (1956), and a Ford Foundation grant-in-aid (1959), Baldwin produced a large body of work, including six novels; a volume of short stories, *Going to Meet the Man* (1965); a children's story, *Little Man, Little Man: A Story of Childhood;* three collections of essays; individually published essays and dialogues; three volumes of plays and scenarios; and two volumes of poetry.

Some have suggested that much of Baldwin's writing career is a long attempt to exorcise "the demons within" and a quest for personal identity. Others regard him primarily as an essayist whose stories and novels are highly autobiographical. Baldwin preferred to identify himself as a "witness" whose responsibility was "to write it all down." There is a strong link between Baldwin's nonfiction and his fiction, and in his novels he attempts to translate into art social issues discussed in his essays (racism, dehumanization, categorization, and the efficacy and redemptive power of love). During the struggle in the United States for civil rights in the 1960s, Baldwin's work became more political, especially after the death of Malcolm X; nevertheless, despite his deep and passionate commitment to the movement, occasionally he found himself at odds with those who he believed were leaning too heavily on ideology and seeking answers in separatism. For a time he was estranged from much of the black American community after Eldridge Cleaver's attack on his homosexuality and accusation that Baldwin had rejected his blackness.

Baldwin's literary reputation has benefited from the passing of time. The distance from the turbulent 1960s and early 1970s has enabled readers and critics to view his work in a clearer light. Few writers have been more in conflict with themselves and with the world around them, and few worked more diligently to maintain their artistic integrity in the face of enormous challenges. In 1986 the French president, François Mitterrand, presented Baldwin with the Legion of Honor. James Baldwin died in St. Paul de Vence, France, on December 1, 1987.

See also "THE ROCKPILE"; "SONNY'S BLUES."

BIBLIOGRAPHY

Baldwin, James. *The Amen Corner: A Drama in Three Acts.* New York: French, 1968.

———. *Another Country.* New York: Dell, 1962.

———. *Blues for Mr. Charlie.* New York: Dell, 1964.

———. *The Devil Finds Work: An Essay.* New York: Dial, 1976.

———. *A Dialogue.* Philadelphia: Lippincott, 1973.

———. *Evidence of Things Not Seen.* Cutchogue, N.Y.: Buccaneer, 1985.

———. *The Fire Next Time.* New York: Dell, 1963.

———. *Giovanni's Room.* New York: Dial Press, 1956.

———. *Go Tell It on the Mountain.* New York: Knopf, 1953.

———. *Gypsy and Other Poems.* Searsmont, Maine: Gehenna Press, 1989.

———. *If Beale Street Could Talk.* New York: Dell, 1974.

———. *Jimmy's Blues.* New York: St. Martin's Press, 1985.

———. *Just above My Head.* New York: Dial Press, 1979.

———. *Nobody Knows My Name: More Notes of a Native Son.* New York: Dial Press, 1961.

———. *No Name in the Street.* New York: Dial Press, 1972.

———. *Notes of a Native Son.* Boston: Beacon Press, 1955.

———. *Nothing Personal.* New York: Dell, 1964.

———. *One Day When I Was Lost: A Scenario Based on Alex Hayley's "The Autobiography of Malcolm X."* New York: Dial Press, 1972.

———. *The Price of the Ticket: Collected Nonfiction, 1948–1985.* New York: St. Martin's/Marek, 1985.

———. *A Rap on Race: Margaret Mead and James Baldwin.* Philadelphia: Lippincott, 1971.

———. *Tell Me How Long the Train's Been Gone.* New York: Dell, 1968.

Bloom, Harold. *James Baldwin.* New York: Chelsea House, 1986.

Campbell, James. *Talking at the Gates: A Life of James Baldwin.* New York: Viking, 1991.

Eckman, Fern Marja. *The Furious Passage of James Baldwin.* Philadelphia: Lippincott, 1966.

Kinnamon, Keneth. *James Baldwin: A Collection of Critical Essays.* Englewood Cliffs, N.J.: Prentice-Hall, 1974.

Leeming, James. *James Baldwin: A Biography.* New York: Knopf, 1994.

O'Daniel, Therman B., ed. *James Baldwin: A Critical Evaluation.* Washington, D.C.: Howard University Press, 1977.

Porter, Harold A. *Stealing the Fire: The Art and Protest of James Baldwin.* Middletown, Conn.: Wesleyan University Press, 1989.

Standley, Fred L., and Louis Pratt, eds. *Conversations with James Baldwin.* Jackson: University Press of Mississippi, 1989.

Standley, Fred L., and Nancy V. Burt, eds. *Critical Essays on James Baldwin.* Boston: G. K. Hall, 1988.

Weatherby, William J. *James Baldwin: Artist on Fire.* New York: Dell Publishing, 1989.

John Unrue
University of Nevada at Reno

BALLAD The traditional or popular ballad is a poem or narrative song that has been passed down orally, appearing in various forms because each poet or singer likely introduced changes. Many folk ballads came to the United States from Great Britain, with the traditional THEMES of love, murder, or the supernatural, but native American forms developed as well, with subjects such as frontiersmen, cowboys, and railroadmen, as in the ballads of Casey Jones and JOHN HENRY. One of the most memorable prose uses of the term is CARSON MCCULLERS's *The BALLAD OF THE SAD CAFE,* a NOVELLA fascinating for the way the author uses musical ALLUSIONS and LEITMOTIFS to highlight the title's significance.

BALLAD OF THE SAD CAFE, THE
CARSON MCCULLERS (1951) A NOVELLA that, as does a BALLAD, tells the ultimately tragic tale of MISS AMELIA EVANS, daughter of one of the most important men in this nameless rural Georgia town. Miss Amelia falls in love with a hunchback, dwarflike stranger who convinces her that he is COUSIN LYMON. Ultimately Miss Amelia's buoyant mood and the cafe she runs become "sad" and begin to wither away after Lymon falls in love with Marvin Macy, Miss Amelia's estranged husband. Together the two men conspire to defeat this powerful, sensitive, eccentric woman in this GROTESQUE yet empathetic story, described by various critics in terms of a FAIRY TALE, MYTH, FABLE, or PARABLE. Above all, it is a love story, a variation of the ageless love triangle.

The story opens in the present with the image of Miss Amelia in self-imprisoned exile in her gray and rotting house. Gradually the story moves backward, revealing Miss Amelia's past, along with her accomplishments: The six-foot-tall Miss Amelia is a shrewd businesswoman who fills the roles of town doctor and bootlegger. Briefly married to Marvin Macy, the local roué, she feels an aversion to sex, cannot bear his demonstrations of love, and kicks him out of her large house. Miss Amelia has numerous so-called masculine characteristics—indeed, the only topic that embarrasses her is that of "female problems"—and one way to interpret her CHARACTER is that she is androgynous or bisexual. (CARSON MCCULLERS and her husband, Reeve McCullers, were both bisexual.)

Whatever her feelings about love, she falls for Cousin Lymon, the hunchback, a TRICKSTER figure who appears in town and charms Miss Amelia, who invites him to stay in her house. Lymon, the archetypical mysterious stranger (see ARCHETYPE), seems to know everything, and the smitten Miss Amelia will do anything he asks. As their relationship grows, Miss Amelia opens the cafe that draws the entire community together in harmony and happiness. But the moment Marvin Macy reenters the scene, Cousin Lymon falls ecstatically in love with him. Some critics point to evidence that perhaps Lymon and Macy knew each other in the penitentiary in Atlanta. Others, however, believe their uniting against Miss Amelia merely demonstrates the capricious nature of love. In an epic battle scene, Miss Amelia beats Marvin Macy in the fight for Lymon but is destroyed when Lymon jumps on her back in a successful effort to help his lover. The two destroy the cafe and run off together, leaving the town a sad and desolate place and Miss Amelia in the self-imprisonment with which the story opened. The only relief—if indeed it is relief—in the tragedy is a final brief description of 12 men on a chain gang outside town: They sing a song both mournful and joyful, perhaps suggesting the inescapable nature of the human condition.

BIBLIOGRAPHY
Carr, Virginia Spencer. *The Lonely Hunter: A Biography of Carson McCullers*. Garden City, N.Y.: Doubleday, 1975.
McCullers, Carson. *The Ballad of the Sad Cafe: Collected Stories of Carson McCullers*. Boston: Houghton Mifflin, 1987, 195–254.

BAMBARA, TONI CADE (1939–1995)

Born and raised in New York City, Toni Cade adopted the name *Bambara* from the signature on a sketchbook she found in her great-grandmother's trunk. She was a linguist who believed that language determined how one perceived the world but could just as often be used to misinform, to misdirect, and to intimidate as to inform. The era in which she matured and wrote, the 1960s and 1970s, was the time of the struggle for civil rights in America by African Americans, and many of Bambara's observations and concerns are politically motivated, but her understanding of racial and interracial, gender, and generational conflicts is often tempered with humor. She uses African-American diction and syntax to give rhythm to her stories about ordinary people in situations described without condescension or sentimentality. According to the critic Eleanor W. Traylor, her importance as a writer was as much the consequence of Bambara's significant role among African-American writers who gained prominence in the 1960s—known as the Black Arts Movement—as it was the consequence of her own style (2703). Cade published two story collections, *Gorilla, My Love* (1972) and *The Seabirds Are Still Alive* (1977).

BIBLIOGRAPHY
Bambara, Toni Cade, ed. *The Black Woman: Anthology*. New York: New American Library, 1970.
———. *Gorilla, My Love*. New York: Random House, 1972.
———. *Raymond's Run*. Mankato, Minn.: Creative Education, 1990.
———. *The Salt Eaters*. New York: Random House, 1980.
———. *The Seabirds Are Still Alive: Collected Stories*. New York: Random House, 1977.
———. *State of the Art*. Minneapolis: Minnesota Center for Book Arts/Tournesol Press, 1987.
———, ed. *Tales and Stories for Black Folks*. Garden City, N.Y.: Zenith Books, 1971.
Bambara, Toni Cade, ed., with Leah Wise. *Southern Black Utterances Today*. Chapel Hill N.C.: Institute of Southern Studies, 1975.
Burks, Ruth Elizabeth. "From Baptism to Resurrection: Bambara and the Incongruity of Language." In *Black Women Writers (1950–1980): A Critical Perspective*, edited by Mari Evans. Garden City, N.Y.: Anchor Books, 1984.
Hargrove, Nancy D. "Youth in Bambara's *Gorilla, My Love*."
Hull, Gloria. "'What It Is I Think She's Doing Anyhow:' A Reading of Bambara's *The Salt Eaters*." In *Conjuring Black Women, Fiction, and Literary Tradition*, edited by Marjorie Pryse and Hortense J. Spillers. Bloomington: Indiana University Press, 1985.
Parini, Jay, ed. *American Writers: A Collection of Literary Biographies*. Supplement 9, *Toni Cade Bambara to Richard Yates*. New York: Scribner, 2002.
Prenshaw, Peggy Whitman, ed. *Women Writers of the Contemporary South*. Southern Quarterly Series. Jackson: University Press of Mississippi, 1984.
Reuben, Paul P. "Chapter 10: Toni Cade Bambara." *PAL: Perspectives in American Literature—a Research and Reference Guide*. Available online. URL: http://www.csustan.edu/english/reuben/pal/chap10/bambara.html. Accessed December 3, 2008.
Traylor, Eleanor W. "Toni Cade Bambara." In *The Heath Anthology of American Literature*. Vol. 2, 3rd ed. New York: Houghton Mifflin, 1998, 2,702–2,703.
Vertreace, Martha M. "The Dance of Characters and Community." In *American Women Writing Fiction: Memory, Identity, Family, Space*, edited by Mickey Pearlman. Lexington: University Press of Kentucky, 1989.
Willis, Susan. "Problematizing the Individual: Bambara's Stories for the Revolution." In *Specifying Black Women Writing the American Experience*, edited by Susan Willis. Madison: University of Wisconsin Press, 1987.

BANKS FAMILY

The Banks family is one of many who dwell in the heavenly valley where JOHN STEINBECK's *The Pastures of Heaven* (1932) is set: "Of all the farms in the Pastures of Heaven the one most admired was that of Raymond Banks" (131). Raymond owns the most beautiful land in the valley and has covered it with chickens and ducks. People admire not only the farm but also Raymond and the parties he throws.

Raymond loves children, who often watch him kill his chickens. Instead of killing them quickly by breaking their necks, Raymond prefers to stab them with a knife. Although the hearts are still beating when Raymond spills their entrails, he explains to the children that the chickens really are already dead.

Only Bert Munroe, Raymond's old schoolmate, discovers Raymond's most disturbing hobby: A couple of times a year, Raymond witnesses hangings at the San Quentin Penitentiary, where Bert is a warden. These are Raymond's only vacations, and he finds them enjoyable and invigorating. After Raymond invites Bert to an execution, Bert spends a great deal of time thinking about it and decides not to go. He knows that if he goes, he will be unable to sleep another night in his life. When Bert tells Raymond how sick his hobby is, he not only hurts Raymond's feelings but also ruins whatever pleasure Raymond derived from his little escapades.

Throughout the work, the Munroe family maintains the pattern illustrated by this episode between Bert and Raymond: They consistently yet inadvertently ruin the dreams, aspirations, and often twisted but happy lives of the other members of the community. This is a common theme that runs throughout many of Steinbeck's other works: Dreams are just delusions that can never be realized.

BIBLIOGRAPHY
Mann, Susan Garland. *The Short Story Cycle: A Genre Companion and Reference Guide.* New York: Greenwood Press, 1989.
Steinbeck, John. *The Pastures of Heaven.* New York: Penguin Books, 1995.

Kathleen M. Hicks
University of Texas at El Paso

"BARN BURNING" WILLIAM FAULKNER (1938)

WILLIAM FAULKNER'S complex father-son story details the emotional effects of combined poverty, exclusion, and revenge, made poignant and painful because the POINT OF VIEW is that of a nine-year-old boy, Colonel Sartoris (Sarty) Snopes (see SNOPES FAMILY). Set in the 1890s, the story exudes the depression and poverty in Faulkner's mythical YOKNAPATAWPHA COUNTY in the post–CIVIL WAR years. The main characters are ABNER SNOPES, Civil War veteran (who participates in Miss Rosa Millard's mule-stealing business with the Yankees during the Civil War in the connected short story collection The UNVANQUISHED). Ab Snopes, Sarty's father, is both an unpleasant and a sympathetic CHARACTER. The title may at some level allude (see ALLUSION) to one of Faulkner's favorite activities in the teens and '20s, barnstorming in his private plane. More significantly, however, the burning and the fires clearly suggest the unabated rage Snopes feels in this complicated tale of class hierarchy. Although in the 1930s many writers published proletarian fiction (see PROLETARIAN LITERATURE), "Barn Burning" rises above the genre and still speaks to readers across class and family lines, remaining remarkably contemporary.

The story opens in a country store with Ab Snopes facing the local and informal jury that has charged him with arson. He is guilty, and Sarty's interior thoughts show a boy conflicted between loyalty to his father and humiliation over his behavior. Snopes is aggrieved at his life as an itinerant farmer who never owns his own land but works for monied plantation owners. After he burns their barns, he moves on to still another job, remaining only briefly until he burns again. Faulkner takes pains to delineate the social structure in this story: Because Ab Snopes is "white trash," at the bottom of the social scale and, to his mind, even worse off than the black butler who works for the wealthy Major de Spain, he strictly enforces his own hierarchy within his family, as illustrated through his treatment of them as well as the clearly metaphorical sleeping arrangements (see METAPHOR). Ab, his wife, and his eldest son (the infamous Flem Snopes of the Snopes Trilogy), have beds, while Sarty, his daughters, and his unmarried and nameless sister-in-law sleep on pallets. Indeed, this powerless spinster figure appears in numerous Faulkner works.

Few readers can help sympathizing with Ab, the man without a future, the man who teaches his sons that blood is more important than any abstract value. Yet somehow Sarty (named for Colonel Sartoris of *Flags in the Dust* and several Faulkner short stories) has imbibed such values as truthfulness, decency, and respect for others. When Ab and Sarty visit the de Spain house with its big white columns and Ab deliberately smears his dung-covered boots on Mrs. de Spain's French rug, then nearly destroys the rug with his vicious scrubbing, Sarty still tries to defend his father. Only when he sets fire to the barn does Sarty break free to warn Major de Spain. In the ambiguous ending (see AMBIGUITY), we hear the gunshots, but we are not sure whether Ab has been killed. He is dead to Sarty, however, who still demonstrates his desire to believe in his father's bravery but sets out alone in the opposite direction. His overriding values are those of his mother rather than those of his father. Sarty's journey away from his father's moral deficiencies resembles those of NICK ADAMS in ERNEST HEMINGWAY's "INDIAN CAMP" or James in ERNEST GAINES's "The SKY IS GRAY."

BIBLIOGRAPHY

Blotner, Joseph. *Faulkner: A Biography.* New York: Random House, 1984.

Carothers, James. *Faulkner's Short Stories.* Ann Arbor: University of Michigan Research Press, 1985.

Faulkner, William. "Barn Burning." In *American Short Stories.* 6th ed. Edited by Eugene Current-García and Bert Hitchcock. New York: Longman, 1997, 377–390.

Ferguson, James. *Faulkner's Short Fiction.* Knoxville: University of Tennessee Press, 1991.

BARNES, DJUNA (1892–1982)

Djuna Barnes was born in rural New York and was educated by her grandmother, the journalist and author Zadel Barnes. Barnes spent the 1910s in Greenwich Village, where she established a reputation as a brilliant and daring journalist. She also published short fiction, poetry, and plays in a number of periodicals and illustrated many of her writings. In the early 1920s, Barnes went to Paris, where she became a dashing figure in the expatriate literary scene of the Left Bank. Her novel *Nightwood* (1936) is notable for its experimental style and earned Barnes her greatest literary fame. T. S. Eliot edited *Nightwood* and wrote an introduction for it. Barnes returned to America in the late 1930s and lived in New York until her death in 1982.

Most of Barnes's short stories were written before she went to Europe in the 1920s and depict the immigrant population of New York. An atmosphere of NATURALISM pervades many of the stories in that the narrator is detached from, yet observant of, the forces at work in shaping CHARACTERS' destinies and records the often-sordid details of their lives. Barnes tempers naturalism with richly elaborate description, her strength in these stories. Her dense METAPHORS and witty EPIGRAMS combine incongruous elements; for example, a balding man's head sheds its hair as instinctively as a beautiful woman's clothes fall from her body. Barnes's THEMES include sin and death and the seemingly hopeless human desire for transcendence or redemption. "A Night among the Horses" (1918) and "Beyond the End" (1919, later retitled "Spillway"), both first published in the *Little Review,* are among Barnes's finest stories. "Aller et Retour" (1924), in which a strong and sophisticated woman futilely encourages her estranged daughter to acquire worldly knowledge, is also highly acclaimed.

BIBLIOGRAPHY

Barnes, Djuna. *Collected Stories of Djuna Barnes.* Edited by Philip Herring. Los Angeles: Sun & Moon Press, 1995.

Kannenstine, Louis F. *The Art of Djuna Barnes: Duality and Damnation.* New York: New York University Press, 1977.

Karen Fearing
University of North Carolina

"BARON OF PATRONIA, THE" GERALD VIZENOR (1988)

One of the stories in *The Trickster of Liberty: Tribal Heirs to a Wild Baronage,* "The Baron of Patronia" is an introduction to GERALD VIZENOR's comical patriarch, Luster Browne, and his family, who live on a reservation in northern Minnesota. Luster inherits a mysterious and uninhabited plot of land on the reservation, thought by the government to be worthless. The estate turns out to be lucrative and magical, a place where mallards remain in winter and mysterious "panic holes" provide outlets for man and beast to unload stress. Luster finds a wife in Novena Mae, and the two create a large family that prospers on the land. The nontraditional education the children receive from their parents is incorporated into their daily lives: Luster tells creation and TRICKSTER stories as he works, jumps, and walks; Novena Mae teaches the children to read by writing on leaves and the hard snow.

As in much NATIVE AMERICAN fiction, humor goes hand in hand with adversity. An undercurrent in this comic tale (see COMEDY) is a lesson in how to deal with the harsh realities of life. Luster gives his children names like Shadow Box, Mouse Proof, and China to enable them to "endure the ruthless brokers of a tragic civilization." Vizenor writes in dense trickster fashion as he pokes fun at everyone from somber government officials to highbrow audiences at colleges, who earnestly consume ludicrous "wild shoe" stories, to lowbrow audiences, who purchase instruction manuals entitled "How to Be Sad and Downcast and Still Live in Better Health than People Who Pretend to Be So Happy."

Calvin Hussman
St. Olaf College

BARRY, LYNDA (1956–)

Lynda Barry is a contemporary artist and writer best known for her creative and effective use of the comic strip, combining art and storytelling in her narrative. A product of divorce and an unstable childhood, Barry draws on her background in much of her work and chronicles the challenges, frustrations, and delights of childhood.

She is best known for her serial *Ernie Pook's Comeek* (found in weekly city newspapers), which chronicles the lives of Maybonne, Marlys, and Freddy, the not-quite-wanted young children of a lower socioeconomic background. Barry captures the essence of childhood in a form that is distinctly youthful—her playful drawings and characters' syntax are awkward and childlike. Not popular in school, the children are often troubled, yet earnest, loyal, and honest. The stories are reminiscent of J. D. SALINGER's *Catcher in the Rye* in that children on the fringes witness and articulate the "phoniness" of adults' actions. Barry takes this concept further by showing from a child's eye (see POINT OF VIEW) the frustration of their inability to rectify problems brought on by adults, including molestation, rape, running away from home, and racial and homophobic prejudice. Although often troubled, unlike Salinger's Holden Caulfield, Barry's characters are optimistic. Her stories and other work range from the gut-wrenching, to the teen angst world of dating, to the hilarious and whimsical. Also an essayist, Barry has written for national magazines and newspapers, focusing mainly on the special perspectives of children and the challenges that face them.

Recently, Linda Barry discussed her latest book, *What It Is,* a fusing of numerous media, including painting, collage, sketching, memoir, text, comics, and portraiture. To the *Washington Post Express* contributor Tim Follos, she addressed the issue of what she terms "the slightly creepy": "I think the 'slightly creepy' is always with us. It's certainly part of the things that make up the back of the mind. I have a lot of collages that are really scary—ones I wouldn't put in a book, not because I would be worried about people knowing how dark the back of my mind can be, but because I would be worried about scaring them."

BIBLIOGRAPHY

Barry, Lynda. *Big Ideas.* Seattle: Real Comet Press, 1983.
———. *Cartoon Collections Girls + Boys.* Seattle: Real Comet Press, 1981.
———. *Come Over Come Over.* New York: HarperPerennial, 1990.
———. *Cruddy.* New York: Simon & Schuster, 1999.
———. *Down the Street.* New York: Perennial Library, 1989.
———. *Everything in the World.* New York: Perennial Library, 1986.
———. *The Freddie Stories.* Seattle: Sasquatch Books, 1999.
———. *The Fun House.* New York: Perennial Library, 1987.
———. *Girls and Boys.* Seattle: Real Comet Press, 1981.
———. *The Good Times Are Killing Me.* Seattle: Real Comet Press, 1988.
———. *The Greatest of Marlys.* Seattle: Sasquatch Books, 2000.
———. *It's So Magic.* New York: Harperperennial, 1994.
———. *My Perfect Life.* New York: Harperperennial, 1992.
———. *Naked Ladies, Naked Ladies, Naked Ladies.* Seattle: Real Comet Press, 1984.
———. *One Hundred Demons.* Seattle: Sasquatch Books, 2002.
———. *Shake, Shake, Shake a Tail Feather.* New York: Harper & Row, 1989.
Follos, Tim. "Mixing Up Her Media: Lynda Barry." *Washington Post Express* (October 2, 2008). Available online. URL: http://www.expressnightout.com/content/2008/10/mixing_up_her_media_lynda_barry.php. Accessed May 6, 2009.

Grossman, Pamela. "Barefoot on the Shag: An Interview with Cartoonist, Novelist Lynda Barry" (May 21, 1999). Available online. URL: http://www.salon.com/books/int/1999/05/18/barry. Accessed May 6, 2009.

Kino, Carol. "How to Think Like a Surreal Cartoonist." *New York Times* (May 11, 2008). Available online. URL: http://www.nytimes.com/2008/05/11/arts/design/11kino.html?_r=1. Accessed May 6, 2009.

Calvin Hussman
St. Olaf College

BARTH, JOHN (JOHN SIMMONS BARTH)

(1930–   )   John Barth has been described as a master of contemporary fiction. Born in Cambridge, Maryland, he briefly studied jazz at the Juilliard School of Music before he entered Johns Hopkins University as a journalism major. He received his B.A. in creative writing from Johns Hopkins University in 1951 and his M.A. degree one year later. Barth has combined his long writing career with teaching at Pennsylvania State University, the State University of New York at Buffalo, and his alma mater, where he was Alumni Centennial Professor of English and Creative Writing from 1973 to 1990. In his retirement, Barth continues to publish fiction.

Although he is best known for his novels, Barth's stories "Night-Sea Journey," "LOST IN THE FUNHOUSE," "Title," and "Life-Story" from his collection of short fiction, *Lost in the Funhouse: Fiction for Print, Tape, Live Voice,* are widely anthologized. The book consists of 14 stories operating in a cycle that begins with the anonymity of origins and ends with the anonymity of a death and, withal, the narrator's exhaustion of his art. Three stories, "Ambrose His Mark," "Water Message," and "Lost in the Funhouse," reveal turning points in the life of Ambrose, a developing character throughout the collection. The three stories depict his naming as an infant; his first consciousness of fact, in both conflict and alliance with a romanticized truth; and a larger apprehension of life suffused with his first sexual consciousness. Barth's characters, or voices, are all natural storytellers compelled to make sense of their observations and experiences; they become METAPHORS for states of love, art, and civilization. As they quest, the author joins them so that

Barth's consciousness of his artistic technique often conforms with his consciousness of his characters and his subject matter.

In 1968 *Lost in the Funhouse* was nominated for the National Book Award, but *Chimera* won it in 1973. *Chimera* (1972) contains three NOVELLAS, each of which retells a MYTH. As is Barth, the HEROes of the three myths—Scheherazade, Perseus, and Bellerophon—are in the process of reorientation to discern their future. Although many reviewers see *Lost in the Funhouse* and *Chimera* as proof that Barth has been swallowed up by his own self-conscious obsession, others maintain that subsequent books demonstrate Barth's ability to invent new work by recycling both traditional literature and his own.

On with the Story, published in 1996, is a collection of short stories ostensibly told by one spouse to another while they are vacationing. Many of the stories involve middle-age academics and writers. His next collection, published in 2004, is entitled *The Book of Ten Nights and a Night: Eleven Stories.* Although the stories had been previously published, Barth links them with new commentary written soon after the events of September 11, 2001, and sets them against *A Thousand and One Nights.* The following year, in *Where Three Roads Meet: Novellas.* Barth writes three long stories linked partially by the three main characters, all nicknamed Fred (Alfred, Winifred, and Wilfred). Formerly college classmates in the 1950s, the three played jazz together and join now to aid Barth in his self-mockery of both his serious readers and his alter ego, the writer Manfred F. Dickson, Sr., who reveals that his muses are three erotic sisters who used prostitution to pay their college tuition. *The Development* (2008), Barth's most recent collection, contains loosely linked stories that begin with a voyeur who has slipped through the security guards at an Eastern Shore gated community. With his trademark perspective of humor and irony, Barth presents the insular preoccupations of the White Anglo-Saxon Protestant (WASP) seniors and retirees who deliberately live within rather than without the walls of their last community. In 2001 he published a novel entitled *Coming Soon!!!: A Narrative,* another postmodern examination of the fate of the writer, in this case, the old one versus the young electronically oriented one.

BIBLIOGRAPHY

Barth, John. *The Book of Ten Nights and a Night: Eleven Stories.* Boston: Houghton Mifflin, 2004.

———. *Coming Soon!!!: A Narrative.* Boston: Houghton Mifflin, 2001.

———. *The Development.* Boston: Houghton Mifflin, 2008.

———. *Where Three Roads Meet: Novellas.* Boston: Houghton Mifflin, 2005.

Bolonik, Kera. "BookForum Talks to John Barth." July 1, 2004. Available online. URL: http://www.highbeam.com/doc/1P3-651745121.html. Accessed December 4, 2008.

Edelman, Dave. Review of *Coming Soon!!!.* The John Barth Information Center, October 4, 2006. Available online. URL: http://www.davidlouiseedelman.com/barth. Accessed December 4, 2008.

Lindsay, Alan. *Death in the Funhouse: John Barth and Poststructural Aesthetics.* New York: Peter Lang, 1995.

Shulz, Max F. *The Muses of John Barth: Tradition and Metafiction from "Lost in the Funhouse" to "The Tidewater Tales."* Baltimore: Johns Hopkins University Press, 1980.

Harriet P. Gold
LaSalle College
Durham College

BARTHELME, DONALD (1931–1989)

Although born in Philadelphia and raised in Texas, Barthelme moved to New York in 1962 and essentially became a New York writer who focused on the complexities, confusions, violence, and apathy of urban life, but from an absurdist's viewpoint (see ABSURD). Often using disjointed prose and employing collagelike clichés, television ads, items from popular journalism, and media jargon, his short stories have been called "verbal objects," the written equivalent of pop art, reflecting his belief that contemporary reality can be described only in fragments. He was one of the most celebrated of the experimental writers to emerge in the 1960s, and his distinctive style is often imitated. One of the few postmodernist writers to focus almost exclusively on short fiction, Barthelme published most of his best work in the NEW YORKER prior to book publication.

Barthelme's characteristic themes and methods appear as early as his first story collection, *Come Back, Dr. Caligari* (1964), and are clearly in evidence in such stories as "BASIL FROM HER GARDEN." Barthelme's penchant for witty SATIRE and PARODY, as well as an imaginative, irreverent sense of the comedy of contemporary life, make him one of the most significant of the AVANT-GARDE writers of the late 20th century. In addition to humor, however, Barthelme demonstrated an increasing interest in MYTH, building on his readers' familiarity with heroic stories and characters and reinventing them in contemporary ways. *Sixty Stories* (1981) collects many of his best short fictions to that date and the posthumously published *Flying to America: 45 More Stories* (2007) contains a number of uncollected and in some cases unfinished or experimental tales to round out Barthelme's oeuvre.

BIBLIOGRAPHY

Barthelme, Donald. *Amateurs.* New York: Farrar, Straus & Giroux, 1976.

———. *City Life.* New York: Farrar, Straus & Giroux, 1970.

———. *Come Back, Dr. Caligari.* Boston: Little, Brown, 1964.

———. *The Dead Father.* New York: Farrar, Straus & Giroux, 1975.

———. *The Emerald.* Los Angeles: Sylvester & Orphanos, 1980.

———. *Flying to America: 45 More Stories.* Edited by Kim Herzinger. Emeryville, Calif.: Shoemaker & Hoard, 2007.

———. *Forty Stories.* New York: Putnam, 1987.

———. *Great Days.* New York: Farrar, Straus & Giroux, 1979.

———. *Guilty Pleasures.* New York: Farrar, Straus & Giroux, 1974.

———. *The King.* New York: Harper & Row, 1990.

———. *Overnight to Many Distant Cities.* New York: Putnam, 1983.

———. *Paradise.* New York: Putnam, 1986.

———. *Presents.* Dallas, Tex.: Pressworks, 1980.

———. *Sadness.* New York: Farrar, Straus & Giroux, 1972.

———. *Sam's Bar.* Garden City, N.Y.: Doubleday, 1987.

———. *Sixty Stories.* New York: Putnam, 1981.

———. *The Slightly Irregular Fire Engine; or The Thinking, Dithering Djinn.* New York: Farrar, Straus & Giroux, 1971.

———. *Snow White.* New York: Atheneum, 1967.

———. *The Teachings of Don B: The Satires, Parodies, Fables, Illustrated Stories, and Plays of Donald Barthelme.* Edited by Kim Herzinger. New York: Turtle Bay Books, 1992.

———. *Unspeakable Practices, Unnatural Acts.* New York: Farrar, Straus & Giroux, 1968.

"Barthelme Issue" of *Critique* vol. 16, no. 3, 1975.

Couturier, Maurice, and Regis Durand. *Donald Barthelme.* New York: Methuen, 1982.

Gordon, Lois. *Donald Barthelme.* Boston: Twayne, 1981.

Klinkowitz, Jerome. *Barthelme: An Exhibition.* Durham, N.C.: Duke University Press, 1991.

McCaffery, Larry. *The Metafictional Muse: The Works of Robert Coover, Barthelme, and William H. Gass.* Pittsburgh: University of Pittsburgh Press, 1982.

Molesworth, Charles. *Donald Barthelme's Fiction: The Ironist Saved from Drowning.* Columbia: University of Missouri Press, 1982.

Provan, Alexander. Review of Donald Barthelme's *Flying to America. StopSmiling* Magazine (March 1, 2008). Available online. URL: http://stopsmilingonline.com/story_detail.php?id=988. Accessed December 4, 2008.

Roe, Barbara L. *Donald Barthelme: A Study of the Short Fiction.* New York: Twayne, 1992.

Stengel, Wayne B. *The Shape of Art in the Stories of Barthelme.* Baton Rouge: Louisiana State University Press, 1985.

Trachtenberg, Stanley. *Understanding Barthelme.* Columbia: University of South Carolina Press, 1990.

BARTHES, ROLAND (1915–1980)

It is difficult to overestimate Roland Barthes's impact on current trends in contemporary literary theory (see POSTMODERNISM), including theory related to the criticism of short fiction. His influence has profoundly reshaped literary theory, not only in Europe, but also throughout the English-speaking world, particularly the United States. Born and raised in Bayonne, France, Barthes went on to become a professor, France's highest academic position, at the Collège de France, where he taught literature and semiotics until his accidental death in 1980. If for no other reason, Barthes's career is intriguing in that he recurrently revised and renewed his thinking, constantly broadening the range of his inquiries while embracing further developments in literary theory. His wide-ranging intellectual capacity and interests led him, throughout his career, to adopt and subsequently reject several schools of literary criticism. The deepening philosophical inquiries that motivate literary theory can be traced in the movement of Barthes's own essays, from STRUCTURALISM to popular culture studies and POSTSTRUCTURALISM with its investigations into new models of understanding the act of reading.

Barthes's highly idiosyncratic thinking is marked by two relatively consistent concerns. The first is the reader's participation in the authorship of the literary text. In one highly influential essay, Barthes proclaims the death of the author, by which he means that the reader has supplanted the author as the creator of meaning. A text has meaning, he suggests, only in relation to the mind of the reader, whom Barthes encourages to be as playful and creative as possible.

Barthes's second major concern is intellectual honesty. "I advance indicating my mask" was his mantra as a literary critic. In Barthes's view, all acts of interpretation are loaded with assumptions or, more precisely, with ideologies. This does not mean, however, that interpretation is a hopeless task; instead, it suggests that the interpreter must acknowledge and subsequently understand the way his or her own ideology affects the reading of a text. Failure to understand this amounts to intellectual bad faith. Therefore criticism, for Barthes, "is not an homage to the truth . . . [but] a construction of the intelligibility of our own times."

With his first book, *Writing Degree Zero* (1953), an extended response to Jean Paul Sartre's *What Is Literature?* (see EXISTENTIALISM), Barthes established himself as a high structuralist, employing the ideas of form and structure of grammar suggested by the linguistic pioneers Ferdinand de Sausseur and Roman Jakobson to interpret the poetry of the French symbolists. Barthes argued that the French symbolists believed in the act of writing as an end unto itself, not merely as a means of expressing information. With his *Mythologies* (1957), Barthes broadened his field of inquiry from French literature to the "grammar" or codes that inform European cultural ideas: in short, the "functions" at work not only in literature but in other social and cultural mores as diverse as advertising and the striptease. Barthes applied the methodologies of sociolinguistics and structural anthropology to various cultural manifestations in order to give an empirical and scientific rigor, if not objectivity, to the act of interpretation.

Language was Barthes's primary theme throughout his career, whether the literary language of Balzac's NOVELLA *Sarrasine,* the cinematic language of Sergei Eisenstein's *Rasputin,* or even the social language of the fashion industry. The premise that meaning is a process, not a static, qualitative essence, lies at the heart of Barthes's work. Arguably Barthes's most exciting work deals with ideas of textuality, or what constitutes a text, as distinct from a work of literature, and the eroticism of the act of reading and writing. In his later work, Barthes saw all reading as an act of rewriting a text, a way of actively engaging and producing meaning within the limits of a text's language. The text is a field of possibilities and ambiguities, Barthes argued, which a reader does not so much consume as participate in. A text, because of its many meanings, asks the reader to become an active collaborator in interpreting it. Because of this new model of literary writing and the shift of emphasis from literature as product to the newly foregrounded process of reading, Barthes declared in such essays as "From Work to Text" and "The Death of the Author" that the traditional practice of defining a work in terms of the author and the author's oeuvre was no longer relevant.

Over the years, Barthes's own writing shifted from the lively but densely academic style of his early career to an essay form that blended criticism with the type of style that characterized the literature he wrote about: fragmentary, nonlinear, and often self-reflexive, or self-absorbed. Clearly, Barthes, as he matured, illustrated by example his belief that criticism was a way of actively participating with a text, criticism was itself a process, and he strove to blur the boundaries between art and criticism. Indeed, in Barthes's last work he focused on the eroticism inherent in the process of reading, that union of reader and text, and turned from philosophical insights on literature to himself, in *Roland Barthes on Roland Barthes* and *Camera Lucida.* Barthes's influence on contemporary theories remains formidable and can be seen in the work of Susan Sontag, Paul de Man, and countless others.

BIBLIOGRAPHY

Barthes, Roland. *A Barthes Reader.* New York: Hill & Wang, 1982.
———. *The Grain of the Voice: Interviews, 1962–1980.* New York: Hill & Wang, 1985.
———. *Roland Barthes.* Translated by Richard Howard. Berkeley: University of California Press, 1994.
———. "What Is Criticism?" In *Critical Essays.* Chicago: Northwestern University Press, 1978.
Brown, Andrew. *Roland Barthes: The Figures of Writing.* New York: Oxford University Press, 1992.
Knight, Diana. *Barthes and Utopia: Space, Travel, Writing.* New York: Oxford University Press, 1997.
Martinsson, Yvonne. *Eroticism, Ethics and Reading.* Stockholm: Almquist & Wiksell International, 1996.
Miller, D. A. *Bringing Out Roland Barthes.* Berkeley: University of California Press, 1992.

Richard Deming
Columbus State Community College

Shannon Zimmerman
University of Georgia

"BARTLEBY THE SCRIVENER" HERMAN MELVILLE **(1856)** Originally appearing in *Putnam's Monthly* in 1853 and later published as part of the 1856 collection entitled *The Piazza Tales,* "Bartleby" is arguably HERMAN MELVILLE's strongest work of short fiction and is often placed alongside his novel *Moby-Dick* as representative of the author's rich, complex genius. The story, with its subtitle "A Story of Wall Street," is narrated by an elderly Wall Street lawyer who specializes in bonds, mortgages, and title deeds, eschewing juries and trial law. He is, as he himself says, an "eminently safe man," one who has come to know all that he cares to about the world beyond his office and practice. The narrator employs two law copyists, Turkey and Nippers, who, because of their idiosyncratic temperaments, are both effective for only half of any given workday. To increase the office's productivity, the narrator hires Bartleby as a new copyist.

Bartleby begins his tenure strongly, voraciously throwing himself into the work, but soon his behavior begins to change. By the third day, when asked to help out on a tedious bit of proofreading, Bartleby declines, saying, "I would prefer not to." As the weeks progress, Bartleby meets more and more requests from his employer and coworkers with his stock response, until finally he does no work at all and yet seems to have taken up residence at the office. Throughout the story Bartleby's behavior and response change not at all, even as the circumstances around him do. Bartleby's staunch passivity forces the employer finally to move his office. He leaves Bartleby, who would not leave the premises even after being fired, behind. The new tenants have the scrivener tossed into debtor's prison, where he later dies.

Clearly, the story is less about Bartleby than it is about the narrator, who when initially introduced is entirely passive and complacent. Indeed, the narrator discovers very little about Bartleby other than a rumor that he had once worked in the dead letter office. In response to Bartleby's fate, however, the narrator becomes capable of feeling pity and compassion. In this way, the scrivener acts as a FOIL, allowing the reader to learn about the narrator and to see the way he develops throughout the story. As the narrator changes, so does the tone of the story he relates. At first Bartleby's behavior seems comical, as does the narrator's emotional inability to force Bartleby to comply with his requests. When Bartleby's response fails to change even as his situation becomes more dire, however, Bartleby himself seems locked into his fate, unable to be anything but passively resistant. The tone turns bleaker as Bartleby draws further into an impenetrable wall of unresponsiveness, and the narrator's outlook becomes more and more existential (see EXISTENTIALISM).

There is no shortage of varied readings of "Bartleby." Some argue that the scrivener represents Melville himself, whose fame diminished the more he moved away from writing the South Sea romances on which he had begun his literary career and toward the more challenging experiments in narrative modes found in *Pierre* and *Moby-Dick*. Other readings emphasize the story's intrinsic existentialism. Jorge Luis Borges even has argued that Melville's story prefigures the KAFKAESQUE use of psychological tensions in fiction. At the very least, "Bartleby" is Melville's most cohesive and ultimately most moving work,

perhaps because it focuses not on grand epic or social tragedy, as is found in BENITO CERENO or *BILLY BUDD, SAILOR,* but instead on the personal and tragic plight of an individual and the narrator's inability truly to understand him. As always, Melville's characteristic use of SYMBOLISM and resonant IMAGERY makes this text particularly open to various critical and theoretical approaches.

BIBLIOGRAPHY

Bloom, Harold. *Modern Critical Interpretations: Billy Budd, "Benito Cereno," "Bartleby the Scrivener," and Other Tales.* New York: Chelsea House, 1987.

Inge, M. Thomas. *Bartleby the Inscrutable: A Collection of Commentary on Herman Melville's Tale, "Bartleby the Scrivener."* Hamden, Conn.: Archon Books, 1979.

McCall, Dan. *The Silence of Bartleby.* Ithaca, N.Y.: Cornell University Press, 1989.

Melville, Herman. *Great Short Works of Herman Melville.* New York: Perennial Library, 1969.

Richard Deming
Columbus State Community College

BASIL AND JOSEPHINE STORIES, THE

F. SCOTT FITZGERALD (1973)   Between 1928 and 1931, when F. SCOTT FITZGERALD had trouble making progress on his novel *Tender Is the Night,* he returned to memories of his adolescence and young manhood to compose two story sequences for the *SATURDAY EVENING POST.* For several years during and after their composition, Fitzgerald considered publishing the stories as a book. His hesitation was the result of the dilemma that more than any other defined his career: If he published successful stories in popular magazines he could support himself financially, but he risked being considered a popular entertainer instead of a serious artist. He decided not to rework the stories for a book in part because he wanted his novel to make its debut unencumbered by associations with his lighter fiction.

In his fourth story collection, *Taps at Reveille* (1935), he published five of the Basil stories and three stories from the Josephine (see JOSEPHINE PERRY) sequence. In 1973 Jackson R. Bryer and John Kuehl collected all 14 of the stories in one volume as *The Basil and Josephine Stories.*

BASIL DUKE LEE is modeled closely on Fitzgerald himself, and Josephine Perry is a fictionalized version of Genevra King, the wealthy debutante from Chicago with whom Fitzgerald had a brief, disappointing romance during his Princeton years. Both story sequences are romantic (see ROMANTICISM) in TONE and style, as Fitzgerald contrasts the urgent, narcissistic desires of young people with the harsh limitations of reality they encounter. Fitzgerald describes the humiliations and disillusionments that accompany the maturation process with the same emotional precision he used in his early fiction, such as "BERNICE BOBS HER HAIR" and the novel *This Side of Paradise.*

The Basil stories begin in 1909 with Basil at age 11 and follow him as he attends boarding school in the East, ending with his departure for Yale. Although the stories reflect comfortable middle-class life in the conservative Midwest, Basil's yearnings and his foolish mistakes in managing them make him at moments a sympathetic and universally recognizable adolescent on the brink of manhood. Only eight of the nine stories were published in the *Post.* "That Kind of Party," which describes kissing games played by 10- and 11-year-old children, was apparently considered inappropriate for publication by the editors, according to Arthur Mizener. In other stories, Basil learns the difference between romantic illusions and reality in his relationships with both women and men and in his literary accomplishments. Basil is a character divided between romantic exuberance and a moral honesty that allows him, by slow degrees, to develop a saving pragmatism. As a study of the effect of American middle-class mores on a romantic, artistic boy as he grows up, the Basil stories identify the rebellions and concessions necessary for the preservation of an individuality that avoids egotism.

Josephine, of the five Josephine Perry stories, is the spoiled and snobbish daughter of a wealthy, established family. The stories, which begin when she is 16 and end just before she turns 18, reveal the sexual politics of the time: A woman considered "speedy" was popular; once she became "fast," however, her reputation was ruined. Josephine narrowly avoids acquiring the latter label in "A Woman with a Past," and in other stories she deftly makes her way through a succession of men, whom she regards as objects for acquisition and display. Once she has kissed them, all the excitement of the chase subsides immediately as she looks to the next conquest.

In the last story in the sequence, "Emotional Bankruptcy," Josephine experiences her only moment of insight into her reckless pursuit of self-satisfaction as she realizes, in the company of a man she ought to love, that she is incapable of feeling anything anymore. This is the first story in which Fitzgerald developed the concept he would return to later in fiction and in his three autobiographical pieces for *ESQUIRE* collectively referred to as "The Crack-Up" essays. People have limited emotional capital, he believed; spending it recklessly all at once leaves one depleted for later experiences.

BIBLIOGRAPHY

Bryer, Jackson R., and John Kuehl, eds. "Introduction." In *The Basil and Josephine Stories.* New York: Collier Books, 1973.

Eble, Kenneth. *F. Scott Fitzgerald.* Rev. ed. Boston: Twayne, 1977.

Nagel, James. "Initiation and Intertextuality in The Basil and Josephine Stories." In *New Essays on F. Scott Fitzgerald's Neglected Stories,* edited by Jackson R. Bryer. Columbia: University of Missouri Press, 1996.

Piper, Henry Dan. *F. Scott Fitzgerald: A Critical Portrait.* New York: Holt, Rinehart & Winston, 1965.

Frances Kerr
Durham Technical Community College

BASIL DUKE LEE

Basil Duke Lee is the PROTAGONIST of F. SCOTT FITZGERALD's short story sequence about a boy growing up in the conservative Midwest at the turn of the 20th century. Over the course of the nine stories, Basil develops the multidimensional quality of a CHARACTER in a novel. Basil demonstrates "negative capability"—John Keats's terms for the ability to hold in one's mind two opposing ideas at the same time. Basil can experience his romantic exuberance while perceiving it objectively, a capacity that teaches him to separate illusion from reality. This learning process occurs in all nine stories as he experiences disillusionment in romances with girls, in social competition among the boys at his boarding school, and in his literary pursuits and love of fantasy. His ability to perceive the moral consequences of his urgent desires brings him to the realization that "life for everybody is a struggle"—a discovery necessary for maturation. (See BASIL AND JOSEPHINE STORIES, *The.*)

BIBLIOGRAPHY
Eble, Kenneth. *F. Scott Fitzgerald.* New York: Macmillian, 1977.

Frances Kerr
Durham Technical Community College

"BASIL FROM HER GARDEN" DONALD BARTHELME (1985)

"Basil from Her Garden," first published in the *NEW YORKER* on October 21, 1985 and reprinted in *The Best American Short Stories 1986* (see appendix I), is a postmodernist tale (see POSTMODERN-ISM) using METAFICTIONAL, minimalist techniques. (See MINIMALISM.) Barthelme's presentation of a disconnected dialogue between two PROTAGONISTS, identified only as Q and A, raises unresolved ethical issues. This dialogue simultaneously suggests a question-and-answer—a Q and A—interview and a therapy session. Oddly, however, A always seems to raise the ideas essential to the story's meaning, whereas Q seems to be the respondent: Although A literally appears in the role of patient or client, Q appears to question his own sense of depression in a world whose values no longer seem certain. Thus A provides the answers to Q's questions about his—and, the text implies, the modern reader's—dilemma. Another possibility is that A and Q are merely two sides of one personality, DOPPELGANGERS.

Together, A and Q consider such human foibles as adultery and guilt. A tells Q about his eclectic interests, including bowhunting, environmentalism, adultery, and the CIA. Their discussion, at times both comic (see COMEDY) and ABSURD, ranges across philosophical and moral fields, and when Q observes that the Bible's seventh commandment forbids adultery, A defends his extramarital activities, which, he explains, are in fact confined to one woman, Al Thea. Indeed, to make his point about various human connections, A refers to several women: Al Thea, with whom he is having an affair; his wife, Grete, who, he says, does

not deserve his philandering; his hair cutter, Ruth, a "good" person; and his unnamed neighbor, for whom he feels the sort of friendship that consists in neighborly good deeds, as he fixes her dead car batteries, and she, in return, offers him her fresh garden-grown basil. Although for Q many questions remain (he reveals his fantasy solution of working in pest control), the story's final note of qualified optimism and possibility recalls the ending of EDWARD ALBEE's play *Who's Afraid of Virginia Woolf?* The critic Barbara L. Roe suggests that "Basil from Her Garden" be read in conjunction with Barthelme's story "Kierkegaard Unfair to Schlegel" (Roe 62).

BIBLIOGRAPHY
Barthelme, Donald. "Basil from Her Garden." In *The Best American Short Stories 1986,* edited by Raymond Carver and Shannon Ravenel, 1–9. Boston: Houghton Mifflin, 1986.
Klinkowitz, Jerome, with Asa Pictatt and Robert Murray Davis. *Donald Barthelme: A Comprehensive Bibliography and Annotated Secondary Checklist.* Hamden, Conn.: Shoestring Press, 1977.
Roe, Barbara L. *Donald Barthelme: A Study of the Short Fiction.* New York: Twayne, 1992.

"BATH, THE" RAYMOND CARVER (1981)

Published in RAYMOND CARVER's short story collection *What We Talk about When We Talk about Love,* "The Bath" marks the height of Carver's minimalist style, with its precise language and sparse detail. "The Bath" centers on Ann and Howard Weiss, simply referred to in the narration as "the mother" and "the father," as they struggle to cope with the possible loss of their son, Scotty, who is referred to as "the boy."

At the beginning of the story, the mother orders a cake for her son's eighth birthday party. The baker notes her contact information, and his interaction with her is businesslike: "No pleasantries, just this small exchange, the barest information, nothing that was not necessary" (48). Such a description further emphasizes Carver's minimalism and later exchanges with the baker. On his birthday the boy is tragically hit by a car and taken to the hospital, where his parents sit at his bedside, waiting for him to wake. After hours of waiting, the father returns home to take a bath to alleviate his fear and is greeted by the telephone ringing. A voice tersely informs him about a cake that needs to be picked up and paid for, but the father, unaware of his wife's order, fails to comprehend and hangs up the phone. His bath yields little relief, his soak interrupted by the ringing telephone, which he rises out of the tub to answer. Again, the baker confuses the father with a cryptic "It's ready" (50).

At the hospital, the father and mother attempt to reassure each other that their son will soon wake from sleep. The doctor's examination sheds little light on the child's condition, and the doctor hesitates to confirm the parents' fear that the boy is in a coma. With no words for their son's state, the mother and father continue their wait and seek refuge in prayer, but additional doctor visits and hours of waiting do little to ease their anxiety.

Her fear palpable, the mother decides to return home for a bath. As she searches for an elevator at the hospital, she encounters another family, who mistake her as a nurse to give them news of their son, Nelson. She briefly tells them of her own son hit by a car. The other father in his grief shakes his head and says his son's name. At home, the mother feeds the dog and prepares herself tea before her bath. The phone disturbs her attempt to relax, and she answers, expecting news from the hospital. She fails to recognize the voice of the baker and asks whether the call is about Scotty: "'Scotty,' the voice said. 'It is about Scotty,' the voice said. 'It has to do with Scotty, yes'" (56). The story abruptly ends with no knowledge of Scotty's fate or any resolution of the conflict with the baker. As Adam Meyer notes, "Here Carver's minimalistic method achieves maximum impact on the reader," and the story "exemplifies the Carveresque mode of *What We Talk about When We Talk about Love,* the minimalist style that made him famous" (Campbell 100). The abrupt ending heightens the tension and leaves the reader with an uncomfortable uncertainty about what may happen. The baker's words are almost chilling in a story where words give little comfort and do not fully convey grief and fear.

Carver returns to Ann and Howard Weiss's plight in "A Small, Good Thing," essentially a revision of "The Bath." "The Bath" and "A Small, Good Thing" make for an interesting comparison and illustrate Carver's move away from minimalism. From the latter and more descriptive story, the reader learns of Scotty's fate and the conflict with the baker is resolved, yet the minimalism of the original story and its ambiguous ending continue to resonate.

BIBLIOGRAPHY
Campbell, Ewing. *Raymond Carver: A Study of the Short Fiction.* Twayne's Studies in Short Fiction. New York: Twayne, 1992.
Carver, Raymond. "The Bath." In *What We Talk about When We Talk about Love.* New York: Vintage, 1989, 47–56.
Gearhart, Michael WM. "Breaking the Ties That Bind: Inarticulation in the Fiction of Raymond Carver." *Studies in Short Fiction* 26, no. 4 (1989): 439–446.
Meyer, Adam. "Now You See Him, Now You Don't, Now You Do Again: The Evolution of Raymond Carver's Minimalism." *Critique* 30 (1989): 239–251.
———. *Raymond Carver.* Twayne's United States Authors Series. New York: Twayne, 1995.

Dana Knott
Columbus State Community College

BATHOS Originating with the Greek critic Longinus, the word, meaning "depth," was parodied by Alexander Pope in 1727 in his essay "On Bathos, or Of the Art of Sinking in Poesy." Ever since, the word has been used for an unintentional descent in literature when, straining to be pathetic or passionate or elevated, the writer overshoots the mark and drops into the trivial or the ridiculous. ANTICLIMAX is sometimes used as an equivalent for bathos.

"BATTLE ROYAL" RALPH ELLISON **(1948)** RALPH ELLISON's "Battle Royal," also published as the first chapter of *Invisible Man* (1952), previews the major THEMES that arise in much 20th-century African-American fiction. (See AFRICAN-AMERICAN SHORT FICTION.) The story uses first-person narration, but Ellison chooses to leave the narrator nameless, suggesting his invisibility to white culture and his ongoing attempt to construct an identity.

The first-person narrator (see POINT OF VIEW) is the adult man recalling a scene from his youth from a perspective of 20 years. Referring twice in one paragraph to a time "eighty-five years ago," he simultaneously alludes to the Emancipation Proclamation (see CIVIL WAR) and belatedly honors his grandparents, particularly his grandfather, who came of age during both the war and RECONSTRUCTION. On his deathbed, his grandfather revealed that he had been a "traitor" and a "spy": He might have seemed an "Uncle Tom," but in fact he had fought a covert "war" and hoped that his son, the narrator's father, would continue to fight (1,519). Establishing the battle IMAGERY, then, the narrator describes the horrors of his "battle royal" before he proudly delivers his high school graduation speech.

As a youth, the narrator had believed that his grandfather was crazy, that his words were a "curse" (1,520), and that a young black man could achieve success only by pleasing the town's white leaders. When these "big shots" invite him to deliver his graduation speech at the best hotel in town, he naively agrees, but when he arrives, he is plunged into a version of hell. As does Nathaniel Hawthorne's YOUNG GOODMAN BROWN, he sees a gathering of the town's most prominent white men—educators, merchants, pastors, judges—all of whom participate in the liquor-ridden, smoke-filled rite called the "battle royal." Through his description, Ellison succinctly demonstrates the way the white men use women and African Americans to remind them of their "place." A young blonde woman with a tattoo of the American flag on her belly dances nude for the pleasure of the men. The tattoo makes her the PERSONIFICATION of the AMERICAN DREAM—a dream that the narrator and nine other black youths are forced to look at, but must never touch. In another sense, of course, the woman represents the symbol of sacred white womanhood whom blacks gaze upon only at their peril, evoking the white male fears of black sexuality that resulted in the lynching of so many black men. Near the end of the performance, as the men obscenely prod and probe this "circus kewpie doll," tossing her into the air like a toy, the narrator notes the "terror and disgust" in her eyes, which mirror his own, thereby implicitly equating the subjugation of American women with that of African Americans.

In the actual battle, the white men force these "boys" to fight among themselves. Yelling racial slurs, the white men enjoy pitting black against black, casually betting on them as they would bet on racehorses or other animals. The narrator's realization that he must fight Tatlock, the biggest "boy" of all, is the first subtle hint that he has inherited his grandfather's subversive tendencies: He suggests that they only pretend to fight. Tatlock, however, fails to understand that by fighting the narrator he is only pleasing the white men, and he naively takes pride in his victory, transferring to the narrator the hostility that should be directed at the white men. In the final stage of the battle, the youths are forced to fight each other for coins scattered on an electrified rug so that they suffer shocks each time they try to acquire the money. At the conclusion of this episode, the white men toss one of the black boys in the air just as they had the white woman, demonstrating their power. As Bernard Bell has explained, the bizarre scenes dramatize "a pattern of behavior designed by whites to emasculate and humiliate black men: reinforcing the taboo against sexual contact between black men and white women, duping young blacks into fighting each other rather than their primary oppressors, and encouraging them to sacrifice moral values for material gain" (197).

When the bloodied narrator delivers his Booker T. Washington–inspired speech, it is anticlimactic; no one cares what he has to say, although when he inadvertently uses the phrase *social equality*, the white men force him to retract the words. Although at this point he hastily acquiesces, his use of the words foreshadows more subversive activities to come. First, however, as he says at the end, he must acquire a college education, and thus he accepts the scholarship to the black state college. Nonetheless, his dream of his resisting grandfather stays with him and will ultimately help him not only to use the system but also to understand that his grandfather was correct: Subservience will not take African Americans out of slavery, 20th-century style.

BIBLIOGRAPHY
Bell, Bernard. *The Afro-American Novel and Its Tradition.*
    Amherst: University of Massachusetts Press, 1989.

Ellison, Ralph. "Battle Royal." In *The American Tradition of Literature,* edited by George Perkins and Barbara Perkins, 1,519–1,528. Boston: McGraw Hill, 1999.

Amy Strong
University of North Carolina at Chapel Hill

BAYARD SARTORIS A young boy in the first of the interconnected stories in WILLIAM FAULKNER'S *The UNVANQUISHED,* "Ambuscade," Bayard grows from boyhood to young manhood. He is the son of Colonel John Sartoris, who is away fighting in the CIVIL WAR during many of the stories. Bayard enacts a coming-of-age ritual when he seeks to avenge Miss Rosa Millard's death and then another when he refuses to avenge his father's death, firmly ignoring the code of vengeance demanded of him by the traditions of the Old South. He also becomes one of Faulkner's sensitive men who feel drawn to but refuse the attentions of attractive women. (See also GAVIN STEVENS.) In "An Odor of Verbena," Bayard rejects the attentions of DRUSILLA HAWKE, a young widow now married to his father. After the Civil War Bayard becomes president of the bank in Jefferson and survives until, in Faulkner's novel *Flags in the Dust,* his grandson and namesake, a WORLD WAR I veteran, drives him in a fast car and old Bayard suffers a heart attack.

"BEAR, THE" WILLIAM FAULKNER (1942) The most frequently anthologized story from the interconnected stories in *Go DOWN, MOSES,* "The Bear" details the profoundly moving relations among the young white boy Ike McCaslin, the Chickasaw Indian Sam Fathers, and several other black and white characters, including Ash, the black cook, and Major de Spain, the prominent white landowner, who also appears in Faulkner's story "BARN BURNING." The story concerns Ike's coming-of-age hunt for the bear, which he finally kills. Considered one of Faulkner's greatest stories, "The Bear" contains passages of lyrically haunting intensity as civilization and nature metaphorically clash in the encounters between humans and woods, and between humans and animals. As critics belatedly realized, however, "The Bear" can be better understood not as an isolated story, but as one significant story interrelated with six others. Only in this context does the reader understand why Ike, although he successfully kills Old Ben, the bear, can fulfill the role of neither savior nor hero: As the other stories amply attest, Ike cannot rid himself of his heritage of racism.

Trained for years by Sam Fathers, Ike is at his peak when he enters the woods, his skills second only to those of the Chickasaw. By the time we see him in "The Bear," he confidently decides that he needs none of the accoutrements of civilization and, as he enters the woods, discards his gun, his watch, his compass. While tracking Old Ben, Ike displays courage and, through some of the finest language in the 20th-century short story, experiences a spiritual union with nature. Before Ben dies, the unarmed Ike has moved close enough to see a tick on Ben's leg and to breathe in the odor of his hide. This day will live forever in Ike's memory, but by the end of the story its potential has already diminished: Sam Fathers dies shortly after Old Ben, and loggers move ever more swiftly to destroy the woods.

Although Ike understands the Indians and nature and has respect for both, his weaknesses have to do with women and with blacks, as revealed in his final appearance, in the story "Delta Autumn." In this story the 80-year-old Ike—who as a boy in "The Bear" showed such promise for respecting all races as well as the environment—displays racism and sexism when he rejects the loving overtures of a nameless black woman who reveals her kinship to him. Significantly, old Ike's action occurs during WORLD WAR II: The world is in chaos, and he cannot relinquish the ways of the Old South. The ideal union with nature and his fellow creatures that Ike so passionately sought in "The Bear" is, to use one of the story's most recurring words, doomed.

"BEAST IN THE JUNGLE, THE" HENRY JAMES (1903) HENRY JAMES's "The Beast in the Jungle" (1903) is unusual in its concentration of focus. Although the story is relatively long (about 50 pages), it contains only two characters. The narrative is not continuous, but rather a series of dramatic scenes, always limited to meetings of the two characters. Their names, *May* Bartram and John *March*er, suggest the sustained motif of the seasons, rendered as the passage from late youth to old age and death. Marcher believes that he is "being kept for something rare and strange, possibly prodigious and terrible," a fate that is figured by the "beast" of the title. May waits in vain for some response from Marcher. After May's death, Marcher concludes, "The escape would have been to love her; then, then he would have lived." Instead, "no passion had ever touched him."

Marcher is part of a tradition of passive aesthetes in American literature, from Coverdale in NATHANIEL HAWTHORNE's *The Blithedale Romance* to Prufrock in T. S. Eliot's "The Love Song of J. Alfred Prufrock." Many traditional readings of this late tale link its THEMES to the famous passage in James's novel *The Ambassadors,* where Strether exclaims, "Live! live all you can! It's a mistake not to!" In these interpretations Marcher, who is apparently indifferent to May's desire, does not live, or at least does not live well, or self-interrogatively. Leon Edel, a biographer of James, claims that the tale has a biographical basis in James's indifference to the writer CONSTANCE FENIMORE WOOLSON. According to Edel, James had "taken her friendship, and never allowed himself to know her feelings" ("Introduction" 10).

In a famous essay, Eve Kosofsky Sedgwick argues against such a romanticized reading as Edel's—which she terms homophobic because it imagines heterosexuality as the exclusive solution to the absence of love. Sedgwick situates Marcher in the tradition of the Victorian bachelor, the unmarried man of leisure and, frequently, the aesthete. She sees in these figures an example of what would soon be created as the homosexual, for the moment just on the cusp of coming into being. Sedgwick argues that we should look not for homosexual acts or consciousness in the text but rather for the unsaid, for the gaps of language that avoid precision. In this sense, to readers interested in the history of sexuality, homosexuality is present through its panicked absence in "The Beast in the Jungle."

BIBLIOGRAPHY

Edel, Leon, ed. *The Complete Tales of Henry James.* Vol. 11, *1900–1903.* Philadelphia: Lippincott, 1964.

Sedgwick, Eve Kosofsky. "The Beast in the Closet: James and the Writing of Homosexual Panic." In *Sex, Politics, and Science in the Nineteenth-Century Novel,* edited by Ruth Bernard Yeazell, 148–186. Baltimore: Johns Hopkins University Press, 1986.

Robert K. Martin
Université de Montréal

BEAT GENERATION   The writers celebrated as the creators of a "Beat generation" never thought of themselves as establishing or perpetuating an organized movement. As Gary Snyder observed after receiving the PULITZER PRIZE in poetry in 1974, the term properly applies only to a small circle of friends, particularly Neal Cassady, Allen Ginsberg, John Clellon Holmes, and JACK KEROUAC, who gathered around William Burroughs in New York City in 1948. Burroughs remained a close friend of the group, but his own experimental work is greatly different in style and purpose from that of the beats. Holmes introduced the term *beat generation* in his little-noticed first novel *Go* (1952). Earlier that year Kerouac had already published his first novel, *The Town and the City,* a conventional romantic BILDUNGSROMAN influenced by Thomas Wolfe that gave no hint of Kerouac's later work. He completed the third version of ON THE ROAD in 1951, but publishers quickly rejected it.

The "movement" became news after a public poetry reading at the Six Gallery in San Francisco on October 13, 1955, by Philip Whalen, Philip LaMantia, Gary Snyder, Michael McClure, and Allen Ginsberg, who crowned the evening by reading the just completed first part of his poem *Howl.* He scored a howling success, and Lawrence Ferlinghetti, proprietor of the local City Lights bookshop, immediately offered to publish the finished poem in his new Pocket Poets series of paperbacks. The first edition, printed in London, where production costs were lower then, attracted enough attention to sell out locally. When a second printing arrived on March 25, 1957, it was held up by U.S. Customs as obscene. Although Customs released the pamphlet in May, city police stepped in to institute condemnation proceedings against Ferlinghetti as the publisher. A nationally publicized trial ensued, at which distinguished poets and academics spoke in defense of Ferlinghetti and Ginsberg. The testimony of the University of California professor Mark Schorer particularly influenced Municipal Court Judge Clayton Horn's decision on October 3, clearing the poem of not possessing, as the prosecution charged, "the slightest redeeming social importance."

This verdict was followed up by two articles by the poet Kenneth Rexroth, leader of the long-established San Francisco renaissance group: "San Francisco Letter" in the second issue of New York City's *Evergreen Review*, which also contained the text of the poem, and "Disengagement: The Art of the Beat Generation," in Arabel Porter's influential *New World Writing*, a semiannual publication in the New American Library. *On the Road* was then published at last in October 1957 and received a tremendous and sales-promoting controversial reception.

Ginsberg's and Kerouac's writings attracted hordes of dissatisfied young people from all over the country to San Francisco's North Beach, where poetry readings flourished in coffeehouses and Rexroth and Ferlinghetti hosted poetry-jazz sessions that they believed gave the movement its greatest importance in a merging of the arts at popular nightclubs.

The city, and especially the police, who still smarted from losing the "Howl" case, however, grew increasingly aggravated by the presence on the streets of a motley crew of camp followers who the popular columnist Herb Caen labeled "beatniks," especially since drugs had become a significant part of communal rituals. The poet and University of California professor Thomas Parkinson, who championed the Beat movement, prepared in 1961 *A Casebook on the Beat*, a popular book providing materials for college research papers on the subject. In it he expressed great annoyance at the poets' being lumped together with sensation seekers and drew a useful distinction between the Beats as serious, dedicated, hardworking artists and the beatniks as untalented loafers for whom life was one long party. Finally complaints from tourists about panhandlers and local pressure groups drove the police to begin a series of raids that drove many of the serious Beats, led by Pierre DeLattre, poet and novelist proprietor of the popular Bread and Wine Mission, to Mexico, especially San Miguel Allende, where Neal

Cassady later died. The Beat scene shifted back to New York City, dominated by Leroi Jones (who later changed his name to *Amiri Baraka*) and Diane di Prima, who later abandoned the movement for greater involvement in 1960s activism that the original Beats eschewed.

During the high years on North Beach, the movement that denied being a movement engendered only one publication suggesting a central focus, *Beatitude* (pronounced *beat*-i-tude), a mimeographed poetry journal that produced 15 issues at irregular intervals in 1959 and early 1960, supported by Lawrence Ferlinghetti. He selected from them a *Beatitude Anthology*, which contained only 25 poems and few prose pieces (mainly letters, no short stories), warning that even all of these were not "on the beat frequency."

There certainly was no Beat "movement" if one thinks of "movements" in terms of groups organized around programs for collective action. The originators' concept of the high-minded but elusive aim of their writing was best summarized in 1982 by Allen Ginsberg at a small convocation that celebrated the 25th anniversary of the publication of *On the Road*. Ginsberg took exception to some remarks by the dynamic activist Abbie Hoffman: "I think there was one slight shade of error in describing the Beat movement as primarily a protest movement. . . . That was the thing that Kerouac was always complaining about; he felt that the literary aspect or the spiritual aspect or the emotional aspect was not so much protest at all but a declaration of unconditioned mind beyond protest, beyond resentment, beyond loser, beyond *winner—way* beyond winner." This was the "disengagement" from conventionally received ideas that Kenneth Rexroth had first noted characterized the Beat generation.

If this movement did constitute any kind of youthful rebellion, it was the last one so far to have its origins in a literary tradition. Ginsberg and Kerouac were well read in both CLASSIC and AVANT-GARDE literature. Their works were contemplative, not action-provoking. Subsequently passingly fashionable groups such as the hippies and Yippies derived their impetus from rock music and activist paintings. The Beats were the last defenders of the word, seeking uncompromised language to transcend the propaganda of the brainwashers.

Movement or not, the Beat remains a living force at Naropa Institute, founded in 1975 in Boulder, Colorado. There the 1982 convocation was one of many events sponsored by the Jack Kerouac School of Disembodied Poetics, long lovingly administered by Allen Ginsberg and Anne Waldman. It seeks to keep alive the tradition of mystical transcendence rather than activist triumph as the aim of human striving.

Warren French
University of Swansea

BEAT LITERATURE If indeed there was a Beat movement that left a landmark legacy of American writings of the mid-20th century, short stories constituted no part of it. The Beats produced few short stories. John Clellon Holmes, one of the original Beat contingent in New York City in the early 1950s, published a few short stories in AVANT-GARDE magazines that have become virtually unobtainable, but these have never been collected, and Holmes considered himself not so much as a Beat writer as the historian of his circle.

The three major retrospective anthologies of Beat writing contain two very short stories by William S. Burroughs ("What Washington? What Orders?" [*The Beat Book,* 186–188] and "My Face" [*The Beat Book,* 188–194]) and one by Ed Sanders from *Tales of Beatnik Glory* ("A Book of Verse" [*The Portable Beat Reader,* 511–516]). The only writer known principally for his short stories included in Ann Charters's two-volume contribution to the *Dictionary of Literary Biography, The Beats,* subtitled *Literary Bohemians in Postwar America* (1983), is Michael Rumaker, and he is primarily associated with the Black Mountain school, a group whose often-downbeat writings testified to its affinities with the Beats but lacked the emphasis on mystic transcendence, "the unconditioned mind" that Allen Ginsberg stressed.

Charters's later *Portable Beat Reader* (1992) contains nothing that can be considered a short story; the prose pieces scattered throughout the text are excerpts from novels or autobiographies, personal letters, and confessions. Brenda Knight's *Women of the Beat Generation* (1996) similarly contains representative works from this long-neglected and important group, also primarily excerpts from autobiographies. The only short story is Hettie Jones's previously unpublished "Sisters, Right!" the touching account of strangers' perception of a white mother's relationship to her black daughter; Jones was married to the black Beat poet Leroi Jones before he changed his name to *Amiri Baraka.* Like Jack Kerouac's novel *On the Road,* the three-page story is thinly disguised autobiography, similar in style and content to Leroi Jones's poetry.

The lack of interest in the short story form amongst the Beats may be explained by the similarity of their novels and confessional autobiographies to their poetry, which is generally intensely personal and free in form, influenced principally by the enormously influential 19th- and 20th-century poets Walt Whitman and William Carlos Williams.

Short story writing in the United States in the 1950s was dominated by tight construction, tersely clipped wording, and an impersonal, ironic story line (see IRONY) fostered by Whit Burnett's STORY magazine and the NEW YORKER, widely emulated by avant-garde little magazines and academic reviews. Part of the "disengagement" that the Beats sought was from the editors and readers of these publications, who prized values that the Beats distrusted. Rather than the ironic impersonality of the stories of WILLIAM FAULKNER, Robert Penn Warren, and other influential members of the southern-based New Critical school (see NEW CRITICISM), the Beats sought inspiration in the loquacious, sometimes embarrassingly confessional outpourings of Whitman and Hart Crane. Principal Beat works were marked by torrents of words, pointing a finger of guilt at a money-worshipping society and seeking self-absolution. Since WORLD WAR I, beginning with SHERWOOD ANDERSON, ERNEST HEMINGWAY, and F. SCOTT FITZGERALD, in the United States the short story form had become the most disciplined form of American creative writing, especially under the tutelage of the developing university creative writing programs.

Allen Ginsberg in *Howl* saw Moloch, an ancient biblical god to whom children were sacrificed, not only in "endless oil and stone" but also as the evil force that frightened the poet out of his "natural ecstasy," which the Beats sought through their disengagement from the "academies" that expelled "the best minds" of the generation for "publishing obscene odes on the windows of the skull." At the time when curiosity about the Beats was at its peak, the possibilities of the short story form held no attraction for them.

Ironically, it is in two unprecedently long short stories published in the *New Yorker* that the Beat concepts of "disengagement" and "unconditioned mind" were most strikingly projected. Even though J. D. SALINGER dismissed the "Dharma Bums" condescendingly in the second of these two stories, in both "Zooey" and "Seymour: An Introduction," climactic episodes (see CLIMAX) in his Glass family saga, he shared through them the Beats' central concepts of "the unconditioned mind, beyond protest, beyond resentment, beyond loser, . . . *way* beyond winner." Fictional fantasies sometimes inspire unrecognized companions.

BIBLIOGRAPHY
Ann Charters, ed. *The Beats: Literary Bohemians in Postwar America.* Vol. 16, Parts 1 and 2 of *Dictionary of Literary Biography.* Detroit: Gale Research, 1983.
———, ed. *The Portable Beat Reader.* New York: Penguin Books, 1992.
Cherkovski, Neeli. *Ferlinghetti: A Biography.* Garden City, N.Y.: Doubleday, 1979.
French, Warren. *The San Francisco Poetry Renaissance, 1955–1960.* Boston: Twayne, 1991.
Holmes, John Clellon. *Passionate Opinions.* Fayetteville: University of Arkansas Press, 1988.
Jones, Leroi. *The Moderns: An Anthology of New Writing in America.* New York: Corinth Books, 1963.
Knight, Arthur, and Kit Knight. *The Unspeakable Visions of the Individual.* Vols. 5–14. California, Pa.: A. W. Knight, 1977–1984.
Knight, Brenda, ed. *Women of the Beat Generation: The Writers, Artists, and Muses at the Heart of Revolution.* Berkeley, Calif.: Conari Press, 1996.
Parkinson, Thomas, ed. *A Casebook on the Beat.* New York: Thomas Y. Crowell, 1961.
Tytell, John. *Naked Angels: The Lives and Literature of the Beat Generation.* New York: McGraw-Hill, 1976.
Waldman, Anne, ed. *The Beat Book: Poems and Fiction of the Beat Generation.* Boston: Shambhala, 1995.

Warren French
University of Swansea

BEATTIE, ANN (1947–) Establishing herself as a talented chronicler of the generation reared in the 1960s, Ann Beattie has earned praise for both novels and short fiction, particularly for her ability to reproduce the ambience of contemporary life. Born in Washington, D.C., she graduated from American University in 1969, earned an M.A. from the University of Connecticut the following year, began publishing stories in the *NEW YORKER,* and, in 1979, published her first collection of stories, *Distortions,* and her first novel, *Chilly Scenes of Winter.* Since then she has published eight additional short fiction collections and six novels. In 2001 she was awarded the PEN/Malamud Award for Excellence in Short Fiction.

The hallmarks of Beattie's fiction include emphatically realistic dialogue and the physical details as well as the specter of spiritual emptiness in contemporary life. Headlines, current soap operas, popular music, and even accurate depictions of weather contribute to the realism of her fiction, and she acknowledges a debt to ERNEST HEMINGWAY for the laconic exchanges between and among her characters. Often compared to RAYMOND CARVER for her minimalist style (see MINIMALISM), Beattie portrays middle-aged children of the 1960s who attempt to discover meaning behind the vacant facade of their lives.

Beattie's work is not completely bleak, however. She has a wry, satiric sense of humor, although often so subtle that the reader may miss it altogether. Beattie's fictional people do not suggest NIHILISM but appear to value the bonds of friendship, and, through their genuine attempts to communicate with others, they attempt to invest their lives with meaning.

Perfect Recall (2001) collects 11 long stories, typically set in Beattie's Key West or Beattie's Maine, portraying imperfect (and now older) characters, from war veterans and master chefs to artists and scholars. In her most recent collection, *Follies: New Stories* (2006), the Charlottesville and Washington, D.C., areas provide ample settings for the novella *Fléchette Follies,* with its Vietnam War veteran and CIA agent characters; and the eight stories that follow depict Beattie's middle-aged characters from New York to Los Angeles.

Ann Beattie, currently the Edgar Allan Poe Chair of the Department of English and Creative Writing at the

University of Virginia, says of the short story, "It's always evolving. Probably it's more various than the novel. The short story is often praised by critics for the wrong reason, though—for the subject matter. There are a lot of writers now writing short stories who don't much interest me, because their stories are no more than shoehorning overtly weird stuff into the form. You know all those reviews that praise the story and say: 'The cross-dressing leprechaun with TB turns out to be the second wife of the King of Sweden, and both are having a secret affair with Prince Charles.' Too many story writers feel they have to add MSG. The best stories have to be searched out: they're in *Narrative* and *Tin House* and *Mississippi Review*" (Athitakis).

See also "FIND AND REPLACE," "THE SNOW."

BIBLIOGRAPHY

Athitakis, Mark. "Mark Athitakis' American Fiction Notes." Available online. URL: http://americanfiction.word-press.com/2008/09/18/links-wallace-robinson-beattie. Accessed December 27, 2008.

Beattie, Ann. *Backlighting.* Worcester, Mass.: Metacom Press, 1981.

———. *The Burning House.* New York: Random House, 1982.

———. *Chilly Scenes of Winter.* Garden City, N.Y.: Double-day, 1976.

———. "Coping Stones." *The New Yorker,* September 12, 2005. Available online. URL: http://www.newyorker.com/archive/2005/09/12/050912fi_fiction. Accessed December 14, 2008.

———. *Distortions.* Garden City, N.Y.: Doubleday, 1976.

———. *The Doctor's House.* New York: Scribner, 2002.

———. *Falling in Place.* New York: Random House, 1980.

———. *Follies: New Stories.* New York: Scribner, 2005.

———. *Love Always.* New York: Random House, 1985.

———. *My Life, Starring Dara Falcon.* New York: Alfred A. Knopf, 1997.

———. *Park City: New and Selected Stories.* New York: Alfred A. Knopf, 1998.

———. *Perfect Recall.* New York: Scribner, 2001.

———. *Picturing Will.* New York: Vintage, 1991.

———. *Secrets and Surprises.* New York: Random House, 1978.

———. *What Was Mine: Stories.* New York: Random House, 1991.

———. *Where You'll Find Me and Other Stories.* New York: Linden Press/Simon & Schuster, 1986.

Gelfant, Blanche H. "Beattie's Magic Slate or The End of the Sixties." *New England Review* 1 (1979).

Gerlach, John. "Through 'The Octoscope': A View of Beattie." *Studies in Short Fiction* 17 (Fall 1980).

Montresor, Jaye Berman. *The Critical Response to Ann Beattie.* Westport, Conn.: Greenwood Press, 1993.

Murphy, Christina. *Ann Beattie.* Boston: Twayne, 1986.

Rainwater, Catherine, and William J. Scheick, eds. *Contemporary American Women Writers: Narrative Strategies.* Lexington: University Press of Kentucky, 1985.

Samway, Patrick H. "An Interview with Ann Beattie." *America,* 12 May 1990, pp. 469–471.

"BECAUSE MY FATHER ALWAYS SAID HE WAS THE ONLY INDIAN WHO SAW JIMI HENDRIX PLAY 'THE STAR-SPANGLED BANNER' AT WOODSTOCK" SHERMAN ALEXIE (1993)

"Because My Father Always Said He Was the Only Indian Who Saw Jimi Hendrix Play 'The Star-Spangled Banner' at Woodstock" was first published in SHERMAN ALEXIE's short story collection *The LONE RANGER AND TONTO FISTFIGHT IN HEAVEN* (1993). Each of the stories in this collection narrates life, love, struggle, and searching on and around the Spokane Indian Reservation in Washington State, where Alexie was raised. As do many of the other stories in the volume, "Because My Father Always Said He Was the Only Indian Who Saw Jimi Hendrix Play 'The Star-Spangled Banner' at Woodstock" further develops many of the themes and characters introduced in Alexie's earlier work.

The story is narrated by one such character, Victor, as he reflects on his father, his parents' tumultuous relationship, what it means to be "Indian," and, through that, his own place in the world. Victor's memories of his family's individual and collective histories, both real and idealized, highlight the complexities of Native American lives and relationships in the face of external pressures and inner demons. The tug of war between Native American ways of being and the corrosive vices, racism, and social strife gripping America in the 1960s reverberates in the characters' lives, like the cords from Hendrix's guitar as it played the song that tore at his father's soul.

Victor's life on the reservation highlights a number of issues that are critical to the lives of First Nations people—colonialization, assimilation, and the struggle to safeguard cultural identity. Each of these repeatedly comes into play in the lives of Victor and his parents, as they collide with each other, the world outside the reservation, memories of the past, and the uncertainties of the future. Taken as a whole, this constellation of issues problematizes the characters' survival—not only in a physical sense, but psychologically, existentially, and culturally, as well. In her winter 2000/2001 *Ploughshares* article, Lynn Cline comments that Alexie's work "carries the weight of five centuries of colonization, retelling the American Indian struggle to survive, painting a clear, compelling, and often painful portrait of modern Indian life" (197).

While these issues may be seen as specifically in play for Native Americans and other indigenous groups, they may also be considered in light of the more broadly applicable, intertwined themes of intimacy and identity, and the ways in which knowledge, memory, and ritual are used as tools to create a sense of self through reference to, and interconnection with, others. As his parents rapidly become more estranged, Victor is inwardly torn between the Native American traditions embraced by his mother and the world of rock music, motorcycles, and alcohol that has laid claim to his father. He struggles to make connections, and succeeds at times, by escaping with his father into his idealized memories of the past.

Victor's yearnings for intimacy are thinly veiled, if at all, in the ways in which he communicates his own memories. He draws comfort and communion from the familiar sounds of his parents' lovemaking: "It makes up for knowing exactly what they sound like when they're fighting" (30–31). His visceral knowledge of both intense emotional extremes allows him to share vicariously in the atmosphere of intimacy they create—for better or worse—an antidote to silence. Similarly, listening to Jimi Hendrix play "The Star-Spangled Banner" makes him want to learn the guitar—not to perform, but to "touch the strings, hold the guitar tight against my body . . . come closer to what my father knew" (24). Or simply, to be closer to his father.

Victor's relationship with his father is cemented by "ceremonies"—rituals that structure and ensure their communication. On nights when Victor's father had been out drinking, their common bond of ritual eased his transition back home to sleep it off. Victor would hear his father's truck pull in, run downstairs to put on his Jimi Hendrix tape, and, as his father wept with the music and passed out on the table above, Victor would fall asleep on the floor beneath, with his head near his father's feet. These shared moments of understanding and unspoken acknowledgment of need give intimacy to Victor's relationship with his father—an intimacy of both present and past: "The days after, my father would feel so guilty that he would tell me stories as a means of apology" (26). Embedded in his father's stories were knowledge, memory, identity—a personal heritage, both real and ideal—and, for Victor, the strength of an ever-deepening understanding of his father and himself. Throughout the narrative, Victor engages with these stories and memories, not only to establish a sense of intimacy with them, but also to understand his own place in the world better. He acknowledges their flawed nature—his father has already admitted; "I ain't interested in what's real. I'm interested in how things should be" (33)—but accepts that his personal heritage resides equally in their flaws.

"Because My Father Always Said He Was the Only Indian Who Saw Jimi Hendrix Play 'The Star-Spangled Banner' at Woodstock" was published at a time of significant conflict and upheaval for First Nation peoples in the United States. Native Americans in the 1990s were among the poorest population groups in the country, suffering from one of the lowest higher education rates and an incidence of alcoholism triple that of the overall population. As with Alexie's earlier works, *I Would Steal Horses* (1992) and the 1992 *New York Times Book Review* Notable Book of the Year *The Lone Ranger and Tonto Fistfight in Heaven* acknowledged and decried the realities weighing on Native Americans but also contextualized them in a cultural richness, dignity, and humor that drew him critical recognition and propelled many late 20th-century Native American authors into wider recognition.

BIBLIOGRAPHY

Alexie, Sherman. "Because My Father Always Said He Was the Only Indian Who Saw Jimi Hendrix Play 'The Star-Spangled Banner' at Woodstock." In *The Lone Ranger and Tonto Fistfight in Heaven*. New York: Atlantic Monthly Press, 1993, 24–36.

Baxter, Andrea-Bess. Review of "Old Shirts and New Skins, First Indian on the Moon," and *The Lone Ranger and Tonto Fistfight in Heaven*. *Western American Literature* 29, no. 3 (November 1994): 277.

Beauvais, Fred. "American Indians and Alcohol." *Alcohol Health and Research World*, 22, no. 4 (1998): 253.

Cline, Lynn. "About Sherman Alexie." *Ploughshares* 26, no. 4 (Winter 2000–2001): 197–202.

Cynthia J. Miller
Emerson College

"BEHIND A MASK" LOUISA MAY ALCOTT (1866)

"Behind a Mask: or, A Woman's Power," perhaps more than any other work, stimulated the reconsideration of LOUISA MAY ALCOTT's career that has taken place since 1975. The tale, originally published anonymously in *The Flag of Our Union* in four installments (October–November 1866), was the title piece of Madeleine Stern's first collection of recovered Alcott sensation tales in 1975. The dark, GOTHIC tone; the complex nature of its HEROINE; and the barely suppressed rage against the condition of 19th-century women made it an ideal piece with which critics could begin to explore other dimensions of Louisa May Alcott, "The Children's Friend."

"Behind a Mask" owes much to Alcott's reading of Charlotte Brontë's *Jane Eyre* and perhaps also of William Thackeray's *Vanity Fair,* while lodging a distinctly American protest against the British class system and celebrating America as the land of opportunity, or at least opportunism. It follows the exploits of Jean Muir, who, as the tale opens, meekly enters the Coventry mansion to report for employment as governess to 16-year-old Bella. Jean is received by the Coventrys with typical condescension. When Jean retires to her room for the evening, however, the reader learns she is not the 19-year-old waif she claims to be but a 30-year-old divorced former actress with false teeth, a wig, and a drinking problem. Jean's acting skills are tested and

found equal to the task as she works her way into and through the hearts of the younger Coventry son, Ned (Edward), and the elder son, Gerald, finally marrying their uncle, the elderly Lord Coventry. Tension builds as Jean seeks to secure her future before her former lovers can expose her. The power of this story rests largely on Alcott's characterization of her complex heroine. On one hand, Jean is undoubtedly deceitful and manipulative. She already has led one family to the brink of ruin, but they discover her sordid past just in time to prevent her marriage to their young son. The IMAGERY in the tale casts her at least as a calculating actress (when the family enacts a number of tableaux for entertainment, Jean is the only one of the women not worn out by the experience, suggesting how accustomed she is to acting), and often as a witch. Alcott also allows us to see another side of Jean, however: a young woman who longs for family and security, who tried the life of governess and companion before turning to acting in an attempt to support herself, and who is desperate as often as she is powerful. Further, Jean introduces life, laughter, and conversation to the dull Coventry household. She encourages Gerald to gain a commission for Ned in order to give him something to do (only partly to get him out of the way), and she inspires Gerald himself to take charge of his lands. Significantly, both the servants (who see through Jean more readily than the upper-class characters) and the Coventrys themselves grow to appreciate her lively presence.

While the unsavory nature of her heroine prevented Alcott from claiming the story as her own when it was first published, Jean's activeness and determination make her a heroine who could be if not a sister to *Little Women*'s Jo March or *Work*'s Christie Devon, at least a distant relative. In other ways, too, this tale contains familiar Alcott THEMES. A belief in hard work and a disdain for class consciousness (although Alcott herself was not totally immune to such attitudes) permeate much of Alcott's work. The story also highlights Alcott's longtime interest in the theater. She acted in community groups, wrote plays for such groups, and attended as many performances in Boston as she could. Her visions of actresses and acting in this tale and others ("V.V.: or, Plots and Counterplots" [1865],

"A Double Tragedy: An Actor's Story" [1865], *Work* [1873], and *Jo's Boys* [1886]) are nearly always sympathetic and frequently positive, unlike those in most fiction of the time. Real performances in Alcott's work, as do the tableaux in "Behind a Mask," frequently reveal rather than conceal. This tightly plotted tale with its memorable heroine is one of the best of the short stories Alcott dared not put her name to during her lifetime, and one that has helped readers and critics know her better a century later.

BIBLIOGRAPHY

Elliott, Mary. "Outperforming Femininity: Public Conduct and Private Enterprise in Louisa May Alcott's 'Behind a Mask.'" *American Transcendental Quarterly* 8 no. 4 (December 1994): 299–310.

Fetterley, Judith. "Impersonating 'Little Women': The Radicalism of Alcott's 'Behind a Mask.'" *Women's Studies* 10 no. 1 (1983).

Keyser, Elizabeth. *Whispers in the Dark: The Fiction of Louisa May Alcott.* Knoxville: University of Tennessee Press, 1993.

Smith, Gail K. "Who Was That Masked Woman? Gender and Form in Louisa May Alcott's Confidence Stories." In *American Women Short Story Writers: A Collection of Critical Essays,* edited by Julie Brown. New York: Garland, 1995.

Stern, Madeleine. "Introduction." In *Behind a Mask: The Unknown Thrillers of Louisa May Alcott.* New York: William Morrow, 1975.

Christine Doyle Francis
Central Connecticut State University

BELLOW, SAUL (1915–2005)

Born in Lachine, Quebec, Canada, Saul Bellow was the son of Russian Jewish immigrants. He learned Yiddish, Hebrew, English, and French as he grew up in Montreal. In 1924, Bellow moved with his family to Chicago; after earning a B.A. at Northwestern University in 1937 and serving in the merchant marine during World War II, he lived in Paris and taught English at Princeton and New York University before returning to live in Chicago. A Distinguished Professor at the University of Chicago for many years, Bellow was one of the most respected contemporary writers in the United States. His numerous awards culminated in the Nobel Prize in literature and the Pulitzer Prize in 1976. Although primarily known as a novelist, Bellow wrote two collections of short stories, *Mosby's Memoirs and Other Stories* (1968) and *Him with His Foot in His Mouth and Other Stories* (1989), as well as several NOVELLAS and plays. His *Collected Stories* appeared in 2001.

Along with other post–World War II American writers, Bellow focused on the problems of the modern urban man in search of his identity. His early rootless heroes are convinced of the need for freedom, yet in their searches they frequently find loneliness and despair. As many critics have pointed out, however, after his pessimistic characters of the 1940s, Bellow became disillusioned with modernist angst (see MODERNISM), and Bellow's subsequent characters in both novels and short fiction appear more affirmative, more cheerful, able to confront the vicissitudes of modern life by asserting the worth and dignity of the individual human spirit.

In "Mosby's Memoirs," for example, the title story of the collection, Dr. Willis Mosby is in Mexico, trying to write his memoirs. After brooding over his past, he realizes that he needs to inject some humor into the manuscript and so writes the story-within-a-story, about Lustgarden, a New Jersey shoe salesman, lately turned capitalist. His luck as an entrepreneur, however, is no better than it was as a Marxist. At first the Lustgarden story serves as COMIC RELIEF, but then it becomes serious as we realize that Lustgarden is a sort of psychic double, or DOPPELGANGER, for Mosby. Other stories in the collection—"A Father-to-Be," for instance, in which the father projects a nightmarish future for his relationship with his son-in-law, serves the same ALTER EGO function.

Him with His Foot in His Mouth, a collection of five stories, evokes the vitality and humor of characters who survive and endure partly by engaging in conversations with willing listeners. In one of the most striking, "What Kind of a Day Did You Have?" Bellow presents a moving portrait of the intellectual—although readers may find, as have feminist critics, that this, and other, male protagonists are better delineated than female ones. Victor Wulpy, ill and knowing that death is imminent, can still engage in the excitement of intellectual thought and thus, in essence, cheat death a little longer. By continuing to confront the major human issues and conflicts—artistic, philosophic, sexual, and mortal—about art and morality, sex and death, he lives on, and in this role Wulpy is emblematic of Bellow's main characters in these two collections of short stories. Unlike the work of some of his contemporaries, Bellow's short fiction, as well as his celebrated longer work, demonstrates that the antidote to modern ills is to assume responsibility for them and to celebrate one's humanity.

See also "LOOKING FOR MR. GREEN."

BIBLIOGRAPHY

Bellow, Saul. *The Adventures of Augie March.* New York: Viking, 1953.

———. *Dangling Man.* New York: New American Library, 1944.

———. *The Dean's December.* New York: Harper & Row, 1982.

———. *Henderson the Rain King.* New York: Viking, 1959.

———. *Herzog.* New York: Viking, 1964.

———. *Him with His Foot in His Mouth and Other Stories.* New York: Harper & Row, 1984.

———. *Humboldt's Gift.* New York: Viking, 1975.

———. *More Die of Heartbreak.* New York: William Morrow, 1987.

———. *Mosby's Memoirs and Other Stories.* New York: Viking, 1968.

———. *Mr. Sammler's Planet.* New York: Viking, 1970.

———. *Seize the Day, with Three Short Stones and a One-Act Play.* New York: Viking, 1956.

———. *A Theft.* New York: Penguin, 1989.

———. *The Victim.* New York: New American Library, 1947.

Bradbury, Malcolm. *Saul Bellow.* London: Methuen, 1982.

Braham, Jeanne. *A Sort of Columbus: The American Voyages of Saul Bellow's Fiction.* Athens: University of Georgia Press, 1984.

Clayton, John Jacob. *Saul Bellow: In Defense of Man.* Bloomington: Indiana University Press, 1968; revised edition, 1979.

Cohen, Sarah Blacher. *Saul Bellow's Enigmatic Laughter.* Urbana: University of Illinois Press, 1974.

Detweiler, Robert. *Saul Bellow: A Critical Essay.* Grand Rapids, Mich.: Eerdmans, 1967.

Dutton, Robert R. *Saul Bellow.* New York: Twayne 1971; revised edition, 1982.

Fuchs, Daniel. *Saul Bellow: Vision and Revision.* Durham, N.C.: Duke University Press, 1984.

Goldman, L. H. *Saul Bellow's Moral Vision: A Critical Study of the Jewish Experience.* New York: Irvington, 1983.

Kulshrestha, Chirantan. *Saul Bellow: The Problem of Affirmation.* Atlantic Highlands, N.J.: Humanities Press, 1979.

Malin, Irving, ed. *Saul Bellow and the Critics.* New York: New York University Press, 1967.

———. *Saul Bellow's Fiction.* Carbondale: Southern Illinois University Press, 1969.

Newman, Judie. *Saul Bellow and History.* New York: St. Martin's, 1984.

Porter, M. Gilbert. *Whence the Power? The Artistry and Humanity of Saul Bellow.* Columbia: University of Missouri Press, 1974.

Rodrigues, Eusebio L. *Quest for the Human: An Exploration of Saul Bellow's Fiction.* Lewisburg, Pa.: Bucknell University Press, 1981.

Rovit, Earl. *Saul Bellow.* Minneapolis: University of Minnesota Press, 1967.

———, ed. *Saul Bellow: A Collection of Critical Essays.* Englewood Cliffs, N.J.: Prentice Hall, 1975.

Scheer-Schazler, Brigitte. *Saul Bellow.* New York: Ungar, 1973.

Tanner, Tony. *Saul Bellow.* New York: Barnes & Noble, 1967.

Trachtenberg, Stanley, ed. *Critical Essays on Saul Bellow.* Boston: G. K. Hall, 1979.

BENÉT, STEPHEN VINCENT (1898–1943)

Born in Bethlehem, Pennsylvania, Benét lived in Paris from 1926 to 1929 and during the 1930s and early 1940s was an active lecturer and radio propagandist for democracy. Recipient of poetry prizes, he also was awarded the Pulitzer Prize in 1929 and 1944; the O. HENRY MEMORIAL AWARD in 1932, 1937, and 1940; and an American Academy Gold Medal the year of his death. One of America's most famous poets during his lifetime and a prolific writer of numerous books, plays, movie scripts, and opera libretti, Benét is best known for *John Brown's Body,* his epic narrative poem of the CIVIL WAR, and "The DEVIL AND DANIEL WEBSTER," a short story. His work is characterized by his interest in FANTASY and American themes, including stories of American history, stories celebrating the country's ethnic and cultural diversity, and contemporary narratives. The patriotic and romantic themes of Benét's work (see ROMANTICISM) became less fashionable after his death and led some critics to label him an old-fashioned, quaint, and chauvinistic writer who wrote "formula stories" designed to appeal to mainstream readers. However, his use of fantasy and of American historical and folk events and his idealized, lyrical style created a subgenre of writing known as "the Benét short story" that continues to attract readers in the early 21st century.

See also "BY THE WATERS OF BABYLON."

BIBLIOGRAPHY

Benét, Stephen Vincent. *The Barefoot Saint.* Garden City, N.Y.: Doubleday, Doran, 1929.

———. *The Devil and Daniel Webster.* New York: Readers' League of America, 1937.

———. *The Last Circle: Stories and Poems.* New York: Farrar, Straus, 1946.

———. *The Litter of Rose Leaves.* New York: Random House, 1930.

———. *O'Halloran's Luck and Other Short Stories.* New York: Penguin Books, 1944.

———. *Selected Poetry and Prose.* Edited by Basil Davenport. New York: Holt, Rinehart & Winston, 1960.

———. *Short Stories: A Selection.* New York: Council on Books in Wartime, 1942.

———. *Tales before Midnight.* New York: Farrar & Rinehart, 1939.

———. *Thirteen O'Clock: Stories of Several Worlds.* New York: Farrar & Rinehart, 1937.

Benét, William Rose. *Stephen Vincent Benét: My Brother Steve.* New York: Saturday Review of Literature and Farrar & Rinehart, 1943.

Fenton, Charles A. *Benét: The Life and Times of an American Man of Letters.* New Haven, Conn.: Yale University Press, 1958.

Holditch, W. Kenneth. "Stephen Vincent Benét." In *Reference Guide to Short Fiction,* edited by Noelle Watson, 66–68. Detroit: St. James Press, 1994.

Stroud, Parry Edmund. *Benét.* New York: Twayne, 1962.

"BENITO CERENO" HERMAN MELVILLE (1856)

First appearing in *Putnam's Monthly Magazine* and later published as one of the stories collected in *The Piazza Tales,* HERMAN MELVILLE's "Benito Cereno" stands as one of the author's strongest and darkest works. Melville uses elements of suspense and mystery to tell the story of the *San Dominick* and its captain, Don Benito Cereno. As is often the case with Melville's fiction, the title character is not so much the story's main PROTAGONIST but instead serves as the FOIL for the narrative's true focus. In this case the protagonist is Captain Amasa Delano, American commander of *The Bachelor's Delight,* a large trader ship off the coast of South America, who comes across the *San Dominick,* a Spanish merchant ship carrying slaves and apparently lost and adrift. After boarding the ship, Delano quickly discerns that all is not as it appears, as he is greeted by Don Benito Cereno, an inebriated captain who can barely stand and seems not at all fit to command, and Babo, Cereno's personal slave, whose fawning over Cereno seems to mask his control of the captain. As the story unfolds, it becomes increasingly clear to Delano that Babo is really the one in command and that the slaves have taken over the ship. In the years immediately before the CIVIL WAR, such a slave uprising embodied a powerful political and personal threat to Melville's American audience. The volatile racial, moral, and cultural tensions on board the ship create a claustrophobic setting in which the story's events unfold.

As morally complex as any of Melville's other work, this story juxtaposes the worldly and broken Don Cereno, who seems complicit in his own fallen state, and Captain Delano, who in his relative trust and innocence is blind to the portent of Cereno's fate. The circle of deception arising in the exchanges of Babo, Cereno, and Delano forces the reader to doubt even the possibility of any objective truth. Melville's taut prose is punctuated here, as elsewhere, with a resonant SYMBOLISM culminating in the hauntingly poignant IMAGERY of the *San Dominick* and its figurehead, a skeleton wrapped in canvas with "Follow the Leader" scrawled on the hull beneath it.

As he does in such longer works as *Pierre, Moby-Dick,* and *The Confidence Man,* Melville merges many different GENRES and modes in "Benito Cereno" in order to subvert the reader's expectations. With this story he combines elements of the South Sea adventure tale, by which he established his career with *Typee* and *Omoo,* and the suspense and psychological tension of the mystery. He further complicates the story by including in the DENOUEMENT extracts from a legal deposition that tells the "facts" in a light very different from the preceding narrative. By doing this, Melville calls into question the authority of history, which is itself, at least in his story, as much an artifice as any fiction.

The blurring of genres and types of discourse that occurs in "Benito Cereno," together with its moral ambiguity, makes this a particularly rich story that invites interpretation by contemporary literary theorists, particularly those in POSTSTRUCTURALISM and postcolonial studies. Although not well received by his contemporaries, Melville's "Benito Cereno," as does the rest of the author's work, continues to gain recognition among modern readers.

BIBLIOGRAPHY
Bloom, Harold. *Modern Critical Interpretations: Billy Budd, "Benito Cereno," "Bartleby the Scrivener," and Other Tales.* New York: Chelsea House, 1987.
Burkholder, Robert E., ed. *Critical Essays on Herman Melville's "Benito Cerino."* New York: G. K. Hall, 1992.
Melville, Herman. *Great Short Works of Herman Melville.* New York: Perennial Library, 1969.
Nnolim, Charles E. *Melville's "Benito Cerino": A Study in Name Symbolism.* New York: New Voices, 1974.

Richard Deming
Columbus State Community College

"BERNICE BOBS HER HAIR" F. Scott Fitzgerald (1920)

"Bernice Bobs Her Hair" is one of F. Scott Fitzgerald's signature pieces about the savage underside of the privileged classes. First published in the SATURDAY EVENING POST, it was included in Fitzgerald's first story collection, *Flappers and Philosophers* (1920). The story's style is light, charming, and precise in its evocation of a world of car rides and country club dances where girls compete with each other for the flattering attention of bland young men. When Bernice visits her cousin Marjorie, her social awkwardness makes her the object of gossip and pity. After instruction from Marjorie in how to appear charming and sincere while engaging in empty banter, Bernice becomes so accomplished a social actress that she threatens to surpass her cousin in popularity. When Marjorie retaliates, her viciousness concealed under charm, Bernice loses her popularity at once. Bernice has the final word, however, with a retaliatory act in which she forgoes all pretense of social grace.

That the shy and awkward Bernice could suddenly become a master of repartee is part of the story's visible machinery. Fitzgerald, however, worked within the magazine fiction formula to present a scathing portrayal of upper-class society. The story sometimes is described as an anatomy of young women's social competition, but its scope is much larger. The narrative opens with a panoramic scene of the country club at night under a black sky and then moves in to the "largely feminine" balcony, where "a great babel of middle-aged ladies with sharp eyes and icy hearts" (116) oversees the flirtations of the young couples below. No fathers are visible in the story. Bernice's aunt Josephine dispenses old-fashioned advice just before she falls asleep, suggesting the exhausted state of her narrow view of the world. As did other modernist writers of the early 20th century, Fitzgerald mockingly feminized the conservative middle class. When Bernice bobs her hair, she becomes a symbol of a new masculine vigor and independence. Her hair is associated throughout the story with feminine charm and beauty. By cutting it, she symbolically rejects and escapes the small-minded world of her social class. The story is an example of Fitzgerald's modernist vision and his skill at using popular magazine fiction for thoughtful social analysis.

BIBLIOGRAPHY
Beegel, Susan F. "'Bernice Bobs Her Hair': Fitzgerald's Jazz Elegy for Little Women." In *New Essays on F. Scott Fitzgerald's Neglected Short Stories,* edited by Jackson R. Bryer. Columbia: University of Missouri Press, 1996.
Bruccoli, Matthew. "On F. Scott Fitzgerald and 'Bernice Bobs Her Hair.'" In *The American Short Story,* edited by Calvin Skaggs. New York: Dell, 1977.
Fitzgerald, F. Scott. "Bernice Bobs Her Hair." In Fitzgerald, *Flappers and Philosophers.* New York: Charles Scribner's Sons, 1920, 116–140.

Frances Kerr
Durham Technical Community College

BERRIAULT, GINA (1926–1999)

Earning high praise in 1983 from her fellow writer Andre Dubus, who called her second story collection (*The

Infinite Passion of Expectation) "the best book of short stories by a living American writer" (qtd. in Berriault, Lyons, and Oliver 714), the Californian Gina Berriault was a critically acclaimed writer whose work has yet to receive the popular attention that it deserves. Her stories appeared in such publications as *Paris Review, ESQUIRE, SATURDAY EVENING POST, Mademoiselle,* and *Harper's Bazaar.* Although she was a highly respected novelist as well as story writer, it is for the stories that Berriault is most revered: She received the National Book Critics Circle Award, the PEN/FAULKNER AWARD, and her third O. HENRY MEMORIAL AWARD for her 1996 collection *Women in Their Beds.* Her stories have been collected in three volumes: *The Mistress, and Other Stories* (1965), *The Infinite Passion of Expectation: Twenty-five Stories* (including "The Stone Boy" [1982]), and *Women in Their Beds: New and Selected Stories.*

Gina Berriault was born Arline Shandling on January 1, 1926, in Long Beach, California, to Russian Jewish immigrant parents. After graduating from high school, she was married briefly to John V. Berriault, a musician. In the 1950s she began publishing short stories in periodicals; her sensitive, almost gemlike prose attracted critical attention, as did her subject matter, ordinary Americans coping with life's misfortunes, losses, failed relationships, and pain. Critics have noted that she writes in the tradition of the 19th-century Russians Leo Tolstoy, Fyodor Dostoevsky, and Anton Chekhov, whom Berriault revered. Philosophically, however, she has been described as an existentialist reminiscent of such 20th-century European and Latin American writers as Albert Camus and Pablo Neruda. Her characters are frequently marginalized working-class or rural folk, some of whom are callous and self-absorbed, others compassionate. Undoubtedly her best-known story is "The Stone Boy" from *The Infinite Passion of Expectation.* It features Arnold, a nine-year-old boy who accidentally shoots his brother, Eugene, and is so utterly traumatized that he is unable to speak or express himself, metaphorically becoming a boy of stone.

Berriault's novels include *The Descent* (1960), *Conference of Victims* (1962), *The Son* (1966), *The Lights of Earth* (1984), and *The Great Petrowski* (1999). In 1984 Berriault wrote the screenplay for *The Stone Boy,* a Twentieth-Century Fox feature-length film based on her short story of the same name and starring Glenn Close and Robert Duvall. She died on July 15, 1999, in Sausalito or Greenbrae, California.

BIBLIOGRAPHY
Amdahl, Gary. "Making Literature." *The Nation,* 24 June 1996, pp. 31–32.
Berriault, Gina. *Conference of Victims.* New York: Atheneum, 1962.
———. *The Descent.* New York: Atheneum, 1960.
———. *The Great Petrowski.* San Pedro, Calif.: Thumbprint Press, 1999.
———. *The Infinite Passion of Expectation: Twenty-Five Stories.* San Francisco: North Point, 1982.
———. *The Lights of Earth.* San Francisco: North Point, 1984.
———. *The Mistress, and Other Stories.* New York: Dutton, 1965.
———. *The Son.* New York: New American Library, 1966.
———. *The Son and Conference of Victims.* San Francisco: North Point Press, 1985.
———. *The Stone Boy.* (screenplay; adapted from Berriault's short story of the same title), Twentieth Century-Fox, 1984.
———. *Women in Their Beds: New and Selected Stories.* Washington, D.C.: Counterpoint, 1996.
Berriault, Gina, with Bonnie Lyons and Bill Oliver. "'Don't I Know You?': An Interview with Gina Berriault." *Literary Review* 37 (Summer 1994): 714–723.
George, Lynell. "Secrets Accidentally Spilled." *Los Angeles Times Book Review,* 26 May 1996, p. 7.
Harshaw, Tobin. "Short Takes." *New York Times Book Review,* 5 May 1996.
Heller, Janet Ruth. Review of *Women in Their Beds: New and Selected Stories. Library Journal,* 1 March 1996, pp. 107–108.
McQuade, Molly. "Gina Berriault's Fiction." *Chicago Tribune Book World,* 6 February 1983, pp. 10–12, 22.
Milton, Edith. Review of *Women in Their Beds. New York Times Book Review,* 5 May 1996, p. 22.
Seaman, Donna. "The Glory of Stories." *Booklist,* 15 March 1996, p. 1,239.
Shelnutt, Eve, ed. *The Confidence Woman, Twenty-Six Women Writers at Work.* Atlanta: Long Street, 1991, 129–132.

BESTIARIES   A popular form during the medieval period in England, these stories made allegorical (see ALLEGORY) use of the traits of beasts, birds, and reptiles, often assigning human attributes to animals who talk and act like the human types they actually represent. (See PERSONIFICATION.) Most of these animal FABLES were didactic as well as entertaining, clearly including moral and religious lessons. AESOP'S FABLES provide a classic example of the medieval bestiary. In the United States, African-American writers have long used the bestiary, early examples of which appear in the UNCLE REMUS tales published by JOEL CHANDLER HARRIS. Although in Euro-American literature a more common form for children, they exist in numerous other writings for adults, as in, for example, Don Marquis's stories and verses about a cockroach and a cat, *archie and mehitabel*. NATIVE AMERICAN writers have a long history of using a form of bestiary, from early tales in the oral tradition through Mourning Dove's coyote stories to SHERMAN ALEXIE's story collection, *The LONE RANGER AND TONTO FISTFIGHT IN HEAVEN*. (See COYOTE STORY.)

BEST OF SIMPLE, THE   See SIMPLE STORIES.

BETTS, DORIS (1932–   )   A native of Statesville, North Carolina, Doris June (Waugh) Betts attended the Women's College of the University of North Carolina (now UNC–Greensboro, 1950–53) and the University of North Carolina at Chapel Hill (1954). She began a journalism career at 18, writing and eventually editing for several North Carolina newspapers between 1950 and 1975. She married Lowry Matthews Betts in 1952 and, while rearing three children, continued to work as a journalist and fiction writer. Betts began teaching creative writing at UNC–Chapel Hill in 1966. She has written essays, served on several university commissions and writing panels, and is Alumni Distinguished Professor of English at the University of North Carolina at Chapel Hill.

Betts's first collection of short stories, *The Gentle Insurrection* (1954), won the G. P. Putnam–University of North Carolina Fiction Award. Her fiction writing career spans over four decades and includes five novels (including *The River to Pickle Beach* [1972] and *Heading West* [1981]) and two other story collections (*The Astronomer and Other Stories* [1966] and *Beasts of the Southern Wild and Other Stories* [1973]). She received a Guggenheim Fellowship in fiction in 1958 and was a National Book Award Finalist in 1974 for her surrealistic collection *Beasts*. (See SURREALISM.) Betts's fiction is set predominantly in small southern towns and concerns local, unexceptional people struggling between a search for personal identity and a commitment to family. Her allusive writing (see ALLUSION) contains elements of southern GOTHIC and GROTESQUE and has been compared to that of Walker Percy, FLANNERY O'CONNOR, Wallace Stevens, and EUDORA WELTY. More than a regional southern writer (see REGIONALISM), Betts explores such universal THEMES as racial prejudice, love, aging, mortality, and time. Critics praise her rich talent for CHARACTERIZATION, her feel for time and place, and her gift for depicting the treasures of the commonplace with humor, simplicity, and tough objectivity. Betts is a master of the short story; "The Astronomer," "The Mother-in-Law," and "The Hitchhiker" are considered three of her best. In recent years she has challenged herself to master the novel form. Each of Betts's succeeding novels has received greater scholarly acclaim. Her novel *Souls Raised from the Dead* (1994) affirms human courage as a child succumbs to a fatal disease and the members of her fractured, far-from-perfect family find some compassion for one another. Her most recent novel is *The Sharp Teeth of Love* (1997).

BIBLIOGRAPHY

Evans, Elizabeth. "Another Mule in the Yard: Doris Betts' Durable Humor." *Notes on Contemporary Literature* (March 1981).

Holman, David M. "Faith and the Unanswerable Questions: The Fiction of Doris Betts." *Southern Literary Journal* (Fall 1982).

Inge, Tonette Bond, ed. *Southern Women Writers: The New Generation*. Tuscaloosa: University of Alabama Press, 1990.

Brenda M. Palo
University of North Carolina at Chapel Hill

BIERCE, AMBROSE (AMBROSE GWINNET BIERCE) (1842–1914?)   At the age of 19, Bierce joined the Ninth Indiana Infantry and fought through the entire CIVIL WAR, serving with distinction despite suffering severe wounds at the Battle of

Kenesaw Mountain. He never lost the overwhelming memories of those years, and his story collections, *In the Midst of Life* (first titled *Tales of Soldiers and Civilians;* 1893) and *Can Such Things Be?,* include his finest war tales with their descriptions of the misery, ghastliness, and shocking brutality of war. The 15 stories in *Tales of Soldiers* combine violent and contrived naturalism with realistic and factual descriptions of combat life, each story concerning the death of the good and the brave. Bierce was a clear master of the short story, and war, with its own framework of irony, foreshortening of time, and rapid transitions and confrontations, provided the setting and structure in an appropriate form. The war stories—a major contribution to fiction—show Bierce as one of the best military short story writers in American literary history. Post–WORLD WAR I writers such as Erich Maria Remarque and ERNEST HEMINGWAY later emulated the tone of disillusionment embodied in Bierce's work. Bierce was also a scathing satirist (see SATIRE), and many of his most witty and sardonic observations of the American scene appeared as a collection of aphorisms in *The Devil's Dictionary* (1911), first published as *The Cynic's Word Book* (1906). He also wrote ghost and horror stories, in which he used local color as background and darkly disturbing analysis of the human psyche in his plots. Bierce had a notable ability to establish an atmosphere of horror through realistic, suggestive detail, but few of these works are as successful as the war stories with their realistic ironies. Bierce traveled to Mexico in 1913, served with Pancho Villa's forces, and is presumed to have been killed in battle in 1914.

See also "CHICKAMAUGA."

BIBLIOGRAPHY
Bierce, Ambrose. *Can Such Things Be?* New York: Cassell, 1893.
———. *Cobwebs from an Empty Skull.* New York: Routledge, 1874.
———. *Collected Works.* 12 vols. New York: Walter Neale, 1909–1912.
———. *Complete Short Stories.* Edited by and with introduction by Ernest Jerome Hopkins. New York: Ballantine, 1970.
———. *The Devil's Advocate: A Reader.* Edited by Brian St. Pierre. San Francisco: Chronicle Books, 1987.
———. *Fantastic Fables.* New York: Putnam, 1899.
———. *Nuggets and Dust Panned Out in California.* London: Chatto and Windus, 1873.
———. *The Stories and Fables.* Edited by and with introduction by Edward Wagenknecht. Owings Mills, Md.: Stemmer House, 1977
———. *Tales of Soldiers and Civilians.* San Francisco: Steele, 1891; as *In the Midst of Life,* London: Chatto and Windus, 1892; revised edition, New York: Putnam, 1898.
Davidson, Cathy N., ed. *Critical Essays on Bierce.* Boston: G. K. Hall, 1982.
———. *The Experimental Fictions of Bierce: Structuring the Ineffable.* Lincoln: University of Nebraska Press, 1984.
Fatout, Paul. *Bierce, The Devil's Lexicographer.* Norman: University of Oklahoma Press, 1951.
———. *Bierce and the Black Hills.* Norman: University of Oklahoma Press, 1956.
McWilliams, Carey. *Bierce: A Biography.* Boston: Little, Brown, 1929.
O'Connor, Richard. *Bierce: A Biography.* Boston: Little, Brown, 1967.
Saunders, Richard. *Bierce: The Making of a Misanthrope.* San Francisco: Chronicle Books, 1985.
Wiggins, Robert A. *Bierce.* Minneapolis: University of Minnesota Press, 1964.
Woodruff, Stuart C. *The Short Stories of Bierce: A Study in Polarity.* Pittsburgh: University of Pittsburgh Press, 1964.

"BIG BLACK GOOD MAN" RICHARD WRIGHT (1957)

Initially published in *ESQUIRE* in November 1957, this frequently anthologized story—the last one RICHARD WRIGHT wrote—reappeared in his 1960 collection *Eight Men.* As Ann Charters has noted, the story, set in Copenhagen, reflects Wright's expatriate experience (1,374). For American readers especially, the geographical distance from the American South initially gives the story an emotional distance, too, as does the Danish PROTAGONIST Olaf Jenson, who speaks eight languages. Yet Wright makes Olaf—who spent 10 years living in New York City—a symbol for white ignorance and bias. By the end of the story, Wright has not only illustrated the THEME of racism—of white prejudice toward African Americans—but also driven home the point that racism has no national boundaries. Further, by employing Lena, a Danish prostitute, as a foil to Olaf, Wright implies intriguing gender differences vis-à-vis racism: White women lack the sexual fears that contribute to white men's biases toward black men. Jim, the American black man, embodies white male fears of the African-American male threat.

Olaf personifies whiteness in notably unpleasant ways (see PERSONIFICATION). Significantly, his "watery grey" eyes cannot see clearly, despite his thick glasses, and the third-person narrator (see POINT OF VIEW) describes him as "pasty-white" and harmlessly idiotic (1,375; 1,381). Olaf, an ex-sailor who is now the night porter in a waterfront hotel, clearly views himself as a man's man, who understands and aids the students and sailors in their need for whiskey and women. Yet when the black stranger appears and asks for a room, a bottle of whiskey, and a woman, Olaf recoils in fear and disgust: Hypocritically thinking that he views all people equally, he singles out this black man as inhuman. Jim, whom Olaf views as a black giant, a black mountain, a black beast, makes Olaf feel "puny" and worthless. Nor can Olaf resist asking Lena about the first of numerous nights she will spend with Jim. Lena, however, who truly views Jim as simply "a man" without Olaf's adjectives denoting his size and color, turns to Olaf furiously: "What the hell's that to you!" she snaps (1,380).

Wright injects some humor into the scene when Jim puts his hands around Olaf's throat, so terrifying the little white man that he loses control of his sphincter muscles. The next year when Jim returns, his action becomes clear: He was measuring Olaf's throat to establish his neck size. He now presents to Olaf six perfectly fitting white nylon shirts in thanks for Olaf's introducing Jim to Lena. Yet when Jim calls Olaf a good man, Olaf cannot return the compliment without adding the adjectives *big* and *black*—and on his way out, Jim grinningly tells him to "drop dead." Cognizant of Olaf's seemingly incurable prejudice, Jim is on his way to see Lena, who, we learn, has left her profession and has been waiting for Jim to return. The ironic twist is that Olaf is correct in fearing Jim's attractiveness to the white woman, not because he embodies sex or animalism, but because Jim is a good man, an adjective we cannot apply to Olaf.

BIBLIOGRAPHY

Charters, Ann. "Richard Wright." In *Major Writers of Short Fiction: Stories and Commentary,* edited by Ann Charters, 1,392–1,375. Boston: St. Martin's, 1993.

Wright, Richard. "Big Black Good Man." In *Major Writers of Short Fiction: Stories and Commentary,* edited by Ann Charters, 1,375–1,385. Boston: St. Martin's, 1993.

"BIG BLONDE"   See PARKER, DOROTHY.

"BIG BOY LEAVES HOME" RICHARD WRIGHT **(1936)**   "Big Boy Leaves Home" was first published in the 1936 anthology *The New Caravan,* the first of RICHARD WRIGHT's stories to receive critical attention in the mainstream press. Reviews in the *New York Times,* the *Saturday Review of Literature,* and the *New Republic* agreed that it was the best piece in the anthology. With THEMES, characters, and a plot that would typify Wright's protest fiction, this graphically violent, naturalistic story (see NATURALISM) follows a young black boy whose trouble with the law forces him to grow up too quickly.

In a scene reminiscent of MARK TWAIN's *Huckleberry Finn,* the story begins as four truant black boys in a sunny southern countryside "play the dozens" (trade rhyming insults), sing songs, wrestle, and discuss trains, the North, and racism. The group's leader, Big Boy, incites the others to go swimming in a creek forbidden to blacks. Their idyll is disrupted when a white woman stumbles upon the naked boys; her screams draw her husband, Jim, who shoots two of the four. Big Boy wrestles with Jim for the gun, shooting him in the struggle. In this scene, Wright draws up an African-American literary STEREOTYPE, one that reverses the JIM CROW–era stereotype of the black male rapist: the white woman as a sexual predator, life-threatening to black men because her cry of rape (or in this case, her mere presence) inevitably results in their deaths.

Upon Big Boy's arrival home, his family summons the church elders, who quickly arrange for the boys to hide in a kiln until morning, when Elder Peters's son will drive them to Chicago. Concealed in the kiln, Big Boy must witness the whites' extended, brutal torture and murder of his friend Bobo, who becomes the third of the four boys to die. By the time the truck arrives, Big Boy has grown numb and detached; Wright uses terse, simple sentences reminiscent of those of ERNEST HEMINGWAY to indicate Big Boy's transition from naive boy to wanted criminal, a change next experienced by Wright's well-known PROTAGONIST Bigger Thomas in the novel *Native Son*.

BIBLIOGRAPHY

Fabre, Michel. *The Unfinished Quest of Richard Wright*. New York: Morrow, 1973.

Joyce, Joyce Ann. *Richard Wright's Art of Tragedy*. Iowa City: University of Iowa Press, 1986.

Kinnamon, Keneth. *The Emergence of Richard Wright: A Study in Literature and Society*. Ann Arbor, Mich.: UMI Books on Demand, 1972.

Margolies, Edward. "The Short Stories: Uncle Tom's Children, Eight Men." In *Critical Essays on Richard Wright*, edited by Yoshinobu Hakutani. Boston: G. K. Hall, 1982.

Kimberly Drake
Virginia Wesleyan College

"BIG TWO-HEARTED RIVER" ERNEST HEMINGWAY (1925)

"Big Two-Hearted River" is a story without dialogue, yet most readers admire ERNEST HEMINGWAY's often praised CHARACTERIZATION of his protagonist, NICK ADAMS, and the way Nick seeks and faces experience. One of Hemingway's best-known characters, Nick appears in many of the stories in IN OUR TIME (published as a brief series of vignettes in 1924 as *in our time,* and published the following year in an expanded version as *In Our Time*). After Hemingway's death, "Big Two-Hearted River" was republished along with those selected by the editor Philip Young for *The Nick Adams Stories* (1972). In one of his letters to his publisher, Hemingway hinted at the creative impulse within him that worked to produce his fiction: He admired people who know they must eventually die but behave very well along the way (see HEMINGWAY CODE). As numerous critics have pointed out, "Big Two-Hearted River" contains all the elements to make it a quintessential Hemingway tale. According to the short story critic Ann Charters, these include the focus on the woods, its creatures, and fishing; the carefully honed sentences; the characteristic understatement; the meticulous

attention Nick devotes to the rituals of camping and fishing; "the repetitions of key words (*good, satisfactory, fine, pleasant, tighten, alive*)"; and the mysterious sense of unease that threatens to unbalance the protagonist (74).

The story opens as Nick, recently returned from the Italian battlefields of WORLD WAR I, steps off the train at the town of Seney, Michigan. The town's life-filled river contrasts sharply with the desiccated landscape (an apparently deliberate evocation of the motif of *The WASTE LAND*) through which Nick has passed on his train ride, and he is immediately drawn to the exquisitely described trout steadying themselves in the current of the river. The two "hearts" of the river are, on one level, the two "parts" of the story; on another level they are the two "hearts" of Nick, who according to some critics suffers from a divided conscience. Nick's fishing trip is really a flight from his past rather than a journey toward his future. We sense that Nick, who admires the trout's ability to steady itself in the current, emulates this activity in his own ritualistic enactment of the rites of camping and fishing—from his mastery of location by reading natural signs, to his methodical camp making, coffee brewing, and cooking and his elaborate preparations for fishing. Nick derives satisfaction from predictability and control rather than good fortune or surprise. He apparently thinks of every detail to which the camper or fisherman might attend, demonstrating a keen awareness that grows from experience.

Problems arise for Nick when he ceases his activities. Even as Nick conceives of his newly pitched tent as his home, a good place, he becomes almost panic-stricken. He regains mastery of his feelings by preparing dinner in the same ritualistic way and with the same careful attention to detail he engages in when fishing: Nick feels content as long as he believes he can control the details of his life. Part I ends tranquilly with a quiet night that gives no hint of the confusion that will arise on the following day's fishing expedition. A single mosquito slips through the netting Nick has affixed to the tent's entrance, but he immediately takes a match to the insect, extinguishing the problem (74). He will not so easily solve the larger problems that will enter his life.

Hemingway's use of sexual innuendo and META-PHOR to describe Nick's encounter with the trout and the river becomes another Hemingway trademark (as in "The Last Good Country," for example). Fishing allows Nick to penetrate a completely different world. As the trout bites the bait and pumps against the current, Nick's rod becomes a living thing, bending in "jerks" against the pull of the trout and then tightening into "sudden hardness" as the trout leaps upward (551, 552). The excitement of hooking the fish leaves him shaken, slightly nauseous, and unprepared for the feeling of dread that overcomes him when he stops to rest near where the river narrows into swamp. The tangled fauna there would confound any methodical attempts at traversal. He wishes he had something to read to occupy his mind and feels a sharp aversion to wading into the murky water. The threat of loss of control—and perhaps of the dark thoughts intruding on his activity—so frightens Nick that he abruptly stops fishing to return to the safe haven of his camp. He reassures himself that he has many more days when he can fish in the swamp, but at this stage of his development he appears unwilling to accept that challenge. While some critics see the DENOUEMENT in a positive light that suggests Nick's recovery, the swamp metaphorically implies, at the very least, a future fraught with danger and difficulty.

"Big Two-Hearted River," with its deliberate dearth of explanation for Nick's sense of unease and dread, provides a near-perfect example of Hemingway's oft-cited "iceberg" technique (like an iceberg, only one-eighth of the story's meaning is visible on the surface) and continues to tantalize readers and critics alike. Equally plausible interpretations include Nick as wounded war veteran, as the author contemplating his own suicide, as a modern frontier hero, and as a Waste Land figure. Readers may also gain further understanding by reading "A Way You'll Never Be," the story that precedes "Big Two-Hearted River" in *The Nick Adams Stories.*

BIBLIOGRAPHY

Benson, Jackson J., ed. *New Critical Approaches to the Short Stories of Ernest Hemingway.* Durham, N.C.: Duke University Press, 1990.

————. *The Short Stories of Ernest Hemingway: Critical Essays.* Durham, N.C.: Duke University Press, 1975.

Brenner, Gerry, and Earl Rovit. *Ernest Hemingway.* Rev. ed. Boston: Twayne, 1990.

Charters, Ann, ed. *The Story and Its Writer.* New York: Bedford, 2002.

Flora, Joseph M. *Ernest Hemingway: A Study of the Short Fiction.* Boston: Twayne, 1989.

Hemingway, Ernest. *In Our Time.* New York: Scribner's, 1925.

————. "Big Two-Hearted River." In *The Nick Adams Stories,* edited by Philip Young. New York: Scribner's, 1972.

Lynn, Kenneth S. *Hemingway.* New York: Simon & Schuster, 1988, pp. 102–108.

Reynolds, Michael S., ed. *Critical Essays on Ernest Hemingway's "In Our Time."* Boston: G. K. Hall, 1983.

BILDUNGSROMAN   A term used to classify a novel that takes as its main subject the moral, intellectual, and psychological development of a PROTAGONIST. Usually such novels trace the maturation of a youthful protagonist into adulthood. Contemporary examples of bildungsroman range from RALPH ELLISON's *Invisible Man* and TILLIE OLSEN's *Yonnondio* to Paul Auster's *Mr. Vertigo.* For examples of short stories as bildungsroman, see, for instance, CARSON MCCULLERS's "Wunderkind," KATHERINE ANNE PORTER's "The Grave," Tillie Olsen's "O, YES," and Zelda Fitzgerald's "Miss Ella."

Richard Deming
Columbus State Community College

BILLY BUDD, SAILOR HERMAN MELVILLE **(1924)**   *Billy Budd, Sailor* is HERMAN MELVILLE's final piece of writing. It is a NOVELLA left unpublished at the time of Melville's death in 1891. The narrative relates the story of Billy Budd, a 21-year-old sailor serving aboard the British merchant vessel *Rights-of-Man.* Billy is forced aboard the H.M.S. *Bellipotent,* whose name means "war power," to fight in the king's service against the French in 1797. Billy is one of several Melville characters portrayed as "handsome sailors." He is a good seaman and well liked by the officers and crew of the *Bellipotent*—except by the master at arms, John Claggart, who bears an ill-defined malice toward Billy. Strangely, Claggart is both attracted to and repulsed by Billy's youth and beauty, and his animosity toward the young sailor seems to stem from an inherent source of evil. As Merton Sealts aptly points out, Billy and Claggart "stand in sharp contrast as types of innocence and worldly experience" ("*Billy Budd, Sailor,*" in John Bryant, ed., *A Companion to Melville Studies* [1986], 408).

Seeking to entrap Billy, Claggart has one of his men attempt to bribe him into participating in a mutiny, but Billy refuses. Claggart responds by going to Captain Vere and formally accusing Billy of mutiny. Billy, who stutters, is called to the captain's cabin, and when he is confronted by the charges facing him, he is unable to answer them because of his stammer. Powerless to voice his indignation, Billy turns to his accuser and strikes Claggart a deadly blow to the head. A battlefield court-martial ensues, and, against his nobler feelings but in accord with military law, Captain Vere condemns Billy to hang for striking and killing a superior officer. The crew is assembled and, neck in the noose and just moments before he is hoisted to the yardarm, Billy calls out, "God Bless Captain Vere" (123). Christlike, "Billy ascended; and, ascending, took the full rose of the dawn" (124). We learn at the end of the narrative that Captain Vere, mortally wounded in battle, called out with his final breath, "Billy Budd, Billy Budd" (129).

Melville's work was left, unpublished, in 351 manuscript leaves written in both pencil and pen and heavily corrected and revised. The author left no directions for its publication, and, as far as we know, he never mentioned the work. *Billy Budd* was not published until 1924, when Raymond Weaver included it in the *Complete Works of Melville.* In 1928 Weaver produced an altered version, and F. Barron Freeman followed in 1948 with yet another rendering of the text. The text edited by Harrison Hayford and Merton M. Sealts, Jr., for the University of Chicago Press entitled *Billy Budd, Sailor (An Inside Narrative)* (1962) is now generally accepted as the standard. Critical reception of *Billy Budd* reflects the problematic nature of the text itself, and the novella has been variously interpreted. Some have read it as Melville's final testament, accepting the inevitability of evil; in the 1950s the prevailing readings of *Billy Budd* foregrounded irony as Melville's dominant concern. Current work focuses more on religious, social, political, and historical

readings of *Billy Budd*. That the text is susceptible to so many readings points to its complexity as a work of art. One point is clear: Melville lived through an age that saw sailing ships replaced by steam-powered vessels and that saw an array of technological improvements, particularly in implements of warfare. That Melville, as witness to these changes, should temper his ROMANTICISM in *Billy Budd,* the only prose he wrote after 1857, seems inevitable. To claim that the work demonstrates Melville's acceptance of change fails to acknowledge the complexity of his views, for at the end of his life Melville apparently concluded that a future mediated by his earlier romantic perception was severely flawed, perhaps impossible. After viewing the carnage of the American CIVIL WAR, Melville probably found it impossible to portray the earthly superiority of an innocent figure like Billy Budd. Nevertheless, in the final pages of the novella, Billy's spirit does indeed survive long after his death in the lore of his fellow sailors.

BIBLIOGRAPHY

Bryant, John. *A Companion to Melville Studies.* Westport, Conn.: Greenwood, 1986.

Hayford, Harrison, and Merton M. Sealts, Jr., eds. *Billy Budd, Sailor (An Inside Narrative).* Chicago: University of Chicago Press, 1962.

Parker, Hershel. *Reading Billy Budd.* Evanston, Ill.: Northwestern University Press, 1990.

Cornelius W. Browne
Ohio University

"BINGO VAN" LOUISE ERDRICH (1990) First published in the *NEW YORKER* and later anthologized in *Talking Leaves: Contemporary Native American Short Stories* (1991), "Bingo Van" is the seventh chapter in *Bingo Palace,* the fourth book in LOUISE ERDRICH's series of novels. In the story Erdrich plays with the concept of luck, questioning the fundamental meaning of fortune, and hints at the tensions between reservation residents and surrounding nonreservation communities. The narrator, Lipsha Morrisey, a well-meaning and lackluster "healer," uses his power to win a van at the Bingo Palace. The van enables Lipsha to become involved with an attractive young single mother and puts him in contact—and subsequently in conflict—

with the non-Indian world off the reservation. As the story plays out, the van turns out to be far from a lucky prize, and Lipsha is better off without it.

Calvin Hussman
St. Olaf College

BIRTHA, BECKY (1948–   )   Born in Hampton, Virginia, in 1948, Becky Birtha graduated from the State University of New York at Buffalo in 1973 and taught preschool children for 10 years. Her first collection of short stories, *For Nights Like This One: Stories of Loving Women,* was published in 1983. After receiving an M.A. in fine arts from Vermont College in 1984, she was awarded a fellowship from the Pennsylvania Council of the Arts. She completed a second volume of short stories, *Lovers Choice,* in 1987. Central to her fiction is the lesbian experience, in which relationships between women are depicted as part of a "normal, familiar, and comfortable reality."

"BIRTH-MARK, THE" NATHANIEL HAWTHORNE **(1843)**   Similar to NATHANIEL HAWTHORNE'S "RAPPACINI'S DAUGHTER" in its presentation of a beautiful woman who lives with a scientist obsessed with perfection, "The Birth-mark" features Aylmer, who, aspiring to perfection and divinity, falls in love with and marries Georgiana, whose beauty he increasingly believes is marred by a tiny birthmark. Under her husband's influence, Georgiana's diminishing beliefs in her own beauty, normalcy, and self-worth make this story as relevant—and as depressing—today as it was in Hawthorne's time. Indeed, the narrator's statement about Aylmer's journals could easily be Hawthorne's self-reflexive comment about the story itself: "as melancholy a record as mortal hand had ever penned" (10:49). Despite the protests of Aminadab, his laboratory assistant (who, as FOIL to the spiritually superior Aylmer, clearly represents earthiness), Aylmer believes not only that the birthmark is a flaw in his wife's perfection but also that his removal of it—his ability to control nature—will provide him proof of his absolute power. By the time the operation begins, Georgiana acquiesces: She has moved from anger at her husband for having married her in the first place

to a total identification with his views of her flaw, her humanity. Although Aylmer successfully removes the birthmark, Georgiana will die, but not before she absolves him of all guilt, submitting to his higher spiritual and scientific power.

"The Birth-mark" yields intriguing results from both religious and FEMINIST perspectives. Critics have long noted the Christian implications of human fallibility in this story and see Aylmer as mistakenly playing God, failing to understand that God created the flaws as well as the beauty of nature and humanity. Georgiana, sacrificed for her husband's spiritual transcendence, may be seen as a Christ figure. From a feminist viewpoint, however, her increasing reliance on her husband and her view of him as superior make her a perfect symbol of woman—in this case, wife—as victim of male arrogance and power. Numerous narrative intrusions suggest clearly the author's agreement with this interpretation.

BIBLIOGRAPHY
Bunge, Nancy. *Nathaniel Hawthorne: Studies in the Short Fiction.* New York: Twayne, 1993.
Hawthorne, Nathaniel. "The Birth-mark." In *Mosses from an Old Manse: The Centenary Edition of the Works of Nathaniel Hawthorne.* Vol. 10, edited by William Charvatt, 38–56. Columbus: Ohio State University Press, 1962–1968.

"BLACKBERRY WINTER" ROBERT PENN WARREN **(1946)**   On the surface, ROBERT PENN WARREN'S most widely acclaimed short story, "Blackberry Winter," appears to be yet another story of boyhood innocence. "Blackberry Winter" is told through the eyes of a nine-year-old boy, Seth; the action takes place when Seth is nine, although in present time the narrator is over 40 years old. Seth recalls how cold the day is for June (hence the title) and begins his day trying to avoid wearing shoes. Throughout the narrative, Seth makes various stops on his parents' farm, and readers learn that the small Tennessee town has experienced a small flood, which leads to the series of events that guide the story. Even though Seth reminisces about this day in his childhood, Warren's use of time serves as the structure for the story itself.

To begin, Warren's primary means of retelling the story, as a man reminiscing about one day in his boyhood, emphasizes the role time plays in "Blackberry Winter." Much of the time, looking back makes experiences more vivid, more vibrant. And Seth's recollection of events is no different. From his morning skirmish with his mother about not wearing shoes to meeting the tramp (who eventually takes what money he can from the family and threatens to cut Seth's throat), Seth's retelling surrounding the events of this June day are clear and insightful. However, Seth's insightfulness has a price—he has learned from this blackberry winter day because he is older and, with the assistance of time, has the ability to reflect on the day's events.

Early in the text, Seth tells us just what time is and how it functions for him. Warren writes, "Nobody had ever tried to stop me in June as long as I could remember, and when you are nine years old, what you remember seems forever; for you remember everything and everything is important and stands big and full and fills up Time and is so solid that you can walk around and around it like a tree and look at it" (63). Seth goes on to explain that time exists, although it is not movement: "You are aware that time passes, that there is movement in time, but that is not what Time is. Time is not a movement, a flowing, a wind then, but is, rather, a kind of climate in which things are, and when a thing happens it begins to live and keeps on living and stands solid in Time like the tree that you can walk around" (63–64). Thus, Seth's memory of this blackberry winter day functions, at least for Seth, as an immovable object, as a tree that he can continually see, touch, and walk around. And this day is exactly that: a part of Seth's past that he sometimes visits, a day that is embedded in his memories.

Readers see this recurrence of time in the text when Big Jebb discusses Dellie's sickness with Seth. Because Seth is nine and too young to understand the concept of menopause, Big Jebb simply tells him, "'Time come and you find out everything'" (82). Here again, Warren emphasizes time by showing how Seth will only learn about certain events, such as menopause, when he has grown and matured, when the time is right. Even when Jebb attempts to explain menopause to Seth, Jebb himself states that "'Hit just comes on 'em when the time comes'" (82), implying that everyone—

even adults—has to respect time and be aware that all events happen when the time is right. Jebb even goes so far as to suggest that this event changes both women's lives and time itself. Warren writes, "'Hit is the change of life and time'" (82). Here, Warren suggests that when a monumental event occurs, the event both changes people's lives and makes a treelike addition to time.

Perhaps the strongest indicator of time's function in "Blackberry Winter" occurs at the end of Warren's short story. When Seth admits that he has followed the tramp all the years of his life, Seth himself reinforces time's importance, for the event when the tramp threatens to cut Seth's throat and warns Seth not to follow him eventually frames both the short story itself and, consequently, Seth's life. Warren writes, "That was what he said, for me not to follow him. But I did follow him, all the years" (87). This one event— the idle threat made by the tramp—is a strong and immovable tree in Seth's concept of time, one that frames this blackberry winter day in June and, perhaps, most of the narrator's life.

Although "Blackberry Winter" is a story about the adventures of a nine-year-old Tennessee boy one cool summer day in June, the narrative itself is a function of Seth's concept of time. Each event that he recalls is one of his trees in this conception of how time functions. From his reluctance to wear shoes and socks to his recollection of his father on horseback to the tramp threatening to cut his throat, every event functions as a placeholder both in Seth's mind and in the narrative structure of "Blackberry Winter."

BIBLIOGRAPHY
Warren, Robert Penn. "Blackberry Winter." In *The Circus in the Attic and Other Stories*. New York: Harcourt, 1931, 63–87.

Chris L. Massey
Wright State University

"BLACK CAT, THE" EDGAR ALLAN POE (1843) While living in Philadelphia, EDGAR ALLAN POE published "The Black Cat" shortly after "The TELL-TALE HEART" (1843). Both are psychological studies using first-person POINT OF VIEW to explore

mental instability, obsession, murder, and the inability of characters to conceal feelings and actions. Although the narrator is reflecting on past events through writing, the sentence structure and rhythm of "The Black Cat," as in many of Poe's tales, replicate speech, and the inverted syntax—or untraditional word placement in sentences—represents the confused and illogical mental state of the alcoholic narrator. This tale is also linked with Poe's "The Imp of the Perverse" (1845), as both are examinations of condemned men who do evil simply because they know they should not.

The tale begins with the obsessed and/or UNRELIABLE NARRATOR, a familiar device in Poe's stories, who assures readers that he will relate a common tale of ordinary events. Furthermore, he insists that he has no interest in cause and effect. Yet the events he describes are far from ordinary: Becoming obsessed with his cat, he first gouges out its eye and later hangs it. When the narrator's house burns down, the GOTHIC image of the cat with the noose around its neck remains imprinted on a bedroom wall. Shortly thereafter another cat appears that resembles the first. The man's affection for the new cat soon turns to disgust. When the man's wife stops him from killing the cat, he turns the ax on her instead. He then conceals her corpse behind a brick cellar wall. Shortly afterward, feeling absolutely no guilt over the brutal murder of his wife, the man brags to police investigators about the solid structure of his house, taps the cellar wall, and hears the cat's spine-tingling howling from behind it. In this use of IRONY, the murderer's confidence and jubilation, along with the mysterious cat, are his undoing. Or, to use Charles E. May's words, "It is not guilt that undoes him, but glee, as he raps on the very wall behind which his wife's body rots upright" (75).

"The Black Cat" is one of Poe's sharpest psychological profiles, starkest statements about human motivation, and most unified tales. Indeed, in the very explication of the narrator's motive—his paradoxical obsession with both the exultation and agony of damnation—lies the impressively rendered unity of the story. It was included in a new edition of his tales in 1845 and has since been reprinted in subsequent collections, anthologies, and school readers.

BIBLIOGRAPHY
Hammond, J. R. *An Edgar Allan Poe Companion: A Guide to the Short Stories, Romances and Essays.* Totowa, N.J.: Barnes & Noble Books, 1981.
May, Charles O. *Edgar Allan Poe: A Study of the Short Fiction.* Boston: Twayne, 1991.
Poe, Edgar Allan. "The Black Cat." In *Collected Works of Edgar Allan Poe.* Vol. 3. Edited by Thomas O. Mabbott. Cambridge, Mass.: Harvard University Press/Belknap Press, 1978, 849–859.

Anna Leahy
Ohio University

BLACK HUMOR   A 20th-century technique that achieves morbidly humorous effects through the use of sardonic wit and morbid or GROTESQUE situations. The narrator's tone often evokes resignation, anger, or bitterness. Similarly to the literature of the ABSURD, black humor frequently depicts a farcical, fantastic world—either dreamlike or nightmarish—featuring naive characters who play out their roles in a world in which the events are simultaneously comic, brutal, horrifying, or absurd. Short stories using black humor include JOHN BARTH's "LOST IN THE FUNHOUSE" and FLANNERY O'CONNOR's "A GOOD MAN IS HARD TO FIND." Novels frequently used to exemplify black humor include KURT VONNEGUT's *Slaughterhouse-Five* and Joseph Heller's *Catch-22.* EDWARD ALBEE's play *Who's Afraid of Virginia Woolf?* provides an example of black humor in modern drama.

BLACK MASK   The first HARD-BOILED FICTION magazine in the DETECTIVE SHORT FICTION vein. Founded in 1919 by the editor Joseph T. Shaw, *Black Mask* published such now-CLASSIC detective fiction writers as RAYMOND CHANDLER and DASHIELL HAMMETT and established the hard-boiled formula that many critics trace to the early work of ERNEST HEMINGWAY. Characterized by crime, sordid environments, and a clipped, terse, often crude dialogue, *Black Mask* stories enjoyed immense popularity in the 1920s and 1930s. In 1946 Shaw collected many of them in *The Hard-Boiled Omnibus: Early Stories from Black Mask.*

"BLUE HOTEL, THE" STEPHEN CRANE (1898)

"The Blue Hotel" is justifiably one of STEPHEN CRANE's most famous and most frequently anthologized stories. The brilliantly blue color of the hotel, standing prominently in the prairie town of Fort Romper, Nebraska, creeps into the imagination as more than merely the bizarre backdrop for the action. Its very color suggests something out of place in the middle of the prairie. The blue hotel itself is a METAPHOR for the inexplicable but violent human emotions enacted both within and without its walls, where the fury of the snowstorm echoes the anger that erupts among the men who remain sheltered at the hotel.

Early in the story, a train interrupts the quiet of the town and the peaceful social order represented by the hotel. Disembarking is a nervous-looking Swede whose head is filled with dime-novel accounts of the Wild West. On entering the hotel he meets the other characters: Pat Scully, owner of the hotel; Mr. Blanc, a diminutive easterner; a nameless cowboy; and Johnnie, Scully's excitable son. From the beginning, the Swede announces that he expects to be killed; of course, by the end of the story his prophecy is fulfilled. Either entirely or half-crazy and hysterical throughout most of the action, the Swede refuses to be calmed by Scully or the others, eventually making them feel somewhat hysterical as well. The story dramatizes the reasons for and the results of uncontrolled human behavior. Part of Crane's considerable achievement here, according to Chester L. Wolford, lies in the complex misperceptions the characters exhibit in relation to one another, misleading the readers as well as themselves (30). Does Scully realize the effect of his liberal pouring of liquor for the nervous Swede? Does Mr. Blanc understand the ramifications of not telling the others that Johnnie is cheating in the card game? Does the cowboy realize his role in inciting the Swede's violence? When the Swede kills Johnnie and survives, only to be killed himself when he attacks another hotel customer for cheating, has he brought on his own death, or were all of the others complicit? The easterner believes that they all collaborated in the two murders. Crane leaves the reader to ponder the connection between order and chaos, free will and DETERMINISM, the individual and the group—and the blue of the hotel compared with the white of the snowstorm.

BIBLIOGRAPHY

Crane, Stephen. "The Blue Hotel." In *University of Virginia Edition of the Works of Stephen Crane.* Vol. 5. Edited by Fredson Bowers. Charlottesville: University of Virginia Press, 142–170.

Kazin, Alfred. "On Stephen Crane and 'The Blue Hotel.'" In *The American Short Story.* Vol. 1. Edited by Calvin Skaggs. New York: Dell, 1977, 77–81.

Wolford, Chester L. *Stephen Crane: A Study of the Short Fiction.* Boston: Twayne, 1989.

"BLUES AIN'T NO MOCKIN' BIRD, THE" TONI CADE BAMBARA (1971)

A silent, subtle violence stirs within the narrative of TONI CADE BAMBARA's "The Blues Ain't No Mockin' Bird." The violence on which Bambara's story turns is a deep, abiding assault on dignity and authenticity—on the essential humanity of its characters.

Originally published in 1971, but most commonly found in Bambara's highly acclaimed collection, *Gorilla, My Love,* published the following year, "Blues Ain't No Mockin' Bird" offers a glimpse—a snippet of time on a winter's day—of a rural African-American family, whose lives have been intruded upon by two white outsiders with a movie camera. As children play in the yard, and Granny ladles rum over freshly baked Christmas cakes on the back porch, the unblinking camera films relentlessly, appropriating landscapes, lives, and objects on its own terms, for its own uses. Granny Cain's cold dismissal of the invasive pair has little impact—they retreat a bit, but the camera films on, "buzzin'" at everything in its gaze. The two claim to be from the county, making a film as "part of the food stamp campaign," but the camera merely serves as an extension of their intrusive aura of entitlement and racism.

When Mister Cain—Granddaddy—returns from hunting with a bloody chicken hawk over his shoulder, his powerful presence commands attention, from both the county men and the reader. His utterances are sparse, yet definitive; his will brooks no argument. As he holds out his hand, silent and still, awaiting the county man's forfeiture of his camera, the power in that hand is described by the young narrator as "not at all a hand but a person in itself." With one move of those powerful hands, Granddaddy Cain destroys the camera and returns the broken bits to the filmmaker. The two beat a hasty retreat, and the rhythm of life at the Cain house returns to normal.

The events of the day are narrated by a young African-American girl, whose "puddle stompin'" with Cathy, her intuitive third cousin, is interrupted by the arrival of the two strangers. Cathy just knows things, but the narrator is not as perceptive, so her narration, at times, forms a disjointed collage. Yet, it is through her unsynthesized bits and pieces of context that the reader gleans the deepest perspective on the violence and objectification embedded within the encounter with the county men—a perspective that might have been mitigated or muddied by a more analytical, self-aware narrator. Through her eyes, the reader also gains awareness of the Cain family's larger-than-life dynamics: from the newly arrived Cathy, who exhibits a wisdom and call to story that will later undoubtedly earn her the mantle of family sage and scribe, to Granny, the family caretaker and teacher, with a fierce pride and an explosive temper, and finally, Mister Cain, a quiet man, yet unnerving in his powerful presence and the finality of his actions.

The violence that insidiously seeps through "The Blues Ain't No Mockin' Bird" is an intricate interweaving of racism and representation. The Cain family, their home, and their lifeways are appropriated as objects by the two county men—an archetypical rural (and hence, disadvantaged) African-American family, hunting and gardening for sustenance. Suitable images for a film on the food stamp program, indeed. Granny Cain immediately recognizes their arrogant assumptions, as the two take liberties with the family images and property, without care or permission. "Go tell that man we ain't a bunch of trees," she instructs the children. They are not "scenery" or "primitives" to be essentialized and objectified by those with social and economic privilege.

The focal point of the story's conflict, Granny challenges their assumptions of knowledge and access at every turn, admonishing, "I don't know about the thing, the it, and the stuff. . . . Just people here is what

I tend to consider"—a sharp reclamation of the family's humanity. When the cameraman calls her "Aunty," Granny recoils at his patronizing, racist address and retorts, "Your mama and I are not related." She then seizes this moment to tutor the children about the inhumanity of turning misery into spectacle, channeling her anger and indignation into a life lesson and portraying one of Bambara's strongest female figures—a teacher, a storyteller, and a resister.

And resistance in the face of racism and appropriation is the battle cry of "The Blues Ain't No Mockin' Bird." Granny and Granddaddy Cain serve as embodiments of the defiance that permeated society in the 1960s and 1970s, when "The Blues" was written. The social impacts of the black power movement were felt most strongly during this era, as movement leaders urged African Americans to take pride in their cultural distinctiveness and actively assume responsibility for their own political and social destinies, through community control and political activism. Rather than be subject to the definitions and representations of others, African Americans were exhorted to utilize and defend their own abilities to interpret social and historical events and assumptions—and Bambara, a former civil rights worker, portrays the Cains as firmly rejecting representation by their cultural "others."

Similarly, the author has received wide acclaim for her own representations, particularly for her use of DIALECT in "The Blues," and has been compared to ZORA NEALE HURSTON and MARK TWAIN for her use of contemporary dialect in literature to create cultural awareness. Ruth Elizabeth Burks describes Bambara as a storyteller who "perpetuates the struggle of her people by literally recording it in their own voices." In "The Blues," Bambara has fashioned a story that not only perpetuates the struggle but speaks the struggle and is the struggle. The blues, after all, are strains of defiance, not the pacifying melodies of a songbird.

BIBLIOGRAPHY

Bambara, Toni Cade. "The Blues Ain't No Mockin' Bird." In *Gorilla, My Love.* New York: Random House, 1972.

Burks, Ruth. "From Baptism to Resurrection: Toni Cade Bambara and the Incongruity of Language." In *Black Women Writers, A Critical Evaluation, 1950–1980,* edited by Mari Evans. New York: Anchor Books, 1984.

Evans, Mari, ed. *Black Women Writers, A Critical Evaluation, 1950–1980.* New York: Anchor Books, 1984.

Cynthia J. Miller
Emerson College

BONNER, SHERWOOD (KATHERINE SHERWOOD BONNER MCDOWELL) (1849–1883)

Katherine Sherwood Bonner McDowell grew up in Holly Springs, Mississippi, the daughter of a sometime physician whose first responsibility was managing the family plantation. After a brief marriage, she moved in 1873 to Boston, where she wrote for HARPER'S, *Harper's Weekly,* and *Lippincott's.* Befriended by Henry Wadsworth Longfellow, she worked for a time as his secretary. Much of her writing is of high quality, demonstrating a fine ear for DIALECT. Had she not died of cancer at age 34, her promising career might have led her to greater fame.

Her work includes *Like unto Like* (1878), a novel of CIVIL WAR and RECONSTRUCTION days, and two collections of short stories, *Dialect Tales* (1883) and *Suwanee River Tales* (1884). Although a number of her sketches of blacks seem the tales of a novice rather than of a fully developed and self-confident writer, Bonner's stories of Tennessee moonshiners and her tales of rural folk on the Illinois prairie reveal a notable talent for grimly realistic portrayals of both characters and action. Ironically, one of her most powerful stories, "A Volcanic Interlude" (1880), was published in *Lippincott's* but never in either of her collected volumes.

BIBLIOGRAPHY

Bonner, Sherwood. *Dialect Tales.* New York: Harper, 1883.
———. *Gran'mammy. Little Classics of the South: Mississippi.* New York: Purdy, 1927.
———. *Like unto Like.* New York: Harper, 1878. As *Blythe Herndon,* bound with *Janetta* by Julia Chandler. London: Ward, Lock, 1882.
———. *Suwanee River Tales.* Boston: Roberts, 1884.
Frank, William L. *Sherwood Bonner.* Boston: Twayne, 1976.
McAlexander, Hubert H. *The Prodigal Daughter: A Biography of Sherwood Bonner.* Baton Rouge: Louisiana State University Press, 1981.

BONNIN, GERTRUDE SIMMONS   See ZITKALA-ŠA.

BOWLES, PAUL (PAUL FREDERIK BOWLES) (1910–1999)

Born in New York City, Paul Bowles lived in Tangier, Morocco, from 1947. Since the publication of his first novel, *The Sheltering Sky* (1949), Bowles has been viewed as undeniably talented, because of his style, but controversial, because of his subject matter. Some readers regard him as a cult figure, noting his ties to and influence on writers of the BEAT GENERATION; others find his work difficult to read, focused as it often is on the horror, violence, and NIHILISM of 20th-century life. The appeal of his work lies chiefly in Bowles's adroit manipulation of language, and in his determination to explore—as did EDGAR ALLAN POE, the American writer whom he most admired—the depths of the human soul. Bowles is also frequently linked with European EXISTENTIALIST writers like Jean-Paul Sartre, whose *No Exit* Bowles translated in 1946.

Bowles wrote a number of tales based on FOLKLORE and rendered in images and techniques of SURREALISM or MAGICAL REALISM, such as "The Scorpion," in which a cave-dwelling woman's divided attraction to both independence and a man of the outer world is ultimately depicted in a dream in which she swallows the scorpion, suggesting in this instance either sex or death or both. In addition to these sorts of stories, and to those of brutality and perversion—"A Distant Episode" and "The Delicate Prey," for example—Bowles wrote "The Garden," one of his most admired stories. An impressive and artistically wrought PARABLE about social intolerance and individual human difference, it demonstrates the way a man's neighbors and even his wife turn on him because, unlike them, he finds genuine pleasure in tending his garden.

BIBLIOGRAPHY

Bertens, Hans. *The Fiction of Paul Bowles: The Soul Is the Weariest Part of the Body.* Atlantic Highlands, N.J.: Humanities Press, 1979.
Bowles, Paul. *Collected Stories 1939–1976.* Santa Barbara, Calif.: Black Sparrow Press, 1979.
———. *The Delicate Prey and Other Stories.* New York: Random House, 1950.
———. *The Hours after Noon.* London: Heinemann, 1959.
———. *A Hundred Camels in the Courtyard.* San Francisco: City Lights, 1962.

————. *In the Red Room.* Los Angeles: Sylvester and Orphanos, 1981.

————. *Let It Come Down.* New York: New Directions, 1949.

————. *A Little Stone.* London: Lehmann, 1950.

————. *Midnight Mass.* Santa Barbara, Calif.: Black Sparrow Press, 1981.

————. *Pages from Cold Point and Other Stones.* London: Owen, 1968.

————. *The Sheltering Sky.* New York: New Directions, 1949.

————. *The Spider's House.* New York: Random House, 1955.

————. *Things Gone and Things Still Here.* Santa Barbara, Calif.: Black Sparrow Press, 1977.

————. *Three Tales.* New York: Hallman, 1975.

————. *The Time of Friendship.* New York: Holt Rinehart, 1967.

————. *Up above the World.* New York: Simon & Schuster, 1966.

————. *Without Stopping: An Autobiography.* New York: Putnam, 1972.

Caponi, Gena Dagel. *Paul Bowles,* Twayne's United States Authors 706. New York: Twayne; Prentice Hall International, 1998.

Dillon, Millicent. *You Are Not I: A Portrait of Paul Bowles.* Berkeley: University of California Press, 1998.

Evans, Oliver. "Paul Bowles and the Natural Man." In *Recent American Fiction.* Boston: Houghton Mifflin, 1963.

Mottram, Eric. *Paul Bowles: Staticity and Terror.* London: Aloes, 1976.

"Paul Bowles Issue." *Review of Contemporary Fiction* 2, no. 3 (1982).

Pounds, Wayne. *Paul Bowles: The Inner Geography.* Bern, Switzerland: Peter Lang, 1985.

Sawyer-Lauçanno, Christopher. *An Invisible Spectator: A Biography of Paul Bowles.* New York: Grove Press, 1989.

Stewart, Lawrence D. *Paul Bowles: The Illumination of North Africa.* Carbondale: Southern Illinois University Press, 1974.

"BOX SEAT" JEAN TOOMER (1923)

"Box Seat" is perhaps the most provocatively ambiguous short story included in the African-American writer JEAN TOOMER's *CANE,* a collection of poems, sketches, and dramatic vignettes. It includes such strange lyricisms as "shy girls whose eyes shine reticently upon—the gleaming limbs and asphalt torso of a dreaming nigger" (59). It is therefore not surprising that even so sensitive an analyst of African-American "double consciousness" as W. E. B. DuBois could say that the story "muddles me to the last degree" (171).

Dan Moore walks in a middle-class African-American neighborhood of a northern city, suffused with anticipation of seeing Muriel, an object, but not the only object, of his desire. His impressions are objectified as audial and visual perceptions so vivid as to seem hallucinatory, such that the natural world becomes a springtime dream of universal eroticized animation and prospective union. A frustrated would-be prophet of a transformative salvific consciousness, Moore exhorts himself, as Toomer simultaneously exhorts himself: "Stir the root-life of a withered people. Call them from their houses, and teach them to dream" (59). But the denizens fail to emerge, just as his soul-song falters. Hyperconscious of being an outsider and fleeting worry that the neighborhood might suspect him of trying to break in, Moore must go inside, penetrate the confines of the bourgeoisie, to deliver Muriel from the sheltering that keeps these houses "virginal."

The dialectical clash of apparently contradictory opposites that governs Toomer's pattern of imagery intensifies once Moore enters the house, a domain characterized by spatial arrangements and structural designs that produce and maintain separation and stagnation under the oppressive weight of genteel propriety and conformist values. Persistent references to what is cold, sharp, heavy, and metallic serve to evoke the stasis and rigidity, at once self-protecting and constricting, of the many kinds of enclosure constructed by the judgmental yet timid, up-tight, and bolted-down African-American urban bourgeoisie. Toomer depicts this class as fearful of losing its hard-won place in the social hierarchy and contemptuous of those who have been locked out. He orchestrates a sound imagery of ratchets and the mechanistic "clicks" of things being put and kept in their place. This is meant to conflict, dialectically, with his, and Moore's, belief that spontaneous impulses are desirable because they manifest what is authentically human, free of the constraints of social conventions, sentimental platitudes, and the "technical intellect" of the machine age. Thus, newspaper reading signifies complicity in binding the self to myopic preoccupations and mundane concerns that serve to displace any creative encounter with the reality of idiosyncratic desire. This activity has produced the paradoxically "watery" yet metallic, piercing eyes of the landlady, Mrs. Pribby, and it is therefore indicative that the admonishing rustle of her newspaper from an adjacent room dispels the moment of greatest intensity between Muriel and Moore.

Moore is convinced he is contact with a truth, a reality, that has been lost or at least obscured, and he bitterly excoriates Mrs. Pribby in his mind: "Dare I show you? If I did, delirium would furnish you headlines for a month" (60). Toomer uses Moore's discomfort with and antagonism toward bourgeois domesticity to address the difficulty of creatively organizing hypersensitive attunements amid the emotional and spiritual obtuseness of others. This problem morphs into another: the struggle to maintain a lyrical, life-giving consciousness against the temptation to prosaic pontification and arrogant and pugnacious grandstanding. Bearing a first name that is Hebrew for "he who judges," Moore possesses the self-righteous mean streak of the unheeded prophet. "Get an ax and smash in . . . their faces," he tells himself. Rejecting the bourgeois preoccupation with happiness, he exhorts Muriel to embrace life's fusion of joy and pain, yet he wants to kill "whats weak" in all of them. This motivation is not easily reconciled with his belief that "I am come to a sick world to heal it," but the seeming contradiction is inherent in the gospel tradition. Speaking more out of vainglory or megalomania than divine inspiration, Moore thinks, "I'll show em" (59).

It is not possible to state conclusively in what sense Moore is more. His perceptions might be authentically visionary or the product of an emerging psychosis. He has, or imagines he has, intimations of a "new-world Christ" who will not descend from the sky but emerge from a subterranean system of arboreal roots—Afro-southern rural roots—that lies beneath the urban concrete of the North. He transmutes the mechanical rumble of a streetcar into the fleshy throb of Earth, which he feels is the repressed legacy of his race and the source of the instinctual spontaneity that offers the only possibility of redemption. This arising god is subtly linked to Moore's own erotic arousal, prompted not just by the hint of Muriel's latent "animalism, still unconquered by zoo-restrictions and keeper-taboos" but by his "impulse to direct her" (62). Different desires and impulses converge: an elevating desire to create and to liberate creativity in others; sexual desire, cruder but obstinate to the point of absurdity; and the desire to compel people to transform themselves through contact with chthonic powers. The stubborn incapacity of others to comprehend him has frustrated and tainted his artistic temperament into resentful wrath and apocalyptic fantasy. As the Messiah arises in his imagination, so too "a continent sinks down," requiring "consummate skill to walk upon the waters where huge bubbles burst" (60). Within the terms of this ambiguous confusion of impulses, attitudes, and motives, it is perhaps worth noting that folk tradition has identified the tribe of Dan, one of the 10 lost tribes of Israel, with the origins of the Antichrist, probably because the tribe fell into idolatry according to the biblical Book of Judges. At the least, a measure of disquiet is produced by the pointed contrast between the impaired, watery eyes of other characters and Moore's feeling that his own eyes "could burn clean—burn clean—BURN CLEAN!" (67).

The development of established imagery and the continuation of his stream-of-consciousness technique in the second and concluding section give "Box Seat" a structural symmetry and thematic integrity its sketchiness might otherwise lack. The Lincoln Theater is ironically named for a liberator of those who do not want to be liberated too much or from all forms of bondage. It is repeatedly designated "the house," which is to say, a place where the potential ravaging revelations of art are domesticated or displaced by meretricious and savage forms of distraction. Nothing can be recreated at the bourgeois site of recreation. Wanting to affirm her genteel sensibility, Muriel tries to believe that she is going to enjoy the show, and yet she also registers annoyance at "This damn tame thing" (64).

Toomer's description of the seating is particularly relevant. Its linearity implicitly contrasts with the unruliness of roots that grow, and sustain life, according to their own logic of necessity; the uprightness of the seats reflects the desire for respectability that keeps people like Muriel morally upright. Moore, who cannot "fit in," as both he and Muriel know, must squeeze his body between those already in their places. With regard to the implications of the story's title, a box seat purports to give access, by virtue of proximity, to the scene of the action, the staged events of culture. By virtue of this proximity it might make those actions and events more vivid—something Moore, who wants to vivify the terms of existence, might endorse if it were less passively spectatorial. Yet a seat that functions as a box functions in the same oppressive manner as the chairs in Muriel's house. Such seats click people into place. Even if the Day of Judgment were to occur, Moore observes: "Each one is a bolt that shoots into a slot, and is locked there. The seats are slots. The seats are bolted houses" (64). Moore's beamed thought to Muriel, "Prop me in your brass box" (66), slights her supposed sexual frigidity by punning on "Rock me in your big brass bed," a well-known blues refrain.

Moore sits next to a fat woman, who seems to exude the vitality of rooted earthiness he requires. His growing unruliness and need to dominate others culminate in a grandiose fantasy of revenge, in which he, as the biblical Samson—the blinded hero of the tribe of Dan—pulls down the girders of the theater around them all. Unruliness and the need to dominate seem the order of the day onstage as well. The battle of the dwarfs and its aftermath constitute a sequence of events and a complex of symbols that are the most ambiguous, if not enigmatic, in the story. The dwarfs perform aggression with bulging heads that are compared to boxing gloves. This might constitute a grotesque allegory of instinctual consciousness deformed into passive aggression by middle-class intellectualization. Such a reading would need to be reconciled with the fact that the conflict "pounds the house" with excitement, and with the fact that many folklore traditions associate dwarfs with chthonic power and wisdom. The triumphant dwarf who sings sentimental songs to a feminine chosen few, illuminates them with a flashing pocket mirror, and presents Muriel with a blood-stained emblem of wounded desire may represent Moore's aspirations and pretensions debased and deformed in accord with his diminished sense of self as he sees himself through the reductive eyes of those who judge him crazy. Moore's capacity to bear witness to the coidentity of him and all misfits as incarnations of Christ may well be authentic, but even this permits a diagnosis of desperate megalomania and romanticized abjection.

At this point the story becomes nebulous, petering out just as Moore has found "an enemy—he has long been looking for" (66). Moore and Toomer may both seem insufficiently concentrated, guilty of Muriel's charge, "Starts things he doesn't finish." It is not clear whether Moore drifts away from the fight because he is impassive in the face of aggression, on the model of the Christian redeemer, or because his rapt obliviousness is less otherworldly than psychologically dissociative. The odor of garbage and rancid flowers seems to testify to the insufficiency of his vegetal vision, as the natural world has reached the decay inherent in it. Whether or not Moore has found his roots, he is now but "a green stem that has just shed its flower." He has proved ineffectual: He has not called Muriel into a vivid sensuality that for him constitutes a redemptive sensibility. The girlish eyes of houses "blink out" (69).

Moore leaves the reader as if called elsewhere, as Toomer would forsake literature for a period shortly after the publication of *Cane.* Toomer's dawning conviction that the artist must first integrate his own being in order to be able to produce art capable of healing the ravages of modernity led him to sustained training in techniques developed by F. M. Alexander and by G. I. Gurdjieff for eliminating habitual thought processes and behavior with the objective of completely spontaneous, yet orderly living.

BIBLIOGRAPHY
DuBois, W. E. B. "Sexual Liberation in Cane." In *Cane: Norton Critical Edition,* edited by Darwin T. Turner. New York/London: W. W. Norton, 1988.
Flowers, Sandra Hollin. "Solving the Critical Conundrum of Jean Toomer's 'Box Seat.'" *Studies in Short Fiction* 25, no. 3 (Summer 1988): 301–306.

Schultz, Elizabeth. "Jean Toomer's 'Box Seat': The Possibility for 'Constructive Crisises[sic].' *Black American Literature Forum* 13, no. 1 (Spring 1979): 7–12.

Toomer, Jean. "Box Seat." In *Cane: Norton Critical Edition,* edited by Darwin T. Turner. New York/London: W. W. Norton, 1988.

Turner, Darwin T. "Introduction [to the 1975 Edition of *Cane*]." In *Cane: Norton Critical Edition*, edited by Darwin T. Turner. New York/London: W. W. Norton, 1988.

BOYLE, KAY (1902–1992)

Born in Ohio, but a resident of Europe for 30 years, Kay Boyle was an expatriate writer of the 1930s who won the O. HENRY MEMORIAL AWARD for the short story in 1935 and 1941. Although she wrote novels, poetry, essays, and memoirs, she is known chiefly as a writer of short fiction. Many of her stories appeared in the NEW YORKER before World War II and were subsequently published as *Wedding Day and Other Stories* (1930), *First Lover and Other Stories* (1933), and *The White Horses of Vienna and Other Stories* (1936). The best of these prewar tales, collected in *Thirty Stories* (1946), treat such subjects as love, marriage, and death. Boyle is well known, too, as a writer who drew on war and political confrontation for subject matter. Critically acclaimed are the stories of postwar Germany in *The Smoking Mountain: Stories of Germany during the Occupation* (1951).

Boyle's prose has a lyric intensity that vividly depicts specific scenes and images: Whether she is describing scenes of natural beauty, the atrocities of war, or individual suffering, her powerful evocations remain with the reader.

As an expatriate living in Europe and writing about the Americans she observed there, Boyle has been compared with such writers as HENRY JAMES and EDITH WHARTON, and in fact she shares with them the thematic motifs of innocents abroad. Indeed, as the critic James G. Watson has observed, undergirding a great deal of Boyle's short fiction is the AMERICAN ADAM, the idealist from EDEN poised to fall from innocence. Illustrative of this theme is Boyle's "Kroy Wen," a story originally appearing in the *New Yorker*: The title (*New York* spelled backward) provides the clue to the reversal of roles as well as of myth in the story, in which the Europeans are the innocents, the American the world-weary cynic. Unlike either James or Wharton, moreover, Boyle additionally infused her writing with political concerns and issues with which she was actively and personally concerned. She unflinchingly addresses American racism, for instance, just as she addresses the racism of Hitler.

"The White Horses of Vienna" is probably Boyle's most frequently anthologized story. In Austria in the mid-1930s, the Austrian doctor and his wife live in a white house on a hill above the tensions and political disarray that infect Europe. When the doctor is injured, however, he and his wife have no choice but to let the newly arrived physician—Dr. Heine, a Jew—tend to him. The patient relates a tale of a crippled Lippizaner stallion at the Spanish Riding School of Vienna, clearly symbolic of the destruction of Austrian ideals and clearly equated with the now crippled Austrian doctor. He has fallen just as all Europe will fall—as will Dr. Heine, who endures anti-Semitic insults of the Austrian doctor's wife. At the end of the story, she serves Heine pork and actually sets him on fire. All three characters will pay a terrible price for their sins—whether of commission or omission—against the individual, the community and country, and the human spirit.

BIBLIOGRAPHY

Bell, Elizabeth S. *Kay Boyle: A Study of the Short Fiction.* New York: Twayne, 1992.

Boyle, Kay. *Avalanche.* New York: Simon & Schuster, 1944.

———. *The Crazy Hunter: Three Short Novels.* New York: Harcourt Brace, 1940.

———. *Death of a Man.* New York: Harcourt Brace, 1936.

———. *Fifty Stories.* New York: Doubleday, 1980.

———. *The First Lover and Other Stories.* New York: Cape and Smith, 1933.

———. *A Frenchman Must Die.* New York: Simon & Schuster, 1946.

———. *Generation without Farewell.* New York: Knopf, 1960.

———. *Gentlemen, I Address You Privately.* New York: Smith, 1933.

———. *His Human Majesty.* New York: McGraw Hill, 1949.

———. *Life Being the Best and Other Stories.* Edited by Sandra Whipple Spanier. New York: New Directions, 1988.

———. *Monday Night.* New York: Harcourt Brace, 1938.

———. *My Next Bride*. New York: Harcourt Brace, 1934.

———. *1939*. New York: Simon & Schuster, 1948.

———. *Nothing Ever Breaks Except the Heart*. New York: Doubleday, 1966.

———. *Plagued by the Nightingale*. New York: Cape and Smith, 1931.

———. *Primer for Combat*. New York: Simon & Schuster, 1938.

———. *The Seagull on the Step*. New York: Knopf, 1955.

———. *Short Stories*. Paris: Black Sun Press, 1929.

———. *The Smoking Mountain: Stories of Post War Germany*. New York: McGraw Hill, 1951.

———. *Thirty Stories*. New York: Simon & Schuster, 1946.

———. *Three Short Novels*. Boston: Beacon Press, 1958.

———. *The Underground Woman*. Garden City, N.Y.: Doubleday, 1975.

———. *Wedding Day and Other Stories*. New York: Cape and Smith, 1930.

———. *The White Horses of Vienna and Other Stories*. New York: Harcourt Brace, 1936.

———. *Year before Last*. New York: Smith, 1932.

Boyle, Kay, with Robert McAlmon. *Being Geniuses Together*. New York: Doubleday, 1968.

Elkins, Marilyn. *Metamorphosing the Novel: Kay Boyle's Narrative Inventions*. New York: Peter Lang, 1993.

Elkins, Marilyn, ed. *Critical Essays on Kay Boyle*. New York: G. K. Hall, 1997.

Spanier, Sandra Whipple. *Boyle: Artist and Activist*. Carbondale: Southern Illinois University Press, 1986.

Watson, James G. "The American Short Story, 1900–1945: A Critical History." In *The American Short Story, 1900–1945*, edited by Philip Stevick, 103–146, 116. Boston: Twayne, 1984.

BOYLE, T. CORAGHESSAN (1948–)

T. Coraghessan Boyle was born in Peekskill, New York, in 1948. Although he turned to literature relatively late (Boyle claims he did not read serious fiction until he was 18), he quickly established himself as a literary star once he began writing. After earning a Ph.D. from the Iowa Writer's Workshop and after serving, for a time, as the fiction editor at the *Iowa Review*, Boyle received a series of prestigious awards. In 1977 his stories earned the writer a Coordinating Council of Literary Magazines Award for Fiction as well as a National Endowment for the Arts Fellowship. *Descent of Man* (1977), a collection of Boyle's early short stories, won the St. Lawrence Award for Short Fiction, while sections of his first novel, *Water Music* (1981), received the Aga Kahn Award. *Greasy Lake and Other Stories* (1985), Boyle's second collection of short fiction, was generally well received by critics, and in 1988 Boyle won the prestigious PEN/FAULKNER AWARD in fiction for his novel *World's End* (1987). *The Road to Wellville* (1993) was published to enthusiastic reviews and was subsequently made into a feature film.

Frequently compared to such writers as Thomas Pynchon and DONALD BARTHELME, Boyle creates energetic, erudite, and highly self-conscious fiction marked by an irreverent style of narration, a style befitting the writer's frequently ABSURDist inclinations. "DESCENT OF MAN," for instance, reports the experience of a man whose girlfriend casts him aside in favor of an especially intelligent chimpanzee who translates Nietzsche at the primate research center where she works. Boyle presents a similarly skewed character in "GREASY LAKE." Attempting to explain his unlikely participation in a near-rape, the unnamed narrator of this widely anthologized coming-of-age tale compares his would-be victim to "the toad emerging from the loaf in [Bergman's film] *Virgin Spring*, lipstick smeared on a child: she was already tainted."

Prominent thematic concerns (see THEME) in Boyle's fiction include the impact of history on the present (*World's End*), the misplaced priorities of contemporary society ("Bloodfall," "Greasy Lake"), and the triumph of nature over civilization ("Descent"). Religion, politics, and popular culture are frequent targets of the writer's satire. Boyle's most recent collections include *After the Plague* (2001) and *Tooth and Claw* (2005). He has also published a collection of young-adult stories, *The Human Fly and Other Stories* (2005).

BIBLIOGRAPHY

Bery, Ashok, ed. *'It's a Free Country': Visions of a Hybridity in the Metropolis*. New York: Macmillan–St. Martin's, 2000.

Boyle, T. Coraghessan. *After the Plague*. New York: Viking, 2001.

———. *Budding Prospects: A Pastoral*. New York: Viking, 1984.

———. *The Collected Stories of T. Coraghessan Boyle*. New York: Granta Books, 1993.

———. *Doubletakes: Pairs of Contemporary Short Stories.* Boston: Thomson/Wadsworth, 2004.

———. *Drop City.* New York: Viking, 2003.

———. *A Friend of the Earth.* New York: Viking, 2000.

———. *The Human Fly and Other Stories.* New York: Speak, 2005.

———. *If the River Was Whiskey: Stories.* New York: Viking, 1989.

———. *Tooth and Claw.* New York: Viking, 2005.

———. *Without a Hero.* New York: Viking, 1994.

———, and Kerrie Kvashay-Boyle, eds. *The Inner Circle.* New York: Viking, 2004.

Carnes, Mark. *Novel History: Historians and Novelists Confront America's Past (and Each Other).* New York: Simon & Schuster, 2001.

Crunden, Robert. *A Brief History of American Culture.* New York: Paragon House, 1994.

DeCurtis, Anthony. *Rocking My Life Away: Writing about Music and Other Matters.* Durham, N.C.: Duke University Press, 1998.

Dewey, Joseph. *Novels from Reagan's America: A New Realism.* Gainesville: University Press of Florida, 1999.

Douglas, Christopher. *Reciting America: Culture and Cliché in Contemporary U.S. Fiction.* Urbana-Champagne: University of Illinois Press, 2001.

Hart, James David. *The Oxford Companion to American Literature.* New York: Oxford University Press, 1995.

Hume, Katherine. *American Dream, American Nightmare: Fiction since 1960.* Carbondale: University of Southern Illinois Press, 2000.

Kurth, Peter. "T. Coraghessan Boyle." In *The salon.com Reader's Guide to Contemporary Authors,* edited by Laura Miller and Adam Begley, 56–57. New York: Penguin Books, 2000.

Miller, Laura, with Adam Begley, eds. *The salon.com Reader's Guide to Contemporary Authors.* New York: Penguin Books, 2000.

Utley, Sandye. "List of nearly 100 interviews with T. Coraghessan Boyle. All About Boyle Resource Center" (February 16, 2003). Available online. URL: http://www.tcboyle.net/intrviews.html. Accessed December 4, 2008.

Shannon Zimmerman
University of Georgia

BRADBURY, RAY (RAYMOND DOUGLAS BRADBURY) (1920–)

Born in Waukegan, Illinois (an idealized version of which appears in some of his fiction as Green Town, Illinois), Bradbury established an early reputation as a writer of short fiction with sinister and sensational plots dealing with the freaks, magicians, and exotic creatures of carnivals and circuses and the fiends and monsters of the movies, incorporating themes of FANTASY, horror, and the macabre.

With the publication of *The Martian Chronicles* in 1950, Bradbury also established himself as a premier writer of SCIENCE FICTION, although as previous and later works show, space fantasies are only one of the vehicles he uses for an allegorical expression of humankind's hopes and fears. Space fantasy in which technology plays a major role also allows Bradbury to address one of his major social concerns, that of humans' relationship to machines and to each other in the modern world. In much of his work, Bradbury shows his compassion for people struggling against tragic ironies, often successfully, in the belief that there is a vital, spiritual dimension to the banal world of daily existence. A prolific writer, Bradbury has also published novels, children's stories, and poetry and written plays, screenplays, and television plays.

See also "The VEIDT"; "THERE WILL COME SOFT RAINS."

BIBLIOGRAPHY

Bradbury, Ray. *The Autumn People.* New York: Ballantine, 1965.

———. *The Best of Bradbury.* New York: Bantam, 1976.

———. *Dandelion Wine.* New York: Doubleday, 1957.

———. *Dark Carnival.* Sauk City, Wisc.: Arkham House, 1947.

———. *The Day It Rained Forever.* London: Hart Davis, 1959.

———. *Death Is a Lonely Business.* New York: Knopf, 1985.

———. *Dinosaur Tales.* New York: Bantam, 1983.

———. *Fahrenheit 451.* New York: Ballantine, 1953.

———. *The Golden Apples of the Sun.* New York: Doubleday, 1953.

———. *I Sing the Body Electric!* New York: Knopf, 1969.

———. *The Illustrated Man.* New York: Doubleday, 1951.

———. *The Last Circus, and The Electrocution.* Northridge, Calif.: Lord John Press, 1980.

———. *Long after Midnight.* New York: Knopf, 1976.

———. *The Machineries of Joy.* New York: Simon & Schuster, 1964.

———. *The Martian Chronicles.* New York: Doubleday, 1950.

———. *A Medicine for Melancholy*. New York: Doubleday, 1959.

———. *A Memory for Murder*. New York: Dell, 1984.

———. *The October Country*. New York: Ballantine, 1955.

———. *Selected Stories*. Edited by Anthony Adams. London: Harrap, 1975.

———. *Silver Locusts*. London: Hart Davis, 1951.

———. *The Stories of Ray Bradbury*. New York: Knopf, 1980.

———. *To Sing Strange Songs*. Exeter, England: Wheaton, 1979.

———. *Something Wicked This Way Comes*. New York: Simon & Schuster, 1962.

———. *Tomorrow Midnight*. New York: Ballantine, 1966.

———. *Twice Twenty-Two: The Golden Apples of the Sun. A Medicine for Melancholy*. Garden City, N.Y.: Doubleday, 1966.

———. *The Vintage Bradbury*. New York: Random House, 1965.

Bradbury, Ray, with Robert Bloch. *Bloch and Bradbury*. New York: Tower, 1969.

Indick, Benjamin P. *The Drama of Ray Bradbury*. Baltimore: T-K Graphics, 1977.

Johnson, Wayne L. *Ray Bradbury*. New York: Ungar, 1980.

Mengeling, Marvin E. "Ray Bradbury's *Dandelion Wine*: Themes, Sources, and Style." *English Journal* (October 1971).

Nolan, William F. *The Ray Bradbury Companion*. Detroit: Gale, 1975.

Olander, Joseph D., and Martin H. Greenberg, eds. *Ray Bradbury*. New York: Taplinger, 1980.

Slusser, George Edgar. *The Bradbury Chronicles*. San Bernardino, Calif.: Borgo Press, 1977.

Toupence, William F. *Ray Bradbury and the Poetics of Reverie: Fantasy, Science Fiction, and the Reader*. Ann Arbor, Mich.: UMI Research Press, 1984.

BRAUTIGAN, RICHARD GARY (1935–1984)

Richard Brautigan began writing as a teenager in his hometown of Tacoma, Washington. He spent the first two decades of his life in the Pacific Northwest—primarily in Washington and Oregon—a region featured in much of his fiction. His adult years were divided among Montana's Paradise Valley, Tokyo (his work contains a special affection for Japan and the Japanese), and California. While still in his 20s, he was estranged from his mother and sisters, and his absent father first heard of his existence after Brautigan committed suicide in a secluded house in Bolinas, California, north of San Francisco. He was married for a short time and had one daughter.

Brautigan began publishing poetry in San Francisco in 1955, during the heyday of the BEAT GENERATION. Over a 25-year period, he produced one collection of short stories, *Revenge of the Lawn: Stories 1962–1970* (1971); eight collections of poetry and several single poems; and 10 novels. Genre distinctions often blur in his work, and some of his novels can be read structurally as SHORT STORY CYCLES. Brautigan's greatest critical and popular success occurred in the 1960s, when his first three novels, *A Confederate General from Big Sur* (1964), *Trout Fishing in America* (1967), and *In Watermelon Sugar* (1968), made him a literary hero and a prominent counterculture voice. Brautigan fell from critical favor in the 1970s and 1980s, although he was more popular in Japan, France, and Germany. He has been compared to the French writers Appolinaire, Baudelaire, and Rimbaud, and the Americans ERNEST HEMINGWAY, KURT VONNEGUT, and JOHN BARTH. Brautigan's writing is part of "new fiction" and features a first-person, self-reflexive narrator who examines cultural myths with wry humor and irreverence and determines finally that America is located only in the imagination. His METAFICTIONAL texts comprise startling, extreme METAPHORS and are concerned with death, childhood, loneliness, heterosexual imagery, lost time, identity, and memory. His narrator often takes a naive, whimsical, or surrealistic (see SURREALISM) view of life's small details. Recently scholarly attention to Brautigan's fiction has increased, as his writing is reexamined within its postmodern context.

BIBLIOGRAPHY

Chenetier, Marc C. *Richard Brautigan*. New York: Methuen, 1983.

Foster, Edward Halsey. *Richard Brautigan*. Boston: Twayne, 1983.

Brenda M. Palo
University of North Carolina at Chapel Hill

"BRIDE COMES TO YELLOW SKY, THE" STEPHEN CRANE (1898)

Critics generally agree that, along with "The BLUE HOTEL," "The Bride Comes to Yellow Sky" marks a new maturity in STE-

PHEN CRANE in which history plays a significant role in the story's meaning. A long-held view is that in this story Crane provides a PARODY, a mock-epic treatment of the demise of the Wild West, invaded and tamed by easterners. As parody, it mocks the Wild West expectations of readers, and, as mock-epic, it reverses presumptions about western heroes. Samuel I. Bellman goes one step further and sees the story as a BURLESQUE, a vaudeville scene enacted by clowns (656). The plot is deceptively simple: Marshall JACK POTTER, riding into town not on a stallion but in a train, has told none of the townsfolk, including Scratchy Wilson, his deputy, that he aims to become domesticated and therefore has married the woman who accompanies him home to Yellow Sky. A married marshall is, of course, unthinkable in the CLASSIC western tale: As do Leatherstocking, the Lone Ranger, and their DETECTIVE FICTION descendants, SAM SPADE and PHILIP MARLOWE, heroes should ride off into the sunset after a gun battle—and ride off single. This comic tale upsets every component of the western formula: Not only does the HERO marry, but he marries a rather plain and dutiful middle-aged woman. Both newlyweds seem awkward and out of their element on the train.

Once they arrive in town, the narrator describes Scratchy Wilson to a newcomer—and to the reader: Scratchy is drunk, wielding his pistol and ready for a shoot-up. But Crane clearly has no intention of allowing a classic gun duel. When Scratchy and Jack have their confrontation, we find no blazing guns, no clipped, witty dialogue. To the contrary, Scratchy is so drunk that he drops his pistol; Jack tells him he is no longer carrying one and intends to settle down peaceably with his wife. Scratchy shuffles off down the sandy road. If Scratchy represents the old West and Jack the new, the old has lost its glamour and the new seems regrettably tame. In the words of Chester L. Wolford, implicitly alluding to T. S. Eliot, the Wild West dies not "with a bang, but with a whimper" (30).

BIBLIOGRAPHY

Bellman, Samuel I. "Stephen Crane." In *Reference Guide to Short Fiction,* edited by Noelle Watson, 655–656. Detroit: St. James Press, 1994.

Crane, Stephen. "The Bridge Comes to Yellow Sky." In *University of Virginia Edition of the Works of Stephen Crane,* vol. 5. Edited by Fredson Bowers. Charlottesville: University of Virginia Press, 109–120.

Wolford, Chester L. *Stephen Crane: A Study of the Short Fiction.* Boston: Twayne, 1989.

"BRIGHT AND MORNING STAR" RICHARD WRIGHT (1938)

In 1938, when RICHARD WRIGHT published "Bright and Morning Star" in the magazine *New Masses,* and in 1940, when he added it as the last of the stories in a collection entitled *Uncle Tom's Children,* he did not yet anticipate the fame and critical acclaim he would later garner for his novel *Native Son* (1940) or his autobiography *Black Boy* (1945). In fact, he knew he had written the story to declare that Uncle Tom—the leading and sympathetic, deferential, self-sacrificing slave character in Harriet Beecher Stowe's novel *Uncle Tom's Cabin* (1851)—was dead and that racism in America had become a plague, but he felt the story had failed. He feared he had relied too heavily upon sentiment and had missed his intended aim: to announce that a necessary change would occur in America, that African Americans needed to and would reject the past roles and traditions that helped propagate oppression. Yet critics agreed that he had judged his work too harshly, that the story—and the collection—contained a satisfying unity and did successfully use literature as protest. It displayed what ultimately became Richard Wright's trademark techniques: a use of religion in a way that applied not to the afterlife but to life in this world, a use of allusion to religious songs and hymns (one of which provides the title of this story), a use of black folklore, a use of naturalism, and a use of the tension between nationalism and integrationism. In employing these literary tropes, Wright hoped to convey a sense of creative resistance grounded in a communal spirit and to break the silence surrounding the racism and exploitive economic forces that prevailed in America.

The America of Richard Wright's era becomes vividly portrayed through the tale of Sue, Johnny-Boy, Reva, and Booker as they grapple with life in a South free of slavery but not free of the JIM CROW laws that prescribe how African Americans can live and make legal white advantage over and abuse of black citizens. Johnny-Boy, like the brother now in jail for his participation in such a group—and like Richard Wright, himself—serves as an organizer of a Communist Party group that believes the principles and practices of the party will give all Americans equality and economic parity and will finally topple "a cold white mountain, the white folks and their laws" (224). The members of the group are blacks and whites, including the white Reva, a young woman devoted to Johnny-Boy and whose relationship with Johnny-Boy represents the tension surrounding interracial relationships. Johnny's aging and tired mother, Sue, already grieving because of the loss of her first son, Sug, fears for Johnny-Boy but nonetheless tries to help him. When Johnny discovers a spy has infiltrated their ranks and has told the white authorities about a planned meeting, Johnny-Boy knows he must go back out into the driving rainstorm and warn his compatriots not to attend the meeting.

While Johnny-Boy tries to prevent attendance at that meeting, a group of white men led by a sheriff arrives looking for him, and Sue must face them alone. Years of resentment about mistreatment by the whites suddenly boil over in her, and she resists them by standing up for herself, by taunting them and demanding they leave her property. She suffers a brutal beating for what they label her sass, and after they have left, as she regains some level of consciousness, the white Booker, a new member of the Communist Party group, questions her. Fearful because the sheriff and his men have told her Johnny-Boy will be caught and killed, she mistakenly trusts Booker and gives him the names of the party members who must be warned. Only a few minutes after Booker leaves does Sue realize her mistake when Reva visits and tells her that Booker is the spy, whom Sue labels "'somebody done turned Judas'" (228).

At this point, Sue has an epiphany. She moves from fear to a realization that she must act; she converts fully from Christianity to communism and truly views the party as "another resurrection" (225), the solid hope for poor black people. Battered, bruised, and ailing in every possible way, she forms a plan to beat

Booker to the group of white men hounding her son. She conquers a hostile nature—the pelting rain and the flooding river—to get to her son and to triumph over Booker by hiding a gun underneath a sheet she has taken ostensibly to cover her dying son. After a torturous witnessing of the brutality the men inflict on her son, she finally achieves her goal and shoots Booker before he can reveal the party members' names. As she and her son lie dying, Sue murmurs her final words of defiance: "'Yuh didn't git whut yuh wanted! N yuh ain gonna nevah get it!'" (263). Though she and her son die, they stand as martyrs to the cause, and in their deaths, by refusing to talk, they keep that cause alive. They represent a racial solidarity that matters more than any individual life. As the story ends, Sue gazes up to the sky and feels not the hard rain of most of the setting for this story but a soft, gentle rain that symbolizes both her triumph over nature and her spiritual triumph over oppression. She has found her salvation not in an afterlife but in the here and now. She has become the bright and shining star of a hope for an improved future for her people.

BIBLIOGRAPHY

Brignano, Russell C. *Richard Wright: An Introduction to the Man and His Works.* Pittsburgh: University of Pittsburgh Press, 1970.

Fabre, Michel. *The Unfinished Quest of Richard Wright.* New York: Morrow, 1973.

Giles, James R. "Richard Wright's Successful Failure: A New Look at *Uncle Tom's Children.*" *Phylon* 34, no. 3 (1973): 256–266.

Graves, Neil. "Richard Wright's Unheard Melodies: The Songs of *Uncle Tom's Children.*" *Phylon* 40, no. 3 (1979): 278–290.

Hakutani, Yoshinobu, ed. *Critical Essays on Richard Wright.* Boston: G. K. Hall, 1982.

Jan Mohammed, Abdul R. *The Death-Bound-Subject: Richard Wright's Archeology of Death.* Durham, N.C.: Duke University Press, 2005.

Kinnamon, Keneth. *The Emergence of Richard Wright.* Urbana: University of Illinois Press, 1986.

Maxwell, William J. "'Is It True What They Say about Dixie?': Richard Wright, Zora Neale Hurston, and Rural/Urban Exchange in Modern African-American Literature." In *Knowing Your Place: Rural Identity and Cul-*

tural Hierarchy, edited by Barbara Ching and Gerald W. Creed, 71–104. New York: Routledge, 1997.

Reed, Brian D. "Wright Turns the Bible Left: Rewriting the Christian Parable in *Uncle Tom's Children.*" *Xavier Review* 24, no. 2 (2004): 56–65.

"Richard Wright: A Webpage." Available online. URL: home.gwu.edu/~cuff/wright/. Accessed January 13, 2009.

Wright, Richard. "Bright and Morning Star." In *Uncle Tom's Children.* New York: HarperPerennial, 1993.

Yarborough, Richard. "Introduction." In *Uncle Tom's Children.* New York: HarperPerennial, 1993, ix–xxix.

Patricia J. Sehulster
State University of New York
Westchester Community College

BROKEBACK MOUNTAIN Annie Proulx (1997, 1999)

"It is a love story," remarks Annie Proulx in an interview with Sandy Cohen, "an old, old story." She has also said that she believes "the country is hungry for this story." After appearing in the *New Yorker* on October 13, 1997, and receiving an O. Henry Award the following year, Proulx's novella *Brokeback Mountain* became the final tale in her 1999 *Close Range: Wyoming Stories* and has repeatedly been dubbed the finest in the collection. It is a story of love between two cowboys who meet on Brokeback Mountain while working as sheepherders. It took Proulx twice the time to write it that she normally allows for a novel, "because I had to imagine my way into the minds of two uneducated, rough-spoken, uninformed young men, and that takes some doing if you happen to be an elderly female person" (Cohen). Conceivably, however, the story owes its success to her gender: As the author and critic David Leavitt notes, "Perhaps it takes a woman to create a tale in which two men experience sex and love as a single thunderbolt, welding them together for life; certainly Proulx's story is a far cry from such canonical gay novels as Edmund White's *The Farewell Symphony* or Allan Hollinghurst's *The Swimming Pool Library,* which poeticize urban promiscuity and sexual adventuring." The success of the story led to the award-winning feature-length film of the same title, starring Heath Ledger as Ennis Del Mar and Jake Gyllenhaal as Jack Twist.

The story opens in 1983 with the middle-aged Ennis, who has a married daughter and is between jobs. As he awakens, he recalls his dream about Jack Twist and "the old, cold time on the mountain when they owned the world and nothing seemed wrong" (253). This Edenic rendering of the past contrasts directly to the cold, roaring windy day of the present and serves to "rewarm" Ennis. The story then reverts to 1963, the year the two 20-year-olds met each other and lived one summer of bliss on Brokeback Mountain before succumbing to the conventional world of marriage, wives, and children.

Their time on Brokeback Mountain, when they engage in a romantic sexual affair that they believe is invisible to the outside world, lasts for about seven pages; the remaining 22 pages invoke the increased misery and frustration resulting from Ennis's inability to agree to live with Jack. Brokeback Mountain thus looms in their imaginations as a metaphor for long-ago youthful happiness. These two rough-mannered high school dropouts, along with "the dogs, horses, and mules, a thousand ewes and their lambs," enter "the great flowery meadows and the coursing, endless wind of the mountain" (256). For a time, lost in nature, they confide in each other, respect each other's opinions, sing, care for the animals, and make love, Ennis telling Jack, "I ain't no queer" and Jack agreeing, "Me neither. A one-shot thing. Nobody's business but ours" (260). The outside world is already against them, however, in the form of Joe Aguirre, their employer, who views their sexual antics through his binoculars and will refuse to rehire Jack when he reapplies the following year. Homophobic men will destroy all chances for Ennis and Jack to share a life together.

Off the mountain at the end of the summer, the two pretend that their parting means nothing, but Ennis actually vomits, feeling "about as bad as he ever had" as he drives off to begin married life with Alma Beers. After bearing two children, she persuades him to move into town away from the ranch work and horses that he loves. After four years, he is surprised by a letter from Jack—also married with a child—who proposes a visit. When Ennis sees Jack stepping out of his truck, a "hot jolt scalded" him and the two merge in a passionate embrace, unaware that Ennis's wife is watching them. This renewal of their affair results in Jack's proposal that if they could have "a little ranch together, little cow and calf operation, your horses, it'd be some sweet life" (268). As Leavitt notes, "What both men want, it becomes clear, is what Ennis is afraid to let them have: the steadiness of each other's companionship."

Indeed, Ennis does not want to be "like them boys you see around sometimes. And I don't want a be dead" (268). Ennis's father had purposely taken his nine-year-old son to see the bloody corpse of a homosexual who had been dragged, beaten with a tire iron, and castrated before he died. Likewise, Jack had been marked by his own father, who urinated on him to punish him for mild incontinence; during the act, Jack noticed that he was "different" in that he was circumcised and his father was not. Both Ennis and Jack are products of homophobic fathers, but whereas those taboos are firmly ingrained in Ennis, who limits his liaisons with Jack to once or twice a year, Jack finally, in frustration with Ennis's refusal to join him in their version of the AMERICAN DREAM, takes another lover and ends his life in a male American nightmare: As was the murdered homosexual Ennis's father had forced him to view, Jack, too, is beaten to a bloody pulp with a tire iron. When Ennis learns the news, "The huge sadness of the northern plains rolled down on him" (278).

Too late, Ennis visits the ranch owned by Jack's parents, the ranch he and Jack might have had to themselves had Ennis not been so stubborn. He realizes, however, that, like Alma and Jack's wife, Lureen, Jack's father is aware of his and Jack's homosexuality. In Jack's boyhood room, Ennis finds that Jack had fitted one of Ennis's old shirts inside one of his own and kept them together on a hanger. Ennis takes the shirts, buys a 30-cent postcard of Brokeback Mountain, and hangs them together in his trailer. As Jack had said to him at their last meeting, "We could a had a good life together, a fuckin real good life. You wouldn't do it, Ennis, so what we got now is Brokeback Mountain. Everything built on that. It's all we got, boy, fuckin all" (276). And Ennis must survive with the knowledge of Jack's early demise, his own pent-up sexuality, and the belief that "if you can't fix it you've got to stand it" (283).

Annie Proulx sees *Brokeback Mountain* as a "reminder that sometimes love comes along that is strong and permanent, and that it can happen to anyone" (Cohen). When Proulx's story was transformed into a feature-length film, the script was written by LARRY MCMURTRY and Diana Ossana, and it garnered three Academy Awards in 2005: Best Director, Best Adapted Screenplay, and Best Original Score.

BIBLIOGRAPHY

Cohen, Sandy. "Annie Proulx Tells the Story behind 'Brokeback Mountain.'" *Entertainment News,* 17–19 December 2005.

D'Souza, Irene. "Review of *Close Range,* by Annie Proulx." *Horizons* 14, no. 1 (Summer 2000): 32.

Edelstein, David. "Lasso Me Tender: Ang Lee's 'Brokeback Mountain': and a Season of Gay Cinema." *Slate Magazine* (December 8, 2005). Available online. URL: http://www.slate.com/id/2131264/. Accessed May 6, 2009.

Kirn, Walter. "True West." *New York Magazine,* 24 May 1999, p. 69.

Leavitt, David. "Men in Love: Is 'Brokeback Mountain' A Gay Film?" *Slate Magazine* (December 8, 2005). Available online. URL: http://www.slate.com/id/2131865/. Accessed May 6, 2009.

Lehmann-Haupt, Christopher. "Lechery and Loneliness in the Hazardous West." *New York Times,* 12 May 1999, p. E8.

Proulx, Annie. *Brokeback Mountain.* In *Close Range: Wyoming Stories.* New York: Scribner, 1999.

Rood, Karen L. *Understanding Annie Proulx.* Aiken: University of South Carolina Press, 2001.

BROTHER   Main CHARACTER of JAMES BALDWIN's "Sonny's Blues," whose life is imperfectly perceived by his older brother, who is also the first-person narrator. Brother gets into trouble because of hard times at home; eventually he is caught with drugs and completes a jail sentence. The narrator, who has had his own problems and has worked hard to carve out his own career as a teacher, realizes he has not listened to his brother. Ironically, Brother becomes teacher to the narrator when he invites him to a nightclub to listen to him play blues music. The narrator finally understands not only the racism that has shaped both their lives but the brotherly love that can strengthen them.

BROWN, CHARLES BROCKDEN (1771–1810)

Born in Philadelphia to a prosperous Quaker family, Brown attended Friend's Latin School and then studied law from 1787 to 1793, although he abandoned the profession without ever practicing. Brown fled Philadelphia in 1793 during the yellow fever epidemic. The fifth installment of his serial fiction, "The Man at Home," recounts the experience of a family suffering during the epidemic. In the same year Brown encountered in New York members of the Friendly Club, who were committed to furthering a distinctly American literature and who included William Dunlop, Brown's biographer. In 1798 Brown began publishing short essays and fragments in a number of periodicals, including the Philadelphia *Weekly Magazine.*

Traditional critical wisdom holds Brown to be the first American author to attempt to make a living from his writing, and critical appraisals of his art vary widely, although none denies his historical importance. He is known primarily for his novels, gothic romances that show an obvious debt to Samuel Richardson, William Godwin, and Anne Radcliffe. Critics have gone so far as to insist that all his work aside from his novels is outside the domain of serious study of American literature.

But such a critical stance unnecessarily hinders a full evaluation of Brown's work. The shorter pieces and essays demand attention in their own right, in particular "Somnambulism," a proto–detective story with a sleepwalking protagonist; "Lesson on Concealment"; and "The Man at Home." Some of his stories—"Thessalonica," for example—are characterized by didactic historical writing that tends to put off the modern reader and that too often obscures a deeper underlying sociological awareness. Scott and Keats both gladly read Brown, and Shelley lauded him, but at times Brown's work seems overwhelmed by a sense of longing and despair that he attempts to transpose onto an American landscape. An unhappy tension often exists between the European forms and the American setting. Although Brown advocated high critical standards for American fiction, his own work seems overly indebted to European influences, and his language sometimes seems artificially or hastily conceived. These problems aside, his work is psychologically probing and gives loose rein to a deep curiosity about the forces that prompt human action, especially those pathologies that tend to provoke evil or destroy human happiness.

Brown produced most of his fiction over five years and then turned his interest to publishing journals, among them the *Literary Magazine and American Register* and the *American Register, or General Repository of History Politics, and Science.* He also edited the *Monthly Magazine and American Review.* Brown's work, flawed though it is, shows concern for the emerging state of American letters, and his fascination with the darker corners of the human psyche opened the way for later American writers such as NATHANIEL HAWTHORNE and EDGAR ALLAN POE.

BIBLIOGRAPHY

Ringe, Donald A. *Charles Brockden Brown.* New York: Macmillan, 1991.

Rosenthal, Bernard, ed. *Critical Essays on Charles Brockden Brown.* Boston: G. K. Hall, 1981.

Warfel, Harry R., ed. *The Rhapsodist and Other Uncollected Writings by Charles Brockden Brown.* New York: Scholars' Facsimiles & Reprints, 1943.

Weber, Alfred, ed. *Somnambulism and Other Stories.* New York: Peter Lang, 1987.

Cornelius W. Browne
Ohio University

BROWNE, CHARLES FARRAR   See WARD, ARTEMUS.

BUCK, PEARL S. (1892–1973)

Pearl Sydenstricker Buck, the daughter of American missionaries to China, was born in West Virginia and educated in Shanghai, China, until she returned to the United States at age 17 to attend Randolph-Macon Woman's College. Widely known as a prolific novelist who wrote fiction based on her experiences while living in China, Buck wrote her best-known novel, *The Good Earth,* in 1931. She received the Pulitzer Prize in 1932, the William Dean Howells Medal for Distinguished Fiction in 1935, and the Nobel Prize in literature in 1938. Despite her fame as a novelist, with more than

60 books to her credit, Pearl Buck was a prolific writer of short stories and NOVELLAS. Indeed, one could argue that her first impulse was to write shorter rather than novel-length works, for evidence exists that she—as were numerous other writers of her time—was under pressure from publishers to produce longer work: Her first story, "A Chinese Woman Speaks," published in *Asia* magazine in 1925, became her first book, *East Wind: West Wind* (1930), when combined with another short story. It told the tale of a Chinese husband who wishes his wife to unbind her feet and become his equal, and of the wife's brother, who shocks the family by marrying an American woman who in due course gives birth to a mixed-race child. Even her next novel, *The Good Earth,* began as a short story, published in *Asia* magazine in 1928 and entitled "The Revolutionist."

Buck published numerous short story collections in her lifetime, always preferring CHARACTER and PLOT—the simple lines of a story she believed her reader wanted—to the literary techniques of MODERNISM. In her fiction as well as her numerous nonfiction essays and articles, she wrote passionately about East-West issues as well as about black-white relations in the United States. She significantly influenced the work of such writers as TILLIE OLSEN. In 1949, with her husband, Richard Walsh, Buck established Friendship House for orphans from various Asian countries. During the VIETNAM WAR, the house grew to include mixed-race, or Amerasian, children. After her death it became the Pearl Buck Foundation.

BIBLIOGRAPHY

Buck, Pearl. *East Wind: West Wind*. New York: John Day, 1930.
———. *Far and Near: Stories of Japan, China and America*. New York: John Day, 1947.
———. *The First Wife and Other Stories*. New York: John Day, 1933.
———. *Fourteen Stories*. New York: John Day, 1961.
———. *Stories of China*. New York: John Day, 1964.
———. *The Story of Dragon Seed: Twenty-Seven Stories*. New York: John Day, 1944.
———. *Today and Forever: Stories of China*. New York: John Day, 1941.

BUKOWSKI, CHARLES (1920–1994)

A counterculture writer of novels and short stories, Bukowski depicts the "lower end" of America in his work. His prose style is simple and straightforward, although he experiments with third- and first-person POINTS OF VIEW and a varying use of capital letters: In some stories no proper nouns are capitalized, and in others every letter of dialogue is in capital letters. The language he uses is blunt and often crude, and much of his work is infused with dark humor.

Bukowski's work was published primarily by small underground presses and LITTLE MAGAZINES. He wrote a weekly column, "Notes of a Dirty Old Man," for the underground newspaper *Open City,* a collection of which was published in 1973. His first collection of short stories, entitled *Erections, Ejaculations, Exhibitionists and General Tales of Ordinary Madness,* was published in 1972.

BIBLIOGRAPHY

Bukowski, Charles. *Bring Me Your Love*. Santa Barbara, Calif.: Black Sparrow Press, 1983.
———. *Erections, Ejaculations, Exhibitionists and General Tales of Ordinary Madness*. San Francisco: City Lights, 1972: abridged edition, as *Life and Death in the Charity Ward,* London: London Magazine Editions, 1974; selections, edited by Gail Chiarello, as *Tales of Ordinary Madness* and *The Most Beautiful Woman in Town and Other Stories*. San Francisco: City Lights, 2 vols., 1983.
———. *Hot Water Music*. Santa Barbara, Calif.: Black Sparrow Press, 1983.
———. *Notes of a Dirty Old Man*. North Hollywood, Calif.: Essex House, 1969.
———. *South of No North*. Los Angeles: Black Sparrow Press, 1973.
———. *There's No Business*. Santa Barbara, Calif.: Black Sparrow Press, 1984.
"Charles Bukowski Issue." *Review of Contemporary Fiction* (Fall 1985).
Fox, Hugh. *Charles Bukowski: A Biographical Study*. Somerville, Mass.: Abyss, 1968.
Sherman, Jory. *Bukowski: Friendship, Fame, and Bestial Myth*. Augusta, Ga.: Blue Horse Press, 1982.

BULOSAN, CARLOS (1911–1956)

Carlos Bulosan was born in Binanlon, the Philippines, to poor and illiterate parents. His father was a farmer;

his mother sold dried fish in the local market. At the age of 17 he left the Philippines permanently for the United States, although he never became a U.S. citizen.

Bulosan's most popular work remains his autobiographical memoir, *America Is in the Heart* (1946). Short stories published during his lifetime, however, appeared in the NEW YORKER, *Harper's Bazaar,* SATURDAY EVENING POST, *Town and Country,* the *Arizona Quarterly,* and *New Masses.* His short story collection, *The Laughter of My Father* (1944), which he wrote in 12 days, was also a best seller during the year it appeared and contributed significantly to his international reputation. Three posthumous works collected additional stories: *On Becoming Filipino* (1975), *The Philippines Is in the Heart* (1978), and *The Power of Money and Other Stories* (1990). Bulosan also wrote the novel *The Cry and the Dedication* (published posthumously in 1995), three books of poetry, and numerous essays.

At least three THEMES are crucial to Bulosan's fiction: first, the immigrant's unattainable longing to find acceptance in America as an American; second, the grievous plight of the poor and disenfranchised around the world and in America itself; and third, the necessity of learning from all life experiences, especially tragic, violent, and horrifying ones. Bulosan's writing is characterized by a compelling sense of intimacy and immediacy, so that all he wrote feels autobiographical even when it is not.

Bulosan's first 14 years in the United States were, in his own words, "violent years of unemployment, prolonged illnesses and heart-rending labor union work on the farms of California" (Kunitz 144). And although he nearly died of tuberculosis at the age of 31, he gradually recovered to become a famous writer and editor. Most of his writing was squeezed into what he called "two restless years" between 1944 and 1946; the final 10 years of his life constituted "a decline into poverty, alcohol, loneliness, and obscurity" (Kim 45)—at least in part because of changing political winds that left Filipino-Americans somewhat out of favor after World War II. Bulosan died in Seattle of pneumonia (which probably resulted in part from his earlier struggles against tuberculosis and cancer) at the age of 42.

BIBLIOGRAPHY

Bulosan, Carlos. *The Laughter of My Father.* London: Michael Joseph, 1945.

———. *On Becoming Filipino: Selected Writings of Carlos Bulosan.* Philadelphia: Temple University Press, 1995.

———. *The Philippines Is in the Heart: A Collection of Stories.* Quezon City: New Day, 1978.

———. *The Power of Money and Other Stories.* Manila: Kalikasan Press, 1990.

Kim, Elaine. *Asian American Literature: An Introduction to the Writings and Their Social Context.* Philadelphia: Temple University Press, 1982, 43–57.

Kunitz, Stanley, ed. *Twentieth Century Authors.* New York: Wilson, 1955, 144–145.

Leon, Ferdinand M. de. "The Legacy of Carlos Bulosan." (September 13, 2002). Available online. URL: http://community.seattletimes.nwsource.com/archive/?date=19990808&slug=2976103. Accessed May 6, 2009.

San Juan, E., Jr. "Introduction." In *On Becoming Filipino: Selected Writings of Carlos Bulosan.* Philadelphia: Temple University Press, 1995.

University of Singapore Society. *The Filipino Short Story.* Singapore: 1980.

Keith Lawrence
Brigham Young University

BURLESQUE A form of COMEDY that contrives to arouse amusement rather than contempt by the use of distortion, exaggeration, and imitation. The essence of burlesque is the apparent discrepancy between the subject matter and the manner of presentation, in that a style ordinarily serious may be used for a nonserious subject, or vice versa.

BUSCH, FREDERICK (1941–2006) Frederick Busch was a humanist with an unwavering focus on the family. He was not alone in this late 20th-century emphasis on the most consistent source of consolation many people know: His THEME has been pursued by such contemporaries as RAYMOND CARVER, GRACE PALEY, PETER TAYLOR, and JOHN UPDIKE. Busch celebrated the tenaciousness with which his characters grapple with and relate to blood kin as a bulwark against the anxiety and fear of death that pervade nearly all his stories, collected in *Breathing Trouble* (1973), *Domestic Particulars* (1976),

Hardwater Country (1979), and Too Late American Boyhood Blues (1984). His last two collections of stories are Don't Tell Anyone (2000) and Rescue Missions (2006). He won the PEN/MALAMUD Award for Excellence in Short Fiction in 1991 and the Lifetime Achievement Award from the American Academy of Arts and Letters in 2001.

Few writers attempt to narrate from as many POINTS OF VIEW—male as well as female, adult's as well as child's. Busch's imagistic and carefully detailed depictions are equally catholic, whether of countryside or city. Natural SETTINGS can provide salvation, as in "Trail of Possible Bones" (Domestic Particulars), or evoke fear, as in "What You Might as Well Call Love" (Hardwater Country). Busch conveys his characters' actions in meticulous detail, from hooking up a television to performing pediatric duties.

Domestic Particulars contains 13 linked stories that follow the life of one New York City family from 1919 to 1976, with Clair Miller and her son, Harry, as focal characters. Busch describes Brooklyn, the Upper West Side, and Greenwich Village with extraordinary clarity in these stories, which attempt to define the essence of family both literally and figuratively. After teaching at Colgate University from 1966 to 2003, Frederick Busch, Edgar W. B. Fairchild Professor of Literature, Emeritus, died on February 23, 2006, of a heart attack, at the age of 64.

BIBLIOGRAPHY

Busch, Frederick. Breathing Trouble and Other Stories. London: Calder and Boyars, 1974.
———. Domestic Particulars: A Family Chronicle. New York: New Directions, 1976.
———. Don't Tell Anyone. New York: W. W. Norton, 2000.
———. Hardwater Country. New York: Knopf, 1979.
———. Invisible Mending. Boston: Godine, 1984.
———. I Wanted a Year without Fall. London: Calder and Boyars, 1971.
———. Manual Labor. New York: New Directions, 1974.
———. A Memory of War. New York: W. W. Norton, 2003.
———. The Mutual Friend. New York: Harper & Row, 1978.
———. The Night Inspector. New York: Harmony Books, 1999.
———. North. New York: W. W. Norton, 2005.
———. Take This Man. New York: Farrar, Straus & Giroux, 1981.
———. Too Late American Boyhood Blues. Boston: Godine, 1984.
———. Rescue Missions. New York: W. W. Norton, 2006.
———. Sometimes I Live in the Country. Boston: Godine, 1986.

"BY THE WATERS OF BABYLON" STEPHEN VINCENT BENÉT (1937) STEPHEN VINCENT BENÉT's "By the Waters of Babylon," first published in 1937, is a prescient science fiction story set in an indeterminate, postapocalyptic era, not uncommon for this genre; this lack of detailed setting suggests an unstable physical and social environment. Only gradually do we learn some detail about the setting and get a sense of the time of the story. The narrative concerns a boy, the son of a priest who will become a priest himself, growing into manhood. The use of titles for places (Dead Places, Forest People) rather than names suggests that his is a primitive culture. At times the narrator finds himself having to make a decision that challenges the "law" (as he understands it); he tells us that he "is a priest and the son of a priest," as though this mantra justifies his mission and his title. This kind of naming and establishing of position suggests a tribal culture.

Benét allows the narrator to tell us what he sees and thinks; he does not supply an authorial voice to explain what has happened, or where in time or place the story is set. This is most effective; science fiction that has to explain itself, or feels the need to explain the science behind its gadgetry or story, often betrays its GENRE. The narrator simply describes his feelings and observations as he begins his quest to become a man and a priest, assuming that role for his band of people.

In the tradition of tribal tales, he has a vision; his father interprets his vision, and the son must complete his quest before he can return to the tribe. This all seems indicative of a generic tribal or native tale, but Benét plants clues to indicate this story might be set in the future, not in the past.

The quest itself sends the boy to the east, where he is forbidden to go, and to the City of the Gods, which is also forbidden. We come across rather typical symbolic devices here: He must cross the river that divides one land from another (or, one state of consciousness from another); he realizes that many of the legends he has heard are not true (tangible experience replaces myth); he finds hieroglyphs he can only partly read (the past trying to communicate with the future; truth is written as a text only a few can read). In his capacity as a priest, he will have to "read" the signs as they appear. Benét allows this; in a kind of typography (which also supports the primitive setting), the narrator reads the will of God through nature; also, nature becomes personified (the river grips, as with hands), demonstrating a culture connected to the world in which nature is a living, active force in lives.

We expect the story to reveal where the narrator is, that is, we sense, and begin to look for, the trick. This is a convention of the genre, and as we read, we get the sense that Benét is telegraphing the end of the story. It is hard not to feel as though, in the story's final paragraph, we will learn which city he has stumbled into, and exactly the condition of the nuclear apocalypse that has reduced civilization to rubble (and set the scene for the rise of a new civilization). In a sense, this does happen; this adherence to the convention works against any rising tension in the story, especially for modern readers. We have seen this often enough to know the trick.

However, Benét does not allow the trick to outrun the narrative. We do learn the secret of the location—New York—and we can figure out some details, but Benét is not interested in the trick as much as he is in his message: that a high civilization has destroyed itself; that the gods were men, just as the narrator is a man; and finally that "we must rebuild." The message is apparent (if a little heavy-handed) to modern readers, but only because it has become well worn. If we can read through the conventions to which Benét adheres, observe the fine descriptive passages, and recognize the less apparent tensions in the text—the boy's entering manhood, his struggle to determine whether he should observe the law, whether the priests are above the law—the story offers more subtle grounds for discussion than the conventional postapocalyptic tale.

BIBLIOGRAPHY

Benét, Stephen Vincent. "By the Waters of Babylon." In *The Devil and Daniel Webster and Other Writings,* edited by Townsend Ludington. New York: Penguin, 1999.

Izzo, David Garrett, and Lincoln Kankle, eds. *Stephen Vincent Benét: Essays on His Life and Work.* Jefferson, N.C.: McFarland, 2002.

Stroud, Perry Edmund. *Stephen Vincent Benét.* Boston: Twayne, 1962.

Bill R. Scalia
St. Mary's University, Baltimore

C

CABLE, GEORGE WASHINGTON (1844–1925)

The American novelist and short story writer who probably gave Americans their most memorable view of 19th-century Louisiana life in all its multiculturalism and diversity, particularly New Orleans Creole life. Born in New Orleans of a New England Puritan background on his mother's side and of a Virginia slaveholding family of German descent on his father's side, Cable had to leave school at age 14 when his father died. He worked in the customhouse, fought with the Fourth Mississippi Cavalry during the CIVIL WAR, contracted malaria, and began his writing career as a columnist for the *New Orleans Picayune*. Cable achieved national attention with his publication of "'Sieur George" in SCRIBNER's *Monthly* in 1873. Within the next three years *Scribner's* published the stories that would gain Cable a national reputation as a LOCAL COLOR realist (see REALISM).

Those stories—"Belles Demoiselles Plantation," "'Tite Poulette," "Madame Delicieuse," "Jean-ah Poquelin," and others—were collected in *Old Creole Days* in 1879. Cable was adept at conveying the language, speech patterns, and character of the region. Particularly notable was "Jean-ah Poquelin," composed during the final period of RECONSTRUCTION in the South: Cable set the story in the period after the Louisiana Purchase in 1803, dramatizing the conflict between the old French colonial civilization, represented by Poquelin, and the new American order in New Orleans. A parallel could be seen then, and may be seen now, between the older French and the current Yankee intrusion. Soon afterward Cable wrote two novels, *The Grandissimes* in 1880 and *Madame Delphine* in 1881, which examine pre–Civil War New Orleans life, with particular attention to black-white relations and the unfair treatment of African Americans.

Successful enough to become a full-time writer, Cable wrote essays and novels more and more sympathetic to the situation of exploited blacks and to reform of the prison system. Indeed, the growing resentment of his treatment of these issues led to his decision to move in 1885 to Northampton, Massachusetts, where he became friendly with MARK TWAIN and continued to urge reform in both his writing and his speeches. Today he is viewed as a thoughtful writer who depicted the moral dimensions of interethnic relations, imaginatively understood the impact of the past on the present, and displayed a sensitivity to the exotic aspects of his region. Cable helped prepare the ground for WILLIAM FAULKNER, EUDORA WELTY, FLANNERY O'CONNOR, and other modern southern writers.

BIBLIOGRAPHY

Bikle, Lucy Leffingwell C(able). *George W. Cable: His Life and Letters.* New York: Scribner, 1928.

Butcher, Philip. *George W. Cable.* New York: Twayne, 1962.

Cable, George Washington. *Dr. Sevier.* Boston: Ticknor and Company, 1884. Reprint, New York: Scribner, 1974.

———. *The Grandissimes.* New York: Charles Scribner's Sons, 1880. Rev. ed. 1883. Reprint, Athens, Ga.: University of Georgia Press, 1988.

————. *John March, Southerner.* New York: Scribner, 1894. Reprint, New York: Garrett Press, 1970.

————. *Madame Delphine.* New York: Scribner, 1881. Reprint, St. Claire's Shores, Mich.: Scholarly Press, 1970.

————. *The Negro Question.* Edited by Arlin Turner. New York: Norton, 1968.

————. *Old Creole Days.* New York: Scribner, 1879. *Old Creole Days: Stories of Creole Life.* Gretna, La.: Pelican, 1991.

Payne, James Robert. "George Washington Cable's 'My Politics': Context and Revision of a Southern Memoir." In *Multicultural Autobiography: American Lives,* edited by James Robert Payne. Knoxville: University of Tennessee Press, 1992.

Petry, Alice Hall. *A Genius in His Way: The Art of Cable's "Old Creole Days."* Rutherford, N.J.: Fairleigh Dickinson University Press, 1988.

Turner, Arlin. *George W. Cable: A Biography.* Baton Rouge: Louisiana State University Press, 1956.

————, ed. *Critical Essays on George W. Cable.* Boston: G. K. Hall, 1980.

CAIN, JAMES M. (JAMES MALLAHAN CAIN) (1892–1977)

Born in Annapolis, Maryland, James M. Cain received B.A. and M.A. degrees from Washington College; served with the American Expeditionary Force in France during WORLD WAR I; worked as a reporter for the *Baltimore American,* the *Baltimore Sun,* and the *New York World;* and wrote pieces for the *American Mercury* and the NEW YORKER. During the GREAT DEPRESSION, Cain moved to California, where he worked briefly for Paramount movie studios before becoming the author of popular murder mysteries and "tough-guy" novels, including *The Postman Always Rings Twice* (1934) and *Double Indemnity* (1943), both of which were made into successful films. Cain also wrote scores of short stories, 17 of which were published in such magazines as the *American Mercury, Redbook, ESQUIRE,* and *LADIES' HOME JOURNAL,* of those nine are collected, along with essays and sketches, in *The Baby in the Icebox,* published in 1981.

Two of Cain's stories, "Pastorale" (1928) and "The Baby in the Icebox," attracted considerable critical and popular attention. Both use a HARD-BOILED FICTION–style first-person narrator; Cain was an admirer of RING LARDNER and consciously imitated his narrative style when writing "Icebox." H. L. Mencken, editor of the *American Mercury,* praised the story and published it in 1933, and in that same year it was made into a film, entitled *She Made Her Bed.*

As do RAYMOND CHANDLER and DASHIELL HAMMETT, Cain belongs to the "tough-guy" tradition, and as they do, Cain writes about the working classes of California and the seamier side of life, the other side of the mythic "golden land." A number of critics have pointed out the value of these writers—popular entertainers all—who not only depict the violence always close to the surface in American life, but also shed light on the urgent problems of social history. In short, they demonstrate one way to understand society.

As did the naturalists (see NATURALISM), Cain made full use of his familiarity with specific areas of knowledge such as the law and even of the intricacies of the restaurant business, as in "Postman" and "Icebox," among others. Along with Hammett and Chandler, Cain used California to his advantage: While Chandler focused on Los Angeles and Hammett on San Francisco, Cain set his stories in Glendale, a Los Angeles suburb. "The Baby in the Icebox" realistically describes the garish stretches of highway dotted with gas stations that have become endemic to the entire country.

As did his peers, Cain writes in the tradition of PROLETARIAN LITERATURE. He is less interested in social criticism, however, than in an examination of his characters themselves, who, as David Madden notes, "add up to an impressive gallery of American public types" (Madden 164). The genre's concern with violence, love, and money not only produces a perspective of the 1930s and 1940s, but also "provides insights into the AMERICAN DREAM–turned–nightmare and into the all-American boy–turned–tough guy" (Madden 165).

BIBLIOGRAPHY

Cain, James M. *The Baby in the Icebox and Other Short Fiction.* Edited by Roy Hoopes. New York: Holt, Rinehart & Winston, 1981.

————. *The Butterfly.* New York: Alfred A. Knopf, 1947.

————. *Cain × 3: Three Novels.* Alfred A. Knopf, 1969.

————. *Career in C Major.* New York: Alfred A. Knopf, 1943.

———. *Double Indemnity.* New York: Alfred A. Knopf, 1943.

———. *The Embezzler.* New York: Alfred A. Knopf, 1943.

———. *Galatea.* New York: Knopf, 1953.

———. *The Government.* New York: Knopf, 1930.

———. *Jealous Woman.* New York: Avon Book, 1950.

———. *Love's Lovely Counterfeit.* New York: Knopf, 1942.

———. *The Magician's Wife.* New York: Dial Press, 1965.

———. *Mignon.* New York: Dial Press, 1965.

———. *Mildred Pierce.* New York: Knopf, 1941.

———. *The Moth.* New York: Knopf, 1948.

———. *Past All Dishonor.* New York: Knopf, 1946.

———. *The Postman Always Rings Twice.* New York: Knopf, 1934.

———. *The Root of His Evil.* New York: Avon Book, 1951.

———. *Serenade.* New York: Knopf, 1937.

———. *Sinful Woman.* New York: Avon Editions, Inc., 1947.

———. *Three of a Kind.* New York: Knopf, 1943.

Madden, David. *James M. Cain.* New York: Twayne, 1970.

CALDWELL, ERSKINE (ERSKINE PRESTON CALDWELL) (1903–1987)

After a series of menial jobs and a stint as a professional football player, Caldwell began his writing career around 1930. Judging by the many millions of copies of his novels and short story collections sold in paperback editions in several countries, within 20 years, Caldwell was probably the most popular writer of fiction in the world. The books and stories that established his reputation deal primarily with life among sharecroppers and blacks in his native Georgia. His earthy and starkly tragic representations (see TRAGEDY) of southern depravity and racial injustice initially earned him acclaim as a social critic. The novels *Tobacco Road* (1932) and *God's Little Acre* (1933), incorporating a mix of violence, deformed characters, subhuman lack of compassion, and an almost mystical interpretation of human potential, became phenomenally successful, as did his short story collection *Jackpot*, published in 1940 with 75 stories from the previous decade. Caldwell's remarkable success led to a growing critical attitude that he was not so much exposing the bleak actualities of life in the South among characters who were often helpless, spiritually castrated, and sadistic, as he was exploiting them for publicity and financial gain. Caldwell was a master teller of TALL

TALES who wrote in a direct style. His impeccable ear for DIALECT is evident in the bulk of his stories, as are the lilt of BLACK HUMOR and the stab of black melodrama.

BIBLIOGRAPHY

Arnold, Edwin T., ed. *Caldwell Reconsidered.* Jackson: University Press of Mississippi, 1990.

Caldwell, Erskine. *American Earth.* New York: Scribner, 1931; as *A Swell-Looking Girl,* New York: New American Library, 1951.

———. *The Black and White Stories of Caldwell.* Edited by Ray McIver. Atlanta: Peachtree, 1984.

———. *The Caldwell Caravan: Novels and Stories.* New York: World, 1946.

———. *Certain Women.* Boston: Little, Brown, 1957.

———. *The Complete Stories of Erskine Caldwell.* Boston: Little, Brown, 1953.

———. *The Courting of Susie Brown.* Boston: Little, Brown, 1952.

———. *A Day's Wooing and Other Stories.* New York: Grossett & Dunlap, 1944.

———. *Georgia Boy.* New York: Duell, Sloan & Pearce, 1943.

———. *Gulf Coast Stories.* Boston: Little, Brown, 1956.

———. *The Humorous Side of Caldwell.* Edited by Robert Cantwell. New York: Duell, Sloan & Pearce, 1951; as *Where the Girls Were Different and Other Stories,* 1962.

———. *Jackpot: The Short Stories.* New York: Duell, Sloan & Pearce, 1940; abridged ed., as *Midsummer Passion,* 1948.

———. *Kneel to the Rising Sun and Other Stories.* New York: Viking, 1935.

———. *Mama's Little Girl: A Brief History.* Portland, Maine: The Bradford Press, 1932.

———. *Men and Women: 22 Stories.* Boston: Little, Brown, 1961.

———. *A Message for Genevieve.* Portland, Maine: Old Colony Press, 1933.

———. *Midsummer Passion and Other Tales of Maine Cussedness.* Edited by Charles G. Waugh and Martin H. Greenberg. Boston: Yankee Books, 1990.

———. *The Pocket Book of Erskine Caldwell Stories.* New York: Pocket Books, 1947.

———. *The Sacrilege of Alan Kent.* Portland, Maine: Falmouth, 1936.

———. *Southways: Stories.* New York: Viking, 1938.

———. *Stories.* Edited by and with introduction by Henry Seidel Canby. Duell, Sloan & Pearce, 1944; as *The Pocket*

Book of Stories of Life: North and South. New York: Pocket Books, 1983.

———. *We Are the Living: Brief Stories.* New York: Viking, 1933.

———. *When You Think of Me.* Boston: Little, Brown, 1959.

———. *Where the Girls Were Different and Other Stories.* Edited by Donald A. Wollheim. New York: Avon, 1948.

———. *A Woman in the House.* New York: Signet Books, 1949.

Cassill, R. V. "Erskine Caldwell." In *Reference Guide to Short Fiction,* edited by Noelle Watson, 96–98. Detroit: St. James Press, 1994.

Devlin, James E. *Caldwell.* Boston: Twayne, 1984.

Korges, James. *Caldwell.* Minneapolis: University of Minnesota Press, 1969.

MacDonald, Scott, ed. *Critical Essays on Caldwell.* Boston: G. K. Hall, 1981.

McIlwaine, Shields. *The Southern Poor-White from Lubberland to Tobacco Road.* Norman: University of Oklahoma Press, 1939.

Sutton, William A. *Black Like It Is/Was: Caldwell's Treatment of Racial Themes.* Metuchen, N.J.: Scarecrow Press, 1974.

CALISHER, HORTENSE (1911–2009)

Although she wrote novels as well as short stories, Calisher was perhaps best known for her anthologized stories, such as "In Greenwich There are Many Gravelled Walks." She typically developed a story by hints and subtleties and information that the characters themselves reveal. Calisher, a master of style and language, used precise, powerful verbs to give scenes life and immediacy. Although her stories are not primarily stories of character but of complex situations, Calisher nonetheless offers intricately drawn insights into her fictional people. The full range of her short fiction is contained in *Collected Stories* (1975). *The Novellas of Hortense Calisher* was published in 1997.

BIBLIOGRAPHY

Brophy, Brigid. *Don't Never Forget: Collected Views and Reviews.* London: J. Cape, 1966.

Brown, Kathy. "Hortense Calisher." *Current Biography* (November 1973).

Calisher, Hortense. *The Collected Stories of Hortense Calisher.* New York: Arbor House, 1975.

———. *Extreme Magic: A Novella and Other Stories.* Boston: Little, Brown, 1964.

———. *In the Absence of Angels: Stories.* Boston: Little, Brown, 1964.

———. *The Railway Police, and The Last Trolley Ride.* Boston: Little, Brown, 1966.

———. *Saratoga, Hot.* Garden City, N.Y.: Doubleday, 1985.

———. *Sunday Jews.* New York: Harcourt, 2002.

———. *Tale for the Mirror: A Novella and Other Stories.* Boston: Little, Brown, 1962.

———. *Tattoo for a Slave.* New York: Harcourt, 2004.

"Interview with Hortense Calisher." *Paris Review* (Winter 1987).

CALLAGHAN, MORLEY (MORLEY EDWARD CALLAGHAN) (1903–1990)

One of Canada's finest writers, Morley Callaghan wrote two plays, more than a dozen novels, and more than 100 short stories that appeared in the little magazines of Paris and in such periodicals as SCRIBNER's, the NEW YORKER, *Harper's Bazaar, Maclean's,* ESQUIRE, *Cosmopolitan,* the SATURDAY EVENING POST, and *Yale Review.* Fourteen of these stories of ordinary individuals who face up to their intimidating and sometimes aggressive environs appeared in nearly half of Edward O'Brien's 26 annual anthologies entitled *Best Short Stories.* Briefly a member of the lost generation in Paris, Callaghan is also familiar as the writer who bested ERNEST HEMINGWAY in the now-famous 1929 Paris boxing match refereed by F. SCOTT FITZGERALD. Callaghan's recounting of the event occurs in his book *That Summer in Paris: Memories of Tangled Friendships with Hemingway, Fitzgerald and Some Others* (1963). Unlike many of his cohorts, however, Callaghan eschewed the modernist creed to "make it new," resisting the faddish or voguish literary techniques in favor of a straightforward and largely nonmetaphorical prose that communicated his stories directly to the reader.

He was born on February 22, 1903, in Toronto, Canada, to Thomas and Mary Dewan Callaghan, Roman Catholic Irish immigrants. In 1929, after earning his bachelor's degree at the University of Toronto (1925) and his law degree at Osgoode Hall Law School (1928), Callaghan married Loretto Florence Dee. His first story, "A Girl with Ambition," a sensitive portrayal of a romance between a well-bred Harry and the working-class Mary Ross, had appeared in 1926. Two years later, the Scribner's editor Maxwell Perkins had published two of Callaghan's stories in a special issue of *Scribner's Magazine* in July 1928. On the cover of the issue, a yellow band reminded readers that the last time Scribner's had published two stories by one author in the same issue, that writer had been Ernest Hemingway. Callaghan's first collection of short stories, *A Native Argosy,* was published in 1929. Although largely set in Canada, Callaghan's tales are unquestionably universal in their appeal. His stories feature complex characters in ordinary situations in search of fulfillment without compromising individual dignity or personal morality.

In 1931, Callaghan published a controversial novella, *No Man's Meat,* a tale of a love triangle among Bert Beddoes; his wife, Teresa; and their lesbian lover, Jean. The subject matter prevented the book from selling well, but it was later republished with another novella as *No Man's Meat & The Enchanted Pimp* (1978). In the meantime, he published numerous novels in the 1930s along with his second collection, *Now That April's Here and Other Stories* (1936). Then followed a fallow period with the onset of WORLD WAR II. He began writing novels and stories again in the late 1940s, including the novella *The Man with the Coat,* winner of the 1955 *Maclean's* magazine $5,000 fiction prize. Callaghan's third story collection, entitled *Morley Callaghan's Stories,* was published in 1959; it was followed in 1989 by *The Lost and Found Stories of Morley Callaghan,* comprising tales written between 1930 and 1950 and assembled by Callaghan's son, Barry, a literature professor. Many of the stories are set during the GREAT DEPRESSION, and a number contain coming-of-age themes. Callaghan's personal favorite (Conron 105) is "The Fisherman," the tale of Thomas Delaney, an upstanding citizen who kills the man who molested his wife, and Michael Foster, the reporter who judges Smitty, one of the hangmen, but reaches a tolerant understanding of the events.

In 1958, Callaghan's story "Now That April's Here" was adapted for film by Klenman-Davidson Productions. Morley Callaghan received the Governor General's Literary Award in 1951 and in 1960 was awarded the Lorne Pierce Medal for literature by the Royal Society of Canada. He died on August 25, 1990, in Toronto. In the words of the writer James T. Farrell,

reminiscing on the lost generation writers, Callaghan may have been "the best of the lot."

Callaghan's papers are distributed among the Metropolitan Toronto Library and the Public Archives of Canada in Ottawa and the libraries of several Canadian universities, including York, Toronto, Concordia, Queen's, and McMaster Universities.

BIBLIOGRAPHY

Allen, Walter. *The Short Story in English.* Oxford: Clarendon, 1981.

Bartlett, Donald R. "Callaghan's 'Troubled (and Troubling)' Heroines." *University of Windsor Review* 16 (Fall–Winter 1981): 60–72.

Boire, Gary A. *Morley Callaghan and His Works.* Toronto: ECW Press, 1990.

———. *Morley Callaghan: Literary Anarchist.* Toronto: ECW Press, 1994.

Callaghan, Morley. *An Autumn Penitent.* Toronto: Macmillan, 1973.

———. *It's Never Over.* New York: Scribner, 1930.

———. *The Lost and Found Stories of Morley Callaghan.* Toronto: Lester & Orpen Dennys/Exile, 1985.

———. *More Joy in Heaven.* New York: Random House, 1937.

———. *Morley Callaghan's Stories.* Vol. 1. Toronto: Macmillan, 1959; Vol. 2. London: MacGibbon & Kee, 1962, 1964.

———. *A Native Argosy.* New York: Scribner, 1929.

———. *No Man's Meat.* Paris: Edward W. Titus, At the Sign of the Black Manikin, 1931.

———. *No Man's Meat and The Enchanted Pimp.* Toronto: Macmillan, 1978.

———. *Now That April's Here and Other Stories.* New York: Random House, 1936; Toronto: Macmillan, 1936.

———. *Strange Fugitive.* New York: Scribner, 1928.

———. *Such Is My Beloved.* New York and London: Scribner, 1934.

———. *That Summer in Paris: Memories of Tangled Friendships with Hemingway, Fitzgerald and Some Others.* New York: Coward-McCann, 1963.

———. *They Shall Inherit the Earth.* New York: Random House, 1935.

Conron, Brandon. *Morley Callaghan.* New York: Twayne, 1966.

———. "Morley Callaghan as a Short Story Writer." *Journal of Commonwealth Literature* 3 (July 1967): 58–75.

———, ed. *Morley Callaghan, Critical Views on Canadian Writers.* Toronto: McGraw-Hill Ryerson, 1975.

Cude, Wilf. "Morley Callaghan's Practical Monsters: Downhill from Where and When?" In *Modern Times: A Critical Anthology,* edited by John Moss, 69–78. Toronto: NC, 1982.

Dooley, D. J. "The Leopard and the Church: The Ambiguities of Morley Callaghan." In *Moral Vision in the Canadian Novel*. Toronto: Clarke, Irwin, 1979, 61–77.

Hoar, Victor. *Morley Callaghan*. Toronto: Copp Clark, 1969.

Journal of Canadian Studies, special issue on Callaghan, edited by Ralph Heintzmann, 15 (Spring 1980).

"Morley Callaghan." *Journal of Canadian Fiction* 1 (Summer 1972): 39–42.

Morley, Patricia. *Morley Callaghan*. Toronto: McClelland & Stewart, 1978.

Staines, David, ed. *The Callaghan Symposium*. Ottawa: University of Ottawa Press, 1981.

Sutherland, Fraser. *The Style of Innocence: A Study of Hemingway and Callaghan*. Toronto: Clarke, Irwin, 1972.

Walsh, William. "Morley Callaghan." In William Walsh, *A Manifold Voice: Studies in Commonwealth Literature,* 185–212. New York: Barnes & Noble, 1970.

Wilson, Edmund. "Morley Callaghan of Toronto." *New Yorker* 26 November 1960, pp. 224–237.

CANE JEAN TOOMER (1923)   Considered a highly influential work in the formative stages of the HARLEM RENAISSANCE, JEAN TOOMER's *Cane,* a montage of short stories, prose vignettes, folk songs, poetry, and drama, looks at the ways erotic relationships, racism, and class stratification prevent black men and women from achieving either social acceptance or a positive connection with their southern folk heritage. Along with other prominent Harlem Renaissance writers of the 1920s and 1930s, such as LANGSTON HUGHES, Countee Cullen, Claude McKay, ZORA NEALE HURSTON, and Arna Bontemps, Toomer examines black history in America, Africa as an important part of black cultural identity, and the role of folk culture in African-American society. Stylistically, *Cane*'s fragmentary and experimental structure, as well as its STREAM OF CONSCIOUSNESS narration, places it in the context of such modernist works as SHERWOOD ANDERSON's *WINESBURG, OHIO,* ERNEST HEMINGWAY's *IN OUR TIME,* and WILLIAM FAULKNER's *GO DOWN, MOSES*. (See MODERNISM.)

Cane has a three-part structure. The first part, set in the fictional town of Sempter, Georgia, focuses on women characters who struggle against social limitations. The male narrators of "Karintha" and "Fern," for example, see these women as sexual objects, and, throughout much of *Cane,* women are objectified and victimized by the men who desire to possess them. At the same time, physical beauty empowers these women: "Men had always wanted her, this Karintha, even as a child, Karintha carrying beauty, perfect as dusk when the sun goes down." On the other hand, "Blood-Burning Moon" overtly explores issues of racism and the ramifications of MISCEGENATION (interracial marriage) in the South. Louisa, caught between two men battling for her affections, watches Bob Stone, who is white, and Tom Burwell, who is black, destroy each other. After Tom kills Bob in a fight, the white community executes him. As the flames engulf Tom and the portentous folk singing dies away in the community, Toomer presents a terrifying and somewhat mythical image of racism in the early 20th century.

The second part, primarily set in Washington, D.C., depicts the ineffectual relationships between black men and women resulting from the harmful impact of urban materialism. In "Rhobert," for example, Toomer shows how the PROTAGONIST suffers under the burdens and financial pressures of urban life: "Rhobert wears a house, like a monstrous diver's helmet, on his head" (40). Burdened by the weight of the unaccustomed ways of white city life, these rural black men nonetheless affirm their masculine sensibilities. The cost to black women, however, is enormous. In the story "Avey," men have ostracized the female protagonist by relegating her identity to that of a prostitute, and as with Karintha and Fern, Avey does not have the opportunity to tell her own story. In "Box Seat" Dan Moore, as do so many of the male narrators and characters in *Cane,* admires and seeks some connection with the past. He feels alienated from the black heritage of the South. Dan also perceives Muriel (like the character of Dorris in "Theater") as trapped by her desire for acceptance in a higher social class. Even though he thinks he can potentially save her from the influence of class, he does not change anything. As Susan Blake suggests, "Dan can dream, but he cannot act" (205).

In the third part, the drama "Kabnis" takes the reader back to Georgia. Ralph Kabnis, a northern-educated black man, has moved south to teach. Frustrated with the meaninglessness he perceives in religion, the educational system, and black American history, Kabnis seeks meaning in his relationships with both men and women. In his search for some connection with his cultural heritage, Kabnis, having lost his job as a teacher, tries to fit into the unaccustomed southern blue-collar world of Halsey's shop, only to realize that he is still an outsider. A "completely artificial man," Kabnis cannot respond to the glory of his heritage. Unlike Kabnis, Father John Lewis is the visionary who appeals to Carrie Kate, the young woman character; she sees in Father John the redemptive vision of the African-American heritage. At the end of the play, however, when Father John speaks and Kabnis falls to his knees before Carrie Kate, Toomer suggests that spiritual redemption is possible for Kabnis: "Light streaks through the iron-barred cellar window. . . . Outside, the sun arises from its cradle in the tree-tops of the forest" (116).

BIBLIOGRAPHY
Baker, Houston, Jr. *Singers of Daybreak: Studies in Black American Literature.* Washington, D.C.: Howard University Press, 1974.

Blake, Susan. "The Spectatorial Artist and the Structure of *Cane.*" In *Jean Toomer: A Critical Evaluation,* edited by Therman B. O'Daniel. Washington, D.C.: Howard University Press, 1988.

Byrd, Rudolph P. *Jean Toomer's Years with Gurdjieff: Portrait of an Artist 1923–1936.* Athens: University of Georgia Press, 1991.

Toomer, Jean. *Cane.* New York: Liveright, 1975.

Thomas Fahy
University of North Carolina at Chapel Hill

CANIN, ETHAN (1961–)

Canin has been praised for the clean, classic tone and the shape of his stories, which have appeared in such magazines as ESQUIRE and the ATLANTIC MONTHLY. In 1985 and 1986, two were reprinted in *Best American Short Stories.* His first story collection, *Emperor of the Air,* contains nine carefully crafted tales that demonstrate the mystery and knowledge awaiting those who try to illuminate the meaning of their everyday existence. The characters range from children—"Star Food," for instance, depicts a young boy whose curiosity protects a thief—to adults—for example, the man in "The YEAR OF GETTING TO KNOW US" who confronts his father's infidelity, or the retired couple in "We Are the Nightime Travelers" who fall in love with each other for the second time. Canin's book *The Palace Thief: Stories,* published in 1995, contains four long short stories, or NOVELLAS, in which Canin presents characters who muse on the past, often focusing on humiliating moments and trying, with varying degrees of success, to understand why they seemed helpless as their lives took them in unforeseen directions.

BIBLIOGRAPHY
Canin, Ethan. *America America.* New York: Random House, 2008.

———. *Blue River.* New York: Warner Books, 1992.

———. *Carry Me across the Water.* New York: Random House, 2001.

———. *Emperor of the Air: Stories.* New York: HarperCollins, 1989.

———. *For Kings and Planets.* New York: Random House, 1998.

———. *The Palace Thief: Stories.* New York: Picador USA, 1995.

Canin, Ethan, and Diane Sterling, eds. *Writers Harvest 2.* New York: Harcourt Brace, 1996.

CAPITALISM

An economic system characterized by private ownership of property and the means of production, and embodying the concepts of individual initiative, competition, supply and demand, and the profit motive. The importance and impact of capitalism grew with the Industrial Revolution, which began in Great Britain in the mid-18th century and gained impetus in the United States after the CIVIL WAR. By the early 20th century, unbridled capitalism had created vast credit, manufacturing, and distributing institutions, and the social and economic aspects of the system had transformed much of the world. The attendant abuses, however, particularly the exploitation of labor, social dislocation, and monopolistic practices, caused pure capitalism to be circumscribed in the early 1900s by the growth of labor unions and by laws enacted to break up and prevent monopolies and to address social and labor concerns, environmental problems, and product and worker safety.

CAPOTE, TRUMAN (1924–1984)

The acclaimed author of *A Tree of Night and Other Stories* (1949), *Breakfast at Tiffany's: A Short Novel and Three Stories* (1958), and a variety of works in other genres, including *In Cold Blood* (1966), Truman Capote set all his fiction either in his native Alabama or in his adopted home, New York City. Capote is most revered, however, for his dark themes and his lonely characters, whose subtly and intricately depicted psychology reverberates with readers. Despite his relatively sparse output as a short fiction writer, therefore, Capote—winner of three O. HENRY MEMORIAL AWARDS (1946, 1948, 1951), among numerous others—seems assured an established place among important 20th-century American short story writers.

A Tree of Night contains many of Capote's best stories. Somewhat reminiscent of KATHERINE ANNE PORTER's work in tone, Capote's stories reveal the internal realities of his protagonists as the author uses lyrical symbolism to blend identity issues, dreams, illusions, and disillusion. Also characteristic of Capote's technique is the use of SURREALISM and fantasy and southern GOTHIC to evoke the presence of evil. In the title story, "A Tree of Night," a young woman named Kay takes a train in which the eerie old couple seated next to her alarm her by their attentions, particularly the old man, who touches her on the cheek. In a stunning DENOUEMENT, in which the old man becomes the wizard of Kay's childhood, the old woman takes Kay's purse and draws Kay's raincoat over her head. The story leaves many unanswered questions as Kay ponders her childhood and identity. Other bleak tales in the collection include "Master Misery," in which the young protagonist, Sylvia, leaves her Ohio home to live in New York. When Sylvia discovers that she can sell her dreams to a man who specializes in collecting those of others, her lonely lot is given temporary meaning. Master Misery, however, finally strips Sylvia of all her dreams, leaving her about to be violated by a literally dirty old man. The bizarre story reaches mythic proportions as it narrates a depressing romance for modern times. In this same vein is "Miriam," whose middle-aged protagonist, Mrs. Miller, is haunted by Miriam, a strange child dressed all in white who ultimately moves into Mrs. Miller's apartment and appropriates her most personal belongings.

BIBLIOGRAPHY

Brinnin, John Malcolm. *Truman Capote: Dear Hearty, Old Buddy.* New York: Lawrence/Delacorte, 1986.

Capote, Truman. *Answered Prayers: The Unfinished Novel.* Edited by Joseph M. Fox. New York: Random House, 1987.

———. *Breakfast at Tiffany's: A Short Novel and Three Stories.* New York: Random House, 1958.

———. *A Christmas Memory.* New York: Random House, 1966.

———. *The Dogs Bark: Public People and Private Places.* New York: Random House, 1973.

———. *The Grass Harp.* New York: Random House, 1951.

———. *In Cold Blood: The True Account of a Multiple Murder and Its Consequences.* New York: Random House, 1965.

———. *Jug of Silver.* Mankato, Minn.: Creative Education, 1986.

———. *Local Color.* New York: Random House, 1950.

———. *The Muses Are Heard.* New York: Random House, 1956.

———. *Music for Chameleons.* New York: Random House, 1980.

———. *Observations.* New York: Simon & Schuster, 1959.

———. *One Christmas.* New York: Random House, 1983.

———. *Other Voices, Other Rooms.* New York: Random House, 1948.

———. *The Thanksgiving Visitor.* New York: Random House, 1968.

———. *A Tree of Night and Other Stories.* New York: Random House, 1949.

———. *Trilogy: An Experiment in Multimedia,* with Eleanor and Frank Perry. New York: Macmillan, 1969.

———. *The White Rose.* Newton, Iowa: Tamazunchale, 1987.

Clarke, Gerald. *Capote: A Biography.* New York: Simon & Schuster, 1988.

Creeger, George R. *Animals in Exile: Imagery and Theme in Capote's "In Cold Blood."* Middletown, Conn.: Wesleyan University Center for Advanced Studies, 1967.

Dunphy, Jack. *"Dear Genius . . .": A Memoir of My Life with Truman Capote.* New York: McGraw-Hill, 1987.

Garson, Helen S. *Truman Capote.* New York: Ungar, 1980.

Nance, William L. *The Worlds of Truman Capote.* New York: Stein & Day, 1970.

Reed, Kenneth T. *Truman Capote.* Boston: Twayne, 1981.

Rudisill, Marbie, and James Simmons. *Truman Capote: The Story of His Bizarre and Exotic Boyhood.* New York: Morrow, 1983.

Walker, Jeffrey. "1945–1956: Post–World War II Manners and Mores." In *The American Short Story, 1945–1980: A Critical History,* edited by Weaver, 22–24. Boston: Twayne, 1983.

Windham, Donald. *Lost Friendships: A Memoir of Truman Capote, Tennessee Williams, and Others.* New York: Morrow, 1987.

CARICATURE   Any fictional representation of a person or fictional character that exaggerates, distorts, and aims to amuse. The term may also be used pejoratively, as when a critic finds an author's CHARACTERIZATION flat, thin, or clichéd.

See also CHARACTER.

CARVER, RAYMOND (1938–1988)   Raymond Carver's untimely death in August 1988 at the age of 50 cut short the career of one of the most influential and talented short story writers in contemporary America. At the time of his death, Carver had published four collections of short fiction: *Will You Please Be Quiet Please* (1976), *Furious Seasons* (1977), *What We Talk about When We Talk about Love* (1981), and *Cathedral* (1983). Most of the stories in these collections as well as some new material were gathered for the posthumously published *Where I'm Calling From* (1988), which contains virtually all of his major fiction. Carver also wrote five collections of poetry, although his reputation as a poet has lagged behind the view of him as the major short story craftsman of his generation.

Born in 1938 to Clevie and Ella Beatrice Carver in Clatskanie, Oregon, Carver had a childhood that was anything but serene. His father's alcoholism and the scenes that it provoked remained etched in his mind all his life and provided material for several of his stories, told from a boy's perspective. In "Nobody Said Anything," for example, after the child narrator hears his mother and father arguing, he plays hooky from school and goes fishing to put his troubled family life out of his mind. He encounters another boy along the river, and together they catch a fairly large fish. They divide the fish in half and when the boy, proud of his catch, takes his portion home to show to his father, the father screams, "Take that goddamn thing out of here! . . . Take it the hell out of the kitchen and throw it in the goddamn garbage!" The story contrasts the child's innocence and sense of wonder about the world with the discordant, dysfunctional adult world in which the child is forced to live.

Characters loosely based on Carver's father or mother appear in "The Third Thing That Killed My Father Off," "Boxes," "So Much Water So Close to Home," and especially "Elephant," one of his best stories, in which the narrator considers his father nostalgically from the perspective of a middle-aged divorced man who is being badgered for money by his ex-wife, his two children, his mother, and his brother. In a dream the narrator sees his father, pretending to be an elephant, carrying his son on his shoulders. He remembers this as a carefree time, in contrast to the reality of his present as a recovering alcoholic, whose own family sees him only as a source of money. He plays the roles of father, son, husband, and brother with only the burdens of those roles and none of the pleasures. In the end, however, the narrator embraces his life for what it is rather than continuing to complain about it.

In 1957 Carver married Maryann Burk, his teenage sweetheart—he was 19 and she was 16 at the time of the wedding—and their tumultuous marriage lasted for 20 years. They were separated in 1977, and shortly thereafter Carver began a long relationship with the poet Tess Gallagher that culminated in their marriage in 1988, the year of Carver's death. The period of his marriage to Maryann provided material for his best and most characteristic stories.

Carver had a watershed year in 1977. Although he had already published his first collection of stories and established a reputation as a "minimalist" writer (see MINIMALISM), he was drinking heavily and had been hospitalized a number of times for alcohol toxicity. When a doctor told him that he would die if he continued drinking, Carver faced his alcoholism squarely, gave up drinking, and began attending Alcoholics Anonymous meetings. Alcohol became a prominent "character" in his fiction and figures centrally in such stories as "Chef's House," "A Serious Talk," "WHAT WE TALK ABOUT WHEN WE TALK ABOUT LOVE," "Careful," "Vitamins," "Where I'm Calling From," "Menudo," and "Elephant," among others.

Although Carver's consciousness of alcohol's impact on individual lives is an important feature of much of his fiction, it is not alcohol but human relationships, particularly those of heterosexual couples, that are his abiding theme.

Carver wrote a significant number of "multiple couple" stories, where two or more heterosexual couples spend some time together socializing, usually drinking, often flirting, and almost always miscommunicating. Stories of this type include "Feathers," "Neighbors," "Put Yourself in My Shoes," "What's in Alaska," "Tell the Women We're Going," and "After the Denim," to name the most prominent.

"What We Talk about When We Talk about Love," one of his most often anthologized, carefully structured, and engaging stories, combines the alcohol motif with the dual couple THEME. Two couples, Mel and Terri and Nick and Laura, sit around a kitchen table drinking gin and talking about love. Mel and Terri's tumultuous and volatile history is explicitly contrasted with that of Nick and Laura, who are also in a second marriage but have known one another for just a year and are still in the flush of a new love. The couples are further contrasted with their previous partners as well as with a long-married elderly couple who have had a serious automobile accident: Their van was broadsided by a drunk driver. Mel, who is a heart surgeon, tells the story of the old couple, who clearly symbolize enduring monogamous love, and finds it hard to comprehend such devotion. The world he lives in and represents consists of "serial" replaceable relationships, and even though the two couples are supposedly "in love," the story raises the question of what love means in a world that no longer regards it with the sanctity of previous generations. As Mel's long quasi-monologue continues, the couples consume two bottles of gin and the kitchen gets darker and darker. The story, which had begun in a brightly lit kitchen with four sober individuals trying to dissect the ways of the heart, ends in total darkness, with four drunks totally in the dark about what it is that we do talk about when we talk about love.

A few of Carver's masterpieces do not quite fit into this pattern of multiple (often alcoholic) couple stories. "A Small Good Thing" deals with a couple's grief over the accidental death of their eight-year-old son; in "Cathedral," a socially withdrawn, resentful narrator who views the world stereotypically awakens to the possibility of connections with other human beings through a lesson he learns from a blind man. And in his last story, "Errand"—one of Carver's least characteristic but most memorable—the death of Anton Chekhov becomes a meditation on the narrator's own impending death.

In all, Carver's influence on the American short story in the late 20th century has been nearly as large as ERNEST HEMINGWAY's influence on an earlier generation. Carver disliked the term *minimalist,* and it is surely a misleading way to characterize his work. That work gave great clarity and precision to the way people lived in the fragmented world of late 20th-century America and deals with those most enduring of subjects: relationships between men and women, loss, love, and death. He wrote about these themes not minimalistically but with economy, grace, and insight.

See also "The BATH"; "The STUDENTS' WIFE."

BIBLIOGRAPHY

Campbell, Ewing. *Raymond Carver: A Study of the Short Fiction.* Twayne; Maxwell Macmillan Canada; Maxwell Macmillan International, 1992.

Carver, Raymond. *Cathedral.* New York: Knopf, 1983.

———. *Elephant.* Fairfax, Calif.: Jungle Garden, 1988.

———. *Fires.* Santa Barbara, Calif.: Capra, 1983.

———. *Furious Seasons and Other Stories.* Santa Barbara, Calif.: Capra, 1977.

———. *If It Please You.* Northridge, Calif.: Lord John, 1984.

———. *The Pheasant.* Worchester, Mass.: Metacom, 1982.

———. *Put Yourself in My Shoes.* Santa Barbara, Calif.: Capra, 1974.

———. *The Stories of Raymond Carver.* London: Picador/Pan, 1985. Reprint. Ridgewood, N.J.: Babcock & Koontz, 1986.

———. *Those Days: Early Writings.* Edited by William L. Stull. Elmwood, Conn.: Raven, 1987.

———. *What We Talk about When We Talk about Love.* New York: Knopf, 1981.

———. *Where I'm Calling From.* New York: Atlantic
   Monthly, 1988.
———. *Will You Please Be Quiet, Please?* New York:
   McGraw-Hill, 1976.
Helpert, Sam. *Raymond Carver: An Oral Biography.* Iowa
   City: University of Iowa Press, 1985.
Meyer, Adam. *Raymond Carver.* New York: Twayne, 1995.
Nesset, Kirk. *The Stories of Raymond Carver: A Critical
   Study.* Athens: Ohio University Press, 1995.
Runyon, Randolph. *Reading Raymond Carver.* Syracuse,
   N.Y.: Syracuse University Press, 1992.
Saltzman, Arthur. *Understanding Raymond Carver.* Colum-
   bia, S.C.: University of South Carolina Press, 1988.

Fred Moramarco
San Diego State University

CASEY, JOHN (1939–) Born in 1939 in
Worcester, Massachusetts, to Constance Dudley
Casey, a political activist, and Joseph Edward Casey, a
lawyer, John Casey completed law school at Harvard
University in 1965 and was admitted to the bar in
Washington, D.C., the following year. Apparently
encouraged by the writer PETER TAYLOR, Casey
attended the Iowa Writer's Workshop at the Univer-
sity of Iowa, where he then earned an M.F.A. in 1968.
In 1972, he began teaching at the University of
Virginia.

Casey had stories published in the *NEW YORKER* and
Sports Illustrated before writing his first novel, *An American Romance,* in 1977. Many of his published stories
from the *New Yorker,* including the title story, were collected in *Testimony and Demeanor* in 1979 and received
praise from such reviewers as the critic Jonathan Yardley and the author JOYCE CAROL OATES. Casey's second
novel, *Spartina,* the metaphorical story of a man engaged
in an affair and building a boat that would outlast a
hurricane, won the National Book Award in 1989. The
critic Susan Kenney called *Spartina* "just possibly the
best American novel about going fishing since *The Old
Man and the Sea,* maybe even *Moby Dick.*" Casey's third
novel is *The Half-Life of Happiness.*

Casey has since published in the *New Yorker,* the
New York Times Magazine, ESQUIRE, and *HARPER's.* He
has received numerous awards, including the Strauss
Living Award from the American Academy of Arts
and Letters and the O. HENRY MEMORIAL AWARD. In
addition to his teaching at the University of Virginia,
Casey regularly teaches creative writing at the Sewanee
Writers Conference at the University of the South. He
enjoys building boats in Rhode Island and fishing in
Narragansett Bay.

BIBLIOGRAPHY
Casey, John. *An American Romance.* New York: Atheneum,
   1977.
———. *The Half-Life of Happiness.* New York: Knopf, 1998.
———. *South Country.* New York: Knopf, 1988.
———. *Spartina.* New York: Knopf, 1989.
———. *Testimony and Demeanor.* New York: Knopf, 1979.

Jay Pluck
Brooklyn, New York

CASH A wonderfully memorable young black man
(in Eudora Welty's story "LIVVIE") who dresses in the
colors of the rainbow and falls in love with the young
Livvie, whose life is drab and constrained while she is
married to old Solomon. Cash, who proclaims to Livvie, "I been to Nashville—I ready for Easter!" represents all the possibilities ahead of them when,
fortuitously, Solomon dies. Cash's name (suggestive of
his willingness to spend money, unlike the cautious
Solomon), together with his joyful approach to life
and disregard of time (he breaks Solomon's watch),
provides clues to Livvie's bright future with him.

**"CASK OF AMONTILLADO, THE" EDGAR
ALLAN POE (1846)** First published in *Godey's Lady's
Book* in November 1846, EDGAR ALLAN POE's well-
known short story "The Cask of Amontillado" is a
carefully crafted tale of revenge and retribution. The
story contains one of Poe's most common motifs, that
of being buried alive. Borne down by the weight of the
"thousand injuries" of the ironically named Fortunato,
MONTRESOR carefully concocts the ultimate scheme for
revenge (666). In the Italian season of Carnival, Montresor wittingly lures Fortunato, his detested enemy,
the intoxicated connoisseur of wines, down into his
family's ancient Gothic vaults, supposedly to sample a
cask of Amontillado. Fortunato is led deep into the
niter-encrusted catacombs, where Montresor unexpectedly chains him in a deep recess and quickly
walls him in. The horror of the situation is ironically

juxtaposed with the pathetic jingling of the bells on Fortunato's jester's cap. Montresor's remorselessness in the face of his terrible deed is astonishing. One should expect this, however, from a member of a family whose motto is *Nemo me impune lacessit,* or "No one provokes me with impunity" (667). The tale is an apt demonstration of Poe's ability to capture the terror of confinement and being buried alive. Poe explored this THEME further in other stories, most notably in the NOVELLA *The FALL OF THE HOUSE OF USHER* (1839).

A. N. Stevens suggests that Poe first heard the anecdote on which he might have based this story when he was a private in the army in 1827. While stationed at Fort Independence in Boston Harbor, Poe saw a gravestone erected to the memory of a Lieutenant Massie, who had been unfairly killed in a duel by a bully named Captain Green. According to the story, Captain Green had been so detested by his fellow officers that they decided to take a terrible revenge on him for Massie's death. They pretended to be friendly and plied him with wine until he was helplessly intoxicated. Then, carrying the captain, the officers forced his body through a tiny opening that led into the subterranean dungeons. His captors shackled him to the floor, then, using bricks and mortar, sealed him up alive inside. Captain Green undoubtedly died a horrible death within a few days.

BIBLIOGRAPHY

Hammond, J. R. *An Edgar Allan Poe Companion.* Totowa, N.J.: Barnes & Noble Books, 1981.

Poe, Edgar Allan. "The Cask of Amontillado." In *The Complete Tales and Poems of Edgar Allan Poe.* New York: Barnes & Noble, 1992.

Stevens, Austin N., ed. *Mysterious New England.* Dublin, N.H.: Yankee, 1971.

Kathleen M. Hicks
University of Texas at El Paso

CASSILL, R. V. (RONALD VERLIN CASSILL) (1913–2002)
Born in Cedar Falls, Iowa, Cassill began his artistic career as a painter and teacher of art. The most noteworthy literary quality of his prose fiction is its "visual" nature: the use of color, the precise visual detail, and sensitivity to proportion.

Although he is primarily a novelist, Cassill's most sustained work is often in short fiction, such as stories in *The Father* (1965) and *The Happy Marriage* (1965) about the family and the provincial qualities of the Midwest, Iowa in particular.

BIBLIOGRAPHY

Cassill, R. V. *The Father and Other Stories.* New York: Simon & Schuster, 1965.

———. *The Happy Marriage and Other Stories.* West Lafayette, Ind.: Purdue University Press, 1967.

———. *Three Stories.* Oakland, Calif.: Hermes House, 1982.

"R. V. Cassill Issue." *December* 23, nos. 1–2 (1981).

Walkiewicz, E. P. "1957–1968: Toward Diversity of Form." In *The American Short Story,* 1945–1980, edited by Gordon Weaver, 35–76. Boston: Twayne, 1983.

CATASTROPHE Corresponding to the more common modern word DENOUEMENT, catastrophe is the Greek word for the unwinding of the plot at the end of a play. Because it frequently involved the death of the HERO, it usually implied a dramatically unhappy or tragic ending. The word may be applied to any sort of literature, including short stories in which the ending involves a horrific upset of balance and order.

"CATBIRD SEAT, THE" JAMES THURBER **(1945)** Based on a famous METAPHOR used by the sports radio announcer Walter (Red) Barber, the title refers to an advantaged position in human relationships. Red Barber, the well-known baseball commentator and "Voice of the Dodgers" during the 1940s, often used his native South Florida expressions, such as "He's in the catbird seat," meaning one has ideally positioned oneself for victory. JAMES THURBER's story involves Mr. Martin, a "Walter Mitty" type of man (see "The SECRET LIFE OF WALTER MITTY"), who confronts Mrs. Ulgine Barrows, a large, overbearing woman, the story's source for Barber's expressions such as "catbird seat" and "tearing up the pea patch." Because Mrs. Barrows threatens Mr. Martin's position and plans to reorganize his department, the story offers a humorous and immensely satisfying if vicarious solution to harassment in the workplace.

The major difference between Mr. Martin and Walter Mitty is that Martin actually copes with his problem through action, whereas Mitty merely escapes his domineering wife by entering heroic daydreams. Conducting a mental trial of Mrs. Barrows, the mild-mannered Martin pronounces her guilty and demands the death penalty. Even better than the murder he initially plans, however, is the "strange and wonderful" idea to blow up her department: It literally explodes, catapulting Mrs. Barrows through the door and effectively eliminating her as a threat. The story entertainingly dramatizes the difficulties individuals face in the modern business world and champions the individual who in the end outwits the system.

"CATHEDRAL" RAYMOND CARVER (1982)

Appearing first in ATLANTIC MONTHLY and reprinted in *Best American Short Stories, 1982,* RAYMOND CARVER's "Cathedral" exemplifies his departure from the minimalist style (see MINIMALISM) of his earlier three collections. It is also acclaimed as one of the finest efforts from one of our greatest short story writers. Carver himself seemingly sensed as much; in an interview with Mona Simpson, he remarked: "When I wrote 'Cathedral' I experienced this rush and I felt, 'This is what it's all about, this is the reason we do this'" (quoted in Mona Simpson interview, "The Art of Fiction" 76 *Paris Review* [1983]: 207).

The story opens with the agitated narrator awaiting the visit of Robert, an old friend of the narrator's wife. Robert, who is blind, has recently suffered the death of his wife. The narrator resents Robert's visit, in part because the blind man represents a connection to his wife's past: She worked for Robert as a reader in Seattle, during her relationship with a childhood sweetheart that ended badly. Because his wife and Robert communicate (via audiotape), the blind man also represents a part of his wife's current life from which the narrator is excluded. The narrator's unwillingness to welcome Robert into his home "exposes his own rather repellent insularity and lack of compassion" (Saltzman 152).

Yet Robert's arrival initiates the narrator's transformation. After a hearty meal, the wife falls asleep; Robert and the narrator—"Bub," as Robert calls him—turn their attention to a television show about cathedrals. The narrator asks Robert whether he knows what a cathedral looks like, and after Robert answers that he does not, the host attempts to describe one. The narrator feels that he cannot adequately help Robert envision a cathedral, but at Robert's suggestion, he gathers a pen and some heavy paper. With Robert's hand on top of his own, the narrator begins to draw an intricate cathedral.

A brief comparison with "Fat," the opening story of *Will You Please Be Quiet, Please?* Carver's first collection, illuminates why critics heralded "Cathedral" as a turning point in Carver's writing. Both stories involve unnamed first-person narrators (see POINT OF VIEW) who encounter an "other": In "Fat," it is a grotesquely fat diner; in "Cathedral," it is Robert. Furthermore, both narrators seek to identify with that person. Yet while "Fat" concerns the failure of the imagination (the narrator's lover, Rudy, and her friend, Rita, fail to comprehend the significance of the narrator's encounter), "Cathedral" suggests the capacity of the imagination. As the blind man encourages the narrator to close his eyes but to keep drawing, the narrator gains a greater understanding not only of Robert but of himself as well. In the midst of this shared, epiphanic (see EPIPHANY) experience, the narrator confesses: "It was like nothing else in my life up to now" (228).

BIBLIOGRAPHY
Campbell, Ewing. *Raymond Carver: A Study of the Short Fiction.* New York: Twayne, 1992.

Gentry, Marshall Bruce, and William L. Stull, eds. *Conversations with Raymond Carver.* Ann Arbor: University of Michigan Press, 1990.

Meyer, Adam. *Raymond Carver.* New York: Macmillan, 1995.

Saltzman, Arthur M. *Understanding Raymond Carver.* Columbia: University of South Carolina Press, 1988.

Michael Hogan
University of North Carolina at Chapel Hill

CATHER, WILLA (WILLELA SIBERT CATHER) (1873–1947)

Willela (Willa) Sibert Cather was born in Back Creek Valley, Virginia, in 1873. At the age of nine, she moved with her family to a homestead on the Nebraska plains. The dramatic change of lifestyle and landscape provided the adult

Cather with many of the THEMES that recur in her fiction: the soul-searing nature of life on the land, the confluence of cultures in the settlement of the Midwest, and the power of memory. As an adult, Cather lived in Pittsburgh and New York City. Ironic or tragic contrasts between rural and urban culture frequently drive the conflicts in her stories; many of her characters are artists, especially composers or singers, who find both opportunity and exploitation in big cities. Although Cather's stature as a major American writer rests primarily on her 12 novels, she produced short fiction for 20 years before attempting her first long work. At her death in 1947, she had published more than 60 stories in LITTLE MAGAZINES as well as the most popular periodicals of the day, including *SCRIBNER'S*, *Smart Set*, and *MCCLURE'S*.

Cather's distinctive stylistic trait is a precision with evocative details, both physical and psychological; consequently, her work has been placed in the American realist (see REALISM) and romantic traditions. Like her mentor SARAH ORNE JEWETT, Cather is frequently described as a regional writer (see REGIONALISM). She also has been compared to modernists like Fitzgerald and Hemingway (see MODERNISM) for her laconic indirection and her lament for the loss of shared values and traditions in the modern world. Irony and ambiguity are regular features in her fiction. Cather's gallery of complex women characters, many of whom display an androgynous transcendence of traditional women's roles, makes her a major contributor to women's literary traditions. Recent studies have examined Cather's life and work in the context of a closeted lesbian identity.

Cather's writing career began when she was a student at the University of Nebraska (1890–95) with the publication of the short story "Peter" in 1892, the first of four early stories about Nebraska notable for their grim naturalistic vision (see NATURALISM). By 1896 she had published nine stories while attending college and working for the *Nebraska State Journal* as a feature columnist and theater critic. From 1896 to 1900, Cather established an arduous lifestyle as a serious short fiction writer who earned her living as a part-time journalist and full-time editor, first at *Home Monthly* and then at the Pittsburgh *Leader*. In the sto-

ries of this period, she began to explore her interest in both exceptionally gifted individuals and ordinary people whose dignity and perseverance she admired. "Nanette, An Aside" (1897) examines a performing artist who lives intensely in and for her music, sacrificing human relationships for art. "The Sentimentality of William Tavener" (1900) is Cather's first realistic portrait of a strong-willed Nebraska farm woman. In a romantic vein, "Eric Hermannson's Soul" (1900) presents the primitive nature of sexual, aesthetic (see AESTHETICISM), and religious impulses as both dangerous and redemptive.

In 1899, when Cather met Isabelle McClung, the daughter of a Pittsburgh judge, she was invited to live in the McClung mansion, where she was given a quiet study in which to write. During the next six years, Cather became a high school teacher of Latin and English. She continued to publish stories, produced a book of poetry (*April Twilights,* 1903), and brought out her first story collection, *The Troll Garden* (1905). The seven stories in the latter volume concern the demands of creativity and commitment in both art and human relationships. Her most anthologized story, "Paul's Case," clarifies art's potential to corrupt as well as enrich when used to escape reality. "The Sculptor's Funeral" and "A Wagner Matinee" are generally ranked with her best work. Commentators have noted that most of the marriages in this volume are unhappy because of one partner's dominance over the other. Cather neither married nor formed romantic attachments to men. Her strong commitments were to art and three women: Louise Pound, Isabelle McClung, and her domestic partner, Edith Lewis, with whom she lived for nearly 40 years.

From 1906 to 1912, Cather held an editor's position at *McClure's* magazine and continued to mature as an artist. In "The Enchanted Bluff" (1909) she established the complex attitude toward the past she would later develop in novels about Nebraska. "Behind the Singer Tower" (1912) is overt social criticism: It challenges the American corporate mentality and its potential to nourish individual ambition at the expense of compassion and honesty. In "The Bohemian Girl" (1912) she created archetypal Nebraska characters whose conflicts she later incorporated in two novels, *O Pioneers!* and *My Ántonia*.

The year 1912 was a turning point in Cather's life: She published her first novel, *Alexander's Bridge,* and she left *McClure's* to become a full-time writer. With her success as a novelist, Cather's story production declined but never ceased entirely. From 1913 to 1920, she published three stories about urban business professionals, a psychological GHOST STORY, and her second collection, *Youth and the Bright Medusa* (1920), which contained four stories, revised, from *The Troll Garden* and four recently published in magazines. Three of the latter stories concern singers whose talent is easily exploited by family and friends in a society that commodifies art. The strongest work in the collection is "COMING, APHRODITE!" (originally bowdlerized and published as "Coming, Eden Bower!"), a bold representation of sexual attraction between two artists who confront the temptations of fame.

From 1922 to 1932, most of Cather's creative effort went to producing six novels, but she also wrote the story "Uncle Valentine" (1925), a tragic tribute to a family of gifted, eccentric individuals who endure loneliness rather than accept conformity. The story also presents industrialization as a destructive force on the American scene. In "DOUBLE BIRTHDAY" (1929) two men look back with insight on the atypical choices that have made them true individuals. In 1932 Cather published her third collection, *Obscure Destinies,* which consists of three stories about death, loss, and intergenerational legacies: "OLD MRS. HARRIS," "NEIGHBOR ROSICKY," and "TWO FRIENDS." From the Library Edition of her collected works (1937–41) she excluded most of her early stories, judging them not worth preserving. Three stories composed near the end of her life were collected and published posthumously in 1948 as *The Old Beauty and Others.*

BIBLIOGRAPHY

Arnold, Marilyn. *Willa Cather's Short Fiction.* Athens: Ohio University Press, 1984.

Cather, Willa. *Uncle Valentine and Other Stories: Willa Cather's Uncollected Short Fiction, 1915–1929.* Edited by Bernice Slote. Lincoln: University of Nebraska Press, 1973.

———. *Willa Cather's Collected Short Fiction, 1892–1912.* Edited by Virginia Faulkner. Lincoln: University of Nebraska Press, 1965.

Gerber, Philip. *Willa Cather.* Rev. ed. New York: Twayne, 1995.

O'Brien, Sharon. *Willa Cather: The Emerging Voice.* New York: Oxford University Press, 1987.

Wasserman, Loretta. *Willa Cather: A Study of the Short Fiction.* Boston: Twayne, 1991.

Woodress, James. *Willa Cather: A Literary Life.* Lincoln: University of Nebraska Press, 1987.

Frances Kerr
Durham Technical Community College

"CAT IN THE RAIN" ERNEST HEMINGWAY (1924)

In a rare moment in "Cat in the Rain," first published in the Paris edition of *in our time,* ERNEST HEMINGWAY seems to show concern for the unfulfilled female. Like many of his other works of fiction, the story is about Americans abroad. An unnamed American woman and her husband are cooped up in their hotel room as the rain beats down outside the window. Looking down, the woman sees a cat crouched under an outdoor table, trying not to get wet. She decides she wants to have that cat. When she goes down to rescue it, however, the cat has disappeared. The woman returns unsatisfied and unhappy. She thinks about all the changes she wishes to make in her life. When she begins to tell her husband about her aspirations, all he says is "Oh, shut up and get something to read" (170). At that moment the *padrone,* or innkeeper, she so admires sends up the maid with the cat. Hemingway suggests the woman now realizes that she will have to look outside her marriage to find fulfillment.

BIBLIOGRAPHY

Flora, Joseph. *Ernest Hemingway: A Study of Short Fiction.* Boston: Twayne, 1989.

Hemingway, Ernest. "Cat in the Rain." In *The Short Stories of Ernest Hemingway.* New York: Collier Books, 1986.

Kathleen M. Hicks
University of Texas at El Paso

"CAT WHO THOUGHT SHE WAS A DOG & THE DOG WHO THOUGHT HE WAS A CAT, THE" ISAAC BASHEVIS SINGER (1973, 1984)

Although the author never saw himself as a children's writer, "The Cat Who Thought She Was a Dog & the Dog Who Thought He Was a Cat" is one of the many stories ISAAC BASHEVIS SINGER wrote after his editor, Elizabeth Shub, encouraged him to write stories specifically for children. The story first appeared in the collection titled *Naftali the Storyteller and His Horse* (1973) before being reprinted in *Stories for Children* (1984).

In this story, the omniscient narrator tells about a poor peasant named Jan Skiba, who lives in a sparsely furnished one-room, straw-roofed hut with his wife, three daughters, a dog named Burek, and a cat named Kot. Because there are no other animals around, the dog and the cat have only each other to which to compare themselves; therefore, as the title indicates, the cat thinks she is a dog, and the dog thinks he is a cat. Even though Jan Skiba seldom has anything to sell, a peddler stops by one day. Marianna, Jan's wife, desires the mirror the peddler has among his trinkets, so she strikes an agreement with the peddler to purchase the mirror on an installment plan. The mirror, however, winds up causing multiple problems in the Skiba household, especially among the women, who become intimately aware of their various visual defects, which ruin their self-esteem (the daughters are certain they will never find husbands) and prevent them from doing their daily chores. The animals are also affected, as the cat is startled by her image, and the dog tries to fight the other dog he sees to the point that they finally attack each other. Seeing the disruption the mirror is causing in his formerly peaceful household, Jan Skiba decides that they really do not need the mirror, which he puts away in the woodshed. When the peddler returns the next month for the second payment, the mirror is returned to him in exchange for more useful items, and the household returns to normal. The story ends with the village priest's providing a moral for the story in the vein of one of AESOP'S FABLES.

BIBLIOGRAPHY

Allison, Alida. *Isaac Bashevis Singer: Children's Stories and Childhood Memories.* New York: Twayne–Simon & Schuster Macmillan, 1996.

Singer, Isaac Bashevis. "The Cat Who Thought She Was a Dog & the Dog Who Thought He Was a Cat." Translated by Joseph Singer. In *Stories for Children.* New York: Farrar, Straus & Giroux, 1984.

Peggy J. Huey
University of Tampa

C. AUGUSTE DUPIN One of the earliest detectives in American fiction, Dupin's appearance in EDGAR ALLAN POE's tales of "ratiocination" established the formula, still imitated today, of the intellectual detective using meticulous detail and his powers of deduction to solve the crime. His amateur status (not affiliated with the police) and cold logic have become familiar characteristics of the literary detectives modeled on him, from Agatha Christie's Hercule Poirot and Sir Arthur Conan Doyle's Sherlock Holmes to RAYMOND CHANDLER's Philip Marlowe and DASHIELL HAMMETT's SAM SPADE. Dupin's bewildered, nameless friend and narrator—to whom he explains his brilliant deductions—also started the trend of the FOILS to these detectives, most celebrated in the relationship between Holmes and his puzzled sidekick, Dr. Watson.

CHAN, JEFFERY PAUL (1942–) Jeffery Paul Chan was born and raised in Stockton, California. Although he is known primarily as a critic and literary historian, his short stories are increasingly influential, particularly within the Asian-American community. He has published in the *Yardbird Reader,* the *Amerasia Journal,* and a number of regional periodicals. Currently a professor of Asian-American studies at San Francisco State University, Chan lives with his wife and two children in Marin County, north of San Francisco. In terms of the politics of ASIAN-AMERICAN LITERATURE, he is closely aligned with FRANK CHIN.

Chan's best-known story is "The Chinese in Haifa" (1974), whose blintz-eating Chinese-American PROTAGONIST initiates an affair with his Jewish neighbor's blonde wife after his own marriage goes awry. Using somewhat exaggerated depictions of sexual prowess, the story seeks to undercut STEREOTYPES of Asian-American males as effeminate and impotent—as nonmale and non-American—while suggesting the alienation of Asian-American males in a society that refuses to acknowledge them fully.

BIBLIOGRAPHY

Chan, Jeffery Paul, et al., eds. *The Big Aiiieeeee! An Anthology of Chinese American and Japanese American Literature.* New York: Meridian, 1991.

Kim, Elaine. *Asian American Literature: An Introduction to The Writings and Their Social Context.* Philadelphia: Temple University Press, 1982.

Keith Lawrence
Brigham Young University

CHANDLER, RAYMOND (RAYMOND THORNTON CHANDLER) (1888–1959) A

DETECTIVE FICTION writer fully considered the equal of DASHIEL HAMMETT and JAMES M. CAIN. Born in Chicago and educated in Great Britain, Chandler put the city of Los Angeles on the literary map (and the geographical map for Europeans) with his realistic depictions of the mean and dirty along with the rich and famous. Known for his CLASSIC novels such as *The Big Sleep* (1939) and *Farewell My Lovely* (1940), Chandler also wrote short stories; in fact, *The Big Sleep* comprises two short stories, "Killer in the Rain" and "The Curtain," he had first published in the BLACK MASK, the leading pulp magazine of the 1930s, which also published Cain, Hammett, and others now viewed as classic writers of detective stories and novels.

Chandler's stories are collected in two volumes, *The Simple Art of Murder* (1950) and *Killer in the Rain* (1964). *The Big Sleep* became a film hit, with WILLIAM FAULKNER as one of the scriptwriters and Humphrey Bogart and Lauren Bacall playing the leads. Chandler's HERO, PHILIP MARLOWE, had his genesis in numerous stories wherein Chandler invented a detective less interested in solving murders than in righting social wrongs. As had EDGAR ALLAN POE, Chandler created guidelines for the murder mystery and the detective hero in his classic essay "The Simple Art of Murder." His dictates influenced not only his own fiction but also that of countless others after him.

BIBLIOGRAPHY
Chandler, Raymond. *The Big Sleep.* New York: Knopf, 1939.
———. *Farewell My Lovely.* New York: Knopf, 1940.
———. *The High Window.* New York: Knopf, 1940.
———. *Killer in the Rain.* New York: Ballantine, 1964.
———. *The Lady in the Lake.* New York: Knopf, 1943.
———. *Little Sister.* New York: Ballantine Books, 1949.
———. *The Long Goodbye.* Boston: Houghton Mifflin, 1954.
———. *Playback.* New York: Ballantine, 1958.
———. *The Simple Art of Murder.* Boston: Houghton Mifflin, 1950.
Durham, Philip. *Down These Mean Streets a Man Must Go: Raymond Chandler's Knight.* Chapel Hill: University of North Carolina Press, 1963.

CHAON, DAN (1964–)   Dan Chaon (pronounced "Shawn"), born in Nebraska, began sending off short stories for publication when in high school. Reginald Gibbons, at *TriQuarterly,* responded to Chaon's "You Are Requested to Close the Eyes" and encouraged him to attend Northwestern University, where he graduated with a bachelor's degree in 1986. His first short story collection, *Fitting Ends,* was published in 1996 and exhibited his careful, nuanced, and impressively articulate style—a crystallized version of what he has described as "a subconscious exercise in which I'm trawling for some kind of entryway into fiction," compelling scenes set in relief to plausible, hyperaccurate, and emotionally resonant environments. His second short story collection, *Among the Missing,* was published in 2001 and was a finalist for the National Book Award and named one of the 10 best books of the year by the American Library Association, the *Chicago Tribune,* the *Boston Globe,* the *Las Vegas Mercury,* and *Entertainment Weekly;* it was cited as a Notable Book by *Publishers Weekly,* the *Washington Post,* and the *New York Times,* and has been translated into several languages. Chaon has won the RAYMOND CARVER Memorial Award, Special Mention in the PUSHCART PRIZE, and an O. HENRY MEMORIAL AWARD.

Some characters from *Fitting Ends* and *Among the Missing* appear in his first novel, *You Remind Me of Me.* He is currently working on another novel, *Sleepwalk,* in which Lake McConaughy, Sean, his mother, and the Morrison family—all from the story "Among the Missing"—play a role. He is also at work on a third collection of short stories. In the meantime, his stories have been published in *Best American Short Stories* (1996), *Best American Short Stories* (2003), *The Pushcart Prize* (2000, 2002, and 2003), *TriQuarterly,* *Ploughshares, American Short Fiction,* and numerous other LITTLE MAGAZINES. Among many other interests for Chaon is the relationship between the literary and the visual arts, and he cites Lynda Barry, Charles Burns, and Daniel Clowes as influences. He is a professed fan of pop surrealism and has called the ideas of Peter Straub a significant influence on his work. He writes mostly in his attic. Dan Chaon teaches creative writing at Oberlin College and is married to the writer Sheila Schwartz, author of the Pushcart Prize Editor's Award–winning novel *Imagine a Great White Light*. The couple and their children live in Cleveland Heights, Ohio.

BIBLIOGRAPHY

Barbash, Tom. "Dan Chaon." Available online. URL: http://www.believermag.com/exclusives/?read=interview_chaon. Accessed August 14, 2006.

Chaon, Dan. *Among the Missing*. New York: Ballantine Books, 2001.

———. *Fitting Ends*. Evanston, Ill.: Triquarterly Books/Northwestern University Press, 1995.

———. *You Remind Me of Me*. New York: Ballantine Books, 2005.

Jay Pluck
Brooklyn, New York

CHAPPELL, FRED (1936–   )

Born in Canton, North Carolina, and formerly a professor at the University of North Carolina at Greensboro, Chappell has published 14 volumes of poetry (the best known of which is *Midquest,* 1981); he received the Bollingen Prize in Poetry in 1985. His short stories, five of which have been included in *Best American Short Stories,* often fuse the LYRIC language of his award-winning poetry with the vernacular tradition and BURLESQUE elements of oral storytelling. While most often credited with only two collections of short stories—*Moments of Light* (1980) and *More Shapes Than One* (1991)—Chappell has also published three unified collections of short fiction that his publisher labels as novels.

All three of these SHORT STORY CYCLES contain related stories unified by Chappell's narrative PERSONA, Jess Kirkman, and by the North Carolina mountain setting; while most stories in these collections can be read independently, they are clearly enriched by the context the others provide. *I Am One of You Forever* (1985) is a BILDUNGSROMAN loosely structured around a series of visits by Jess's strange uncles and his close relationship with Johnson Gibbs, who lives with the family. In the process of telling these stories, Jess chronicles his own emergence as a storyteller, who discovers his niche in the family and the region as well as the importance of both to his art. *Brighten the Corner Where You Are* (1989) episodically traces a day of misadventure in the life of Jess's father, who must testify before the local school board concerning charges that he has been teaching evolution—but not until he has chased a devil-possum, encountered a talking goat on the school roof, and held a Socratic dialogue on the theory of evolution with his class. *Farewell, I'm Bound to Leave You* (1996) complements the previous works by focusing on female strategies for survival in stories that Jess relates in his mother's and grandmother's voices. As do the other works in this trilogy, this latest volume comprises an artistic rescue and celebration of a vanishing mountain realm, transcending LOCAL COLOR in its exploration of the ordinary world's mystery.

More Shapes than One begins with a cluster of stories concerning historical characters and the epiphanies (see EPIPHANY) that revitalize their vision. In the remainder of the volume, Chappell experiments with a variety of voices and genres, ranging from SCIENCE FICTION to horror to the TALL TALE, most often verging into SURREALISM and burlesque. Chappell's poetic talents animate his best short fiction, which explores the nature of the imagination and the connection to one's place of origin. METAPHOR informs his vision of the world, transforming the facts of everyday existence into a lyrical and often magical realm in such stories as "The Beard," "The Storytellers," "Bacchus," and "Linneaus Forgets." The lyric prose of his stories blends erudition, epiphany, and an elegant style with the earthiness of Appalachian DIALECT and the burlesque of the tall tale.

BIBLIOGRAPHY

Campbell, Hilbert. "Fred Chappell's Urn of Memory: *I Am One of You Forever.*" *Southern Literary Journal* 25, no. 2 (1993): 103–111.

Chappell, Fred. *Brighten the Corner Where You Are*. New York: St. Martin's Press, 1989.

———. *Farewell, I'm Bound to Leave You*. New York: Picador USA, 1996.

————. *I Am One of You Forever: A Novel.* Baton Rouge: Louisiana State University Press, 1985.

————. *Moments of Light.* New York: New South, 1980.

————. *More Shapes than One.* New York: St. Martin's Press, 1991.

Edgerton, Clyde, et al. "Tributes to Fred Chappell." *Pembroke Magazine* 23 (1991): 77–92.

Garrett, George. "A Few Things about Fred Chappell." *Mississippi Quarterly* 37, no. 1 (1983–84): 3–8.

Gray, Amy Tipton. "Fred Chappell's *I Am One of You Forever*: The Oneiros of Childhood Transformed." In *The Poetics of Appalachian Space,* edited by Parks Lanier. Knoxville: University of Tennessee Press, 1991.

Hobson, Fred. *The Southern Writer in the Postmodern World.* Athens: University of Georgia Press, 1991.

Powell, Dannye Romine. *Parting the Curtains: Voices of the Great Southern Writers.* Winston-Salem, N.C.: John F. Blair, 1994.

Stuart, Dabney. "'What's Artichokes?': An Introduction to the Work of Fred Chappell." *The Fred Chappell Reader.* New York: St. Martin's Press, 1987.

Robert M. Luscher
University of Nebraska at Kearney

CHARACTER

A fictional person in literature or drama. In *Aspects of the Novel* (1927), E. M. Forster introduced the now widely accepted distinction between two-dimensional or "flat" characters, who have little individualizing detail, and "round" characters, whose complexity echoes that of real-life human beings. Although flat characters may perform an important function in the work (as METAPHOR or FOIL, for instance), the reader does not view them as realistic. In NATHANIEL HAWTHORNE's story "YOUNG GOODMAN BROWN," for example, Brown appears as a central figure in an ALLEGORY. In his growing disillusion with his beliefs and with the townspeople, Brown remains clearly indispensable to the tale, yet he is flat, not round. Round characters possess a complexity of temperament, motivation, thought, and dialogue that reminds readers of real people. EUDORA WELTY's narrator in "WHY I LIVE AT THE P.O.," ERNEST HEMINGWAY's NICK ADAMS, and RAYMOND CARVER's myriad short story characters, for example, convincingly replicate the foibles, the yearnings, and the recognizable responses of modern people.

CHARACTERIZATION

The methods authors use to depict the characters they create. An author's major approaches to characterization include showing and telling. In showing, or the dramatic method, characters—seemingly independent of the author—may behave in such a way that they speak and act as believable, or "round" (see CHARACTER). In telling, the author presents characters, usually intervening with some commentary or evaluation, illustrating with action from time to time; or allows characters to tell their own stories.

"CHARLES" SHIRLEY JACKSON (1948)

SHIRLEY JACKSON's short sketch "Charles" is frequently anthologized primarily because of the appeal of its protagonist, Laurie Hymen, whose first days at kindergarten prefigure his rebellion against the school system and against authority figures in general. First published in *Mademoiselle* in 1948, this tale of domestic realism was later reprinted in Jackson's 1953 collection entitled *Life among the Savages.* In this series of short stories, Jackson concentrates on more humorous and lighthearted material, moving away from the gothic and horrific modes that she had employed in the short story "The Lottery" and the novels *The Haunting of Hill House* and *We Have Always Lived in the Castle.*

Narrated by Laurie Hymen's mother, "Charles" relates the story of the boy Laurie's first schoolday and his transformation from precocious toddler to self-sufficient schoolboy who relates his daily adventures to his family, especially the escapades of his classmate Charles, who is daily punished for his pranks. Charles hits or kicks the teacher, is "fresh," and gets other students in trouble.

Fascinated by Charles's acting out, the Hymans began to use the child's name whenever anyone in their extended family does anything bad or inconsiderate. It is no wonder the Hymans are shocked when, during the third week of school, Laurie reports that Charles has transformed himself into the teacher's helper and into a model student. The parents are fascinated by his sudden change but hardly surprised when Charles reverts to his original rebellious self shortly before the parent-teacher meeting.

Since Laurie reports to his parents that Charles has tremendous power in the classroom and that his rebellious actions are followed and admired by his classmates, it is no wonder that Mrs. Hymen is anxious to discover all she can about this little boy who has so impressed her son. However, the teacher reveals that there is no child named Charles in the class and instead voices her concerns about Laurie's lack of adjustment to the classroom environment.

This ironic twist suggests that, in order to draw attention to himself, the precocious Laurie has created an alter ego who will take the blame for his own acting out. In short, Laurie's shift from negative to positive behavior indicates his dilemma about what role he wants to fulfill.

While not her most famous story, "Charles" remains one of Jackson's most appreciated works.

Michael J. Meyer
De Paul University

CHARLES (CHICK) MALLISON

Chick is a young boy and man who appears in WILLIAM FAULKNER's novels and stories. In addition to playing key roles in such novels as *Intruder in the Dust* and *The Mansion,* Chick appears in stories with his uncle GAVIN STEVENS, the majority of which are in the collection *KNIGHT'S GAMBIT.* In addition to the humor Chick's behavior provides, his POINT OF VIEW sustains the perspective of an amusing and only partially informed narrator and commentator. Chick thus becomes one of Faulkner's UNRELIABLE NARRATORS. In a sense, as successor to Gavin, he is the last of the narrators, including ISAAC (IKE) MCCASLIN and Horace Benbow, but without their tortured sensibilities. He is morally sound, however, and performs some heroic acts as he aligns himself with blacks and women to correct wrongs and to illuminate bigotry. Chick is thus aligned with the modern South.

CHARLIE WALES

In F. SCOTT FITZGERALD's "BABYLON REVISITED," Charlie Wales enters the story as a reformed alcoholic PROTAGONIST. A third-person narrator provides us with information on his background when he lived the profligate expatriate life in Paris, the "Babylon" of the story. He desperately wishes to reclaim his honor—as signified in the name of his daughter, Honoria, who is being withheld from him by a disapproving sister-in-law, Marion, until he proves himself a fit father. There are at least two ways to view Charlie: first, as a sympathetic character who has truly repented of his formerly wicked ways and is now being unfairly judged by Marion; second, as a man who is not being honest with himself and still has not come to terms with his own responsibility for Helen's death. Many critics also view him as an alter ego for Fitzgerald, who lived a similarly dissolute life in the Paris of the 1920s and who suffered similar reversals after the 1929 stock market crash and the GREAT DEPRESSION that ensued. This biographical viewpoint is not without problems, however, as the real Fitzgerald had to cope not with his wife's death but instead with her collapse into madness. (Zelda Fitzgerald outlived her husband by seven years.) As the ambiguous DENOUEMENT implies, the careful reader must consider this character in all his complexity: Will he stop drinking altogether? Will he regain his daughter—and his honor? Critics have reached no consensus on these issues.

CHEEVER, JOHN (JOHN WILLIAM CHEEVER) (1912–1982)

Born in Quincy, Massachusetts, in 1912, John Cheever published more than 200 stories before his death in 1982. His remarkable writing career began at age 18 with the publication of his first story, "Expelled," in the *New Republic,* based upon his expulsion from Thayer Academy in South Braintree, Massachusetts. Determined to fulfill a long-held ambition to make his living as a writer, Cheever lived a bohemian life in New York City during the 1930s, publishing stories in the *NEW YORKER,* the *ATLANTIC MONTHLY, COLLIER'S* and *STORY.* While serving four years in the army during World War II, he maintained his remarkable output, publishing his first collection of stories, *The Way Some People Live,* in 1942. After the appearance of five more story collections, four novels, and numerous *New Yorker* stories, he published the retrospective *The Stories of John Cheever* in 1978, the first short story collection ever to appear on the *New York Times* best-seller list: It won the PULITZER PRIZE in literature, the National Book Critics Circle Award, and an American Book Award.

Cheever's second book, *The Enormous Radio and Other Stories* (1953), earned him a reputation, reaffirmed over the decades, as one of the most talented American short story writers of the second half of the 20th century. *The Housebreaker of Shady Hill and Other Stories* (1958) focuses on the personal problems of wealthy but troubled American suburbanites. The settings of *Some People, Places, and Things That Will Not Appear in My Next Novel* (1961); *The Brigadier and the Golf Widow* (1964); and *The World of Apples* (1973) range from contemporary America to Italy.

Because he wrote deceptively simple stories, critics and readers alike have found Cheever's literary techniques difficult to classify. Over the course of hundreds of stories, Cheever clearly became less concerned with the restrictions of GENRE and increasingly experimental in terms of literary technique. He experimented in various and complex ways, and, although not a postmodernist (see POSTMODERNISM), he developed a notably lyrical style and infused his stories with SATIRE, REALISM, MAGICAL REALISM, FANTASY, and even modern GOTHIC qualities. "The ENORMOUS RADIO," for example, one of his best-known stories, seems conventional and realistic as it introduces a complacently successful New York couple, but with the intrusion of the fantastic radio into the lives of Jim and Irene Wescott, their middle-class existence shatters to reveal deep wounds and insecurities beneath their patina of respectability.

Cheever has also demonstrated a keen eye and a clear penchant for examining the fabric that holds together or destroys relationships between characters who, at first glance, seem respectable and unremarkable. Another of his most frequently anthologized stories, "The FIVE FORTY-EIGHT," displays his sympathetic sensitivity to women and family members who are used and abused by powerful men—and his obvious, though subtly expressed, delight in describing Miss Dent's revenge on Blake, her abuser. Moral retribution awaits a number of his other characters—Neddy Merrill, in "THE SWIMMER"; Cash Bentley, in "O Youth and Beauty"; Charlie Pastern in "The Brigadier and the Golf Widow"; and various expatriate Americans in his Italian stories.

Cheever also invented the mythical setting of SHADY HILL, an affluent suburb that frequently seems to be EDEN gone awry. Since his death, Cheever, a writer whose talents critics have compared to those of EDGAR ALLAN POE, NATHANIEL HAWTHORNE, STEPHEN CRANE, and ERNEST HEMINGWAY, has held his own as one of the most talented chroniclers of 20th-century American life.

See also "The COUNTRY HUSBAND."

BIBLIOGRAPHY

Avedon, Richard. "John Cheever, 1981." *The New Yorker,* 20–27 February 1995, p. 202.

Baumgartner, M. P. *The Moral Order of a Suburb.* New York: Oxford University Press, 1988.

Cheever, John. *The Brigadier and the Gold Widow.* New York: Harper & Row, 1964.

———. *The Enormous Radio and Other Stories.* New York: Funk & Wagnalls, 1953.

———. *The Housebreaker of Shady Hill and Other Stories.* New York: Harper, 1958.

———. *The Journals of John Cheever.* New York: Knopf, 1991.

———. *Some People, Places, and Things That Will Not Appear in My Next Novel.* New York: Harper. 1961.

———. *The Stories of John Cheever.* New York: Knopf, 1978.

———. *Thirteen Uncollected Stories.* Chicago: Academy Chicago Publishers, 1994.

———. *Uncollected Stories.* Chicago: Academy Chicago Publishers, 1988.

———. *The Way Some People Live: A Book of Stories.* New York: Random, 1943.

———. *The World of Apples.* New York: Alfred A. Knopf, 1973.

Cheever, Susan. *Home before Dark.* Boston: Houghton, 1984.

———. *John Cheever.* New York: Ungar, 1977.

Coale, Samuel. "Cheever and Hawthorne: The American Romancer's Art." In *Critical Essays on John Cheever,* edited by R. G. Collins. Boston: G. K. Hall, 1982.

Collins, Robert G., ed. *Critical Essays on John Cheever.* Boston: G. K. Hall, 1982.

Donaldson, Scott. *John Cheever: A Biography.* New York: Delta, 1988.

Greenberg, Clement. "Avant-Garde and Kitsch." In *Perceptions and Judgements, 1939–1944,* edited by John O'Brian. Chicago: Chicago University Press, 1986.

Hausdorff, Don. "Politics and Economics: The Emergence of the *New Yorker* Tone." In *Studies in American Humor* 3, no. 1 (1984): 74–82.

Hunt, George W. *John Cheever: The Hobgoblin Company of Love.* Grand Rapids, Mich.: Eerdmans, 1983.

Hutcheon, Linda. *A Theory of Parody.* New York: Methuen, 1985.

Irvin, Rea. *Good Morning, Sir: The Sixth New Yorker Album.* New York: Harper and Brothers, 1933.

MacDonald, Dwight, ed. *Parodies: An Anthology from Chaucer to Beerbohm—and After.* New York: Random House, 1960.

Morace, Robert A. "John Cheever." In *Reference Guide to Short Fiction,* edited by Noelle Watson, 118–119. Detroit: Gale Press, 1994.

O'Hara, James Eugene. *John Cheever: Study of the Short Fiction.* Boston: Twayne, 1989.

Rovit, Earl. "Modernism and Three Magazines: An Editorial Revolution." *The Sewanee Review* 18, no. 4 (1985): 541–553.

Waldeland, Lynne. *John Cheever.* Boston: Twayne, 1979.

Warren, Austin. *The New England Conscience.* Ann Arbor: Michigan University Press, 1966.

Whyte, William. *The Organization Man.* New York: Simon & Schuster, 1956.

CHESNUTT, CHARLES WADDELL

(1858–1932) Charles Waddell Chesnutt was born in Cleveland, Ohio, the son of free blacks who returned to their home of Fayetteville, North Carolina, after the CIVIL WAR. Chesnutt became a teacher but by 1883 moved back to Cleveland, where he passed the bar exam and began his own court reporting business. Despite his social and economic success, Chesnutt still desired to make a living by the pen and devoted much of his time to writing. He concentrated on what he knew best: the history and African-American folklore that he had heard as a child. He found an audience in 1887 when the prestigious ATLANTIC MONTHLY published his story "The Goophered Grapevine." It marked the first time that an African-American writer's fiction had appeared in the magazine. In 1899 two collections of his short stories were published, *The Conjure Woman* and *The Wife of His Youth and Other Stories of the Color Line.* Following the success of these two books, Chesnutt closed his business to focus on writing full time.

The DIALECT stories of *The Conjure Woman* placed it in early criticism as a representative work of REGIONALISM and REALISM popular in the late 19th century.

Chesnutt used the stories to subvert the romantic vision of plantation literature (which extolled the lost plantation society and longed for the antebellum era) written by JOEL CHANDLER HARRIS and Thomas Nelson Page, and as social commentary on the problems of the Reconstructionist South. (See RECONSTRUCTION.) The stories are told by the ex-slave Uncle Julius McAdoo, an ironic counterpart of Harris's UNCLE REMUS. Each story (with the exception of "Dave's Neckliss") is a conjure tale designed to illustrate Uncle Julius's cleverness and wit at the expense of the narrator, John, a Northern businessman. CONJURE STORIES drew on the superstitions of folk characters and used blacks in often witty ways against "white folks" as a means of amusement on the surface but as a means of survival at a far more serious level. The tales share another characteristic. Set in the days of slavery, they illustrate the tragic lives of slaves and the imagination and faith that they had to possess in order to preserve themselves and their community. Stories such as "The Goophered Grapevine," "The Conjurer's Revenge," and "Po Sandy" showed slaves turned into trees, plants, and animals through conjuring. Chesnutt's bitterly ironic implication is that African Americans were not considered "human" before slavery was abolished and that because of racist laws and attitudes, nothing had changed for them in the late 19th century.

Also published in 1899, the stories in *The Wife of His Youth and Other Stories of the Color Line* focus primarily on the psychological and social problems facing mixed race people, those living on "the color line." Countering the stereotypical (see STEREOTYPE) picture of the tragic mulatto, Chesnutt analyzed the results of MISCEGENATION and mob violence in such works as "The Sheriff's Children." Chesnutt's realistic portrayal of class and color prejudice within the African-American community can be found in stories such as "The Wife of His Youth" and "The Matter of Principle." One of the most well-received stories in the collection is "The Passing of Grandison." The story reveals the true nature beneath a seemingly docile slave who dupes his master, Dick Owens, and helps his family escape to the North.

Chesnutt published his last piece of short fiction, "Baxter's Procrustes," in 1904. He was largely overlooked by critics in the early 20th century in favor of the writers of the HARLEM RENAISSANCE but has since gained respect for illustrating the broad and diverse range of African-American experience and for drawing attention to the nation's continuing problems of racism.

He published his first novel, *The House behind the Cedars,* in 1900. His novel *The Marrow of Tradition* appeared in 1901. Its social realism and plea for racial tolerance garnered high praise from the critic WILLIAM DEAN HOWELLS, but it angered many other reviewers. Chesnutt's last novel, *The Colonel's Dream,* was published in 1905 to little fanfare. No longer able to support his family entirely from his writing, he reopened his business. Recently Chesnutt has received recognition for his outstanding contribution to the development of African-American fiction, particularly in the short story.

See also AFRICAN-AMERICAN SHORT FICTION.

BIBLIOGRAPHY

Andrews, William. *The Literary Career of Charles W. Chesnutt.* Baton Rouge: Louisiana State University Press, 1980.

Render, Sylvia Lyons. *Charles Chesnutt.* Boston: Twayne, 1980.

Sundquist, Eric J. *To Wake the Nations.* Cambridge, Mass.: Belknap Press of Harvard University Press, 1993.

Tracie Guzzio
Ohio University

CHICAGO RENAISSANCE (a.k.a. "LITTLE RENAISSANCE")

The term *Chicago Renaissance* describes the artistic and literary renewal associated with two distinct groups of principally midwestern writers and artists. The first was an avant-garde group of writers in the 1910s that included the novelists and short fiction writers SHERWOOD ANDERSON, Floyd Dell, THEODORE DREISER, and James T. Farrell; the poets Carl Sandburg, Vachel Lindsay, and Edgar Lee Masters; and the LITTLE MAGAZINE editors Harriet Monroe (of the Chicago-based *Poetry*) and Margaret C. Anderson (*The Little Review*). These writers and others, whom outsiders considered rebels and bohemians, openly criticized the provincialism and materialism they perceived in American society and culture.

This group existed more or less separately from the African-American exponents of the Chicago Renaissance, flourishing from the end of the HARLEM RENAISSANCE in about 1935 to the civil rights era of the early 1950s. This group contributed significantly to increased recognition of black women writers, particularly Gwendolyn Brooks, Lorraine Hansberry, Margaret Walker, and DOROTHY WEST. Interaction between the black and the white Chicago Renaissance did occur, particularly among younger African-American writers and Dreiser, Farrell, Masters, and Sandburg, and under the editorship of Monroe, *Poetry* magazine advanced the careers of LANGSTON HUGHES and Gwendolyn Brooks.

"CHICKAMAUGA" AMBROSE BIERCE (1889)

Chickamauga is Cherokee for "bad water," the name a branch of the tribe gave to the creek alongside which they lived in the northwest corner of Georgia when they were decimated by an outbreak of smallpox. Subsequent historians dubbed Chickamauga Creek the "River of Death" (Morris 56); the Civil War's Battle of Chickamauga on September 19–20, 1863, was "the largest battle in the western theater of operations and the bloodiest two-day encounter of the entire war" (Morris 61), with Union and Confederate casualties estimated at 16,000 and 20,000, respectively (McPherson 674–675).

AMBROSE BIERCE (born 1842), an Indiana farm boy who had enlisted on the Union side in 1861, took part in this battle, and in his story "Chickamauga" (1889) he not only accurately describes the tactical military aspects of the terrain but also captures the horrors of war in gruesome detail. Bierce accomplishes this with the expertise he had gained as an advance scout and topographical engineer (cf. "A Little of Chickamauga" [1898], *Collected Works* I, 275) and with the dual-narrative perspective he uses in having an adult tell the story of a six-year-old farm boy's first and shattering experience of war.

This "child" strays "one sunny autumn afternoon" from his "home in a small field" and enters "a forest unobserved." He is "the son of a poor planter," who "in his younger manhood . . . had been a soldier," in whom "the warrior-fire survived" and from whose "military books and pictures" the boy has made himself "a wooden sword," which he now recklessly brandishes as he advances with ease in the forest against "invisible foes." Here Bierce (cf. "A Little of Chickamauga," *Collected Works* I, 271, 274) has the boy duplicate the Union general William S. Rosencrans's tactical blunder when he incautiously advanced south from Chattanooga, by noting that the boy was committing "the common enough military error of pushing the pursuit to a dangerous extreme," arriving at "a wide but shallow brook," whose "rapid waters" he nevertheless crosses and vanquishes "the rear-guard of his invisible foe." However, he is then frightened by "a rabbit," from which he flees, "calling with inarticulate cries for his mother," and eventually sobs himself to sleep between two rocks near the stream. Meanwhile, "the wood birds sing merrily above his head," and "somewhere far away was a strange, muffled thunder."

When he awakens at twilight, he sees "before him a strange moving object which he took to be some large animal—a dog, a pig—he could not name it; perhaps it was a bear." But as it nears, he gains courage, "for he saw that at least it had not the long menacing ears of the rabbit." Then he notices that "to right and to left were many more; the whole open space about him was alive with them—all moving toward the brook." The narrator identifies these creatures as wounded soldiers dragging themselves away from the battle site, seeking a place to drink or die: "They were men. They crept upon their hands and knees. . . . They came by the dozens and by hundreds. . . . Occasionally one who had paused did not again go on, but lay motionless. He was dead. Some, pausing, made strange gestures with their hands, erected their arms and lowered them again, clasped their heads, spread their palms upward. . . ." The boy jumps on one of the crawling soldiers, thinking he can ride him as he had often ridden his father's slaves "for his amusement." The soldier collapses but turns "a face that lacked a lower jaw," and "from the upper teeth to the throat was a red gap fringed with hanging shreds of flesh and splinters of bone," which gave him "the appearance of a great bird of prey." Meanwhile, the soldiers "moved forward down the slope like a swarm of great black beetles." The narrator reinforces the

animal imagery by comparing the trail of their discarded equipment to "the 'spoor' of men flying from their hunters."

Fire "on the farther side of the creek" was "now suffusing the whole landscape," and the boy, ahead of the crawling soldiers, crosses the creek and heads for the fire "across a field," where he recognizes "the blazing building as his own home" and finds the body of his mother, "the white face turned upward, the hands thrown out and clutched full of grass, the clothing deranged, the long dark hair in tangles and full of clotted blood," and "The greater part of the forehead was torn away, and from the jagged hole the brain protruded, overflowing the temple, a frothy mass of gray, crowned with clusters of crimson bubbles—the work of a shell." "Looking down upon the wreck," the boy utters "a series of inarticulate and indescribable cries—something between the chattering of an ape and the gobbling of a turkey." The "child," only now revealed to be "a deaf mute," is brutally brought face to face with the horrific reality of war in ironic contrast to his war games in the forest.

In its review (February 20, 1892), the *London Atheneum* objected to Bierce's focus on "the minutest details of bodily and mental pain," most gruesomely in "Chickamauga," in which the reviewer mistakenly notes that the child "was struck deaf and dumb" by the sight of his dead mother. The *Atheneum* found this "extremely unsuitable for young readers, to whom it is surely more wholesome to present the nobler side of war" (*Critical Essays* 15–16). Indeed, whether in Victorian England or in the United States, where the Civil War had been portrayed for decades "through a halo of civilian romance" (Grattan 137), Bierce's Civil War stories shocked readers. In its review (March 1898) of *In the Midst of Life* (New York, 1898), however, the *Nation* praised "Chickamauga" as "an allegory" and noted that "this volume could not have been revived at a more opportune moment," just before the outbreak of the Spanish-American War (April–August 1898), and that it therefore deserved "the widest circulation as a peace tract of the first order, in the present craze for bloodshed" (*Critical Essays* 16). After the republication of the English edition (1915) during World War I, the *London Opinion* cited Bierce "as one of the greatest masters in depicting the horrors of war" and called him "the veritable Goya of literature" (*Critical Essays* 47). Although he has remained in the shadow of Stephen Crane (1871–1900), whose novel *The Red Badge of Courage* (1895) has become a classic, Bierce, too, is a worthy forerunner of such 20th-century American war writers as ERNEST HEMINGWAY or Tim O'Brien.

BIBLIOGRAPHY

Bierce, Ambrose. "Chickamauga" (1889). In *Tales of Soldiers and Civilians*. San Francisco, Calif.: Steele, 1892.

———. "Chickamauga." *The Collected Works of Ambrose Bierce*. Vol. 2. New York/Washington: Neale, 1909.

———. "Chickamauga." In *The Civil War Stories of Ambrose Bierce*, edited by Ernest J. Hopkins. Lincoln/London: University of Nebraska Press (Bison Books), 1988.

———. *In the Midst of Life—Tales of Soldiers and Civilians*. London: Chatto & Windus, 1892.

———. "A Little of Chickamauga" (1898). In *The Collected Works of Ambrose Bierce*. Vol. 1. New York/Washington: Neale, 1909.

Crane, Stephen. *The Red Badge of Courage and Selected Short Fiction*. Edited by Richard Fusco. New York: Barnes & Noble Classics, 2003.

Davidson, Cathy N., ed. *Critical Essays on Ambrose Bierce*. Boston: G. K. Hall, 1982.

Gale, Robert L. *An Ambrose Bierce Companion*. Westport, Conn.: Greenwood Press, 2001.

Goya, Francisco. *The Disasters of War*. Edited by Philip Hofer. New York: Dover, 1967. (Translation of *Los Desastres de la Guerra*, Madrid, 1863.)

Grattan, C. Hartley. *Bitter Bierce: A Mystery of American Letters*. Garden City, N.Y.: Doubleday, Doran, 1929.

McPherson, James M. *Battle Cry of Freedom: The Civil War Era*. 1988. Reprint, New York: Ballantine Books, 1989.

Morris, Roy, Jr. *Ambrose Bierce: Alone in Bad Company*. New York/Oxford: Oxford University Press, 1998.

Frederick Betz
Southern Illinois University Carbondale

"CHILDREN ARE BORED ON SUNDAY" JEAN STAFFORD (1948)

JEAN STAFFORD'S first *NEW YORKER* story and one of only two (along with "An Influx of Poets") emerging from her marriage to the poet Robert Lowell, this story is not anthologized as frequently as one would expect. Judged as a brilliant tale by virtually all Stafford critics, it has contemporary resonances with all who have experienced a sense of loneliness or marginalization and its destructive aspects. Ironically, as Mary Ann Wilson notes, the story's reception replicates the very subject of the story itself: Stafford's literary acquaintances derided her for appearing in a middle-brow publication such as the *New Yorker*, just as her young woman in the story is "excoriated" by the literati (63).

Biographical parallels aside, however, Stafford's story, a "PARABLE of a lost soul," movingly depicts Emma, the young woman, judged by the same people whose standards she rejects. Emma, the third-person narrator and controlling consciousness in the story, by chance encounters at the Metropolitan Museum of Art a man named Alfred Eisenstein, whom she recalls as an artist who had made her feel inferior at a recent cocktail party. The story is divided into three sections: a flashback to the superficial New York artists' party; Emma's current observations of young boys in the museum and her connection of them with Alfred as a first-generation immigrant who, like her, is an outsider driven to alcoholism and nervous collapse; and finally, Emma and Alfred's meeting outside the museum, greeting each other like long-lost friends. Together they enter a Lexington Avenue bar, clinging to each other like children, and order martinis. The LYRICally romantic ending may be viewed literally or cynically, depending on how seriously the reader takes the final ALLUSION to a Van Eyck painting of souls in hell.

BIBLIOGRAPHY

Stafford, Jean. *Children Are Bored on Sunday*. New York: Harcourt Brace, 1953.

Wilson, Mary Ann. *Jean Stafford: A Study of the Short Fiction*. New York: Twayne, 1996.

CHILDREN OF LONELINESS ANZIA YEZIERSKA (1923)

In *Children of Loneliness*, ANZIA YEZIERSKA presents nine poignant stories about Jewish immigrants living on the East Side of New York City: "Children of Loneliness," "Brothers," "To the Stars," "An Immigrant among the Editors," "America and I," "A Bed for the Night," "Dreams and Dollars," "The Song Triumphant," and "The Lord Giveth." She introduces these works of fiction with "Mostly about Myself," a nonfiction chapter about her writing, in which she claims, "My one story is hunger. Hunger driven by loneliness" (12).

Yezierska's style is simple and emotional (some say sentimental). DIALECT and autobiographical material permeate the stories, giving them the raw, realistic edge that typifies the author's work. Characters such as Hanneh Breineh, the gritty boardinghouse manager, appear in multiple stories, unifying the collection. What seem at first to be straightforward, even simplistic THEMES become, in Yezierska's hands, revelations of the paradoxes inherent in the immigrant experience. In the title story, for example, the PROTAGONIST, Rachel Ravinsky, a newly Americanized teacher, abandons her self-sacrificing mother and otherworldly rabbi father for an American-bred college beau, Frank Baker, who, she believes, will scorn their old country ways. She soon discovers, however, that she feels uncomfortable with Frank, a social worker who sees her people as "picturesque" and romanticizes their poverty (51). Rachel fits nowhere, and that is the irony of the book.

The author examines the immigrants' conflicts, pitting economic and spiritual needs, communal and individual expectations, and the yearning for both assimilation and ethnic identity one against the other; she provides no easy middle ground for her characters. The conflicts of the artist reflect the conflicts of the immigrant in such stories as "The Song Triumphant," whose subtitle, "The Story of Berel Pinsky, Poet of the People, Who Sold His Soul for Wealth," introduces two of Yezierska's recurring themes: the necessity of artistic integrity and the fact that inspiration is gained from one's own people. The struggle to maintain a pure aesthetic while attaining a public voice is conflated with the effort to retain one's own identity in an alien world (themes also seen in "To the Stars" and "An Immigrant among the Editors").

Other stories that deal with selling one's soul for money emphasize the crass materialism that surfaces as a reaction to years of deprivation. Yezierska claims in her introductory chapter that "the dollar fight that grew up like a plague in times of poverty, killing the souls of men, still goes on in times of plenty" (22). In "Dreams and Dollars" the card table and the "King of Clothing," Moe Mirsky, represent the ugly competition of the consumer culture that often replaces the "hunger driven by loneliness."

Yezierska seeks a third option, the compromise finally reached by Pinsky in "The Song Triumphant." Pinsky rejects Broadway and returns to the East Side, where he works at a machine for his living and writes honest poetry about his fellow workers. Pinsky thus alleviates his loneliness while satisfying both his physical and artistic hunger.

BIBLIOGRAPHY

Henriksen, Louise Levitas. *Anzia Yezierska: A Writer's Life.* New Brunswick, N.J.: Rutgers University Press, 1988.
Shapiro, Ann R. "The Ultimate Shaygets and the Fiction of Anna Yezierska." *MELUS* 21, no. 2 (Summer 96): 79–88.
Yezierska, Anzia. *Red Ribbon on a White Horse.* New York: Scribner, 1950.

Gwen M. Neary
Santa Rosa Junior College
Sonoma State University

"CHILD WHO FAVORED DAUGHTER, THE" ALICE WALKER (1973)

First published in 1973 in the collection *In Love & Trouble: Stories of Black Women,* this story offers a GOTHIC tale of love, lust, and dismemberment in three parts, told in a lyric prose style interspersed with bits of poetry. "The Child Who Favored Daughter" begins in the same way that it concludes: An unnamed black man with a shotgun waits on his porch for a school bus. In the first section, he awaits his own daughter's return from school in order to confront her about an intercepted love letter written to a white lover who has spurned her to marry a white woman.

The second section sketches the psychological makeup of the father, which includes an incestuous desire for his sister (ironically and confusingly named "Daughter"), virulent racism, a fear of sexually liberated women, and a history of physical abuse in his own childhood home. The events surrounding his sister's life and death form the character of the young brother, who presumes that everyone will disappoint and betray him and therefore must be punished accordingly. This young man grows into the older abusive husband (he beats his wife into a cripple who eventually deserts her family) and father of a daughter who, unfortunately for her, is "a replica in every way" of his dead sister, Daughter.

The father's sadism toward women culminates on the day that he finds his daughter's letter. She will not deny that she loves a white man, even after her father beats her with a belt (a fairly regular occurrence). In the face of his daughter's refusal to deny her love for the white man, the father suddenly hacks off her breasts with his pocket knife and "flings what he finds in his hands to the yelping dogs." The story's elliptical final paragraph concludes with the father back on his porch once again waiting for the school bus with his shotgun, only now he waits in vain. All the daughters are dead. In the beginning of the story Walker hints that the father-daughter bond implicitly involves violence when daughters come of age and prefer other men to their own fathers. The conclusion of her story suggests an ironic twist on the OEDIPAL MYTH, in which the Greek Oedipus killed his father and married his mother, lighting a tragic fuse that burns until his wife, Jocasta, and, later, his daughter, Antigone, commit suicide. In Walker's story, the father has slain his own Antigone.

BIBLIOGRAPHY
Boose, Lynda E., and Betty S. Flowers, eds. *Fathers and Daughters.* Baltimore: Johns Hopkins University Press, 1989.

S. L. Yentzer
University of Georgia

CHIN, FRANK (1940–)

Frank Chin was born in Berkeley, California, and grew up in the Chinatowns of Oakland and San Francisco. He earned his B.A. from the University of California at Santa Barbara and his M.F.A. from the Writer's Workshop at Iowa State University, where he attended on a Writer's Workshop fellowship. His stories have appeared in *Panache,* the *Carolina Quarterly, City Lights Journal,* and the *Chouteau Review;* eight of them are collected in *The Chinaman Pacific & Frisco R.R. Co.* (1988). He is also the author of personal essays; literary criticism; several award-winning plays, including *The Chickencoop Chinaman* (1981); and the novels *Gunga Din Highway* (1995) and *Donald Duk* (1991). He lives in the Los Angeles area.

In his stories, Chin argues that, as a group, Chinese-American males are dressed in a fake identity created by white Americans and by illusory memories of what it is to be "Chinese." Chin's PROTAGONISTS struggle for a unique identity that is self-created and that is neither Chinese nor American but Chinese American. Contrary to Asian-American paradigms established by TOSHIO MORI and others, Chin believes the Asian-American community is claustrophobic and self-destructive. As Elaine Kim has observed, Chin's notion of valid identity is "built around the Asian American man's being accepted as American," and to be accepted, the Asian-American male finds it necessary "to challenge the STEREOTYPE of quaint foreigners, to reject the notion of the passive, quiet Asian American, and to move away from the stultifying limitations of the glittering Chinatown ghetto." Thus Chin's protagonists are at odds with those of many other Asian-American writers, who value the strong ethnic identity that provides security, stability, and a strong sense of community.

As with the fiction of JEFFERY PAUL CHAN, the writings of Frank Chin often employ an exaggerated sexuality. Chin's male protagonists METAPHORICALLY establish their identities—sometimes ironically, sometimes not—through sexual conquests, often of white women. This, together with Chin's mean-spirited dismissal of Asian-American women writers in his literary criticism and in the afterword to *The Chinaman Pacific & Frisco R.R. Co.,* has persuaded some readers that Chin is misogynistic and even racist.

Writers and scholars who embrace his politics of ASIAN-AMERICAN LITERATURE believe that Chin, in distancing himself from writers like MAXINE HONG KINGSTON, AMY TAN, GISH JEN, and David Henry Hwang by labeling them "fake" writers who distort or destroy Asian culture and perpetuate white stereotypes of Asians and Asian Americans, is courageously staking out a moral high ground that "real" Asian Americans eventually may occupy. The more cynical of his detractors believe such a position is both arbitrary and illogical, especially in its naive or false understanding of basic principles of folklore, oral narratives, and cross-cultural discourse, and that it unsuccessfully masks a profound jealousy of writers who have been far more influential than he.

BIBLIOGRAPHY

Chin, Frank. "Come All Ye Asian American Writers of the Real and the Fake." *The Big Aiiieeeee! An Anthology of Chinese American and Japanese American Literature,* edited by Jeffery Paul Chan, et al. New York: Meridian, 1991.

Kim, Elaine. *Asian American Literature.* Philadelphia: Temple University Press, 1982.

Li, David Leiwei. "The Formation of Frank Chin and Formations of Chinese American Literature." In *Asian Americans,* edited by Shirley Hune, et al. Comparative Global Perspectives. Pullman: Washington State University Press, 1991.

Keith Lawrence
Brigham Young University

CHOPIN, KATE (1850–1904)

Although Kate Chopin is known primarily for her 1899 novel *The Awakening,* in her lifetime she was celebrated as the author of LOCAL COLOR stories set in Louisiana. Born in St. Louis in 1850 to an Irish father and French Creole mother, Chopin experienced two tragedies in her early childhood: the death of her father in 1855 and the loss of her half brother, a Confederate soldier, to typhoid in the CIVIL WAR. She married Oscar Chopin, a French Creole from Louisiana, in 1870, and they lived in New Orleans until 1879, when business losses forced them to relocate to a family farm near Natchitoches, Louisiana. The Chopins had six children. When her husband died of yellow fever in 1883, Kate Chopin managed his businesses until she moved to St. Louis to reside with her mother. After the death of her mother in 1885, Chopin began to write, encouraged by her physician friend Dr. Kohlenbeyer. In 1890 she published her first novel, *At Fault,* at her own expense. Her first literary successes were children's stories, published in *Youth's Companion* and *Harper's Young People.*

The 1894 publication of *Bayou Folk,* a collection of 23 tales and sketches, by Houghton Mifflin & Co., earned Chopin national fame as a master of REGIONALISM. Set exclusively in Louisiana, primarily Natchitoches and New Orleans, the stories centered on the lives of Creoles and Cajuns. Reviewers praised her keen ear for DIALECT and the picturesque evocations of rural life. William Marion Reedy (*Sunday Mirror* April 15, 1894) judged her Louisiana stories superior to those of GEORGE WASHINGTON CABLE and declared the volume "the best literary work that has come out of the Southland in a long time."

In 1897 Chopin's second volume of short stories, *A Night in Acadie,* was published by Way and Williams. *Acadie* is, in some ways, a continuation of *Bayou Folk;* the second volume shares the same Louisiana locales and even some of the same characters featured in the first collection. However, as Barbara Ewell notes, in *Acadie* "Chopin's bayou world persists, but its romance and charm seem diminished, its happy endings muted" (94). The influence of the French realists (see REALISM), most notably Guy de Maupassant, whose work Chopin translated, sets these stories apart from conventional local color stories such as those by JOEL CHANDLER HARRIS.

Although Chopin received several enthusiastic reviews for *Acadie,* critics objected to the "unnecessary coarseness" of some of the material (*Critic* April 16, 1898), a charge that would be leveled at her masterpiece, *The Awakening,* the following year. According to one reviewer, "Like most of her work . . . *The Awakening* is too strong drink [sic] for moral babes and should be labelled 'poison'" (*St. Louis Post-Dispatch* May 21, 1899). Although it is widely claimed that the novel was banned, Emily Toth refutes those charges (422–425).

Chopin published little in the final years of her life. Her last volume of stories, entitled *A Vocation and a Voice,* was slated for publication, but the manuscript was returned. On August 20, 1904, after a strenuous day at the St. Louis World's Fair, Chopin collapsed. She died two days later, apparently of a brain hemorrhage.

The past few decades have witnessed a revival of interest in Chopin, in part initiated by the publication in 1969 of Per Seyersted's *Kate Chopin: A Critical Biography* and *The Complete Works of Kate Chopin* and by the burgeoning FEMINIST movement. In addition to examining gender issues in Chopin's works, scholars are investigating her treatment of race, the cultural contexts of her fiction, and her position in the literary canon. Chopin has been associated with a variety of late 19th-century literary groups or movements: impressionism, realism, regionalism, AESTHETICISM, and NATURALISM. Her fiction also anticipates MODERNISM and MINIMALISM.

See also "DESIREE'S BABY."

BIBLIOGRAPHY

Boren, Lynda S., and Sara de Saussure Davis, eds. *Kate Chopin Reconsidered: Beyond the Bayou.* Baton Rouge: Louisiana State University Press, 1992.

Chopin, Kate. *The Complete Works of Kate Chopin.* Baton Rouge: Louisiana State University Press, 1969.

Ewell, Barbara. *Kate Chopin.* New York: Ungar, 1986.

Koloski, Bernard. *Kate Chopin: A Study of the Short Fiction.* New York: Twayne, 1996.

Seyersted, Per. *Kate Chopin: A Critical Biography.* Baton Rouge: Louisiana State University Press, 1969.

Toth, Emily. *Kate Chopin.* New York: Morrow, 1990.

Mary Anne O'Neal
University of Georgia

"CHOPIN IN WINTER" STUART DYBEK (1990, 1994)

This short story from STUART DYBEK's second collection, titled *The Coast of Chicago* (1990), explores the life of a family living in one of Chicago's ethnic enclaves. While ethnicity provides a background for much of Dybek's writing, "Chopin in Winter" is actually one of the few Dybek stories to consider what it means to be of Polish descent. That the author is a poet as well as a storyteller accounts for the LYRICAL quality that is apparent in his stories; in several interviews he has admitted that approximately one-third of his short stories are really failed poems. The other admitted influence on his writing is music; he listens to music when he writes, and the music of Chopin (especially the nocturnes) provides a central theme and a motif for this particular story. As is seen in other of Dybek's stories that deal with childhood events, the father figure is absent—in this instance, because he died in WORLD WAR II.

The story begins as two significant events happen: a young boy's grandfather (referred to as *Dzia-Dzia*) arrives to live with the family, and the landlady's daughter, Marcy, returns home pregnant from New York, where she had been at college studying music. The boy, Michael, slowly gets to know his grandfather, who had emigrated from Poland and had kept on the move looking for work in cold and hazardous situations while the family settled in Chicago. Most of their interaction occurs as they are sitting in the kitchen in the evenings—Michael doing his homework and Dzia-Dzia soaking his swollen, calloused feet, telling the story of his life, while they both listen to Marcy playing her piano on the floor above them. As the evenings pass by, Marcy plays Chopin's waltzes, nocturnes, preludes, and polonaises, which Dzia-Dzia teaches Michael to identify in order to appreciate his heritage as a Pole. Then one day as the weather starts to change, Marcy disappears, leaving only a note telling her mother not to worry. Finally, a few months later, after Marcy informs her mother that she and her son are "living on the South Side in a Negro neighborhood near the university" (160), all of her music, the essence of which had lingered in the house, slowly fades away.

BIBLIOGRAPHY

Dybek, Stuart. "Chopin in Winter." In *The Vintage Book of Contemporary American Short Stories,* edited by Tobias Wolff, 141–161. New York: Vintage Contemporaries–Random House, 1994.

Gladsky, Thomas S. "From Ethnicity to Multiculturalism: The Fiction of Stuart Dybek." *Melus* 20, no. 2 (1995): 105–118.

Nickel, Mike, and Adrian Smith. "An Interview with Stuart Dybek." *Chicago Review* 43, no. 1 (1997): 87–101.

Peggy J. Huey
University of Tampa

"CHRYSANTHEMUMS, THE" JOHN STEINBECK (1938)

Although critical attention now focuses on numerous stories by JOHN STEINBECK as his reputation as a short story writer continues to grow, "The Chrysanthemums" is generally considered not only his best but among the very best in 20th-century American literature. This remarkable work, first published in *The Long Valley,* presents a complex, sensitive portrait of 35-year-old Elisa Allen, the repressed wife of a SALINAS VALLEY rancher. Set during the years of the GREAT DEPRESSION, the story takes place on a Saturday, the last weekday of the last month of the year, and focuses on a woman in middle life who can coax blooms from chrysanthemums, the last flowers of the year. A wealth of critical commentary has examined every aspect of this tale, noting the bleak fog that enshrouds the valley, the constricting fence that surrounds Elisa's tidy house, and Steinbeck's artful use of SYMBOLISM and IMAGERY to evoke Elisa's situation.

At the opening of the story, the narrator juxtaposes Elisa, who is tending to her chrysanthemums, to the mechanistic world outside her fenced garden: It is a man's world, peopled by her husband and his male clients associated with cars and tractors. This metallic imagery prepares us for the arrival of the itinerant tinker who travels the country fixing such household items as knives, scissors, and pots. At first Elisa firmly resists his request for repair work, but this unkempt and pronouncedly grimy man—apparently a perversion of the archetypal romantic dark stranger (see ARCHETYPE)—slyly compliments her chrysanthemums, causing Elisa to believe he shares her interest in her creative talents, and she invites him into her enclosed yard. Her explanation of the needs of the chrysanthemums becomes sexually charged as Elisa's breast swells with passion, and she makes METAPHORS of the nighttime stars that drive their points into one's body, producing a "hot and sharp and—lovely" sensation (400). The tinker deflates this figuratively sexual crescendo by reminding her that nothing is pleasurable if "you don't have no dinner," shaming Elisa into giving him some saucepans to mend. He leaves with an obviously false promise to deliver Elisa's pot of chrysanthemums to a "lady" down the road.

From a Freudian perspective, Steinbeck's use of sexual innuendo seems fairly obvious: Both the valley and the pots suggest female sex, whereas the knives and scissors suggest the male. Mere hours later, on her way out to dinner with Henry, the emotionally and sexually recharged Elisa understands almost immediately that the dark spot on the road is the chrysanthemums: The tinker has thrown away the symbols of

female creative potential and kept the pot with its generic female shape. Just as he has no use for the late-blooming chrysanthemums, he has no use for her, the 35-year-old individual woman. Critics continue to debate Elisa's future: whether she has been defeated or whether, like the chrysanthemums, she will bloom again.

BIBLIOGRAPHY

Steinbeck, John. "The Chrysanthemums." In *American Short Stories.* 6th ed. Edited by Eugene Current-García and Bert Hickock. New York: Longman, 1997.

"CHURCH MOUSE, A" MARY E. WILKINS FREEMAN (1891)

Published in *A New England Nun and Other Stories,* "A Church Mouse" portrays a poor but rebellious New England spinster, Hetty Fifield, who loses her home and moves into the church meetinghouse, appointing herself sexton, a position typically held by a male. After the male officials try unsuccessfully to evict her, Mr. Gale, a church deacon and town selectman, solicits his wife's help. Mrs. Gale, recognizing Hetty's desperation and determination to stay, puts a stop to the uncharitable attempt to oust her and offers her Christmas dinner the next day. Hetty rings the church bells to celebrate the holiday that finally has given her peace and independence after a lifetime of caring for and depending on others. The bells, then, symbolize New World "liberty" bells as well as the echo of Old World traditions long forgotten in the pinch-penny Puritan village.

Mrs. Gale, too, declares her independence from narrow-minded bigotry when she tells Hetty, "Of course, you can stay in the meetin'-house" (416). The narrator describes her as follows: "Mrs. Gale stood majestically, and looked defiantly around; tears were in her eyes" (416). She also finds other women sympathetic to Hetty; together, these women overwhelm the "masculine clamor" (415) and "the last of the besiegers" (417) to introduce a bit of Christmas peace to their tiny corner of the earth.

Critics often group this story with other Freeman stories that examine the "strong but healthy will" of the New England woman (Westbrook 50), who, as a feminist critic reminds us, is a descendant of the nonconformist Anne Hutchinson (M. Pryse, "Afterword," in M. Pryse, ed., *Selected Stories of Mary Wilkins Free-man* [1983], 340). Other critics view "A Church Mouse" as a comment on the effects of poverty, a FEMI-NIST THEME, since "the poorest of the poor in the Free-man village are women" (Reichardt 53).

BIBLIOGRAPHY
Freeman, Mary E. Wilkens, and Sarah Orne Jewett. *Short Fiction of Sarah Orne Jewett and Mary Wilkins Freeman.* Edited by Barbara H. Solomon. New York: New American Library, 1979.
Reichardt, Mary R. *Mary Wilkins Freeman: A Study of the Short Fiction.* New York: Twayne, 1997.
Tutwiler, Julia. "Two New England Writers in Relation to Their Art and to Each Other." In *Critical Essays on Mary Wilkins Freeman,* edited by Shirley Marchalonis. Boston: G. K. Hall, 1991.
Westbrook, Perry. *Mary Wilkins Freeman.* Boston: Twayne, 1988.

Gwen M. Neary
Santa Rosa Junior College
Sonoma State University

"CIRCUMSTANCE" HARRIET PRESCOTT SPOF-FORD (1860, 1863)

First published in the *ATLANTIC MONTHLY* in May 1860, this story was included in HAR-RIET PRESCOTT SPOFFORD's first collection of short stories, *The Amber Gods and Other Stories* (1863). The unnamed female PROTAGONIST's captivity by an "Indian Devil" panther is supposedly based on the experience of Spof-ford's maternal great-grandmother, but the story, a symbolic romance, can be read on several levels.

The woman's nightmarish experience in the forest depicts a test of faith, a journey into a psychic wilder-ness, and a confrontation with sexuality and death. The sexual violence represented by the panther's "sav-age caresses" both suggests the woman artist's sense of vulnerability and exposure and provides a female counterpart to initiation tales such as NATHANIEL HAWTHORNE's "YOUNG GOODMAN BROWN." The protag-onist, a SCHEHERAZADE-like figure whose song saves her life but who ultimately must please the beast, rep-resents the trials of the 19th-century woman artist, whose voice was necessary for survival but also was controlled by a potentially hostile reading public. In addition to portraying the protagonist as EVERY-WOMAN, Spofford particularizes her experience as American. Through the frontier setting and depiction of the "Indian Devil" as well as the protagonist's fear of violation and cannibalism and search for providen-tial meaning—all of which echo Indian captivity nar-ratives—Spofford explores the importance of myth in the creation of national identity. Concluding with a reference to the last lines of John Milton's *Paradise Lost,* in which Adam and Eve depart from the garden, the story recasts the newly liberated protagonist as a New World Eve who has endured the initiation through which Americans gained imaginative posses-sion of the landscape.

BIBLIOGRAPHY
Dalke, Anne. "'Circumstance' and the Creative Woman: Harriet Prescott Spofford." *Arizona Quarterly* 41, no. 1 (Spring 1985): 71–85.
Fetterley, Judith. *Provisions: A Reader from 19th-Century American Women.* Bloomington: Indiana University Press, 1985.

Paula Kot
Niagara University

CISNEROS, SANDRA (1954–)

Perhaps one of the best known Chicana writers (see HISPANIC-AMERICAN SHORT FICTION), Sandra Cisneros gained national recognition when, in 1989, Random House published a revised version of her 1984 novella *The House on Mango Street.* In addition, *Bad Boys* (1980), *My Wicked, Wicked Ways* (1987), and most recently *Loose Woman* (1995) attest to Cisneros's talent as a poet. In 1995 she was awarded a MacArthur "Genius" Fellowship, and she is currently working on a novel. The publication of *Woman Hollering Creek and Other Stories* (1991) marked Cisneros's entry into the short story genre, and it was, indeed, a celebrated entry: The collection received both the Lannan Foundation 1991 Literary Award for Fiction and the PEN Center West Award for best fiction of 1991.

Divided into three sections—"My Lucy Friend Who Smells Like Corn," "One Holy Night," and "There Was a Man, There Was a Woman"—*Woman Hollering Creek* charts, through a number of characters, the develop-ment from youth to womanhood, making it a BILDUNG-SROMAN of sorts. *The House on Mango Street* uses both the narrative voice and vignette form in the opening section, as Cisneros gives us a child's account of growing up Chicana. One of the more frequently anthologized selections, "Barbie-Q," for instance, humorously delves into the race, class, and gender anxieties of growing up with the Mattel Barbie doll and the role it has played in constructing beauty norms and gender roles. The second section, which comprises two stories—"One Holy Night" and "My *Tocaya*"—examines sexual awakening from the perspective of two adolescent girls and critiques the way in which adults and schools tend to mystify and circumnavigate sex education discussions, often at the children's own peril. It is in the final section that the title story appears; among other things, it contests the representation of women in the popular media (namely, in the telenovela) and in cultural myths like the story of La Llorona, the woman who allegedly killed her children and now spends her evenings crying and searching for them.

These representational conflicts move to the fore in the abusive marriage of the principal female character, Cleófilas, and in her meeting with Felice, her independent, self-determined female savior. The conflict between man and woman in this story represents an overarching THEME for this final section, in which Cisneros explores the relationship struggles between men and women, including a tour-de-force story of the Mexican revolutionary leader Emiliano Zapata and his wife and lovers.

Cisneros's narrative experimentation deserves note, for her formal theatrics transcend rigid classifications of the short story. While many of her stories conform to more traditional definitions of the genre, Cisneros also includes, for instance, a five-page dialogue between two women over the Marlboro man's sexuality, with absolutely no narrative exposition: That is, we read only the conversational exchange between these women. Also, the distribution of the names of Tejanas and Tejanos, who sacrificed their lives in the Battle of the Alamo, throughout "Remember the Alamo" disrupts its narrative flow and rewrites the historical record, which has effaced their names and misrepresented the battle as an Anglo versus Mexican event. Finally, the collection of *milagritos,* or prayers,

to a number of saints that composes "Little Miracles, Kept Promises" demonstrates the formal range of the story form and Cisneros's uncanny ear for dialogue. Her most recent work, *Caramelo* (2003), is a novel based on the stories of her father and her family both in Mexico and in the United States.

BIBLIOGRAPHY

Cisneros, Sandra. *Caramelo.* New York: Knopf, 2002.

Eysturoy, Annie O. *Daughters of Self-Creation: The Contemporary Chicana Novel.* Albuquerque: University of New Mexico Press, 1996.

Kanellos, Nicolás, ed. *The Hispanic Literary Companion.* New York: Visible Ink Press, 1997.

———. *Hispanic American Literature: A Brief Introduction and Anthology.* New York: HarperCollins College Publishers, 1995.

López, Tiffany Ana, ed. *Growing Up Chicana/o.* New York: William Morrow, 1993.

Moraga, Cherríe, and Gloria Anzaldúa, eds. *This Bridge Called My Back: Writings by Radical Women of Color.* Watertown, Mass.: Persphone Press, 1981.

Quintana, Alvina E. *Home Girls: Chicana Literary Voices.* Philadelphia: Temple University Press, 1996.

Rodríguez Aranda, Pilar E. "On the Solitary Fate of Being Mexican, Female, Wicked and Thirty-Three: An Interview with Writer Sandra Cisneros." *Americas Review* 18, no. 1 (1991): 64–80.

Simmen, Edward, ed. *North of the Rio Grande: The Mexican American Experience in Short Fiction.* New York: Mentor, 1992.

Ralph E. Rodriguez
Pennsylvania State University

CIVIL WAR (1861–1865)

Also known as the War of Rebellion, the War of Secession, and the War between the States, the Civil War broke out between the Northern United States (the Union) and 11 Southern states that seceded to form the Confederate States of America (the Confederacy). The war resulted from deep-seated differences over economic and social issues, particularly those of tariff regulations and the extension of slavery. The principal objective of the North was to maintain the Union, but after 1862 the emancipation of slaves became a secondary objective.

In reaction to Abraham Lincoln's election to the presidency in 1860, South Carolina seceded, followed by 10 other Southern states that formed the Confederacy and elected Jefferson Davis as its president in 1861. Although the Union suffered a setback when routed by the Confederates at the Battle of Bull Run, and although the most brilliant generals led the Confederate troops, the superior forces of the North ultimately prevailed. Despite the best efforts of ROBERT E. LEE and Thomas (Stonewall) Jackson, the South was eventually defeated at the BATTLE OF GETTYSBURG, Pennsylvania, and at Vicksburg, Mississippi, in 1863. In 1864 the Union general Ulysses S. Grant laid siege to Richmond, Virginia, and General William Tecumseh Sherman destroyed the Confederates in his famous and controversial march to the sea through Georgia. General Lee surrendered to General Grant at Appomattox Courthouse, Virginia, on April 9, 1865.

With the possible exception of the Napoleonic Wars, the Civil War has produced the most writing and the greatest number of books of any conflict in history. Among the most famous novellas and novels are STEPHEN CRANE's *The Red Badge of Courage,* WILLIAM FAULKNER's *Absalom, Absalom!,* and Margaret Mitchell's *Gone with the Wind.* Various aspects of the conflict are depicted in numerous short stories by AMBROSE BIERCE, SHERWOOD BONNER, GEORGE WASHINGTON CABLE, WILLIAM FAULKNER, F. SCOTT FITZGERALD, ELLEN GLASGOW, Barry Hannah, JOEL CHANDLER HARRIS, WILLIAM DEAN HOWELLS, Thomas Nelson Page, and MARK TWAIN.

CLASSIC Originally used to describe artistic works of the Greeks and Romans, in the 21st century the term was customarily applied to any work that has achieved recognition for its superior quality or for its place in an established tradition. In American literature, for instance, NATHANIEL HAWTHORNE's *The Scarlet Letter* is commonly recognized as a "classic" American novel, and WASHINGTON IRVING's "The LEGEND OF SLEEPY HOLLOW" as a classic American story. The term may also be applied to works in terms of literary genre; thus, HENRY JAMES's *The TURN OF THE SCREW* is a classic American GHOST STORY, and FLANNERY O'CONNOR's "A GOOD MAN IS HARD TO FIND" is a classic tale in the genre of American southern GOTHIC. *Classic* also may be applied to authors.

Although the obvious meaning is generally accepted outside academia, much recent criticism questions not only the components—what constitutes a "classic" work?—but also the people who make the decisions. Scholars and critics help make or break a work by publishing reviews and commentary, but sometimes the public acclaim of and demand for a work are so great that, despite the disapproval of intellectuals, a work continues to be read. Publishers, too, play a significant role: If a book is allowed to go out of print, it cannot be bought and read. Until the past two decades, this has been the case with much of women's literature. It is also the case with literature by so-called minorities, who until relatively recently had difficulty finding publishers. In terms of short fiction, yet another major issue is the academic tendency to prefer longer works, such as novels, to short fiction. Thus the term *classic* is in a constant state of evaluation.

"CLEAN, WELL-LIGHTED PLACE, A"

ERNEST HEMINGWAY (1933)   Two waiters, one young and one older, discuss an old man who sits, late at night, drinking brandy in the cafe. We learn from their dialogue that he attempted suicide the week before. A soldier and a girl pass by in the street. The younger waiter is impatient, eager to go home to his wife. The older waiter speaks his understanding of the old man's needs and despair. After closing the cafe, the older waiter thinks of the nothingness of life that creates the need for some light and cleanliness. He goes to a bodega and then home, where, sleepless till daylight, he thinks about the need for a clean, well-lighted place. He discounts his insomnia, which he is sure many others must suffer from as well.

Commonplace reading of the story sees the older waiter as sympathetic, empathizing with the old man. The younger waiter, who is married, is more callous and wants only to go home. He spills the old man's drink; he says an old man is a "nasty thing." Critics have long disagreed, however, about the consistency of each waiter's perspective, a confusion created by ERNEST HEMINGWAY's technique of using dialogue without always identifying his speakers precisely.

Spare and short, "A Clean, Well-Lighted Place" develops almost entirely by dialogue. The narrative depends on the reader's ability to provide the framework of existential despair (see EXISTENTIALISM) and NIHILISM, the encounter with the cultural wasteland, and loss of faith. For many it is the seminal story in Hemingway's short story catalog, the quintessential illustration of his theory of omission. It is one of his most anthologized short stories. A. E. Hotchner quotes the author as saying it "may be my favorite story."

It was first published in *Scribner's Monthly* in 1933 and then in Hemingway's short story collection *Winner Take Nothing.* Since that time it has been widely anthologized, as it is a quintessential example of Hemingway's spare and dramatic style and nihilistic vision. This is distilled in the older waiter's PARODY of the Lord's Prayer, as he substitutes the Spanish word *nada* (nothing) for all the key terms: "Our nada who art in nada, nada be thy name. . . . Give us this nada our daily nada. . . ." The effect is powerful: the loss of faith, the despair, the lonely encounter with the nothingness of existence. The phrase "a clean, well-lighted place" has become a code for whatever refuge modern beings choose to help them make it through the night and withstand the enveloping darkness.

BIBLIOGRAPHY

Bennett, Warren. "The Manuscript and the Dialogue of 'A Clean, Well-Lighted Place.'" *American Literature* (1979): 613–624.

Flora, Joseph M. *Ernest Hemingway: A Study of the Short Fiction.* Boston: Twayne, 1989.

Gabriel, Joseph F. "The Logic of Confusion in Hemingway's 'A Clean, Well-Lighted Place.'" *College English* (May 1961): 539–546.

Hoffman, Steven K. "Nada and Clean Well-Lighted Place: The Unity of Hemingway's Short Fiction." *Essays in Literature* (1979): 91–110.

Johnston, Kenneth G. *The Tip of the Iceberg: Hemingway and the Short Story.* Greenwood, Fla.: Penkevill, 1987.

Kerner, David. "The Ambiguity of 'A Clean, Well-Lighted Place.'" *Studies in Fiction* (1992): 561–573.

———. "The Foundation of the True Text of 'A Clean, Well-Lighted Place.'" *Fitzgerald-Hemingway Annual* (1979): 279–300.

Mimi Reisel Gladstein
University of Texas at El Paso

CLIMAX   The rising action that leads to the culmination of the HERO's or HEROINE's fortunes. (See PLOT.)

CLOSE READING   The cornerstone of NEW CRITICISM, which advocated the explication of a text through close attention to its literary techniques, particularly image, symbol, and IRONY. Despite the demise of New Criticism among scholars and critics, many still believe that its legacy of close reading remains the key to understanding a novel or story.

CLOSURE   A term that has been adopted relatively recently to indicate an ending to a literary work that may or may not "end" in a definitive way; thus a short story may or may not achieve closure by the end of the tale. For instance, F. SCOTT FITZGERALD's "BABYLON REVISITED" ends on an ambiguous note as CHARLIE WALES ponders his future. Fitzgerald withholds closure: We never learn whether Charlie's sister-in-law allows his daughter to return to him or whether Charlie truly acknowledges his reprehensible past behavior.

COFER, JUDITH ORTIZ (1952–   )   Judith Ortiz Cofer was born in Hormigueros, Puerto Rico, and grew up there and in Paterson, New Jersey, until her family moved to Augusta, Georgia, in 1968. When her father went on tours of duty in the navy, Ortiz Cofer, her mother, and her brother lived in Puerto Rico with her maternal grandmother. Moving between the urban, English-speaking Paterson and the rural, Spanish-speaking Hormigueros gave Ortiz Cofer the major THEMES that inform her novel, short stories, creative nonfiction, and poetry. Ortiz Cofer uses this variety of genres to examine what she knows intimately: the lives of Puerto Rican women on the island and on the mainland, the resulting bicultural conflicts and strengths, and the role of storytelling in both Spanish-speaking and English-speaking cultures.

Her first publications were books of poetry, beginning with *Latin Women Pray* (1980). Her first novel, *The Line of the Sun* (1989), was nominated for a Pulitzer Prize. In 1990 she published *Silent Dancing: A Partial Remembrance of a Puerto Rican Childhood,* an autobiographical work of creative nonfiction and poetry. Ortiz Cofer called the prose pieces *ensayos*—Spanish for "essay" and "rehearsal"—to define her own attempts to blend the essay with her slightly fictionalized reconstructions of memory (12). In *The Latin Deli* (1993), the creative nonfiction, poetry, and short stories illustrate the lives of Puerto Ricans living in a New Jersey barrio, a residential area comprising one ethnic group. Finally, *An Island Like You: Stories from the Barrio* (1996) is a collection of short stories written about young adults living in a Puerto Rican barrio. In 2003 she published a novel entitled *The Meaning of Consuelo*.

BIBLIOGRAPHY

Bruce-Novoa, Juan. "Judith Ortiz Cofer's Rituals of Movement." *The Americas Review* 19 (Winter 1991): 88–99.

Cofer, Judith Ortiz. *An Island Like You: Stories of the Bario.* New York: Puffin Books, 1995.

———. *The Latin Deli: Prose and Poetry.* Athens: University of Georgia Press, 1993.

———. *Latin Woman Pray.* Fort Lauderdale, Fla.: Florida Arts Gazette Press, 1980.

———. *The Line of the Sun.* Athens: University of Georgia Press, 1989.

———. *The Meaning of Consuelo.* New York: Farrar, Straus & Giroux, 2003.

———. *The Native Dancer.* Bourbonnais, Ill.: Lieb/Schott, 1981.

———. *Peregrina.* Golden, Colo.: Riverstone Press, 1986.

———. *Silent Dancing: A Partial Remembrance of a Puerto Rican Childhood.* Houston, Tex.: Arte Público Press, 1990.

———. *Woman in Front of the Sun: On Becoming a Writer.* Athens: University of Georgia Press, 2000.

———. *The Year of Our Revolution: New and Selected Stories and Poems.* Houston: Tex.: Piñata Books, 1998.

———, ed. *Riding Low on the Streets of Gold: Latino Literature for Young Adults.* Houston, Tex.: Arte Público Press, 2003.

Nancy L. Chick
University of Georgia

COLD WAR

The name given to the political and economic competition and military confrontation between the United States and other democratic capitalist countries and the Soviet Union and other communist countries from the end of WORLD WAR II to the disintegration of the Soviet Union and its empire in the 1980s. Most of this period was marked by strained diplomatic relations, nuclear terror, unparalleled espionage and intrigue, and the "exporting of revolution." The period of greatest tensions and danger was from the late 1940s to the late 1960s; at this time disputes between the Soviet Union and the Allies over the occupation policies and reunification plans of Germany caused the Soviets to tighten military, political, and economic control over the occupied countries (Poland, Czechoslovakia, Hungary, Romania, Bulgaria, and East Germany) of Eastern Europe, virtually annexing them to the Soviet Union. That portion of the cold war included the Berlin airlift (1948–49); the beginning of the arms race after the Soviets exploded an atomic bomb in 1949 and a hydrogen bomb in 1952; the communist takeover of China (1949); the KOREAN WAR (1950–53); the construction of the Berlin Wall (1961), which divided Germany into a communist East and noncommunist West until 1989; the Cuban Missile crisis (1962); and the VIETNAM WAR (1954–75). By the late 1960s, relations had become less strained in a period of detente and the signing of various nuclear nonproliferation and strategic arms limitation treaties.

COLLIER'S

From 1888 to 1957, *Collier's* was one of the leading mass-circulated, illustrated magazines in the country. In the early 20th century, *Collier's* followed the lead of MCCLURE'S magazine and took up campaigns against various social ills, such as child labor, and in favor of rights such as women's suffrage. Throughout its history, the magazine was known for superb illustrations and the strength of the fiction it published. Fiction writers of consequence included EDITH WHARTON, P. G. Wodehouse, Frank Norris, HENRY JAMES, JACK LONDON, H. G. Wells, BRET HARTE, Conan Doyle, O. HENRY, Kathleen Norris, PEARL BUCK, and JOHN STEINBECK. *Collier's* remained popular in the 1950s but suffered continuing financial losses and ceased publication in 1957.

COLTER, CYRUS (1910–2002)

Born in Noblesville, Indiana, Colter published his first collection of short stories, *The Beach Umbrella,* in 1970. He wrote in the style of modern REALISM and keeps his authorial self unobtrusive while using colloquial dialogue and developing the story by entering briefly into the minds of characters. The subject of each story is often an apparently small event, as in "Rescue," which tells of a woman who agrees to marry a man she does not love. Colter's style is masterly and his imagination for situation is fertile.

BIBLIOGRAPHY

Colter, Cyrus. *The Amoralists and Other Tales: Collected Stories.* New York and St. Paul, Minn.: Thunder's Mouth Press, 1988.

———. *The Beach Umbrella and Other Stories.* Iowa City: University of Iowa Press, 1970.

———. *A Chocolate Soldier.* New York and St. Paul, Minn.: Thunder's Mouth Press, 1988.

———. *City of Light: A Novel.* New York and St. Paul, Minn.: Thunder's Mouth Press, 1993.

———. *The Hippodrome.* Chicago: Swallow Press, 1973.

———. *Night Studies: A Novel.* Chicago: Swallow Press, 1997.

Colter, Cyrus, and Michael Anania, eds. *The Rivers of Eros.* Chicago: Swallow Press, 1972.

Reilly, John M. "Cyrus Colter." *Contemporary Literature* (1986).

COMEDY A term originally applied only to drama, and then in medieval times to nondramatic prose fiction, today any prose fiction that entertains, delights, or amuses the reader through its wit, humor, or ridicule may be recognized as comedy. Unlike TRAGEDY, comedy nearly always provides a happy ending for characters and readers. Comedy also may take the form of farce or BURLESQUE, or of COMIC RELIEF in stories with ultimately serious themes. The comic form is variously employed in such stories as MARK TWAIN's "The Jumping Frog of Calaveras County," JAMES THURBER's, "The SECRET LIFE OF WALTER MITTY," WILLIAM FAULKNER's, "Mule in the Yard," DOROTHY PARKER's "The Waltz," and PHILLIP ROTH's "The CONVERSION OF THE JEWS."

See also BLACK HUMOR.

COMIC RELIEF A device used to lighten the tragic effect or to alleviate the tension in a somber or tragic work. Although sometimes merely intrusive and amusing, in the best stories humorous characters,

dialogues, or situations actually function to illuminate and deepen the ultimately serious meaning of the work. Although classic examples occur in Shakespeare (the gravediggers' scene in *Hamlet* [5.1], the drunken porter scene in *Macbeth* [2.3], the speeches of the Fool in *King Lear*), the use of comic relief continues in American fiction. A primary example of comic relief occurs in FLANNERY O'CONNOR's "GOOD COUNTRY PEOPLE."

"COMING, APHRODITE!" WILLA CATHER **(1920)** First published in the magazine *Smart Set* (August 1920) as "Coming, Eden Bower!" and included in the collection *Youth and the Bright Medusa* (1920), the story relates the brief, passionate love affair between a painter and an opera singer in Washington Square, a bohemian section of New York City during the early 20th century. The story is Cather's most explicit treatment of sexual passion, but it is equally concerned with two different kinds of artistic success. The painter, Don Hedger, is willing to forgo friends, fame, and material comfort to pursue groundbreaking originality in his art. The singer, Eden Bower, wants a large, appreciative audience for her stunning but standard portrayal of heroic characters. Many years after their affair, both artists have found success on their own terms. The story pursues one of Cather's persistent ironic THEMES: The production of art, whether for human enrichment or entertainment, necessitates isolation.

A good example of Cather's craftsmanship, the story uses references to Greek myth along with the archetypal images of birds, light, and darkness to create a dense visual and symbolic tapestry, with AMBIGUITY a dominant effect. Is Don Hedger, whose name implies the trimming of natural growth, an artist whose disciplined labor produces works of excellence, or is he meant to suggest that romantic love prunes too much of the artistic soul? Some commentators have described Eden Bower as an exquisite representation of the eternal feminine principle, but others see her as an Eve-like temptress who threatens to seduce Hedger away from his high aesthetic ideals. She also can be seen as one of Cather's many strong, androgynous women who defy traditional gender expectations.

The magazine version of the story, published first, was altered to avoid offending censorship crusaders at a time when more than one publisher had been taken to court. Besides the title change, in this bowdlerized version Eden Bower's nudity was deleted from one scene, as were a number of descriptions with sexual overtones.

BIBLIOGRAPHY
Arnold, Marilyn. *Willa Cather's Short Fiction*. Lincoln: University of Nebraska Press, 1984.
Cather, Willa. *Uncle Valentine and Other Stories: Willa Cather's Uncollected Short Fiction, 1915–1929*. Edited by Bernice Slote. Lincoln: University of Nebraska Press, 1973.

Frances Kerr
Durham Technical Community College

"CONFESSION, THE" EDITH WHARTON (1936)

"The Confession," adapted from EDITH WHARTON's incomplete and unpublished play *Kate Spain* and published in *The World Over*, alludes to the notorious case of Lizzie Borden. It recounts the romance of two American travelers, Mr. Severance and Kate Ingram, who meet in a European hotel. Severance, a convalescing American banker, and Ingram, a quiet, pale woman with "unquiet" hands, an unknown past, and the power to monopolize Severance's heart and mind, must negotiate with Ingram's companion, Cassie Wilpert, a heavy, unrefined Irish woman who attempts to prevent the couple's growing affection. Severance successfully woos Ingram but is disconcerted when she becomes agitated by the appearance of an American journalist. Later this journalist, whom Severance had known in New York, tells him that Ingram is really Kate Spain, who was acquitted of a murder charge in a much-publicized trial three years earlier. Severance denies this possibility, although he recalls receiving strange looks from the hotel staff whenever he has been with her. He discounts the journalist's comments and eagerly plans to propose marriage. When he learns that Kate and Cassie have unexpectedly fled, he traces them to a small pension in Italy and declares his love to Kate. She confesses that she is Kate Spain and sadly rejects his offer because she knows that they would be hounded by people curious about her role in the murder and because Cassie would never permit her to marry.

The story thus implies that Kate Spain has left the prison of her tyrant father's house for that of her present captivity with her companion Cassie. The next morning Cassie goes to Severance's room and angrily insists that he leave Kate. When he refuses, she warns him that she is going to tell him details that will kill him. The moment she reaches for a document in her purse, she collapses from a stroke. She never regains consciousness, and within a month, she is dead. Severance reassures Kate that Cassie told him nothing and suggests that she remove any papers in Cassie's purse that might embarrass her. Later she insists that he read the document that Cassie had meant to show him and repeats that she cannot marry him. To ease her concern, he refuses to read the document but agrees to take it with him.

The last section of the tale is narrated by Severance seven years later. He reports that he and Kate were married for five years of uncommon happiness. Now that she is dead, he plans to burn Cassie's unopened document. He argues that Kate's insistence that he read it marks her an honest woman.

Barbara White, who has written extensively on Wharton's short fiction, notes the emphasis on a secret, hidden past in the period in which Wharton wrote this story. White finds evidence of incest in Wharton's life and suggests that the author tried to exorcise it in stories such as "Confession." Particularly in this story, written in her last decade, Wharton appears to have survived and, perhaps, triumphed: Kate has killed her father, and although she feels divided into two selves, one-half can marry the man whose name suggests her severed life and who exonerates her from her past (White 104).

BIBLIOGRAPHY
Lewis, R. W. B., and Nancy Lewis, eds. *The Letters of Edith Wharton*. New York: Macmillan, 1988.
White, Barbara. *Edith Wharton: A Study of the Short Fiction*. New York: Macmillan, 1991.

Sandra Chrystal Hayes
Georgia Institute of Technology

"CONFESSIONAL, THE" EDITH WHARTON (1901)

First published in a volume entitled *Crucial Instances* (1901), "The Confessional" weaves together Italian political intrigue, religious questions, and domestic relationships in a manner similar to EDITH WHARTON's novel *The Valley of Decision*. Its four shifts of confessors and confessants could serve as a study of punishment, silence, and power and can be listed among Wharton's stories of voiceless women and loveless marriages. It is told by an American narrator, an accountant who listens to the confession of a dying priest, Don Egidio.

Egidio relates his ties to the aristocratic Da Milano family, who adopted and reared him as a brother to the scholarly Count Roberto Siviano Da Milano, a man committed to improving the conditions of peasants and to promoting the cause of Italian liberty. The count had married a young woman he had observed at mass whom he saw as the embodiment of his beleaguered country, now degraded by Austrian invaders. His much-younger bride, exchanged by her family for appropriate compensation, finds entertainment with the count's half brother and sister-in-law and with their cousin, a handsome Austrian officer.

Crucial personal and political battles converge as ambitions divide the family. On the eve of the count's departure to the revolution, his half brother and wife "confess" that they know the countess has had an adulterous relationship with the Austrian soldier. Assuming that the count will discredit his wife and that he will then name his nieces and nephews successors to the family fortune, the two propose that the count disguise himself as Egidio in order to hear the countess's confession. After quarreling with the priest, the count impersonates him and hears his wife's confession. The next morning he meets with the family to announce her innocence. He leaves for Milan, heroically engages in battles for several months, and then disappears. Meanwhile his wife gives birth to a daughter, but her "marble breast" gives no milk. Don Egidio, who had permitted the deceitful confession, confesses his own guilt in so doing to his bishop and is sent to New York as penance.

Four years later, when the priest is called to tend to an ailing professor, he realizes that the man is Count Roberto. The count teaches Italian and shares his meager income with other Italian expatriates. The two agree never to discuss the past and live as close friends for another eight years. Don Egidio concludes his tale with the justification for his own sin: "[The Count's] just life and holy death intercede for me, who sinned for his sake alone."

The many Wharton readers who find evidence and implications of incest in her fiction point to this early story, with its apt title, as a primary example. This THEME of past secrets continues and intensifies in Wharton's later works. Notably, the count (clearly a father figure) has under false pretences listened to the confession of his young wife (clearly a daughter figure) when in fact a man, not she, has sinned. The transference of guilt to another man at least suggest that Wharton may have been "confessing" and also reassigning the blame to a male figure.

BIBLIOGRAPHY

Lewis, R. W. B. *Edith Wharton.* New York: Scribner's, 1975.

Singley, Carol. *Edith Wharton: Matters of Mind and Spirit.* New York: Cambridge University Press, 1995.

White, Barbara. *Edith Wharton: A Study of the Short Fiction.* New York: Macmillan, 1991.

Sandra Chrystal Hayes
Georgia Institute of Technology

CONFLICT

In a work of fiction, the struggle between the main character and opposing forces. External conflict occurs between the protagonist and another character or force. Internal conflict occurs within the character himself or herself.

CONJURE STORIES

Conjure is a blend of religion and magic with roots in Africa and was taken to the New World by those who were forcibly removed from Africa and enslaved. Since their Christian oppressors did not allow the practice of traditional African religions, conjure was practiced secretly by slaves without the knowledge of masters and overseers. In North America, South America, and the Caribbean, conjure was rooted in African views on magic and spirituality and based on the belief that forces and spirits beyond the visible world influence events. In practice, the person performing conjure was usually a woman, and it was believed that her skills allowed her to cast a spell upon a chosen victim. The items used by the conjurer to create a spell varied widely, from hair to roots to grave dust. Carol S. Taylor Johnson has noted the origins of conjure visible in Olaudah Equiano's 1789 narrative *The Life of Olaudah Equiano, or Gustavus Vassa, the African*. In this slave narrative, the multiple roles held by priests as religious figures, healers, and magicians in African culture are readily visible. For Africans thrust into an antagonistic culture in America, conjure persisted as a social link to African beliefs and offered a means of binding slave communities outside the religious systems of European-American culture.

In American short fiction, perhaps the most successful and well-known conjure writer is CHARLES W. CHESNUTT. In his popular *The Conjure Woman* (1899), Chesnutt provides a glimpse into the beliefs and practice of conjure while also recognizing its subversive potential. In the stories of this collection, Uncle Julius is an old black caretaker of a North Carolina plantation who relays vivid tales of conjure from his days as a slave. In "The Goophered Grapevine," for example, Uncle Julius attempts to convince John, a white Northerner, not to purchase an abandoned vineyard. Julius tells John that the vineyard had been conjured by the local conjure woman Aunt Peggy so that anyone who eats the grapes will die within a year. John buys the vineyard nonetheless and discovers Julius's ulterior motive for the story—his own sale of the grapes, which provided a "respectable revenue." The remaining stories in *The Conjure Woman* follow a similar pattern—portraying both the power of conjure in the black oral tradition and white disregard for and misunderstanding of its practice. Conjure fiction has not been limited to African-American writers, however. In his 1929 story "THAT EVENING SUN," for example, WILLIAM FAULKNER also explores conjure, but instead focuses on the power that conjuring holds in the African-American imagination. In this story Nancy, a black woman, appears to have been conjured by Jesus, a male conjurer or "badman" who is preparing to kill her. While Nancy is nearly paralyzed with fear, the white Compson family does not understand the situation she is confronting. They simply dismiss her behavior as erratic and urge her to continue her work as housekeeper. Both examples here illustrate the gap in white and black attitudes toward conjure and its lingering cultural presence, particularly in the American South.

BIBLIOGRAPHY

Brodhead, Richard H. "Introduction." In *The Conjure Woman and Other Tales,* edited by Richard H. Brodhead. Durham, N.C.: Duke University Press, 1993.

Chesnutt, Charles Waddell. *The Conjure Woman and Other Tales.* Edited by Richard H. Brodhead. Durham, N.C.: Duke University Press, 1993.

Faulkner, William. "That Evening Sun." In *Collected Stories of William Faulkner.* New York: Random House, 1950.

Taylor, Carol S. "Conjuring." In *The Oxford Companion to African American Literature,* edited by William L. Andrews, et al. New York: Oxford University Press, 1997.

Chris McBride
California State University at Los Angeles

CONNELL, EVAN S., JR. (EVAN SHELBY CONNELL, JR.) (1924–)

As a writer of short fiction, Connell has a reputation that rests mainly on the characters of Mr. and Mrs. Bridge, who appeared first in several sketches collected in *The Anatomy Lesson* (1957). The Bridges are affluent upper-middle-class suburbanites who live near Kansas City, Missouri, and are "vaguely baffled" by life. To Connell, they represent a kind of person found in a sterile, provincial culture, such as the Midwest, who have achieved wealth but lack the sophistication to enjoy their lives. *The Collected Stories of Evan S. Connell* was published in 1999.

BIBLIOGRAPHY

Blaisdell, Gus. "After Ground Zero." *New Mexico Quarterly* (Albuquerque) (Summer 1966).

Connell, Evan S. *The Anatomy Lesson and Other Stories.* New York: Viking, 1957.

———. *At the Crossroads: Stories.* New York: Simon & Schuster, 1965.

———. *Deus Lo Volt! Chronicle of the Crusades.* New York: Counterpoint, 2000.

———. *St. Augustine's Pigeon: The Selected Stories.* Edited by Gus Blaisdell. Berkeley, Calif.: North Point Press, 1980.

CONNIE   Adolescent girl in JOYCE CAROL OATES'S "WHERE ARE YOU GOING, WHERE HAVE YOU BEEN?" who, with some valid reasons, deplores and ignores her parents. The results for her are horrific: From the evil personified in ARNOLD FRIEND, who has correctly chosen her as someone incapable of resisting his power, she learns that she has nothing to depend on, nothing to protect her. Particularly notable are Oates's depiction of the realistic details of Connie's life, her teenage interests, her small, quiet signs of rebellion—and finally her appalled realization that she is utterly powerless to defend herself.

CONNOTATION AND DENOTATION   In literature, *denotation* refers to the concrete meaning or dictionary definition of a word or words, while *connotation* refers to the emotional implications and associations that words may suggest. A standard example involves the difference between *house* and *home*: *House* denotes the place where one lives, but *home*—in addition to denoting one's residence—connotes coziness, intimacy, familial values, and privacy. The distinction between the two words achieved widespread recognition with the publication of I. A. Richards's *Principles of Literary Criticism* (1924).

CONSPICUOUS CONSUMPTION   Term coined by the American economist Thorstein Veblen (1857–1929) in his influential book *The Theory of the Leisure Class* (1899) to describe the human tendency—particularly of the monied class—to purchase and own goods that set people apart from their peers. Numerous American short stories have fruitfully explored the theme: for example, WILLA CATHER'S "PAUL'S CASE: A STUDY IN TEMPERAMENT," JOYCE CAROL OATES'S "Shopping," and F. SCOTT FITZGERALD'S "The DIAMOND AS BIG AS THE RITZ" and "BABYLON REVISITED."

"CONVERSATION WITH MY FATHER, A" GRACE PALEY (1974)   GRACE PALEY has stated that this story is autobiographical, and, although she never wrote a story for her father about a neighbor, as the narrator does in this story, Paley's father once asked her: "Why can't you write a regular story, for God's sake?" (qtd. in Charters 1,158). The first-person narrator in "Conversation with My Father," faced with her 86-year-old father's approaching death, visits him in the hospital. Although neither speaks of the short time that remains for him, most readers are aware of the undercurrents lying just beneath the surface of the banter and joking between father and daughter.

In response to her father's request to write a story for him in the manner of Chekhov or de Maupassant, the narrator, who is also a writer, brings him the skeleton of a story she wishes to tell about her neighbor across the street. The unadorned bare bones state merely that in an attempt to join her son in his drug addiction, the mother becomes a junkie as well—but when her son cures himself, she remains at home, alone and still addicted.

When the narrator's father tells her that she cannot compose a real story as the Russian and French writers can, she returns with a second draft, this time adding touches of COMEDY and REALISM. We realize that Paley is writing not in the 19th-century mode of Chekhov and de Maupassant but in the 20th-century mode of POSTMODERNISM. On one level, the narrator, as does SCHEHEREZADE, attempts to entertain her father through her storytelling, putting off not her death but his. On another, self-reflexive level, Paley the author is telling a story about telling a story. The difference between her way and her father's way signals a generational difference that separates the two as well as his Russian birth as opposed to her American birth. Experientially, too, father and daughter see different endings to this story: The father sees tragedy, whereas the daughter-writer sees hope and possibility. There is also an intriguing element of control in this American-born daughter's role as writer: She can make the story end in whatever way she chooses. In her love for her father, however, after speaking her mind, she keeps her promise to her family and lets him have the last word: He believes she will never see tragedy head on. Although some critics view this ending as evidence of the daughter's inability to face her father's imminent death, an alternative view is that the daughter, despite her recognition of misfortune around her, has lived a life so different from her father's that she can truthfully put her faith in a more optimistic outcome.

BIBLIOGRAPHY

Charters, Ann. "Grace Paley: A Conversation with Ann Charters." In *Major Writers of Short Fiction: Stories and Commentary,* edited by Ann Charters, 1,156–1,160. Boston: Bedford Books/St. Martin's Press, 1993.

Paley, Grace. "A Conversation with My Father." In *Enormous Changes at the Last Minute.* New York: Farrar, Straus & Giroux, 1974.

"CONVERSION OF THE JEWS, THE"

PHILIP ROTH (1959)   Although PHILIP ROTH's *Goodbye, Columbus and Five Short Stories,* published in 1959, received the Jewish Book Council's Daroff Award in that year and the National Book Award in 1960, the Jewish community vehemently accused Philip Roth of, among other things, condemning his own people. In *Reading Myself and Others,* Roth's attempt to defend himself against such attacks, he asserts that "the STEREOTYPE as often arises from ignorance as from malice; deliberately keeping Jews out of the imagination of Gentiles, for fear of the bigots and their stereotyping minds, is really to invite the invention of stereotypical ideas" (166).

Throughout *Goodbye, Columbus,* Roth, as did ERNEST HEMINGWAY in IN OUR TIME, wrote from his experiences. For Roth, growing up in a Jewish neighborhood, attending Hebrew school, and joining the army, for example, provided a colorful landscape for exploring the struggles and conflicts of assimilated Jews in a predominantly Christian American society. In "The Conversion of the Jews," a FABLE about religious hypocrisy and abuse, Ozzie Freedman, a young boy in Hebrew school, questions the teachings and authority of Rabbi Binder. The names *Freedman* and *Binder* have a humorously allegorical resonance (see ALLEGORY) in that neither realizes he is bound and restricted by the rigid blinders of orthodox religion.

If God could create the world in six days, Ozzie muses, "He [could] let a woman have a baby without intercourse" (*GC* 141). As Ozzie continues to question some of the tenets of Judaism, the tension escalates until Rabbi Binder hits him. With memories of his mother, who had struck him the previous night for the first time, Ozzie locks himself on the school's rooftop and threatens to jump. In an ironic inversion of the religious and, more specifically, adult oppression imposed on Ozzie, he forces his peers, the firemen trying to save him, Rabbi Binder, and his mother to kneel and proclaim a belief in Jesus Christ.

Although Ozzie begins by questioning Jewish dogma, his story tries to give us a larger understanding that religion should be about love, not coercion: "Don't you see . . . you should never hit anybody about God" (*GC* 158). Like many of Roth's characters who struggle against coercion, from religion, women, families, or government, Ozzie feels both the strength and the limitations of his cultural heritage. As he jumps into the firemen's net, he reenters a world of moral AMBIGUITY—one where struggles with his identity as a Jew are just beginning.

BIBLIOGRAPHY

Baumgarten, Murray, and Barbara Gottfried. *Understanding Philip Roth.* Columbia: University of South Carolina Press, 1990.

Cooper, Alan. *Philip Roth and the Jews.* Albany: State University of New York, 1996.

Halio, Jay L. *Philip Roth Revisited.* New York: Twayne, 1992.

Roth, Philip. *Goodbye, Columbus and Five Short Stories.* Boston: Houghton Mifflin, 1959.

———. *Reading Myself and Others.* New York: Farrar, Straus & Giroux, 1961.

Thomas Fahy
University of North Carolina

COOVER, ROBERT (ROBERT LOWELL COOVER) (1932–)

Born in Charles City, Iowa, Coover was reared in several midwestern states. He attended Southern Illinois University and Indiana University and later spent a three-year tour in Europe as a naval officer. On his return, he attended the University of Chicago and became intrigued with the work of Samuel Beckett and Alain Robbe-Grillet, among others. Coover's first stories were published in the *Evergreen Review,* the LITTLE MAGAZINE in the forefront of publishing metafictional experimental tales by such writers as John Hawkes, Joseph Heller,

Thomas Pynchon, DONALD BARTHELME, and JOHN BARTH. Like many of his generation, Coover was strongly influenced by the experimental fiction of such South American writers as Jorge Louis Borges and Julio Cortázar, evident in his use of MAGICAL REALISM, the ABSURD, and the self-conscious attention to the devices of storytelling.

In 1969 Coover published his first short story collection, *Pricksongs and Descants,* which bears comparison with other experimental writing of the period—Barth's *LOST IN THE FUNHOUSE,* for instance. As author and critic Jerome Klinkowitz points out, both seem indebted to the way Borges exploits the fictive components of what one normally views as reality (138). In his most frequently anthologized story, "The BABYSITTER," Coover appears to describe in realistic terms (see REALISM) a familiar middle-class evening: The parents leave their children in the charge of a babysitter. Coover's introduction of multiple perspectives into the story, however, calls reality into question, for he clearly demonstrates the chasms between one person's reality and another's. This story aptly demonstrates Coover's ability to ground the reader in reality, then remove most of its recognizable aspects through his use of FABLE and METAFICTION, MAGICAL REALISM, and ABSURDITY. Coover's other collections of short fiction include *A Night at the Movies* (1987) and *A Child Again* (2005).

BIBLIOGRAPHY

Coover, Robert. *Aesop's Forest*. Santa Barbara, Calif.: Capra Press, 1986.

———. *Charlie in the House of Rue*. Lincoln, Mass.: Penmaen Press, 1980.

———. *The Convention*. Northridge, Calif.: Lord John Press, 1982.

———. *Gerald's Party: A Novel*. New York: Linden Press/Simon & Schuster, 1986.

———. *In Bed One Night and Other Brief Encounters*. Providence, R.I.: Burning Deck, 1983.

———. *A Night at the Movies; or, You Must Remember This*. New York: Linden Press/Simon & Schuster, 1987.

———. *The Origin of the Brunits: A Novel*. New York: Putnam, 1966.

———. *Pinocchio in Venice*. New York: Linden Press/Simon & Schuster, 1991.

———. *A Political Fable*. New York: Viking, 1980.

———. *Pricksongs and Descants*. New York: Dutton, 1969.

———. *The Public Burning*. New York: Viking, 1977.

———. *Spanking the Maid*. New York: Grove Press, 1982.

———. *The Universal Baseball Association, Inc., J. Henry Waugh, Prop*. New York: Random House, 1968.

———. *Whatever Happened to Gloomy Gus of the Chicago Bears?* New York: Linden Press/Simons & Schuster, 1987.

Cope, Jackson I. *Coover's Fictions*. Baltimore: Johns Hopkins University Press, 1986.

Gass, William H. *Fiction and the Figures of Life*. New York: Harper & Row, 1970.

Gordon, Lois. *Coover: The Universal Fictionmaking Process*. Carbondale: Southern Illinois University Press, 1983.

Gunn, Jessie. "Structure as Revelation: Coover's *Pricksongs and Descants*." *Linguistics in Literature* 2, no. 1 (1977).

Hansen, Arlen J. "The Dice of God: Einstein, Heisenberg, and Coover." *Novel* 10 (1976).

Heckard, Margaret. "Coover, Metafictions, and Freedom." *Twentieth Century Literature* 22 (1976).

Klinkowitz, Jerome. "Robert Coover." In *Reference Guide to Short Fiction*, edited by Noelle Watson, 138–139. Detroit: St. James Press, 1994.

McCaffery, Larry. *The Metafictional Muse: The Works of Coover, Donald Barthelme, and William H. Gass*. Pittsburgh: University of Pittsburgh Press, 1982.

Schmitz, Neil. "Coover and the Hazards of Metafiction." *Novel* 7 (1974).

Schulz, Max. *Black Humor Fiction of the Sixties*. Athens: Ohio University Press, 1973.

Shelton, Frank W. "Humor and Balance in Coover's *The Universal Baseball Association, Inc.*" *Critique* 17 (1975).

"COUNTRY HUSBAND, THE" JOHN CHEEVER (1958)

One of Cheever's most frequently anthologized stories (along with "The SWIMMER"), "The Country Husband" is the author's modern take on the English bawdy Restoration comedy William Wycherly's *The Country Wife* (1675). It was first published in Cheever's collection *The Housebreaker of Shady Hill* (1958). Protagonist Francis Weed's predicament may be viewed as the now-classic rendition of an American male midlife crisis—and, as such, is a serious topic. The story is also profitably read, however, as a seriocomedy containing many of the elements of the humorous picaresque. Critics and readers alike are divided over whether to interpret Weed as a flawed hero who overcomes his peccadilloes, a comic figure reduced to a Casper Milquetoast by story's end, or a 1950s chauvinist with a reprehensible attitude toward women. Although the plot is slim and the dialogue sparse, the story has been praised for its third-person narrative, which reveals Weed's journey from a near-death experience through a mild rebellion against his suburban marriage to his return to the confines of his marriage and the conventions of his suburb.

The story opens as Weed is flying from Minneapolis to the East Coast, presumably New York. The plane has engine trouble and makes a forced landing in an Iowa cornfield, but the passengers are so expeditiously rounded up and sent on their way that he arrives at his home in Shady Hill at the usual time. Because his family cannot fathom the upheaval he has suffered, they behave normally: Weed's wife, Julia, lights candles for the dinner table, and his children engage in childish bickering and rebellious teen behavior. Weed sees his world through the eyes of one who nearly rendezvoused with death, and he now sees his family as conventional and uncaring, his world as cloying and petty, with its parties, its barbecues,

A great deal of criticism has focused on Cheever's use of metaphor in this story, particularly in the imagery of war: His house is a "battlefield" as he invokes the "war cries of Scottish chieftains" (201), and, at the party the next evening, he believes that the Farquarsons' maid is the woman he saw stoned for sleeping with a Nazi during his WORLD WAR II sojourn in France. Another major metaphor is that of the "thread" that links Weed's experiences together, from plane crash to suburban battlefield to sexual upheaval, and the implicit comparison of Weed to the other disruptive forces in the story: the irrepressible Labrador retriever Jupiter, the unconventional and unpredictable child Gertrude, and Weed's childish feelings, which, as does the Beethoven sonata played by his neighbor, constitute "an outpouring of tearful petulance, lonesomeness, and self-pity—everything it was Beethoven's greatness not to know" (202).

On one level, Weed is a sad case, a man misunderstood by his wife and children and one who thus naturally gravitates toward the charms of Anne Murchison, the teenaged babysitter, whose beauty seems perfect as he breathes in "her light, her perfume, and the music of her voice" (207). On another, Weed seems a comic figure as, overcome with lust, he denies the clichéd nature of his response to the teenager and wants "to sport in the green woods, scratch where he itched, and drink from the same cup" (209). He becomes the fool as he "salivated, sighed and trembled" (212), then childishly and jealously argues with Anne's boyfriend, Clayton Thomas. On still another level, Weed is not comic at all, but self-centered and imperious in his dealings with women: He inappropriately squabbles with his teenaged daughter Helen, tries to force himself on Anne Murchison, speaks rudely to his older and less attractive neighbor Mrs. Wrightson, and fantasizes about the Farquarsons' maid, imagining her naked and humiliated, just as he fantasizes about a woman in a passing train, imagining her naked and Venus-like. When Julia accuses him of childishness, he strikes her across the face; Julia threatens to leave but reverses herself at the last minute. Miss Rainey, his secretary, tells him she wishes to "leave as soon as possible" (218).

Toward the end, Weed realizes that he "is in trouble" (218), caught between his family, imaged in the photograph on his desk, and the sexual coils of the Laocoon, imaged in his firm's letterhead. He chooses to see the psychiatrist Dr. Herzog, who encourages him to take up a hobby. In the final paragraphs, Shady Hill shows no signs of change: In this 20th-century version of America's "country," the suburb is a far cry from the paradise set forth in myth. Francis sits happily in his basement with his woodworking equipment and builds a coffee table. "Then it is dark; it is a night where kings in golden suits ride elephants over the mountains" (221). The contrast between the subdued Francis Weed and the elevated language is comic or ironic or just plain sad, depending on one's interpretation.

BIBLIOGRAPHY

Cheever, John. "A Country Husband." In *Contemporary American Short Stories*. Greenwich, Conn.: Fawcett, 1967.

COUNTRY OF THE POINTED FIRS, THE

SARAH ORNE JEWETT (1896)   Initially serialized in the ATLANTIC MONTHLY—the leading literary periodical when SARAH ORNE JEWETT was most prolific—*The Country of the Pointed Firs* is, according to many critics (as well as authors such as WILLA CATHER), her strongest and most representative work. Critics praised the NOVELLA, her 17th book, for having an exquisite writing style; for capturing New England life, land, and language; and for using REGIONALISM, the picturesque, and NATURALISM.

The Country of the Pointed Firs consists of semirelated sketches of people and place, interconnected by an outsider narrator who enters a pastoral, preindustrial region from an industrialized city. Jewett had been concerned with people and place since she began publishing in 1868; in *Country,* perhaps her most masterful attempt at this sort of writing, small crosssections of the lives of an insular, stereotypically (see STEREOTYPE) New England community based in the fictional town of Dunnet Landing, Maine, intersect and comment on one another. Some of the residents of Dunnet Landing, notably Almira Todd, later appeared in Jewett's short stories, such as "The Foreigner" (1900).

The residents of Dunnet Landing are long-term Maine residents. Jewett tells their stories in a style most often described as weblike, or artistically connected in a complex pattern. These characters have a very close community, and, not surprisingly, their closeness has a somber as well as a communal quality: They frequently exclude those who are not of Dunnet Landing and of European (generally French) descent. As has any small town, Dunnet Landing has characters (in all senses of the word) who refuse to conform to town standards; William Blackett, Captain Littlepage, and Joanna Todd, for instance, attain almost mythic status for their deviance. Those who, as Marie Harris, do not blend in racially, also refuse to adhere to community morals and thus appear coarse and uncivilized.

The narrative pointedly deviates from a traditional, patriarchal way of storytelling, instead almost always weaving outward from Almira Todd's home. (The female METAPHOR of weaving appears apt here.) Dun-

net Landing also focuses on women's friendships: Mrs. Todd and Mrs. Fosdick, lifelong friends, discuss each other's families as if they were their own; Mrs. Todd and Mrs. Blacket share an emotional trip to Green Island; and, in a pivotal scene, Mrs. Todd and the narrator gather pennyroyal, a medicinal herb, for Mrs. Todd's homemade medicine. The land is pastoral, industry is absent, and the trees—firs and spruces—are mentioned as frequently as town locales, like the Bowden farm and Elijah Tilley's fish house. The town, cast as fiercely regional, lies notably distant from the urban landscape where the female narrator used to live.

Many conversations and storytelling moments occur, such as long semidivergent anecdotes by Captain Littlepage and Elijah Tilley, but other stories explicitly address the significance of tradition. Mrs. Todd and Mrs. Fosdick relate the tale of Joanna Todd, who disappeared into self-imposed exile. The narrator—as participant, observer, and the reader's way into the story—travels to Shellheap Island, stands at Joanna's grave, and, as the character frequently does, philosophizes about life inside and outside the world of Dunnet Landing. Ultimately, although the stories of *Country* feature moments of suffering, particularly of women under the subtly present arm of patriarchy, the majority of the tales connect through Jewett's meticulously artistic examinations—often expressed through scenes of EPIPHANY—of love, community, understanding, discovery, and individual fulfillment (Heller xxii).

BIBLIOGRAPHY

Heller, Terry. "Introduction." In *Sarah Orne Jewett: The Country of the Pointed Firs and Other Fiction.* New York: Oxford University Press, 1996.

Howard, June, ed. *New Essays on "The Country of the Pointed Firs."* New York: Cambridge University Press, 1994.

Jewett, Sara Orne. *The Country of the Pointed Firs and Other Fiction.* New York: Oxford University Press, 1996.

Anne N. Thalheimer
University of Delaware

COUSIN LYMON   The hunchbacked dwarf in CARSON MCCULLER's *The Ballad of the Sad Cafe* with whom Miss AMELIA EVANS becomes utterly and

irretrievably smitten. In terms of his appearance, we learn how misshapen and physically unappealing he is; in terms of his character, we learn how self-centered, selfish, and lazy he is. Thus his purpose, as a grotesque character, is to personify the beloved, which McCullers famously describes in her classic passage on the characteristics of and differences between the lover and the recipient of that love. Cousin Lymon uses Miss Amelia, of course and, in the end, is himself smitten by Marvin Macy, who cares nothing for Lymon but uses him to defeat Miss Amelia—who has wounded him indelibly by throwing him out of the house. The NOVELLA introduces the possibility that Lymon and Macy first met each other in prison. Whether literally true or not—and there is evidence both for and against a previous acquaintance—McCullers unquestionably demonstrates through the personalities of both men that they recognize the evil thoughts in one another.

"COYOTE STEALS THE SUN AND MOON" ANONYMOUS   This story, like many other stories from Native American cultures, is based on the centuries-old concept of the oral tradition. Before cultures worldwide invented and/or used writing, stories were told to explain natural occurrences, to teach religious or moral principles, and to provide basic entertainment. It is not uncommon to find Native American stories that were put in writing by cultural anthropologists in the late 19th and early 20th centuries, and this example from the Zuni culture is probably one of those. Richard Erdoes and Simon Ortiz, who edited the collection of Native American stories titled *American Indian Myths and Legends,* point out that this particular story is based on one told by Ruth Benedict in 1935. Readers must assume that Benedict wrote the story down and reproduced it in that fashion but must never forget that the story's true essence can only be experienced orally.

In this particular myth Coyote, who is a typical character in stories found in many Native American cultures, becomes involved in a scheme to steal the Sun and Moon from the Kachinas, a group of Pueblo deities. Coyote, who is described as a "bad hunter who never kills anything" (140), is jealous of Eagle, who

hunts so well that much of what he kills goes to waste. Coyote suggests to Eagle that the two of them collaborate and that way both get what they want—Coyote would get to eat, and Eagle would not be as wasteful. While they are hunting, Coyote realizes that his problem is that there is not enough light in the world for him to see his prey (there is no Sun or Moon at this point), so the two set out to find the Kachinas, who have power over light. When they find the Kachinas, Coyote and Eagle steal the Sun and Moon while the Kachinas are distracted. After arguing about who should carry the box, Coyote makes the mistake of looking to see what is inside and releases the Sun and Moon into the sky.

There are several points being made in the story. The first involves a creation myth—an explanation for the existence of the Sun and Moon. The story is set before the creation is complete, and the actions of Coyote and Eagle contribute to the world that we all know. Their releasing the Sun and Moon not only gives light and heat but also influences the pattern of the seasons. Thus several phenomena are explained at once in the story. There is also a moral lesson to be found in it: Coyote is lazy and jealous of Eagle, and his jealousy leads to his losing the Sun and Moon. Coyotes are often silly or comical figures in Native American stories, often interfering with people, playing tricks (thus the term *trickster*), and getting into mischief. Coyote's foolishness makes the story entertaining, but there is more to it. Eagle, who is superior to Coyote, carries the box containing the Sun and Moon after the two have stolen it. Coyote is curious about what is in the box and suspects that Eagle will keep its contents to himself and not share with him. He asks Eagle whether he can carry the box himself, and Eagle refuses. Coyote uses a scheme to change Eagle's mind, telling him that since Eagle is superior, it would not be right for him to carry the box himself. Again, Eagle refuses, but once Coyote has asked four times, Eagle relents. Four is a symbolic number in many Native American cultures, as it represents the four cardinal directions—often, in Native American tales, deities and mortals alike repeat actions and sayings four times. After Eagle turns over the box to Coyote, Coyote's curiosity, jealousy, and foolishness get the better of him. He opens the box, and the Sun and Moon escape, giving not only light to the world but also summer and winter. As the footnote to the story points out, "the release of the moon brings death and desolation to the world" (142). The story thus ends by becoming primarily focused on the origins of the seasonal cycle. The storyteller points out that without Coyote's meddling, we could be enjoying summer all the time.

BIBLIOGRAPHY

Allen, Paula Gunn. *The Sacred Hoop: Recovering the Feminine in American Indian Traditions.* Boston: Beacon Press, 1986.

Erdoes, Richard, and Alfonso Ortiz, eds. *American Indian Myths and Legends.* New York: Pantheon Books, 1984, 140–143.

Erdoes, Richard, and Alfonso Ortiz, eds. *American Indian Trickster Tales.* New York: Penguin, 1999.

Velie, Alan R. *Native American Perspectives on Literature and History.* Norman: University of Oklahoma Press, 1995.

James Mayo
Jackson State Community College

COYOTE STORY

Coyote is a character in numerous Native American TRICKSTER tales (see also NATIVE AMERICAN STORYTELLING). A complex figure, Coyote has been described as more ANTIHERO than HERO, a Native American version of the European EVERYMAN, a flawed character whose greatest weaknesses are vanity and pride. Coyote stories vary from tribe to tribe, but in general Coyote is credited with shaping the past—especially in creation stories—and with embodying hope for the future. Jay Miller notes that the best Coyote stories are heard at wakes, "helping to relieve the grief and keep everyone awake" (Miller ix). Simultaneously edifying and entertaining, Coyote stories have a kinship with traditional European beast FABLEs and with the African-American tales told by UNCLE REMUS. Examples of Coyote stories occur in Peter Blue Cloud's 1990 collection *The Other Side of Nowhere: Contemporary Coyote Tales* and in Mourning Dove's *Coyote Stories,* first published in 1933.

BIBLIOGRAPHY

Blue Cloud, Peter. *The Other Side of Nowhere: Contemporary Coyote Tales.* Fredonia, N.Y.: White Pine Press, 1990.

Miller, Jay. "Introduction to the Bison Book Edition." In *Coyote Stories,* by Mourning Dove and edited by Heister Dean Guie, v–xvii. Lincoln: University of Nebraska Press, 1990.

Mourning Dove. *Coyote Stories.* Edited by Heister Dean Guie. Lincoln: University of Nebraska Press, 1990.

CRANE, STEPHEN (1871–1900)

Stephen Crane was born on November 1, 1871, the 14th and youngest child of a Methodist minister, Jonathan Townley Crane, and his wife, Mary Helen Peck Crane. Young Stephen attended various colleges, but he did not take his higher education very seriously. His talent for writing appeared at an early age, and his first article, on the explorer Henry M. Stanley, was published in the February 1890 issue of *Villette.* In 1891 and 1892 he assisted an older brother on stories for the New York *Tribune* to gain further experience in journalistic writing. The writing style Crane developed while working for the newspaper remained with him throughout his career.

Although Stephen Crane is perhaps most remembered for his NOVELLA of the CIVIL WAR *THE RED BADGE OF COURAGE* (1895), his short stories also show his flair for narrative and description. One of his notable stories is "The OPEN BOAT," which first appeared in the June 1897 issue of *SCRIBNER'S.* This short story grew from the author's personal involvement in the sinking of the *Commodore,* a tugboat that was taking weapons to Cuba. In this story of four men striving toward shore in a dinghy after their ship has gone down, Crane combines his talent as a journalist with his fiction-writing skill. The resulting tale draws together the "personal and [the] universal" (Davis 191), allowing Crane to tell his own story of that horrific event while also illuminating the struggle of man against the forces of nature.

Other short stories by Crane reveal his strong background in newspaper writing and his ability to combine fact and fiction. His urge toward REALISM in his creation of characters and their situations led him to stand in a breadline without a winter coat when working on "The Men in the Storm" (1894), so that he could accurately describe how it felt to be cold. Crane also voluntarily slept in a flophouse while he was writing

"An Experiment in Misery" (1894) in order to gain a sense of his characters' sufferings in that environment. While some have criticized this element of Crane's writing, claiming that its realism is overly harsh, his ability to write of other people's trials and emotions in such a direct way is one of the characteristics that draws readers to his work. Besides writing of societal ills, Crane also had a passion for history, specifically war history. Although he did not witness the Civil War firsthand, with *Red Badge* Crane proved he could write accurately and poignantly about the experience of battle.

Considered one of his best works on this THEME, "The Upturned Face" (1900) captures the scene of a small group of soldiers and their commanding officer burying a fallen comrade in the midst of combat. In just a handful of pages Crane creates the sounds and emotions of the battle raging both around and within the men as they hesitate to cover their dead friend's cold blue face with dirt. Crane makes the scene immediate for the reader by describing the "windy sound of bullets," the "button . . . brick-red with drying blood," and the "plop" the earth makes as it covers the body of the dead man. This characteristic use of sensory details also operates powerfully in Crane's "Death and the Child" (1898), "The Price of the Harness" (1898), and "An Episode of War" (1899), which are counted among the best of his later war stories.

Crane wrote *Whilomville Stories* (1900), his last major collection of short fiction, while he was battling tuberculosis near the end of his life. These 14 stories center on scenes of small town life, and many of them have children and childhood as their central theme. Crane's ability to write of human struggles and their accompanying emotions is shown as masterfully in these vignettes of the agonies and ecstasies of childhood as in the war stories that made him famous. For example, "His New Mittens" gives the reader a glimpse inside the mind of a young boy caught between his mother's order not to ruin his red mittens and the taunts of a group of boys playing in the snow. Crane raises the conflicts suffered by this child and the children in the other tales in this collection to the level of the conflict of the men in "The Open Boat" or "The Upturned Face," and he shows the same desire for

realism as he does in "An Experiment in Misery." Perhaps Crane's desire to show realistically the significance of childhood events stemmed from his knowledge of his own impending death.

Stephen Crane died in Badenweiler in the Black Forest on June 5, 1900, after a long illness and multiple hemorrhages; he was only 28. During his brief life, Crane's writing had a great impact not only on the general public but also on other writers. In October 1897 Crane had met and befriended the novelist Joseph Conrad. Conrad greatly respected and admired Crane's work, and he recognized his new friend's incredible talent for capturing events and places he had not actually experienced. The two authors shared their work with each other and remained close friends until Crane's death. Although Crane died at 28, he produced a fairly large body of work. In the four years before his death, he wrote five novels, two collections of poetry, two volumes of war stories, three other story collections, and a variety of journalistic pieces. Stephen Crane's place in the canon of American literature is firmly established, and his short stories remain of interest in studies of such issues as realism and the effects of journalism on fiction writing.

See also "The LITTLE REGIMENT."

BIBLIOGRAPHY

Adams, Richard P. "Naturalistic Fiction: 'The Open Boat.'" *Tulane Studies in English* 4 (1954): 137–146.

Bais, H.S.S. *Stephen Crane: A Pioneer in Technique*. New Delhi: Crown, 1988.

Bergon, Frank. *Stephen Crane's Artistry*. New York: Columbia University Press, 1975.

Berryman, John. *Crane*. New York: Sloane, 1950.

Bloom, Harold, ed. *Stephen Crane*. New York: Chelsea House, 1987.

Cady, Edwin H. *Stephen Crane*. New York: Twayne, 1962; revised ed., 1980.

Colvert, James B. *Crane*. San Diego: Harcourt Brace, 1984.

Crane, Stephen. *The Complete Short Stories and Sketches of Stephen Crane*. Edited by Thomas A. Gullason. Garden City, N.Y.: Doubleday, 1963.

———. *The Little Regiment and Other Episodes of the American Civil War*. New York: Appleton, 1896.

———. *The Monster and Other Stories*. New York: Harper, 1899; augmented ed. New York: Harper, 1901.

————. *The Open Boat and Other Tales of Adventure.* New York: Doubleday and McClure, 1898.

————. *The Portable Crane.* Edited by Joseph Katz. New York: Viking, 1969.

————. *Prose and Poetry* (Library of America). Edited by J. C. Levenson. New York: Library of America, 1984.

————. *The Sullivan County Sketches.* Edited by Melvin Schoberlin, Syracuse, N.Y.: Syracuse University Press, 1949; revised ed. published as *Sullivan County Tales and Sketches.* Edited by R. W. Stallman. Ames: Iowa State University Press, 1968.

————. *Whilomville Stories.* New York: Harper, 1900.

————. *The Works of Stephen Crane.* 10 vols. Edited by Fredson Bowers. Charlottesville: University of Virginia Press, 1969–76.

————. *Wounds in the Rain: War Stories.* New York: Stokes, 1900.

Davis, Linda H. *Badge of Courage: The Life of Stephen Crane.* Boston: Houghton Mifflin, 1988.

Gibson, Donald B. *The Fiction of Crane.* Carbondale: Southern Illinois University Press, 1968.

————. *The Red Badge of Courage: Redefining the Hero.* Boston: Houghton Mifflin, 1988.

Haliburton, David. *The Color of the Sky: A Study of Crane.* Cambridge: Cambridge University Press, 1989.

Holton, Milne. *Cylinder of Vision: The Fiction and Journalistic Writing of Crane.* Baton Rouge: Louisiana State University Press, 1972.

Kissane, Leedice. "Interpretation through Language: A Study of the Metaphors in Crane's 'The Open Boat.'" *Rendezvous* 1 (1966).

Metzger, Charles R. "Realistic Devices in Crane's 'The Open Boat.'" *Midwest Quarterly* 4 (1962).

Mitchell, Lee Clerk, ed. *New Essays on The Red Badge of Courage.* New York: Cambridge University Press, 1986.

Nagel, James. *Crane and Literary Impressionism.* University Park: Pennsylvania State University Press, 1980.

Pizer, Donald, ed. *Critical Essays on Stephen Crane.* Boston: G. K. Hall, 1990.

Stallman, R. W. *Stephen Crane: A Biography.* New York: George Braziller, 1968.

Tibbets, A. M. "Crane's 'The Bridge Comes to Yellow Sky.'" *English Journal* 54 (1965).

Weatherford, Richard, ed. *Stephen Crane: The Critical Heritage.* Boston: Routledge, 1973.

Wolford, Chester L. *The Anger of Crane: Fiction and the Epic Tradition.* Lincoln: University of Nebraska Press, 1983.

————. *Stephen Crane: A Study of the Short Fiction.* San Diego, Calif.: Greenhaven Press, 1989.

Sara J. Triller
University of Delaware

CYBERPUNK   A popular GENRE named for its computer cowboy heroes and related to SCIENCE FICTION. Cyberpunk stories are set in a futuristic, dystopic environment—the opposite of utopian—in which computer technology plays an important role. Although the cyberpunk world can be described as postmodern, the genre is distinguished from literary POSTMODERNISM by a more traditionally realistic style. The PROTAGONISTS of cyberpunk stories are technologically proficient, lonely adventurers struggling with issues of identity and forced to use computer skills to fight menacing forces of domination. WILLIAM GIBSON, whose collection of short stories *Burning Chrome* is exemplary of cyberpunk, is the genre's best-known author.

Karen Fearing
University of North Carolina at Chapel Hill

D

DADA Originating from the French word for hobbyhorse, the term was chosen randomly from the dictionary for the literary and artistic movement founded in 1916 in Zurich by Tristan Tzara, the artist Hans Arp, the poet Hugo Ball, and the medical student Richard Huelsenbeck. The movement intentionally rejected all traditional philosophical and artistic values. Its leaders intended dadaism as a protest against WORLD WAR I and its awesome destruction of civilization. The *Dada Review* proclaimed its intention to replace logic and reason with deliberate madness and to substitute intentionally discordant chaos for established notions of beauty or harmony in the arts. Dadaists mocked conventional behavior; some dada meetings turned into riots; art exhibits were mocking hoaxes. The artist and writer André Breton and his followers became interested in the subconscious, breaking with Tzara in 1921 and officially founding SURREALISM in 1924. GERTRUDE STEIN's radical experiments with language have roots in dadaism. Revived in the 1930s in parts of England and the United States, certain aspects of dadaism survive in the "theater of the ABSURD." In retrospect critics recognize much of dadaism's shock value in certain forms of POSTMODERNISM, and, although the term is normally applied to art and poetry, it can usefully describe radical experiments in short fiction in both the early and the late 20th century.

"DADDY GARBAGE" JOHN EDGAR WIDEMAN **(1981)** "Daddy Garbage" is the second story in JOHN EDGAR WIDEMAN's collection *Damballah,* the second book in Wideman's Homewood Trilogy. "Daddy Garbage" follows "DAMBALLAH," a tale of an African slave who, before his murder in 1852, transfers the African spiritual legacy to a young American slave. "Daddy Garbage" is set in 20th-century Homewood and features John French, grandfather of the narrator and usually seen as a surrogate for Wideman himself. The writer, the intellectual, must get the story right so that he can use his gifts to illustrate and communicate the communal links stretching across seas and generations of black history. At first glance, "Daddy Garbage" seems very different from "Damballah," but a main theme in both tales is, in fact, conflicting views of the worth of a black life.

Typical of Wideman's contemporary style, "Daddy Garbage" moves in and out of time sequences. In the opening scene, set during the summer of the mid-20th century, an aged Lemuel Strayhorn sells iceballs from his cart on Homewood Avenue. His customer is Geraldine French, daughter of his friend John French, who is buying iceballs for her great nieces and nephews and recalling Strayhorn's dog Daddy Garbage, long deceased. Although Strayhorn says he cannot remember his reason for naming the dog *Daddy Garbage,* Geraldine replies, "I bet you still remember what you want to remember" and tells him he will live for centuries (30). In the next scene, however, it is snow-ing and Daddy Garbage is the young dog who makes a discovery in a garbage can beyond a row of low-income housing: Vexed and thinking to himself, "Nigger garbage ain't worth shit" (32), Strayhorn unwraps the package and thinks he has discovered a "little, battered, brown-skinned doll" until he realizes to his horror that she was a newborn baby, wrapped in newspaper, whom someone had tossed on the trash heap.

Cradling the dead baby under his arm, he first thinks to ask advice from Freeda French, John's wife, but she sends one of her daughters to turn him away from the door. In her view, Strayhorn influences John to gamble and drink wine. Strayhorn puts the little corpse on the pile of mattresses he uses for a bed and joins French in the Bucket of Blood. If French's major flaw is his alcoholism, his major gift is his love of all his children and grandchildren; he is as appalled as Strayhorn: "Ain't nobody could do that. Ain't nobody done nothing like that," he protests, but Strayhorn swears that he and Daddy Garbage found the baby "laid in the garbage like wasn't nothing but spoilt meat" (36). Together they decide that, despite the snow and the cold, they must give the infant the decent burial it deserves. Strayhorn agrees that even Daddy Garbage deserved a burial; he would never consider throwing him in the trash.

The baby's identity is never resolved and the perpetrator never identified, but after considering possibilities, French decides that it does not matter: "Black or white. Boy or Girl. A mongrel made by niggers tipping in white folks' beds or white folks paying visits to black. Everybody knew it was happening every night. Homewood people every color in the rainbow and they talking about white people and black people like there's a brick wall tween them and nobody don't know how to get over" (38). The cold and somber scene is juxtaposed to another hot July one, in which French's daughter, Gertrude, tells Strayhorn that her older sister, Lizabeth, wants her father in the hospital where she has just given birth to a baby boy. Even though she is embarrassed to note her father's drunken singing of "an ignorant darky song" (41), she still loves him and thinks of him as "Daddy John" (42). The warm summer scene shifts again to the cold burial of the abandoned child and a conversation between Strayhorn

and French. Therein they compare the heartless life of the cold urban North to the warm communal life of the South that, despite slavery and economic deprivation, is part of African-American culture. The two men, with Daddy Garbage in attendance, bury the infant in a full six feet of earth, telling it to "sleep in peace" (43) and laying it to rest on a cushion of snow.

BIBLIOGRAPHY
Coleman, James W. "Damballah: The Intellectual and the Folk Voice." In *Blackness and Modernism: The Literary Career of John Edgar Wideman.* Jackson: University Press of Mississippi, 1989.
Wideman, John. "The Architectonics of Fiction." *Callaloo* 13 (Winter 1990): 42–46.
———. "Daddy Garbage." In *Damballah.* New York: Avon Books, 1981.
———. "Defining the Black Voice in Fiction." *Black American Literature Forum* 2 (Fall 1977): 79–82.
———. "Frame and Dialect: The Evolution of the Black Voice in Fiction," *American Poetry Review* 5, no. 5 (1976): 34–37.
———. "Of Love and Dust: A Reconsideration." *Callaloo* 1 (May 1978): 76–84.

"DAEMON LOVER, THE" Shirley Jackson (1949)

In "The Daemon Lover," James (Jamie) Harris, a handsome author, deserts his dowdy 34-year old fiancée. The plot of this short story may be indebted to "The Demon Lover" by Elizabeth Bowen, whom Jackson ranked with Katherine Anne Porter as one of the best contemporary short story writers. When Jamie Harris disappears, he shatters his bride's dreams of living in a "golden house in-the-country" (DL 12). Her shock of recognition that she will never trade her lonely city apartment for a loving home mirrors the final scenes of "The Lottery" and "The Pillar of Salt" as well as many other stories in which a besieged woman suffers a final and often fatal blow.

In "The Daemon Lover," the second story in *The Lottery and Other Stories,* Jackson's collection of 25 tales, the reader sees James Harris only through his fiancée's eyes as a tall man wearing a blue suit. Neither the reader nor anyone in the story can actually claim to have seen him. Nonetheless, this piece foreshadows the appearance of Harris in such other stories in the collection as

"Like Mother Used to Make," "The Village," "Of Course," "Seven Types of Ambiguities," and "The Tooth." As James Harris wanders through the book, he sheds the veneer of the ordinary that covers his satanic nature.

The IRONY in "The Daemon Lover" is that the female PROTAGONIST becomes suspect as she hunts for the mysterious young man "who promised to marry her" (DL 23). Everywhere she searches, she encounters couples who mock her with not-so-subtle insinuations that she is crazy. Indeed, at the end of the story she may well have become insane; the narrative is ambiguous on this point. Significantly, however, if the nameless woman has indeed lost her mind, it is James who is responsible. Although some critics speculate that the disruptive male figure—both in this story and in the others in the collection—is a hallucination of a sexually repressed character, the epilogue to *The Lottery,* a ballad entitled "James Harris, The Daemon Lover," suggests otherwise: He is, in fact, the devil himself.

For Jackson, *The Lottery* is more than a GHOST STORY; "The Daemon Lover" in particular and the collection in general critique a society that fails to protect women from becoming victims of strangers or neighbors. As in "The Lottery," Jackson's shocking account of a housewife's ritualistic stoning, or in "The Pillar of Salt," which traces a wife's horror and growing hysteria when she has lost her way, the threatened characters are women. Although many of Jackson's stories are modern versions of the folk tale of a young wife's abduction by the devil, and although her characters are involved in terrifying circumstances, the point is that these tales seem true: They are rooted in reality. Thus, Jackson exposes the threat to women's lives in a society that condones the daemon lover.

BIBLIOGRAPHY

Jackson, Shirley. "The Daemon Lover." *In the Lottery and Other Stories.* Modern Library Series. New York: Random House, 2000.

Oppenheimer, Judy. *Private Demons: The Life of Shirley Jackson.* New York: Putnam, 1988.

Wylie, Joan. *Shirley Jackson: A Study of the Short Fiction.* New York: Twayne, 1994.

Harriet P. Gold
LaSalle College
Durham College

DAHLBERG, EDWARD (1900–1977) Dahlberg's early life hardly portended his emergence as a novelist, essayist, poet, and critic. Born to an unmarried woman, he spent much of his childhood in orphanages and at age 17 was on the road as a hobo. His first novels, *Bottom Dogs* (1929) and *From Flushing to Calvary* (1932), drew on personal experience and were examples of PROLETARIAN LITERATURE, which included novels and short stories sympathetic to the struggles and plights of the working class. Both of Dahlberg's novels received critical attention and a significant readership. Although Dahlburg wrote these novels in the style of NATURALISM, however, the style of his later work became more allusive and epigrammatic. (See ALLUSION and EPIGRAM.) His POINT OF VIEW was intensely personal and moral, and his criticism considered incisive. His critical works, which include *Do These Bones Live?* (1941; rev. as *Can These Bones Live?* 1960), *The Flea of Sodom* (1950), and *The Sorrows of Priapus* (1957), attacked modern culture and criticized such American literary icons as WILLIAM FAULKNER, ERNEST HEMINGWAY, and F. SCOTT FITZGERALD. Among the few writers whom he praised were Henry David Thoreau, SHERWOOD ANDERSON, and THEODORE DREISER. Dahlberg's views are echoed in such stories as those in Anderson's WINESBURG, OHIO, HAMLIN GARLAND'S "Under the Lion's Paw," RICHARD WRIGHT'S "The MAN WHO WAS ALMOST A MAN," and—somewhat ironically given his lack of admiration for Faulkner—Faulkner's "BARN BURNING."

DAISY MILLER: A STUDY HENRY JAMES (1878, 1879)
HENRY JAMES'S NOVELLA—or *nouvelle,* as he called it—literally took the reading public by storm when it appeared in serial form in the British magazine *Cornhill* in 1878. It features an unsophisticated, strikingly lovely young woman from Schenectady, New York, who travels to Europe and defies the conventions of a group of Europeanized Americans who enforce the rules of the older European community with unthinking severity. Published in book form in 1879 and as a play in 1883, *Daisy Miller* aroused a good deal of controversy, some reviewers calling it a libel on American manners, but it later became one of the most popular of James's writings. WILLIAM DEAN

HOWELLS reportedly said that members of society divided themselves into "Daisy Millerites" or "Anti–Daisy Millerites," and Daisy Miller hats appeared everywhere (Hocks 32). Today the story still appears as a standard in American literature anthologies and continues to arouse readers' interest.

The story is told through a nominal first-person narrator, but all the information is filtered through the central consciousness of Frederick Winterbourne, a young expatriate American who has lived in Europe since age 12. On meeting Daisy; her mother, Mrs. Miller; and her brother, Randolph, at a hotel in Vevey, Switzerland, he finds himself fascinated with Daisy but somewhat shocked at her disregard of European customs regarding the proper behavior for a young unmarried woman. Throughout the story he seeks to discover whether Daisy is essentially "innocent," but in the process he—and the reader—learns a good deal about his own prejudices and motivations. Winterbourne learns the answer at the end of the story, but too late: Daisy dies, and he must share some of the responsibility for her death.

Winterbourne's name suggests his coldness, and, indeed, he lives most of the year in Geneva, Switzerland, characterized in the novella as a dark, grim, brooding locus of Protestantism. James uses locale to point up differences in temperament, and Rome—the site of Daisy's death—is in some senses Geneva's opposite, suffused in sunshine and color, attractive with its cathedrals but also implicitly dangerous with its pre-Christian sites of antiquity. Winterbourne never comes to terms with his rather hypocritical view of sex: He pays lip service to the proprieties espoused by his aunt, Mrs. Costello, and her coterie, yet the narrator reminds us more than once that he constantly "studies" in Geneva, an apparent euphemism for his affair with a safely married foreign woman. Winterbourne ignores or fails to recognize his sexual response to Daisy; her obstreperous 12-year-old brother (the same age as Winterbourne when he moved to Europe) provides an intriguing male counterpart to Winterbourne with his Freudian brandishing of his "alpenstock," a hiking stick, as they discuss American girls.

Most critics find Daisy Miller perplexing, difficult to pin down. Many see her as frivolous, as indeed in some sense she is. But she is natural, good, and, as we learn with Winterbourne (whose viewpoint we find difficult to shake) at the end, completely innocent. The very fact that her innocence is an issue makes Daisy a sympathetic figure: Roman fever, or malaria, is the ostensible cause of her death, but it becomes a METAPHOR for the attitude toward and preoccupation with her innocence, her virtue. Daisy dies precisely because the concept means so much to Winterbourne and his wealthy social group. A FEMINIST perspective helps to illuminate this story's complexity and to decipher the reprehensible nature of the men like Winterbourne—and the women like his aunt who help them perpetuate the standards of behavior for young women. Daisy Miller's fate provides a fascinating contrast to the women in EDITH WHARTON's "ROMAN FEVER," almost surely a woman writer's response to James's novella.

BIBLIOGRAPHY

Hocks, Richard A. *Henry James: A Study of the Short Fiction.* Boston: Twayne, 1990.

James, Henry. *Daisy Miller: A Study.* In *The Complete Tales of Henry James.* Vol. 18. Edited by Leon Edel. Philadelphia: Lippincott, 1961–64.

"DAMBALLAH" JOHN EDGAR WIDEMAN (1981)

Through its 12 stories, the first of which is "Damballah, *Damballah* traces the earliest tales of the characters who eventually play roles in the so-called Homewood Trilogy; some are even named after Wideman's family members. On one level, the book is a storyteller's achievement, developing relationships and linking generations. On another, it is about the storytelling process itself: Wideman dedicates the book to his own brother, Robby; models Tommy, one of the characters in both *Hiding Place* and *Damballah*, on him; and demonstrates the connections that can be forged through the sharing of stories across time. It is also a way to portray two very different brothers—one intellectual but for a long time uncomfortable with his blackness, one jailed for murder, but more attuned to his blackness. John French, featured in several stories, including "DADDY GARBAGE," gathers stories of African-American family history, cultural tradition, folk ritual, myth, and song to link himself to family members both in the past and in the present and in the community memory that links them all.

As the critic James W. Coleman points out, *Damballah* views African-American tradition as tied closely to African tradition: It is "a river flowing back and forth in black history" (79). Wideman deliberately blurs time lines as the African slave Orion looks directly into the eyes of the American slave and, later, wills the word *Damballah* into the American to form links among past, present, and future. Much of the tradition is supernatural, communicated by ghosts and spirits, dreams and magic.

Damballah is the second book in the Homewood Trilogy, preceded by *Hiding Place* (1981), a novel, and followed by *Sent for You Yesterday* (1983). The epigraph explains that the god Damballah, or "good serpent of the sky," is the ancient and venerable father, who gathers the family together and gives peace. His association with family and community tradition suggests a link among all the stories; indeed, the book's interconnected tales, from the "ancient origin of the race" (*Damballah* 11) to Pittsburgh's inner-city neighborhood of Homewood, form a short story cycle that critics have compared to WILLIAM FAULKNER's GO DOWN, MOSES, ERNEST HEMINGWAY's IN OUR TIME, RICHARD WRIGHT's UNCLE TOM'S CHILDREN, and ERNEST GAINES's *Bloodline*.

The story "Damballah" opens on a cane plantation in 1852 as the solitary African slave Orion bathes in the river. After the white men stole him from his village and took him over the sea to this plantation, this "blood-soaked land" (18), he realizes that he can bear slavery no longer. He refuses to speak another word of English, the language of "the white people who had decided to kill him" (18), or to touch another portion of the white man's food. Orion—called Ryan by the African-American slaves—knows that one of them, a young boy, is watching him as he bathes, and Orion has determined that he will pass on his African spirit and wisdom to this boy: "He could be the one. This boy born so far from home. This boy who knew nothing but what the whites told him. This boy could learn the story and tell it again" (18). And so, on the eve of his death, Orion bores his eyes into the boy, who feels him "boring a hole into his chest and thrusting into

that space the word *Damballah*. Then the hooded eyes were gone" (20). Orion draws a cross in the dust and speaks the word again.

The boy is clearly fascinated with Orion and, despite warnings from Aunt Nissy, the slave who cooks for the whites, he insists on repeating the word *Damballah*. This is the word that Orion apparently yelled in the middle of the sermon preached by Jim, the African-American Christian preacher. Orion's final act of insubordination occurs as he violently pulls the plantation overseer off his horse, breaking half of his bones, a crime that dooms him to death. Observed by the boy, four men drag Orion to the barn, from which he hears one single scream, "A bull screaming once that night and torches burning in the barn and Master and the men coming out and no Ryan" (24). In a deliberate blurring of events, the Master spends the night with Patty in the slave quarters, causing the weeping Mistress to lock herself in her room; in the morning—but which morning?—Mistress sees the naked Orion on the porch—or was it his spirit?—and no one dares call the Master back from slave row, and no one but the boy dares approach the barn. Once inside, he finds Orion's head brutally severed from his body. The boy recalls the stories Orion has told him, draws a cross in the dust, repeats the word, and settles in to wait for Orion's spirit: "Damballah said it be a long way a ghost be going and Jordan chilly and wide and a new ghost take his time getting his wings together. Long way to go so you can sit and listen till the ghost ready to go on home" (25). Mixing African and Christian references together in anticipation of African-American cultural history, the boy eventually sees the spirit rise from Orion's body. Moving full circle, he throws the head into the river.

The mythic aura of the story is enhanced by the dual perspectives, both African and African-American, and the slightly uncertain time sequence: Orion, recalling his independence in his African village, is willing his own death. He was kidnapped, taken to the United States, sold to another owner, returned to the cane plantation after being repeatedly beaten for "misconduct" (22), refused to eat or speak English, and deliberately attacked the overseer. At the opening of the story, though, he recalls his African village and is certain that when he dies, his African fathers will "sweep him away, carry him home again" (18). Wideman's depiction of his refusal to adapt to slavery contrasts sharply with his evocation of those who succumbed. Aunt Lissy calls "Ryan" a "wild African nigger" (18) and slaps the boy when he repeats the word *Damballah*: "Don't you ever, you hear me, ever let me hear that heathen talk no more. You hear me, boy? You talk Merican, boy" (21). Preacher Jim prays that God will forgive Orion's "heathen ways" (25). Wideman sketches in the horrors of slavery with brief but vivid detail: Orion is sent back by the white man who beats him, finds him "brutish" and "a flawed piece of the Indies" unfit even for his kennels; significantly, he finds Orion utterly lacking both human qualities and a soul (22). The nameless African-American boy is locked in a room all day to polish silver, and the slave Patty is at the beck and call of her white Master. Orion becomes Wideman's prototype of the slave who escapes and flies home to Africa, while the others, if they are lucky, endure slavery and produce progeny who move north in the 20th century and populate such areas as Homewood.

BIBLIOGRAPHY

Coleman, James W. "Damballah: The Intellectual and the Folk Voice." In *Blackness and Modernism: The Literary Career of John Edgar Wideman*. Jackson: University Press of Mississippi, 1989.

Wideman, John. "The Architectonics of Fiction." *Callaloo* 13 (Winter 1990): 42–46.

———. "Damballah." In *Damballah*. New York: Avon Books, 1981.

———. "Defining the Black Voice in Fiction," *Black American Literature Forum* 2 (Fall 1977): 79–82.

———. "Frame and Dialect: The Evolution of the Black Voice in Fiction." *American Poetry Review* 5, no. 5 (1976): 34–37.

———. "Of Love and Dust: A Reconsideration." *Callaloo* 1 (May 1978): 76–84.

D'AMBROSIO, CHARLES (1960–   ) Charles

D'Ambrosio's emergence into contemporary literature began in the early 1990s when he graduated from the Iowa Writer's Workshop in 1991. Since that time his work has appeared in the *New Yorker,* the *Paris Review,* *Zoetrope All-Story,* and *Best American Short Stories*. His work blends the tender and compassionate nature of humanity with its darker side, often within the same character. His stories are alive with detail; he paints pictures of contemporary society with its beauty, its ugliness, and, ultimately, a sense of hope that prevails over tragedy.

D'Ambrosio has published two collection of short stories. His most recent publication, *The Dead Fish Museum* (Knopf, 2006), is particularly noteworthy, as seven of the eight stories were previously published in the *New Yorker*. This collection features "The High Divide," which won the O. HENRY MEMORIAL AWARD in 2005. The stories feature a broad mix of characters and situations including a screenwriter in a mental institution ("Screenwriter") and a carpenter building a set for a porn film ("The Dead Fish Museum"). His first short story collection, *The Point: And Other Stories* (Little, Brown, 1995), features characters in the Puget Sound, Washington, area, who face difficulties with personal relationships, alcoholism, and abusive behavior. The highlighted story, "The Point," selected for inclusion in *Best American Short Stories 1991,* reveals the inner thoughts of Kurt Pittman, whose mother turned to alcoholism after Kurt's father committed suicide. This collection was also a *New York Times* Notable Book of the Year and a finalist for the PEN/Hemingway Award.

Although primarily known for his short stories, D'Ambrosio is also a prolific essayist, publishing a collection entitled *Orphans* (Clear Cut Press, 2005). He continues to demonstrate his interest in human behavior through his essays, which contain such topics as his own personal history ("Documents"), a Russian orphanage in Svirstroy ("Orphans"), and contemporary public interest in Mary Kay Letourneau ("Mary Kay Letourneau"). Through the 11 essays in the collection D'Ambrosio shows that his skill as writer extends beyond the borders of the United States and of his own imagination into the corners of the world.

The list of awards D'Ambrosio has received for his writing is numerous, with no sign of slowing in the future. He has been the recipient of the PUSHCART PRIZE, the Paris Review Aga Khan Fiction Prize (1993), a James Michener Fellowship, among other awards.

D'Ambrosio was born and grew up in Seattle, Washington. Prior to receiving his M.F.A. from the Iowa Writer's Workshop in 1991, he was educated at Oberlin College, where he received his B.A. in 1980, and was a Humanities Fellow at the University of Chicago. He has resided in a number of states, including California, Montana, and Oregon, where he currently makes his home in Portland. He teaches in the M.F.A. programs at the University of Montana in Missoula and Warren Wilson College in North Carolina.

BIBLIOGRAPHY

D'Ambrosio, Charles. *The Dead Fish Museum.* New York: Knopf, 2006.

———. *Orphans.* Portland, Ore.: Clear Cut Press, 2005.

———. *The Point: And Other Stories.* Boston: Little, Brown, 1995.

Starr, Karla. "The Tragically Happy Life of Charles D'Ambrosio." *Willamette Week Online,* 10 May 2006. Available online. URL: http://www.wweek.com/editorial/3227/7516. Accessed February 16, 2007.

"DARE'S GIFT" ELLEN GLASGOW (1917)

"Dare's Gift" was completed by January 5, 1917, and published in *Harper's Magazine* in March of that same year (Kelly 117). The story was later included in *The Shadowy Third and Other Stories,* published in 1923, and is included in *The Collected Stories of Ellen Glasgow,* published in 1963. It was the second in a series of short stories, many drawing upon supernatural themes, written after the death of several of ELLEN GLASGOW's family members. Glasgow had moved back into her Richmond family home, which she felt "belonged to the dead" (*Woman Within* 222), and she was particularly drawn to the "ghosts" of her sister Cary, her brother Frank, and her mother (*Woman Within* 222). She was also in the midst of a courtship with Henry Anderson, to whom she became engaged six months later (Goodman 148). Glasgow had had a problematic relationship with her mother, "who personified the Southern Lady" (Ammons 169), and she believed that her father had betrayed her mother by committing adultery (Godbold 27). Probably as a result of the adultery, Glasgow's mother had suffered from long periods of mental illness.

Betrayal, a "haunted" house, mental illness, and fears about marriage converge in "Dare's Gift," as does fascination with southern culture, which Glasgow was reexperiencing after living for some time in the North.

Dare's Gift, from which the story gets its name, is a southern colonial mansion in Virginia to which Harold Beckwith takes his wife, Mildred, for a rest cure. Supposedly mentally unbalanced, possibly by inhabiting the political hothouse of Washington, D.C., Mildred has been advised by a "great specialist" to leave the city ("Dare's Gift" 48). The implication is that Mildred needs to renew her hold on "domestic space": her private, female sanctuary of home and garden (Matthews 112). But this space is figured as dark and foreboding, its box hedges walling her in, its stale air giving her "a sudden feeling of faintness" ("Dare's Gift" 60) as she arrives at the mansion.

Glasgow constructs the story in two parts: the first about Mildred, the author's contemporary, who leaks her attorney husband's secrets to his adversary, and, hence to the newspapers; the second about Lucy Dare, an occupant of Dare's Gift, who, near the end of the Civil War, betrays her Northern lover by pointing out his hiding place to Confederate soldiers—although those soldiers, as true Southern gentlemen, had previously decided not to search the house out of respect for Lucy and for her father, the typical Southern "Colonel." Mildred's revelation causes only a rift in the marital bond while Lucy's brings on the death of her lover, who is shot trying to escape. However, both women sacrifice personal relationships for political causes. Lucy's costly and desperate act serves a lost cause, as the narrator makes clear. Mildred's violation of her husband's confidence, however, makes public the corporate crimes of a large railway. History may validate Mildred's courage.

Both women defy the stereotype of the emotional female, shielded from and hesitant to enter the public realm. Both "break out" of the traditions of southern womanhood as Ammons claims Glasgow desired to do (169). Both strongly assert, "I had to do it. I would do it again" ("Dare's Gift" 73, 100).

Both, moreover, are motivated by "an idea" (77). Dr. Lakeby, the narrator of Lucy's story, sees "every act as merely the husk of an idea." He claims, "The act dies; it decays like the body, but the idea is immortal" (77). Lakeby believes the idea of "treachery" is embedded in the "haunted" house. He also refers to "the idea of the Confederacy" (81): the most significant historic betrayal of the nation-state. Lakeby, in retrospect, recognizes the insubstantiality of the "dream . . . that commanded the noblest devotion, the completest self-sacrifice" (81), yet he valorizes the ability to subordinate personal welfare to the public good; he compares Lucy to a medieval saint (79) and to Antigone (80).

Glasgow, who hated the crimes of the South against blacks and against those who, as her brother Frank, did not fit into the southern cultural mold, seems in this story to come to terms with her Southern heritage. The cause of the Confederacy, wrongheaded and damaging as she knew it was, elicited the kind of idealism and selflessness that she admired. Her own mother's endurance through war, poverty, and a difficult family life must have seemed noble to Glasgow, as did the code of the southern gentleman. Devotion to an idea might not be so terrible if that idea were worthy. Mildred's defining action is to contact a philanthropist/watchdog, and she refuses to take her "share of the spoils" from her husband's defense of a corrupt corporation (63). According to Catherine Rainwater, Mildred's rebellion demonstrates "tentative progress." Rainwater suggests that Glasgow believed with H. G. Wells in a "spiral" of progress, in "the gradual evolution of humanity" (131). Mildred is further evolved than Lucy, and Glasgow's story itself attempts to redefine Southern idealism and to show how it might be used to change the course of history to encourage humane evolution. As Rainwater claims, "The Chinese-box arrangement of stories within stories" models the way in which "storytelling itself" facilitates the escape from historical repetitions (130).

Recent scholarship tends to focus on the "storytelling itself," on the two-part narrative structure, and on the two unreliable male narrators. Part 1 is told by Mildred's husband, who considers his wife and her action insane. Part 2 is told by Dr. Lakeby, a superstitious country physician, who condemns Lucy's choice but excuses her because he believes the house influenced her decision. Pamela Matthews accurately points out that Beckwith "denies [Mildred] the agency" that she finds to act independently of him because he imputes her action to mental illness (127). Lakeby, in blaming the house for Lucy's betrayal, likewise denies her agency. In addition, the male narrators silence the women; the reader never hears their stories in their own words and must negotiate his or her way through various male prejudices. Furthermore, Mildred never hears Lucy's whole story; Lakeby tells it to Beckwith. The narrative structure thus represents, according to Matthews, "the insufficiency in the telling of women's stories by anyone other than themselves" (126).

But let us back up a bit to examine how Dare's Gift became haunted. Sir Roderick Dare, the first owner, is rumored to have betrayed Bacon, the leader of Bacon's Rebellion, a precursor of the American Revolution. Sir Roderick, a presumed royalist, seems to have backed the losing side; he opposed the evolutionary forces that impelled America toward democracy. His descendant Lucy also supports an aristocracy the country has outgrown: a regressive, slaveholding, economically stratified society. But Glasgow includes two other stories within the story. Duncan, the present owner of Dare's Gift, is personally betrayed by his secretary, who embezzles "cash and securities" (56); and Duncan has also alienated the community, perhaps "by putting on airs" (55). The woman who precedes the Beckwiths as a tenant has experienced a similar personal betrayal: Her husband has run off with her sister.

Critics mention, but do not discuss in depth, the relationships among these four betrayals, three of which concern marriage and all of which touch on delicate personal issues. Matthews relates Masse's concept of "gothic repetition" to the "two-part structure" and to "the doubled female protagonists" (124), but not to the dual betrayals of the sister and husband or of the secretary and neighbors. Further study might elucidate these "repetition[s]."

Also deserving further study is Glasgow's use of Poe. Critics note that the name *Roderick* may allude to Poe's Roderick in "The Fall of the House of Usher" (Rainwater 130; Meeker 12). Glasgow no doubt had in mind Poe's story when she had her narrator describe the "heavy cedars" and light-sucking windows of Dare's Gift (49). However, Beckwith also insists, "Nowhere could I detect a hint of decay or dilapidation" (49). On the contrary, the house has taken on "wanton excrescences in the modern additions" (61). The "idea" persists and has taken further odd forms. This could be the "idea" of Southern ROMANTICISM, the "idea" of a corrupt and devolutionary social and economic power structure, or the "idea" of the glory of war.

In fact, Lucy herself still lives; Lakeby has seen her recently in an old ladies' home, where she sits "knitting—the omnipresent dun-colored muffler for the war relief associations," this time for the "War to End All Wars," the war of Glasgow's own generation. An "idea" dies hard.

BIBLIOGRAPHY

Ammons, Elizabeth. *Conflicting Stories: American Women Writers at the Turn into the Twentieth Century.* New York: Oxford University Press, 1992.

Glasgow, Ellen. "Dare's Gift." In *The Shadowy Third and Other Stories.* New York: Doubleday, 1923.

———. *The Woman Within.* New York: Harcourt, Brace, 1954.

Godbold, E. Stanly, Jr. *Ellen Glasgow and the Woman Within.* Baton Rouge: Louisiana State University Press, 1972.

Goodman, Susan. *Ellen Glasgow: A Biography.* Baltimore: Johns Hopkins University Press, 1998.

Kelly, William W. *Ellen Glasgow: A Bibliography.* Charlottesville: University of Virginia Press, 1964.

Matthews, Pamela R. *Ellen Glasgow and a Woman's Traditions.* Charlottesville: University of Virginia Press, 1994.

Meeker, Richard. "Introduction." In *The Collected Stories of Ellen Glasgow.* Baton Rouge: Louisiana State University Press, 1963.

Rainwater, Catherine. "Ellen Glasgow's Outline of History in 'The Shadowy Third.'" In *The Critical Response to H. G. Wells,* edited by William J. Scheick. Westport, Conn.: Greenwood Press, 1995.

Gwen M. Neary
Santa Rosa Junior College

"DARING YOUNG MAN ON THE FLYING TRAPEZE, THE"   See SAROYAN, WILLIAM.

DARWIN, CHARLES ROBERT (1809–1882)   An English naturalist, Charles Darwin published *On the Origin of Species* (1859), which sets forth his theory of natural selection, to angry reactions and bitterly controversial reviews. Darwin's observations of animals led to his now-famous statement that only the "fittest" of any species survive; the process is nature's way of weeding out the weakest of any species so that only the strongest remain to propagate their kind. This theory, known as Darwinism, has had a profound influence on human concepts of life, and the book is considered one of the most important works ever written in the field of natural philosophy. His ideas were generated on the H.M.S. *Beagle* on an expedition (1831–36) to southern Pacific islands, South American coasts, and Australia. Darwin's theories have influenced stories by such writers as JACK LONDON and Tennessee Williams.

DAVIS, REBECCA HARDING (REBECCA BLAINE HARDING DAVIS) (1831–1910)   Rebecca Davis is considered one of the first American realist writers. (See REALISM.) Although Davis was reared in a well-to-do household in industrial Wheeling, West Virginia, her first published story, "LIFE IN THE IRON MILLS," which appeared in ATLANTIC MONTHLY in April 1861, grimly portrayed the sordid lives of iron-mill workers, who were depicted doing brutally hard work and living in a world devoid of emotional or spiritual uplift, hope, or justice. This work was a precursor to the "muckraking" literature (see MUCKRAKERS) that would be published at the turn of the century. This story, which introduced new elements of NATURALISM and realism to American literature, drew Davis fame and the acquaintance of other professional authors, including NATHANIEL HAWTHORNE. She continued to write, addressing such problems as racial bias and political corruption, but none of these efforts equaled her first work in imaginative power. "Life in the Iron Mills" influenced TILLIE OLSEN to such a degree that she introduced and republished the story in 1972. Davis was also an associate editor of the *New York Tribune,* and some critics have reassessed her as a more talented

and more important writer than her renowned son, RICHARD HARDING DAVIS.

BIBLIOGRAPHY

Davis, Rebecca Harding. *Life in the Iron Mills and Other Stories.* Edited by and with an afterword by Tillie Olsen. New York: Feminist Press, 1972.

Rose, Jane Atteridge. "Reading 'Life in the Iron Mills' Contextually: A Key to Rebecca Harding Davis's Fiction." In *Conversations: Contemporary Critical Theory and the Teaching of Literature,* edited by Charles Moran and Elizabeth F. Penfield. Urbana, Ill.: National Council of Teachers of English, 1990.

DAVIS, RICHARD HARDING (1864–1916)

The son of REBECCA HARDING DAVIS, Richard Davis was a journalist who covered wars all over the world and was among the leading reporters of his time. He is typically associated with the MAUVE DECADE of the 1890s, and although his fiction is largely viewed as superficial, he was a talented storyteller; indeed, he was one of the highest-paid and most popular short story writers of his era. Davis wrote novels, plays, and stories in which he created such notable characters as Gallegher, the enterprising office boy, and the good-deed-doer Cortland Van Bibber. Davis's fiction often depicted the superficial nature of turn-of-the-century society, of which he was a prominent member.

DAY, CLARENCE, JR. (CLARENCE SHEPHARD DAY, JR.) (1874–1935)

Clarence Day primarily wrote humorous stories. His best-known works were based on reminiscences of his parents. One of these, "Life with Father" (1937), was made into a long-running Broadway play in 1939 by Russel Crouse and Howard Lindsay. With a gentle humor, Day recalls his rather domineering father and his soft-spoken mother, whose will nearly always prevailed.

BIBLIOGRAPHY

Day, Clarence, Jr. *God and My Father.* New York: Knopf, 1932.

———. *Life with Father.* New York: Knopf, 1935.

———. *Life with Mother.* New York: Knopf, 1937.

"DAY I GOT LOST: A CHAPTER FROM THE AUTOBIOGRAPHY OF PROFESSOR SCHLEMIEL, THE" ISAAC BASHEVIS SINGER (1975, 1984)

Although the author apparently never saw himself as a children's writer, "The Day I Got Lost: A Chapter from the Autobiography of Professor Schlemiel" is one of the many stories ISAAC BASHEVIS SINGER wrote after his editor, Elizabeth Shub, encouraged him to write stories specifically for children. The story first appeared in *The Puffin Annual* (1975) before being reprinted in the collection titled *Stories for Children* (1984).

In this story, the first-person narrator, an absent-minded philosophy professor named Schlemiel, is in a cab on his way to his New York City home when he realized that he does not remember his address. The taxi driver drops him off at a drugstore so that he can look up the address; however, because the professor's wife had insisted that they get an unlisted phone number so that the professor's students could not call him at home, he is unable to find the information. He tries calling a few friends and discovers that they apparently are all waiting for him at his house in order to celebrate his birthday. The professor wanders back out to the street, where it is now raining heavily; he, of course, has left his umbrella somewhere and lost his galoshes. So he stands under an overhang and ponders the eternal question—which came first, the chicken or the egg? A big black soaking-wet dog wanders up; the look in the dog's eyes tells the professor that the dog, too, has forgotten where he lives. They are standing there, giving each other some comfort with their companionship, when a taxi drives by and splashes them both. The cab stops because the passenger has recognized Schlemiel; since he is on his way to the professor's house for the party, he gives the professor and his newfound friend a ride home. After a minor ruckus involving a cat and two parakeets, the dog, now named "Bow Wow" (120), joins the professor's household, with all of the animals becoming friends. The story of the entire experience will become the first chapter of the professor's book, "The Memoirs of Schlemiel," if he manages not to lose the manuscript.

A character named Schlemiel also appears in Singer's story titled "Schlemiel the Businessman"; however, unlike "The Day I Got Lost," this other story takes place in Chelm, Poland, and the character exemplifies the connotations traditionally associated with the name *Schlemiel*: an ineffectual, inept person who is easily victimized. In contrast, Professor Schlemiel is represented more within the story as the prototypical absent-minded professor, even being described by the author with those exact words. This schlemiel loses a lens from his glasses, his briefcase (which he left in the taxi that dropped him at the drugstore when he could not remember his address), and his umbrella, among other things. He is never victimized; he is merely a victim of his own ineptitude—his inability to focus on the mundane things of daily life while pondering the great philosophical questions such as whether the chicken or the egg came first.

BIBLIOGRAPHY

Allison, Alida. *Isaac Bashevis Singer: Children's Stories and Childhood Memories.* New York: Twayne–Simon & Schuster Macmillan, 1996.

Singer, Isaac Bashevis. "The Day I Got Lost: A Chapter from the Autobiography of Professor Schlemiel." In *Stories for Children.* Translated by I. B. Singer and Elizabeth Shub. New York: Farrar, Straus & Giroux, 1984.

Peggy J. Huey
University of Tampa

"DAY'S WAIT, A" ERNEST HEMINGWAY (1927)

ERNEST HEMINGWAY's "A Day's Wait," which was published in his 1927 collection *The Snows of Kilimanjaro and Other Stories,* is representative of Hemingway's short fiction in that it encompasses the subject matter and one of the more prevalent themes that Hemingway sought to capture in his writing—facing death with bravery. This time, however, death is not being confronted by a soldier on the front lines, a WORLD WAR I veteran dealing with his psychological wounds, a boxer being hunted by the mob, or a matador facing a bull. In this story, the character bravely facing death is "a very sick and miserable boy of nine years" (332).

Told in the first person, the story's plot revolves around a simple misunderstanding with complicated consequences. The boy of nine, sick with influenza, is convinced that he is going to die because he is confused about a reading of his temperature. Having attended school in France, the boy has been told that any reading above 44 degrees is deadly, and his reads 102. The boy's father, unaware of his son's confusing the Celsius and Fahrenheit scales, has no idea that his young son has been waiting to die all day (thus the story's title). When the father explains it as being like the difference between "miles and kilometers," the boy is able to release the "hold over himself" and begin his recovery.

Many have argued that "A Day's Wait" is another in the long line of NICK ADAMS stories written by Hemingway, in which Adams is a kind of ALTER EGO for the author himself. It is true that the story has some of the earmarks of a Nick Adams story—it deals with the relationship between a father and a son, much as Hemingway's early Michigan stories do, only with Nick playing the role of a father instead of a son, and it includes a brief hunting scene. However, there are important aspects of this story that seem to indicate that it is not one of the Nick Adams stories. The first is simple enough—we do not know the father's name, so we cannot be sure that it is Nick Adams. The second is that, with one exception, the Nick Adams stories are written in the third person. This allows readers to identify characters by name through the narrative. The one exception is "Now I Lay Me," which is narrated from Nick's point of view. In this story, Hemingway tells us Nick's name in a flashback scene. Philip Young, who is responsible for the collection known as *The Nick Adams Stories,* chose not to include "A Day's Wait" in the collection, yet he did choose to include "In Another Country," a story that offers no direct evidence of being a Nick Adams story. The theory, then, seems inconclusive at best.

One could argue that the plot of "A Day's Wait" lacks any sort of credibility, as it may seem very difficult to imagine that a young boy of nine, even in Hemingway's world of bravery and machismo, would face his death so bravely, even telling his father that he could leave the room so he would not have to witness the death scene. But the story does seem to be set up around the idea of life and death and the thin line between the two. The father, who is unaware of his son's confusion and fear, decides to leave him alone and go hunting. An ice storm had passed the night before, making it difficult for the father and his dog to move around, but he is able to flush out a covey of quail. The father is pleased that he killed four but is even happier that "there were so many left to find on another day" (333). The idea of having another day (and the birds' survival) represents life, while the setting (winter, ice) and the killing of the four birds suggest death. The ice that covers the ground and trees, making them look "varnished with ice" (333), suggests that thin balance (not to be confused with "thin ice," which would be a cheap pun) that we walk every day between life and death.

Hemingway has often been criticized for romanticizing bravery and masculinity, and it does seem rather difficult to accept the notion that a nine-year-old boy could face death so bravely only to become completely childlike again when he finds out he is not dying, but Hemingway is after a much larger point—the thin and slippery line between life and death that he wrote about so often.

BIBLIOGRAPHY

Benson, Jackson J., ed. *New Critical Approaches to the Short Stories of Ernest Hemingway.* Durham, N.C.: Duke University Press, 1991.

Bloom, Harold, ed. *Ernest Hemingway: Modern Critical Views.* New York: Chelsea House, 1985.

Hemingway, Ernest. "A Day's Wait." In *The Complete Short Stories of Ernest Hemingway: The Finca Vigía Edition.* New York: Charles Scribner's Sons, 1987.

Oliver, Charles M. *Ernest Hemingway A to Z: The Essential Reference to the Life and Work.* New York: Facts On File, 1999.

Tyler, Lisa. *Student Companion to Ernest Hemingway.* Westport, Conn.: Greenwood Press, 2001.

Wagner-Martin, Linda, ed. *Ernest Hemingway: Six Decades of Criticism.* East Lansing: Michigan State University Press, 1988.

James Mayo
Jackson State Community College

"DEATH BY LANDSCAPE" Margaret Atwood (1989)

In "Death by Landscape," Atwood rewrites early American stories about the wilderness from her own trenchant perspective. At the same time, the story finds literary ancestors in Edgar Allan Poe's detective stories, especially the locked-room mystery ("The Murders in the Rue Morgue") and those in which the answer is hidden in plain sight ("The Purloined Letter"). Other themes in this story are the relationships between girls (see *Cat's Eye*), sexuality and its dangers, and art and the artist (see *The Blind Assassin* and "True Trash," also in *Wilderness Tips*).

"Death by Landscape" begins by juxtaposing wilderness and civilization, only to reveal how they overlap. Lois, the main character, has a new apartment "now that the boys are grown up and [her husband] is dead" (127). The apartment is crowded with landscape paintings, which themselves show this overlap: Lois imagines "a tangle, a receding maze, in which you can become lost almost as soon as you step off the path" (152). It is impossible, of course, to step off a path in a painting, but for Lois, the idea is quite real and terrifying.

Lois "is relieved not to have to worry about the lawn, or the squirrels gnawing their way into the attic and eating the insulation off the wiring, or about strange noises. The building has a security system" (127). Even the tamer, more cultivated forms of nature presented on the story's first page—lawns, squirrels, and plants—are presented as things that encroach, that endanger one's safety and security; indeed, Lois seems to believe that her security system will keep not just human nature but nature itself at bay.

Lois has collected these paintings out of a compulsion to recapture something from her girlhood experiences at Camp Manitou. What she is trying to capture is unnamed—indeed, the unnamed, the hidden, and the wordless take center stage in this story—but by the end of the story, we suspect that what she is trying to recapture is Lucy, the friend she made in her second year at camp. As an American, Lucy seems exotic to Lois, both more wild and more sophisticated than she. The two become fast friends, even pretending to be twins. Indeed, Atwood, who is fond of word games (she copyrights her works under the name O. W. Toad, an anagram of *Atwood*), suggests that they, too, overlap, by giving them names that are phonetic anagrams of each other: Rearrange the sounds of *Lois* and you get something like *Lucy*. The girls only see each other in the summer. Lucy changes from year to year: One year, her parents have divorced and she has a stepfather; the next, she begins to have periods; and the next, when she is marked by the heightened sexual nature of her home and her own budding sexuality, Lois's and Lucy's group go on a canoe trip.

The canoe trip is meant to be a rite of passage, and "Lois feels as if an invisible rope has broken. They're floating free, on their own, cut loose" (140). But the entire experience is supervised and carefully planned, crafted to present a specific and misleading understanding of both the society these young women are passing into and the roles they will take in it. The camp portrays itself as a return to nature, but clues abound that the canoe trip, like the rest of the camp, is not as "pure, and aboriginal" as the characters would like to believe. The most important clues we are given are the "burned tin can and a beer bottle" in the fireplace that await them at the first campsite.

Beneath the surface of events at the camp is the suggestion that real womanhood should not be openly addressed or even admitted. In a ceremony before the canoe trip, for instance, Cappie, who runs the camp, calls the campers "braves" (139). Unlike Cappie's ceremony, about which Lois is deeply ambivalent and "Lucy rolls up her eyes" (138), Lois and Lucy's private ceremony, when Lois and Lucy "burned one of Lucy's used sanitary napkins" (136), is a more genuine rite of passage, both "wordless" and filling Lois with "deep satisfaction" (136). Also not talked about are the hints of sexual inappropriateness and even danger. By not saying anything outright, Atwood recreates both the social rules of post–WORLD WAR II society and the ignorance they create in Lois's own consciousness.

Descriptions of the camp mostly center on its rules, both spoken and unspoken—rules that translate into the real world, as "Lois thinks she can recognize women who went to these camps, and were good at it. They have a hardness to their handshakes, even now; a way of standing, legs planted firmly and farther apart than usual; a way of sizing you up" (130). The rules are one way the camp socializes young women, and Lois, though at first uncomfortable with the rules, is herself socialized by them, culminating in her realization, shortly before Lucy disappears, "that they've

traveled so far, over all that water, with nothing to propel them but their own arms. It makes her feel strong. There are all kinds of things she is capable of doing" (144). This, of course, is only partly true; she is propelled, in part, by the social obligations Cappie felt to keep the camp going, by the obligations the "Old Girls" (131) felt to send their daughters there, by the money that bought the canoes, and so on. As soon as Lois has this equivocal epiphany, Atwood shatters it: The girls are not alone and not as powerful as they think but are subject to the vagaries not of nature, but of human nature.

At the second campsite, Lois and Lucy leave the group to hike up to Lookout Point. When Lucy leaves the path, she disappears. *Lookout Point,* like many other names in the story, is meaningful. Since "what you were supposed to see from there was not clear" (143), Atwood is suggesting that we consider the other meaning of *lookout*: to be careful.

In a way, Lucy's disappearance happens to Lois as well. Indeed, the two are close enough that when Lois tells Cappie that just before Lucy disappeared, "She said you could dive off there. She said it went straight down" (148), Cappie deftly turns this hint of a suicide wish into proof of Lois's own guilt—and Lois, in a way, accepts it. Cappie, she understands later, did this to Lois out of "desperation, her need for a story, a real story with a reason in it" (149). But Lois herself never finds the reason and is so deeply affected by what happened that she seems perpetually both guilty and victimized. She misses the wilderness tip, the clue that, as does Poe's purloined letter, lies in plain sight: As in "The Murders in the Rue Morgue," the perception of the locked door—that nature is safe and the camp is secluded—is misleading. Humanity, if not civilization, pervades the camp and the canoe trip. The only death by landscape is Lois's. Landscape, Atwood tells us, is a lie about nature: a convention that, by turning nature into an aesthetic object, leaves too much—including human nature itself—out of the picture.

To get the most out of this story, readers must rebuild the "real story" from clues embedded in Lois's understanding. Readers must also make sense of the "Indian" names used at the camp, which are oddly appropriate, since the camp, in trying to signify a return to nature, overlooks both that "Indians" had their own civilization and that the camp is still closely tied to the rules of society at large. They must consider what Lois sees when she looks at Lucy as an American and when, from her apartment, she looks across Lake Ontario at America (150). They must investigate Lois's guilt, where it might come from, and what it leads to. And they must examine how nature is presented in the story: as a reflection of the characters' feelings, as a repository for the characters' wishes, and as a scapegoat.

BIBLIOGRAPHY

Atwood, Margaret. *Survival: A Thematic Guide to Canadian Literature.* Toronto: Anansi, 1972.

Hammill, Faye. "'Death by Nature': Margaret Atwood and Wilderness Gothic." *Gothic Studies* 5, no. 2 (November 2003): 47–63.

Howells, Coral Ann, ed. *The Cambridge Companion to Margaret Atwood.* New York: Cambridge University Press, 2006.

"The Margaret Atwood Society." Available online. URL: http://www.mscd.edu/~atwoodso/. Includes bibliographies of Atwood's work and criticism on Atwood. Accessed May 1, 2009.

Kerry Higgins Wendt
Emory University

"DEATH IN THE WOODS" SHERWOOD ANDERSON (1926, 1933)

First published in *American Mercury* in 1926 and later in SHERWOOD ANDERSON's collection *Death in the Woods* in 1933, "Death in the Woods" is his most frequently anthologized story, and Anderson considered it his best. Readers find it bleak, because it depicts the unrelenting hardship of Ma Grimes's life and death, and instructive, because the death of this farm woman is described by a man struggling to understand and express the reasons it has haunted him since boyhood. Although interpretations of the story are diverse, primary readings see it from KUNSTLERROMAN, BILDUNGSROMAN, and FEMINIST perspectives.

The story opens as Ma Grimes trudges into town to buy provisions for her husband, her son, and the farm animals. This act is self-defining because, as the narrator repeatedly tells us, her role is to "feed animal life": "horses, cows, pigs, dogs, men" (384). She speaks to no one and carries the load of food without help: "People drive right down a road and never notice an old woman like that" (390, 380). We learn that Ma Grimes, as both girl and woman, is a composite of various farm women the narrator observed while growing to manhood. She was an orphan, a "bound girl" beholden to a German farmer, a slave to him and later to her husband and son. She has suffered sexual abuse at the hands of the men, whose coarse habits have taught her to remain silent; throughout the story, she never speaks.

Although we learn that she is not yet 40 years old, she is consistently referred to as "the old woman." On her way home, she is followed by a pack of dogs, whom the men likewise "kick and abuse" (385). As she sinks wearily to the ground and dies soon afterward, it is the animals who define her by imprinting a circle around her. And they never touch her, despite the narrator's emphasis on their descent from wolves. Dogs, not men, outline her circular space as though she were a goddess who, freed from her imprisonment, has finally risen to her rightful place, leaving behind a body transformed from that of an old woman to that of a young girl. After the hunter accidentally stumbles on her corpse, a variety of men go together to look at her, from an aged Civil War veteran to the boy narrator and his brother.

It is the sight of her frozen white partially clothed body that so impresses the narrator that, as an adult man, he feels impelled to tell the story over again. "A thing so complete has its own beauty" (390), he says. Numerous critics see his reactions as those of the artist who creates beauty out of ordinary or even degraded circumstances. Certainly, there inheres in the gaze of the boy and his brother an awed baptism into the mysteries of sex as they gaze at the half-clad body that now looks youthful and beautiful. This scene may also be viewed as an example of male voyeurism and the story as one more instance of a male writer's finding poetry in the "DEATH OF A BEAUTIFUL WOMAN." Whatever the reader's interpretation, with each rereading of the story, Ma Grimes is freed from her death in the woods to live again for us and to give us pause.

BIBLIOGRAPHY
Anderson, Sherwood. "Death in the Woods." In *American Short Stories.* 4th ed. Edited by Eugene Current-Garcia and Walton R. Patrick. Glenview, Ill.: Scott, Foresman, 1982.

"DEATH OF A BEAUTIFUL WOMAN"

EDGAR ALLAN POE's famous (or infamous, according to many FEMINIST critics) dictum was first set out in his essay "The Philosophy of Composition," originally published in *Graham's Magazine* in April 1846. Poe contends that beauty is the province of poetry and death the most melancholy of poetical topics; hence, when the poet combines the two concepts, "the death of a beautiful woman" is the world's most poetical topic. Further, the best person to tell the story of her death is the grieving lover. The THEME occurs in many Poe stories, such as "LIGEIA" and "The FALL OF THE HOUSE OF USHER," but as critics have pointed out, it also occurs in much literature of both the 19th and 20th centuries. See, for example, NATHANIEL HAWTHORNE's "RAPPACCINI'S DAUGHTER" and "The BIRTHMARK," HENRY JAMES's *DAISY MILLER: A STUDY*, KATE CHOPIN's "DESIREE'S BABY," and DOROTHY PARKER's "Big Blonde."

DECADENCE   A term used in both literary and art history for the decline that marks the end of a great artistic period. The term is relative to the particular period it identifies, and the general characteristics of decadence are often self-consciousness, artificiality, overrefinement, and perversity. (See MAUVE DECADE.)

"DEER IN THE WORKS" KURT VONNEGUT (1955)

In this story the family man David Potter contemplates giving up his own weekly small-town newspaper in favor of taking a public relations job at the Ilium Works of the Federal Apparatus Corporation. The Works is a sprawling maze of clanking machinery and pollution. Potter fears that his newspaper income may not continue to support his growing family, so he tries to convince himself that he will be better off as a company man, with the life insurance, health insurance, and future pension that accompany a long-term commitment to the Works.

After learning that a deer is loose on the grounds, his new supervisor sends Potter off to cover the story. The plan is to snap some photos, write a press release, then serve the venison at the company's Quarter-Century Club, where 25-year veterans dine and smoke cigars.

Along the way, David becomes hopelessly lost. By the time he stumbles upon the scene, the overwhelming environment has numbed his spirit and sickened his body. Potter finds himself between the deer—its antlers broken and its coat smeared with soot and grease—and a gate leading to lush, green pine woods. With little hesitation he opens the gate, releasing the deer into the woods. As the deer's white tail disappears into the trees, David follows it, leaving the Ilium Works behind without looking back.

What is most interesting about this story beyond its message of following one's heart and the familiar THEME of the dehumanizing effect of the Big Corporation is that it is largely an autobiographical FANTASY. Before making a living as a writer, Vonnegut had a public relations job with General Electric, which he openly loathed. It is entirely possible that Vonnegut's experience at GE was a major contributing factor to his pursuit of short stories as a means to write his way out of his day job. While his stories later financed the writing of his novels, they first provided him an escape from the corporate world. One has to wonder whether most (or any) of Vonnegut's short stories would have come to be had he instead owned a small-town weekly newspaper.

David Larry Anderson

"DEFENDER OF THE FAITH" PHILIP ROTH (1959)

PHILIP ROTH's "Defender of the Faith" raises questions about identity and identification, and the complexities that arise when different aspects of a person's self-concept are in conflict with one another. The story also invokes the ethical dilemmas that identification creates, forcing its characters and the audience to confront competing allegiances. Published in 1959 as part of Roth's first collection, the story takes place in 1945, as WORLD WAR II is winding down. The issues that it addresses are equally salient right now, when, in a time of war and increased tensions over immigration, ethnic Americans seek to maintain their identities while feeling pressured to prove their patriotism.

The narrator of "Defender of the Faith" is Nathan Marx, a Jewish noncommissioned officer who has returned from a two-year tour of duty in Europe to serve out his time with a training company in Missouri. As Marx's name suggests, his situation is humorous (Groucho and Harpo) but also potentially dangerous (Karl), as he finds himself serving as an unwilling mediator between his American superiors and his ethnic subordinates. Marx's doppelganger and nemesis is a trainee with the noticeably Jewish name of *Sheldon Grossbart*. A character whose behavior is as repellant and over-the-top as his name implies, Grossbart appeals to a shared sense of heritage to manipulate Marx into giving special accommodations to him and two other Jewish boys, Halpern and Fishbein. These privileges include excused absences from cleaning details, special leave, and even a favorable duty assignment. Although some action does occur over the weeks that the trainees spend preparing to ship out, the story takes place mostly in Marx's head as he seeks to cope with Grossbart's shenanigans and to justify his methods to himself.

Two fundamental ambiguities occupy the heart of the story: Who is the defender and what is he defending? A case can be made for both Marx and Grossbart as the defender, for both Judaism and American patriotism as the faith. Furthermore, speech is an important medium in the text, which features both actual dialogue and internal conversations. Indeed, it is language itself that provides the chink in the armor that lets Grossbart know that Marx is indeed "one of them" (165), as Marx slips into using the Yiddish term *shul* to refer to the Jewish house of worship, as opposed to "Jewish church" or "Jewish Mass" as the gentiles on the base call it. Chain-of-command issues are also significant and arise through language, as Grossbart tricks Marx into calling him by his first name and stubbornly refuses to stop calling Marx "sir."

In challenging us to untangle the questions raised by the title, Roth forces us to pay particular attention to the questions of who speaks for whom and in what

capacity. In his initial interactions with Grossbart, Marx finds himself taking on the role of military superior: "My tone startled me. I felt I sounded like every top sergeant I had ever known" (163). Grossbart, however, is not intimidated; he seems to have appointed himself the defender of Judaism and the spokesman for his fellows who are too shy or inept to speak for themselves. And yet Jewish though he might be, Grossbart is not religiously observant. He does not pray during the evening service he insists on being able to attend, and he marks the service's end by chugging down the ritual wine. Similarly, when he prevails upon Marx to arrange for him to celebrate a religious meal with a relative, he takes Marx an egg roll instead of the promised gefilte fish, a parody of the unofficial American Jewish ritual of getting Chinese food on Christmas. Furthermore, Grossbart literally (and dishonestly) speaks for his father by forging a letter in his father's name, writing to his congressional representative to protest the Jewish boys' treatment. For his part, Marx is made to speak for Jews in general when his superior asks him to account for Grossbart's dietary requests and the behavior of his parents. As distasteful as it is to him, Marx finds himself defending Grossbart to the non-Jewish military officials. Against his will, Marx is led to accept a responsibility to his fellow Jew.

If Grossbart is parading his religious faith (or at least his religious affiliation), Marx is not exactly passing passing for gentile. He does not hesitate to affirm his Jewish heritage when confronted by his commanding officer. And yet Marx is also a red-blooded American boy, the pitcher for the camp's softball team. When Marx seeks to subterfuge the special arrangement Grossbart makes for his assignment by manipulating a Corporal Shulman (another recognizably Jewish name, and a play on the Yiddish word for synagogue, *shul* man), Marx calls on his teammate, Wright, who begins the conversation by asking, "How's the pitching arm?" (198). It is true that Grossbart embodies some of the worst stereotypes about Jews: He is manipulative, cunning, and deceitful. But if Marx is Jewish, then Grossbart serves to some extent as a mirror. Interacting with Grossbart forces Marx to confront the negative parts of his own personality;

hating Grossbart analogously becomes a form of self-hatred.

By the end, Marx has become polarized. Philip Roth once said, "I am not a Jewish writer; I am a writer who is a Jew" (qtd. in Ozick 158). At the beginning of the story, Nathan Marx might have correspondingly offered, "I am not a Jewish soldier; I am a soldier who is a Jew." By the end, however, Marx has allowed the Jewish aspect of his identity to override the neutrality of the American soldier of the story's opening pages and he singles out a Jewish trainee. Was it fair for the first man in the alphabet randomly to get the favorable assignment? Assuredly. But Marx does not orchestrate it to be fair. He does it to get even, to use Grossbart's manipulations against him, something the Marx of the beginning would not have done. The final sentences of the story move from faith to fate: "With a kind of quiet nervousness, [the trainees] polished shoes, shined belt buckles, squared away underwear, trying as best they could to accept their fate. Behind me Grossbart swallowed hard, accepting his. And then, resisting with all my will an impulse to turn and seek pardon for my vindictiveness, I accepted my own" (200). Grossbart's fate, however, is not ordained by mysterious and unknowable forces, but rather by Marx himself. Marx's desire to seek pardon suggests a need for atonement, and yet his acceptance of his fate suggests a recognition that his experiences have changed him—paradoxically not his experiences in Europe fighting the enemy but his experiences in Missouri, fighting with one of his own. Like it or not, Marx's fate and Grossbart's are intertwined.

BIBLIOGRAPHY

Roth, Philip. "Defender of the Faith." In *Goodbye, Columbus and Five Short Stories.* 1959. Reprint, New York: Vintage International, 1993.
Ozick, Cynthia. *Art and Ardor.* New York: Knopf, 1983.

Jessica G. Rabin
Anne Arundel Community College

"DELTA AUTUMN" WILLIAM FAULKNER (1942)

The sixth chapter of WILLIAM FAULKNER's GO DOWN, MOSES, "Delta Autumn" tells the story of Ike McCaslin's last hunting trip into the Mississippi Delta.

While earlier chapters record young Isaac's rite of passage in the big woods, in this chapter we are presented with an older Uncle Ike, who "no longer told anyone how near eighty he actually was because he knew as well as they did that he no longer had any business making such expeditions" (336). Ike's age, however, is not so much at issue here as is his heritage when he discovers that his nephew Roth fathered a child by a mulatto woman in the Delta during their hunting trip the year before. While the hunting party jokes with Roth about his interest in hunting does instead of bucks, Uncle Ike is filled with "amazement, pity, and outrage" (361). For Ike discovers that he knows the mother of the child: She is the granddaughter of James Beauchamp, or Tennie's Jim, a black descendant of Ike's grandfather, Lucius Quintus Carothers McCaslin, whose sins Ike discovers in "The BEAR." Thus, says the Faulkner critic Cleanth Brooks, "Isaac knows that once more a descendant of old Carother's McCaslin's slave Eunice has been injured by a descendant of old Carothers" (272).

The confrontation between Ike and this young woman, which is the most important exchange in the story, provides Faulkner with the dramatic setting within which to explore further Ike's repudiation of his land and of his heritage because of the sins of Carothers. Ultimately, Faulkner seems to call into question Ike's decision to repudiate the young woman and her baby, characterizing it as one borne more out of irresponsibility than honor.

BIBLIOGRAPHY

Brooks, Cleanth. *William Faulkner: The Yoknapatawpha Country.* New Haven, Conn.: Yale University Press, 1963.
Faulkner, William. *Go Down, Moses.* New York: Random House, 1942.

H. Collin Messer
University of North Carolina at Chapel Hill

DE MAN, PAUL (1919–1983)

One of the foremost architects of the school of literary criticism known as deconstruction, de Man was born in Antwerp in 1919. He received a Ph.D. from Harvard University in 1960 and subsequently became a professor of English at Yale University, where he, Geoffrey Hartman, and J.

Hillis Miller became known as the Yale school critics. Although De Man's reputation has been tarnished by the discovery of early articles written for the pro-Nazi newspaper *Le Soir,* he articulated the practice of deconstruction with passion and intelligence.

De Man once provocatively told an interviewer that he never had an idea on his own. His ideas, he claimed, always originated in a text. In this way, De Man meant to draw attention to his own rigorous form of close reading. Unlike the close readings of the NEW CRITICISM, which were to be conducted with certain predetermined issues in mind, De Man's characteristic practice is to expose the "aporia" (ambivalence) of literary texts by following the logic (or, more precisely, the antilogic) of the text in question without recourse to extratextual resources. In a famous example, De Man criticizes literary scholars who have always read the last lines of William Butler Yeats's "Among School Children" ("How can we know the dancer from the dance?") as a rhetorical question. What textual evidence do critics have for such a view, De Man asks, and what happens if we read these lines as a question about which the poet is genuinely curious? Such a view is demonstrably more faithful to the text in question. Moreover, as De Man goes on to show, it significantly alters any interpretation of the poem by pointing to the ways in which a text's "official" meaning is undermined by the rhetorical (i.e., figural) properties of language—the unstable and alien symbol system in which that meaning is constituted.

BIBLIOGRAPHY

De Man, Paul. *Blindness and Insight: Essays in the Rhetoric of Contemporary Criticism.* 2nd ed. Minneapolis: University of Minnesota Press, 1983.

————. *The Resistance to Theory.* Minneapolis: University of Minnesota Press, 1986.

Graef, Ortwin de. *Titanic Light: Paul de Man's Post-Romanticism, 1960–1969.* Lincoln: University of Nebraska Press, 1995.

Lehman, David. *Signs of the Times: Deconstruction and the Fall of Paul De Man.* New York: Poseidon Press, 1991.

Norris, Christopher. *Paul de Man, Deconstruction and the Critique of Aesthetic Ideology.* New York: Routledge, 1988.

Shannon Zimmerman
University of Georgia

DENOUEMENT   From the French word for "untying," in fiction and drama, *denouement* refers to the final unwinding of the tangled elements of the plot that ends the suspense; it follows the CLIMAX. The word is also applied to the resolution of complicated sets of actions in life. See CATASTROPHE and SURPRISE ENDING.

DESANI, G. V. (GOVINDAS VISHNOODAS DESANI) (1909–2000)

G. V. Desani's published fiction consists of one novel, *All about H. Hatten,* and a small number of short stories, collected as *Hali and Collected Stories.* In *Hali,* Desani, born in Kenya, educated in India, and formerly professor emeritus at the University of Texas at Austin, offers 23 stories and FABLES, along with a dramatic prose poem, "Hali," that range from bleakness to ironic COMEDY and from supernatural tales to highly mannered satires. The prose poem—which tells the story of Hali, who loves Rooh, whose death plunges Hali into grief and a mystical journey—is most noteworthy as an example of private mythology turned into accessible invocation. The supernatural element in many of the other fictions is strong: "The Valley of Lions," for example, is short and visionary; "Mephisto's Daughter" concerns a narrator who has access to "Old Ugly's daughter"; and "The Lama Arupa" follows the holy man of the title through "several states of consciousness" after his death, until he returns as a chicken. "The Merchant of Kisingarh" is told by a deceased merchant speaking through his son, a sometime medium. These pieces manage to be both wry and penetrating by turns. "A Border Incident," more traditional, tells of a man punished for deserting his post to save a boy's life. Desani also offers a mock lecture ("Rudyard Kipling's Evaluation of His Own Mother") on one of Kipling's more ludicrous compositions, and he closes with the phantasmagoric "The Mandatory Interview of the Dean," a hilarious satire of bureaucracy and officiousness. Desani's varied collection is impressive in its use of religious and personal mythology—and lushly descriptive of a sensibility and a culture that is part English, part Indian, and uniquely Desani's own.

"The Last Long Letter" records the ecstatic visions of a young man, a suicide who casts his soul back into the opaque void of the universe, where it had been a light, as he has previously cast his jeweled ring into the depths of the sea to symbolize his belief that from time to time spirit illuminates matter but then withdraws, leaving all in chaos and darkness until its next coming. Taken together, these stories, mainly satires and fantasies, further exemplify the talent that made *All about H. Hatten* one of the 20th century's major contributions to the literature of the ABSURD.

Desani immigrated to the United States and became a U.S. citizen in 1979. He shared a professorship in oriental philosophy at the University of Texas with Professor Raja Rao until his retirement in 1978. G. V. Desani died at age 91 on November 15, 2000, in Fort Worth, Texas.

BIBLIOGRAPHY

Desani, G. V. *All about H. Hatten: A Novel.* New Paltz, N.Y.: McPherson, 1986.

———. *Hali and Collected Stories.* New York: McPherson, 1991.

"DESCENT OF MAN" T. CORAGHESSAN BOYLE (1977)

T. CORAGHESSAN BOYLE's "Descent of Man" is not the first American short story to carry the title of Darwin's controversial study of the evolutionary development of man. However, EDITH WHARTON's "The Descent of Man" (1904) uses the title of Darwin's work only to satirize a professor who betrays his scientific research by publishing fraudulent but popular scientific books in order to pay off his son's debts. The scientist is a professor at the university in the fictional New England town of Hillbridge, which is also the setting for "Xingu" (1911) and several other stories, in which Wharton satirizes the intellectual or cultural pretensions of her day.

Boyle's satirical story is narrated by Mr. Horne (16), whose lover, Jane Good (4, 6), a primate researcher, will leave him for a chimpanzee. "I was living," he begins, "with a young woman who suddenly began to stink" (3). The first time he confronts her about it, she merely smiles and replies, "Occupational hazard" (3). One evening, "just after her bath (the faintest odor still lingered . . .)," he is startled to see an insect cross

her belly and "bury itself in her navel." "Louse," she explains, "picked up" so that Konrad, her chimpanzee, "can experience a tangible gratification of his social impulses during the grooming ritual" (4). He cannot sleep and takes three Doriden (5). The next afternoon, he goes to the Primate Center to pick her up and meets an African-American janitor, who tells him about Konrad: "He can commoonicate de mos esoteric i-deas in bof ASL and Yerkish, re-spond to and translate English, French, German, and Chinese." In fact, "Konrad is workin right now on a Yerkish translation ob Darwin's De-scent o Man"; last fall, "he done undertook a Yerkish translation of Chomsky's *Language and Mind* [1968] and Nietzsche's *Jenseits von Gut und B se* [1886]" (7). "Stuff and nonsense," the narrator replies. "No sense in feelin personally treatened . . ., mah good fellow—yo's got to ree-lize dat he is a genius" (8).

That evening, they go out to dinner, but Jane wears her work clothes and wishes he would not insist that she bathe every night, as she is "getting tired of smelling like a coupon in a detergent box" and finds it "unnatural" and "unhealthy" (8). At the restaurant, they dine with the Primate Center director, Dr. U-Hwak-Lo, and his wife. The director's wife and the narrator smile at each other, while the director and Jane discuss "the incidence of anal retention in chimps deprived of Frisbee co-ordination during the sensorimotor period" (10); during the meal of delicacies the narrator cannot identify, she tells the director about the "Yerkish epic" Konrad is "working up" (12). The following day, the narrator misses work and has to take five Doriden to fall asleep (12); when he awakes in the afternoon, he finds a note indicating that Jane is bringing Konrad home for dinner. She serves "watercress sandwiches and animal crackers as hors d'oeuvres" (13), while they watch the evening news. Konrad starts to react violently to a war story, and she translates his comments while telling the narrator not to worry, that "it's just his daily slice of revolutionary rhetoric," that "he'll calm down in a minute—he likes to play Che, but he's basically nonviolent" (14). When the narrator returns from work the next day, Jane has moved out. He feels "alone, deserted, friendless," and he begins "to long even for the stink of her" (15). He looks for her at the Primate Center, pushes the director and his wife out of the way, but is knocked across the room by Konrad, and as Jane escapes, he can only look up "into the black eyes, teeth, fur, rock-ribbed arms" (16).

Boyle's satire includes ironic allusions to historical or contemporary figures and literary or film characters. The model for Jane Good is the British primatologist Jane Goodall (born 1934), the world's foremost authority on chimpanzees, who has observed their behavior in East Africa since the 1960s, as documented in *In the Shadow of Man* (1971) and many other publications. Dr. U-Hwak-Lo appears to be an anagram of *Hugo van Lawick,* who married Goodall in 1964 and served as her photographer. They divorced, however, in 1974, and in 1975 Goodall married Derek Bryceson (died 1980), who was the director of the national parks in Tanzania. The model for Mr. Horne may be Brian Herne, whose love affair with Goodall in 1957 foundered on his ambition to become a big game hunter (Goodall, *Africa in My Blood* 82). The model for Konrad is Konrad Lorenz (1903–89), whose most famous work, *On Aggression* (1966), studies "the fighting instinct in beast and man" (ix) and who is cited in Goodall's *In the Shadow of Man* (288). The Primate Center is the one named after the American psychobiologist Robert M. Yerkes (1876–1956) in Atlanta; Goodall opposed the way chimps were studied there in captivity instead of in their natural habitat (Goodall, *Beyond Innocence* 218).

Among the items Jane takes with her when she moves out is "her Edgar Rice Burroughs collection" (15), which suggests another set of allusions to Tarzan and Jane in Burroughs's novels *Tarzan of the Apes* (1914) and *The Return of Tarzan* (1915). Quoted on the dedication page in *Descent of Man: Stories* (1979), however, is the yell "Ungowa" by Johnny Weismuller in the film *Tarzan Finds a Son* (1939), and the allusions in Boyle's story are to the characters in the films *Tarzan the Ape Man* (1932) and *Tarzan and His Mate* (1934) rather than to the novels, for while Jane Porter in the novels is from Baltimore, Jane Parker in the films, like Jane Goodall, is from England. In both sources, Jane rejects her father's younger big game hunting partner, because she falls in love with the "ape man" Tarzan.

Also quoted on the dedication page to Boyle's collection is Franz Kafka's "free ape," who gives "A Report to an Academy" (*The Complete Stories* [1971] 250) about how, after being captured in Africa (251) by the German "Hagenbeck firm" (which pioneered in the hunting and marketing of wild animals for zoos and circuses), he found "a way out" of his cage by learning to "imitate" (ape!) his captors. He did not want "freedom" (253), for there was no way back to the jungle. Nor did he like behaving as a human (257), but "it was so easy to imitate these people" (255), and he even managed "to reach the cultural level of an average European" (258). The "free ape" opted for performing on the "variety stage" rather than remaining in captivity in a zoo (258).

Whether Kafka's story is a satire on man as animal or on the "Jew who has allowed himself to be converted to Christianity" as "a way out" of the ghetto (Rubenstein 135), its savage (!) irony and humor clearly inspire Boyle's "Descent of Man." As is Josef K. in *The Trial* or Gregor Samsa in *The Metamorphosis,* Mr. Horne is confronted at the outset with a bizarre situation with which he cannot cope, and his downfall (descent) is precipitated by his refusal to acknowledge Konrad's intellectual abilities and sealed by his vain attempt to fight the chimpanzee physically over Jane Good, who has also opted to be a "free ape." Boyle's Kafkaesque satire continues in his later story "The Ape Lady in Retirement" (1989), in which Konrad reappears with Beatrice Umbo (whose name is an anagram of Gombe Stream Research Center, where Jane Goodall worked in Tanzania), "the world's foremost authority on the behavior of chimpanzees in the wild," who has "come home to retire in Connecticut" (194) but who cannot adjust to the "civilized" world.

BIBLIOGRAPHY

Boyle, T. Coraghessan. "The Ape Lady in Retirement." *The Paris Review* 110 (1989): 98–117.

———. "Descent of Man." *The Paris Review* 69 (1977): 16–28.

Brownell, Charles F. "Marketing Wild Animals." *Leslie's Monthly Magazine* 60, no. 3 (July 1905): 287–295.

Goodall, Jane. *Africa in My Blood: An Autobiography in Letters: The Early Years.* Edited by Dale Peterson. Boston: Houghton Mifflin, 2000.

————. *Beyond Innocence: An Autobiography in Letters: The Later Years.* Edited by Dale Peterson. Boston: Houghton Mifflin, 2001.

————. *In the Shadow of Man.* Rev. ed. Photographs by Hugo van Lawik. Boston: Houghton Mifflin, 1971.

Herne, Brian. *White Hunters: The Golden Age of African Safaris.* New York: Holt, 1999.

Kafka, Franz. *The Complete Stories.* Edited by Nahum N. Glatzer. New York: Schocken Books, 1971.

Lorenz, Konrad. *On Aggression.* Translated by Marjorie Kerr Wilson. New York: Harcourt, Brace & World, 1966.

Leonard Maltin's Movie and Video Guide. New York: Signet, 1998, 1,326–1,330.

Rubenstein, William C. "A Report to an Academy." In *Explain to Me Some Stories of Kafka,* edited by Angel Flores, 132–137. New York: Gordian Press, 1983.

Ullery, David A. *The Tarzan Novels of Edgar Rice Burroughs: An Illustrated Reader's Guide.* Jefferson, N.C., and London: McFarland, 2001.

Wharton, Edith. "The Descent of Man." *Scribner's Magazine* 35 (1904): 313–322.

Frederick Betz
Southern Illinois University Carbondale

"DESIRE AND THE BLACK MASSEUR"

TENNESSEE WILLIAMS (1946)   This TENNESSEE WILLIAMS short story, written in 1946, was first published in the 1948 volume *One Arm and Other Stories.* The tale is at once a sadomasochistic fantasy and a homosexual ALLEGORY of religious atonement. Anthony Burns is a 30-year-old clerk in an unnamed city that seems to be New Orleans; he is an "incomplete" and timid creature about to achieve and atone for his previously unrealized masochistic desire. When his coworker recommends a massage to help cure his backache, Burns encounters a huge "Negro" masseur who senses in Burns "an unusual something" and assaults Burns's body with blows of increasing violence that eventually bring Burns to orgasm. For Burns, suffering is intrinsically tied to sexual release, and with his first massage, Burns fulfills his desires. The story moves swiftly to its inevitable conclusion as his massages escalate in their level of violence. Burns and the masseur are evicted from the bathhouse after the masseur breaks Burns's leg, so they continue at the masseur's home. The CLIMAX of the story takes place during the week of Lent (this celebration of "human atonement"), when the Negro masseur slowly beats Burns to death with the latter's full consent, and then, in a symbolic act of cannibalistic communion, takes "twenty-four hours to eat the splintered bones clean." In the tale's DENOUEMENT the masseur obtains another job in a massage parlor and is "serenely conscious of fate bringing toward him another, to suffer atonement as it had been suffered by Burns."

Atonement in "Desire and the Black Masseur" is defined as the "surrender of self to violent treatment by others." The ceremonial violence of Burns's destruction and the fact that his death coincides with Easter seem to point to a concept of Christ as an anonymous EVERYMAN with unconscious erotic desires who is crucified for our sins while "the earth's whole population twisted and writhed beneath the manipulation of the night's black fingers and the white ones of day with skeletons splintered and flesh reduced to pulp, as out of this unlikely problem, the answer, perfection, was slowly evolved through torture." Exactly what the sins of the world are remains ambiguous: Is it "incompletion," whether sexual or spiritual, or is it desire in itself? Spirituality, desire, and even death are inseparable in the GOTHIC love story of Anthony Burns and his black giant, and so, too, Williams seems to say, is our own redemption through the death of this masochistic Christ figure.

BIBLIOGRAPHY

Vannatta, Dennis. *Tennessee Williams: A Study of the Short Fiction.* New York: Macmillan, 1988.

S. L. Yentzer
University of Georgia

"DESIREE'S BABY" KATE CHOPIN (1892)

KATE CHOPIN's brief but mesmerizing story opens in medias res, with Madame Valmonde preparing to visit her adopted daughter, Desiree, recently married to the wealthy Louisiana plantation owner Armand d'Aubigny and even more recently delivered of a baby girl. Then, in a series of FLASHBACKS, the narrator reveals Desiree's uncertain origins as a foundling, her beauty as she grew to womanhood, and Armand's passionate proposal of marriage. The narrator then returns to the present and, using briefly effective images, sketches the hierarchical plantation system of whites, quadroons, and blacks. Using Mme. Valmonde's perspective, the narrator reveals that the baby does not look white—and so the tragedy of this story moves rapidly to its completion.

It is difficult to imagine a reader who would not be horrified and disgusted by the results of the racism and sexism that permeate this story. No one could believe that Armand Aubigny's inhuman cruelty to his wife, Desiree, and his child is warranted. The only real uncertainty for the reader concerns Armand's foreknowledge of his own parentage: Did he know that his mother had Negro blood before he married Desiree, or did he discover her revealing letter later on? If he *did* know beforehand (and it is difficult to believe that he did not), his courtship of and marriage to Desiree were highly calculated actions, with Desiree chosen because she was the perfect woman to be used in an "experimental" reproduction. If their child(ren) "passed" as white, Armand would be pleased and would keep the marriage intact. If not, Desiree, the foundling, would be the perfect victim to take the blame.

This may seem to be judging Armand too harshly, because the narrator does describe his great passion for Desiree, so suddenly and furiously ignited. Certainly Armand behaves as a man in love. But Chopin inserts a few subtle remarks that allow us to question this, at least in hindsight: "The wonder was that he had not loved her before; for he had known her since his father brought him home from Paris, a boy of eight, after his mother died there." It does seem unlikely that a man of Armand's temperament would conceive this sudden intense desire for "the girl next door," a sweet, naive young woman whom he has known for most of his life. Right from the beginning, Chopin also reveals details about his character that are unsettling, even to the innocent and loving Desiree. The basic cruelty of Armand's nature is hinted at throughout the story, particularly regarding his severe treatment of "his negroes," which is in notably sharp contrast to his father's example.

Armand's reputation as a harsh slave master supports the presumption that he has known about his own part-Negro ancestry all along. He did not learn this behavior from his father, who was "easy-going and indulgent" in his dealings with the slaves. The knowledge that some of his own ancestors spring from the same "race of slavery" would surely be unbearable to the proud, "imperious" Armand, and the rage and shame that this knowledge brings would easily be turned against the blacks around him. In much the same way, when Armand realizes that his baby is visibly racially mixed, he vents his fury viciously on his slaves, the "very spirit of Satan [taking] hold of him."

Modern readers will find many disturbing aspects to this story. The seemingly casual racism is horrifying. Feminists are likely to take exception (as they sometimes do to Chopin's *The Awakening*) to Desiree's passive acceptance of Armand's rejection of her and his child and her apparently deliberate walk into the bayou. Suicide is not the strong woman's answer to the situation, but Desiree is definitely not a strong woman. What she does have is wealthy parents who love her and are willing to take care of her and the baby. Why does she feel that she has to end her life? Gender and class roles and structures were so rigid in this period that it was impossible for a woman to cross those lines very far; the racial barrier was the most rigid of all. No mixing of black and white blood would ever be condoned in that society, so Desiree's baby would never find acceptance anywhere. Desiree is not able to see a viable way out of her terrifying situation, and her view is not entirely unrealistic, considering her time and place. As she has done in her other stories, Kate Chopin realistically depicts the cruelty and horror of a social structure that totally denies power to women, children, the poor, and most of all, blacks.

BIBLIOGRAPHY

Chopin, Kate. *The Complete Works of Kate Chopin*. Edited by Per Seyersted. Baton Rouge: Louisiana State University Press, 1969.

Koloski, Bernard. *Kate Chopin: A Study of the Short Fiction*. New York: Twayne, 1996.

DE SPAIN   Always signifying a "man's man" in WILLIAM FAULKNER's stories, Manfred de Spain appears in Faulkner's *The Town* and *The Mansion* as the true love of the earth goddess Eula Varner. He also appears in numerous short stories, such as "BARN BURNING," in which he displays a degree of sympathy and a sense of justice to such benighted characters as the hapless ABNER SNOPES. He is Faulkner's only SPANISH-AMERICAN WAR hero.

DETECTIVE SHORT FICTION

The detective story is often defined narrowly to prevent confusing it with the crime story or the puzzle story. Frederic Dannay, writing as his ALTER EGO Ellery Queen in 1942, summed it up most succinctly when he called it "a tale of ratiocination, complete with crime and/or mystery, suspects, investigation, clues, deduction, and solution; in its purest form the chief character should be a detective, amateur or professional, who devotes most of his (or her) time to the problems of detection" (Queen, *The Detective Short Story: A Bibliography* v).

The pure detective story begins with the crime (murder, robbery, or blackmail, for instance) during which the criminal makes mistakes and inadvertently leaves clues that the detective must be clever enough to recognize. The detective fits together the evidence and identifies the perpetrator of the crime. This formula differs from that of the crime story in which the criminal may be the central figure and the story concerns his motive for committing the crime. He may or may not escape the law. The puzzle story involves the solution to a mystery or quandary; a crime may not even have occurred. (EDGAR ALLAN POE's "The Gold Bug," 1843, is an example of a puzzle story.) The suspense story, meanwhile, has no central detective to solve the mystery but may have a protagonist who becomes involved in events and situations that must be resolved by the end of the story. There are also variants of the detective story, such as the police procedural in which the police solve the mystery by the use of official police methods. Many readers refer to all of these stories as murder mysteries, even when there is no murder and little mystery. The pure detective story resembles a crossword puzzle and involves the reader in attempting to discover the solution to the mystery along with the detective.

The earliest example of a detective story appears in "The History of Bel" in the apocryphal Scriptures: Daniel spreads ashes on the floor of the temple and, by identifying the footprints left behind, reveals who has been stealing the offerings from the altar. Other early literary examples featuring crime solvers are Boccaccio's *Decameron,* Chaucer's *The Canterbury Tales, The Arabian Nights,* and Voltaire's *Zadig; or, The Book of Fate.*

The detective story as we have come to recognize it owes its creation to Poe, whose influence may be one reason for considering the short form preferable to the long form. Indeed, probably because of Poe's major role in defining the form, early writer-critics such as Howard Haycraft, Ronald Knox, Dorothy L. Sayers, Vincent Starrett, H. Douglas Thomson, Charles Honce, G. K. Chesterton, Charles Bragin, and E. C. Bentley argued for the short story as the proper form for detective fiction. The short detective story centers on one intensive idea (the crime committed and the detective's solution) where the situation must be resolved quickly to maintain the desired effect. There is little room for depth of characterization or a change of setting as in the novel.

In three short stories—"The MURDERS IN THE RUE MORGUE" (1841), "The Mystery of Marie Roget" (1842), and "The PURLOINED LETTER" (1844)—Poe set down most of the elements now considered necessary for the true detective story. These include the omniscient private citizen–detective; his less-than-astute assistant, who sometimes serves as narrator; and an official police representative, who may offer a theory that the detective proves wrong. Other elements include the discovery of false clues, or "red herrings," and the gradual unraveling of the solution to the mystery that culminates in a dramatic scene in which the explanation is provided. Robert A. W. Lowndes has actually identified 32 of these elements central to the detective story in Poe's three tales about C. AUGUSTE DUPIN, the first fictional detective to appear in a series of stories.

Fifty years later, Sir Arthur Conan Doyle in the Sherlock Holmes stories for the *Strand* magazine (beginning in 1891) adapted Poe's elements and created a more realistic relationship between Holmes, the detective, and Dr. Watson, the narrator. Doyle also created the trademark element of the enigmatic phrase by which the detective hints at the solution, toying with both the narrator and the reader, without making the solution explicit. The most famous is the passage about the "dog in the night time" in Doyle's "Silver Blaze" (collected in *The Memoirs of Sherlock Holmes,* 1982), in which the dog's failure to bark or attack in the night suggests that the criminal was someone with whom the dog was familiar.

The success of the Sherlock Holmes short stories in particular, and the popularity of detective fiction in general, inspired the editors of general fiction magazines to add series about detectives to their schedules. A succession of stories with a continuing central character brought readers back for each succeeding issue and sold magazines. Each editor wanted his own Sherlock Holmes who could entice the customers. Few of these fictional detectives are remembered today, but there was a time when *Cosmopolitan,* the SATURDAY EVENING POST, COLLIER'S, LADIES' HOME JOURNAL, and other publications included detective stories in their pages on a regular basis. Among these were the scientific detective stories featuring Craig Kennedy (e.g., "The Silent Bullet," [1912]), by Arthur B. Reeve (1880–1936); the Thinking Machine stories (e.g., "The Problem of Cell 13" [1907]), by Jacques Futrelle (1875–1912); stories of Average Jones, fraudulent advertising investigator (e.g., "The Man Who Spoke Latin" [1911]), by Samuel Hopkins Adams (1871–1958); of Uncle Abner, Virginia squire (e.g., "Doomdorf Mystery" [1918]), by Melville Davisson Post (1871–1930); of Jim Hanvey (e.g., "Common Stock" [1923]), by Octavus Roy Cohen (1891–1959); and of Professor Poggioli (e.g., "A Passage to Benares" [1929]), by the Pulitzer Prize–winning author T. S. Stribling (1881–1965). These stories appeared in addition to serialized detective novels in the same periodicals.

The most significant change in the development of the genre was in the 1920s in the pages of the American pulp magazine BLACK MASK. The first important author in the pages of *Black Mask* was DASHIELL HAMMETT, the father of the hard-boiled detective story (see HARD-BOILED FICTION). Hammett spun fairy tales inhabited by real people. In the words of his most significant successor, RAYMOND CHANDLER, in "The Simple Art of Murder" (1944), Hammett "gave murder back to the people who commit it for reasons, not just to pro-

vide a corpse" and did not use fancy poisons or weapons either (Chandler 234). The two of them, working independently, revitalized the genre with stories of detectives SAM SPADE, the Continental Op, Hammett's earliest series detective, a nameless operative for the Continental Detective Agency, and PHILIP MARLOWE, Chandler's private eye. Other writers followed, and emulated, but never duplicated the achievements of Hammett and Chandler. Eventually the two (along with Ross MacDonald) became a triumvirate representing the hard-boiled school. Other pulp magazines such as *Dime Detective* and *Detective Fiction Weekly* imitated the format and content of *Black Mask.*

The hard-boiled detective story is the urban equivalent of the western in American fiction. As do other stories of REALISM, the detective story deals with human problems but in a world in which the problems can be solved. The situations are often fantastic; their authors render them realistic through their writing styles, especially the believable dialogue and the detailed descriptions of actual places.

During his lifetime Hammett published only five novels but dozens of short stories. In spite of the popularity of these stories in both the pulp and slick magazines, the recognition of Hammett's contribution to the short story did not really occur until various presses began to collect and publish his short stories in the 1940s, making them as available as his novels to a wider public.

Chandler's first story, "Blackmailers Don't Shoot," appeared in *Black Mask* in December 1933. Other stories were published in *Dime Detective* and *Detective Story.* His first short story collection, *Five Murderers,* was published in 1944 by Avon Murder Mystery Monthly (which released in trade paperback format a monthly collection featuring a different author, either a novel or a collection of short stories). Chandler's stories were also collected belatedly in both hardcover and paperback editions, and eventually two volumes that included all of his stories were published in England. Some writers of the genre—JAMES M. CAIN, for instance—were never published in the pulp magazines and are better known for their novels than their short stories, although recently Cain's stories have been collected and republished.

Ellery Queen's contribution to the genre was two-fold: as writer of the detective stories about Ellery Queen (with the famous Challenge to the Reader—to solve the crime just before the denouement) and as editor of what became the premiere specialist publication after BLACK MASK, *Ellery Queen's Mystery Magazine* (*EQMM*), which began in 1914. Countering the not-quite-"respectable" reputation of most detective magazines, Queen intended *EQMM* to be the equivalent of a high-brow literary magazine for readers of popular fiction. The editor set out to publish the best of the old stories as well as to encourage new writers. To this end he celebrated the "first" story by a new writer in each issue and ran contests for the best new detective and crime fiction. Editor Queen was a stern and objective judge. In 1946 WILLIAM FAULKNER submitted "An Error in Chemistry," a story in his sequence about GAVIN STEVENS (the short stories were collected in 1949 as *KNIGHT'S GAMBIT*), and received second prize.

The editor boasted of having launched several significant writers on a career of crime. Stanley Ellin's famous "The Specialty of the House" first appeared in its pages in 1948; so did Robert L. Fish's Holmesian pun-filled parodies about detective Schlock Homes; individual issues published stories by international authors. In 1948, the Argentinean writer Jorge Luis Borges's (1899–1986) "The Garden of Forking Paths" was published in a translation by the mystery writer and critic Anthony Boucher.

Book collections of detective stories from these and other periodicals preserved the works of many writers. Collections of stories by a single author often represented an interesting quirk in publishing. Publishers found that short stories in book form did not sell as well as novels, so the collections were sometimes disguised as novels by breaking the individual episodes up into chapters and numbering them sequentially throughout the entire book. Examples of these include Jack Boyle's *Boston Blackie* (1919), Richard Harding Davis's *In the Fog* (1901), T. W. Henshaw's *Cleek: The Man of the Forty Faces* (1910), and Frank L. Packard's *The Adventures of Jimmie Dale* (1917).

Anthologies of stories by many writers have made unique contributions to the detective short story not only by preserving some of the best examples of the form, but by providing the editors with a forum, in the introductions, for examining the history and development of the genre. Some of the more significant ones are *The Omnibus of Crime* (1929), edited by Dorothy L. Sayers; *The World's Great Detective Stories* (1927), edited by Willard Huntington Wright (better known as the author of the Philo Vance detective novels, signed S. S. Van Dine); and Ellery Queen's centennial volume *101 Years' Entertainment: The Great Detective Stories 1841–1941* (1941). Queen enjoyed editing "theme" anthologies with contents following a common motif, stories marking a first appearance in the United States or stories by writers not known for writing detective fiction (such as Sinclair Lewis's "The Post-Mortem Murder" [1921] and RING LARDNER's "Haircut" [1926]; ERNEST HEMINGWAY's "The KILLERS" [1926] is often cited as well).

Recent anthologies edited by other authorities include the annual collection sponsored by the Mystery Writers of America and the annual collection of the best stories of the year drawn from several periodicals. *The Best Detective Stories of the Year* began in 1946 with 15 volumes edited by David E. Cooke, followed by two more volumes edited by mystery writer Brett Halliday, then six edited by Anthony Boucher, and six edited by Allen J. Hubin. In 1976 Edward D. Hoch assumed the editorship of the series, which in 1982 changed its title and focus to *The Year's Best Mystery & Suspense Stories*.

Ellery Queen became a critic, as well as a writer of fiction, with a number of essays on different aspects of the genre in *EQMM* and two significant bibliographies: *The Detective Short Story: A Bibliography* (1942) and *Queen's Quorum: The 101 Most Important Books of Detective-Crime Short Stories* (1948; revised and expanded, 1969). The latter contains a running commentary and history of the genre. It has also influenced collectors to acquire first editions of the volumes Queen recommends.

Perhaps ironically, then, a form that began in the mass media has now become a very specialized and almost elite genre. The market for such periodical fiction has shrunk appreciably, and many writers lack the incentive to write for the minimal fees offered for short stories as opposed to full-length novels. The only newsstand magazines to publish detective fiction are the two specialist publications *Alfred Hitchcock's Mystery Magazine* and *Ellery Queen's Mystery Magazine,* and *Playboy.* In the place of the once voluminous periodicals, only a few publishers include anthologies of detective fiction on their regular lists or specialize in collections of detective short stories. Since September 1994, the firm of Crippen and Landru has issued a collection of short works by contemporary writers at the rate of four volumes a year. Among the authors have been Edward D. Hoch, Margaret Maron, Marcia Muller, Bill Pronzini, and James Yaffe.

Indeed, perhaps the key to the detective short fiction market lies in the scores of recent minority and women writers who in the last two decades, especially, have reshaped the classic hard-boiled detective into a different breed. Acclaimed Chicana/o writers include Rolando Hinojosa, featuring his detective Rafe Buenrostro; Michael Nava and his gay amateur sleuth Henry Rios; Manuel Ramos and his hardboiled Luis Montez; Lucha Corpi and her activist crime solver Gloria Damasco; and Rudolfo Anaya and his private investigator Sonny Baca. Cuban-American Carolina Garcia-Aguilera, with her detective Lupe Solano, has been compared favorably with Patricia Cornwell and Sara Paretsky. Among the most acclaimed African-American mystery writers are Walter Mosley, with his hard-boiled Los Angeles private detective Easy Rawlins, and Valerie Wilson Wesley, who features a liberated private investigator, Tamara Hayle. Notable, too, are Gar Anthony Haywood and his sleuth Aaron Gunner, Grace F. Edwards (Mali Anderson), Eleanor Taylor Bland (Marti MacAlister), Barbara Neely (Blanche White), and Hugh Holton (Larry Cole). To date, however, these writers have not written short stories. Leading the field are the *Sisters in Crime* anthologies, publishing since 1989 award-winning detective stories by women.

The number and popularity of women writers in the genre have grown dramatically, with notable portraits of such female private investigators as Sue Grafton's Kinsey Milhone and Diane Mott Davidson's Goldy Bear. The most recently published anthology, *The Best of Sisters in Crime* (1997) includes stories by aforementioned Grafton, Davidson, Maron, and Muller, as well as Mary Higgins Clark, Joan Hess, Sharyn McCrumb, JOYCE CAROL OATES, Nancy Pickard, Sara Paretsky, and Julie Smith. In a recently published study of women detective fiction writers, *Busybodies, Meddlers, and Snoops* (1998), Kimberly J. Dilley notes the changing view of fictional women detectives: No longer seen as stereotypic and passive and certainly no longer overlooked by critics, women mystery writers and their women characters over the last two decades have begun creating a new type of hero—the modern female detective, an independent, intelligent, witty, and compassionate woman who can take care of herself. Dilley analyzes the new female serial detectives and explores their struggles with issues of gender and FEMINISM in their day-to-day lives and the ways they have profoundly altered the genre's standard plotlines and protagonists.

Detective fiction continues to gain in popularity in the 21st century. Notable recent anthologies range from the general *Longman Anthology of Detective Fiction* (2004) to the specifically ethnic *Mystery Midrash: An Anthology of Jewish Mystery & Detective Fiction* (1999) to the specifically thematic *Death Dines at 8:30* (2001) to the specifically contemporary *Killer Year: Stories to Die For . . . From the Hottest New Crime Writers* (2008). The latter, edited by veteran mystery writer Lee Childs, contains stories by established writers (Ken Bruen, Allison Brennan, and Duane Swiercynski) and newcomers to the crime scene. Clearly, interest in the genre continues to increase and the number of short-story writers interested in it continues to expand.

BIBLIOGRAPHY

Bakerman, Jane. *Then There Were Nine: More Women of Mystery.* Bowling Green, Ohio: Bowling Green State University Popular Press, 1985.

Bargainnie, Earl F. *Ten Women of Mystery.* Bowling Green, Ohio: Bowling Green State University Popular Press, 1981.

Barzun, Jacques, and Wendell Hertig Taylor. *A Catalogue of Crime.* Rev. ed. New York: Harper & Row, 1989.

Bishop, Claudia. *Death Dines at 8:30.* New York: Berkley, 2001.

Burke, James Lee. *The Convict and Other Stories.* New York: Pocket, 2007.

———. *Jesus Out to Sea: Stories.* New York: Simon & Schuster, 2007.

Chandler, Raymond. "The Simple Art of Murder." In *The Art of the Mystery Story,* edited by Howard Haycraft. New York: Simon & Schuster, 1946.

Cox, J. Randolph. *Masters of Mystery and Detective Fiction: An Annotated Bibliography.* Englewood Cliffs, N.J.: Salem Press, 1989.

Dilley, Kimberly J. *Busybodies, Meddlers, and Snoops.* Greenwich, Conn.: Greenwood, 1998.

Ellroy, James. *Destination: Morgue!: L.A. Tales.* New York: Vintage, 2004.

Haycraft, Howard. *Murder for Pleasure: The Life and Times of the Detective Story.* New York: D. Appleton-Century, 1941.

———, ed. *The Art of the Mystery Story.* New York: Simon & Schuster, 1946.

Killer Year: Stories to Die For . . . From the Hottest New Crime Writers. Edited by Lee Child. New York: Minotaur: 2008.

Klein, Kathleen Gregory. *Diversity and Detective Fiction.* Madison, Wisc.: Popular Press, 1999.

Lowndes, Robert A. W. "The Contributions of Edgar Allan Poe." In *The Mystery Writer's Art,* edited by Francis M. Nevins, Jr. Bowling Green, Ohio: Popular Press, 1970.

Mansfield-Kelley, Deane. *The Longman Anthology of Detective Fiction.* New York: Longman, 2004.

Mundell, E. H., Jr., and G. Jay Rausch. *The Detective Short Story: A Bibliography and Index.* Manhattan: Kansas State University Library, 1974.

O'Shaunessy, Perri. *Sinister Shorts.* New York: Bantam, 2006.

Pronzini, Bill, and Marcia Muller. *1001 Midnights: The Aficionado's Guide to Mystery and Detective Fiction.* New York: Arbor House, 1986.

Queen, Ellery, ed. *The Detective Short Story: A Bibliography.* Boston: Little, Brown, 1942; reprint with new introduction by editor. New York: Biblo & Tannen, 1969.

———. *101 Years' Entertainment: The Great Detective Stories 1841–1941.* Boston: Little, Brown, 1941.

———. *Queen's Quorum: A History of the Detective-Crime Short Story as Revealed in the 106 Most Important Books Published in this Field since 1845: Supplements through 1967.* New York: Biblo & Tannen, 1969.

Raphael, Lawrence W. *Mystery Midrash: An Anthology of Jewish Mystery & Detective Fiction.* Woodstock, Vt.: Jewish Lights Publishing, 1999.

Shaw, Joseph Thompson. *The Hardboiled Omnibus: Early Stories from "Black Mask."* New York: Simon & Schuster, 1946.

Wallace, Marilyn, ed. *The Best of Sisters in Crime.* New York: Berkeley Prime Crime, 1997.

J. Randolph Cox
St. Olaf College

DETERMINISM   The word is a shortened version of the scientific term *biological determinism,* which describes the belief that one's destiny is "determined" by heredity and environment, not good deeds, faith, God's "grace," or adherence to the precepts of organized religions, such as Christianity, Judaism, or Islam. Determinism emerged as a result of the scientific discoveries by Charles Darwin and others in biology, geology, and astronomy in the mid-19th century. Another major influence was rapid industrialization, especially of the United States. These developments shattered the previously held concept that the individual was the center of the universe and instead posited the idea that human beings are insignificant players in a cruel, ironic world where there are no longer any heroes or villains, only unfeeling nature. This deeply pessimistic philosophy is present in such turn-of-the-20th-century authors as AMBROSE BIERCE, STEPHEN CRANE, and O. HENRY. It remained a THEME throughout 20th-century American literature, reflected in the works of SHERWOOD ANDERSON, ERNEST HEMINGWAY, SAUL BELLOW, JOHN CHEEVER, JOHN BARTH, and others. It is often discussed as an aspect of literary NATURALISM.

BIBLIOGRAPHY

Conron, John. *The American Landscape.* New York: Oxford University Press, 1964.

Cowley, Malcom. "A Natural History of American Naturalism." In *Documents of Modern Literary Realism,* edited by George J. Becker. Princeton, N.J.: Princeton University Press, 1967.

Hofstadter, Richard. *Social Darwinism in American Thought.* Boston: Allyn & Bacon, 1964.

Horton, Rod W., and Herbert W. Edwards. *Backgrounds of American Literary Thought.* 3rd ed. Englewood Cliffs, N.J.: Prentice-Hall, 1974.

Howard, June. *Form and History in American Naturalism.* Chapel Hill: University of North Carolina Press, 1985.

Michaels, Walter Berm. *The Gold Standard and the Logic of Naturalism: American Literature at the Turn of the Century.* Berkeley: University of California Press, 1987.

Pizer, Donald. *Realism and Naturalism in Nineteenth-Century American Literature.* Rev. ed. Carbondale: Southern Illinois University Press, 1984.

———, ed. *Cambridge Companion to American Realism and Naturalism.* Cambridge: Cambridge University Press, 1995.

Carol Hovanac
Ramapo College

DEUS EX MACHINA

From the Latin meaning "god from a machine." In Greek tragedy this practice involved a god literally appearing at the last moment to provide the solution to the tangled problems of the main characters. The god is let down from the sky on a sort of crane. The phrase has come to have a pejorative ring, particularly in short fiction, where it is criticized as the writer's inability to resolve problems without resorting to the crutch of a sometimes hastily introduced character.

"DEVIL AND DANIEL WEBSTER, THE"

STEPHEN VINCENT BENÉT (1937) A popular short story first published in the SATURDAY EVENING POST and then in the collection *Thirteen O'Clock,* it was adapted as an opera (1938) with music by Douglas S. Moore and later as a play (1931) and a film (1941, under the title *All That Money Can Buy*). The story involves Jabez Stone, a New England farmer, who sells his soul to the Devil in exchange for riches. The eloquent Daniel Webster argues Stone's case before a devilish and prejudiced jury and saves him from having to pay his debt.

DE VOTO, BERNARD A. (BERNARD AUGUSTINE DE VOTO) (1897–1955)

American historian and critic who first gained recognition for his *Mark Twain's America* (1932), a rebuttal of Van Wyck Brooks's *The Ordeal of Mark Twain* (1920). De Voto taught at Northwestern University and Harvard University and wrote for HARPER'S magazine (1935–55). His most respected work is his historical study of the American West in three volumes, one of which (*Across the Wide Missouri*) won the PULITZER PRIZE in 1947. His view of the frontier as a richly diverse source of FOLKTALE, MYTH, and song helped popularize the concept of the West and helped encourage writers whose stories focused on the West.

DEVRIES, PETER (1910–1993)

After working at *Poetry* magazine from 1938 to 1944, DeVries began a long association with the NEW YORKER, in which most of his short fiction was published. A comic writer in the *New Yorker* tradition of JAMES THURBER and S. J. Perelman, DeVries was funny, witty, and unfailingly clear. He is a satirist (see SATIRE) who applied his antic humor to the foibles and excesses of affluent middle-class exurbanites.

DEXTER GREEN

Dexter Green, in F. SCOTT FITZGERALD's "Winter Dreams," is an important figure in modern literature, representing the effect on the individual of the American dream of unlimited opportunity. He is a caddie for the wealthy patrons of a country club, and his winter dreams are off-season fantasies about the "glittering things" in life. As does Fitzgerald's character BASIL DUKE LEE, Dexter Green appears to be both a romantic and a realist (see ROMANTICISM and REALISM): His imagination and hard work together enable him to leave his humble beginnings to become a successful Wall Street financier by the time he reaches his mid-30s. As do other young men in Fitzgerald's fiction, Dexter Green falls in love forever with Judy Jones, a beautiful woman who appears indifferent to her many admirers; for years, however, she remains his fertile image of ideal love and the possibility of life's promises. When he learns by chance that she has become a matronly housewife married to an abusive philanderer, he collapses in tears, understanding that with the loss of his idea of her, he has lost his youthful belief in the freshness of life's possibilities—and the motive for acquiring his "glittering things." Recent interpretations have described Dexter Green as a pitiful rather than a tragic romantic figure. He cannot accept the unexciting fact that Judy Jones is average; instead, he idealizes her physical beauty emotionally to finance his materialism.

BIBLIOGRAPHY
Burhans, Clinton S., Jr., "'Magnificently Attuned to Life': The Value of 'Winter Dreams.'" *Studies in Short Fiction* 6 (1968–69).
McCay, Mary A. "Fitzgerald's Women: Beyond 'Winter Dreams.'" In *American Novelists Revisited: Essays in Feminist Criticism,* edited by Fritz Fleischmann, 1982.

Frances Kerr
Durham Technical Community College

DIAL, THE A magazine founded in Concord, Massachusetts, in 1840, by Theodore Fuller and Ralph Waldo Emerson as the organ of the New England TRANSCENDENTALISM movement. Fuller served as its editor from 1840 to 1842, and Emerson, with Henry David Thoreau's help, took over until 1844, when the magazine ceased publication. During its short history, it wielded a great deal of influence in literary, philosophic, and religious thought. Since 1844 other magazines have taken the same name. In 1880 a conservative group founded the third *Dial* in Chicago. When the magazine moved to New York in 1918, it became the outstanding literary review of its time. Until 1920, with the aid of CONRAD AIKEN, Randolph Bourne, and Van Wyck Brooks, it published articles by leading radical thinkers, including John Dewey and Thorsten Veblen. After 1920 the magazine was devoted to the encouragement of AVANT-GARDE authors. The poet Marianne Moore became editor in 1925. The magazine ceased publication four years later. A fourth *Dial,* first a literary quarterly edited by James Silberman, then an annual, ran from 1959 to 1962.

DIALECT According to the *Oxford English Dictionary,* the word *dialect* entered the English language in 1577 and is etymologically related to the Greek *dialektos.* The Greek term means "conversation" or "discourse," but it connotes (see CONNOTATION AND DENOTATION) a regional variety of a particular language. This, of course, is the most familiar meaning of *dialect,* but the word also can refer to a specialized discourse based on factors other than geography. Thus, one may speak of a scholarly dialect or the dialect of a certain scientific community. In the most general sense, then, a dialect is merely one variant of a standardized language system.

Some scholars, however, have been troubled by the notion of a "standard" language. In his widely cited *Keywords,* for instance, Raymond Williams points out that languages exist only in dialect form, and he thus dismisses the belief in a standard language from which all variants derive as a "metaphysical notion." A dialect, then, is perhaps best thought of as one language strand among many which, taken together, constitute the language itself.

Ever since MARK TWAIN famously used the dialects of both white and black Americans in *The Adventures of Huckleberry Finn,* writers have been employing dialects to establish a further sense of realism in their characters' speech. Such writers include DOROTHY ALLISON, WILLIAM FAULKNER, JOEL CHANDLER HARRIS, ZORA NEALE HURSTON, and RICHARD WRIGHT, to name only a few of the many writers who employ this technique.

Shannon Zimmerman
University of Georgia

"DIAMOND AS BIG AS THE RITZ, THE" F. SCOTT FITZGERALD (1922) This story's unusual mixture of FANTASY and REALISM made it hard for F. SCOTT FITZGERALD to find a publisher, and this blending of genres bewildered or disturbed its first readers. The story appeared originally in *The Smart Set* in 1922 under the title "The Diamond in the Sky" and in a shorter version in Fitzgerald's story collection *Tales of the Jazz Age.* Some commentators have called it a modern FAIRY TALE about the moral education of John Unger, who visits the Washington Braddock family on their fantastic underground estate in Montana. The Braddocks hoard a monstrous diamond and kill all visitors to prevent them from revealing its presence. Some critics have described the story as a satire on American materialism that also incorporates the traditional boy-girl romance PLOT. In its unusual mixture of genres, the story holds a unique position in Fitzgerald's canon and confirms the range of his fictional interests.

BIBLIOGRAPHY
Buell, Lawrence, "The Significance of Fantasy in Fitzgerald's Short Fiction." In *The Short Stories of F. Scott Fitzger-*

ald: New Approaches in Criticism, edited by Jackson R. Bryer. Madison: University of Wisconsin Press, 1982.

Frances Kerr
Durham Technical Community College

DIASPORA   Exile or dispersion, used in the past almost invariably with reference to the exile of the Jewish people from the land of Israel. Diaspora can refer not only to the state of being in exile but also to the place of exile—any place outside Israel where Jews are living—to the communities in exile, and the state of mind that results from living in exile. Inherent in the term is usually the Jew's feeling of living as a member of a relatively defenseless minority, subject to injustice if not to outright persecution; of an unfulfilled life and destiny as a Jew, and of living in an unredeemed—although not unredeemable—world.

In the last decade the term *diaspora* has been applied with increasing frequency to members of the African community, with nearly identical connotations. (See CONNOTATION AND DENOTATION.) Thus, for example, the term can refer to stories by CYNTHIA OZICK, on one hand, as well as to those by RALPH ELLISON, JOHN EDGAR WIDEMAN, and RICHARD WRIGHT, on the other.

DÍAZ, JUNOT (1968–   )   Born in the Dominican Republic, Junot Díaz spent the first six years of his life without a phone, television, or plumbing; his family had to cart its own water. In 1974 the family immigrated to the United States and settled in Perth Amboy, New Jersey—beside one of the country's largest landfills, where Díaz spent the rest of his formative years in a primarily African-American and Puerto Rican neighborhood.

Díaz grew up immersed in the conditions that would become thematically central to his writing: poverty, racism, language barriers, immigration, and marginalization. He has had a variety of jobs, including pool table delivery man, dishwasher, copy shop assistant, and steelworker. After a short stint at a community college, Díaz transferred to Rutgers University, where he earned a B.A. in literature and history. It was there that he took his first creative writing class and discovered his passion for storytelling. He earned an

M.F.A. from Cornell University in 1995 and published his first book of short stories, *Drown,* which was an instant literary sensation, in 1996.

The NEW YORKER magazine placed Díaz on a list of the top 20 writers for the 21st century, and his work has been featured in the *Best American Short Stories* anthology many times. In 1998 he won the MIT Eugene McDermott Award and the PUSHCART PRIZE, in 2000 the Lila Wallace–Reader's Digest Writer's Award, and the PEN/Malamud Award for short fiction in 2002.

Díaz's stories have appeared in the *New Yorker, Paris Review, Time Out, Glimmer Train, African Voices, Story,* and elsewhere. His long-awaited first novel, *The Brief Wondrous Life of Oscar Wao,* won the Pulitzer Prize in 2008. Díaz currently teaches creative writing at the Massachusetts Institute of Technology.

See also "The SUN, THE MOON, THE STARS."

BIBLIOGRAPHY

Díaz, Junot. "Contributors Notes." In *The Best American Short Stories 1999,* edited by Amy Tan and Katrina Kenison, 378. Boston: Houghton Mifflin, 1999.

Feldman, Orna. "Literary Sensation: Young author meets new challenges at MIT." *Spectrum,* Fall 2003. Available online. URL: http://spectrum.mit.edu/issue/2003-fall/literary-sensation. Accessed May 1, 2009.

Guthmann, Edward. "It's a Scary Time for Latin American Immigrants and Junot Díaz Feels the Pressure to Help." *San Francisco Chronicle.* 22 April 2006, p. E1.

Solomita, Olga. "Swimming Lessons: Junot Díaz, Author of *Drown,* Visits Cambridge Harvard Summer Academy Students." *Harvard University Gazette,* 21 August 2003, p. 3.

Iver Arnegard

DIDION, JOAN (1934–   )   Born in Sacramento, California, Joan Didion has worked as a columnist for *Vogue, SATURDAY EVENING POST, ESQUIRE,* and the *National Review,* among others. Her nonfiction views on American life have been taken up by many contemporary fiction writers. Didion's insight into the culture of the 1960s focuses on her native California as a METAPHOR for the lost AMERICAN DREAM. Her novels and short stories, too, depict the disorder, loss, anxiety, and human and cultural disintegration of modern life. In Didion's books, the pioneering American spirit is replaced by a lack of belief, a creed of "me-ism," and eternal motion without direction. These same observations can be seen in the fiction of such writers as JOYCE CAROL OATES, BOBBIE ANN MASON, JOHN BARTH, and others.

Although much of her writing focuses on California, Joan Didion is not provincial. She uses her immediate milieu to envision, simultaneously, the last stand of America's frontier values pushed to their limits and the manifestations of craziness and malaise that have initiated their finale. Thus her THEMES in both short fiction and nonfiction appear in her novel *Play It As It Lays,* set in Los Angeles: Her characters—whose pasts have been completely obliterated—have problems with failed marriages, abortion, mental instability, and freeway phobias. Didion's short fiction was published in the volume *Telling Stories* in 1978.

BIBLIOGRAPHY

Didion, Joan. "California Blue." *Harper's,* October 1976.
———. *Fixed Ideas: America since 9.11.* New York: New York Review of Books, 2003.
———. *Political Fictions.* New York: Knopf, 2001.
———. *Vintage Didion.* New York: Vintage Books, 2004.
———. "The Welfare Island Ferry." *Harper's Bazaar,* June 1965.
———. *We Tell Ourselves Stories in Order to Live: A Collected Nonfiction.* New York: Knopf, 2006.
———. "When Did the Music Come This Way? Children Dear, Was It Yesterday?" *Denver Quarterly,* Winter 1967.
———. *Where I Was From.* New York: Knopf, 2003.
———. *The Year of Magical Thinking.* New York: Knopf, 2005.
Eggers, Dave. Interview with Joan Didion (July 10, 2003). Available online. URL: http://www.salon.com/oct96/didion961028.html. Accessed May 1, 2009.
Henderson, Katherine Usher. *Joan Didion.* New York: Ungar, 1981.

DIES IRAE   From the Latin for "day of wrath." A famous medieval hymn about the Last Judgment, it is used in the Roman Catholic Mass for the Dead and on All Souls' Day, religious occasions liberally employed by such writers as EDWARD ALBEE, Tennessee Williams, Anne Rice, and others, to suggest the threatening cloud hanging over modern characters doomed by their superficial obsessions and lack of spiritual beliefs.

DIONYSIAC   See APOLLONIAN AND DIONYSIAC.

DISCOURSE   Used as a word for discussion, or to describe a form of conversational expression, *discourse* traditionally has been separated into direct (She said, "I feel sad") or indirect (She said that she was sad). A more explicit theoretical use of the term has occurred in the last few decades, however, in reference to the heavily weighted way that all of us communicate with one another. The French linguist Emile Benveniste divided the terms *language* and *discourse,* with *language* referring to speech or writing used objectively and *discourse* emphasizing the implications of the understanding—or lack thereof—between speaker or writer, on one hand, and listener or reader, on the other. Thus in fiction, for example, although the text may seem to describe a person, a situation, or an idea—and may in fact do so—its most important function is "performative" (Eagleton 118), that is, to achieve certain effects on the reader.

BIBLIOGRAPHY

Eagleton, Terry. *Literary Theory: An Introduction.* Minneapolis: University of Minnesota Press, 1983.

"DISPLACED PERSON, THE" FLANNERY O'CONNOR (1954)   Generally agreed to be one of FLANNERY O'CONNOR's best stories as well as an excellent entrée to her work, "The Displaced Person" offers all the major hallmarks of the first-rate story. It first appeared in *Sewanee Review* in 1954. Echoing throughout the story is the phrase *displaced person:* Although the term initially refers to Mr. Guizac, the literal so-called D.P., a refugee from Poland, by the end of the story we realize that everyone—including the reader—is a displaced person at some point, severed by race, class, or gender prejudice from the mainstream community. Other major O'Connor THEMES support the story, as well: the South, the Catholic faith, and her use of the grotesque.

"The Displaced Person" begins as Mr. Guizac, the displaced foreigner, appears in a southern rural area where class and color lines are already in place. He finds work with Mrs. McIntyre, who, as owner of the farm, considers herself superior to Mr. and Mrs. Shortley, the poor whites, and to the "Negroes," Sulk and Astor, all four of whom work for her. The Shortleys dislike and distrust the industrious Mr. Guizac, who, they fear, will take their place on the farm. As Ann Charters notes, their suspicious, fear-driven attitude is the American version of those in Europe who would put people like Mr. Guizac in concentration camps. Mrs. Shortley thus forms an unlikely alliance across color lines with Sulk and Astor in an attempt to shore up the position of her and her husband.

Mrs. Shortley's fears prove well grounded. Mrs. McIntyre, impressed with Mr. Guizac's willing devotion to farm work, decides to fire the Shortleys and replace them permanently with Mr. Guizac. Initially the two women seem to be FOILS; O'Connor gradually reveals to us, however, that despite their different social positions, Mrs. McIntyre (ironically, "entire" only in her complete self-interest) and Mrs. Shortley (short on compassion) are linked through their egotism and selfishness (Paulson 64). Mrs. Shortley, on the verge of escaping the farm before she is literally replaced, dies a violent death that recalls the concentration camp pictures she has seen in a newsreel. In her displacement and violent death, she begins to understand suffering.

With Mrs. Shortley's death, Mrs. McIntyre's problems would appear to have ended: Mr. Guizac is helping her to modernize the farm into a model of efficiency. However, she learns that, to save his niece from the concentration camp, he plans to bring her over to marry Sulk. Since Mrs. McIntyre cannot abide the thought of interracial marriage (racism temporarily overrides self-interest here), she forms another unlikely alliance, this time with Mr. Shortley, on whom devolves the responsibility to devise a way to kill Mr. Guizac. As we hear the sounds of the dying Mr. Guizac, crushed under the tractor wheel, we see Mrs. McIntyre and Mr. Shortley joined in their responsibility for Guizac's death. Their collaboration is short-lived, though, and Mrs. McIntyre ultimately is left with no one to help her but Astor and his wife, and the priest. Forced to sell off all the farm equipment, she is literally left with nothing but a place.

Many critics view the priest as the central consciousness of this tale. He, along with the revelatory images of the peacock, always associated with Christ in O'Connor's stories, provides some sense of the redemptive meaning of Christianity. Seeing Shortley as a devil figure and Guizac as a Christ figure might seem an easy way out, but O'Connor's stories are too complex for easy ALLEGORY, in which the characters represent pure good or pure evil. Indeed, even Mrs. Shortley, in death, finally has her vision, in which the meaning of the peacock is revealed to her. And O'Connor extends the possibility that Mrs. McIntyre, alone on her farm with a black couple and a priest, may learn true equality and humility. In addition to a Christian and humanitarian message is a historical or sociological one. Mr. Guizac, the displaced person, was the truest American of all: Having emigrated from his own country, he arrived in America determined to succeed and was too busy working and helping others to succumb to either class or race prejudice. In this sense, as nearly always occurs in O'Connor's stories, Georgia—or the South—becomes a microcosm for the United States, in all its horror and all its possibility.

BIBLIOGRAPHY

O'Connor, Flannery. "The Displaced Person." In *Flannery O'Connor: The Complete Stories*. New York: Farrar, Straus & Giroux.

———. "The Displaced Person." *Sewanee Review,* 62, no. 4 (October–December 1954): 634–635.

Paulson, Suzanne Morrow. *Flannery O'Connor: A Study in the Short Fiction*. Boston: Twayne, 1988.

DIVAKARUNI, CHITRA (1956–)

Chitra Banerjee Divakaruni was born in Calcutta, India, and lived in several cities in India before immigrating to America at the age of 19 to pursue graduate studies in English. She earned her M.A. degree from Wright State University in Dayton and her Ph.D. from the University of California at Berkeley. Divakaruni's first collection of short stories, *Arranged Marriage* (1995), won a 1996 American Book Award as well as two regional awards given to authors from the Bay Area. An accomplished poet who has written several volumes of poetry, Divakaruni is also the author of an acclaimed first novel, *The Mistress of Spices* (1997). Involved in a variety of women's causes, since 1991 Divakaruni has been president of MAITRI, a support service for South Asian Women in the San Francisco area. Divakaruni lives near San Francisco with her husband and two sons; she teaches creative writing at Foothill College.

The title of Divakaruni's story collection becomes a METAPHOR for the immigrant experience in contemporary America, particularly the experience of women from South Asia. But while the collection insists on the powerless subservience of immigrant women in their "arranged marriage" with American culture, it also affirms their capacity for renewal and rebirth, suggesting that subservience may be transcended through self-knowledge and compassion. Divakaruni's most recent publications include one story collection, *The Unknown Errors of Our Lives: Stories* (2001), and three novels, *The Vine of Desire: A Novel* (2002), *Queen of Dreams: A Novel* (2004), and *The Place of Illusions* (2008).

BIBLIOGRAPHY

Chitra Banerjee Divakaruni Home Page. Available online. URL: http://chitradivakaruni.com/. Accessed July 16, 2009.

Divakaruni, Chitra. *Queen of Dreams: A Novel.* New York: Doubleday, 2004.

———. *The Unknown Errors of Our Lives: Stories.* New York: Doubleday, 2001.

———. *The Vine of Desire: A Novel.* New York: Doubleday, 2002.

Mehta, Julie. "Arranging One's Life: Sunnyvale Author Chitra Divakaruni Talks about Marriages and Stereotypes." *Metro: Santa Clara Valley's Weekly Newspaper,* October 3, 1996. Available online. URL: http://www.metroactive.com/papers/metro/10.03.96/books-9640html. Accessed May 1, 2009.

Keith Lawrence
Brigham Young University

DIXIE   The name for the pre–CIVIL WAR American South and for the name of the popular song entitled "I Wish I Was in Dixie's Land," composed by Daniel Decatur Emmett in 1859. A great favorite in the South, the song was taken up by the soldiers in the Confederate army during the Civil War. Fanny Crosby wrote a Union version of the text in 1861, known as "Dixie for the Union."

The origin of the word *Dixie* is obscure. It has been suggested that it is related to the Mason-Dixon line separating the North and the South during the Civil War; others believe that a Louisiana bank, printing its pre–Civil War bills in French with the word *DIX* (French for "ten") in the middle of the ten-dollar notes, made the South the land of "dixies." A further, ironic derivation is from the name of a slaveholder on Manhattan Island in the late 18th century; so benevolent was he that when his slaves were moved down south, they pined for "Dixie's land" up north.

DIXON, STEPHEN (1936–   )   Born in New York City, Stephen Dixon is a prolific, often humorous writer who has attracted a large and loyal readership. Although it was his novel *Frog* (1991) that was nominated for both the National Book Award and the PEN/ FAULKNER AWARD, Stephen Dixon is even better known as one of the finest experimental modern American short story writers. While stopping short of the anti-realistic experiments of authors such as ROBERT COOVER, Dixon nevertheless writes strikingly innovative fiction. In books like *Fourteen Stories, Movies, No Relief,* and *Long Made Short,* to name only a few, he portrays with great humor and insight the peculiar anxieties of contemporary urban life as well as the precarious conduct of our modern relationships.

Dixon's reputation is built on his short stories, and, in addition to his collections of short fiction, in 1994 he published *The Stories of Stephen Dixon,* which contains the stories Dixon himself considers to be his best over the years from 1963 to 1993. All his major themes are contained in this work, including his concern with the tenuous stability of human relationships and characters who feel trapped, cheated, or terrified by the urban scene in which so many of them must live. As a result, many of his characters speak in either incomplete, coded exchanges or non sequiturs.

His stories are both fabulous and rooted in the specific detail of everyday existence, written in a style both experimental and realistic (see REALISM) that has prompted comparisons to such early AVANT-GARDE 20th-century writers as the novelist Franz Kafka and the dramatist Samuel Beckett—and even to the imaginative writer Lewis Carroll, author of *Alice in Wonderland.* His is a prolific talent that often produces varied perceptions of Dixon as a stylist who experiments with such techniques as BLACK HUMOR, FANTASY, MAGICAL REALISM, and SURREALISM, yet who remains accessible and, to numerous readers, addictive. He has been praised for his "unpredictable" and "disturbing" qualities, his surrealism, yet also for his gifts for dialogue and narrative technique that convincingly portray the absurdities of complex, contemporary urban life, and the melancholy realities of human relationships. Although he has published no short story collections recently, Stephen Dixon has published five novels since 2000.

BIBLIOGRAPHY

Anonymous interview with Stephen Dixon (January 7, 2008). Available online. URL: http://www.failbetter.com/21/DixonInterview.php. Accessed May 1, 2009.

Barry, John. "The End of U." Interview with Stephen Dixon (July 7, 2007). Available online. URL: http://www.citypaper.com/news/story.asp?id=13229. Accessed May 1, 2009.

Chang, Young. "JHU's Stephen Dixon Reflects on His Life's Work" (October 16, 1997). Available online. URL: http://www.mcsweeneys.net/authorpages/dixon/dixon17.html. Accessed May 1, 2009.

Dixon, Stephen. *End of I.* San Francisco: McSweeney's, 2006.

———. *Falls and Rise: A Novel.* San Francisco: North Point Press, 1985.

———. *Fourteen Stories.* Baltimore: Johns Hopkins University Press. 1980.

———. *Frog.* Latham, N.Y.: British American, 1991.

———. *Gould: A Novel in Two Novels.* New York: Holt, 1997.

———. *I.* San Francisco: McSweeney's, 2002.

———. *Long Made Short.* Baltimore: Johns Hopkins University Press, 1994.

———. *Man on Stage: Play Stories.* Davis, Calif.: Hi Jinx, 1996.

———. *Meyer.* Hoboken, N.J.: Melville House, 2007.

———. *Movies.* Berkeley, Calif.: North Point Press, 1983.

———. *No Relief.* Ann Arbor, Mich.: Street Fiction Press. 1976.

———. *Old Friends.* Hoboken, N.J.: Melville House, 2004.

———. *Phone Rings.* Hoboken, N.J.: Melville House, 2005.

———. *Quite Contrary: The Mary and Newt Story.* New York: Harper, 1979.

———. *The Stories of Stephen Dixon.* New York: Holt, 1994

———. *30: Pieces of a Novel.* New York: Holt, 1999.

———. *Time to Go.* Baltimore: Johns Hopkins University Press, 1984.

———. *Tisch.* Palmdale, Calif.: Red Hen Press, 2000.

Epstein, Lee. "Stephen Dixon Week: For Intensity, an Interview with Stephen Dixon, on His Writing and His New Book." Interview with Stephen Dixon (June 11, 2002). Available online. URL: http://www.mcsweeneys.net/2002/06/13lennon.html. Accessed May 1, 2009.

Klinkowitz, Jerome. *The Self-Apparent Word.* Carbondale: Southern Illinois University Press, 1984.

———. "Stephen Dixon: Experimental Realism." *North American Review,* March 1981.

"Stephen Dixon Issue." *Ohio Journal* (Fall–Winter) 1983–84.

Stephens, Michael. *The Dramaturgy of Style.* Carbondale: Southern Illinois University Press, 1985.

Teicher, Craig Morgan. "Looking Backwards, Forward, and All Around: On Stephen Dixon" (March 4, 2008). Available online. URL: http://quietbubble.typepad.com/quietbubble/2008/03/lookingbackward.html. Accessed May 1, 2009.

"DOCTOR AND THE DOCTOR'S WIFE, THE" ERNEST HEMINGWAY (1924, 1925)

As with so many of ERNEST HEMINGWAY's short stories, "The Doctor and the Doctor's Wife" (first published in the *Transatlantic Review* and later in his collection IN OUR TIME [1925]) offers certain highly autobiographical details from Hemingway's life. In particular, the story reflects his early life growing up in the Michigan woods, as Hemingway explains in a letter to his father: "I put Dick Boulton and Billy Tabeshaw as real people with their real names because it was pretty sure they would never read the *Transatlantic Review.* I've written a number of stories about the Michigan country—the country is always true—what happens in the stories is fiction" (*Letters,* March 20, 1925, 153). Despite the apparent disclaimer, many biographers have found autobiographical parallels between the depiction of Dr. Adams and his wife and Hemingway's own father and mother.

The opening scene of the story sets the stage for the conflict between Dr. Adams and the Indian men he has hired to cut up logs for him. Dick Boulton, Billy Tabeshaw, and Eddy emerge from the wilderness heavily armed, Eddy with the long crosscut saw, Billy Tabeshaw with two large cant hooks, and Dick with three axes, and they enter a gated area that marks off Dr. Adams's territory. The ensuing conflict over who is the rightful owner of the "driftwood" logs can be seen as one more incident in the ongoing struggle for land between whites and Indians. Dr. Adams eventually backs down from the threat of violence posed by Dick Boulton and goes inside his own home, only to have his authority challenged again—this time by his wife, a practicing Christian Scientist whose faith denies the importance of his medical profession. The strain of their marriage is further symbolized by the sexual impotence underlying Dr. Adams's gesture with his gun: "He was sitting on his bed now, cleaning a shotgun. He pushed the magazine full of the heavy yellow shells and pumped them out again. They were scattered on the bed."

NICK ADAMS enters this story only in the final scene, after his mother asks Dr. Adams to send Nick to see her. Both father and son reject her request in favor of heading into the wilderness together. What they leave behind (the woman) and what they embrace (the wilderness) fulfill a pattern that will be replayed many times in Hemingway's later works.

BIBLIOGRAPHY
Baker, Carlos, ed. *Ernest Hemingway: Selected Letters, 1917–1961.* New York: Scribner's, 1981.
Smith, Paul. *A Reader's Guide to the Short Stories of Ernest Hemingway.* Boston: G. K. Hall, 1989.

Amy Strong
University of North Carolina at Chapel Hill

DOCTOROW, E. L. (EDGAR LAWRENCE DOCTOROW) (1931–)

E. L. Doctorow cannot be readily assigned to any single school of contemporary fiction; rather, his works synthesize various important strains in postmodernist writing. (See POSTMODERNISM.) Doctorow's formal inventiveness, wit, and covertly apocalyptic philosophy link him with such practitioners of METAFICTION as THOMAS PYNCHON, DONALD BARTHELME, and JOHN BARTH; his fascination with "facts"—invented or real—links him with new journalists and "nonfiction novelists." The new journalists, who reported on news stories using a first-person narrative voice (see POINT OF VIEW) as well as writerly observation, insight, and wit, included such practitioners as TRUMAN CAPOTE, NORMAN MAILER, and Tom Wolfe; nonfiction novelists used all the tools of fiction to write about an actual event, as exemplified in Capote's *In Cold Blood* (1966). But Doctorow decries the self-reflexivity of much contemporary fiction.

Although best known as a novelist, particularly for *Ragtime* (1975), a historical work set in the 1920s, and *The Book of Daniel* (1971), based on the execution of Julius and Ethel Rosenberg, Doctorow has also written "The Songs of Billy Bathgate" (1968) and *Lives of the Poets* (1984), a story collection focusing on the characters' inner tensions between past and present, memory and reality. The concluding novella, containing a writer whose life resembles Doctorow's, unifies the entire collection with its suggestion that contemporary literature lacks purpose and that the writer exists on the fringes as a marginal entity. Since 2000, E. L. Doctorow has written two novels (including the award-winning Civil War novel *The March*), essays, screenplays, and a story collection entitled *Sweet Land Stories* (2004).

Born in New York City, Doctorow is a recipient of the National Book Critics Circle Award and an American Academy Award, both in 1976.

BIBLIOGRAPHY
Bloom, Harold, ed. *E. L. Doctorow.* Philadelphia: Chelsea House, 2002.
Doctorow, E. L. *City of God.* New York: Random House, 2000.
———. *Creationists: Selected Essays, 1993–2006.* New York: Random House, 2006.
——— *Lamentation 9/11.* Photographs by David Finn. New York: Ruder-Fin Press, 2002.
———. *Lives of the Poets: Six Stones and a Novella.* New York: Random House, 1984.
———. *The March.* New York: Random House, 2005.
———. *Reporting the Universe.* Cambridge, Mass.: Harvard University Press, 2003.
———. "The Songs of Billy Bathgate." In *New American Review,* Vol. 2. Edited by Theodore Solotaroff. New York: New American Library, 1968.
———. *Sweet Land Stories.* New York: Random House, 2004.
Doctorow, E. L., and Katrina Kenison, eds. *The Best American Short Stories 2000.* Boston: Houghton Mifflin, 2000.
Levine, Paul. *E. L. Doctorow.* London: Methuen, 1985.
Trenner, Richard, ed. *E. L. Doctorow: Essays and Conversations.* Princeton, N.J.: Ontario Review Press, 1983.

DOERR, HARRIET (1910–2002) The acclaimed author of *Stones for Ibarra,* a widely praised collection of interlocking short stories that won the American Book Award in 1984, Harriet Doerr also wrote a well-reviewed novel entitled *Consider This, Senora* and, in 1996, *The Tiger in the Grass,* a collection of 15 stories and "inventions," as Doerr called them. She died on November 24, 2002, of complications of a broken hip, in Pasadena, California. The granddaughter of the railroad tycoon Henry Edwards Huntington, whose estate now encompasses the Huntington Library, Art Collections, and Botanical Gardens, Harriet Doerr made a literary name for herself and a deep impression on the reading and television-viewing public for her artistically rendered tales of Mexicans and Americans confronting each other's similarities and differences. Doerr composed the majority of her stories by drawing on her memories of her many years in Mexico.

Stones for Ibarra is comprised of the stories that result when Richard and Sara Everton move from San Francisco to an old family home and abandoned mine in Mexico. The mood of the entire collection is established in the opening story, in which Richard and Sara lose their way. The tales involve a sense of rootlessness and also an intimacy with death: The narrator reveals that Richard is dying of cancer and segues into a LYRICAl but realistic (see REALISM) comparison of the American and Mexican attitudes toward death. Related to the THEMES of death and loss is the Evertons' desire to connect the present with the past. Although at first they have trouble understanding the Mexicans' very different attitudes toward these issues, the stories gradually reveal the way the Evertons learn life-changing lessons from their neighbors.

One of the most memorable images—in a work renowned for its lyrical, imagistic style—is of the window into Sara and Richard's house. Doerr invites the reader, along with the Mexican neighbors, to peer into the windows of the foreigners, the Evertons, and watch them gradually reveal themselves. The timelessness of the stones of the landscape, too, and their association with death and eternity provide another central METAPHOR that links these stories. Doerr is adept at humor as well, presenting all her characters, Mexican and American, in both their ignorance and their wisdom.

Critics have observed that the story of Richard, Sarah, and their Mexican friends is set on a landscape that remains both constant and surprising, described in a narrative tone of affectionate and patient wisdom. Perhaps the cumulative effect results from the author's long germination period: Harriet Doerr received her B.A. at age 67 and published this (her first) book a year later. *The Tiger in the Grass,* her most recent story collection, again uses memory as a LEITMOTIF. This collection reveals the same startling sensitivity and sculpted prose with which Doerr habitually conjures the light, smells, and sounds of Mexico with enrapturing clarity, creating characters both amusing and tragic. Reviewers note that the precision of Doerr's style is probably the felicitous result of her having kept her stories to herself for so long, polishing every image, every story, with striking and unforgettable gemlike clarity.

BIBLIOGRAPHY
Doerr, Harriet, *Consider This, Senora.* New York: Penguin, 1993.
———. *Stones for Ibarra.* New York: Penguin, 1984.
———. *The Tiger in the Grass: Stories and Other Inventions.* New York: Penguin, 1996.

"DOE SEASON" DAVID MICHAEL KAPLAN (1985) Originally published together with 11 other DAVID MICHAEL KAPLAN stories, all dealing with parent-child relationships, in a collection entitled *Comfort,* "Doe Season" was selected for the volume *Best American Short Stories* for the year 1985. Set in Pennsylvania's snowy winter woods, it is a classic coming-of-age story, focusing both on the steps in nine-year-old Andrea's rite of passage as well as on the existential issues of how we discover who we are and how we find our place in the world.

A rite of passage, traditionally meant to mark a new and significant phase in an adolescent's life, consists of three major segments: separation from the familiar and isolation, frequently in a "wild" or "natural" setting; a task to be performed or obstacle to be overcome, often including interaction with a totem animal; and the eventual return to society with a changed status. Andrea's 48-hour experience follows each of these steps closely. Nicknamed *Andy,* she leaves the comforts of home, represented by her mother's rather stereotyped figure and behavior, to go hunting in the woods with her father; she finds herself in a position where she must shoot the doe that she has found and then reflect on the meaning of her act; aided by an owl and the deer itself, both of which are totem animals revered in Native American cultures, she gains insight into her own identity, rejects the nickname *Andy,* and accepts her return home and her feminine nature. It is even interesting to contemplate whether or not Andrea's dream encounter with the deer and her subsequent flight from the dawn gutting of the animal might reflect the physically demanding all-night vigil and running at dawn required by the Navajo for a girl-child to be considered a woman.

The dream sequence itself has definite overtones of magic realism: "Kaplan infuses his stories with another reality; apparitions and magic, a demon and a witch, mystical events that seem like dreams but may not be" (Gold). The author himself has said that "encounters with an animal that is surrealistic . . . are very primal ones, in other words, pulling something deep and chthonic from one's unconscious" (http://faculty.nwacc.edu/ljlovell/Kaplan.htm). And the meaning of the dream? An ecocritical reading might claim that when we touch the heart of nature, we discover who we really are.

But "Doe Season" is also a story built around mirror images, the most obvious of which are male-female, woods-ocean, life-death, light-dark, morning-night, sleep-wake, and summer-winter. Although seemingly opposites, these issues provide a strong sense of continuity, since all are in fact part of a larger whole, part of the cycle of life. Reinforcing such an ecocritical reading is the vision of Gaia, the female representing or connecting with nature versus the traditionally male sport of killing. Throughout the story Andrea is deeply aware of the enormity and beauty of the woods; animals approach her without fear; she is reluctant to shoot the doe and wills it to run away; after shooting it, she feels instant remorse, "What have I done?" (97). In a 2003 virtual conference with students at Northwest Arkansas Community College, Kaplan predicts that Andrea will "pull more and more away from her father's world and move more and more toward her ultimate biological/psychological destiny as a young woman. That after all is what the greater hunt of 'Doe Season' has been, really" (http://faculty.nwacc.edu/ljlovell/Kaplan.htm).

BIBLIOGRAPHY

Gold, Sarah. *Village Voice,* 2 June 1987, p. 50.
Kaplan, David Michael. "Doe Season." In *Comfort.* New York: Viking, 1987.
Levy, Laurie. Review of *Comfort. Chicago Magazine,* September 1987.
"Q & A with David Michael Kaplan." Available online. URL: http://faculty.nwacc.edu/ljlovell/Kaplan.htm. Accessed May 1, 2009.
Soete, Mary. Review of *Comfort. Library Journal,* January 1987, pp. 107–108.
Steinberg, Sybil. Review of *Comfort. Publishers Weekly,* 26 December 1986, p. 47.
Wood, Susan. Review of *Comfort. New York Times Book Review,* 14 June 1987, p. 41.

Jeri Pollock
Our Lady of Mercy School
Rio de Janeiro, Brazil

DON JUAN   The archetype of the romantic lover, the "Don Juan type" has evolved and appeared in many forms, but his most enduring is that of his first appearance in Tirso de Molina's *El Burlador de Sevilla,* which gave the HERO the identity that he has retained ever since: Don Juan, a nobleman of Seville. The internal complications of his nature have endlessly fascinated writers and composers, and the name of Tirso's hero quickly became a synonym for an obsessive and unscrupulous pursuer of women. The most famous of all forms of the story is undoubtedly Mozart's great opera *Don Giovanni* (1787), written to a libretto by Lorenzo da Ponte. Another noteworthy musical work is Richard Strauss's tone poem *Don Juan* (1888). In literature, Byron immortalized him in the poem *Don Juan,* begun in 1819 and unfinished at his death. Many short fiction writers allude (see ALLUSION) directly or indirectly to Don Juan–like characters, as in ZORA NEALE HURSTON's "The Gilded Six-Bits," or use such contemporary ironic inversions as ARNOLD

FRIEND in JOYCE CAROL OATES's "WHERE ARE YOU GOING, WHERE HAVE YOU BEEN?," Manley Pointer in FLANNERY O'CONNOR's "GOOD COUNTRY PEOPLE," or COUSIN LYMAN in CARSON MCCULLERS's "THE BALLAD OF THE SAD CAFE."

DON QUIXOTE MIGUEL DE CERVANTES (1605, 1615)

A novel by MIGUEL DE CERVANTES credited by many as the first Western novel. Alonso Quijano is a country gentleman, kindly and dignified, who lives in the province of La Mancha. His mind is so crazed by reading chivalric romances that he believes himself called on to redress the wrongs of the whole world. Changing his name to *Don Quixote de la Mancha,* he asks Sancho Panza, an ignorant rustic, to be his squire, with whom he enjoys various adventures. Although it is generally agreed that Cervantes meant his novel to be a SATIRE on the exaggerated chivalric romances of his time, some critics have interpreted it as an ironic story of an idealist frustrated and mocked in a materialistic world, while others see it more specifically as a commentary on the Catholic Church, contemporary Spain, or the Spanish character. Many American writers have used the story, both humorously and satirically, from WASHINGTON IRVING's Ichabod Crane in "The LEGEND OF SLEEPY HOLLOW" to WILLIAM FAULKNER's GAVIN STEVENS in KNIGHT'S GAMBIT to JAMES THURBER's "The SECRET LIFE OF WALTER MITTY."

"DON'T TELL ME YOU DON'T KNOW" DOROTHY ALLISON (1988)

"Those twin emotions, love and outrage, warred in me. . . . Nothing was clean between us, especially not our love." In these two sentences, the narrator of "Don't Tell Me You Don't Know" gives the reader a snapshot of what it means to live in the push-pull of a working-class family where women value their daughters more than anything but cannot or will not save them from the abuses of their abused men. The narrator is DOROTHY ALLISON herself, and her story is a testimony to both the strength of her female family and her own strength in seeking both her own safety and her own bond with those she loves.

The plot of the story centers on Allison's aunt, Alma, driving hundreds of miles to fetch Allison back home, where her mother is pining away for her. Allison is living a life of her own construction, born out of her politics and personal desires: She is living in a small lesbian commune, with a commitment to her writing and a refusal to participate in any of the elements of domesticity that she felt so oppressive to her and her aunts and mother. Aunt Alma arrives in righteous contempt, seeing Allison as living an empty life because it seems to be about personal pleasure and ambition, with no valuing of what should be the cornerstone of her existence—family devotion. Alma wants to know why Allison has stopped talking to her mother, and why her mother has turned to such deep despair. Alma, if she cannot rescue her dear niece, is determined to take that niece back to restore her sister.

The revelation of what has driven Allison to cut ties with her aunts and mother is unveiled as the aunt plays pool with herself as she lectures Allison. Allison watches her aunt, admiring her incredible strength and confidence, lamenting that she has needed all that strength and more to endure the way poverty has destroyed men and women in her family, longing for the love the woman gives and at the same time furious that she did not use that strength to protect Allison when she was a child. Allison has told her mother exactly why she cannot have the babies that her family tells her it is her duty to have—a duty to love and family endurance: Allison's stepfather raped her for years when she was a child, and her mother did nothing to protect her or acknowledge the problem because she could not raise the kids without his income, and because doing so would disrupt the family. Because Allison's stepfather had a venereal disease that he passed on to Allison, she found out that she is sterile. But she is also ravaged by violation and betrayal in a way that makes her at all costs want to escape her family—especially the women who colluded to keep her rape a dirty secret. When her mother's nagging about the importance of children pushes Allison to the edge, she rips into her mother with the truth, that the mother's betrayal of her daughter is what led to her not only to be unable to produce more children but also to see her family as sacrificing female children to hold on to men undeserving of loyalty.

Aunt Alma pushes Allison to a confession she had left in order not to upset her family even more, and Allison, tired of being shamed as antifamily, lashes at her for being a hypocrite: "Don't tell me you don't know" is implicit in her accusation of her mother and her aunt. Allison feels most betrayed not even by the rape but by the way the women she loved sacrificed her in the name of the survival of the family as a whole. Throughout the story to its end, what tears the narrator apart is the unbreakable bond of love she has for the women in her family, the knowledge that the will to survival and the courage to face pain pour like a river from them into her being, and the inescapable fact that working-class women will do anything, even let their children be hurt, in order to support and maintain their men in a world that is out to destroy them physically and psychologically.

A shallow interpretation of this story would be to call it an incest narrative, but Allison is adamant that her work is political, not merely confessional. In the preface to the collection *Trash,* in which this story appears, she writes: "I write stories. I write fiction. I put on the page a third look at what I've seen in life—the condensed and reinvented experience of a cross-eyed working-class lesbian . . . who has made a decision to live, is determined to live, on the page and in the street, for me and mine." Most incest narratives are framed in terms of the individual striking back at the family and branching out on her or his own. Allison, however, insists on solidarity, on an economic analysis of the forces distorting the strength of the working-class family. Her lesbianism, she makes clear in this story and others, is not the main source of her alienation—indeed, it is her solace in its offer of love and community. When she titles the story "Don't Tell Me You Don't Know," it is also an accusation to the reader, asking whether we, too, refuse to see how we collude in the trashing of people, the victimizing of the most vulnerable.

Her work has the key feature of most working-class writing: to argue against the middle-class impulse to dismiss the poor as deserving of their oppression and as solely responsible for their problems (in a word, that they are "trash"), and to offer a testimonial to the family as courageous and committed in spite of strife.

When Aunt Alma and Allison reconcile but do not resolve their division, they share a single word to say what each is worth to the other, both saying, "Precious." Aunt Alma says it to mean that Allison, even if she does not become a mother, is deeply loved as a daughter, and always wanted. Allison, in saying it, affirms that the love for her mother and aunts, even though not "clean" and riven with a sense of betrayal, is inescapable, is essential, and is life itself to her.

BIBLIOGRAPHY
Allison, Dorothy. "Don't Tell Me You Don't Know." In *Trash*. Ithaca, N.Y.: Firebrand Books, 1988.

Carolyn Whitson
Metrostate University

DOPPELGANGER   From the German "double" and "walker," an apparition that generally represents another side of a CHARACTER's personality. The doppelganger can personify one's demonic counterpart (as in E. T. A. Hoffman's *The Devil's Elixirs*, 1816), or an ALTER EGO, as in EDGAR ALLAN POE's "William Wilson" (1839). Frequently the appearance of the apparition presages imminent death. For suggestive modern variations on the doppelganger THEME, see also WILLIAM FAULKNER's "Elly," PETER TAYLOR's "First Confession," and M. Evelina Gulang's "Talk to Me, Milagros" in *Her Wild American Self.*

"DOUBLE BIRTHDAY" WILLA CATHER (1929)
First published in *Forum,* "Double Birthday" is one of many stories by WILLA CATHER that celebrate idiosyncrasy while contemplating its costs. Two Albert Engelhardts, an uncle and his nephew, born on the same day 25 years apart, value art, beauty, and intense emotional experiences over the disciplined life that produces social approval and material security. Pitied needlessly by their old friends in prestigious circles, the two bachelors share unusual priorities and the top floor of a shabby house in a working-class district. At 80, Dr. Engelhardt's life is animated by memories of a young German singer he discovered and in whom he invested money and faith, believing her destined for brilliance until her death of cancer at age 26. The loss left him desolate but deeply gratified to have experi-

enced the extremity of passion that leads to sacrifice. One of the ironies in the story's romantic vision (see ROMANTICISM) is that what one loses can become a permanent treasure. The younger Albert, now 55, spent his share of the family fortune on art and travel, enjoying every moment completely but never planning financially for the future. On their shared birthday, they toast their past devotions, not without a sense of loneliness. In their company is Margaret Parmenter, a wealthy friend from the past that Cather uses to register the men's odd sincerity, which moves her to renew their lapsed friendship despite her vastly different social class.

Told in dialogue and third-person description (see POINT OF VIEW), the story includes FLASHBACKS that unite the characters' past and present lives. Rather than nostalgic, the story's mood is vigorous, almost insistent, in its romanticism, suggesting that Cather's purpose is not to evoke the charm of old memories but to assert the simultaneous and vigorous appearance of both past and present in these characters' recollections.

BIBLIOGRAPHY

Arnold, Marilyn. *Willa Cather's Short Fiction.* Athens: Ohio University Press, 1984.

Cather, Willa. *Uncle Valentine and Other Stories: Willa Cather's Uncollected Short Fiction, 1915–1929.* Edited by Bernice Slote. Lincoln: University of Nebraska Press, 1973.

Frances Kerr
Durham Technical Community College

DOUGLASS, FREDERICK (1817?–1895)

The son of a slave and a white man, Douglass, an American abolitionist, orator, and journalist, escaped to the North in 1838. A speech he delivered at an antislavery convention in Nantucket in 1841 made such an impression that he was soon in great demand as a speaker. Mobbed and beaten because of his views, he described his experiences in the outspoken *Narrative of the Life of Frederick Douglass* (1845). He also founded and for 17 years published the *North Star,* a newspaper that advocated the use of black troops during the CIVIL WAR and civil rights for freedmen. Douglass was the first African American to speak publicly and to write about his experiences.

DREISER, THEODORE (1871–1945)

Born in Terre Haute, Indiana, Theodore Dreiser grew up in a poor family that was forced to move often and, as Dreiser later told his friend and literary adviser H. L. Mencken, could not always afford shoes for all 10 children. Dreiser's siblings had a reputation for being tough, wild, and flirtatious. His father, although briefly successful as a wool manufacturer, was destitute after his factory burned down and he could not repay the debt for fleece and machinery bought on credit. Dreiser's fiction draws on this background: It breaks with conventional literary gentility, and it chronicles with accuracy and compassion the economic struggles and intimate lives of men and women.

Dreiser is primarily known as a novelist, but his best short stories show a sophisticated understanding of the short story form, perhaps because Dreiser worked in journalism throughout his life. After a string of odd jobs in Chicago, Dreiser finally escaped his family's poverty by working as a reporter. As a freelancer, he wrote popular pieces, including portraits of famous people and places. For several years he edited the *Delineator,* a popular women's magazine published by Butterick, the sewing pattern company.

Dreiser's experience in journalism did not, however, guarantee success for his stories. HARPER'S and ATLANTIC MONTHLY published some of his nonfiction work, but they repeatedly rejected his stories. "The Last Phoebe" (1914), a sad tale of an old man searching vainly for his dead wife, was rejected by more than 10 magazines, even though Dreiser reduced his asking price from $600 to less than $200. Editors judged that Dreiser's stories were not what the public wanted. After publishing "Free" (1918), a story about an unhappily married man, the SATURDAY EVENING POST received many complaints from readers who thought the story promoted divorce. In 1918 *Redbook* rejected a story because the characters were German.

Dreiser's best short fiction explores THEMES similar to those in his novels—the allure of big cities, the power of sexual desire, the appeal of money, and the erosion of traditional mores. Dreiser's first novel, *Sister Carrie,* portrays the rise of a poor girl to stardom in Broadway musicals and the decline of a well-to-do businessman into homelessness. The novel is based, in part, on the life of his sister Emma, and Dreiser describes without judgment the sexual liaisons of his unmarried HEROINE. The sexuality of young women is also the subject of Dreiser's second novel, *Jennie Gerhardt,* and of the short story "OLD ROGAUM AND HIS THERESA."

Dreiser was often accused of immorality in his life as well as his work. He was married twice, had several affairs, and was charged with adultery while in Kentucky reporting on a coal miners' strike. Dreiser insisted that sexual desire should not be judged by conventional mores, and although the publishing house of Doubleday effectively suppressed *Sister Carrie,* publishing it but never advertising it, Dreiser continued to write honestly, although never crudely, about sexuality.

Dreiser's training as a journalist is evident in much of his work. In "NIGGER JEFF," a disturbing tale of a cub reporter sent to cover a lynching, Dreiser suggests that good journalism requires a strong aesthetic sense (see AESTHETICISM). His most acclaimed novel, *An American Tragedy* (1925), is a fictional reworking of a much-publicized trial of a young man who murdered his pregnant working-class girlfriend. Dreiser's style is often reportorial, thick with details and facts.

Many of Dreiser's best short stories are collected in *Free and Other Stories* (1918), and many of his best CHARACTER sketches are in *Twelve Men* (1919). Other collections include *Chains: Lesser Novels and Stories* (1927) and *A Gallery of Women* (1929).

Dreiser was deeply influenced by the social philosophers of the day, in particular Herbert Spenser, and his work is often considered part of American literary NATURALISM. Dreiser's fiction does not, however, describe only determined lives. He also portrays with great compassion the inchoate yearnings of characters who are pushed and pulled by the forces of desire, nature, and society. Dreiser's style and philosophy have, at times, been maligned as clumsy and unsophisticated. Nevertheless, he was a major influence on young writers, and his fiction offers astute, realistic (see REALISM), and moving representations of the desires and lives of ordinary people.

BIBLIOGRAPHY

Dreiser, Theodore. *An American Tragedy.* New York: Boni & Liveright, 1925.

———. *Chains: Lesser Novels and Stories.* New York: Boni & Liveright, 1927.

———. *Free and Other Stories.* New York: Boni & Liveright, 1918.

———. *A Gallery of Women.* New York: Horace Liveright, 1929.

———. *Jennie Gerhardt.* New York: Boni & Liveright, 1911.

———. *Sister Carrie.* New York: Doubleday, Page & Copy, 1900.

———. *Twelve Men.* New York: Boni & Liveright, 1919.

Gerber, Philip L. *Theodore Dreiser.* New York: Twayne, 1964.

Griffin, Joseph. *The Small Canvas: An Introduction to Dreiser's Short Stories.* Rutherford, N.J.: Fairleigh Dickinson University Press, 1985.

Lingeman, Richard. *Theodore Dreiser.* 2 vols. New York: Putnam, 1986.

Menken, H. L. "Theodore Dreiser." In *A Book of Prefaces.* Garden City, N.Y.: Doubleday 1917.

Swanberg, W. A. *Dreiser.* New York: Scribner, 1965.

Stephanie Browner
Berea College

"DR. HEIDEGGER'S EXPERIMENT"
NATHANIEL HAWTHORNE (1837) A mendicant, a hedonist, a ruined politician, and a scandalous widow all answer the summons of their friend, a doctor, in NATHANIEL HAWTHORNE's 1837 tale "Dr. Heidegger's Experiment." He calls these aging friends to his study to participate in an experiment—one that intrigues them because "They were all melancholy old creatures" (67) and because the experiment Dr. Heidegger has in mind appeals to their vanity. Watching them experience its results seems to appeal to his sense of entertainment. Is that entertainment a mere masquerade, a magician's trick, an evening of intoxication due to alcohol and vivid imaginations, or something more than any of these labels suggests? Does the tale offer a cynical statement about humans and their history, or does it actually comment upon the magical effects of fiction?

The magic of the evening centers around the age-old quest for the Fountain of Youth. Dr. Heidegger—a bachelor whose fiancée died on the eve before their wedding because she accidentally took one of his medicines, who practices his science not in a laboratory but in a study complete with a mirror and a big black book of magic, and who has somehow managed to age gracefully—invites to his home the friends he labels "venerable" (67). Those supposedly respectable individuals, however, include Mr. Medbourne, a once-successful merchant who has lost everything because of risky speculation; Colonel Killigrew, who has made a life of pleasure seeking and now suffers the physical ailments of the debauched; Mr. Gascoigne, a politician who has lost all credibility because of his disreputable deals; and the widow Clara Wycherly, a once-beautiful woman of questionable sexual morals who once was lover to all three men but now has become a wrinkled recluse. Dr. Heidegger announces that he would like to share with them another of his "experiments with which I amuse myself" (67) and even offers a convincing preview to persuade them to agree to participate. Dr. Heidegger restores a withered, dead rose to life by dipping it in what he calls the Water of Youth. In spite of Dr. Heidegger's performance, the group believes it can be nothing more than "a very pretty deception" (70), and as if to emphasize that point for Hawthorne, the narrator asks the reader twice, "Was it illusion?" (72, 75).

But before Dr. Heidegger's guests have the opportunity to contemplate the validity of the results, he pours them large wine glasses full of the Waters of Youth, and they imbibe. He, however, remains but a scientific observer, a voyeur of sorts, for he says—or perhaps warns—"For my part, having had much trouble in growing old, I am in no hurry to grow young again" (70). He also issues an explicit edict before he allows them to drink heartily of the waters: "It would be well that, with the experience of a lifetime to direct you, you should draw up a few general rules for your guidance, in passing a second time through the perils of youth. Think what a sin it would be if, with your peculiar advantages, you should not become patterns if virtue" (71). But they barely heed his words or his sarcasm or even pause to consider the fact that he refuses to join them. Instead, immediately

after the first round, they begin to feel the effects of the concoction and beg for another round because they want to feel and look even younger. They begin to see each other and themselves as much younger and begin to act accordingly. The narrator says of the politician's ramblings that no one could tell whether they were "relating to the past, present, or future . . . since the same ideas and phrases have been in vogue these fifty years" (72). His emphasis on time—and repetition—seems calculated to slant the reader toward a view that the text demonstrates that the present is no better than the future. An accentuation of such a conclusion is the behavior of all four: They repeat the unwise actions of their youth, for the men begin fighting over Clara. In their struggling, they knock over the vase containing the Water of Youth, and all of its contents spill on the floor, where it revives a dying butterfly.

To restore the civility of his friends, Dr. Heidegger must step in and break up the fight. As he does so, the rose—now out of the water—withers and dies and the butterfly, too, falls to its death again. They only foreshadow what soon becomes of the four guests: They too revert to their aged status. Dr. Heidegger announces that they have taught him a lesson: "I would not stop to bathe my lips in [the Water]" (75). He expresses pure dismay at their actions, their mere repetition of the past, as if their life knowledge has had no effect upon their second chance at youth. They, however, have learned nothing—either from their lives or from their recent experience with the experiment. They tell Dr. Heidegger that they will themselves go to Florida and find and drink constantly the Waters of Youth. They seek a recaptured vitality that Dr. Heidegger has already proven they will waste. Or has the tale merely woven its magic for a fleeting time to suspend its players and its readers in the land of imagination? Have the artist and his art been but illusion, with no moral to convey?

BIBLIOGRAPHY

Bell, Millicent, ed. *New Essays on Hawthorne's Major Tales.* Cambridge: Cambridge University Press, 1993.

Cameron, Sharon. *The Corporeal Self: Allegories of the Body in Melville and Hawthorne.* Baltimore: Johns Hopkins University Press, 1981.

Crews, Frederick C. *The Sins of the Father: Hawthorne's Psychological Themes.* New York: Oxford University Press, 1966.

Fogle, Richard Hurter. *Hawthorne's Fiction: The Light and the Dark.* Norman: University of Oklahoma Press, 1964, pp. 41–58.

Hawthorne, Nathaniel. "Dr. Heidegger's Experiment." In *Selected Short Stories,* edited by Alfred Kazin, 67–76. Greenwich, Conn.: Fawcett, 1966.

Kazin, Alfred. "Introduction." In *Selected Short Stories,* edited by Alfred Kazin. Greenwich, Conn.: Fawcett, 1966.

Male, Roy. *Hawthorne's Tragic Vision.* Austin: University of Texas Press, 1957.

Miller, Edwin Haviland. *Salem Is My Dwelling Place: A Life of Nathaniel Hawthorne.* Iowa City: University of Iowa Press, 1991.

Scanlon, Lawrence E. "The Very Singular Man, Dr. Heidegger." *Nineteenth-Century Fiction* 17 (December 1962): 253–263.

Stein, William Bysshe. *A Study of the Devil Archetype.* Gainesville: University of Florida Press, 1953.

Von Frank, Albert J. *Critical Essays on Hawthorne's Short Stories.* Boston: G. K. Hall, 1991.

Wallace, James D. "Stowe and Hawthorne." In *Hawthorne and Women: Engendering and Expanding the Hawthorne Tradition,* edited by John L. Idol, Jr., 92–103. Amherst: University of Massachusetts Press, 1999.

Patricia J. Sehulster
State University of New York,
Westchester Community College

DRUSILLA HAWKE One of WILLIAM FAULKNER's finest and most sympathetic, if enigmatic, characters, Drusilla appears in several stories in *The UNVANQUISHED.* On one level it is possible to view her, with her tragic destiny, as metaphoric of the American South during and after the CIVIL WAR; on another she becomes emblematic of Faulkner's many heroic women who, although technically defeated by outside (male) forces, remain defiantly "unvanquished." She is the prototypical young woman who runs races faster and rides horses better than any man, and who actually joins the Confederate army disguised as a man, yet is beaten by "those skirts" she is forced to wear. Her name, vaguely reminiscent of Druids and pre-Christian rituals combined with the warlike bird, makes her an astonishingly strong and unique character in the Faulkner canon of short stories and novels alike.

DUBOIS, W. E. B. (WILLIAM EDWARD BURGHARDT DUBOIS) (1868–1963) W. E. B. DuBois was an American civil rights leader and writer. The descendant of a French Huguenot and an African slave, DuBois received his B.A., M.A., and Ph.D. degrees from Harvard. Among the first important leaders to advocate complete economic, political, and social equality for blacks, DuBois cofounded the National Negro committee (later the NAACP) in 1909. He taught history and economics at Atlanta University from 1897 to 1910 and from 1932 to 1944. In the intervening years, he served as editor of the NAACP magazine, *Crisis.* He lived the last two years of his life in Ghana, joined the Communist Party, and edited the *African Encyclopedia for Africans.* Among his many influential writings are *The Souls of Black Folk* (1903), *John Brown* (1909), and *The Black Flame* (1957). His *Autobiography* appeared posthumously in 1968. Often called the intellectual father of black Americans, DuBois was a significant factor in shaping the aims of the writers connected with the HARLEM RENAISSANCE. His influence also can be seen in the work of LANGSTON HUGHES and ZORA NEALE HURSTON.

DUBUS, ANDRE (1936–1999) Although he began writing in the early 1960s, Dubus shares little with the magical realists (see MAGIC REALISM) or even the postmodernists (see POSTMODERNISM)—writers such as JOHN BARTH and ROBERT COOVER—whose fiction manipulates language, logic, and reality, flouting the boundaries of writing. Dubus's fiction, instead, concerns itself with ordinary people enduring, sometimes suffering through, ordinary lives. His characters are largely blue-collar people: construction workers, bartenders, waitresses, and mechanics. They inhabit the Merrimack Valley, a cluster of dying mill towns and old farms located north of Boston.

Andre Dubus, the son of André Jules and Katherine (Burke) Dubus, was born August 11, 1936, in Lake Charles, Louisiana. After graduating from Christian Brothers High School, Lafayette (1954), and McNeese State College, Lake Charles (1958), he was commissioned a second lieutenant in the U.S. Marine Corps. In 1963 Captain Dubus resigned his commission and enrolled in the University of Iowa's Writers' Workshop program. After completing both his M.F.A. (1965) and a brief teaching assignment in Louisiana, Dubus began teaching at Bradford College in Massachusetts, where he remained until retiring to write full time in 1984. Over a half-dozen story collections, two novels, and an essay collection later, Dubus was one of the most highly regarded American short story writers of the late 20th century. His awards include two National Endowment for the Arts Grants (1978 and 1985), two Guggenheim Grants (1977 and 1986), and the MacArthur Fellowship (1988).

Dubus's stories are emotionally bruising accounts of shattered marriages, fractured families, and daily struggles with faith. While there is much of the Hemingway tradition in Dubus's language, his female characters are fellow sufferers. And although his fiction is often compared to that of RAYMOND CARVER, Dubus's fictional landscape is more spiritually lush, his humanism more forgiving. In "A Father's Story," for example, a father chooses to protect his daughter by covering up her crime, an accidental vehicular homicide. Both Dubus's Catholicism and his Marine Corps experience seem to infuse his stories: His characters often either struggle for structure or hunger for spirituality as they grapple with the messiness of their lives.

In July 1986, while going to the aid of a stranded motorist, Dubus was struck by a car and lost his left leg in the accident. Many of the essays in *Broken Vessels* (1991) concern the implications of his accident. They are without self-pity but can be as wrenching as his fiction: In one Dubus relates how he watches helplessly as his baby daughter crawls away from his wheelchair toward an exercise bicycle and, disregarding his shouts of warning, inserts her finger into the cycle's sprocket, severing her finger.

But Dubus was primarily a short story writer, and in *Broken Vessels* he explains his affection for the genre in which he excelled: "I love short stories because I believe they are the way we live. They are what our friends tell us, in their pain and joy, their passion and rage, their yearning and their cry against injustice" (104).

See also "The FAT GIRL."

BIBLIOGRAPHY

Dubus, Andre. *Adultery and Other Choices*. Boston: Godine, 1977.

———. *Broken Vessels*. Boston: Godine, 1991.

———. *Dancing After Hours*. New York: Knopf, 1996.

———. *Finding a Girl in America: Ten Stories and a Novella*. Boston: Godine, 1980.

———. *In the Bedroom*. New York: Vintage, 2002.

———. *The Last Worthless Evening: Four Novellas and Two Stories*. Boston: Godine, 1986.

———. *The Lieutenant*. New York: Dial Press, 1967.

———. *Separate Flights*. Boston: Godine, 1975.

———. *The Times Are Never So Bad: A Novella and Eight Short Stories*. Boston: Godine, 1983.

———. *Voices from the Moon*. Boston: Godine, 1984.

———. *We Don't Live Here Anymore*. New York: Crown, 1984.

Kennedy, Thomas E. *Andre Dubus: A Study of the Short Fiction*. Boston: Twayne, 1988.

Michael Hogan
University of North Carolina at Chapel Hill

DUNBAR, PAUL LAURENCE (1872–1906)

Poet and short story writer noted for his use of African THEMES and DIALECT, Dunbar wrote during the time REGIONALISM was in vogue and was almost unquestionably influenced by Thomas Nelson Page (see AFRICAN-AMERICAN SHORT FICTION). The son of former Kentucky slaves, Dunbar was fascinated to hear his mother's stories and his father's tales of his experiences as a Union soldier during the CIVIL WAR. This love of stories translated into the publication of his first story and, shortly afterward, with the financial help of his former schoolmates Orville and Wilbur Wright, the collection *Oak and Ivy* in 1893. Dunbar's poetry lacks the bitterness of the work of later black writers. He also wrote novels, including *The Uncalled* (1898) and *The Sport of the Gods* (1902).

Dunbar's best story collection is probably *The Strength of Gideon and Other Stories,* published in 1900. Its 20 narratives cover a broad range. Some treat the imagined loyalty of former slaves both tenderly and sarcastically; others examine the hostility of the Northern environment and the shortcomings of urban life. The tales of RECONSTRUCTION, set in a time when blacks were attempting to become part of the body politic, remain pertinent today. Perhaps nowhere is the indifference of the white political structure more poignantly presented than in "Mr. Cornelius Johnson, Office Seeker." Johnson is both a believing fool and a sad figure of a man who is not only a victim but also a victimizer. His hope for a political future in payment for his support of white politicians understanding of the political process are told with an admirable economy of language—as in the ironic use of *Mr.* in the title.

BIBLIOGRAPHY

Brawley, Benjamin. *Paul Laurence Dunbar: Poet of His People.* Chapel Hill, N.C.: University of North Carolina Press, 1936.

Cunningham, Virginia. *Paul Laurence Dunbar and His Song.* New York: Dodd, Mead, 1947.

Dunbar, Paul Laurence. *The Fanatics.* New York: Dodd, Mead, 1901. Reprint, Salem, N.H.: Ayer, 1991.

———. *Folks from Dixie.* New York: Dodd, Mead, 1898. Reprint, Freeport, N.Y.: Books for Libraries, 1971.

———. *The Heart of Happy Hollow.* New York: Dodd, Mead, 1904. Reprint, Freeport, N.Y.: Books for Libraries Press, 1970

———. *In Old Plantation Days.* New York: Dodd, Mead, 1903, 1967.

———. *The Love of Landry.* New York: Dodd, Mead, 1900. Reprint, Upper Saddle River, N.J.: Gregg Press, 1969.

———. *Lyrics of Love and Laughter.* New York: Dodd, Mead, 1903, 1979.

———. *Lyrics of Lowly Life.* New York: Dodd, Mead, 1896.

———. *Lyrics of Sunshine and Shadow.* New York: Dodd, Mead, 1905. Reprint, Salem, N.H.: Ayer, 1991.

———. *Lyrics of the Hearthside.* New York: Dodd, Mead, 1899. Reprint, New York: AMS Press, 1972.

———. *Majors and Minors: Poems.* Toledo, Ohio: P. L. Dunbar, Hadley & Hadley, 1895.

———. *Oak and Ivy.* Dayton, Ohio: United Brethren Publishing House, 1893; N.Y.: Doubleday, 1971.

———. *The Sport of the Gods.* New York: Dodd, Mead, 1902. Reprint, Salem, N.H.: Ayer, 1990.

———. *The Strength of Gideon and Other Stories.* New York: Dodd, Mead, 1900. Reprint, Salem, N.H.: Ayer, 1990.

———. *The Uncalled.* New York: Dodd, Mead, 1898. Reprint, New York: AMS Press, 1972.

Dunbar-Nelson, Alice Moore. *Paul Laurence Dunbar: Poet Laureate of the Negro Race.* Philadelphia: Reverdy C. Ransom, 1914.

Gayle, Addison, Jr. *Oak and Ivy: A Biography of Paul Laurence Dunbar.* Garden City, N.Y.: Doubleday, 1971.

Gould, Jean. *That Dunbar Boy: The Story of America's Famous Negro Poet.* New York: Dodd, Mead, 1958.

Lawson, Victor. *Dunbar Critically Examined.* Washington, D.C.: The Associated Publishers, 1941.

Martin, Jay, ed. *A Singer in the Dawn: Reinterpretations of Paul Laurence Dunbar.* New York: Dodd, Mead, 1975.

Revell, Peter. *Paul Laurence Dunbar.* Boston: Twayne, 1979.

Wiggins, Lida Keck. *The Life and Works of Paul Laurence Dunbar: Containing His Complete Poetical Works, His Best Short Stories, Numerous Anecdotes and a Complete Biography of the Famous Poet.* Naperville, Ill.: L. Nichols, 1907.

DUNBAR-NELSON, ALICE MOORE

(1875–1935)   Born of mixed black, NATIVE AMERICAN, and white ancestry into upper-class Creole society in New Orleans, Alice Nelson attended Straight College (later named Dilliard University). In 1898 she married the poet and short story writer PAUL LAURENCE DUNBAR. She was a teacher of English, an activist for racial causes, and a feminist. Her first novel, *Violets, and Other Tales,* was published when she was 20. Dunbar-Nelson was a prolific writer of short stories, plays, poems, newspaper columns, speeches, and essays in black journals and anthologies. She was a presence in the HARLEM RENAISSANCE. In her stories, she developed her fictional characters in pointed contrast to the traditional STEREOTYPES of blacks in the minstrel roles and plantation stories prevalent in turn-of-the-century literature and thus helped establish the short story form in African-American literature (see also AFRICAN-AMERICAN SHORT FICTION).

BIBLIOGRAPHY

Dunbar-Nelson, Alice Moore. *The Goodness of St. Rocque and Other Stories.* New York: Dodd, Mead, 1899.

———. *Violets, and Other Tales.* Boston: Monthly Review, 1895.

DUPIN, C. AUGUSTE   See C. AUGUSTE DUPIN.

DYBEK, STUART (1942–)

The noted fiction writer and poet Stuart Dybek was born in 1942 in Chicago, the oldest of the three sons of Stanley, a truck-plant foreman, and Adeline, a truck dispatcher. In 1964, after graduating from Loyola University of Chicago, Dybek—the first in his family to attend college—briefly worked with the Cook County Department of Public Aid. In the early 1970s, after teaching stints in Chicago and the Virgin Islands, Dybek enrolled in the writing program at the University of Iowa, joining a group of classmates who would distinguish themselves in literary circles, including T. COR-AGHESSAN BOYLE, Tracy Kidder, Thom Jones, and Denis Johnson. Upon finishing the M.F.A., Dybek focused on a career as a teacher and a writer. He has taught in the English Department at Western Michigan University in Kalamazoo since 1974.

Dybek first published *Brass Knuckles,* a book of poems, in 1979 and has since received, among other honors, a Whiting Writers' Award for the fiction collection *Childhood and Other Neighborhoods* (1980), a Guggenheim Fellowship, a National Endowment for the Arts Fellowship, two O. HENRY MEMORIAL AWARDS (for "Hot Ice" in 1985 and "Blight" in 1987), and a lifetime achievement award from the American Academy of Arts and Letters. His work calls to mind that of his fellow Chicagoans SAUL BELLOW, Carl Sandburg, Nelson Algren, Gwendolyn Brooks, and James T. Farrell in its ability to evoke the magic of a specific time and place—in this case, the gritty, diverse southwest side of Chicago so indelibly part of the author's worldview. Although Dybek appreciates such comparisons, he sees his work as something apart from the REALISM of previous generations, a LYRICAL mélange of prose and poetry informed by his reading of Eastern European and Hispanic writers and his passion for jazz and classical music. "If somebody asked me what I thought my subject was, the answer wouldn't be Chicago, and it probably wouldn't be childhood: it would be perception," Dybek says. "I think that what I'm always looking for is some door in the story that opens on another world. . . . Childhood for me is one of those doorways. To me, childhood seems like a state of extraordinary perception, and to inhabit that

state or that neighborhood means that you're perceiving the world in a different way than is defined as ordinary" (Nickel and Smith 88). That "state of extraordinary perception" is the basis for *Childhood and Other Neighborhoods,* 11 stories that have in common the characters' loss of innocence and a coming of age into a wondrous and difficult world, themes examined in stories such as "Blood Soup" and "Sauerkraut Soup," as well as "The Palatski Man," a sleight-of-hand piece rejected by more than a dozen literary journals before being published—Dybek's first fiction credit—in *The Magazine of Fantasy and Science Fiction.*

The Coast of Chicago (1990) has been compared to the work of ERNEST HEMINGWAY and SHERWOOD ANDERSON. Consisting of 14 stories—seven brief vignettes or "short-shorts" and seven more traditional short stories—*The Coast of Chicago* combines realism with a fabulist edge influenced by the author's fascination for Eastern European classical music and the fiction of Franz Kafka and Isaac Babel. The stories resonate with memories of a childhood in a neighborhood peopled largely by immigrants, particularly in "CHOPIN IN WINTER," in which the young protagonist discovers the heartbreaking beauty of music thanks to Dzia Dzia, an aged relative who has come to live with the family, as the two listen to the accomplished, plaintive piano playing of a young woman destined never to fulfill her potential as an artist.

The short-story cycle *I Sailed with Magellan* (2003) is narrated by Perry Katzek, a denizen of Chicago's South Side who collects butterflies and enjoys music (autobiographical echoes of the author himself) and recalls with preternatural clarity the events of his childhood and adolescence, bringing the neighborhoods, taverns, churches, schools, and gangs (before that term became the pejorative that it is today) to life. In the opening story, "Song," Perry visits the neighborhood's taverns with his uncle Lefty, signing for beer and observing men who have been deeply affected by war and long years of hard work and hard living. In "We Didn't," the narrator nearly loses his virginity on a local beach but, at a crucial moment, learns the consequences of his sin when police nearby discover the body of a pregnant woman washed ashore, the victim of homicide. The collection's title and its intimation of far-flung adventure neatly illustrate the author's thoroughgoing nostalgia and his sense of wonder, all played out through characters who understand the world in the microcosm of their beloved Chicago neighborhoods.

BIBLIOGRAPHY

Dybek, Stuart. *Childhood and Other Neighborhoods.* New York: Viking, 1980.
———. *The Coast of Chicago.* New York: Knopf, 1990.
———. *I Sailed with Magellan.* New York: Farrar, Straus & Giroux, 2003.
Lee, Don. "About Stuart Dybek." *Ploughshares* 24, no. 1 (Spring 1998): 192–198.
Nickel, Mike, and Adrian Smith. "An Interview with Stuart Dybek." *Chicago Review* 43, no. 1 (Winter 1997): 87–101.

Patrick A. Smith
Bainbridge College

E

EASTER In Christianity, Easter is the spring season when Jesus is said to have risen from the grave after his crucifixion. It follows a much older tradition of fertility, renewal, and rebirth as the earth returns to life. Following MODERNISM's lead, T. S. Eliot's *The Waste Land* featured a post–World War I perverse spring in which April is "cruel" and corpses "bloom." Numerous writers make METAPHORical use of the springtime to indicate renewal of their characters. EUDORA WELTY, for instance, uses the death of an old man to make way for the new and younger lover of the title character in "LIVVIE." Other writers use Easter symbolism inversely to show an ironic malaise in their characters; as in for example, SHERWOOD ANDERSON's "The EGG" and JOHN UPDIKE's "SEPARATING."

EASTLAKE, WILLIAM (WILLIAM DERRY EASTLAKE) (1917–1977) William Eastlake appears initially to be a writer of utmost paradox. Although he was born in New York City and grew up in New Jersey, and although after WORLD WAR II he traveled in Europe and lived for a time in Los Angeles, he purchased land and lived for some years as a rancher and writer in a remote area of New Mexico. Eastlake developed into an ardent regionalist (see REGIONALISM) and a shrewd observer of contemporary Native American life, interests apparent in his artistically wrought fiction. His stories have been reprinted in *The O. Henry Awards: Prize Stories* and *Best American Short Stories* (see APPENDIX).

The subjects of his art are Native Americans, tourists, and cattlemen; the settings, the glitzy towns and the sagebrush. Beneath this carefully detailed, naturalistic surface (see NATURALISM), the themes include the values implicit in the behavior and moral attitudes of the protagonists, yet these are frequently treated with irony, humor, and compassion, suggesting Eastlake's niche in the American literary tradition. His move to the West, his stints as war correspondent in Vietnam, and his concern with cultural and political issues identified him with such 19th-century writers as STEPHEN CRANE and JACK LONDON. ERNEST HEMINGWAY, however, seems the dominant influence on Eastlake's use of terse dialogue and understatement as well as the protagonists' search for value in times of both war and peace. Eastlake received favorable critical attention for his short fiction; of the stories in his collection *Jack Armstrong in Tangier* (1984), at least four have been included in major anthologies. These works demonstrate Eastlake's penchant for vividly detailed description and a genuine if pessimistic perspective on contemporary life.

BIBLIOGRAPHY
Bamberger, W. C. *The Work of William Eastlake: An Annotated Bibliography and Guide.* San Bernardino, Calif.: Borgo Press, 1993.
Eastlake, William. *The Bamboo Bed.* New York: Simon & Schuster, 1969.
———. *The Bronc People.* New York: Harcourt Brace, 1958.
———. *Castle Keep.* New York: Simon & Schuster, 1966.

———. *A Child's Garden of Verses for the Revolution.* New York: Viking, 1970.

———. *Dancers in the Scalp House.* New York: Viking, 1975.

———. *Go in Beauty.* New York: Harper & Row, 1956.

———. *Jack Armstrong in Tangier.* Flint, Mich.: Bamberger, 1984.

———. *The Long, Naked Descent into Boston: A Tricentennial Novel.* New York: Viking, 1977.

———. *Lyric of the Circle Heart: The Bowman Family Trilogy.* American Literature Series. Normal, Ill.: Dalkey Archive Press, 1996.

———. *Portrait of an Artist with Twenty-six Horses.* New York: Simon & Schuster, 1963.

———. *Prettyfields: A Work in Progress.* Santa Barbara, Calif.: Capra Press, 1987.

———. "Three Heroes and a Clown." In *Man in the Fictional Mode.* Evanston, Ill.: McDougal, Littell, 1970.

Haslam, Gerald W. *William Eastlake.* Austin, Tex.: Steck-Vaughn, 1970.

ECCLESIASTES

A book of the Old Testament, once believed to have been written by Solomon because of the opening textual reference to "the words of the preacher, the son of David, king in Jerusalem" but since generally assigned to an unknown author in the third century B.C. The book has a somewhat despairing tone, with an emphasis on the evil in man and the universality of death. In a world of despotism and oppression, the one good reserved for man is to "rejoice in his labor, for this is the gift of God." Ecclesiastes appealed to many writers of the 1920s, notably T. S. Eliot and ERNEST HEMINGWAY, who alluded (see ALLUSION) to its passages in such works as *The WASTE LAND* and *The Sun Also Rises,* respectively. Many modernists (see MODERNISM) took their cue from these definitive fictions and adopted in their works the gloomy mood and the inevitability of death.

EDEN

In the Old Testament Book of Genesis, Eden is the garden in which Adam and Eve lived before the Fall of Man. In Eden, the first couple lived a carefree life until, in disobedience of God's command, they ate the forbidden fruit from the tree of knowledge. God expelled Adam and Eve from the garden, and since that time man font has had to live "by the sweat of his brow." In the Book of Genesis, however, the Bible makes clear that the garden was not destroyed after their expulsion but only barred to them by an angel with a flaming sword. It was widely believed in the Middle Ages that the earthy paradise, sometimes identified with the Garden of Eden, a place of beauty, peace, and immortality, existed on earth in some undiscovered land. The word *eden* often is used to describe an idyllically beautiful place. Subtle and not-so-subtle ALLUSIONS to gardens exist in many American short stories from NATHANIEL HAWTHORNE's "RAPPACCINI'S DAUGHTER" to SANDRA CISNEROS's *The HOUSE ON MANGO STREET.*

"EGG, THE" SHERWOOD ANDERSON (1921)

SHERWOOD ANDERSON published his third short story collection, *The Triumph of the Egg,* which contains "The Egg," in 1921. Narrated retrospectively by the nameless son, now an adult, the story of his father contains in its first paragraph the seeds of the unhappy tale that follows: His father, says the narrator, was perfectly happy with his life as a farmhand until he learned ambition. Quite logically, the son suggests that the father probably learned this American trait when he married, late in life, the taciturn schoolteacher who induced her new husband to start a chicken farm. From this point on, the narrator uses eggs and chickens to chronicle the unhappy and downward-spiraling movement of his family's life in and near Bidwell, Ohio.

Anderson's narrative strategy in this story is to reverse the traditional, life-affirming symbol of the egg in parallel with his reversal of the traditional American myth that hard work yields success, a rise in fortunes, and happiness. Eggs, traditionally a symbol of new life, are associated in Christian cultures with EASTER and the resurrection of Christ; in other cultures they have the same meaning, associated with spring and rebirth. Yet the narrator seems not to see that his own birth—from an egg—also plays a role in the failure of his parents' farm and, after the move to town, of their restaurant. He tells us that his mother wanted nothing for herself but, once her son was born, had great ambition for her husband and son. The narrator surmises that she probably had read of

ABRAHAM LINCOLN's and James Garfield's mythic rise from impoverishment to the presidency and may have wished the same success for her own son. Indeed, in later life he knows that she had hoped he could leave the farm and the small town and rise in the world.

In any event, in his recollection of his youth on the chicken farm, the offspring of the eggs bring nothing but worry, disease, and death; the young son has brooding and somber memories of his childhood and at one point speaks directly to the readers, warning that whatever we do, we should never put our trust in chickens. Any alternative is better: prospecting for gold in Alaska, trusting a politician, or believing that goodwill eradicates evil.

For a time, because they work hard, the mother and father's business realizes a small profit. Foolishly, however, the father decides that he will achieve even more success if he can entertain his customers. He tries to force a customer to look at the grotesque freak chickens—those born with two heads or five legs—that he keeps in a jar of alcohol behind the restaurant counter. The man is, predictably, sickened by the sight. When this endeavor fails, the nervous but determined father attempts two silly egg tricks in front of the reluctant customer, who tries to ignore him. When the tricks fail, the final blow occurs, literally, when the frustrated father throws an egg at the customer, who barely makes his escape. The pathetic father breaks down completely; the narrator son still remembers joining his father in an outpouring of wailing and grief. Apparently the sadness continues into the narrator's adulthood, for, as he contemplates the reason for the cycle of chicken-egg-chicken, he notes that, even all these long years later, he is his father's son. The pessimism of those early years, along with its sense of defeat, remains in the narrator's tone: The AMERICAN DREAM remains unattainable for those who are not Lincoln or Garfield.

BIBLIOGRAPHY

Anderson, Sherwood. *The Triumph of the Egg: A Book of Impressions of American Life in Tales and Poems.* New York: B. W. Huebsch, 1921.

Crowley, John W., ed. *New Essays on Winesburg, Ohio.* New York: Cambridge University Press, 1990.

EGGERS, DAVE (1971–)

Dave Eggers was catapulted to fame with the publication of his memoir, *A Heartbreaking Work of Staggering Genius* (2000). As the title implies, personal tragedy and loss lie at the bottom of Egger's work: After losing both his parents to cancer within a few weeks of each other during his final year of college, Eggers raised his eight-year-old brother Christopher ("Toph"). The experience forms the basis for the best-selling memoir. Eggers is also the author of a collection of short stories entitled *How We Are Hungry;* a novel entitled *You Shall Know Our Velocity* (2002); a novel based on the real-life experiences of a Sudanese refugee, *What Is the What: The Autobiography of Valentino Achak Deng; A Novel* (2006); and *The Wild Things* (2009), a novel based on the children's book *Where the Wild Things Are.*

Raised in the suburb of Lake Forest, Illinois, Eggers was founder and editor of the short-lived *Might Magazine,* as well as editor at ESQUIRE and *Timothy McSweeney's Quarterly Concern.* The stories in *How We Are Hungry* vary in length and range in locale from Scotland to Costa Rica to Egypt to Tanzania. It has received mixed reviews, one critic, Ed Caesar, claiming that the story entitled "There Are Some Things He Should Keep to Himself," consisting of five blank pages, "might be the best of the lot" (Caesar). The reviewer Jeff Torrentino makes the perhaps inevitable comparison to JOHN BARTH's short stories, which seemed AVANT-GARDE when first published in the 1960s "but now seem precious" (Torrentino). At their best, however, as Roger Clarke notes, they showcase Eggers's formidable talent. Torrentino singles out "UP THE MOUNTAIN COMING DOWN SLOWLY" as the longest and most conventionally rewarding of these stories. In it, a young woman climbs Kilimanjaro and enjoys the experience briefly before tumbling back down into the somewhat more sordid world of reality.

BIBLIOGRAPHY

Caesar, Ed. "You Mean, Both Water and Oil Are Wet?" Review of *How We Are Hungry* by Dave Eggers. *Independent* (June 5, 2005). Available online. URL: http://www.highbeam.com/doc/1P2-1936340.html. Accessed May 2, 2009.

Clarke, Roger. "The Tuesday Book: A Protege with Plenty to Learn from His Master": Review of *How We Are Hungry* by Dave Eggers. *Independent* (May 17, 2005).

Available online. URL: http://www.highbeam.com/
doc/1G1-132496205.html. Accessed May 2, 2009.

Eggers, Dave. *A Heartbreaking Work of Staggering Genius.*
New York: Simon & Schuster, 2000.

———. *How We Are Hungry.* San Francisco: McSweeney's,
2004.

———. *What Is the What: The Autobiography of Valentino
Achak Deng.* San Francisco: McSweeney's, 2006.

———. *You Shall Know Our Velocity.* San Francisco:
McSweeney's, 2002.

———, ed. *The Best American Nonrequired Reading 2004.*
Boston: Mariner Books, 2004.

———. *For the Love of Cheese: The Editors of Might Magazine.* New York: Boulevard Books, 1996.

Eggers, Dave, ed., with Michael Cart. *The Best American
Nonrequired Reading.* Boston: Houghton Mifflin, 2002.

Eggers, Dave, ed., with others. *Created in Darkness by Troubled Americans: The Best of McSweeney's Humor Category.*
New York: Knopf, 2004.

Eggers, Dave, ed., with Zadie Smith. *The Best American
Nonrequired Reading.* Boston: Houghton Mifflin, 2003.

Fill, Grace. Review of *A Heartbreaking Work of Staggering
Genius. Booklist,* 1 January 2000, p. 860.

Green, John. Review of *How We Are Hungry. Booklist,* 15
December 2004, p. 707.

Theiss, Nola. Review of *How We Are Hungry: Stories. Kliatt*
40, no. 3 (2006): 28.

Turrentine, Jeff. "Animal Appetites." Review of *How We
Are Hungry* by Dave Eggers. *Washington Post* (December
5, 2004). Available online by subscription. URL: http://
www.highbeam.com/doc/1P2-221779.html. Accessed
July 24, 2009.

"EIGHTY-YARD RUN, THE" Irwin Shaw
(1941) Published in Esquire magazine in 1941,
this remains one of Shaw's most famous and enduring short stories. A seemingly simple tale of a 1920s
college football player who cannot adjust to everyday life out of the limelight, nor to the Great Depression and the professional and marital havoc it
creates, "The Eighty-Yard Run" contains subtleties
and depths that remain underappreciated. Shaw,
often dismissed as a popular novelist, has yet to
receive his critical due even for his best work,
including this story.

This story is told in a circular fashion, beginning
and ending at the same spot and time: Christian Darling, at age 35, walking alone in the stadium where,
15 years earlier, he had made an 80-yard run in practice, a run that launched him into (temporary) football stardom and into the arms of his girlfriend,
Louise Tucker. This narrative form mirrors the story's
dominant theme—namely, Christian's inability to
grow or mature, remaining stuck in the same midwestern collegiate track, while Louise becomes a
smart, successful, and sophisticated New York City
woman. He is trapped in a circle of arrested development, while Louise experiences rapid linear progression. Why?

The reader gets an answer of sorts at the end
when Christian reflects that "he had practiced the
wrong thing, perhaps" (11). As do many idolized
and insulated star athletes, Christian made no provisions for the future, living in the immediate world
of sense and ego satisfaction; this is artfully revealed
in the description of how Christian luxuriates in the
physical details of his run and in the shower and
dressing afterward, as well as in the reports of his
serial sexual conquests. Christian, as does the
sports-obsessed culture he inhabits, never anticipates the time when the stadium lights go out; he is
convinced he will always be an "important figure,"
as Louise says to him during the college years. But
of course it is a mirage: Even Diederich, the genuine
football star who supplanted Christian, has no
future after his neck is broken in a professional football game. Christian—whose second-rung adult life
is foreshadowed by his being reduced to a mere
blocker who "open[s] up holes for Diederich"—is
similarly helpless. He, as do so many athletes, "practiced" for a game rather than for real life (Giles
22–23).

And that reality, in the form of the 1929 crash and
the subsequent depression years, has in effect broken
his neck; he is left to half-survive in a brace of his own
egocentricity and poor education, his own pathetic
dreamworld of former athletic stardom. Here, the
character of Cathal Flaherty is instructive: He is a
similarly tough, manly figure, his nose broken from
earlier struggles as if he were a former athlete, yet
because he is also intellectually vibrant, he is able to
shine in the real adult world of work, art, and conver-

sation (and have women on his arms). People like him, Louise, and the people they talk to and about at parties are now the "important figures," while Christian stands voiceless in their midst or finds someone to talk football with in the corner.

Christian's circular stagnation, if not deterioration, is contrasted by Louise's growth into womanhood, symbolized by her chic hat and the fact that it is only in this later stage of the story that her last name is revealed: She has now earned full-named woman status, rather than clinging, adoring girlfriend status. The story, then, not only has a circular form but also a crossing X pattern, with the two principals exchanging positions—Christian sliding from the top left to the bottom right, Louise ascending from the bottom left to the upper right. By the end, Louise is the "man of the house," who pays the bills, has the responsible and demanding job, not to mention affairs (clear revenge for, and reversal of, his philandering days), while Christian humbly and dumbly abides. Louise's habit of calling him "Baby" illustrates this repositioning: That word, as does the chic hat, infuriates Christian for reasons he cannot quite articulate. He has become infantilized if not emasculated, a condition also perhaps foreshadowed by the repeated use of the adjective *girlish* to describe the way he runs (Reynolds).

In another one of the many deft touches in this story, Christian finally gets a decent job toward the end but as a sales representative for a line of clothing designed to create a collegiate look. He is hired not only because of his former repute of being in the same backfield with Diederich, but also because he is a man "who as soon as you look at him, you say, 'There's a university man'" (10). That capsulizes Christian's failing: He is all appearances. He practiced only the superficial things of athletic ability and good collegiate looks, things that will not endure and will not counter the brutal realties of aging and economic dislocation. He is a "university man," not an adult man (Shnayerson 113).

Recreating his 80-yard run at the end of the story, he finds himself gasping and sweating, even though "his condition was fine and the run hadn't winded him" (12). Clearly, it is the realization of having practiced the wrong thing—and recognition that the bright fresh hopes of that fine fall day 15 years earlier are forever gone—that is painfully squeezing his chest and strangling his neck.

Shaw believed that this story, which was his favorite, had larger implications as well. "It's an allegory," he said, "a symbol for America, because it begins in the boom times of the 1920s when Americans thought they were sitting on top of the world and nothing would ever stop them, and then the plunge into the Depression, and the drab coming to the realization of what the Depression meant. I used the symbol of the athlete who in the 1920s had this great day. The one great day—in practice, even—and then the long decline into his own private depression which coincided with the Depression of the United States" (qtd. in Shnayerson 113).

BIBLIOGRAPHY

Giles, James R. *Irwin Shaw: A Study of the Short Fiction.* Boston: Twayne, 1991.

Reynolds, Fred. "Irwin Shaw's 'The Eighty-Yard Run.'" *Explicator* 49, no. 2 (Winter 1991): 121–124.

Shaw, Irwin. "The Eighty-Yard Run." In *Short Stories: Five Decades.* New York: Delacorte Press, 1978.

Shnayerson, Michael. *Irwin Shaw: A Biography.* New York: Putnam, 1989.

Quentin Martin
University of Colorado at Colorado Springs

EISENBERG, DEBORAH (1945–   )

Deborah Eisenberg has been consistently lauded for her psychologically probing portrayals of restless, rootless characters in her O. HENRY MEMORIAL AWARD–winning (1986, 1995, 1997) short stories: from her stunning debut collection *Transactions in a Foreign Currency* (1986) to her deftly executed and sometimes witty *Under the 82nd Airborne* (1992), to her most recent exploration of silences, *All around Atlantis* (1997). Eisenberg seems to cock her head to gain her unique and edgy perspective on her men and women, who frequently need to travel in order to experience the epiphany of self-recognition. Her characters vacillate between intense relationships and profound loneliness as they journey toward an understanding of self, a state that cannot be achieved until they are alone, frequently in a strange or foreign place.

Eisenberg was born on November 20, 1945, in Chicago, Illinois, to George Eisenberg, a pediatrician, and Ruth Lohen Eisenberg. After graduating from New York's New School for Social Research with a bachelor of arts degree in 1968, Eisenberg tried her hand at playwriting, and the result was *Pastorale,* performed in 1981 at the Second Stage Theatre in New York. After traveling frequently in the early and mid-1980s, visiting nearly every country in Latin America, she turned to short story writing, a genre that, she says, challenges her because of its possibilities. In 1992, Eisenberg told the interviewer Nancy Sharkey that she uses the short story form because therein one can condense "something down to the point where it almost squeaks" (11). In "Traveling Light," one of the most frequently discussed stories in *Transactions in a Foreign Currency,* the narrator travels across country in a van with her lover Lee until the end of the relationship, when the story ends with the image of the narrator alone in a vast and empty parking lot, waiting for a bus that will take her somewhere new. Similarly, in *Under the 82nd Airborne,* Eisenberg's characters painstakingly grope their way toward self-definition. In the title story, Caitlin, an actress who has just broken up with her boyfriend, travels to Tegucigalpa to reunite with her daughter, Holly. Instead of the reception she had imagined, Holly is hostile and resentful of the mother who walked out on her in childhood, and Caitlin literally walks her way to a new understanding of herself and the reality of her situation. And in *All around Atlantis,* another rootless woman, the daughter a Holocaust survivor, searches to understand her relationship with her enigmatic mother, whose experiences she will fathom only incompletely, at best. As the reviewer Paula Friedman has noted, Eisenberg defines her characters not only through their actions, but through their thoughts and the sometimes "most stifling silences" (25).

Eisenberg has also written *Air, 24 Hours: Jennifer Bartlett* (1994), a monograph on the artist she admires and with whom she shares some affinities. She supports herself through her writing and through professorships at various universities. Currently, Eisenberg teaches in the fall semester at the University of Virginia and then returns to Manhattan to write.

BIBLIOGRAPHY

Eisenberg, Deborah. *Air, 24 Hours: Jennifer Bartlett.* New York: H. N. Abrams, 1994.
———. *All around Atlantis.* New York: Farrar, Straus & Giroux, 1997.
———. *Pastorale.* New York and London: French, 1983.
———. *The Stories (So Far) of Deborah Eisenberg.* New York: Farrar, Straus & Giroux, 1996.
———. *Transactions in a Foreign Currency.* New York: Knopf, 1986.
———. *The Twilight of the Superheroes.* New York: Farrar, Straus & Giroux, 2006.
———. *Under the 82nd Airborne.* New York: Farrar, Straus & Giroux, 1992.
Friedman, Paula. Review of *All around Atlantis. Houston Chronicle,* 14 December 1997, p. 25.
Gamerman, Amy. Review of *The Designated Mourner. Wall Street Journal.* 17 May 2000, p. A24.
Harlan, Megan. Review of *All around Atlantis. Entertainment Weekly,* 10 October 1997, p. 87.
Hickman, Christie. "Where Brevity Meets Profundity: From Waitress to Doyenne of the American Short Story." *Independent* (London), 2 April 1998, p. 4.
Kellaway, Kate. Review of *All around Atlantis. Observer,* 8 March 1998, p. 17.
Klepp, L. S. Review of *Under the 82nd Airborne. Entertainment Weekly,* 13 March 1992, p. 46.
Leiding, Reba. Review of *All around Atlantis. Library Journal,* August 1997, p. 137.
Liebmann, Lisa. Review of *Air, 24 Hours: Jennifer Bartlett. Artforum International,* November 1995, p. S9.
Manning, Jo. Review of *The Stories (So Far) of Deborah Eisenberg. Library Journal,* January 1997, p. 151.
Novak, Ralph. Review of *Transactions in a Foreign Currency. People,* 14 April 1986, p. 18.
Seaman, Donna. Review of *Air, 24 Hours: Jennifer Bartlett. Booklist,* 1 November 1995, p. 447.
———. Review of *All around Atlantis. Booklist,* August 1997, p. 1877.
Sharkey, Nancy. "Courting Disaster." *New York Times Book Review,* 9 February 1992, p. 11.
Sheppard, R. Z. Review of *All around Atlantis. Time,* 15 September 1997, p. 108.

"ELI, THE FANATIC" PHILIP ROTH (1959)

With "Eli, the Fanatic," the last and longest short story in *Goodbye, Columbus and Five Short Stories* (1959), PHILIP ROTH became one of the first Jewish American writers to explore "the repressed shame and guilt Western Jews felt about the HOLOCAUST" (Baumgarten and Gottfried 54). Because of their dissociation with European Jews and their lack of involvement in WORLD WAR II, the assimilated Jews of Woodenton have turned to a sheltered community life to avoid facing both their guilt and the atrocities of the war. As Leo Tzuref—the head of a nearby Orthodox community that comprised 18 refugee children and one Hasidic Jew—explains to Eli during their second meeting: "What you call law, I call shame. . . . They hide their shame" (266).

As do the PROTAGONISTS in "The CONVERSION OF THE JEWS" and "Defender of the Faith," Eli Peck struggles with his religious and cultural identity. As a lawyer, he unwittingly becomes a liaison between the yeshivah (a traditional school of Judaism) and Woodenton, whose Jews want to oust the Orthodox group for violating a zoning code. Torn by his sympathies for both communities, he proposes a solution that will allow the yeshivah to remain on Woodenton property so long as the Hasidic Jew wears secular, "American" clothing. Essentially, this stipulation asks the Hasid to surrender his religious and cultural identity: "The suit the gentleman wears is all he's got . . . Tzuref, father to eighteen, had smacked out what lay under his coat, but deeper, under the ribs" (263, 265).

When the Hasid and Eli exchange clothing, Eli, by putting on this black outfit, must literally and symbolically confront his own religious identity: "Eli looked at what he wore. And then he had a strange notion that he was two people. Or that he was one person wearing two suits" (289). Even though he tries to embrace the spiritual component of his Jewish identity, his attempts are extreme and superficial. Finally, while looking at his newborn son through a glass window at the hospital, Eli experiences his second breakdown and must be carried away by the attendants. Even though he wears the Hasid's clothing, he is trying to fit into a tradition he is not part of and does not understand. As many of Roth's other works do, this story raises many questions about "Jewish" identity in America without providing any answers.

BIBLIOGRAPHY

Baumgarten, Murray, and Barbara Gottfried. *Understanding Philip Roth.* Columbia: University of South Carolina Press, 1990.

Brent, Jonathan. "'The Job,' Says Roth, 'Was to Give Pain Its Due,'" In *Conversations with Philip Roth,* edited by George J. Searles. Jackson: University of Mississippi Press, 1992.

Cooper, Alan. *Philip Roth and the Jews.* Albany, N.Y.: State University of New York Press, 1996.

Halio, Jay L. *Philip Roth Revisited.* New York: Twayne, 1992.

Roth, Philip. "Eli the Fanatic." In *Goodbye, Columbus and Five Short Stories.* New York: Vintage Books, 1993.

———. *Reading Myself and Others.* New York: Farrar, Straus & Giroux, 1961.

Thomas Fahy
University of North Carolina at Chapel Hill

"ELIZABETH STOCK'S ONE STORY" KATE CHOPIN (1894)

This story begins with the announcement that Elizabeth Stock, an unmarried postmistress of Stonelift, died of consumption (tuberculosis) at St. Louis City Hospital. The narrator, a visitor in the village, was permitted to examine the contents of Elizabeth's desk and found a manuscript. The bulk of the story is that manuscript, Elizabeth Stock's one story, an account of how she lost her position as postmistress. As she was sorting mail one day, she read an urgent post card addressed to a businessman. She admits she often read postcards, reasoning that it is human nature to be inquisitive and that anyone writing anything personal would use a sealed envelope. Recognizing the importance of the message, she walked in the rain to deliver the mail personally, contracting in the process the illness that led to her eventual death. Although she went to great lengths to perform her duties, she was promptly dismissed from her position, ostensibly because of her negligence. The real reason she was fired, however, was that an official in St. Louis wanted to give the job to his son.

Barbara Ewell describes Elizabeth Stock as "one of Chopin's strongest, most self-possessed females" (168) and argues that the story "conceals a high degree of technical contrivance and sophistication in its artlessness" (168). Emily Toth regards this tale as "one of [Chopin's] most bitter and hopeless stories," a "somber version" of BRET HARTE's popular "Postmistress of Laurel Run" (315). An example of literary REALISM, "Elizabeth Stock's One Story" also resembles the fiction of MARY E. WILKINS FREEMAN in its unsentimental depiction of village life.

BIBLIOGRAPHY

Chopin, Kate. "Elizabeth Stock's One Story." In *The Complete Works of Kate Chopin.* Baton Rouge: University of Louisiana Press, 1969.

Ewell, Barbara. *Kate Chopin.* New York: Ungar, 1986.

Toth, Emily. *Kate Chopin.* New York: Morrow, 1990.

Mary Anne O'Neal
University of Georgia

ELKIN, STANLEY (STANLEY LAWRENCE ELKIN) (1930–1995)

Born in Brooklyn, New York, Elkin has won acclaim for his three NOVELLAS in *Searches and Seizures,* and his stories in *Criers and Kibitzers, Kibitzers and Criers* have appeared in numerous anthologies. In *The Living End,* a triad of long stories about heaven and hell, Elkins creates a whole cosmos, laced and grained with detail. The most widely read of Elkin's books, *The Living End* ranges from the life of a Minneapolis–St. Paul liquor salesman to the secrets God held back from man: PROTAGONISTS question, for example, why dentistry holds a higher place in the sciences than astronomy, or why biography is more admired than dance. These stories encompass the banalities of conventional wisdom and the profundities of larger issues. Elkin's gifts are primarily, however, those of the novelist. Shorter forms do not allow Elkin room for the accretion of CHARACTER that marks the novels, so situations and people in the stories—with the significant exceptions just noted—can seem simply eccentric. In the novels, repetition of image and action, rhetorical intensity, even digressions and included tales have a cumulative effect difficult to achieve in the stories.

BIBLIOGRAPHY

Bailey, Peter J. *Reading Stanley Elkin.* Boston: Houghton Mifflin, 1985.

Bargen, Doris G. *The Fiction of Stanley Elkin.* Bern, Switzerland: Peter Lang, 1980.

Elkin, Stanley. *Criers and Kibitzers, Kibitzers and Criers.* New York: Random House, 1966.

———. *Early Elkin.* Flint, Mich.: Bamberger, 1985.

———. *Eligible Men.* London: Gollancz, 1974; as *Alex and the Gypsy,* London: Penguin, 1977.

———. *The Living End.* New York: Dutton, 1979.

———. *The Making of Ashenden.* London: Covent Garden Press, 1972.

———. *Searches and Seizures.* New York: Random House, 1973.

Guttman, Allen. *The Jewish Writer in America.* New York: Oxford University Press, 1971.

Lebowitz, Naomi. *Humanism and the Absurd.* Evanston, Ill.: Northwestern University Press, 1971.

Olderman, Raymond. *Beyond the Wasteland.* New Haven, Conn.: Yale University Press, 1972.

Tanner, Tony. *City of Words.* New York: Harper & Row, 1971.

ELLISON, HARLAN (1934–   )

Harlan Ellison, often labeled a SCIENCE FICTION writer, rejects that term and prefers to regard his work as "MAGIC REALISM." Joseph McLellan of the *Washington Post* has called him a "lyric poet, satirist, explorer of odd psychological concerns, moralist, one-line comedian, purveyor of pure horror and of black comedy." He writes in a highly personal literary language, infused with his own interpretations of myth and moral ALLEGORY. The critic Ben Bova has said that Ellison has an "electromagnetic aura that strikes sparks" but that "underneath all his charisma, behind all the shouting and fury, is one simple fact: he can write circles around most of the people working in this business" (8).

A native of Cleveland, Ohio, Ellison is the son of Louis Laverne Ellison, a dentist and jeweler, and Serita Rosenthal Ellison. He published his first story at the age of 13 and, when he was 16, founded a science fiction society. In 1953 he began publishing the *Science Fantasy Bulletin,* which later became *Dimensions.* He attended Ohio State University for two years, then took on miscellaneous jobs while establishing his writing career. He served in the U.S. Army and has had several marriages.

Ellison edited *Roque Magazine,* was the founder and editor of Regency Books, and has lectured at various colleges and universities. He worked in television in the 1960s, writing scripts for *The Alfred Hitchcock Hour, Star Trek, The Outer Limits,* and other programs. His biographer George Edgar Slusser has stated that his own PERSONA serves "as the means of binding and unifying collections" (qtd. in Dillingham 162) and humanizing his short fiction by means of autobiographical comments. Known as a critic of mass culture, he edited the anthologies *Dangerous Visions: 33 Original Stories* (Doubleday, 1967) and *Again, Dangerous Visions* (Doubleday, 1972). His film criticism has been compiled in *Angry Candy* (Houghton Mifflin, 1988). His other books include *I Have No Mouth and I Must Scream* (Pyramid, 1967), *Paingod and Other Delusions* (Pyramid, 1975), *Phoenix without Ashes* (Fawcett, 1975), *Deathbird Stories: A Pantheon of Modern Gods* (Harper & Row, 1975), *The Illustrated Harlan Ellison* (Baronet, 1978), *Strange Wine: Fifteen New Stories from the Nightside of the World* (Harper, 1978), *Shatterday* (Houghton Mifflin, 1980), *The Deadly Streets* (Ace Books, 1983), *Harlan Ellison's Watching* (Underwood-Miller, 1989), and *Mefisto in Onyx* (Mark V. Ziesing Books, 1993). He has won the HUGO AWARD and the NEBULA AWARD and special achievement awards of the World Science Fiction Convention.

Ellison also writes under various pseudonyms, including Lee Archer, Robert Courtney, E. K. Jarvis, and Clyde Mitchell (magazine pseudonyms); Phil ("Cheech") Beldone, C. Bird, Cordwainer Bird, Jay Charby, Price Curtis, Wallace Edmondson, Landon Ellis, Sley Harson, Ellis Hart, Al[lan] Maddern, Paul Merchant, Nabrah Nosille, Bert Parker, Jay Solo, and Derry Tiger.

Slusser has called Ellison a "tireless experimenter with forms and techniques" and believes he has produced "some of the finest, most provocative fantasy in America today" (170). Ellison's characters are often Americans living at the psychological edge of civilization, turning to attack the status quo, the accepted order of the universe. An example is "Shatterday"; in the introduction to this story, Ellison states bleakly

that each person must assume responsibility for both past and future. In this story, he refers to such Jungian archetypes as "shadow," "persona," "anima," and "animus." In much of his fiction, Ellison makes use of CLASSIC myths. For example, "The Face of Helene Bournow" reflects the LEGEND of Persephone, queen of the underworld and goddess of reviving crops. "I have No Mouth and I Must Scream" may be traced to the Prometheus myth, and some of the tales in *Deathbird Stories* echo Norse myths.

One of his more famous stories, widely reprinted, is "'Repent, Harlequin,' Said the Ticktockman," which reveals the futility of protest in effecting social change. Ellison uses as an epigraph a passage from Thoreau's essay "Civil Disobedience," beginning

> The mass of men serve the state thus, not as men mainly, but as machines, with their bodies. . . . A very few, as heroes, patriots, martyrs, reformers in the great sense, and men, serve the state with their consciences also, and so necessarily resist it for the most part; and they are commonly treated as enemies by it. (1,754)

The Ticktockman is the Master Timekeeper, guardian of the state-as-machine. The HERO, Harlequin (whose real name is Everett C. Marm), tries to instigate reforms but is ultimately subdued and brainwashed. His name recalls the commedia dell'arte, the improvisatory Italian street theater in which Harlequin, dressed in motley, is the stock figure of pathos and COMEDY, the satirist who is much loved by others but is unlucky in love. The critic Thomas Dillingham has remarked that such a figure "may well be diverse enough to encompass the complexities of Ellison's presentation of himself." The sense of identity is a strong component of much of Ellison's work; often, as in "'Repent, Harlequin!'" a person with a weak sense of self awakens and tries to oppose the evils about him, often caused by invidious exterior forces.

The critic J. G. Ballard has described Ellison as "an aggressive and restless extrovert who conducts his life at a shout and his fiction at a scream" (169). This assessment seems particularly apt in view of Harlequin's unattainable utopia. It is also relevant to the story "I Have No Mouth, and I Must Scream," a modern FABLE about AM, a computer system made up of the remnants of the computerized weapon systems of World War III. It decides to destroy all life: "One day AM woke up and knew who he was, and he linked himself, and he began feeding all the killing data, until everyone was dead." It spares five humans, playing with them like balls in a pinball machine. One of them, Ted, kills his companions to release them from AM, but then, like Everett Marm, hero of "Repent, Harlequin!" becomes imprisoned inside himself. He realizes that he is human but is powerless to express it and is doomed to suffer indefinitely. Darren Harris-Fain suggests that although the machine is portrayed as anthropomorphic and also divine, it is really only Ted who is "both fully human and fully godlike in the story" (144) "Delusion for a Dragon Slayer" shows the effects of a flawed subconscious, when a man is not equal to his dreams and is unable to correct his errors. One of Ellison's later stories, "The Whimper of Whipped Dogs," was based on the story of Kitty Genovese (a young woman who was murdered in New York City while onlookers failed to help her). Ellison writes from the POINT OF VIEW of one of the witnesses, who later must face the possibility of violence in her own life and discards the sentimentality she once possessed.

Beginning as early as the 1960s, Ellison expressed his concern about society's readiness to grapple with the implications of our technological future. Today, in light of the Internet, mammoth electronic databases, and the burgeoning use of personal computers, his remarkable insights seem more relevant, perhaps, than at any time in the past four decades.

BIBLIOGRAPHY

Ballard, J. G. *Contemporary Reviews.* In *Literary Criticism,* vol. 13, edited by Dedria Bryfonski. Florence, Ky.: Gale, 1980.

Bova, Ben. "Electromagnetic Aura": "Fagin, & Other Harlan Ellisons." In Swigart, *A Bibliographical Checklist,* 8.

Crow, John, and Richard Erlich. "Mythic Patterns in Ellison's *A Boy and His Dog.*" *Extrapolation* 18 (1977): 162–166.

Dillingham, Thomas F. "Harlan Ellison." *Dictionary of Literary Biography* 8: 8, 162.

Ellison, Harlan. *Again, Dangerous Visions.* New York: Doubleday, 1972.

———. *Angry Candy.* New York: Houghton Mifflin, 1988.

———. *Dangerous Visions: 33 Original Stories.* New York: Doubleday, 1967.

———. *The Deadly Streets.* New York: Ace Books, 1983.

———. *Deathbird Stories: A Pantheon of Modern Gods.* New York: Harper & Row, 1975.

———. *Harlan Ellison's Watching.* Los Angeles, Calif.: Underwood-Miller, 1989.

———. *I Have No Mouth and I Must Scream.* New York: Pyramid, 1967.

———. *The Illustrated Harlan Ellison.* New York: Baronet, 1978.

———. "Magic Realism." In *Contemporary Reviews,* New Revision Series, vol. 5, 169.

———. "Memoir: I Have No Mouth, and I Must Scream." *Starship: The Magazine about Science Fiction* 17, no. 3: 6–13.

———. *Mefisto in Onyx.* Shingletown, Calif.: Mark V. Ziesing Books, 1993.

———. *Paingod and Other Delusions.* New York: Pyramid, 1975.

———. *Phoenix without Ashes.* New York: Fawcett, 1975.

———. *Shatterday.* Boston: Houghton Mifflin, 1980.

———. *Strange Wine: Fifteen New Stories from the Nightside of the World.* New York: Harper & Row, 1978.

Harris-Fain, Ted. "Created in the Image of God: The Narrator and the Computer in Harlan Ellison's 'I Have No Mouth, and I Must Scream,'" 144.

Malekin, Peter. "The Fractured Whole: The Fictional World of Harlan Ellison." *Journal-of-the-Fantastic-in-the-Arts,* 1, no. 3: 21–26.

McLellan. *Washington Post: Contemporary Reviews,* New Revision Series, vol. 5, 169.

Rubens, Philip M. "Descents into Private Hells: Harlan Ellison's 'Psy-Fi.'" *Extrapolation* 20 (1979): 378–385.

Slusser, George Edgar. *Contemporary Reviews,* New Revision Series, vol. 5, 170.

Thoreau, Henry David. "Resistance to Civil Government." [Reprinted in 1866 as "Civil Disobedience."] In *The Norton Anthology of American Literature.* 5th ed., vol. 1. Edited by Nina Baym. New York: W. W. Norton, 1998, 1,752–1,767.

White, Michael D. "Ellison's Harlequin: Irrational Moral Action in Static Time." *Science Fiction Studies* 4 (1977): 161–165.

Sarah Bird Wright

ELLISON, RALPH (RALPH WALDO ELLISON) (1914–1994)

Born in Oklahoma City, Oklahoma, and recipient of diverse honors, Ellison won the National Book Award for his novel *Invisible Man* (1952). In a poll conducted in 1965 by *Book Week,* a group of critics selected *Invisible Man* as the most distinguished work of fiction to appear in the post–WORLD WAR II period. In the opinion of the scholars George Perkins and Barbara Perkins, "That poll may be taken as a tribute not only to the power of the novel but also to the continuing literary reputation of a man who, although past 50, had published only one other volume, a collection of essays called *Shadow and Act*" (1964) (69). In addition to *Invisible Man,* Ellison's skill in fiction is apparent in a number of short stories that remained uncollected until after his death but were published as *Flying Home and Other Stories* in 1996.

From the time of his earliest published writing Ellison was interested in the universal THEME of identity, but he always conceived the theme in the context of black culture. "Slick Gonna Learn," for instance, which tells of an aborted beating of a black working man, describes experiences typical of the special circumstances of African-American life. Several stories ("Afternoon," "That I Had the Wings," "Mister Toussan," "A Coupla Scalped Indians"), which represent young black boys contending with fear and guilt, learning of sex, and fantasizing retaliation on whites who despise them, might describe the nameless HERO of *Invisible Man* in adolescence, while "Flying Home," in which Todd, a young black aviator, discovers his kinship to a black peasant, employs race and culture as the basic terms for self-discovery. Todd, one of the black eagles from the Negro air school at Tuskeegee, is a descendant of Icarus, of the Greek myth, and of James Joyce's Stephen Daedalus. When he falls to earth in rural Alabama, Todd is saved by an old black peasant who uses folktales to help the young man understand his identity.

"A Party Down at the Square," unpublished in Ellison's lifetime, is a tour de force. By narrating a lynching in the voice of a Cincinnati white boy visiting his uncle in Alabama, Ellison compels the reader to experience the worst of human situations. The white boy's most telling response arises from his insides when, to his shame, he vomits.

See also "KING OF THE BINGO GAME."

BIBLIOGRAPHY

Bloom, Harold, ed. *Ralph Ellison.* New York: Chelsea House, 1986.

Bluestein, Gene. *The Blues as a Literary Theme.* Indianapolis: Bobbs-Merrill, 1967.

Dietze, Rudolf F. *Ralph Ellison: The Genesis of an Artist.* Nuremberg: Carl, 1982.

Ellison, Ralph. *The Collected Essays of Ralph Ellison.* Edited by John F. Callahan. New York: Random House, 1995.

———. *Conversations with Ralph Ellison.* New York: Modern Library, 1995.

———. *Flying Home and Other Stories.* New York: Random House, 1996.

———. *Going to the Territory.* New York: Random House, 1986.

———. *Invisible Man.* New York: Random House, 1952.

———. *Juneteenth.* New York: Random House, 1999.

———. *Shadow and Act.* New York: Random House, 1954.

Fischer-Hornung, Dorothea. *Folklore and Myth in Ralph Ellison's Early Works.* Stuttgart: Hochschul, 1979.

Frank, Joseph. "Ralph Ellison and Dostoevsky." *New Centerion* (September 1983).

Gibson, Donald B. *Five Black Writers: Essays.* New York: New York University Press, 1970.

Hersey, John, ed. *Ralph Ellison: A Collection of Critical Essays.* Englewood Cliffs, N.J.: Prentice-Hall, 1973.

"Interview with Ralph Ellison." *Atlantic,* December 1970.

O'Meally, Robert G. *The Craft of Ralph Ellison.* Cambridge, Mass.: Harvard University Press, 1980.

———. "The Rules of Magic: Hemingway as Ellison's 'Ancestor.'" *Southern Review,* Summer 1985.

Perkins, George, and Barbara Perkins, eds. *Contemporary American Literature.* New York: Random House, 1968, 69–70.

"Ralph Ellison Issue." *CLA Journal,* March 1970.

"END OF SOMETHING, THE" ERNEST HEMINGWAY (1925)

Perhaps one of the most enigmatic of ERNEST HEMINGWAY's stories, "The End of Something" was first published in the 1925 collection *In Our Time,* Hemingway's first major literary effort and, as some would argue, his best individual collection of short fiction.

One of the famous "NICK ADAMS stories," "The End of Something" has a plot that focuses on the breakup of Marjorie and Nick. The story begins with the two trolling for trout in the deep water off Horton's Bay and then making a camp for night fishing on the shore. Nick is detached and verbally short with Marjorie, and when she asks what is wrong for the second time, Nick tells her, "It isn't fun any more" (81). Marjorie, upset but not making the scene that Nick expected, takes the boat and leaves Nick to walk home around the point. After she has gone, Nick buries his head in the blanket and is approached by his friend Bill, obviously waiting in the wings for the breakup to take place. Bill asks how things went, and Nick tells him to leave for a while.

Hemingway establishes the setting and mood for the story, as he usually does, in the first paragraph. In fact, the story could be called "The End of Two Things," as Hemingway begins by describing the short boomtown history of Horton's Bay. The town had once been the site of a major logging operation, but once the logs were gone, the company packed up the mill and moved on, leaving behind the relics of their buildings, what Marjorie calls "our old ruin" (79).

The setting is certainly symbolic of the breakup that takes place in the story, but the symbol is heavier than the breakup itself. When the lumber mill closed, a town (and thus a society) died. However, when the relationship between Nick and Marjorie ends, readers may feel a certain sense of apathy. In the Hemingway canon, readers encounter many strong male characters, some often strong and masculine to a fault, and Nick Adams, the protagonist of several Hemingway short stories, is in many cases one of these strong characters. However, in "The End of Something" Nick comes across to readers as childish and immature. It is true that we are not told Nick's age in the story, but he is old enough to night fish unchaperoned with a girl and he is old enough to be involved in a relationship with Marjorie. But instead of discussing the end of the relationship with Marjorie in a direct and mature fashion, Nick is passive-aggressive. His responses to her questions and comments are short ("There it is"; "I can just remember"; "I don't feel like eating"). In fact, most of Nick's lines of dialogue are from three-to-five words in length. His longest, 23 words in two sentences, occurs when he is teaching Marjorie how to cut a bait fish properly. The pending breakup is palpable, considering the title and the symbolic beginning, but Nick's dialogue suggests what is coming perhaps more than anything else.

It is worth noting that feminist critics panned the work of Hemingway for decades, primarily because of his characters' machismo as well as his own projected manly image. However, Nick Adams, at least in this story, is presented in a manner that may lead readers to side with Marjorie. Nick is a fine example of the typical Hemingway male, who hunts, fishes, fights wars, writes prose, drinks hard, and has many relationships with women. But there is little redeeming about Nick in this story. Marjorie, who is trying hard to please him and take part in activities that he likes, draws the sympathy of readers. Nick is overbearing and knows it all, except how to have a mature relationship. Nick says the fish are not biting, and Marjorie says, "They're feeding" (80). Nick reiterates his point immediately: "But they won't strike." It is also only natural that Nick's longest line of dialogue involves his teaching Marjorie something, how to cut a bait fish properly.

Marjorie, knowing something is wrong and perhaps knowing "the end" is near, uses Nick's know-it-all personality combined with flattery to lighten Nick's mood. Nick has noticed that the hills "were beginning to sharpen against the sky" (81), which tells him that the moon is rising. Apparently, at some point Nick took the opportunity to explain (perhaps condescendingly) to Marjorie how to recognize this herself, and she uses this knowledge, but to no avail: "'Oh, shut up,' Marjorie says. 'There comes the moon'" (81). Within a few lines of dialogue, the relationship has ended.

Hemingway claimed more than once that there was little symbolism in his work, but almost any reader could have a field day with the symbols in this rather short and simple story. And it should be no surprise that Nick, throughout the entire Nick Adams stories, has problems with personal relationships. This story may indeed be the beginning rather than the end of this issue for Nick.

BIBLIOGRAPHY

Benson, Jackson J., ed. *New Critical Approaches to the Short Stories of Ernest Hemingway.* Durham, N.C.: Duke University Press, 1991.

Bloom, Harold, ed. *Ernest Hemingway: Modern Critical Views.* New York: Chelsea House, 1985.

Hemingway, Ernest. "The End of Something." In *The Complete Short Stories of Ernest Hemingway: The Finca Vigía Edition.* New York: Charles Scribner's Sons, 1987.

Oliver, Charles M. *Critical Companion to Ernest Hemingway.* New York: Facts On File, 2007.

Tyler, Lisa. *Student Companion to Ernest Hemingway.* Westport, Conn.: Greenwood Press, 2001.

Wagner-Martin, Linda, ed. *Ernest Hemingway: Six Decades of Criticism.* East Lansing: Michigan State University Press, 1988.

James Mayo
Jackson State Community College, Tennessee

"ENORMOUS RADIO, THE" JOHN CHEEVER (1953)

Opening with a description of a New York City couple, Jim and Irene Wescott, who aspire someday to move to Westchester, "The Enormous Radio"—first published in the NEW YORKER before reappearing in the 1953 collection *The Enormous Radio and Other Stories*—begins as a realistic story (see REALISM) about people who, a few decades later, would be called "yuppies." Irene and Jim, the uninvolved, third-person narrator tells us, fit the profile of successful couples with reasonably good incomes, a reasonably fashionable address, and the prescribed total of two children. They differ from their neighbors only in their serious interest in classical music.

Almost immediately, however, in a move that today we call MAGIC REALISM, JOHN CHEEVER introduces a new radio into their lives, a radio described as powerful, uncontrollable, and more than faintly disturbing. (See PERSONIFICATION.) Unlike nonmagic radios, this one tunes in to neighbors' private conversations. Irene identifies these people because she can recognize their voices. She becomes mesmerized by the way the radio transmits the marital arguments, conversations of drunken revelers, angry words spoken to children, disclosures of dishonest behavior, and secret liaisons she never would have imagined. In Irene's reactions to the worry, hypocrisy, and even violence among her neighbors, the story portrays her desperately clinging to a belief in Jim and herself as different from all the others with their sordid secrets.

Voyeuristically, the reader sees into Irene's and Jim's lives just as Irene eavesdrops, through the radio, on the lives of their neighbors. Despite Irene's pleas for reassurance that they are different from the others, Jim finally snaps and angrily contradicts her rosy and complacent view of their relationship. He yells furiously at her—and Jim's words and tone sound exactly like those of other men shouting at their wives, those angry voices Irene has listened to through the radio. As do the other men, he complains to her that he is tired and overworked, feeling already old at age 37. He then criticizes Irene's extravagance and inability to manage finances, accusing her of stealing jewelry from her dead mother, cheating her sister, and hypocritically forgetting her visit to an abortionist, an act he now discloses he has always thought of as out-and-out murder.

Irene feels humiliated and ill after Jim's outburst but, significantly, makes no move to contradict him. Our final view of her shows her standing by the radio, childishly hoping for loving, kind words, obviously still in denial of the reality of Jim's accusations. Jim continues to yell at her through the door. Because we know that Irene fears that the malevolent radio might transmit their voices just as it has transmitted those of her neighbors, we cannot be sure that the radio is not doing exactly that. In any case, the radio has done its work, and a return to innocence is impossible. The story itself, like an enormous radio, has transmitted to readers the ugly facts that, like Irene, we would prefer not to confront. Instead, we may just listen to the calm voice of the radio announcer in the final lines of the story, hearing impersonally the headlines about good deeds and ill and an hourly report on the weather.

BIBLIOGRAPHY

Cheever, John. *The Enormous Radio and Other Stories.* New York: Harper & Row, 1953.

O'Hara, James Eugene. *John Cheever: A Study of the Short Fiction.* Boston: Twayne, 1989.

"ENTROPY" THOMAS PYNCHON (1960) THOMAS PYNCHON's early short story "Entropy" heralds many of the thematic concerns and stylistic features that were to make his novels *The Crying of Lot 49, V.,* and *Gravity's Rainbow* central to the canon of American POSTMODERNISM. Most notable of these, as the title indicates, is his deployment of self-consciously recondite and comically extravagant metaphors drawn from scientific concepts that threaten to disintegrate and render absurd the established humanistic worldview. Entropy serves as the organizing (and disorganizing) principle of the story inasmuch as many of Pynchon's metaphors and images derive from his conflation of two somewhat different, but related, conceptions of the term—one arising out of thermodynamics and the other arising out of cybernetics, the science of information and what the text refers to as "communication theory" (75).

The second law of thermodynamics states that "for the universe as a whole, or an isolated part of it, processes forward in time tend to increase disorder," the maximal degree of which is entropy (Friedman 84). Within a closed system, energy (in this case, heat) disperses from areas of higher concentration to those of lesser, ultimately producing an equilibrium of evenly distributed energy throughout the system such that no work can be done (physics conceives energy as the capacity to do work) and no change can occur. Entropy, a condition of "form and motion abolished," is, then, metaphorically comparable to the theological concept of limbo (Pynchon 69). As Pynchon's story implies, the slow heat death of the universe generally is unnoticed because of daily and seasonal temperature fluctuations, but these are better understood as variations on a developing theme. This is the contextual significance of the unchanging temperature upon which the character Callisto fixates. The entropic state of maximal disorder due to minimal energy is accompanied by disintegration of structures inasmuch as structures, particularly biological structures, constitute sites of consolidated energy. The fact that entropic processes produce chaos in any system authorizes Callisto to reformulate the laws of thermodynamics in more human terms as, "You can't win, things are going to get worse before they get better, who says they're going to get better" (72).

Narrative elements of the story are also typical of Pynchon's operating procedures, notably a predilection for characters with ridiculous, ostentatiously contrived names (Meatball Mulligan, Callisto, Aubade) and abrupt cross-cutting among parallel actions performed by a contingent of eccentrics (the "crew") converged, seemingly, by contingency but perhaps drawn together by a hypothetical, certainly unknowable, sorting mechanism. This mechanism has been designated "Maxwell's demon" by theoretical physics after James Clerk Maxwell's thought experiment challenging the second law of thermodynamics. Traces of a mechanism that sorts highly energized atoms from less energized ones into adjacent spaces might be discerned in the story's reversal of this process, as the surging incursions and noisy turbulence of Meatball's downstairs party seep through the floorboards of consciousness into the hermetic confines of Callisto and Aubade's apartment upstairs. The ambiguity of the relationship between these lower and upper worlds becomes more apparent on considering the fact that, according to thermodynamics, "any particular system *can* become more ordered and energetic if it does so at the expense of greater disorder and loss of energy in the rest of the universe" (Friedman and Puetz 70). (The impairment of seemingly inviolate structures by entropic incursions is probably the metaphorical import that also dictates Pynchon's allusion to WILLIAM FAULKNER's novel *Sanctuary,* which concerns the violation of the aptly named *Temple* Drake.) In Pynchon's fictions the figure of Maxwell's demon can generally be seen in the sudden surprising entry or unexpected disruptive act of a seemingly minor character, whose interruption deflects and redirects the trajectory of the narrative and causes its constituent elements, such as the behavior of the other characters, to be reordered (Friedman 87). The fact that many physics textbooks used to depict the demon as "opening and closing doors" as it sorts atoms into the compartments "of a divided box" (88) may warrant interpreting the crew of sailors who barge through a door into Meatball Mulligan's lease-breaking party as a personification of this mechanism. Their incursion necessitates that Meatball expend a great deal of energy to sort things out in the attempt to prevent the party from "deteriorating into total chaos" (Pynchon 84), although even before this he had resorted to tequila as a means of "restoring order to his nervous system" (70).

The fact that entropy is only tendentially true authorizes the presence of a thematic element in the story derived from the convergence of physics and mathematics, another source of metaphor prevalent in Pynchon's novels. Statistical mechanics, "a branch of physics that was recognized at the end of the nine-teenth century as the mathematical base to the entropy concept" (Friedman 78), attempts to establish the principle of likelihood—a hypothetical average or mean, a convenient indication of typicality—after first calculating predictable deviations. Callisto speaks from this perspective when he articulates the principle "that the isolated system—galaxy, engine, human being, culture, whatever—must evolve spontaneously toward the Condition of the More Probable" (Pynchon 73). This principle has compelled him "in the sad dying fall of middle age, to a radical reevaluation of everything he had learned up to then" (73). One of his recognitions is that cosmological entropy has a social analog: conformity, the institutionalization of same-ness, and the growing unlikelihood of deviation and uniqueness. This is especially evident in the area of consumerism, where he "discovered a similar ten-dency from the least to the most probable, from differ-entiation to sameness, from ordered individuality to a kind of chaos" (74). The end result of social confor-mity will be a cultural manifestation of heat death "in which ideas, like heat-energy, would no longer be transferred, since each point in it would ultimately have the same quantity of energy; and intellectual motion would, accordingly, cease" (74). Despite Cal-listo's proclaimed awareness of "the dangers of the reductive fallacy," despite his desire to remain "strong enough not to drift into the graceful decadence of an enervated fatalism," and despite his former conviction that "the forces of *virtù* [the manly capacity to inter-vene and control] and *fortuna* [fortune or chance]" have always been equal (73), Callisto begins to believe that "a random factor [had] pushed the odds to some

unutterable and indeterminate ratio which he found himself afraid to calculate" (73).

It should be noted at this point that Callisto shares Pynchon's penchant for reading prevailing cultural practices as signs to be connected into revelatory patterns, although it is also the case that the author satirizes the search for symptomatic indices as itself symptomatic of a culturally pervasive apocalyptic paranoia. He also tends to overwhelm the reader's semiotic and diagnostic attempt to ascertain or con-struct patterns with a plethora of allusions amalgam-ating elite and mass cultures (ranging, in this instance, from Roman and medieval philosophical concepts to jazz saxophonists and popular songs from the 1920s–40s). That said, on the evidence of "Entropy" no less than the novels, Pynchon is as prone as Callisto is to scrutinizing fin de siecle deca-dence and the period of the two world wars for pro-phetic signs of the jejune condition that will typify postmodernity. Thus, pondering the popularity of the tango and Igor Stravinsky's incorporation of that "sad, sick dance" into classical music, Callisto won-ders, "What had tango music been for them after the war, what meanings had he missed in all the stately coupled automatons in the *cafés-dansants,* or in the metronomes which had ticked behind the eyes of his own partners?" (79). It is highly significant that Stravinsky's tango is said to have "managed to com-municate . . . the same exhaustion, the same airless-ness one saw" in the indifferent, conformist, and imitative youth of the 1920s: Music, for both Callisto and Pynchon, is "information" (80).

The second conception of entropy deployed by Pynchon is derived from cybernetics's understand-ing that information is constituted as a patterned organization of recognizable, coherent signals and that the entropic process is discernible in the degree of randomness, unpredictability, and lack of formal coherence or disorganization in such signals. Infor-mation being transferred in messages is subject to signal breakup, while noise constitutes an extreme degree of signal dissipation and randomness. By fig-urative extension, entropy, or noise, is also present in misunderstanding, which constitutes an ineffi-cient reception of the signals. Whatever seems garbled or meaningless is entropic. However, signals organized into unfamiliar and therefore unrecognizable, unpredictable patterns—such as AVANT-GARDE jazz improvisation—may also seem to be noise because of the intricacy of their coherence. Jazz improvisation exemplifies how some information systems, notably biological systems, are self-monitoring and self-adjusting; they resist information entropy by utilizing feedback loops that allow information output to be introduced back into the system as input. From the perspective of cybernetics, the human mind and culture are patterned continuities of information feedback taking the form of memory. (Note in this regard Callisto's preoccupation with his past.) Feedback is central to the reversal of information entropy (signal breakup and communication breakdown) by the ongoing correction (compensatory reordering) of noise into meaningful signals. Examples of the compensatory reordering of signals can be heard in the conversation Meatball has with Duke di Angelis, an avant-garde musician, which in part entails the correction of memory lapses regarding the names of songs and the venue where a song was played in the wrong key (itself an example of signal distortion).

Music is a major source of Pynchon's metaphoric exploration of communication breakdown and noise as a ramification of entropic processes, and a music vocabulary figures significantly throughout the story. As a two-part invention that counterpoints entropic processes occurring in two apartments, the story is organized along the lines of a simplified fugue, a form in which a theme and tonic key is announced by an initial instrumental voice and then harmoniously developed, through contrapuntal variation, by succeeding instrumental voices. The sentence linking "a *stretto* passage in the year's fugue" with "months one can easily spend in fugue" (67) indicates that Pynchon also has in mind what psychology designates a *fugue state,* a state of mental disorganization characterized by the disintegration of memory regarding an environmental situation that has been unconsciously rejected and physically evaded. Metaphorically speaking, the fantastical closed refuge of Callisto and Aubade—an artificial

"hothouse" in both the thermodynamic and ecological senses of the term—might be said to represent just such a state. Counterpointing Meatball's open house, the outside rarely enters the couple's "[h]ermetically sealed . . . enclave of regularity in the city's chaos," and therefore it is "alien to the vagaries of the weather [and to] any civil disorder" (68).

The quasi-autistic Aubade lives "on her own curious and lonely planet," where all physical sensations "came to her reduced inevitably to the terms of sound: of music which emerged at intervals from a howling darkness of discordancy" (69). Thus, she can hear "a motif" of tree sap rising in an "unresolved anticipatory theme of . . . blossoms, which, it is said, insure fertility" (79). But she feels under unremitting threat of the noisy "hints of anarchy . . . to which she had continually to readjust lest the whole structure shiver into disarray of discrete and meaningless signals" (73). Reiterating the signal of his cybernetic theme, Pynchon writes that Callisto has designated "the process . . . a kind of 'feedback'" (73). Aubade's acute sensitivity makes it hard for her to modulate the world, and her desperate, exhaustive "vigilance" requires an expenditure of energy that is in diminishing supply. She is subliminally disturbed by the sounds generated by Meatball's lease-breaking party, hearing the music rise "in a tangled tracery: arabesques of order competing fugally with the improvised discords [that] peaked sometimes in cusps and ogees of noise . . . [a] signal-to-noise ratio whose delicate balance required every calorie of her strength" (79). Aubade breaks a window to allow the apartment heat to disperse toward "equilibrium" with the outside so that she and Callisto will eventually be "resolve[d] into a tonic of darkness and the final absence of all motion" (85–86). Given that "the soul (*spiritus, ruach, pneuma*) is nothing, substantially, but air" and that, therefore, "it is only natural that warpings in the atmosphere should be recapitulated in those who breathe it" (67), Aubade's suicidal act is also a liberating counterentropic improvisation in which the noisy act of breaking barriers introduces "disorganization" into the "airless void," the closed circuit, the set piece, she and Callisto have made their lives.

Loud noises and instances of breaking—beginning with the party-crashing sailors and culminating in Aubade's window—take some of their meaning from intervening conversations that Meatball has with his friends Saul and Duke. Saul reports that his wife threw a *Handbook of Chemistry and Physics* through a window during an argument about, absurdly, "communication theory." The point of Saul's commentary on this conversation is that often the information in the intended message breaks up in reception because the denotative sign has different connotative significations. Saul introduces another aspect of entropic communication, "leakage," illustrating this phenomenon through reference to communiqués of love, "that nasty four-letter word" that destructively intervenes between an erotically closed circuit of an "I" and a "you," thereby producing "Ambiguity. Redundancy. Irrelevance" (76). Saul continues, "All this is noise" that "screws up your signal, makes for disorganization in the circuit" (77). Meatball protests, but the repetitive, inelegant form of his protest demonstrates a degrading signal-to-noise ratio: "What it is is, most of the things we say, I guess, are mostly noise" (77). Referring to the difficulty of discussing the esoteric impenetrability of communication theory, Saul also introduces conspiracy theory, a Pynchon staple: "You get where you're watching all the time for security cops . . . MUFFET [Multi-unit factorial field electronic tabulator] is top secret" (75). A subsequent conversation between Meatball and Duke constitutes a more oblique reference to the breakdown of communication by extrapolating to absurdity the logic of 1950s artistic experimentation. Just as the jazz avant-garde's abandonment of "root chords" has compelled the deprived listener to *think* them back into the music (82), Duke's group now plays its tunes with imaginary instruments—a groovy variant on "the reductive fallacy" (73).

Pynchon's convergence of the thermodynamic and the cybernetic conceptions of entropy is most explicitly signified when he describes Callisto's failure to "transfer" his body heat to the dying bird as a failure to "communicat[e] life" to it (85). As the sky proceeds toward an entropic "uniform darkening," a disruptive noise from below shatters the torpor upstairs, causing the awakened Callisto's pulse "to pound more fiercely, as if trying to compensate" for the pulse of the dying bird. But bird and story settle toward "a graceful diminuendo down at last into stillness" (85). Considering that an aubade is a poem or song that either celebrates daybreak or laments the parting of lovers at daybreak, the story ends on an ambiguous note. Callisto thinks he has discovered that love and power are "identical" inasmuch as love really does "make the world [and "the nebula precess"] go round," as the pop song claims (69). That being the case, the ensuing entropic equilibrium might be thought to entail not the death of love, but the inability of anything to love any longer.

BIBLIOGRAPHY
Barth, John. "The Literature of Exhaustion." In *The Friday Book*. Baltimore: Johns Hopkins University Press, 1984.
Friedman, Alan J. "Science and Technology." In *Approaches to 'Gravity's Rainbow,'* edited by Charles Clerc. Columbus: Ohio State University Press, 1983.
Pynchon, Thomas. "Entropy." In *Slow Learner*. New York: Bantam Books, 1985.
Tanner, Tony. *Thomas Pynchon*. London/New York: Methuen, 1982.

David Brottman
Southern Indiana University

EPIGRAM   In Greek, *epigram* means "inscription," but its meaning has been extended to include any very short poem that is polished, condensed, and pointed. Often an epigram ends with a surprising or witty turn of thought. The epigram was especially popular as a literary form in classic Latin literature after Martial, the Roman epigrammist, established the enduring model for the caustically satiric epigram. It was also used by European and English writers of the Renaissance and neoclassical periods. Samuel Coleridge wrote of it: "What is an epigram? A dwarfish whole, Its body brevity, and wit its soul."

EPILOGUE   *Epilogue*, from the Greek meaning "to say in addition," is the final part that completes and rounds off the design of a work of literature. An epilogue is the opposite of a prologue, the author's brief remarks to the reader that appear before the beginning of a work of fiction.

EPIPHANY   In Christian theology, an epiphany is the manifestation or appearance of Jesus Christ in the world. The feast of the Epiphany celebrates the coming of the magi as Christ's first manifestation to the gentiles. The Irish writer James Joyce adapted the term to secular experience to mean a sudden revelation of the essential nature of a person, object, or scene. This moment of sudden recognition is an epiphany. Thus, a fictional character may experience a revelation—or an epiphanic moment—when all becomes radiantly clear.

"EPSTEIN" PHILIP ROTH (1959)   Lou Epstein, the eponymous narrator of "Epstein," is having a hard time. At age 59, he finds himself experiencing a postmidlife crisis. His once-beautiful wife, Goldie, sags and nags; his daughter, Sheila, "a twenty-three-year old woman with 'a social conscience!'" (205), and "her fiance, the folk singer" (203), fail to share his values; his brother and one-time business partner has become estranged, moving out of town "with words" (206); and the son who would succeed him, carrying on the family name and taking over the family business, died of polio as a child. When Epstein discovers that his nephew Michael, a soldier on leave from a nearby army base, is sexually involved with a young woman across the street, Epstein is driven to melancholy reflection over what was and what might have been; he takes Michael's youth and vigor as a challenge, offering us an early glimpse at Roth's most fully developed dirty old man, Mickey Sabbath of *Sabbath's Theater*.

The story is full of shifting sets of opposing pairs. Epstein is contrasted with his brother, Sol. Epstein's two children (Herbie, who dies at 11, two years before the age of religious maturity, and Sheila, the rebellious socialist) are contrasted with Sol's son and daughter (Michael, the soldier, and Ruth, who is pretty and presumably obedient). Epstein's character is also developed in relation to Michael, who seems to be a younger version of Epstein himself. Indeed, Epstein's affair commences in what appears to be an attempt to compete with his nephew. Having discovered Michael's relationship with Linda Kaufman, Epstein takes up with Linda's mother, Ida.

Another important structuring device in the story is the biblical motif that runs through it, as Roth carefully blends elements of the Book of Genesis with the MYTH of the AMERICAN DREAM. Epstein's concern with succession echoes the focal tension of the Book of Genesis, continuity versus crisis, as time and again viable heirs prove hard to produce (barren and/or elderly parents) and harder to sustain (murderous brothers and natural disasters). Hence Epstein's despair echoes that of the patriarch Abraham: "Does a man of fifty-nine all of a sudden start producing heirs?" (205). Further, Epstein's daughter Sheila and the folk singer (who remains nameless until two-thirds of the way through the story) fly in the face of Epstein's hard-won American success; they are socialists and, as Epstein observes with typically American opprobrium, the singer is "a lazy man" (205). Epstein had pursued the American capitalist route to success with the Epstein Paper Bag Company: "He had built the business from the ground, suffered and bled during the Depression and Roosevelt, only, finally, with the war and Eisenhower to see it succeed" (205). His daughter the socialist, however, has no interest in the business's fate. Clearly succession is in crisis.

In the face of such futility, Epstein finds himself picking up Ida Kaufman at a bus stop, joking with her, and soon enough, sleeping with her. When he finishes his first day with Ida by "squeeze[ing] a bill into her hands" (211), the exchange takes the quality of prostitution. Is Ida a concubine like Abraham's Hagar? Or is she more like Tamar, Judah's daughter-in-law, who orchestrates the continuation of his line by standing on a street corner and pretending to be a harlot? In either case, Epstein quickly discovers that he has contracted syphilis, marked by a telltale rash in his genital area. Epstein's affliction is a symbolic one, in both the biblical and the American canon. "His blemish" (212) appears at the site of circumcision, the locus of the biblical covenant between God and Abraham (and all of Abraham's male descendants). The redness of the rash further calls up images of the focal symbol of NATHANIEL HAW-THORNE's *The Scarlet Letter,* as it constitutes a bodily inscription of sin and of adultery in particular. In addition, the rash is a physical manifestation of Epstein's metaphorical itch. His discomfort and dissatisfaction with his life—his desire to break free of his life's monotony, to return to a time of greater promise, vigor, and hopefulness—is embodied by the "prickly heat" (212) he experiences.

When Epstein's wife discovers the rash (and infers the infidelity), the ensuing confrontation continues in a biblical vein. Epstein and his wife confront each other "naked as Adam and Eve" (212), and Epstein quickly tries to cover his nakedness. When he drops "the fig leaf of his hands" (213), his wife recognizes Epstein's indiscretions and begins assigning blame, leading to a screaming match. The shouting brings Sheila, the folk singer, and Michael running. Epstein invokes filial piety—"Respect your father!" (215)—but to no avail. During a physical confrontation, Epstein drops his sheet, "and the daughter looked on the father" (216), suggesting the sin of Noah's three children, who viewed their father's nakedness. The result is exile: Epstein is unceremoniously banned from his own bedroom. In spite of indications otherwise, Epstein insists on his innocence, trying to convince Michael, who nevertheless seems to view him as "Uncle Lou the Adulterer." Epstein tells him he has no right to judge: "Who are you, what are you, King Solomon!" (220). This reference to the biblical king known for his wisdom is also a play on the name of Epstein's brother and Michael's father, Sol. Michael is not Sol; he is Sol's son, and judge he does. Epstein's exile continues as he finds himself supplanted by the folk singer, who is referred to by his name *(Martin)* for the first time in the story when he takes over Epstein's accustomed Sunday morning tasks.

Paradoxically, Epstein's downward spiral is halted by a catastrophe; he has a heart attack, and it soon becomes clear that this is the best possible thing that could have happened to him. Instead of banishing him and asking for a divorce, Goldie reaffirms her status as his wife. She assures him that Marvin and Sheila will marry and take over the business. And the young doctor confirms that if Epstein acts his age, the doctor can treat the "irritation. . . . So it'll never come back" (230). One can only hope Epstein's metaphorical itch will prove similarly responsive to his family's intervention.

BIBLIOGRAPHY
Roth, Philip. "Epstein." In *Goodbye, Columbus and Five Short Stories.* 1959. Reprint, New York: Vintage International, 1993.

Jessica G. Rabin
Anne Arundel Community College

ERDRICH, LOUISE (1954–   )

Louise Erdrich, the eldest of seven children, grew up in Wahpeton, North Dakota, where her parents, Ralph Louis Erdrich (a German American) and Rita Joanne Gourneau (a Chippewa), taught at the Bureau of Indian Affairs school on the Turtle Mountain reservation. She received a B.A. from Dartmouth College in 1976 and an M.A. in Creative Writing from Johns Hopkins University in 1979. While she was a student at Dartmouth, she began her writing career with poetry when *Ms.* magazine published one of her poems, which later won the 1975 American Academy of Poets Prize. Her first major publication was a collection of poems entitled *Jacklight* (1984). She had also begun the stories that later became *Tracks* (1988), one of which she published under the title "Fleur."

After receiving her master's degree, Erdrich returned to Dartmouth as the Native American writer in residence. There she met the writer and professor Michael Dorris, the head of Dartmouth's Native American Studies Program. They married in 1981 and began a writing partnership that involved conceptualizing, revising, and editing each other's work. Using the pseudonym *Milou North,* they first published a series of stories that gained recognition for the authors. One story, "The World's Greatest Fisherman," later became the opening for Erdrich's first novel, *Love Medicine* (1984). The immediate and overwhelming success of this book, which won the National Book Critics Circle Award for fiction, earned Erdrich a Guggenheim Grant to write *The Beet Queen* (1986).

In these two works plus *Tracks* (1988) and *The Bingo Palace* (1993), covering the years 1860 to 1864,

Erdrich presents an epic story of a group of interrelated families that reflected her own heritage. In and around the fictional town of Argus, North Dakota, live the Pillagers, Nanapushes, Kashpaws, and Puyats of the Chippewa people; the Lazarres and the Morriseys, half-breeds; and the Adares and Jameses, the whites of Argus. Erdrich's stories revolve around the tangled lives of her characters on the reservation, in Argus, and beyond. Both internal and external forces threaten the Chippewa with extinction, yet certain tribal members promise that their culture will survive, even if they cannot remain on their homeland. These works are multiple-narrator novels, or SHORT STORY CYCLES. They contain chapters (some of which may appear independently as short stories) narrated by different characters, and they often disrupt the traditional chronological sequence of novels with cyclical or nonlinear narrative time.

Erdrich and Dorris also coauthored *The Crown of Columbus* (1991), a novel that reexamines the anniversary of Christopher Columbus's voyage to the New World told from the modern perspectives of a Native American woman named Violet Twostar and a New England Protestant poet named Roger Williams. Since then Erdrich has published another novel in the short story cycle mode, entitled *Tales of Burning Love* (1996), a departure from her focus on the Native American tribal community; and *The Antelope Wife* (1998). Her short stories have appeared in the ATLANTIC MONTHLY, *Ms.*, *Mother Jones*, *Chicago*, and the *Paris Review*. She had separated from Michael Dorris shortly before he committed suicide in 1997. In 2009, Erdrich published the story collection *The Red Convertible: Selected and New Stories 1978–2008*. The reviewer Liesl Schillinger of the *New York Times* called the book "a keepsake of the American experience" and Erdrich "a wondrous short story writer."

BIBLIOGRAPHY

Chavkin, Allan, and Nancy Feyl Chavkin. *Conversations with Louise Erdrich and Michael Dorris*. Jackson: University of Mississippi Press, 1994.

Dorris, Michael, and Louise Erdrich. *The Crown of Columbus*. New York: HarperCollins, 1991.

Erdrich, Louise. *The Antelope Wife*. New York: HarperCollins, 1998.

———. *The Beet Queen: A Novel*. New York: Henry Holt, 1986.

———. *The Bingo Palace*. New York: HarperCollins, 1993.

———. *The Blue Jay's Dance: A Birth Year*. New York: HarperCollins, 1995.

———. *Four Souls*. New York: HarperCollins, 2004.

———. *The Last Report on the Miracles at Little No Horse*. New York: HarperCollins, 2001.

———. *Love Medicine: A Novel*. New York: H. Holt, 1984.

———. *Love Medicine: New and Expanded Version*. New York: H. Holt, 1993.

———. *The Master Butchers Singing Club*. New York: HarperCollins, 2003.

———. *Original Fire: New and Selected Poems*. New York: HarperCollins, 2003.

———. *A Plague of Doves*. New York: HarperCollins, 2008.

———. *A Reader's Guide to the Fiction of Louise Erdrich: "Love Medicine," "The Best Queen," "Tracks," "The Bingo Palace."* New York: HarperPerennial, 1994.

———. *Tales of Burning Love*. Rockland, Mass.: Wheeler, 1996.

———. *Tracks*. New York: Harper & Row, 1988.

———. "Whatever Is Really Yours: An Interview with Louise Erdrich." In *Survival This Way: Interviews With Native American Poets*, edited by Joseph Bruchac. Tucson: Sun Tracks–University of Arizona Press, 1987.

Jacobs, Connie A. *The Novels of Louise Erdrich: Stories of Her People*. New York: Peter Lang, 2001.

Lyons, Rosemary. *A Comparison of the Works of Antonine Maillet of the Acadian Tradition of New Brunswick, Canada, and Louise Erdrich of the Ojibwe of North America with the Poems of Longfellow*. Lewiston, N.Y.: Edwin Mellen Press, 2002.

Peterson, Nancy J. *Against Amnesia: Contemporary Women Writers and the Crises of Historical Memory*. Philadelphia: University of Pennsylvania Press, 2001.

Scott, Steven D. *The Gamefulness of American Postmodernism: John Barth and Louise Erdrich*. New York: Peter Lang, 2000.

Spillman, Robert. "The Creative Instinct." Interview with Louise Erdrich (August 23, 2004). Available online. URL: http://www.salon.com/weekly/interview960506.html. Accessed December 6, 2008.

Stookey, Lorena L. *Louise Erdrich: A Critical Companion*. Westport, Conn.: Greenwood Press, 1999.

Wong, Hertha D. "Adoptive Mothers and Thrown-Away Children in the Novels of Louise Erdrich." In *Narrat-

ing Mothers: Theorizing Maternal Subjectivities, edited by Brenda O. Daly and Maureen T. Reddy. Knoxville: University of Tennessee Press, 1991.

Nancy L. Chick
University of Georgia

ESQUIRE   An instant success when introduced in 1933, *Esquire* magazine was directed at a previously neglected audience, males—specifically college-educated, professional men aged 25 to 45. With full-page cartoons; articles on business, sports, and fashion; and features on a wide range of issues as well as fiction, *Esquire* in its heyday was slick, informative, and humorous. The tone was one of quality in all respects, from clothing to fiction. Its first issue, which included contributions by ERNEST HEMINGWAY, John Dos Passos, RING LARDNER, ERSKINE CALDWELL, George Ade, and DASHIELL HAMMETT, set the tone for its writing. Subsequently the magazine published many, if not most, well-known and noted American authors.

"ETHAN BRAND: A CHAPTER FROM AN ABORTIVE ROMANCE" NATHANIEL HAWTHORNE (1851)

If readers accept the thinking that much of early American fiction presents a story about American reinvention and redemption, then they must consider NATHANIEL HAWTHORNE's "Ethan Brand: A Chapter from an Abortive Romance" a nonredemptive tale that contradicts that interpretation. Published as part of *The Snow Image* in 1851, "Ethan Brand" stands as a story that gets only halfway to redemption and envelops only the first step of Hawthorne's philosophy that mankind must redeem the past before it can positively affect the future. Certainly, the story represents Hawthorne's writing philosophy of conveying not necessarily the realistic details so commonly employed by the fiction of his era but instead the inward, psychological, and spiritual realities of humankind. It also portrays the typical Hawthorne themes of guilt, an examination of the self, the evil nature of man, and the isolation of the individual. Yet the story's moral message emerges as ambiguous and offers several possibilities: It may serve as a tale about the artist figure, as a cautionary tale about the dangers of divorcing the mind from the heart and humanity, as a story about the perils of obsessive dreams based on self-delusion, and as a morality narrative about the sin of pride. These themes emerge as different pieces of the same fabric: Hawthorne's focus upon human beings' internal struggles with appearances versus realities of their own and others' making.

The text's own ambiguities emphasize Hawthorne's play with appearances versus realities. The story's very title might imply a romance the author abandoned and aborted, or a romance Ethan has with an idea that has aborted his life. The reader does not know for certain what constitutes exact rendering of the legend, for the words *seemed, appeared,* and *looked* proliferate in the tale. The point of view—Bartram's—becomes questionable, for as the story progresses, Bartram becomes drunk. The commentary with the seemingly deepest significance is that of the child, Joe, who is labeled as excitable and impressionable, and Ethan himself is identified by the doctor and Bartram as a madman. On every level, the story makes the reader question what merely appears versus what is actually real.

The story begins with Ethan Brand, a former lime-kiln stoker—just as Bartram is now—essentially returning to his home on Mount Graylock to tell his tale. He comes upon Bartram and his child, Joe, in the darkness of night and frightens them as he explains that he has found "the Unpardonable Sin," and it lies within his own heart. Bartram then recognizes Ethan as the man who has become a legend in their town and sends Joe to get the townspeople. As these people gather to greet Ethan and discover their chiding cannot alter his convictions, they depart as quickly as they have arrived. Ethan then tells Bartram and Joe to sleep and he will tend the kiln. Instead, he ascends the kiln's tower and throws himself into it. In the morning, Bartram and Joe discover in the kiln a perfect batch of lime, and in its center, a skeleton with a heart of marble.

Ethan's death surely opens itself to several readings. Certainly, he could represent an artist (writer), for he spends 18 years following "The Idea" as a form of education and as a "cold observer" who converts "man and woman to be his puppets and pulling wires that moved them to such degrees of crime as were demanded for his study" (233). Just as the marble becomes subjected to the kiln to create lime, the people in Ethan's life become the raw material thrown into the kiln of his intellect to create a story. His journey to find out what lies within the hearts of men and women from a detached observer's point of view parallels the artist's journey to flesh out a theme.

But if that theme surfaces as the understanding of evil, then the tale also conveys the spiritual and moral danger of living only with the mind and without the heart, which considers—and is part of—humanity. Ethan becomes just such an individual, for as his quest continues, "Then ensued that vast intellectual development, which, in its progress, disturbed the counterpoise between his mind and his heart. . . . [His heart] had withered,—had contracted,—had hardened,—had perished" (233). In expanding his intellect, Ethan has ignored his heart and alienated himself from humanity.

Yet equally dangerous is the obsessive pursuit of his dream, his "one thought that took possession of his life" (222) and has led him to 18 years of doing nothing but focusing on his journey, deliberately experimenting with others' lives and turning them to corrupt ways. His life parallels the action of the symbolic dog that appears among the group and chases his tail until exhaustion "in pursuit of an object that could not possibly be attained" (231). Like that dog, Ethan has but come full-circle, returning to exactly where he started, a lonely and disillusioned man.

In spite of that broken condition, however, Ethan can also not rid himself of a dangerous sense of pride that makes him proclaim haughtily that regardless of his "sin of an intellect that triumphed over sense of brotherhood with man and reverence for God," he "sacrificed everything to its own mighty claims! . . . Freely, were it to do again, would I incur guilt" (226). He feels no repentance for his acts but, rather, takes pride in them. He sees himself and his intellect as mightier than God.

That might ultimately burns away to lime as the broken Ethan decides he no longer wants to live. He commits the physical act of destroying his life, or has he merely become the same raw material the artist uses to become a part of his own art? Hawthorne does not clearly say.

BIBLIOGRAPHY

Bell, Millicent, ed. *New Essays on Hawthorne's Major Tales.* Cambridge: Cambridge University Press, 1993.

Bliss, Perry. "Hawthorne at North Adams." In *The Amateur Spirit.* New York: Books for Libraries Press, 1969.

Brown, Christopher. "'Ethan Brand': A Portrait of the Artist." *Studies in Short Fiction* 17 (1980): 171–174.

Crews, Frederick C. *The Sins of the Father: Hawthorne's Psychological Themes.* New York: Oxford University Press, 1966.

"Ethan Brand" by Nathaniel Hawthorne. Available online. URL: www.classicshorts.com/stories/ebrand.html. Accessed August 14, 2006.

Fogle, Richard Hurter. *Hawthorne's Fiction: The Light and the Dark.* Norman: University of Oklahoma Press, 1964, 41–58.

Harris, Mark. "A New Reading of 'Ethan Brand': The Failed Quest." *Studies in Short Fiction* 31 (1994): 69–77.

Hawthorne, Nathaniel. "Ethan Brand: A Chapter from an Abortive Romance." In *Selected Short Stories,* edited and with an introduction by Alfred Kazin. Greenwich, Conn.: Fawcett, 1966.

"Hawthorne in Salem." Available online. URL: http://hawthorneinsalem.org/Literature/ AlienationOfTheArtist/ ethanbrand/Criticism.html. Accessed August 14, 2006.

Kazin, Alfred, ed. "Introduction." In *Selected Short Stories.* Greenwich, Conn.: Fawcett, 1966.

Male, Roy. *Hawthorne's Tragic Vision.* Austin: University of Texas Press, 1957.

Miller, Edwin Haviland. *Salem Is My Dwelling Place: A Life of Nathaniel Hawthorne.* Iowa City: University of Iowa Press, 1991.

"Nathaniel Hawthorne (1804–1864)." Available online. URL: www.wsu.edu/~campbelld/amlit/hawthor.htm. Accessed August 14, 2006.

Stein, William Bysshe. *A Study of the Devil Archetype.* Gainesville: University of Florida Press, 1953.

Stock, Ely. "The Biblical Context of 'Ethan Brand.'" *American Literature: A Journal of Literary History, Criticism, and Bibliography* 37, no. 2 (May 1965): 115–134.

Way, Brian. "Art and the Spirit of Anarchy: A Reading of Hawthorne's Short Stories." In *Nathaniel Hawthorne: New Critical Essays,* edited by Robert A. Lee, 11–30. London: Vision Paperbacks, 1982.

Patricia J. Sehulster
Westchester Community College,
State University of New York

"EUROPE" HENRY JAMES (1900) "Europe," originally published in the story collection *The Soft Side,* is a useful encapsulation in short story form of the symbolic use of Europe that HENRY JAMES had employed so successfully in the novella *DAISY MILLER* and later in a number of his novels. The tale opens with a nameless and now expatriate American male character who, during his visits to his family in Boston, followed with amused interest the lives of the three Rimmle sisters and their mother, Mrs. Rimmle. Introduced to the Rimmles by his sister-in-law, the narrator confesses that in the long hall of his memory, their collective story is worthy of an anecdote. Any reader the least bit familiar with James immediately grows alert: If the tale of these women merits nothing more in his memory than an anecdote, a parenthesis, will this narrator be trustworthy, or will we ultimately find him unreliable? (See UNRELIABLE NARRATOR.)

The narrator says that he enjoyed his visits to Brookbridge, a thinly veiled renaming of Cambridge. There, in a square white house with a neat brick walk, live the Rimmle family of women, Mr. Rimmle having passed on before the narrator entered the scene (although the narrator somewhat wittily places Mr. Rimmle's birth around the time of the Battle of Waterloo). Having established his own youth at the time of meeting—and having established the Rimmles as the acme of New England culture and Puritanism—he begins the chronologically sequenced story of Rebecca (Becky), Maria, and Jane.

From the earliest time anyone can recall, Mrs. Rimmle has been telling her daughters that as soon as her health permits, she shall accompany them to Europe, where she had once traveled with her eminent husband. The promise of Europe dangles in front of these girls for decades, for Mrs. Rimmle's health is never quite good enough. All three of the daughters have familiarized themselves with the idea of Europe, Becky, the literary sister, most of all. The scholar of the family, she has edited and translated all the letters from associates who praised her father's many professional achievements. On first meeting the sisters, the narrator learns that since Mrs. Rimmle cannot be left alone, their idea is that Becky and Jane, the pretty sister, should be the first to go. The narrator, obliquely attracted to Jane, senses her submerged and restless passion. When he receives a letter from his sister-in-law telling him that the trip never materialized, he feels sympathy for them and acknowledges his genuine feeling for the young women.

The years wear on; the narrator travels to Europe several times and continues to visit the Rimmles whenever he is in Boston. He refers to himself and his sister-in-law as "students" of the "case," recalling the subtitle "A Study" in Winterbourne's narrative about Daisy Miller. Although he jokes with his sister-in-law that the sisters should hasten their mother's death, he privately admits that if only two could go, he would choose Maria as the one to stay, and if only one could go, he would choose Jane, who he thinks should burst free and go on her own. Then, without warning, he learns that Jane has gone and stubbornly refuses to leave Florence, Italy. Indeed, she intends to travel to Asia and has become a flirt. Moreover, says the sister-in-law, Becky is sending her money.

When the narrator travels to Boston, an unrecognizable Becky visits him—unrecognizable because she has so aged that she looks exactly like her mother. She surprises him with the news that Jane will never leave Europe, and Mrs. Rimmle, although alive, is dead. He finds Mrs. Rimmle looking like a mummy; she tells him Jane is dead and now Becky is going. To Europe? the narrator asks. But for Becky, Europe seems to have become a private METAPHOR for death. Only the thought of it had kept her alive, and the implication is that with the realization that she will never see Europe, Becky has no reason to continue living. When he next visits, Becky is dead, but the shrunken mother remains seated in the midst of the shrinelike tributes to her husband. Maria looks even older than Becky had. The mother repeats to him that Jane will never come back and he imagines Jane in the flush of a second youth. The mother, now called a witch, says that Becky has gone to Europe. Clearly, then, the differing equations of Europe—with death by the mother and with sex and passion by the daughters, two of whom, failing to experience either, succumb to death literally or figuratively—reflect a discrepancy that the narrator reports but fails to understand. The mother has a terrible tale to tell, for after returning from Europe with her husband, she lived a death-in-life existence and tries to prevent her daughters from sharing her fate. But the exact nature of that fate—and marriage to the man whose presence still rules the house—can only be surmised by the reader, for the narrator, who classifies the women as so many museum specimens, can never fathom that even he has missed the point.

BIBLIOGRAPHY
James, Henry. "Europe." In *American Short Stories*. 4th ed. Edited by Eugene Current-Garcia and Walton R. Patrick. Glenview, Ill.: Scott, Foresman, 1982.

"EVENING SUN, THAT" See "THAT EVENING SUN."

"EVER FALL IN LOVE WITH A MIDGET?"

WILLIAM SAROYAN (1938) Saroyan's "Ever Fall in Love with a Midget?" was first published in his 1938 collection *Love, Where Is My Hat?* A Fresno native, Saroyan explored American folk culture of the depression. "Ever Fall in Love with a Midget?" relates the beer-fueled conversation of two men in a western bar. An unnamed narrator listens to the increasingly sensationalistic life adventures of his companion, the 56-year-old cowboy Murph, who enters his stories through intriguing questions. In addition to the title question, Murph asks, "Don't suppose you ever had to put on a dress to save your skin, did you?" and "Ever try to herd cattle on a bicycle?" (21). Murph's adventures are punctuated by the narrator's repeated urging to "have another beer." As he drinks, Murph tells of card games, fights, a daring escape dressed in drag, the challenges of herding on bicycle, and a (meteorologically impossible) hurricane in Toledo, Ohio. In spite of the narrator's urging, Murph never returns to the tale of the midget. As it becomes clear that Murph's adventures are exaggerated or entirely fictional, the narrator enters into playful participation. When he repeats Murph's question, asking whether the cowboy has ever fallen in love with a midget, the cowboy seems to have forgotten his original discussion of the topic and responds, "Can't say that I have" (25). In the final line, the narrator offers, "Let *me* tell *you* about it"

(25). As a result, the "amazon of small proportions" (20) at the heart of the story is never actually described. Her unusual body, and presumably the other strange subjects of Murph's tales, exists only for sensational effect. Saroyan's work thus reflects the freak-show culture pervasive in 1930s rural America, in which difference and disability served as forms of entertainment, sometimes at the expense of true knowledge of the disabled individual. "Ever Fall in Love with a Midget?" is ultimately a story about storytelling, and not about love or physicality.

Saroyan revisited the story's barroom setting and some of its content in the 1939 play *The Time of Your Life* (which was awarded the Pulitzer Prize, although Saroyan objected to prizes as status symbols in the arts and refused the award). Prolific both as a playwright and a story writer, Saroyan builds his fiction around dialogue. Saroyan is moderate in his representation of dialect—he avoids phonetic spelling, for instance—but nevertheless endows Murph with a distinctive and colorful voice in which pronoun references are vague and the subject of a sentence is often omitted. This grammatical style parallels the work's theme of tall tales and its celebration of a good story over factual knowledge.

BIBLIOGRAPHY
Foster, Edward Halsey. *William Saroyan: A Study of the Short Fiction*. Twayne's Studies in Short Fiction, 26. New York: Twayne, 1991.
Saroyan, William. *Love, Here Is My Hat*. London: Faber & Faber, 1938, 19–25.

Lillie Craton
Kennesaw State University

"EVERYDAY USE" ALICE WALKER (1973)

Probably ALICE WALKER's most frequently anthologized story, "Everyday Use" first appeared in Walker's collection *In Love and Trouble: Stories by Black Women*. Walker explores in this story a divisive issue for African Americans, one that has concerned a number of writers, Lorraine Hansberry, for instance, in her play *Raisin in the Sun* (1959). The issue is generational as well as cultural: In leaving home and embracing their African heritage, must adults turn their backs on their

African-American background and their more traditional family members? The issue, while specifically African-American, can also be viewed as a universal one in terms of modern youth who fail to understand the values of their ancestry and of their immediate family. Walker also raises the question of naming, a complicated one for African Americans, whose ancestors were named by slaveholders.

The first-person narrator of the story is Mrs. Johnson, mother of two daughters, Maggie and Dicie, nicknamed Dee. Addressing the readers as "you," she draws us directly into the story while she and Maggie await a visit from Dee. With deft strokes, Walker has Mrs. Johnson reveal essential information about herself and her daughters. She realistically describes herself as a big-boned, slow-tongued woman with no education and a talent for hard work and outdoor chores. When their house burned down some 12 years previous, Maggie was severely burned. Comparing Maggie to a wounded animal, her mother explains that she thinks of herself as unattractive and slow-witted, yet she is good-natured too, and preparing to marry John Thomas, an honest local man. Dee, on the other hand, attractive, educated, and self-confident, has left her home (of which she was ashamed) to forge a new and successful life.

When she appears, garbed in African attire, along with her long-haired friend, Asalamalakim, Dee informs her family that her new name is *Wangero Leewanika Kemanio*. When she explains that she can no longer bear to use the name given to her by the whites who oppressed her, her mother tries to explain that she was named for her aunt, and that the name *Dicie* harkens back to pre–CIVIL WAR days. Dee's failure to honor her own family history continues in her gentrified appropriation of her mother's butter dish and churn, both of which have a history, but both of which Dee views as quaint artifacts that she can display in her home. When Dee asks for her grandmother's quilts, however, Mrs. Johnson speaks up: Although Maggie is willing to let Dee have them because, with her goodness and fine memory, she needs no quilts to help her remember Grandma Dee, her mother announces firmly that she intends them as a wedding gift for Maggie. Mrs. Johnson approvingly tells Dee that Maggie

will put them to "everyday use" rather than hanging them on a wall.

Dee leaves in a huff, telling Maggie she ought to make something of herself. With her departure, peace returns to the house, and Mrs. Johnson and Maggie sit comfortably together, enjoying each other's company. Although readers can sympathize with Dee's desire to improve her own situation and to feel pride in her African heritage, Walker also makes clear that in rejecting the African-American part of that heritage, she loses a great deal. Her mother and sister, despite the lack of the success that Dee enjoys, understand the significance of family. One hopes that the next child will not feel the need to choose one side or the other but will confidently embrace both.

BIBLIOGRAPHY
Walker, Alice. "Everyday Use." In *Major Writers of Short Fiction: Stories and Commentary,* edited by Ann Charters. Boston: St. Martin's, 1993, 1,282–1,299.

EVERYMAN/EVERYWOMAN   This term is from the medieval morality play entitled *Everyman* (ca. 1500), in which the protagonist, Everyman, receives a summons from Death and attempts to persuade his friends—named for various items and virtues such as Worldly Goods, Kindred, Fellowship, and Beauty—to accompany him on his journey. Various life-changing experiences occur along the way, with the help of other wayfarers such as Knowledge and Confession. In modern fiction, *Everyman* and *Everywoman* apply to any character who represents us in his or her recognition and employment of his or her weaknesses and strengths along life's pathway. HARRIET PRESCOTT SPOFFORD'S "CIRCUMSTANCE," for instance, features an Everywoman character, and NATHANIEL HAWTHORNE'S "YOUNG GOODMAN BROWN," an Everyman.

"EVERYTHING THAT RISES MUST CONVERGE" FLANNERY O'CONNOR (1965)   As do many of FLANNERY O'CONNOR's short stories, "Everything That Rises Must Converge" deals with the Christian concepts of sin and repentance. The specific sin O'Connor focuses on in this story is pride. As a Catholic, O'Connor considered this offense against

God a venial sin, an attempt to place human power and ability above God's. O'Connor's portrayal is set in the South, centering on two white characters: an elderly woman living in the past glories of her racial heritage and her college-educated son, Julian, who considers himself liberated from such stereotypical (see STEREOTYPE) racist views of life. The story begins with the two embarking on a bus journey to an exercise class for the mother. As they travel, each character reveals not only racial prejudice but also severe antagonism toward the other.

Julian Godhigh, as part of a "new" generation, prides himself on the fact that he is unlike his mother in applying racial stereotypes: Such actions are obsolete echoes of a distant past, and he considers himself above them. Embarrassed constantly by his mother's egotistical attitude (a fact emphasized by her overweight condition), Julian decides he will use the bus trip to "cut her down to size." By attempting to make his mother see her own flaws instead of those of an "inferior" race, he will force her to come face to face with "who she really is." Such self-discovery in spite of self-deception then becomes the major thematic (see THEME) emphasis of this tale. Ironically, however, both Julian and his mother progress from inaccurate self-images to the stark realization that the character traits they so prize are in fact petty and worthless.

Julian's way of forcing self-discovery in his mother includes fraternizing with black people on the bus, an act that his mother considers outrageous but that Julian perceives as evidence of his tolerance and lack of racial bias. He feels his mind is obviously superior to hers, and thus he alone can see her flagrant mistakes. Mother, on the other hand, emphasizes the value of the heart over the head and insists that human feelings and emotions are more important than intelligence. Since she "feels" superior, she must be so, and Julian's actions are therefore both insensitive and inconsiderate.

O'Connor reveals the flaws of both Godhighs through repeated imagery and through the use of DOPPELGANGERS, or doubles. Using the phrase "Rome wasn't built in a day," O'Connor suggests the tottering world of Julian and his mother: Their existence is truly not the "Julian" age of Rome's expansion and success but rather an indication of its ultimate fall. In addition, through the use of doppelgangers, O'Connor points out the similarities of the seeming disparate races by introducing a black woman who boards the bus wearing the same purple hat that Julian's mother has picked out earlier in the day. Carrying a small boy, the woman is the mirror image of her white counterpart. Julian, duly noting only part of the parallel, sees this as a delicious put-down of his mother's arrogance but fails to note the parallels to himself in the little boy, who is also cowed and dominated by a fiercely aggressive parent.

Mother, fascinated by the young boy's cuteness, is pleased when he sits down next to her, and symbolically O'Connor suggests that the mothers have exchanged sons. As the bus ride continues, Julian must watch as his mother continues to try to attract the young black boy's attention, all the while fostering the condescending attitude to another race that Julian so despises. Eventually, when both parent/child pairs depart the bus at the same stop, Julian's mother offers the child a shiny new penny, an indication of her insensitivity and her feelings of superiority. Julian exults when his mother receives a fierce blow from the black mother's purse that knocks her to the ground. With prideful lack of pity and forgiveness, Julian believes his mother has received only the punishment she deserves. When, however, he notes that the blow has resulted in a heart attack or stroke that threatens his mother's life, Julian finally understands that sin must be met with mercy and that his own self-centered attitude has prohibited him from ministry until it is too late.

O'Connor's intriguing title for the story seems to suggest that all of life (classes, races, and religions) eventually will have to intersect, just as pure laws of physics would predict that everything on Earth that rises eventually will converge somewhere in space. Whether this action causes a disastrous collision or a peaceful merging of equals is left to the characters and to the reader.

Michael J. Meyer
DePaul University

EXISTENTIALISM A philosophical theory that gained a great deal of attention during and after WORLD WAR II, especially in Europe. Based on the premise that one simply exists in a meaningless world before one can acquire a defined character, existentialism asserts the twin concepts of free will and responsibility. Because we are born into a valueless world in which no God exists, each individual must bear the responsibility for making meaning out of an ABSURD, lonely, anxiety-producing existence. In the process, one must often overcome feelings of anguish and despair. Existentialism, particularly as expressed and made popular by the French writer-philosopher Jean-Paul Sartre, was persuasively used in the novels of such European writers as Albert Camus, Simone de Beauvoir, Fyodor Dostoyevski, and Franz Kafka (see KAFKAESQUE) and aroused the interest of numerous American writers. ERNEST HEMINGWAY, for instance, thematically incorporates existentialism into his celebrated story "A CLEAN, WELL-LIGHTED PLACE."

EXODUS In the Old Testament of the Bible, the story of the liberation of the people of Israel from slavery in Egypt in the 15th century B.C. and their safe passage through the Red Sea, led by Moses, to Mount Sinai. Direct and indirect ALLUSIONS to Exodus occur in such stories as RALPH ELLISON's "King of the Bingo Game" and WILLIAM FAULKNER's GO DOWN, MOSES.

"EXPENSIVE MOMENT, THE" GRACE PALEY **(1985)** Although GRACE PALEY has written a comparatively small body of work, publishing primarily short stories and poetry, she figures prominently among late 20th-century fiction writers. Part of her third collection of short stories, *Later the Same Day* (1985), "The Expensive Moment" features Faith Asbury, a protagonist who appears in many of her other stories, creating an "ongoing story cycle" (Arcana 3). Faith is a figure whom many readers have identified with the author herself, because of similarities to Paley's life and political activism, but "this factor has increasingly distorted some interpretations of the stories" (Isaacs 3–4). In fact, many readers "feel that they have been tricked because the author has been so

good at making up Faith" (Arcana 3). In "The Expensive Moment," told in Paley's distinctive narrative style, Faith, a wife and mother of two grown children, moves through the story in a series of conversations, in particular one she continues with her friend Ruth. In these conversations, Paley makes distinctions between men and women, as she depicts the contrasts between the language and values of both genders in the story. In "The Expensive Moment," as in other Paley stories, the author's protest against women's oppression manifests when Faith connects to a Chinese woman "from half the world away who'd lived a life beyond foreignness and had experienced extreme history" (374) and creates a bond more mutual and effective than the relationships she has with several of the men in the story.

Before Faith meets Xie Feng, who is from China, she visits her lover, Nick Hegestraw, "the famous sinologist," a man who studies Chinese language and culture. Her friend Ruth guesses Faith is having an affair from the way she describes Nick, with whom Faith discusses politics and culture. She asks Nick about China's "rotten foreign policy" (369), a question that receives a series of theoretical answers from Nick and other people, including her own son Richard.

Although she understands political theory and cultural issues, Faith has other, more practical, more humane issues on her mind. She imagines the "beauty of trade, the caravans crossing Africa and Asia, the roads to Peru through the terrible forests of Guatemala, and then especially the village markets of underdeveloped countries" (369–370). These thoughts contrast with Richard's beliefs, as he mocks his mother's ideas of beauty. He is a product, she thinks, of "the Free Market, which costs so much in the world" (370). She compares her son to herself during an adolescent argument she had with her own father and then compares him to the serious young men she met during draft counseling. She realizes that "not one of them was trivial, and neither was Richard," as she recognizes the intensity and promise of his youth (370).

Richard stands at a metaphoric intersection of two paths, "the expensive moment when everyone his age is called but just a few are chosen by conscience or passion or even only love of one's own agemates" to do something meaningful for humanity (370–371). From Faith's perspective, he is of the age when he could try to improve the world either by doing something destructive, like destroying a missile or setting off a bomb, or by doing something constructive, like becoming a lawyer or a doctor. She thinks, "He could have done a lot of good, just as much that way, healing or defending the underdog" (371).

When Faith meets Xie Feng, a Chinese woman Ruth has met earlier, they spend the day together, because the woman wishes to see her world—the world of the community and the home. Faith shows her around her home, pointing out its rooms, where her sons and her husband live with her. Then she takes her out into the neighborhood: "They walked east and south to neighborhoods where our city, in fields of garbage and broken brick, stands desolate, her windows burnt and blind. Here, Faith said, the people suffer and struggle, their children turn round and round in one place, growing first in beauty, then in rage" (376). The Chinese woman seems to understand Faith's meaning; she, too, is interested in the lives of the next generation, her own children, her sister's children. She asks the question Faith herself has contemplated earlier in the story; she, too, wonders about the best way to raise children: "Shall we raise them to be straightforward, honorable, kind, brave, maybe shrewd, self-serving a little? What is the best way to help them in the real world? We don't know the best way" (376).

Paley demonstrates the connections between women—here between two women from opposite sides of the Earth—when Faith recognizes her own uncertainty in the woman's questioning. The Chinese woman talks to Faith about the things Faith is truly interested in: the day-to-day business of living and raising families. With Xie Feng, Faith engages in the way one Paley biographer claims the author engaged with other mothers in her own neighborhood, who "in those days inspired her to. . . . think global/work local" (Arcana 64). This conversation, like the conversations with Ruth, contrasts the discussions Faith has with her lover Nick, who does not engage in the same

kind of mutual exchange she shares with women friends. On the contrary, he lives in the world of ideas, removed from the lives of the community: "He was writing in his little book—thoughts, comments, maybe even new songs for Chinese modernization—which he planned to publish as soon as possible" (373). Soon, Faith loses interest in him; her interest is held by her new Chinese friend, suggesting the mutual concern among women is more meaningful to her than the preoccupations of men, which have caused "the colossal failures of patriarchy—war, ecological destruction, world hunger" (Taylor 18).

BIBLIOGRAPHY

Arcana, Judith. *Grace Paley's Life Stories: A Literary Biography.* Urbana: University of Illinois Press, 1993.

Isaacs, Neil D. *Grace Paley: A Study of the Short Fiction.* Boston: Twayne, 1990.

Paley, Grace. "The Expensive Moment." In *The Collected Stories.* New York: Farrar, Straus & Giroux, 1994, 365–377.

Taylor, Jacqueline. *Grace Paley: Illuminating the Dark Lives.* Austin: University of Texas Press, 1990.

Heather Ostman
Empire State College, State University of New York

"EYES, THE" EDITH WHARTON (1910) One of EDITH WHARTON'S most respected ghost stories (see GHOST STORY), "The Eyes" is a modern GOTHIC tale that illustrates a haunted inner consciousness. The external horror of the tale is a reflection of internal evil, much as it is in HENRY JAMES'S "The TURN OF THE SCREW." As does James, Wharton uses ghostly encounters as a setting for psychological study and personal discovery.

The story begins after a gathering at Andrew Culwin's home, where friends have been telling ghost stories. The narrator describes Culwin as a rationalist who does not believe in ghosts. Culwin sees himself as mentor to young male artists. After everyone else leaves, Phillip Frenham, a young intellectual, asks his host to tell a ghost story of his own. Culwin reveals to the narrator and Frenham the tale of ghostly eyes that have haunted him on several occasions. The framing narrative of "The Eyes" allows the reader to understand the source of these visitations, while revealing Culwin's misogynistic, detached, and cruel character.

Culwin is first visited by the eyes after his marriage proposal to his cousin, Alice. He has pursued her out of scientific curiosity, to "find out the secret of her content." Culwin is awakened that evening by the glowing eyes. He is so frightened that he leaves for Europe without a word to Alice. Months later Alice asks Culwin to befriend her cousin, Gilbert, a young man who wants to be a writer. Culwin lies to Gilbert about his talent in order to satisfy his own selfish desire to impress the young man. Afterward Culwin is again haunted by the eyes. Once Gilbert learns how Culwin has used him, the eyes disappear. After Cul-win finishes his story, Frenham realizes that he is the next victim of Culwin's manipulation, and Culwin finally sees that he himself is the source of the hideous eyes.

BIBLIOGRAPHY

Fedorko, Kathy A. *Gender and the Gothic in the Fiction of Edith Wharton.* Tuscaloosa: University of Alabama Press, 1995.

Wharton Edith. *Collected Short Stories.* 2 vols. Edited by R. W. B. Lewis. New York: Scribner, 1968.

White, Barbara. *Edith Wharton: A Study of the Short Fiction.* New York: Twayne, 1991.

Tracie Guzzio
Ohio University

F

FABLE A short story or tale, usually epigrammatic (see EPIGRAM), exemplifying a moral thesis or demonstrating correct or "good" behavior. A fable's characters can include gods, people, animals, or even inanimate objects, and the fable itself illustrates a moral, usually stated at the end in the form of an epigram by either the narrator or one of the characters. Most common is the beast fable, in which animals talk and act like the human types they represent. (See PERSONIFICATION.) In the fable of the race between the hare and the tortoise, for example, the hare runs quickly but has no stamina; the tortoise finishes the race ahead of the hare, illustrating the moral "Slow and steady wins the day." An early set of beast fables was attributed to Aesop, a Greek slave of the sixth century B.C.; in the 17th century the Frenchman Jean Fontaine wrote a set of witty fables in verse. In *Animal Farm* (1945), the British writer George Orwell expanded the beast fable into a sustained satire on the political and social conditions of the age. See also, for example, Geoffrey Chaucer's "The Nun's Priest's Tale," and JAMES THURBER's *Fables for Our Time* (1940). A form of beast fable occurs in NATIVE AMERICAN stories; MOURNING DOVE, for instance, writes COYOTE stories that include many tales in which animals demonstrate human characteristics.

See also AESOP'S FABLES, COYOTE STORY.

"FACTS IN THE CASE OF M. VALDEMAR, THE" EDGAR ALLAN POE (1845) The

seriocomic tale "The Facts in the Case of M. Valdemar" first appeared in *American Review* in December 1845 as "The Facts of M. Valdemar's Case." The revised tale was reprinted with an introductory note by Poe that noted the connection to *American Review* in the December 20, 1845, issue of *Broadway Journal,* the only journal over which Poe managed to gain complete editorial control. The story evolved out of Poe's earlier attempt to relate a Mr. Vankirk's experience with mesmerism that was titled "Mesmeric Revelation," which first appeared in August 1844 in *Columbian Magazine.*

The unidentified first-person narrator begins his tale by explaining that, for the past three years, he has been interested in the subject of mesmerism, a form of hypnotism that renders the subject unable to feel pain, which was developed by Franz Anton Mesmer, an 18th-century Austrian physician. In the course of his studies, the narrator realizes that no one has tried to mesmerize someone "in articulo mortis" (480), at the moment of death. Therefore, he devises an experiment designed to answer the following questions: whether a person nearing death would be susceptible to being mesmerized, what effect being close to death would have on the process of being mesmerized, and how long actual death might be staved off by being mesmerized. To assist with his experiment, he recruits a friend from Harlem, New York, the well-known author M. Ernest Valdemar, who is in the late stages of tuberculosis and whom the narrator has previously been able to hypnotize.

When M. Valdemar is nearing death, seven months prior to the time of the story, he sends for the narrator. Because the cryptically identified physicians Doctors D___ and F___ predict the patient's demise by midnight of the next day, the narrator sends for a medical student, Mr. Theodore L___l, who arrives to record the proceedings, from which the narrator tells this story. After M. Valdemar verbally agrees to allow the narrator to proceed (providing an early example of gaining informed consent from a patient before a procedure is done), the narrator then mesmerizes the patient, who first says he is asleep, then a few hours later that he is dying, then a little bit later that he is dead. For seven months Valdemar persists in this final state, until the narrator, in consultation with the physicians, decides that the humane thing to do would be to take the patient out of the trance. As the narrator makes the movements associated with drawing someone out of a trance, Valdemar's tongue keeps saying, "Dead! dead!" (490) until the body crumbles away into a putrid mess and the story ends.

Critics see the irony of the story as another example of a characteristic way that Poe approaches obsessive themes in his work. In what can be seen as a parody of some of the experiments being legitimately reported during his lifetime, Poe applies the well-regarded age-old scientific method to the relatively new psychological approach that was ambivalently received in the scientific and medical community of the 19th century. Poe himself admitted in letters written to Arch Ramsay and George W. Eveleth that the story of M. Valdemar was a hoax, though critics have argued that the public uproar after his story was first published forced Poe to make this statement.

BIBLIOGRAPHY

The Edgar Allan Poe Society of Baltimore. Available online. URL: http://www.eapoe.org/works/index.htm. Accessed August 14, 2006.

Poe, Edgar Allan. "The Facts in the Case of M. Valdemar." In *Great Short Works of Edgar Allan Poe,* edited by G. R. Thompson. New York: Perennial Classic–Harper, 1970.

Ware, Tracy. "The 'Salutary Discomfort' in the Case of M. Valdemar." *Studies in Short Fiction* 31 (1994): 471–480.

Peggy J. Huey
University of Tampa

FAIRY TALE The fairy is a mythical being with a diminutive human form, a mischievous temperament, and magical powers. The description of these tiny creatures varies from the graceful, delicate English pixie to the gnarled, old Irish leprechaun. Other types of fairies are Arabian genies, Scandinavian trolls, and German elves. The fairy tale is a simple narrative that usually includes fairies but might also include giants, ogres, and other supernatural beings in magical or fantastic settings written for the amusement of children. The Danish writer Hans Christian Andersen wrote many original fairy tales, and the German Brothers Grimm published a well-known collection.

"FALL OF THE HOUSE OF USHER, THE" EDGAR ALLAN POE (1839)

Long considered EDGAR ALLAN POE's masterpiece, "The Fall of the House of Usher" continues to intrigue new generations of readers. The story has a tantalizingly horrific appeal, and since its publication in *Burton's Gentleman's Magazine,* scholars, critics, and general readers continue to grapple with the myriad possible reasons for the story's hold on the human psyche. These explanations range from the pre-Freudian to the pre–Waste Land and pre-Kafka-cum-nihilist (see KAFKAESQUE and NIHILISM) to the biographical and the cultural. Indeed, despite Poe's distaste for ALLEGORY, some critics view the house as a METAPHOR for the human psyche (Strandberg 705). Whatever conclusion a reader reaches, none finds the story an easy one to forget.

Poe's narrative technique draws us immediately into the tale. On a stormy autumn (with an implied pun on the word *fall?*) evening, a traveler—an outsider, like the reader—rides up to the Usher mansion. This traveler, also the first-person narrator and boyhood friend of Roderick Usher, the owner of the house, has arrived in response to a summons from Usher. We share the narrator's responses to the gloomy mood and the menacing facade of the House of Usher, noticing, with him, the dank lake that reflects the house (effectively doubling it, like the Usher twins we will soon meet) and apprehensively viewing the fissure, or crack, in the wall. Very soon we understand that, whatever else it may mean, the house is a metaphor for the Usher family itself and that if the house is seriously flawed, so are its occupants.

With this foreboding introduction, we enter the interior through a Gothic portal with the narrator. With him we encounter Roderick Usher, who has changed drastically since last the narrator saw him. His cadaverous appearance, his nervousness, his mood swings, his almost extrahuman sensitivity to touch, sound, taste, smell, and light, along with the narrator's report that he seems lacking in moral sense, portrays a deeply troubled soul. We learn, too, that his twin sister, Madeline, a neurasthenic woman like her brother, is subject to catatonic trances. These two characters, like the house, are woefully, irretrievably flawed. The suspense continues to climb as we go deeper into the dark house and, with the narrator, attempt to fathom Roderick's malady.

Roderick, a poet and an artist, and Madeline represent the last of the Usher line. They live alone, never venturing outside. The sympathetic narrator does all he can to ease Roderick's hours, recounting a ballad by Roderick, which, entitled "The Haunted House," speaks figuratively of the House of Usher: Evil and discord possess the house, echoing the decay the narrator has noticed on the outside. During his stay Roderick tells the narrator that Madeline has died, and together they place her in a vault; she looks deceptively lifelike. Thereafter Roderick's altered behavior causes the narrator to wonder whether he hides a dark secret or has fallen into madness. A week or so later, as a storm rages outside, the narrator seeks to calm his host by reading to him a romance entitled "The Mad Trist." The title could be evidence that both the narrator's diagnoses are correct: Roderick has a secret (perhaps he has trysted with his own sister?) and is now utterly mad. The tale unfolds parallel to the action in the Usher house: As Ethelred, the hero of the romance, breaks through the door and slays the hermit, Madeline, not dead after all, breaks though her coffin. Just before she appears at the door, Roderick admits that they have buried her alive and that she now stands at the door. Roderick's admission is too late. Just as Ethelred now slays the dragon, causing the family shield to fall at his feet, Madeline falls on her brother (the hermit who never leaves the house),

killing them both and bringing down the last symbol of the House of Usher. As the twins collapse in death together, the entire house disintegrates into the lake, destroying the double image noted at the opening of the story.

The story raises many questions tied to gender issues: Is Madeline Roderick's female double, or DOP-PELGANGER? If, as many critics suggest, Roderick is Poe's self-portrait, then do Madeline and Roderick represent the feminine and masculine sides of the author? Is incest at the core of Roderick's relationship with Madeline? Is he (like his creator, some would suggest) a misogynist? FEMINISTS have for some time now pointed to Poe's theory that the most poetic subject in the world is the "DEATH OF A BEAUTIFUL WOMAN." Is Madeline's return from the tomb a feminist revenge story? Does she, as the Ethelred of the romance does, adopt the male role of the hero as she slays the evil hermit and the evil dragon, who together symbolize Roderick's character? Has the mad Roderick made the narrator complicit in his crime (saying *we* rather than *I* buried her alive)? If so, to what extent must we view him as the UNRELIABLE NARRATOR? Is the narrator himself merely reporting a dream—or the after-effects of opium, as he vaguely intimates at points in the story? Or, as the critic and scholar Eugene Current-Garcia suggests, can we generally agree that Poe, like NATHANIEL HAWTHORNE, was haunted by the presence of evil? If so, "perhaps most of his tales should be read as allegories of nightmarish, neurotic states of mind" (Current-Garcia 81). We may never completely plumb the psychological complexities of this story, but it implies deeply troubling questions and nearly endless avenues for interpretation.

BIBLIOGRAPHY

Current-Garcia, Eugene. *The American Short Story before 1850.* Boston: Twayne, 1985.

May, Charles E. *Edgar Allan Poe: Studies in the Short Fiction.* Boston: Twayne, 1991.

Poe, Edgar Allan. "The Fall of the House of Usher." In *The Heath Anthology of American Literature.* Vol. 1, 3rd ed. Edited by Paul Lauter. Boston: Houghton Mifflin, 1998.

Strandberg, Victor. "The Fall of the House of Usher." In *Reference Guide to Short Fiction,* edited by Noelle Watson. Detroit: Gale Press, 1994.

FALSE DAWN Edith Wharton (1924)

One of EDITH WHARTON's many stories of New York, *False Dawn* was published with the subtitle *The 'Forties* in 1924 as the first of four volumes in a set entitled *Old New York*. This NOVELLA recounts the experiences of Lewis Raycie, son of an old New York family. As a young man departing on his European grand tour, he is given $5,000 by his father to spend on artwork for the family collection. Instead of buying what is popular at the time, however—such as works by Carlo Dolce, Salvator Rosa, and, ideally, Raphael—Lewis becomes aware of a "revolution in taste" in Europe through meeting the English writer and critic John Ruskin. Following Ruskin's pre-Raphaelite tastes, Lewis instead purchases works by the primitive artists Giotto de Bondone, Carpaccio, Mantegna, and Piero della Francesca. His father, furious with his choices, disowns him and dies within a year. Lewis marries his childhood sweetheart, Beatrice Kent, and in order to make a living, they attempt to charge admission to see the collection but are unsuccessful.

In the conclusion of the novella, set several years later, a young narrator learns of how the Raycies, shamed, went off to live alone in the country and died at an early age, along with their daughter, Louisa. The collection was passed on and finally found, 50 years later, in the attic of the elderly Miss Alethea Raycie's house. It was now priceless, "one of the most beautiful collections of Italian Primitives in the world" (367), but the inheritor of the collection, Netta Cosby, sold the works to various museums in order to buy jewels, Rolls-Royces, and a house on Fifth Avenue.

The novella exhibits Wharton's masterful use of IRONY, a pervasive characteristic of her work, in treating the division between crass new-money values, which Wharton often identified with Americans, and aesthetic taste and connoisseurship, traits Wharton herself valued and often associated with Europeans. The novella also illustrates REALISM in its careful detailing of life in New York of the 1840s. R. W. B. Lewis notes a connection to Wharton's own life in the novella; she "wove an account of her parents' courtship" (458) into the work when she described Lewis Raycie's, in the face of family disapproval, sailing an improvised boat down Long Island Sound in the early morning to meet his sweetheart, as Wharton's father, George Frederic Jones, had done in order to meet her mother, Lucretia Rhinelander.

BIBLIOGRAPHY

Brooks, Van Wyck. *The Dream of Arcadia: American Artists and Writers in Italy 1760–1915*. New York: Dutton, 1958.

Lewis, R. W. B. *Edith Wharton: A Biography*. New York: Scribner, 1975.

Rae, Catherine M. *Edith Wharton's New York Quartet*. Lanham, Md.: University Press of America, 1984.

Wharton, Edith. *False Dawn (The 'Forties)*. In *Wharton: Novellas and Other Writings*. New York: Literary Classics of the United States, 1990.

Charlotte Rich
University of North Carolina at Chapel Hill

FANTASY

A narrative or situation in fiction with no basis in the real world. Authors may use fantasy for pure entertainment, or for serious commentary, direct or implied, on real-world issues and situations. Much SCIENCE FICTION and UTOPIAN fiction employs fantasy, as in the stories of Isaac Asimov or RAY BRADBURY, for instance. Fantasy is a major component of the fairy tale or the FABLE. It may also be an element of MAGICAL REALISM in contemporary American fiction, as in the stories of JOHN BARTH, for example, and in numerous stories by African-American, Hispanic-American, and Native American writers.

FARRELL, JAMES T.   See STUDS LONIGAN.

FASCISM

A political philosophy that exalts nation and race at the expense of the individual. Major concepts include dictatorial leadership, a one-party system, an aggressive military policy, control at all levels of individual and economic activity, and the use of special police forces to instill fear and suppress opposition. The modern term derives from the party led by Benito Mussolini, who ruled Italy from 1922 until the Italian defeat in WORLD WAR II, and was later applied to include ADOLF HITLER's regime in Germany and Francisco Franco's government in Spain, among others.

"FAT GIRL, THE" ANDRE DUBUS (1979) ANDRE DUBUS, a Louisiana native and devout Catholic, created fiction often noted for its psychological realism and gentle morality. His short fiction emphasizes character study and examines moments of affection, violence, and self-discovery in American life. Dubus's straightforward narrative contrasts with the postmodern styles explored by his contemporaries in the 1960s and 1970s. "The Fat Girl," first published in the 1977 collection *Adultery and Other Choices,* imagines the interior life of the overweight Louise, who begins to eat secretly at age nine in response to a strict diet imposed by her image-conscious mother. Eating little in public, Louise enjoys snacking as a private and sensual pleasure. Her extra weight causes parental disapproval and awkwardness with her peers. In high school, Louise's social life is limited to the company of other outsiders: a plain girl and an anxious smart girl. In college, Louise forms a deep friendship with her roommate Carrie, who notices and accepts Louise's secret eating. As they near graduation, Carrie begins dating and urges Louise to diet to increase her chances of finding romantic love. Carrie offers structure and affectionate encouragement (far more nurturing than the discipline imposed by Louise's mother) to help Louise shrink to 113 pounds over the course of a year. The process is difficult and painful, one that Louise will "remember always, the way some people remember having endured poverty" (50). Now the darling of her mother and the country club circles that once eluded her, Louise marries Richard, a partner in her father's law firm, and settles into affluent life. When she becomes pregnant with a son, however, Louise begins to loosen the self-restraint that has kept her thin. In spite of her husband's displeasure, she refuses to diet during or after the pregnancy and regains much of her weight. Enraptured with her son and feeling misunderstood by her husband, she embraces her return to food as truer expression of her selfhood. In the story's conclusion, Louise decides to eat a candy bar in front of her husband, excited by the prospect that he will soon leave her and she can be alone with her child.

Louise's relationship to her weight is inextricably tied to her understanding of identity and love. Though self-conscious about her body (she will neither eat in public nor be seen with other fat girls), Louise finds both food and her fat body appealing to the senses and diets only for social acceptance. As a child, she imagines that fat actresses are "fat because they chose to be" (46). After losing weight, she feels that her friends and husband cannot truly know her without understanding her struggle with fat. She feels like an imposter in her new life: "There were times . . . when she was suddenly assaulted by the feeling that she had taken the wrong train and arrived at some place where no one knew her" (55). When discussing her childhood with her husband, "she felt as though she were trying to tell a foreign lover about her life in the U.S., and if only she could command the language he would know and love all of her and she would feel complete" (56). Until the birth of her son, none of her new relationships rivals the acceptance and affection of her friendship with Carrie. As a mother, she finds that the surface-driven relationships in her life, including her marriage, pale in comparison with her feelings for her child. Her decision to regain weight at the expense of her marriage strikes readers not as a reflection of a troubled mind but an act of assertion. By eating in the presence of Richard, she both changes her childhood pattern of secret eating and rejects social rules in favor of her own standards of pleasure and beauty. In this tribute to a woman's self-determination in the face of restrictive social norms, Dubus's story seems linked to the feminist ideology gaining strength in the years leading up to the collection's publication. More generally, "The Fat Girl" offers a detailed portrait of a character outside the social mainstream and explores the resonance of her decisions and longings.

BIBLIOGRAPHY

Dubus, Andre. "The Fat Girl." In *Adultery and Other Choices.* Boston: David R. Godine, 1977, 45–59.
Kennedy, Thomas E. *André Dubus: A Study of the Short Fiction.* Twayne's Studies in Short Fiction, 1. Boston: Twayne, 1988.

Lillie Craton
Kennesaw State University

FAULKNER, WILLIAM (WILLIAM CUTHBERT FAULKNER) (1897–1962) For many critics and readers, William Faulkner remains the most significant writer of the 20th century: He invented a unique voice, a highly charged, rhetorical, compelling one of urgent intensity. Known as one of the greatest and most genuinely innovative modernists (see MODERNISM), Faulkner published 19 novels and more than 75 short stories between 1926 and 1962. Like other CLASSIC American authors, NATHANIEL HAWTHORNE or HENRY JAMES, for instance, Faulkner is best known for his groundbreaking novels: *The Sound and the Fury; As I Lay Dying; Light in August; Absalom, Absalom!;* and GO DOWN, MOSES. His short stories, however, have been regularly anthologized and have attracted an enormous amount of critical attention. Indeed, contemporary readers are probably as familiar with "A ROSE FOR EMILY" or "The Bear" as they are with the novels. Like the novels, a majority of Faulkner's stories are set in the South, particularly in YOKNAPATAWPHA COUNTY, which Faulkner invented and peopled with fictional black and white residents. In both novels and stories, moreover, many of the same individuals and families appear. Some of Faulkner's major fictional families include the Sartoris, SNOPES, DE SPAIN, Compson, Sutpen, McCaslin, and Carothers families. Throughout Faulkner's canon, these characters appear and reappear, carefully delineated, their family histories often spanning several generations.

Faulkner was born in Oxford, Mississippi, and lived there for most of his life, except for brief trips, until he moved to Charlottesville, Virginia, where he was writer in residence at the University of Virginia. Thus the Deep South is the locus of most of his stories: By setting them in Yoknapatawpha County; reintroducing characters; filling in gaps of MYTH, LEGEND, THEME, situation, and CHARACTER; and continually experimenting with these and other techniques, Faulkner extended the world of the short story. Faulkner, KATHERINE ANNE PORTER, ERNEST HEMINGWAY, EUDORA WELTY, and F. SCOTT FITZGERALD in his later years formed the core of the modernist short story writers. Faulkner wrote some stories that rank among the best in the world: "A Rose for Emily," "Dry September," and "BARN BURNING," to name just three.

"A Rose for Emily" is one of the most frequently anthologized, along with "THAT EVENING SUN" and "Barn Burning." A number of the stories from *Go Down, Moses* have been published separately ("The Bear" is the most famous), and stories collected in *The UNVANQUISHED* are important CIVIL WAR stories that also give the background of the major families. Faulkner's short story collections published during his lifetime include *These 13: Stories* (1931), *Doctor Martino and Other Stories* (1934), *Go Down, Moses, and Other Stories* (1942), KNIGHT'S GAMBIT (1949), *Collected Stories* (1950), *Big Woods* (1955), *Jealousy and Episode: Two Stories* (1955), *Uncle Willy and Other Stories* (1958), and *Selected Short Stories* (1961). Posthumously published are *Barn Burning and Other Stories* (1977) and *Uncollected Stories* (1979). Two individual stories, "Barn Burning" and "A Courtship," won the O. HENRY MEMORIAL AWARD in 1939 and 1949, respectively, and *Collected Stories* won the National Book Award for fiction in 1950.

The critic James G. Watson makes a key point when he says that although Faulkner was first and foremost a writer of novels that range over and define an entire locale, it is also true that the short stories play a critical role in explaining and in amplifying that world; indeed, in some cases the novels are indebted to the stories (Watson 126). For instance, "Wash" and "Evangeline," although published after the novel, contain the seeds of *Absalom, Absalom!* (1936), whereas *The Hamlet* (1940) actually incorporates a number of revisions of five previously published stories. Both *The Unvanquished* (1938) and *Go Down, Moses* (1942) are novels consisting entirely of short stories as chapters, the majority of them previously published.

The range of Faulkner's stories extends in many directions, featuring NATIVE AMERICANS, blacks, and whites, with attention to the larger issues with which the United States continues to grapple. Some of his most memorable stories about Native Americans include "Red Leaves," concerned with two Indians in pursuit of a slave who does not wish to die with his master, a tribal chief, and "A Justice," which depicts two interracial love affairs, the Indian Pappy's with a slave woman and Ikkemotubbe's with a Creole woman. The "yellow" child of Ikkemotubbe and the slave woman is named *Had-Two-Fathers,* but as critics have pointed out, it should be *Had-Three-Fathers,* since Pappy does not know that the slave woman's child is actually Ikkemotubbe's. The child reappears as the adult Sam Fathers in "The Bear." Faulkner wrote an entire SHORT STORY CYCLE about Yoknapatawpha blacks, published as *Go Down, Moses.* His stories about blacks are counterpointed by those about poor whites, most famously exemplified in "Barn Burning." And his stories about women are legion, ranging from background stories to women in novels (for example, "There Was a Queen" provides insight into Narcissa Benbow, featured in *Flags in the Dust* and *Sanctuary*), to those that examine gender restrictions and the way they can warp one's humanity ("A Rose for Emily," for instance, and "Dry September"). This theme reappears in Faulkner's tribute to DRUSILLA HAWKE in the stories of *The Unvanquished.*

One significant fact about Faulkner's story collections is that he envisioned them contrapuntally—that is, he arranged them in an order that, far from being random, evoked a special kind of unity. This unity is easier to see in the short story cycles such as *Go Down, Moses, The Unvanquished,* and even *Knight's Gambit,* in which the same characters reappear in stories that are more or less sequential. This order is less easy to discern in larger collections, such as *These Thirteen,* and even less so in *Collected Stories.* Faulkner, however, insisted that the order was there, and critics continue to study the connections among the stories. In *Dr. Martino and Other Stories,* the author even divided the book into six subsections that juxtapose past and present, Yoknapatawpha and the world outside. For *Big Woods,* five years later, he gathered together his hunting stories.

In many ways the unity of Faulkner's stories complements the unity of his novels; in fact, they are indispensable in assessing the unity of his entire oeuvre. As the novels do, the stories stand alone—and, as do the novels, when viewed as part of the entire Yoknapatawpha saga, they contribute to our understanding of the people, the history, the region, the changing eras, and, ultimately, Faulkner's artistic rendering not only of a microcosm of the United States but also of humanity at large.

BIBLIOGRAPHY

Faulkner, William. *Absalom, Absalom!* New York: Random House, 1936.

———. *As I Lay Dying.* New York: Random House, 1930.

———. *Big Woods.* New York: Random House, 1955.

———. *Collected Stories.* New York: Random House, 1950.

———. *Doctor Martino and Other Stories.* New York: Smith and Haas, 1934.

———. *A Fable.* New York: Random House, 1954.

———. *Father Abraham.* Edited by James B. Meriweather. New York: Random House, 1984.

———. *The Faulkner Reader.* Edited by Saxe Commins. New York: Random House, 1954.

———. *Go Down, Moses, and Other Stories.* New York: Random House, 1942.

———. *The Hamlet.* New York: Random House, 1940; excerpt, as *The Long Hot Summer.* New York: New American Library, 1958.

———. *Intruder in the Dust.* New York: Random House, 1948.

———. *Jealousy an Episode: Two Stories.* Minneapolis, Minn.: Faulkner Stories, 1955.

———. *Knight's Gambit.* New York: Random House, 1949.

———. *Light in August.* New York: Smith and Haas, 1932.

———. *The Mansion.* New York: Random House, 1959.

———. *Miss Zilphia Gant.* Dallas, Tex.: Book Club of Texas, 1932.

———. *Mosquitoes.* New York: Boni and Liveright, 1927.

———. *Notes on a Horsethief.* Greenville, Miss.: Levee Press, 1950.

———. *Novels 1930–1935.* Edited by Joseph Blotner and Noel Polk. New York: Literary Classics of the United States. 1985.

———. *Novels 1936–1940.* Edited by Joseph Blotner. New York: Library of America, 1990.

———. *The Portable Faulkner.* Edited by Malcolm Cowley. New York: The Viking Press, 1967.

———. *Pylon.* New York: Smith and Haas, 1935.

———. *Requiem for a Nun.* New York: Random House, 1951.

———. *The Reivers: A Reminiscence.* New York: Random House, 1962.

———. *Sanctuary.* New York: Cape and Smith, 1931.

———. *Sartoris.* New York: Harcourt Brace, 1929. *As Flags in the Dust.* Edited by Douglas Day. New York: Random House, 1973.

————. *Selected Short Stories*. New York: Modern Library, 1961.

————. *Soldiers' Pay*. New York: Boni and Liveright, 1926.

————. *The Sound and the Fury*. New York: Cape and Smith, 1929.

————. *These Thirteen: Stories*. New York: Cape and Smith, 1931.

————. *The Town*. New York: Random House, 1957.

————. *Uncle Willy and Other Stories*. London: Chatto and Windus, 1958.

————. *Uncollected Stories*. Edited by Joseph Blotner. New York: Random House, 1979.

————. *The Unvanquished*. New York: Random House, 1938.

————. *The Wild Palms*. New York: Random House, 1939.

Watson, James G. "The American Short Story: 1930–1945." In *The American Short Story 1900–1945,* edited by Philip Stevick, 103–146. Boston: Twayne, 1984.

FAUSTIAN   Pertaining to either the historical Georg Faust, a 15-century German magician and astrologer, or to the various subsequent literary works by Christopher Marlowe, Goethe, Thomas Mann, and others loosely based on his life. According to legend, Faust sold his soul to the devil in exchange for youth and all personal and worldly experience. In modern usage, striking a "Faustian bargain" implies using any means, including unsavory ones, to attain one's goal.

"FEATHER BEHIND THE ROCK, THE"
ANNE TYLER (1967)   ANNE TYLER recalls that as a young child she often made up stories, "Westerns, usually," in which she pretended to be other people. "So far as I can remember," she says, "mostly I wrote first pages of stories about lucky, lucky girls who got to go West in covered wagons," and later, "I was truly furious that I'd been born too late to go west in a covered wagon" (Petry, ed., CritEss 42; Petry, "Intro" 5; Tyler, "SJW" 13). Although she never attempted to fulfill that early yen for a covered-wagon journey west, Tyler obviously never forgot it either. She refers to it at times when asked about her childhood, and an inkling of it occasionally appears in her fiction, as in "The Feather behind the Rock." By the time this title first appeared in the August 12 issue of the *NEW*

YORKER in 1967, Tyler already had two novels and 15 other stories to her credit. Although she had moved two months earlier to Baltimore, which would become the principal setting for her fiction to follow, "The Feather behind the Rock" had been written while she still resided in North Carolina, where the story begins.

It relates Joshua's experience as a recent high school graduate on a cross-country drive from Wilmington to San Francisco with his elderly grandparents, Charles and Lucy Hopper, who have invited him to join them, specifying "no reason for the trip" (Tyler, "Feather" 154). Because the story is narrated from a limited third-person perspective, readers know what Joshua sees, hears, and thinks, yet nearly all the dialogue is that of his grandparents. By perceiving everything that Joshua does as well as the way he responds to the experience, readers can consider his POINT OF VIEW from their own vantage point and recognize along with his patience and kindliness toward his grandparents, a misunderstanding of their seemingly peculiar behavior, especially toward each other. As they travel, the flow of gentle words between them, mostly a reiteration of familiar old memories, appears as endless to Joshua as the countless stream of miles they leave behind. They travel in an aging car towing a small trailer at a steady 35 miles an hour, never stopping to see sights along the way.

If the Hoppers appear a little odd, they typify Tyler's characterization. She says, "I write about . . . off-beat characters and the blend of laughter and tears because in my experience, that's what real life consists of" (Petry, *UAT* 6). "People have always seemed funny and strange to me, and touching in unexpected ways," she admits; "even the most ordinary person . . . will turn out to have something unusual at his center" (Teisch 22). She plumbs her characters for their extraordinary core and celebrates that in portraying and individualizing them.

Joshua does not mind the drive or the constant drone of voices in a dialogue to which he can contribute little, but he is disturbed to the point of anger over the Hoppers' practice of seeing western films at local theaters every evening when they stop overnight. Even then Mrs. Hopper continues to speak in an ordinary tone of voice to her husband as he holds her arthritic hand. She describes what they can all see for themselves on the screen and what it obviously suggests: The Indian cannot be trusted, and the man with "a mean face" is the villain ("Feather" 156). Joshua is embarrassed by the loudness of her voice in the otherwise quiet theater and the simplemindedness of her responses to movies that leave nothing to guesswork. One evening he becomes so upset that he abruptly leaves the theater, then feels ashamed.

Because they travel in summer, the daily temperature is so high in the car that Mrs. Hopper faints when they stop at an isolated roadside café for water. Joshua, dreadfully afraid, urges his grandfather to take her home; a passing doctor offers to help, but being touched on her cheeks with the water revives her, and she insists on continuing the ride. On returning to the car, Mr. Hopper restarts the "the tide of his words," and again they set off "along straight unchanging roads, . . . rounding the curve of the globe" (162). Watching another western that evening, the two oldsters hold hands as usual while Mrs. Hopper again describes what appears on the screen. "That last wagon is dropping too far behind. Yes, there. I see a pony on the ridge, I see a feather behind the rock. I expect the Apaches are lining up now, Charles. I can hear the war cries" (162).

Because the incident earlier that day frightens Joshua but not his grandparents, their journey continues as if uninterrupted. Still preoccupied with their bygone days together and their devotion to formula westerns, they continue feeding their obsession with the past while Joshua eagerly looks forward not only to the road but also to college soon after their return home.

Yet this journey eventually will prove more significant to him than he can realize as he rides, because he is in the presence, for days on end, of his grandparents' undying love for each other, two people who have been together for most of a lifetime, long enough to accept each other as they are and share each other's eccentricities without complaint. Robert W. Croft's observation that "Tyler's love for her grandparents is apparent in her treatment of elderly characters in her work" (Croft 7) applies well to this story. Joshua, sensitive and tolerant as he is, has "a sort of protective feeling toward" his grandparents ("Feather" 157), but he cannot see yet, as readers can, that their long drive toward the setting sun is a ride that parallels life's journey as it carries them past familiar representations of the past, western by western, across the land. Tyler implies that it may end soon, at least for Mrs. Hopper, who observes shortly after fainting beside the road that "the last wagon is dropping too far behind" and that "a feather behind the rock" foreshadows harm or death to its occupants, perhaps even to her. By the time Joshua begins college, he will have learned through his experience with the Hoppers that words may be a facade for love as well as an expression of it and that its presence alone constitutes a manner of communication that may be superior to any other.

To be sure, Tyler has had reservations for years about verbal communication. She asserts, "I don't think it's necessary or desirable in a lot of cases" (Petry, CritEss 39). She would surely agree that the loving relationship of the Hoppers speaks for itself and that their words are less significant as communication than as mutual recollection, in Joshua's presence, of a long, full life together. Eventually he will appreciate the mutual support that underlies the love of his garrulous grandparents for each other.

BIBLIOGRAPHY

Croft, Robert W. *Anne Tyler: A Bio-Bibliography.* Westport, Conn.: Greenwood Press, 1995.

Evans, Elizabeth. *Anne Tyler.* New York: Twayne, 1993.

Petry, Alice Hall, ed. "Introduction." In *Critical Essays on Anne Tyler.* New York: G. K. Hall, 1992.

———. *Understanding Anne Tyler* [UAT]. Columbia: University of South Carolina Press, 1990.

Tyler, Anne. "The Feather behind the Rock." In *A Duke Miscellany: Narrative and Verse of the Sixties.* Durham, N.C.: Duke University Press, 1970.

———. "Still Just Writing [SJW]." In *The Writer on Her Work,* edited by Janet Sternburg. New York: W. W. Norton, 1980.

Teisch, Jessica. "Anne Tyler." In *Bookmarks,* November–December 2006, pp. 22–27.

Voelker, Joseph C. *Art and the Accidental in Anne Tyler.* Columbia: University of South Carolina Press, 1989.

Sanford E. Marovitz
Kent State University

FEMINISM/FEMINIST CRITICISM

Often used synonymously with the term *women's movement,* feminism in its largest sense is concerned with political and social equality for women. Historically, the women's, or feminist, movement in the United States is divided into roughly three eras: the antebellum period (1830–60), the Progressive era (1900–WORLD WAR I), and the 1960s and 1970s, when the study of women became a major focus. Today, most critics generally agree that there is no one kind of feminism; the study of women recognizes individual differences but has attempted to find common subjects of agreement: for instance, that patriarchal society oppresses women and minorities, among whom a close link exists; that women have been marginalized; and that texts by women must be recovered, reissued, publicized, studied, and interpreted.

Growing out of the post–WORLD WAR II women's movement—three of whose founding works, Simone de Beauvoir's *The Second Sex* (1949), Betty Friedan's *The Feminine Mystique* (1963), and Kate Millett's *Sexual Politics* (1969), included sustained analyses of the representation of women in literature—feminist criticism has pursued what Elaine Showalter calls "feminist critique" (analysis of the works of male authors, especially in the depiction of women and their relation to women readers), on the one hand, and "gynocriticism" (the study of women's writing), on the other. Feminist critiques provide new and illuminating ways to interpret male authors' work. In WILLIAM FAULKNER's "A ROSE FOR EMILY," for instance, a traditional interpretation views Emily, the protagonist, as a grotesque metaphor for the decaying southern aristocracy. A feminist critique, however, reveals Emily as a casualty of patriarchy and literally of her own father and lover; her unconventional way of fighting back reveals her sense of identity and makes her portrait much more sympathetic. Relatedly, gynocriticism has been responsible for resurrecting numerous "lost" women writers—KATE CHOPIN, EDITH WHARTON, and ZORA NEALE HURSTON. Feminist critics who worked to rediscover and recover women writers' works include Patricia Meyers Spacks (*The Female Imagination,* 1975), Ellen Moers (*Literary Women,* 1976), Elaine Showalter (*A Literature of Their Own,* 1978), and Nina Baym (*Women's Fiction,* 1978).

In addition to recovering neglected works by women authors through the ages and creating a canon of women's writing, feminist criticism has become a wide-ranging exploration of the construction of gender and identity, the role of women in culture and society, and the possibilities of women's creative expression. The 1970s spawned a wealth of ways to approach both images of women in literature by men and books written by women. Some of the most influential texts that call into question the old male-oriented literary criticism include Adrienne Rich's essay "When We Dead Awaken: Writing as Re-vision" (1971) and Carolyn Heilbrun's "Feminist Studies: Bringing the Spirit Back to English Studies" (1979). Near the end of the decade, feminist critics began to focus less on patriarchy and more on issues of gender differences, suggesting that women's reading, writing, and criticism differ from men's. Significant voices in this recent phase of feminist criticism include Rich (*Of Woman Born,* 1976), Nancy Chodorow (*The Reproduction of Mothering,* 1979), Judith Fetterly (*The Resisting Reader,* 1978), Janice Radway (*Reading the Romance,* 1984), Annette Kolodny (*The Lay of the Land,* 1976, and *The Land before Her,* 1984), and Jane Tomkins (*Sensational Designs,* 1985).

One strongly debated issue in current feminist criticism is the difference between the American school and the French school, as argued in Toril Moi's influential book *Sexual/Textual Politics: Feminist Literary Theory* (1985). Moi opposes such American feminist critics as Showalter and coauthors Sandra Gilbert and Susan Gubar of *The Madwoman in the Attic* (1979) for what she perceives as a naive treatment of texts and for participation in the liberal humanist—and patriarchal—tradition. On the other hand, Moi praises such French feminists as Julia Kristeva, Hélène Cixous, and Luce Irigaray, who view texts from a psychoanalytic perspective and interpret women and the feminine through close examination of the problems of language.

Although in the 1970s an increasing number of women of all colors perceived the cultural and academic marginalization of women, white women paid little attention to the differences among women. Much of the important work in researching differences, recovering texts, and staking new literary ground in the 1980s was being performed by women of color, including ALICE WALKER (*In Search of Our Mothers' Gardens: Womanist Prose,* 1983), Gloria Anzaldua (*Borderlands/La Frontera: The New Mestiza,* 1987, and *Making Face, Making Soul—Haciendo Caras,* 1990), Cherrie Moraga (*This Bridge Called My Back: Writings by Radical Women of Color,* with Gloria Anzaldua, 1981), Paula Gunn Allen (*The Sacred Hoop,* 1986, and *Spider Woman's Granddaughters,* 1989), and numerous others. From the 1980s, women of all colors began focusing on differences among women, resulting in the current views of a much more diverse and individualized feminism and feminist criticism.

BIBLIOGRAPHY

Davidson, Cathy N., and Linda Wagner-Martin. *The Oxford Companion to Women's Writing in the United States.* New York: Oxford University Press, 1995.

Gilbert, Sandra M., and Susan Gubar. *The Madwoman in the Attic.* New Haven, Conn.: Yale University Press, 1979.

———, eds. *The Norton Anthology of Literature by Women: The Tradition in English.* New York: Norton, 1985.

Moers, Ellen. *Literary Women.* New York: Oxford University Press, 1976.

Moi, Toril. *Sexual/Textual Politics: Feminist Literary Theory.* New York: Routledge, 1985.

Showalter, Elaine. *A Literature of Their Own.* Princeton, N.J.: Princeton University Press, 1977.

———, ed. *The New Feminist Criticism: Essays on Women, Literature, and Theory.* New York: Pantheon, 1985.

Vandell, Kathy Scales. "Literary Criticism." In *The Oxford Companion to Women's Writing in the United States,* edited by Cathy N. Davidson and Linda Wagner-Martin, 524–527. New York: Oxford University Press, 1995.

Warhol, Robyn R. "Feminism." In *The Oxford Companion to Women's Writing in the United States,* edited by Cathy N. Davidson and Linda Wagner-Martin, 307–314. New York: Oxford University Press, 1995.

FERBER, EDNA (1887–1968)

A prolific writer of novels, plays, and stories, Edna Ferber actually launched her long career as a popular and highly successful writer of fiction with several collections of short stories. Her story "No Room at the Inn" was issued as a GIFT BOOK in 1941 and was included in the 1947 collection of Ferber stories entitled *One Basket.* In 1925 she won the PULITZER PRIZE for her novel *So Big* (1924), and a classic musical play was created from her novel *Showboat* (1926). Many of Ferber's works were also made into movies.

BIBLIOGRAPHY

Ferber, Edna. *Buttered Side Down.* New York: Frederick A. Stokes, 1912.

———. *Cheerful, by Request.* Garden City, N.Y.: Doubleday, Page, 1918.

———. *Emma McChesney & Co.* New York: Frederick A. Stokes, 1915.

———. *Gigolo.* Garden City, N.Y.: Doubleday, Page, 1922.

———. *Half Portions.* Garden City, N.Y.: Doubleday, Page, 1920.

———. *Mother Knows Best: A Fiction Book.* Garden City, N.Y.: Doubleday, Page, 1927.

———. *No Room at the Inn.* Garden City, N.Y.: Doubleday, Doran, 1941.

———. *Old Man Minick: A Short Story.* Garden City, N.Y.: Doubleday, Page, 1924.

———. *One Basket: Thirty-One Short Stories.* New York: Simon & Schuster, 1947.

———. *Personality Plus: Some Experiences of Emma McChesney and Her Son, Jock.* New York: Frederick A. Stokes Company, 1914.

———. *Roast, Beef, Medium: The Business Adventures of Emma McChesney.* New York: Frederick A. Stokes, 1913.

———. *So Big.* Cleveland, Ohio: World, 1924.

———. *They Brought Their Women: A Book of Short Stories.* Garden City, N.Y.: Doubleday, Doran, 1933.

———. *Your Town.* Cleveland, Ohio: World, 1948.

FEVER JOHN EDGAR WIDEMAN (1989)

Fever, JOHN EDGAR WIDEMAN's second short story collection, contains some of his most anthologized and respected work. The title reverberates through many of the stories as a symbol of the disease of racism in America, past and present. The stories are also characterized by a distinctive postmodern style. (See POSTMODERNISM.) Included in the collection are "Surfiction," "Little Brother," "Doc's Story," and "Valaida," a story inspired by the life of the jazz trumpeter Valaida Snow (ca. 1900–1956) that illustrates the connections among victims of hate and oppression across time and the world. The hallmark of the collection is the title story "Fever." Based on historical accounts of the yellow fever epidemic in Philadelphia in 1798, the story traces the exploits of Richard Allen, an African-American minister, and Dr. Benjamin Rush, a local physician credited with halting the epidemic. Allen and members of his congregation helped to aid the sick and bury the dead. City leaders questioned the motives of the sacrifices made by Allen and his followers, and accused them and others of African descent of causing and carrying the disease. This event is also the source of Wideman's novel *The Cattle Killing* (1996). "Fever" and other stories in the collection question the ways that traditional history has silenced the lives and achievements of marginalized people, thus continuing racist attitudes and perceptions.

Tracie Guzzio
Ohio University

"FIND AND REPLACE" ANN BEATTIE (2005)
This story is part of ANN BEATTIE's seventh collection of short stories in which she explores issues raised by adult children who are attempting to make sense of their aging parents. In "Find and Replace," the first-person narrator, identified as "Ann," tries to understand her mother's decision to move in with another man after the death of the narrator's father. While the story reads more like an extended vignette (the first words, for example, are "True story" [113]), Beattie's trademark style is evident in the deft humor and the carefully chosen language that help her define her characters through their relationship and their habits.

Though the narrator's father had died on Christmas Day, her work schedule did not allow her to go home to observe the event until the following July, at which time she flies down to Fort Myers, rents a car, and drives up to Venice to see her mother. The two ladies, having developed a habit of not answering any direct question asked by the other person, primarily make small talk until the mother reveals that her neighbor, Drake Dreodadus, has asked her to move in with him. She shocks her daughter by agreeing to make the move because she and Drake are "compatible" (116). When Ann questions the decision, her mother retaliates by questioning Ann's pre-

vious decisions regarding a relationship she had had. That evening, Ann and her mother sit down to a dinner lit by cinnamon-scented candles, snack on M&M's, then go to bed. The next morning Ann leaves for the airport without meeting the new man in her mother's life.

When Ann arrives at the car rental place, she has to go inside to the car rental counter, where she meets a trainee, Jim Brown. She explains to him how she writes from real life, using the "find and replace" feature of a word processing program to change the names so that the people she is writing about do not recognize themselves. Then, on a whim, she winds up renting a red Mustang convertible (having already returned her sensible Mazda) and driving back to Venice. As she approaches her mother's yard, she sees the mother walking slowly, bent over like an old woman, to the door being held open by Drake. The daughter drives on by, leaving them to their new life, and returns to Fort Myers to return the car and get on with her life.

BIBLIOGRAPHY
Beattie, Ann. "Find and Replace." In *Follies: New Stories.* New York: Scribner, 2005.
Schwarz, Christina. "A Close Read: What Makes Good Writing Good." *Atlantic Monthly,* April 2005, p. 104.

Peggy J. Huey
University of Tampa

"FIRE AND CLOUD" RICHARD WRIGHT (1938)
"Fire and Cloud" was among the first of RICHARD WRIGHT's literary efforts to give him critical attention and praise. In 1938 it won first prize of $500 among 600 entries in a *Story Magazine* contest; that same year it won an O. HENRY MEMORIAL AWARD ($200) and was included in Wright's *Uncle Tom's Children: Four Novellas* (1938). Wright explained that he wrote this story out of a "desire on my part to depict in dramatic fashion the relationship between leaders of both races." Wright's communist affiliation is visible in his portrayal of a successful interracial protest march, although his PROTAGONIST is ultimately more of a Christian black nationalist than a communist.

Set in the rural South of Wright's childhood, "Fire and Cloud" is influenced by both proletarian REALISM and NATURALISM; its protagonist, the Reverend Dan Taylor, is poor, uneducated, and controlled by the white leadership, but in order to defend the lives of his oppressed people, he forges an alliance with local communists and develops a proletarian consciousness. The story depicts a small town in a depression era crisis: Landowning whites have refused to let impoverished blacks farm their property, and town leaders will not provide food relief, leaving the black community hungry and desperate enough to join a communist protest march. At the beginning of the story, Wright builds dramatic tension by placing members of each of the factions pressuring Taylor in different rooms of his house: In one room are the mayor, chief of police, and head of the anticommunist Red Squad; in another are the communists Hadley and Green; in another are a group of starving parishioners begging Taylor to help them; in the basement is the deacon board, including Deacon Smith, who wants to run Taylor out of the church so that he can take his place. Unable to take a stand, Taylor frantically placates each group, trying to defuse the potentially explosive conflict among the whites, the blacks, and the communists. Wright accurately depicts the nuances of racial tensions in these scenes: The mayor and the communists both use a form of psychological blackmail on Taylor, holding him accountable for the lives of the black community threatened by hunger on one side and by lynching on the other.

After being whipped into unconsciousness by a group of whites who also beat other parishioners, Taylor realizes that his attempts to keep the various factions at bay have resulted in his isolation and vulnerability. Telling his son that God is in the people, he incites his congregation to march, and when the protest is a success, he renews his faith both in God and in the power of the people. Critics have viewed this ending as too ideological and the characters as unrealistic STEREOTYPES. (Wright's awkward use of DIALECT contributes to this impression.) Others argue that Wright finds a nice balance between ideology and story. Either way, "Fire and Cloud" is one of the rare Wright stories with a happy ending.

BIBLIOGRAPHY

Fabre, Michel. *The Unfinished Quest of Richard Wright.* New York: Morrow, 1973.

Gibson, Donald. *The Politics of Literary Expression: Essays of Major Black Writers.* Westport: Conn.: Greenwood Press, 1981.

Joyce, Joyce Ann. *Richard Wright's Art of Tragedy.* Iowa City: A University of Iowa Press, 1986.

Kinnamon, Keneth. *The Emergence of Richard Wright: A Study in Literature and Society.* Urbana: University of Illinois Press, 1972.

Margolies, Edward. "The Short Stories: *Uncle Tom's Children, Eight Men.*" In *Critical Essays on Richard Wright,* edited by Yoshinobu Hakutani. Boston: G. K. Hall, 1982.

Writer's Club Bulletin (Columbia University). 1 (1938).

Young, James O. *Black Writers of the Thirties.* Baton Rouge: University of Louisiana Press, 1973.

Kimberly Drake
Virginia Wesleyan College

"FIRST SEVEN YEARS, THE" BERNARD MALAMUD (1950)

BERNARD MALAMUD's "The First Seven Years" was initially published in the *Partisan Review* (September–October 1950). In 1958 it was published as the first story in Malamud's first collection of short fiction, *The Magic Barrel.*

In the long opening paragraph Malamud provides a comprehensive foreword to the story by introducing the setting, characters, and narrative POINT OF VIEW. It even hints at the problematic situation, but that does not become clear until later. The plot can be described briefly. Feld, a Polish immigrant living with his wife and daughter, Miriam, owns a small shoemaker's shop, presumably in Brooklyn, where Malamud himself was reared; his trusted assistant, Sobel, also a Polish immigrant, has worked for him about five years. Feld worries for his 19-year-old daughter, who shows no interest in going to college or dating. Instead she has turned to the thirtyish Sobel to be her mentor; a prolific reader, he recommends and lends classic books to her that he accompanies with written expositions and critiques. Feld arranges a date for Miriam with Max, a drab college student who gives him a pair of shoes for repair, but their two evenings together lead only to mutual boredom. Having overheard Feld's request of Max, however, Sobel rushes enraged from the shop without a word and does not return, leaving the aging, ailing Feld to work alone. The effort is excessive, so he hires another assistant, who proves capable but untrustworthy, so his wife persuades him to find Sobel and plead for his return. When he confronts Sobel in a meagerly furnished rooming house, the assistant refuses to return regardless of higher pay. Only then does Feld learn that his assistant has been laboring not for money but for Miriam. At first, he is incredulous, outraged, so he responds harshly, but on learning that Miriam accepts Sobel's devotion, Feld relents and asks him to work for two more years until she is 21; then he leaves before receiving an answer. The next morning, however, when Feld drags himself downstairs for another exhausting day alone in the shop, he finds Sobel there "already seated at the last, pounding leather for his love" (16).

As its title suggests, Malamud's story is based loosely on the scriptural account of Jacob's desire to wed Rachel, the younger daughter of his mother's brother, Laban (Genesis 29:10–30). Laban consents to their marriage if Jacob will agree to give him in return seven years of labor. Jacob concurs, and when the time has passed, Laban hands him his veiled daughter. Not until the following morning does Jacob discover that he has been deceived into marrying Rachel's elder sister, Leah. According to the law of the land, Laban tells him, the eldest daughter must be the first to marry. Only after seven more years may Jacob take Rachel to wife. Again Jacob agrees, and after the next seven years pass, he and Rachel are wed.

In neither the Genesis version nor "The First Seven Years" does the courted maiden speak to her father about the pending betrothal. Miriam replies to Feld's questions about Max but says nothing in the reader's presence about Sobel; her affection for him is revealed only indirectly and implicitly by Sobel himself in response to Feld's questioning. Moreover, aside from the disagreeable portrait of Max, who appears but briefly, the sole well-defined character in this story is Feld; he alone awakens to experience, whereas the others are fixed in their aims and attitudes, so they undergo no change. In contrast, during Feld's confrontation with his obstinate assistant, he experiences an EPIPHANY, a sudden awakening to a truth that had long been evident but to which he had been blind, the deepening relationship between Sobel and Miriam. Once this realization occurs to him, his mind clears, and he no longer foresees a bleak future for his daughter but a happy one with Sobel, who loves her deeply. With this new understanding gained almost instantaneously on leaving Sobel's room, Feld heads home through the snow, walking "with a stronger stride" (15).

Much of the story's effectiveness, as is true of nearly all of Malamud's early fiction, is achieved through the subtle stylistic variations he applies in his language. Known chiefly for his imaginative portraits of Jewish characters, communities, and themes, Malamud takes advantage of the Yiddish he learned from his parents as a child and adapts it to suit his aim of being an American and indeed a universal author as well as a Jewish one. Consequently, he often blends Yiddish and English into Yinglish, a style that includes Yiddish syntax and phrasing without necessarily incorporating actual Yiddish words, which he uses but sparingly in his fiction. By shifting, often quickly, among standard English, colloquial English, and Yinglish, Malamud achieves the sense of a Yiddish-speaking environment in an English narrative like "The First Seven Years" and several other stories in *The Magic Barrel* and *Idiot's First* (1963), as well as in such novels as *The Assistant* (1957). The opening paragraphs of "The First Seven Years," for example, are rendered in standard English; Feld's share of the dialogue with Max is chiefly Yinglish; Max himself speaks colloquially with such terms as "She's all right" to look at, and he asks whether she is "the flighty kind"; paraphrasing Max, the narrator says, "it was okay with him if he met her" (6). Malamud's diversified style conveys an impression of authenticity in a situation that borders on myth among his earthy, romanticized East-European Jewish immigrants in urban America who fret and suffer but truly come to life as they speak.

BIBLIOGRAPHY

Astro, Richard, and Jackson J. Benson, eds. *The Fiction of Bernard Malamud.* Corvallis: Oregon State University Press, 1977.

Field, Leslie A., and Joyce W. Field, eds. *Bernard Malamud: A Collection of Critical Essays.* Englewood Cliffs, N.J.: Prentice-Hall, 1975.

Giroux, Robert, ed. "Introduction." In Bernard Malamud's *The People and Uncollected Stories.* New York: Farrar Straus & Giroux, 1989.

Malamud, Bernard. "The First Seven Years." In *The Magic Barrel.* New York: Farrar, Straus & Cudahy, 1958.

Solotaroff, Robert. *Bernard Malamud: A Study of the Short Fiction.* Boston: Twayne, 1989.

Sanford E. Marovitz
Kent State University

FISHER, DOROTHY CANFIELD (1879–1959)

Unlike many American writers with turbulent lives and tumultuous relationships, Dorothy Fisher was born to loving, responsible parents, who encouraged her literary ambitions. After enjoying a happy and productive childhood, she married John Fisher, a man with whom she was in love and in whose company she was able to be productive: Between 1907 and 1958 she published 40 books, including many volumes of short stories. Her husband shared her commitments to education, peace, feeding the hungry, healing the hurt, and ending prejudice, concerns Fisher incorporated into her fiction. Dorothy Fisher introduced Americans to the type of education practiced by Maria Montessori, now known as Montessori schools. Fisher's stories are often set in small towns in Vermont, where she lived. Her most esteemed stories are collected in *The Bedquilt and Other Stories* (1995).

FITZGERALD, F. SCOTT (FRANCIS SCOTT KEY FITZGERALD) (1896–1940)

Born into the upper middle class in 1896 in St. Paul, Minnesota, F. Scott Fitzgerald was fascinated by the paradoxes of the American class system. In stories and novels, he fictionalized his own experiences as an outsider attempting to enter the privileged world of the wealthy. He was among the expatriate writers in Paris in the 1920s whose fiction reflected the cultural transformations in Europe and America in the early 20th century. As a realist (see REALISM), he is sometimes called a social historian in fiction, but his work incorporates romantic THEMES (see ROMANTICISM) as well, such as the distance between imagination and reality and the impossibility of recreating the past.

Fitzgerald enjoyed extraordinary popularity in the first decade of his career, beginning with the novel *This Side of Paradise* (1920), which he followed immediately with a collection of stories, *Flappers and Philosophers.* His depiction of glamorous young people in pursuit of excitement, love, or a dream of the moment captured a mood that, for many readers, epitomized the Jazz Age. In addition to four novels, he published over 150 short stories in popular magazines, such as *Redbook* and *MCCALL'S* MAGAZINE. As a regular contributor to the *SATURDAY EVENING POST,* he received $4,000 per story at the height of his career. Fitzgerald published four collections of stories, each of which was timed to appear in conjunction with a novel. In 1922 *The Beautiful and Damned* was followed by *Tales of the Jazz Age.* After *The Great Gatsby* was *All the Sad Young Men* in 1926, and *Tender Is the Night* followed the collection *Taps at Reveille* in 1935.

In the 1930s Fitzgerald's reputation began to fade dramatically as troubles in his personal life interfered with his productivity. His wife, Zelda, was hospitalized permanently, suffering from schizophrenia; his own alcoholism became life-threatening. In the 1920s the couple had lived an extravagant life of international travel, expensive homes, and lavish parties; the subsequent decade was characterized by illness and debt. After 1935 *ESQUIRE* was the only magazine that published his stories consistently—at about 10 percent of the price he had commanded in his prime. Nonetheless, Fitzgerald continued to write, although he feared he had become a relic consigned to the past. In 1937 he was under contract as a scriptwriter for M-G-M, but he also began work on a fifth novel, *The Last Tycoon,* while continuing to produce stories. In 1940 he died suddenly of a heart attack at age 44.

In the years since his death, reassessments of Fitzgerald's life and work have restored him to his former stature as an important American author. The critic Malcolm Cowley inspired new interest in the stories in 1951 when he collected 28 of them in *The Stories of F. Scott Fitzgerald.* At that time, most of Fitzgerald's short fiction was uncollected and without published commentary. Since Cowley's volume, several new collections have appeared, followed by a slow but steady stream of critical reappraisal.

Fitzgerald made a number of disparaging remarks about his magazine stories, but he also expressed pride in their craftsmanship. Their quality is uneven because he produced many surprisingly quickly, in order to earn money. Others deserve the serious critical attention they have begun to receive.

The stories display Fitzgerald's versatility. As do the novels, they often combine social realism with a romantic theme of loss or disillusionment; however, Fitzgerald also used his stories to experiment with fantasy and humor, including farce and BURLESQUE. In "The Curious Case of Benjamin Button" (1922), he created a character who was born an old man instead of an infant. "Head and Shoulders" (1920) resembles a burlesque COMEDY routine as the husband and wife—a philosopher and acrobat, respectively—switch professions as well as traditional gender roles in marriage. Fitzgerald's stories are sometimes hard to classify because he often mixed techniques from different genres in the same story. In "Gretchen's Forty Winks" (1924), stage comedy devices combine with serious social criticism when a husband drugs his wife in order to pursue the advertising accounts that will give them financial comfort.

Many of Fitzgerald's stories achieve a complex irony with this combination of opposing tones. Sometimes Fitzgerald used his stories to develop themes he did not explore in the novels, such as differences between the American North and South. In "The Ice Palace" (1920) a Georgia woman discovers that her personality has been permanently shaped by southern culture: Life in the North with her future husband is impossible. "The Baby Party" (1924) and "The Adjuster" (1924) describe the trials of domestic life with young children, a theme that receives no extended attention in the novels.

Biographical criticism is the most common approach to the stories as readers continue to find in the fiction correlations with Fitzgerald's personal life. Bibliographical approaches include the examination of story-and-novel clusters to track the way a theme or character from a short story ends up in a novel. The short story "WINTER DREAMS" (1922), for example, has

been described—along with several others—as the basis for *The Great Gatsby:* The midwestern PROTAGONIST of the story bears a striking resemblance to Jay Gatsby, who, despite his move to New York City and his fabulous business success, never marries the woman he has idealized all his life.

Fitzgerald wrote three long stories sometimes called NOVELLAS or novelettes: "The Rich Boy" (1926), "The DIAMOND AS BIG AS THE RITZ" (1922), and "May Day" (1920). Along with "BABYLON REVISITED" (1931), these three stories are usually considered his best work in the genre. In "The Rich Boy" Fitzgerald developed his trademark theme of the effect of wealth on character. He used fantasy and SATIRE in "The Diamond as Big as the Ritz" to explore the same theme. "May Day" sometimes is described as Fitzgerald's foray into NATURALISM; others see Marxist overtones in its anatomy of the American class structure. "Babylon Revisited," Fitzgerald's most anthologized story, has been described as an autobiographical atonement for his extravagance in the 1920s and a reflection on expatriate life in Paris. A number of stories have an international theme that recalls the work of HENRY JAMES, including "The Swimmers" (1929) and "One Trip Abroad" (1930).

Fitzgerald published three successful story sequences. From 1928 to 1931 the *Saturday Evening Post* published the BASIL DUKE LEE stories, featuring a fictionalized version of Fitzgerald in his youth, and the JOSEPHINE PERRY stories, which were based on the author's memories of Genevra King, a wealthy socialite he fell in love with during his Princeton years. At the time of his death, *Esquire* was publishing his light, satirical story sequence about a Hollywood hack writer named PAT HOBBY. The 17 stories were collected posthumously in 1962 as the *PAT HOBBY stories.* In 2004, *The Great Gatsby* was published in serial form in its entirety in the Metro Section of the *New York Times.*

See also "An ALCOHOLIC CASE."

BIBLIOGRAPHY

Bryer, Jackson R., ed. *New Essays on F. Scott Fitzgerald's Neglected Short Stories.* Columbia: University of Missouri Press, 1996.

———, ed. *The Short Stories of F. Scott Fitzgerald: New Approaches in Criticism.* Madison: University of Wisconsin Press, 1982.

Bryer, Jackson R., and Cathy W. Barks, eds. *Dear Scott, Dearest Zelda: The Love Letters of F. Scott and Zelda Fitzgerald*. New York: St. Martin's Press, 2002.

Cline, Sally. *Zelda Fitzgerald: Her Voice in a Paradise*. New York: Arcade, 2003.

Curnutt, Kirk, ed. *A Historical Guide to F. Scott Fitzgerald*. Oxford: Oxford University Press, 2004.

Fitzgerald, F. Scott. *All the Sad Young Men*. New York: Scribner, 1926.

———. *Flappers and Philosophers*. New York: Scribner's, 1920.

———. "*The Great Gatsby*: The Great Summer Read: *The New York Times* Free Book Series." Serial format. *New York Times,* Metro Section, 12 July 2004.

———. *The Stories of F. Scott Fitzgerald*. Edited by Malcolm Cowley. New York: Scribner, 1951.

———. *Tales of the Jazz Age*. New York: Scribner, 1922.

———. *Taps at Reveille*. New York: Scribner, 1935.

Kuehl, John, ed. *F. Scott Fitzgerald: A Study of the Short Fiction*. Boston: Twayne, 1991.

Mellow, James R. *Invented Lives: F. Scott and Zelda Fitzgerald*. Boston: Houghton Mifflin, 1984.

Petry, Alice Hall. *Fitzgerald's Craft of Short Fiction: The Collected Stories, 1920–1935*. Tuscaloosa: University of Alabama Press, 1989.

Piper, Henry Dan. *F. Scott Fitzgerald: A Critical Portrait*. New York: Holt, Rinehart & Winston, 1965.

Prigozy, Ruth, ed. *The Cambridge Companion to F. Scott Fitzgerald*. Cambridge: Cambridge University Press, 2002.

Frances Kerr
Durham Technical Community College

"FIVE-FORTY-EIGHT, THE" JOHN CHEEVER (1954)

JOHN CHEEVER's story, first published as part of the collection *The Housebreaker of Shady Hill* (1958), is notable for the way it presents, through an apparently uninvolved, objective third-person narrator, a man's callous and reprehensible treatment of a female employee. The story's powerful impact is due in part to the narrator's nonjudgmental tone but also to the details this narrator presents by limiting the POINT OF VIEW so that the action unfolds through Mr. Blake's thoughts, allowing the reader to decipher the meaning of his behavior and to applaud Miss Dent when, at the end of the story, she bests him. In brief, Cheever has given us a tale of sexual harassment, 1950s style.

The story opens with Blake's startled recognition of Miss Dent as he steps out of the elevator in his office building. At first he cannot recall her name, and we follow him along the street, momentarily wondering whether she is a stalker, wondering whether we should sympathize with him. Through a series of FLASHBACKS the story provides the information we need: Miss Dent, a shy and timid temporary employee, falls in love with Blake when she goes to work for him. After he engages in sex with her, he feels distaste for her powerlessness and her poverty. Clearly, Blake is a powerful businessman, accustomed to using people to achieve his goals.

He thinks he has eluded her as he boards the commuter train home to SHADY HILL. He recognizes two of his neighbors seated in the same car, but neither greets him with friendliness. We learn that the woman neighbor knows about Blake's shameful treatment of his wife, Louise, who has turned to her for sympathy. The other neighbor offends Blake because of his casual way of dressing and because Blake's son spends nearly all his time with this man's kind and amiable family. Apparently neither Louise nor Blake's son has the power to speak out against him and he has punished them both, ceasing to sleep with or speak to his wife and forbidding his neighbors to entertain his son. Blake feels angry at these personal betrayals by both his wife and his son; ironically, of course, he fails to reckon with his own betrayal of them.

His superiority and power wielding are about to end, however, as Miss Dent boards the train, shoves a concealed pistol into his side, and tells him why and how he has wrecked her life. Although she has been institutionalized for emotional problems and has been unemployed since Blake fired her six months earlier, she demonstrates a newfound strength and a self-confident voice as she castigates him for his arrogance, his superficiality, his self-centeredness. Not only does she know more about love than he, she says, but she knows she is a better person than he. The story ends in an act that is more self-affirmation than punishment of Blake: Miss Dent forces him to kneel at her feet and put his face in the dirt, thereby avenging herself and attaining self-respect (Charters 35). Timid no longer, Miss Dent understands the phallic power of the gun and the authority of a self-confident voice: Cheever has artfully constructed the story so that readers feel justified in approving Blake's humiliation and applauding Miss Dent's newfound confidence.

BIBLIOGRAPHY

Charters, Ann. *Resources for Teaching: Major Writers of Short Fiction.* Boston: St. Martin's Press: 1993, 34–36.

Cheever, John. *The Stories of John Cheever.* New York: Knopf, 1978.

O'Hara, James E. *John Cheever: A Study of the Short Fiction.* Boston: Twayne, 1989.

FLASHBACK   The interruption of the chronological sequence in a literary, theatrical, or cinematic work by the interjection of events that occurred earlier. The technique may be a memory, a reverie, or a confession by a character.

"FLEUR" LOUISE ERDRICH (1986)   Originally published in *ESQUIRE* in August 1986, "Fleur" later appeared as the first chapter of *Tracks,* published in 1988. It exemplifies LOUISE ERDRICH's blend of REALISM and magic (see MAGICAL REALISM). Narrated in the first person by Pauline (see POINT OF VIEW), a character in her own right who appears in Erdrich's *Love Medicine,* the story focuses on Fleur Pillager, a Chippewa Indian of the Ojibway tribe (see NATIVE AMERICAN SHORT FICTION) who lives in various locales on and around the Chippewa reservation in North Dakota. Fleur has powers that even her own community find upsetting. Indeed, Pauline frequently talks with the voice of the reservation, using *we* in a way reminiscent of WILLIAM FAULKNER's narrator in "A ROSE FOR EMILY." Pauline tells us that Fleur has drowned twice, can turn into a bear at night, and kills any man who tries to interfere in her life.

To illustrate this last trait, Pauline—who views herself as unattractive and invisible—relates the unforgettable story of Fleur in Argus, North Dakota, in the summer of 1920. While working for a butcher, Fleur proves adept at playing poker with three unpleasant white men (the character named Lily, for instance, is pasty white, with cold flat eyes like those of a snake), and they cannot bear the thought of losing to this "squaw," who plays and wins steadily throughout the summer. One particular steamy midwestern night Fleur captures the jackpot from the men, who, in a nightmarish scene filtered through Pauline's confused memory, retaliate by raping Fleur. According to Pauline, Fleur avenges herself by conjuring up a tornado, and the girl, feeling guilty for failing to prevent Fleur's rape, locks the men in the icehouse. The tornado destroys the men while miraculously avoiding the possessions of the innocent.

Fleur and Pauline eventually return to the reservation, where stories swirl around Fleur in mythic fashion. Whether or not she really does "mess with evil" (657), as Pauline and the community believe, Fleur earns our admiration and respect: Still connected to the old, traditional tribal medicines and ways, Fleur lives a proudly independent life and answers to no one, especially to men.

BIBLIOGRAPHY

Erdrich, Louise. "Fleur." In *American Short Stories.* 6th ed. Edited by Eugene Current-García and Bert Hitchcock. New York: Longman, 1997.

"FLIGHT" JOHN STEINBECK (1938)   JOHN STEINBECK's "Flight" first appeared in his collection of short stories *The Long Valley* in 1938. It is a carefully constructed coming-of-age tale that chronicles a 19-year-old boy's ascent to manhood, quick regression to hunted animal, and thence to his "manly" and untimely death. The PROTAGONIST in the story is Pepe, whom his mother refers to as nothing more than a "lazy peanut." Apparently Pepe has spent his entire life in indolent ease, basking in the warm sunshine on his mother's small farm in California. One beautiful day Mama decides to send Pepe to Monterey to fetch medicine for the family. Pepe, excited that his mother is allowing him to make such a journey alone, takes her decision as a sign that he will finally become a man and assume the responsibilities of his deceased father. Mama even lets Pepe wear his father's hat and green silk scarf tied around his neck. Pepe promises Mama that he will be careful, for he is a man now. Mama merely scoffs and reminds him that he is a young boy. The third-person narrator indicates, however, that Mama realizes and fears that Pepe will become a man too soon, although she does not realize how soon.

When Pepe returns that night, he has killed a man with his father's beautiful knife. Mama, devastated and fearing for her son's life, sends him away. As the narrator describes Pepe's flight into the hills, the depiction becomes increasingly animalistic—a pattern of imagery Steinbeck frequently returns to in many of his works—as the snake and wild cat, he crawls and slithers among the rocks and brush to flee his pursuers. Not until the very end of the story, however, does Pepe enact his one truly manly deed. No longer able to run, he stands high on top of a rock and faces his pursuers' bullets head on. Thus, according to the precepts of his family and his culture, Pepe dies a "man."

The artistry of the story undercuts Pepe's naive view. It invites us to question the meaning of manhood, to regret that Pepe learns nothing of the irony of his view of manhood, to mourn the loss of a youth with such bright potential, and to reevaluate these devastating social codes. "Flight" is not the only story in which Steinbeck ridicules society's conventions and beliefs about the meaning of manhood. Disgust with society's absurd rituals and conventions, as well as the callousness of such institutions as banking and business, runs throughout most of his work.

BIBLIOGRAPHY

Steinbeck, John. "Flight." In *The Long Valley*. New York: Book-of-the-Month Club, 1995.

Timmerman, John. *The Dramatic Landscape of Steinbeck's Short Stories*. Norman: University of Oklahoma Press, 1990.

———. "Introduction." In *The Long Valley*. New York: Book-of-the-Month Club, 1995.

Kathleen M. Hicks
University of Texas at El Paso

FLOWERING JUDAS KATHERINE ANNE PORTER (1930)

In this NOVELLA from her first collection, *Flowering Judas and Other Stories,* published in 1930, KATHERINE ANNE PORTER creates a totally rootless character, an American expatriate in Mexico with ties to neither the past nor the future. Laura finds no reason to recall her previous life or to think back to her former country. In the opinion of many critics, Laura herself is the Judas of the title—a title that takes its symbolism from the ALLUSION to the biblical Judas,

betrayer of Christ. Others see the tale as a PARABLE of the effects of revolution and renunciation, with several contenders for the role of betrayer. The dreamlike aura of the story adds to the difficulty of interpreting its meaning. The critic Charles E. May points out that Laura is named for the lovely and unattainable—and thus idealistic—HEROINE of Petrarch's sonnets (710).

The story opens with Laura paying polite attention to Braggacio, revolutionary hero and the other main character in the story. The disgusting physical description of Braggacio, a coarse, gross, lustful man who embodies the sexist qualities of machismo, contrasts with Laura's more ethereal qualities. Laura, by refusing to flee, and Braggacio, by revoking his formerly ascetic behavior, have already betrayed the ideals of the revolution. Laura rejects her three suitors, finding none of them attractive; she seems zombielike, unable to act and unable to say yes to anyone who needs her. Indeed, the narrator makes clear that the one word that characterizes Laura is *no*. The conflicts within Laura are readily apparent: She hides her voluptuous body beneath a shapeless and nunlike dress, she pays lip service to the revolution but sneaks into the Catholic chapel, and she facilitates the suicide of Eugenio, the imprisoned revolutionary to whom she takes poison. In the critic James G. Watson's summation, Laura is "lovely without love, Catholic without faith, a socialist without ideals" (141).

At the end of the story, Laura dreams of the dead Eugenio, who offers her the fruit of the flowering Judas tree, also known as the redbud tree, into which Judas is supposed to have metamorphosed (Charters 154). In the end, in her refusal to participate in the literal and figurative communion of life and in her passive participation in death, Laura becomes the quintessential modern woman, the counterpart of T. S. Eliot's *WASTE LAND* characters. Porter takes her title from Eliot's poem "Gerontion" and clearly, in creating Laura, had his paralyzed ANTIHEROES in mind.

BIBLIOGRAPHY

Charters, Ann. *Resources for Teaching Major Writers of Short Fiction*. Boston: St. Martin's Press, 1993.

May, Charles E. *Flowering Judas*. In *Reference Guide to Short Fiction*, edited by Noelle Watson. Detroit: St. James Press, 1994, 710.

Porter, Katherine Anne. *Flowering Judas.* In *The Collected Stories of Katherine Anne Porter.* New York: Harcourt, Brace and World, 1965.

Watson, James G. "The American Short Story: 1930–1945." In *The American Short Story, 1900–1945,* edited by Philip Stevick. Boston: Twayne, 1984.

"FLOWERS FOR ALGERNON" DANIEL KEYES (1959)

"Flowers for Algernon," first published in 1959, is considered a landmark work in both science fiction and disability literature. It was expanded into a novel of the same name, which was published in 1966. Both the short story and the novel consist of a series of progress reports that track Charlie Gordon, a 37-year-old man suffering from mental retardation, through an experimental procedure designed to triple his I.Q. Charlie is the first human to receive the operation, though it has been successfully completed on a laboratory mouse, Algernon. Charlie's early reports are riddled with spelling and grammatical errors; a month after the operation, the reports are grammatically correct. Within two months Charlie complains that the doctors in charge of the experiment cannot read Hindustani and Chinese. This rapid growth in intelligence from an I.Q. of 68 to triple that figure is accompanied by a crippling isolation from other people. A decline in his intelligence is first predicted by Algernon's rapid regression, and Charlie soon conducts experiments into his own condition. He finds that his regression will be as rapid as his ascent to genius. The last progress reports are similar in style to those at the beginning, and Charlie closes the story by telling the doctors that he will be leaving New York, presumably to enter a state-operated home.

Experimentation is the predominant theme in "Flowers for Algernon." At the height of his intelligence, Charlie complains that Dr. Strauss and Dr. Nemur, the doctors conducting the experiment, are not the mental giants he once perceived them to be. Some of his complaining can be accurately perceived as hubris—his aforementioned complaint about the professors' knowledge of foreign languages is certainly unreasonable, considering their wide reading knowledge in Western languages. Much of Charlie's obser-

vations about the doctors, though, can be interpreted as a nuanced critique on the medical establishment. The doctors argue at several points in the story, and the arguments reveal that they are often more interested in self-advancement than in Charlie's development. Dr. Nemur is especially held to ridicule because he is primarily driven by his wife's prodding. If the doctors are in a certain sense using Charlie, then the parallelism between him and Algernon takes on more significance. In the short story, Charlie is implicitly similar to Algernon because the doctors use him for advancement of their careers. The novel makes this theme more explicit through confrontations between Charlie and Dr. Nemur about the latter's attitude toward the former. Dr. Nemur states that Charlie is a new creation of sorts, that he has achieved personhood through the experiment.

Charlie's status as experimental subject comes into focus at the end of "Flowers for Algernon," when he researches the consequences of the experiment conducted that made him a genius. The turning point in both the short story and the novel happens in a diner: A retarded young man breaks a plate and the customers, including Charlie, laugh at him. The moment defines the rest of the story because Charlie realizes how deeply he has isolated himself from other people during his ascent to genius. Although he has gained many gifts, he has also lost his meaningful relationships; thus, the connection with the retarded young man motivates Charlie to pursue research for the betterment of all who suffer from retardation. His research is set in opposition to the research of Dr. Strauss and Dr. Nemur because it is conducted solely to improve the lives of other people. Moreover, Charlie readily accepts his discouraging conclusion— namely, that the experiment conducted on him has no practical value because of the swift regression into retardation—and asks that the results be published. Charlie's research can be read, therefore, as a commentary on medical experimentation and a call to consider the subjects involved—particularly those with limited abilities—as individuals.

The emphasis on experimentation in "Flowers for Algernon" can largely be explained by its roots in science fiction. Critics have observed that the experiment conducted on Charlie and his subsequent regression into mental retardation indicate that "Flowers for Algernon" properly belongs in the science fiction genre. Moreover, the short story and the novel won the most prestigious awards in science fiction (respectively, the HUGO AWARD and the NEBULA AWARD).

"Flowers for Algernon" can also be classified as disability literature because its explorations delve into fundamental questions about the place of disabled people in modern American society. Charlie's descriptions of other retarded people are telling—he speaks of vacant smiles and empty eyes. This perception is remarkably similar to Dr. Nemur's assertion in the novel that Charlie did not properly exist as a person before the experiment. Disability remains an important public policy issue, which contributes to the enduring popularity of "Flowers for Algernon."

BIBLIOGRAPHY

Biklen, Douglas. "Constructing Inclusion: Lessons from Critical, Disability Narratives." *International Journal of Inclusive Education* 4 (2000): 337–353.

Clareson, Thomas D. *Understanding Contemporary American Science Fiction: The Formative Period, 1926–1970.* Columbia: University of South Carolina Press, 1990, 231–233.

Keyes, Daniel. *Algernon, Charlie, and I: A Writer's Journey.* New York: Harvest-Harcourt, 2004.

Moser, Patrick. "An Overview of Flowers for Algernon." In *Exploring Novels.* Farmington Hills, Mich.: Thomson Gale, 1998.

Rabkin, Eric S. "The Medical Lessons of Science Fiction." *Literature and Medicine* 20 (2001): 13–25.

Scholes, Robert. *Structural Fabulation: An Essay on Fiction of the Future.* Notre Dame, Ind.: University of Notre Dame Press, 1975.

Small, Robert, Jr. "Flowers for Algernon by Daniel Keyes." In *Censored Books: Critical Viewpoints,* edited by Nicholas J. Karolides, Lee Burress, and John M. Kean, 249–255. Metuchen, N.J.: Scarecrow, 1993.

Whittington-Walsh, Fiona. "From Freaks to Savants: Disability and Hegemony from *The Hunchback of Notre Dame* (1933) to *Sling Blade* (1997)." *Disability & Society* 17 (2002): 695–707.

Tim Peoples
Texas State University—San Marcos

FOIL   Any fictional character who, through appearance or behavior, contrasts with and thereby underscores the distinctive characteristics or actions of another. A foil is often (but not always) a minor character who sets off the opposite traits of a major character.

FOLKLORE   Since the mid-19th century, the term *folklore* has been the general word applied to traditional stories, myths, and rituals handed down primarily by example and through oral rather than written form. Folklore can include LEGENDS, superstitions, songs, tales, spells, riddles, proverbs, nursery rhymes; pseudoscientific lore about the weather, plants, and animals; customary activities at births, marriages, and funerals; and traditional dances and forms of drama performed on holidays or at communal gatherings.

FORD, RICHARD (1944–)   Known for his frequently anthologized stories and his award-winning novels, Richard Ford has been compared to WILLIAM FAULKNER, ERNEST HEMINGWAY, WALKER PERCY, BARRY HANNAH, and RAYMOND CARVER, with whom he shares some affinities in short fiction. As critics are quick to point out, however, Ford's stories lack the existential pessimism common in Carver's work. Indeed, in his three collections—*Rock Springs: Stories* (1987), *Women with Men: Three Stories* (1997), and *A Multitude of Sins: Stories* (2002)—Ford differs not only from his friend Carver but also from many of his contemporaries in his optimistic belief that his characters can prevail over modern rootlessness, isolation, loss, and grief. The *New York Times* reviewer Michiko Kakutani, speaking of *Rock Springs,* praised Ford's "wholly distinctive narrative voice," which could produce both "neat, staccato descriptions and rich lyrical passages" (Kakutani, "Books of the Times" 1). Ford has also received praise for his six novels, one of which, *Independence Day* (1995), became the first novel to win both the PEN/FAULKNER AWARD and the PULITZER PRIZE.

Richard Ford was born on February 16, 1944, to Parker Carrol Ford, a salesman, and Edna Akin Ford, in Jackson, Mississippi, where he was reared in a house across the street from EUDORA WELTY. He also spent periods of time with his grandparents in Arkansas. After graduating from Michigan State University with a bachelor's degree in 1966, he married Kristina Hensley, a research professor, in 1968, before earning his master of fine arts degree from the University of California at Irvine in 1970. After publishing three novels, Ford received acclaim for the 10 stories in *Rock Springs* (the title refers to a town near Great Falls, Montana) and for the characters he depicts in constant motion as they leave one life or one set of circumstances—alcoholism, debt, infidelity, violence, divorce—for another. It is these middle-class characters—in this collection, all white males—who have drawn praise from the critics as each alienated person seeks connection with another.

Women with Men, a collection containing three novellas—*The Womanizer,* set in Paris; *Jealous,* in Montana; and *Occidentals,* again in Paris—has been linked with Hemingway's short story collection *Men without Women,* a connection that Ford denies: "I'm not going to sacrifice a good title for my book because of something some guy did seventy or eighty years ago," he told Huey Guagliardo in a 1998 interview. Each of these novellas explores the loneliness and damages resulting from infidelity or desertion: In *Occidentals,* for instance, Helen Carmichael commits suicide in their Paris hotel as her lover Charley Matthews roams the streets, callously ignoring the reappearance of her cancer and seeking another woman. Ford's most recent collection, *A Multitude of Sins,* consists of nine stories and a novella, nearly all depicting characters involved in extramarital affairs. Ford's stories were collected in 2003 and issued under the title *Vintage Ford.*

Although Ford does not necessarily prefer the short story to the novel, averaging only about one story a year, he is unquestionably gifted in his storytelling abilities. As the reviewer Julie Myerson writes, "Ford's sheer mastery of the short-story form is jaw-dropping," noting further that "each of these tales boasts the satisfying density of a novel" and nearly each "character is rounded enough to carry 300 pages," even though we lose them after a half hour or so (20). Ford's story "Communist" was adapted for the stage and produced in San Francisco in 1999.

His papers are housed at Michigan State University Libraries in Lansing, Michigan. He and his wife, Kristina, continue to live and work in one or another of their locales—a house in Chinook, Montana; an apartment in Paris; a Bourbon Street town house in New Orleans; and a plantation house in Mississippi.

BIBLIOGRAPHY

Bemrose, John. "State of the Sinful Union: Two Authors Take the Pulse of Uncle Sam." *Maclean's* 114, no. 44 (October 29, 2001): 60–61.

Bone, Martyn. "The 'Southern' Conundrum, Continued: Barry Hannah and Richard Ford." *Mississippi Quarterly* 53, no. 3 (Summer 2000): 459–466.

Bonetti, Kay. "An Interview with Richard Ford." *Missouri Review* 10, no. 2 (1987): 71–96.

Brookner, Anita. "Adrift in the Male Doldrums." *Spectator* 279, no. 8824 (September 13, 1997): 36–37.

Falbe, John de. "Crafted with Too Much Care." *Spectator* no. 9039 (November 3, 2001): 57–58.

Flower, Dean. "In the House of Pain." *Hudson Review* 41, no. 1 (1988): 209–217.

Folks, Jeffrey J. "Richard Ford's Postmodern Cowboys." In *Perspectives on Richard Ford,* edited by Huey Guagliardo, 141–156. Jackson: University Press of Mississippi, 2000.

Ford, Richard. *Independence Day.* New York: Knopf, 1995.

———. *The Lay of the Land.* New York: Bloomsbury, 2006.

———. *A Multitude of Sins: Stories.* New York: Knopf, 2002.

———. *A Piece of My Heart.* New York: Harper, 1976.

———. *Rock Springs: Stories.* New York: Atlantic Monthly Press, 1987.

———. *The Sportswriter.* New York: Vintage, 1986.

———. *The Ultimate Good Luck.* Boston: Houghton Mifflin, 1981.

———. *Vintage Ford.* New York: Vintage, 2003.

———. *Wildlife.* New York: Atlantic Monthly Press, 1990.

———. *Women with Men: Three Stories.* New York: Knopf, 1997.

Ford, Richard, and Bonnie Lyons. "Richard Ford: The Art of Fiction CXLVII." *Paris Review* 38, no. 140 (Fall 1996): 42–77.

Ford, Richard, and Huey Guagliardo. "A Conversation with Richard Ford." *Southern Review* 34, no. 3 (Summer 1998): 609–620.

Ford, Richard, Jennifer Levasseur, and Kevin Rabalais. "Invitation to the Story: An Interview with Richard Ford." *Kenyon Review* 23, nos. 3–4 (Summer–Fall 2001): 123–143.

Ford, Richard, with Molly McQuade. "Richard Ford." *Publisher's Weekly* 237, no. 20 (May 18, 1990): 66–67.

Ford, Richard, with Susan Larson. "Novelist's View: Real Estate and the National Psyche." *New York Times,* 5 November 1995, sec. 9, p. 7.

Ford, Richard, *Paris Review,* and others. "The Man in the Back Row Has a Question VII." *Paris Review* 43, no. 158 (Spring–Summer 2001): 297–304.

Gornick, Vivian. "Tenderhearted Men: Lonesome, Sad, and Blue." *New York Times Book Review,* 16 September 1990, pp. 32–35.

Guagliardo, Huey, ed. *Perspectives on Richard Ford.* Jackson: University Press of Mississippi, 2000.

———, ed. *Conversations with Richard Ford.* Jackson: University Press of Mississippi, 2001.

Herd, David. "Nailing People." *Times Literary Supplement* no. 5139 (September 28, 2001): 24.

Hugo, Richard. *The Triggering Town: Lectures and Essays on Poetry and Writing.* New York: Norton, 1979.

Iftekharuddin, Farhat, Mary Rohrberger, and Maurice Lee, eds. *Speaking of the Short Story: Interviews with Contemporary Writers.* Jackson: University Press of Mississippi, 1997.

Kakutani, Michiko. "Afloat in the Turbulence of the American Dream." *New York Times,* 22 June 1995, p. 1.

———. "Books of the Times." *New York Times,* 16 September 1987, p. 1.

Lyons, Bonnie, and Bill Oliver, eds. *Passion and Craft: Conversations with Notable Writers.* Urbana: University of Illinois Press, 1998.

Myerson, Julie. Review of *A Multitude of Sins. Guardian* (London), 28 February 2003, p. 20.

Orr, Phillip. "Rock Springs." *Northwest Review* 26, no. 2 (1988): 143–147.

Schroth, Raymond. "America's Moral Landscape in the Fiction of Richard Ford." *Christian Century,* 1 March 1989, pp. 227–230.

Walker, Elinor Ann. *Richard Ford.* New York: Twayne, 2000.

Weber, Bruce. "Richard Ford's Uncommon Characters." *New York Times Magazine,* 10 April 1988, pp. 59–65.

FORESHADOWING

FORESHADOWING The inclusion of material in a work to hint, suggest, or prepare for later action and events. The technique sometimes may also produce in the reader a feeling of anxiety or suspense. For example, in Edgar Allan Poe's *The Fall of the House of Usher,* the crack or fissure in the wall of the house noted near the beginning of the tale foreshadows the splitting and ultimate demise of the entire Usher family. After reading any story that uses foreshadowing, readers may recall or look back to see when they first anticipated the outcome.

"FRANNY" AND "ZOOEY" J. D. Salinger (1955, 1957)

"FRANNY" AND "ZOOEY" J. D. Salinger (1955, 1957) "Franny" (first published in the New Yorker on January 29, 1955) and its companion short story "Zooey" (also published in the *New Yorker,* on May 4, 1957) detail the lives of two members of J. D. Salinger's epic Glass family. The stories of Francesca (Franny) Glass and her older brother, Zachary (Zooey) Martin Glass, were published together in book form in September 1961 as *Franny and Zooey,* which reached the top of the *New York Times* best-seller list in the year it was published.

Each sibling is troubled by religion. Franny finds too much ego and phoniness (two things Salinger was transfixed with, ascribing the same characteristics to *Catcher in the Rye*'s Holden Caulfield) in herself and those around her. Zooey tries to assist her by way of a telephone call in which he disguises his voice and leads her to a sort of inner peace. Franny is often seen as a hopeless romantic searching for faith, while Zooey is cast as the realistic intruder on this fantasy land. Zooey is all intellect and sharp wit, while Franny is the fragile character—her dialogue is reminiscent of Holden Caulfield—who seemingly suffers at the hands of the world. Franny and Zooey, like many of Salinger's characters, are unhappy with the way the world is. Franny's personal discontent is most manifest in her predilection for self-absorption and fakery, which she sees in everyone around her. Zooey sees mental problems in his associates and considers quitting his job.

"Franny" begins with Franny meeting her boyfriend at a coffeehouse. They talk, eventually digressing into a tangent about religion and philosophy, in which Franny reveals her hypersensitivity and withdrawal from her daily activities. Her only joy and source of relief is found in her "Jesus Prayer," which distracts her from the egocentric people in her life, including her professors and her boyfriend. She eventually faints and is taken home.

Zooey, in his section, explains his sister's breakdown, his own ulcer, and their shared religious preoccupation as a result of their torturous childhood. Their education was received via two older siblings: Seymour (whose suicide was described in Salinger's 1948 story "A Perfect Day for Bananafish") and Buddy (a self-described neurotic). Before the educational basics began, Franny and Zooey were deeply steeped in religion and philosophy in all its various forms.

The joint moral of each story seems to be tolerance and understanding, but at a certain price. These stories explore religion, psychology, familial relationships, and the ever-present human quest not only for a sense of purpose but also for a unique understanding of life, the world, and one's own place. In this way Franny and Zooey both seem typical Salinger characters in that they question the world and their place in it, while turning as equally critical eye to those surrounding them. Religion, however, seems more central an issue here than in other Salinger short stories, although family connections—and connections to other people—remain constant THEMES in Salinger's work.

Anne N. Thalheimer
University of Delaware

FREEMAN, MARY E. WILKINS (MARY ELEANOR WILKINS FREEMAN) (1852–1930)

An impressively prolific author, the Massachusetts-born Mary E. Wilkins Freeman published 14 novels and 15 collections of short fiction during her 50-year career as an author. Writing of her native New England and its folk, she excelled at the short story form and was a popular success in her own time. Although praised for her use of atmosphere, setting, and mood, Freeman herself focused on people and CHARACTER. Indeed, recent critics have resisted the traditional classification of Freeman as a LOCAL COLOR writer and find this classification far too narrow for "her profound insights into human nature and social relationships" (Westbrook, "Mary E. Wilkins Freeman" 290). Recognized as a realist (see REALISM) by such critics and writers as WILLIAM DEAN HOWELLS and HAMLIN GARLAND, Freeman chronicled the changing New England of her era, including Brattleboro, Vermont, where she lived from ages 15 to 31, and Randolph, Massachusetts, where she spent the subsequent two decades before marrying Charles Freeman and moving with him to Metuchen, New Jersey.

Freeman began selling stories to such magazines as *Harper's Bazaar* and established herself as a significant voice with the publication of *A Humble Romance* (1887), set in rural Vermont, and *A New England Nun and Other Stories* (1891), containing some of her best stories; these stories continue to be widely anthologized. She wrote plays, poetry, and novels as well, but with the possible exceptions of two novels—*Pembroke* (1894) and *The Shoulders of Atlas* (1908)—her talent lies in her short fiction, much of which displays impressive psychological depth.

Because Freeman wrote a large number of stories that feature strong and determined women, recently she has become the object of a good deal of attention from feminist scholars. As did EDITH WHARTON, together with whom in 1926 Freeman was elected to the National Institute of Arts and Letters, Freeman did not consider herself a feminist—but again, as with Wharton, much of that attitude mirrored those of other women of her time. Leah Glasser positions Freeman's voice between the bold protesting voice of CHARLOTTE PERKINS GILMAN and the softer, calmer voice of SARAH ORNE JEWETT: In Glasser's words, Freeman's stories "offer women strategies of subterfuge, methods of coping and surviving through seeming compromise" (xx), yet some of her strongest stories, such as "Sister Liddy," demonstrate the confining, conflicted choices women still face today.

"Sister Liddy" focuses on Polly, who has been locked away in an asylum for the insane. In this image of the imprisoned woman who has resisted conformity, the trope of The MADWOMAN IN THE ATTIC comes to mind. The asylum's female inmates, all women or children, spend hopeless and meaningless lives against the backdrop of random and chaotic noise.

Glasser compares Polly to Charlotte Perkins Gilman's narrator in "The YELLOW WALL-PAPER," because Polly creates a double, or DOPPELGANGER—but Polly's double is Sister Liddy, a conventional and successful young woman for whom life seems perfectly balanced and blissful. Yet one can see a second sister to Polly in Sally, the screaming, violent madwoman, possibly a METAPHOR for all the women who rebel against society's insistence that they shape themselves after the ideal married woman symbolized in Sister Liddy (Glasser 230–231).

More successfully rebellious women appear in such stories as "Louisa." Louisa is a young woman who has lost her job as a schoolteacher. Refusing her widowed mother's wish that she marry a rich suitor whom she does not love, she works as a field hand on neighboring farms and independently farms the family land, thereby supporting herself, her mother, and her senile grandfather. Likewise, in the more widely known "The REVOLT OF MOTHER," the wife rebels against her husband in order to acquire a better home and better living conditions than he had managed to provide. A similarly strong woman is celebrated in "A CHURCH MOUSE."

BIBLIOGRAPHY

Foster, Edward. *Mary E. Wilkins Freeman.* New York: Hendricks House, 1956.

Freeman, Mary E. Wilkins. *The Best Stories.* Edited by Henry Wysham Lanier. New York: Harper, 1927.

———. *The Copy-Cat and Other Stories.* New York: Harper, 1914.

———. *Edgewater People.* New York: Harper, 1918.

———. *The Fair Lavinia and Others.* New York: Harper, 1907.

———. *The Givers: Short Stories.* New York: Harper, 1904.

———. *A Humble Romance and Other Stories.* New York: Harper, 1887. As *A FarAway Melody and Other Stories.* Edinburgh: D. Douglas, 1892.

———. *The Love of Parson Lord and Other Stories.* New York: Harper, 1900.

———. *A New England Nun and Other Stories.* New York: Harper, 1891.

———. *Selected Short Stories of Mary E. Wilkins Freeman.* Edited by Marjorie Pryse. New York: Norton, 1983.

———. *Silence and Other Stories.* New York: Harper, 1898.

———. *Six Trees: Short Stories.* New York: Harper, 1903.

———. *Understudies: Short Stories.* New York: Harper, 1901.

———. *The Wind in the Rose-Bush and Other Stories of the Supernatural.* New York: Doubleday, Page, 1903.

———. *The Winning Lady and Others.* New York: Harper, 1909.

Glasser, Leah. *In a Closet Hidden: The Life and Work of Mary E. Wilkins Freeman.* Amherst: University of Massachusetts Press, 1996.

Westbrook, Perry D. *Mary Wilkins Freeman.* Rev. ed. Boston: Twayne, 1988.

———. "Mary E. Wilkins Freeman." In *Reference Guide to Short Fiction,* edited by Noelle Watson, 189–190. Detroit: Gale Press, 1994.

FREUD, SIGMUND (1856–1939)

An Austrian psychiatrist, Freud is considered founder of psychoanalysis. He devised the technique of free association in which patients under the guidance of an analyst allowed material, such as emotional episodes in their past that had been repressed in the unconscious, to emerge to conscious recognition. He also used dream interpretation, in which he analyzed patients' dreams for their symbolic content, because he believed dreams were a person's means of expressing repressed emotions, and repression was the cause of neurotic behavior. His most controversial work dealt with his theories about the sexual instinct, or the libido: Freud maintained that a primary motivating factor in human behavior, including that of children, was sexual in nature and ascribed most neuroses to the repressive influence of social and individual inhibitions about sex. Freud's ideas had a great impact on the thinking of the 20th century, influencing anthropology, education, and especially the fine arts and literature.

FRONTIER HUMORISTS

For several decades before the CIVIL WAR these early humorists were keen-eyed observers of the human scene. For the most part they were not professional writers, and they probably thought of themselves as recording rather than imaginatively creating the tales they wrote. Although they play a minor part in the development of the short story because their metier was generally the sketch or anecdote, collections like A. B. Longstreet's *Georgia Scenes* (1835), W. T. Thompson's *Major Jones's Courtship* (1843), J. J. Hooper's *Some Adventures of Captain Simon Suggs* (1845), and G. W. HARRIS's *SUT LOVINGOOD: YARNS SPUN* (1867) contain selections that show a drift toward plotted narrative.

The humorous anecdote or TALL TALE was essentially an oral genre, and when transferred to print it usually retained the voice and verbal mannerisms of the teller. Sut Lovingood, for instance, tells of his scrapes and his practical jokes in a vernacular that identifies him as a Tennessee hill-country boy, a "nat'ral born durn'd fool." If the language is comic, the DIALECT is reasonably accurate and gives the story an immediacy much greater than if it had been told in literary language.

BIBLIOGRAPHY

Harris, George Washington. "Sut Lovingood: Yarns Spun by a 'Nat'ral Born Durn Fool.'" In *The Harper American Literature*. Vol. 1, edited by Donald McQuade. New York: Harper & Row, 1987.

FUGITIVES, THE   See AGRARIANS, THE.

G

GAINES, ERNEST (1933–) Born on River Lake Plantation near New Roads, Louisiana, Ernest Gaines moved from the locale that would become the animating force behind his fiction to Vallejo, California, with his parents when he was 15. Before graduating from San Francisco State College in 1957, he published his first short story. After completing a year of graduate work at Stanford on a creative writing fellowship, Gaines began writing novels—a critic advised him that they were more marketable than short stories. In addition to his 1968 collection of stories, *Bloodline,* Gaines has written six novels: *Catherine Carmier* (1964), *Of Love and Dust* (1967), *The Autobiography of Miss Jane Pittman* (1971), *In My Father's House* (1978), *A Gathering of Old Men* (1983), and *A Lesson before Dying* (1993), which won the National Book Critics Circle Award. In 2005 Gaines published *Mozart and Leadbelly: Stories and Essays.*

Gaines's works all share a common setting—Bayonne, Louisiana—a locale comparable to WILLIAM FAULKNER's fictional YOKNAPATAWPHA COUNTY, although, unlike Faulkner, Gaines has not created characters that appear in more than one work. Influenced by ERNEST HEMINGWAY, Faulkner, and the Russian novelist Ivan Turgenev, Gaines depicts the African-American experience in the changing South; his fiction is thoroughly grounded in region and community.

Bloodline collects five stories concerning young black male PROTAGONISTs, struggling to transcend the limitations imposed by their environment and their past. Beyond physical setting, this SHORT STORY CYCLE is unified by various THEMEs that develop concurrently as the stories progress: the definition of black manhood through conflict with white social institutions, the role of women and the community in relation to social progress, the failure of traditional religion, and the importance of visionary characters in defining the nature of change. Arranged chronologically according to the age of the protagonists, these stories depict a progressive awareness of the nature of racial oppression and its individual and communal implications. "A Long Day in November" (revised and published separately as a children's book in 1971) chronicles the separation and reconciliation of six-year-old Sonny's parents through the child's viewpoint. (See POINT OF VIEW.) "THE SKY IS GRAY" (filmed for public television in 1980) presents the trials posed by segregation from the viewpoint of a nine-year-old whose mother takes him to town for a dental appointment. Both stories portray the black male's struggle to achieve manhood in the context of a female-dominated community and within the barriers erected by the dominant white society.

"Three Men" depicts the spiritual and ethical growth of Proctor Lewis, whose encounter with two other men and a young boy in prison spurs his decision to break the cycle of powerless dependence and misdirected anger by enduring suffering in prison instead of allowing the paternalistic plantation owner

262

to bail him out. In "Bloodline," Copper, a mulatto veteran, returns home to the plantation on which he was born to claim his legacy from the white uncle who owns it. While Copper's adamant militancy is not presented as the ultimate solution, Copper does obtain recognition of kinship from his uncle, who suffers a similar lack of compassion and vision. "Just Like a Tree" concludes the collection on a hopeful note when Emmanuel, a young civil rights activist engaged in nonviolent resistance, moves away. He is not motivated by hatred or by the community's more conservative feminine elements but instead by his aunt Fe, who preserves the memory of historical oppression. A composite of 10 different narrative voices—black and white—this final story mirrors the unresolved tension of the collection's other voices. Read as a short story cycle, Gaines's collection depicts a community in the process of dissolution, struggling to preserve a communal past (that is, its bloodline) as individuals move toward self-realization that threatens to erase it.

BIBLIOGRAPHY
Babb, Valerie Melissa. *Ernest Gaines*. Boston: Twayne, 1991.
Bryant, Jerry H. "Ernest J. Gaines: Change, Growth, and History." *Southern Review* 10 (1974): 851–864.
Byerman, Keith E. *Fingering the Jagged Grain: Tradition and Form in Recent Black Fiction*. Athens: University of Georgia Press, 1985.
Callahan, John F. "Hearing Is Believing: The Landscape of Voice in Ernest Gaines's *Bloodline*." *Callaloo* 7 (1984): 86–112.
Doyle, Mary Ellen. "Ernest J. Gaines: An Annotated Bibliography, 1956–1988." *Black American Literature Forum* 24 (1990): 125–150.
Duncan, Todd. "Scene and Life Cycle in Ernest Gaines's *Bloodline*." *Callaloo* 1 (1978): 85–101.
Estes, David C. *Critical Reflections on the Fiction of Ernest J. Gaines*. Athens: University of Georgia Press, 1994.
Gaines, Ernest. *Bloodline*. New York: Dial, 1968.
Gaudet, Marcia, and Carl Wooton. *Porch Talk with Ernest Gaines: Conversations on the Writer's Craft*. Baton Rouge: University of Louisiana Press, 1990.
Hicks, Jack. "To Make These Bones Live: History and Community in Ernest Gaines's Fiction." *Black American Literature Forum* 11 (1977): 9–19.
Lowe, John. *Conversations with Ernest Gaines*. Jackson: University Press of Mississippi, 1995.
Rowell, Charles. "The Quarters: Ernest Gaines and the Sense of Place." *Southern Review* 21 (1985): 733–750.
Werner, Craig Hansen. *Paradoxical Resolutions: American Fiction since Joyce*. Urbana: University of Illinois Press, 1982.

Robert M. Luscher
University of Nebraska at Kearney

GALE, ZONA (1874–1938)

Stark REALISM characterizes the writing of Zona Gale in her novels and stories. A native of Wisconsin, Gale primarily wrote about small-town life in the Midwest. Her four-volume collection of short stories, *Friendship Village* (1908), focuses on the citizens of a small town based on her hometown of Portage, Wisconsin.

GALLANT, MAVIS (1922–)

Mavis Gallant is one of the great short story specialists of our time. Critics compare her to a wide range of authors, including Katherine Mansfield, HENRY JAMES, Anton Chekov, George Eliot, and KATHERINE ANNE PORTER. Her stories have been appearing in the NEW YORKER for six decades, and she continues to present psychologically complex yet ordinary individuals who struggle to come to terms with—and frequently to overcome—the onus of history and the recent past. No character remains unscathed by the political turmoil and upheavals of the 20th century. The aftermath of WORLD WAR II is one of Gallant's great subjects, and in fact, her first collection, *The Other Paris* (1956), contains tales peopled with disillusioned British, American, and Canadian expatriates living in both physical and spiritual exile in Western Europe, and *From the Fifteenth District: A Novella and Eight Short Stories* (1979) focuses on American expatriates in post–World War II Europe. *My Heart Is Broken: Eight Stories and a Short Novel* (1964) likewise depicts despairing exiles living in seedy European hotels.

Gallant was virtually ignored in Canada until the late 1970s. By her own account, the *New Yorker* enabled her to earn a living and "the United States was my career. Canada paid no attention to me until 1979" (qtd. in Bernrose 66). Conditions changed in 1981, when Gallant published *Home Truths: Selected Canadian Stories,* a portrayal of Canadians in general and Montreal in particular, and gained a huge readership in her home country as well as the Governor General's Award, Canada's highest literary honor. Particularly admired is her Linnet Muir cycle, a first-person narrative about a Montreal childhood. In other stories Gallant portrays German characters in the post-Hitler era and French characters during and after the 1968 student uprisings in Paris. One of her most popular works is *The Pegnitz Junction,* a series of interconnected stories that depict what the critic Geoff Hancock calls "the small possibilities [of fascism] in people" (41). A resident of Paris for the past 50 years, she has written numerous stories of Parisian life, most recently in *Overhead in a Balloon: Stories of Paris* (1985) and *Paris Stories* (2002).

Mavis Gallant was born Mavis de Trafford Young on August 11, 1922, in Montreal, Quebec, Canada, to an Anglo-Scottish father and an American mother. Because her father died and her mother remarried, she was shunted back and forth to attend 17 different schools in both Canada and the United States. Numerous critics have linked this constant state of transition to the rootlessness and exile characteristic of so many of Gallant's fictional people and to her interest in portraying dislocated and unloved children. After graduating from high school in New York City, she returned to Canada and became a journalist for the *Montreal Standard,* was briefly married to the pianist John Gallant, and in 1950 moved permanently to Paris, where she has remained for over half a century. In that same year the *New Yorker* accepted her story entitled "Madeline's Birthday," and Gallant has been a regular contributor to the magazine ever since. *In Transit* (1988) contains 20 stories that appeared in the *New Yorker* in the 1950s and 1960s and focuses on preadolescent and adolescent children and their parents.

The 11 stories appearing in *Across the Bridge* (1993) are set in Montreal or Paris and contain Gallant's dislocated and alienated modern characters. Of this collection, the reviewer Barbara Gabriel observes, "As always in Gallant, the main protagonist in these stories is history itself," again showcasing Gallant as "one of the great chroniclers of the human fallout of World War II and its redrawn borders" (38). She continues to be lauded for her caustic irony, her wit, her expatriate perspective, and her distinctly Canadian sensibilities. Gallant attributes her feel for the "rhythm of English prose" to the English and American children's books she read as a child (Gallant, preface xvi). And it is precisely and invariably through this use of language, argues the reviewer Judith Farr, "that we approach Gallant's troubled, traveled but never serenely urbane men, women and children" (33).

The 900-page *Collected Stories of Mavis Gallant* appeared in 1996, demonstrating the breadth and depth of six decades of writing, and the *Paris Stories,* edited by the author Michael Ondaatje, was published in 2002. Although best known for her short stories, Gallant has written two novels: *Green Water, Green Sky* (1959) and *A Fairly Good Time* (1970). She has written one play, *What Is to Be Done,* dramatizing two young Canadians with communist sympathies, and one nonfiction work, *The Affair of Gabrielle Russier* (1971).

BIBLIOGRAPHY

Allen, Brooke. "Brownout in the City of Light." *New Criterion* 15, no. 4 (December 1996): 69–72.

Bell, Pearl K. "Rara Mavis." *New Republic* 215, no. 22 (25 November 1996): 42–45.

Besner, Neil. "A Broken Dialogue: History and Memory in Mavis Gallant's Short Fiction." *Essays on Canadian Writing,* no. 33 (Fall 1986): 89–99.

Bieler, Zoe. "Visiting Writer Finds Montreal Changed in the Past Five Years." *Montreal Star,* 30 August 1955, p. 26.

Blodgett, E. D. "Heresy and Other Arts: A Measure of Mavis Gallant's Fiction." *Essays on Canadian Writing* 42 (Winter 1990): 1–8.

Clement, Lesley D. "Mavis Gallant's Stories of the 1950s: Learning to Look." *American Review of Canadian Studies* 24, no. 1 (Spring 1994): 57–73.

Farr, Judith. Review of *The Collected Stories of Mavis Gallant. America* 176, no. 4 (February 8, 1997): 33–34.

Gallant, Mavis. *Across the Bridge: Stories.* New York: Random House, 1993.

———. *The End of the World and Other Stories.* Toronto: McClelland & Stewart, 1974.

———. *A Fairly Good Time.* New York: Random House, 1970.

———. *From the Fifteenth District: A Novella and Eight Short Stories.* New York: Random House, 1979.

———. *Green Water, Green Sky.* Boston: Houghton Mifflin, 1959.

———. *Home Truths: Selected Canadian Stories.* Toronto: Macmillan, 1981; New York: Random House, 1985.

———. *In Transit.* New York: Random House, 1988.

———. *The Moslem Wife and Other Stories.* Edited by Mordecai Richler. Toronto: McClelland & Stewart, 1994.

———. *My Heart Is Broken: Eight Stories and a Short Novel.* New York: Random House, 1964; republished as *An Unmarried Man's Summer* (London: Heinemann, 1965); republished under original title (Don Mills, Ontario: Paperjacks, 1974).

———. *The Other Paris.* Boston: Houghton Mifflin, 1956.

———. *Overhead in a Balloon: Stories of Paris.* New York: Random House, 1985.

———. *The Pegnitz Junction: A Novella and Five Short Stories.* New York: Random House, 1973.

———. Preface to *The Collected Stories of Mavis Gallant.* New York: Random House, 1996.

———. *The Selected Stories of Mavis Gallant.* Toronto: McClelland & Stewart, 1996.

———. *What Is to Be Done?* Dunvegan, Ontario: Quadrant, 1983.

Gallant, Mavis, and Daphne Kalotay. "Mavis Gallant: The Art of Fiction CLX." *Paris Review* 41, no. 153 (Winter 1999–2000): 192–211.

Gallant, Mavis, and Leslie Schenk. "Celebrating Mavis Gallant." *World Literature Today* 72, no. 1 (Winter 1998): 19–26.

Grant, Judith Skelton, and Douglas Malcolm. "Mavis Gallant: An Annotated Bibliography." In *The Annotated Bibliography of Canada's Major Authors.* Vol. 5, edited by Robert Lecker and Jack David. Downsview, Ontario: ECW, 1984.

Hancock, Geoff. "An Interview with Mavis Gallant." *Canadian Fiction Magazine,* no. 28 (1978): 1,867.

Hatch, Ronald. An excerpt from a review of *"Home Truths: Selected Canadian Stories." Canadian Fiction Magazine,* no. 43 (1982): 125–129.

———. "Mavis Gallant and the Creation of Consciousness." In *Present Tense,* edited by John Moss, 45–71. Toronto: NC Press, 1985.

———. "Mavis Gallant and the Expatriate Character." *Zeitschrift der Gesellschaft für Kanada-Studien* 1 (1981): 133–142.

———. "Missing Connections." *Essays on Canadian Writing* 41 (Summer 1990): 21–25.

———. "The Three Stages of Mavis Gallant's Short Fiction." *Canadian Fiction Magazine* no. 28 (1978): 92–114.

Merler, Grazia. *Mavis Gallant: Narrative Patterns and Devices.* Ottawa: Tecumseh, 1978.

O'Rourke, David. "Exiles in Time: Gallant's 'My Heart Is Broken.'" *Canadian Literature* 93 (Summer 1982): 98–107.

Schaub, Danielle. "'Small Lives of Their Own Creation': Mavis Gallant's Perception of Canadian Culture." *Critique* 34, no. 1 (Fall 1992): 33–46.

———. "Structural Patterns of Alienation and Disjunction: Mavis Gallant's Firmly-Structured Stories." *Canadian Literature* 136 (Spring 1993): 45–57.

Wyile, Herb. "Home and Abroad." *Canadian Literature* 131 (Winter 1991): 235–236.

GARDNER, ERLE STANLEY (1889–1970)

A practicing lawyer for many years, Gardner initially wrote stories published in pulp magazines under several pseudonyms, including A. A. Fair. He proceeded to write over 100 books and became one of the most successful writers of DETECTIVE SHORT FICTION in American publishing history. Most of his stories employed either Perry Mason, perhaps the most famous lawyer in American fiction, or the district attorney Douglas Selby. Gardner's stories are noted for their fast action, clever legal devices, and ingenious plotting.

BIBLIOGRAPHY

Gardner, Erle Stanley. *The Case of the Murderer's Bride and Other Stories.* New York: Davis, 1969.

———. *Ellery Queen Presents Erle Stanley Gardner's The Amazing Adventures of Lester Leith.* New York: Davis, 1981.

———. *The Human Zero, The Science Fiction Stories of ESG.* New York: Morrow, 1981.

———. *Pay Dirt and Other Whispering Sand Stories of Gold Fever and the Western Desert.* New York: Morrow, 1983.

———. *Whispering Sands: Stories of Gold Fever and the Western Desert.* New York: Morrow, 1981.

GARLAND, HAMLIN (HANNIBAL HAMLIN GARLAND) (1860–1940)

Born in rural poverty in Wisconsin and reared on a succession of farms in Iowa and South Dakota, Garland moved to Boston in 1884. Despite loneliness and poverty, he educated himself at the public library, found a teaching position, and met WILLIAM DEAN HOWELLS and others in the Boston literary circle. Influenced by the realistic techniques of Howells, who encouraged him in his literary efforts, and by a return visit to his family in South Dakota, where he observed the loneliness and drudgery of farm life from a new perspective, Garland found his subject. He published his first story in *Harper's Weekly* in 1888 and published a collection of stories about rural prairie life entitled *Main-Travelled Roads: Six Mississippi Valley Stories* in 1891. These stories about the poverty and heroic, silent endurance of ordinary folk in the "Middle Border" states (Wisconsin, Minnesota, Nebraska, and the Dakotas) launched his career as a full-time writer. The collection was one of the first to contain the stories linked by a common theme and location, a link later honed by such writers as SARAH ORNE JEWETT in *THE COUNTRY OF THE POINTED FIRS* and SHERWOOD ANDERSON in *WINESBURG, OHIO*.

Although today critics view Garland's writings as early contributions to NATURALISM, as well as talented illustrations of REGIONALISM and LOCAL COLOR, in 1894 he published *Crumbling Idols,* in which he explains his own literary theory. Garland uses the term *veritism* to describe his particular version of realism: He based his observation about the actual lives of the midwestern characters in a knowledge of sociology and a use of local color firmly rooted in a sense of place. His technique is evidenced in two other story collections, *Prairie Folks* (1893) and *Wayside Courtships* (1897), both later edited to form the collection *Other Main-Travelled Roads,* published in 1910.

Of the many fine stories in *Main-Travelled Roads,* Garland's frequently anthologized "Under the Lion's Paw" exemplifies the author's reformist beliefs that the lives of the rural poor are needlessly exploited by profit-seeking absentee landlords who give the lie to the AMERICAN DREAM. Tim Haskins and his wife, Nettie, driven out of Iowa in the depression of the 1880s, seek a better life in Kansas. The Haskinses are befriended by Steven Council and his wife, Sarah, who demonstrate to the newcomers the feasibility of owning and successfully farming their own land. Tim and Nettie and their children

do find a farm, but when Tim—after spending three years on improvements—is finally ready to purchase it, he and his family suffer the exploitations of the capitalist (see CAPITALISM) land speculator Jim Butler, who raises the price. When Tim, enraged almost to the point of committing murder, nearly impales Butler on his pitchfork, some critics see him as the lion trapping Butler under his paw. Nonetheless, when Tim eventually consents to Butler's increased price, he clearly falls under the "paw" of Butler.

Other notable stories include "Among the Corn Rows," a rural romance, and "A Branch Road," both of which employ rescue plots inspired by Garland's sympathy for his mother's life of hopeless drudgery (and hence his active support of FEMINIST causes). "Up the Coulee," another often-published story, in which a son returns from the city to find his mother and younger brother living in rural poverty, provides still another example of Garland's concern with his mother's lot and his impulse to recreate it, illustrate her plight, and give her a better life. "The Return of a Private" explores the homecoming of a Union CIVIL WAR veteran who, having fought for an ideal, must now contend with poverty and the harshness of nature on his Wisconsin farm, along with the injustice of his fellow humans.

In an almost metaphorically American way, Garland found himself drawn to both the comfortable existence and literary establishment of the East, and then to the hope and possibilities of the West. From his eastern perspective, he created the stories illuminating the hard lives of rural midwestern farm folk, and, as the critic Robert Franklin Gish notes, from his western perspective, writing his Klondike and Dakota gold rush adventures, Garland "more or less discovered, and certainly advanced, the Western novel" with its faith in the American dream (Gish 203). Besides the short stories on which his reputation firmly rests, Garland wrote a number of novels and autobiographical narratives. In 1922 he received the Pulitzer Prize in biography for *A Daughter of the Middle Border,* which, together with the frontier story of his wife, traces his family's progress from early pioneer times until WORLD WAR I.

BIBLIOGRAPHY

Bryer, Jackson R., and Eugene Harding. *Hamlin Garland and the Critics: An Annotated Bibliography.* Troy, N.Y.: Whitston, 1973.

Garland, Hamlin. *The Book of the American Indian.* New York: Harper, 1923.

———. *Crumbling Idols.* Chicago: Stone and Kimball, 1894.

———. *Hamlin Garland's Diaries.* Edited by Donald Pizer. San Marino, Calif.: Huntington Library, 1968.

———. *Jason Edwards: An Average Man.* Boston: Arena, 1892.

———. *Main-Travelled Roads: Six Stories of the Mississippi Valley.* Boston: Arena, 1891.

———. *Other Main-Travelled Roads.* New York: Harper, 1910.

———. *Prairie Folks.* Chicago: F. J. Schulte & Company, 1893; revised edition: New York: Macmillan, 1899.

———. *Rose of Dutcher's Coolly.* Chicago: Stone and Kimball, 1895.

———. *A Son of the Middle Border.* New York: Macmillan, 1917.

———. *They of the High Trails.* New York: Harper & Brothers, 1916.

———. *Wayside Courtships.* New York: D. Appleton and Company 1897.

Gish, Robert Franklin. *Garland: The Far West.* Boise, Idaho: Boise State University, 1976.

———. "Hamlin Garlin." In *Reference Guide to Short Fiction,* edited by Noelle Watson, 202–203. Detroit: St. James Press, 1994.

Holloway, Jean. *Garland: A Biography.* Austin: University of Texas Press, 1960.

McCullough, Joseph B. *Garland.* Boston: Twayne, 1978.

Nagel, James, ed. *Critical Essays on Garland.* Boston: G. K. Hall, 1982.

Pizer, Donald. *Garland's Early Work and Career.* Berkeley: University of California Press, 1960.

Silet, Charles L. P., Robert E. Welch, and Richard Boudreau, eds. *The Critical Reception of Garland 1891–1978.* Troy, N.Y.: Whitston, 1985.

GARRISON, WILLIAM LLOYD (1805–1879)

A prominent abolitionist—from Massachusetts who in 1831 founded the *Liberator,* a weekly newspaper in which he campaigned for the immediate and complete abolition of slavery. Garrison advocated Northern succession from the Union, because the Constitution permitted slavery, and he opposed the CIVIL WAR until ABRAHAM LINCOLN issued the Emancipation Proclamation in 1862. The *Liberator* ceased publication in 1865 after slavery was abolished with passage of the Thirteenth Amendment to the Constitution. Garrison's sharing the lecture platform with the African-American abolitionists and writers FREDERICK DOUGLASS and FRANCES HARPER exemplified his indirect support of their literary endeavors. The abolitionists' consciously active role in promoting literature, however, did not occur until they recruited such intellectuals as William Ellery Channing, his fellow transcendentalist Ralph Waldo Emerson (see TRANSCENDENTALISM), and the poets Henry Wadsworth Longfellow and James Russell Lowell. In 1899, Garrison's son, Francis J. Garrison, in his role as editor at Houghton Mifflin Company, encouraged CHARLES W. CHESNUTT and helped publish his first collection of stories, *Conjure Woman and Other Stories.*

GAVIN STEVENS

Gavin Stevens has been variously described as WILLIAM FAULKNER's "Favorite," his "Good Man," and his "Footloose Knight." Truly an admirable, albeit quixotic, figure, Stevens is arguably one of Faulkner's most important characters: He plays an active role in more of the author's works than any other character. In six novels and nearly a dozen short stories, Faulkner uses Gavin Stevens, a YOKNAPATAWPHA COUNTY attorney, to explore many of his chief concerns as a writer.

Nearly all of the Gavin Stevens stories can be grouped into one of three categories. The short stories and NOVELLA that compose *KNIGHT'S GAMBIT* (1949) consistently focus on the vital role that language plays in Stevens's life as well as his earnest efforts as county attorney to discover and execute humane truth and justice. The second grouping, which consists primarily of *Light in August* (1932), *GO DOWN, MOSES* (1941), *Intruder in the Dust* (1948), and *Requiem for a Nun* (1951), present Gavin's (and Faulkner's) increasingly honest confrontation with the issue of race in the South. These are arguably the most important of the Gavin Stevens stories because they reflect, through Gavin, the development of Faulkner's increasingly liberal and sympathetic view of "the race problem in the South." Consisting of "By the People" (1955), *The Town* (1957), and *The Mansion* (1959), the final grouping could be appropriately titled "Stevens *v.* SNOPES," as they tell about the noble attorney's decades-long struggle against Faulkner's most notorious family of characters, who symbolize the unscrupulous rapacity of the post-RECONSTRUCTION South.

BIBLIOGRAPHY

Faulkner, William. *Faulkner in the University*. Edited by Joseph L. Blotner and Frederick L. Gwynn. Charlottesville: University of Virginia Press, 1959.

Watson, Jay. *Forensic Fictions: The Lawyer Figure in Faulkner*. Athens: University of Georgia Press, 1993.

H. Collin Messer
University of North Carolina at Chapel Hill

GAY MALE SHORT FICTION

Just as fiction can be about anything, so, too, is gay male fiction not necessarily just about gay men; rather, as David Leavitt explains, a gay male short story can be one "that illuminates the experience of love between men, explores the nature of homosexual identity, or investigates the kinds of relationships gay men have with each other, with their friends, and with their families" (*Penguin Book of Gay Short Stories*, xxiii). That is, gay male short fiction is not just fiction that is written by gay men but actually encompasses all of the relationships gay men have—relationships that include all readers, regardless of sexual identity.

While relationships between women can be found in American short fiction during the 19th century, relationships between men are harder to come by, even though the short story as a genre was blossoming at this time. One reason for the lack of gay male representation could be the societal prohibition against such relationships: Male-male relationships verging on the homoerotic were vehemently discouraged and outlawed by the sodomy laws of the time. Examples of homosexual/homosocial bonding can be found in novels and poetry from the 19th century, such as in HERMAN MELVILLE's sea novels and Walt Whitman's *Calamus* poems, but these relationships are almost always placed in settings and institutions dominated by men, such as the military, the sea, or boarding schools, or in imaginary/utopian spaces. In these settings, the gay male relationship could be read simply as a close friendship, while codes and symbols also could point to an underlying homosexual THEME.

Not surprisingly, then—since the concept of homosexuality as identity rather than behavior is relatively contemporary—gay male presence in the American short story does not really emerge until the turn of the 20th century. One example can be found in HENRY JAMES's short story "The Great Good Place." James presents a bachelor who falls asleep amid all the pressures of his business and social engagements and dreams of a halcyonic place of harmony and happiness. In this place he finds only men, and he attaches himself to one man in particular, who is identified only as "Brother." They determine that this special place will always be perfect, because "not everyone will find it, there would never be too many." Rather than assigning a traditional name to the place, the men call it "The Great Good Place" as well as "The Great Want Met." When the PROTAGONIST awakes, he finds his sleep has lasted only a few hours, although it seemed like weeks. The story ends with the protagonist affirming that what he felt and experienced in the dream "*was* all right"; it is perhaps James's most open affirmation of homosexuality in all of his works.

Even after some short story writers ventured to present gay male relationships away from the ship or the barracks, they still placed their characters in faraway places, perhaps in order to distance the threat of the homosexual relationship from the reality of American culture: Gay males could be represented more openly in these spaces but were still not allowed to be a part of American culture. Therefore, in the 1950s, PAUL BOWLES, in "Pages from Cold Point," and Gore Vidal, in "Pages from an Abandoned Journal," are able to tell stories detailing homosexual relationships, which are allowed to flourish only in the Caribbean and Europe. These stories also point to a common theme for stories of gay men prior to the 1960s and 1970s: In both stories the gay male lives a tortured existence, ultimately leading to death or persecution. As in films and popular fiction of the time, gay men were shown to be troubled by their sexuality and to live unhappy, unfulfilled lives. Although perhaps this was the only way gay men could be represented in a culture that outwardly condemned them—that is, homosexuality could exist in fiction only as long as it was ultimately shown to be wrong—these works nonetheless demonstrate the struggles gay men encountered on their way to achieving happiness and acceptance.

In the summer of 1969 New York City police raided the Stonewall Inn, a gay bar in Greenwich Village, because of an alleged liquor license violation. People from the bar and the surrounding neighborhood fought back against the police for two days. In the weeks and months following what soon became known as the Stonewall riots (or even just "Stonewall"), gays and lesbians across the nation and the world began to organize a more cohesive and effective effort against the kind of abuse and oppression typified by Stonewall. The Stonewall riots and the subsequent gay rights movement provided writers with the opportunity to change the negative image of the gay man. As gay males began to find more acceptance in mainstream American society, and as representations of their lives increased, outlets for these new stories proliferated as well. In the 1970s, still lacking mainstream publication sources, magazines, journals, and newspapers devoted to gay and lesbian issues and culture sprouted in major American cities: Such publications as *Gay Sunshine, Mouth of the Dragon,* and *Christopher Street* provided outlets for gay and lesbian fiction as well as information for gays and lesbians. Related small presses, such as the Gay Sunshine Press, the Sea Horse Press, and Calamus Press, emerged, providing another opportunity for fiction related to gay and lesbian issues to be printed and read.

One of the most popular themes to emerge in these forums was the "coming-out" story, where the gay male protagonist comes "out of the closet" into a homosexual identity. Edmund White has argued that gay and lesbian identity requires the construction of a coming-out narrative. To this day gay male short

stories focus heavily on the process of coming out and the resulting effects on the gay male and those around him.

Once the gay male was able to "come out" in short fiction, the opportunities for an expansion of the roles available to him increased. Before Stonewall, gay men were represented in fiction as either effeminate or macho, nymphomaniacal or frigid, in denial or suicidal. After Stonewall, gay men in short stories could have more than just one-night stands; they could have lasting relationships with other men and could even survive happily until the end of the story. Gay male fiction showed that gay men are everywhere in American society: They are uncles, fathers, nephews, and sons (as in Christopher Coe's story "Gentlemen Can Wash Their Hands in the Gents'") and fellow coworkers (as in Daniel Curzon's "Victor," a story as much about the struggles of being a teacher as the struggles of being a gay man).

For years artists masked references to gay sexual acts by using codes or subtexts. For example, physical affection between men often has been hidden under the guise of hypermasculine activity, as in the intense wrestling scene in D. H. Lawrence's *Women in Love* or on film in the Roman war epics of *Ben Hur* and *Spartacus*. Gay male short story writers began to describe sex in sometimes shockingly explicit ways. Just as authors of postmodern fiction (see POSTMODERNISM) were pushing the boundaries of sexual propriety in fiction, so, too, were authors of gay fiction using their newfound but still limited acceptance to explore sexuality in their works.

As AIDS entered the lives of gay men in the 1980s, this harrowing disease become a major theme in gay male short fiction. Indeed, it can be argued that literature devoted to the impact of AIDS on American gay male society developed into its own subgenre as authors attempted to respond to this crisis. Most stories dealing with acquired immune deficiency syndrome (AIDS) have centered on the impact of the illness on relationships—those between lovers, as in Michael Cunningham's story "Ignorant Armies," where a man deals with his lover's death and then his own, or between friends, as in David Leavitt's story "A Place I've Never Been," told through the eyes of a woman coming to terms with her friend's impending death. As AIDS has persisted as a disease that knows no boundaries, however, so have authors expanded their view past the sorrowful stories of urban gay men: Sam Rudy, in his story "Sheet Music," chronicles the story of a married man caring for another man dying of AIDS in a small town, while David Feinberg looks at AIDS through a comic lens in his story "Despair."

Although the stories of white gay men predominate, the stories of gay men of color have begun to come to the fore with their own anthologies, such as Essex Hemphill's *Brother to Brother: New Writings by Black Gay Men* (1991). In addition, stories of other groups of gay men, whose voices have been silenced or ignored by both heterosexuals and homosexuals, such as stories about sadomasochistic relationships or of gay men with disabilities, also have begun to appear in both gay publications and mainstream media.

While the history of anthologies of gay male short fiction is relatively short, the number and diversity of anthologies are impressive. The anthologizing of gay male short fiction began with *The Other Persuasion* (1977) and Ian Young's *On The Line: New Gay Fiction* (1981) and was continued by the highly successful Men on Men series, begun in 1986 by George Stambolian. Major publishers soon joined this trend, with anthologies by Penguin and Faber and the annual *Best American Gay Fiction* by Little, Brown.

Many writers continue to believe that coming to terms with one's own homosexuality and its perception and reception will always inform gay fiction, but in recent years, another point of view has been expressed: Andrew Holleran, in his introduction to *Fresh Men 2* (2005), suggests that "being gay seems no longer to be an urgent matter; we now have the freedom to be bored." Not everyone agrees. However, somewhat along these lines, critic Richard Canning believes that the new and younger writers who do not recall the pre-AIDS period are therefore freer to express themselves. According to Canning, because AIDS is an established fact to these writers, "they don't have to confine themselves to gay fiction and gay experiences. They are helping to extend the boundaries of gay fiction by using their imaginations more broadly" (191).

A plethora of gay magazines now exist, and many smaller book presses have stepped forward to publish gay fiction, including Serpent's Tail, Soft Skull, Suspect's Thoughts, Clear Cut, Terrace Books (from the University of Wisconsin Press), and Carroll & Graf. Notable recent work includes Byrne R. S. Fone's *The Columbia Anthology of Gay Literature* (2001), Greg Herren's *Shadows of the Night: Queer Tales of the Uncanny and Unusual* (2007), and the award-winning new series *Fresh Men: New Voices in Gay Fiction*.

BIBLIOGRAPHY

Bao, Quang, Hanya Yanagihara, and Timothy Lui, eds. *Take Out: Queer Writing from Asian Pacific America.* Asian American Writers' Workshop, 2001.

Bergman, David. *The Violet Quill Reader: The Emergence of Gay Writing after Stonewall.* New York: St. Martin's Press, 1995.

Berman, Steve, ed. *Best Gay Stories 2008.* Maple Shade, N.J.: Lethe Press, 2008.

———. *Wilde Stories 2008.* Maple Shade, N.J.: Lethe Press, 2008.

Bouldrey, Brian, ed. *Best American Gay Fiction.* Boston: Little, Brown, 1996.

Bowles, Paul. "Pages from Cold Point." In *The Delicate Prey and Other Stories.* New York: Random House, 1950.

Carbado, Devon, Dwight McBride, and Done Weise, eds. *Black Like Us.* San Francisco: Cleis, 2002.

Coe, Christopher. "Gentlemen Can Wash Their Hands in the Gents.'" In *The Penguin Book of Gay Short Stories,* edited by David Leavitt and Mark Mitchell. New York: Penguin, 1994.

Cooper, Bernard, ed. *Best American Gay Fiction.* Vol. 2. Boston: Back Bay Books, 1997.

Cunningham, Michael. "Ignorant Armies." In *The Penguin Book of Gay Short Stories,* edited by David Leavitt and Mark Mitchell. New York: Penguin, 1994.

Curzon, Daniel. "Victor." In *Human Warmth and Other Stories.* San Francisco: Grey Fox Press, 1981.

Drake, Robert, and Terry Wolverton, eds. *His 3: Brilliant New Fiction by Gay Writers.* New York: Faber & Faber, 1999.

Feinberg, David B. "Despair." In *Spontaneous Combustion.* New York: Viking, 1991.

Fone, Byrne R. S., ed. *Columbia Anthology of Gay Literature.* New York: Columbia University, 2001.

————. *A Road to Stonewall: Male Homosexuality and Homophobia in English and American Literature, 1750–1969.* Boston: Twayne Publishers, 1995.

Fuss, Diana, ed. *Inside/Out: Lesbian Theories, Gay Theories.* New York: Routledge, 1991.

Harris, E. Lynn. *Freedom in this Village: 25 Years of Black, Gay Men's Writing.* New York: Carroll & Graf, 2005.

Hemphill, Essex. *Brother to Brother: New Writings by Black Gay Men.* Boston: Alyson, 1991.

Herren, Greg, ed. *Shadows of the Night: Queer Tales of the Uncanny and Unusual.* New York: Southern Tier, 2004.

Herren, Greg, and Paul J. Willis, eds. *Love, Bourbon Street.* New York: Alyson, 2006.

Herring, Scott. *Queering the Underworld: Slumming, Literature, and the Undoing of Lesbian and Gay History.* Chicago: University of Chicago Press, 2007.

James, Henry. "The Great Good Place." *Scribner's Magazine* 27 (January–June 1900).

Kleinberg, Seymour. *The Other Persuasion: Short Fiction about Gay Men and Women.* New York: Vintage, 1977.

LAMBDA Awards. URL: http://www.lambdaliterary.org/awards/current_nominees.html. Accessed February 8, 2009.

Laurence, Craig. *Sea, Swallow Me and Other Stories.* Maple Shade, N.J.: Lethe Press, 2008.

Leavitt, David. "A Place I've Never Been." In *A Place I've Never Been.* New York: Viking, 1990.

Leavitt, David, and Mark Mitchell, eds. *The Penguin Book of Gay Short Stories.* New York: Penguin, 1994.

Malinowski, Sharon, ed. *Gay and Lesbian Literature.* Detroit: St. James Press, 1994.

Malinowski, Sharon, Christa Brelin, and Malcolm Boyd, eds. *The Gay and Lesbian Literary Companion.* Detroit: Visible Ink Press, 1995.

Manrique, Jaime, and Jesse Dorris, eds. *Besame Mucho: New Gay Latino Fiction.* New York: Painted Leaf Press, 1999.

Mars-Jones, Adam, ed. *Mae West Is Dead: Recent Lesbian and Gay Fiction.* Boston: Faber & Faber, 1983.

Maustbaum, Blair, and Will Fabrom, eds. *Cool Thing: The Best New Gay Fiction from Young American Writers.* New York: Running Press, 2008.

Nolan, James. *Perpetual Care: Stories.* Chattanooga, Tenn.: Jefferson Press, 2008.

Porter, Joe Ashby. *All Aboard: Stories.* New York: Turtle Point Press, 2008.

Quinn, Jay. *Rebel Yell: Stories by Contemporary Southern Gay Authors.* New York: Harrington Park, 2001.

Rudy, Sam. "Sheet Music." In *The Gay Nineties: An Anthology of Contemporary Gay Fiction,* edited by Phil Willkie and Greg Baysans. Freedom, Calif.: Crossing Press, 1991.

Sedgwick, Eve Kosofsky. *Epistemology of the Closet.* London: Harvester Wheatsheaf, 1991.

Somerville, Siobhan B. *Queering the Color Line: Race and the Invention of Homosexuality in American Culture.* Durham, N.C.: Duke University Press, 2000.

Soucy, Stephen, ed. *Nine Hundred & Sixty-Nine: West Hollywood Stories.* New York: Modernist Press, 2008.

Summers, Claude J. *Gay Fictions: Wilde to Stonewall: Studies in a Male Homosexual Literary Tradition.* New York: Continuum, 1990.

————, ed. *The Gay and Lesbian Literary Heritage: A Reader's Companion to the Writers and Their Works, From Antiquity to the Present.* New York: Routledge, 2002.

Vidal, Gore. "Pages from an Abandoned Journal." In *A Thirsty Evil: Seven Short Stories.* New York: The Zero Press, 1952.

Weise, Donald, ed. *Fresh Men: New Voices in Gay Fiction.* New York: Carroll & Graf, 2004.

White, Edmund, ed. *The Faber Book of Gay Short Fiction.* Boston: Faber & Faber, 1991.

Willkie, Phil, and Greg Baysans, eds. *The Gay Nineties: An Anthology of Contemporary Gay Fiction.* Freedom, Calif.: Crossing Press, 1991.

Woods, Gregory. *A History of Gay Literature: The Male Tradition.* New Haven, Conn.: Yale University Press, 1999.

Young, Ian, ed. *On the Line: New Gay Fiction.* Trumansburg, New York: Crossing Press, 1981.

Gregory M. Weight
University of Delaware

GENRE Stemming from the French word meaning "kind" or "type," *genre* traditionally has been used to describe the separate sorts of fiction: comedy, epic, lyric, pastoral, and tragedy. It is also the word used to designate distinct categories of literature: short story, novel, play, poem, or essay. Television play and film scenario are also considered genres, as are DETECTIVE FICTION and SCIENCE FICTION. In the 20th century, particularly, the concept of genre stimulated controversy as numerous writers deliberately blurred the distinctions and tended to use several genres in one work.

GEORGE WILLARD The reporter in SHER-WOOD ANDERSON'S SHORT STORY CYCLE WINESBURG, OHIO, who becomes involved with the chief characters in various stories but often fails to understand the import of the human lessons contained therein. A character in his own right, George also may be viewed as the PROTAGONIST of a BILDUNGSROMAN, for the linked stories demonstrate his gradual coming of age. Appearing in the first short story cycle in American literature in 1919, George presages such other protagonists as ERNEST HEMINGWAY'S NICK ADAMS, WILLIAM FAULKNER'S ISAAC (IKE) MCCASLIN (see "The BEAR" and GO DOWN, MOSES), and KATHERINE ANNE PORTER'S MIRANDA RHEA.

GERONIMO (1829?–1909) Born in what is now the state of Arizona, Geronimo became a leader of the Chirichua Apache Indians. After the Chirichua Reservation was abolished in 1876, Geronimo led repeated raids against United States government forces. He and his followers finally surrendered in 1886 and were transported to Florida, where they were incarcerated as prisoners of war. Later sent to Fort Sill, Oklahoma, Geronimo eventually converted to Christianity and lived as a prosperous farmer. He is featured in LESLIE SILKO'S "A Geronimo Story" in The Man to Send Rain Clouds, edited by Kenneth Rosen (New York: Viking Press, 1974).

GETTYSBURG, BATTLE OF Fought from July 1 to 3, 1863, this battle was a major turning point in the American CIVIL WAR and is considered the high-water mark for the Confederacy in its war with the Union. In late June, General ROBERT E. LEE led the Army of Northern Virginia across the Rappahannock River and invaded the North. Union forces at first believed his intended aim was to attack Washington, D.C. When they belatedly learned Lee's army was continuing to move north toward Pennsylvania, they sent units of the Army of the Potomac in pursuit. Representatives of the two armies met by accident on July 1 near the small town of Gettysburg, and both commanders decided to fight there. By the end of the first day, Union forces under General George G. Meade had taken a strong defensive position on a ridge to the south of the town. Lee attacked the left flank of these defenses on July 2, but after initial successes his forces were thrown back. On the following day Lee sent his forces against the Union center in an attack that ended with the famous charge by General George E. Pickett, whose troops briefly penetrated the Union lines before being thrown back. The battle was over, and Lee withdrew his battered army back to Virginia. Of 75,000 men, his army suffered nearly 23,000 casualties (killed, wounded, missing, or captured). The Northern army of 90,000 had an almost equal number of casualties.

Considered a major victory for the North, this battle also generated the most controversy for the remainder of the war and years afterward. For Southerners, the debate centered on Lee's decision to stand and fight in a place not of his choosing against a well-entrenched Northern army, and, especially, the role of Lee's cavalry under General J. E. B. Stuart, who left the Confederate army without "eyes" for several maddening days while he was raiding Union facilities near Harrisburg, Pennsylvania. For Northerners, the debate centered on General Meade's decision not to pursue and perhaps annihilate the battered Army of Northern Virginia, which may have needlessly prolonged the war. On November 19, 1863, ABRAHAM LINCOLN dedicated the cemetery on the battlefield and delivered his brief but famous speech known as the Gettysburg Address.

Numerous references to this battle and to these controversial generals occur in stories by AMBROSE BIERCE and WILLIAM FAULKNER.

GHOST STORY The ghost story, which flowered in America from 1870 to 1930, arises from a long oral tradition grounded in folk beliefs and quasi-religious teachings (or speculations). In these contexts, ghosts often have been presented as arbiters or recipients of a crude form of social justice in a world in which such justice seems lacking. For example, a ghost will identify a murderer or provide a reason for a slave to evade a master's demands. A bully will be forced to wander the earth in chains in the afterlife. The oral tradition has established certain ghostly conventions: Ghosts are pale, for example; they leave no footprints; they seldom speak; and only chosen, sensitive mortals can perceive their presence.

British authors of the late 18th and early 19th century popularized ghosts in GOTHIC fiction. Horace Walpole and Anne Radcliffe wrote novels that strongly influenced the short supernatural fiction that followed. Some of the novels are episodic in form, with many subplots. Each episode (such as the story of Emily and the bandits in *Mysteries of the Castle Udolpho*) can be viewed as a kind of short story, woven into the main plot.

German romantics (see ROMANTICISM) also contributed to the development of the American ghost story. Tales by E. T. A. Hoffman, Ludwig Tieck, Friedrich Novalis, and others, painted eerie, supernatural landscapes and haunted medieval castles, explored psychological and theological concepts, and presented the spirit guide and the DOPPELGANGER as significant figures. SIGMUND FREUD's essay "The Uncanny" analyzes "The Sandman" by E. T. A. Hoffmann and attributes its power to disturb to repressed desires and family secrets. The German influence can be seen in later stories by EDGAR ALLAN POE and NATHANIEL HAWTHORNE.

Modern readers associate ghost stories with Halloween. However, ghost stories were, until recently, closely allied with Christmas traditions. They were read around the fire on long winter nights during the holiday season. In addition, wandering spirits were believed to be a part of the misrule or disorder said to occur during the Christmas season. Spirits, benign or malignant, embodied all the forces mortals could not control.

Victorian writers capitalized on this idea, often questioning the established social order in their ghost stories. Almost everyone knows the plot of Dickens's "A Christmas Carol," which portrays the transformation of Scrooge from a greedy businessman into a man full of Christmas spirit. Other Dickens ghost stories, such as "The Body Snatchers," also warn readers against the single-minded pursuit of wealth and progress. Dickens and publishers such as Mary Braddon made the Victorian ghost story available to large numbers of subscribers, who avidly read the Christmas

issues of *Household Words, Belgravia Temple Bar,* and other periodicals.

The December and January issues of *Scribner's, HARPER's* and *ATLANTIC MONTHLY* also contained ghost stories. Several factors contributed to their development.

The first of these was the spiritualist movement, the belief that humans can communicate with the parted souls, which began in 1848. This movement became associated with other progressive causes, including feminism (see FEMINIST), nonauthoritarian religion, and abolition. Prominent Americans such as WILLIAM LLOYD GARRISON, William James, and Lydia Maria Child were attracted to spiritualist circles. By the 1870s, however, many spiritualists were discredited—some discovered to be outright frauds. The public imagination turned to fiction for its accounts of spirits. A strong reform element permeates the fiction as it did the religion. Ghosts provide justice to women, children, and the poor in stories by MARY WILKINS FREEMAN, Georgia Wood Pangborn, and EDITH WHARTON.

REGIONALISM and its spirit of place also contributed to the American ghost story. Hawthorne set the stage early with his tales of New England Puritan life. His characters in "YOUNG GOODMAN BROWN" are reflected in Freeman's "The Little Maid at the Door"; both are based on regional, historical THEMES. ELLEN GLASGOW's ghost stories are similarly steeped in history, that of a defeated and haunted South (see her "DARE'S GIFT" and "Whispering Leaves"). Western TALL TALES seem to have influenced stories by western writers; the folktale is never far beneath the surface, no matter how sophisticated the author may be.

The new psychology also influenced the ghost story. Alienists (physicians who treat mental disorders) hold central roles in many stories, including the feminist work of Freeman, Glasgow, and CHARLOTTE PERKINS GILMAN. Some of the tales respond to ideas promulgated by Oliver Wendell Holmes and S. Weir Mitchell, prominent doctors who also wrote fiction (not ghost fiction, however) based on their practices. Many writers sought to find a relationship between science and theology. William James, for instance, sought to substantiate the presence of spirits through his American Society for Psychic Research and established psychology as an economic discipline. His brother, HENRY JAMES, on the other hand, explored the individual psyche through stories such as "The JOLLY CORNER" and "The TURN OF THE SCREW" and left science to others. In so doing, he wrote some of the best 19th-century ghost stories. Psychological themes continued to be popular during the 20th century in stories by JOYCE CAROL OATES, SHIRLEY JACKSON, and Lester del Rey.

The feminist critic Nina Auerbach argues that social change and its accompanying instability led to the evocation of ghosts in 19th-century fiction (in *Private Theatricals: The Lives of the Victorians* [1990], 53–83). The late 20th century saw a renewed interest in tales of the supernatural. Stories published today often are influenced by modern technology, space exploration, and Einstein's theories of time and energy. Many contemporary ghost stories (such as those by HARLAN ELLISON, Lisa Tuttle, and Phyllis Eisenstein) merge the ghost story with SCIENCE FICTION.

With all their technological trappings, however, ghost stories still serve an age-old purpose. Our environment alienates us, our machines intimidate us, and our social systems fail to deliver the justice we feel we deserve. Therefore, our imaginations suspend reality as we know it and explore the liminal regions in which spirits confront and sometimes transcend the terrors of this world and those beyond.

BIBLIOGRAPHY
Carpenter, Lynette, and Wendy K. Kolmar, eds. *Haunting the House of Fiction: Feminist Perspectives on Ghost Stories by American Women.* Knoxville: University of Tennessee Press, 1991.

Kerr, Howard, John W. Crowley, and Charles L. Crow, eds. *The Haunted Dusk: American Supernatural Fiction, 1820–1920.* Athens: University of Georgia Press, 1983.

Lundie, Catherine A., ed. *Restless Spirits: Ghost Stories by American Women, 1872–1926.* Amherst: University of Massachusetts Press, 1996.

McSherry, Frank D., Jr., Charles G. Waugh, and Martin Greenberg, eds. *Great American Ghost Stories.* Vol. 1. Nashville, Tenn.: Rutledge Hill Press, 1991.

Robillard, Douglas, ed. *American Supernatural Fiction: From Edith Wharton to the Weird Tales Writers.* New York: Garland, 1996.

Salmonson, Jessica Amanda, ed. *What Did Miss Darrington See? An Anthology of Feminist Supernatural Fiction.* New York: Feminist Press, 1989.

Gwen Neary
Santa Rosa Community College/
Sonoma State University

GIBBSVILLE, PENNSYLVANIA   Based on Pottsville, Pennsylvania, the town where JOHN O'HARA was reared, Gibbsville provides the backdrop for O'Hara's numerous so-called Pennsylvania novels and for a large number of his more than 400 short stories. O'Hara uses Gibbsville to present his often satiric contempt for the shallow values of his suburbanite characters. Gibbsville, once the heart of the anthracite fields, suffered from the coal miners' strike in 1925 and never completely recovered: by the 1930s, mired in the GREAT DEPRESSION, Gibbsville is also the source of psychological depression in its rootless, dissatisfied characters, who seek release in alcohol, adultery, and sometimes suicide. Often compared with WILLIAM FAULKNER'S YOKNAPATAWPHA COUNTY, Gibbsville provides the literary map for O'Hara's depiction of the realities of suburban life and becomes the symbol of the failure of the AMERICAN DREAM.

GIBSON, WILLIAM (1944–)   Gibson, who is often called the founder of the CYBERPUNK genre, became famous for his first novel, *Neuromancer* (1985), for which he was awarded the HUGO AWARD, THE NEBULA AWARD, and Philip K. Dick awards. Gibson wrote the short stories collected in *Burning Chrome* (1986) before *Neuromancer,* and they are classic examples of cyberpunk. Although they share some features with DETECTIVE FICTION and western film, Gibson's stories are futuristic and, in some respects, postmodernist. (See POSTMODERNISM.) The future according to Gibson is a world of technological domination, corporate and syndicated crime, stark economic contrasts, and fierce struggles for survival. Another, virtual world, that of the "matrix" or "cyberspace" formed by the connections between the world's computers, exists alongside the actual world in *Burning Chrome,* and cyberpunk HEROes adeptly navigate it. Many of the characters'

bodies have been technologically altered so that they have computerized eyes, enhanced muscular or neural capabilities, or weapons implanted in their fingers. Plastic surgery and drug use abound. Bonds of family and community have been fractured or destroyed, and the hero, although cautious and suspicious, sometimes makes human contacts and bonds as he tries to buck the system. The hostile environment complicates the establishment of a stable identity, an implicit goal of Gibson's heroes. Most of the stories are narrated in first person (see POINT OF VIEW), and the dialogue is gritty and realistic, exhibiting the slang of the fictional world. There are frequent references to late 20th-century popular culture. The first story in *Burning Chrome*, "Johnny Mnemonic," in which the title character makes a living by storing and transporting computerized information in his brain, was made into a feature film in 1994.

BIBLIOGRAPHY

Gibson, William. *All Tomorrow's Parties*. New York: Putnam, 1999.

———. *Pattern Recognition*. New York: Putnam, 2003.

———. *Spook Country*. New York: Putnam, 2007.

Karen Fearing
University of North Carolina, Chapel Hill

GIBSON GIRL

The slim-waisted American beauty with a pompadour hairstyle created by the illustrator Charles Dana Gibson (1867–1944) came to portray the Gay Nineties' looks and manners of the ideal woman. Although Dana was a successful illustrator for various magazines, including *HARPER'S* and *SCRIBNER'S,* and many books, he is best known for this creation, for which his wife, Irene Langhorne, was the model.

GIFT BOOK

Popular in both the United States and England in the 19th century, these annually published collections contained stories, poems, and essays on sale as gifts around Christmastime. Of genuine significance in American literary history, gift books were the single best market for short fiction in the United States during the first half of the 19th century.

"GIFT OF THE MAGI, THE" O. HENRY (1906)

Although many critics do not view O. HENRY's stories as first-rate literature, some of his many hundreds of tales have become CLASSIC. "The Gift of the Magi," touching as it does a common human cord, is one of those stories. Not tragic, perhaps sentimental or a little didactic, it combines the THEMES of married love and selflessness with the techniques of suspense and the O. Henry SURPRISE ENDING.

Della Dillingham Young and her husband, Jim, on the edge of poverty but deeply in love, wish to purchase Christmas gifts that will surprise and please the other. The narrator focuses on Della as she tries to figure a way to find enough money to buy her husband a fine gift. Each of them has a prize possession: Jim's is a gold watch that belonged to his father and his grandfather, and Della's is her long, thick, luxuriant hair. Suddenly Della realizes that she could sell her hair for enough money to buy Jim a gold chain for his watch. The touches of realistic detail (see REALISM) add to the poignancy of her sacrifice: She had only $1.87 but, with the sale of her hair, she receives the $20 to buy the watch chain.

At home, feeling shorn and sheepish, Della greets Jim with her schoolboyish haircut. Because the narrator has focused on Della's thoughts rather than Jim's, readers feel suspense in waiting for his response. Not only does he tell her that he will love her no matter what she does with her hair, but he gives her two beautiful jeweled, tortoiseshell combs that she had admired. When Della gives him the watch chain, he suggests putting their fine presents away for a while: He has sold his watch so that he could buy Della the combs for her hair. The narrator points out that the two may have unwisely sacrificed their valuable possessions, but they are the wisest gift givers of all. Despite the moral and the sentiment—or perhaps because of them—"The Gift of the Magi" in its very simplicity appeals to a love and loyalty for which many modern readers, no matter how sophisticated, may still yearn.

BIBLIOGRAPHY

Blansfield, Karen Charmaine. *Cheap Rooms and Restless Hearts: A Study of the Formula in the Urban Tales of Porter.*

Bowling Green, Ohio: Bowling Green State University Press, 1988.

Henry, O. "The Gift of the Magi." In *Stories,* edited by Harry Hansen. New York: Heritage Press, 1965.

GILDED AGE A name given to the post–CIVIL WAR era of economic expansion, greed, and gaudy wealth typified by the Vanderbilts, Morgans, Goulds, and other "captains of industry," financiers, and tycoons. The term is from the book *The Gilded Age* (1873) by Charles Dudley Warner in collaboration with MARK TWAIN. STEPHEN CRANE and EDITH WHARTON, for instance, wrote of the effects of this wealth on the individual.

"GILDED SIX-BITS, THE" ZORA NEALE HURSTON (1933) Appearing in *STORY* magazine and traditionally considered ZORA NEALE HURSTON's most accomplished story, "The Gilded Six-Bits" had a favorable reception that helped call Hurston to the attention of critics and publishers and resulted in the publication of her first novel, *Jonah's Gourd Vine* (1934). Whether readers and critics have actually plumbed the story to its full extent, however, is called into question with the recent rise in popularity of her earlier story "SWEAT"" and its sympathetic portrayal of a wife's situation. Although "The Gilded Six-Bits" clearly addresses the themes of hypocrisy, money, infidelity, and marital love, a reading of Hurston's themes in earlier stories, along with a feminist critical perspective, suggests that the third-person narrator implicitly criticizes marriage and depicts it as a subtle form of prostitution. Readers who interpret the story this way can connect Hurston with the social and gender concerns of such other contemporaries as EDITH WHARTON.

Hurston depicts Missie May and Joe, a young married couple, as sharing a happy and loving relationship. Beneath the surface of their EDENIC bliss, however, the alert reader notes that Hurston portrays Missie May as childlike (even her name sounds babyish) and pointedly illustrates Joe's superior attitude toward her. Each Saturday he returns home from work and hurls, throws, and chunks silver dollars at the door, having trained Missie May to pick them up and pile them beside her plate at dinner. As a father does, he "indulgently" allows his wife to search his pockets for hidden treats (568); contradicts her when she says she is hungry, because only men, he implies, work hard enough to have an appetite; and insists that he "parade" his pretty wife in front of Otis, the big spender from Chicago. Missie May resists the trip, protesting that Joe is all the man she needs, but he unwittingly sets her up for adultery by praising Otis, whom he tries to emulate, and extolling his pieces of gold and envying all his "pretty womens" (567). The equation of money, sex, and maleness cannot but filter dimly into Missy May's consciousness.

When Joe arrives home early one night and surprises Missy May in bed with Otis, she confesses that Otis promised the gold in return for sex. Missie May is grateful that, rather than leaving her, Joe allows her to continue to cook for and wait on him and perform the services of a masseuse. Moreover, he gives her the gold piece he had ripped from Otis's vest when he struck him, and Missie May, feeling like a prostitute, returns the money—which in any case turns out to be only a gilded half-dollar. When, months later, Missie May gives birth to a baby boy that looks exactly like Joe, she has redeemed herself: He uses the gilded coin to buy candy for her and the baby.

As with many Hurston stories and novels, the African-American characters are sympathetically treated, especially when they interact with whites. When Joe buys the candy from the clerk and pridefully tells him that Otis never fooled him, the clerk's reaction is like the white sheriff's in WILLIAM FAULKNER's "PANTALOON IN BLACK": The clerk insensitively and erroneously remarks that "these darkies" never have problems; they just laugh "all the time" (574). Yet when Hurston refocuses on the couple, her narrator remains implicitly critical of the unequal nature of the relationship: Joe returns home and chunks 15 silver dollars at the door. Still weak from childbirth and unable to run, but clearly grateful for her reinstatement in Joe's good graces, Missie May "crept there as quickly as she could" (574). The complexity of the story and the ways readers continue to interpret it assure it a long-lasting place in 20th-century literature.

BIBLIOGRAPHY
Hurston, Zora Neale. "The Gilded Six-Bits." In *Major Writers of Short Fiction: Stories and Commentary,* edited by Ann Charters. Boston: St. Martin's, 1993.

GILMAN, CHARLOTTE PERKINS (CHARLOTTE ANNA PERKINS STETSON) (1860–1935)

The great-niece of the author and abolitionist advocate Harriet Beecher Stowe, Charlotte Perkins Gilman was born in Hartford, Connecticut, and is best remembered today for her autobiographically inspired short story "THE YELLOW WALL-PAPER" (1892), which chronicles the nervous breakdown of a young wife and mother. Gilman was able to write with authority about the terrifying consequences of chronic depression because, from early adulthood, she struggled with episodes of severe melancholia. After her engagement and subsequent marriage in 1884 to her first husband, Charles Walter Stetson, her depression deepened. After the birth of her daughter, Katharine, in 1885, Gilman underwent a rest cure for neurasthenia—a term used to describe a condition of depression accompanied by feelings of helplessness and uselessness—and subsequently suffered a nervous breakdown. She gradually recovered her health after separating from Stetson in 1888 and divorcing him six years later.

Gilman moved to Pasadena, California, in 1888; she began writing short fiction in 1890. By the end of her long career, she had published nearly 200 short stories. Regrettably, although she remained remarkably prolific, she would never again write a story that rivaled the power and poignancy of "The Yellow Wall-Paper," which is superior to her other literary works in artistry and execution. With the notable exception of this story, in fact, critics generally have not been enthusiastic about Gilman's fiction, citing as deficiencies its heavy didacticism, its uneven quality, and its tendency to resist easy classification.

Owing to the constant pressure of deadlines, Gilman wrote hastily and without revision. Always on the brink of poverty, she frequently subordinated quality to quantity, turning work out quickly in an effort to secure a much-needed income. Early in her career, she experimented with tales in the popular GOTHIC tradition. In addition to "The Yellow Wall-Paper," published in *New England Magazine* and originally characterized as a horror story, other stories by Gilman in the gothic tradition include "The Giant Wistaria" (1891), "The Rocking Chair" (1893), and "The Unwatched Door" (1894). After her conversion in the early 1890s to nationalism, a movement promoting an end to capitalism and advancing the peaceful, progressive, ethical, and democratic improvement of the human race, Gilman's literary style changed, and she began to emphasize THEMES of social reform. Both the nationalist movement and her support of reform Darwinism—a philosophy advocating conscious intervention in the evolutionary process for the purpose of controlling human destiny—profoundly shaped her fictional landscape. In most of her works published after 1895, Gilman recreated the world according to her vision of the ideal. Through her fiction, she attempted to illustrate tangible solutions to problems arising from a patriarchal society in which women often were expected to assume obsequious roles.

Among the themes that emerge in Gilman's reform fiction are the need for women to become economically self-sufficient (as in "Making a Change," 1911; "Mrs. Beazley's Deeds," 1911; and "Mrs. Elder's Idea," 1912); the importance of sisterhood (as in "Turned," 1911; "Being Reasonable," 1915; and "Dr. Clair's Place," 1915); the promotion of human rights issues (as in "The Boys and the Butter," 1910, and "Joan's Defender," 1916); and the value of utopian communities (as in "Maidstone Comfort," 1912, and "Bee Wise," 1913). Gilman constructed stories around such provocative topics as sexual harassment, blackmail, bribery, venereal disease, streetcar safety, tainted milk, social motherhood, and yellow journalism—subjects that she also addressed in her poetry and essays.

Gilman experimented briefly with other fictional styles in 1894 and 1895, when she served as editor of the *Impress,* a literary weekly published by the Pacific Coast Women's Press Association. Sixteen of her stories appeared in "Studies in Style," a series that featured works written in imitation of such well-known authors as LOUISA MAY ALCOTT, HAMLIN GARLAND, NATHANIEL

HAWTHORNE, HENRY JAMES, EDGAR ALLAN POE, MARK TWAIN, and MARY E. WILKINS FREEMAN. The experiment, however, was little more than a gimmick used to promote the ailing newspaper, and Gilman quickly abandoned the practice once the *Impress* folded.

In the first decade of the 20th century, Gilman turned her attention to book-length theoretical treatises; during this time she published only a handful of stories. When she returned to fiction writing, however, in the years prior to WORLD WAR I, she found that editors did not share her enthusiasm for reform fiction, and her work became increasingly difficult to place. She decided, therefore, single-handedly to write, edit, and publish her own monthly magazine, the *Forerunner.* In circulation from 1909 until 1916, the *Forerunner* was the most ambitious project of Gilman's long career and the forum in which the majority of her fiction appeared.

Although Gilman's goal of publishing a separate volume of her stories was never realized, dozens of her works have been collected and reprinted in recent years. In addition to her fiction, Gilman produced close to 500 poems, a handful of plays, nine novels, hundreds of essays, and a posthumously published autobiography. By 1925, however, her writings no longer appealed to the postwar generation, and she virtually disappeared from the public eye.

In 1934 her second husband and first cousin, George Houghton Gilman, whom she married in 1900, died suddenly of a cerebral hemorrhage. In 1935, after battling inoperable breast cancer for three years, Gilman—an advocate of euthanasia—ended her life by inhaling chloroform. Gilman's death, like her life, was meant to be instructive.

Although Gilman feared that she would be forgotten by later generations, her legacy has been ensured as a result of her 1994 induction into the National Women's Hall of Fame in Seneca Falls, New York. A critical reevaluation of her fiction continues as her work becomes increasingly available.

BIBLIOGRAPHY

Davis, Cynthia J., and Denise D. Knight. *Charlotte Perkins Gilman and Her Contemporaries: Literary and Intellectual Contexts.* Tuscaloosa: University of Alabama Press, 2004.

Gilman, Charlotte Perkins. *The Yellow Wall-Paper and Selected Stories of Charlotte Perkins Gilman.* Edited by Denise D. Knight. Newark: University of Delaware Press, 1994.

Hill, Mary A. *Charlotte Perkins Gilman: The Making of a Radical Feminist, 1860–1896.* Philadelphia: Temple University Press, 1980.

Karpinski, Joanne B. "The Economic Conundrum in the Lifewriting of Charlotte Perkins Gilman." In *The Mixed Legacy of Charlotte Perkins Gilman,* edited by Catherine J. Golden and Joanne S. Zangrando. Newark: University of Delaware Press, 2000.

Knight, Denise D. *Charlotte Perkins Gilman: A Study of the Short Fiction.* Boston: Twayne, 1997.

Lane, Ann J., ed. *The Charlotte Perkins Gilman Reader.* New York: Pantheon Books, 1980.

Long, Lisa A. "Herland and the Gender of Science." In *MLA Approaches to Teaching Gilman's The Yellow Wall-Paper and Herland,* edited by Denise D. Knight and Cynthia J. David, 125–132. New York: Modern Language Association of America, 2003.

Scharnhorst, Gary. *Charlotte Perkins Gilman.* Boston: Twayne, 1985.

Tuttle, Jennifer S. "Rewriting the West Cure: Charlotte Perkins Gilman, Owen Wister, and the Sexual Politics of Neurasthenia." In *The Mixed Legacy of Charlotte Perkins Gilman,* edited by Catherine J. Golden and Joanna Schneider Zangrando. Newark: University of Delaware Press, 2000.

Weinbaum, Alys Eve. "Writing Feminist Genealogy: Charlotte Perkins Gilman, Racial Nationalism, and the Reproduction of Maternalist Feminism." *Feminist Studies* 27 (Summer 2001): 271–230.

Denise D. Knight
SUNY Cortland

"GIMPEL THE FOOL" ISAAC BASHEVIS SINGER (1957)

Widely regarded as ISAAC BASHEVIS SINGER's masterpiece as well as one of his most frequently anthologized stories, the Yiddish version of "Gimpel the Fool" appeared in the *Jewish Daily Forward* (1953) before SAUL BELLOW translated it into English for publication in the *Partisan Review* (1957). Although set in Singer's native Poland, "Gimpel the Fool" continues to enjoy international success because of Reb Gimpel, its universally sympathetic character. Readers have not only seen Gimpel as the cuckolded husband whose wife makes him into a fool but also as an innocent and childlike naïf whose quest for truth makes him into an EVERYMAN; a little man, or a schlemiel; a scapegoat, a shaman, a trickster, and the archetypical figure of "the wandering Jew" (Siegel 170). The devout Gimpel questions and confronts his faith in God and finds that, in the long run, it sustains him.

The story opens as Gimpel, the first-person narrator, explains that ever since childhood he has been the butt of the town jokes, when he was called "imbecile, donkey, flax-head, dope, glump, ninny, and fool. The last name stuck" (26). The town of Frampol looks to Reb Gimpel for entertainment, telling him outrageous lies and playing humiliating tricks on him. Stung too often, he at one point resolves to believe nothing that the townspeople tell him, but that technique serves only to confuse him. When Gimpel seeks advice from the rabbi, the one sane voice in his life, the rabbi responds, "Better to be a fool all your days than for one hour to be evil. You are not a fool. They are the fools" (27). Gimpel continues to be fooled until he actually marries Elke, the pregnant town prostitute: "I realized I was going to be rooked," he tells us, but "what did I stand to lose?" (28).

He stands to lose a great deal, of course, as he loves not wisely but too well: Despite Elke's giving him "bloody wounds," he "adored her every word" (30). When her baby is born, the townsfolk make fun of Gimpel, but he loves the child "madly, and he loved me too" (29). Gimpel loves children and animals—and Elke—with little or no reservation. He is the town baker, and his association with bread, the source of human sustenance, aligns him with life, spirituality, and optimism; even when he discovers a man in bed with his wife, his anger is short-lived ("You can't live without errors" [31]), and he withdraws his request for a divorce. In denial of his wife's infidelity—even after discovering his apprentice in her bed—he lives equably with her for 20 years. In the critic and scholar Alfred Kazin's words, even after learning of Elke's adultery, he "ignores his own dignity for the sake of others" (61).

It is only with her deathbed confession that he is not the father of any of their children that Gimpel succumbs to the Evil Spirit, who urges him to take revenge on the entire town that has conspired against him. Persuaded that there is no God and no afterlife, he agrees to contaminate all his bread with buckets of urine so that the townsfolk of Frampol will eat "filth" (34). Just in time, Elke appears to him in a dream: "You fool! Because I was false is everything false too? . . . I'm paying for it all, Gimpel. They spare you nothing here" (34). Realizing the irretrievable act he nearly committed, the baker believes that God is helping him, and he buries the ruined bread in the frozen earth. When people ask where he is going, he replies, "Into the world."

Gimpel wanders for the rest of his life, exchanging stories and concluding that truth is as strange as, if not stranger than, fiction: "I understood that there were really no lies. Whatever doesn't really happen is dreamed at night. It happens to one if it doesn't happen to another, tomorrow if not today, or a century hence if not next year" (35). And so he becomes a storyteller, still longing for the time he can rejoin Elke and living with the belief that "the world is entirely an imaginary world, but it is only once removed from the true world" (35). Indeed, at the end he becomes a prophet, a visionary, "a shaman of sorts, someone who mediates between worlds" (Drunker 35). Living to a ripe white-haired old age, Gimpel has gained infinite wisdom and has eluded evil with his belief in goodness still intact.

BIBLIOGRAPHY

Allentuck, Marcia, ed. *The Achievement of Isaac Bashevis Singer*. Carbondale: Southern Illinois University Press, 1969.

Buber, Martin. "The Master of Prayer." In *The Tales of Rabbi Nachman,* retold by Martin Buber. New York: Horizon Press, 1956.

Clasby, Nancy Tenfelde. "Gimpel's Wisdom: I. B. Singer's Vision of the 'True World.'" *Studies in American Jewish Literature* 15 (1996): 90–98.

Drucker, Sally Ann. "I. B. Singer's Two Holy Fools." *Yiddish* 8, no. 2 (1992): pp. 35–39.

Farrell Lee, Grace. *From Exile to Redemption: The Fiction of Isaac Bashevis Singer*. Carbondale: Southern Illinois University Press, 1987.

Fraustino, Daniel V. "Gimpel the Fool: Singer's Debt to the Romantics." *Studies in Short Fiction* 22, no. 2 (Spring 1985): 228–231.

Friedman, Lawrence S. *Understanding Isaac Bashevis Singer.* Columbia: University of South Carolina Press, 1988.

Grebstein, Sheldon. "Singer's Shrewd 'Gimpel': Bread and Childbirth." In *Recovering the Canon: Essays on Isaac Bashevis Singer,* edited by David Neal Miller, 58–65. Leiden: Brill, 1986.

Hennings, Thomas. "Singer's 'Gimpel the Fool' and the Book of Hosea." *Journal of Narrative Technique* 13 (Winter 1983): 11–19.

Howe, Irving. "I. B. Singer." In *Critical Views of Isaac Bashevis Singer,* edited by Irving Malin, 100–120. New York: New York University Press, 1969.

Kazin, Alfred. "The Saint as Schlemiel." In *Critical Essays on Isaac Bashevis Singer,* edited by Grace Farrell, 61–65. New York: G. K. Hall, 1996.

Malin, Irving, ed. *Critical Views of Isaac Bashevis Singer.* New York: New York University Press, 1969.

Miller, David Neal, ed. *Recovering the Canon: Essays on Isaac Bashevis Singer.* Leiden: Brill, 1986.

Pinsker, Sanford. *The Schlemiel as Metaphor.* Carbondale: Southern Illinois University Press, 1971.

Radin, Paul. *The Trickster: A Study in American Indian Mythology.* New York: Philosophical Library, 1956.

Sholem, Gershom. *Kabbalah.* New York: NAL, 1978.

———. *Major Trends in Jewish Mysticism.* New York: Schocken Books, 1961.

Siegel, Ben, ed. *Critical Essays on Isaac Bashevis Singer.* New York: G. K. Hall, 1996.

Siegel, Paul N. "Gimpel and the Archetype of the Wise Fool." In *The Achievement of Isaac Bashevis Singer,* edited by Marcia Allentuck, 159–174. Carbondale: Southern Illinois University Press, 1969.

Singer, Isaac Bashevis. "Gimpel the Fool." In *Contemporary American Literature,* edited by George Perkins and Barbara Perkins. New York: Random House, 1988.

———. "Gimpel the Fool." In *A Treasury of Yiddish Stories.* Translated by Saul Bellow and edited by Irving Howe and Eliezer Greenberg. New York: Schocken, 1973.

Wisse, Ruth. *The Schlemiel as Modern Hero.* Chicago: Chicago University Press, 1971.

"GIRL" JAMAICA KINCAID (1978)

JAMAICA KINCAID's "Girl" is a SHORT-SHORT STORY; it is only one paragraph in length, and that paragraph is actually punctuated as one long sentence, a series of dependent and independent clauses separated by semicolons. The story's details provide insight into a young girl's relationship with her judgmental and domineering mother. The story's POINT OF VIEW is unusual and effective: The tale consists of a catalog of advice given to the daughter by the mother. The cumulative effect of this listing is to show the way the mother attempts to shape every area of the daughter's life ("Wash the white clothes on Monday . . . soak salt fish overnight before you cook it . . . you mustn't speak to wharf-rat boys . . . this is how to sew on a button . . . this is how you grow okra."). In this list Kincaid uses a technique similar to STREAM OF CONSCIOUSNESS, presenting the mother's litany filtered through the daughter's consciousness. More disturbing than the mother's advice, though, is her judgment; ostensibly she intends her advice to prevent her daughter from being "the slut you are so bent on becoming." Twice the daughter interrupts the mother's listing, but the mother's catalog of the daughter's "faults" continues.

This story addresses many of the THEMES of *At the Bottom of the River* (1983), Kincaid's first short story collection: disconnection between mothers and daughters, role conflicts, lack of communication, and isolation in the midst of community. Its fragmented style is also typical of the experimental narratives and dreamlike imagery of other stories in this collection.

Karen Weekes
University of Georgia

GLASGOW, ELLEN (ELLEN ANDERSON GHOLSON GLASGOW) (1873–1945)

Ellen Glasgow was born in Richmond, Virginia, the eighth in a family of 10 children. Too sickly to attend school, she was educated at home, where she read science and philosophy voraciously. In her autobiography, *The Woman Within,* published in 1954 long after her death, she describes an isolated and unhappy childhood that was partly exacerbated by growing deafness. She identified with her frail mother and resented her overbearing father; much of her later work deals with women who suffer in unequal relationships with men.

Glasgow's first publication, a short story titled "A Woman of Tomorrow" (1895), describes a woman's choice of her career over love. In the end, although she briefly regrets never having children, the HEROINE is happy with her life's decision.

Glasgow is best known for her novels, most of which are set in Queensborough, Virginia, the fictional Richmond, and deal with the uneasy relationship between the Old South and the New South and the troubled relationships between men and women. At the beginning of her career, critics viewed Glasgow as a rebel because she portrayed the South as it really was instead of idealizing and romanticizing it as most other southern writers of her time did. (See REALISM.) By the end of her career, however, more revolutionary writers such as Thomas Wolfe and WILLIAM FAULKNER had taken her place and the literary public saw her as staid and conservative. She wrote 20 novels and was awarded the PULITZER PRIZE for the last one published during her lifetime, *In This Our Life* (1941), partly in recognition of her past achievements.

Glasgow's decision to focus on the novel rather than the short story was a conscious one made after a publisher and friend, Walter Hines Page, told her she would be more successful as a novelist. But she did publish 13 stories in various magazines, seven of which were collected into a volume entitled *The Shadowy Third and Other Stories* (1923). Most of these stories were written between 1916 and 1924 during a period when she needed money but did not have the emotional energy for a longer work.

As did her contemporary EDITH WHARTON, Glasgow wrote two main types of stories: those that deal with marriage and those that focus on the supernatural. The marriage stories reflect many of the same THEMES that appear in her novels. For instance, in "JORDAN'S END" (1923) an aristocratic but worn-out southern family slowly decays as their mansion decays around them, and a southern lady gets away with murder. Similar situations occur in the later novels *Barren Ground* and *In This Our Life.*

The supernatural stories often reflect the author's unhappy childhood. In the title story of her collection, "The SHADOWY THIRD" is the ghost of the wife's recently dead child, offspring of a previous marriage, who can be seen only by sensitive characters. The overbearing husband cannot see the child, but the frail and mournful mother can. Assuming that his wife is insane, the husband commits her to an asylum, where she soon dies, but the ghost child gets her

revenge by tripping her stepfather on the stairs and causing him to fall to his death. Although Glasgow's reputation does not rest on these stories, many are excellent examples of her work and offer insights into her novels' themes and into her own life.

Two of her most famous novels, *Virginia* (1913) and *Barren Ground* (1925), present opposite ways that women cope with trying relationships. Virginia, the heroine of the novel that bears her name, represents the traditional lady of the Old South. After being abandoned by a philandering husband, she becomes a pathetic shell. Dorinda Oakley, the heroine of *Barren Ground,* is abandoned by the father of her baby; after losing the baby, she becomes a stronger woman, who successfully runs her own farm and vows to live without love.

See also "DARE'S GIFT."

BIBLIOGRAPHY

Inge, M. Thomas, ed. *Ellen Glasgow: Centennial Essays.* Charlottesville: University Press of Virginia, 1976.

Meeker, Richard K. "Introduction." In *The Collected Stories of Ellen Glasgow.* Baton Rouge: Louisiana State University Press, 1963.

Thiebaux, Marcelle. *Ellen Glasgow.* New York: F. Ungar, 1982.

Betina I. Entzminger
University of North Carolina at Chapel Hill

GLASPELL, SUSAN (1882–1948)

Born in Davenport, Iowa, Susan Glaspell was reared with traditional midwestern values and graduated from Drake University in 1899. As a reporter for the *Des Moines Daily News,* she began writing stories in the LOCAL COLOR tradition, seeking, as did her contemporaries ZONA GALE and Mary French, to preserve those special qualities of place, speech, and thought that made her region unique. Unlike Glaspell, her husband, George Cram Cook, whom she married in 1913, resisted what he saw as the provinciality of Davenport and the ROMANTICISM he perceived in his wife's works.

She and her husband moved to Provincetown, Massachusetts, and summered in Greenwich Village. In 1915, with a small group of Greenwich Village friends, they established the Provincetown Players, an experimental theater designed to present new drama and combat the commercialism of Broadway. Among playwrights whose work was introduced by this theater was Eugene O'Neill. Although Glaspell went on to become a professional playwright herself and won the Pulitzer Prize for *Alison's House* (1930), based on the life of Emily Dickinson, she also wrote novels, the best known of which is *Judd Rankin's Daughter* (1945), and short stories, including "A JURY OF HER PEERS" (1917), a story based on her play *Trifles* (1916).

BIBLIOGRAPHY

Glaspell, Susan. *Alison's House: A Play in Three Acts.* New York: S. French, 1930.

———. *Ambrose Holt and Family.* New York: Stokes, 1931.

———. *Inheritors: A Play in Three Acts.* New York: Dodd, 1921.

———. *Judd Rankin's Daughter.* New York: Grosset & Dunlap, 1945.

———. *Plays.* New York: Dodd, Mead, 1920.

———. *The Verge: A Play in Three Acts.* Boston: Small, Maynard, 1922.

Waterman, Arthur E. *Susan Glaspell.* New York: Twayne, 1966.

———. "Susan Glaspell." *American Literary Realism* 4 (Spring 1971): 183–191.

GLOSS   A brief explanation of a difficult or obscure word or expression in the margin or between the lines of a text. Glosses can provide a running commentary and explanation of a difficult text or can be an interlinear (between-the-lines) translation. A glossary is a collection or list of textual glosses.

GO DOWN, MOSES WILLIAM FAULKNER (1942)

Go Down, Moses, WILLIAM FAULKNER's 12th novel, is generally ranked as one of his greatest—not least because it doubles as a unique collection of short stories. Most of these stories had been published separately between 1935 and 1942, in such popular magazines as HARPER'S, COLLIER'S, and the SATURDAY EVENING POST. Their middlebrow magazine audience differed greatly from the tiny highbrow public interested in Faulkner's novels. Thus, the genesis of this text—the transformation of what Faulkner at first derisively called "stories about niggers" (Grimwood 228) into tragic tales of racial torment, each an unexpected prism on the others—is virtually a story in its own

right. Delayed recognitions that vividly recast all that has gone before are a signature event in Faulkner's work. In like manner, the making of *Go Down, Moses* is premised on his discovery (with almost all the individual pieces already done) that he has on his hands the saga of a single seven-generational black and white family. Their interlocking lives—humorous, abusive, guilt-driven, above all inextricable—convey his version of the haunted South itself.

Although the formal structure of *Go Down, Moses* is unique, SHERWOOD ANDERSON's WINESBURG, OHIO (1919) and James Joyce's *Dubliners* (1914) may well have served as models. Anderson was Faulkner's first mentor, and Joyce was his great modernist (see MODERNISM) precursor. Both of them deploy the multiple stories of stymied individual lives to suggest the contours of a larger shared malaise. For Anderson and Joyce the community in distress is a town. For Faulkner it is both less and more: a family but also a culture and a history. The seven stories of individual lives join to produce a novel of Faulkner's entire race-tormented region.

The opening story, "Was," is whimsical in tone (its narrator is a nine-year-old boy), and it revolves around a series of hunts. Two white brothers (Uncle Buck and Uncle Buddy) are chasing their escaped "nigger" (Tomey's Turl), another white man (Hubert) is trying to marry off his sister (Sophonsiba) to Uncle Buck, the black man (Tomey's Turl) is escaping his owners in order to court his sweetheart (Tennie, one of Hubert's slaves), and the unmarried white woman (Sophonsiba) is trying to snare Buck for a husband. These hunts merrily echo each other, CLIMAXing in a game of poker between Hubert and Buck that will determine who pairs off with whom and (literally) at what price. Only later will the reader recognize that Turl is Buck and Buddy's half brother (concealed MISCEGENATION is at the heart of this text) and that the year of these shenanigans is 1859—just before the outbreak of the CIVIL WAR and the end of innocence.

In the next story, "The Fire and the Hearth," set in the 1940s, Faulkner painstakingly explores the perspective of the black characters. Lucas Beauchamp (offspring of Turl and Tennie) ceases to be a stereotypical (see STEREOTYPE) "nigger." Faulkner devotes page after page to Lucas's memories, ordeals, and desires. These poetic passages reveal the fineness of Lucas's mind, and although he remains a black man caught up in the racist South, he is agile enough to outwit the various whites who would exploit him. Despite his restless schemes, Lucas manages to preserve his marriage with Molly. The title of this story points to a domestic warmth outside the reach of any white family in Faulkner's work. Lucas heroically accommodates all the pressures—racial, domestic, gendered—that surround him. In this he is the counterpart for Faulkner's other heroic figure (yet to appear): ISAAC (IKE) MCCASLIN, a dreamer, idealist, and hunter who finds sustenance in the unspoiled wilderness.

"Pantaloon in Black," the next story, may be the most moving story about race that Faulkner ever wrote. He positions us inside the mind of Rider, the grief-stricken black man whose young wife has just died. (See POINT OF VIEW.) Inconsolable, inarticulate, suffocating, Rider moves through the woods at an almost epic pace, desperately seeking release in liquor or violence. Our bond with this character is so intimate that we watch, hypnotized, as Rider finally seals his fate by killing with a razor the white man who has just cheated him with crooked dice. Then, suddenly, after this moment-by-moment intensity, the story switches from Rider's mind to that of the deputy who has tried unsuccessfully to jail him and has seen his body once the white man's family has taken its revenge. The deputy understands nothing of what he has witnessed, for Faulkner has rendered a distress no white person in Rider's world can understand when it rages inside a black body.

The next pair of stories—"The Old People" and "The BEAR"—build on each other, as they gradually introduce the boy Ike McCaslin to his twin heritage: the guilt-saturated inheritance of McCaslin property and the liberating ritual of the wilderness hunt. Ike's childhood is structured on the promise, and then the reality, of participating in the autumnal hunt in the big woods. For this development a further cast is needed: Sam Fathers, part Indian and part black, Ike's guide in both the art of the hunt and the communal sharing with the wild that it permits; Old Ben, the legendary bear; Lion, the wild dog that is alone capable of bring-ing the bear down; and Boon Hogganbeck, part Indian, wholly untamed. In a climactic encounter that is both embrace and murder, celebration and farewell, Boon and Lion and Old Ben merge in an act of pure beauty and violence. Ike watches as Boon bestrides the beleaguered bear, "working and probing the buried blade," finally taking them all down together.

Four of the five sections of "The Bear" rise to and descend from this climactic moment in which the figures of the wilderness—Old Ben, Lion, Sam Fathers—embrace, deal out their death, and die themselves. The wilderness enters its autumnal phase, yet Ike McCaslin will be shaped by this scene forever. Five years later, at age 21, he renounces his McCaslin property and heritage, telling his cousin quietly that "Sam Fathers set me free" (286). Indeed, this narrative of renunciation fills the experimental fourth section of "The Bear," in which Faulkner explores the widest cultural ramifications of the hunt. Ike discovers, in the ledgers of the McCaslin commissary, the race-tormented history of his family, sees that Tomey's Turl is actually his grandfather's son by a black woman and realizes that the old man evaded this bond by giving money instead: "*I reckon that was cheaper than saying My son to a nigger* he thought" (258). Brooding on his family's refusal to acknowledge their own black offspring, Ike rejects his blood heritage, becoming "uncle to half a county and father to no one" in his lifelong retreat to the woods.

Faulkner treats Ike's withdrawal with compassion, yet he shows, in the next story, "DELTA AUTUMN," that the family's racist history continues unabated. In this last hunt (dated 1940s) Ike encounters a mysterious woman with a child; she is looking for Ike's great-nephew Roth. As in a dream, it turns out that, although her skin does not reveal it, she is black (is in fact the great-granddaughter of Tomey's Turl) and that her fleeing lover is Roth. Miscegenation upon miscegenation, the 1940s nonacknowledgment echoing that of the 1830s, Ike sees the futility of his attempt to escape, as he gazes on the woods ruined by loggers and their machinery.

Futility is likewise the THEME of the last story, "Go Down, Moses," which centers on a ceremonial return-ing of the corpse of the black Samuel Worsham

Beauchamp to his grieving southern family. Roth had earlier "exiled" Samuel from the plantation for theft. The young man had moved to the urban North, turned criminal, and been caught and executed. Samuel's family awaits the return of his body, singing of Roth's casting out of Samuel as betraying him to Pharaoh—"'Sold him in Egypt and now he dead.' 'Oh yes, Lord. Sold him in Egypt.'" (363). If this 150-year history is powerless to envision black life freed from white Pharaoh's grasp, it at least acknowledges the pathos of black death, the community (white and black) bringing one of their own home to be laid to rest. On this note of ceremonial grief, Faulkner concludes *Go Down, Moses*.

BIBLIOGRAPHY

Faulkner, William, *Go Down, Moses*. New York: Random House, 1942.

Grimwood, Michael. *Heart in Conflict: Faulkner's Struggles with Vocation*. Athens: University of Georgia Press, 1987.

Harrington, Evans, and Ann J. Abadie, eds. *Faulkner and the Short Story*. Jackson: University of Mississippi Press, 1992.

Matthews, John T. *The Play of Faulkner's Language*. Ithaca, N.Y.: Cornell University Press, 1982.

Snead, James. *Figures of Division: William Faulkner's Major Novels*. New York: Methuen, 1986.

Sundquist, Eric. *Faulkner: The House Divided*. Baltimore: Johns Hopkins University Press, 1983.

Wagner-Martin, Linda, ed. *New Essays on Faulkner's Go Down, Moses*. New York: Cambridge University Press, 1996.

Weinstein, Philip M., ed. *The Cambridge Companion to William Faulkner*. New York: Cambridge University Press, 1995.

Philip M. Weinstein
Swarthmore College

"GOLD" ISAAC ASIMOV (1995) "Gold," the title story of *Gold: The Final Science Fiction Collection*, fittingly mirrors ISAAC ASIMOV's half-century writing career. Asimov's work has defined science fiction as a multilayered genre, ranging from the simple rearrangement of history to more complex manipulation of reality. *Gold* is a collection of stories and essays that explain Asimov's perception of the genre and the craft involved. The title story is a "drama about a writer

who gambles everything on a chance at immortality: a gamble Asimov himself made—and won" (cover).

Orson Scott Card observes that America has "two levels of language," one for communicating and one for making an impression (Introduction). He presents Isaac Asimov as "the purest, clearest, most fluid, most effective writer of the American Plain Style" (x). Asimov's purposefully transparent language and intolerance for unexplored mysteries make his work seem artless, but his preference for the plain style of writing was fundamentally the result of expunging "all fanciness from his writing" to produce a telescopically clear view of distant or fuzzy possibilities (xi). Appropriately, "Gold," characteristic of Asimov's fiction, clearly addresses Asimov's purposefully plain style of writing. In the same manner that he explicitly addressed his views of machines in earlier works, Asimov in "Gold" focuses the telescope on a more personal target, Isaac Asimov, the writer, his stories, and his values.

Many of the themes of the earlier Robot stories, in print for half a century, are also directly or indirectly represented in "Gold." For example, the stories "Robbie" (1939) and "Runaround" (1942) established the Laws of Robotics, prompting readers to expect Asimov's machines to do the work they are programmed to do. Asimov's First Law of Robotics states that a robot may not injure a human through action or inaction; the Second Law states that a robot must obey human orders except those that conflict with the First Law; the Third Law states that a robot must protect itself except where doing so conflicts with the First or Second Law. In "Gold," as in "The Inevitable Conflict" (1950), the computer is a valuable extension of the imagination but is also understood to be merely a "computerized machine" or a "mobile computer" that efficiently generates and adapts desired sounds and images to accompany dialogue and action in computerized theater productions (131).

Familiar with the existence of computers at the time he wrote "Franchise" (1955), Asimov created the computer "Multivac," an enormous machine. He acknowledges missing the opportunity to predict the miniaturization and etherealization of computers, an oversight that is corrected in "The Last Question"

(1956), the story that followed (204). Asimov notes that his robots are almost always masculine, in name and pronoun, but "not necessarily in an actual sense of gender" (205). At the suggestion of a female editor, he wrote "Feminine Intuition" (1969), about a robot that is still metal but has "a narrower waistline" and a feminine voice. In "Gold," Meg Cathcart, representative of Asimov's efforts to be inclusive, is the woman in charge of background and works with Jonas Willard through the glitches of compudrama.

Asimov's comments regarding "Little Lost Robot" are that while his machines tend to be "benign entities" and tend to gain moral and ethical qualities as his stories progress, he has not confined himself to "robots as saviors" but has followed "the wild winds" of imagination to address even the risky elements of the "robot phenomena" (203). For example, in "The Feeling of Power" (1958), Asimov deals with fictional pocket computers almost two decades before their counterparts were marketed. The story also addresses the social implications of dependency on technology, before data supporting these implications had begun to accumulate (208).

In "Gold," readers may recognize echoes of similar concerns regarding the future of the arts. Asimov conjectures, regarding utopianism, that since the 19th century scientific and technological advances make it easier to imagine a utopia imposed from without, while society remains "as irrational and imperfect as ever"; the scenario includes scientific advances that supply food, cure diseases, and reprogram irrational human impulses (241–242). However, as a rational humanist who prefers the reasonableness of occupying a position somewhere "between the extremes of utopia and dystopia," Asimov imagines and explores such a world by creating stories involving conflict between two forces that are mixtures of good and evil (244).

SELECTED BIBLIOGRAPHY

Asimov, Isaac. *Gold: The Final Science Fiction Collection.* New York: HarperCollins, 1995.

Card, Orson Scott. *How to Write Science Fiction and Fantasy.* Cincinnati: Writer's Digest, 1990.

Stella Thompson
Prairie View A&M University

GOLDEN APPLES, THE EUDORA WELTY **(1949)**   When EUDORA WELTY published *The Golden Apples* in 1949, critics did not know whether to treat it as an experimental novel or as a collection of interconnected short stories. But Welty included the separate pieces from *The Golden Apples* in her *Collected Stories of Eudora Welty* (1980), making it clear that she intended them as stories. This seven-piece cycle (see SHORT STORY CYCLE) covers 40 years in the life of the small community in Morgana, Mississippi. Each story focuses on different central characters, who also appear on the periphery in other stories at different stages of their lives. In the first story, Katie Rainey, mother of the rebellious Virgie Rainey, introduces the reader to Morgana's residents, especially the promiscuous and wandering King McLain. In the final story, "The Wanderers," Katie's funeral takes place and Virgie, who at the funeral recognizes a kinship with the now aged King McLain, finally gets her chance to escape Morgana, completing the cycle.

In depicting the residents of Morgana, Welty alludes to Greek, Roman, Celtic, and Germanic MYTHS and LEGENDS, Welty's thematically demonstrating the relatedness of all human communities, regardless of time and place (see THEME). As all people, mythic or mundane, ancient or modern, do, the characters in *The Golden Apples* seek beauty, love, contentment, and passion, each in his or her own way. The title of the cycle is found in William Butler Yeats's poem "The Song of the Wandering Aengus," which describes the Celtic hero Aengus's quest for eternal happiness in the form of a beautiful girl. And the Golden Apples also refer to the Greek legend in which the apples, as symbols of perfect beauty and passion, were awarded by Paris to Aphrodite, causing jealousy among the goddesses, who became partially responsible for beginning the Trojan War. We also find counterparts for many of Welty's characters in myth. King McLain, who has many love affairs and children throughout Mississippi, and who first appears to us in "A Shower of Gold," is a Zeus figure. Loch Morrison, the heroic boy who saves a drowning orphan in "Moon Lake," is a youthful Perseus. Cassie Morrison, Loch's older sister, gains deep understandings of the other characters that she is unable to express in "June Recital" and is, as her name indicates, a Cassandra figure.

In "June Recital" we also meet Virgie Rainey, the rebellious but talented young girl, and Mrs. Eckhart, the misunderstood artist and piano teacher. These characters, while seemingly opposite, have much in common as they learn to understand themselves in relation to the world, and both are linked to a portrait of Perseus slaying the Medusa that hangs above Mrs. Eckhart's piano. As Virgie Rainey reflects in "The Wanderers," in order for there to be heroes, there also must be victims, and she and her piano teacher contain qualities of both figures.

Although all these characters have mythic counterparts, *The Golden Apples* is not merely an ALLEGORY. The characters are also real, 20th-century southerners, described in vivid detail, making the reader feel that even the most ordinary of us has a connection to myth.

BIBLIOGRAPHY
Evans, Elizabeth. *Eudora Welty.* New York: Ungar, 1981.
Vande Kieft, Ruth M. *Eudora Welty.* Boston: Twayne, 1987.

Betina I. Entzminger
University of North Carolina at Chapel Hill

GONZALEZ, N. V. M. (1915–1999)

N. V. M. Gonzalez was born in Mindoro, the Philippines. He began writing as soon as he finished high school, but it would be more than 10 years before the publication of his first book of short stories, *Seven Hills Away* (1947). This collection was deeply admired in the Philippines and attracted enough international attention that two years later Gonzalez was offered a writing fellowship at Stanford University, where he studied under Wallace Stegner. Gonzalez was a professor emeritus of English literature at California State University at Hayward; he was also the international writer in residence at the University of the Philippines, Manila.

Although Gonzalez lived in the United States from 1949, most of his story collections—including *Children of the Ash-Covered Loam, and Other Stories* (1954); *Look, Stranger, on This Island Now* (1963); and *Mindoro and Beyond: Twenty-one Stories* (1979)—and the major-

ity of his separately published stories appeared exclusively in the Philippines. Most American readers know Gonzalez only through *The Bread of Salt and Other Stories* (1993), which collects 19 representative stories spanning the length of Gonzalez's writing career. Gonzalez also wrote several novels and numerous essays.

A postcolonial writer in perspective and THEMES, Gonzalez used a compassionate TONE and gentle IRONY to explore the subjugation of the Filipinos by the West and especially by America, grieving over Filipinos' loss of myth and of traditional connections to the land and the utter absence of any kind of substitute culture.

BIBLIOGRAPHY
Campomanes, Oscar V. "Filipinos in the United States and Their Literature of Exile." In *Reading the Literatures of Asian America,* edited by Shirley Geok-lin Lim and Amy Ling. 1992.
Gonzalez, N. V. M. *The Bread of Salt and Other Stories.* Seattle: University of Washington Press, 1993.
———. *Children of the Ash-Covered Loam, and Other Stories.* Manila: Benipayo Press, 1954.
———. *Look, Stranger, on This Island Now.* Manila: Benipayo Press, 1963.
———. *Mindoro and Beyond: Twenty-one Stories.* Quezon City: University of the Philippines Press, 1979.
———. *Seven Hills Away.* Denver: A. Swallow, 1947.

Keith Lawrence
Brigham Young University

"GOOD ANNA, THE" GERTRUDE STEIN (1909)

Throughout *Three Lives,* in which "The Good Anna" appears, GERTRUDE STEIN explores the heterosexual and lesbian relationships of three common women, Anna, Melanctha, and Lena. In her attempts to capture the thoughts and consciousness of these women, Stein uses a number of stylistic innovations that contributed significantly to the development of MODERNISM, influencing such writers as ERNEST HEMINGWAY. In "The Good Anna," for example, Stein employs inverted grammatical patterns, repetition, and simple language to characterize Anna, the PROTAGONIST, as a stubborn, matter-of-fact, hardworking German immigrant. At the same time, the ironic and understated narration, which creates a humor that is often incongruous with the story's events, suggests some of Stein's larger social criticisms.

The good Anna works for numerous men and women who seemingly take advantage of her kindness. As she tries to enforce her own moral code of "good" and "bad" on the world (including her dogs Peter, Baby, and Rags), Anna struggles with her own lesbian desires for Mrs. Lehntman: "The widow Mrs. Lehntman was the romance in Anna's life" (30). Ironically, Anna's attempts to gain moral and emotional control over others prevent the fulfillment of her own emotional needs, leaving her "bitter with the world . . . for its sadness and wicked ways of doing" (65, 69). Unable to change those around her, she loses her money, friends, and health. Having defined herself by her work ethic, she eventually works herself to death running a boardinghouse. Stein subtly uses the story of Anna to make a powerful critique of the destructiveness of a society that locks women into restrictive, "feminine" roles even as it represses homosexuality.

BIBLIOGRAPHY

DeKoven, Marianne. *A Different Language: Gertrude Stein's Experimental Writing.* Madison: University of Wisconsin Press, 1983.

Fahy, Thomas. "Iteration and Narrative Control in Gertrude Stein's 'The Good Anna.'" *Style* 34, no. 1 (2000).

Wagner-Martin, Linda. *"Favored Strangers": Gertrude Stein and Her Family.* New Brunswick, N.J.: Rutgers University Press, 1995.

Thomas Fahy
University of North Carolina at Chapel Hill

"GOODBYE, COLUMBUS" PHILIP ROTH

(1959) Sometimes called a NOVELLA, PHILIP ROTH's "Goodbye, Columbus" offers a thorough introduction to some of the key themes, techniques, and character types that will populate Roth's subsequent novels. While "Goodbye, Columbus" provides sharp social criticism, it is equally resonant on a surface level as a classic story of summer love. The story is narrated by Neil Klugman, a 23-year-old graduate of Newark Colleges of Rutgers, a secular Jew, and an employee of the Newark Public Library. Over the course of a summer, Neil dates Brenda Patimkin, a wealthy Radcliffe student and stereotypical Jewish-American princess whose family lives in the ritzy suburb of Short Hills; the relationship seems to have potential as more than just a summer fling but dissolves soon after Brenda returns to school.

Although "Goodbye, Columbus" is about social class and Americanization, it does not present the entrenched polarities that audiences are trained to seek. Neil and Brenda are of the same race and the same religion; both have or will obtain a college degree; their families have nothing against each other. What separates the two is simply that they are at different stages on the path to seeking and achieving the AMERICAN DREAM and have conflicting attitudes about the compromises such a journey entails. Most prominently among its themes, "Goodbye, Columbus" offers a reexamination of the American dream, questioning its attainability and whether its benefits are worth its costs. While the trajectory of Neil's relationship with Brenda comprises the main plot of the story, several interlocking subplots evolve in parallel ways; each features a foil for Neil and sheds light on Neil's dilemma, ultimately suggesting a cost or limitation of the American dream: the African-American boy in the library and his romance with Gauguin, Ron Patimkin and his mother, and Leo Patimkin's unsuccessful marriage to Harriet, the relationship between Brenda and pursuit of the American dream.

The nameless little boy in the library is a foil for Neil and a source of irony in the story. While Neil is keenly aware of the challenges the boy faces—he is treated with suspicion, has difficulty making himself understood, and does not understand how the system works—Neil remains remarkably obtuse about recognizing the parallels between the boy's situation and his own in Short Hills. The boy's misplaced confidence in the continued presence of his Gauguin book is analogous to Neil's lack of awareness of the fragility of his relationship with Brenda. What the boy shows us is that the myth of the American dream is precisely that—a myth.

A second foil is Brenda's brother, Ron, an All-American athlete who is marrying his mother-approved girlfriend and going into the family business, right on schedule. One has the sense, however, that Ron's glory days have already passed him by. Although Ron had planned to become a gym teacher, a fitting profession and one in which he would excel, he follows his father into a business for which he is unsuited and that he will not enjoy. Ron's acceptance of "responsibilities" (61) and his plans to defer his own gratification to give greater possibilities to his yet-unborn children constitute another casualty of the American dream, the loss of personal dreams.

While Ron sacrifices his personal dreams to comply with the goal of success his parents have ordained for him, the disintegration of the relationship between Brenda and her mother suggests that family can become a casualty of success. The three major sources of tension between Mrs. Patimkin and her eldest daughter all originate in the family's material success: loss of ethnic identity, different attitudes toward money, and failure to share values. Mrs. Patimkin maintains her sense of herself as Jewish, but Mr. Patimkin pays for the nose job that will remove the inscription of ethnic identity from his daughter's face; Mrs. Patimkin laments: "[Brenda] was the best Hebrew student I've ever seen . . . but then, of course, she got too big for her britches" (89). Money itself has also become divisive, as Mrs. Patimkin frets that Brenda does not appreciate it, while Brenda counters that her mother cannot enjoy it. Finally, financial success has driven a wedge between the two women because they do not share core values. While Mrs. Patimkin achieved her status through hard work, her daughter takes maids and lawn services for granted.

If Brenda's nuclear family shows Neil what he might have to sacrifice in order to "become a Patimkin" (120) and live the American dream, another Patimkin serves as a cautionary tale about what happens to a person whose dream quest fails. Like the Ancient Mariner, Leo Patimkin corners Neil at Ron's wedding and tells a tale of failed aspirations, adjuring Neil, "Don't louse it up" (108). His discontent suggests that it might be better not to reach beyond one's grasp than to live with regret.

What Neil ultimately realizes is that the relationship with Brenda requires him to give up too much of his personal identity. If Short Hills is indeed paradise, it is a troubled one; Neil's innocence, like Brenda's virginity, is lost. Defying audience expectations, Neil

breaks up with Brenda. The ending also suggests an irony, that perhaps what Neil took for a serious relationship was actually just Brenda's using Neil to get her mother's attention. Certainly this would be a very different story if told from the point of view of either of the Patimkin women. Ultimately, the story's title proves prophetic. A play on Ron's alumni album from Ohio State University, the title foreshadows both the dissolution of the relationship and the protagonist's return to his homeland. Indeed, the story begins almost exactly where it left off. Brenda is back at Radcliffe (with a new coat to console her for her losses), the little African-American boy is on the street, and Neil is back at the library. Clearly Brenda is a static character, remaining essentially unchanged in outlook and behavior despite the events of the text, and although Neil might not know exactly what he wants, he does seem more clear about what price he is and is not willing to pay to pursue his dreams.

BIBLIOGRAPHY

Rabin, Jessica. "Still (Resonant, Relevant and) Crazy after All These Years: *Goodbye, Columbus and Five Short Stories.*" In *Philip Roth: New Perspectives on an American Author,* edited by Derek Parker Royal, 9–23. Westport, Conn: Praeger, 2005.

Roth, Philip. "Goodbye, Columbus." In *Goodbye, Columbus and Five Short Stories.* New York: Vintage International, 1993.

Jessica G. Rabin
Anne Arundel Community College

"GOOD COUNTRY PEOPLE" FLANNERY O'CONNOR (1955)

In a memorable contribution to her stories that use the GROTESQUE, FLANNERY O'CONNOR's "Good Country People" ironically reverses the old saying that country people are good and its corollary, simple. Set in Georgia, the story features three women and a Bible salesman.

As in most of O'Connor's stories, the unselfconscious third-person narrator injects comic (see COMEDY) overtones or, more accurately, those of BLACK HUMOR, to entertain readers as they become acquainted with these markedly peculiar characters. Mrs. Hopewell, the initiator of the "good country people" idea, speaks in clichés equivalent to "Have a good day." Her FOIL is her maid, Mrs. Freeman, who, in her fascination with all forms of sickness, disease, and abnormality, tells revolting tales about her daughters (Glynese and Carramae) and exhibits a perverse fascination with Mrs. Hopewell's large, hulking, 32-year-old daughter, Joy. Joy had lost her leg at age 10; she lumbers and stumps around on a wooden one and has changed her name to *Hulga*. JOY-HULGA brags to the two older women about her doctorate in philosophy, boasting that she believes in nothing at all.

When MANLEY POINTER arrives on the scene with his Bibles and his humorously phallic name, the reader expects that Hulga will exert her strong will on him and seduce him. But he has only been playing the part of a simple, good country person, and his briefcase contains a false bottom under which he keeps liquor, condoms, and items he steals from women with deformities. He has, he informs Hulga as he runs off with her wooden leg, believed in nothing since birth. Hulga, for all her degrees and pride in her intellectual power, has been played for a fool, losing not her virginity but her carefully cultivated outward sense of superiority to others less educated. As Ann Charters points out, "However dastardly Pointer's actions, he forces Hulga to feel and acknowledge her emotions for the first time," and our final impression is that Hulga may learn from this humbling experience, becoming "less presumptuous and closer to psychic wholeness" (136). Hulga and her mother must correct and surmount their complacency and naïveté, for the story suggests that without a strong philosophy and spiritual beliefs, they remain at the mercy of the Manley Pointers and Mrs. Freemans, significantly connected through their similar names, who also believe in nothing but have less difficulty surviving.

BIBLIOGRAPHY

Charters, Ann. *Resources for Teaching: Major Writers of Short Fiction.* Boston: Bedford Books/St. Martin's, 1993.

O'Connor, Flannery. "Good Country People." In *Contemporary American Literature,* edited by George Perkins and Barbara Perkins. New York: Random House, 1988.

GOOD HOUSEKEEPING

A monthly magazine directed primarily at women and homemakers that has offered household advice, recipes, articles, and fiction since 1885. Among writers published in the magazine have been W. Somerset Maugham, James Hilton, Mary Roberts Rinehart, Sinclair Lewis, Daphne du Maurier, and John P. Marquand.

GOODMAN BROWN See "YOUNG GOODMAN BROWN."

"GOOD MAN IS HARD TO FIND, A"

FLANNERY O'CONNOR (1952) Frequently anthologized, "A Good Man Is Hard to Find" exemplifies FLANNERY O'CONNOR's southern religious grounding. The story depicts the impact of Christ on the lives of two seemingly disparate characters. One is a grandmother joining her son's family on a trip to Florida. Accompanied by a silent daughter-in-law, a baby, two unpleasant children, and her smuggled cat, she wheedles the son into making a detour to see a plantation that she remembers from an earlier time.

Moments of recognition and connection multiply as the seemingly foreordained meeting of the grandmother and the killer she has read about in the paper takes place. She upsets the basket in which she has hidden her cat; the cat lands on her son's neck, causing an accident. Soon three men appear on the dirt road, and the grandmother recognizes one of them as the notorious killer the Misfit.

O'Connor weaves the notion of punishment and Christian love into the conversation between the Misfit and the grandmother while the grandmother's family is being murdered. Referring to the similarity that he shares with Christ, the Misfit declares that "Jesus thrown everything off balance" (27), but he admits that unlike Christ, he must have committed a crime because there were papers to prove it. When the grandmother touches his shoulder because she sees him as one of her own children, she demonstrates a Christian love that causes him to shoot her.

This story typifies O'Connor's mingling of COMEDY, goodness, banality, and violence in her vision of a world that, however imperfect, most readers inevitably recognize as part of their own. O'Connor views the world as a place where benevolence and good intentions conflict with perversity and evil, and her PROTAGONISTS frequently learn too late that their lives can crumble in an instant when confronted by the very real powers of darkness.

BIBLIOGRAPHY

Kessler, Edward. *Flannery O'Connor and the Language of Apocalypse.* Princeton, N.J.: Princeton University Press, 1986.

Orvell, Miles. *Flannery O'Connor: An Introduction.* Jackson: University Press of Mississippi, 1991.

Sandra Chrystal Hayes
Georgia Institute of Technology

GORDON, CAROLINE (1895–1981)

A talented novelist and short story writer, Caroline Gordon both celebrates the stability of the past and details the complex social, psychological, and political transition from the Old South to the New. Although she has a distinctive voice and vision, her studies of middle-class southerners and the passing of the old cultured agrarian way of life link her with writers like EUDORA WELTY or PETER TAYLOR. Her stories, which take place in Kentucky and Tennessee, include "The Captivity," a well-known Native American captivity story, as well as several CIVIL WAR tales about the Union army's invasion of the rural South (for instance, "Hear the Nightingale Sing," "The Forest of the South," and "The Ice House"). Gordon is probably best known, however, for her insightful and meticulously crafted stories about ALECK MAURY, southern sportsman, which have prompted comparison to the hunting and fishing tales of ERNEST HEMINGWAY and WILLIAM FAULKNER (Schaefer 214). The episodic novel *Aleck Maury, Sportsman* contains most of the Maury material, as do numerous stories from *The Forest of the South* (1945), including the acclaimed "Old Red."

These related stories feature Aleck, a.k.a. Professor Maury, classics teacher, gentleman farmer, and, above all else, avid sportsman. Gordon makes Maury into a central consciousness similar to that used by HENRY JAMES. He understands that he devotes himself to fishing because, as with Hemingway's NICK ADAMS, it provides a way for confronting and coming to terms with his own identity. Essentially at war with his family and others who represent a constricted and socialized life, Maury understands that they are like hunters engaged in the sport of capturing him as he, as does Old Red, the fox, desperately seeks his freedom. With "The Presence," "One More Day," "To Thy Chamber Window, Sweet," and "The Last Day in the Field," Gordon completes the saga of the Professor; in "The Last Day in the Field," she depicts an aging Aleck, whose failing health instigates his ritual farewell to the hunt.

BIBLIOGRAPHY

Fraistat, Rose Ann C. *Gordon as Novelist and Woman of Letters.* Baton Rouge: Louisiana State University Press, 1984.

Gordon, Caroline. *Aleck Maury, Sportsman.* New York: Charles Scribner's Sons, 1934. As *The Pastimes of Aleck Maury: The Life of a True Sportsman.* London: Dickson & Thompson, 1935.

———. *Collected Stories.* New York: Farrar, Straus & Giroux, 1981.

———. *The Forest of the South.* New York: C. Scribner's Sons, 1945.

———. *The Garden of Adonis.* New York: C. Scribner's Sons, 1937.

———. *The Glory of Hera.* Garden City, N.Y.: Doubleday, 1972.

———. *Green Centuries.* New York: Scribner, 1941.

———. *The Malefactors.* New York: Harcourt Brace, 1956.

———. *None Shall Look Back.* New York: C. Scribner's Sons, 1937.

———. *Old Red and Other Stories.* New York: Scribner, 1963.

———. *Penhally.* New York: Scribner, 1931.

———. *The Strange Children.* New York: Scribner, 1951.

———. *The Women on the Porch.* New York: Scribner, 1944.

Gordon, Caroline, and Allen Tate, eds. *The House of Fiction: An Anthology of the Short Story.* New York: Scribner, 1950; revised edition, 1960.

Landess, Thomas H., ed. *The Short Fiction of Gordon: A Critical Symposium.* Irving, Tex.: University of Dallas Press, 1972.

Makowsky, Veronica A. *Gordon: A Biography.* New York: Oxford University Press, 1989.

McDowell, Frederick P. W. *Gordon.* Minneapolis: University of Minnesota Press, 1966.

Schaefer, William J. "Caroline Gordon." In *Reference Guide to Short Fiction,* edited by Noelle Watson, 214–215. Detroit: St. James Press, 1994.

Stuckey, W. J. *Gordon.* New York: Twayne, 1972.

Waldron, Ann. *Close Connections: Gordon and the Southern Renaissance.* New York: Putnam, 1987.

GOTHIC A term used to describe fiction whose major characteristics include magic, chivalry, mystery, terror, the irrational, and the perverse—and often a villain pursuing a helpless virgin. The word *gothic* originally referred to the Goths, a Germanic tribe, and later signified "Germanic," and then "medieval." The British writer Horace Walpole is credited with writing the first gothic novel (*The Castle of Otranto,* 1764). Set in a medieval castle, it features elements we have come to associate with the fictional gothic: trap doors, winding underground tunnels, dark staircases, and mysteriously slamming doors. Mary Shelley's *Frankenstein* (1818), with its monster and its dark horrors, provides another example of the typical gothic novel. The popular form—a subgenre of romanticism—spread throughout Europe, particularly Germany, and reached the United States, where its earliest practitioner was CHARLES BROCKDEN BROWN. In the short story, EDGAR ALLAN POE practiced gothic horror; an excellent example is "The CASK OF AMONTILLADO," in which the vengeful MONTRESOR leads his victim down a long tunnel under a castle and then walls him up alive, the better to enjoy his revenge.

In the 21st century, the term *gothic* is often applied to stories that, although lacking the medieval atmosphere, achieve the effect of dark mystery and terror. WILLIAM FAULKNER'S "A ROSE FOR EMILY" is frequently referred to as "southern gothic," as is much of the work of FLANNERY O'CONNOR and CARSON MCCULLERS. In modern literature, the term *gothic*—including southern gothic—is frequently associated with the grotesque, or a focus on the weird, bizarre, or fantastic. To some writers, both the gothic and the GROTESQUE—as in SHERWOOD ANDERSON'S *WINESBURG, OHIO* or ERSKINE CALDWELL'S "A Mid-Summer Passion"—appear an appropriate metaphor for the modern human condition. The 20th-century movement of SURREALISM also claims the gothic mode as a forerunner.

BIBLIOGRAPHY
Eisenger, Chester E. "The Gothic Spirit in the Forties." In *Fiction of the Forties,* edited by Chester E. Eisenger. Chicago: University of Chicago Press, 1963.

Harmon, William, and C. Hugh Holman. *A Handbook to Literature.* 7th ed. Upper Saddle River, N.J.: Prentice Hall, 1995, 237–238, 239–240.

"GRAVE, THE" KATHERINE ANNE PORTER (1935) In the mid-1930s, KATHERINE ANNE PORTER's early work was attracting the favorable attention of America's burgeoning New Critics, whose techniques of close literary analysis to this day remain useful for reading Porter's tightly written, symbol and image-laden fiction. Her story "The Grave," for example, first appeared in the *Virginia Quarterly,* which was edited at that time by Allen Tate, and additional titles by Porter were selected for publication in the *Southern Review* by then-coeditors Robert Penn Warren and Cleanth Brooks.

In exemplary New Critical readings, the two latter critics wrote important responses to Porter's work, Warren in "Katherine Anne Porter: Irony with a Center" and Brooks in "On 'The Grave.'" Warren, for example, praises the body of Porter's work, citing its adherence to the New Critical hallmarks of controlling irony, balance through paradox, contradiction, and dialectic, not to mention "the underlying structure of contrast and tension" and the "counterpoint of incident and implication" (62). Brooks, writing expressly on "The Grave," provides additional New Critical touchstones omitted from his colleague's observations: Not only is "The Grave" an initiation story (a form favored by the New Critics), but its patterns of imagery admirably serve the purposes of objective correlative, ultimately unifying the story by reconciling its conflicts and "bringing into focus its underlying theme" (176). Indeed, Porter's "The Grave" seemed uniquely fitted for New Critical explication by virtue of its symbolism of womb and tomb, ring and dove; by its juxtaposition of sweetness with corruption, flight with boundaries, intuition with experience, philosophical depth with childlike simplicity; and by its conflation of life, death, sex, and maternity.

Even read on its own, "The Grave" is a story of motherless children; reading it in the context of the several accompanying stories among which Porter eventually placed it in *The Old Order* (1955), we know nine-year-old Miranda and 12-year-old Paul as doubly bereft, not only through the long-ago death of their mother, but also through the more recent death of their matriarchal grandmother, who even in her absence is simply and definitively "the Grandmother." The Grandmother's death has the effect on Miranda of relaxing the demands for ladylike dress and comportment that would otherwise have directed her behavior. On the other hand, implied in the story are the financial difficulties into which the Grandmother's passing has plunged Miranda along with her father, her brother Paul, and her sister Maria. Although relishing her "summer roughing" attire, Miranda is still aware of the special economies that make roughing it and thus saving her good clothes a necessity. Pondering the problem of her late grandmother's expectations of and for her and the joys and trials freedom from them gives, Miranda hardly knows which to embrace and which to discount.

An additional economy structuring the narrative is the need to sell long-held farm acreage, causing the displacement of several coffins from the family's small private cemetery. The now-emptied graves prove irresistible to the children, who must trespass on land no longer theirs in order to achieve the thrill of self-imposed fear as they dig about in space that has once held dead family members. In their play, they discover the two objects that bespeak the destinies and desires of which the children are only vaguely aware: a silver coffin screw and a gold wedding ring. Paul glories in what he feels is his unique possession of the dove-shaped coffin screw with a "deep round hollow" (363) where the breast should be. Miranda claims the intricately carved ring, only to know immediate dissatisfaction with her roughing about clothes as she places it on her thumb. Wearing the ring produces a desire for a cold bath and a becoming dress and sash in which she might display herself "in a wicker chair under the trees" (365), and she actually considers wordlessly abandoning Paul to seek them out. Then, as she hesitates between her newly formulated vision of self-identity and her more accustomed fraternal loyalty, Paul flushes a rabbit from the brush, shooting and killing it.

This final act is the most significant of the day, forcing the two children from the liminal space of unvoiced and unacknowledged intuitions—those hints toward actual knowledge they had each responded to in claiming the dove and the ring—into experiential knowledge. Skinning the rabbit, Paul finds that it carries unborn young, themselves now forever liminal—unborn and thus untouched by death, having neither past nor future. The image is of a closed circuit, like the ring we know Miranda still wears on her thumb but of which no further mention is made in the story. When Paul and Miranda agree never to speak to anyone of the incident, they leave behind the rabbit babies, and a part of their childhood, wrapped within the dead body of the mother and hidden away in the sage bushes.

The irony that Warren claims as the center of this work relies in actuality on the disruption of gender expectations that we experience with our final view of Miranda, 20 years older and "in a strange city of a strange country" (367). Her vision of the cool wicker chair under the trees has failed to materialize, giving way to a busy foreign marketplace, the sights and smells of which—particularly a tray of sweets in the shapes of little animals—evoke for her that long-ago memory of the graves and the unborn rabbits. And like the image of the dove with the hollowed out center, "The Grave" as narrative is itself unexpectedly "decentered" by her final vision of Paul, 12 once more, examining the coffin screw, the symbol by which Miranda has lived her life in spite of her initial choice of the ring on that now-distant summer day.

BIBLIOGRAPHY

Brooks, Cleanth. "On 'The Grave.'" *Yale Review* 55 (Winter 1966): 275–279.

Porter, Katherine Anne. "The Grave." In *The Collected Stories of Katherine Anne Porter.* New York: Harcourt Brace, 1979.

Warren, Robert Penn. "Katherine Anne Porter (Irony with a Center)." *Kenyon Review* 4 (Winter 1942): 29–42.

Patricia L. Bradley
Middle Tennessee State University

"GRAVEN IMAGE" JOHN O'HARA (1943)

"Graven Image" first appeared in the NEW YORKER (March 13, 1943) and then in O'Hara's collection of short stories, *Pipe Night* (1945). In his review (March

18, 1945), Lionel Trilling praised O'Hara as having, "more than anyone now writing," "the most precise knowledge of the content of our subtlest snobberies, of our points of social honor and idiosyncrasies of personal prestige," for example, "of how secretly profound is the feeling which many modern Americans have about their college lives." It seemed to Trilling that "no other writer could have projected the story 'Graven Image,' in which the New Deal bigwig, even at the moment of his greatest power, cannot forgive or forget his exclusion from the Harvard Club he had wanted to make." Indeed, O'Hara was "the first writer . . . to deal fictionally with the social and emotional possibilities of the New Deal dignitaries" (*Critical Essays on John O'Hara* 41–43).

The "New Deal bigwig," an undersecretary in the Roosevelt administration, arrives for lunch at an exclusive men's club in Washington with a former Harvard classmate, who seeks a high-level federal appointment. The undersecretary, "a little man," is called "Joe" by "the man he was to meet, Charles Browning." He is surprised to have heard from Browning, who thanks him for having answered his "letter so promptly." "Well, frankly, there wasn't any use in putting you off. . . . I don't where I'll likely be in a month from now. In more ways than one. I may be taking the Clipper to London, and then of course I may be out on my can! Coming to New York and asking you for a job. I take it that's what you wanted to see me about." Browning replies, "Yes, and with hat in hand." The undersecretary cannot see Browning "waiting with hat in hand" for anybody, "not even for The Boss." Browning laughs and explains to the puzzled undersecretary, "Well, you know how I feel about him, so I'd say least of all The Boss." The undersecretary concedes that Browning has "plenty of company in this goddam town," and therefore wonders why he has come to him.

Why did he not go instead to one of his "Union League or Junior League or whatever-the-hell-it-is pals," for example, "that big jerk over there with the blue suit and the striped tie." Browning looks and the two men nod. "You know him?" the undersecretary asks. "Sure I know him [from New York], but that doesn't mean I approve of him." But "you're not one of our team," the undersecretary observes" and "yet you'd ask me a favor. I don't get it." "Oh, yes you do, Joe. You didn't get where you are by not being able to understand a simple thing like that." Grinning reluctantly, the undersecretary admits that he was "baiting" Browning, who had expected him to do so, for he had "always been against you fellows," even "in 1932." "But that's water under the bridge—or isn't it?" The undersecretary asks why it should be, to which Browning replies, "For the obvious reason." "My country, 'tis of thee?" the undersecretary conjectures. "Exactly. Isn't that enough?" "It isn't enough for your [New York] Racquet Club friend over there." "You keep track of things like that?"

"Certainly," the undersecretary declares, "I know every goddam club in this country, beginning back about twenty-three years ago." He had "had ample time to study them all, objectively, from the outside." Noting that Browning is wearing a wristwatch, the undersecretary asks what happened to "the little animal." Browning pulls out of his pocket a key chain with "a small golden pig," but the undersecretary notes that "a lot of you fellows put them back in your pockets about five years ago, when one of the illustrious brethren closed his downtown office and moved up to Ossining." "Are you still sore at the Pork?" Browning asks, and "Do you think you'd have enjoyed being a member of it? . . . You'd show the bastards. O.K. You showed them. Us. If you hadn't been so sore at the Porcellian so-and-so's, you might have turned into just another lawyer." Mollified, the undersecretary thinks he can help Browning, who wants to order drinks to celebrate. The undersecretary orders a cordial, which he sips, while Browning takes a scotch, half of which he drinks while noting that he had been worried about that "club stuff," adding, "I don't know why fellows like you—you never would have made it in a thousand years," realizing at that moment that he has "said exactly the wrong thing, haven't I?" "That's right, Browning," replies the undersecretary, who leaves, "all dignity."

This conversation occurs in 1943, as can be inferred from the allusion to Richard Whitney (1888–1974), born into a wealthy family in Boston, educated at Groton and Harvard (B.A., 1911), elected to the Porcellian

Club, president of the New York Stock Exchange (1930–35), convicted of embezzlement, and sent to Sing Sing Prison (Ossining, New York) in 1938. The undersecretary, who attended Harvard around 1920 ("about twenty-three years ago"), may be a composite of Sumner Welles, Adolf A. Berle, and FDR. Welles (1892–1961), scion of a rich and socially prominent family in Boston, was educated at Groton and Harvard (B.A., 1914) and served as undersecretary of state (1937–43). Berle (1895–1971), also born in Boston and educated at Harvard (B.A., 1913), served in FDR's "Brain Trust" and then as assistant secretary of state (1938–44). Neither Welles, who was a nonconformist, nor Berle, who lacked the wealth and social status, cared about not being elected to Porcellian. O'Hara's undersecretary is "a little man," but Undersecretary Welles was tall, while Assistant Secretary Berle was short. Welles was forced to resign in August 1943, and Berle was dismissed in November 1944. FDR (1882–1945) was also educated at Groton and Harvard (B.A., 1904) and rejected by Porcellian and confessed later that it was "the greatest disappointment of my life" (Ward 236). Such unnamed historical models (even FDR is referred to only as "The Boss") lend authenticity to O'Hara's undersecretary and Charles Browning, who, as did Richard Whitney (released from Sing Sing in 1941), appears to have worked on Wall Street. In 1940, O'Hara defended FDR against "the fascist bastards who like to say that Roosevelt is a traitor to his class" and contrasted the journalist Heywood Broun (1888–1939), who "honored Harvard by going there," with "a Richard Whitney, who naturally went to Harvard and was a member of the Pork and the crew, and hunted, and did this and that" (*Selected Letters* 157). But in "Graven Image," O'Hara seems to suggest that both the undersecretary and Browning are blinded by their reverence for the Porcellian's "golden pig."

BIBLIOGRAPHY

O'Hara, John. "Graven Image." *New Yorker,* 13 March 1943, pp. 17–18.

———. *Selected Letters of John O'Hara.* Edited by Matthew J. Bruccoli. New York: Random House, 1978.

"Richard Whitney (1888–1974)." Available online. URL: http://wiki.whitneygen.org/wrg/index.php/Archive:Richard_Whitney_(1888–1974). Accessed July 23, 2009.

Schwarz, Jordan A. *Liberal: Adolf A. Berle and the Vision of an American Era.* New York: Free Press, 1987.

Trilling, Lionel. "John O'Hara Observes Our Mores" (review of *Pipe Night*). *New York Times Book Review,* 18 March 1945.

Ward, Geoffrey C. *Before the Trumpet: Young Franklin Roosevelt, 1882–1905.* New York: Harper & Row, 1985.

Welles, Benjamin. *Sumner Welles: FDR's Global Strategist. A Biography.* New York: St. Martin's Press, 1997.

Wolff, Geoffrey. *The Art of Burning Bridges: A Life of John O'Hara.* New York: Knopf, 2003.

Frederick Betz
Southern Illinois University Carbondale

"GREASY LAKE" T. CORAGHESSAN BOYLE (1987)

T. CORAGHESSAN BOYLE's widely anthologized coming-of-age tale, initially published in *Greasy Lake and Other Stories,* tells the story of three young men—Digby, Jeff, and an unnamed narrator—who are abruptly ushered into adulthood through a painful experience at the lake of the story's title on the third night of summer vacation. The story is set in an era that no longer values manners and polite behavior, the narrator tells us. Consequently, the characters strike "elaborate poses" designed to demonstrate how dangerous they are. *Poses* is the operative term here, though, for we quickly learn that these three young men are actually innocent, suburban upper-middle-class college boys whose fascination with an idealized form of DECADENCE demonstrates how far removed they are from the real thing. These boys favor Hollywood movies and the novels of André Gide, while their wildest exploits typically involve drinking excessively and hurling raw eggs at random mail boxes. At Greasy Lake, however, the boys participate in real evil for the first time and are profoundly altered by the experience. In short, they are ushered from the world of innocence to that of experience.

After mistakenly identifying a car parked at Greasy Lake as that of their friend Tony Lovett, Digby, Jeff, and the narrator decide to play a practical joke and harass Lovett, who they suspect is having an intimate moment with his girlfriend. As they begin to flash the lights and honk the horn of the narrator's mother's station wagon, however, it dawns on the narrator that this car is not Lovett's. Indeed, it is the car of a "bad greasy character" with whom the boys soon fight. During the fight, which Boyle depicts as a ritual, the narrator hits the man with a tire iron and assumes he has killed him. The boys then turn to the man's girlfriend. As they are about to attack her, however, another car pulls into the lot and the boys disperse. The narrator dives into the lake, where he encounters a dead body and recoils in horror.

As the narrator and his friends hide in the woods, the "bad greasy character" regains consciousness; he and the boys from the second car then demolish the station wagon. Just after the vandals leave, another car drives into the lot. Two young, drug-addled women step out of the car, one of them saying to the boys, "You guys look like some pretty bad characters" (71). One woman offers the boys drugs, but the narrator, indicating his revulsion at the decadence that had once seemed so appealing, declines the offer, thinking that he "was going to cry" (71). The story concludes as he puts the wrecked and barely drivable car in gear and "creep[s] back toward the highway" (71), back toward a world of innocence that is now, we are led to believe, largely inaccessible to him.

BIBLIOGRAPHY
Boyle, T. Coraghessan. "Greasy Lake." In *An Introduction to Fiction*. 4th ed. Edited by X. J. Kennedy. Boston: Little, Brown.

Shannon Zimmerman
University of Georgia

GREAT DEPRESSION, THE   The Great
Depression began in the United States with the stock market crash of October 1929. Thousands of stockholders, including banks, lost large sums of money, and within a short time many banks, factories, and businesses closed, causing millions of Americans to become jobless. The national unemployment rate, which was 3 percent in 1925, reached 25 percent in 1933. Americans were not the only ones affected; a worldwide business slump in the 1930s made this depression the worst and longest period of high unemployment and low business activity in modern times. It also caused a sharp decrease in world trade as each country tried to protect its own industries by raising

tariffs on imports. The conditions brought on by the depression were a factor in ADOLF HITLER's consolidation of power in Germany and Japan's decision to invade China.

In the United States, farmers were severely affected. The farm depression of the 1920s caused by low prices for farm products became even worse in the 1930s. From 1929 to 1933 prices fell about 50 percent, partly because farmers produced a surplus of crops and partly because high tariffs made exports unprofitable. Severe droughts and dust storms in parts of the Midwest and Southwest created what became known as the Dust Bowl, which destroyed thousands of farms. Many farmers migrated west to seek work in the fertile agricultural areas of California.

Shortly after being sworn in as president in 1933, Franklin D. Roosevelt called Congress into a special session, known as the Hundred Days, to pass a massive legislative package to relieve the depression. This program, called the New Deal, established relief programs such as the Civilian Conservation Corps (CCC) and Works Progress Administration (WPA) and recovery programs including the National Recovery Administration (NRA) and the Public Works Administration (PWA). It also created agencies to supervise banking and labor reforms: the Federal Deposit Insurance Corporation (FDIC) to insure bank deposits, the National Labor Relations Board (NLRB) to prevent unfair labor practices and monitor union elections, and the Securities and Exchange Commission (SEC) to protect investors from buying unsafe stocks and bonds. The Social Security Act (1935) provided money to retired and unemployed persons.

Although the New Deal programs may have increased the confidence of many Americans in their government, the depression continued, and about 15 percent of the workforce was still unemployed in 1940. The Great Depression did not end in the United States until 1942, with the nation's entry into WORLD WAR II.

The depression gave rise to such groups as the American Writers' Congress of 1935, many of whose members advocated PROLETARIAN LITERATURE, and to magazines such as *Partisan Review, New Masses,* and the *Anvil.* The era provides a powerful backdrop for numerous stories by such writers as SAUL BELLOW, JAMES BALDWIN, F. SCOTT FITZGERALD, ERNEST HEMINGWAY, LANGSTON HUGHES, ZORA NEALE HURSTON, MERIDEL LESUEUR, TILLIE OLSEN, DOROTHY PARKER, and JOHN STEINBECK.

"GREENLEAF" FLANNERY O'CONNOR (1956)

By emphasizing intense archetypal imagery, FLANNERY O'CONNOR raises her short story "Greenleaf" to a complex level. O'Connor's choice of symbolic names, her suggestion of mythological fertility cults, and her use of light and dark images all serve to raise the reader's consciousness regarding class prejudice, and to paint an accurate picture of the New South, where individuals of little heritage have begun a systematic takeover from those landowners once identified as aristocrats.

O'Connor uses a third-person limited omniscient POINT OF VIEW to tell the story of Mrs. May (a questionable aristocrat with limited potential) and her two sons, Wesley and Scofield. These sons are contrasted with the earthy Greenleaf, a lower-class hired man whom Mrs. May has employed to look after her property, and to Greenleaf's twin boys, O. T. and E. T. Mrs. Greenleaf also serves as a FOIL to Mrs. May as the hopeless widow who, forced to undergo a self-evaluation, tries at the same time to come to terms with the changing conditions of her environment. Her former feelings of power in her household have shifted strangely, and the rise of individuals like the Greenleaf family (whose name suggests progress and growth) suggests to her that the control she so values is gradually being subsumed by "white trash" people whose social heritage is questionable at best.

O'Connor uses a scrub bull ordinary and lacking in pedigree, belonging to O. T. and E. T. as a symbol for the encroaching aggression of this "lower" class. The archetypal bull (indicative of mythical sexuality, as in the Minoan culture in general and the Greek myth of Europa in particular), having escaped from the Greenleaf boys' pasture, first appears outside Mrs. Greenleaf's house, devouring her foliage. Mrs. May views its escape as a threat to her own herd of cattle, indeed to her very existence. If the bull, with its inferior genes, is allowed to breed with her herd, the offspring will no doubt be inferior as well. The bull's desire to mate

and its less-than-satisfactory breeding quality suggest a parallel to the Greenleafs, who also pose a threat to the "superior" May family. While her two sons dissipate their lives with disappointing occupations (Scofield sells "nigger" insurance and Wesley teaches at a second-rate university), Mrs. May observes that the Greenleaf boys have had distinguished military careers, married French wives, and produced offspring as well as developed a state-of-the-art milk farm. Automated and advanced by its owners' persistence and determination, the Greenleaf farm is shown to be productive, as opposed to the sterility represented by the Mays. The narrator implies the takeover of a lazy, unconcerned society by a tough (although genealogically less impressive) new working class.

Once again O'Connor centers on the sin of pride. As Mrs. May egotistically bewails her fate at the hands of inferiors, it becomes obvious that despite her so-called iron hand, her farm has withered and her own offspring have lost respect for her. Their sarcastic and mocking back talk suggests their own awareness of their mother's flaws, while their apathy toward their own situations implies that there are real reasons behind their failure to obtain the success attained by their doubles.

Mrs. May shows her determination to regain control and assert her power in her attempt to force Mr. Greenleaf into killing the scrub bull and eliminating its potential to "romance" her. Combining light and dark imagery (Mrs. May's growing insight is suggested through recurring sun images), O'Connor asks a PROTAGONIST to confront who she really is as opposed as to whom she mistakenly identifies with and who she desires to be. Unfortunately, Mrs. May persists in her delusions, seeing herself as her own God and dismissing the primitive religiosity of Mrs. Greenleaf as meaningless ritual rather than a true trust in a higher power.

Mr. Greenleaf is expected to perform his god's/employer's every demand, and, as he reluctantly contemplates the task of tracking down and shooting the bull, Mrs. May is ironically led to confront her tormentor and nemesis face to face. O'Connor again employs light imagery as Mrs. May appears deliberately to close her eyes to the truth despite the brightness that encompasses her. Instead she envisions Mr. Greenleaf being gored to death by the bull and thus removed as a potential threat. Because of her impatience with Greenleaf's hesitancy, she attempts to summon him by honking a truck horn, an act that infuriates the bull, which not only charges Mrs. May but inflicts an ironic reversal on her by goring her to death, burying its horns in her lap. This act completes the sexual merger that O'Connor's imagery has implied throughout the story and reiterates a frequent O'Connor THEME: Only in death does understanding of self become complete. O'Connor closes by describing Mrs. May as one who has regained her sight but who cannot bear looking at the brilliant light. As her life expires, her final discovery is shown to be in vain: Human pride is revealed as the most destructive element in the effort to discover one's true self.

Michael J. Meyer
DePaul University

"GREVILLE FANE" HENRY JAMES (1892)

Written in 1892, HENRY JAMES's short story "Greville Fane" depicts the troubled and tumultuous relationship between a popular novelist, Greville Fane, and her two ungrateful children, Lady Ethel Luard and Leolin. The short story begins with the narrator's receiving news of Greville Fane's impending death and then chronicles the unsettled connection that exists between the children and their mother. Clearly, Greville Fane—whose real name is *Mrs. Stormer*—wants the best for her children, mainly entry into society for Ethel and a life of luxury for Leolin. Both children, however, only use their mother to further their own desires, so much so that the narrator doubts the innocence of Greville Fane's death, implying that both Leolin and Lady Luard had motive to assist in the old woman's death. On the surface, James seems to focus on this rocky relationship between the mother and her daughter and son. However, a closer read suggests that James uses "Greville Fane" to wrestle with his own demons about authorship.

Early in the story readers learn that *Greville Fane* is the pseudonym Mrs. Stormer uses to write her popular fiction, fiction that—at least for James—bor-

ders on the formulaic. James makes it clear that Fane is not a very good writer: "Her [Fane's] table was there, the battered and blotted accessory to innumerable literary lapses, with its contracted space for the arms (she wrote from the elbow down) and the confusion of scrappy, scribbled sheets which had already become literary remains" (218). James's narrator reminds the reader that Fane has written many stories: "The dear woman had written a hundred stories" (219).

For James's narrator, Fane's writing is an escape from literature. That narrator states, "This was why I liked her—she rested me so from literature. To myself literature was an irritation, a torment; but Greville Fane slumbered in the intellectual part of it like a Creole in a hammock" (219–220). But the narrator does not end here in his condemnation of Fane, and by implication, popular fiction. For James's narrator, Fane lacks language skills, and this shows in Fane's inherent ability to develop plot with no attention to the English language. James writes, "She could invent stories by the yard, but she couldn't write a page of English. She went down to her grave without suspecting that though she had contributed volumes to the diversion of her contemporaries she had not contributed a sentence to the language" (220).

James tells his readers early in the text that Fane does not pretend to write great novels. According to James, "She made no pretence of producing works of art, but had comfortable tea-drinking hours in which she freely confessed herself a common pastrycook, dealing in such tarts and puddings as would bring customers to the shop" (221). Thus, James's narrator criticizes Fane for catering to her audience, which enables her to sell so many books. For the narrator—and James—this type of selling out was to be avoided at all costs, and the selling out was the division between popular works and great literature. James's narrator even gives us a glimpse of Fane's inability to capture accents in dialogue in her novels. James writes, "Greville Fane's French and Italian were droll; the imitative faculty had been denied her, and she had an unequalled gift, especially pen in hand, of squeezing big mistakes into small opportunities. She knew it, but she didn't care; correctness was the virtue in the world, that, like her heroes and heroines, she valued least" (226). So for Fane, the emphasis is on selling the novel, not on the correctness of form, even if it means selling out.

At the end of "Greville Fane," we learn that Fane is writing novels to support her children. The narrator tells us that he discovers Fane's fiction at his club: "She kept it up amazingly, and every few months, at my club, I saw three new volumes, in green, in crimson, in blue, on the book-table that groaned with light literature" (233). So, not only is Fane supporting her children, but she is supporting them by composing popular fiction—or light literature—at an alarming rate. By calling attention to Fane's ability to write this popular fiction at such an old age and in such a rapid progression, James—through his narrator—obviously questions the validity of such works.

On the surface, "Greville Fane" presents a story of sour relationships between a writer and her children. However, James cleverly uses this setting and plot to establish and work out his own frustrations with writers of popular fiction. Frequently referred to as the father of the modern novel, James himself never published a best seller in his time. In fact, James at one point used money from what he thought was an advance on his work but was actually money fronted by his contemporary and friend EDITH WHARTON. Is it any wonder that he resented the popularity of a certain kind of fiction?

BIBLIOGRAPHY
James, Henry. "Greville Fane." In *Henry James: Complete Stories 1892–1898*. New York: Penguin, 1996.

Chris L. Massey
Wright State University

GROTESQUE Originally used to describe ancient paintings and decorations found in the *grotte,* or underground chambers, of Roman ruins, the term *grotesque* in fiction applies to fantastic (see FANTASY), bizarre, often ugly or unnatural presentations of characters, themes, and moods. It is widely perceived as an American genre, dating back to EDGAR ALLAN POE's 19th-century *Tales of the Grotesque and Arabesque,* continuing into the 20th century in SHERWOOD ANDERSON's *WINESBURG, OHIO [A Book of the Grotesque]* and in stories by such writers as ERSKINE CALDWELL, WILLIAM FAULKNER, FLANNERY O'CONNOR, and EUDORA WELTY.

GUGGENHEIM GRANT (JOHN SIMON GUGGENHEIM MEMORIAL FOUNDATION FELLOWSHIP) Established by U.S. senator and Mrs. Simon Guggenheim as a memorial to their son, who died on April 26, 1922, the Guggenheim grant recognizes men and women of high intellectual and personal qualifications who have already demonstrated a capacity for productive scholarship or exceptional creative ability in the arts.

H

"HAIRCUT" RING LARDNER **(1925)** Literary small-town life at its most positive is crafted in ways that celebrate community, collaboration, and the gentle accommodation of vulnerability and eccentricities. RING LARDNER's "Haircut," however, once referred to as "one of the cruelest pieces of American fiction" (Hardwick 1963), uses small-town life to expose the weaknesses, irony, and coldhearted self-interest inherent in the social contract of relationships. Lardner, well recognized for his bitter and cynical stories overflowing with greed, dishonesty, and cruel humor, created a small fictitious town somewhere in Michigan; opened a barbershop; filled it with locals; and sat a stranger down in the chair for a haircut. The narrative that follows, rendered as close to fiction as to reality from one moment to the next, is delivered by "Whitey," the town barber, who slowly winds his way—from one point of divergence to another—along the story of the murder of the town prankster, Jim Kendall.

The story's narration takes place entirely in the barbershop—perhaps as the day's entertainment—since the shop is a much less lively place, the stranger is told, without Jim. During the course of the visitor's haircut, Whitey pays homage to Jim, his death, and his practical jokes, drawing in the town's main characters, all of whose lives have been touched by his malicious humor: Hod Myers, Jim's former partner in crime, who tries his best to carry on without him; Doc Stair, the town's handsome new young doctor; Julie Gregg, the too-smart-to-fit-in local girl secretly in love with him; young Paul Dickson, who, brain damaged in a fall, is an easy target for Jim; and of course, Jim's wife and children, who bear the brunt of his cruelty. All of these characters are linked in a web of emotions and interactions that ultimately lead to Jim's demise.

In ways similar to Lardner's prior work (for example, the satirical "Alibi Ike" [1915], *You Know Me, Al* [1916], and *Gullible's Travels, Etc.* [1917]), "Haircut" excavates the moral codes of everyday life—the mundane yet complex negotiations of relationships carried out over time, and the intentions behind them—in order to condemn the flaws and shortcomings found in one and all. No character remains untainted. There is no portrayal that is fully good or fully bad, no right or wrong, black or white: merely a pack of moral dalmatians. In this story, Lardner's focus is on the town's collective give and take—the shared habits and rationalizations that maintain the status quo and allow its inhabitants to rest comfortably in the "the way things have always been." But there is purpose to Lardner's irony and satire, for with it, he constructs an examination of values, social strategies, power, and acquiescence within this muddled social setting, constructing a morality tale and providing "social correction" for the reader—life lessons admonishing against the flaws found unchecked in the author's characters (Cowlishaw 1994).

But in "Haircut," the exact intention of those life lessons has been left open for debate. As Whitey narrates the tale of Jim Kendall's death, he appears to look back on Jim's cruel brand of practical jokes with a sense of fondness. As the barber gradually reveals tales of Jim's malicious pranks against total strangers, his heartless behavior toward his wife and children, and the attempted rape of the town's eye-catching young Julie Gregg, Whitey ritualistically concludes each episode's telling by reaffirming that yes, indeed, Jim was a "card"—a "character" who "just couldn't resist no kind of a joke, no matter how raw" (30–31). Jim's humor was menacing, victimizing all who received its attention, and yet appears to have received the approval of his Saturday morning audience at the barbershop. Lardner forces the reader to consider these responses, and the range of possible motivations for them. Is Whitey, a seemingly benign character, so cruel, himself, as to be truly indifferent to Jim's malice? Does he lack the critical abilities or intelligence to recognize the difference between humor and brutality? Or is Whitey far less obtuse than he appears and, in fact, one of many participants in a dance between a small town and its bully (May 1973)? Jim's practical jokes wield the power of indifference—abusing friend and foe, the hearty and the helpless. Jim's behavior, while part of the town's everyday life, is bubbling with potential for destroying the social contract—the comfort of certainty. Rather than risk confrontation, the townspeople give Jim his way—allowing him territorial rights to his own special chair in the barbershop and forcing smiles at his cruel tricks and jabs. What appears to be amused approval of Jim's antics, might, as May points out, be capitulation—going along to get along—because the universe of small-town America, with its dependence on intimacy and face-to-face relationships, is ill suited to discord. Cleanth Brooks and Robert Penn Warren also recognize these "ripples of complicity" that inhere in the townspeople's reactions to Jim—other than those of Paul, who by virtue of being "crazy" is at least partially excluded from the normative social contract that binds the town and shoots Jim.

Once Jim has been killed, the town creates yet another sort of complicity or contract—the agreement that his death was accidental. It is here that Lardner leads the reader into complicity, as well—guaranteeing fulfillment of the author's cynical expectations that the worst of human nature will rise to the surface. At best, readers believe, with Whitey, that "Jim was a sucker" for handing his gun over to an inexperienced hunter, and at the worst, they believe he had it coming (May). Through this strategy, Lardner redirects the critical gaze, from the story's characters to the readers, as a reminder that they are deserving of his critical social commentary.

BIBLIOGRAPHY

Blythe, Hal, and Charlie Sweet. "The Barber of Civility: The Chief Conspirator of Haircut." *Studies in Short Fiction* 23 (1986): 450–453.

Brooks, Cleanth, and Robert Penn Warren. *Understanding Fiction.* New York: Appleton, Century, Crofts, 1959.

Cowlishaw, Brian. "The Reader's Role in Ring Lardner's Rhetoric." *Studies in Short Fiction* 31, no. 2 (Spring 1994): 207.

Hardwick, Elizabeth. "Ring." *New York Review of Books* 1, no. 1, 1963.

Gilead, Sarah. "Lardner's Discourses of Power." *Studies in Short Fiction* 22 (1985): 331–337.

May, Charles E. "Lardner's Haircut." *Explicator* 31, no. 9 (1973): 133–135.

Cynthia J. Miller
Emerson College

HAMMETT, DASHIELL (SAMUEL DASHIELL HAMMETT) (1894–1961)

A leading exponent of the "hard-boiled" school of detective writing, Hammett used his eight years of experience as a Pinkerton detective to give his stories authenticity. (See HARD-BOILED FICTION.) His stories are fast paced and intricately plotted, frequently violent, and realistic (see REALISM), although his style is spare. Many critics credit him with elevating the detective story to the level of literature in terms of sophisticated plot and original characterization. Most of his more than 75 stories first appeared in the popular magazine BLACK MASK, and his most famous work, *The Maltese Falcon,* was first published in that magazine as a five-part serial. In that novel he introduced the classic tough, realistic, hard-boiled detective, SAM SPADE. Virtually all of Hammett's published writing was done between 1922 and 1934, but in that time he transformed the genre of detective fiction and strongly influenced later writers in the field such as RAYMOND CHANDLER, Horace McCoy, and ERLE STANLEY GARDNER.

See also DETECTIVE SHORT FICTION.

BIBLIOGRAPHY

Edenbaum, Robert I. "The Poetics of the Private Eye: The Novels of Hammett." In *Tough Guy Writers of the Thirties,* edited by David Madden. Carbondale: Southern Illinois University Press, 1968.

Durham, Philip. "The Black Mask School." In *Tough Guy Writers of the Thirties,* edited by David Madden. Carbondale: Southern Illinois University Press, 1968.

Gregory, Sinda. *Private Investigations: The Novels of Hammett.* Carbondale: Southern Illinois University Press, 1984.

Hammett, Dashiell. *The Adventures of Sam Spade and Other Stories.* Edited by Ellery Queen. New York: Dell, 1944. As *They Can Only Hang You Once,* 1949; selection, as *A Man Called Spade,* 1945.

———. *The Big Knockover: Selected Stories and Short Novels.* New York: Random House, 1966. As *The Hammett Story Omnibus.* Edited by Lillian Hellman. London: Cassell, 1966.

———. *The Continental Op.* New York: Dell, 1945.

———. *The Continental Op: More Stories from the Big Knockover.* New York: Dell, 1925.

———. *The Creeping Siamese.* New York: Dell, 1950.

———. *Dashiell Hammett Omnibus.* New York: Grosset & Dunlap, 1930.

———. *Dead Yellow Women.* New York: Dell, 1947.

———. *Hammett Homicides.* New York: Dell, 1946.

———. *The Maltese Falcon.* New York: Knopf, 1930.

———. *A Man Named Thin, and Other Stories.* New York: Ferman, 1962.

———. *Nightmare Town.* New York: Dell, 1948.

———. *Red Harvest.* New York: Knopf, 1929.

———. *The Return of the Continental Op.* New York: Dell, 1945.

———. *Woman in the Dark.* New York: Lawrence E. Spivak, 1951.

Hellman, Lillian. *An Unfinished Woman.* Boston: Little, Brown, 1969.

———. *Pentimento.* Boston: Little, Brown, 1973.

———. *Scoundrel Time.* Boston: Little, Brown, 1976.

Johnson, Diane. *The Life of Dashiell Hammett.* London: Chatto and Windus, 1983. As *Dashiell Hammett: A Life.* New York: Fawcett Columbine, 1985.

Layman, Richard. *Shadow Man: The Life of Hammett.* New York: Harcourt Brace, 1981.

Marling, William. *Dashiell Hammett.* Boston: Twayne, 1983.

Nolan, William F. *Hammett: A Casebook.* Santa Barbara, Calif.: McNally & Loftin, 1969.

———. *Hammett: A Life at the Edge.* New York: Congdon and Weed, 1983.

Symons, Julian. *Hammett.* San Diego: Harcourt Brace, 1985.

Wolfe, Peter. *Beams Falling: The Art of Hammett.* Bowling Green, Ohio: Bowling Green University Popular Press, 1980.

"HANDS" SHERWOOD ANDERSON SHERWOOD ANDERSON's story "Hands" might be called a portrait. Like a formal painted portrait, it not only depicts Wing Biddlebaum, the central figure, as he exists but also uses background props to reveal his past and define his circumstances. Wing's hands are the focal image of the portrait. The story also depends for effect on a series of painterly tableaux, from the sunset landscape with berry pickers with which it begins to the silhouette of Wing as a holy hermit, praying over and over the rosary of his lonely years of penance for a sin he did not commit. The use of synecdoche in which a part becomes representative of the whole, in the title keeps the tale of the unfortunate Wing in the reader's memory; we recall his hands far longer than we do his name.

Part of Anderson's SHORT STORY CYCLE *WINESBURG, OHIO* (1919), "Hands" also features GEORGE WILLARD, the reporter in the tales who, as a character in his own right, may be viewed as the progenitor of ERNEST HEMINGWAY's NICK ADAMS. George is one of the few people in Winesburg who feel sympathetic to the peculiar Wing, and Wing will speak to no one but George. Wing had arrived in Winesburg two decades previously under unexplained circumstances. Gradually the unnamed third-person narrator reveals Wing's background: He had been a teacher in Pennsylvania, popular and well liked by the boys who attended his school. Wing treated them gently, touching their shoulders or tousling their hair. Through a series of misunderstandings, a half-witted boy accuses Wing of making sexual advances on him, and Wing barely escapes the boys' outraged fathers. Neither Wing nor George Willard experiences any clear revelation or makes any climactic decision. Wing never understands why he was driven out of Pennsylvania—he realizes only dimly that his hands were somehow to blame—and George is afraid to ask the questions that might lead them both to a liberating understanding of Wing's experience.

The reader, however, is not permitted to remain in the dark. With the clear understanding of the way the crudity and narrow-minded suspicion of his neighbors have perverted Wing's selfless and innocent love for his students into a source of fear and shame comes a poignant sorrow for the waste of a good man's life. Wing's hands may be the pride of Winesburg for their agility at picking strawberries, but the nurturing love that they betoken is feared by everyone, including George and even Wing himself, whose loneliness is as great as his capacity to love, and from which, by a cruel irony, it arises.

"HAPPY ENDINGS" MARGARET ATWOOD (1983)

An innovative and oft-anthologized story that demonstrates the arbitrariness of any author's choice of an ending, "Happy Endings" offers six different endings from which the reader may choose. "Happy Endings" was first published in the Canadian collection *Murder in the Dark* (1983) and then became available in the United States in *Good Bones and Simple Murders* (1994). Intentionally written in only 1,500 words, the story contains little plot, little character development, and little motivation. Readers, however, should not be deceived: MARGARET ATWOOD is, according to the critic Reingard M. Nischik, "a chronicler of our times, exposing and warning, disturbing and comforting, opening up chasms of meaning as soon as she closes them, and challenging us to question conventions and face up to hitherto unarticulated truths" (159). "Happy Endings" is a story about writing a story, with thoughtful advice to both readers and would-be writers. In this unusual tale she demonstrates why "who and what" are insufficient; the reader must ask (and the writer must supply) "how and why." In addition to analyzing the appropriateness of the six endings, the reader might profit from comparing "Happy Endings" to ROBERT COOVER's "THE BABYSITTER," in which the author offers several possibilities of

what happens to the babysitter, leaving the decision to the reader's imagination; and Akira Kurosawa's 1951 film *Roshomon,* which depicts the rape of a bride and the murder of her husband through various eyewitness accounts; it demonstrates the near-impossibility of arriving at the actual "truth" of the events.

Atwood's technique differs from that of Coover and Kurosawa, however, in that she fleshes out nothing: Indeed, the six possible endings to the story of John and Mary are written as a skeletal outline. She opens with the words, "John and Mary meet. What happens next? If you want a happy ending, try A." (1).

In A, John and Mary live a richly fulfilling life in terms of careers, sex life, children, vacations, and retirement, until they die. In Ending B, however, Mary loves John but he does not return her love, instead using and abusing her in classical doormat fashion. When Mary learns of John's affair with Madge, she commits suicide, John marries Madge, and we are told to move to Ending A.

In Ending C, John is an older man married to Madge and the father of two children. He falls for the 22-year-old Mary, but when he finds her in the arms of James, he shoots all three of them. Madge marries a man named Fred and proceeds to Ending A. In Ending D, Fred and Madge are the sole survivors of a tidal wave, and, despite the loss of their home, they are grateful to have survived the calamity that killed thousands and continue to Ending A.

Ending E follows Fred to his death of a "bad heart." Madge soldiers on with charity and volunteer work in Ending A, until she dies of cancer—or, if the reader prefers, becomes guilt-ridden or begins bird-watching. Finally, for those who find Endings A through E "too bourgeois," Atwood suggests making John and Mary spies and revolutionaries. Still, though, they will end up at Ending A because, after all, "this is Canada" (3). The only authentic ending, says Atwood, is this one: *"John and Mary die. John and Mary die. John and Mary die."* As the critic Nathalie Cooke points out, "For Atwood, writing is a fascinating but dark art—one where shadows lurk, not only in the subject matter . . . but also in the author's role as a double being, and in the writing process itself, in which the writer must not only face the darkness, but learn to see in and through it" (19). As Atwood suggests to the readers at the conclusion of "Happy Endings," that process is achieved by understanding motivation through asking "how" and "why."

BIBLIOGRAPHY

Atwood, Margaret. "Happy Endings." In *Murder in the Dark*. Dallas, Tex.: Bookman, 1996. Available online. URL: http://users.ipfw.edu/ruflethe/endings.htm. Accessed May 2, 2009.

Cooke, Nathalie. *Margaret Atwood: A Critical Companion*. Westport, Conn.: Greenwood Press, 2004.

Nischik, Reingard M. "Margaret Atwood's Short Stories and Shorter Fictions." In *The Cambridge Companion to Margaret Atwood,* edited by Coral Ann Howells, 145–160. New York: Cambridge University Press, 2006.

HARA, MARIE (1943–)

Born and raised in Honolulu, where she currently lives, Marie Hara is a writer, teacher, journalist, and publicist. Her stories have been published in *Bamboo Ridge, Chaminade Literary Review,* and *Honolulu Magazine*; they appear with increasing frequency in anthologies of adolescent and ASIAN-AMERICAN LITERATURE and were published as a collection entitled *Bananaheart* in 1994. Hara has been active in promoting literature and the arts in Hawaii, working for the Hawaii Literary Arts Council and codirecting the first Talk Story Conference in 1978.

Her stories, as do those of her fellow Hawaiian DARRELL H. Y. LUM, often employ Hawaiian Creole English; Hara is especially gifted in hearing how people of all ages talk and, largely through dialogue, creating sharply delineated and convincing CHARACTERs in her stories. An important THEME is that despite Hawaii's multicultural society, not all cultures are equally valued or respected.

BIBLIOGRAPHY

Hara, Marie. *Bananaheart and Other Stories: A Collection of Short Stories*. Honolulu: Bamboo Ridge Press, 1994.

Hara, Marie, and Nora Okja Keller. *Intersecting Circles: The Voices of Hapa Women in Poetry and Prose (Bamboo Ridge, No. 76)*. Honolulu: Bamboo Ridge Press, 1999.

Keith Lawrence
Brigham Young University

HARA, MAVIS (1949–)

Mavis Hara was born and raised in Honolulu. She received her B.A. from the University of Hawaii and her M.A. in education from the University of California, Santa Barbara. In addition to working as a freelance and professional writer, she has taught English in Japan. Her fiction has appeared in *Bamboo Ridge* and in several anthologies.

Because many of her stories have teenage PROTAGONISTS, she has acquired a reputation and following as an author of adolescent literature. Her characters are vivid, funny, and absolutely convincing. Beneath the casual tone, however, Hara's fiction is invariably concerned with significant ethnic THEMES: America's cultural colonization of much of the world, racial and gender inequity, the perpetuation of Eurocentric ideals in Asian-American communities, the plight of contemporary Hawaiians, and the continuing dilution of Hawaiian culture. Indeed, most of these themes may be found in her most recent story collection, *An Offering of Rice* (2007).

Keith Lawrence
Brigham Young University

HARD-BOILED FICTION

A type of American crime story, closely associated with the magazine *BLACK MASK* (founded 1919), this genre is characterized by a strong sense of REALISM generated by laconic, often crude dialogue; the depiction of cruelty and bloodshed at close range; and the use of sordid environments. DASHIELL HAMMETT, who wrote his stories for *Black Mask,* is the acknowledged founder and chief proponent of this type of writing, which subsequently was used by others, including RAYMOND CHANDLER and ERLE STANLEY GARDNER. Early works in this genre were critically acclaimed as serious literature, and Hammett was frequently compared to ERNEST HEMINGWAY, but later novels of this type, by such writers as Mickey Spillane, degenerated into sensationalism and gratuitous violence.

"HARD RIDING" D'ARCY McNICKLE

Most of D'ARCY McNICKLE's short fiction was published posthumously in a 1992 collection titled *"The Hawk Is*

Hungry" and Other Stories, yet McNickle is still seen as an important and influential person in American Indian literary studies. His most widely known work of fiction, his novel *The Surrounded,* was published in 1936, and he was also the author of important works dealing with American Indian culture, including his popular work titled *Native American Tribalism* (1962).

It is impossible to date the story "Hard Riding," but it made its first appearance in print in the 1980s. The story concerns the experiences of Brinder Mather, a government agent living on the reservation of a fictional tribe called the Mountain Indians (McNickle often used fictional tribes in his work). Specifically, the story focuses on Brinder's attempt to convince the tribal elders to set up a tribal court to prosecute and punish those on the reservation who have been stealing cattle. He had previously convinced the tribe to establish a "stock association," whereby all members of the tribe contribute to the work of raising and selling cattle and all benefit from the profits. However, there are some who will not do their share of the work and steal cattle instead. His goal is to convince the tribe to take this matter into their own hands by establishing a court that will punish those offenders. Most of the story's plot concerns the meeting he has with the Tribal Council, which basically ends with the Indians' making a fool of Mather.

Brinder Mather represents a stock character found in many examples of American Indian writing. He is the semisympathetic white, and in this case, he is a sympathetic white government official (similar to the agent in McNickle's novel *Wind from an Enemy Sky*). He seems to want to work with and help the tribe that is his responsibility. For example, his convincing the tribe to set up a stock association so that the tribe can be financially responsible for itself does not seem to be a bad idea. The problem, though, with many of the sympathetic whites like Mather and even those in real life is that they lack a true understanding of American Indian ways of life. To Mather, and others like him, the concept is simple: Join the mainstream white culture by pursuing economic interests, leave the reservations and go to the cities to find jobs, learn English, learn a trade—the list goes on and on. But the fact

remains that many of the ideas of the mainstream culture do not gel with tribal culture.

It is true that Mather has had success reaching out to the Mountain Tribe. In order to persuade them to form a stock association, he pretends to understand their culture. He tells them: "Indians don't know, more than that don't give a damn, about dragging their feet behind a plow. Don't say as I blame 'em. But Indians'll always ride horses. They're born to that. And if they're going to ride horses they might as well be riding herd on a bunch of steers. It pays money" (5). Thinking that Mather is on their side, the Indians are willing to go along with his scheme. But his idea of a tribal court, which will try and prosecute other Indians, fails miserably because it runs counter to the Indian sense of community.

Thus the title, "Hard Riding," becomes important. Mather is known as a person who pushes his horse too hard when he rides, as McNickle points out: "It was a habit with the rider" (3). And the story begins with Mather riding hard on his way to the meeting with the Tribal Council. But his attempts to push his way of thinking by riding over the tribe do not work. The tribe cannot be tricked into giving up their native traditions. Mather knows that when they are presented with a new concept, the Indians will take their time absorbing and considering it, will ask questions, and will attempt to stall the process. And he attempts to push his agenda quickly this time, telling himself not to stall and give them the upper hand. Ironically, he begins the meeting by telling the tribe that they "have learned a lot since I been with you" (5), but Mather himself has not learned. Once they are presented with the idea of the court, the tribe begins to ask questions, and he knew, or at least thought, "that they hadn't the least idea what he was driving at" (7). The tribal elders then speak, and they slowly begin to undermine his idea. The basic problem they have is deciding who would serve as a judge on the tribal court. The real problem may be that the idea of prosecuting someone for stealing cattle instead of starving does not make sense to them. Finally, the tribe presents their nominees for judges: "an aged imbecile dripping saliva," another who is "stone deaf and blind," and another who is "an utter fool, a half-witted clown, to whom no one listened" (10). Mather realizes then that he is the butt of a joke. With all his experience dealing with Indians, he has let this group fool him. In a classic example of the Indian sense of humor, Mather's idea falls apart.

But it fails, not because the Indians are vindictive, but because Mather's idea is one that is alien to their culture. Mather has good intentions, but that is not enough. What he lacks is understanding.

BIBLIOGRAPHY

Allen, Paula Gunn. "Whose Dream Is This Anyway?" In *The Sacred Hoop: Recovering the Feminine in American Indian Traditions.* Boston: Beacon Press, 1986.

McNickle, D'Arcy. "Hard Riding." In *"The Hawk Is Hungry" and Other Stories,* edited by Birgit Hans. Tucson: University of Arizona Press, 1992.

Owens, Louis. "Maps of the Mind: John Joseph Mathews and D'Arcy McNickle." In *Other Destinies: Understanding the American Indian Novel.* Norman: University of Oklahoma Press, 1992.

James Mayo
Jackson State Community College

HARLEM RENAISSANCE   This historical period, also known as the New Negro Renaissance, refers to the proliferation of literature, music, visual arts, and political essays by African-American and African-Caribbean writers and artists living or working in the Harlem neighborhood of New York City in the 1920s. Most cultural historians designate 1925 as the inaugural year of the Harlem Renaissance. In March 1924, Charles Johnson, editor of *Opportunity* magazine, hosted a dinner at the racially integrated Civic Club. Known as the "dress rehearsal" of the Harlem Renaissance, the dinner gathered together black writers and white editors and publishers to recognize a number of emerging black writers, such as ZORA NEALE HURSTON and JEAN TOOMER. Their work was the first to receive serious critical attention since James Weldon Johnson's *Autobiography of an Ex-Coloured Man* (1916) and W. E. B. DuBois's *Darkwater* (1920). Among the white guests was Paul Kellogg, editor of the *Survey Graphic,* who offered to devote an entire issue of his magazine to black arts and letters. Kellogg's special edition "Harlem: Mecca of the New Negro" appeared in March 1925 and included articles on race prejudice, jazz, and Harlem as well as poetry and short stories such as DuBois's "The Black Man Brings His Gifts" and Rudolph Fisher's "The South Lingers On." The *Opportunity* dinner (and its subsequent literary contest) as well as the *Survey Graphic* issue inspired Alain Locke to edit *The New Negro,* an anthology of drawings, essays, poetry, and short stories, which was published at the end of 1925. Most of the black fiction writers whose names have become nearly synonymous with the Harlem Renaissance contributed short stories to *The New Negro.* The anthology includes Rudolph Fisher's "The City of Refuge" and "Vestiges"; two sections of Jean Toomer's lengthy prose poem *CANE*; and Zora Neale Hurston's "Spunk."

The editor Alain Locke was known, along with Charles Johnson, as one of the "midwives" of the Harlem Renaissance. In his introduction to *The New Negro* he rallied black and white intellectuals, artists, and writers to recognize that "for the present, more immediate hope [for alleviating race prejudice] rests in the reevaluation by white and black alike of the Negro in terms of his artistic endowments and cultural contributions, past and prospective" (15). Locke's statement marks the spirit of optimism and the focus on artistic production associated with Harlem in the 1920s. However, it also points to several disputes within the Harlem community. First, Harvard-educated Locke and other "midwives" were criticized for being elitist, for ignoring and silencing the working class by granting black intellectuals alone the responsibility for uplifting the race. Second, W. E. B. DuBois voiced the concern that the kind of interracial collaboration Locke called for would result in black writers' pandering to the desires of a white publishing industry that continued to market less-than-uplifting representations of blacks. (The most extreme criticism of interracial relations during this period was that of Marcus Garvey, whose back-to-Africa campaign attracted thousands of mostly working-class Harlemites.) Although DuBois shared Locke's goal of using artistic production to uplift the race, he was concerned that black writers would strip their work of any overtly political content in order to make it more palatable to white audiences and critics.

DuBois represented the older generation of intellectuals who, from the turn of the century through the 1920s, helped to set the stage for the Harlem Renaissance. Locke, Hurston, LANGSTON HUGHES, and Claude McKay were part of the younger generation whose writing reflected a departure from didactic conventions devoted to conservative or "middle-class" representations of the black community. *Fire!!* a journal "Devoted to the Younger Artists," which, because of lack of funding, saw only one printing, promised a more AVANT-GARDE forum than the literary department of DuBois's *Crisis*. Younger-generation writers often included in their fiction representations of the working class through rural South folk THEMES or gritty urban settings, thinly veiled sexual references, and the speakeasy/cabaret life in Harlem. *Fire!* gave the writer Richard Bruce Nugent his Harlem Renaissance debut with his short story "Smoke, Lilies, and Jade," which further fueled DuBois's fear that the new writers would "turn the Negro renaissance into decadence." Other short story contributions to *Fire!!* included Hurston's "SWEAT," Wallace Thurman's "Cordelia the Crude," and Gwendolyn Bennet's "Wedding Day."

Many cultural histories and criticism of the period associate the beginning of the GREAT DEPRESSION in 1929 with the end (and the "failure") of the Harlem Renaissance. Some critics judge the movement a failure because of writers' and artists' inability to ameliorate race prejudice, and their economic dependence on white patrons and publishers. This criticism tends to overlook the important alliances that the period fostered between black writers and publishers such as Alfred Knopf, Albert Boni, and Horace Liveright, as well as the mutual cultural and intellectual borrowing between black and white writers and the movement's social, economic, political, and geographic context. The 1920s was marked not only by the excesses and optimism of the Jazz Age but also by an influx of European immigrants as well as urban migration from the rural South; by a spirit of nativism (manifested in immigration restriction acts and a resurgence of the KU KLUX KLAN, even in northern cities); and by massive industrial development, which put individuals within the city in closer contact. Although Harlem itself bore the imprint of racial violence and systematic segregation, the Harlem Renaissance marks an extraordinary effort toward racial tolerance and revolutionary cultural forms that extended even beyond the geographic boundaries of New York—to Paris, Chicago, and the West Coast—and that resonates through the later works of such writers as RICHARD WRIGHT, RALPH ELLISON, TONI MORRISON, and ANN PETRY.

Other Harlem Renaissance short stories include Nella Larsen's "The Wrong Man" (1926), "Freedom" (1926), and "Sanctuary" (1930); Eric Walrond's GOTHIC collection *Tropic Death* (1926); Claude McKay's *Gingertown* (1932); and Langston Hughes's *The Ways of White Folk* (1934).

BIBLIOGRAPHY

Anderson, Jervis. *This Was Harlem: A Cultural Portrait, 1900–1950.* New York: Farrar, Straus & Giroux, 1982.

Douglass, Ann. *Terrible Honesty: Mongrel Manhattan in the 1920s.* New York: Farrar, Straus & Giroux, 1995.

Huggins, Nathan. *Harlem Renaissance.* New York: Oxford University Press, 1971.

———. *Voices from the Harlem Renaissance.* New York: Oxford University Press, 1994.

Hurston, Zora Neale. *The Complete Stories.* New York: HarperCollins, 1995.

Hutchinson, George. *The Harlem Renaissance in Black and White.* Cambridge, Mass.: Belknap Press of Harvard University Press, 1995.

Larsen, Nella. *An Intimation of Things Distant: The Collected Fiction of Nella Larsen.* New York: Anchor Books, 1992.

Lewis, David Levering. *When Harlem Was in Vogue.* New York: Oxford University Press, 1981.

———, ed. *The Portable Harlem Renaissance Reader.* New York: Viking, 1994.

Locke, Alain. *The New Negro: Voices of the Harlem Renaissance.* New York: Atheneum, 1992.

Wall, Cheryl. *Women of the Harlem Renaissance.* Bloomington: Indiana University Press, 1995.

Jennifer L. Schulz
University of Washington

HARPER, FRANCES ELLEN WATKINS
(1825–1911)   Poet, novelist, short story writer, abolitionist lecturer, agent on the Underground Railroad, leader in the women's and temperance movements, and magazine columnist, FRANCES E. W. HARPER was born free in Baltimore, Maryland. Her short story

"THE TWO OFFERS," now recognized as the first story published by an African-American woman, appeared in the *Anglo-African Magazine* in 1859. The two protagonists—the conservative, traditional Laura and the activist writer Janette—represent the choices open to women: following convention and marrying or following personal interests and not marrying. Laura feels the disappointing loss of her failed marriage, having followed society's conventions, while Janette, like Harper, embodies the feminist perspective of a woman committed to her political beliefs and her art.

Orphaned by the age of three, Harper was raised by an uncle who operated a school for free blacks. Her talents in writing and elocution surfaced early, as did her interest in radical politics and religion. At approximately age 25 she became the first female teacher at the Union Seminary, established by the African Methodist Episcopal Church in Columbus, Ohio. Interactions with fugitive slaves, along with her own tenuous status, led Harper to abandon the classroom for the abolitionist platform, which she often shared with FREDERICK DOUGLASS and WILLIAM LLOYD GARRISON, and she was well known for her fiery lectures and such poignant poems as "The Slave Mother" and "Bury Me in a Free Land." In 1854 Harper published her first collection of poems, *Poems on Miscellaneous Subjects,* a book that many critics argue pioneered a tradition of African-American protest poetry. Her best-known novel, *Iola Leroy; or, Shadows Uplifted,* was published in 1892.

BIBLIOGRAPHY

Ammons, Elizabeth. "Legacy Profile: Frances Ellen Watkins Harper (1825–1911)." *Legacy: A Journal of American Women Writers* 2, no. 2 (Fall 1985): 61–66.

Harper, Frances Ellen Watkins. *A Brighter Coming Day: A Frances Ellen Watkins Harper Reader.* Edited by Frances Smith Foster. New York: Feminist Press, 1990.

———. *Iola Leroy; or, Shadows Uplifted.* Philadelphia: Garrigues, 1892.

———. *Minnie's Sacrifice; Sowing and Reapin; Trial and Triumph: Three Rediscovered Novels.* Edited by Frances Smith Foster. Boston: Beacon Press, 1994.

———. *Moses: A Story of the Nile.* Philadelphia: Merrihew & Son, Printers, 1869.

———. *Sketches of Southern Life.* Philadelphia: Merrihew & Son, Printers, 1872.

Riggins, Linda N. "The Works of Frances E. W. Harper: An 18th-Century Writer." *Black World* 22, no. 2 (1972): 30–36.

Rosenthal, Debra J. "Deracialized Discourse: Temperance and Racial Ambiguity in Harper's 'The Two Offers' and *Sowing and Reaping.*" In *The Serpent in the Cup: Temperance in American Literature,* edited by David S. Reynolds, 153–164. Amherst: University of Massachusetts Press. 1997.

Scheick, William J. "Strategic Ellipses in Harper's 'The Two Offers.'" *Southern Literary Journal* 23, no. 2 (Spring 1991): 14–18.

Wilfred D. Samuels
University of Utah

HARPER'S   First published in 1850 as *Harper's New Monthly Magazine,* it became *Harper's Monthly Magazine* after 1900 and *Harper's Magazine* in 1925. Until the 1920s it was an illustrated literary magazine devoted to the publication of essays, poetry, and fiction, including the serialization of novels by popular English and American authors. A column called "The Easy Chair," in which important and influential articles on contemporary fiction appeared, was written by a series of distinguished editors, including WILLIAM DEAN HOWELLS and G. W. Curtis. After WORLD WAR I, *Harper's* abandoned the illustrated format and increased its economic, political, and social analysis, although it retained an emphasis on poetry, fiction, and reviews.

HARRIS, GEORGE WASHINGTON (1814–1869)

The southern humorist George Washington Harris does not enjoy the reputation of regionalists such as JOEL CHANDLER HARRIS or A. B. LONGSTREET, but he was read and appreciated by such writers as MARK TWAIN, FLANNERY O'CONNOR, HAMLIN GARLAND, and Robert Penn Warren. WILLIAM FAULKNER, when asked by the *Paris Review* to list his favorite literary characters, listed Falstaff and Prince Hal, Don Quixote and Sancho Panza, and Huck Finn and Jim but composed his longest discussion on Harris's SUT LOVINGOOD. However, while F. O. Matthiessen in *American Renaissance* chose Harris as "representative of the comic response to the national myth of the common man," Edmund Wilson wrote that *Sut Lovingood's Yarns* is "the most repellant book of any literary merit in American literature." Harris is not for all tastes, but the character of Sut Lovingood survives in American literature, and Harris studies continue today (principally in the form of the Sut Society).

George Washington Harris was born March 20, 1814, in Allegheny City, Pennsylvania, but was taken to Knoxville, Tennessee, by his half brother, Samuel Bell, when Harris was five years old. Harris would find inspiration for his writing in his beloved East Tennessee hill country. In Knoxville, Harris grew to become a skilled metalworker and a steamboat captain. His earnings allowed him to purchase 375 acres of farmland in Blount County, at the gateway to the Great Smoky Mountains. It is here that Harris, in 1839, began to write for the first time, submitting political articles to the Knoxville *Argus.*

In 1843 Harris left his farm, returned to the city of Knoxville, and opened a metalworking shop, earning a reputation as a skilled craftsman. He began contributing what he calls "sporting epistles" to William T. Porter's New York *Spirit of the Times,* under the pseudonym of *Mr. Free.* Harris's first important piece of literary work—a sketch titled "The Knob Dance—A Tennessee Frolic"—appeared in the *Spirit* in 1845. "The Knob Dance" is a colorful sketch of life in the Tennessee hills, and Harris displays a talent for LOCAL COLOR and DIALECT. Because of the success of "The Knob Dance," Harris began to consider writing a book on "the manners and customs of East Tennessee." In 1849 Harris became a superintendent of the Holston Glass Works; this proved to be an important position, because it represented a steady income with which Harris could support his family, and because at the glass works he met Sut Miller, who would become the inspiration for Harris's best known literary character: Sut Lovingood.

A key to Harris's comedy is the nature of the East Tennessee dialect in which he writes. As is that of many regionalist writers, Harris's writing is close to a musical performance; he is attentive to the cadence and rhythm of Sut's language:

Hit am on orful thing, George, tu be a natral born durn'd fool. Yu'se never 'sperienced hit pussonally, hev yu? Hits made pow'fully agin our famerly, am all owin tu dad. I orter bust my head open agin a bluff ove rocks, an' jis' wud du hit, ef I warnt a cussed coward. All my yearthly 'pendence is in these yere laings—d'ye see 'em? Ef they don't fail, I may turn human, sum day, that is sorter human, enuf tu be a Squire ur a school cummisiner.

Harris captures the expressions and the rhythm of Sut's talk through diction and spelling, as when using the aspirated *h* at the beginning of *it,* or *enuf* for *enough.* (In 1954 Brom Weber issued a Harris anthology titled *Sut Lovingood.* However, Weber compromises Harris's artistic effects, and much of the comedy, by regularizing the language.)

In 1854 Harris contributed to the *Spirit* his first Sut Lovingood tale, "Sut Lovingood's Daddy 'Acting Horse.'" The tale involves a poor Tennessee family whose horse has died; the no-account father decides to hitch himself to the plow, with disastrous results. This sketch introduces Sut Lovingood, as well as exhibits Harris's first attempt at characterization. The style of the sketch is similar to that of "The Knob Dance," but the tone is darker, and the descriptions of the Lovingood family suggest a more violent, GROTESQUE forcefulness than the lighter country frolic of "The Knob Dance."

By 1858 Harris had developed the character of the Lovingood family further and had introduced several minor characters who would resurface in the Lovingood tales, most notably Sicily Burns, the object of Sut's amorous attention. As Sut's character began to develop, Harris's intention for his central theme becomes clearer: Sut is driven by an intense desire for freedom and is opposed to forms of organized social restraints, such as religion and law. These traits remain true over the course of the Sut Lovingood tales.

Also feeding Harris's rejection of social controls was the fact of the declining economy of the South in the years leading to the CIVIL WAR. Harris took part in the intensifying political debate that strained southern unity in East Tennessee, causing him to reaffirm his dedication to the cause of southern secession.

Over the next four years Harris wrote several more Sut stories; also, he began writing political satire and planning for a collection of Sut Lovingood stories.

Knoxville was a town divided by the growing debate between pro-Union and secession powers. Harris, concerned that his efforts to direct the will of the South against the North (in war if necessary), found himself further disillusioned by what he saw as a dissolving spirit of southern unity in East Tennessee. After leaving Unionist Knoxville for Nashville, Harris's secessionist activities, including writing three anti-Lincoln sketches for the Nashville *Union & American,* continued. In 1862 Harris fled Nashville with his family before advancing Union troops arrived. For the duration of the Civil War, Harris lived and worked in several southern cities.

After the war, Harris continued writing anti-Republican, anti-Yankee newspaper pieces. Finally, in April 1867, the book Harris has been planning for 20 years appeared as *Sut Lovingood. Yarns Spun by a "Nat'ral Born Durn'd Fool." Warped and Wove for Public Wear.* The book includes the popular Sut tales "Sut Lovingood's Daddy 'Acting Horse,'" "Old Burn's Bull Ride," "Sut Lovingood Blown Up," "Sicily Burns' Wedding," and "Mrs. Yardley's Quilting." The tales Harris selected for the book demonstrate the vulgar humor typical of the Sut sketches (which is even more alarming in the context of the high mannerisms of Victorian literature), but the comedy is not as violent as the newspaper sketches. More than half of the tales include comedy instigated by practical jokes rather than violent, malicious planning.

Revisions to the sketches in the *Yarns* best demonstrate Harris's picaresque narrative style and his increased focus on characterization. Harris's strength as a writer was creating characters propelled by their own energies rather than in plot creation. Throughout the tales, Sut remains an outsider driven by lust and his desire for freedom, narrating his adventures to a similarly disposed audience.

Harris published 11 more sketches in the two years between the publication of the *Yarns* and his death in 1869, though these sketches (such as "Sut Lovingood, a Chapter from His Autobiography" and "Sut Lovingood Reports What Bob Dawson Said after Marrying a Substitute") show no demonstrable improvement over the Sut tales in the *Yarns.* These tales may have been part of a larger plan for another book and, given similar attention to revision as the earlier *Yarns,* might perhaps have developed into more fully realized sketches.

In October 1869 Harris remarried after the death of his first wife (in 1867) and settled in Decatur, Alabama, having bought the right-of-way for the Wills Valley Railroad. While on railroad business Harris traveled to Lynchburg, Virginia, with his new manuscript, *High Times and Hard Times,* to plan for the publication of his second book. On the return trip Harris died on the train, having taken ill suddenly, and reportedly whispering one word—*poison*—before his death. The doctor at the scene attributed the death to apoplexy. However, the attending physician noted no apparent signs of poisoning, and no autopsy was ordered. The mysterious circumstances surrounding Harris's death were never resolved—one theory suggests he was poisoned by rival political factions—but he probably succumbed to natural causes. The manuscript Harris had with him remains undiscovered

Bill R. Scalia
St. Mary's University, Baltimore

HARRIS, JOEL CHANDLER (1848–1909)

Born near Eatonton, Georgia, in 1848, Joel Chandler Harris is most famous for his humorous adaptations of African-American folk LEGENDS in the UNCLE REMUS stories. Many of these 220 tales first appeared in the *Atlanta Constitution* before being published as collections in *Uncle Remus, His Songs and His Sayings* and *Nights with Uncle Remus.* Although the tales were about animals, Harris also used them as vehicles for his conciliatory THEME, having the kindly former slave, Uncle Remus, electing to remain on the plantation of his former mistress and her Yankee husband after the CIVIL WAR and relating these tales to their young son.

Perhaps more significantly, these stories depict the efforts of African Americans to preserve their humanity through these often allegorical animal tales (see ALLEGORY), many of which describe the triumph of the seemingly powerless, through intelligence and wit, over superior and often brutal force. These tales had been transmitted orally by slaves for several generations before Harris preserved them in written form. One of the most famous is the CLASSIC story of the Tar Baby; other characters who have entered American MYTH include B'rer Rabbit and B'rer Fox. In these and many other stories, Harris tried to preserve the best of the Old South as well as promote reconciliation during the post–Civil War RECONSTRUCTION period. Reconciliation between the North and the South, between whites and former slaves, and even between southern social classes was a common theme in Harris's writing.

BIBLIOGRAPHY

Bickley, R. Bruce. *Joel Chandler Harris*. Boston: Twayne, 1978.

———, ed. *Critical Essays on Joel Chandler Harris*. Boston: G. K. Hall, 1981.

Cousins, Paul M. *Joel Chandler Harris: A Biography*. Baton Rouge: Louisiana State University Press, 1968.

Harlow, Alvin F. *Joel Chandler Harris: Plantation Storyteller*. New York: J. Messner, 1941.

Harris, Joel Chandler. *Aaron in the Wildwoods*. Boston: Houghton Mifflin, 1897.

———. *Balaam and His Master: And Other Sketches and Stories*. Boston: Houghton Mifflin, 1891.

———. *The Bishop and the Boogerman*. New York: Doubleday, Page, 1909. As *The Bishop and the Bogie-Man*. London: Murray, 1909.

———. *The Chronicles of Aunt Minervy Ann*. New York: Scribner, 1899.

———. *The Complete Tales of Uncle Remus*. Edited by Richard Chase. Boston: Houghton, Mifflin, 1955.

———. *Daddy Jake and the Runaway and Short Stories Told after Dark*. New York: Century 1889.

———. *Free Joe and Other Georgian Sketches*. New York: Scribner, 1887.

———. *Little Mr. Thimblefinger and His Queer Country: What the Children Saw and Heard There*. Boston: Houghton Mifflin, 1894.

———. *A Little Union Scout: A Tale of Tennessee during the Civil War*. New York: McClure, Phillips, 1904.

———. *The Making of a Statesman and Other Stories*. New York: McClure, Phillips, 1902.

———. *Mingo and Other Sketches in Black and White*. Boston: Osgood, 1884.

———. *Mr. Rabbit at Home*. Boston: Houghton Mifflin, 1895.

———. *Nights with Uncle Remus: Myths and Legends of the Old Plantation*. Boston: Houghton Mifflin, 1883.

———. *Old Plantation*, 1880; as *Uncle Remus and His Legends of the Old Plantation*. New York: Appleton, 1881. As *Uncle Remus: or, Mr. Fox, Mr. Rabbit, and Mr. Terrapin*. New York: Routledge, 1881. Rev. ed., 1895.

———. *On the Wing of Occasions*. New York: Doubleday, Page, 1900.

———. *Plantation Pageants*. Boston: Houghton Mifflin, 1899.

———. *A Plantation Printer: The Adventures of a Georgia Boy during the War*. New York: Appleton, 1892. As *On The Plantation*. Boston: Houghton Mifflin, 1892.

———. *Stories of Georgia*. New York: American Book Company, 1896.

———. *Tales of the Home Folks in Peace and War*. Boston: Houghton Mifflin, 1898.

———. *Told by Uncle Remus: New Stories of the Old Plantation*. New York: McClure, Phillips, 1905.

———. *Uncle Remus and Brer Rabbit*. New York: F. A. Stokes, 1907.

———. *Uncle Remus and His Friends: Old Plantation Stories, Songs, and Ballads, with Sketches of Negro Character*. Boston: Houghton Mifflin, 1892.

———. *Uncle Remus and the Little Boy*. Boston: Small, Maynard, 1910.

———. *Uncle Remus: His Songs and His Sayings: The Folklore of the Old Plantation*. New York: Appleton, 1880.

———. *Uncle Remus Returns*. Boston: Houghton Mifflin, 1918.

———. *Wally Wanderoon and His Story-Telling Machine*. New York: McClure, Phillips, 1903.

———. *The Witch Wolf: An Uncle Remus Story*. Cambridge, Mass.: Bacon & Brown, 1921.

Harris, Julia Collier. *The Life and Letters of Joel Chandler Harris*. Boston: Houghton Mifflin, 1918.

HARRISON, JAMES THOMAS (JIM HARRISON) (1937–)

The fiction writer, poet, and essayist Jim Harrison was born on December 11, 1937, in Grayling, Michigan, the second of five children. He received B.A. and M.A. degrees from Michigan State University and taught briefly at the State University of New York at Stony Brook. In 1960 he married and worked for the next several years as a carpenter, a well digger, and a block mason to support his family. Harrison and his family later moved to a farm in Lake Leelanau, Michigan.

Much of Harrison's fiction is recognizably autobiographical: In 1945, during his first sexual experience, Harrison was blinded in his left eye; in 1962 his father and younger sister were killed in a car accident. The THEMES of blindness and alienation, loss and relationships, as well as a preoccupation with food and the outdoors, figure prominently in his narratives. He is closely associated with the fiction writer THOMAS MCGUANE, the writer/painter Russell Chatham, and the adventurer Guy de la Valdene, all of whom are world-class gourmands and sportsmen. Harrison has published short fiction and essays in *Sports Illustrated* and *ESQUIRE* (including a long-running column titled "The Raw and the Cooked"), and he is perhaps the most prolific American NOVELLA writer. He has published nine novellas in three collections: *LEGENDS OF THE FALL* (1979), *The WOMAN LIT BY FIREFLIES* (1990), and *JULIP* (1994). The novellas have gained critical attention for their sketches of uniquely American characters and the range of PROTAGONISTS and landscapes they describe: from the estranged wife Clare in *The Woman Lit by Fireflies* to the contemporary American rogue Brown Dog, who is featured in both *Brown Dog* (from *The Woman Lit by Fireflies*) and *The Seven-Ounce Man* (from *Julip*); from the wilderness of Upper Peninsula Michigan to the desert of the American Southwest. After *The Beast God Forgot to Invent* (2000), Harrison's most recent novella collection is *The Summer He Didn't Die,* published in 2005. The title novella features Brown Dog, in which the main character faces up to the conflict between his love for a lesbian social worker and the needs of his mentally challenged daughter. The novella *Republican Wives* features three women who muse on the death of a man who pursued all three of them, and *Tracking* features a writer and a poet.

Harrison's narratives are grounded in the deepest traditions of American and European literature: The works of MARK TWAIN, WILLIAM FAULKNER, GERALD VIZENOR, Rainer Maria Rilke, and Loren Eiseley, among others, have influenced his writing. While Harrison's fiction is often darkly humorous and ironic, the novellas seriously detail the encroachment of a complex society on a decreasing physical and psychic wilderness.

BIBLIOGRAPHY

Harrison, Jim. *The Beast God Forgot to Invent.* New York: Atlantic Monthly Press, 2000.

———. *The Boy Who Ran into the Woods.* New York: Atlantic Monthly Press, 2000.

———. *Julip.* Boston: Houghton Mifflin, 1994.

———. *Legends of the Fall.* New York: Delacorte Press, 1979.

———. *Letters to Yesenin.* Port Townsend, Wash.: Copper Canyon Press, 2007.

———. *Off to the Side: A Memoir.* New York: Atlantic Monthly Press, 2002.

———. *Returning to Earth.* New York: Grove, 2006.

———. *Saving Daylight.* Port Townsend, Wash.: Copper Canyon Press, 2006.

———. *The Summer He Didn't Die.* New York: Atlantic Monthly Press, 2005.

———. *True North.* New York: Grove, 2004.

———. *The Woman Lit by Fireflies.* Boston: Houghton Mifflin, 1990.

Harrison, Jim, with Ted Kooser. *Braided Creek: A Conversation in Poetry.* Port Townsend, Wash.: Copper Canyon Press, 2003.

Reilly, Edward C. *Jim Harrison.* New York: Twayne, 1996.

Patrick A. Smith
Ohio University

"HARRISON BERGERON" KURT VONNEGUT (1961)

KURT VONNEGUT is celebrated more for his longer fiction than for his short stories. Nonetheless, Vonnegut's "Harrison Bergeron," originally published in the *Magazine of Fantasy and Science* in October 1961, and currently available in the author's collection, *Welcome to the Monkey House,* is a very popular short story and is often cited as an example of dystopian science fiction with an emphasis on egalitarianism. One segment of the 1972 teleplay *Between Time and Timbuktu* was based on the story, and it was later adapted into a TV movie, *Harrison Bergeron* (1995), with Sean Astin in the title role.

Set in 2081, the story depicts society's vain search for absolute equality. Specifically, this new world does not attempt to raise standards for the disabled or handicapped but rather chooses to implement a more onerous solution: to impede those who have superior intellect, beauty, or strength. This solution deprives individuals of their talents by employing masks, loud noises, and weights in an attempt to level the playing field for the less talented. Actually the government is attempting to place all members of society at the level of the lowest common denominator, a process that is overseen by the United States Handicapper General, the shotgun-toting Diana Moon Glampers, whose primary goal is to rid society of anyone who might threaten mediocrity and inadequacy. A similar (though less developed) version of this character and idea appeared in Vonnegut's earlier novel, *The Sirens of Titan*.

In this brave new world, the exceptional are consistently repressed, arrested, thrown into mental institutions, and ultimately killed for failing to be average. The central and title character, Harrison Bergeron, is, of course, a threat to this community since he is physically fit, handsome, intellectual, and, what is worse, rebellious. As a result, he is forced to bear enormous handicaps. These include distracting noises, 300-pounds of excess weight, eyeglasses to give him headaches, and cosmetic changes to make him ugly. Despite these handicaps, however, he is able to invade a TV station and declare himself the new emperor. He then strips himself of his handicaps and begins to dance with a ballerina whose amazing beauty and skills have also been distorted by the authoritarian government in an attempt to restrict her advancement and recognition as a superior individual. As the couple dance in defiance of the "rules," the two defy gravity as they "kiss" the ceiling and assert their artistic independence as well as their refusal to be controlled by an outside authority. The story ends abruptly with two shotgun blasts, suggesting to the reader that there is no forgiveness for those who defy society's demand for conformity to the ordinary. Added poignancy is created by the framing story, in which Bergeron's parents are watching TV and observe their son's demise but cannot concentrate enough to remember the incident or assess its importance. Vonnegut's point seems to be that without the nonconformists, the dreamers, and the different, society is doomed. The good intention of equality is marred by the way society decides to maintain it. To be fair to one group, it must necessarily be unfair to another. Yet if the brilliant and talented are hindered, society will be unable to improve, and the status quo will be all it can hope for.

Vonnegut's more pessimistic view of life may be termed absurdist. In this future society, growth and experimentation are no longer fostered, and science and technologies are devised to hurt rather than to help humankind. The complacency of Harrison's parents who witness his murder and yet cannot remember why they are so sad indicates they both have submitted to a world where rebellion is not tolerated and where sameness is fostered and encouraged.

While many critics have considered Vonnegut's story as an attack on the attempt to level all individuals, what Vonnegut is really assailing is the public's understanding of what that leveling entails. Critics like Roy Townsend and Stanley Shatt seem to have missed the underlying irony of "Bergeron," as well as its UNRELIABLE NARRATOR, preferring to stress the obvious and ignore the fact that the story line offers an assessment of the foolishness that is "common sense." Common sense is shown to be ridiculous in its assumptions about equality and in its belief that a sense of morality and ethics is intuitive. Moreover, since Vonnegut's politics were Leftist in nature, it is unlikely that he would attack the concepts of communism and socialism.

In fact, it is Harrison himself who embodies the past oppression of a dominant culture, and readers should remember his desire is to be emperor, to reassert his superiority and the power it entitles him to wield. Instead Vonnegut seems to satirize society's limited view of egalitarianism as only intelligence, looks, and athleticism. He never addresses income distribution (the separation between rich and poor) or class prejudice (the difference between the powerful and the powerless) even though both are significant issues for America. The mediocrity Vonnegut decries is not a result of the future but a continuation of past practices, an antiintellectualism that is depicted in Harrison's parents, Hazel and George, whose ideas seem to be shaped by what they see on TV and little else. Controlled by a corrupt value system that says to ignore sad things and be satisfied with normality, it is their world that is condemned more than the world of Diana Moon Glampers. They have facilitated her rise to power with all the coldness and sterility that one might associate with the lunar goddess. Freedom is not the greatest good for the smallest number; nor does it hold that a class-ruled society will promulgate economic success. Though the story's message appears quite simple, its moral is rather complex, forcing individual readers to think twice before they reduce its meaning to a sentence or two. Vonnegut was clearly not just trying to side with the radical Right's objections to big government, and "Harrison Bergeron" is definite evidence of how his convoluted texts beg for more contemplation than they have been previously given.

Michael J. Meyer
De Paul University

HARTE, BRET (FRANCIS BRETT HARTE) (1836–1902)

Although he was born and reared in New York, Bret Harte's best work is associated with California. He arrived there in 1855 at age 19 and mined for gold before becoming a schoolteacher and, later, a journalist. During the 1860s Harte wrote most of his most durable fiction, including the stories "M'Liss," "The Luck of Roaring Camp," "THE OUTCASTS OF POKER FLAT," and the poem "Plain Language from Truthful James." His collection of poetry, *The Last Galleon and Other Tales,* and a satirical work, *Condensed Novels,* were published in 1868. Harte gained a national reputation with these stories of the West that combined humor and sentimentality, vivid characterization, and colorful dialogue. He returned east in 1871 and continued to write extensively, but his work was deemed to lack originality and his reputation declined sharply. His best work is still anthologized, however, and Harte is credited as a pioneer in western LOCAL COLOR writing.

BIBLIOGRAPHY

Duckett, Margaret. *Mark Twain and Harte.* Norman: University of Oklahoma Press, 1964.

Harte, Bret. *The Ancestors of Peter Atherly and Other Tales.* Leipzig: B. Tauchnitz, 1897.

———. *Barker's Luck and Other Stories.* Boston: Houghton Mifflin, 1896.

———. *The Bell-Ringer of Angels and Other Stories.* Boston: Houghton Mifflin, 1894.

———. *The Best Short Stories of Bret Harte.* Edited by Robert N. Linscott. New York: Modern Library, 1967.

———. *California Stories.* Franklin Center, Pa.: Franklin Library, 1984.

———. *Drift from Two Shores.* Boston: Houghton, Osgood, 1878. As *The Hoodlum Bard and Other Stories.* London: Ward, Lock and Co., 1878.

———. *An Episode of Fiddletown and Other Sketches.* London: Routledge, 1873.

———. *Flip and Other Stories.* London: Chatto & Windus, 1882.

———. *An Heiress of Red Dog and Other Sketches.* Leipzig: B. Tauchnitz, 1879.

———. *The Heritage of Dedlow Marsh and Other Tales.* New York: Macmillan, 1889.

———. *Jeff Briggs's Love Story and Other Sketches.* Leipzig: B. Tauchnitz, 1880.

———. *Jinny.* New York: Routledge, 1878.

———. *The Lost Galleon and Other Tales.* San Francisco: Towne & Bacon, 1867.

———. *The Luck of Roaring Camp and Other Sketches.* Rev. ed. Boston: Fields, Osgood. 1871.

———. *The Man on the Beach.* London: Routledge, 1878.

———. *Mr. Jack Hamlin's Mediation and Other Stories.* Boston: Houghton Mifflin, 1899.

———. *Mrs. Skaggs's Husbands and Other Sketches.* Boston: Osgood, 1873.

———. *My Friend, the Tramp.* New York: Routledge, 1877.

———. *On the Frontier.* New York: Routledge, 1884.

———. *A Protegeé of Jack Hamlin's and Other Stories.* Boston: Houghton Mifflin, 1894.

———. *Representative Selections.* Edited by Joseph B. Harrison. New York: American Book Company, 1941.

———. *Sally Dows, and Other Stories.* Boston: Houghton Mifflin, 1893.

———. *A Sappho of Green Springs and Other Tales.* Boston: Houghton Mifflin, 1891.

———. *Stories in Light and Shadow.* Boston: Houghton Mifflin, 1898.

———. *Stories of the Sierras and Other Sketches.* London: J. C. Hotten 1872.

———. *Tales of the Argonauts and Other Sketches.* Boston: Houghton Mifflin, 1875.

———. *Tales of Trail and Town.* Boston: Houghton Mifflin, 1898.

———. *Trent's Trust and Other Stories.* Boston: Houghton Mifflin, 1903.

———. *The Twins of Table Mountain.* Boston: Houghton Osgood, 1879.

———. *Wan Lee, the Pagan and Other Sketches.* London: Routledge, 1876.

———. *The Writings of Bret Harte.* 20 vols. Boston, Houghton Mifflin, 1914.

Morrow, Patrick D. *Bret Harte.* Boise, Idaho: Boise State College, 1972.

Nissen, Axel. *Bret Harte: Prince and Pauper.* Oxford: University Press of Mississippi, 2000.

O'Connor, Richard. *Harte: A Biography.* Boston: Little, Brown, 1966.

Pemberton, Thomas Edgar. *The Life of Bret Harte.* Honolulu, Hawaii: University Press of the Pacific, 2004.

Scharnhorst, Gary. "Introduction." In *Bret Harte: The Luck of Roaring Camp and Other Writings.* New York: Penguin Books, 2001.

Stewart, George Rippey. *Harte, Argonaut and Exile.* Boston: Houghton Mifflin, 1931.

HAWTHORNE, NATHANIEL (1804–1864)

Nathaniel Hawthorne, perhaps best known—at least to the general American public—as the author of *The Scarlet Letter* (1850), was, in fact, a prodigious author of short stories before ever writing a novel. Hawthorne began his career by anonymously writing the GIFT BOOKS popular in the early half of the 19th century; at the urging of a friend, he collected his short stories into a book. He published this first collection, *Twice-Told Tales,* in 1837. By the time of its reprinting five years later, with additional material, EDGAR ALLAN POE and Henry Wadsworth Longfellow had written glowing reviews of his work, and HERMAN MELVILLE had firmly backed Hawthorne as a major talent.

Twice-Told Tales included stories of varying length, such as "The Gray Champion" (originally published in the *New-England Magazine,* 1835) and "The Prophetic Pictures" (in *Token,* 1837), both of which feature Hawthorne's fascination with religion, sin, and issues of redemption combined with his historically accurate, realistic depiction of New England Puritanism. (See REALISM.) The most widely known story from this collection, "THE MINISTER'S BLACK VEIL" (*Token,* 1836), prefigures the connected issues of identity, hypocrisy, and sin so central to *The Scarlet Letter*; members of a New England congregation find themselves transfixed by their minister, who refuses to remove the black veil that hides his face. Because they cannot see beneath the veil, the congregation believes that evil lurks under it, while the minister believes that evil walks among everyone: Their spiritual devoutness, however, may vary widely beneath the METAPHORICAL veil that masks their true nature. The minister wears a physical manifestation of the moral AMBIGUITY inherent in all human beings regardless of their perceived public piety or religious fervor. His congregation wants him to lift the veil to prove he is neither evil nor disfigured, but the minister refuses to do so. This tension between the actual and the perceived—between reality and hypocrisy—drives the story.

The unknown, whether a physical object, scientific conjecture, or moral ambiguity, constitutes a major factor in all of Hawthorne's works, and the author presents it through ALLEGORY and symbolism. Hawthorne's works frequently address the human condition and the capacity of mortal man to sin. Hawthorne felt deep concern with the human capacity for self-isolation and a prideful, distorted sense of superiority; his characters, both in his novels and short stories, fall prey to this disturbing state.

Hawthorne's three most widely anthologized stories, "YOUNG GOODMAN BROWN" (initially published in the *New-England Magazine* in 1835), "The BIRTH-MARK" (in *Pioneer,* 1843), and "RAPPACCINI'S DAUGHTER" (in *Democratic Review,* 1844), eventually reappeared in *Mosses from an Old Manse* (1846), his best-known collection of short stories. "The Birth-mark" is the story of a man, a woman, and one fatal flaw, the latter represented by a heavily symbolic birthmark. Ironically, the fatal flaw lies not in the so-called physical deformity of the birthmark but in those who overlook true beauty (both spiritual and physical) as they pridefully attempt to imitate God, or even usurp his power, in their effort to attain perfection, whether through the technological or the spiritual.

In "The Birth-mark," a scientist strives to improve his wife, Georgiana—a devout woman whose great beauty he finds marred only by her birthmark—to the point of perfection. However, his attempt to improve on God's work, the human form, ultimately proves disastrous: The scientist ultimately destroys and loses exactly what he has tried unnecessarily to improve. In "Rappaccini's Daughter," Hawthorne uses the same plot with only slight variation. Again, a beautiful woman dies because, despite—or because of—her great beauty, the men in the tale believe that she harbors a fatal flaw. Dr. Rappaccini attempts to keep his daughter Beatrice to himself by slowly feeding her plant poison; eventually she becomes as lethal as the plants her famous father cultivates to boil down into medicines. Because she becomes poisonous, Beatrice can have no more suitors, and thus her father preserves her purity and innocence for himself alone.

Both Georgiana, in "The Birth-mark," and Beatrice, the title character of "Rappaccini's Daughter," die at the hands of men of science: Georgiana from her husband's attempt to remove the birthmark, and Beatrice from consuming an antidote to the poison coursing through her veins. In these stories Hawthorne implicitly indicts technological advancement and science, along with the masculine attitudes of superiority and knowledge that literally give men the power of life and death over women. Clearly, Georgiana and Beatrice die because they are women and therefore, from the male perspective, associated with danger. Beatrice's crisis and eventual death directly result from her awakening desire and the entrance of her first (and only) suitor, while Georgiana's results from her innocent but misplaced trust in her husband, whose feverish attempt to remove the "stain" from her face eventually kills her. Both women also share an inexorable link to nature, a popular 19th-century metaphor for femininity; Georgiana's successful testing of her fatal drink on a plant leads her to believe it will also succeed with her, while Beatrice, in essence, becomes nature through the plant toxins that conquer her body.

"Young Goodman Brown" presents these same problematic questions regarding gender roles and purity, although the ostensible emphasis lies on a spiritual rather than a physical plane. Feminism has long cast a skeptical eye on Hawthorne's representations of women as evil temptresses or innocent victims; while a FEMINIST reading of Hawthorne's works has a wealth of material to draw from, readers should also consider the era in which Hawthorne wrote and note that he often presents ethically and morally suspect male characters as well. These men pay heavily for their sins, as does Young Goodman Brown, who follows his wife, the aptly named Faith, into the New England woods one dark night. As he walks, joined by a character astute readers may recognize as the devil, he sees—or thinks he sees—that the numerous pious, pure townspeople actually engage in witchcraft. Brown's disillusionment heightens as he believes he has misjudged not only town elders, teachers, and men and women of the church but, finally, Faith herself. Brown's sin is not that he doubts God but, instead, that he becomes morally superior and isolationist; he ruins his life not because of religion but because he believes so unflinchingly in his own moral and ethical rightness.

In the opinion of most critics, later stories and sketches, collected in *The Snow Image and Other Thrice-Told Tales* (1852) and *Tanglewood Tales* (1853), lack the compelling force of Hawthorne's earlier work, although his signature preoccupations infiltrate stories such as "Alice Doane's Appeal" (*Token,* 1835) and "The Antique Ring" (*Sargent's New Monthly Magazine,* 1843). Hawthorne himself never intended to include these works in collections, but his editor did so after Hawthorne's death.

On June 26, 2006, after a century and a half in a London cemetery, the remains of Hawthorne's wife, Sophia, and daughter, Una, were taken to Concord and, in a ceremony attended by Hawthorne family descendants, laid to rest alongside their husband and father in the Sleepy Hollow Cemetery. A reception for friends and family followed at the Old Manse, where Hawthorne's great-great-granddaughter, Alison Hawthorne Deming, delivered remarks on behalf of the Hawthorne family. In the words of the critic Mary Joseph: "One can only wonder at what the intensely private Nathaniel would have thought had he known that the story was reported not only in local newspapers and television stations but also in the *London Times* and on National Public Radio, the Canadian Broadcasting Company, and the BBC, which broadcast it as far away as India. In the end, however, one can be certain that he would have rejoiced to know that he was at last reunited with his 'best beloved.'"

See also "DR. HEIDEGGER'S EXPERIMENT" and "ETHAN BRAND: A CHAPTER FROM AN ABORTIVE ROMANCE."

BIBLIOGRAPHY

Arvin, Newton. *Hawthorne*. Boston: Little, Brown, 1929.

Bell, Millicent. *New Essays on Hawthorne's Major Tales*. New York: Cambridge University Press, 1993.

Bunge, Nancy L. *Hawthorne: A Study of the Short Fiction*. New York: Twayne, 1993.

Cheever, Susan. *American Bloomsbury: Louisa May Alcott, Ralph Waldo Emerson, Margaret Fuller, Nathaniel Hawthorne, and Henry David Thoreau; Their Lives, Their Loves, Their Work*. Detroit: Thorndike Press, 2006.

von Frank, Albert J., ed. *Critical Essays on Harthorne's Short Stories*. Boston: G. K. Hall, 1991.

Hawthorne, Julian. *Nathaniel Hawthorne and His Wife*. Boston: Osgood, 1884.

Hawthorne, Nathaniel. *The Centenary Edition of the Works of Nathaniel Hawthorne*. Vol. 14. Edited by William Charvat, et al. Columbus: Ohio State University Press, 1962.

———. *The Complete Works of Nathaniel Hawthorne*. 12 vols. Boston: Houghton Mifflin 1883. Vol. XIII added about 1891.

———. *The Complete Writings of Nathaniel Hawthorne*. 22 vols. Boston and New York: Houghton Mifflin, 1900.

———. *The Complete Writings of Nathaniel Hawthorne*. 22 vols. Boston and New York: Houghton Mifflin, 1903.

———. *Hawthorne's Short Stories*. Edited by Newton Arvin. New York: Knopf, 1946. Reprint, Columbus: Ohio State University Press, 1963.

James, Henry. *Hawthorne*. London: Macmillan, 1879.

Joseph, Mary. "Nathaniel and Sophia Reunited after 142 Years. (Nathaniel Hawthorne and Sophia Hawthorne)." *Nathaniel Hawthorne Review,* 13 December 2008.

McFarland, Philip. *Hawthorne in Concord*. New York: Grove Press, 2004.

Mellow, James R. *Nathaniel Hawthorne and His Times*. Boston: Houghton Mifflin, 1980.

Newman, Lea Bertani Vozar. *A Reader's Guide to the Short Stories of Nathaniel Hawthorne*. Boston: G. K. Hall, 1979.

Payne, Tom, ed. *Encyclopedia of Great Writers*. New York: Barnes & Noble, 1997.

Wagenknecht, Edward. *Nathaniel Hawthorne: Man and Writer*. New York: Oxford University Press, 1961.

———. *Nathaniel Hawthorne: The Man, His Tales and Romances*. New York: Continuum, 1989.

Waggoner, Hyatt. *Hawthorne: A Critical Study*. Rev. ed. Cambridge, Mass.: Harvard University Press, 1963.

Young, Philip. *Hawthorne's Secret: An Untold Tale*. Boston: Godine, 1984.

Anne N. Thalheimer
University of Delaware

"HEALTH" JOY WILLIAMS (1990) An anonymous *Boston Globe* reviewer once described JOY WILLIAMS as "Annie Dillard bumping into Cotton Mather." She is also routinely compared with such contemporary writers as JOYCE CAROL OATES, ANN BEATTIE, RAYMOND CARVER, FLANNERY O'CONNOR, as well as the film director Roman Polanski and the Russian author Anton Chekhov. She is particularly distinguished by her tone, which the writer-reviewer Carolyn See has described as one of "elegant melancholia"; ultimately her fellow writer Gail Godwin notes, "Joy Williams writes like nobody but Joy Williams" (Godwin). Her technique is described as KAFKAesque and minimalist (see minimalism), allied with the so-called K-Mart realism. Her story "Health," appearing in the collection entitled *Escapes* (1990), provides an excellent example of Williams's techniques and concerns. Williams's stories frequently center on families and the complexities of loss, absence, uncertainty, disease, death, and the layer of fear and uneasiness underlying the surface lives of her characters. Pammy, the central character in "Health," is no exception.

Williams's BILDUNGSROMAN, or coming-of-age story, opens as Morris drops off his daughter, the stocky blonde-haired 12-year-old Pammy, at an unnamed Texas city spa for one of her tanning sessions, a birthday gift from Morris and his wife, Marge. Pammy likes to be tanned and knows the various types: "golden tans, pool tans, even a Florida tan which seemed yellow back in Texas" (114). We learn that Pammy, an aspiring racing skater, is a privileged child accustomed to traveling to such vacation spots as Mexico, Padre Island, and the Gulf beaches. Unlike her friend Wanda, who is adopted and has an alcoholic stepfather, Pammy apparently has decent, caring parents; her science professor father teaches her to drive, and Marge, her 35-year-old mother, studies art history and film at the university where Morris teaches. Pammy, however, is beset with adolescent uncertainties and fears: Even before she reaches the spa, the narrator reveals her belief that "behind words were always things, sometimes things you could never tell anyone, certainly no one you loved, frightening things that weren't even true" (113). On the freeway, the impermanence, unreliable technology, and violence of the contemporary world inhabited by Pammy and her family are symbolized in the truck that carries thrown-away televisions sets. The set facing them has a bullet hole in the exact center of the screen.

Williams's often wounded and always vulnerable characters wander through a land metaphorically littered with rusting cars and broken television sets. Two weeks ago Pammy became infected with tuberculosis, a disease that her friend Wanda sees as the romantic illness that infects artists, poets, and other "highly sensitive individuals" (116). And she does seem extraordinarily observant and perceptive. As the narrator notes with characteristic precision the receptionist's "scratched metal desk" and "black jumpsuit and feather earrings" (115), the tanning room's "ultraviolet tubes" and "black vinyl headrest," Pammy turns on the tanning bed timer "and the light leaps out, like an animal in a dream, like a murderer in a movie" (116). The coffinlike shape of the tanning bed and the uneasy atmosphere are intensified as Pammy, lying in the tanning bed, thinks of Snow White in her "glass coffin," suggesting the solitary young woman who was surrounded by men and poisoned by a scheming woman. Pammy further recalls "ugly" things that would "break her parents' hearts": One school friend stole green stamps from her mother to buy a personal massager, another has a cross-dressing brother, while a third attacked his father and left him unconscious.

A short story, according to Joy Williams, "should break your heart and make you feel ill at ease. It should be swift and damaging" (Catapano). During Pammy's 25 tanning minutes she not only reminisces but also overhears conversations through the paper-thin walls, tales of disease and suicide, thievery and trickery. In such a decadent mood, readers are not really surprised when the door opens and the terrified Pammy sees a man silently stare at her nakedness and then walk out again. He does not respond to her frightened "What?" (120). In panic, she hurriedly dresses, staring at herself in the mirror and wondering about a world where "she can be looked at and not discovered . . . speak and not be known" (121). As she walks out into the rain, she is aware of grime and neon palm trees and obscenely shaped candy and "a

clump of bamboo with some beer cans glittering in its ragged, grassy center" (121). A moment later her mother unlocks the car door to admit Pammy and then locks her safely inside, but the mother is too late: Pammy will see the sinister male figure over and over as she grows older in a world "infinite in its possibilities, and uncaring" (122).

BIBLIOGRAPHY
Catapano, Peter. "The Dark at the End of the Tunnel." *New York Times*, 21 January 1990, p. 9.

Godwin, Gail. Review of "Escapes." *Chicago Tribune*, 14 January 1990, xiv, p. 1.

See, Carolyn. *Los Angeles Times*, 25 December 1989, p. E12.

Williams, Joy. "Health." In *Escapes*. New York: Atlantic Monthly Press, 1990.

HEMINGWAY, ERNEST (1899–1961)   Born in Oak Park, Illinois, Ernest Hemingway grew up in comfortable circumstances as the oldest son and second of the six children of Grace Hall, an accomplished singing teacher, and Dr. Clarence Hemingway, a well-loved physician. He began writing early, publishing in his high school newspaper and literary magazine. Rather than go to college, Ernest took a job with the *Kansas City Star*, where, it is argued, he honed his skills by developing the recommended journalistic virtues of writing in short, declarative sentences; avoiding adjectives; and telling interesting stories. Readers of his fiction, however, have come to understand that this writing style, while it may make his works disarmingly accessible, is also, as the title of one study of his short fiction informs us, only "the tip of the iceberg": That is, seven-eighths of the story's meaning lies submerged while only one-eighth is visible on the surface.

In WORLD WAR I Hemingway enlisted in the Red Cross Ambulance Corps and was badly wounded while distributing chocolate and cigarettes to troops on the Italian front. During his hospital recuperation, he fell in love with Agnes von Kurowsky, a nurse. She was the first mature romance of his life, and her subsequent rejection of him was a great blow. He recovered, however, to marry four times.

Literary recognition occurred early, and Hemingway benefited from the sponsorship and support of significant literary figures such as SHERWOOD ANDERSON, F. SCOTT FITZGERALD, Ezra Pound, and GERTRUDE STEIN. With his first wife, Hadley Richardson, he lived in Paris and traveled through Europe, working as a correspondent for the *Toronto Star*. Living in the center of the artistic ferment that was at the heart of the modernist movement (see MODERNISM), Hemingway explored narrative strategies and thematic concerns (see THEME) in his early fiction that put him in its vanguard. His was a style so distinctive that it is credited with informing 20th-century prose; it is, in the words used to present him the NOBEL PRIZE in literature, a "powerful, style-making mastery of the art of modern narration."

Early critical recognition occurred first with the limited edition of *Three Stories and Ten Poems* (1923) and then the commercial publication of *IN OUR TIME* (1925), an unusual juxtaposition of stories and vignettes in the form of a literary collage, or of fragments that achieve a sort of ironic unity. *In Our Time* contains a number of stories featuring NICK ADAMS, the character some critics view as Hemingway's ALTER EGO. Once Hemingway achieved some fame, his writing, both fiction and nonfiction, garnered a wider audience from initial publication in mass-audience magazines such as *ESQUIRE, Cosmopolitan,* and *ATLANTIC MONTHLY. The Old Man and the Sea* was first serialized in *Life*. Other important story collections include *Men without Women* (1927), *Winner Take Nothing* (1933), and *The Fifth Column and the First Forty-nine Stories* (1938). His most famous novels are *The Sun Also Rises* (1926), *A Farewell to Arms* (1929), *For Whom the Bell Tolls* (1940), and *The Old Man and the Sea* (1952). Several posthumous works have also gained wide readership, including *A Moveable Feast* (1964), *Islands in the Stream* (1970), and *The Garden of Eden* (1986).

The short story was Hemingway's natural milieu and the genre most unequivocally admired by his readers. Carlos Baker, his first biographer, calls it his early and hardest kind of discipline, one that taught him his craft. Whatever else about Hemingway has come under attack—his personality, his problematic sexuality, his "macho" perspective, his self-glorification—he wrote short stories that are many critics and

readers acclaim among the best of the 20th century. Late in his career he wrote an essay, originally meant as the introduction to an anthology for students of his most popular stories, called "The Art of the Short Story." In it he rearticulated his credo that "if you leave out important things or events that you know about, the story will be strengthened" (quoted in Lynn). His caveat, of course, was that you can leave out only what you know, not what you don't know.

As Fitzgerald was called the chronicler of the Jazz Age, so Hemingway was the historian for the lost generation. Living with a loss of faith, in a world of insecurities, and dealing with disillusionment, his characters try to create coping mechanisms to get them through, trying to divert their attention from the pain and—in the words of a nameless character in "A CLEAN, WELL LIGHTED PLACE"—from the "nada." Jake Barnes, the main character in *The Sun Also Rises,* voices the basic existential concern of most of Hemingway's PROTAGONISTS in both the long and the short fiction: "I did not care what it was all about. All I wanted to know was how to live in it. Maybe if you found out how to live in it you learned from that what it was all about."

Hemingway lived life at a high pitch, traveling the world and hobnobbing with the rich and famous. After his first divorce, he married Pauline Pfeiffer, whose wealth made possible their adventurous life together. One of his books, *The Green Hills of Africa,* is about their African safari with friends. Word of these and similar adventures was trumpeted in the world press, and as Hemingway grew older and more celebrated, his grizzled countenance, instantly recognizable, was known by many who had never read a word he wrote. He was the writer as superstar, a world celebrity, who achieved a mythic status in which he was confused with the characters he created. This biographical reading of his works extended till well after his death. Still, his star quality was such that he created tourist attractions of the places he celebrated in his writing, be they towns such as Pamplona or restaurants such as Botins in Madrid.

In his public PERSONA, Hemingway fed the myth. It has been suggested that he began to believe his own publicity, a situation that proved deleterious for his writing. Although he remained loyal to many old friends, many others who helped him rise became casualties of his cruelty and competitiveness.

The complexity and controversy of Hemingway's life has inspired an inordinate number of biographies and memoirs, from the authorized and meticulously researched *Ernest Hemingway: A Life Story* by Carlos Baker to the controversial psychological reading of his struggle with an ambiguous sexual identity in Kenneth S. Lynn's *Hemingway*. Friends, siblings, and sons also have written their remembrances of what it was like to know Ernest Hemingway. He attracted; he repelled. In 1954, after two successive plane crashes in Africa, he was reported dead but in fact had survived. In the same year he won the Nobel Prize in literature. His later years were plagued by health problems and accidents, made worse by his heavy drinking. After a series of physical and mental problems, he killed himself in Ketchum, Idaho, in 1961.

See also "A Day's Wait"; "The End of Something"; "In Another Country"; "The Killers"; and "Up in Michigan."

BIBLIOGRAPHY

Baker, Carlos. *Hemingway: The Writer as Artist.* Princeton, N.J.: Princeton University Press, 1980.

Beegel, Susan F., ed. *Hemingway's Neglected Short Fiction: New Perspectives.* Ann Arbor, Mich.: UMI Research Press, 1989.

Benson, Jackson J., ed. *New Critical Approaches to the Short Stories of Ernest Hemingway.* Durham, N.C.: Duke University Press, 1990.

Donaldson, Scott. *The Cambridge Companion to Hemingway.* Cambridge: Cambridge University Press, 1996.

Flora, Joseph M. *Ernest Hemingway: A Study of the Short Fiction.* Boston: Twayne, 1989.

Hemingway, Ernest, and A. E. Hotchner. *Dear Papa, Dear Hotch: The Correspondence of Ernest Hemingway and A. E. Hotchner.* Edited by Albert J. Defazio III. Columbia: University of Missouri Press, 2005.

Johnston, Kenneth G. *The Tip of the Iceberg: Hemingway and the Short Story.* Greenwood, Fla.: Penkevill, 1987.

Lynn, Kenneth S. *Hemingway.* New York: Simon & Schuster, 1987.

Mellow, James R. *Hemingway: A Life without Consequences.* Reading, Mass.: Addison-Wesley, 1992.

Wagner-Martin, Linda. *A Historical Guide to Ernest Hemingway.* New York: Oxford University Press, 2000.

Mimi Reisel Gladstein
University of Texas at El Paso

HEMINGWAY CODE Ernest Hemingway advocated a particular code of behavior through various characters in his novels and short stories. The Hemingway hero tries to show loyalty to his friends, to behave well in difficult situations (with "grace under pressure"), to behave with courage and stoicism, to lose well, and to avoid loquacity. The character Robert Wilson, the hunting guide in "The Short Happy Life of Francis Macomber," for example, acts according to this code.

HENRY, O. (WILLIAM SYDNEY PORTER) (1862–1910)

William Sydney Porter's career as the legendary O. Henry spanned the mere eight years between his arrival in New York in 1902 and his death there in 1910. During that time he published more than 300 stories in such popular magazines as *Everybody's, McClures', Munsey's, Smart Set,* and the New York *Sunday World,* for which he wrote a story per week for several years. His stories have been collected in nearly 20 volumes, 13 of them published within his lifetime. The enormous impact of O. Henry's work—despite changing tastes and trends in critical opinion—remains pervasive and indisputable. Admired by millions of Americans and translated into a welter of foreign languages, O. Henry and his "all-American" short stories inspired the debut, in 1919, of the O. Henry Memorial Awards, an honor still coveted by contemporary writers, whose winning stories are published annually in a single volume. Over the years, O. Henry stories have been used in or adapted to radio, television, film, and stage, and today the World Wide Web boasts numerous sites and scores of pages devoted to the author, his work, and his critical reception.

As the scholar and critic Eugene Current-García has demonstrated, the central question for contemporary readers is the one that has excited critical debate since the decade after O. Henry died: "Was he a genuine literary artist or a literary mountebank, a creative innovator of narrative prose fiction or an artful dodger and con man?" (xi). Critical opinion has ranged from the adulatory, comparing him with the likes of Joseph Conrad, Thomas Hardy, HENRY JAMES, Guy de Maupassant, and EDITH WHARTON, to the virtual dismissal by critics and scholars from 1930 to the present. Despite his pronounced absence from the indexes of all major university literary anthologies, however, bookstores and public libraries attest to the continued enthusiasm for the O. Henry story with its characteristic SURPRISE ENDING.

Although O. Henry gained much of his fame by writing about the lives of the "four million" inhabitants of the New York City of his era, his American qualities inhere also in his post-RECONSTRUCTION southern roots and in his western sojourn: His life and work spanned much of the vast country. Some 30 of Porter's stories are set in and deal directly with the South, 80 with the West, and 26 with Central America, where he lived for some months. Among his best southern stories are "Vareton Villa: A Tale of the South," which LAMPOONS the excessive biases of both northerners and southerners and emanates from the TALL TALE tradition of FRONTIER HUMOR; "The Rose of Dixie," a satiric treatment of southern journalism, replete with the characteristic surprise ending; the hilarious "The Ransom of Red Chief," another example of O. Henry's use of the tall tale; and "The Municipal Report," one of his most critically acclaimed stories, demonstrating his use of LOCAL COLOR description and DIALECT.

The southwestern stories are based on his experiences while living in Texas and in prison, where he served three years of a five-year sentence on conviction of embezzlement, an indisputably traumatic force in O. Henry's life. In a number of these stories one sees his belief in DETERMINISM, his characters as mere pawns in a large, indifferent world; encounters between criminals and law enforcement officials; and the theme of "reformation or rehabilitation" (Current-García 41). The most famous of these is "A Retrieved Reformation," the story of Jimmy Valentine, a burglar whose safe-cracking wizardry was later dramatized in both play and film. Another of his finest tales is "Caballero's Way," a perennially popular story involving the Cisco Kid and a Texas ranger. With this tale,

O. Henry's talents have been compared to those of STEPHEN CRANE, and versions of "the Kid's" exploits continue as part of American mythology.

After his release from prison and his move to New York, O. Henry wrote more than 140 stories about the people he daily observed on subways, in restaurants, on park benches. He liked to choose a few who captured his attention and then create stories about them. Current-García has noted the irony of O. Henry's move to Irving Place and his respectful pilgrimage to the home of WASHINGTON IRVING, the first American writer to capture the New York scene. Notable similarities exist between these two city-life chroniclers, not least their lack of interest in moralizing or politicizing the circumstances and characters they portrayed. Both writers, moreover, favored SATIRE, humor, romance, BURLESQUE, and both made innovative contributions to the short story form (see COMEDY and ROMANTICISM) (Current-García 58). Of the many memorable New York stories, O. Henry is almost surely best remembered for "The GIFT OF THE MAGI" and "The LAST LEAF," tales of human love and generosity that have attained classic status and can move even most postmodern readers, despite some critics' charges of sentimentalism. "Let Me Feel Your Pulse," the last story he ever wrote as he wasted away from an incurable disease, continues to receive praise as one of his finest.

Although numerous critics have accused O. Henry of romanticizing such issues as poverty—in "The Cop and the Anthem," "A Madison Square Arabian Night," "The Unfinished Story," "The Unfurnished Room," for example—others view him as a writer who believes in a common human bond that unites us all: Far from thinking as an idealist, then, he is a man who believes in ideals. In this sense, the unresolved controversy over O. Henry's talents is one of philosophy rather than literary criticism. Whatever perspective the critical reader holds, O. Henry has made an indelible mark on the American short story, and his tales promise to reach into the next century.

BIBLIOGRAPHY
Arnett, Ethel Stephens. *O. Henry from Polecat Creek.* Greensboro, N.C.: Piedmont Press, 1962.
Blansfield, Charmaine. *Cheap Rooms and Restless Hearts: A Study of Formula in the Urban Tales of Porter.* Bowling

Green, Ohio: Bowling Green State University Popular Press, 1988.

Current-García, Eugene. *O. Henry*. New York: Twayne, 1965.

———. *O. Henry: A Study of the Short Fiction*. New York: Twayne, 1993.

Davis, Robert H., and Arthur B. Maurice. *The Caliph of Bagdad*. New York: Appleton, 1931.

Ejxenbaum, Boris Mikhailovich. *O. Henry and the Theory of the Short Story*. Translated by I. R. Titunik. Ann Arbor: University of Michigan Press, 1968.

Gallegly, Joseph. *From Alamo Plaza to Jack Harris's Saloon: O. Henry and the Southwest He Knew*. The Hague: Mouton, 1970.

Henry, O. *The Best of O. Henry: One Hundred of His Stories*. London: Hodder and Stoughton, 1929.

———. *The Best Short Stories of O. Henry*. Edited by Bennett Cerf and Van H. Cartmell. New York: Modern Library, 1945.

———. *Cabbages and Kings*. New York: A. L. Burt, 1904.

———. *Complete Works*. New York: Doubleday, Page, for Funk & Wagnalls, 1926.

———. *Complete Writings*. 14 vols. Garden City, N.Y.: Doubleday, Page, 1917.

———. *Cops and Robbers: O. Henry's Best Detective and Crime Stories*. New York: L. E. Spivak, 1948.

———. *The Four Million*. New York: A. L. Burt, 1906.

———. *The Gentle Grafter*. Garden City, N.Y.: Doubleday, Doran, 1908.

———. *Heart of the West*. New York: McClure Company, 1907.

———. *Let Me Feel Your Pulse*. New York: Doubleday, Page, 1910.

———. *More O. Henry: One Hundred More of the Master's Stories*. London: Hodder and Stoughton, 1933.

———. *O. Henryana: Seven Odds and Ends: Poetry and Short Stories*. Garden City, N.Y.: Doubleday, Page, 1920.

———. *O. Henry Westerns*. Edited by Patrick Thornhill. London: Methuen, 1961.

———. *Options*. New York: Grosset & Dunlap, 1909.

———. *The Pocket Book of O. Henry Stories*. Edited by Harry Hansen. New York: Pocket Books, 1948.

———. *Roads of Destiny*. New York: Doubleday, Page, 1909.

———. *Rolling Stones*. New York: Collier, 1912.

———. *Selected Stories of O. Henry*. Edited by C. Alphonse Smith. Garden City, N.Y.: Doubleday, Page, 1922.

———. *Sixes and Sevens*. Garden City, N.Y.: Doubleday, Page, 1911.

———. *The Stories of O. Henry*. Edited by Harry Hansen. New York: Heritage Press, 1965.

———. *Strictly Business: More Stories of the Four Million*. New York: Collier, 1910.

———. *The Trimmed Lamp and Other Stories of the Four Million*. New York: A. L. Burt, 1907.

———. *The Two Women*. Boston: Small, Maynard, 1910.

———. *The Voice of the City: Further Stories of the Four Million*. Garden City, N.Y.: Doubleday, Doran, 1908.

———. *Waifs and Strays: Twelve Stories*. Garden City, N.Y.: Doubleday, 1917.

———. *Whirligigs*. New York: Collier, 1910.

Kramer, Dale. *The Heart of O. Henry*. New York: Rinehart, 1954.

Langford, Gerald. *Alias O. Henry: A Biography of William Sidney Porter*. New York: Macmillan, 1957.

Long, Eugene Hudson. *O Henry: American Regionalist*. Austin, Texas: Steck-Vaughn, 1969.

———. *O. Henry: The Man and His Work*. New York: Russell & Russell, 1949.

O'Connor, Richard. *O. Henry: The Legendary Life of William S. Porter*. Garden City, N.Y.: Doubleday, 1970.

Smith, C. Alphonse. *O. Henry Biography*. Garden City, N.Y.: Doubleday, Page, 1916.

HERO/HEROINE In a literary or dramatic work, the main character on whom one's interest is focused. Many FEMINIST critics now eschew the term *heroine*: All central figures in fiction, female or male, are called heroes. Also called the PROTAGONIST.

"HILLS LIKE WHITE ELEPHANTS"

ERNEST HEMINGWAY (1927) The frequently anthologized "Hills Like White Elephants" first printed in *transition* magazine in 1927 is often read and taught as a perfect illustration of ERNEST HEMINGWAY's minimalist (see MINIMALISM), self-proclaimed "iceberg" style of writing: In much of Hemingway's fiction what is said in the story often is less important than what has not been said. Like the iceberg—only one-eighth of which is visible above the surface—Hemingway's fiction is much richer than its spare language suggests. Hemingway has great faith in his readers and leaves them to discern what is truly happening from the scant facts he presents on the surface of his story. On a superficial level, *Hills* is merely about a man, a woman, and an "awfully simple operation" (275). What the narrator never actually tells the reader, however, is that "awfully simple operation" is an abortion, a taboo subject in 1925. Underneath the surface of this story are THEMES and motifs that are characteristic of many of Hemingway's other works as well. As do many of those works, "Hills" tells the story of an American abroad and depicts the strained relationships between men and women that clearly intrigued the author. As with many of the relationships Hemingway portrays, this man and woman apparently have nothing in common but sex and the heavy consumption of alcoholic beverages.

"Hills" is also a story of avoidance. Instead of having a significant, rational conversation about the issue at hand, the "girl," Jig, says only that the hills of Spain look like white elephants. "Wasn't that clever?" she asks the unnamed man (274). This rather inconsiderate male companion agrees, but he actually wants to talk about the procedure. Jig would rather not discuss it. When he pressures her, she replies, "Then I'll do it. Because I don't care about me." Jig is the typical Hemingway female, selfless and sacrificial. She is prepared to have the abortion, but the reader is left with the distinct impression that any previous magic between the couple is gone. "It isn't ours anymore," Jig tells the American (276). The unfortunate accident of pregnancy has ruined the relationship; it will never be the same. Hemingway explores many of the same themes in his important war novel *A Farewell to Arms* and in *The Sun Also Rises*.

BIBLIOGRAPHY
Hemingway, Ernest. "Hills Like White Elephants." 1927. Reprinted in *The Complete Short Stories of Ernest Hemingway: The Finca Vigía Edition*. New York: Scribner, 1987.

Johnston, Kenneth. "'Hills Like White Elephants': Lean, Vintage Hemingway." *Studies in American Fiction* (1982).

Renner, Stanley. "Moving to the Girl's Side of Hills." *The Hemingway Review* (1995).

Kathleen M. Hicks
University of Texas at El Paso

HISPANIC-AMERICAN SHORT FICTION

Hispanic-American fiction, also called Latino fiction, is published by writers of Mexican, Puerto Rican, Dominican, and Cuban descent as well as by authors with ties to Central and South America. Latino fiction represents diverse cultural situations and is published by such storytellers as the Chicano author RUDOLFO ANAYA, the Puerto Rican writer Nicholasa Mohr, the Cuban-American writer Virgil Suárez, and the Dominican-American author JUNOT DÍAZ. Though not belonging to one ethnic community, Latino writers often engage in dialogue with one another as they take inventory of their colonial past with Spain and their sometimes difficult or frustrating experiences in the United States. As a whole, Latino fiction reflects a search for identity and belonging at the same time as it affirms the individual spirit within a family and community. One can understand the Latino short story by considering its historical roots, the venues in which it is published, and the techniques and themes used by Hispanic-American writers.

Latino short fiction has its roots in Spanish colonial writing such as the travelogues of Christopher Columbus and Cabeza de Vaca, the treatises of the priest and Indian emancipator Bartolome de las Casas, and the accounts of conquest by the soldier-historian Bernal Díaz. Exploration narratives, royal mandates, and colonial directives constitute the majority of Hispanic-American literature from the 1490s to the 19th century. But by the 1800s several significant developments took place: the Treaty of Guadalupe Hidalgo, the emancipation of slaves throughout Latin America and in the United States, the liberation of Latin American colonies from Spanish rule, and the spread of print culture. The dissemination of periodicals at this time gave rise to serialized fiction and essays, and it created audiences ranging from San Juan to New York, from Havana to Miami, and from San Miguel de Allende to San Antonio.

By the 20th century, many writers capitalized on the memoir, novel, and short story form to explore their cultural heritage—especially after the civil rights movement. By the 1980s literary journals such as *Revista Chicano-Riqueña* and *Americas Review* provided a venue for Latino writers, and by the 1990s academic presses and mainstream publishers issued single volumes of fiction and anthologies. Arte Público Press is perhaps the largest publisher of Latino fiction, coordinating with the "Recovering the U.S. Hispanic Literary Project," directed by Nicolas Kanellos at the

University of Houston. But Random House and Harcourt have also emerged as major corporate presses interested in Latino authors.

As in other kinds of ethnic writing, the issue of language is an important one. Depending on the degree of assimilation or the ideology associated with language use, Latino fiction writers express themselves in English, Spanish, or a combination of the two. The Texan novelist Tomás Rivera, one of the foundational figures of Chicano letters, wrote *. . . y no se lo tragó la tierra [And the Earth Did Not Devour Him]* (1971) in Spanish. Yet Spanish continues to be a problematic means of asserting identity because, like English, it is a colonial inheritance. Increasingly, we find Latino authors such as René Saldaña, Jr., and Junot Díaz injecting Spanish into English prose; this code switching underscores divided allegiances between mainstream and "peripheral" communities—though increasingly Spanish speakers are becoming more populous throughout the United States. In addition to code switching between English and Spanish, writers such as HELEN MARÍA VIRAMONTES and Nicholasa Mohr sometimes employ slang or ghetto speech, echoing African-American rhythms, which, in turn, represent the linguistic dynamics of ethnically diverse urban communities. Language, in turn, shapes the authorial techniques and themes of Latino fiction.

TECHNIQUES AND THEMES

Techniques used in the short story include code switching (moving back and forth between English and Spanish), the incorporation of Spanglish (words that are neither wholly Spanish nor English but a combination of both), and narration about one's place in a family or community. Often biographical and autobiographical, Latino short stories give us memorable images of Cuban enclaves in Miami, the bustling tenements of New York City, and the working-class barrios of the Southwest. Accounts of the complexity and conflict of community relations can be found in such stories as the Texas-born Lionel Garcia's "The Day They Took My Uncle," set in Texas, and the Puerto Rican writer Magali Garcia Ramis's "Fritters and Moons" (in Olmos and Paravisini-Gebert). Plots generally depend on one or a few episodes in order to preserve the economy of scope found in short fiction. Such episodes might involve a narrator's real or imagined visit to the past or the exploration of one's heritage through a journey or movement across the border, as in Oscar Casares's *Brownsville Stories* (2003). Episodes also may involve an encounter with a strong or unusual character that brings about an important perspective—often this is a grandmother or person of wisdom. So, too, are cultural encounters with white mainstream culture a significant plot detail in short fiction—as in Daniel Chacón's "Andy the Office Boy" in *Chicano Chicanery* (2000). In this story, an attractive Mexican-American lawyer living on a tight budget is told to buy the law firm's office boy a gift. In an interesting and playful turn of events, she buys a fuzzy baby blue sweater and displays to Andy—in private—her voluptuous figure underneath the sweater. He is pleased with the office gift, and she has undermined the snub of her colleagues by giving her such a menial task. Chacón's most recent collection of stories can be found in *Unending Rooms* (2008).

As one of many plot devices, short story writers will often describe a trip abroad—whether to Mexico, Cuba, Puerto Rico, the Dominican Republic, or any number of geographies that give rise to Hispanic-American culture. For example, both Lisa Hernandez's *Migrations and Other Stories* (2007) and Daniel Chacón's *Chicano Chicanery* describe a character's trip from the United States to Mexico and the feeling of being out of place in, respectively, Guadalajara and Mexico City. Chacón writes about a Mexican-American graduate student who wants to stay in his La Zona Rosa hotel room and watch television rather than experience historically rich—and also dangerous—red light districts of Mexico City.

Another major concern in Latino fiction is coming of age as in SANDRA CISNEROS's collection of short stories *WOMAN HOLLERING CREEK AND OTHER STORIES* (1991) and *HOUSE ON MANGO STREET*. Contributing to the experience of coming of age is the passing on of wisdom from one generation to another. Viola Canales—author of the collection *Candy Slices and Other Tales* (2001)—observes in an interview with Nell Porter Brown that "if we don't, as Asians, African Americans, and Latinos, pass our stories amongst each other and down to our kids, we're going to lose the kids." . . . "We are already losing many of them at around 12 and 13; they drop out of school, join gangs, get pregnant, et cetera, Stories need to be told; they anchor us" (Brown). Canales and her counterparts Gary Soto and René Saldaña, Jr., use short fiction as a way of both representing and reaching out to the young. Soto appeals to young readers with stories about the self-consciousness of adolescence and the awkwardness of dating with *Baseball and Other Stories,* and Saldaña explores the conflicts of coming of age for teenage boys in *Finding Our Way.*

Along with coming of age, the political and economic landscape of Latin America—including the Caribbean—shapes Latino fiction. Dominicans, El Salvadorans, Guatemalans, and Chileans, who fled harsh military regimes in their own countries, write about their experiences growing up or adapting to life in the United States—as in Mario Bencastro's *Tree of Life: Stories of Civil War* (1996). This collection of stories about El Salvador reveals the successful integration of the historical and the uniquely personal.

MEXICAN-AMERICAN SHORT FICTION

The Treaty of Guadalupe-Hidalgo of 1848 converted Mexican land into U.S. territory—now the Southwest—and demanded new approaches and eventually new languages in literary production. According to the critic Raymund A. Paredes, 19th-century memoirists and novelists responded to their U.S. citizenry through criticism, introspection, or nostalgia. By the mid-20th century, Mexican-American authors such as Josephina Niggli and José Villarreal articulated assimilationist concerns in, respectively, *Mexican Village* (1945) and *Pocho* (1959), both of which are widely excerpted and anthologized (Paredes 40–41). At the same time Latino communities felt the pressure to assimilate, they also participated in the civil rights movement to fight for civil liberties. Chicano authors—such as Rudolfo Anaya and Tomás Rivera—used their writing in the 1970s and 1980s to create awareness of the need for fair labor practices and equal access to education and the right to speak Spanish in order to preserve Mexican traditions and ways of being.

Along these same lines, Chicana writers such as Helen María Viramontes, Sandra Cisneros, and Alma Luz Villanueva draw on Mexican traditions in their narrative details, which include prayers, recipes, and *remedios* (cures). Even in, or perhaps especially in, urban settings the routines of the past are important. Helen María Viramontes's "The Moths" (1985) demonstrates this through the dying grandmother figure, Abuelita (little grandmother), and the 14-year-old narrator (Augenbraum and Olmos 433). Together, the women—one old and sage, one young and rebellious—save old coffee cans, puncture them, and garden with the newly made pots. This horticultural activity contrasts sharply with the narrator's insulting and violent family. Abuelita provides an alternative to her granddaughter's dysfunctional home life and its compulsory Catholicism, which appears merely as an empty form, not a sincere belief. When Abuelita dies, the narrator takes careful measures to preserve the past. The narrator gathers clean linen, gently washes Abuelita, and cradles her frail torso.

The grandmother is also an important figure in Alma Luz's "Weeping Woman: La Llorona and Other Stories." "La Llorona," the first story of the collection depicts Nina's life in the care of her reserved but loving grandmother, and as a point of contrast, it reveals the abusiveness of Nina's mother. The relationship—as do many of those portrayed in Latino fiction—depends on the passing down of stories and legends: In this case, Isidra tells her granddaughter about La Llorona. In Villanueva's imagination, La Llorona has lost her children and is crying for them at the water's edge. Nina and her grandmother go to the beach of San Francisco and hear the lament of the weeping woman: "There was a dark figure moving along the beach, slowly. Her shawl covered her head. She looked tall and strong as she came toward them, weeping and singing" ("La Llorona" 7). La Llorona is a person of fortitude, and while a protective figure, she is also somewhat menacing; she reappears at the end of the collection in the story entitled "El Alma/ The Soul, Four." Here Nina reflects on her calling as a poet and the life of pain, hardship, and emancipation she feels as a 50-year-old woman. For Nina, such feelings of freedom are hard won after a life of struggle—including rape, parental abuse, and living paycheck to paycheck as a writer.

PUERTO RICAN SHORT FICTION

Puerto Ricans form the second major group of Latino authors. Living on the island or on the mainland, they have views on American culture that differ accordingly. Indeed, when Puerto Rico became a U.S. Commonwealth in 1898, its writers regarded this new imperial presence with interest and trepidation. We see this in Ana Roqué's epistolary novel *Luz y sombra* (1903), which explores two women's lives as they attempt to deal with European influences and U.S. policies. Yet Puerto Rico's distance from the United States and its Spanish influences have tended to make its literature somewhat inaccessible to American readers until recently, when translations have become more common, as in *Reclaiming Medusa: Contemporary Short Stories by Puerto Rican Women Writers* (1997), where readers can find the short stories of Rosario Ferré, Carmen Luggo Filippi, Mayra Montero, and Ana Lydia Vega.

As did Mexican-American literature, Puerto Rican writing gained momentum after the civil rights movement. Short story writers include Abraham Rodriguez, Jr.; JUDITH ORTIZ COFER; Jack Agüeros; and Nicholasa Mohr, all of whom cross cultures in their depiction of Puerto Rican life. In "Mr. Mendelsohn," Nicholasa Mohr captures the essence of the Bronx barrio as a cross section between the young and old, the Latino and Jewish (Augenbraum and Stavans 131). A sharp contrast is the drug-based gang murder of a young pregnant woman in Abraham Rodriguez, Jr.'s "Roaches" (Poey and Suárez 267). The premise of this story is that watching real life is more gripping than watching television. Rodriguez reveals his range as a writer in his quieter, though no less hopeful, story of teenage sex, pregnancy, and high school attrition in "The Lotto" (1992) (Gonzalez 36). Both stories show the tough, merciless side of Puerto Rican life in the Bronx and reveal an apathetic disconnection with society. Thus Puerto Rican short stories span the humanitarian, nostalgic outlook to a perhaps more troubling postmodern passivity.

CUBAN-AMERICAN SHORT FICTION

As do their counterparts in Puerto Rico (which is a U.S. Commonwealth), Cuban-American and Dominican-American writers represent life in the Caribbean, but their stories center on issues of immigration rather than migration. The Cuban-American literary tradition began, in part, with the revolutionary José Martí, who was one of the first Cuban exiles to publish in the United States. His essay "Nuestra America" (1891) helped his compatriots, and indeed Latin Americans more broadly, to understand mestizo cultures, cultures threatened by the effects of European colonialism and U.S. intervention. Fidel Castro's assumption of military power in 1959 took up Martí's rallying cry to make Cuba resistant to U.S. hegemony. But this occurred at the price of Cubans, who sought repatriation to the United States. For Cuban-American writers such as Ana Menendez and Virgil Suárez, relationships to family and the island are vexed, for at the same time there is more civil freedom in the United States, many Cubans suffer a loss of status in their exile from the island. Menendez reflects on this loss in her short story collection *In Cuba I Was a German Shepherd* (2002).

As with many short stories by Latino writers, the fast pace of the American city and changes to the nuclear family are important because of a general movement from an agricultural situation to an urban one. The change in the nuclear family is central to Virgil Suárez's story "Miami during the Reagan Years" (1994) because the narrator's mother intends to remarry. The narrator's father has no major objections, for he is living with someone himself (Gonzalez 384). This collapse of the nuclear family is paralleled by divisions of education and class in other works. Cecilia Rodríguez-Milanés's "Abuelita Marieleta" (1992) exposes the pretensions of middle-class Cuban Americans living in Miami and recent *marieletas* who hide their "boat people" status (Poey and Suárez 287).

A common technique for Cuban-American writers is to use an instigatory moment in the present to review the past or anticipate the future. This allows readers to examine opposing values between a conservative, patriarchal Spanish-American society and a Westernized, commercialized, and fiercely individual society. For example, in Marisella Veiga's Caribbean vignette "Fresh Fruit" (1992), the housewife-narrator spies on her young single neighbor, Susana (Poey and Suárez 349). From the narrator's perspective, Susana has adopted "American ways" that are troubling; she lives alone, drives alone, works alone, and eats alone, buying ready-made food. We learn through the narrator's criticism—and perhaps through her envy—that Susana is not interested in saving money or in "forming a home with a husband." For the narrator, Susana's life seems socially empty, but when the housewife-narrator admits her own restlessness and her husband's infidelities, we see a validation of those "American ways," ways that liberate women from the confines of their homes. Latino fiction, therefore, has much to contribute to larger discourses of women's roles in a changing society.

About her fiction, she explains, "I have lived in Puerto Rico and briefly in the Dominican Republic. As a result, I have a sense of what it means to be an islander. Many of my adventures contain archetypical Spanish Caribbean characters. I can now sit with a group of 'those who remember' in Miami and conjure whatever scene is called for. I know the cool privacy of a Spanish colonial home, what fried fish and plantains taste like at a sea-side stand, how old women hobble to the cathedral" (Hobbler et al. 108). Her stories "The Mosquito Net" and "Liberation in Little Havana" can be found in, respectively, *A Century of Cuban Writers in Florida: Selected Prose and Poetry* (1996) and *Little Havana Blues: A Cuban American Literature Anthology.*

DOMINICAN-AMERICAN SHORT FICTION

The two major contributors to Dominican-American short fiction are the award-winning novelists Julia Alvarez and Junot Díaz. Alvarez is most widely known for her novels such as *How the Garcia Girls Lost Their Accents* and she has recently published a short story in the *Washington Post,* "The Dictator's Ex-Wife Writes Him a Letter" (2008). In this story, as in her novels *In the Time of the Butterflies* and *How the Garcia Girls Lost Their Accents,* Alvarez writes of the former wife of Trujillo: "Only she knew how he checked himself constantly in the mirror. How he ordered platform shoes to make himself taller, applied whiteners

to his skin. How he was always preoccupied, forming a nation out of a rude people. The Americanos had left him in charge." Alvarez, too, writes of the U.S. complicity in supporting right-wing military leaders such as Trujillo—though the subject is often taboo in the Dominican Republic, so fierce and brutal was his legacy.

As is Alvarez, Díaz is also considered a novelist (most recently of *The Brief Wondrous Life of Oscar Wao*), but he has published his works individually in the *New Yorker* and elsewhere. His award-winning book *Drown* (1996) can be read either as a short story cycle or as a novel. For Díaz and Alvarez (as well as for other authors), the difference between a collection of short stories and a novel is often blurred because short stories eventually contribute to novels and novels are excerpted in anthologies as short stories. In any case, Díaz's stories contemplate the disjunction between rural experiences on a tropical island and the gritty, cold, urban Northeast.

One final consideration in Latino short fiction is its scholarly reception. Author-specific criticism relevant to the short story can be found in Ramirez's *The Encyclopedia of Hispanic-American Literature* (2008), an overview of the long history shaping Latino fiction can be found in Kanellos's *Herencia: The Anthology of Hispanic Literature of the United States*; and insight about the political forces driving fiction by Cuban-American, Puerto Rican, and Dominican-American writers can be found in Olmos and Paravisini-Gebert's *Remaking a Lost Harmony: Stories from the Caribbean.*

BIBLIOGRAPHY

Agueros, Jack. *Dominoes: and Other Stories from the Puerto Rican.* Willimantic, Conn.: Curbstone Press, 1995.

Alvarez, Julia. "The Dictator's Ex-Wife Writes Him a Letter." *Washington Post Magazine,* Valentine's Fiction Issue, 10 February 2008.

Augenbraum, Harold, and Ilan Stavans, eds. *Growing Up Latino: Memoirs and Stories.* Boston: Houghton Mifflin, 1993.

Augenbraum, Harold, and Margarite Fernández Olmos, eds. *Latino Reader: An American Literary Tradition from 1542 to the Present.* Boston: Houghton Mifflin, 1997.

Bencastro, Mario. *Tree of Life: Stories of Civil War.* Houston: Arte Público Press, 1997.

Brown, Nell Porter. "The Beauty of Beans: A Mexican-American Girl Grows Up." *Harvard Magazine* (January–February 2006). Available online. URL: http://harvardmagazine.com/2006/07/the-beauty-of-beans.html. Accessed May 2, 2009.

Casares, Oscar. *Brownsville Stories*. Back Bay Books, 2003.

Chacón, Daniel. *Chicano Chicanery*. Houston: Arte Público Press, 2000.

———. *Unending Rooms*. Black Lawrence Press, 2008.

Cisneros, Sandra. *Woman Hollering Creek and Other Stories*. New York: Vintage Books, 1991.

Dalleo, Raphael, and Elena Machado Saez, eds. *The Latino/a Canon and the Emergence of Post-Sixties Literature*. Palgrave Macmillan, 2007.

Garcia, Lionel. *The Day They Took My Uncle and Other Stories*. Texas Christian University Press, 2001.

Gaspar de Alba, Alicia. *The Mystery of Survival and Other Stories*. Bilingual Review Press, 1993.

Gilb, Dagoberto. *Magic of Blood*. Grove Press, 1994.

Gonzalez, Ray, ed. *Mirrors beneath the Earth: Short Fiction by Chicano Writers*. Willimantic, Conn.: Curbstone Press, 1995.

Gutierrez, Ramón, and Genero Padilla, eds. *Recovering the U.S. Hispanic Literary Heritage*. Houston: Arte Público Press, 1993.

Hernandez, Lisa. *Migrations and Other Stories*. Houston: Arte Público Press, 2007.

Hoobler, Dorothy, and Thomas Hoobler, eds. *Cuban American Family Album*. Oxford University Press, 1996.

Horno-Delgado, Asunción, and Eliana Ortega, et al., eds. *Breaking Boundaries: Latina Writing and Critical Readings*. Amherst: University of Massachusetts Press, 1989.

Hospital, Caroline, and Jorge Cantera, eds. *A Century of Cuban Writers in Florida: Selected Prose and Poetry*. Sarasota, Fla.: Pineapple Press, 1996.

Kanellos, Nicolás, ed. *Herencia: The Anthology of Hispanic Literature of the United States*. Oxford University Press, 2002.

Martí, José. *Nuestra America*. Havana: Casa de las Americas, 1974.

Menendez, Ana. *In Cuba I Was a German Shepherd*. Grove Press, 2002.

Ortiz Cofer, Judith. *An Island Like You: Stories of the Barrio*. Puffin, 1996.

Poey, Delia, and Virgil Suárez, eds. *Iguana Dreams: New Latino Fiction*. New York: HarperPerennial, 1992.

———. *Little Havana Blues: A Cuban-American Literature Anthology*. Houston: Arte Público Press, 1996.

Quintana, Leroy. *La Promesa and Other Stories*. Norman: University of Oklahoma Press, 2002.

Ramirez, Luz Elena, ed. *The Encyclopedia of Hispanic-American Literature*. New York: Facts On File, 2008.

Ríos, Alberto Alvaro. *The Iguana Killer*. Albuquerque: University of New Mexico Press, 1999.

Rivera, Carmen, ed. *Kissing the Mango Tree: Puerto Rican Women Rewriting American Literature*. Houston: Arte Público Press, 2002.

Rivera, Tomás. *. . . y se no lo tragó la tierra. /. . . And the Earth Did Not Devour Him*. Translated by Evangelina Vigil-Pinón. Houston: Arte Público Press, 1971.

Rodriguez, Abraham. *Boy without a Flag: Tales of the South Bronx*. Milkweed Editions, 1999.

Saldaña, Jr., René. *Finding Our Way*. Laurel Leaf, 2004.

Simpson, Victor C. *Afro-Puerto Ricans in the Short Story: An Anthology*. Peter Lang, 2006.

Soto, Gary. *Baseball in April and Other Stories*. Harcourt, 2000.

———, ed. *Pieces of the Heart: New Chicano Fiction*. San Francisco: Chronicle Books, 1993.

Trevino, Jesus. *Fabulous Sinkhole and Other Stories*. Houston: Arte Público Press, 1995.

Vélez, Diana, ed. *Reclaiming Medusa: Contemporary Short Stories by Puerto Rican Women Writers*. Aunt Lute Books, 1997.

Villaseñor, Victor. *Walking Stars: Stories of Magic and Power*. Piñata Books, 2003.

Luz Elena Ramirez
California State University, San Bernardino

HITLER, ADOLF (1889–1945)

Adolf Hitler was born in Austria and served in the Bavarian Army in WORLD WAR I. He blamed Germany's defeat in that war on Jews and Marxists, and with others founded the National Socialist (Nazi) Party in 1920. In 1923 the Nazis unsuccessfully attempted to overthrow the Bavarian government, and Hitler was imprisoned. While in jail, he wrote *Mein Kampf* (My Struggle), a book filled with anti-Semitism, power worship, disdain for morality, and his strategy for world domination. The GREAT DEPRESSION gained his Nazi movement mass support after 1929. A spellbinding orator, Hitler understood mass psychology and proved himself a master of deceitful strategy. He manipulated virulent anti-Semitism and anticommunism to gain support of workers as well as bankers and industrialists. He became chancellor in 1933, and soon afterward the Reichstag (legislature) gave him dictatorial powers.

Hitler's aggressive and ruthless foreign policy was appeased by Western nations until he invaded Poland in 1939 and war was declared. Hitler's equally brutal internal policies included the "Final Solution," which aimed to eliminate targeted minorities, primarily Jews, in the infamous concentration camps. Millions were killed in what is known as the HOLOCAUST. WORLD WAR II ended in 1945 with Germany defeated and the country in ruins. Hitler committed suicide before being captured, leaving as a legacy the memory of the most dreadful and evil tyranny of modern times. ALLUSIONS to Hitler occur directly or indirectly in such stories as CYNTHIA OZICK's "The Shawl" and WILLIAM FAULKNER's GO DOWN, MOSES.

HOFFMAN, ALICE (1952–)

Although known primarily as a prolific and talented prose writer with 17 novels to her credit, Alice Hoffman has contributed stories to such magazines as *Ms., Redbook, Fiction,* and *American Review* and has published two story collections: *Local Girls* (1999) and *Blackbird House* (2004), both containing stories linked either by character or by setting. Hoffman's penchant for FANTASY, MAGICAL REALISM, FOLKLORE, SYMBOL, and MYTH has earned her comparisons with such writers as Angela Carter, Bruno Bettelheim, and MARGARET ATWOOD, along with the Latin Americans Gabriel García Márquez and Isobel Allende. Hoffman's main characters are always strong women, often iconoclasts and eccentrics, who are nonetheless attracted to the wrong sort of men. The writer was nurtured on *Grimm's Fairy Tales* and names TILLIE OLSEN and GRACE PALEY, who are both authors and activists, as her models.

Hoffman was born on March 16, 1952, in New York City. She earned her bachelor's degree in 1973 from Adelphi University and her master's degree in 1975 from Stanford University. She married Tom Martin, a writer. With her debut collection, *Local Girls,* Hoffman received praise for her supple and evocative prose style as her teenage protagonist, Gretel Samuelson, takes center stage. Set on Long Island, the linked stories of the Samuelson family—a family rent asunder by divorce and dysfunction—feature

intelligent young Gretel and the three remarkable girls and women who help her face tragedy: her best friend Jill, her cousin Margot, and her mother, Franny, who, despite the divorce and a diagnosis of breast cancer, helps them navigate the journey to physical and emotional health. The reviewer Rose Martelli observes that Hoffman transforms the ordeals and trials "into a celebration of family" (G1). Hoffman donated the proceeds from the book to breast cancer research and care.

Blackbird House is named for the small Cape Cod farm, built in 1800, that remains haunted by former inhabitants, including a white blackbird. Beginning just after the American Revolution, each story focuses on a different inhabitant of Blackbird House. In each generation, strong women emerge to take charge, to sustain the family, and, frequently, to behave with courage and wisdom. In the reviewer Elaine Showalter's words, "The farmhouse on the 'edge of the world' with its summer kitchen, red-pear tree, ghost-birds and lush wild gardens, [becomes] a powerful metaphor for regeneration."

BIBLIOGRAPHY

Alice Hoffman Web site. Available online. URL: http://www.alicehoffman.com. Accessed August 25, 2004.

Frechette, Zoe. "Talking with Alice Hoffman." *Story Quarterly* 38 (2002): 228–236.

Gaines, Judith. "Alice Hoffman." *Yankee* 67, no. 10 (2003): 18.

Hoffert, Barbara. Review of *Local Girls. Library Journal,* 15 May 1999, p. 130.

Hoffman, Alice. *Blackbird House.* New York: Doubleday, 2004.

———. *Local Girls.* New York: Putnam, 1999.

Hooper, Brad. Review of *Local Girls. Booklist,* 15 March 1999, p. 819.

Kanner, Ellen. "Making Believe: Alice Hoffman Takes Her Practical Magic to the River." BookPage.com. Available online. URL: http://www.bookpage.com/. Accessed August 6, 2004.

McCay, Mary. Review of *Local Girls, Practical Magic,* and *Angel Landing. Booklist,* 15 March 2000, pp. 1,396–1,397.

O'Hara, Maryanne. "About Alice Hoffman." *Ploughshares* 29, no. 2–3 (2003): 194–198.

Ratner, Rochelle. Review of *Local Girls. Library Journal,* December 1999, p. 205.

Reichl, Ruth. "At Home with Alice Hoffman: A Writer Set Free by Magic." *New York Times,* 10 February 1994, p. C1.

Showalter, Elaine. "Learning to Lie with Loss," *Guardian* (London), 14 August 2004, p. 1.

HOLMES, OLIVER WENDELL (1809–1894)

A physician and a professor at the Harvard Medical School, Holmes also wrote important medical papers, essays, and novels. He is best remembered for the series of sketches he wrote for the ATLANTIC MONTHLY under the title *The Autocrat of the Breakfast Table*. The stories in this series, notable for their wit and originality, combined fiction, essay, conversation, drama, and verse and were collected in book form (*The Autocrat of the Breakfast Table,* 1858). Other essays were published as *The Professor at the Breakfast Table* (1859) and *The Poet at the Breakfast Table* (1872).

HOLOCAUST

Soon after ADOLF HITLER was named chancellor of Nazi Germany in 1933, anti-Semitism was enacted into law and ceased only with the crushing defeat of Germany at the end of WORLD WAR II in Europe in 1945. Most Jews who did not flee Germany were sent to concentration camps, and, after World War II began in 1939, the Nazis implemented Hitler's "final solution of the Jewish question," which called for the extermination of all Jews in any country conquered by the Germans. By the war's end, more than 6 million Jews had been systemically murdered in what became known as the Holocaust.

HOMOSEXUALITY IN LITERATURE

With the increasing impact of the gay rights movement and acceptance of gays in mainstream society, gay studies and gay literature are emerging as respected fields. Defining *gay literature* is sometimes difficult, given the frequent vague and subtle references to gay characters or THEMES found in works. Not all gay literature deals specifically with sex; most focuses on emotion. The writer Christopher Isherwood said it best when he explained that being gay does not involve the act of sex; instead, it is the proclivity or the ability to fall in love with another member of the same gender.

In general, however, fiction is termed gay when it incorporates a gay theme or gay character into its narrative. Thus, not all gay literature is written by gay authors; nor do all gay authors write gay fiction. No single piece of gay fiction can claim to be emblematic of the "gay experience," for as the growing numbers of gay short stories shows, this "experience" is different in each story. Further, gay literature also can share traits of other thematic clusters of literature, such as FEMINISM/FEMINIST, NATIVE AMERICAN, and AFRICAN-AMERICAN and such genres as DETECTIVE SHORT FICTION, the GHOST STORY, and the COMEDY.

From the early days of civilization, there have always been gay thinkers and writers. Among them is the Greek philosopher Plato, who has been among the most influential historically in the fields of philosophy and literature. Despite the much-heated debate over William Shakespeare's sexuality, many critics believe his work—littered with cross-dressing characters and same-sex affectionate themes—strikes a definite gay or bisexual cord. In premodern America, Walt Whitman and HERMAN MELVILLE were reputed to have been gay. In general, their better-known works do not contain overt sexual references, but their sexuality has been the subject of much biographic and bibliographic research and scholarly debate and has led to new interpretations of their works in recent years.

Historically, literary greats have been a driving force of the modern gay movement, which began in the late 1800s. As the example of Oscar Wilde shows, the road for these writers was far from easy. In his infamous 1895 trial for homosexuality, the British courts found the prolific and prize-winning Wilde guilty and sentenced him to a two-year jail term of hard labor. In both his writings and the notoriety of his personal life, Wilde drew international focus to the issue.

For the first part of the 1900s, gays were more or less "invisible," living underground lives in the United States. Gay men and women organized a vast network through friends, businesses, and bars. Numerous laws targeted homosexuals. Gays lived with the constant threat of the police raids on gay establishments, which entailed brutality, arrests, and public embarrassment.

The gay lives of the literary giants Virginia Woolf and GERTRUDE STEIN were widely known in literary circles, yet until recently scholarship about their sexuality or any subtle gay themes in their work has been minimal. Stories such as HENRY JAMES's "The Pupil" (1891) are so subtle that the unsuspecting reader would not realize the underlying gay theme. In other stories, such as WILLA CATHER's widely anthologized "Paul's Case" (1905), the homoeroticism and sexuality of the characters are elusive yet present. Given the public intolerance of homosexuality, much of Stein's writing that was overtly lesbian in theme was withheld from publication until later in the century.

At midcentury psychological associations told Americans that homosexuality was abnormal behavior, thereby contradicting the *Kinsey Report,* which indicated that nearly 10 percent of Americans were homosexual. At this point the literary world began to note and accept more direct gay references in fiction. The African-American writer JAMES BALDWIN introduced gay themes in his novel *Go Tell It on the Mountain* (1953) and later—more boldly—in *Giovanni's Room* (1956). Central to the BEAT movement and preceding the "free love" years of the 1960s, Allen Ginsberg gave an "in-your-face" homoerotic sexuality to his poetry. Other gay American authors writing early to midcentury include the poet H. D. (Hilda Doolittle); the playwrights Tennessee Williams, EDWARD ALBEE, and Christopher Isherwood; and the fiction writers Gore Vidal and JOHN CHEEVER.

The birth of the contemporary gay rights movement was heralded in 1969 at a small gay bar in the Greenwich Village section of New York City (see GAY MALE SHORT FICTION). Although it did not gain the momentum of the civil rights and women's rights movements of the time, this marked the beginning of an age when gays stopped hiding underground and became advocates for their rights. Later that year the National Institute of Mental Health recommended that the United States repeal laws against homosexual sex between consenting adults.

With the onslaught of acquired immune deficiency syndrome (AIDS) in the early 1980s, the gay community became one of the hardest-hit groups. During the early years of AIDS, a panic swept through the gay community since doctors and researchers did not know exactly how the disease was contracted. As AIDS became more prevalent, its threat acted as a mobilizing force for the community. The specter of AIDS is present in most recent literature, whether directly or lurking in the shadows.

Gay literature made a significant impact in the literary landscape in the 1980s and 1990s. Universities offered courses in gay and lesbian literature and culture, and the number of gay-themed books being published increased considerably. Numerous anthologies of short gay fiction include *The Faber Book of Gay Short Fiction* (1991), *Penguin Book of Gay Short Stories* (1994), *Penguin Book of Lesbian Short Stories* (1994), the series Men on Men (beginning in 1988) and Women on Women (beginning in 1990), and even an anthology of gay and lesbian SCIENCE FICTION, *Kindred Spirits* (1984). In addition, many nonfiction compilations of stories about being gay have been published, including coming-out stories and reflections on definitions of families and hometowns. Most bookstores now have sections devoted to gay, lesbian, and bisexual literature; indeed, some are devoted almost entirely to the topic.

Bisexual literature often is included in this gay category, yet it has a foot in both sexual camps. ALLUSIONs to the complex sexuality of bisexuals can be found in writings by CARSON MCCULLERS, especially in her "BALLAD OF THE SAD CAFE" (1951), or LOUISE ERDRICH's *The Beet Queen* (1986).

In recent years, awards for homosexual-themed literature have become increasingly prominent. The LAMBDA awards (Lesbian, Gay Male, Bisexual, and Transgender Awards) have swelled to 22 categories, including story collections and anthologies, poetry, memoirs, cultural studies, public policy, law, history, spirituality, and gender studies. These awards have gone not only to exclusively homosexual or transgender writers but also to those who win awards in both gay and straight categories, such as Jeffrey Eugenides, the Pulitzer Prize–winning novelist and short story writer.

LAMBDA first-place prizes have been awarded to some critically well-received anthologies and short story collections, including *Fresh Men: New Voices in Gay Fiction* (2004) and *Freedom in This Village: 25 Years of Black, Gay Men's Writing* (2005). Among the LAMBDA finalists during the last decade are several story collections: *Shadows of the Night: Queer Tales of the Uncanny and Unusual* (2004); *Best Lesbian Love Stories 2003* and *Best Lesbian Love Stories 2004; Everything I Have Is Blue: Short Fiction by Working-Class Men* (2005); and *No Margins: Writing Canadian Fiction in Lesbian* (2006).

The literature of homosexuality has evolved to the point where it is often grouped not only according to ethnicity and genre, for example, Latina and Chicana, African-American, Asian and Native American, but also into sorts of sexuality, such as gay, transsexual, and bisexual not to mention the literary genres that represent it, including MYSTERY, science fiction, and detective fiction, and even geographic region.

In addition to myriad small presses, important publishers of homosexual literature include the University of Wisconsin Press, Duke University Press, and Ohio State University Press. Moreover, many online magazines publish and critique homosexual short fiction, *Blithe House Quarterly* and the *Canadian Review of Gay & Lesbian Writing,* to name just two.

See also LESBIAN THEMES IN SHORT STORIES.

BIBLIOGRAPHY

Berman, Steve, ed. *Best Gay Stories 2008.* Philadelphia: Lethe Press, 2008.

Brown, Angela. *Best Lesbian Love Stories 2004.* New York: Alyson Books, 2004.

Burton, Peter. *A Casualty of War: The Arcadia Book of Gay Short Stories.* Mt. Pleasant, S.C.: Arcadia Books, 2008.

Currier, Jameson. *Still Dancing: New and Selected Stories.* Maple Shade, N.J.: Lethe Press, 2008.

Fone, Byrne R. S. *A Road to Stonewall: Male Homosexuality and Homophobia in English and American Literature, 1750–1969.* Boston: Twayne, 1995.

Harris, E. Lynn. 2005. *Freedom in This Village: 25 Years of Black, Gay Men's Writing.* New York: Carroll & Graf, 2005.

Herren, Greg, ed. *Shadows of the Night: Queer Tales of the Uncanny and Unusual.* New York: Southern Tier, 2004.

LAMBDA Awards. Available online. URL: http://www.lambdaliterary.org/awards/current_nominees.html. Accessed February 8, 2009.

Malinowski, Sharon, and Christa Brelin, eds. *The Gay and Lesbian Literary Companion.* Canton, Mich.: Visible Ink Press, 1995.

Maustbaum, Blair, and Will Fabrom, eds. *Cool Thing: The Best New Gay Fiction from Young American Writers.* Philadelphia: Running Press, 2008.

Meyers, Jeffrey. *Homosexuality and Literature: 1890–1930.* London: Athlone Press, 2000.

Miner, Valerie. *Lavender Mansions: 40 Contemporary Lesbian and Gay Short Stories.* Boulder, Colo.: Westview Press, 1994.

Nestle, Joan, and Naomi Holoch, eds. *Women on Women: An Anthology of American Lesbian Short Fiction.* New York: NAL Dutton, 1990.

Nolan, James. *Perpetual Care: Stories.* Chattanooga, Tenn.: Jefferson Press, 2008.

Porter, Joe Ashby. *All Aboard: Stories.* New York: Turtle Point Press, 2008.

Ricketts, Wendell, ed. *Everything I Have Is Blue: Short Fiction by Working-Class Men.* San Francisco: Suspect Thoughts, 2005.

Soucy, Stephen, ed. *Nine Hundred and Sixty-Nine: West Hollywood Stories.* Los Angeles & New York: Modernist Press, 2008.

Summers, Claude. *Gay and Lesbian Literary Heritage.* 2nd ed. New York: Routledge, 2002.

Weise, Donald, ed. *Fresh Men: New Voices in Gay Fiction.* New York: Carroll & Graf, 2004.

White, Edmund, ed. *The Faber Book of Gay Short Fiction.* Boston: Faber & Faber, 1991.

Woods, Gregory. *A History of Gay Literature: The Male Tradition.* New Haven, Conn.: Yale University Press, 1999.

Calvin Hussman
St. Olaf College

HOOD, MARY (1946–)

The Georgia native and resident Mary Hood established herself as an important new southern writer with her first short story collection, *How Far She Went* (1984), which won the Flannery O'Connor Award for short fiction and several other prestigious awards.

Often compared in subject and style to other southerners, FLANNERY O'CONNOR, CARSON MCCULLERS, and EUDORA WELTY, Hood writes stories usually set in rural Georgia and peopled with conflicted, struggling, and often isolated local residents. She has a direct, unstinting approach to her subject and, as O'Connor and WILLIAM FAULKNER, does not flinch in depicting the violence and confusion inherent in modern life. Hood presents dialogue as storytelling southerners truly speak it: rich with colloquialisms, full of humor and detail. "How Far She Went," the often-anthologized title story of her first collection, tells of a woman raising her granddaughter and trying to protect her from a brutal encounter. The granddaughter learns the surprising depth of her grandmother's strength and courage; when a pistol-wielding tough tells the old woman to go to hell, "'Probably will,' her granny told him. 'I'll save you a seat by the fire.'"

Hood is a prolific writer, frequently contributing fiction and nonfiction to periodicals including the *Georgia Review*, HARPER'S, and the *KENYON REVIEW*. She has published a second collection of short stories, *And Venus Is Blue* (1986), and a novel, *Familiar Heat* (1995).

BIBLIOGRAPHY

Hood, Mary. *And Venus Is Blue.* New York: Ticknor & Fields, 1986.

———. *How Far She Went.* Athens: University of Georgia Press, 1984.

———. "A Stubborn Sense of Place." *Harper's,* August 1986, pp. 35–45.

Pope, Dan. "The Post-Minimalist American Story; or, What Comes after Carver?" *Gettysburg Review* 1 (Spring 1988): 331–342.

Karen Weekes
University of Georgia, Athens

HOPKINSON, FRANCIS (1737–1791)

Francis Hopkinson was born and reared in Philadelphia, the son of a prominent lawyer. Professionally, Hopkinson followed in his father's footsteps upon receiving the first diploma from the Academy of Philadelphia (now the University of Pennsylvania) in 1757. Although his work was to remain in politics, law, and trade, Hopkinson became known in the 1760s through his poetry, musical works, and, more important, essays on politics. A staunch supporter of American independence, Hopkinson scathingly satired loyalist politicians and supporters in pamphlets and in popular periodicals, such as the *Pennsylvania Magazine,* often

embroiling himself in public battles that resulted in a somewhat tarnished reputation. At the same time, Hopkinson's writings enjoyed popular acclaim and notice, particularly "A PRETTY STORY," an allegorical (see ALLEGORY) rendering of the tense state of British-American relations. Hopkinson's stature in colonial American literary and political culture was such that he was elected to represent New Jersey at the Continental Congress, where he signed the Declaration of Independence.

During and after the AMERICAN REVOLUTION, Hopkinson continued his support of the American side by using his scathing wit against the British cause. He purportedly also used his artistic flair to design the American flag. After the war, Hopkinson continued to write social and political SATIRE and commentary for popular magazines and was appointed a district court judge in Pennsylvania. The news of his sudden death of a stroke was largely ignored by the press, who both loved and hated this talented and patriotic, although often bombastic, man of letters.

BIBLIOGRAPHY

Hastings, George Everett. "Francis Hopkinson." In *Dictionary of American Biography,* edited by Allen Johnson, Dumas Malone, et al. New York: Charles Scribner's Sons, 1932.

———. *The Life and Works of Francis Hopkinson.* Chicago: University of Chicago Press, 1926.

Levernier, James A. "Francis Hopkinson." In *Reference Guide to American Literature,* edited by Jim Kamp. 1994.

Marshall, George N. *Patriot with a Pen: The Wit, Wisdom, and Life of Francis Hopkinson, 1737–1791, Gadfly of the Revolution.* West Bridgewater, Mass.: C. H. Marshall, 1993.

Zall, Paul M. *Comical Spirit of Seventy-six: The Humor of Francis Hopkinson.* San Marino, Calif.: Huntington Library, 1976.

Gregory M. Weight
University of Delaware

HOUSE ON MANGO STREET, THE SANDRA CISNEROS (1984)

Categorized by critics as a NOVELLA, SHORT STORY CYCLE, or collection of prose poems, *The House on Mango Street* (1984) employs a unique, cross-genre form that characterizes the work as postmodern.

(See POSTMODERNISM.) In it SANDRA CISNEROS captures the diverse voices and stories that she has encountered in the Chicano/Chicana community.

The House on Mango Street is unified by the voice of its narrator, a young Latina named Esperanza. The work is in many ways a typical BILDUNGSROMAN. It centers on the development of Esperanza's artistic voice as she experiences the confusing and often harsh world around her. Many vignettes focus on the problems facing young Latina women in the community and the forces that prevent them from finding creative and personal fulfillment. The work concludes as most bildungsroman do, with the artist's withdrawal from the community. Esperanza, however, unlike most other artist-HEROes, promises to return for those in her neighborhood who do not have the opportunities that she has had—those whose voice cannot be heard except through her art.

BIBLIOGRAPHY

Cahill, Susan. *Writing Women's Lives.* New York: HarperPerennial, 1994.

Cisneros, Sandra. *The House on Mango Street.* Houston: Arte Público Press, 1984.

McCracken, Ellen. "Sandra Cisneros' *The House on Mango Street*: Community-Oriented Introspection and the Demystification of Patriarchal Violence." In *Breaking Boundaries: Latina Writing and Critical Readings,* edited by Asuncion Horno-Delgado, Eliana Ortega, Nina M. Scott, Nancy Saporta Sternbach, and Elaine N. Miller, 62–71. Amherst: University of Massachusetts Press, 1989.

Olivares, Julian. "Sandra Cisneros' *The House on Mango Street,* and the Poetics of Space." In *Chicana Creativity and Criticism: New Frontiers in American Literature,* edited by Maria Herrera-Sobeck and Helena Maria Viramontes, 233–244. Albuquerque: University of New Mexico Press, 1996.

TuSmith, Bonnie. *All of My Relatives: Community in Contemporary Ethnic American Literatures.* Ann Arbor: University of Michigan Press, 1993.

Tracie Guzzio
Ohio University

HOWELLS, WILLIAM DEAN (1837–1920)

An editor and prodigious writer of novels, short stories, drama, poetry, essays, criticism, reviews, biographies, autobiography, and travel books, William Dean Howells was probably the most influential person in American literature during his lifetime. Howells's vast output was widely read and appreciated by a large audience, he promoted prominent and emerging American writers, and he promulgated seminal international arts and their concepts in America. Thus, Howells was known to his admirers as the "dean" of American letters.

Born in March 1837 in a still mostly rustic Ohio, Howells was the second of eight children in a close-knit, economically humble but proud, respectable, and culturally aware family. Particularly close to his mother, Howells was also shaped by his father, whose politics and religion made him an abolitionist and a follower of the Swedish philosopher-theologian, Emmanuel Swedenborg (1688–1772), whose mystical visions influenced numerous writers. Howells's initiation to letters occurred early by setting type for his father, who owned newspapers in several Ohio locations. In part because those papers did not succeed, the family moved often.

Lacking extensive formal education, the autodidactic Howells was nevertheless well read and deeply ambitious as a writer. Howells published a poem when he was only 15 and a story the following year, but his first significant writing was as a journalist. In 1860 this work took Howells to New England, where he met many giants of American literature, including James Russell Lowell, OLIVER WENDELL HOLMES, Ralph Waldo Emerson, Henry David Thoreau, Walt Whitman, and NATHANIEL HAWTHORNE.

Journalism also led to his first important book, an 1860 biography of ABRAHAM LINCOLN. In turn, the Lincoln book earned Howells the American consulship at Venice in 1861, where he remained during the CIVIL WAR. Upon his return to the United States, Howells began work as an editor, eventually serving in that capacity at some of the finest magazines of his day: ATLANTIC MONTHLY, *Harper's Monthly,* and the *Nation.* Howells relished this role, because it allowed him to encounter and further the careers of other writers.

The many, many writers whom Howells supported or celebrated were diverse both in background and in emphasis and included controversial writers, women writers, and writers of color. Most were younger than Howells, including Abraham Cahan, CHARLES WADDELL CHESNUTT, STEPHEN CRANE, Emily Dickinson, PAUL LAURENCE DUNBAR, MARY E. WILKINS FREEMAN, HAMLIN GARLAND, CHARLOTTE PERKINS GILMAN, Frank Norris, and EDITH WHARTON. As for his contemporaries, Howells was very close to both HENRY JAMES and MARK TWAIN.

As advocate and practitioner of literary REALISM, or the accurate portrayal of everyday life of ordinary people, Howells was opposed to popular sentimental and romantic fiction. He was convinced that literature should do more than just entertain; it also should instruct and uplift, but gracefully and not by means of didacticism. His concerns included many of the major phenomena of the time: urbanization, industrialization, and social and economic inequality and injustice. Over time Howells began to espouse socialism.

His commitment to an accurate account of the human condition did not completely extend to sexuality as a motivating force; Howells largely dealt with it indirectly in his fiction. This restraint, along with other of his more conservative propensities, contributed to the derision and dismissal of Howells's work late in his career. Among others, Frank Norris, AMBROSE BIERCE, H. L. Mencken, Sinclair Lewis, and Van Wyck Brooks complained that his fiction was too optimistic and wanting in vitality and insight.

In the 1930s, however, his reputation underwent revision and revival, which have continued to the present. Howells is once again recognized for his impact on American literature. He is best known as a novelist, and his finest contributions in this genre are usually seen as *A Modern Instance* (1882), *The Rise of Silas Lapham* (1885), *A Hazard of New Fortunes* (1890), and *The Landlord at Lion's Head* (1897). These works reveal his skill and scope in subject, treatment, and technique.

His 36 works of drama are in *The Complete Plays of W. D. Howells* (1960), while some of Howells's observations on literature can be found in *Criticism and Fiction* (1891) and the three-volume *Selected Criticism* (1992). *My Mark Twain* (1910) is probably his most distinguished biography, and his travel books include *Venetian Life* (1866). As for autobiography, *Years of My Youth* (1916) stands out. Much of his correspondence is collected, in *Life in Letters of William Dean Howells* (1928).

Often overlooked if not unknown, the short stories are an important reflection on Howells's biography. In *Selected Short Stories of William Dean Howells* (1997), Ruth Bardon points out that Howells's 46 works in this genre span his career and reflect both his biography and the development of his literary theories and practice; they include popular romance, realism, psychological realism, and psychic romance. The most often anthologized of Howells's short fiction is "Editha" (1905).

Those of Howells's collections that contain at least one short story are *Suburban Sketches* (1871), *A Day's Pleasure and Other Sketches* (1881), *A Fearful Responsibility and Other Stories* (1881), *Christmas Every Day and Other Stories Told for Children* (1893), *A Pair of Patient Lovers* (1901), *Questionable Shapes* (1903), *Between the Dark and the Daylight* (1907), and *The Daughter of the Storage and Other Things in Prose and Verse* (1916).

BIBLIOGRAPHY

Abeln, Paul. *William Dean Howells and the Ends of Realism.* New York: Routledge, 2005.

American Literary Realism. Special Issue on Howells 38, no. 2 (Winter 2006).

Baum, Rosalie Murphy. "Editha's War: 'How Glorious.'" In *War and Words: Horror and Heroism in the Literature of Warfare,* edited by Sara Munson Deats, Lagretta Tallent Lenker, and Merry G. Perry, 145–163. Lexington, Md.: Lanham, 2004.

Cady, Edwin. *The Realist at War: The Mature Years, 1885–1920.* Westport, Conn.: Greenwood, 1986.

———. *The Road to Realism: The Early Years, 1837–1885.* Syracuse, N.Y.: Syracuse University Press, 1956.

Campbell, Donna M. "Howells' Untrustworthy Realist: Mary Wilkins Freeman." *ALR* 38, no. 2 (Winter 2006): 115–131.

Carrington, George, Jr. *The Immense Complex Drama: The World and Art of the Howells Novel.* Columbus: Ohio State University Press, 1966.

Crowley, John. *The Mask of Fiction: Essays on W. D. Howells.* Amherst: University of Massachusetts Press, 1989.

Davidson, Rob. *The Master and the Dean: The Literary Criticism of Henry James and William Dean Howells.* Columbia: University of Missouri Press, 2005.

Eble, Kenneth. *William Dean Howells.* 2nd ed. Boston: Twayne, 1982.

Marovitz, Sanford. "W. D. Howells: Realism, Morality, and Nostalgia." In *Transatlantic Cultural Contexts: Essays in Honor of Eberhard Brüning,* edited by Hartmut Keil, 9–20. Stauffenberg: Verlag, 2005.

Petrie, Paul. *Conscience and Purpose: Fiction and Social Consciousness in Howells, Jewett, Chesnutt, and Cather.* Tuscaloosa: University of Alabama Press, 2005.

Prioleau, Elizabeth. *The Circle of Eros: Sexuality in the Work of William Dean Howells.* Durham, N.C.: Duke University Press, 1983.

Wray, Sarah. "Light and Darkness in Howells's 'Editha': A Feminist Critique." *Explicator* 65, no. 3 (2007): 157–159.

Geoffrey C. Middlebrook
California State University at Los Angeles

"HOW THE GRINCH STOLE CHRISTMAS" DR. SEUSS (1957)

Having gone through 53 printings, translations into more than 20 languages, sales of more than 200 million copies, and transformation into a much-loved 1966 television Christmas classic, Dr. Seuss's justly revered 1957 story "How the Grinch Stole Christmas" shares the moral framework of that other famous Christmas story Charles Dickens's "A Christmas Carol." Seuss's plot focuses on the emotional growth of one solitary creature, the Grinch, who has a heart "two sizes too small" and lives in a cave just north of Who-ville, friendless save for his much-abused dog, Max. Loathing the feasting and singing and sheer happiness of Christmas, the Grinch garbs himself as St. Nick with poor Max in tow as a reindeer and steals every present, every decoration, and every tree in Who-ville on Christmas Eve. Poised to drop the Christmas goodies off a cliff, the Grinch waits for the sounds of Whos wailing; instead, he hears singing. Amazed by the possibility that perhaps Christmas will come to Whos even without decorations and presents, the Grinch experiences an EPIPHANY during which his "small heart / Grew three sizes that day!" He returns all the treats and trimmings to the Whos and participates in the holiday revelry.

Told in 52 brief pages with the simple patterns and repetitions of nursery school rhymes and wonderfully invented words (the word *grinch* has irrevocably entered the commonplace vernacular to describe any stingy or crabby person), the story is deceptively simple. Like the rest of Dr. Seuss's tales, it is as much for adults as for children. Where Seuss's "The Lorax" warns against the destruction of the environment and *The Butter Battle Book* warns against the danger of weapons proliferation, this story teaches us that Christmas is a feeling, not a sale. Long before the era of malls in which Christmas displays go up in August, "Grinch" speaks without didacticism against the commodification of the holiday spirit and for the genuine sentiment of love and togetherness.

BIBLIOGRAPHY
MacDonald, Ruth K. *Dr. Seuss.* New York: Twayne, 1988.

S. L. Yentzer
University of Georgia

"HOW TO TELL A TRUE WAR STORY" TIM O'BRIEN (1990)

TIM O'BRIEN's "How to Tell a True War Story" is an often-anthologized metafictional short story that provides, among many surprises, an important literary representation of the Vietnam War and the trauma it inflicted upon individuals. The story is part commentary on the nature of truth in storytelling and part illumination on the character's experiences in war. In fact, the narration is divided into 15 sections that range from commenting on how a war story ought to be told to the story itself. In one sense, O'Brien appears to be experimenting with POSTMODERNISM through the deconstruction of his tale, which bears witness to the death of a comrade into so many fragmentary episodes, some that repeat particular details. In another sense, O'Brien is commenting on the traumatic impact war has upon those who survive it. In fact, O'Brien's narrator explains that "a war story is never moral" (68) but that "you can tell a true war story by its absolute and uncompromising allegiance to obscenity and evil" (69).

Although the criticism of O'Brien's story ranges from canonization to cautious reverence, many scholars agree that he uses metafiction effectively, and his depiction of trauma is a central theme. Catherine Calloway lauds O'Brien's use of metafiction in which form "perfectly embodies its theme" (255). This linkage of form and theme is also praised by Daniel Robinson, who declares that O'Brien's "truths lie as much in the fragmented, impressionistic stories he tells as in the narrative technique he chooses for the telling" (257). Heberele goes one step further in specifying how the theme and form unite as a "brilliant representation of trauma writing," in which the 14 sections of the story raise awareness of "the validity of fiction and its relationship to trauma" (187).

O'Brien uses metafiction as a device to fragment the trauma that his narrator experienced during his service in Vietnam. The narrator/protagonist seeks to fragment, hide, and tell his story only in piecemeal fashion. The narrator is traumatized by essentially witnessing the death of Curt Lemon and by being involved in the cleanup of the body parts. This story finds a central metaphor in the blown-up body parts of the deceased soldier, Curt Lemon, hanging from a tree that the narrator has to climb to retrieve it. Like the fragmented body of Lemon, the narrator's story is broken into parts consisting of story and commentary as representative of his trauma. He tells the story of Lemon's death four times, and it is this retelling, in various ways, that reflects an attempt by the narrator to reveal, however slyly, his own inexpressible traumatic reaction.

The commentary about the episode seems as important as the episode itself, as if O'Brien's goal here is to recreate the sense of disbelief that accompanies shocking events. For example, the narrator laments, "When a guy dies, like Curt Lemon, you look away and then look back for a moment and then look away again" (71). The narrator is so traumatized that in his telling of the episode the first time, he seeks to find a description of the episode that will allow him an acceptable way to remember the horror. He describes the death as "almost beautiful, the way the sunlight came around him and lifted him up and sucked him high into a tree full of moss and vines

and white blossoms" (70). There are no gory details on this first telling. The next time he tries to tell the story in a journalistic manner by keeping to facts: "Curt Lemon stepped on a booby-trapped 105 round. He was playing catch with Rat Kiley, laughing, and then he was dead. The trees were thick; it took nearly an hour to cut an LZ for the dustoff" (78). Up to that point in the narrative, O'Brien describes the death scene but never with as much vigor and detail as he describes Rat Kiley's vengeful butchering of a water buffalo. Then, as if the detailing of the water buffalo's destruction has freed him to render gore more fully, the narrator's third description of the episode includes more details:

> Then he [Lemon] took a peculiar half step, moving from shade into bright sunlight, and the booby-trapped 105 round blew him into a tree. The parts were just hanging there, so Dave Jensen and I were ordered to shinny up and peel him off. I remember the white bone of an arm. I remember pieces of skin and something wet and yellow that must've been the intestines. (83)

Yet the narrator claims it is not the gore that wakes him up 20 years later, but instead it is the memory of Jensen singing "'Lemon Tree' as we threw down the parts" (83). O'Brien's telling of the scene will not end on the graphic reality of the episode. His fourth description finally openly merges memory with incident as he begins, "Twenty years later, I can still see the sunlight on Lemon's face" (84). He attempts once again to make sense of the scene while describing it, curiously aware of his own artifice by saying,

> But if I could ever get the story right, how the sun seemed to gather around him and pick him up and lift him high into a tree, if I could somehow re-create the fatal whiteness of that light, the quick glare, the obvious cause and effect, then you would believe the last thing Curt Lemon believed, which for him must've been the final truth. (84)

By ending with this description, O'Brien's narrator connects the traumatic incident with the mysteries of human thoughts and emotions. O'Brien is healing trauma with story. Is it finally more important to accept the impossibility of knowing a dead man's thoughts than to accept the memory's unreliability in rendering specific physical details? By clearly denouncing the mimetic fallacy, O'Brien is offering a revision of Vietnam War stories that pivot on the mechanism of artifice—not reality.

O'Brien's story foregrounds the structure as metafiction, and yet that same structure is found to replicate the central metaphor and theme of trauma. O'Brien's story is a powerful reminder of how fiction writing comes down to the choices a writer makes and how those choices shape the reader's experience.

BIBLIOGRAPHY

Calloway, Catherine. "'How to Tell a True War Story': Metafiction in 'The Things They Carried.'" *Critique* 36, no. 4 (1995): 249–257.

Heberle, Mark A. *A Trauma Artist: Tim O'Brien and the Fiction of Vietnam.* Iowa City: University of Iowa Press, 2001.

O'Brien, Tim. "How to Tell a True War Story." In *The Things They Carried.* Boston: Houghton Mifflin, 1990.

Robinson, Daniel. "Getting It Right: The Short Fiction of Tim O'Brien." *Critique* 40, no. 3 (1999): 257–264.

Smith, Lorrie N. "'The Things Men Do': The Gendered Subtext in Tim O'Brien's *Esquire* Stories." *Critique* 36, no. 1 (1994): 16–40.

Tal, Kali. "The Mind at War: Images of Women in Vietnam Novels by Combat Veterans." *Contemporary Literature* 21, no. 1 (1990): 76–96.

Mark Fabiano
Columbus State Community College

HUBRIS   In Greek tragedies, hubris (from the Greek *hybris,* meaning "pride" or "insolence") was the character flaw of pride or overweening self-confidence that led a person to disregard a divine warning or to violate a moral law, resulting in the hero's downfall. In general use, the term has come to mean wanton arrogance. Instances of hubris abound in short fiction, from JOEL CHANDLER HARRIS's UNCLE REMUS tales to JACK LONDON's "TO BUILD A FIRE."

HUGHES, LANGSTON (JAMES LANGS-TON HUGHES) (1902–1967)   Perhaps best known today as the major poet of the HARLEM RENAISSANCE and as one of the major American poets of the 20th century, Langston Hughes nonetheless produced impressive work in a wide variety of genres, including essays, dramas, autobiography, and newspaper columns. Less well known is that Hughes wrote stories for such mainstream publications as *Esquire* and *Scribner's* and published eight collections of short stories between 1934 and 1965. Hans Ostrom points out that one reason Hughes's stories are not better known lies in the critical tendency to associate AFRICAN-AMERICAN SHORT FICTION with novels (ix). (Witness the attention paid to novels by Claude McKay, RICHARD WRIGHT, RALPH ELLISON, JAMES BALDWIN, TONI MORRISON, and ALICE WALKER.)

Hughes's first collection, *The Ways of White Folks* (1934), implicitly announced his effort to examine the gap between the white and African-American views of life in general and the hypocrisy of white Americans in race relations in general. Using an ironic, unsentimental TONE, he overturns, in Phillip A. Snyder's words, "the traditional white/black power structure," managing not to gloss over the human weaknesses of his African-American characters and their own cultural foibles, and using "blues" humor (257). Showing a Marxist influence (Hughes wrote some of the tales while in the Soviet Union), the stories dramatize such issues as lynching, white promiscuity, and slavery. The essentially political nature of his stories sets them apart from those of such other practitioners as James Joyce, Katherine Mansfield, and ERNEST HEMINGWAY (Ostrom 18).

Laughing to Keep from Crying (1952), Hughes's second short fiction collection, contains stories that originally appeared in such magazines as the NEW YORKER, *Esquire,* and STORY. Although they continue to illuminate such realities as "passing"; segregation, particularly in hotels and restaurants; and the racism and hypocrisy that still so pointedly exist in American society, these stories are more optimistic in tone than most of the earlier stories, ultimately suggesting that African Americans have a richer future ahead.

Perhaps related to the lightening in tone from the first to the second collection, Hughes had already published the first SIMPLE STORIES; a total of four collections featuring the popular JESSE B. SIMPLE would subsequently appear. In his use of blues cynicism, weariness, and humor; in his devotion to African-American FOLKLORE; and in his clear devotion to the working class in his stories, Hughes made a lasting contribution to American short fiction.

BIBLIOGRAPHY

Bernard, Emily. *Remember Me to Harlem: The Letters of Langston Hughes and Carl Van Vechten, 1925–1964.* New York: Knopf, 2001.

Berry, Faith. *Hughes: Before and beyond Harlem.* Westport, Conn.: Lawrence Hill, 1983.

Emmanuel, James A. *Langston Hughes.* New York: Twayne, 1967.

Hughes, Langston. *The Best of Simple.* New York: Hill & Wang, 1961.

————. *Laughing to Keep from Crying.* New York: Holt, 1952.

————. *Simple Speaks His Mind.* New York: Simon & Schuster, 1950.

————. *Simple Stakes a Claim.* New York: Rinehart, 1957.

————. *Simple's Uncle Sam.* New York: Hill & Wang, 1965.

————. *Simple Takes a Wife.* New York: Simon & Schuster, 1953.

————. *Something Uncommon and Other Stories.* New York: Hill & Wang, 1963.

————. *The Ways of White Folk.* New York: Knopf, 1934.

Hughes, Steven C. *Langston Hughes and the Blues.* Normal: University of Illinois Press, 1988.

Joyce, Joyce A. "Hughes and Twentieth-Century Gender-racial Issues." In *A Historical Guide to Langston Hughes,* edited by Steven C. Tracy, 119–140. New York: Oxford University Press, 2004.

Meltzer, Milton. *Hughes: A Biography.* New York: Harper & Row, 1968.

Miller, R. Baxter. *The Art and Imagination of Hughes.* Lexington: University Press of Kentucky, 1991.

O'Daniel, Therman B., ed. *Langston Hughes, Black Genius: A Critical Evaluation.* New York: Morrow, 1971.

Ostrom, Hans. *Langston Hughes: A Study of the Short Fiction.* New York: Twayne, 1993.

Rampersad, Arnold. *The Life of Langston Hughes: I, Too, Sing America (1902–41).* Vol. 1. New York: Oxford University Press, 1986.

————. *The Life of Hughes: I Dream a World (1941–1967).* Vol. 2. New York: Oxford University Press, 1988.

Rummel, Jack. *Langston Hughes.* New York: Chelsea House, 1988.

Snyder, Phillip A. "Langston Hughes." In *Reference Guide to Short Fiction,* edited by Noelle Watson, 256–258. Detroit: Gale Press, 1994.

HUGO AWARD The Science Fiction Achievement Award given annually since 1955 in honor of Hugo Gernsback (therefore referred to almost exclusively as the Hugo). It is an "amateur" award: Recipients are chosen by SCIENCE FICTION readers and fans, as opposed to other science fiction awards, such as the NEBULA AWARD, which are awarded at the recommendation of professional panels or readers.

"HUNTERS IN THE SNOW" TOBIAS WOLFF (1981) One of the most penetrating and riveting of the 12 stories in TOBIAS WOLFF's 1981 collection *In the Garden of the North American Martyrs,* "Hunters in the Snow" was selected as the title story of the British edition that appeared in the following year. Wolff's story features three men on a hunting trip, but the friendships among the three men evolve in a complex, ironic, and contradictory manner so that the concepts of hunters and hunted, men and animals, seem to exchange places. Removed from the apparently safe haven of their homes and jobs in Spokane, Washington, each of the men seeks some sort of self-validation through the masculine ritual of the hunt, and if their discoveries seem not to alarm them, they surely distress the reader. The relentlessly falling snow and the numbing cold suffuse this story of flawed friendships gone irreversibly awry.

The story opens in the driving snow as Tub, who has been waiting over an hour for his friends Frank and Kenny, is forced to leap out of the path of the truck that jumps the sidewalk and nearly kills him. The truck is driven by Kenny, who looks at Tub and remarks, "He looks just like a beach ball with a hat on, doesn't he? Doesn't he, Frank?" This opening with its suggestion of aggression, insults, violence, and near-misses sets the mood for the rest of the story. Frank and Kenny share a close relationship from which they exclude Tub; they insult him and push him to his limit. Kenny is the most aggressive of the three, probing the weaknesses in Tub, who is overweight and is self-conscious about and denies his condition, and Frank, who feels defensive and guilty about and denies the immorality of his affair with a teenage babysitter. When they see deer tracks and realize they must ask permission to hunt it from the farmer who owns the land, Kenny, accompanied by Frank, accelerates the truck so that Tub barely makes it into the truck bed, where "he lay there, panting" in the freezing wind. In the words of the scholar and critic Dean Flower, Wolff is a master at presenting "insecure and immature adults. The effect is less [J. D.] SALINGER than, say, RAYMOND CARVER, with its special emphasis on passivity and sublimation" (278).

After gaining permission from the farmer, Kenny, kneeling on all fours, cannot resist ridiculing even the farmer's incontinent old dog, who slinks away from him. Later, angry that for the first time in 15 years he has not shot a deer, Kenny points to a post; smiles; says, "I hate that post"; and shoots it. He looks at a tree; repeats, "I hate that tree"; and shoots it. When the farmer's dog barks at him, he says, "I hate that dog" and shoots it between the eyes. As most critics and readers note, this is the turning point in the story. Tub protests that the dog has done nothing to deserve being killed; Kenny says, "I hate you"; and Tub shoots Kenny in the stomach. Frank and Tub discuss calling an ambulance and, with Kenny rather than Tub lying in the truck bed, they return to the farmhouse. After learning that the nearest hospital is 50 miles away and that the farmer had asked Kenny to shoot his old, sick dog because he could not do so himself, they return to the truck and Tub asserts himself: Grabbing Frank by the collar, he orders him to stop taunting him about his weight. Frank acquiesces and they drive off, ignoring the wounded Kenny in the back of the truck.

Because they are cold, they stop at a tavern to warm up, and they warm to each other, Frank confessing to Tub his obsession with the babysitter, apparently the daughter of a mutual friend, and Tub confessing to Frank his obsessive gluttony. As each man not only accepts but also sympathizes with the other's need to lie to his wife and family about his secret compulsions, Frank orders Tub four plates of pancakes smothered in butter and syrup and tells him to eat them all. When they return to the truck, they find the freezing and semiconscious Kenny jackknifed over the tailgate, but neither seems concerned. They know that they have lost the directions to the hospital. And it no longer matters. As the story concludes, Kenny still thinks they are taking him to the hospital, but as the narrator remarks, "He was wrong. They had taken a different turn a long way back." In the words of the reviewer Bruce Allen, Tobias Wolff "is a really rather frighteningly accomplished writer" (486) as he dispassionately presents the way individuals cope with moments of crisis in their lives. They prove themselves no better than the animals they hunt. Actually, in retrospect, the animals, lacking the urges of cruelty and vengeance, are more admirable than these human males.

BIBLIOGRAPHY

Allen, Bruce. "American Short Fiction Today." *New England Review* 4, no. 3 (Spring 1982): 486–488.

Challener, Daniel D. *Stories of Resilience in Childhood: The Narratives of Maya Angelou, Maxine Hong Kingston, Richard Rodrigues, John Edgar Wideman, and Tobias Wolff.* New York: Garland, 1997.

Flower, Dean. "Fiction Chronicle." *Hudson Review* 35, no. 2 (Summer 1982): 278–279.

Gates, David. "Our Stories, Our Selves." *Newsweek,* 23 January 1989, p. 64.

Hannah, James. *Tobias Wolff: A Study of the Short Fiction.* New York: Twayne, 1996.

Lyons, Bonnie, and Bill Oliver. "An Interview with Tobias Wolff." *Contemporary Literature,* 31 (Spring 1990): 1–16.

Wolff, Tobias. "Hunters in the Snow." In *In the Garden of the North American Martyrs.* New York: HarperPerennial, 1996.

HURSTON, ZORA NEALE (1891?–1960)

Born in Eatonville, Florida, Zora Neale Hurston—although she died in poverty and obscurity—is recognized today as the best African-American woman writer before WORLD WAR II. Despite her abusive father, who often mistreated his wife and eight children, Hurston had a mother who encouraged achievement and success and grew up in a town devoid of racism: Eatonville was an all-black town. Hurston's successes were remarkable. She studied at Howard University with Alain Locke, whose anthology *The New Negro,* published in 1925, was to revolutionize the black arts, and at Barnard College with Franz Boas, a prominent anthropologist, who encouraged Hurston's interest in African and African-American FOLKLORE. With LANGSTON HUGHES and Wallace Thurman, Hurston established *Fire!!* a magazine devoted to black literature; the magazine also published "SWEAT," one of Hurston's best stories.

With the publication of some of her earlier stories, Hurston embarked on a career of folklorist and fiction writer, merging both interests in her stories and novels, most of which are characterized by realistic details of African-American culture and DIALECT (see REALISM). Her two most frequently anthologized stories are "The GILDED SIX-BITS" and "Sweat," tales that present a complex portrait of African-American characters and culture. Indeed, Hurston was criticized by a number of men with whom she was associated in the HARLEM RENAISSANCE: Both Langston Hughes and RICHARD WRIGHT deplored her refusal of allegiance to racial and political causes, and, in return, the resolutely nonideological Hurston called the major intellectuals and artists in Harlem culture "the niggerati."

Her iconoclastic vision produced an admirable body of work, including eight short stories. Three of the most notable appeared in *Opportunity*: "Drenched in Light" depicts a young girl similar to Hurston; "Muttsy" portrays a marriage that seems doomed to fail, and "Spunk," in which Hurston deploys MAGICAL REALISM, is actually a GHOST STORY relating the haunting of a husband who has just murdered his wife's lover. Hurston wrote four novels (*Jonah's Gourd Vine,* published in 1934; *Moses, Man of the Mountain,* in 1935; the acclaimed *Their Eyes Were Watching God,* in 1937; and *Seraph on the Suwanee,* in 1948) and numerous essays, articles, and literary reviews for newspapers and magazines. Her two folklore collections are *Mules and Men*

(1935) and *Tell My Horse* (1938), and in 1942 she published her much admired autobiography, *Dust Tracks on a Road,* for which Hurston's picture appeared on the cover of the *Saturday Review of Literature.* After the 1930s, however, and with the GREAT DEPRESSION effectively ending the Harlem Renaissance, Hurston, whose seemingly conservative views alienated her from the black community and the black press, supported herself by working as a maid. She died in the poorhouse in Saint Lucie County, Florida, and was buried in a grave that remained unmarked until the writer ALICE WALKER discovered it and placed a gravestone on it. As Hurston's biographer Robert Hemenway points out, more of her work is in print today than at any point during Hurston's lifetime ("ZNH" 1,537).

BIBLIOGRAPHY

Awkward, Michael, ed. *New Essays on Their Eyes Were Watching God.* New York: Cambridge University Press, 1990.

Bloom, Harold, ed. *Zora Neale Hurston.* New York: Chelsea House, 1986.

Curry, Renee R. "Zora Neale Hurston." In *Reader's Guide to Short Fiction,* edited by Noelle Watson. Detroit: St. James Press, 1993.

Hemenway, Robert E. *Zora Neale Hurston: A Literary Biography.* Normal: University of Illinois Press, 1977.

———. "Zora Neale Hurston." In *The Heath Anthology of American Literature.* Vol. 2, 3rd edition. Edited by Paul Lauter. Lexington, Mass.: D. C. Heath, 1998.

Hurston, Zora Neale. *Dust Tracks on a Road: An Autobiography.* Philadelphia: Lippincott, 1942.

———. *Every Tongue Got to Confess: Negro Folk Tales from the Gulf States.* New York: HarperCollins, 2001.

———. *Jonah's Gourd Vine.* Philadelphia: Lippincott, 1934.

———. *I Love Myself When I Am Laughing . . . and Then Again When I Am Looking Mean and Impressive: A Hurston Reader.* Edited by Alice Walker. Old Westbury, N.Y.: Feminist Press, 1979.

———. *Moses, Man of the Mountain.* Philadelphia: Lippincott, 1939.

———. *Mules and Men.* Philadelphia: Lippincott, 1935.

———. *Seraph on the Sewanee.* New York: Scribner, 1948.

———. *Spunk: The Selected Stories.* Berkeley, Calif.: Turtle Island, 1985.

———. *Tell My Horse.* Philadelphia: Lippincott, Berkeley, Cal.: Turtle Island, 1938; as *Voodoo Gods: An Inquiry into*

Native Myths and Magic in Jamaica and Haiti. London: Dent, 1939.

————. *Their Eyes Were Watching God.* Philadelphia: Lippincott, 1937.

————, ed. *Caribbean Melodies for Chorus of Mixed Voices and Soloists.* Philadelphia: Ditson, 1947.

Kaplan, Carla, ed. *Zora Neale Hurston: A Life in Letters.* New York: Doubleday, 2002.

Menefee, Samuel Pyeatt. "Zora Neale Hurston (1891–1960)." In *Women and Tradition: A Neglected Group of Folklorists,* edited by Hilda Ellis Davidson and Carmen Blacker, 157–172. Durham, N.C.: Carolina Academic Press, 2000.

Nathiri, N. Y., ed. *Zora! A Woman and Her Community.* Orlando, Fla.: Sentinel Communications, 1991.

Turner, Darwin T. *In a Minor Chord: Three Afro-American Writers and Their Search for Identity.* Carbondale: Southern Illinois University Press, 1971.

HYPERBOLE This figure of speech, which in Greek means "overshooting," is bold overstatement, or extravagant exaggeration of fact, used for either serious or comic effect. Understatement is the opposite of hyperbole.

I

"I'M A FOOL" Sherwood Anderson (1923)
The myth about Sherwood Anderson—that in the middle of a successful advertising career he repudiated the moneymaking ethics and the regimentation of business in order to realize himself as a writer—has become part of our literary tradition, an ironic reversal of the Horatio Alger myth. After working in advertising for 12 years, he realized that he was being dishonest with words and dishonest with himself. He wanted to uproot himself, to walk out the door and out of that baleful phase of his life. Thus he walked away from his desk and out of town. The central concern of the stories for which Anderson is celebrated today is that of young boys growing into manhood. This theme links his classic cycle of related stories about Winesburg, Ohio, and the subject of *Horses and Men* (1923) and its three famous monologues that recapture his summers at the race tracks: "I Want to Know Why," "The Man Who Became a Woman," and "I'm a Fool."

In these oral narratives, the racetrack setting and the sounds and earthy smells of the stables, the closeness of horses and men, represent the easy, intimate, and idyllic relationship that Anderson was convinced existed between human beings and the natural world before the onslaught of the machine. Like the raft and the river in Mark Twain's *Huckleberry Finn,* the stables and the racetrack are places of contentment and escape, Edenic oases for the Adamic adolescent. Horses in this context embody the noble fulfillment of purposeful nature; they are dependable, honest, and fine, while adults are ambiguous, devious, and phony. Each of these three monologues is a tale of resistance to the loss of boyhood innocence and of reluctant initiation into the complexities of manhood, especially the shadowy complexities of adult sexuality.

The emotional tone of these tales, on which so much of their lasting appeal is based, mixes boyish bewilderment, frustration, and vulnerability. The boy-man in each suffers from feelings of inferiority (social and sexual), and he speaks from the depths of his being, confessing his burden of guilt and confusion in order to come to terms with it and to subdue it forever. His pitiful search for the meaning of the experience, for understanding, is his reason for telling the story, for taking us into his confidence.

Although the main incident in "I'm a Fool" has occurred some time before the telling of the tale, the big lumbering fellow who confesses it still fails to understand why it happened. He had told a lie to impress the young woman with whom he is in love, but he blames his foolishness on "the dude in the Windsor tie" and on being slightly drunk, not on the unresolved conflict of values that is tearing him up inside, the conflict between life in the stables and life in the grandstand. He is in mild revolt against the dude's false air and against the false respectability of his middle-class mother and his schoolteacher sister—respectability imposed by a binding morality and a restrictive society where money and position are at stake. Yet even he capitulates to the social importance of appearances when he meets the girl in the soft blue dress. And when he must, he, too, can put up a good front; deceiving comes easily when he is at the mercy of economic and social forces beyond his control. It is only afterward, on the beach, against the background of a clump of roots sticking up like arms, that he realizes that his denial of his origins, of his identity, will hold him back from the fulfillment of the tenderness and love that he feels. But he never understands why.

Anderson's main techniques in dramatizing the story are to convert the oral monologue into a dialogue and a series of incremental dramatic scenes, and to rearrange time in an orderly manner. The unskilled speaker in the story, unable to control his responses, rambles and runs on, in and out of time, relating events that occurred in the past, events that occurred on the day of the races (which was some time ago, before PROHIBITION), and disclosing his present, compulsive desire to make himself look cheap. That the story should adapt to a dramatic form as faithfully as it does attests to Anderson's painstaking, original craftsmanship and to his finesse in making colloquial conversation—essentially, an ancient way of storytelling—serve the needs of modern fiction and drama. In Anderson's dramatic monologue, the artless rambling of the boy-man, not only continuously reveals his CHARACTER in ways he does not even suspect but also artfully pushes the action forward.

Anderson sold "I'm a Fool" to the literary magazine the DIAL for less than $100 because he could not successfully sell it to the mass market, where editors found it unfinished and vague. But so was life, Anderson argued, and he continued to write stories that an admiring Virginia Woolf was later to call "shell-less"—stories that exposed the vulnerable areas and the secrets of thwarted lives and that illuminated the obscure realm of personal relationships.

By the example of the crisis in his own life, Sherwood Anderson is said to have liberated man from timetable servitude to business; by the example of his art, he is said to have liberated the short story from its previous dependence on slick plots and trick endings. Generations of writers have followed and will continue to follow his example in both areas. Almost all good modern fiction writers, including ERNEST HEMINGWAY and WILLIAM FAULKNER, whom Anderson so generously helped at the beginning of their literary careers, are beholden to him. Although Sherwood Anderson was a provincial in his choice of subject matter, in his concentration on the limited lives of limited human beings, he was a pioneer in his narrative techniques. (See POINT OF VIEW.)

BIBLIOGRAPHY

Anderson, Sherwood. *The Portable Sherwood Anderson.* Edited by Horace Gregory. New York: Viking, 1949.

———. *Sherwood Anderson: Short Stories.* Edited by Maxwell Geismar. New York: Hill & Wang, 1962.

———. *Winesburg, Ohio.* Edited by Malcolm Cowley. New York: Viking, 1960.

Papinchak, Robert Allen. *Sherwood Anderson: A Study of the Short Fiction.* New York: Twayne, 1992.

Small, Judy Jo. *A Reader's Guide to the Short Stories of Sherwood Anderson.* New York: G. K. Hall, 1994.

IMAGERY   The term refers to the collection or pattern of images, the representations of the sensory details in a literary work. Images typically employ one or more of the five senses (sight, sound, touch, taste, smell). For example, NATHANIEL HAWTHORNE'S "RAPPACCINI'S DAUGHTER" relies heavily on visual and olfactory (evoking the sense of smell) imagery to evoke the alluring but poisonous beauty of Dr. Rappaccini's garden.

"IN ANOTHER COUNTRY" ERNEST HEMINGWAY (1927)   There is something unique about the way ERNEST HEMINGWAY begins a short story, and readers will find no better example of this than "In Another Country," first published in 1927 as part of the collection *Men without Women.* It seems that the first paragraph of a Hemingway story functions one of three ways: It gives some sense of movement or action (for example, "The rain stopped as Nick turned into the road"); it begins with dialogue or conversation ("'All right,' said the man. 'What about it?'"); or, as is the case with "In Another Country" and many others, it creates a sense of place and/or mood. Often, these beginnings are poignant and painfully descriptive, by Hemingway standards at least.

"In Another Country" begins thus:

In the fall the war was always there, but we did not go to it any more. It was cold in the fall in Milan and the dark came very early. Then the electric lights would come on, and it was pleasant along the streets looking in the windows. There was much game hanging outside the shops, and the snow powdered in the fur of the foxes and the wind blew their tails. The deer hung stiff and heavy and empty, and small birds blew in the wind and the wind turned their feathers. It was a cold fall and the wind came down from the mountains. (206)

The story, set in WORLD WAR I Italy, begins with an echo of Hemingway's famous novel of that time and place, *A Farewell to Arms* (1929):

In the late summer of that year we lived in a house in a village that looked across the river and the plain to the mountains. In the bed of the river there were pebbles and boulders, dry and white in the sun, and the water was clear and swiftly moving and blue in the channels. Troops went by the house and down the road and the dust they raised powdered the leaves of the trees. The trunks of the trees too were dusty and the leaves fell early that year and we saw the troops marching along the road and the dust rising and leaves, stirred by the breeze, falling and the soldiers marching and afterward the road bare and white except for the leaves.

It is difficult to consider one of these paragraphs without thinking about the other, and even though there are differences in the two (one describes fall, the other summer; one suggests damp and cold, the other aridity and heat), they share the same quality, the poignant creation of place and mood. The sentences have the same surface simplicity, directness, and rhythm that most Hemingway sentences have, but in spite or perhaps because of their directness and simplicity, the reader at once embarks on a journey into a familiar place with the narrator. This familiarity that Heming-

way creates between his narrators and readers has often been commented upon, but in "In Another Country," it serves a different purpose. Readers feel as if they are there fishing the river on the plain with NICK ADAMS or watching the bullfights in Pamplona with Jake and Brett in other Hemingway works, but in this story the narrative familiarity serves as irony.

"In Another Country" is the story of an American soldier receiving physical therapy for wounds he has received in combat. Far from the front in Milan, the narrator and four other patients make their way through the streets of the city on their way to the hospital to receive treatment. There the patients are exposed to revolutionary treatments using new machines, and they naturally have doubts about the efficacy of the new treatments. The wounded veterans are naturally bitter about their wounds and the treatments they receive. The American later learns that the major is suffering emotionally because his young wife had died recently, and the story ends with the patients' continuing the cycle of pointless treatment at the hospital, the major staring out the window.

Perhaps the key to the story is the expression given by the narrator as he describes the mental condition of his fellow patients. Speaking of the lieutenant, the most decorated of the group, the narrator points out that "he had lived a very long time with death and was a little detached. We were all a little detached" (207). The idea of detachment naturally fits the story, as readers would expect that the veterans, now far from the front and dealing with their physical and emotional wounds, would feel separated from the rest of society, and readers may also expect Hemingway's terse style to suggest detachment itself. The American is detached from the Italian soldiers in his group, mainly because he received his decorations only "because I was an American" (208). He is learning Italian and is not very good at it, and that also makes him detached from the group. The doctor and his patients mainly participate in idle chat, instead of meaningful conversation.

However, in light of the mood and sense of place established in the story's opening lines as well as the relationship between the American and the major, which strengthens toward the end of the story, the idea of detachment becomes somewhat ironic. The American and the major are anything but detached when the major explains that his wife had died recently, and the sense of place established in the opening lines is so detailed and poignant that readers experiencing the narrative familiarity that Hemingway is famous for feel a strong sense of attachment and immediacy.

BIBLIOGRAPHY

Benson, Jackson J., ed. *New Critical Approaches to the Short Stories of Ernest Hemingway.* Durham, N.C.: Duke University Press, 1991.

Bloom, Harold, ed. *Ernest Hemingway: Modern Critical Views.* New York: Chelsea House, 1985.

Hemingway, Ernest. "In Another Country." In *The Complete Short Stories of Ernest Hemingway: The Finca Vigía Edition.* New York: Charles Scribner's Sons, 1987.

Oliver, Charles M. *Ernest Hemingway A to Z: The Essential Reference to the Life and Work.* New York: Facts On File, 1999.

Tyler, Lisa. *Student Companion to Ernest Hemingway.* Westport, Conn.: Greenwood Press, 2001.

Wagner-Martin, Linda, ed. *Ernest Hemingway: Six Decades of Criticism.* East Lansing: Michigan State University Press, 1988.

James Mayo
Jackson State Community College, Tennessee

"INDIAN CAMP" ERNEST HEMINGWAY (1924)

Originally printed in the April 1924 *Transatlantic Review* as "Work in Progress" and published the following year as part of IN OUR TIME, "Indian Camp" is ERNEST HEMINGWAY's earliest NICK ADAMS story. It focuses primarily on the relationship between father and son, and on its attendant rites of initiation into the world of adult experience: childbirth, loss of innocence, suicide.

The boy, Nick Adams, accompanies his doctor father to the Indian camp where a pregnant woman has serious complications as she labors to give birth. Dr. Adams ultimately saves her life and that of the baby by performing a cesarean section, but, shortly afterward, the woman's husband commits suicide. A number of specific questions have puzzled critics for decades: Why does the Indian husband kill himself? What is Uncle George's role, and why does he disappear by the end of the story? How are we supposed to feel toward Dr. Adams? Though the story is consistently read as a father-son initiation tale, these sorts of questions encourage readers to look beyond the simple and benevolent fact that Dr. Adams almost surely saved the life of the Indian woman and her baby, and focus attention on some of the more disturbing aspects of the story. First, the Indian woman's screams have been going on for a long time, so long that the men of the village have purposely moved out of earshot; but Dr. Adams tells Nick that the screams "are not important" (68) and chooses not to hear them. As a doctor, he may adopt this attitude as a professional necessity in order to accomplish the difficult task of performing the operation without anesthetic. Conversely, it may indicate his callousness to the woman's evident pain.

Readers' views of Dr. Adams may then influence the way they interpret the Indian husband's suicide: Why does he slit his throat moments after Dr. Adams has operated and the baby is successfully delivered? Do readers see a connection between the presence of Uncle George and the husband's decision to kill himself? Is Uncle George the father of the baby, as some critics suggest? Readers must also decide whether Uncle George's remark to Dr. Adams, "Oh, you're a great man, all right" (69), is meant seriously or sarcastically. Hemingway's oblique and sparse writing style encourages such open-ended questions, and his ending to the story refuses to settle on a single, clear resolution. A short burst of questions from Nick to his father on the significance of life and death leave him with this final thought: "he felt quite sure he would never die" (70). Nick's reflections on immortality, here in the protective warmth of his father's arms, may represent his last moments of youthful innocence before he falls into such adult experiences as romance and war in the later chapters of *In Our Time*.

BIBLIOGRAPHY

Hemingway, Ernest. "Indian Camp." In *The Complete Short Stories of Ernest Hemingway: The Finca Vigía Edition.* New York: Charles Scribner's Sons, 1987.

Smith, Paul. *A Reader's Guide to the Short Stories of Ernest Hemingway.* Boston: G. K. Hall, 1989.

Amy Strong
University of North Carolina at Chapel Hill

IN OUR TIME ERNEST HEMINGWAY (1925, 1930)

The publishing dates, the authoritative text, even the genre of the text all prove intensely problematic, for Ernest Hemingway's early stories and arguably his best sustained work. Published in Paris in 1924 as *in our time*, a series of vignettes, it was published in New York in 1925 in an expanded version entitled *In Our Time*. When either literary scholars or the popular audience refers to the "Hemingway style," it is the style of *in our time* (and of *The Sun Also Rises*, published one year later) that people have in mind. Among the best-known stories in the collection are "BIG TWO-HEARTED RIVER" and "Indian Camp," featuring NICK ADAMS, their modernist PROTAGONIST. (See MODERNISM.)

Sometimes regarded as a mere collection of short stories, sometimes seen as a SHORT STORY CYCLE in the vein of James Joyce's *Dubliners*, sometimes heralded as the literary descendant of SHERWOOD ANDERSON'S *WINESBURG, OHIO*, Hemingway's *in our time* has more in common with JEAN TOOMER'S *CANE*—another textually and generically complicated work—than with any other well-known work. In fact, the "pretty good unity" (to cite Hemingway's own words about *in our time*; Baker 26) that characterizes both *in our time* and *Cane* might accurately be described as an ironically fragmentary unity, in which dissonance is an integral part of both structure and THEME. In other words, the fragments themselves contribute to a peculiar sort of unity.

The best discussion of the complicated publishing of the works that finally constitute *in our time* is Michael J. Reynolds's "Hemingway's *In Our Time*: The Biography of a Book." Beginning with "My Old Man" and "Out of Season" (the first of which is clearly indebted to Anderson), portions of what would finally make *in our time* were published as *Three Stories & Ten Poems* in 1923. The same year, six of the vignettes or "interchapters" that would finally be interlaced between the nominal 14 stories of the 1925 publication were published in *little review*, one of the most influential of the LITTLE MAGAZINES. The following year 18 sketches (two of which would be retitled as short stories in the 1925 version) were published as a small chapbook entitled *in our time* (Paris: Three Mountains

Press). Over 1924 and the first half of 1925, numerous individual short stories that would be collected in *in our time* also appeared in a variety of journals. However, in 1925 the first major version of *In Our Time* as we know it was published by Boni & Liveright, including 16 sketches (called "chapters" but unlisted on the contents page) and 14 short stories. In 1930 a new piece (similar in tone to the vignettes or chapters) prefaced the work and was called "An Introduction by the Author"; it would later be retitled as "In the Quai at Smyrna" (first in *The First Forty-Nine Stories*) and later in the republication of *In Our Time* by Scribner in 1955.

It is little wonder that Hemingway's highly influential and earliest sustained artistic work has proven so critically elusive. Of the individual short stories comprising *in our time*, possibly "Indian Camp" and the two-part "Big Two-Hearted River" are the best known. As these two short stories might suggest, many of the nominal short stories in *In Our Time* roughly tell the story of Nick Adams (sometimes considered to be a surrogate for Hemingway himself), first growing up in Michigan (with a doctor for a father), rejecting early relationships with women, exploring Europe, then facing both WORLD WAR I and its aftermath. These stories—as well as others, such as "Mr. and Mrs. Elliot," "Soldier's Home," or "Cat in the Rain"—have much in common with Hemingway's subsequent work, *The Sun Also Rises*, the work that became known as the hallmark of the "Lost Generation" (a phrase that GERTRUDE STEIN used dismissively and that Hemingway reproduced as the epigraph to *Sun*). At least superficially, the stories seem to record a certain ennui, a loss of faith in traditional ideals and values, and a certain resignation to an emasculated and impoverished modern world. Taken with the interchapters, a series of vignettes appearing between longer stories, (at least one of which, "Chapter VI," includes Nick), however, the collected stories and volume *In Our Time* make a heavy indictment against the war, violence, even misogyny that the stories alone appear partially to record, if not condone. In fact, the brutal violence of bullfighting and war depicted in the interchapters seems the logical extension of the accounts of fishing or boxing found in the stories.

Read as a collective work, *In Our Time* ironically dismantles the patriarchal, if not sexist, assumptions that past scholarship wrongly attributed to the author as the "HEMINGWAY CODE," and strongly suggests that the supposedly innocent age preceding World War I was not so innocent after all.

Despite the controversies and complications of *in our time,* stylistically this work changed modern American prose. The rigorous, terse, realistic style that Hemingway created in this work (albeit with notable and unusual uses of repetition—all stylistic strategies he may have learned from Gertrude Stein) has been imitated frequently but rarely matched. How Hemingway accomplished this artistic feat is at least partially recorded in his posthumously published *A Moveable Feast,* an autobiographical narrative (and partial fiction) that records his life during the writing of *in our time.*

BIBLIOGRAPHY

Frye, Northrup. *Anatomy of Criticism.* Princeton, N.J.: Princeton University Press, 1957, 365.

Hemingway, Ernest. *In Our Time.* New York: Boni & Live-right. 1925, 1930. Reprint, New York: Scribner, 1958, 1970.

———. Letter to E. Wilson, October 18, 1924, p. 26, in Carlos Baker. *Ernest Hemingway: A Life Story.* New York: Scribner, 1967.

Moddlemog, Deborah. "The Unifying Consciousness of a Divided Conscience: Nick Adams as Author of *In Our Time.*" *American Literature* (1988): 591–610.

Reynolds, Michael. *Critical Essays on Hemingway's In Our Time.* Boston: G. K. Hall, 1983.

———. "Hemingway's *In Our Time*: The Biography of a Book." In *Modern American Short Story Sequences,* edited by Gerald Kennedy. New York: Cambridge University Press, 1995.

Smith, Paul. *A Reader's Guide to the Short Stories of Ernest Hemingway.* New York: Macmillan, 1989.

Wagner-Martin, Linda. "Toomer's *Cane* as Narrative Sequence." In *Modern American Short Story Sequences,* edited by Gerald Kennedy. New York: Cambridge University Press, 1995.

Winn, H. "Hemingway's *In Our Time*: 'Pretty Good Unity'." *Hemingway Review* (1990): 124–140.

Jacqueline Vaught Brogan
University of Notre Dame

INTENTIONAL FALLACY   A critical term that means the author's stated or implied intentions may well be fallacious, misleading, or even useless for the reader who interprets the author's work, because the author's design or plan in writing the work may not correspond to what was actually produced. In other words, a reader's reliance on an author's intention when writing the piece may lead to an erroneous interpretation. Intentional fallacy suggests that the true meaning of a work should be found only by analyzing the actual text without any reference to the author's avowed or supposed purpose, which may introduce factors personal to the author, such as state of mind, that could be irrelevant to the actual work.

"INTERVENTION"   JILL MCCORKLE (2003)
In an age of plastic surgery, stomach stapling, and laser treatments, American culture has placed its focus not on only hiding flaws but erasing them entirely in the quest for perfection. "Intervention," by JILL MCCORKLE, was first published in *Ploughshares* in 2003 and uses a distinct trait of southern writing, an emphasis on family, to show that perfection is far from ideal; it is through flaws and weaknesses that the greatest love can be shown. McCorkle says of southern writing: "Somewhere woven into the history and detail, the asides that often carry us into left field, there is a plotline—something actually happened—but there are other stories as well, slipping like bright threads in all directions. You follow first this one and then that one, but if you listen long enough, they begin to come clear. There is indeed a pattern and a texture" ("Preface" ix).

"Intervention" is more than a story of the aging couple Sid and Marilyn. It is also the story of their children, Sally and Tom, and their spouses, Rusty and "Snow Bunny." While the central plotline of the story is Sid's pending intervention, readers are rewarded with a multilayered entity containing several stories.

After Marilyn expresses concern to Sally about Sid's drinking—"there were times when she watched Sid pull out of the driveway only to catch herself imagining that this could be the last time she ever saw him"—Sally begins to plan an intervention (276). "Marilyn has never heard the term intervention before her daughter, Sally, introduces it and showers her with a pile of literature" (275). Marilyn immediately regrets sharing her concerns with her children, and readers experience her unease with keeping a secret from Sid. As she waits for the intervention day to arrive, her feelings are of guilt rather than hope as she reflects on her own flaws, which Sid has carefully helped her erase.

Marilyn and Sid are a strong family unit who have stayed together in spite of a number of potentially fatal mistakes, largely Marilyn's. Her struggle to forgive herself for an affair that took place when Sally and Tom were young children exists even at the time of the intervention: "Whenever anything in life—the approach of spring, the smell of gin, pine sap thawing and reviving to life—prompts her memory, she cringes and feels the urge to crawl into a dark hole. She does not recognize that woman. That woman was sick. A sick, foolish woman, a woman who had no idea that the best of life was in her hand" (285).

In the style of southern literature, the family pulls together in times of crisis and protects itself against outside forces. In this case, the "outside forces" are their own children. "If you live long enough, your children learn to love you from afar, their lives are front and center and elsewhere. Your life is only what they can conjure from bits and pieces. They don't know how it all fits together. They don't know all the sacrifices that have been made" (288). The children and their spouses do not understand the delicate balance of their parents' marriage, that they are like two playing cards leaning up against one another with the perfect amount of stability. Marilyn's realization of how much she depends on both the steady presence of Sid and the strength of their history together shows that the survival of a family involves occasionally closing out the surrounding world.

When the family gathers on intervention day, Sid acknowledges their concern and shows Marilyn that familial love is that in which love exists because flaws are embraced and not "fixed." He makes a show of pouring several bottles of bourbon and Scotch down the kitchen sink. "She [Marilyn] nods and watches him pour out some cheap Scotch he always offers to cheap friends. He keeps the good stuff way up high behind her mother's silver service" (289). After the children leave, Marilyn fixes them both a drink with the "good stuff" Sid kept hidden. She reflects again on the events surrounding her affair, on their grandchildren, and finally surmises of herself and Sid, "It is their house. It is their life" (290).

While readers are focused on Sid and Marilyn, on their past and future, and on the intervention, McCorkle weaves in elements of Sally and Tom's lives as well. Sally is married to Rusty, who has been promoted and is thinking about going back to school. Tom's thread focuses on his former wife and the grandchildren who live in Minnesota and Sid and Marilyn never see but speak to on the phone. Tom and his wife, referred to by Sid and Marilyn as "Snow Bunny," want to have a child. Tom and Marilyn's relationship is explored through Marilyn's recollections of her own drinking history. "She has always wanted to ask him what he remembers from those horrible days. Does he remember finding her there on the floor?" (288–289). The addition of these separate story lines, while not fully developed, provides rich depth of character and the pattern and texture McCorkle suggests are highly characteristic of southern storytelling.

Contemporary southern writing, while shifting into a decidedly "modern" framework, maintains the core characteristics of the foundation established by WILLIAM FAULKNER, EUDORA WELTY, and FLANNERY O'CONNOR. While McCorkle weaves many separate story threads together, the pattern they form is one of family and of love. The support of family in spite of life's tribulations, while seemingly lost in American culture, is still paramount in southern literature, both CLASSIC and contemporary.

BIBLIOGRAPHY

McCorkle, Jill. "Intervention." In *Best American Short Stories 2004,* edited by Katrina Kenison. New York: Houghton Mifflin, 2004.
———. "Preface." In *New Stories from the South 2005,* edited by Shannon Ravenel. Chapel Hill, N.C.: Algonquin Books of Chapel Hill, 2005.

Kelly Flanigan

"IN THE CEMETERY WHERE AL JOLSON IS BURIED" AMY HEMPEL (1985)

"In the Cemetery Where Al Jolson Is Buried" initially appeared in AMY HEMPEL's first collection of short stories titled *Reasons to Live* (1985), a group of stories that address various scenarios of coping, with this story, according to Hempel, providing the foundation for the rest. Ever since it was first published, the story has been well received critically, including being reprinted in many collections such as the Norton Anthologies, which are frequently used in college classrooms. Hempel's style of writing is considered minimalistic, because she does not focus on the character and plot development traditionally associated with stories; instead, the focus is on presenting an experience as it happens without any editorial comments by one of the characters or the story's narrator. Classification with MINIMALISM places her squarely with Mary Robison as an heir to RAYMOND CARVER, working in a narrative voice that echoes the voices of writers such as Anton Chekhov, ERNEST HEMINGWAY, and Samuel Beckett in his early works. Her uniqueness, however, lies in her use of humor to lighten the darkness of the situation that she is portraying.

This story centers on an unidentified first-person narrator, who is the best friend of a similarly unidentified terminally ill patient in an intensive care ward at a generically identified hospital in the Hollywood area (the hospital is described as the one appearing under the opening credits of the *Marcus Welby, M.D.* television show, which ran from 1969 to 1976). The narrator makes small talk to distract her friend, telling her, for example, about the first chimp that was taught to talk using sign language but was caught in a lie. The narrator had taken two months to visit her friend because she had feared looking death in the face, yet the two friends joke about topics such as the "Five stages of grief" defined by Dr. Elisabeth Kübler-Ross in 1969. When the friend finally dies or, as the narrator euphemistically puts it, is "moved to the cemetery, the one where Al Jolson is buried" (349), the narrator starts to face her own fears by enrolling "in a 'Fear of Flying' class" (349). As the story ends, the narrator ponders how she might retell the events of her friend's death in the future by adjusting the details that she chooses to include as part of her own "language of grief" (350).

BIBLIOGRAPHY

Hallett, Cynthia Whitney. "Amy Hempel." In *Minimalism and the Short Story—Raymond Carver, Amy Hempel, and Mary Robison.* Lewiston, N.Y.: Edwin Mellon, 1999, 67–99.

Hempel, Amy. "In the Cemetery Where Al Jolson Is Buried." *The Scribner Anthology of Contemporary Short Fiction,* edited by Lex Williford and Michael Martone, 343–350. New York: Scribner–Simon & Schuster, 1999.

Peggy J. Huey
University of Tampa

"IN THE FIELD" TIM O'BRIEN (1990)

In the short story cycle *The Things They Carried* (1990), TIM O'BRIEN cemented his reputation as one of the most powerful chroniclers of the VIETNAM WAR, joining the conversation alongside Philip Caputo (*A Rumor of War*), Michael Herr (*Dispatches*), David Halberstam (*The Best and the Brightest*), and the poet Bruce Weigl (*Song of Napalm*), among others. Comprising 22 pieces—some little more than vignettes, others more "traditional" stories—the collection details the experiences of the soldier Tim O'Brien, who returns to his native Minnesota after a tour of duty in Vietnam. In his subsequent role as author, O'Brien records his recollections in a false memoir of sorts as a way of reconstructing the war's elusive "truth." O'Brien's goal in *The Things They Carried,* he tells Michael Coffey, "was to write something utterly convincing but without any rules as to what's real and what's made up. I forced myself to try to invent a new form. I had never invented form before" (60).

"In the Field" follows Lieutenant Jimmy Cross and his platoon of 17 remaining men as they search a Vietnamese muck field for Kiowa, a lost comrade. Cross, who figures prominently in several of the book's pieces—including the eponymous "The Things They Carried," the collection's most anthologized story—feels tremendous guilt over Kiowa's death, not the least because the previous evening, just before an ambush, Cross refused to disobey orders and to move his men to higher, and therefore safer, ground. Kiowa, buried when a fellow soldier inadvertently gave away the platoon's position to the enemy, was a popular soldier. Out of respect for their fallen comrade, the men dutifully wade through waist-deep sewage searching for his remains; they sustain themselves with a morbid sense of humor, making light of the situation in order to quell their fear of random, sudden death at the hands of a faceless enemy. Cross quickly realizes that he is ill suited for the military, having been shipped to Vietnam after joining the officer training corps in college only to be with friends and to collect a few college credits. "[Cross] did not care one way or the other about the war," O'Brien intones, "and he had no desire to command, and even after all these months in the bush, all the days and nights, even then he did not know enough to keep his men out of a shit field" (168).

War is a great leveler in O'Brien's fiction. In the field where Cross and his men search for Kiowa, "The filth seemed to erase identities, transforming the men into identical copies of a single soldier, which was exactly how Jimmy Cross had been trained to treat them, as interchangeable units of command" (163). The young lieutenant, however, suspends his humanity only with great difficulty. Ruminating on Kiowa's death, he imagines writing a letter to the soldier's father before deciding that "no apologies were necessary, because in fact it was one of those freak things, and the war was full of freaks, and nothing could ever change it anyway" (176). Cross's rationalization may absolve him (at least in part) of his guilt over Kiowa's death, though it is also a tacit admission of his lack of control over the war's daily life-and-death struggles. Cross's desire to organize the details of Kiowa's death in his own mind is an extension of O'Brien's attempt in *The Things They Carried* to construct a coherent narrative that finds the essential truth of war (a notion that the author confirms in the ironically titled "How to Tell a True War Story," which acts as an interpretive key to his recollections).

Upon the discovery of Kiowa's body, the men properly mourn the loss of their fellow soldier, though "they also felt a kind of giddiness, a secret joy, because they were alive, and because even the rain was preferable to being sucked under a shit field, and because it was all a matter of luck and happenstance" (175).

Cross, yearning for war's end, imagines himself on a golf course in his New Jersey hometown, free of the burden of leading men to their deaths. O'Brien examines the onus of responsibility often, and in the related story "Field Trip," which details the author's return to Vietnam two decades later to the field where Kiowa died, O'Brien finds a world barely recognizable as the one he left behind. "The field remains, but in a form much different from what O'Brien remembers, smaller now, and full of light," Patrick A. Smith writes of O'Brien's visit. "The air is soundless, the ghosts are missing, and the farmers who now tend the field go back to work after stealing a curious glance in his direction. The war is absent, except in O'Brien's memory" (107). But it is memory, O'Brien makes clear, that supersedes experience and haunts soldiers long after the shooting has stopped.

BIBLIOGRAPHY
Coffey, Michael. "Tim O'Brien: Inventing a New Form Helps the Author Talk about War, Memory, and Storytelling." *Publishers Weekly,* 16 February 1990, pp. 60–61.
O'Brien, Tim. "In the Field." In *The Things They Carried.* Boston: Houghton Mifflin, 1990.
Smith, Patrick A. *Tim O'Brien: A Critical Companion.* Westport, Conn.: Greenwood Press, 2005.

Patrick A. Smith
Bainbridge College (GA)

"IN THE HEART OF THE HEART OF THE COUNTRY" William H. Gass (1968)

William H. Gass is an eminent theorist and practitioner of postmodern *metafiction,* self-reflexive, performative fictions that emphasize the writing process itself by directing the reader's attention to the author's shaping presence in the showy deployment of literary strategies and conventions. But "In the Heart of the Heart of the Country" is perhaps more indebted to the older tradition of the prose poem for its relatively plotless alternations of preoccupation and mood and its intricate pattern of recurring verbal phrases and imagery (eyes, windows, wings, wires, worms, flies, flying, and spilling—all of which are implicated in a sustained dialectic of the prepositions *beyond* and *in*). A monologic narration, it has the sketchy, notational structure of a poet's daybook, and it might seem a hodgepodge of lyrical reveries; aphoristic, even gnomic, maxims about love and loss; and more prosaic quasi-ethnographic comments on a deteriorating small Indiana community where the narrator, a poet, spent his happy boyhood and youth and to which he has returned in order to recover emotional and artistic virility.

Feeling "spilled, bewildered, quite mislaid," the narrator adjures, "I must pull myself together . . . there is nothing left of me but mouth" (202). He feels "bereft" with multiple, interrelated losses: of love, family, job, youth, health, self-respect, and sense of vocational purpose or inspiration ("wings withering . . . I've fallen" 179). His ostensibly jotted, but often lapidarian, notes seem intended as a vehicle of recovery, being addressed both to himself and to a lost lover who is also in some sense his lost best self—the boy in him. "In retirement from love," he claims, "the fool's position of having love left over which I'd like to lose" and asks scornfully, "What good is it now to me" (173). He also mocks poetry as lying and derides the objects of its rhetorical inflation. Thus "Childhood is a lie of poetry" (205) and his lost beloved a "fiction," a mere literary trope (179). And yet he cannot resist repeatedly evoking the "perpetual summer" of his love affair in terms of a literary child, Huckleberry Finn: "I dreamed my lips would drift down your back like a skiff on a river" (179); "we are adrift on a raft; your back is our river" (188). He knows he must restrain his poet's predilection for hyperbole, "another lie of poetry" (202). Realizing that he is too prone to poetic posturing and embellishing even the minutest details, he tells himself, "I must stop making up things. I must give myself to life; let it mold me," rather than vice versa. Yet he also realizes in his self-conscious pride as an intellectual that such platitudes are "what they say in *Wisdom's Monthly Digest* every day" (187). Poetry is archaic, perpetrating and perpetuating myths that belie contemporary reality. For example, the Nature it extols hardly exists and no longer matters as a standard by which to evaluate human endeavor, superseded, even among farmers, by machinery, chemistry, and accounting (194). Poetic images are but cenotaphs on emotions, "stones . . . memorials" laid over the things in themselves; the "wild flood of words" that

bursts from the dam of loneliness cannot adequately apprehend the world as it is: "Beneath this sea lies sea" (179, 195).

The inadequacies of poetry and the deceits of poets partially explain why some of the narrator's descriptive observations seem projections of his inner state, as when he calls telephone wires "where sparrows sit like fists" (190). These wires "offend" because they fence off the landscape, "enclosing the crows," yet not feeling free himself and resenting what escapes him, he resents "all the beyond birds" (174). That said, the narrator's own acutely felt condition also heightens fellow feeling, giving him empathetic intimations of the human condition he shares with his neighbors, Billy Holsclaw and Mrs. Desmond. This conflation of projection and empathetic *feeling-into* is exemplified by the way he describes dilapidated, decaying houses as reflections of the afflicted condition of their inmates: "These houses are now dying like the bereaved who inhabit them; they are slowly losing their senses," becoming blind, decrepit, and insecure (181). The ubiquity of this imagery confesses the narrator's obsessive preoccupation with a debilitated and rehabilitated willingness to see: "Our eyes have been driven in like the eyes of the old men. And there's no one to have mercy on us" (176). (It should also be noted that he endorses an early 19th-century account of small-town Indiana that indicts the "wormish blindness" of its inhabitants [178]). The narrator acknowledges that there is "no way of knowing . . . whether [Billy is] as vacant and barren and loveless as the rest of us are—here in the heart of the heart of the country" (180). But Billy seems to return to his attention as a dark ALTER EGO and portent: "His house and his body are dying together," and, suffering from glaucoma, "His windows are boarded" (200–201). The writer's, perhaps any writer's, ambivalence—a combination of compassionate sensitivity and exploitative desire to make use—can be heard in his annotation: "I'm not sure what his presence means to me . . . or to anyone. Nevertheless, I keep wondering whether given time, I might not someday find a figure in our language which would serve him faithfully, and furnish his poverty and loneliness richly out" (190).

Both Billy and Mrs. Desmond are in their loneliness greedy talkers, just as the narrator is in his journal. Mrs. Desmond, a habitually fretful "life-deaf old lady," reminisces compulsively in an unsuccessful attempt to draw down the shade and fence off an equally compulsive awareness of death lurking in time. It is noteworthy that Mrs. Desmond is disturbed by Mr. Tick, the poet's cat. Much like the poet Christopher Smart's cat Jeoffrey (in *Jubilate Agno*), Mr. Tick is, in his electric mobility, an embodiment of poetry as it might be, "his long tail rhyming with his paws" (183). His strong, practical application of his tongue is implicitly contrasted to the poet's stymied and impotent use of his own (185). More fundamentally, Mr. Tick is the very embodiment of *living in*—a mode of being undisturbed by the superfluity of consciousness. Thus, the narrator addresses him with a mixture of praise and lament: "You are alive, alive exactly, and it means nothing to you—much to me. . . . You are a cat so easily. Your nature is not something you must rise to. You, not I, live in: in house, in skin, in shrubbery" (184). This complete occupation of one's being—famously celebrated in and exemplified by the late poetry of Rainer Marie Rilke, whom Gass has translated and sympathetically analyzed—seems the goal of the narrator's life project: "That is poetry: to bring within about, to change" (197). This is the significance of the narrator's reference to "my house, this place and body, I've come in mourning to be born in" (179). His observations trigger reminiscences that in turn heighten his perceptions so that present and past conflate. He begins to occupy the past in the present, asserting, somewhat hopefully, "I am learning to restore myself, my house, my body, by paying court to gardens, cats," and other aspects of everyday life (183). Momentarily recovering lost modes of being and feeling states, he realizes, "This country takes me over in the way I occupy myself when I am well . . . completely—to the edge of both my house and body" (179). On such occasions he feels, "I've lost my years . . . as though I were living at last in my eyes, as I have always dreamed of doing" (173).

It is within the terms of the narrator's preoccupation with the way looking may or may not promote being that his persistent evocations of windows must be understood. These are his parameters: "the world beyond my window, me in front of my reflection, above this page, my shade" (i.e., the pall cast by self-awareness, generally, and, more particularly, by awareness that he is dead in the spirit). Scrutiny blurs into uncanny directives: "And my blear floats out to visible against the glass, befog its country and bespill myself" (195). Windows are many things to the narrator. They are ambiguous symbols of passive, promiscuous receptivity: "What do the sightless windows see, I wonder, when the sun throws a passerby against them?" (189). In this sense they are extensions of his eyes inasmuch as they too "see what blunders into them . . . I'm empty or I'm full . . . depending; and I cannot choose" (182). And, in keeping with the poetic convention that eyes are the windows to the soul, he avers, "My window is a grave, and all that lies within it's dead" (195). Yet windows can also be wings when they become vehicles for transcending the petty cares and inadequacies of a petty self through acts of dynamized attention. This is because movement—the leaves that "move in the glass" (175), the transports of the gaze—constitutes the essence of being that has been liberated and redeemed: "Let out like Mr. Tick, my eyes sink in the shrubbery. I am not here: I've passed the glass . . . flown by branches" (183). However, in the deceptive transparency that offers the mirage of vistas, "bewitching windows" can also be barriers that protectively shut the narrator in by shutting life out (179). The narrator captures this conflation of promise and delusion, this dialectic of connection and divorcement, in the enigmatic remark "We meet on this window, the world and I, inelegantly, swimmers of the glass; and swung wrong way round to one another, the world seems in" (196). All of these shifting meanings are implicit in the ambivalence that characterizes the narrator's claim that even as a child, "after the manner approved by Plato, I had intercourse by eye" (202).

Contemplating how he had gone wrong, the narrator indicates, through a pun that turns mouth into genital, that misdirected energy has led to his present impotence: "It's there where I fail—at the roots of my experience" (202). Elsewhere he deploys more explicitly visceral images. He castigates the arrogant ambition and vindictive pettiness that drove him to use writing to raise himself above others so that "when I shit I won't miss anybody" (189). He even describes poetry itself as a mode of excretion. Neither poets nor teachers are true lovers, he suggests, because their verbal paeans displace the pulsations of being like those who "faucet-off while pissing heartily to preach upon the force and fullness of that stream, or pause from vomiting to praise the purity and passion of their puke" (175). He mocks his former posturing, self-deluded aspiration to be "a [poet] of the spiritual," evidently having recognized that "poetry, like love, is—in and out—a physical caress. I can't tolerate any more of my sophistries about spirit, mind, and breath. Body equals being" (202). And yet the compulsive palaver of the poet proceeds apace despite the fact that status as a lover, as must other aspects of merely bodily being, must die away, leaving "love-ill fools like me lying alongside the last bone of their former selves, as full of spirit and speech, nonetheless" (201). He concludes that pastiche of decadent romantic declamation with the morose assertion that "though my inner organs were devoured long ago, the worm which swallowed down my parts still throbs and glows like a crystal palace"—by which he seems to mean "the endless worm of words I've written, a hundred million emissions" in a lifetime of spilled, masturbatory "spew" (201).

But the narrator's notes emerge from the heart of the heart of the country, not from a Dostoevskian underground, and therefore the images of worms and flies that swarm the penultimate section of his journal are ultimately not pestiferous. The narrator's description of infestation is virtually a parable in which an EDENIC fullness of being is momentarily retrieved as a consequence of untenable innocence. Amid his apple and pear trees, the narrator discovers with horror the "falls" of fruit. He recognizes that "the worms had them all" because aesthetic preoccupations led him to overlook the need for practical vigilance; he had "acclaimed the blossoms" but had failed to spray them (202–203). He begins to "gather remains" as if to pull himself together, and this in turn returns him via childhood memories of swatting flies to a "small

Dakota town I knew as a kid; knew as I dreamed I'd know your body, as I've known nothing, before or since; knew as the flies knew, in the honest, unchaste sense" (203). The pure carnality of their mode of being appeals to him; such "flies have always impressed me; they are so persistently alive" (203). They become figures for the actualized authentic poet *living in*, at home in, the contingency of things: "Inside, they fed. . . . apples like a hive for them" (204). Coating his juice-drenched hands with their dynamic presence, flies and beetles give him "indifferently complete" caresses that "despite my distaste" left "my arm . . . never . . . more alive" (204–205).

It is useful to compare the poet's metaphorical description of insects "explosively ris[ing], like monads . . . windowless, certainly, with respect to one another, sugar their harmony" (205) and his subsequent description of "neighbors" at a basketball game "joining in to form a single pulsing ululation—a cry of the whole community" as "each body becomes the bodies beside it, pressed as they are together, thigh to thigh, and the same shudder runs through all of them, and runs toward the same release" (205). However, the story does not end with any affirmation of community or thigh-to-thigh carnality. It concludes, again parabolically, with the narrator's description of himself alone among the "bedizened" windows and vacated streets of downtown during the Christmas season. He thinks he hears "Joy to the World," but though he tries to pay attention, he cannot be certain: "Perhaps the record's playing something else" (206). Gass seems to imply, by analogy, that the usefulness of literary musings as a guide to living remains equivocal and dubious, as much for the writer as for any other reader.

BIBLIOGRAPHY

Gass, William H. *In the Heart of the Heart of the Country and Other Stories.* New York: Harper & Row, 1968.
———. "The Origin of Extermination in the Imagination." In *Habitations of the Word: Essays.* New York: Touchstone Books/Simon & Schuster, 1985.
———. *Reading Rilke: Reflections on the Problems of Translation.* New York: Basic Books, 2000.
Hix, H. L. *Understanding William Gass.* Columbia: University of South Carolina Press, 2002.

Saltzman, Arthur. *The Fiction of William Gass: The Consolation of Language.* Carbondale: Southern Illinois University Press, 1986.

David Brottman
Southern Indiana University

"IRONING THEIR CLOTHES" Julia Alvarez (1984)

"Ironing Their Clothes" belongs to *Homecoming,* the first poetry collection published by Julia Alvarez, a collection of narrative poems that focus on domestic life, where the author uses family images to reconstruct her family's past. This poem—a short story in prose—first appeared in an issue of the journal *13th Moon,* devoted to American women's writing.

The collection is narrated by an adult female voice trying to recompose scenes from her childhood and coming to terms with current events in her present life. Alvarez creates an ALTER EGO to review her childhood, contemplating it from the distance that age provides. The first part of *Homecoming,* entitled "Housekeeping," to which "Ironing Their Clothes" belongs, is composed of sketches. These sketches deal exactly with doing the family housework: she sweeps, dusts, makes the beds, does laundry, and, in this story, irons the laundry of her family both literally and symbolically. She presses the wrinkles of her parents' clothing, trying to liberate them from their problems, pains, and conflicts while she maps her childhood in a household too busy for love.

The story does not talk directly about immigration but has a strong smell of exile, fear, and frustration, voiced mainly in the silence of the father and the bad temper of the mother, a woman forced to spend her life doing the housework with the sole help of her daughters, for she cannot afford to hire someone to take care of domestic tasks for her because of her social and economic position. The protagonist breathes all those feelings while growing up and translates them into words to make a portrait of her childhood home: a household full of worries. At the same time, she reveals, through the choice of words of her narrative voice, how, even in her adult life, she has proven unable to overcome most of these feelings of impotence and disappointment, which are expressed consciously and nostalgically in the lines of her narrative.

The feminine character of the narrative voice is heard clearly as she becomes an individual woman, in a process of acquiring an identity of her own, separated from her mother; the *I* speaks aloud, detached from her mother's voice, yearning for a personal space inside the household and within the love of her family.

The domestic scene is transformed into a time of longing and reflection upon the history written on the family's bodies. The clothes she irons still carry the imprint of overworked bodies, yelling for a long night's rest and showing the history of a long life of effort and hard labor.

The memory of this narrator, undoubtedly Alvarez's alter ego, moves to the fore images of her father's back "cramped and worried with work," of "the collapsed arms" waiting to be hugged by his loved ones in the first stanza or part of the poem. The second stanza recalls memories of an always busy mother, doing strenuous domestic work that occupies a precious time her daughter claims as hers. Thus, the narrative voice does not complain about the absence of love in her family but their lack of time to express it, a working routine that makes her feel abandoned and alienated from the other members of the family. The narrator highlights the importance of her task, her responsibility to her family, who are expecting her contribution to the domestic tasks, so that they can wear freshly ironed clothes every morning. Paradoxically, her care and diligence seem to be unnoticed; her housework is constantly taken for granted by her family, who apparently only establish communication with the narrator to scold and warn her of the possible consequences of getting distracted from her daily routine.

The feeling of alienation overcomes the protagonist of the poem; she feels detached from reality and clings to her family clothing and familiar scenes of her past in an attempt to come to terms with her present life, a reflection for the most part of her lonely childhood. Because of this detachment and feeling of displacement, she gives higher value to domestic scenes and sees ironing as a refuge, as a way to express the emotions and feelings restrained by the circumstances of her family. The narrator has no contact with the outside world; she does not question her parents' decisions and submissively accepts her role in the house, a secondary position that distances her from true human contact except with their clothing.

Coming to terms with her solitude, the girl caresses the clothes she irons, compares their wrinkles with her mother's aging fast; her love is like the soft and warm touch of the iron that kisses the lines of time, tiredness, and concern. The clothes she irons receive the most precious expressions of love, those she hopes her family will eventually receive when they wear those fabric pieces on their skin. Finally, in the last stanza, she finds comfort and a certain sense of fulfilment, dreaming of her power to heal the pains of her relatives, transmitting it through the pieces of clothing, "all needing a touch of my iron," in order to remove any trouble that could possibly become attached to them while being worn.

BIBLIOGRAPHY
Alvarez, Julia. *Homecoming: New and Collected Poems.* New York: Plume, 1996.
Johnson, Kelli Lyon. *Julia Alvarez: Writing a New Place on the Map.* Albuquerque: University of New Mexico Press, 2005.
Sirias, Silvio. *Julia Alvarez: A Critical Companion.* Westport, Conn.: Greenwood Press, 2001.

Imelda Martín-Junquera
Universidad de León

IRONY
An author's use of a reality different from the one that the fictional characters apprehend. Irony is normally divided into two types: verbal irony, in which the tone of the narrator or speaker contradicts the spoken words, and dramatic irony, in which the reader understands a state of affairs more fully than the character or characters do; it is usually the reverse of the reality the characters perceive.

IRVING, WASHINGTON (1783–1859)
Born in New York City and named after the Revolutionary War hero and first president of the United States, Washington Irving is considered the first American author and short story writer. His life roughly spanned the period between the Revolutionary War and the CIVIL WAR. Although he was trained for a profession in law and worked in business for a time, Irving's real interest was writing. In 1808–09, he wrote much of *Salamagundi,* a satirical magazine, in collaboration with his brother, William, and brother-in-law, James Kirke Paulding, demonstrating his talent and potential. *Diedrich Knickerbocker's History of New York,* published in 1809, a BURLESQUE account of Dutch colonists in New York, earned him literary recognition. The work solidified the term for the KNICKERBOCKER school, a literary circle influenced by the wits associated with *Salamagundi;* it included William Cullen Bryant, James Fenimore Cooper, and Clement Clark Moore.

It was Irving's *The Sketch Book,* however, published serially in both England and the United States from 1819 to 1820, that became the first American book to win international recognition. Cooper, considered the first significant American novelist, provided Irving's only competition, and Irving remains secure in his position as the first significant short story writer. Moreover, his belief that the new country provided a unique opportunity for a national literature, and his recognition of the story as a distinct form of fiction, helped pave the way for such great writers as NATHANIEL HAWTHORNE and HERMAN MELVILLE in the generation that succeeded him. Groups such as the southwestern humorists, tellers of TALL TALES, learned from Irving to use details from American country life to achieve noteworthy effect in their writings.

The Sketch Book, also narrated by Diedrich Knickerbocker but set in rural New York, is a collection of the short tales, essays, and occasional pieces, including "The LEGEND OF SLEEPY HOLLOW" and "RIP VAN WINKLE," the two stories that have entered the realm of American MYTH. In both tales Irving employs the supernatural in a comic way to achieve the resolution of the action and uses these techniques again in "The Specter Bridegroom," another well-known tale from *The Sketch Book.* When a bridegroom dies on the way to his wedding, a friend impersonates him. The bride's family subsequently learns that the bridegroom has died, but they believe simply that they have seen his ghost. Ultimately, the "specter" returns and elopes with the bride.

The Sketch Book was written during the 17 years that Irving lived abroad, finding an international audience. During these expatriate years, Irving wrote *Bracebridge Hall,* a series of sketches about British country life and characters, published in 1822, and the less successful *Tales of a Traveller,* published in 1824. Its best known story is "The Adventure of a German Student," a bizarre GHOST STORY set in Paris during the French Revolution. Irving used the pseudonym Geoffrey Crayon when writing these three books of stories. Though some are more successful than others, taken together they illustrate his comprehensive vision of the components of the American tale: clear, engaging prose; sharp visual images; and a conscious use of native material. Moreover, he understood the significance of the role of the imagination and the relative insignificance of the artist in a materialistic society, the vacuum created in a culture that looked only to the present, and the need for American fiction to identify a specific historical context (McQuade 788). By creating Sleepy Hollow, Irving became the first of numerous American writers to invent a mythic locus for his stories, just as WILLIAM FAULKNER later invented in his YOKNAPATAWPHA COUNTY, JOHN STEINBECK his SALINAS VALLEY, or EUDORA WELTY her MORGANA, MISSISSIPPI.

During his years in Spain, Irving published *The ALHAMBRA,* another collection of tales published in 1931 and commonly known as "the Spanish Sketch Book." Irving actually lived in the Alhambra, in Granada, while writing these tales, and they were very well received, particularly "The Legend of the Rose of Alhambra" and "The Legend of the Moors." This collection marked the end of Irving's career as a fiction writer, however. While in Spain he had also written a biography of Christopher Columbus, and with his return to the United States—cloaked with an international reputation and an honorary degree from Oxford University—he channeled his talents into history and biography.

Although he was first and foremost a writer, over the years Irving served in many positions, including magazine editor, New York State militia colonel, businessman, and diplomat. During the final years of his life, while living at Sunnyside, the house he had purchased in Tarrytown, New York, this quintessential American writer wrote a five-volume biography of George Washington. Irving died shortly after publishing the first volume.

BIBLIOGRAPHY

Alderman, Ralph, ed. *Washington Irving Reconsidered: A Symposium.* Hartford, Conn.: Transcendental Books, 1969.

Antelyes, Peter. *Tales of Adventurous Enterprise: Irving and the Poetics of Western Expansion.* New York: Columbia University Press, 1990.

Bowden, Mary Weatherspoon. *Washington Irving.* Boston: Twayne, 1981.

Brooks, Van Wyck. *The World of Washington Irving.* New York: E. P. Dutton, 1944.

Burstein, Andrew. *The Original Knickerbocker: The Life of Washington Irving.* New York: Basic Books, 2006.

Dorsky, Jeffrey Rubin. *Adrift in the Old World: The Psychological Pilgrimage of Irving.* 1988.

Hedges, William L. *Irving: An American Study 1802–1835.* Baltimore: Johns Hopkins University Press, 1965.

Irving, Pierre M. *Life and Letters of Irving.* 4 vols. New York: Putnam, 1862–1864.

Irving, Washington. *The Complete Tales of Washington Irving.* Edited by Charles Neider. Garden City, N.Y.: Doubleday, 1975.

———. *Complete Works.* Edited by Richard Dilworth et al., Boston: Twayne; Madison: University of Wisconsin Press, 1969–1989.

———. *The Sketchbook of Geoffrey Crayon, Gent.* Edited by Haskell Springer. Boston: Twayne, 1978.

———. *Washington Irving: History, Tales and Sketches.* Edited by James W. Tuttleton. New York: Library of America, 1983.

Jones, Brian Jay. *Washington Irving: An American Original.* New York: Arcade, 2008.

Kime, Wayne R. *Pierre M. Irving and Washington Irving: A Collaboration in Life and Letters.* Waterloo, Ont.: Wilfred Laurier University Press, 1977.

Leary, Lewis. *Irving.* Minneapolis: University of Minnesota Press, 1963.

McQuade, Donald, ed. "Washington Irving." In *The Harper American Literature.* Vol. 1. New York: Harper & Row, 1987.

Myers, Andrew B., ed. *A Century of Commentary on the Works of Irving.* Tarrytown, N.Y.: Sleepy Hollow Restorations, 1976.

———. *The Worlds of Irving.* Tarrytown, N.Y.: Sleepy Hollow Restorations, 1974.

Reichart, Walter A. *Irving and Germany.* Ann Arbor: University of Michigan Press, 1957.

Roth, Martin. *Comedy and America: The Lost World of Irving.* Port Washington, N.Y.: Kennikat, 1976.

Rubin-Dorsky, Jeffrey. *Adrift in the Old World: The Psychological Pilgrimage of Irving.* Chicago: University of Chicago Press, 1988.

Wagenknecht, Edward. *Irving: Moderation Displayed.* New York: Oxford University Press, 1962.

Williams, Stanley T. *The Life of Irving.* 2 vols. New York: Oxford University Press, 1935.

Woodress, James. "Washington Irving." In *Reader's Guide to Short Fiction,* edited by Noelle Watson, 262–265. Detroit: St. James Press, 1993.

ISAAC (IKE) MCCASLIN

The chief character of WILLIAM FAULKNER's GO DOWN, MOSES, Isaac McCaslin matures from boyhood to manhood in this SHORT STORY CYCLE. A curious figure in the BILDUNGSROMAN, Ike easily captures our sympathy as he tests and ultimately proves his manhood in a series of hunts for Old Ben, the bear in the story "The BEAR." Therein Ike learns that ownership of property (nature) is analogous to owning slaves, and therefore wrong; he firmly rejects both courses. Ike also forfeits his wife and all possibility of children, however. As he grows older, his limitations become increasingly noticeable until, in "DELTA AUTUMN," his rejection of the nameless black woman and distant relative ultimately displays his inability to surmount racial prejudice, and, feminist critics would argue, a latent misogyny.

"I STAND HERE IRONING" TILLIE OLSEN

(1956) "I Stand Here Ironing," first published in *Prairie Schooner* as "Help Her to Believe," became the opening story of TILLIE OLSEN's collection *Tell Me a Riddle* (1961). It is a mother's monologue, instigated by a school counselor's request that she go in to discuss her daughter Emily. She recalls the obstacles she faced as a single mother during the GREAT DEPRESSION and their inevitable consequences for her firstborn. She was forced to send Emily to live with her in-laws on two different occasions when she could not find work. When she was working and they were able to be

together, she had to leave her daughter in inadequate day care with indifferent caretakers. She regrets the effect of her worries on Emily, especially when she compares Emily's good behavior to the stubborn demands of the younger children in the family. Even after her second marriage, when circumstances improved, mother and daughter were again separated when she was convinced to send Emily, who was not recovering well from the measles, away to convalesce. But the convalescent home's rules, which restricted parental contact and discouraged close attachments, only taught Emily isolation.

Thin and awkward as a young girl, labeled "slow" at school, Emily faced difficulties and disappointments in her peer world that were exacerbated by her family's frequent moves. She resented her younger, more attractive, and more outgoing sister, Susan. She had to help care for her four younger siblings, whose needs often took precedence over her, leaving little time for her to attend to her schoolwork or for her mother to attend to her. Forced to become self-sufficient at an early age, she learned not to need attention and grew to shun her mother's efforts to nurture her.

Her talent as an actor gained her attention and success: Audiences loved her humor and charisma. But her mother lacked the means to support her daughter's talent with acting lessons, and Emily was left to develop her gift on her own. The mother knows Emily probably will never realize her full potential. Emily's happiness when she bounds in at the end of the story reassures her mother, but the fatalism of her daughter's final remark—that she is not going to take her midterm examinations because "in a couple of years when we'll all be atom-dead they won't matter a bit" (11)—depresses her. Within her realistic resignation to the circumstances of her daughter's life lies her decision "Let her be" and her hope "Help her to know," she asks, "that she is more than this dress on the ironing board, helpless before the iron" (12).

BIBLIOGRAPHY

Bauer, Helen Pike. "'A Child of Anxious, Not Proud, Love': Mother and Daughter in Tillie Olsen's 'I Stand Here Ironing.'" In *Mother Puzzles: Daughters and Mothers in Contemporary American Literature,* edited by Mickey Pearlman. Westport, Conn.: Greenwood, 1989.

Coiner, Constance. *Better Red: The Writing and Resistance of Tillie Olsen and Meridel Le Sueur.* New York: Oxford University Press, 1995.

Faulkner, Mara. *Protest and Possibility in the Writing of Tillie Olsen.* Charlottesville: University Press of Virginia, 1994.

Frye, Joanne S. "'I Stand Here Ironing': Motherhood as Experience and Metaphor." In *The Critical Response to Tillie Olsen,* edited by Kay Hoyle Nelson and Nancy Huse. Westport, Conn.: Greenwood, 1994.

———. *Tillie Olsen: A Study of the Short Fiction.* New York: Macmillan, 1995.

Olsen, Tillie. "I Stand Here Ironing." In *Tell Me a Riddle.* Chicago: Lippincott, 1961.

Orr, Elaine Neil. *Tillie Olsen and a Feminist Spiritual Vision.* Jackson: University Press of Mississippi, 1987.

Pearlman, Mickey, and Abby H. P. Werlock. *Tillie Olsen.* New York: Twayne, 1991.

Kelley Reames
University of North Carolina at Chapel Hill

"I WANT TO KNOW WHY" SHERWOOD ANDERSON (1919)

"I Want to Know Why" is a coming-of-age story by SHERWOOD ANDERSON that first appeared in November 1919 in H. L. Mencken's avant-garde magazine *Smart Set* and was later anthologized in the collection *The Triumph of the Egg,* published in 1921. It was reprinted in *Redbook* in 1937 and was included in collections of Anderson's short stories published in 1947, 1963, 1982, and 1993. Judy Jo Small suggests that the story grew out of several of Anderson's own adolescent experiences, citing the author's personal passion for horses and recalling events that occurred at Saratoga and Churchill Downs racetracks during the 1918 racing season.

In "I Want to Know Why," a young man, the unnamed protagonist of the story, relates events that occurred a year previously, just before his 15th birthday. Trying to sort out how these events have impacted his life, the boy initially experiences only confusion and desperation in his struggle to comprehend their meaning. In order to get on with his life, he believes he must find the answer to the title question, a query that challenges many teenagers even in today's modern-day society.

Growing up in Beckersville, Kentucky, the young man is fascinated by horses and horse racing, and despite his father's prestigious position as the town lawyer, the son dreams solely of being part of the racetrack environment, even trying to stunt his growth by eating cigars in the hope of becoming a jockey. His disappointment at the failure of this effort is evident immediately as the story begins, and the sad mood continues to dominate his feelings as he relates the past events that have so impacted his existence.

Since his jockey dreams seem destined to be dashed, the boy continues to hang around the stables and the racehorses, hoping that his close attention to the scene will serve him well even if he cannot be a rider. As he learns the ropes of horse racing, he especially hones his instinct and appreciation for the animals, initially relying on a black stablehand named Bildad Johnson, who gives the inexperienced and callow youth a deeper awareness of equine beauty and motivates a spiritual appreciation of horseflesh that approaches worship.

The central event of the story occurs when the boy and three of his friends hitch a freight train to see a horse race at Saratoga Downs, New York, where Sunstreak, a stallion, is competing against a gelding named Middlestride. The boy roots for Sunstreak, sensing that the horse represents something in him, a sexual awareness that is simultaneously joyous yet painful.

The stallion's courage, strength, grace, and vitality become even more moving when the young narrator realizes that his sensitive perceptions about the horse are shared by Sunstreak's trainer, Jerry Tilford. When the race finishes (Sunstreak's victory is a forgone conclusion), the narrator desires to be near the trainer, whom he has come to idealize. He seems to transfer his love for the horse, whom he wants to kiss, to the man. Later, however, when he discovers Tilford in an old farmhouse that is really a brothel, the boy is shocked to discover that his heroic figure (almost a surrogate father) treats the prostitutes of the whorehouse with the same sense of awe and admiration that he gave the stallion. For the boy, this seems a real betrayal.

The sensuous but "ugly" and "mean" setting of the brothel is described as "rotten" by the boy, and he is sorely disappointed and disgusted by the lust and blatant sexuality that he observes firsthand as he peeks into the window. He wants to scream and rush into the room and disrupt the proceedings and even kill Tilford. Instead, he retreats into the darkness, and after a night of sleepless unrest, he heads for home, confused and upset by the events he has witnessed. He is no longer an innocent adolescent but has gone through some rite of passage he cannot comprehend.

A year later, as he relates how the past has impacted him, the boy acknowledges that suddenly the air at the tracks now no longer tastes as good or smells as good as it did before. Tilford's actions reflect the corruption inherent in all men, and the initial magical allure of the horses has suddenly diminished. The racetrack fantasy has burst, and the narrator feels betrayed by a man he had previously admired and with whom he had identified.

The sexual content of the story seems sublimated even as teenage sexual longing must sometimes be repressed. The beauty and excitement of racing and an almost perfect equine specimen are somehow equated with masculine sexual urges, and Sunstreak, while remaining a virile stallion, ironically becomes a representative of a beautiful girl that the narrator wishes he could interact with sexually.

When Tilford's spiritual appreciation of Sunstreak (a trait he shares with the narrator) is compromised by the sexual lust for the opposite sex that the boy observes in the brothel, the narrator suddenly comes face to face with his confusing feeling about sex and becoming an adult male. Unfortunately, there are no clean-cut, easy answers to this dilemma of adolescence, and the turmoil the boy experiences is merely representative of the complexities he will face when he has left his childhood innocence behind.

Because of the immediacy of its first-person narrative, readers can easily sense the difficulty the speaker has in expressing what he has observed. His vague childish descriptions of what he has seen seem inadequate and even inaccurate; similarly, his confusion of the meaning of life is typical of Anderson's concern with what it means to be mature. No longer having the option to be naive and inexperienced, the young man can only lament as the story closes: "That's what

I'm talking about. I'm puzzled. I'm getting to be a man and want to think straight and be OK." By wanting to know the why of what has happened to him, the narrator indicates that even though he struggles to understand, he has begun to face the obligations and realities of adulthood.

The critic Ray White credits Anderson with introducing "the honest use of sex into American literature," and this story seems especially to stress an expression of latent homosexual longing within males that causes much distress and questioning. Anderson's biographer, Kim Townsend, relates this sexual confusion to the author's relationship with his mother, whom he idealized and worshipped, forcing him to direct his brutish sexual desires away from women and toward more masculine figures. Townsend even goes so far as to suggest that Anderson thus sought spiritual communication with men, fearing that his sexual urges would debase and defile heterosexual contact and detract from the purity he saw in the feminine. Shifting his desire to men thus precluded his using women and was a way of finding purity in friendship with no sexual undertone present. Ellis's reading of the story speaks of Sunstreak as the embodiment of the feminine idea—beautiful and lovely and yet hard all over—suggestive of his masculinity. Since the narrator is attracted to this hardness, says Ellis, a homosexual undercurrent is being explored in the story's subtext, explaining why the boy expresses a desire to kiss both the horse and the trainer, saying, "I loved the man as much as the horse."

No wonder then that Ellis concludes that the boy is angered when he sees Tilford in a sexual embrace in the brothel. Identifying the prostitute as like the gelding Middlestroke but "not clean," the boy is frustrated when his budding sexuality seems rejected by Tilford in favor of the whore and when his affection seems unreturned and his passion somewhat sullied by the choice the trainer makes.

The onset of adulthood and its attendant sexual awakening and confusion creates in the narrator, and perhaps created in Anderson himself, a feeling that male-to-male attraction is unacceptable, despite the ambiguity that presents itself in longing for what is forbidden. Ellis concludes the boy, in true Oedipal fashion, wants to kill his pseudo–father figure since his attraction to Tilford causes distress and engenders the title question that is left unanswered. If this is the real issue of the story, Anderson may be struggling with how to think "straight" and "become a man" even when one's most primal urge suggests the appeal of the masculine bond and an aversion to the "corruption" men visit upon women by lust. Readers who discover this interest in "I Want to Know Why" will truly understand why the narrator's questioning only begins in earnest a year after the event, and why the answers to his questions may still be a long time in coming.

BIBLIOGRAPHY

Ellis, James. "Sherwood Anderson's Fear of Sexuality: Horses, Men and Homosexuality." *Studies in Short Fiction* 30, no. 4 (Fall 1993): 595–602.

Papinchak, Robert Allen. *Sherwood Anderson: A Study of the Short Fiction.* New York: Twayne, 1992.

Small, Judy Jo. *Readers' Guide to the Short Stories of Sherwood Anderson.* New York: G. K. Hall, 1994.

Townsend, Kim. *Sherwood Anderson.* Boston: Houghton Mifflin, 1987.

White, Ray Lewis. *The Achievement of Sherwood Anderson.* Chapel Hill: University of North Carolina Press, 1966.

Michael J. Meyer
De Paul University

J

JACK POTTER   Potter is the town marshal of Yellow Sky, Texas, in STEPHEN CRANE's "THE BRIDE COMES TO YELLOW SKY." Without disclosing his intentions, Potter has traveled to San Antonio, has taken a bride, and is returning to Yellow Sky feeling he has betrayed his neighbors by marrying. As he sneaks back to his house from the train station with his bride, he accidentally encounters his nemesis, Scratchy Wilson, a gunslinger, the last of a gang who lived in Yellow Sky. In a comical exchange, Potter subdues the dumbfounded Wilson. The encounter represents the domestication of the town, the end of lawlessness, and the promise of civic order.

JACKSON, SHIRLEY (SHIRLEY HARDIE JACKSON) (1919–1965)   Although Shirley Jackson wrote six novels and approximately 100 short stories, she is identified almost exclusively with one story, "The LOTTERY" (1949), which describes the ritualistic murder of a housewife in a small American town. The THEME of this story is a terrifying one, memorable for the way it sweeps aside romantic notions of rural folk, but Jackson's stories covered the spectrum from the fantastic to the realistic to the humorous. Her early fiction often dealt with socially sensitive topics such as racism ("After You, My Dear Alphonse" and "Flower Garden") and mental retardation ("Behold the Child Among His Newborn Blisses"). The stories included in the collection *The Lottery; or, the Adventures of James Harris* often combine REALISM with the fantastic and typically portray a significant threat to at least one character's well-being, usually a woman's. Jackson's later work included stories that explored unbalanced minds and bizarre situations, as well as humorous sketches about family life, many based on personal experience. Her stories appeared in magazines as disparate as the NEW YORKER, LADIES' HOME JOURNAL, *Playboy*, and HARPER'S. Jackson was recipient of the Mystery Writers of America Edgar Allan Poe Award in 1961.

See also "CHARLES."

BIBLIOGRAPHY

Byall, Joan Wylie. *Shirley Jackson: A Study of the Short Fiction*. New York: Twayne, 1993.

Hattenhauer, Darryl. *Shirley Jackson's American Gothic*. Albany: State University of New York Press, 2003.

Hyman, Stanley Edgar, ed. *Come Along with Me*. New York: Viking Press, 1968.

Jackson, Shirley. *Hangsaman*. New York: Farrar, Straus and Young, 1951.

———. *Life among the Savages*. New York: Farrar, Straus and Young, 1953.

———. *The Lottery; or, The Adventures of James Harris*. New York: Farrar, Straus, 1949.

———. *The Magic of Shirley Jackson*. New York: Farrar, Straus & Giroux, 1966.

———. *Raising Demons*. New York: Farrar, Straus and Cudahy, 1957.

———. *The Sundial*. New York: Farrar, Straus and Cudahy, 1958.

———. *We Have Always Lived in the Castle.* New York: Viking Press, 1962.

Joshi, S. T. "Shirley Jackson: Domestic Horror." In *The Modern Weird Tale.* New York: McFarland, 2001.

JACKSON, THOMAS JONATHAN ("STONEWALL") (1824–1863)

A Confederate general in the U.S. CIVIL WAR, Jackson won his sobriquet at the First Battle of Bull Run, when he and his brigade "stood like a stone wall" against Union attacks. He was General ROBERT E. LEE's most able and trusted lieutenant and played a major role in the Confederate victory at the Second Battle of Bull Run, the standoff at Antietam, and the victories at Fredricksburg and Chancellorsville. While returning from a reconnaissance during this latter battle, Jackson was mortally wounded by gunfire from his own troops. Stonewall Jackson is alluded to in stories of the Civil War as well as in more modern war stories such as Barry Hannah's "Midnight and I'm Not Famous Yet."

JAMES, HENRY (1843–1916)

Along with EDGAR ALLAN POE, one of the foremost practitioners of the short story. An American expatriate who had been reared in both New York and Europe, James the writer considered the American scene from afar, most often from Lamb House, his residence in Rye, England. Known today—at least in scholarly circles—as much for his theories of literature as for his writing, James made contributions to the modern story that can hardly be overstated. Although he did in fact write more about the novel than about the short story, his theories apply to all fiction. James was an ardent practitioner of the short story and the NOVELLA—*nouvelle* was his preferred term—publishing 112 stories and novellas between 1864 and 1910. Never known for their fast pace, compression, or dramatic action, James's stories are remarkable for their meticulous psychological shadings and for their use of the author's "central intelligence" device, the gradual revealing of facts, emotion, or action through the thoughts of a character, usually a pivotal one.

Although James has been compared with NATHANIEL HAWTHORNE as an important American writer of short fiction, Hawthorne in no sense developed or evolved in the notable ways that James progressed. Because his work was published over so many decades, James's fiction is customarily divided into three phases or periods: early, middle, and late. In terms of short fiction, *DAISY MILLER: A STUDY* represents work of the early period, "The REAL THING" and *The TURN OF THE SCREW* the middle, and "The BEAST IN THE JUNGLE" the late. The stories also may be grouped under several well-established THEMES. Among the most prominent are the international theme, exemplified in such early stories as *Daisy Miller,* "A Passionate Pilgrim," "A Bundle of Letters," or "An International Episode," and in such late and admired stories as "The Marriages," "The Bench of Desolation," and "The Beast in the Jungle." Another significant theme involves artists and writers, exemplified in, for instance, "The Lesson of the Master," "The Real Thing," and "The Figure in the Carpet." Still other important themes include supernatural or ghostly ones—but always overlaid with the psychological, as in "The Turn of the Screw," "The Altar of the Dead," "The Great Good Place," and "The JOLLY CORNER," which also uses the motif of the double, or DOPPELGANGER. Further, James wrote tales that evoke social COMEDY or TRAGEDY. Some of the previously mentioned stories fall under the rubric of comedy ("An International Episode"); others include "The Point of View," "The Liar," "Lady Barbarina," and "The Birthplace." "EUROPE" and "The Beast in the Jungle" espouse tragic themes, as do such stories as "The Pupil," "Julia Bride," and "A Round of Visits" (Hocks 4–6).

The early James was a proponent of REALISM, or psychological realism, along with such writers as WILLIAM DEAN HOWELLS, SARAH ORNE JEWETT, MARY E. WILKINS FREEMAN, HAMLIN GARLAND, KATE CHOPIN, and others. As he moved beyond realism, or attempted to transcend it, he became less interested in action and increasingly interested in subtlety and nuance, psychology and perception. James became a British subject late in life, largely in reaction to his irritation with the reluctance of the United States to enter WORLD WAR I. He died at his home a year later.

See also "GREVILLE FANE."

BIBLIOGRAPHY

Anderson, Quentin. *The American Henry James.* New Brunswick, N.J.: Rutgers University Press, 1957.

Auchincloss, Louis. *Reading Henry James.* Minneapolis: University of Minnesota Press, 1975.

Bradley, John R. *Henry James's Permanent Adolescence.* New York: Palgrave, 2000.

Dupee, F. W. *Henry James.* New York: Sloane, 1956.

Edel, Leon. *Henry James: A Life.* New York: Harper & Row, 1985.

Fogel, Daniel Mark. *Daisy Miller: A Dark Comedy of Manners.* Boston: Twayne, 1990.

Habegger, Alfred. *Henry James and the "Woman Business."* New York: Cambridge University Press, 1989.

Hall, Richard. "The Sexuality of Henry James." *New Republic,* 28 April and 5 May 1979.

Hocks, Richard A. *Henry James: A Study of the Short Fiction.* Boston: Twayne, 1990.

James, Henry. *The Complete Letters of Henry James, 1855–1872.* 2 vols. Edited by Pierre A. Walker and Greg Zacharias. Lincoln: University of Nebraska Press, 2006.

———. *The Complete Letters of Henry James, 1872–1876.* 3 vols. Edited by Pierre A. Walker and Greg W. Zacharias. Lincoln: University of Nebraska Press, 2008.

———. *The Complete Notebooks of Henry James.* Edited by Leon Edel and Lyall Harris Powers. New York: Oxford University Press, 1987.

———. *Daisy Miller; Washington Square; The Portrait of a Lady; The Bostonians; The Aspen Papers.* London: Chancellor, 2001.

———. *Dearly Beloved Friends: Henry James's Letters to Younger Men.* Edited by Susan E. Gunter and Steven H. Jobe. Ann Arbor: University of Michigan Press, 2001.

———. *Literary Criticism.* 2 vols. Edited by Leon Edel and Lyall H. Powers. Cambridge: Cambridge University Press, 1984.

———. *Novels, 1896–1899.* New York: Library of America, 2003.

———. *The Novels and Tales of Henry James.* New York Edition. 26 vols. New York: Scribner, 1907–1917.

———. *Selected Tales.* Edited, introduction, notes by John Lyon. New York: Penguin, 2001.

———. *The Tales of Henry James.* 3 vols. Edited by Maqbool Aziz. Oxford: Oxford University Press, 1973–1984.

———. *The Turn of the Screw, and In the Cage.* Introduction by Hortense Calisher, notes by James Danly. New York: Modern Library, 2001.

James, Henry, et al., *The Classics of Style.* Cleveland, Ohio: American Academic Press, 2006.

Johnson, Kendall. *Henry James and the Visual.* New York: Cambridge University Press, 2007.

Jones, Vivian. *James the Critic.* New York: St. Martin's, 1985.

Novick, Sheldon M. *Henry James: The Mature Master.* New York: Random House, 2007.

Poole, Adrian. *Henry James.* New York: St. Martin's, 1991.

Springer, Mary Doyle. *A Rhetoric of Literary Character: Some Women of Henry James.* Chicago: University of Chicago Press, 1978.

Tanner, Tony. *Henry James: The Writer and His Work.* Amherst: University of Massachusetts Press, 1985.

Weinstein, Philip M. *Henry James and the Requirements of the Imagination.* Cambridge, Mass.: Harvard University Press, 1971.

JEN, GISH (1955–)

JEN, GISH (1955–) Gish Jen grew up in Scarsdale, New York; her parents had immigrated to the United States from Shanghai during the 1940s. Jen graduated from Harvard with a B.A. in creative writing; she earned her M.F.A. degree from the Writers' Workshop at the University of Iowa in 1983. Before devoting herself to a writing career, she taught English in China and attended business school at Stanford. Her stories have appeared in the *Iowa Review, Yale Review, Southern Review,* NEW YORKER, ATLANTIC MONTHLY, and *Boston Globe Magazine.*

Her two novels and most of her semiautobiographical short stories (including the frequently anthologized "In the American Society" and "What Means Switch") explore the lives of the Chang family. Jen insists that while she is concerned with the phenomenon of outsiderness in American culture, particularly as it characterizes the Asian immigrant condition, her writing is most truly centered on an earnest fascination with America (*Heath* 10).

Her first novel, *Typical American* (1991), incorporated several of her early short stories; it was nominated for the National Book Critics Circle Award. Jen has received writing grants from a number of bodies including the National Endowment for the Arts (NEA), the Guggenheim Foundation (see GUGGENHEIM GRANT), and the Massachusetts Artists Foundation. Her second novel, *The Love Wife,* was published in 2004.

BIBLIOGRAPHY

Jen, Gish. *The Love Wife.* New York: Knopf, 2004.

Kafka, Phillipa. "'Cheap, On Sale, American Dream': Contemporary Asian American Women Writers' Responses to American Success Mythologies." In *American Mythologies: Essays on Contemporary Literature,* edited by William Blazek and Michael K. Glenday, 105–128. Liverpool, Eng.: Liverpool University Press, 2005.

Lee, Don. "About Gish Jen." *Ploughshares* 26 (Fall 2000): 2–3, 217–222.

Lee, Rachel. "Gish Jen." In *Words Matter: Conversations with Asian American Writers,* edited by King-Kok Cheung, 215–232. Honolulu: University of Hawaii Press, with UCLA Asian American Studies Center, 2000.

Madsen, Deborah L. "Artefact, Commodity, Fetish: The Aesthetic Turn in Chinese American Literary Study." In *Querying the Genealogy: Comparative and Transnational Studies in Chinese American Literature,* edited by Jennie Wang, 185–197. Shanghai, China: Shanghai yi wen chu ban she, 2006.

"Profile of Gish Jen." *Heath Anthology of American Literature Newsletter.* 1992. Available online. URL: http://www.georgetown.edu/tamlit/newsletter/numb8tex.html. Accessed May 2, 2009.

Satz, Martha. "Writing about Things that Are Dangerous: A Conversation with Gish Jen." *Southwest Review* (1993).

Keith Lawrence
Brigham Young University

JEREMIAD

In modern times a jeremiad may refer to any work that foretells destruction because of the evil of a group. Originally a severe expression of grief, a prolonged lamentation, or a complaint, the word derives from the biblical prophet Jeremiah, after whom the Old Testament book was named. The Book of Jeremiah contains many autobiographical sections as well as descriptions of Jerusalem during the time of the fall of that city to the Babylonians in 586 B.C. In "Jeremiah's Lamentations," occurring in the midst of havoc and destruction, the prophet expresses his profound sorrow over the capture of Jerusalem and realizes that true religion lies in the heart rather than in the temple.

JESSE B. SIMPLE

Although early on in LANGSTON HUGHES's so-called SIMPLE STORIES Jesse is referred to as Jesse B. Semple, in the bulk of the tales he is called Jesse B. Simple, the name by which he is commonly known and discussed today. Simple has been characterized as Harlem folk hero, African-American EVERYMAN, TRICKSTER, and the black counterpart of MARK TWAIN's Huck Finn. Simple offers his garrulous and comic but wise and perceptive insights into African-American culture in conversations with Boyd, his friend and FOIL, who narrates the tales. Boyd has been variously described as playing Boswell to Simple's Dr. Johnson and Watson to his Holmes. Simple, who uses street talk (see DIALECT), has both wives and girlfriends. Essentially a loner like Hughes himself, Simple, born out of Hughes's imagination during WORLD WAR II, "lived" into the era of civil rights. Through Simple, Hughes helped destroy the false STEREOTYPE of the African-American male created by white society.

"JEWBIRD, THE" BERNARD MALAMUD (1963)

One of the most frequently anthologized of BERNARD MALAMUD's stories, "The Jewbird," from the 1963 collection *Idiots First,* with its original blending of MAGICAL REALISM and humor to demonstrate the serious effects of bigotry and hatred, rarely fails to elicit sympathetic responses from readers. The story opens one August evening in New York City when a black bird flies through the open window into the top-floor apartment where the Cohen family is eating supper. When the bird lands on the kitchen table, the father, Harry Cohen, curses; while his wife Edie admonishes him not to curse in front of their 11-year-old son, Maurie, the bird flies to the top of the kitchen door, opens its mouth, and says, "Gevalt, a pogrom! [Heaven, an anti-Jewish uprising!]" The family is, naturally, stunned to note that it is not only a talking bird but a bird who speaks "Jewish," is named Schwartz, and is fleeing "Anti-Semeets" (191). From this moment on, the four of them converse in a very human, non-birdlike way—and this is Malamud's point, because the family is split between a humane view of the world—represented by Edie and Maurie and Schwartz—and the inhumane, hate-filled one that Cohen so aptly demonstrates. In Cohen, we learn that the anti-Semite is not only without but within the Jewish community.

From the beginning, the battle rages between Cohen and Schwartz, two Jews who are polar opposites. To many critics, Cohen represents the assimilated American Jew who has forgotten his Jewish roots and the meaning of Judaism. His speech is American vernacular: "Poor bird, my ass. He's a foxy bastard. He thinks he's a Jew" (193). In such statements, Cohen reveals his own warped view of Jewish identity (himself, the rough, anti-intellectual frozen foods salesman) and his inability to recognize or appreciate the old values inherent in Schwartz. His resentment of the bird increases despite—and perhaps because of—the affection that develops among Edie, Maurie, and Schwartz; when, with the coming of winter, Schwartz refuses to "hit the flyways" (197), as Cohen puts it, he increases his harassment of Schwartz, beginning with the introduction of a cat into the family and ending with Cohen's brutal, violent attack on the bird.

Schwartz, on the other hand, is the image of the old-fashioned Jew that Cohen has been trying to escape. In Robert Solotaroff's words, Schwartz is "just somebody's cranky, sly, Old World Jewish uncle who moves into crowded quarters for awhile" (78), a slightly unkempt one with a yen for warmth and the smell of cooking, along with a taste for pickled herring. His idiom contrasts sharply with Cohen's: "If you'll open for me the jar I'll eat marinated," he tells Edie, and he would like "to see once in awhile the *Jewish Morning Journal* and have once in awhile a schnapps because it helps my breathing, thanks God" (192, 193). Schwartz also connects the historically ignorant Cohen with centuries of Jewish oppression when he intones the word *pogram* and, in his refusal to "migrate" (197), with a history of escape from persecution (Hanson 1). Edie is afraid to anger her husband but slips food to Schwartz and protects him whenever possible. Maurie's grades at school begin to improve while under Schwartz's tutelage, and Cohen envisions enrolling his son in an Ivy League school.

Both Philip Hanson and J. Gerald Kennedy have drawn intriguing parallels between EDGAR ALLAN POE's "The Raven" and Malamud's "The Jewbird," in that both birds speak and represent selves that are onerous, even horrific, to the humans with whom they converse. Another viewpoint involves Cohen's mother, who, although we never see her, has been ill throughout the story. At her death, Solotariff believes

that the last restraints on Cohen are dissolved (79), and he craftily waits until Edie takes Maurie to his violin lesson and then savagely attacks the bird and hurls him out the window to his death. Although on their return both Edie and Maurie are too cowed to protest Schwartz's disappearance, Maurie deliberately searches for him in spring, when the melting snow reveals Schwartz's violated body, "his two wings broken, his neck twisted, and both bird-eyes plucked clean" (199). When he tells his mother and asks her who would commit such a crime, Edie's response—"Anti-Semeets"—is clearly directed at her husband. Schwartz's death evokes one of his opening remarks, that he has been fleeing the anti-Semites, who will actually "take your eyes out" (191).

BIBLIOGRAPHY

Alter, Robert. "Jewish Humor and the Domestication Myth." In *Veins of Humor,* edited by Harry Levin. Cambridge, Mass.: Harvard University Press, 1972.

Hanson, Philip. "Horror and Ethnic Identity in 'The Jewbird,'" *Studies in Short Fiction* 30 (Summer 1993).

Kennedy, J. Gerald. "Parody as Exorcism: 'The Raven' and 'The Jewbird.'" *Genre* 13 (1980): 161–169.

Malamud, Bernard. "The Jewbird." In *The Signet Classic Book of American Stories,* edited by Burton Raffel. New York: New American Library, 1985.

Solotaroff, Robert. *Bernard Malamud: A Study of the Short Fiction.* Boston: Twayne, 1989.

Watts, Eileen H. "Jewish Self-Hatred in Malamud's 'The Jewbird.'" *MELUS* 21, no. 2 (Summer 1996): 157–163.

JEWETT, SARAH ORNE (1849–1909) Now known mainly as a New England regional writer, Sarah Orne Jewett produced a substantial body of work between 1868 and 1900. Jewett was born in 1849 in South Berwick, Maine, which was to remain her home her entire life. The daughter of a well-to-do physician, for a time she considered a career in medicine, but she was too frail to take on the demands of medical school. Jewett began her writing career at the age of 18.

Her first short story, "Jenny Garrow's Lovers," was published in the magazine *Flag of Our Union* in 1867, and her second, "Mr. Bruce," was accepted by the *ATLANTIC MONTHLY,* whose assistant editor at the time was WILLIAM DEAN HOWELLS. Howells may have sensed some awkwardness in the love stories and is reputed to have asked, "Sarah, was thee ever in love?" To which Jewett replied, "No sir, whatever made you think that?"

Jewett's first novel, *Deephaven,* was published in 1877, after several of the chapters had appeared separately in the *Atlantic Monthly.* Deephaven was a city girl–meets–country girl story about two young women who spend a summer on the seacoast of Maine. Jewett's knowledge of her home state shines through this novel, and many of her colorful characters are stereotypical (see STEREOTYPE) Downeasters. The urban-meets-rural THEME would recur in later stories and novels, including *Marsh Island,* in which a country girl chooses between two suitors, one from the city and one from the farm. Jewett's sentimental attachment to country life is evident; in each of these stories the farm life or rural setting emerges as superior to city or urban dwelling.

Jewett's best-known short story appeared in her second collection, *A White Heron and Other Stories,* which can be considered Jewett's best collection. It contains the two types of stories that are her hallmarks: stories that emphasize the natural environment and those in which Jewett's characters are impecunious old women. "A WHITE HERON" is the tale of an ornithologist who goes to the countryside from the big city in order to find a rare bird specimen for his museum. On his trek through the woods he meets Sylvia, a girl of nine, and asks for her help in locating the nesting place of the white heron. Sylvia has explored the woods and forests near her home and knows that, from a certain treetop, the nest can be seen. The young ornithologist also has offered the princely sum of $10 to Sylvia if she leads him to the nest. She realizes that to share the knowledge of the heron's nesting place would lead to the death of the beautiful bird. Discovering that she is attracted to the young man, Sylvia is torn between pleasing him by revealing the heron's nest and remaining true to herself by preserving a part of her beloved New England natural heritage. This simple story, which contains a moral worthy of today's environmental movement, is Jewett's most popular and has been anthologized often.

Sarah Orne Jewett's most widely read published work was her third, the NOVELLA entitled *The COUNTRY OF THE POINTED FIRS,* published in 1896. It is the tale of a declining New England town, Dunnet Landing, and of its inhabitants. In *Country,* Jewett's maturity as a writer comes into focus. The CHARACTERS are well drawn, especially the women, and she depicts a place and a time that reflect her view of New England and its unique character. Jewett came of age during the American CIVIL WAR and, as a young woman, experienced the expansion of the Industrial Revolution, which was to change New England and its way of life forever, throughout her home region. Dunnet Landing was a town that was experiencing the gradual shifting from a rural to an urban lifestyle, and Jewett depicts the profound changes in people's lives wrought by the change from farm life to factory life.

The second style of story for which Jewett is known concerns elderly women in somewhat reduced circumstances. Although neither elderly nor poor, Jewett was able to depict the lives of these women in stories and sketches. Two in particular stand out: "Miss Tempy's Watchers" and "The Flight of Betsey Lane." Jewett is reported to have said to WILLA CATHER, "When an old house and an old woman come together in my brain with a click, I know a story is under way."

"Miss Tempy's Watchers" is one such sketch, in which not one but two old ladies and an old house come together. Two old friends are reunited at the wake of a third friend, Miss Tempy Dent. As was customary, they sit up throughout the night watching over her coffin. They begin to reminisce about the life of their late friend, whose presence is made to seem very real to her watchers. In describing the departed Miss Dent, Jewett creates the impression that she is in the room with her mourners. Perhaps because of this supernatural presence, the two ladies engage in a spirited discussion of the virtues of Miss Dent and resolve to be better friends to one another—the kind of friend that Tempy had been to them.

This sketch, as Sarah Orne Jewett called many of her stories, is so called because it lacks a dramatic plot. This is not to say the story goes nowhere, rather that it is character-driven, not an action story. It is simply a portrait of three characters, two women finely drawn and a third brought to life through their reminiscences.

A second story in which Jewett portrays the lives of elderly women is "The Flight of Betsey Lane." Here Jewett deftly portrays three old friends who are residents of the Byfleet Poor House, being cared for by the many village residents rather than a few relatives. Betsey Lane, at 69 the youngest of the trio, spent most of her life in the employ of a well-to-do family who left her with a retirement pension. A woman of a generous nature, Betsey Lane soon uses up her pension on lavish gifts for friends and relatives. She is forced by circumstances to take up residence in the town poorhouse, where she quickly befriends Miss Peggy Bond and Mrs. Lavinia Dow.

These three ladies share work at the poorhouse, which consists of planting corn in the adjacent fields. Betsey Lane, bored with work and reduced circumstances, dreams of attending the Philadelphia Centennial Exposition. Her friends tell her this is impossible, until she receives a visit from the daughter of her former employer. The young woman still has a sentimental attachment to Betsey and leaves her with $100 to spend as she pleases. Betsey makes secret plans to go to Philadelphia. Early one morning she slips away to the train station, where she offers to mend the train conductor's jacket in exchange for a ride to Philadelphia on the freight train. This is how Betsey Lane arrives, unobserved, at the Centennial Exposition. She spends three wonderful days there, staying in a rooming house and enjoying the carnival atmosphere. She does not forget her friends and buys them each a gift with her new wealth.

In Byfleet, no one knows what has become of Betsey Lane, and the speculation is that she wandered off and drowned in the great pond on the poorhouse property. Mrs. Dow and Miss Bond are determined to find their missing friend. On the ninth day of her disappearance, they go down to the pond to see whether they can find some trace of her. Just as they arrive at the pond, they spy the figure of their old friend approaching. She has returned home to relate her adventures at the Philadelphia Centennial Exposition and to share her generous gifts with her friends.

Unlike her fictional characters, Sarah Orne Jewett did not lead a restricted life. Although she never married, she maintained a 30-year relationship with Annie Fields, the widow of the editor George Ticknor Fields. The two women made four trips to Europe, where Jewett befriended many of the literary figures of the 19th century, including Rudyard Kipling, Alfred Tennyson, and Christina Rosetti. In the United States, she was on friendly terms with many literary figures of her day, notably Julia Ward Howe, Harriet Beecher Stowe, Willa Cather, William Dean Howells, John Greenleaf Whittier, and Henry Wadsworth Longfellow.

Jewett's last novel, *The Tory Lover,* was published in 1901. It is a sentimental love story set in the time of the AMERICAN REVOLUTION. Some of Jewett's trademarks, notably her description of the physical beauties of New England, are present in this book, but it lacks the substance of *The Country of the Pointed Firs.* In 1902 Jewett was thrown from a horse-drawn carriage, and the resulting injuries put an end to her literary career. In 1909 she suffered a stroke and died at her childhood home in South Berwick, Maine.

BIBLIOGRAPHY

Auchincloss, Louis. *Pioneers and Caretakers: A Study of Nine American Women Novelists.* Minneapolis: University of Minnesota Press, 1961.

Cary, Richard. *Sarah Orne Jewett.* New York: Twayne, 1962.

Jewett, Sarah Orne. *The Best Stories of Sarah Orne Jewett.* Gloucester, Mass.: Houghton Mifflin, 1965.

Matthiessen, Francis Otto. *Sarah Orne Jewett.* Gloucester, Mass.: Houghton Mifflin, 1965.

Nagel, Gwen L. "Sarah Orne Jewett." In *Dictionary of Literary Biography: American Short Story Writers before 1880.* Vol. 74, edited by B. E. Kimbel and W. E. Grant, 208–232. Detroit: Gale, 1988.

"Sarah Orne Jewett." In *Twentieth Century Literary Criticism.* Vol. 22, edited by D. Poupard, 114–115. Detroit: Gale, 1987.

"(Theodora) Sarah Orne Jewett." In *Dictionary of Literary Biography: American Realists and Naturalists.* Vol. 12, edited by D. Pizer and E. Herbert, 326–338. Detroit: Gale, 1987.

Wetzel, Nancy Mayer. "The White Rose Road: Sarah Orne Jewett's Journey to Orris Falls." *Greatworks: The Newsletter of the Great Works Regional Land Trust* (Winter 2003): 5, 11.

Laurie Howell Hime
Miami Dade Community College

JHABVALA, RUTH PRAWER (1927–)

Ruth Prawer Jhabvala was born in Cologne, Germany. Hers was one of the last Jewish families permitted to leave Nazi Germany; the family emigrated to Britain in 1939. Her father committed suicide in 1948 after learning that his entire family, with the exception of his wife and children, had died in the HOLOCAUST.

Jhabvala earned her M.A. in English literature from Queen Mary College in 1951; that same year she married Cyrus Jhabvala, an architect, and the couple moved to Delhi, India. By 1953 Jhabvala had published her first novel, considering herself a full-time writer despite the demands of raising three daughters. She is the author of more than 15 books, including five short story collections: *Like Birds, like Fishes* (1963), *A Stronger Climate* (1968), *An Experience of India* (1972), *How I Became a Holy Mother* (1976), and *Out of India* (1986). A crucial member of the Merchant-Ivory film team, she has written more than a dozen screenplays; she received an Academy Award for her adaptation of E. M. Forster's *A Room with a View* (1987). Her collection *Out of India* was chosen by the *New York Times Review of Books* as one of the Best Books of 1986.

In her most recent story collection, *East into Upper East: Plain Tales from New York and New Delhi* (1998), the "East" refers to India's sprawling metropolis, New Delhi, while the "Upper East" refers to that other big city, New York. In this work, Jhabvala explores the nature of love on two continents. These stories, written over the last 20 years, reaffirm her as a spellbinding urban fabulist. (See FABLE.) The subtitle of the collection is *Plain Tales from New York and New Delhi*, and, indeed, Jhabvala tells her complicated stories in a straightforward, elegant, economic manner, yet her multifaceted CHARACTERS find themselves in complex situations. The first tales take place in New Delhi. The characters are mostly educated and affluent Indians grappling with changes wrought by the former colony's independence. Sumitra, in the story "Independence," becomes a kind of guide and hostess for men who have newly risen to power. In "Expiation," the narrator, an affluent cloth broker, must deal with a much-beloved but mentally unstable younger brother. Many years of closing his eyes to the evidence of his brother's delinquency eventually puts the entire fam-ily at risk. Sunil, in "Farid and Farida," is a new kind of businessman, marketing "Indianness" abroad. A marriage that had soured when transported from India to London comes to life again in an unconventional way when the estranged spouses meet again years later under a banyan tree in India.

Jhabvala moves from the six stories set in India to New York with "The Temptress," a transitional story in which an Indian holy woman is literally imported to the United States by a wealthy American. From there the author delves into the lives of Manhattanites. In "Fidelity," for example, Dave; his wife, Sophie; and his sister, Betsy, live in a symbiotic relationship stronger than betrayal, disappointment, and even death. All but the last of the remaining stories are firmly grounded in the United States, and in these stories Jhabvala's keen insights into the complexities of human relationships become even more evident, showing that human love and need take many different forms. These engrossing domestic tales depict the emotional lives and complex psychologies of intense lovers, quarreling married couples, weary elders, and their restless adult children.

Jhabvala's most recent novel, *My Nine Lives*, appeared in 2004. Because she divides her time between Delhi and New York City, because she writes about India rather than the Europe of her Jewish heritage, and because her perspectives and ideals are decidedly multinational rather than exclusively Indian, she is sometimes claimed as an Asian-American author.

While the style and structure of Jhabvala's fiction have been compared to those of 19th-century European novels, the comparison is rendered inaccurate by her postcolonial stance, her insistent irony, and what might be called her shorthand manner of moving through scenes. While her fiction reveals India and her cultures to the world, it also reveals the profound (and sometimes profoundly tragic) extent to which the world, especially the colonizing influences of Europe and America, is evident in—and represented by—India.

BIBLIOGRAPHY

Bawer, Bruce. "Passage to India: The Career of Ruth Prawer Jhabvala." *The New Criterion* 6, no. 4 (December 1987): 5–19.

Dahr, T. N. "Jhabvala's 'An Experience in India': How True and Right?" *Panjab University Bulletin* (Arts) 21, no. 2 (October 1990): 21–27.

Dudt, Charmazal. "Jhabvala's Fiction: The Passage from India." In *Faith of a Woman Writer,* edited by Alice Kessler-Harris. Westport, Conn.: Greenwood, 1988.

Gooneratne, Yasmine. "Film into Fiction: The Influence of Ruth Prawer Jhabvala's Early Cinema Work upon Her Fiction." In *Still the Frame Holds: Essays on Women Poets and Writers,* edited by Sheila Roberts and Yvonne Pacheco Tevis. San Bernardino, Calif.: Borgo, 1993.

McDonough, Michael. "An Interview with Ruth Prawer Jhabvala." *San Francisco Review of Books* 11, no. 4 (Spring 1987): 5–6.

Mishra, Pankaj, ed. "Ruth Prawer Jhabvala." In *India in Mind: An Anthology.* New York: Vintage Books, 2005.

Newman, Judie. *The Ballistic Bard: Postcolonial Fictions.* London: Edward Arnold, 1995, 29–50.

Rubin, David. "Ruth Jhabvala in India." *Modern Fiction Studies* 30, no. 4 (Winter 1984): 669–683.

Sucher, Laurie. *The Fiction of Ruth Prawer Jhabvala: The Politics of Passion.* London: Macmillan, 1989.

Keith Lawrence
Brigham Young University

"JILTING OF GRANNY WEATHERALL, THE" KATHERINE ANNE PORTER (1929)

"The Jilting of Granny Weatherall" was the first of KATHERINE ANNE PORTER's Texas stories, all drawn from persistent memories of her own impoverished and motherless childhood as well as from her memories of her sternly rigorous and religious grandmother, Catherine Anne Porter of Kyle, Texas. Ellen Weatherall is a character distinctly different from grandmother Sophia Jane Gay, who plays an initially important role in the stories that make up *The Old Order* (1955), but whose influence is beginning to fade in "The GRAVE." As does Sophia Jane, however, Granny Weatherall represents Porter's fascination not with the generation of her prematurely dead mother but with the earlier generation—the women who had weathered first the CIVIL WAR, then the drastically fluctuating social and economic times that followed, and finally the steady challenges to the gender expectations of their young womanhood upon which they had depended but against which practical circumstance dictated resistance. Porter, faced in 1928 with physical breakdown and no stranger herself to economic duress and self-doubts about her own role in a patriarchal society, created in Granny Weatherall a figure who would enact not only the author's personal abhorrence of rejection, loneliness, and passivity but also her marked tendency toward creative self-narrative.

Fear of rejection colors all of Granny Weatherall's adult life after her fiancé, George, fails to claim her at the altar and thus affirm her womanhood. Granny Weatherall's literal response to rejection and the loneliness that threatens to follow it has been action: She marries her second choice, John; bears his children; musters her capabilities both maternal and paternal at his early death; and is in all things "dutiful and good." Or at least she maintains the appearance of being dutiful and good, since it is with those words that she slightingly names the weaknesses of her daughter, Cornelia, weaknesses for which she at 80 is willing to spank her middle-aged child. In reality, her life has been, of necessity, a subtle challenge to the sentimental and romantic standards of her youth.

Her figurative response to rejection and loneliness has been to light a candle rather than curse the darkness. She associates her jilting with dark smoke, a personal image of the spent light of hell that returns decades later to fog her brain as she lies on what she at first refuses to acknowledge as her deathbed. Uncomprehendingly, she watches "a fog [rise] over the valley, . . . marching across the creek . . . like an army of ghosts" (83–84). That vision reminds her of the beauty that lay in "lighting the lamps" (84) as her small children crowd around her to escape the nightly darkness, striking the match that would dispel their nightmares and embodying the strong light of reassurance that the younger generation, whose modern shaded lamps were "no sort of light at all, just frippery" (87), would mourn with her passing.

Her joy at her ability to become the illumination for her own life and the lives of her family is a pragmatic response to the social failure of the cult of true womanhood and the circumstantial failure of her dead husband to see to her needs and the needs of her children. A true woman gives her heart once and forever: If jilted, she remains rejected and unwed, or, if wed and widowed, she mourns for her remaining lifetime. Ellen Weatherall permits herself neither of these cultural prescriptions, choosing instead as a young woman to live on purposefully with John through children birthed, meals cooked, clothes sewn, and gardens made; widowed and without John, she does the work of man and woman, counseling her son on financial matters, post holing and fencing her hundred acres, or seeing to the sick and the lyings-in of other women with equal aplomb. It is not in her to "let good things rot for want of using."

Yet faced with the imminence of her death, Granny Weatherall becomes aware of the ambiguous legacy she will leave behind her. Will her children's memories of her be consistent with the self she has created in her lifelong effort to dispel the dark? Or will she be remembered as the mournful and bereft bride at the altar whose revealing letters to her lover and her husband-to-be lie waiting in the attic to be discovered after her death?

As Robert Brinkmeyer suggests in his reading of this Porter story, the hopeful narratives of self created through public acts are gravely at risk in the face of memory's secret narrative. If Ellen's children discover the letters, they will know the self she has hidden and the setbacks she has worked to overcome through the years, possibly to think less of her as a result. Fearful of the loss of her consciously created selfhood, Granny Weatherall doubts the efficacy of her favorite saints—probably those of the household and of women's concerns—in whom she had entrusted the certainty of her heavenly reward. Instead, she pledges herself yet another time to the bridegroom, in words the ironic overlay of which she seems unaware: "Without thee, my God, I could never have done it. Hail, Mary, full of grace." Expecting God to claim and confirm her at the end of her life, and failing to receive the sign that he will do so, she responds in a manner typical of all her years: Albeit grievingly and sorrowfully, she takes charge of the light once again, blowing it out with the last of her own life's breath.

BIBLIOGRAPHY

Brinkmeyer, Robert H., Jr. *Katherine Anne Porter's Artistic Development: Primitivism, Traditionalism, and Totalitarianism.* Baton Rouge: Louisiana State University Press, 1993.

Givener, Joan. *Katherine Anne Porter: A Life.* Rev. ed. Athens: University of Georgia Press, 1991.

Porter, Katherine Anne. "The Jilting of Granny Weatherall." In *The Complete Stories of Katherine Anne Porter.* New York: Harcourt, 1979.

Stout, Janis. *Katherine Anne Porter: A Sense of the Times.* Charlottesville: University Press of Virginia, 1995.

Patricia L. Bradley
Middle Tennessee State University

JIM CROW   A term, possibly derived from the title of an early black minstrel song, that refers to the segregation of blacks and whites and the policies and laws enforcing it. Although practiced in the South during RECONSTRUCTION with the establishment of "Black Codes" that restricted the civil rights of freed slaves, Jim Crow became formalized in laws after the U.S. Supreme Court ruling in *Plessy v. Ferguson* (1896). According to this ruling, the Fourteenth Amendment to the Constitution mandated political but not social equality, and therefore racially segregated "separate but equal" facilities were constitutional. Even though the Supreme Court overturned *Plessy v. Ferguson* in *Brown v. Board of Education* (1954), widespread segregation—and Jim Crow—continued in the South until the civil rights movement in the early 1960s. This movement, led by Martin Luther King, Jr., and others, resulted in such legislation as the Civil Rights Acts of 1964 and 1968 and the Voting Rights Act of 1965, prohibiting discrimination on the basis of color, race, religion, or national origin in public accommodations, schools, employment, and voting.

JOHN HENRY   The legendary black hero John Henry is the subject of BALLADS, TALL TALES, a novel, and a song. He was a man of prodigious strength who worked as a roustabout on river steamboats or was employed in the building of railroads. In one notable tale, Henry dies of overexertion after winning a contest with a steam drill. The basis for the tales and the man may well have been the exploits of a giant black man who worked on the Chesapeake & Ohio Big Bend Tunnel in the 1870s. Although not mentioned specifically, he may be the inspiration for RICHARD WRIGHT's "BIG BLACK GOOD MAN."

JOHNSON, DOROTHY M. (1905–1984)

Born in Iowa, Dorothy Johnson moved to Montana with her family at age eight. Educated at Montana State University, she moved in 1935 to New York City, where she spent the next 15 years as a magazine editor. Upon returning to Montana, Johnson embarked on a journalism career for local newspapers and subsequently joined the journalism faculty at the University of Montana. Drawing on the stories told to her by her grandparents, she became a prolific writer about the West of the 1800s. Her works include short stories, novels, nonfiction, and juvenile literature.

Johnson seems to have enjoyed popularity at both ends of the literary spectrum: Many of her works received critical praise, and adaptations of several of her short stories became Hollywood film CLASSICS. She received literary awards from the Western Writers of America and the Western Heritage Association. Critics in the *New York Times Book Review* and *Best Sellers* characterize her writing as "historically accurate," "sensitive in avoiding the sensationalized and stereotypical image of the American Indian," and "vivid in her portrayal of Indian customs and practices."

Three of her works were made into films. *The Hanging Tree* (1959) was followed by *The Man Who Shot Liberty Valance* (1962), which was directed by John Ford with John Wayne, Jimmy Stewart, and Lee Marvin as leads. Told as a FLASHBACK, it traces a complex relationship between a U.S. senator (Stewart) and an obscure rancher (Wayne) and their dealings with a gunfighter (Marvin).

Also in the Indian tradition, "A Man Called Horse" was made into a movie starring Richard Harris. Harris plays an English aristocrat captured by the Sioux and forced to endure painful and humiliating rituals to earn acceptance. A highlight of both the film and the story is the realistic depiction of the Sun Vow ceremony.

A recurring THEME in many of Johnson's stories is the capture of white children by hostile Indians and their subsequent integration into tribal life, stories no doubt passed on to her by her grandparents. Unlike most interpretations of her era, which focused on atrocities, Johnson's stories portray the NATIVE AMERICAN lifestyle as appealing, and she takes special care in presenting details of daily life and ceremonial occasions. The tone of her work is reminiscent of the widely successful film *Dances with Wolves,* yet in her time, this portrayal of Indian culture was uncommon. Her sensitivity in this area resulted in her being named an honorary member of the Blackfeet tribe.

BIBLIOGRAPHY

Johnson, Dorothy M. *All the Buffalo Returning.* Lincoln: University of Nebraska Press, 1996, 1979.
———. *The Bloody Bozeman: The Perilous Trail to Montana's Gold.* New York: McGraw-Hill, 1971.
———. *Buffalo Woman.* Thorndike, Maine: G. K. Hall, 1997, 1977.
———. *Famous Lawmen of the Old West.* New York: Dodd, Mead, 1963.
———. *Farewell to Troy.* Boston: Houghton Mifflin, 1964.
———. *Flame on the Frontier: Short Stories of Pioneer Women.* New York: Dodd, Mead, 1967.
———. *Giuliano the Innocent.* London: A. Dakers, 1946.
———. *The Hanging Tree.* New York: Ballantine, 1957.
———. *Indian Country.* New York: Ballantine Books, 1953. Published as *A Man Called Horse.* New York: Ballantine, 1970.
———. *Lost Sister.* New York: Ballantine, 1956.
———. *Some Went West.* New York: Dodd, Mead, 1965.
———. *Warrior for a Lost Nation: A Biography of Sitting Bull.* Philadelphia: Westminister Press, 1969.
———. *When You and I Were Young, Whitefish.* Missoula, Mont.: Mountain Press, 1982.
———. *Witch Princess.* Boston: Houghton Mifflin, 1967.
Johnson, Dorothy M., and Robert Townley Turner. *The Bedside Book of Bastards.* New York: McGraw-Hill, 1973.

Lawrence Czudak
St. Joseph's Academy

"JOLLY CORNER, THE" HENRY JAMES (1908)

First published in the *English Review*, this story, frequently interpreted in conjunction with "The BEAST IN THE JUNGLE" and *The TURN OF THE SCREW*, begins in medias res. Spencer Brydon, age 56, who has just returned to New York from Europe after a 23-year absence, is speaking to Alice Staverton, an old friend whom, we quickly learn, he visits as often as possible. Spencer has returned to oversee two inherited city houses, one a rental property he is renovating, the other, on the "jolly corner," filled with memories of his boyhood and adolescence. Since then he has been a wanderer, a free man who has enjoyed pleasures, frivolities, and infidelities Alice only dimly comprehends. He views Alice as lovely, flowerlike, one who shares memories of their youthful days in a New York far less chaotic than it appears now. They enter the house on the jolly corner that Spencer has decided to keep, having already hired Mrs. Muldoon, a housekeeper, who is pleased with the arrangements as long as she need not enter the premises after dark.

In their conversation, Spencer confesses to Alice that he is drawn to the house as he is drawn to the question of an ALTER EGO, the self he might have become had he not left for Europe. Together they conclude he would have become a billionaire living on the proceeds of the construction of the skyscrapers that now punctuate the city skyline. Spencer is determined to meet his alter ego, or DOPPELGANGER, in the house on the jolly corner, and Alice confesses to him that she has seen that other Spencer twice in her dreams. She refuses, however, to discuss him further.

The rest of the tale is a suspenseful GHOST STORY, one in which Spencer, alone at night in the house, summons the courage to stalk his double and to draw him out. Indeed, the uncharacteristic hunting METAPHORS have prompted at least one critic to note a resemblance to a motif more commonly associated with ERNEST HEMINGWAY. Other critics have noted that Spencer seems a double for the author himself, as James wrote the story after returning to New York after a two-decade-long absence. After so many years in Europe, James might well have wondered what sort of man he might have been had he stayed in the New York of his youth.

After some spine-tingling near-encounters with his alter ego, including one scene in which he briefly appears to consider suicide by jumping from the window, Spencer faces the monstrous, hideous apparition, an utter stranger who looms larger than he, and falls into unconsciousness. Hours later Spencer looks up into the faces of Mrs. Muldoon and Alice. He believes that he has died and that Alice has resurrected him. She reassures him that he never became the dreadful beast he would have been had he not left New York and that by having faced his double, Spencer can understand his true self as it has developed. The depth of Alice's love is measured in her admission that she would have loved him in either form. As the critic Richard A. Hocks points out, Spencer is "saved by the regenerative power of love; in more psychoanalytic terms, his divided self is regenerated with her help" (80). A homosexual interpretation is possible as well, especially if "The Jolly Corner" is compared with recent studies, such as Eve Kosofsky Segwick's on "The Beast in the Jungle." Spencer's numerous ALLUSIONS to "Europe" and to the pleasures he had engaged in as a wandering bachelor at the very least suggest that we should look more closely into the autobiographical connections between James and his PROTAGONIST.

BIBLIOGRAPHY

Hocks, Richard A. *Henry James: A Study of the Short Fiction.* Boston: Twayne, 1990.

James, Henry. "The Jolly Corner." In *Major Writers of Short Fiction,* edited by Ann Charters. Boston: St. Martin's Press, 1993.

Sedgwick, Eve Kosofsky. "The Beast in the Closet: James and the Writing of Homosexual Panic." In *Sex, Politics, and Science in the Nineteenth-Century Novel,* edited by Ruth Bernard Yeazell, 148–186. Baltimore: Johns Hopkins University Press, 1986.

"JORDAN'S END" ELLEN GLASGOW (1923)

"Jordan's End," which first appeared in ELLEN GLASGOW's collection *The Shadowy Third* (1923), shows the influence of EDGAR ALLAN POE's story "The FALL OF THE HOUSE OF USHER," a kinship that Glasgow acknowledged. In Glasgow's story, the ill-fated Jordan family resides in their eerily GOTHIC family estate, Jordan's End, which is similar to the House of Usher. The declining families in both Jordan's End and Usher suffer from mysterious mental and physical ailments, believed to be the result of inbreeding. But in Glasgow's story the main representatives of the Jordan family are husband and wife rather than brother and sister, Mr. Jordan having married a woman from a neighboring town to strengthen the family's failing bloodline.

Recognizing in the development of her husband's incurable madness the fate of his father, grandfather, and uncles, Mrs. Jordan administers an overdose of a narcotic left by the doctor. Unlike Poe's story and contrary to the title's implications, however, the Jordan line does not end at the story's close. Mrs. Jordan, having been brought in from the outside, does not suffer the same fate as her husband, and the couple have a young son whom the mother plans to send away to school, in hope that the family name will survive to begin a new, although less patrician, line. The doctor in "Jordan's End" serves a similar function to the narrator in Usher, as an objective outsider who describes the haunting family situation to the reader.

"Jordan's End" also introduces THEMES that are found in Glasgow's later novels. The decaying Southern aristocracy appears in other works such as *Barren Ground* (1925), *The Sheltered Life* (1932), and *In This Our Life* (1941). The latter two also present the concept of a southern womanhood that is above the law. Although technically Mrs. Jordan murders her husband, she appears otherworldly and untouchable to the doctor, and her crime is unreported.

BIBLIOGRAPHY
Glasgow, Ellen. "Introduction." In *The Collected Stories of Ellen Glasgow,* edited by Richard Kilburn Meeker. Baton Rouge: Louisiana State University, Press, 1963.
Thiebaux, Marcelle. *Ellen Glasgow.* New York: Ungar, 1982.

Betina I. Entzminger
University of North Carolina at Chapel Hill

JOSEPHINE PERRY

Josephine Perry is the PROTAGONIST of F. SCOTT FITZGERALD's five-story sequence (see The BASIL AND JOSEPHINE STORIES) about a beautiful, wealthy socialite. More like the finely drawn sketch of a social type than a fully developed CHARACTER, Josephine has been described as a femme fatale and a vampiric product of upper-class wealth— a beautiful girl without moral conscience, whose sole motive in life is satisfaction of egoistic desires. Josephine also represents the social changes in the 1920s, when young women abandoned the demure femininity of their mothers. She embodies the element of defiant independence that came to be associated in the popular imagination with the New Woman. She is the first of Fitzgerald's characters to be associated with his concept of "emotional bankruptcy": Living from conquest to conquest in a fever of excitement, she exhausts her emotional capacity. On her 18th birthday, she discovers she is no longer capable of feeling anything at all.

BIBLIOGRAPHY
Bryer, Jackson R., and John Kuehl, eds. "Introduction." In *The Basil and Josephine Stories.* New York: Scribner, 1973.
Eble, Kenneth. *F. Scott Fitzgerald.* New York: Twayne, 1963. Rev. ed., 1977.

Frances Kerr
Durham Technical Community College

JOY-HULGA

The central figure in FLANNERY O'CONNOR's story "GOOD COUNTRY PEOPLE" with whom readers easily identify, despite her grotesque characteristics. Wounded as a child, she has a weak heart and an artificial leg, and as a doctor of philosophy, she believes herself superior to those around her. Her lack of spiritual beliefs renders her powerless in her bizarre seduction by an uneducated but street-smart country boy named MANLEY POINTER.

JULIP JIM HARRISON (1994)

The three stories in JIM HARRISON's third NOVELLA collection—*Julip, The Seven-Ounce Man,* and *The Beige Dolorosa*—describe diverse characters and landscapes from three different POINTS OF VIEW. The PROTAGONISTS here, as in Harrison's other novella collections, *The WOMAN LIT BY FIREFLIES* (1990) and *LEGENDS OF THE FALL* (1979), are intimately associated with their surroundings, which range from Florida and the Midwest and Upper Peninsula Michigan to the American Southwest.

Bobby, Julip's brother, is serving seven to ten years in prison for wounding three best friends who had at one time all been Julip's lovers. Julip, a young dog trainer, travels from the Midwest to Florida to have her brother moved from Raiford State Prison to a mental hospital, where he is more likely to obtain early release. Julip's relationship with the three older men is complex and awkward, and they await Julip's return with some trepidation. She finds them and convinces them that they should testify on Bobby's behalf. Julip's burgeoning sexuality and her relationships with her mother, her father, the lovers, and her friend Marcia form a subtext for her journey, which ends as she walks to her own car and heads north, eager to get back to the dogs (82). The story is written in the third-person omniscient point of view and is the most traditional of the three narratives.

In *The Seven-Ounce Man,* Brown Dog, Harrison's American picaro, or adventurer, who appears earlier in *The Woman Lit by Fireflies,* continues to eat, drink, and womanize his way through the Upper Peninsula wilderness. Brown Dog, still on the run from the law, protests the excavation of Indian burial mounds, the site of which Brown Dog has divulged to his former lover, Shelley Thurman (in *Fireflies,* that is; in *Brown Dog,* she is called Shelley Newkirk). The novella's 97 pages are divided into three sections, which alternate from third-person omniscient to Brown Dog's own distinctive voice. The protagonist's journey parallels Huckleberry Finn's as, as does Huck, Brown Dog heads west (182).

In *The Beige Dolorosa,* the English professor Phillip Caulkins moves to the desert to escape the politics of academia, after he is falsely accused of sexual harassment, and to stave off what he believes are the early effects of Alzheimer's disease. In the desert, Caulkins awakens to a nature he has never known. He catalogs the wildlife and plants he finds on his journeys in the Arizona landscape in an attempt to regain control of his life: "When I first began closely observing nature a month ago I found the experience a bit unbalancing, though the concepts weren't new. Notions such as otherness and the thinginess of reality are scarcely new to a literary scholar. What is new is the vividness of the experience" (243). The novella is written in the first person and convincingly portrays the fragmentation Caulkins feels as he fights for clarity.

The protagonists of these three novellas all work within their particular landscapes to remember their pasts and to order their futures. While Harrison's fiction is often comical, his characterization is poignant, his characters human in their shortcomings.

BIBLIOGRAPHY
Harrison, Jim. *Julip.* Boston: Houghton Mifflin, 1994.
Reilly, Edward C. *Jim Harrison.* New York: Twayne, 1996.

Patrick A. Smith
Ohio University

"JURY OF HER PEERS, A" SUSAN GLASPELL (1917)

Originally written and performed in 1916 as a play called *Trifles,* "A Jury of Her Peers" appeared in *Everyweek* on March 5, 1917, and became SUSAN GLASPELL's best-known story. On one level, readers may see it as an evocative LOCAL COLOR tale of the Midwest, but its fame and popularity rest largely on its original PLOT and strongly feminist theme. Indeed, the story anticipates the feature-length film *The Burning Bed* and the legal issues debated in the 1970s and beyond: When is a wife justified in murdering her husband?

When the story opens, Minnie Foster Wright has been taken to jail for the possible murder of her husband, John Wright, names suggesting the diminutive and powerless wife and the confident husband. The PROTAGONISTS of the story are Martha Hale, friend to Minnie since childhood, and Mrs. Peters—whose first name we never learn, married to Sheriff Peters, a blustery overpowering man who seems a double for John Wright. The men—including the sheriff, the county attorney, and Martha's domineering husband, Mr. Hale—comb the house for evidence to convict Minnie of murder. So confident are they in their methods, however, that they fail to search the kitchen, the province of women, whose work they repeatedly criticize and belittle.

Martha and Mrs. Peters, the female sleuths in this story (which actually may be viewed as a form of detective fiction), examine the kitchen and, through such evidence as jam jars, quilts, an empty bird cage, and, finally, a dead bird, deduce the loneliness, poverty, and emotional devastation of Minnie Foster's marriage. The loud, heavy footsteps of the men punctuate the two women's gradual understanding that Minnie Foster murdered her husband in the same way that he had cruelly killed her canary. Although Martha Hale has been sympathetic all along, the little bird corpse is the deciding factor for Mrs. Peters, who recalls a similar incident in her youth: She easily could have killed the boy who destroyed her cat. More important, however, is Mrs. Peter's awakening to the similarities between Minnie's husband and her own. She joins Martha in conspiring to hide the dead bird, thus destroying the only physical evidence of Minnie's motivation to murder. Minnie has been judged by a jury of her peers, and they have found her innocent.

BIBLIOGRAPHY

Glaspell, Susan. "A Jury of Her Peers." In *American Short Stories*. 6th ed. Edited by Eugene Current-García and Bert Hitchcock. New York: Longman, 1997.

K

KADOHATA, CYNTHIA (1956–) Cynthia Kadohata was born in Chicago. Her short stories have been published in the *NEW YORKER,* the *Pennsylvania Review,* and *Grand Street;* they also have been widely anthologized. She is also the author of three novels, *This Floating World* (1989), *In the Heart of the Valley of Love* (1992), and *Dragon Road* (1994), which incorporate previously published stories. In recent years, she has published books for young readers, such as the award-winning *Kira-Kira* (2004). Kadohata currently lives in Los Angeles.

Kadohata's fiction features complex and often surprising characters, evocative details, and warm humor. Her PROTAGONISTS are generally female, but her male characters also are developed in rich and sympathetic ways. While her fiction carefully delineates representative segments of Japanese-American culture, Kadohata's central interest is always the universal quality of human experience.

Keith Lawrence
Brigham Young University

KAFKAESQUE The stories and novels of the Austrian writer Franz Kafka (1883–1924) often depict a nightmarish world of ABSURDity and paradox, of aimlessness and futility, of ethical, philosophic, and religious uncertainty, in which his protagonist is tormented by an unrelieved and unexplained anxiety. Kafka dramatized the alienation of the individual in a fathomless world. The adjective *Kafkaesque* describes a situation in which the goal is difficult or impossible to attain, usually because of the "red tape" of a faceless bureaucracy.

KAZIN, ALFRED (1915–1998) Alfred Kazin was a literary critic whose first book, *On Native Grounds* (1942), traced the development of American prose from the time of WILLIAM DEAN HOWELLS. Subsequent critical works included *The Inmost Leaf* (1955), *Contemporaries* (1962), and *Bright Book of Life* (1973), which traced the development of prose from ERNEST HEMINGWAY to NORMAN MAILER. In *An American Procession* (1984), Kazin presented a critical appraisal of the literary greats of American literature from Henry David Thoreau to WILLIAM FAULKNER and Hemingway.

BIBLIOGRAPHY
Kazin, Alfred. *An American Procession.* New York: Knopf, 1984.
———. *Bright Book of Life.* New York: Dell, 1973.
———. *Contemporaries, From the Nineteenth Century to the Present.* Boston: Little, Brown, 1962.
———. *The Inmost Leaf.* New York: Harcourt, Brace, 1955.
———. *On Native Grounds.* New York: Harcourt, 1942.

KENYON REVIEW, THE (1939–1970, 1979–) Founded in 1939 at Kenyon College in Gambier, Ohio, the *Kenyon Review* quickly became a preeminent scholarly journal of poetry, short stories, and NEW CRITICISM that consistently sought out unpublished and innovative writers. The review was an influential force in literary taste and criticism during its years under John Crowe Ransom, a southern poet and political conservative, who went on to edit the review for 21 years. Through his involvement teaching at Vanderbilt University and in the Fugitive and Agrarian movement (see AGRARIANS), Ransom formed lifelong friendships with Allen Tate and Robert Penn Warren. The two were consistent contributors to the journal, as were many other distinguished writers such as W. H. Auden, Cleanth Brooks, Lawrence Ferlinghetti, Northrop Frye, and Marianne Moore. While the *Kenyon Review* began primarily as a poetry outlet (in its first four years, the journal published only four short stories), after the *Southern Review* expired in 1947, the amount of space devoted to fiction increased seven times over. Thus the *Kenyon* came to be one of the American Big Four of scholarly periodicals along with the *PARTISAN REVIEW,* the *Sewanee Review,* and the *Hudson Review.* PETER TAYLOR was a regular contributor, and the *Kenyon's* first Fellow in Fiction was FLANNERY O'CONNOR; her stories "The Life You Save May Be Your Own" and "The ARTIFICIAL NIGGER" were first published in the spring issues in 1953 and 1955, respectively. While the *Kenyon's* influence waned during the late 1950s when the market for scholarly journals became saturated, it still serves as a hallmark of high-quality poetry, fiction, and criticism.

BIBLIOGRAPHY

Crump, Galbraith M., ed. *The Kenyon Poets: Celebrating the Fiftieth Anniversary of the Founding of the Kenyon Review.* Gambier, Ohio: Kenyon College, 1989.

Janssen, Marian. *The Kenyon Review 1939–1970: A Critical History.* Baton Rouge: Louisiana State University Press, 1989.

S. L. Yentzer
University of Georgia

KEROUAC, JACK (LOUIS) (1922–1969)

Jack Kerouac was born of French-Canadian parents in the textile mill town of Lowell, Massachusetts. Offered football scholarships, he attended Horace Mann School in New York City for his senior year (1939–40) and Columbia College the next. At the outbreak of WORLD WAR II, however, he enlisted in the navy, was discharged for resisting military discipline, and spent the rest of the war in the merchant marine and writing a novel. After the war he briefly studied writing and literature at the New School for Social Research in New York City but then dropped out: He had in effect begun his career as the wandering chronicler of the BEAT GENERATION, along with Allen Ginsberg, William S. Burroughs, and other literary friends with whom he evolved the concept of Beat life and its artistic aims and methods.

Although Kerouac published no short fiction during his lifetime, among his papers exist a number of sketches, short stories, and NOVELLAS, including manuscripts entitled "Book of Sketches," written in 1952 and 1953; "Short Stories, Shorts," written from 1940 to 1953; "Hartford Stories," written in 1941; as well as two novella-length works written in French (Brinkley 63). The Kerouac estate has authorized the historian Douglas Brinkley to edit and publish many of these pieces, along with a new biography of Kerouac (Brinkley 49).

Among the many books Kerouac published in the 1950s, it was ON THE ROAD (1957) that gave him fame. This book, widely accepted as the quintessential Beat novel (see BEAT LITERATURE), recorded Kerouac's travels throughout the United States and Mexico with his friend Neal Cassady and others. By the time he had published *On the Road,* Kerouac was convinced his art could succeed only if it emanated directly from experience, a technique he called "spontaneous prose," similar to jazz, writing "without consciousness" in a pure flow of expression. He consistently maintained that at the heart of the Beat experience was a religious quest. Indeed, Kerouac's book *The Dharma Bums,* featuring the poet Gary Snyder, has been credited with setting off the "rucksack revolution"—young people traveling widely and inexpensively, and, suspicious of Western technology and philosophy, feeling drawn to the religions of the East (Waldman 16). Kerouac died in St. Petersburg, Florida, of complications related to alcoholism.

BIBLIOGRAPHY

Brinkley, Douglas. "In the Kerouac Archive." *Atlantic Monthly* 282, no. 5 (November 1998): 49–76.

Challis, Chris. *Quest for Kerouac*. London: Faber & Faber, 1984.

Charters, Ann. *Kerouac: A Biography*. San Francisco: Straight Arrow, 1973.

Clark, Tom. *Jack Kerouac*. San Diego, Calif.: Harcourt Brace, 1985.

Gifford, Barry, and Lawrence Lee. *Jack's Book: An Oral Biography*. New York: St. Martin's, 1978.

Hipkiss, Robert A. *Jack Kerouac, Prophet of the New Romanticism*. Lawrence: Regents Press of Kansas, 1976.

Hunt, Tim. *Kerouac's Crooked Road*. Hamden, Conn.: Archon, 1981.

Nicosia, Gerald. *Memory Babe: A Critical Biography of Jack Kerouac*. New York: Grove, 1983.

Waldman, Anne. *The Beat Book: Poems and Fiction of the Beat Generation*. Boston: Shambhala, 1966.

Weinrich, Regina. *The Spontaneous Poetry of Jack Kerouac*. Carbondale: Southern Illinois University Press, 1986.

KEYES, DANIEL (1927–)

Daniel Keyes has been compared to Harper Lee, author of the classic *To Kill a Mockingbird,* and to other one-story writers. He catapulted to fame with "FLOWERS FOR ALGERNON" (1959), the emotionally wrenching story of a mentally handicapped 37-year-old janitor named Charlie Gordon that became an international classic. An immensely absorbing story that won a HUGO AWARD in 1960, it portrays the life of kind and good-natured Charlie Gordon, who is treated with intelligence-enhancing drugs to become a genius but who then returns to his original state as the effect of the drugs dissipates. Unfortunately for Charlie, his increased mental powers enable him to see the pettiness and hypocrisy evident in his fellow human beings, as well as cruelties of which he was never previously aware. Because he never judges these people, Charlie remains an innocent, unlike the more intelligent folk who surround him. Parallel to Charlie is Algernon, a laboratory mouse whom the scientists experimented on prior to deciding to explore similar possibilities with Charlie.

The story is also admired for the implicit questions that Keyes raises about genius, intelligence, mental retardation, the ethics of scientific intervention, and simple humanity. Keyes uses the form of a diary, or "progris riport," as Charlie initially spells it, to demonstrate the man's progress as the drugs take effect. As he passes through the normal intelligence phase and rises to the genius phase, he is obviously more intelligent than the scientists who treat him. He realizes that those whom he considered his friends now resent him, for they had considered him only mildly entertaining in his former state. His former teacher, Alice Kinnian, becomes problematic as well, for he discovers his emotional and sexually charged feelings for her, only to be rejected when she, too, resents his superior intelligence. As Charlie realizes that, as does Algernon, he must return to his former state, he learns that Algernon has died, and he asks that flowers be placed on the grave of the little mouse.

Daniel Keyes was born in 1927 in Brooklyn, New York, and studied at Brooklyn College. A high school English teacher when he wrote the story, he then expanded it into a best-selling novel with the same title. A television play of *The Two Worlds of Charlie Gordon,* based on the short story "Flowers for Algernon," was aired on the CBS Playhouse on February 22, 1961. A feature film, *Charly,* based on the novel *Flowers for Algernon,* starred Cliff Robertson, who won an Academy Award for this role in 1968. Although Keyes never replicated the success of "Flowers for Algernon," he has been critically lauded for his nonfiction work on mental illness in the schizophrenic Billy Mulligan, discovered to have 24 multiple personalities, and the mentally ill Claudia Elaine Yasko, who mistakenly confessed to serial murders. "The Daniel Keyes Collection," a repository of papers and manuscripts, is housed at the Alden Library at Ohio University.

BIBLIOGRAPHY

"Daniel Keyes: 40 Years of Algernon." Excerpted from *Locus Magazine,* June 1997. Available online. URL: http://www.locusmag.com/1997/Issues/06/Keyes.html. Accessed January 13, 2009.

Fremont-Smith, Eliot. "The Message and the Maze." *New York Times,* 7 March 1966, p. 25.

Hackett, Alice P. Review of *The Touch*. *Publishers Weekly* (12 August 1968): 46–47.

Keyes, Daniel. *Algernon, Charlie and I: A Writer's Journey.* Boca Raton, Fla.: Challcrest Press Books, 2000.

———. *Daniel Keyes Collected Stories.* Tokyo: Hayakawa, 1993.

———. *Daniel Keyes Reader.* Tokyo: Hayakawa, 1994.

———. *The Fifth Sally.* Boston: Houghton Mifflin, 1980.

———. *Flowers for Algernon.* New York: Harcourt, 1966.

———. *The Touch.* New York: Harcourt, 1968.

"Making Up a Mind." *Times Literary Supplement,* 21 July 1966, p. 629.

"KILLERS, THE" ERNEST HEMINGWAY (1927)

ERNEST HEMINGWAY's "The Killers," first published in *SCRIBNER'S* magazine in 1927 and included in his collection *Men without Women,* which came out later the same year, has everything the Hemingway reader wants and has come to expect. The mood is one of subtle danger and action; the dialogue is snappy and terse; the style is pure Hemingway; NICK ADAMS is a featured character; the story has a modern, one-man-alone-against-the-world feel; and it includes one of the hallmark Hemingway openings.

Hemingway completed the story in Madrid a couple of years before its publication. The plot begins in medias res, establishing a pattern of action while suggesting that the action has been ongoing long before the telling of the story begins:

> The door of Henry's lunch-room opened and two men came in. They sat down at the counter.
>
> "What's yours?" George asked them.
>
> "I don't know," one of the men said. "What do you want to eat, Al?"
>
> "I don't know," said Al. "I don't know what I want to eat."
>
> Outside it was getting dark. The street-light came on outside the window. The two men at the counter read the menu. From the other end of the counter Nick Adams watched them. He had been talking to George when they came in. (215)

It does not take the reader very long to decide that the two men are strangers. They are unfamiliar with the ordering process at the lunch counter and address the other characters in a condescending manner. And soon Nick and George learn that the two strangers have arrived in town to kill Ole Anderson, a boxer who is apparently hiding in the town. He often goes to the café at 6:00 p.m. to eat dinner, and the two plan on killing him when he arrives. In the meantime, Nick and the cook are tied up and kept quiet in the kitchen. When it becomes clear that Anderson is not going to show up for dinner, the two killers leave, and Nick, with the advice of George and against the advice of the cook, decides to go and warn Ole of their presence. Nick warns Ole, who decides to stay and face his killers alone instead of hiding or leaving town. At the end of the story, George tells Nick, who is disturbed by Ole's apathy toward his coming death, to "not think about it" (222).

It could be argued that the dialogue (snappy and rough), the situation (a boxer mixed up with the mob), and the theme are all somewhat clichéd, and it is true that the story does have a 1930s gangster film feel about it. The opposite argument may suggest that Hemingway's hard-boiled prose and plots influenced both the detective fiction/crime GENRE novels and the films of the 1930s. But what is intriguing about the story is something that the critics Cleanth Brooks, Jr., and Robert Penn Warren presented in their groundbreaking textbook *Understanding Fiction* (1943), which helped make the NEW CRITICISM a moving force in both university and even high school literature courses for decades. Brooks and Warren argue that Hemingway's characters are often "tough . . . experienced . . . and apparently insensitive. . . . They are, also, usually defeated men." But from this toughness, insensitivity, and defeat the characters "salvage something. And here we come upon Hemingway's basic interest in such situations and such characters. They are not defeated expect by their own terms." Ole Anderson, along with a host of Hemingway characters, is no exception. Instead of packing his bags and leaving town for his own health, Ole Anderson tells Nick that he "got in wrong" and that he is "through with all that running around" (221). Simply put, he is going to stay and face the music. We are not told exactly what Ole Anderson did to anger the big city mob, but we are left to assume that it involved fixing fights and that now he has to face the consequences of that decision. He is only going to be defeated on his own terms (ironically, Ole Anderson may have been taking dives in the ring).

Hemingway is able to create this sense of impending doom and subtle action and danger in his typical fashion—with a limited amount of description and a heavy dose of dialogue. Of the 232 indented paragraphs, only 26 contain no dialogue. Stereotypes (gangsters, black cooks) abound, but so do symbols (consider the towel in Nick's mouth and the wall Ole turns toward when Nick tells him he is going to die). And at the same time, readers are led to sympathize with Anderson and especially with Nick, who by now is getting his first real taste of life and death that the big world has waiting for him and us all.

BIBLIOGRAPHY

Benson, Jackson J., ed. *New Critical Approaches to the Short Stories of Ernest Hemingway.* Durham, N.C.: Duke University Press, 1991.

Bloom, Harold, ed. *Ernest Hemingway: Modern Critical Views.* New York: Chelsea House, 1985.

Brooks, Cleanth, Jr., and Robert Penn Warren. *Understanding Fiction.* Englewood Cliffs, N.J.: Prentice Hall, 1943.

Hemingway, Ernest. "The Killers." In *The Complete Short Stories of Ernest Hemingway: The Finca Vigía Edition.* New York: Scribner, 1987.

Oliver, Charles M. *Ernest Hemingway A to Z: The Essential Reference to the Life and Work.* New York: Facts On File, 1999.

Tyler, Lisa. *Student Companion to Ernest Hemingway.* Westport, Conn.: Greenwood Press, 2001.

Wagner-Martin, Linda, ed. *Ernest Hemingway: Six Decades of Criticism.* East Lansing: Michigan State University Press, 1988.

James Mayo
Jackson State Community College

KINCAID, JAMAICA (1949–)

Jamaica Kincaid was born Elaine Potter Richardson in St. John's, Antigua, in 1949; she left Antigua in 1965 to become an au pair in New York City. After enrolling in the New School for Social Research, where she studied photography, and Franconia College in New Hampshire, Kincaid became a staff member of the NEW YORKER in 1976 and since then has often published both fiction and nonfiction in that periodical and others. Her Caribbean background figures prominently in her first three books, *At the Bottom of the River* (1983), *Annie John* (1985), and *A Small Place* (1988). *At the Bottom of the River* is a short story collection that presents the day-to-day life of island dwellers in Antigua, often given in a cataloging of tasks; her story "GIRL" is an example of this style and subject. Both *At the Bottom of the River* and *Annie John,* however, have as their thematic core (see THEME) the resistance and conflict that arise between mothers and daughters and the inevitable imposition of the domestic on females in that culture. *A Small Place* is a collection of essays about the exploitation of the Caribbean islands by tourism.

Both *Annie John* and *Lucy* (1990) are novels that also can be considered SHORT STORY CYCLES. Their chapters present narratives complete in themselves that, taken together, trace the development of their titular PROTAGONISTS. *Annie John*'s exotic locale and details are striking—bleached white shirts drying on stones in the yard, breadfruit dishes, a fabulously grimy "red girl" whom Annie adores, monsoon rains—but while these images are fascinating and memorable on a literal level, they also add figurative resonance to the stories. *Lucy* is the tale of an au pair who left the Caribbean in her teens; her resentment toward her mother and her alienation from home are themes that unite *Lucy* with the earlier *Annie John* and to many of the stories in *At the Bottom of the River*.

Kincaid has been overwhelmingly well received by critics, and she continues to be a major figure in New York literary circles. *Autobiography of My Mother* was published in 1995 and *My Brother: A Memoir* in 1997. She also has written the introduction to *Generations of Women* (1998) and edited *My Favorite Plant: Writers and Gardeners on the Plants They Love* (1998). Her novel *Mr. Potter* was published in 2002.

BIBLIOGRAPHY

Cudjoe, Selwyn R. "Jamaica Kincaid and the Modernist Project: An Interview." *Callaloo* 12 (Spring 1989): 396–411.

Edwards, Audrey. "Jamaica Kincaid: Writes of Passage." *Essence* (May 1991): 86–90.

Ferguson, Moira. "A Lot of Memory: An Interview with Jamaica Kincaid." *Kenyon Review* 16 (Winter 1994): 163–188.

Garis, Leslie. "Through West Indian Eyes." *New York Times Magazine,* 7 October 1990, p. 6.

Kincaid, Jamaica. "Putting Myself Together." *New Yorker,* 20 February 1995, pp. 93–101.

Kreilkamp, Ivan. "Jamaica Kincaid: Daring to Discomfort." *Publishers Weekly,* 1 January 1996, pp. 54–55.

Mendelsohn, Jane. "Leaving Home: Jamaica's Voyage round Her Mother." *Village Voice Literary Supplement* (October 1990): 21, 89.

Karen Weekes
University of Georgia

KING, STEPHEN (1947–)

A late 20th-century phenomenon in the genres of GOTHIC horror, fantasy, and SCIENCE FICTION literature, Stephen King has been called the heir to EDGAR ALLAN POE and has been compared with the likes of RAY BRADBURY and H. P. Lovecraft. His fame rests on his novels, yet as all King aficionados know, he has written four collections of short fiction, several of which contain works that have been made into feature films. King has published stories in magazines since the early 1970s and continues to do so in periodicals ranging from *Cavalier, Whispers, Twilight Zone Magazine,* and the *Magazine of Fantasy and Science Fiction,* to such mainstream publications as *Cosmopolitan,* LADIES' HOME JOURNAL, *Penthouse, Playboy, Redbook,* and the NEW YORKER. *Night Shift* (1978), *Skeleton Crew* (1985), and *Nightmares and Dreamscapes* (1993) combine previously published stories with those written especially for the collections, and *Different Seasons* (1982) contains four NOVELLAS.

One of King's most critically acclaimed stories is "The Mist," a Faustian tale first published in *Dark Forces* in 1980 and revised for *The Skeleton Crew* five years later. The characters in the story become engulfed in a terrifyingly opaque mist apparently caused by a malfunction from scientific experiments at a nearby government facility. Conjuring a number of moral dilemmas for his characters as each reacts differently, King subtly injects into the horror story questions about religion, science, and materialism. Set in and around Bridgton, Maine, the tale features the protagonist, David Drayton, who makes his living creating artificial representations of human life. Ultimately pitted against Drayton's attempts to view the mist from a rational, scientific perspective are members of the Flat Earth Society (which includes a New York City attorney), who refuse to believe in the mist at all, and members of a religiously oriented group, who interpret it as God's punishment.

Other notable stories include the four novellas from the collection *Different Seasons. Rita Hayworth and Shawshank Redemption,* one of these novellas, is set in the Shawshank penitentiary in Maine. Told from the POINT OF VIEW of Red, the first-person narrator, the tale examines the theme of innocence. It was later made into a feature film, *The Shawshank Redemption. The Body,* an autobiographical story told from the first-person viewpoint of Gordon Lachance—an ALTER EGO for Stephen King (Winter 120)—is set in Castle Rock, Maine, a fictional locale that King frequently uses. Based on a childhood memory, King's story opens with young Gordon finding a corpse in the woods. This novella, too, was made into a feature film, entitled *Stand by Me.* Still another novella, made into a feature film, in the collection, *The Apt Pupil,* describes a young Todd Bowden's fascination with and final corruption by the HOLOCAUST memories of an aged Nazi war criminal.

Nightmares & Dreamscapes (1993) is a story collection that includes a nonfiction piece, a teleplay, and some poetry. The subjects include vampires, zombies, an evil toy, man-eating frogs, the burial of a mafioso in a Cadillac, a disembodied finger, and an evil stepfather. The style ranges from King's well-honed horror to a Ray Bradbury–like fantasy voice to an ambitious pastiche of RAYMOND CHANDLER and Ross MacDonald. Perhaps both despite and because of the popularity of his work—and thus the traditional hostility among "literary" academics—King's writing has received attention from a number of scholars who have written serious studies of his work, particularly during the last two decades. King's most recent story collection is *Everything's Eventual: 14 Dark Tales,* published in 2002.

BIBLIOGRAPHY
Beahm, George, ed. *The Stephen King Companion.* Kansas City, Mo.: Andrews & McMeel, 1989.

Brooks, Justin. *Stephen King: A Primary of the World's Most Popular Author.* Abingdon, Md.: Cemetery Dance, 2008.

Collings, Michael R. *Stephen King Is Richard Bachman.* Overlook Connection Press, 2008.

King, Stephen. *Cell.* New York: Scribner, 2006.

———. *The Colorado Kid.* New York: Hard Case Crime, 2004.

———. *The Dark Tower.* New York: Scribner, 2005.

———. *The Dark Tower: The Gunslinger.* New York: Amereon, 1976. Revised and expanded edition, New York: Viking, 2003.

———. *The Dark Tower II: The Drawing of the Three.* Illustrated by Phil Hale. New York: New American Library, 1989. Republished, New York: Plume Book, 2003; New York: Viking, 2003.

———. *The Dark Tower III: The Waste Lands.* Illustrated by Ned Dameron. Hampton Falls, N.H.: Donald M. Grant, 1991.

———. *The Dark Tower Trilogy: The Gunslinger; The Drawing of the Three; The Waste Lands.* New York: New American Library, 1993. Republished, New York: Penguin Group, 2003.

———. *The Dark Tower IV: Wizard and Glass.* New York: Plume, 1997.

———. *The Dark Tower V: Wolves of the Calla.* New York: Plume, 2003. Premium edition. Illustrated by Bernie Wrightson. New York: Pocket Books, 2006.

———. *The Dark Tower VI: The Songs of Susannah.* Hampton Falls, N.H.: Donald M. Grant, 2004.

———. *The Dark Tower VII.* New York: Scribner, 2004.

———. *Dreamcatcher.* New York: Simon & Schuster, 2001.

———. *Duma King.* New York: Scribner, 2008.

———. *Everything's Eventual: 14 Dark Tales.* New York: Scribner, 2002.

———. *From a Buick 8.* New York: Scribner, 2002.

———. *Lisey's Story.* New York: Scribner, 2006.

———. *On Writing: A Memoir of the Craft.* New York: Scribner, 2000.

King, Stephen, with Peter Straub. *Black House.* New York: Random House, 2001.

King, Stephen, with Ridley Pearson. *The Diary of Ellen Rimbauer: My Life as Rose Red.* New York: Hyperion, 2001.

King, Stephen, with Stewart O'Nan. *Faithful: Two Die-Hard Boston Red Sox Fans Chronicle the Historic 2004 Season.* New York: Scribner, 2004.

King, Stephen, under name Eleanor Druse. *The Journals of Eleanor Druse: My Investigation of the Kingdom Hospital Incident.* New York: Hyperion, 2004.

Winter, Douglas E. *Stephen King: The Art of Darkness.* New York: New American Library, 1984.

Wood, Rocky, et al. *Stephen King: Uncollected Unpublished.* Abingdon, Md.: Cemetery Dance, 2006.

"KING OF THE BINGO GAME" RALPH ELLISON (1944)

"King of the Bingo Game" registers the crisis in consciousness of an unnamed African-American man who has recently migrated to a northern city, which, he feels, does not provide the communality that his former life down South had afforded him. Unemployed, he has gone to a movie to immerse his worries in fantasy, with the additional hope of winning bingo money to pay the doctor bills for his ailing wife.

Straying from the film he has been watching through repeated screenings, his attention fixes on the cinematic apparatus that must be ignored in order to ensure hermetic encapsulation in the mass-mediated dreams it provides: "It was strange how the beam always landed right on the screen and didn't mess up and fall somewhere else. But they had it all fixed. Everything was fixed." (Ellison 124). This thought conflates a self-assuring conviction of stability, constancy, and security and a subtly bitter recognition of institutionalized unfairness. However, the melodrama on screen stimulates an erotic reverie of narrative rupture that reflects the attractive prospect of conditions going out of control: "If a picture got out of hand like that those guys up there would go nuts" (125). It is unclear—and this blurring is suggestive—whether "up there" refers to the characters on the screen or to the locus of the power that sets the story in motion at the site of *projection* (in both the cinematic and psychological senses of that term). In any case, these two observations introduce the dialectic at the heart of Ellison's story between the need for fixity and the desire to be out of control. This need and this desire will organize the man's cognitive experience as he abandons himself to the Wheel. (Although Ellison does not capitalize the word, designating it by the uppercase serves to emphasize both its iconographic identification with the American socioeconomic system, and the way the man receives his experiences as epiphany and theophany.)

His attention continuing to wander, the man has a nostalgic reverie of walking along a railway trestle as a boy down South, "getting off the trestle to solid ground just in time" as a train looms down on him. But this reverie quickly turns to nightmare as he imagines "that the train had left the track and was following him right down the middle of the street, and all the white people laughing as he ran screaming" (125). This fantasy proves darkly prophetic inasmuch as it constitutes the violation of programmatic fixity (i.e., going off the tracks), just as he will violate the rational order of his mind and has already begun to transgress the regulations and protocols of the game by having played more than the single card each patron is allotted.

The rest of the story records the stages of the man's psychotic break and the conflation of delusion and revelatory higher truth it bestows. His entry into the limelight and before the crowd is described in terms that announce the quasi-mystical experience he is about to undergo. Announced, with some irony, as "one of the chosen people," he is momentarily blinded and feels himself "moved into the spell of some strange, mysterious power" that is nevertheless "as familiar as the sun" (127–128). Even before engaging the Wheel, he has an overawed presentiment of its pervasive influence—that it has "determined" not only his life but also the life of his parents and, by implication, the fate of his race. But as he settles himself, he begins to feel "a profound sense of promise, as though he were about to be repaid for all the things he'd suffered all his life" (129). With fear and trembling he activates the Wheel, soon discovering that he cannot release himself from the mechanism, as though it were "a high-powered line in his naked hand" (129). Absorbed into the power of the wheel's increasing speed of rotation, he feels "a deep need to submit, to whirl, to lose himself in its twirl of color"—to "let it be" (129).

Despite his absorption into pure energy, the man is sundered by self-doubt. He shifts away from thinking about the proper moment to release the button so that the Wheel will stop on the number required to win the prize. He becomes preoccupied with the mechanism itself, convinced that to refrain from releasing the button is the way to control destiny (a feat superior to winning a particular jackpot, however much it is needed). Maintaining control becomes more important than gaining reward (130). As if he were a prophet descended from "a high hill into a valley of people," he receives the mockery of the crowd, who ridicule his evidently delusional state (130). But he is in the grip of a theophanic ecstasy: "This is God! This is really truly God!" Transmogrified into a visionary, he feels they will not let him "tell them the most wonderful secret in the world" (130–131). At the same time, the Wheel is an instrument of self-imposed torture, reminiscent of those in underworld myths. The man feels himself "a long thin black wire that was being stretched and wound . . . until he wanted to scream; wound, but this time himself controlling the winding and the sadness and the shame" (132). At this point he begins to believe that as long as he holds on, his sick wife, Laura, will continue to live. But this fixed idea destabilizes as did those before it, shifting into a paranoid fantasy that literalizes his collapsing ego structure in images of his body being invaded and stomped on.

Ellison scholars who have analyzed the story have tended to read it as a precursor to many of the imaginal motifs and thematic preoccupations of Ellison's great novel *Invisible Man* (begun a year later, in 1945), whose protagonist is another unnamed African American who has journeyed north and is, in existential terms, modernity's EVERYMAN. Ellison's story offers many salient similarities to his novel, although in an abbreviated form that owes as much to the author's still-developing imagination as to the intrinsic limits of the short story form. There is, for example, the theme of racial shame. The man recognizes that he is causing the crowd to feel shame because he, too, has often felt ashamed "of what Negroes did" (132). Furthermore, the shame of recognizing oneself an object that lacks autonomy, agency, and self-determination is an experience that the Invisible Man must learn to resolve. In the short story, Ellison's bingo player desperately clings to the fleeting conviction that "he and only he could determine whether or not it [the prize] was to be his" (130). In both works such convictions are put in dialectical relation with the regenerative possibility that resides in contingency. That is, both works represent the lack of self-determination as namelessness, the unexpected loss of an identity conferred by others. The social aspect of this condition is indicated by the fact that the man cannot find employment because he lacks a birth certificate, an institutional authentication of his existence, but during the crisis it becomes a matter of more intense existential realization: "It was a sad, lost feeling to lose your name, and a crazy thing to do" (132). The man is not aware, as the Invisible Man comes to be, that the absence of identity is an opportunity fraught with perilous, but rich, possibilities for self-definition.

A few other parallels between story and novel may serve to illuminate further the continuity of Ellison's preoccupations. The story converges at the electrifying site of an illusory prospect of reward for the shamefulness of racial abjection and the competitive antagonism it provokes between members of the abjected group ("They wanted the prize, that was it. They wanted the secret for themselves"). Similarly, a memorable incident early in the novel links this abjection and antagonism at the site of a frenzied competition between black youths grabbing false gold coins off an electrified rug. It is also worth noting that the $36.90 jackpot the man aspires to make his own by merging with the spinning wheel of fortune shares an uncanny numerical progression with the 1,369 light bulbs that the Invisible Man keeps lit by tapping into the corporate energy of Consolidated Power and Light. The passage in which the bingo player looks down on a mass of "poor nameless bastards" who "didn't even know their own names" and begins to have "a sense of himself that he had never known before" (133) looks toward the crucial passage in Ellison's novel when the Invisible Man, in the course of orating to a Harlem crowd, recognizes that his vocation is to delineate the uncreated features of his race. The protagonist of the novel, however, does not succumb to a delusion of grandeur under the pressure of his desperation and thus does not feel that "he was running the show, by God!" or that he embodies and vouchsafes the luck of his audience. Neither does the Invisible Man begin to feel, as the bingo player seems to, that he has the thaumaturgic power of kings to make someone "Live!" by his fiat (133).

But there will not be, there cannot be, an analog to the melodramatic climax of the film the bingo player has watched again and again. There will be no heroic rescue of the imperiled beloved from her bed of duress. However, a hint of silent film melodrama can be sensed when the combination of the howling crowd and the fixed rotation of the Wheel conjures back the runaway train of his earlier reverie. He sees himself carrying Laura running down the tracks just ahead of a subway train, which objectifies death's terrible inexorability (134). This is not the only oblique, subtle evocation of the movies. The man's delusional but heightened perceptions cause him momentarily to identify the flashing, spinning Wheel with the film spool in the projection booth. In an almost farcical interlude reminiscent of the Keystone Cops, the man briefly evades the police by "running in a circle" as if he had become the Wheel.

Brought to a halt, the man suffers the blows of police clubs as his totemic deity continues to revolve "serenely above," until coming to rest, inevitably, on double zero, the winner's ambiguous number. Ellison's ironic denouement is as heavy-handed as the cops when, just before the final blow falls, he has the man expect "he would receive what all the winners received." More skilled is Ellison's final sentence, whose phrasing evokes bloodshed without literally showing it: "and he knew even as it slipped out of him that his luck had run out on the stage" (136).

BIBLIOGRAPHY

Deutsch, Leonard J. "Ellison's Early Fiction." *Negro American Literature Forum* 7, no. 2 (Summer 1973): 53–57.

Ellison, Ralph. "King of the Bingo Game." In *Flying Home and Other Stories*. New York: Random House, 1996.

Urquhart, Troy A. "Ellison's 'King of the Bingo Game.'" *Explicator* 60, no. 4 (Summer 2002): 217–219.

David Brottman
Southern Indiana University

KINGSTON, MAXINE HONG (1940–)

Maxine Hong Kingston was born and raised in Stockton, California. She graduated from the University of

California at Berkeley in 1962 with a B.A. in English. Although portions of what Kingston eventually published as the nonfiction *The Woman Warrior* (1976) and *China Men* (1980) appeared earlier in *Viva, Bamboo Ridge, Hawaii Review,* the New Yorker, the *New York Times,* and the *Seattle Weekly,* Kingston did not become famous until after her first book appeared, hit the best-seller lists, and was awarded the National Book Critics Circle Award. *China Men* also sold well and received the National Book Award the year it was published. Kingston is the author of a collection of personal reminiscences, *Hawai'i One Summer* (1998), and two novels, *Tripmaster Monkey, His Fake Book* (1989) and *The Fifth Book of Peace* (2003). Kingston has taught English in both Hawaii and California, living for extended periods in each and claiming both states as her home.

Kingston's importance to the Asian-American short story is twofold. First—as Kingston apparently intended when she wrote them—the frequently anthologized short narratives composing *The Woman Warrior* and *China Men* are neither fiction nor nonfiction. Kingston herself resists labels, asking that she not be classed as an autobiographical, ethnic, or FEMINIST writer but simply a human writer. While Kingston's first two books grew out of real experience, the narratives themselves are shaped as short stories, with plot development, carefully moderated structures, tension between PROTAGONIST and ANTAGONIST, and symbolism. Because of this aesthetic shaping, Kingston's narratives must be considered in any discussion of the Asian-American short story.

Second and more important is Kingston's legacy to other Asian-American authors and to authors in general. Her narrative style, her manipulation and personalization of Asian mythology and culture, her focus on female relationships, and her calculated assessment of a multiracial American audience had an enormous influence on authors of the 1980s and 1990s, especially such Asian-American authors as AMY TAN, David Henry Hwang, GISH JEN, FAE MYENNE NG, CHITRA DIVAKARUNI, Gus Lee, and SIGRID NUNEZ. In *Woman Warrior,* in particular, Kingston's concepts of "talk-story," GHOST STORY, FABLE, and acquiring a voice have had significant impact on understanding the "double binds" around the feet and psyches of the daughters of Chinese-American immigrants. In 2008 she received the Medal for Distinguished Contributions to American Letters from the National Book Foundation, presenter of the National Book Awards.

BIBLIOGRAPHY
"Interview with Maxine Hong Kingston." Sonshi.com. Available online. URL: http://www.sonshi.com/kingston. html. Accessed May 2, 2009.
Kim, Elaine H. *Asian-American Literature.* Philadelphia: Temple University Press, 1982.
Kingston, Maxine Hong. *China Men.* New York: Vintage Press, 1989.
———. *The Fifth Book of Peace.* New York: Knopf, 2003.
———. *Hawai'i One Summer.* Honolulu: University of Hawaii Press, 1998.
———. *To Be the Poet.* Cambridge, Mass.: Harvard University Press, 2002.
———. *Tripmaster Monkey: His Fake Book.* New York: Vintage Press, 1990.
———. *The Woman Warrior: Memoirs of a Childhood among Ghosts.* New York: Vintage Books, 1989.
Ling, Amy. "Maxine Hong Kingston and the Dialogic Dilemma of Asian American Writers." *Bucknell Review* (1995).
Perry, Donna. "Maxine Hong Kingston." In *Backtalk: Women Writers Speak Out.* New Brunswick, N.J.: Rutgers University Press, 1993.
Seshachari, Neila C. "An Interview with Maxine Hong Kingston." *Weber Studies* (1995).

Keith Lawrence
Brigham Young University

KNICKERBOCKER GROUP   Diedrich Knickerbocker was a fictional Dutch character created by WASHINGTON IRVING. The name—associated with New York because of its numerous Dutch residents—was used to describe a group of writers, including Irving, James Fenimore Cooper, and William Cullen Bryant, who lived in or near New York City. Although the group's association was due to proximity and friendship rather than commonly held literary principles, it was significant because it marked the emergence of New York over Boston as a literary and cultural center in the early 19th century.

KNIGHT'S GAMBIT William Faulkner (1949)

Consisting of five short stories and a NOVELLA, WILLIAM FAULKNER's *Knight's Gambit* was published in 1949. Called "the GAVIN STEVENS volume" by Faulkner, *Knight's Gambit* is essentially a collection of murder mysteries in which Stevens, YOKNAPATAWPHA COUNTY attorney and the quixotic knight-errant of the title, plays the role of the clever and winsome country lawyer who successfully solves each case, at times bravely confronting killers and other notorious rascals; in the more intense scenes, often he is threatened; he is even shot once. Beyond the surface concerns of the murders themselves, however, Stevens struggles with some deeper philosophical matters in these stories, particularly regarding the puzzling incompatibility of justice and truth. In one story, "An Error in Chemistry," Stevens and the sheriff discuss this paradox:

> "I'm interested in truth," the sheriff said.
> "So am I," Uncle Gavin said. "It's so rare. But I am more interested in justice and human beings."
> "Ain't truth and justice the same thing?" the sheriff said.
> "Since when?" Uncle Gavin said.

Gavin proceeds to discuss the inconsistent relationship between, and sometimes the corruption of, these two virtues.

All five stories and the title novella, *Knight's Gambit,* appear in chronological order, covering the years 1936 to 1941 in Yoknapatawpha history, and they highlight Steven's efforts to confront the tension created by unjust truth and unscrupulous justice. They also reflect Stevens's necessary, if painful, maturation during a time when the world around him is growing increasingly complex and incompatible with his noble and chilvaric ideals. Ultimately, Stevens is shown to be a man suspended between two worlds—a status symbolized by his Phi Beta Kappa key (received at Harvard and followed by a Ph.D. at Heidelberg University in Germany) and a family heritage that hearkens back to the 18th-century foundations of Yoknapatawpha County. Equal to the tension he feels regarding truth and justice and human beings is his ambivalence—one that Faulkner surely shared—toward his heritage as a southerner and his role in his community.

BIBLIOGRAPHY

Faulkner, William. *Knight's Gambit.* New York: Random House, 1949.

Gresset, Michael, and Patrick Samway, eds. *Faulkner and Idealism: Perspectives from Paris.* Jackson: University of Mississippi Press, 1983.

H. Collin Messer
University of North Carolina at Chapel Hill

KOBER, ARTHUR (1900–1975)

Noted as DIALECT stories set in the Bronx, New York, or Hollywood, Kober's "Bella Stories" and others were first published in the *NEW YORKER* magazine between 1926 and 1958 before being reissued in collected form as *My Dear Bella* (1941) and *Bella, Bella Kissed a Fella* (1951).

KOREAN WAR (1950–1953)

The first major armed confrontation of the COLD WAR occurred when Soviet- and Chinese-backed North Korea invaded U.S.-backed South Korea in 1950. Fighting between the North Korean and Communist Chinese forces and the South Korean U.S. and UN forces ended with an armistice in 1953, with the armies facing each other at the 38th Parallel, as they had before the war began. Perhaps because the Korean War occurred so soon after the cataclysmic events of WORLD WAR II and ended not long before the prolonged and divisive VIETNAM WAR began, it is sometimes referred to as the Forgotten War.

KRISTEVA, JULIA (1941–)

A French literary theorist of Bulgarian origin, Kristeva is also a psychoanalyst, professor of linguistics, and novelist. Under the tutelage of ROLAND BARTHES, her early research defined language as a complex signifying process and culminated in her revolutionary concept, semiotics—a literary theory involving preoedipal processes that subvert and call into question the traditional meaning of language. Kristeva emphasizes the power of poetic language to subvert traditional (male) writing and challenge prevailing social, political, and historical systems. Associated with poststructuralist feminism, Kristeva questions notions of sexual difference, rejects the idea of feminine writing, and proposes a concept of femininity that includes diverse perspectives. (See FEMINISM/FEMINIST, POSTSTRUCTURALISM.)

Brenda M. Palo
University of North Carolina at Chapel Hill

KRUTCH, JOSEPH WOOD (1893–1970)

Joseph Wood Krutch was a critic, essayist, and English professor at Columbia University and elsewhere. His critical works include *Edgar Allan Poe: A Study of Genius* (1926), *Five Masters: A Study in the Mutations of the Novel* (1929), and *The American Drama since 1918* (1939; revised ed. 1957). His essays are collected in *The Modern Temper* (1929), *The Measure of Man* (1954), and *Human Nature and the Human Condition* (1959). His interest in the environment and in psychoanalytical interpretations of literature as well as his pleas for humanistic values in an industrialized, technological society influenced both readers and writers of his day.

KU KLUX KLAN

A white-supremacist secret society that was formed originally in 1866, after the CIVIL WAR, by former Confederates in Pulaski, Tennessee, to intimidate newly enfranchised blacks and prevent them from voting. It was formally disbanded in 1871 after Congress passed acts to suppress it. In 1915 the KKK was revived in Georgia, advocating white supremacy and the maintaining of "pure Americanism." Membership was confined to American-born Protestant whites. The group attacked blacks, Catholics, and Jews as well as ideas such as Darwinism. (See DARWIN, CHARLES ROBERT.) By the early 1920s there were an estimated 20 million clansmen throughout the United States, and the movement was politically significant, especially in some southern states. The Klan's power and size declined precipitously after 1923, with press exposés of its terrorist activities. Attempts to revive the society in the 1940s, 1960s, and 1970s failed, but it remains a small, fringe racist organization. The name derives from the Greek word *kuklos,* which means "band" or "circle."

KUNSTLERROMAN

A German term that means "artist novel," the *Kunstlerroman* is an important subtype of the BILDUNGSROMAN (novel of education). The *Kunstlerroman* is a novel that depicts the development of novelists or other artists into the stage of maturity in which they recognize their artistic destiny and achieve mastery of their artistic craft. Examples of this type of novel are James Joyce's *A Portrait of the Artist as a Young Man* and Marcel Proust's *Remembrance of Things Past*. Despite the term's connection to the novel, it can be used with regard to artist figures in short fiction as well.

L

LADIES' HOME JOURNAL Owing its start to a column in the weekly newspaper *Tribune and Farmer* in the 1880s, the *Ladies' Home Journal* now enjoys an autonomous existence as one of the most widely circulated magazines in the United States.

By November 1889 the *Journal* had reached a circulation of 1 million. Its popularity was due to the short stories and serialized novels it published, written by some of the most popular writers of the day, including Ella S. Wheeler and Margaret S. Harvey. It quickly became a woman's survival manual, featuring departments that offered practical advice on child rearing, useful household hints, instructions for crafts, and inspirational essays on a variety of topics. The magazine had a traditional bias and never editorially endorsed woman suffrage. In 1935 its husband-and-wife editorial team of Beatrice and Bruce Gould fashioned it as the conservative voice to America's women, in the belief that women were wives and mothers first. According to Beatrice, it was "a woman's job to be as truly womanly as possible. I mean to nourish her family, and to rest them, to guide them, and to encourage them."

Despite this editorial creed, not all women were included. Women of color, for instance, generally were overlooked, despite occasional columns by the wife of the civil rights leader Medgar Evers. Second-wave FEMINISTs went so far as to storm the office of the *Journal* in March 1970, demanding a chance to put out a "liberated" issue of the magazine and calling for an end to "exploitative" advertising. The editors heeded the protest and, in the August issue, included an eight-page supplement written by supporters of the feminist/women's movement. Editorial course has shifted as a result, and today, although articles on beauty, fashion, food, child rearing, and home care still predominate, editorials on travel, business, and national and international affairs are prevalent.

Laura S. Behling
Gustavus Adolphus College

"LADY, OR THE TIGER?, THE" FRANK R. STOCKTON (1882) Frank R. Stockton (1834–1902) originally entitled this story "The King's Arena," and after its appearance in 1882, it became the most famous story ever published in *Century Magazine*. Related by a caustic first-person narrator (see POINT OF VIEW) who clearly disagrees with the feudal nature of kings and courtiers who set themselves above commoners, the story takes place in an unnamed barbaric country. The king discovers that a handsome young man, a commoner, whose low social rank prohibits his marrying royalty, has fallen in love with the king's daughter—a crime that, the author remarks wryly, became common enough in later years. The trial of the young man takes place in the king's arena. He must choose to open one of two doors. Behind one waits a ferocious beast who will tear him to pieces; behind the other, is a beautiful maiden who will marry him immediately. If he chooses the beast, he is automatically guilty; if he chooses the maiden, he proves his innocence.

Of all those in the arena—including the king—only the clever princess has discovered the secret of what lies behind each door. She has made her decision to send a signal to the young man, and she does so, indicating the door on the right. In reaching her decision, the princess has agonized between the dreadful images of the savage and bloody death, and of the young man married to the beautiful maiden of whom the princess is intensely jealous. The young man moves immediately to the door the princess has indicated, and the story ends with the narrator's question to the reader: "Which came out of the door,—the lady, or the tiger?" (10). Although similar to a SURPRISE ENDING, the final sentence differs in that it leaves the reader without a DENOUEMENT. Five years later, Stockton followed with "The Discourager of Hesitancy" (1887), which promises to solve the puzzle, but in fact this story, too, leaves the question unanswered.

BIBLIOGRAPHY

Stockton, Frank R. "The Lady, or the Tiger?" In *The Lady, or the Tiger? And Other Stories.* New York: Scribner, 1914.

"LADY OF LITTLE FISHING, THE" CONSTANCE FENIMORE WOOLSON (1875)

Appearing in *Castle Nowhere: Lake-Country Sketches,* "The Lady of Little Fishing" exemplifies Constance Fenimore Woolson's strengths as a writer of both LOCAL COLOR and REALISM. The grandniece of James Fenimore Cooper and friend and possibly the intimate of HENRY JAMES, Woolson produced short stories of Great Lakes and Florida coast life that led the literary scholar and critic Fred Lewis Pattee to call her "the most unconventional feminine writer" to appear in America in the second half of the 19th century (250).

"The Lady of Little Fishing" explores the influence of an itinerant woman preacher on a small Lake Superior logging community in the summer of 1850. Told from the perspective of a former resident, the narrative illustrates how a woman's public speech produces order and temperance in a hitherto lawless male community. On one hand, the lady's irreproachable purity and the desire that it produces in her male listeners cause them to reorganize their previously ill-man-nered and uncouth community so that they distinguish between public and private behavior; on the other, the lady's awakening love for one unregenerate logger finally destroys the community. Published a few years before Henry James wrote *The Bostonians,* Woolson's account of the nature of the female orator's public power may have inspired James's satirical portrayal of Olive Chancellor, the strong-willed Boston FEMINIST of that novel.

BIBLIOGRAPHY

Levander, Caroline. *Voices of the Nation: The Politics of the Female Voice and Women's Public Speech in Nineteenth-Century Literature and Culture.* New York: Cambridge University Press, 1997.

Pattee, Fred Lewis. *The Development of the American Short Story: An Historical Survey.* New York: Harper & Brothers, 1923.

Torsney, Cheryl. *Constance Fenimore Woolson: The Grief of Artistry.* Athens: University of Georgia Press, 1989.

———, ed. *Critical Essays on Constance Fenimore Woolson.* New York: G. K. Hall, 1992.

Woolson, Constance Fenimore. "The Lady of Little Fishing." In *Castle Nowhere: Lake-County Sketches.* New York: Harper, 1875.

Caroline F. Levander
Trinity University

LAFARGE, OLIVER (OLIVER HAZZARD PERRY LAFARGE) (1901–1963)

An anthropologist and writer, Oliver Lafarge was known as a leading authority on NATIVE AMERICANS, particularly the Navajo. He won the PULITZER PRIZE for the novel *Laughing Boy* (1929), which dealt with life among the Navajo. Many of his other novels and stories also concern Native Americans, as does the nonfiction history *As Long as the Grass Shall Grow* (1940). Recent reevaluations, however, particularly by Native Americans such as Louis Owens, see Lafarge's work in the tradition of white "literary colonization" of the vanishing Indian: Thus Lafarge joins the ranks of HERMAN MELVILLE (Queequeg), MARK TWAIN (Injun Joe), and WILLIAM FAULKNER (Chief Doom), all of whom, according to Owens, appropriated the "Indian as the quintessential naturalistic [see NATURALISM] victim" and entered him into "the Vanishing American Hall of Fame" (Owens 23).

BIBLIOGRAPHY

Lafarge, Oliver. *As Long as the Grass Shall Grow.* New York: Alliance Book, and Toronto: Longmans, Green, 1940.

———. *The Enemy Gods.* Boston: Houghton Mifflin, 1939.

———. *Laughing Boy.* Cambridge, Mass.: Houghton Mifflin, 1929.

———. *Raw Material.* Boston: Houghton Mifflin, 1945.

Owens, Louis. *Other Destinies: Understanding the American Indian Novel.* Norman and London: University of Oklahoma Press, 1992.

LAHIRI, JHUMPA (1967–)

Although Lahiri was born in London in and grew up in Rhode Island, her stories are inflected with her Bengali heritage. Her delicately woven stories explore the relationship between India and her diaspora, between Americans and Indians, and even between Indians themselves. In interrogating cultural identity and cultural difference, Lahiri eschews easy binaries, such as those between the self and the Other, or Indian and non-Indian, preferring to examine the conflicts and cultural misunderstandings that arise between generations, between immigrants and children of immigrants, between those who leave and those who stay behind.

For the most part, her fiction is set in the Northeast United States, generally in an upper-middle-class intellectual and cultural milieu, in contrast with those few stories that take place in India. There are not two, but three continents omnipresent in her work: the place of origin (the Indian subcontinent), the destination (North America), and the intermediary place (Europe). It is thus not surprising that the final story in her Pulitzer Prize–winning 1999 collection *Interpreter of Maladies,* entitled "The Third and Final Continent," features a narrator who has passed through London on his way to Boston. This final story takes the themes and tensions of the collection to a resolution, which ultimately values individual experience over collective conflict and embraces a fluid sense of identity, forever changing according to one's experience and context.

Enakshi Chowdhury identifies this as part of a movement toward multiculturalism in the United States starting in the 1990s. "The idea that people are members of different collectivities and there is no such thing as a universal 'we' came to be recognized. Immigration and diaspora were unavoidable contexts," he writes. Lahiri's participation in this evolution is specifically marked by her attention to gender roles; according to Chowdhury, Indian-American women writers such as Lahiri represent "women characters in every piece of fiction they write, for this is the way they, themselves, appraise their own social reality" (127–128).

The Namesake, her first novel, which appeared in 2003, treats many, if not all, of the themes that run through *Interpreter of Maladies,* and it, too, spans the three continents. Gogol, the son of Indian immigrants to America, was named for the Russian writer whose story "The Overcoat" saved his father's life. He wears his name loosely, awkwardly; it prevents him from alighting on just one cultural identity, being neither American nor Indian. He himself feels completely American but cannot throw off his Indian identity. He has difficulty understanding his parents' relationship to India because he himself feels no direct bond at all to the country. He does not understand the way his parents feel the distance from their native land until his college girlfriend spends a semester at Oxford: "It sickens him to think of the physical distance between them. . . . He longs for her the way his parents have longed, all these years, for the people they love in India for the first time in his life, he knows this feeling" (117). Gogol begins to discover that his Indian identity is for him to tailor to his own specifications, based on his own experience of the world.

This is reinforced by his interactions with other children of Indian immigrants. At university he attends a meeting by a group called ABCD: *American-born confused deshi.* In other words, him. He learns that the *C* could also stand for *conflicted.* He knows that *deshi,* a generic term for "countryman," means "Indian"; knows that his parents and all their friends always refer to India simply as *desh.* But Gogol never thinks of India as *desh.* He thinks of it as Americans do, as India (118).

This passage is illustrative of the issues at the heart of Lahiri's work. Gogol is bored, at the meeting, by the panelists' discussion of "marginality"; so is Lahiri. Indian identity is certainly not marginal in her work: It is central, and her characters naturally do not feel themselves to be "marginal" to society but integral parts of it, building it, as Gogol becomes an architect, learning to be compassionate ("When Mr Pirzada Came to Dine"), insisting on an ethics of relationships ("Sexy"), or translating between cultures ("Interpreter of Maladies").

Lahiri's 2008 collection *Unaccustomed Earth* also received great critical acclaim.

Lahiri's stories are not the first to be written about cultural exile, and they are not the last. They do not pretend to present unique experiences; nor do they aspire to represent universal values. They are, rather, picking up, turning around, and wondering at the everyday journeys. "I am aware that my achievement is quite ordinary," says the narrator of "The Third and Final Continent." "I am not the only man to seek his fortune far from home, and certainly I am not the first. Still, there are times I am bewildered by each mile I have traveled, each meal I have eaten, each person I have known, each room in which I have slept. As ordinary as it all appears, there are times when it is beyond my imagination" (198).

BIBLIOGRAPHY

Bess, Jennifer. "Lahiri's *Interpreter of Maladies*." *Explicator* 62, no. 2 (Winter 2004): 125–128.

Brada-Williams, Noelle. "Reading Jhumpa Lahiri's *Interpreter of Maladies* as a Short Story Cycle." *MELUS: The Journal of the Society for the Study of the Multi-Ethnic Literature of the United States* 29, nos. 3–4 (Fall–Winter 2004): 451–464.

Chowdhury, Enakshi. "Facing the Millennium." In *Indian Response to American Literature,* edited by T. S. Anand. New Delhi: Creative Books, 2003.

Cox, Michael W. "Interpreters of Cultural Difference: The Use of Children in Jhumpa Lahiri's Short Fiction." *South Asian Review* 24, no. 2 (2003): 120–132.

Dubey, Ashutosh. "Immigrant Experience in Jhumpa Lahiri's *Interpreter of Maladies*." *Journal of Indian Writing in English* 30, no. 2 (2002): 22–26.

Flaherty, Kate. "Jhumpa Lahiri's *The Namesake*." *Philament,* 5 January 2005. Available online. URL: http://www.arts.usyd.edu.au/publications/philament/issue5_Commentary_Flaherty.htm. Accessed August 14, 2006.

Karim, Rezaul. "Jhumpa Lahiri." In *South Asian Writers in English,* edited by Fakrul Alam. Detroit: Thomson Gale, 2006.

Lahiri, Jhumpa. *Interpreter of Maladies.* Boston: Houghton Mifflin, 1999.

———. *The Namesake.* Boston: Houghton Mifflin, 2004.

———. *Unaccustomed Earth.* Boston: Houghton Mifflin, 2008.

Lewis, Simon. "Lahiri's *Interpreter of Maladies*." *Explicator* 59, no. 4 (2001): 219.

Lauren Elkin
City University of New York Graduate Center

LAMPOON   From the refrain *lampons* ("let's drink") in 17th-century French satirical drinking songs, a lampoon is a malicious, often scurrilous satirical piece of writing that attacks an individual's character or appearance. The lampoon flourished in 17th- and 18th-century England and sometimes took the form of extended satire, as with Alexander Pope's attack on Joseph Addison—a fellow writer whom Pope depicts as a jealous Atticus—in "An Epistle to Dr. Arbuthnot" (1735). The form fell into disuse as a result of public disapproval and the rise of modern libel laws. The term still is used to describe a verbal or written piece of pointed mockery directed at a person or institution, as loosely demonstrated in the *Harvard Lampoon* and the *National Lampoon.*

LARDNER, RING (RING GOLD WILMER LARDNER) (1885–1933)

Ring Lardner was a newspaper humorist, sportswriter, and short story writer known for his satirical stories and sketches about life in early 20th-century America. Lardner had an infallible ear for vernacular (see DIALECT) and an exceptional gift for PARODY. His stories were told in the language of the subject, whether athlete, songwriter, secretary, or chorus girl. He also created a gallery of fictional boobs who commented perceptively on the social scene and the emergence of an avaricious, pretentious, and largely ignorant middle class. A small number of Lardner's 128 short stories have been anthologized regularly.

Lardner's years as a newspaperman—and his famous baseball column, "In the Wake of the News"—

taught him how to hold readers' interest. He understood the importance of a tight narrative; of pace, tone, and voice; and of appeal to eye and ear. Humor and satire were central to his vision. To the 1920s Lardner gave a new kind of short story that emphasized the masculine personality; the world of sports; the wise boob as hero, particularly ALIBI IKE, the crude but endearing baseball player who became an American myth.

Significantly, Lardner introduced to the American literary tradition a new interest in colloquial dialect, colorful and vibrant, if filled with grammatical lapses, malapropisms, and redundancies. Lardner also was especially adept at using the technique of the letter, as he does in his famous novel *You Know Me, Al* (1916) and, especially, the monologue. Two of his most famous stories, "The Golden Honeymoon," and "HAIRCUT," use the monologue in extremely revealing ways. In "The Golden Honeymoon," Lardner uses both dialogue and monologue to develop the story of a couple on a trip to celebrate their 50th wedding anniversary. They are tedious, short-tempered, quarrelsome, and silly; the husband's interior monologue reveals his jealousy when they run into his wife's old beau. Nonetheless, beneath these qualities Lardner reveals the decreasing size of the couple's world, their aging faculties, and their somewhat pathetic attempts to hold onto their love as well as their lives, for they know they have little time remaining.

"Haircut" is told by a barber, the first-person narrator, and the result, as numerous critics have wryly observed, is a story, with a sharp, cutting edge. The barber exposes both the mentality of the small town as well as his own limited reasoning abilities, his insensitivity, and his primitive, shallow PERSONA. This story influenced such writers as ERNEST HEMINGWAY and WILLIAM FAULKNER, who used POINT OF VIEW in a similar way in a number of their stories.

BIBLIOGRAPHY

DeMuth, James. *Small Town Chicago: The Comic Perspective of Peter Dunne, George Ade, and Lardner.* Port Washington, N.Y.: Kennikat Press, 1980.

Elder, Donald. *Lardner: A Biography.* Garden City, N.Y.: Doubleday, 1956.

Evans, Elizabeth. *Lardner.* New York: Ungar, 1979.

Ferguson, Andrew. "Five Best: Some Humor Doesn't Age Well, but These American Classics Remain Funny beyond Compare." *Wall Street Journal,* 2 December 2006, p. P8.

Friedrich, Otto A. *Lardner.* Minneapolis: University of Minnesota Press, 1965.

Geismar, Maxwell. *Lardner and the Portrait of Folly.* New York: Crowell, 1972.

Lardner, Ring. *The Big Town.* Indianapolis: Bobbs-Merrill, 1921.

———. *First and Last.* New York: Scribner, 1934.

———. *How to Write Short Stories.* New York: Scribner, 1924.

———. *Lardner on Baseball.* Guilford, Conn.: Lyons Press, 2003.

———. *Lose with a Smile.* New York: Scribner, 1933.

———. *The Love Nest and Other Stories.* New York: Scribner, 1926.

———. *Own Your Own Home.* Indianapolis: Bobbs-Merrill, 1919.

———. *The Portable Ring Lardner.* New York: Viking Press, 1946.

———. *The Real Dope.* Indianapolis: Bobbs-Merrill, 1919.

———. *The Ring Lardner Reader.* New York: Scribner, 1963.

———. *Round Up.* New York: Scribner, 1929.

———. *Shut Up, He Explained.* New York: Scribner, 1962.

———. *Some Champions.* New York: Scribner, 1976.

———. *What of It?* New York: Scribner, 1925.

———. *You Know Me Al.* New York: George Doran, 1916.

Lardner, Ring, Jr. *The Lardners: My Family Remembered.* New York: Harper & Row, 1976.

Patrick, Walton R. *Lardner.* New York: Twayne, 1963.

Yardley, Jonathan. *Ring: A Biography of Lardner.* New York: Random House, 1977.

LASCH, CHRISTOPHER (1932–1994)

A professor of history, Christopher Lasch was a social critic and cultural historian known for his analyses of contemporary American cultural and political phenomena. *The New Radicalism in America, 1889–1963: The Intellectual as a Social Type* (1965) is a collection of essays dealing with the psychological motivations of 20th-century social activism. *The Culture of Narcissism* (1979) deals with an increasingly self-centered view of the world and its effect on the family and the community. *The Minimal Self* (1984) examines individual freedom and privacy issues. Lasch consistently challenged contemporary Americans' reliance on experts to determine standards of behavior and thought. His criticism leads, sometimes explicitly, sometimes implicitly, to a questioning of the self-reflexive stance taken by many novelists and short story writers whose work falls under the rubric of POSTMODERNISM.

"LAST LEAF, THE" O. HENRY (1907)

One of the most famous of the O. HENRY tales, "The Last Leaf" (1907) not only concludes with the usual O. Henry SURPRISE ENDING, but, like "A Service of Love," is conveyed with a narrative tone of sadness and even despair. Two young women artists, Sue and Joanna (Johnsy), share a brownstone in New York. In a cold and wintry November, Johnsy catches pneumonia (personified as an icy ravager who smites his victims as he strides through Greenwich Village) and has resigned herself to dying; the doctor gives her one chance in 10 unless she can find a reason to live. Johnsy tells the distraught Sue that with the fall of the last leaf on the ivy vine that clings to the wall outside her window, she will die. Sue reveals the situation to their failed artist friend Mr. Behrman; he poses for the sketch of an old hermit miner that Sue must finish for her editor; then Sue lies down to sleep for an hour. When she awakens, she and Johnsy look out the window to see that one leaf has survived the nighttime rains and gusty winds, encouraging Johnsy to disregard her previous "foolish" belief that she is near death. As she recovers, however, the doctor informs them that Mr. Behrman has died of pneumonia. He had been found soaking wet, his body lying next to a ladder, a lantern, and some paint brushes. The clear implication is that Behrman braved the cold and rain while printing the last leaf (which actually had fallen) on the wall so that Johnsy would not die.

This story, as have many of O. Henry's, has been called implausible and sentimental. It nevertheless appeals to readers in the generosity of the selfless Mr. Behrman and in the uniqueness of the plot. The irony of Mr. Behrman's losing his life to save Johnsy's emanates from the same selflessness exhibited in the husband and wife in the well-known O. Henry story "The GIFT OF THE MAGI."

"The Last Leaf" may be interpreted from feminist and lesbian perspectives, too, to produce some intriguing readings (see FEMINISM and LESBIAN THEMES IN SHORT STORIES). From a feminist viewpoint, the skeptical doctor and the male-personified illness try to undermine the women's aspirations. The doctor asks Sue if Johnsy has anything worth thinking about to keep her alive, either a man or an interest in women's fashions. Johnsy's longings lie not in sex or clothing styles, but, Sue responds, in art: She hopes someday to travel to Italy to paint the Bay of Naples. From this perspective, the women emerge victorious: Helped by the old European artist, they defy the illness and the doctor and survive to continue their work as independent women artists. From the lesbian viewpoint, however, the story has a more somber message. Clearly Johnsy and Sue may be viewed as lesbians: Johnsy's name is a masculinized version of *Joanna*; Sue alternately swaggers and whistles, and talks baby talk to Johnsy, calling herself Johnsy's "Sudie." Moreover, the story centers on Johnsy in bed, with Sue leaning her face on the pillow or putting her arm around her. Not only do the male doctor and Mr. Pneumonia attempt to break up the pair, but in the very survival of these women, a man, Mr. Behrman, must die—a plot suggesting a hostility toward lesbian women at the core of the story.

BIBLIOGRAPHY
Henry, O. "The Last Leaf." In *The Collected Works of O. Henry.* Vol. 2. Garden City, N.Y.: Doubleday, 1953.

"LAUREL" ALICE WALKER (1982)

In this story, a discussion of how the political can be made all too personal takes place in the context of a thwarted love affair in the Deep South of the 1960s. Annie, the narrator whom the author invites you to think of as a mirror of herself, is looking back at how an incident has changed her in ways she did not really want to be changed, and how it has failed to change what is perhaps her best characteristic as an author but her worst as a woman in a relationship.

The backdrop of "Laurel" is a time of great political moment: The narrator is a young black radical working to create a new journal on racism and activism in Georgia. People are working for and achieving greater freedom and equality for the disenfranchised, but Annie, though a contributor to this, is still a bored 20-year-old woman who is thrill-seeking and exploring her sexual freedom. The journal's name is *First Rebel*: "The title referred, of course, to the black slave that was rebelling all over the South long before the white rebels fought the Civil War." Annie and Laurel's relationship in the story will eventually deteriorate into a disagreement with each other about what the black rebel owes the white one.

It is in an instance of boredom that Annie encounters Laurel, a white Californian man, whose family has been pickers in apple orchards and grape vineyards; he has come to work on the journal in hopes of starting his own back home. They are immediately drawn to each other, and this attraction seems to be driven by the exoticism of the other and the great danger and shock value of being sexually involved. Annie, who has much more middle-class polish from her education than Laurel, sees the dirt under his fingernails and figures at first that she has the advantage over him: "That's it, I thought. I can safely play here. No one brings such dirty nails home to dinner." Annie feels she can "safely play" because she would never consider a serious (take him home to a family dinner) relationship with a person who has the habits of what she terms a country bumpkin.

But Annie becomes mutually obsessed with Laurel, and in the one week of their relationship the impossibility of having sex with him makes him compelling to the point that she thinks she is in love. Because of the laws of segregation still in effect and their rigorous enforcement, she and Laurel are barred from cheap hotels, their sex-segregated dormitories, and even the woods. Annie romanticizes their unquenched lust. She describes Laurel as a promise of EDENIC pleasure, saying that he smells of apples and May wine. His voice "sounded as if two happy but languid children were slowly jumping rope under apple trees in the sun." They long for each other so—barred from paradise, as it were—that they can hardly eat from choking on their desire. Annie finds this to be "a veritable movie." When their friends and fellow radicals remind them of how they are endangering themselves, their cause, and others, the couple acknowledge the reality

but are numbed by their intoxication. Their story seemed to be a reverse image of a movie very famous for its comment on the place of romance in an unjust world: *Casablanca*. But in the case of Annie and Laurel, they felt that the wants of two little people amounted to much more than a hill of beans in this world, and their acts of activism mostly became about their right to mutual pleasure.

On what they do not know will be their last night together, Laurel, in a fit of guilt, tells Annie that he has a wife back home. Annie does not particularly care—she is too radicalized to feel guilty or obligated, as her romance with Laurel is just part of her self-exploration. But six months later she finds that Laurel's wife and family do feel that Annie should feel obligated to Laurel—he has been grievously injured—it is unknown whether he is the victim of bashers or merely fell asleep at the wheel—while delivering copies of *First Rebel*. Laurel's family ushers her to his hospital bed, but she does not wake the comatose beauty.

Annie begins to take on a more conventional life after Laurel's accident: She settles down, marries a lawyer activist, and has a daughter. She becomes less and less the woman Laurel loved. But Laurel, after two years severely disabled, roars back into Annie's life, like Freud's return of the repressed, and demands that they resume their relationship where it left off. Apparently, Laurel's mind has frozen itself in the delirium of that one week he shared with Annie. Annie does her best to dissuade him, but he will not give up, and as he deteriorates with each rebuff, his desire for her turns to a menacing resentment.

Laurel sees himself as entitled to Annie's devotion because of his injuries, he writes: "I hope you know how I lost part of my brain working for your people in the South." He says of her marrying a Jew: "I guess you have a taste for the exotic though I am not exotic. I am a cripple now with part of my brain in somebody's wastepaper basket." Laurel goes to see her and her blackness as his salvation: "I dream of your body so warm and brown, whereas mine is white and cold to me now. . . . I want you here. We can be happy and black and beautiful and crippled and missing part of my brain together." Laurel wants to own Annie's body because he has lost part of his brain; he has a taste for the exotic and does not see that to Annie he was exotic; and he wants her to join him in his obsession—crippled and missing a part of his brain forever.

Annie wonders whether Laurel's entrapment in his lustful delirium and defiance reflects a way in which she is not as changed by time as she would like to think. She has viewed herself as the first rebel, as if rebellion in itself were her freedom. But Laurel becomes the second rebel, the white man who was fighting still to own a person, to be redeemed by his brain-distorting lust and sense of entitlement to save himself through a black woman. Over a century after the CIVIL WAR, what does a black radical owe a white liberal who is damaged by his joining the fight for her freedom? Apparently, Laurel thinks she owes him the very self she has fought to free.

But Annie's freedom haunts her—she feels that her will to complete freedom keeps her alienated from everyone, even those with whom she sought to make common cause, such as her now-former husband. Years after their divorce and Laurel's destruction, Annie seeks for her husband to assuage her fears and her guilt about Laurel by telling her she was right not to go to Laurel, if only for a while, to give him some happiness. She says that she would have gone to Laurel and temporarily left her husband and child not only "because of the pity—[but] for the adventure."

Her former husband, the voice of rationality, compassion, and commitment, does not tell her that her abandonment of Laurel was right, at least not in a way that Annie can hear, because her doubts and regrets go deeper than what was the right decision: She wonders whether she should have followed her sense of adventure—a great part of her radicalism—even to a destructive turn. She feels that she has lost something of being the first rebel, and in her former husband's response that her staying with her family and adult life was the reasonable thing to do, she feels a kind of nihilism—what can she do when the passion that drives her ceases to be the right impulse?

Carolyn Whitson
Metrostate University

LEAVITT, DAVID (DAVID ADAM LEAVITT) (1961–)

Bursting onto the American landscape as a wunderkind in 1984 with his first short story, "Territory," published in the *New Yorker* in 1982 when he was only 21 years old, and his story collection, *Family Dancing* (1984), winner of the 1984 PEN/FAULKNER AWARD, David Leavitt has continued to prove himself as a writer. His subject matter ranges from family ambiguities and complexities to love, sexuality, and the gay experience. In addition to his three novels, he has published three subsequent story collections: *A Place I've Never Been* (1990), *Arkansas: Three Novellas* (1997), and *The Marble Quilt* (2001).

David Leavitt was born on June 23, 1961, in Pittsburgh, Pennsylvania, to Harold J. Leavitt, a professor, and Gloria Rosenthal Leavitt, and was reared in Palo Alto, California. Before graduating with a bachelor's degree from Yale University in 1983, he saw "Territory" create a stir with its focus on homosexuality. Its main character is a young gay man who takes his lover home to meet his parents; his mother, a sixties radical, is nonetheless horrified to learn of her son's homosexuality. The story is collected in *Family Dancing,* as is "Counting Months," a story that won the 1984 O. HENRY MEMORIAL AWARD. Leavitt's deftly drawn characters are educated and middle class, and his strong women have elicited favorable comment from critics. His second collection, *A Place I've Never Been* (1990), focuses even more consistently on gay relationships, from the loss of a lover to a young man's losing battle with AIDS. The reviewer Harriet Waugh observed of these tales, "Short stories, unlike novels, have to be perfect" and added that *A Place I've Never Been* "very nearly is" (28).

In the stories contained in *Arkansas: Three Novellas,* Leavitt uses autobiography, even depicting a young writer protagonist named David Leavitt in *The Term Paper Artist.* The other two novellas are set in Italy, where Leavitt lived for a time, and portray the ravages of lovers' deaths and the struggles endured by the ones left behind. The year 2001 saw the publication of still another collection, *The Marble Quilt,* which was extremely well received by critics. It includes stories on the British playwright Oscar Wilde, on another tragic case of AIDS, and on death by murder and by plane crash. Leavitt is masterful at both the realistic depiction of his characters and the emotionally charged pain that results from loss and betrayal. His *Collected Stories* appeared in 2003. In addition, together with his companion, Mark Mitchell, he has edited a number of volumes of gay fiction, including the *Penguin Book of Gay Short Stories* (1994). David Leavitt is currently a professor of English at the University of Florida.

BIBLIOGRAPHY

Boatwright, James. "*Family Dancing*: Rich and Touching." *USA Today,* 5 October 1984, p. 3D.

Chase, Clifford. Review of *A Place I've Never Been. Village Voice Literary Supplement,* December 1990, pp. 10–11.

David Leavitt's Web site at the University of Florida. Available online. URL: http://web.english.ufl.edu/faculty/dleavitt. Accessed January 13, 2009.

de Botton, Alain. "Betrayal." *New Republic* 209, no. 4112 (November 8, 1993): 44–45.

Duka, John. "David Leavitt." *Interview* 15 (March 1985): 84–86.

Iannone, Carol. "Post-Counterculture Tristesse." *Commentary* 83, no. 2 (February 1987): 5,761.

"Interview with David Leavitt." *Occident* 102 (1988): 143–151.

Kakutani, Michiko. "Ambition, Manipulation and a Misguided Mother." *New York Times,* 27 March 1998.

———. "The Writing Life: Never Unexamined, Often Nasty." *New York Times,* 29 September 2000.

Leavitt, David. *Arkansas: Three Novellas.* Boston: Houghton Mifflin, 1997.

———. *Collected Stories.* New York: Bloomsbury, 2003.

———. *Family Dancing.* New York: Knopf, 1984.

———. *The Lost Language of Cranes.* New York: Knopf, 1986.

———. *The Marble Quilt.* Boston: Houghton Mifflin, 2001.

———. *Martin Bauman; or, A Sure Thing.* Boston: Houghton Mifflin, 2000.

———. *A Place I've Never Been.* New York: Viking, 1990.

Leavitt, David, and Mark Mitchell. *In Maremma: Life and a House in Southern Tuscany.* Washington, D.C.: Counterpoint, 2001.

Leavitt, David, with Mark Mitchell. *Italian Pleasures,* San Francisco: Chronicle, 1996.

———, eds. *E. M. Forster: Selected Stories.* New York: Penguin, 2001.

———, eds. *Pages Passed from Hand to Hand: The Hidden Tradition of Homosexual Literature in English from 1748 to 1914.* Boston: Houghton Mifflin, 1997.

———, eds. *The Penguin Book of Gay Short Stories.* New York and London: Penguin, 1994.

Lesser, Wendy. "Domestic Disclosures." *New York Times Book Review,* 2 September 1984, pp. 7–8.

Lively, Penelope. "Class, Sex, and History." *New York Times Book Review,* 3 October 1993, p. 14.

Martin, Wendy. "Everybody Loves Somebody Sometime." *New York Times Book Review,* 26 August 1990, p. 11.

Spender, Stephen. "My Life Is Mine, It Is Not David Leavitt's." *New York Times Book Review,* 4 September 1994.

Staggs, Sam. "David Leavitt." *Publishers Weekly* 237, no. 4 (August 24, 1990): 478.

Ullman West, Martha. Review of *Family Dancing. San Francisco Review of Books,* January–February 1985, p. 22.

Waugh, Harriet. Review of *A Place I've Never Been. Spectator,* 9 March 1991, p. 28.

LEE, ROBERT (ROBERT EDWARD LEE) (1807–1870)

At the outset of the CIVIL WAR, Lee was offered command of the U.S. forces, but he declined and returned to his native Virginia after the state seceded from the Union. He took command of the Army of Northern Virginia and, shortly before the war ended, was given command of all Confederate forces. Lee is considered by most historians to be the greatest general of the Civil War; his outnumbered, outgunned army won several major battles with the North before losing the BATTLE OF GETTYSBURG. Lee was a master strategist and an inspirational leader of men. Idolized by his troops and admired in both the North and South, he exhibited the best qualities of a gentleman of the Old South: chivalry, courage, and loyalty to his state and people.

LEGEND

A traditional, unverifiable, usually fabulous (see FABLE) narrative in prose, song, verse, or ballad passed down (often orally) in a community, often conveying the lore of the culture and widely accepted as in some sense true. A legend is distinguished from MYTH by its closer relation to historical fact than to the supernatural.

"LEGEND OF MISS SASAGAWARA, THE" HISAYE YAMAMOTO (1950)

Originally published in the KENYON REVIEW (December 1, 1950), this story depicts CONFLICTS among cultures, genders, and generations. Miss Mari Sasagawara, the 33-year-old unmarried daughter of a Buddhist priest, is a famous Nisei ballerina who suffers the indignities of living with six families in Block 33 of a WORLD WAR II Arizona internment camp. Sensitive and reticent by nature, she must live with little privacy among 15,000 other Japanese Americans. When Miss Sasagawara displays her outrage through several acts of unconventional behavior, she is sent to a Phoenix sanitarium for several months. When she returns, she talks to others in a more relaxed manner and offers a ballet class to the children in the camp. Her previous unorthodox behavior resumes, however, and when her nocturnal wandering frightens a family in her compound, she is sent to a California institution.

The "Legend" is constructed by Kiku, a woman writer able to escape the camp by attending college in Philadelphia but unable to escape the haunting image of Sasagarawa, the imprisoned woman artist. Kiku's tale dismantles notions of American justice, artistic freedom, and gender equity. It indicts Sasagarawa's physical and patriarchal imprisonment when it argues that her father's dedication to meditation supersedes his ability to relate to his daughter. The narrative culls impressions received from a variety of sources: Kiku's friend Elsie, hospital workers, and, finally, a poetry journal in which Kiku reads a poem by the displaced ballerina. Concluding the story, Miss Sasagarawa's poem contrasts gender and generational responses to imprisonment. It juxtaposes an Issei man (first-generation Japanese American) who gains freedom to seek Nirvana when he is released from the constraints of providing for his family against a Nisei woman (second-generation Japanese American), who, unable to express her passions and frustrations, endures a painful existence that she attributes to the man's madness.

BIBLIOGRAPHY

Cheung, King-Kok. "Double-Telling: Intertextual Silence in Hisaye Yamamoto's Fiction." American Literary History 3, no. 2 (1991): 96–113.
———. "Thrice Muted Tale: Interplay of Art and Politics in Hisaye Yamamoto's 'The Legend of Miss Sasagawara.'" MELUS 173 (1991–92): 109–125.
McDonald, Dorothy Ritsuko, and Katherine Newman. "Relocation and Dislocation: The Writings of Hisaye Yamamoto and Wakako Yamauchi." MELUS 63 (1980): 21–38.
Yamamoto, Hisaye. "The Legend of Miss Sasagawara" (1950). In Seventeen Syllables and Other Stories. Latham, N.Y.: Kitchen Table: Women of Color Press, 1988.

Sandra Chrystal Hayes
Georgia Institute of Technology

"LEGEND OF SLEEPY HOLLOW, THE"
WASHINGTON IRVING (1820) WASHINGTON IRVING'S famous opening to this story, which first appeared in The Sketch Book in 1820, evokes the dreamlike, almost mystical quality of the Hudson River Valley. It also takes the reader to Sleepy Hollow, where almost anything might have happened in 1790—the approximate date of the story, now become LEGEND, of Ichabod Crane and the Headless Horseman. Ichabod, we learn, was an awkward, homely, gangling schoolteacher with too great an imagination: He fears that one night on his way home from gossiping and telling ghost stories with the Dutch wives, he might meet a ghost himself.

Ichabod is also smitten with Katrina Van Tassel, the pretty daughter of a well-to-do farmer. Ichabod is not solely interested in her charms: The narrative makes clear that his imagination surveys the munificent crops and livestock on the family farm and covets them as well. Unfortunately for Ichabod, he has a rival in Brom Van Brunt, often called Brom Bones because of his great physical strength. A FOIL to Ichabod as well as his rival for Katrina's hand, Brom Bones is also fun-loving, clever, and skillful on a horse. After a particularly rousing evening at the home of Mynheer Van Tassel, when Ichabod has spent the entire evening dancing with Katrina, he thinks he may have won her affections. We never know the exact nature of his talk with Katrina, but he leaves the party in low spirits. On his way home, Ichabod's nightmares come true: The Headless Horseman pursues him, throws his head at him, and knocks him to the ground. Although the next day the villagers find his horse, his saddle, and a smashed pumpkin, Ichabod is never again seen in Sleepy Hollow. Brom Bones marries Katrina and laughs at the mention of smashed pumpkins.

In addition to providing fine entertainment, the story seems particularly American. One reading is that Ichabod, with his awkwardness and overstimulated imagination, could not fit into the mold of the American male; lacking in the "right" qualities, he is bested by Brom Bones and fails to capture the woman of his dreams. We should remember, however, that although the Dutch women believe Ichabod has been spirited away by ghosts or phantoms, a traveler says that he has seen Ichabod in New York, where he has become a successful lawyer and judge. If one believes this traveler, Ichabod performs yet another American feat, leaving home for the big city and snatching a victory from defeat. Sleepy Hollow might just have been too small for a man of Ichabod's imagination. One also might infer a humorous if wistful comment on the position of male teachers, a historic one in the United States, and one that reappears in WILLIAM FAULKNER'S ALLUSION to Ichabod Crane when describing his schoolmaster character in *The Hamlet* (1949).

BIBLIOGRAPHY

Irving, Washington. "The Legend of Sleepy Hollow." In *The Complete Tales of Washington Irving,* edited by Charles Neider. Garden City, N.Y.: Doubleday, 1975.

Myers, Andrew B. *A Century of Commentary on the Works of Washington Irving.* Tarrytown, N.Y.: Sleepy Hollow Restorations, 1976.

LEGENDS OF THE FALL JIM HARRISON (1979)

Legends of the Fall is the first of Jim HARRISON's three NOVELLA collections and, as the other two, it contains narratives: *Legends of the Fall, Revenge,* and *The Man Who Gave Up His Name.* Harrison recalled, "I always loved the work of Isak Dinesen, and Knut Hampson [*sic*], who wrote three or four short novels, so I thought I would have a try at it" (Bonetti 65). He said his agent told him no one would publish the stories; the collection became the author's first commercial success.

The title story in *Legends of the Fall* details almost a century in the history of the Ludlow family. The narrative focuses on Tristan, who Harrison has suggested is an American Cain, against the backdrop of WORLD WAR I. Tristan Ludlow becomes an odd sort of HERO,

having avenged his brother's death in the war by scalping Germans, going temporarily mad, and marrying Susannah so she can give him a son to take the place of his dead brother. Tristan then goes to sea and leaves his brother Albert to remarry Susannah. Throughout the narrative Tristan is a loner, "much like a LEGENDary western outlaw hero" (Reilly 82). His isolation is made complete by the death of his wife, Isabel Two, when she is struck by a ricochet from the gun of a federal agent. Critics "have been divided about whether *Legends of the Fall* is an epic or a saga" (Reilly 78) despite its brevity. Certainly the novella is epic in its scope and in the depth of the TRAGEDY and redemption of Tristan's life.

Revenge is similar in scope to *Legends of the Fall,* and the outcome is no less tragic: Cochran, a retired fighter pilot, has had an affair with the beautiful wife of his friend, a wealthy Mexican drug lord whose nickname is Tibey (from the Spanish *tiburon,* shark). Cochran is beaten nearly to death, and Miryea, Tibey's wife, is forced to take heroin, raped, cut, and sent to a brothel. Tibey later moves Miryea to an asylum, where she dies. Cochran is left to sort out the motives and means for revenge on his old friend.

Harrison told Kay Bonetti in an interview that he wrote *The Man Who Gave Up His Name* "in a time of extreme duress. I envisioned a man getting out of the life he had created for himself with the same intricate carefulness that he'd got into it in the first place. I suppose I was pointing out that if you're ethical you can't disappear" (65–66). The story line is simple enough, although the underlying THEME of the search for order and meaning goes much deeper: Nordstrom meets his wife at college, marries her, becomes vice president of Standard Oil, and amicably divorces her after they grow apart. In his early middle age, Nordstrom has taken to dancing, as he does at the beginning of the narrative. He searches for an answer to the disintegration of his life, and as do Harrison's other PROTAGONISTS who return to the land and their roots to restore order and purpose in their lives, Nordstrom returns home after the death of his father (Reilly 75). Finally, Nordstrom makes peace with himself by working as a cook in Islamorada, Florida, and dancing with the waitresses.

Critics tend to compare the styles of Harrison and ERNEST HEMINGWAY. While this novella collection contains, as do many Hemingway works, a certain amount of macho posturing, the compression of the rich details of life and death, the diversity of the characters, the originality of the voice, and the intricate analyses of human nature resemble Hemingway's artistic strengths and point up the strengths of Harrison's short fiction.

BIBLIOGRAPHY

Bonetti, Kay. "An Interview with Jim Harrison." *Missouri Review* 8, no. 3 (1985): 65–86.

Harrison, Jim. *Legends of the Fall.* New York: Delacorte, 1979.

Reilly, Edward C. *Jim Harrison.* New York: Twayne, 1996.

Patrick A. Smith
Ohio University

LE GUIN, URSULA K. (1929– 2018)

Ursula K. Le Guin, one of the most distinguished and prolific contemporary SCIENCE FICTION writers working today, grew up in Berkeley, California; she holds an A.B. from Radcliffe College and an A.M. from Columbia University. Her father, Aldred Kroeber, was an anthropologist, and her mother, Theodora Kroeber, a psychologist and writer. The wife of the historian Charles Le Guin, she has three children. Early in her career Le Guin combined writing with teaching French at Mercer University in Macon, Georgia, and at the University of Idaho. She later served as visiting lecturer and writer in residence at several universities, including the University of Reading, England; Tulane University; Portland State University; and the University of California at San Diego.

Le Guin has suggested that her interest in what has been called "world-building," the creation of imaginative parallel universes, derived from her parents' interest in studying diverse cultures; both wrote, for example, on NATIVE AMERICANS and taught her to be willing to "get outside of your own culture" and to understand how "culture affects personality." She has received the NEBULA AWARD, the HUGO AWARD, and Newberry Silver Medal award; a Fulbright Fellowship; and many other honors. She has also written juvenile tales, poetry, and critical essays.

Le Guin gives a special interpretation to the genre of science fiction. She has insisted that its function is not simply the invention and portrayal of distant galaxies or worlds alien to us. Rather, it has a serious narrative mission to raise and examine the larger ethical issues and questions of the age of science. Such concerns, for example, might be the potential misuse of computer technology by the federal government to overregulate and oppress citizens, the THEME of the NOVELLA *The New Atlantis.*

Another well-known story is "Those Who Walk Away from Omelas," which was published in *The Wind's Twelve Quarters* (1975) and won a Hugo award. This story depicts a pastoral utopia, almost within the realm of possibility today, a society with few laws but not "fantastic" in the sense of extraterrestrial. There is only one problem: The society considers happiness stupid and banal; only pain is intellectual and interesting. Yet the society has no guilt, even over an innocent, wretched child, malnourished and living in a dark closet, condemned to eternal emotional and physical torture. The child is the scapegoat, and the behavior of the citizens exhibits man's inhumanity to man. Le Guin explains in a headnote that the central idea for "this psychomyth, the scapegoat," came from an essay by William James, "The Moral Philosopher and the Moral Life." She began the story, however, not by focusing on James's "lost soul" but with one word, *Omelas (Salem, Oregon,* spelled backward).

The title of "Vaster Than Empires and More Slow," also published in *The Wind's Twelve Quarters,* is taken from Andrew Marvell's poem "To His Coy Mistress": "Our vegetable love should grow / Vaster than empires, and more slow." In a headnote, Le Guin states that every individual gets lost, every night, in his or her own forest; we all have "forests in our minds." The phrase *vegetable love* refers to the way in which Osden, the PROTAGONIST, is absorbed into the forest world of the planet he is investigating.

JOHN UPDIKE has stated that the social sciences inform Le Guin's fantasies "with far more earthy substance than the usual imaginary space-flight." Le

Guin refuses to consider evil banal or pain irrelevant; our perception of them determines the moral quality of life itself. Science fiction may, therefore, be called a "literature of ideas." In contrast, what is often called realistic (see REALISM) fiction is more likely to explore individual psyches and personal relationships than the structure and principles of society as a whole.

An important theme in Le Guin's work is the journey, one of the CLASSIC and enduring archetypes of fiction and poetry from the time of Homer and earlier (also known as the *Bildungsreise,* or educational journey into nature and back home again). The process of literal travel reflects humans' inner search for self-knowledge and answers to the meaning of life. "True journey is return," Le Guin writes in one of her journey novels, *The Dispossessed* (1974). The landscape of the journey results in learning that, as Peter Brigg observes, it stands as a "paradigm of all human experience" for both traveler and reader. The journey theme also occurs in many of her short stories, including "Things," published in *The Wind's Twelve Quarters* (originally published in *Orbit* as "The End"). The title signifies the end of the world, but the ending has been called enigmatic; the characters go beyond mere things to board sailboats that will supposedly take them to the islands.

Le Guin received the annual Nebula Award for "The Day before the Revolution," published in *The Dispossessed* (1974). It is the story of Odo, the woman founder of an anarchistic society, depicted in old age on the eve of the revolution she has inspired. Le Guin has called Odo's rejection of the totalitarian state and reliance on mutual aid "the most idealistic . . . of all political theories." After her death, her theories lead to the colonization of the Moon.

The critic James Bittner observes that Le Guin's heroes frequently make circular journeys to fulfill needs they have themselves determined, adding an ethical or moral dimension. In their quests for "home, freedom, and wholeness" the characters learn to disregard "self-regarding individualism" in favor of "cooperative partnership" and to value their roots (33).

Serious science fiction writers, including Le Guin, do not rely simply on evoking an unregulated and fanciful realm of the supernatural but take pride in making plausible deductions from current scientific knowledge, in carrying out research, and in checking facts. The imaginary worlds created by Le Guin include Earthsea, Hainish, Orsinia, and the West Coast. Her mystic visions have caused her to be regarded as a literary successor to J. R. R. Tolkien. Le Guin's fiction "may be filled with wizards, aliens, and clones," write Joseph Olander and Martin Greenberg, but "the vision contained in her stories and novels is, above all, what is most permanent about the human condition" (13).

BIBLIOGRAPHY

Arbur, Rosemarie. "Le Guin's 'Song' of Inmost Feminism." *Science Fiction Studies* 2, no. 5 (1978): 143–155.

Bittner, James W. *Approaches to the Fiction of Ursula K. Le Guin.* Ann Arbor, Mich.: UMI Research Press, 1984, 33.

Brigg, Peter. "The Archetype of the Journey in Ursula K. Le Guin's Fiction." In *Ursula K. Le Guin,* edited by J. D. Olander and M. H. Greenberg, 36. New York: Toplinger, 1979.

Bucknall, Barbara J. *Ursula K. Le Guin.* New York: Frederick Ungar, 1981.

Clareson, Thomas D., ed. Special Ursula K. Le Guin Issue. *Extrapolation* 21 (Fall 1980).

Cummins, Elizabeth. *Understanding Ursula K. Le Guin.* Columbia: University of South Carolina Press, 1990.

De Bolt, Joe, ed. *Ursula K. Le Guin: Voyager to Inner Lands and to Outer Space.* Port Washington, N.Y.: Kennikat Press, 1979.

Le Guin, Ursula K. *Always Coming Home.* New York: Harper & Row, 1986.

———. *The Beginning Place.* New York: Harper & Row, 1980.

———. *Blue Moon over Thurman Street.* Portland, Oreg.: NewSage Press, 1993.

———. *City of Illusions.* New York: Ace Books, 1967.

———. *The Compass Rose.* New York: Harper & Row, 1982.

———. *The Dispossessed: An Ambiguous Utopia.* New York: Harper & Row, 1974.

———. *The Eye of the Heron and Other Stories.* New York: Harper & Row, 1980, 1983.

———. *The Farthest Shore.* New York: Atheneum, 1972.

———. *The Left Hand of Darkness.* New York: Ace Books, 1969.

————. *Orsinian Tales*. New York: Harper & Row, 1976.

————. *Planet of Exile*. New York: Ace Books, 1966.

————. *Rocannon's World*. New York: Ace Books, 1966; Harper & Row, 1977.

————. *Tehanu: The Last Book of Earthsea*. New York: Atheneum, 1990.

————. *The Tombs of Atuan*. New York: Atheneum, 1971.

————. *Unlocking the Air and Other Stories*. New York: HarperCollins, 1996.

————. *The Wind's Twelve Quarters*. New York: Harper & Row, 1975.

————. *A Wizard of Earthsea*. Berkeley, Calif.: Parnassus Press, 1968.

————. *The Word for World Is Forest*. New York: Putnam, 1976.

————, ed. "Introduction." In *The Norton Book of Science Fiction*. New York: Norton, 1993.

Lewis, Naomi. "Earthsea Revisited." *Times Literary Supplement* 28 (April 1972): 284.

Mullen, R. D., and Darko Suivin, eds. *Science Fiction Studies: Selected Articles on Science Fiction 1973–1975*. Boston: Gregg, 1976.

Olander, Joseph D., and Martin Harry Greenberg, eds. *Ursula K. Le Guin*. New York: Taplinger, 1979, 13.

Selinger, Bernard. *Le Guin and Identity in Contemporary Fiction*. Ann Arbor, Mich.: UMI Research Press, 1988.

Shippey, T. A. "The Magic Art and the Evolution of Works: Ursula Le Guin's *Earthsea Trilogy*." *Mosaic* 10 (Winter 1970): 147–163.

Slusser, George E. *The Farthest Shores of Ursula K. Le Guin*. San Bernadino, Calif.: Borgo Press, 1976.

Spivack, Charlotte. *Ursula K. Le Guin*. Boston: Twayne, 1984, 85.

Updike, John. "Imagining Things." *The New Yorker*, 23 June 1980, p. 94.

Sarah Bird Wright

LEITMOTIF

LEITMOTIF A German word meaning a "leading or guiding pattern." In operas, such as those of Richard Wagner, a recurrent musical theme that coincides with each appearance of a given character, problem, emotion, or thought serves as a leitmotif. The term also is applied to a similar device when used in literature and has been notably employed by such authors as Thomas Mann, Virginia Woolf, WILLIAM FAULKNER, and James Joyce.

LESBIAN THEMES IN SHORT STORIES

The historical record of lesbianism in the American short story has not received the same amount and depth of attention from historians and literary critics as has that of male homosexuality. Moreover, critics still disagree about what constitutes lesbian writing. Is the author a known lesbian? Is there evidence of a lesbian relationship within the text? If lesbianism is in disguise and relies on repetitious wordplay and double-entendre, as does GERTRUDE STEIN's "MISS FURR AND MISS SKEENE" (1923), can that text be read as "lesbian" if only a limited number of people understand it? These difficulties are complicated by the imprecision of defining lesbian relationships through history. Terms such as *female friendships* and *Boston marriages,* both commonly used in the 19th century to describe intimacy between women, were quickly discarded in the early decades of the 20th century when sexological theories about the "female invert" reduced woman-to-woman intimacies, emotional or physical, to aberrant sexuality. Today the difficulties remain, although they have changed in focus. No longer is sexual intimacy at issue; rather, many lesbian-feminists, disagreeing with writers of previous generations, argue that no form of sexual expression should be a forbidden subject in lesbian literature.

Perhaps the most inclusive, although by no means uncontroversial, standard by which to identify the lesbian in the American short story is to apply the idea in Adrienne Rich's essay "Compulsory Heterosexuality and Lesbian Existence" that woman-to-woman intimacies can be plotted along a "lesbian continuum." If all attachments between women (emotional, physical, or both) are read as some degree of "lesbianism," then contemporary readers can consider 19th-century stories that only vaguely suggest intimacy as "lesbian texts."

MARY E. WILKINS FREEMAN's "Two Friends" (1887) is one of her many short stories that focus on New England "spinsters" who, despite opportunity to marry, preferred to remain with each other in a "Boston marriage." Abby and Sarah, two friends in their 50s, have lived together happily for their entire adult lives in a small New England town. Thirty years previously, however, Abby's aunt had given Abby permission to marry John Marshall, a message Sarah was supposed to relay to Abby but never did. When Sarah finally confesses, Abby laughingly tells her, "I wouldn't have had John Marshall if he'd come on his knees after me all the way from Mexico!"

SARAH ORNE JEWETT's "Martha's Lady" (1897) details the relationship between a wealthy woman and her maid that is as intimate and permanent as Freeman's portrayal. In "Tommy, the Unsentimental" (1899), WILLA CATHER presents a tomboyish woman whose gender ambiguity prompts her community to judge that "it was a bad sign when a rebellious girl like Tommy took to being sweet and gentle to one of her own sex, the worst sign in the world." Yet Cather keeps Tommy within acceptable sexual behavior; she is even allowed to express some amused affection for men.

Yet as the 20th century approached, "suspicion" and outright rejection of lesbian relationships occurred as psychological and medical theories from men such as Havelock Ellis and Richard von Krafft-Ebing became more thoroughly disseminated and believed in American society. The lesbian in short fiction began to assume some of the "inverted" or "abnormal" qualities that science ascribed to her. Constance Fenimore Woolson's "Felipa" (1876) focuses on an androgynous, "dark-skinned" Felipa and her intense emotional attachment to the "tall, lissome" Christine. When Christine accepts a marriage proposal from Edward Bowne, however, Felipa's love turns self-destructive; in her jealous rage, she stabs Edward. Felipa's grandfather, unable to dismiss the passion as "nothing," knowingly closes the story by judging that Felipa was in love with both Christine and Edward, but her violence against Edward shows the danger of lesbian attachments: "the stronger [love] thrust the knife." Mary E. Wilkins Freeman, who less than ten years before provided a loving portrayal of Sarah and Abby, presents in 1895 "The Long Arm," DETECTIVE SHORT FICTION, in which the murderer is discovered to be a mannish woman, desperate and even demonically possessed. Phoebe Dole kills Martin Fairbanks in an attempt to maintain possession of Maria Woods, to whom Fairbanks was about to propose.

Characterization of the lesbian as an evil obstacle to heterosexual unions continued throughout the early decades of the 20th century. Catherine Wells's "The Beautiful House" (1912) begins with a positive portrayal of a romantic attachment between Mary and Sylvia. But when the handsome Evan Hardie enters the story, the women's relationship is torn apart for the more socially affirming heterosexual relationship between Evan and Sylvia, and Mary is left a heartbroken spinster. Helen Hull's "The Fire" (1917) follows a similar plot. Cynthia is an art student of Miss Egert; it is clear that mutual emotional attraction, if not physical intimacy, exists between them. When Cynthia's mother forbids her to see Miss Egert again for unspoken but easily inferred reasons, the literal bonfire that closes the story also METAPHORically consumes the suggested lesbianism.

Although O. HENRY's "The LAST LEAF" (1907) does not portray lesbianism as a hindrance or precursor to heterosexuality, the characterization of one of the two women friends as deathly ill and determined to die as soon as the last leaf falls from the ivy outside her window signals the unhealthiness of woman-to-woman intimacies, which was proposed as scientific fact in O. Henry's time. Yet John Held, Jr.'s "Ride of the Valkyries" (1930), collected in *Grim Youth,* presents a stereotypical young woman who casually announces to the man seated next to her at her parents' dinner party that she is a lesbian. SHERWOOD ANDERSON's "That Sophistication" (1933) also provides a glimpse of lesbians as they interact among guests of all kinds at a party in Paris. Such nonchalant remarks would seem to suggest that by 1930 lesbianism, even if presented as the sexual novelty of the expatriate moment, was socially acceptable and even sophisticated. But "The Knife of the Times" (1932) by William Carlos Williams removes any pretense of acceptability; lesbianism is the violent "knife" that cuts through social decorum.

During the last decades of the 19th and early decades of the 20th centuries, a particular type of fiction arose that took as its setting, and often its subject, the activities unique to women's colleges, which had only recently been founded. Often the plot focused on one of the seemingly innumerable "crushes" or "smashes" or "spoons" that developed between two female students, usually of different ages. The alternative sexual relationships between schoolgirls in these stories supports Havelock Ellis's 1902 contention that women's colleges were "the great breeding ground" of lesbianism. In "The School-Friendships of Girls," Ellis suggests that lesbianism is an "abnormality" that affected any woman who had a "crush"; according to "authorities," this entailed more than 60 percent of students at women's colleges. Josephine Dodge Daskam's collection of *Smith College Stories* (1900) contains 10 episodes of life at a women's college, including "A Case of Interference," which provide intimate glimpses into the excitement, embarrassment, and despair that accompanied female friendships.

Two stories published in popular periodicals examine liaisons within the girls' school: "The Lass of the Silver Sword" by Mary Constance Dubois (published serially in ST. NICHOLAS in 1908–1909) and Jeanette Lee's "The Cat and the King" (published in the LADIES' HOME JOURNAL in 1919). Dubois's story initially focuses on the boarding school adventures of two women, Carol Armstrong, 18 years old, and the younger Jean Lennox, who has fallen madly in love with Carol "at first sight." But soon after Carol and Jean's pledge of friendship, the story shifts to a summer camp where the girls spend their time plotting playful jokes against the neighboring boys' camp and striking up socially acceptable friendships with the boys. By the end of the story, Carol and Jean still are friends, but the interest of each has shifted to a relationship that is heterosexual. "The Cat and the King" does not end with the same affirmation of heterosexuality, but it is clear that Flora Bailey's crush on the older Annette Osler has been rightfully displaced by her even more passionate interest in science.

In the middle decades of the 20th century, the lesbian in American literature all but disappeared. When she did resurface in American fiction, it was in the pulp novels of the 1950s and 1960s. Relying on the heterosexually modeled gender dichotomies of masculine and feminine, the lesbian was relegated to either a butch or femme role, a time Joan Nestle remembers in "Esther's Story" (1987). If a lesbian

character were able to escape such portrayals, she was most often turned into a sexual predator of vampiric proportions. During the 1970s, however, in the hands of women who were involved in the awakening politics of feminism, civil rights, and gay liberation, the lesbian in the American short story began to enjoy a more liberated existence; through the rise of feminist bookstores, journals, and publishing houses, she was given a space in which to thrive.

In 1970 the New York group Radicalesbians distributed a pamphlet that began with the question "What is a lesbian?" As answer they wrote, in part: "A lesbian is the rage of all women condensed to the point of explosion. . . . She may not be fully conscious of the political implications of what for her began as personal necessity, but on the same level she has not been able to accept the limitations and oppression laid on her by the most basic role of her society—the female role." In their short stories, writers began to dismantle the confusion of sex and gender and allow their characters the full range of gendered expression in their intimate relationships. Moreover, the lesbian in the American short story was offered roles that were traditionally portrayed by heterosexual women: mother, grieving lover, and emotionally and sexually fulfilled woman. Textually, positive images of love between women appeared in relationships that were open and unhidden. In addition, many of these fictional lesbians were the creations of women who proudly identified themselves as women-loving women.

The "romantic friendships" between women at the turn of the 20th century were seemingly benign compared to the defiant expressions of Radicalesbian love. The short stories of the last three decades occupied a far different place on Rich's continuum as authors depicted not only the emotional attraction between women but also, often explicitly, the physical desire. Dorothy Allison's "A Lesbian Appetite" (1988) and Sapphire's "Eat" (1988) together link sexual satiation with the physical contentment that food brings. Allison's PROTAGONIST dreams of throwing a dinner party and inviting all the women in her life: "Everybody is feeding each other, exclaiming over recipes and gravies, introducing themselves and telling stories about great meals they've eaten"; for the first time in her life, the narrator concludes, she is not hungry.

Joan Nestle's "Liberties Not Taken" (1987) suggests that Jean, even though married and mother of three young children, enjoys intimacy with women. Told from the POINT OF VIEW of an adolescent girl who works as nanny for the children one summer, Nestle explores the girl's awakening lesbian sexuality and her physical infatuation with Jean. The sexual awakenings of adolescents receive fictional attention by authors intent on exploring this pivotal time when sexual orientation is often ill-defined. Emma Perez in "Gulf Dreams" (1991) relates the story of a 15-year-old girl whose sexual passions are awakened by an older friend of her sister's. A girls' boarding school provides the setting for Rebecca Brown's story "Bread" (1984), of a strong but unreciprocated adolescent love, told from the first-person point of view. When the narrator unintentionally usurps the authority of her beloved, her love turns ugly and distasteful.

Adolescent coming-of-age stories introduce the numerous accounts of adult women who struggle to maintain the pretense of heterosexuality or marriage despite their lesbian longings. Beth Nugent's "City of Boys" (1992) tells of the passionless acts of heterosexual sex by the woman who dreams of passion with her woman lover. Jane Rule's "His Nor Hers" (1985) examines the successful pretense of one woman who maintains the shell of a marriage so that she may continue her intimacies with women. When her husband requests a divorce, Gillian's sexual appetites suddenly disappear as she realizes that since heterosexual cover no longer exists, "the illusion of freedom that he had given her" also has disappeared.

Confronted with a society that still often denies the lesbian's very existence, authors have been careful to plot the REALISM of love and loss in the lesbian short story. The grieving process after the loss of a lover, either through a breakup, as in Leslie Lawrence's "My Lesbian Imagination" (1987), or death, is poignantly explored in numerous short stories. Pearl, in BECKY BIRTHA's "In the Life" (1987), mourns her lover's death and lives her remaining days remembering and longing for a reunion. In "A Life Speckled with Children" (1987), Sherri Paris poignantly details

the double loss Sabra feels—unlucky in love but also unlucky because of the relationships with her lovers' children she also loses as a result of the breakups. Interweaving a NATIVE AMERICAN past with the narrator's present, Beth Brant explores the loss of children by force in "A Long Story" (1985). Likening the removal of Native American children from their families by the American government to the modern-day reality that sees children stripped from their lesbian mothers, Brant links cultures and generations within the lesbian present.

Some authors, however, prefer to imagine a future where the relationships between women are not only of primary importance but also exist in a world without men. The SCIENCE FICTION writer Joanna Russ, in "When It Changed" (1972), imagines the community of Whileaway where women pairs have children by merging ova and share child rearing and social governance. When "real Earth men" arrive in Whileaway, it is clear to the women that they will lose their way of life; they fear they will be relegated to the ancient inequalities that once existed between men and women—inequalities that are, of course, based on contemporary society. Sarah Schulman envisions a different change in women's relationships; in "The Penis Story" (1986), Ann awakes one morning to find that she has become a "lesbian with a penis." Assumption of the phallus provides Ann with a power she has never felt before as well as awe from women who now want to sleep with her. Eventually, however, Ann desires "to be a whole woman again" by having her penis surgically removed, since, she reflects, "she never wanted to be mutilated again by being cut off from herself." Russ's and Schulman's stories clearly challenge the heterosexual status quo. The visions they articulate, like the controversial sodomasochistic world of Pat Califia's "The Finishing School" (in *Macho Sluts* 1988) and "The Vampire" (1988), broaden the range of the lesbian short story in the late 20th century, transgressing fictional boundaries in order to suggest a more fully articulated and inclusive, albeit conflicting, lesbian world.

In the early 21st century, as lesbian fiction has become more prolific and more diversified, publications devoted to it have been increasingly broken down by ethnicity (e.g., Latina and Chicana, African-American, Asian) and genre (e.g., mystery, science fiction, nonfiction). LAMBDA, the major literary award specifically for gay, lesbian, bisexual, and transsexual (GLBT) writing, has responded similarly and now offers literary awards in 22 categories. Recent LAMBDA short fiction winners include Angela Brown's *Best Lesbian Love Stories 2004,* Katherine Forrest's *Lesbian Pulp Fiction* (2005) and *Women of Mystery* (2005), Catherine Lake and Marine Holtz's *No Margins: Writing Canadian Fiction in Lesbian* (2006), and Harlyn Aizley's *Confessions of the Other Mother* (2007). Furthermore, a plethora of new magazines have entered the scene. In addition to *Blithe House Quarterly,* probably the oldest GLBT magazine, and *Khimairal Ink Magazine,* numerous electronic publications feature lesbian short stories, such as the Canadian *A Room of Her Own: A Dynamic Anthology of Lesbian Fiction* and *Read These Lips,* which features stories by such authors as British Nicola Griffith, Australian Susan Hawthorne, and American Ruthann Robson. Similarly, there are now many publishers of lesbian short fiction, including the two most preeminent lesbian book publishers, the American Bella Books and the Canadian Bold Strokes Books, as well as electronic downloading sites. Since the closing of New York's historic Oscar Wilde bookstore, the largest lesbian and gay bookstore in North America is Toronto's Glad Day.

BIBLIOGRAPHY

Aizley, Harlyn, ed. *Confessions of the Other Mother.* Boston, Mass.: Beacon, 2007.

Blithe House Quarterly. Available online. URL: http://www.blithe.com. Accessed April 10, 2009.

Brand, Dionne, Catherine Lake, and Nairne Holtz, eds. *No Margins: Writing Canadian Fiction in Lesbian.* London, Ontario: Insomniac Press, 2006.

Brown, Angela, ed. *Best Lesbian Love Stories 2004.* New York: Alyson, 2004.

Cahill, Susan Neunzig, ed. *Women and Fiction: Stories by and about Women.* New York: Signet Classics, 2002.

Christopher, Victoria M. *Lesbian Short Stories.* Canton, Ohio: Creative Works Publishing, 2001.

Faderman, Lillian. *Odd Girls and Twilight Lovers: A History of Lesbian Life in Twentieth Century America.* New York: Penguin, 1991.

Forrest, Katherine, ed. *Lesbian Pulp Fiction.* San Francisco, Calif.: Cleis Press, 2005.

————. *Women of Mystery.* Binghamton, N.Y.: Haworth, 2005.

Hart, Lois Cloarec. *Assorted Flavors: Lesbian Short Stories.* Clayton, N.C.: P.D. Publishing, Inc., 2005.

Khimairal Ink Magazine. Available online. URL: http://fictionwriting.wordpress.com. Accessed April 10, 2009.

Lake, Lori. *Shimmer and Other Stories.* Port Arthur, Tex.: Regal Crest, 2007.

McCann, Jeanne. *Love Times Four: Lesbian Love Stories.* Bloomington, Ind.: iuniverse, 2003.

Peters, Julie Anne. *grl2grl: Short fictions.* New York: Little, Brown, 2007.

Ramos, Juanita. *Compañeras: Latina Lesbians.* New York: Routledge, Chapman and Hall, 1994.

ReadtheseLips, vols. 1 and 2. Available online. URL: http://www.readtheselips.com. Accessed April 10, 2009.

Reynolds, Margaret. *The Penguin Book of Lesbian Short Stories.* New York: Viking Penguin, 1999.

Robson, Ruthann. *Struggle for Happiness: Stories.* New York: Stonewall Inn Editions, 2001.

A Room of Her Own: A Dynamic Anthology of Lesbian Fiction. Available online. URL: http://blmiller.net/room. Accessed April 10, 2009.

Trujillo, Carla. *Chicana Lesbians: The Girls Our Mothers Warned Us About.* Berkeley, Calif.: Third Woman Press, 1991.

Wadsworth, Ann. "American Literature: Lesbian, Post-Stonewall." Available online. URL: http://www.glbtq.com/literature/am_lit5_lesbian_post_stonewall,6.html. Accessed April 6, 2009.

Laura L. Behling
Gustavus Adolphus College

LESUEUR, MERIDEL (1900–1996)

Meridel LeSueur wrote about the harsher realities of life, and particularly women's lives, such as pregnancy, abortion, prostitution, sterilization, and physical abuse by men—areas of life ignored or trivialized by the popular writers of her day. She also wrote about immigrants, Native Americans, and ecology decades before such subjects entered literary popularity. Born in February 1900 in Murray, Iowa, LeSueur produced radical literature and held views that took root early through the influence of activist socialist parents. By 1916 LeSueur had quit school and had worked in a variety of jobs including as a dancer, silent screen extra, stuntwoman, and factory worker. She was always writing.

Many of her short stories were published during the 1920s and 1930s, including "Persephone" (*Dial* 82 [1927]); "Laundress" (*American Mercury* [1927]); "Spring Story" (reprinted from *Scribner's Magazine* in O'Brien, *Best Short Stories of the Year 1931*); "The Horse" (*Story* magazine [1935]), and "ANNUNCIATION" (*Best Short Stories of the Year 1936*). In 1940 the short story collection *Salute to Spring* was published; on the jacket were quotes of praise by Sinclair Lewis, ZONA GALE, Carl Sandburg, and NELSON ALGREN. It seemed LeSueur's place in literature was assured. But soon afterward she became yet another victim of MCCARTHYISM in the COLD WAR following WORLD WAR II. Her stories were deemed too radical, and she was blacklisted. Mainstream publishers rejected her work; at one point only Alfred Knopf would publish her children's fiction.

For decades, LeSueur pieced together a living and continued to write short stories, poetry, novels, and journalistic pieces, all in a lyrical style, blending stories of common people with images drawn from nature and myth. With the resurgence of feminism (see FEMINIST) in the 1970s, her work received renewed attention and acclaim. Her work was reprinted, and previously unpublished work was collected and published for the first time. She continued to write in the midst of a schedule filled with speaking engagements and readings. Even in the last year of her life, an experimental novel, *The Dread Road*, was published. LeSueur always remained true to her belief that the writer could and should serve as activist and revolutionary.

BIBLIOGRAPHY

LeSueur, Meridel. *Chanticleer of Wilderness Road: A Story of Davy Crockett*. Duluth, Minn.: Holy Cow! Press, 1990, 1981.
———. *Crusaders*. New York: Blue Heron Press, 1955.
———. *The Dread Road*. Albuquerque: West End Press, 1991.
———. *The Girl: A Novel*. Minneapolis: West End Press, 1985.
———. *Harvest: Collected Stories*. Cambridge, Mass.: West End Press, 1977.
———. *Harvest Song: Collected Essays and Stories*. Albuquerque: West End Press, 1990.
———. *I Hear Men Talking and Other Stories*. Minneapolis: West End Press, 1984.
———. *I Speak from the Shuck*. Browerville, Minn.: Ox Head Press, 1992.
———. *Nancy Hanks of Wilderness Road: A Story of Abraham Lincoln's Mother*. New York: Knopf, 1949.
———. *North Star Country*. New York: Duell, Sloan & Pearce, 1945.
———. *Ripening: Selected Work*. 2nd ed. Edited by Elaine Hedges. New York: Feminist Press, 1990.
———. *Salute to Spring*. New York: International, 1940.
———. *Winter Prairie Woman: A Short Story*. Minneapolis: Minnesota Center for Book Arts, 1990.
———. *Worker Writers*. Minneapolis: Blue Heron Press, 1982.
Schleuning, Neala. *America, Song We Sang without Knowing: The Life and Ideas of Meridel LeSueur*. Mankato, Minn. and Minneapolis: Little Red Hen Press, 1983.

Susan Thurston Hamerski
St. Olaf College

"LIFE IN THE IRON-MILLS" REBECCA HARDING DAVIS (1861) "Life in the Iron-Mills," an account of the squalid life, blighted aspirations, and aborted potential of the Welsh mill worker and primitive artist Hugh Wolfe, is rightly celebrated as both a powerful indictment of unrestrained industrial capitalism and a superior example of the initial phase of American realism. However, for all its evocative documentation of the dismal, polluted mills of Wheeling (in what is now West Virginia) and the spiritual degradation of generations of laborers, REBECCA HARDING DAVIS's story derives much of its continuing poetic impact from its deployment of allegorical strategies perfected by older contemporary American writers: emblematic characters representing clearly demarcated social functions and spiritual conditions, ambiguous and often IRONIC deployment of Christian scripture, and objects that emerge from their ostensibly realistic contexts to acquire the status of complex moral, aesthetic, and spiritual symbols. (NATHANIEL HAWTHORNE's "The Artist of the Beautiful" and HERMAN MELVILLE's "The Paradise of Bachelors and the Tartarus of Maids" provide useful comparisons as meditations on, respectively, the plight of the American artist and the depredations of the factory system.)

The events of the story are told in retrospect by an unidentified narrator unusually familiar with the daily and lifelong misery of the workers: "Not many even of the inhabitants of a manufacturing town know the vast machinery of system by which the bodies of workmen are governed" (909). The intimate knowledge displayed by the narrator is conveyed in a sympathetic manner that distinguishes him/her from would-be reformers who have "gone among" the abject and vice-ridden workers "with a heart tender with Christ's charity, and come out outraged, hardened" (907). This intimate knowledge and sympathy are displayed in the way the workers' manner of speaking is accurately and sensitively reproduced without any intent to caricature and ridicule. The linguistic contortions of the ethnic working class—the twisted and severely truncated pronunciation that renders the Virgin Mary into "the Vargent" (907)—is reproduced as an index, for the middle-class reader, of the thwarted capacity to be or to communicate their being to others exemplified by the sickly, frustrated Hugh and his physically deformed cousin, Deborah.

The opening paragraphs describe "a town of ironworks" (904)—a phrase that suggests the unyielding nature of its social structure and economic undergirding. The perpetual gloom of "thwarted sunshine" possesses a gravitational pull that nothing is sufficiently dynamic to withstand: "The sky sank down before dawn, muddy, flat, immovable" (904, 906). The atmosphere of adjectives and adverbs—*foul, sullenly, slimy, dingy, greasy, reeking, dull, sluggishly, tired* (905)—is similar to that evoked in the widely disseminated British chronicles of urban slums by Charles Dickens and Henry Mayhew (whose *London Labour and the London Poor* was published in the same year as Davis's story). So, too, the mills are described with similarly GOTHIC overtones as the site of "hopeless discomfort and veiled crime"—"a city of fires" with "liquid metal-flames writhing in tortuous streams" and "ghastly wretches . . . looking like revengeful ghosts in the red light" (910). However, the description of the "weary, dumb appeal upon the face of the negro-like river

slavishly bearing its burden day after day" (905) clearly identifies the distinctively American political context in which the story was written and originally read—not just the war over racial emancipation but also the raging debate over so-called wage slavery in the North. Nevertheless, the fact that Hugh's father is said to have already worked half his life in Cornish tin mills establishes a generalized, transatlantic continuity with regard to labor relations under capitalism. This idea of continuity is more explicitly stated by a generic description of past generations of Welsh workers followed by a reference to "their duplicates swarming the streets to-day" (907).

The narrator takes the reader on a Dantesque descent into a living hell to retrieve the unknown lives of two of the mills' myriad anonymous denizens in order to answer the mocking rhetorical question regarding the ostensible depravity of the working class, "Is that all of their lives? . . . nothing beneath?—all?" (907). Wolfe and his fellow workers have been dehumanized by the factory system into creatures that "skulk along like beaten hounds" and sleep in "kennel-like rooms" (907). He has also been emasculated by his fellows, who think of him "as one of the girl-men" and call him "Molly" because, in keeping with the American tradition, they suspect that his (limited) education and artistic inclinations are effeminate (912). Hugh is more abject than the abject, having been ostracized from the brutal society of his kind, in which "to be alive" is nothing but "a drunken jest, a joke—horrible to angels perhaps, to them commonplace enough" (905). However, he is tended to by someone even more abject, the patient yet painfully eager, self-sacrificing Deborah, who "watche[s] him as a spaniel its master" from an unrequited love bordering on worship (912). Although Hugh feels tugs at his conscience, Deborah's "thwarted woman's form" offends his innate aesthetic sensibility, which desperately gropes among the surrounding "grossness" for a modicum of beauty and purity that might bring his latent spirit into being and feed the "soul-starvation" that afflicts him and his class as a "disease" (910–911). Deborah's "waking stupor . . . pain and hunger" (910) might be thought the partial inspiration for the "hideous, fantastic" woman Hugh hews from korl, the flesh-colored refuse of the iron-making process: "a woman, white, of giant proportions, crouching on the ground, her arms flung out in some wild gesture of warning . . . the powerful limbs instinct with some one poignant longing." Yet this woman is also a self-portrait, its "clutching hands, the wild, eager face, like that of a starving wolf's" (916). This allegorical figure is described as mutely posing "the awful question, 'What shall we do to be saved?'" (918).

The turning point in Hugh's life is his encounter with members of what to him is a "mysterious class that shone down on him perpetually with the glamour of another order of being" (913) and whose existence vexes him with the enigma why his lot should be so different from theirs, a gulf "never to be passed" (915). He overhears a conversation between Kirby, an owner of the mill, who is guiding his companions Dr. May and Mr. Mitchell on a tour. Listening "like a dumb, hopeless animal" (915), Hugh fails to understand their conversation, as all of the men express different contemporary attitudes about what can or should be done about the poor. Each of the men is an allegorical representation and as such an object of the author's satire. Mitchell, a "thoroughbred gentleman" and scoffing, dilettantish aesthete, represents the head, an overly refined, essentially frigid, and uncommitted intellect "not rare in the States" (915). He gazes upon the infernal labor fancifully as if it were a theatrical spectacle, and when he turns his scrutiny on Hugh, his "cool, probing eyes" are "mocking, cruel, relentless" (917). However, he is the only one capable of recognizing that Wolfe's sculpture represents spiritual hunger, that it is asking "questions of God," demanding "I have a right to know" (917). And he repeatedly, though always sardonically, refers to Wolfe in terms that identify him with Christ.

According to the acerbic Mitchell, Kirby represents "the pocket of the world"—which is to say, "Money" speaks its ideology through him (918–919). Kirby states that had he been God he would have made "these men who do the lowest part of the world's work" machines, adding, with an appalling logic, that this would be beneficent, since "What are taste, reason, to creatures who must live such lives as that?"

(918). Mitchell designates Dr. May "the heart," although, as his name suggests, that heart is not dependable. May wants to be benign but cannot help revealing the patronizing superiority of his class when he addresses Hugh in tones normally used with a child and displays "the affable smile which kind-hearted men put on, when talking with these people" (917, 919). May asks the author's question, "God help us! Who is responsible?" (918). But to save himself the expense of taking responsibility for Wolfe, he begs off by asking another: "Why should one be raised, when myriads are left?" (920). He satisfies himself that prayer is his only responsibility, and in praying for "these degraded souls" he recognizes his "accomplished duty" (920). He also gives voice to the ideological platitude that the American system provides equal opportunity, assuring Wolfe (and himself), "A man may make himself anything he chooses." Allaying his guilty unease, and "glowing with his own magnanimity," May further assures Hugh that "it is his right to rise" (919, 921), although he labels it ingratitude when Hugh eventually acts on a self-ordained conviction that he deserves "to live the life God meant him to live . . . to live as they" by the exertions of his "unused powers" (924). The narrator concurs, comparing Hugh to the biblical Esau in his having been "deprived of his birthright" (935).

Within the terms of this allegory, and as Kirby himself indicates, Hugh represents the hands; thus the text is replete with references to hands and hand gestures, as when Dr. May asks the crucial question of Kirby, "Have you many such hands as this? What are you going to do with them?" (917). Hugh is no more than hands because he is an intuitive sculptor lacking the guidance of a critical intellect and, more pointedly, because as a factory hand he sells these parts of his being in a fetishistic process analyzed by Davis's contemporary, the philosopher Karl Marx. After being imprisoned for possessing a wallet stolen by Deborah in the hope of giving him the means of liberating himself, Hugh lies "with his hands over his eyes," a man completely "cut down" (927). This metaphorical reference to castration and execution is meant to be linked to Hugh's artistic activity. As if in fulfillment of Kirby's tacit curse, "if they cut korl, or cut each other's throats . . . I am not responsible" (918), Hugh ultimately achieves freedom through suicide, using an implement reminiscent of those he has used to carve his artwork, which he sharpens by scraping against the iron bars of his prison cell. Davis derives additional irony from iron, as Hugh ceases to "fight like a tiger" once shackled in the very material his labor has produced.

The narrator repeatedly addresses the reader as if to shame him or her: "I want you to hide your disgust, take no heed to your clean clothes, and come right down with me,—here, into the thickest of fog and mud and foul effluvia. I want you to hear this story" (905). Direct address is also used to articulate a claim for justice that Hugh is too inarticulate to make for himself: "I want you to come down and look at this Wolfe . . . and see him just as he is, that you may judge him justly" (912). The mocking tone of some of these direct addresses suggests that Davis suspects that some readers, having been compelled to identify with a criminal, might be so discomfited as to seek refuge in the comforting ideological platitudes of their class: "You see the error underlying its argument so clearly,—that to him a true life was one of full development rather than self-restraint? that he was deaf to the higher tone in a cry of voluntary suffering for truth's sake" (925). Davis concludes this passage with pointed ambiguity by blurring whether she is referring to Wolfe or to the reader when she writes, "I only want to show you the mote in my brother's eye: then you can see clearly to take it out" (925).

Davis deploys her allegorical REALISM as a challenge to traditional American Calvinist ideas about sin and salvation, particularly the deeply entrenched conviction that economic failure manifests spiritual unworthiness. This conviction is implicitly challenged as Davis induces the reader to identify with Hugh's puzzlement regarding the source of his seemingly eternal punishment: "His nature starts up with a mad cry of rage against God, man, whoever it is that has forced this vile, slimy life upon him" (913). Similarly, she induces the reader to repudiate Kirby's washing his hands, like Pontius Pilate, "of all social problems" (918). Challenging this Calvinist conviction from the perspective of radical contemporary ideas about economic and environmental determinism, while establishing a pattern of biblical allusions, Davis's story constitutes a harbinger of the social gospel movement of the 1880s–1920s, which sought authority in Christian scripture for governmental regulation of industrial practices, notably labor reform, and for publicly financed protection and rehabilitation of the socially abject or abused.

In significant respects Davis's story is also a radical departure from the sentimental magazine fiction of the period, which generally focused on self-sacrifice, secret emotions, and moral scruples confined within the narrow contexts of familial and courtship relationships. Such fiction served to endorse tacitly an ideology of individual responsibility, the conviction that willpower and rectitude, or lack thereof, is what establishes a person's condition in life. There are, of course, sentimental elements in Davis's story of "what might have been and was not: a hope, a talent, a love" (934). These are most evident with regard to Deborah's conventional womanly devotion to the preoccupied Hugh: "Was there nothing worth reading in this wet, faded thing . . . no story of a soul filled with groping passionate love, heroic unselfishness, fierce jealousy? of years of weary trying . . . to gain one look of real heart-kindness from him?" (911). The narrator deliberately equates these feelings with those of her readers by adding, "One sees that dead, vacant look steal sometimes over the rarest, finest of women's faces . . . and then one can guess at the secret of intolerable solitude that lies hid beneath the delicate laces and brilliant smile" (911). But these familiar, easily recognizable sentiments function to augment and make more acceptable what is Davis's larger set of concerns related to societal indifference and its deleterious effects.

In a sense, the interplay between sentiments and scruples takes place at the site of those challenging addresses to the "you" of the reader: "You laugh at it? Are pain and jealousy less savage realities down here in this place I am taking you to than in your own house or your own heart—your heart, which they clutch at sometimes?" (911). The narrator's reminder of the "unawakened power" of the masses that Hugh represents serves to make the story a cautionary tale of progressivism, a contemporary political movement founded on the recognition that industrialization had enabled a massive accumulation of wealth by a few and that that, practically speaking, had made untenable the constitutional promise of equal opportunity in the pursuit of happiness. The progressives clung to the hope that structural reform would protect the capitalist system from the radical assault posed by union organizers, socialists, communists, and anarchists. Anxieties of this sort are registered throughout the conversation of the visitors to the mill. Kirby, for example, declares, "Let them have a clear idea of the rights of the soul, and I'll venture next week they'll strike for higher wages" (920), and he asks defiantly, "Do you want to banish all social ladders and put us all on a flat table-level" (917). Taking no sides, Mitchell observes that "reform is born of need, not pity. No vital movement of the people's has worked down, for good or evil"; ferment from below has always "carried up the heaving, cloggy mass" (920). Contemporary anxieties about the revolutionary potential of the rootless urban mob can also be registered in the description of Hugh's delirious, short-lived experience of freedom as "the madness that underlies revolution, all progress, and all fall" (925). Davis provides a warning in Hugh's insistence, upon hearing his prison sentence, that "the money was his by rights, and that all the world had gone wrong" (927). At the end of the story Hugh's work of art is still asking its "terrible" questions, as Davis's own work of art goads the reader to take action: "Is this the End? . . . nothing beyond?—no more?" (935).

BIBLIOGRAPHY

Davis, Rebecca Harding. "Life in the Iron-Mills." In *The Norton Anthology of Literature by Women,* edited by Sandra M. Gilbert. New York: W. W. Norton, 1985.

David Brottman
Southern Indiana University

"LIFE YOU SAVE MAY BE YOUR OWN, THE" FLANNERY O'CONNOR (1971)

As a devout Catholic, FLANNERY O'CONNOR felt her calling in life was to convert her readers through her stories. As with many of O'Connor's stories, in "The Life You Save May Be Your Own," readers must struggle to define what is and is not morally correct. This is the story about a drifter who meets an old woman and her feeble-minded daughter living on an isolated farm. Throughout the story, both the vagrant and the old woman have ulterior motives guiding their every action and decision.

The drifter, Mr. Shiftlet, conspicuously resembles a broken Christ figure. He approaches the old woman's yard walking with a sideways slant. One of his arms is missing from the elbow down, and with the other he carries a tin toolbox. We learn later that he is indeed a carpenter, alluding to the biblical image of Jesus. As he greets the two women, the sun is setting over the mountains in the distance, causing him to turn and stare for a prolonged time with outstretched arms, "his figure formed a crooked cross" (146). Despite his broken appearance, Mr. Shiftlet declares, "I'm a man . . . even if I ain't a whole one. I got . . . a moral intelligence!" (149). It is this moral intelligence that he seems to struggle with throughout the story. He claims to be disheartened with the current state of society, disparaging people for being complacent, concerned with money, or promiscuous. Yet all the while he is talking to the old woman, he is assessing the condition of the car he espies jutting out from the barn: "He judged the car to be about a 1928 or '29 Ford" (147).

The old woman, Lucynell Crater, is no better. The entire time Mr. Shiftlet is talking to her, she is making plans of her own. Mr. Shiftlet tries to engage the old woman in philosophical discourse: "He asked her what she thought she was made for but she didn't answer, she only sat rocking and wondered if a one-armed man could put a new roof on her garden house" (148). Finally, after a long diatribe by Mr. Shiftlet, she blurts out, "Are you married or are you single?" (149). It becomes increasingly apparent that the old woman intends to marry off her deaf mute daughter, Lucynell, in order to get a handyman. She makes it clear to Mr. Shiftlet that she would not let a man take Lucynell away but suggests that she would marry her off if the man agreed to stay on the farm.

In this story, Lucynell is the pawn in a game of high-stakes chess. As readers, we know that Mr. Shiftlet is more interested in the car than in Lucynell, but he does seem to have some affection for her. He treats her kindly from the minute he arrives, giving her a stick of gum and teaching her her first word, *bird*. Mr. Shiftlet tells the old woman "that the trouble with the world was that nobody cared, or stopped and took any trouble . . . [and that] he never would have been able to teach Lucynell to say a word if he hadn't cared and stopped long enough" (150). Yet he clearly seems dismayed by the proposition of marrying her. Martin writes, "One has the feeling that [Lucynell's] hilarious antics mysteriously mock the purposes of both [the old woman and Mr. Shiftlet] and that her idiocy is a blessed condition far superior to their calculating devices" (209). Lucynell's innocence ensures her spiritual redemption, as can be evidenced by her likeness to "an angel of Gawd" (154).

Is Mr. Shiftlet a heartless con man, as some critics suggest? This may be suggested by his physical deformity. André Bleikasten claims that in O'Connor's stories "[the] deformity of bodies point[s] to a deeper sickness, invisible but more irremediably tragic, the sickness of the soul" (141). While Mr. Shiftlet preaches his morals and prays to God, he also exhibits some unethical actions: lying, marrying Lucynell in order to obtain the car, and then abandoning Lucynell in a strange place. But if Mr. Shiftlet's professed principles are simply an act, then we must wonder why he continues the charade alone in the car. Once the hitchhiker has jumped out of the car, Mr. Shiftlet "felt that the rottenness of the world was about to engulf him . . . [and cried out] 'Oh Lord! . . . Break forth and wash the slime from this earth!'" (156). Perhaps Mr. Shiftlet is simply a lost soul searching for spiritual grace. Martin claims that Lucynell is the embodiment of grace and as such is Mr. Shiftlet's opportunity at redemption, which he ultimately rejects. Martin writes, "[Mr. Shiftlet's] complete awareness of his action is indicated by his transference of the waiter's phrase from Lucynell to his mother, all the while thinking of his abandonment of the girl: 'My mother was a angel of Gawd. . . . He took her from heaven and giver to me and I left her.' . . . As the title of the story indicates, it is not Lucynell's life that he must save, but his own" (88).

As with most O'Connor tales, at the story's close, we are left to ponder whether the protagonist has made any progress at all toward spiritual redemption.

BIBLIOGRAPHY

Bleikasten, André. "The Heresy of Flannery O'Connor." In *Critical Essays on Flannery O'Connor,* edited by Melvin J. Friedman and Beverly Lyon Clark, 138–158. Boston: G. K. Hall, 1985.

Grimshaw, James A., Jr. *The Flannery O'Connor Companion.* Westport, Conn.: Greenwood Press, 1981.

Martin, Carter. *The True Country.* Kingsport, Tenn.: Kingsport Press, 1969.

O'Connor, Flannery. "The Life You Save May Be Your Own." In *The Complete Stories of Flannery O'Connor.* New York: Farrar, Straus & Giroux, 1971.

Paige Huskey
Wright State University

"LIGEIA" Edgar Allan Poe (1838) Suffused with a gloom reminiscent of that of "The Fall of the House of Usher," "Ligeia" remains one of Edgar Allan Poe's best-known stories. It achieves Poe's goal of the "single effect" through the narrator's focus on Ligeia, his deceased wife. In a tightly knit plot that relies on sensational incidents, the narrator's sharp focus on Ligeia leads to the stunning and ambiguous denouement. In the tale Poe also makes use of the unreliable narrator whom the reader must constantly distrust.

This powerful tale about Ligeia, a strong-willed woman who wills herself back to life in the body of Rowena, the narrator's second wife, may be read, as critic Gordon Weaver observes, as a story of either madness or the occult (Current-García 67). Clearly the narrator is obsessed with Ligeia. Having remarried, he treats his second wife abominably as he recalls for the readers the history of his relationship with Ligeia. We notice Poe's careful references to the narrator's opium habit and the overly rich, sensuous gloom in the castle apartment in which he and Rowena live, but feel mesmerized by the narrator's description of Ligeia. The suspense builds incrementally, and only when we see that Ligeia has entered Rowena's body do we realize the many questions the narrative raises.

Poe leaves many of the details of the story mysterious and unresolved. The narrator cannot remember

Ligeia's surname, for example, nor can he recall the name of the city where they met; these lapses seem distinctly odd in the narrative of an undying love. He may indeed be mad, he may indeed be suffering the extreme effects of opium, and most readers can accept the ghost of Ligeia and her reappearance in another's body. With those interpretations, the story remains a masterpiece of suspense, of horror, of obsessive men. Yet another interpretation is possible, however, from a FEMINIST viewpoint: If one understands the narrator's tone in much the way one understands the tone of the Duke in Robert Browning's later poem, "My Last Duchess," Ligeia's character becomes the reason for the narrator's anger as well as madness. Her erudition, her brilliance, her voluptuousness, as well as her forceful personality may well have plagued her husband until he had no choice but to kill her. Moreover, many critics have pointed to the poem-within-the-story as performing a function similar to that same device in "The Fall of the House of Usher." Indeed, the "Conqueror Worm" of the husband's poem in "Ligeia" has both phallic and murderous connotations. Having killed the strong wife so odious to him, the narrator may then have used Ligeia's fortune to buy the castle and marry her FOIL. Viewed in this way, Ligeia, as does MADELINE USHER, becomes the avenging woman who refuses to allow the narrator a peaceful moment, underscored with his hysterical, desperate calling of her name at the end of the story.

Whatever interpretation the reader chooses, Poe, once again, demonstrates his genius in continuing to puzzle, to terrify, above all to intrigue his readers even a century and a half removed from him. With Poe we always feel that he has more to tell us, could we but fathom the psychological depths of his artistry.

BIBLIOGRAPHY

Current-García, Eugene. *The American Short Story before 1850.* Boston: Twayne, 1985.

May, Charles E. *Edgar Allan Poe: Studies in the Short Fiction.* Boston: Twayne, 1991.

Poe, Edgar Allan. "Ligeia." In *Heath Anthology of American Literature,* 3rd ed. Edited by Paul Lauter. Boston: Houghton Mifflin, 1,450–1,461.

"LIKE A WINDING SHEET" ANN PETRY (1945)

Representative of ANN PETRY's naturalist (see NATURALISM) fiction, "Like a Winding Sheet" portrays the daily experience of racism as a cause of domestic violence. Throughout his degrading workday, the PROTAGONIST Johnson suppresses the urge to strike the faces of the white women who insult him, reiterating his vow never to hit a woman. FORESHADOWING the story's violent end, however, Johnson observes that his hands have developed a separate life of their own. Upon his arrival home, his hands escape his control and release his rage onto his beloved wife, Mae. This frequently anthologized story appears in *Best American Short Stories 1946,* a volume dedicated to Petry, as well as in Petry's *Miss Muriel and Other Stories.*

BIBLIOGRAPHY

Andrews, William L., et al. *The Oxford Companion to African-American Literature.* New York: Oxford University Press, 1997.

Barksdale, Richard, and Keneth Kinnamon, eds. *Black Writers of America: A Comprehensive Anthology.* Englewood Cliffs, N.J.: Prentice Hall, 1972.

Davis, Arthur P., J. Saunders Redding, and Joyce Ann Joyce, eds. *New Calvacade: African-American Writing from 1760 to Present.* Washington D.C.: Howard University Press, 1991.

Ervin, Hazel Arnett. *Ann Petry: A Bio-Bibliography.* 1993.

Holliday, Hilary. *Ann Petry.* New York: G. K. Hall, 1996.

Washington, Gladys J. "A World Made Cunningly: A Closer Look at Ann Petry's Short Fiction." *CLA Journal* 30, no. 1 (September 1986): 14–29.

Kimberly Drake
Virginia Wesleyan College

"LILACS" KATE CHOPIN (1896)

Originally published in the *New Orleans Times-Democrat* (December 20, 1896), "Lilacs" centers on the annual visit of an opera singer, Adrienne Farival, to the Sacré-Coeur convent school she attended in her youth. In the beginning of the story, Adrienne makes a dramatic entrance wearing fashionable clothes and bearing expensive gifts. Despite a cold reception from the mother superior, Adrienne remains in the convent, sharing a room with her childhood friend, now Sister Agathe, and participating in the daily rites. After two weeks of dutiful service, Adrienne returns to her sumptuous apartment in Paris and resumes her life of DECADENCE. She mistreats her servants, pelting one with hothouse roses, and treats her suitors callously. She keeps her yearly retreat a secret, allowing others to believe she is idling at a spa. The next spring when she again smells the lilacs blooming, she makes another pilgrimage to "the haven of peace, where her soul was wont to refresh itself," but this time, she is refused admittance (365). The mother superior returns the expensive gifts Adrienne has given through the years, causing Adrienne to weep at the rejection. The story ends with Sister Agathe crying in her room as the lilacs that Adrienne has left on the convent steps are swept away.

"Lilacs" has interesting biographical relevance, for KATE CHOPIN herself was educated at the Sacred Heart Academy in St. Louis, and her best childhood friend later became a nun. Although critics such as Edmund Wilson have detected a "serene amoralism" in her works (592), Chopin was deeply influenced by her religious upbringing and returned to the church near the end of her life (Seyersted 185). While "Lilacs" may be interpreted as an indictment of Roman Catholicism, the central focus, as Elmo Howell points out, is not the church but "an individual soul at odds with itself" (106). Adrienne's tragic dilemma is that she cannot reconcile her worldly existence with her spiritual longing.

BIBLIOGRAPHY

Chopin, Kate. "Lilacs." In *The Complete Works of Kate Chopin.* Baton Rouge: Louisiana State University Press, 1969.

Howell, Elmo. "Kate Chopin and the Pull of Faith: A Note on 'Lilacs.'" *Southern Studies* (Spring 1979): 103–109.

Seyersted, Per. *Kate Chopin: A Critical Biography.* Baton Rouge: Louisiana State University Press, 1969.

Toth, Emily. *Kate Chopin.* New York: Morrow, 1990.

Wilson, Edmund. *Patriotic Gore.* New York: Oxford University Press, 1966.

Mary Anne O'Neal
University of Georgia

LIM, SHIRLEY GEOK-LIN (1944–) Shirley

Geok-lin Lim was born in Malaysia of Chinese-Malaysian heritage. She moved to America at age 24, beginning a new life as a student and then as a teacher and writer in California.

Lim is the author of three short story collections, *Another Country and Other Stories* (1982), *Life's Mysteries* (1995), and *Two Dreams: New and Selected Stories* (1997). She also has published two volumes of poetry and an autobiography, *Among the White Moon Faces* (1996); edited two anthologies of ASIAN-AMERICAN LITERATURE; and written or edited five volumes of literary criticism. She has also written a novel, *Joss and Gold* (2001).

"Mr. Tang's Girls," one of the stories in the collection in *Another Country,* won the *Asiaweek* short story competition in 1982. The stories are concerned primarily with the domains of women in Chinese-Malaysian society. But for American readers inclined to read Asian stories either from a sense of smugness or to satisfy tastes for the exotic, Lim has a surprise. The weaknesses in the characters of her ANTAGONISTS (often Chinese-Malaysian males) subtly echo telling attributes of Western—and particularly American—society, so that the sensitive reader is made to feel the universality of crucial social flaws, especially those relevant to gender inequity, to sexual arrogance and abuse, to the objectification of girls and women. In "A Pot of Rice," for instance, the PROTAGONIST Su Yu rebels against her husband, Mark, who arrives home from work to find that Su Yu, rather than fixing his dinner, has covered the dining table with food offerings to her recently deceased father. Mark retreats angrily into the bedroom and turns on the television. "'This is the first time,' he said loudly, hoping she would hear in the kitchen, 'you haven't served me first'" (291).

BIBLIOGRAPHY

Edelson, Phyllis. Review of Lim's works. In *The Forbidden Stitch: An Asian American Women's Anthology,* edited by Shirley Geok-lin Lim, et al. Corvallis, Oreg.: Calyx Books, 1989.

Lim, Shirley Geok-lin. *Among the White Moon Faces.* New York: Feminist Press, 1996.

———. *Another Country and Other Stories.* Singapore: Times Books International, 1982.

———. *Joss and Gold.* New York: Feminist Press, 2001.

———. *Life's Mysteries.* Singapore: Times Books International, 1995.

————. *Monsoon History.* London: Skoob, 1994.

————. "A Pot of Rice." In *Home to Stay: Asian American Women's Fiction,* edited by Sylvia Watanabe and Carol Bruchac. Greenfield Center, N.Y.: Greenfield Review Press, 1990.

————. *Sister Swing.* Singapore: Marshall Cavendish Editions, 2006.

————. *Two Dreams: New and Selected Stories.* New York: Feminist Press, 1997.

————, ed. *Tilting the Continent: An Anthology of Southeast Asian American Writing.* St. Paul, Minn.: New Rivers Press, 2000.

————, ed. *Transnational Asian American Literature: Sites and Transits.* Philadelphia: Temple University Press, 2006.

Lim, Shirley Geok-lin, and Amy Ling. *Reading the Literatures of Asian America.* Philadelphia: Temple University Press, 1992.

Lim, Shirley Geok-lin, and Maria Herrera-Sobek, eds. *Power, Race, and Gender in Academe: Strangers in the Tower?* New York: Modern Language Association of America Press, 2000.

Keith Lawrence
Brigham Young University

LIMINALITY

A term originating in anthropological and cultural research on ceremony and ritual, *liminality* indicates that persons, objects, places, events, or times are between one state and another. This ambiguous position of being at a threshold or border, neither completely here nor there, implies suspension and paradox. For example, a mixed-race teenager leaning in a doorway, on New Year's Eve, while riding in a mobile home from the United States to Canada is a multiply liminal figure. Scholars have studied liminality in such short fiction writers as WILLA CATHER, NATHANIEL HAWTHORNE, WASHINGTON IRVING, HENRY JAMES, HERMAN MELVILLE, and EDGAR ALLAN POE.

Brenda M. Palo
University of North Carolina at Chapel Hill

LINCOLN, ABRAHAM (1809–1865)

The 16th president of the United States (1861–65), Lincoln presided over the most divisive period of American history. His eloquence, steadfastness of purpose, and considerable political skills contributed greatly to the North defeating the South in the CIVIL WAR, preserving the Union, and abolishing slavery. He was assassinated within a week after General ROBERT E. LEE surrendered to General Ulysses S. Grant at Appomattox to end the war. Considered with George Washington to be one of the truly great presidents, Lincoln attained the status of LEGEND and folk hero soon after his death.

LITTLE MAGAZINES

Initially appearing in the first two decades of the 20th century and becoming major forces in publishing by about 1920, the little magazines provided a remarkable opportunity for innovative modernist writers (see MODERNISM). Their unofficial role was an adversarial one against official culture. Small, significant, and elite (in that they published the AVANT-GARDE writings of a coterie of new writers), the least successful of these magazines published little that we remember today, but the most successful—even those that lasted only briefly—published stories still considered extraordinary.

Among the most significant of the hundreds of little magazines that sprang up are *Poetry: A Magazine of Verse,* begun in 1912; the *Little Review,* in 1914; *Seven Arts,* in 1916; the *Dial,* in 1917; the *Frontier,* in 1920; *Reviewer* and *Broom,* in 1921; *Fugitive,* in 1922; *This Quarter,* in 1925; *Transition* and *Hound and Horn,* in 1927. Although *Broom,* published in the early 1920s in Rome, Berlin, and New York, ran for less than three years, it featured short stories by SHERWOOD ANDERSON and James Stephens, and criticism by the short story writers CONRAD AIKEN and JEAN TOOMER. The *Little Review* published James Joyce's *Ulysses* (1922) in serial form, and the *Dial* was the first to publish T. S. Eliot's *The WASTE LAND* (1922). On the pages of the *Double Dealer,* published for three and a half years in New Orleans, appeared short fiction by WILLIAM FAULKNER, Carl Van Vechten, and Thornton Wilder. Stories by KATHERINE ANNE PORTER, KAY BOYLE, and ERSKINE CALDWELL ran in *Hound and Horn,* and nearly every significant modernist short fiction writer published in *Story,* which appeared from 1931 through 1948. Although the little magazines paid nothing to contributors and reached a tiny market, they recognized talent and innovation and assured their writers a thoughtful and committed readership.

Several little magazines with left-wing political orientations also appeared during this era, including the *New Masses* (1911–17), the *Liberator* (1918–26), and the *New Masses* (1926–48), publishing works by Philip Gold and TILLIE OLSEN, for example. Combining poetry, short stories, essays, and reviews, quarterlies also arose during this period: The *Prairie Schooner* began in 1927, the *Partisan Review* in 1934, the *Quarterly Review of Literature* in 1943, and the *Hudson Review* in 1948, along with the *Southern Review* (1935–42), the KENYON REVIEW (1939–70), and *Accent* (1940–60). In the 1950s and 1960s appeared little magazines reacting against the quarterlies, most of which had lost their avant-garde status. The most significant include the *Black Mountain Review* (1954–57); the *Evergreen Review* (1957–73); *Yugen* (1958–62), associated with the BEAT MOVEMENT; and *Kulchur* (1960–65). The most successful of this period—the *Paris Review*, begun in 1953, and *Tri Quarterly*, begun in 1958—continue to influence critical and literary opinion.

By the end of the 20th century, little magazines had proliferated, numbering well over 1,000. They continued to provide an important outlet for so-called ethnic writers and for writers of experimental short fiction.

From the last decade of the 20th century through the first of the 21st, numerous quarterly print journals continue to sustain readership—*Georgia Review, Granta, Threepenny Review,* et al.—and the *Pushcart Prize Anthology* continues to rate the top 120 magazines, the top five of 2009 being *Ploughshares, Zoetrope: All Story, Conjunctions, Paris Review* and *Southern Review* (2009 Pushcart Prize Rankings). For many authors, in the words of novelist Francine Prose, the little magazines represent a sort of protest against "corporatization of our culture" (Shapiro). In addition to the print magazines, however, technology has made remarkable inroads into the future of the short story. Many important magazines featuring short fiction are now published solely online. So far, the benefits appear to outweigh the detriments, particularly in terms of accessibility. Thousands of these online magazines have appeared, providing an abundance of opportunity to both readers and previously unpublished authors of every possible background. Some of the best known include *3:AM Magazine, The Barcelona Review, Eclectica Magazine, Fence, Literary Mama, The Little Magazine, McSweeney's Internet Tendency, Ninth Letter, Spike Magazine, storySouth,* and *Tin House.* Some are particularly innovative; for example, *OneStory* sends its subscribers a single story every three weeks.

BIBLIOGRAPHY
Begun, Bret. "Not the Same Ol' Story." *Newsweek,* 14 October 2002. Available online. URL: http://www.highbeam.com/doc/1G1-92743179.html. Accessed May 6, 2009.

Meany, Thomas. "The Little Magazine That Could." *Appreciation,* 15 May 2007. Available online. URL: http://www.nysun.com/arts/little-magazine-that-could/54472/. Accessed May 5, 2009.

Perpetual Folly: 2009 Pushcart Prize Rankings, Saturday, December 7, 2008. Available online. URL: http://perpetualfolly.blogspot.com/2008/12/2009-pushcart-prize-rankings.html. Accessed May 13, 2009.

Shapiro, Gary. "In Search of the Perfect Little Magazine." Knickerbocker, 17 May 2005. Available online. URL: http://www.nysun.com/arts/in-search-of-the-perfect-little-magazine/13955. Accessed May 13, 2009.

"LITTLE REGIMENT, THE" STEPHEN CRANE (1896)

Pressured by his publisher, McClure, to write more CIVIL WAR works after the success of his novel *The Red Badge of Courage,* STEPHEN CRANE crafted with some difficulty "The Little Regiment." The story, which Crane identified as a novelette divided in eight parts, became the title piece in a small collection of war stories titled *"The Little Regiment" and Other Episodes of the American Civil War.* The story signifies "Crane's foray into naturalism: the protagonists are not individualized human beings but representatives of 'humanity'" (Wolford 63). The characters inhabit an indifferent world of war, chaos, and death.

"The Little Regiment" begins with vivid descriptions of fog blanketing a regiment of Union soldiers who lie in wait in the mud, joking and bragging while gun and artillery fire rumble in the distance. As Austin McC. Fox suggests, "Often it is the opening description in Crane's stories that strikes the note of the indifference of the universe," and the fog that pervades the story "becomes a symbol of this indifference" (60). Two brothers, Billie and Dan Dempster, trade barbs and openly express derision to each other, which began when they enlisted on the same day and continues under the eyes of their fellow soldiers, who expect the brothers to come to blows. Billie's promotion to corporal prompts his brother's open defiance of Billie's higher rank. It is not until Dan calls Billie a fool in a "decisive" and "brightly assured" voice that Billie considers severing all ties to his brother (229). In battle, surrounded by gunfire and bloodshed, Billie gains an awareness of his own insignificance: "The terrible voices from the hills told him that in this wide conflict his life was an insignificant fact, and that his death was an insignificant fact. They portended the whirlwind to which he would be as necessary as a butterfly's waved wing" (230). Such knowledge fails to mend the rift between him and Dan and further isolates them. Billie decides to ignore Dan as if his brother no longer exists.

Billie's silent treatment initially dismays and quickly angers Dan, yet it does not damper his spirits as he eagerly awaits the regiment's next engagement of the enemy, certain of victory. Billie is awakened in the middle of the night by a sergeant gathering men for special duty, and Dan is among them. Despite the rancor between them, Billie worries about Dan's safety and is visibly agitated; however, when Dan safely returns, Billie hides his concern and feigns sleep.

The brothers are quickly thrust back into danger. In another skirmish, the regiment blindly fights the enemy in the dense fog. As the fog clears, Dan comes face to face with the enemy, registers the details of the man's appearance, and by chance kills his enemy before his enemy kills him. The next morning, again marked by fog, the regiment marches toward a greater battle in which the soldiers struggle to overcome an enemy that stands its ground and breaks their lines. After the failed onslaught, the Union soldiers rename themselves the *Little Regiment*.

Back at camp, Dan isolates himself from his fellow soldiers, who ask him whether he has received any news of Billie, who has not returned after battle. He finds little comfort from the soldiers, who try to reassure him that Billie may lie among the wounded. Dan struggles to maintain his stony countenance to mask his worry. Billie awakes on the battlefield, surrounded by the dead barely distinguishable through the fog, and discovers he was wounded in the head. The regiment cheers as Billie appears in camp, and Dan struggles to conceal his emotions. The brothers reunite, physically and emotionally: "After a series of shiftings, it occurred naturally that the man with the bandage was very near to the man who saw the flames. He paused, and there was a little silence. Finally he said: 'Hello, Dan.' [and Dan replies], 'Hello, Billie'" (243). Chester L. Wolford notes, "At that point, they realize what they had always known instinctively: that the other's existence increases their own importance, just as the existence of the regiment surpasses in importance the lives of its members" (63). Their simple greeting reveals the affection concealed by their public displays of derision toward one another.

Michael Schaeffer acknowledges that current critical appraisals of the story remain mixed. Critics such as James Colvert view the work as a failure, and others, following suit, point to "Crane's overwriting, editorializing, lack of movement in describing the action of the story, failure to develop the brothers' relationship fully enough," among other problems (Schaeffer 200). On the other side of the spectrum, more favorable critics applaud Crane's use of SYMBOLISM and his growing maturity. Regardless of any negative criticism, no critic or reader can deny the poignancy of the story's final scene, where the brothers once again stand side by side.

BIBLIOGRAPHY

Crane, Stephen. "The Little Regiment." In *The Oxford Book of American Short Stories,* edited by Joyce Carol Oates. New York: Oxford University Press, 1992.

Fox, Austin McC. "Crane Is Preoccupied with the Theme of Isolation." In *Readings on Stephen Crane,* edited by Bonnie Szumski, 56–62. The Greenhaven Press Literary Companion to American Authors. San Diego: Greenhaven, 1998.

Ives, C. B. "'The Little Regiment' of Stephen Crane at the Battle of Fredericksburg." *Midwest Quarterly* 9 (1967): 247–260.

Schaefer, Michael W. *A Reader's Guide to the Short Stories of Stephen Crane*. New York: G. K. Hall, 1996.

Wolford, Chester L. *Stephen Crane: A Study of the Short Fiction*. Twayne Studies in Short Fiction. Boston: Twayne, 1989.

Dana Knott
Columbus State Community College

"LIVVIE" EUDORA WELTY (1942) One of EUDORA WELTY's frequently anthologized stories, "Livvie" focuses on the title character, a 24-year-old African-American woman whose old and ill husband, Solomon, lies dying in their home. Solomon had married Livvie when she was 16, and, although the narrator points out that he has given her everything he thought she wanted, he has kept her a virtual prisoner in the house that he has perfected over his years as a respected farmer. Wise like his Old Testament namesake in terms of owning and operating a cotton farm complete with his own field hands, Solomon echoes him as well in terms of the patriarchal biblical tradition with which he is associated. Contrary to the SYMBOLISM suggested in her name, the protected and naive Livvie has led a static existence lacking experience, vividness, and passion. Because she is trapped at the end of the Natchez Trace, which no one visits either on foot or by car, Livvie has never lived for herself but performs the role of caretaker, first for the white baby she tended before she married, and now for Solomon, whom she increasingly thinks of in terms of a baby himself. Livvie keeps the house spotless and prepares meals for herself (which she devours hungrily) and for Solomon (who loses his appetite as he draws nearer to death). She feels proud of her ability to maintain silence so as never to disturb her husband.

Livvie is associated not only with images of hunger and silence, but also with those of roundness and fertility, in contrast to Solomon, associated with images of rigidity and stasis. Whereas Livvie eats eggs, symbolic of life, Solomon rejects them. Significantly, the story takes place just before EASTER and, in yet another ironic twist to a biblical story, just before Livvie arises from her deadened state, she is visited by a white woman, Miss Baby Marie. Miss Baby Marie, her name a variation of Mary, mother of Christ, and a reminder of the childish state of both Solomon and Livvie, literally opens Livvie's door and causes her to examine herself in the mirror. Livvie, wearing the bright lipstick the white women wishes to sell her, suddenly understands—though she does not articulate the thought—that Solomon is dying and that a potentially bright future awaits her.

In an admirably crafted, tightly knit story replete with FORESHADOWING, Welty has prepared the reader for Livvie's metaphorical ascension. When the young woman meets Cash McCord, one of Solomon's field hands, the passion between them is natural, mutual, and instantaneous. Cash seems destined to cut the umbilical cord between Livvie and her husband, who is at once childish and old enough to be her father. The ANTITHESIS of Solomon, always associated with darkness, Cash has spent money on brightly colored clothing and tells Livvie that he is "ready for Easter." Yet this story contains no villains: Cash resists the impulse to strike Solomon down, and the old man dies naturally, realizing on his deathbed his error in taking Livvie from her home and preventing her from meeting others her own age. The story ends in utter joy as Cash and Livvie embrace under a spring-flowering peach tree: The sun shines, a redbird sings, and Livvie drops the heavy silver watch Solomon has bequeathed her. She is joyously reborn, her life just beginning, and she youthfully ignores the constraints of time.

LOCAL COLOR The speech, DIALECT, customs, and other features characteristic of a certain region provide the local color in a work of fiction. In the late 19th century, a number of American writers consciously incorporated local color to enhance the REALISM of their work. They included BRET HARTE and Joaquim Miller (the West), MARK TWAIN (the Mississippi), JOEL CHANDLER HARRIS and GEORGE WASHINGTON CABLE (the South), HAMLIN GARLAND (the Midwest), and SARAH ORNE JEWETT (New England). O. HENRY and Damon Runyon are further examples of local color writers. The term *local color writing* denotes works that use local color primarily for entertainment by emphasizing or dwelling on the particular and peculiar characteristics of a region or people. It lacks the basic seriousness of realism in that, generally, it does not use locale as a vehicle to explore larger and more universal issues. The term is called into question by some contemporary critics, feminists in particular, because it sometimes is used in a condescending or pejorative manner. Much local color writing was in the form of the sketch or short story and was published in mass-circulation magazines.

LONDON, JACK (JOHN GRIFFITH LONDON) (1876–1916)

Jack London's unique philosophy of life, the work he performed to express it, and his artistic sincerity find their greatest fulfillment in his short fiction. Notwithstanding the merits of his nonfiction and his novels, such as *The Call of the Wild* (1903), which made him America's leading international author; as well as compelling sociological studies such as *The People of the Abyss* (1903), his autobiographical novel, *Martin Eden* (1909); and the haunting visionary fantasy, *The Star Rover,* it is in London's nearly 200 short stories, published from 1899 to his death in 1916, that one finds his finest treasures as a writer. His career reflected the major intellectual currents of his day: socialism and individualism, Darwinism (see DARWIN) and the philosophy of Nietzsche, materialism and spiritual yearning. These conflicting stances found expression in the often startling combinations of NATURALISM and ROMANTICISM in his diverse body of fiction.

London, one of the inventors of the modern American short story, is viewed by many critics as second in importance only to EDGAR ALLAN POE, and his body of work presents an astonishing range of narrative experimentations, diverse characters, and international settings that prepared America's reading public for the advent of literary MODERNISM. Through the existentialism exemplified by the HERO of "TO BUILD A FIRE" (1908), the ragged aesthetic that consumes the heart of the child laborer in "The Apostate" (1911), the awful power of the feminine in "The Night-Born" (1913), and the religious and racial alterity of the old Hawaiian fisherman in "The Water Baby" (1919), London's short stories imagine for us the outlooks and voices of hundreds of characters, from the Indians of the Klondike as they confront the gold-seeking "Sun-landers" to the native peoples of the Pacific Rim encountering their rapacious colonizers, as in "The Red One." London's call for the writer to encompass the world from "magnet to Godhead" was a fitting one; he best embodies Ralph Waldo Emerson's description of the American scholar as one who would learn from nature, learn from books, be a man of action, and, finally, act as a consummate observer. London's famed eclecticism and seemingly inexhaustible energy found their discipline as well as their release in the carefully crafted form of the short story.

London's career may be divided into four roughly chronological concentrations: the Northland tales, which present characters' engagement with nature and each other within the code of brotherhood of the North, as in "To Build a Fire"; the middle socialist period, in which the streets of Oakland and San Francisco, California, are the setting for characters' communal conflicts, as in "South of the Slot"; an experimental phase that saw London breaking out of the "Jack London" formula of adventure and social protest and adventure to work with new subject matter and narrative structures, especially involving racial and sexual others, as in "The Mexican"; and finally the late South Seas stories written during his last few months, as in "The Red One."

Too often in the past, critics have allowed London's adventurous life to obscure the central activity within that life: writing. Living in the great age of the magazine in America and faithfully writing his 1,000 words per day, Jack London spent a majority of his time and thought on crafting the short story. His was an unusual apprenticeship, combining as it did the rigor of library and typewriter with another kind of rigor as he struggled to come to terms with his boyhood illegitimacy and poverty in Oakland. His early life as a child laborer, oyster pirate, hobo, sailor, gold prospector, and even (briefly) college student made way for his true calling, after he found his medium in his first successful short story, "An Odyssey of the North," published in the *ATLANTIC MONTHLY* in 1900. His was a representative voice of his time, with economic uncertainties at home, imperialistic excursions abroad, and emergent movements such as feminism (see FEMINISM/ FEMINIST) and socialism. Fin-de-siècle America had grown impatient with the warmed-over romanticism proffered in the nation's periodicals. In *John Barleycorn* (1913), London said of his entry into the successful magazine market, "Some are born to fortune, and some have fortune thrust upon them. But in my case I was clubbed into fortune, and bitter necessity was the club"—a statement about his own personal sense of REALISM and how that realism was mirrored by the new desires of his audience. London made no secret of his writing for cash, and this fact is connected to the new American realism—literary naturalism—he helped invent. He never lost sight of his own self-described cardinal virtue, his sincerity, and neither did his audience.

Alongside WILLIAM DEAN HOWELLS, MARK TWAIN, STEPHEN CRANE, Frank Norris, THEODORE DREISER, and others, London developed literary naturalism into new and diverse forms, finally reconciling in his late South Seas fiction the DETERMINISM it generated with an inner sense of a world beyond the material, particularly after his reading of the works of the psychologist Carl Jung. Despite his frequent characterization as merely a "red-blooded" naturalist writer for men and boys, his stories reveal that his abiding interest was not in a clichéd notion of "man versus nature" but in human nature—rather like WILLIAM FAULKNER's notion of the "human heart in conflict with itself." As does Faulkner, London places that conflict within both domestic and alien social constructions and contextualizes it within race and gender. Throughout his career London attempts to enter community after community and to show them from the inside, as if his own need to belong, which drove him as a youth, was at last transmuted into a dynamic new art for a new century, particularly in its emphasis on reshaping tradition through his radical social critique.

Many readers are surprised by London's frequent use of strong female characters—as shown, for example, in "The Red One"—and even more by his evident feminist views. In part his thinking about women evolved because of the women in his own life, beginning with his rejection by his own mother and father and his consequent lifelong search for belonging, accompanied by his inner quest for identity as a writer, which caused him to seek the androgynous self of artistic freedom. Fortunately he enjoyed loving relationships with his stepsister, Eliza London Shepard, and his childhood nurse, Virginia Prentiss, but the most important woman in his life was his second wife, Charmian Kittredge London, who, after his divorce from Bess Maddern London (with whom he had two daughters, Joan and Becky London), became his beloved "mate woman." With Charmian he built and ran the Beauty Ranch in Sonoma Valley, California, and undertook his famed adventuring and writing careers.

BIBLIOGRAPHY
Kingman, Russ. *A Pictorial Life of Jack London.* New York: Crown, 1979.
Labor, Earle, and Jeanne Campbell Reesman. *Jack London.* Rev. ed. New York: Twayne, 1994.
London, Jack. *The Complete Stories of Jack London.* 3 vols. Edited by Earle Labor, Robert C. Leitz III, and I. Milo Shepard. Stanford, Calif.: Stanford University Press, 1993.
———. *The Letters of Jack London.* 3 vols. Edited by Earle Labor, Robert C. Leitz III, and I. Milo Shepard. Stanford, Calif.: Stanford University Press, 1988.
Raskin, Jonah, ed. *The Radical Jack London: Writings on War and Revolution.* Berkeley: University of California Press, 2008.
Stasz, Clarice. *Jack London's Women.* Amherst: University of Massachusetts Press, 2001.

Jeanne Campbell Reesman
University of Texas at San Antonio

LONE RANGER AND TONTO FISTFIGHT IN HEAVEN, THE   See ALEXIE, SHERMAN.

LONGSTREET, AUGUSTUS BALDWIN
(1790–1870)   Born in Augusta, Georgia, Longstreet graduated from Yale and studied law in Litchfield, Connecticut, before returning to Georgia, where he was soon appointed a circuit judge on the Ocmulgee District Superior Court. Distraught by the death of his son in 1824, Longstreet abandoned politics, became a Methodist minister, and began editing the *Southern Field and Fireside* and, later, the *State Rights Sentinel.* Both publications allowed him to express his political and moral opinions and to indulge his penchant for

storytelling. A natural raconteur, Longstreet reveled in the tale-telling sessions of the circuit, gleaning plots and characters from the cases and people at the circuit's stops.

Written in the style of WASHINGTON IRVING and Addison and Steele, the first of Longstreet's sketches appeared anonymously in the *Southern Recorder* in Milledgeville, Georgia, in 1833. In 1835, Longstreet collected 19 published sketches; the *Sentinel*, attributing authorship to a "Native Georgian," published these as *Georgia Scenes: Characters, Incidents, &c. in the First Half Century of the Republic.* Longstreet described his characters as both fanciful and real and intended to amuse readers despite their "coarse, inelegant, and sometimes ungrammatical language."

Georgia Scenes proved immensely popular: *Harper* published a second edition, identifying Longstreet as the author, and numerous other editions appeared before and after Longstreet's death in 1870. Although he wrote other sketches, some tracts, and a novel, *Master William Mitten: Or a Youth of Brilliant Talents Who Was Ruined by Bad Luck,* during his tenure as president of several universities including the University of Mississippi and the University of South Carolina, Longstreet's later works never garnered critical acclaim. Lacking the realistic appeal of *Georgia Scenes,* these pieces are heavily didactic, overly cynical, and pointedly religious and political.

Georgia Scenes is recognized as the first collection of southern humor, the first work offering an alternative view of the antebellum plantation tradition, and the first literary impression of early life in Georgia. Two narrators, Lyman Hall and Abram Baldwin, relate the scenes, Hall recounting twice as many as Baldwin. A well-educated country aristocrat, Hall seems genuinely amused by the rough, natural Georgia crackers of his tales. Baldwin, more akin to Longstreet himself, offers a satirical view of the city, one particularly critical of upper-class women.

EDGAR ALLAN POE favorably reviewed *Georgia Scenes,* noting Longstreet's realistic DIALECT, his mastery of style, his sense of the ludicrous, and his exploration of southern bravado. Establishing the standard for what became known as southwestern humor, *Georgia Scenes* was a forerunner of later works, including MARK TWAIN's "The CELEBRATED JUMPING FROG OF CALAVARAS COUNTY," and JOEL CHANDLER HARRIS's UNCLE REMUS tales, and prefigured the LOCAL COLOR movement of the latter part of the 19th century.

Longstreet's tales feature lighthearted humor and generally illustrate the moral superiority of rural folk. Indeed, the joke is often on the narrators, who, despite their superior education, misunderstand the quasi-TRICKSTER figures, the Georgia characters. In "Georgia Theatrics," for example, the narrator's moral superiority precludes his understanding the cathartic effect of a pretend fight. Indeed, despite both narrators' attempts at social bonding, they observe the frontier community and relate their observations to others but are never integrated into the frontier world that values shrewdness and ability to compete. Polly Gibson in "The Dance" cannot (or will not) remember Hall because he sees himself as better than she. The narrators respond to the lower-class dialogue but, once removed, cannot renegotiate the complex hierarchy of one-upmanship.

Georgia Scenes's stereotyping and its racism and sexism often repulse modern readers, but Longstreet's tales clearly prefigure later developments in southern literature. Indeed, Ned Brace, who delights in manipulating others, and Ransy Sniffle, who is described as thrown "quite out of the order of nature," may be the first southern GROTESQUES, precursors to WILLIAM FAULKNER's, ERSKINE CALDWELL's, and FLANNERY O'CONNOR's characters.

Longstreet delights in both the humor and the horror of the primitive frontier's games, sports, and performances, enjoying the loud, rollicking, practical-joking characters while disapproving of moral degenerates. Throughout *Georgia Scenes* appears a tension between the rough frontier's fun and violence and the decadent city, which has lost touch with its natural humanity. In "The Turn-Out," for example, nostalgia for the values of a past era appears in stark contrast to the emerging middle class. *Georgia Scenes* features fast-moving action, men's activities (especially those narrated by Hall), and local, often distasteful rituals such as a gander pulling. Comic understatement, ritualistic put-downs (a kind of playing the dozens), and satire appear in each tale; abundant animal metaphors suggest a thin line between humans' bestial natural and the civilization that holds that nature in check.

The continuing value of *Georgia Scenes* lies in its images of backwoods characters and its recognition that, in the inevitable urbanization of the South, connections must be forged among diverse groups, ideally without losing the admirable qualities of the lower class.

BIBLIOGRAPHY

King, Kimball. *Augustus Baldwin Longstreet.* TUSAS, 474. Boston: Hall, 1984.

Longstreet, Augustus Baldwin. *Georgia Scenes: A Scholarly Text,* edited by David Rachels. Athens: University of Georgia Press, 1998.

Meriwether, James B. "Augustus Baldwin Longstreet: Realist and Artist." *Mississippi Quarterly* 35 (1982): 351–364.

Nimeiri, Ahmed. "Play in Augustus Baldwin Longstreet's Georgia Scenes." *Southern Literary Journal* 33 (2001): 44–61.

Rachels, David. "A Biographical Reading of A. B. Longstreet's Georgia Scenes." In *The Humor of the Old South,* edited by M. Thomas Inge and Edward J. Piacention, 113–129. Lexington: University Press of Kentucky, 2001.

Romine, Scott. *Narrative Forms of Southern Community.* Baton Rouge: Louisiana State University Press, 1999.

Wade, John Donald. *Augustus Baldwin Longstreet: A Study of the Development of Culture in the South.* 1924. Reprint, Athens: University of Georgia Press, 1969.

Wegmann, Jessica. "'Playing in the Dark' with Longstreet's *Georgia Scenes:* Critical Reception and Reader Response to Treatments of Race and Gender." *Southern Literary Journal* (Fall 1997): 13–26.

Gloria A. Shearin
Savannah State University

"LOOKING FOR MR GREEN" SAUL BELLOW (1951)

Originally published in the March 1951 issue of *Commentary* magazine and subsequently included in collections of Bellow's short fiction, "Looking for Mr Green" is one of SAUL BELLOW's best early stories. It anticipates the unmistakable and abundant sense of happy invention in the better-known *Adventures of Augie March* (1953). It is an instance of Bellow's maturing storytelling genius that harnessed to the full the Chicago material that molded his creative imagi-

nation and sharpened his sense of individual American experience. The story has all the strengths one associates with Bellow at his best—REALISM of presentation combined with an ability to evoke the ineluctable mystery of human life rendered in quirky and riveting episodes. The story partakes of all the ingredients of a successful narrative. Set in depression-era Chicago, it describes the first working day in the life of George Grebe, a white employee of the relief bureau entrusted with the job of distributing uncollected checks in a black neighborhood. Bellow works up a steady narrative tempo in the opening paragraphs and goes on to sustain the brisk pace of action in a judicious mixture of description, incident, and reminiscence with a puzzling encounter in the end to conclude the tale on an ambivalent note. In the process the narrative explores important themes like money, race, human survival, and, above all, that recurring Bellovian concern with the problem of appearance and reality in an object-laden world.

Like most other Bellow heroes, Grebe is an intellectual (with a degree in classics) and cast in the role of a seeker. The epigraph of the story is taken from the Book of Ecclesiastes: "Whatsoever thy hand findeth to do, do it with thy might." In a story that predominantly follows a realistic mode of narration, the biblical imperative underscores the inescapability of human effort in the face of uncertain and perplexing life situations and alerts the reader to the tale's serious intentions. What follows is, in effect, a simple story line. Grebe reports for work in his new job at the city relief bureau in the difficult days of the depression. He is asked by his supervisor, Raynor, also white, with the extra benefit of a law degree, to go to a black neighborhood on a bracing wintry day and deliver uncollected checks to their beneficiaries. He is given the usual tips by his boss and sets out with a bunch of information cards. Grebe, puny of stature but resolute of mind, goes about his job with a determined air and has a reasonably fruitful day except for the hard time he has in locating a recipient named Tulliver Green. One of the high points of the story is pitching the frail Grebe against the "high energy" of Chicago, "the giant raw place" (100). Skillful storyteller that Bellow is he succeeds in orchestrating the action between two parallel planes—the thick external world of a desolate urban ghetto with an overwhelming sense of loss and aspiration and the surprised consciousness of an itinerant relief worker unwilling to be intimidated by "the fallen world of appearances" (93). In an eventful first day in the field Grebe manages a series of meetings that sets his nerves on edge but finds himself absolutely clueless about Mr. Green at the end of the day. Reluctant to give up, he stumbles upon a run-down letter box with the name faintly scrawled over it and knocks on the door nearby with the hope of finally discovering Green and bringing his day to a satisfactory end. In a perplexing last paragraph the reader is told that the check is delivered to a drunken naked woman who responds to the knock on the door but refuses to identify herself. Despite his misgivings, Grebe hands over the check to the mysterious emissary: "Whoever she was, she stood for Green, whom he was not to see this time" (105). Grebe retreats with the consoling thought of having found Green. Quite clearly, the ending indicates the elusive nature of Grebe's search. Although Grebe understandably exercises his option to end the search, the mystery lingers. In fact, there is just a hint that the search will resume another time. Thus, far from being clear in purpose and outcome, Grebe's foray into the black ghetto sends out contradictory signals of human frailty and steadfast resilience.

"Looking for Mr Green" is best interpreted as a symbolic quest. Although the story contains a wealth of sociological information and is affiliated to the naturalistic representational style of THEODORE DREISER and JAMES T. FARRELL, there is no mistaking the moments of transcendence in the flow of mundane urban reality. Like his worthy Chicago predecessors Bellow is a master of city facts and harnesses these hard facts to lay the basic groundwork for the story. But what ultimately matters in Bellow's story is the tendency of everyday facts to acquire symbolic resonance without quite losing their specific weight as contingent facts. In sum, the quest of the Bellow hero carries with it the usual burden of worldly trivia, but there is also a distinctive suggestion that this facticity gestures toward a higher wisdom that endows the narrative with a rare sense of ethical urgency. "Looking for Mr Green" is a fine illustration of this principle.

BIBLIOGRAPHY
Bellow, Saul. *"Looking for Mr Green": "Mosby's Memoirs" and Other Stories.* Harmondsworth, Eng.: Penguin Books, 1977, 83–105.
Rodrigues, Eusebio L. "Koheleth in Chicago: The Quest for the Real in 'Looking for Mr Green.'" *Studies in Short Fiction* 11 (Fall 1974): 387–393.

Ram Shankar Nanda
Sambalpur University, India

LOST GENERATION SHORT STORIES

As part of the modernist (see MODERNISM) imperative to "make it new," writers of the 1920s and 1930s consistently wreaked havoc with existing genre conventions. "Poems" no longer rhymed and scanned predictably; essays and reviews had a subjective, even idiosyncratic, slant; plays were anything but three long acts; and the well-made moralizing short story had given way to the "sketch," the prose poem improvisation, some innovative grouping of pages that offended editors and readers alike. Because the short story has become so intrinsically an American province, readers have difficulty appreciating how bold short story writers of the Lost Generation were. Damned (and seldom published) by commercial editors, they persisted in writing in this form—and changed the world's understanding of what a short story might be.

This AVANT-GARDE current was tempered and influenced by the fact that some short story writers of the time were making large sums of money by publishing more conventional stories in slick American magazines. It might be said that the visibly experimental stories of DJUNA BARNES, JEAN TOOMER, ERNEST HEMINGWAY, KAY BOYLE, KATHERINE ANNE PORTER, and others were prompted into being by the possibility of earning good money. The near notoriety of F. SCOTT FITZGERALD's financial success from 1920 on dominated most young writers' imaginations; indeed, during the 1930s, when WILLIAM FAULKNER's novels had been monetary disasters, he set himself the task of writing simple, or at least easily accessible, short fiction to try to recoup his losses on the publication of his first half-dozen novels. His careful records of which stories had been sent to which magazines showed the power of the financial imperative.

The tug of war between aesthetic merit and money-making potential made the struggle for the modern short story form a truly American activity. It also generated a literal flood of short fiction that helped effect the change from the notion that only Guy de Maupassant or EDGAR ALLAN POE could craft a story to a willingness to recognize even the brief prose poem segments of Ernest Hemingway's *in our time* (1924) (and the later *IN OUR TIME,* 1925) as stories. The short story was fast becoming one of the most interesting of literary forms.

F. Scott Fitzgerald's 1920 short story collection, *Flappers and Philosophers,* may have planted the seed of a romanticized disillusion that made the phrase *lost generation* appealing to the post—WORLD WAR I generation. Hemingway, in one epigraph to his 1926 novel *The Sun Also Rises,* wryly quoted GERTRUDE STEIN as having used the phrase (when in reality it was Stein's garage mechanic, speaking of a French prewar generation). The phrase struck many war survivors, especially those living abroad, as a kind of defiant rallying cry. The realists (see REALISM) who had known war were often those who demanded the new in art; just as history could not be repeated, neither could earlier aesthetics (see AESTHETICISM) be effective in modern times.

The best of Fitzgerald's stories blended realism with illusion, and the influence of his first works—"Benediction," "The Ice Palace," even "Bernice Bobs Her Hair"—grew to be as important as that of SHERWOOD ANDERSON's 1919 *WINESBURG, OHIO.* The GROTESQUE, as Anderson described his lost characters, were less picturesque and more real in Fitzgerald and Glenway Wescott (as they had been, somewhat earlier, in AMBROSE BIERCE, JACK LONDON, and STEPHEN CRANE). The first half of the 1920s saw remarkable stories—and collections—peaking in books that were central to readers' views of both the literary form and gender relations in the United States. Fitzgerald's 1926 collection of stories (his third) was *All the Sad Young Men;* Hemingway's 1927 collection of stories (his second) was *Men without Women.* The stories in each drew from the patterns that already existed in both *Winesburg* and Jean Toomer's *CANE* (1923), where women were featured as objects of men's desire rather than as subjects.

Similarly, in these collections of some of the greatest stories of the century ("The RICH BOY," "The Undefeated"), male characters sorted through their lives—analyzing, assessing, dissecting—and placed sexual satisfaction, or romance, low on their list of priorities. In many of these stories men, struggling to find dignity and belief, abandoned any hope of finding love.

Perhaps that paradigm helped to explain the difficulty some other American writers of the time had in finding publication, much less fame. Katherine Anne Porter's stories, like those of Djuna Barnes, ZORA NEALE HURSTON, TILLIE OLSEN, and WILLA CATHER, seemed enigmatic: For readers who understood Fitzgerald and Hemingway, women protagonists led lives that seemed either frustrating or bizarre. By the early 1930s stories by William Faulkner, Thomas Wolfe, William Carlos Williams, Nathanael West, and, somewhat later, JOHN STEINBECK, Albert Maltz, RICHARD WRIGHT, and other male writers, were also finding acceptance. Until assessments that began during the 1980s, the bravura performance of short story writers of the Lost Generation was marked as gendered: crucial to the development of the short story as the world knew it, fascinating in its variation and vitality, and almost exclusively male-oriented in its CHARACTERS and THEMES.

BIBLIOGRAPHY

Clark, Suzanne. *Sentimental Modernism.* Bloomington: University of Indiana Press, 1991.

Dolan, Marc. *Modern Lives, A Cultural Re-Reading of "The Lost Generation."* West Lafayette, Ind.: Purdue University Press, 1996.

Faulkner, Peter, ed. *The English Modernist Reader, 1910–1930.* Iowa City: University of Iowa Press, 1986.

Gilbert, Sandra M., and Susan Gubar. *No Man's Land: The Place of the Woman Writer in the Twentieth Century.* 2 vols. New Haven, Conn.: Yale University Press, 1989.

Ingram, Forrest. *Representative Short Story Cycles of the Twentieth Century: Studies in a Literary Genre.* The Hague: Mouton, 1971.

Kennedy, J. Gerald, ed. *Modern American Short Story Sequences.* New York: Cambridge University Press, 1995.

Kenner, Hugh. *The Proud Era.* Berkeley: University of California Press, 1971.

Koppelman, Susan. "Short Story." In *Oxford Companion to Women's Writing in the United States,* edited by Cathy N.

Davidson and Linda Wagner-Martin. New York: Oxford University Press, 1995.

Lohaffer, Susan, and Jo Ellyn Clarey, ed. *Short Story Theory at a Crossroads*. Baton Rouge: Louisiana State University Press, 1989.

Linda Wagner-Martin
University of North Carolina at Chapel Hill

"LOST IN THE FUNHOUSE" John Barth (1968)

"Lost in the Funhouse" begins with young Ambrose, who was possibly conceived in "Night-Sea Journey," now an adolescent, traveling to Ocean City, Maryland, to celebrate Independence Day. Accompanying him through his eventual initiation are his parents; his uncle Karl; his older brother, Peter; and Magda, a 13-year-old neighbor who is well developed for her age. Ambrose is "at the awkward age" (89) when his voice and everything else are unpredictable. Magda becomes the object of his sexual awakening, and he feels the need to do something about it, if only barely to touch her. The story moves from Ambrose's innocence to his stunned realization of the pain of self-knowledge. John Barth uses printed devices—italics, dashes, and so on—to draw attention to the storytelling technique throughout the presentation of conventional material: a sensitive boy's first encounters with the world, the mysterious "funhouse" of sexuality, illusion, and consciously realized pain.

As the story develops, Barth incorporates comments about the art of fiction into the narrative: "Should she have sat back at that instant, his hand would have been caught under her. . . . The function of the *beginning* of a story is to introduce the principal characters, establish their initial relationship, set the scene for the main action . . . and initiate the first complication or whatever of the rising action" (92). These moments, when the voice seems to shift outside Ambrose's consciousness, actually unite the teller with the tale, Barth with his protagonist, and life with art. As the developing artist, Ambrose cannot forget the least detail of his life, and he tries to piece everything together. Most of all, he needs to know himself, to experience his inner being, before he will have material to translate into art.

When Ambrose is lost in the carnival funhouse, he develops this knowledge. Straying into an old, forgotten part of the funhouse, he becomes separated from the mainstream—the funhouse represents the world for lovers—and has fantasies of death and suicide, recalling the "negative resolve" of the sperm cell from "Night-Sea Journey." Ambrose also finds himself reliving past incidents with Magda and imagining alternative futures.

These experiences lead to Ambrose's fantasy that he is reciting stories in the dark until he dies, while a young girl behind the plyboard panel he leans against takes down his every word but does not speak, for she knows his genius can bloom only in isolation. This fantasy is the artistic parallel to the sperm's union with "Her" in "Night-Sea Journey." Barth thus suggests that the artist's creative force is a product of a rechanneled sexual drive. Although Ambrose prefers to be among the lovers in the funhouse, he is constructing his own funhouse in the world of art.

Harriet P. Gold
LaSalle College
Dawson College

LOST LADY, A Willa Cather (1923)

Like Willa Cather's novels *O Pioneers!* (1913) and *My Antonia* (1918), *A Lost Lady,* a novella-length work, is linked with the landscape of the western American plains. *A Lost Lady* is set in the Colorado prairie town of Sweet Water, where the history of Marian Forrester unfolds, as seen primarily through the eyes of her youthful admirer, Niel Herbert.

As in much of Cather's work, the driving tension in *A Lost Lady* grows out of shifting values as the stewardship of the American West passes from pioneers to speculators and developers. From the outset, we learn that there were two distinct social strata in the prairie states: the homesteaders and hand workers who were there to make a living, and the bankers and gentlemen ranchers who traveled there from the Atlantic seaboard to invest money and to develop the great West (9–10). Nineteen-year-old Marian Ormsby becomes Captain Forrester's bride after he rescues her from a near-fatal fall in the Sierras. He is honorable and compassionate, 25 years her senior, and a member of the first small band of whites to enter the West. He prepared the way for the railroad, and influential members of the western upper class regularly visit the

Forrester home, which, although a bit gaudy, is the finest in town. Financial crisis strikes Captain Forrester when he personally covers deposits made by poor working folk when a bank on whose board he served fails, and his bankruptcy, incurred through honesty and compassion, marks the beginning of his decline. As he physically declines, first falling from his horse, then suffering a stroke, and finally dying, he signifies the passing of his era.

To Niel Herbert, himself part of the new generation of westerners, it is Marian who most effectively mirrors the decline of the West. Physically beautiful and passionate, she seems to him the perfect consort for a past ideal he has not yet perceived as lost. He imagines her the epitome of loyalty until he discovers her in a passionate extramarital affair with Captain Forrester's young bachelor friend, Frank Ellinger. Ivy Peters, pictured at the beginning of the narrative as a cruel adolescent slitting the eyes of a woodpecker, exemplifies the worst of the new West. Peters gradually gains control of the Forrester land, and after Captain Forrester dies, he enters into a crass liaison with Marian Forrester, solidifying her decline in Herbert's eyes.

Men like Ivy Peters see the land primarily as a resource from which to derive material wealth, and degradation of the land also marks the passing era. On the Forrester place, the captain and Marian have always kept a pristine marsh in its natural state. Peters, upon assuming control of the property, drains the wetlands and plants it in wheat, but we learn that he emptied the land of its beauty not because he could grow crops on it but because by doing so he could obliterate a few acres of something he hated, although he could not name it, and could assert his power over the people who had loved those unproductive meadows for their idleness and silvery beauty (106). The West becomes a world in which men like Captain Forrester and land like Sweet Water Marsh cannot survive.

Marian Forrester survives, however, and she returns to her childhood home in California after Peters marries and moves into the Forrester house. She meets a wealthy Englishman living in Buenos Aires, remarries, and moves to South America, where she prospers. Herbert takes years to reconcile his conflicting feelings for Marian Forrester; he cannot forgive her for not passing away with the era she so clearly repre-

sented to him. Recently much insightful critical attention has focused on the shortfalls of Herbert's selective telling of history and on Cather's FEMINIST perception. Although this criticism is valuable, it seems clear that Cather, at least in *A Lost Lady,* remains most deeply concerned with the demise of the western prairie that helped form her life and usher her into art.

BIBLIOGRAPHY
Cather, Willa. *A Lost Lady.* New York: Knopf, 1923.
———. *On Writing: Critical Studies on Writing as Art.* New York: Knopf, 1920.
Murphy, John J., ed. *Critical Essays on Willa Cather.* Boston: G. K. Hall, 1984.
Roskowski, Susan J. "*Willa Cather and the Fatality of Place: O Pioneers!, My Antonia,* and *A Lost Lady.*" In *Geography and Literature: A Meeting of the Disciplines,* edited by William E. Mallory and Paul Simpson-Housely. Syracuse, N.Y.: Syracuse University Press, 1987.
———. "Willa Cather's *A Lost Lady:* The Paradoxes of Change." *Novel* 11, no. 1 (1977).
Urgo, Joseph R. "How Context Determines Fact: Historicism in Willa Cather's *A Lost Lady.*" *Studies in American Fiction* 17, no. 2 (1989).

Cornelius W. Browne
Ohio University

"LOTTERY, THE" SHIRLEY JACKSON (1949)

As were many of SHIRLEY JACKSON's stories, "The Lottery" was first published in the *NEW YORKER* and, subsequently, as the title story of *The Lottery: or, The Adventures of James Harris* in 1949. It may well be the world's most frequently anthologized short story. A modern horror story, it derives its effect from a reversal of the readers' expectations, already established by the ordinary setting of a warm June day in a rural community. Readers, lulled into this false summer complacency, begin to feel horror, their moods changing with the narrator's careful use of evidence and suspense, until the full realization of the appalling ritual murder bursts almost unbearably on them.

The story opens innocently enough, as the townspeople gather for an unidentified annual event connected to the harvest. The use of names initially seems to bolster the friendliness of the gathering; we feel we know these people as, one by one, their names are called in alphabetical order. In retrospect, however, the names of the male lottery organizers—*Summer* and *Graves*—provide us with clues to the transition from life to death. Tessie, the soon-to-be-victim housewife, may allude (see ALLUSION) to another bucolic Tess (in Thomas Hardy's novel *Tess of the D'Urbervilles*), whose promising beginnings transformed into gore and death at the hands of men.

The scholar and critic Linda Wagner-Martin observes that only recently have readers noticed the import of the sacrificial victim's gender: In the traditional patriarchal system that values men and children, mothers are devalued once they have fulfilled their childbearing roles. Tessie, late to the gathering because her arms were plunged to the elbow in dishwater, seems inconsequential, even irritating, at first. Only as everyone in the town turns against her—children, men, other women invested in the system that sustains them—does the reader become aware that this is a ritual stoning of a scapegoat who can depend on no one: not her daughter, not her husband, not even her little boy, Davy, who picks up an extraordinarily large rock to throw at her.

No reader can finish this story without contemplating the violence and inhumanity that Jackson intended it to portray. In the irony of its depiction lies the horror of this CLASSIC tale and, one hopes, a careful reevaluation of social codes and meaningless rituals.

BIBLIOGRAPHY

Jackson, Shirley. *The Lottery: or, The Adventures of James Harris.* New York: Farrar, Straus, 1949.

Wagner-Martin, Linda. "The Lottery." In *Reference Guide to Short Fiction,* edited by Noelle Watson, 783–784. Detroit: St. James Press, 1994.

"LOUDEST VOICE, THE" GRACE PALEY (1956)

GRACE PALEY's autobiographical story is a humorous account of events that transpired when she was a New York City grammar school student chosen to narrate the Christmas play because she had the loudest voice of any child in the school. In the story, she fictionalizes herself as Rose Abramovitch, Rose's immigrant Jewish mother, who is upset at what she thinks is the way the school is indoctrinating the children with Christian traditions. Her father is more tolerant, telling her mother that she is now in America and reminding her that she wanted to emigrate because anywhere else—Palestine, Europe, Argentina—would have been fraught with danger. In humorous understatement, he chides her for fearing Christmas in the United States.

In the second half of the story, the reader realizes that the narrator is cast in the speaking role of Jesus Christ himself. Rose speaks of Christ's childhood as lonely, utters his famous words of the Garden of Gethsemane ("My God, my God, why has thou forsaken me?"), and ends by proclaiming to the largely Jewish audience of parents who have arrived to see their children in the school play, "as everyone in this room, in this city—in this world—now knows, I shall have life eternal" (1,155).

Any shock these words might have held for her parents is defused when they return home after the play. When Mr. Abramovitch kids the Jewish neighbor Mrs. Kornbluh, whose daughter played the Virgin Mary, Mrs. Kornbluh refuses to take the bait and asks instead why the Christian children in the school had such small roles. Mrs. Abramovitch understands why: "You think it's so important they should get in the play? Christmas . . . the whole piece of goods . . . they own it."

In the final paragraphs of the story, as Rose remembers how she fell asleep happily listening to her parents and remembering her success in the play, the hold of her Jewish traditions certainly has not been shaken; indeed, she prays for "all the lonesome Christians." She confidently expects the Jewish God to whom she directs her prayers with the traditional Hebrew salutation, "Hear, O Israel," to hear her. After all, whether speaking Yiddish or English, she knows she has the loudest voice.

BIBLIOGRAPHY

Isaacs, Neil David. *Grace Paley: A Study of the Short Fiction.* Boston: Twayne, 1990.

Paley, Grace. "The Loudest Voice." In *Major Writers of Short Fiction,* edited by Ann Charters, 1,151–1,156. New York: St. Martin's, 1993.

LOUIE, DAVID WONG (1954–)

David Wong Louie was born in Rockville Center, New York. He received his B.A. from Vassar College and his M.F.A. from the University of Iowa, where he attended the Writers' Workshop. His stories have appeared in the *Iowa Review, Ploughshares, Chicago Review,* and *Best*

American Short Stories (1989). His first short story collection, *Pangs of Love* (1991), received the *Ploughshares* First Book Award and the *Los Angeles Times* Award for First Fiction in 1991. Louie has also received fellowships from the National Endowment for the Arts, the California Arts Council, the McDowell Colony, and Yaddo. He currently lives in the Los Angeles area and teaches in the English Department and the Asian American Studies Center at the University of California at Los Angeles. In 2001 he published a novel called *The Barbarians Are Coming.*

Reminiscent of and comparing favorably to the stories of AMY TAN and MAXINE HONG KINGSTON, those in Louie's *Pangs of Love* explore the lives of Asian immigrants and of their American-born children. Many of Louie's stories tend to focus on the alienation of the American male in general and the Asian-American male in particular; METAPHORS for this alienation range from forced sacrifice to denied paternity. Louie also deflates STEREOTYPES of the Asian male as the well-behaved and mild-mannered intellectual by purposely exaggerating the libidos and rebellious natures of certain male characters; these characterizations have garnered praise from FRANK CHIN and JEFFEREY PAUL CHAN. In "Disturbing the Universe," Louie uses the device of the FABLE in a scene near the Great Wall as peasants, criminals, and scholars at a labor camp participate in the invention of baseball. As in other of Louie's stories, his characters try to Americanize each other with names like *Edsel* and *Bagel*. His stories and characters are often quirky and amusing, as Louie dramatizes their often surreal (see SURREALISM) attempts to adapt to a new culture without forgetting the old ways.

Other Louie stories featuring very different male PROTAGONISTS and complex, sensitively portrayed female characters also have won plaudits from critics. "Displacement," reprinted in *Best American Short Stories 1989,* concerns Mrs. Chow, 35, who immigrates to the United States with her husband. Mr. and Mrs. Chow find employment in the home of a widow who has suffered a stroke and who treats the Chows abominably. In a moment of poignant clarity, Mrs. Chow sees a billboard with a rendering of a glamorous American woman and realizes that she must learn to cope with the new country, for she will never return to the old. Similarly, the title piece, about a son and his mother who speaks no English, takes the two in a rented car to another son's house, where the narrator and his mother watch wrestling on television. In another moment of clarity, the mother realizes that the world has changed for good and that she must relearn its shape. Louie uses another female POINT OF VIEW in "Inheritance," where the narrator comes of age after appearing on a television news program in support of a protest against a bombing of an abortion clinic.

BIBLIOGRAPHY

Hirose, Stacey Yukari. "David Wong Louie." In *Words Matter: Conversations with Asian American Writers,* edited by King-Kok Cheung, 189–214. Honolulu: University of Hawaii Press, with UCLA Asian American Studies Center, 2000.

Ho, Wen-ching. "Caucasian Partners and Generational Conflicts—David Wong Louie's *Pangs of Love.*" *EurAmerica: A Journal of European and American Studies* 34, no. 2. (June 2004): 231–264.

Parikh, Crystal. "'The Most Outrageous Masquerade': Queering Asian-American Masculinity." *Modern Fiction Studies* 48, no. 4 (Winter 2002): 858–898.

Wong, David Louie. *The Barbarians Are Coming.* New York: Putnam, 2000.

———. *Pangs of Love: Stories.* New York: Knopf, 1991.

Wong, Sau-ling Cynthia. "Chinese/Asian American Men in the 1990s: Displacement, Impersonation, Paternity and Extinction in David Wong Louie's *Pangs of Love.*" In *Privileging Positions: The Sites of Asian American Studies,* edited by Gary Y. Okihiro, et al. Pullman: Washington State University Press, 1995.

Keith Lawrence
Brigham Young University

LOVE MEDICINE LOUISE ERDRICH (1984)

Winner of the National Book Critics Circle Award in 1984, *Love Medicine* began as a short story. Its author, LOUISE ERDRICH, in close collaboration with her husband, Michael Dorris, planned it as a novel, yet many readers view it as a series of interconnected stories with reappearing characters, themes, and settings; indeed, many of the individual chapters have been anthologized as short stories. *Love Medicine* forms part of a SHORT STORY CYCLE; although published before the others, it chronologically takes place after *Tracks* (1988) and *Tales of Burning Love* (1996). Erdrich's style has been highly praised for its lyricism, on the one hand, and for its crisp, direct clarity, on the other.

The stories in *Love Medicine,* told from different characters' points of view, begin in 1981, move back to 1934, and then conclude in 1948, a fragmentation that obliquely underscores the fragmentation of the Native Americans themselves. Several times the narrators relate the same scene from several different perspectives. Set on the Chippewa reservation in North Dakota, the stories focus on the Kashpaw, the Lamartine/Nanpush, and the Morrisey families. The first and one of the most memorable stories is that of June Kashpaw, who meets her death in a blizzard on EASTER Sunday. The story is told from the perspective of her niece, a college student, who struggles to understand the meaning of June's death. As Louis Owens observes, however, June is something of a TRICKSTER figure, and after her death, she constantly reappears, like Christ, in the subsequent stories, thereby conflating her Native American and Christian background (195). In the subsequent stories appear such unique characters as Lulu Lamartine, a passionately intense woman, also a trickster figure; Marie Lazarre, a strong-willed woman who passes on that strength to her children; Nector Kashpaw, who loves Lulu but married Marie and fathered their child, June; and Sister Leopolda, whose confusion over her identity and her place in the world of the reservation sent her into the convent. (In *Tracks,* we learn that Leopolda, or Pauline, is actually Marie's mother.)

Critics have pointed out that part of Erdrich's success in the stories of *Love Medicine* lies in her refraining from pointing the finger of blame at her white readers, with whom the book has been both a popular and a critical success (Owens 205). Beneath the warmly human tales, some told with a comic voice, some with a deeply tragic one, however, Erdrich provides a complex and compassionate portrait of a dispossessed people.

BIBLIOGRAPHY

Owens, Louis. *Other Destinies: Understanding the American Indian Novel.* Norman: University of Oklahoma Press, 1992.

Wiget, Andrew O. "Louise Erdrich." In *The Heath Anthology of American Literature.* 3rd ed. Edited by Paul Lauter. Boston: Houghton Mifflin, 1997.

"LUCKIEST TIME OF ALL, THE" LUCILLE CLIFTON (1986) This children's story, a part of Clifton's book *The Lucky Stone,* is more about the community that is created by elders sharing stories with children than the plot of those stories themselves. As is often the case in working-class literature and African-American literature, creating community and stability is of higher value than adventure.

The story begins by asserting that two family members, spending time together is what makes a story, and that a story is about not only passing family history and wisdom but also about creating bonds: "Mrs. Elzie F. Pickens was rocking slowly on the porch one afternoon when her Great-granddaughter, Tee, brought her a big bunch of dogwood blossoms, and that was the beginning of a story." The gift of the girl's visit and the dogwood blossoms motivate Mrs. Pickens to relate a story from her youth that will connect her to the girl three generations distant from her. The narration, when gesturing to the reader, keeps the woman distant from us: We regard her respectfully as "Mrs. Pickens," but we watch the process of her becoming closer to the girl, who calls her "Grandmama." The reader is a witness to the relationship and the story, but the participant characters are enclosed in the intimacy of family. Because no dogwoods occur in Mrs. Pickens's story—the only relationship to the story itself is the word *dog,* and there is a dog in the tale—it appears that what begins the story is the being together of the two family members.

Mrs. Pickens's story is charming and seemingly simple: She tells Tee of the day she met Tee's great-grandfather, whom the girl never knew. This story is one of a series that she has been telling Tee throughout *The Lucky Stone.* Mrs. Pickens has passed on to the girl her lucky stone from her girlhood: a "shiny black" stone with "the letter *A* scratched on one side." In giving Tee the stone, Mrs. Pickens, through her stories, is connecting her girlhood to Tee's, just as she is passing on the luck to her. At the same time, by attaching stories to the stone for Tee, she is creating a family object—a tradition for Tee to carry on, by remembering the stories and by passing on her own stories of luck to future generations of the family.

The stone itself, a humble object, is one of great value. In the working-class family of Mrs. Pickens and Tee, the stone, which is not a gem or a crafted thing of great monetary value, is nonetheless an heirloom, and it carries the identity of the family and the tradition it represents as well as any more expensive item might for a wealthy family. The shiny blackness of the stone also enshrines and celebrates the blackness of the family, whereas otherwise being African American has been thought unlucky for people. The etched *A* explained earlier in the collection in this story of Mrs. Pickens signifies the name of her husband: *Amos Pickens*. Thus, she is able to give the girl a memory and an object relating to a family member, blood of her blood, whom she has never met.

Mrs. Pickens tells Tee of when she and her best friend, both teenagers, went to the visiting circus with the idea that they would join and leave their small town behind to see "the world." Mrs. Pickens, then just Elzie, and her friend, Ovella, before signing up, witness a dancing dog act, and the dog is so entertaining and mesmerizing that the girls, after first throwing pennies, start throwing trinkets of value to them. Elzie throws her lucky stone at the dog and regrets it the moment it leaves her fingers. She did not mean to give away her luck.

The lucky stone at first seems to foment disaster: It hits the dog on the nose, and he begins to chase Elzie with hopes of retaliation. Elzie flees but eventually looks back and sees not only the circus dog but also a handsome boy pursuing her. The man Elzie describes as "the fineest fast runnin hero in the bottoms of Virginia." She tells Tee that Mr. Pickens (as Mrs. Pickens refers to him) seemed to her "an angel come to help a poor sinner girl." The *A* of the stone Mrs. Pickens links indirectly to *angel* but directly to Mr. Pickens's first name: *Amos*. Amos saves Elzie from the dog by cradling it gently when he grabs it, and he encourages Elzie to forget her fear of it.

Amos also helps Elzie retrieve her lucky stone and restores it to her. Mrs. Pickens ends the story there, but she has led Tee to ask the right question for her to get the message of the story, "Grandmama, that stone almost got you bit by a dog that time. It wasn't so lucky that time, was it?" and Mrs. Pickens asserts that the stone is what gave her beloved husband, and, therefore, "That was the luckiest time of all." Tee hopes that she will have the same luck with the stone someday, and her great-grandmother wishes that for her. They share the warmth of the memory and their good wishes for each other, speaking no more, but, as the story concludes, "And they rocked a little longer and smiled together."

The stone's luck is multifold: It gets Mrs. Pickens her husband, helping her continue her family and create ongoing love in her life and that of those she loves. The stone makes the future generations possible and now binds them together, closing a circle of experience and memory. But the stone also holds Mrs. Pickens to the greatest working-class and perhaps also the greatest African-American value of all: loyalty to community, with family at its center. Elzie set out that day with her lucky stone to leave her community and family to go off for personal adventure and fulfillment. She was seeking money and recognition—fortune and fame and adventure in the circus. But the stone made her lucky: It rescued her from becoming unrooted, alone, and alien. It was a lucky stone for Elzie's family and community, for her finding love with Amos Pickens kept her at home, in the less glamorous but more loving and more significant life of belonging and responsibility.

Mrs. Pickens, through Lucille Clifton's deft and subtle plotting, uses the lucky stone to keep the true story—not of adventure, but of family continuity—intact. That story is of not storytelling or finding one's true love but of women three generations apart remaining together on the porch, smiling quietly about the future.

Carolyn Whitson
Metrostate University

LUM, DARRELL H. Y. (1950–)

Darrell H. Y. Lum was born and reared in Hawaii. He is the author of two collections of short stories, *Sun* (1980) and *Pass On, No Pass Back!* (1990); a children's book, *The Golden Slipper: A Vietnamese Legend* (1994); and *Pake: Writings by Chinese in Hawaii*, with Erick Chock, winner of the 1997 Hawaii Award in literature. Lum is cofounder of Bamboo Ridge Press, a nonprofit literary and scholarly press established in 1978 to encourage the publication of works by and about the peoples of Hawaii, and also written several plays.

Lum's stories have been widely anthologized; they also have appeared in *Manoa, Bamboo Ridge, Seattle Review, Chaminade Literary Review,* and *Hawaii Review.* Lum is the recipient of a National Endowment for the Arts (NEA) Fellowship; in 1992, *Pass On, No Pass Back!* won the National Book Award from the Association for Asian American Studies.

Although Lum writes more traditional stories as well, many of his stories are written entirely in Hawaiian Creole English, intimately capturing the emotions, energy, and consciousness of his Hawaiian characters. Particularly notable for Lum's use of Hawaiian pidgin DIALECT are "No Pass Back" and "Toads" from *Pake* and "Beer Can Hat" and "Primo Doesn't Take Back Bottles Anymore" from *Sun*. His most commonly anthologized stories are humorous, some of them darkly so, and are typified by a bold defensiveness toward judgmental or condescending non-Hawaiians. Other stories, such as "Streams in the Night," are quietly yet deeply tragic. Through his writing Lum aims to help preserve Asian Hawaiian culture as well as to depict racial and cultural inequities within the larger contexts of Hawaiian and American society.

BIBLIOGRAPHY

Chock, Eric, and Darrell H.Y. Lum, eds. *Best of Bamboo Ridge.* Honolulu: Bamboo Ridge Press, 1987.
———. *Pake: Writings by Chinese in Hawaii.* Honolulu: Bamboo Ridge Press, 1997.
Fujita-Sato, Gayle K. "The Island Influence on Chinese American Writers." *Amerasia Journal* (1990).
Lum, Darrell H. Y.. *The Golden Slipper: A Vietnamese Legend.* Mahwah, N.J.: Troll Association, 1994.
———. *Hot-Pepper-Kid and Iron-Mouth-Chicken Capture Fire and Wind.* New York: Macmillan/McGraw-Hill, 1997.
———. *A Little Bit Like You.* Honolulu: Kumu Kahua, 1991.
———. "On Pidgin and Children in Literature." In *Infant Tongues: The Voice of the Child in Literature,* edited by Elizabeth Goodenough et al. Detroit: Wayne State University Press, 1994.
———. *Pass On, No Pass Back!* Honolulu: Bamboo Ridge Press, 1990.
———. *Sun: Short Stories and Drama.* Honolulu: Bamboo Ridge Press, 1980.

Keith Lawrence
Brigham Young University

"LUST" SUSAN MINOT (1989) The initial story in SUSAN MINOT's 1989 collection *Lust and Other Stories,* this short tale sets the stage in both THEME and subject for the stories that will follow. The 12 stories portray different types of estrangement in heterosexual relationships: shifts in passion and fidelity, the longing for and frustration of true intimacy. Lust rather than love seems to be the chief (or only) possible link, tenuous though it is, between men and women.

"Lust" exemplifies this bleak theme. The story catalogs an unnamed young girl's sexual experiences in a series of isolated scenes, all told in first-person POINT OF VIEW from the perspective of the girl involved. Each experience is related in a short paragraph, separated by a blank line from the next; there is no transition between events. The cumulative effect of this barrage of brief paragraphs is to reinforce the fragmented nature of the girl's sexual encounters; each is short, without any intersection with other areas of her life. A subtle shift in perspective traces her metamorphosis from innocence to cynicism. In her initial encounters, her love interest "had a halo from the campus light behind him. I flipped," but only a few paragraphs later she has become "a body waiting on the rug." In spite of her sometimes gentle lovemaking, tender moments where her lover "rocked her like a seashell," she eventually feels "diluted, like watered-down stew," filled with "an overwhelming sadness." Minot's language is invariably frank and direct, and the story is filled with striking images and details that depict the scenes as well as the isolation of the characters in them.

Karen Weekes
University of Georgia

LYRIC A term used originally to describe a poem sung to music played on a lyre. Now used to describe a subjective, melodic poem that expresses the author's personal emotion or sentiment rather than the straightforward narration of a tale. In prose, the term *lyric* or *lyrical* is applied to a writer whose style expresses emotion with imagination and poetic phrasing.